The Heath Guide to Literature

The Heath Guide to Literature

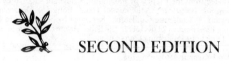

SECOND EDITION

David Bergman
Towson State University

Daniel Mark Epstein
Towson State University

D. C. HEATH AND COMPANY
Lexington, Massachusetts   Toronto

Acknowledgments

FICTION

Margaret Atwood. "Giving Birth" from *Dancing Girls and Other Stories* by Margaret Atwood. Copyright © 1977, 1982 by O. W. Toad, Ltd. Reprinted by permission of Simon & Schuster, Inc.
Isaac Babel. "My First Goose." Reprinted by permission of S. G. Phillips, Inc. from *The Collected Stories of Isaac Babel.* Copyright © 1955 by S. G. Phillips, Inc.
James Baldwin. "Sonny's Blues." Copyright © 1948, 1951, 1957, 1958, 1960, 1965 by James Baldwin. Permission Granted by The Dial Press.
Toni Cade Bambara. "My Man Bovanne." Copyright © 1971 by Toni Cade Bambara. Reprinted from *Gorilla, My Love,* by Toni Cade Bambara, by permission of Random House, Inc.
John Barth. "Autobiography." Copyright © 1968 by John Barth, from *Lost in the Funhouse* by John Barth. Reprinted by permission of Doubleday & Company, Inc.
Samuel Beckett. "fizzle 5" from *fizzles* by Samuel Beckett. Reprinted by permission of Grove Press, Inc. Translated from the French by the author. Copyright © 1976 by Samuel Beckett.
Giovanni Boccaccio. "A Dinner of Hens" from *The Decameron* by Giovanni Boccaccio, trans. by Richard Aldington. © Catherine Guillaume. Reprinted by permission of Rosica Colin Ltd.
Jorge Luis Borges. "The Library of Babel" from *Labyrinth* by Jorge Luis Borges. Copyright © 1962, 1964 by New Directions Publishing Corporation.
Ray Bradbury. "There Will Come Soft Rains." Copyright © 1950 by Ray Bradbury. Reprinted by permission of Don Congdon Associates, Inc.
Italo Calvino. "The Canary Prince" from *Italian Folktales,* selected and retold by Italo Calvino, translated by George Martin, copyright © 1956 by Giulio Einaudi editore, s.p.a., English translation copyright © 1980 by Harcourt Brace Jovanovich, Inc. Reprinted by permission of Harcourt Brace Jovanovich, Inc.
Elias Canetti. "Earwitness" from *Earwitness: Fifty Characters* by Elias Canetti. English translation copyright © 1979 by The Seabury Press, Inc. Used by permission of The Continuum Publishing Company.
Anton Chekhov. "Lady with Lapdog" from *Lady with Lapdog and Other Stories* by Anton Chekhov, translated by David Magarshack (Penguin Classics, 1964) pp. 264–281. Copyright © 1964 by David Magarshack. Reprinted by permission of Penguin Books Ltd.
Arthur C. Clarke. "The Star." Copyright, 1955, by Royal Publications, Inc. Reprinted from *The Nine Billion Names of God* by Arthur C. Clarke by permission of Harcourt Brace Jovanovich, Inc.
William Faulkner. "Spotted Horses" by William Faulkner. Copyright 1931 and renewed 1959 by William Faulkner. Reprinted from *Scribner's* Magazine by permission of Random House, Inc. An expanded version of this story appears as a part of *The Hamlet,* by William Faulkner.

(continued on page 1412)

(continued on page 1412)

Cover: *Still Life With White Boats,* by Fairfield Porter. Private Collection, NJ / Courtesy Tibor de Nagy Gallery.

Preface

To the Student

This book is a record of the bond between writers of literature and their readers. The authors of these stories, poems, and plays had a reader in mind when they set their pens to paper. They had in mind not so much students as readers who would gain pleasure and a certain insight from a thrilling story or a beautiful poem. All of the great writers, as far as we know, began as fascinated readers. Novelists Virginia Woolf and Ernest Hemingway and poets William Carlos Williams and Marianne Moore, among others, have told of this relationship within themselves between reading and writing. To hear them tell it, no excitement in life quite equals the writing of a great book, unless it be the reading of it.

Like most bonds, this one between writers and readers has its times of difficulty, disappointment, and frustration along with its times of calm and delight. There is an African proverb that says: "It is difficult to make friends with an elephant." This piece of wisdom is meant to explain the relationship between a king and his servant, for any creature with enormous power is capable of carrying you or stepping on your toes. Literature, among the arts, has just such force and unpredictability. It communicates the deepest fears and desires of humanity. You probably will not like everything you read in these pages, any more than you would like everyone in your town. Along with enjoyable and uplifting stories and poems you may find some you consider at first ugly, or confusing. At these times, particularly, we hope our introductions and discussion questions will prove useful to you. As students we have known many such moments ourselves. In fact, some of our most exciting experiences in reading have come during these transitions from bewilderment to understanding.

Another pleasure of studying great literature is the development of taste and perception—the ability to recognize excellence and to support your preferences with intelligent reasoning. To aid you in developing this faculty, we have given some attention to general differences between good stories and poems and inferior ones. We love to discuss our likes and dislikes and we encourage you to do the same after careful reading.

The body of literature called the "classics" consists of works that many readers have admired for many years. Most of our selections have gained such admiration. But this is not a museum of precious fossils; it is a living body of literature constantly growing and changing, and nourished by the enthusiasm of new readers. Our reading has led us to include new stories and poems by writers like Toni Cade Bambara and Alice Walker to set alongside monuments like "Young Goodman Brown" and "Ode to a Nightingale." We invite you to exercise your taste and state your preferences. Ultimately it will be you, the reader, who will decide the content of future literary anthologies.

In the course of an academic year you will not have the time to give all these works the attention they deserve. Indeed, an entire lifetime might not suffice. Such works as *Oedipus Rex, Hamlet,* and "The Love Song of J. Alfred Prufrock" are virtually inexhaustible, as are many other selections. You will not be required to read everything, so we invite you to browse through the rest, letting your eye fall upon engaging lines and passages, and reading on as you will. We also suggest, on behalf of the several hundred authors included, that you consider this book not merely the guide for a semester or two of study, but a valuable resource for years to come, a point of departure.

To the Instructor

When we were undergraduates at Kenyon College, we were fortunate enough to study literature with several inspired teachers. The pedagogic atmosphere was still suffused with the New Criticism of John Crowe Ransom (who lived nearby), I. A. Richards, and William Empson. We learned to analyze syntax with reverent calculation and to sift stories and sonnets for metaphysical irony and ambiguity. We learned, in short, to read carefully, to pay attention to the text. But the text itself remained immortal and as aloof from the humble reader (and the author, strangely enough) as the *Book of Job* or the nearly anonymous plays of Shakespeare. Insofar as the study of literature might partake of the exactitude of the sciences, it should. Insofar as it seemed imprecise, this could only betray the inadequacy of our critical instruments.

Yet our teachers were inspired, and inspiration kept jamming those critical instruments. Analyzing a verse paragraph of *Paradise Lost,* our Milton scholar would begin ranting and railing along with Satan; the Donne scholar in reading a love poem showed subtle signs of rather unscholarly enthusiasm; the Conrad expert reciting Kurtz's lines, "the horror, the horror," became truly, unconcealably horrified. And so were we. The literature was obviously a living part of us, and would not lie still upon the examining table while we probed it.

It was then that we realized the study of literature is a passion rather than a discipline. The discipline, too, has its place: the reader must learn to read carefully and critically, must acquire certain tools—but only in the service of human curiosity and sympathy, the desire to hear what a writer has to say. Our teachers began and ended with the text, presuming its acknowledged greatness would compel our attention. We, as teachers, begin with ourselves as readers, passionate readers, and try to communicate our enthusiasms to our students. If we are successful, then our students are motivated, as we were, to obtain the tools of analysis this book has to offer.

Our teachers sometimes neglected the historical contexts of literary works, assuming quite sensibly that everyone who has lived for the past three thousand years is our contemporary. Yet one cannot explain Hamlet's delay without reference to the Renaissance education of noblemen. Nor can one know exactly how rash was Oedipus's murder of three travelers without referring to ancient Greek standards of aristocratic conduct and honor. Although this text does not pretend to be a thorough historical study of literature, we have an eye to history and try to locate works within a historical framework.

We have striven to present authors as human beings, for the most part with normal human concerns, rather than as gods or unworldly eccentrics. The numerous photographs should be helpful in establishing the intimacy between writers and readers we consider so important. Students who have become particularly interested in one author may find it fascinating to see how he or she uses different genres. So we have included both poems and stories by D. H. Lawrence, Stephen Crane, Herman Melville, James Joyce, and Alice Walker.

When students first begin reading serious literature, they often have difficulty because they have not learned how to experience certain literary conventions. They do not know what authors expect of them. For example, many inexperienced readers of stories approach fictional settings as mere filler-facts one may freely ignore. They do not realize that such passages usually have psychological, sociological, or symbolic significance. This book differs from other introductory texts in being explicit about author-reader conventions, helping students develop the reading conventions necessary to a full appreciation of literature.

Another unique feature of this text is that two 90-minute cassette tapes have been developed to serve as classroom aids. One of them includes forty-two poems read by their authors or by famous actors. The symbol • appears in the table of contents and in the text beside the recorded poems. The other tape contains important scenes from the plays and interviews with professional theatre people. We hope that these tapes will communicate some of the excitement of living poetry and drama.

In making our selections we have provided for a vast range of student abilities and classroom situations. In fact, any number of different courses may be taught with these materials, from advanced-placement high school literature to a high-powered college course, without leaving the students baffled or bored. Generally, each chapter begins with a selection that is classic in its simplicity and ends with several that are sophisticated, inexhaustible. The same pattern applies to the questions following a selection: the first questions concern factual information; the last is frequently open-ended. You should find more than enough material to engage and challenge students whatever their level of preparation, and we encourage you to experiment in choosing assignments.

This edition is slightly smaller than the first. We have taken out only what readers from all over the country told us was unnecessary or repetitious. This second edition of *The Heath Guide to Literature* is, therefore, lighter to carry and easier to use. The selections are broader and more up-to-date, but still retain the balance between classic works students of literature should know, and newer, exciting works that may become classics in the future. In this edition we have included for the first time plays by Sam Shepard and Beth Henley, both of whom have won recent Pulitzer Prizes in drama. In addition, there are stories by Alice Walker, Bobbie Ann Mason, and Anne Tyler—writers who only now are beginning to emerge as major figures. We hope we have packed a few surprises, works that even the most voracious readers may not know but will come to love.

The Instructor's Manual contains discussion of important thematic and technical aspects of each work, teaching suggestions, and selected bibliographies.

We are grateful to the many people who have helped us in the preparation of this book. It certainly would not have come to be written without the help of Gordon Lester-Massman, Paul Smith, and Holt Johnson. Linda Vlasak and Sylvia Mallory helped us improve the style. We wish to thank Charles Haller, Jennifer Isaacs, Helen Jones, and Jane Rosenthal, who typed the manuscript and further advised us on style. Diskin Clay, Thomas Curley, Richard Howard, Hugh Kenner, David St. John, and Richard Wilbur graciously answered our questions. Elaine Hedges and Donald H. Craver shared their knowledge and experience, as did John E. Connolly and the research staffs of the Albert S. Cook Library and the Milton S. Eisenhower Library. We wish to thank John Irwin, Mary Camerer, and Dorothy De Witt for their many kindnesses during the preparation of the manuscript. We are also grateful to the Township of Heath, Massachusetts, for providing working space, to Johanna Ruth Epstein and Madeleine Irvine for help in organization and proofreading, and to Wendy Roberts for advice and support.

The following individuals also generously helped us with their suggestions: David Allen, Citadel Military College of South Carolina; Chris Antonides, Lansing Community College; Tom Barthel, Herkimer County Community College; John Bassett, North Carolina State University; Alan Bickford, Macon Junior College; Peter Brier, California State—Los Angeles; Dorothy Brown, Macon Junior College; Jerald Butler, San Diego State University; Alice Carter, Ohio State University, Columbus; Joan Doggrell, Clark County Community College; Richard Dowell, Indiana State University; Janice Edens, Macon Junior College; Alan Ehmann, University of Texas, El Paso; Gaye Elder, Abraham Baldwin Agricultural College; Leon Gatlin, University of North Carolina, Charlotte; Ernest Giordani, Broome Community College; Harriet Herlihy, Glendale Community College; David Hilton, Anne Arundel Community College; Ralph D.

Howell, Mississippi College, Clinton; Leon Jacobson, Lake City Community College; Ejner Jensen, University of Michigan, Ann Arbor; Yvonne Jones, Shelby State Community College; Michael Joyce, Jackson Community College; Andrew Kelly, Shelby State Community College; Paulino Lim, California State University, Long Beach; Amy Ling, Rutgers University; Steve Liu, Clark County Community College; Emery Maiden, Appalachian State University; Bill Martin, Armstrong State College; Tom McDermott, Southern Connecticut State University; Terry Miller, Indian River Community College; Larry Mobley, Macon Junior College; Chadyeane Neuman, Prince George's Community College; Douglas A. Pearson, Jr., University of Wisconsin, Eau Claire; Les Perelman, Tulane University; William Pierce, Prince George's Community College; David Piwinski, Herkimer County Community College; Nancy Posselt, Midland Technical College; Richard Raymond, Armstrong State College; Phyllis Read, Bronx Community College-CUNY; Douglas Rose, SUNY A & T, Canton; Arthrell Sanders, North Carolina Central University; George Scott, Abraham Baldwin Agricultural College; Jack Selzer, Pennsylvania State University; Robert Tapply, Fitchburg State College; Ethel Taylor, North Carolina A & T State University; J. Chesley Taylor, Washington State University; Dennis Thompson, Macomb Community College; Jean Turner, Anne Arundel Community College; Gilbert Vaughan, Wayne State College; Thomas Waldrep, University of South Carolina; Barclay M. Wheeler, Evergreen Valley College; Johnnie Williams, St. Petersburg Junior College.

Finally we must acknowledge many students, who, by their excitement, confusion, understanding, and impatience, have led us to improve ourselves as teachers and to grow as individuals.

David Bergman

Daniel Mark Esptein

Topical Contents

POETRY

Contents

5 Dramatic Poetry: The Poet as Actor   477

8 The Idea Dresses Up: Personification, Allegory, Symbol   538

DRAMA

Fiction

1 🌿 The Worlds of Fiction

Children happily act out their fantasies. Left alone, they will immerse themselves in day-long dramas of cowboys and Indians, or a battle of superheroes. Even before children can speak, they will sit quietly and listen to grownups read bedtime stories, following the pictures as the pages turn. One of our most vivid childhood memories is sitting around a campfire, the summer evening air suddenly chilled, listening to ghost stories that raised gooseflesh on our arms and the hairs on the back of our necks. Children don't have to be persuaded to like stories or the make-believe world of the imagination. They crave a good tale and search out the best storytellers, pestering them to tell their longest and most exciting tales.

The autobiographies of writers are filled with early delight and enchantment in stories and books. Jean-Paul Sartre, the French novelist, playwright, and philosopher, recalls in his memoir, *The Words*, how his mother told him stories:

> While she spoke, we were alone and clandestine, far from men, gods and
> priests, two does in a wood, with those other does, the Fairies. I simply could
> not believe that someone had composed a whole book to tell episodes of our
> . . . life, which smelled of soap and eau de Cologne.

The magic of these stories colored his attitude toward books. Sartre had, he remembers, the irrational feeling that his "family's prosperity depended on them," and he prophesies, "I began my life as I shall no doubt end it: amidst books."

Why do children enjoy stories so much? As Sartre suggests, part of the enjoyment is the listener's physical closeness to the storyteller. But the psychologist Bruno Bettleheim, who has made a lengthy study of fairy tales, says there are other reasons. He contends that stories tell the child that life has its difficulties which can be met and overcome. The heroes of fairy tales "master all obstacles

3

and emerge victorious." Bettleheim insists that fairy tales are not "escape" reading—stories read to avoid reality—rather they "confront the child squarely with the basic human predicaments."

Of course, children may not be aware of the reason why one story holds their attention and why they want to hear it over and over again. Later on, we may explain our preference by saying that one story seems more exciting, more romantic, or more moving than another one. But as long as the basis of our interest remains unconscious or semiconscious, we are not fully enjoying what we read, not deriving the full pleasure and appreciation of the storyteller's art.

The Fictional World and the Real World

The world of fiction differs from the one we live in, and the study of fiction differs from the study of science. The sciences try to uncover the way things are or were: the facts and principles that govern our world and our lives. But fiction does not uncover facts. A story is a construction of language and a projection of the imagination. Although some writers restrict themselves to stories that conceivably could be true, their stories are still not "fact." Whether an author writes, "The cowboy rode into the sunset," or "The unicorn flew toward the sun," the sentences are still imaginative products, and it would be foolish to ask for proof of the cowboy's existence or the unicorn's present whereabouts.

Consequently, the storyteller has much greater freedom than ·the scientist. When scientists describe a chemical compound, a geologic formation, or the symptoms of a disease, they must describe things as faithfully and objectively as possible. A storyteller, however, can describe magic potions, enchanted islands, and fantastic diseases. The scientific report is an objective, rational survey of data. But for a storyteller, a book can contain all sorts of magical properties. In the folktale "The Canary Prince," retold by Italo Calvino, a witch gives a princess an enchanted book inscribed with the instructions: "Turn the pages forward, and the man becomes a bird; turn them back, and the bird becomes a man." A scientist would not explain events through magic.

Does it make any sense to complain that magic books are untrue? Italo Calvino would agree that no such books exist except in his imagination when he wrote about one and in our own minds when we read about it. But we would be naive to say that Calvino has lied to us or told us a falsehood. Because the work of fiction does not claim to be true, it cannot be said to be false. It exists in an imaginary space cut off from truth and falsity, fact and verification.

Fictional Conventions

Critics and students, however, sometimes say that stories contain improbable actions, inconsistent characters, or inappropriate material. Since a storyteller is free to narrate any action—flying carpets, life on stars, people the size of ants, ants the size of people—why are some stories improbable, inconsistent, or made with inappropriate materials?

The answer is that literature is governed by certain *conventions*. Conventions are agreed-upon rules, decisions, or practices. The Geneva Convention, for example, set up procedures for countries to handle prisoners-of-war. Literary conventions are practices that artists choose to follow in constructing their stories, plays, and poems. Just as athletes agree to certain rules of the game, so, too, do writers respect certain practices of their craft. Of course, there are many different games, each with its own conventions, and there are many different types of stories, each with its own particular set of expectations. Such restrictions do not, however, limit the pleasure of athletics or fiction. To the contrary, a game in which no one obeyed the rules would degenerate into chaotic action. So, too, a story that corresponds to no recognizable convention is impossible to follow or enjoy.

Thus, when we say a work is inconsistent, improbable, or inappropriate, we mean that the work has not followed its own chosen conventions, its own rules of procedure. For example, a *realistic* work—a story in which characters and action conform to natural laws and recognizable human behavior—cannot include magic books that turn men into canaries and canaries into men. Such a magical book would be inconsistent with the conventions of realistic fiction and inappropriate in a realistic story. Similarly, if an author creates an all-powerful character like Superman, the author would be breaking his own convention if the character were hurt in a car accident. Superman might pretend to be injured, but readers would assume from the conventions of the story that he is "really" well.

We might put it this way: each story has its own imaginative "facts" and "rules." As long as a story obeys its own conventions, it is consistent and appropriate. We get upset only when we notice that the imaginative rules are changed in mid-story.

The Variety of Fictional Worlds

So far we have mentioned "realistic" stories and supernatural stories such as folk stories and fairy tales. But these two sorts of fiction are merely extremes in a large range of possible fictions. For example, Jean Rhys's story, "I Used to Live Here Once" is generally "realistic," except for a ghost who is surprised by its own existence. Maxine Hong Kingston's "On Mortality" begins as history but ends as fantasy. Because each story is governed by its own rules, readers must be attentive and flexible. Readers are like spectators who must figure out the rules of the game by watching it being played. Although other stories might help one figure out the basic principles of construction, each story must be judged on its own terms.

The Lessons of Fiction

If stories are not factual, why should we study them? What could we possibly learn from literature? After all, when we study history we gain a better sense of the past; we have a more accurate understanding of what happened.

When we study biology, we learn how organisms function. But what do we gain by reading stories that are neither true nor possessed of facts? What benefit is derived from literary studies?

Philosophers since Aristotle have been asking these questions, and they have developed several answers. First, by showing how things *might* be, *could* be, or *ought* to be, writers indicate the consequences of actions. Arthur C. Clarke's science fiction story "The Star" shows us a solar system that has died. Indirectly, Clarke cautions us about our own fate. But authors can also show us examples of an ideal world. Boccaccio's tale from *The Decameron* depicts how an ideal wife rebuffs the amorous advances of a king and still remains a polite hostess. Stories are a helpful and enjoyable way to learn lessons in proper behavior. The moral tale instructs us how to be better people, and the political story can convey a potent message.

Literature can also show us how the mind works. Psychology and philosophy both concern themselves with mental processes. But students of literature have their own way of learning how the mind works: by observing one of its most fascinating products—stories and the fictional world they create.

For those of you who need a more practical justification for studying literature, consider this: American business and industry is known for its ingenuity, inventiveness, and imaginative use of resources. The wealth of America is based on its imagination. But the imagination is not a mental process that can be ignored until you need it. Like any bodily process, it must be exercised and cultivated to be in ready working condition. The person who comes up with a new product, method of production, marketing strategy, or design is using much the same type of imagination and inventive power as the writer. We have all heard stories of the poor, impractical artist. Such stories disguise the fact that many writers have also been successful business persons. Wallace Stevens is one outstanding example: a man who was simultaneously one of America's most celebrated poets and a successful insurance executive, as comfortable in the board room as in the literary salon. Hawthorne became in later life a fine diplomat; Chekhov was a physician. The successful professional or business person can look beyond present conditions and envision how things might be in the future. This demands imagination.

But perhaps the best reason for studying literature is that reading the best works is fun. Our horizons are widened; our capacity to understand and delight in life is greatly enhanced. Reading, of course, is not like the passive pleasure of watching television or listening to some sorts of "background" music. Reading is an activity. The enjoyment we get from literature is akin to the enjoyment we get from swimming, jogging, painting, or playing a musical instrument. All these activities demand time, concentration, patience, and knowledge. Reading demands more than passing your eyes across the page, just as playing the piano demands more than pressing down a few keys. The rewards of reading make up for the effort. A great story, poem, or play can leave an impression that lasts for life, an excitement that you can take with you, and thoughts always worth considering.

Suggestions for Essayists

1. We usually think of reality and fantasy as two distinct categories. Write an essay showing how in life that distinction is blurred.
2. Describe some of the benefits of studying literature.
3. Describe some of the social conventions that govern your life and discuss your thoughts about them.

Suggestions for Fiction Writers

1. Take a fairy tale and rewrite it to make it as realistic as possible. (For example, do away with the magic book in "The Canary Prince.") Observe just where the fantastic occurrences are necessary for the story to make sense.
2. Write down one of the stories you were told as a child. Make up any details you can't remember.
3. Narrate a dream as though it were reality.
4. Narrate an incident that really happened to you as though it were a fairy tale, using as many of the conventions of fairy tales as you can.

ITALO CALVINO (1923–)

The Canary Prince

There was a king who had a daughter. Her mother was dead, and the stepmother was jealous of the girl and always spoke badly of her to the king. The maiden defended herself as best she could, but the stepmother was so contrary and insistent that the king, though he loved his daughter, finally gave in. He told the queen to send the girl away, but to some place where she would be comfortable, for he would never allow her to be mistreated. "Have no fear of that," said the stepmother, who then had the girl shut up in a castle in the heart of the forest. To keep her company, the queen selected a group of ladies-in-waiting, ordering them never to let the girl go out of the house or even to look out the windows. Naturally they received a salary worthy of a royal household. The girl was given a beautiful room and all she wanted to eat and drink. The only thing she couldn't do was go outdoors. But the ladies, enjoying so much leisure time and money, thought only of themselves and paid no attention to her.

Every now and then the king would ask his wife, "And how is our daughter? What is she doing with herself these days?" To prove that she did take an interest in the girl, the queen called on her. The minute she stepped from her carriage, the ladies-in-waiting all rushed out and told her not to worry, the girl was well and happy. The queen went up to the girl's room for a moment. "So you're comfortable, are you? You need nothing, do you? You're looking well, I see; the country air is doing you good. Stay happy, now. Bye-bye, dear!" And off she went. She informed the king she had never seen his daugher so content.

On the contrary, always alone in that room, with ladies-in-waiting who didn't so much as look at her, the princess spent her days wistfully at the window. She sat there leaning on the windowsill, and had she not thought to put a pillow under them, she would have got calluses on her elbows. The window looked out on the forest, and all day long the princess saw nothing but treetops, clouds and, down below, the hunters' trail. Over that trail one day came the son of a king in pursuit of a wild boar. Nearing the castle known to have been unoccupied for no telling how many years, he was amazed to see washing spread out on the battlements, smoke rising from the chimneys, and open casements. As he looked about him, he noticed a beautiful maiden at one of the upper windows and smiled at her. The maiden saw the prince too, dressed in yellow, with hunter's leggings and gun, and smiling at her, so she smiled back at him. For a whole hour, they smiled, bowed, and curtsied, being too far apart too communicate in any other way.

The next day, under the pretext of going hunting, the king's son returned, dressed in yellow, and they stared at each other this time for two hours; in addition to smiles, bows, and curtsies, they put a hand over their hearts and waved handkerchiefs at great length. The third day the prince stopped for three hours, and they blew each other kisses. The fourth day he was there as usual, when from behind a tree a witch peeped and began to guffaw: "Ho, ho, ho, ho!"

"Who are you? What's so funny?" snapped the prince.

"What's so funny? Two lovers silly enough to stay so far apart!"

"Would you know how to get any closer to her, ninny?" asked the prince.

"I like you both," said the witch, "and I'll help you."

She knocked at the door and handed the ladies-in-waiting a big old book with yellow, smudgy pages, saying it was a gift to the princess so the young lady could pass the time reading. The ladies took it to the girl, who opened it at once and read: "This is a magic book. Turn the pages forward, and the man becomes a bird; turn them back, and the bird becomes a man once more."

The girl ran to the window, placed the book on the sill, and turned the pages in great haste while watching the youth in yellow standing in the path. Moving his arms, he was soon flapping wings and changed into a canary, dressed in yellow as he was. Up he soared above the treetops and headed straight for the window, coming to rest on the cushioned sill. The princess couldn't resist picking up the beautiful canary and kissing him; then remembering he was a young man, she blushed. But on second thought she wasn't ashamed at all and made haste to turn him back into a youth. She picked up the book and thumbed backward through it; the canary ruffled his yellow feathers, flapped his wings, then moved arms and was once more the youth dressed in yellow with the hunter's leggings who knelt before her, declaring, "I love you!"

By the time they finished confessing all their love for one another, it was evening. Slowly, the princess leafed through the book. Looking into her eyes the youth turned back into a canary, perched on the windowsill, then on the eaves, then trusting to the wind, flew down in wide arcs, lighting on the lower limb of a tree. At that, she turned the pages back in the book and the canary was a prince once more who jumped down, whistled for his dogs, threw a kiss toward the window, and continued along the trail out of sight.

So every day the pages were turned forward to bring the prince flying up to the window at the top of the tower, then turned backward to restore his human form, then forward again to enable him to fly away, and finally backward for him to get home. Never in their whole life had the two young people known such happiness.

One day the queen called on her stepdaughter. She walked about the room, saying, "You're all right, aren't you? I see you're a trifle slimmer, but that's certainly no cause for concern, is it? It's true, isn't it, you've never felt better?" As she talked, she checked to see that everything was in place. She opened the window and peered out. Here came the prince in yellow along the trail with his dogs. "If this silly girl thinks she is going to flirt at the window," said the stepmother to herself, "she has another thought coming to her." She sent the girl for a glass of water and some sugar, then hurriedly removed five or six hairpins from her own hair and concealed them in the pillow with the sharp points sticking straight up. "That will teach her to lean on the window!" The girl returned with the water and sugar, but the queen said, "Oh, I'm no longer thirsty; you drink it, my dear! I must be getting back to your father. You don't need anything, do you? Well, goodbye." And she was off.

As soon as the queen's carriage was out of sight, the girl hurriedly flipped over the pages of the book, the prince turned into a canary, flew to the window, and struck the pillow like an arrow. He instantly let out a shrill cry of pain. The yellow feathers were stained with blood; the canary had driven the pins into his breast. He rose with a convulsive flapping, trusted himself to the wind, descended in irregular arcs, and lit on the ground with outstretched wings. The frightened princess, not yet fully aware of what had happened, quickly turned the pages back in the hope there would be no wounds when he regained his human form. Alas, the prince reappeared dripping blood from the deep stabs that had rent the yellow garment on his chest, and lay back surrounded by his dogs.

At the howling of the dogs, the other hunters came to his aid and carried him off on a stretcher of branches, but he didn't so much as glance up at the window of his beloved, who was still overwhelmed with grief and fright.

Back at his palace, the prince showed no promise of recovery, nor did the doctors know what to do for him. The wounds refused to heal over, and constantly hurt. His father the king posted proclamations on every street corner promising a fortune to anyone who could cure him, but not a soul turned up to try.

The princess meanwhile was consumed with longing for her lover. She cut her sheets into thin strips which she tied one to the other in a long, long rope. Then one night she let herself down from the high tower and set on the hunters' trail. But because of the thick darkness and the howls of the wolves, she decided to wait for daylight. Finding an old oak with a hollow trunk, she nestled inside and, in her exhaustion, fell asleep at once. She woke up while it was still pitch-dark, under the impression she had heard a whistle. Listening closely, she heard another whistle, then a third and a fourth, after which she saw four candle flames advancing. They were four witches coming from the four corners of the earth to their appointed meeting under that tree. Through a crack in the trunk the princess, unseen by them, spied on the four crones carrying candles and sneering a welcome to one another: "Ah, ah, ah!"

They lit a bonfire under the tree and sat down to warm themselves and roast a couple of bats for dinner. When they had eaten their fill, they began asking one another what they had seen of interest out in the world.

"I saw the sultan of Turkey, who bought himself twenty new wives."

"I saw the emperor of China, who has let his pigtail grow three yards long."

"I saw the king of the cannibals, who ate his chamberlain by mistake."

"I saw the king of this region, who has the sick son nobody can cure, since I alone know the remedy."

"And what is it?" asked the other witches.

"In the floor of his room is a loose tile. All one need do is lift the tile, and there underneath is a phial containing an ointment that would heal every one of his wounds."

It was all the princess inside the tree could do not to scream for joy. By this time the witches had told one another all they had to say, so each went her own way. The princess jumped from the tree and set out in the dawn for the city. At the first secondhand dealer's she came to, she bought an old doctor's gown and a pair of spectacles, and knocked at the royal palace. Seeing the little doctor with such scant paraphernalia, the servants weren't going to let him in, but the king said, "What harm could he do my son who can't be any worse off than he is now? Let him see what he can do." The sham doctor asked to be left alone with the sick man, and the request was granted.

Finding her lover groaning and unconscious in his sickbed, the princess felt like weeping and smothering him with kisses. But she restrained herself because of the urgency of carrying out the witch's directions. She paced up and down the room until she stepped on a loose tile, which she raised and discovered a phial of ointment. With it she rubbed the prince's wounds, and no sooner had she touched each one with ointment than the wound disappeared completely. Overjoyed she called the king, who came in and saw his son sleeping peacefully, with the color back in his cheeks, and no trace of any of the wounds.

"Ask for whatever you like, doctor," said the king. "All the wealth in the kingdom is yours."

"I wish no money," replied the doctor, "Just give me the prince's shield bearing the family coat-of-arms, his standard, and his yellow vest that was rent and bloodied." Upon receiving the three items, she took her leave.

Three days later, the king's son was again out hunting. He passed the castle in the heart of the forest, but didn't deign to look up at the princess's window. She immediately picked up the book, leafed through it, and the prince had no choice but change into a canary. He flew into the room, and the princess turned him back into a man. "Let me go," he said. "Isn't it enough to have pierced me with those pins of yours and caused me so much agony?" The prince, in truth, no longer loved the girl, blaming her for his misfortune.

On the verge of fainting, she exclaimed, "But I saved your life! I am the one who cured you!"

"That's not so," said the prince. "My life was saved by a foreign doctor who asked for no recompense except my coat-of-arms, my standard, and my bloodied vest!"

"Here are your coat-of-arms, your standard, and your vest! The doctor was none other than myself! The pins were the cruel doing of my stepmother!"

The prince gazed into her eyes, dumbfounded. Never had she looked so beautiful. He fell at her feet asking her forgiveness and declaring his deep gratitude and love.

That very evening he informed his father he was going to marry the maiden in the castle in the forest.

"You may marry only the daughter of a king or an emperor," replied his father.

"I shall marry the woman who saved my life."

So they made preparations for the wedding, inviting all the kings and queens in the vicinity. Also present was the princess's royal father, who had been informed of nothing. When the bride came out, he looked at her and exclaimed, "My daughter!"

"What!" said the royal host. "My son's bride is your daughter? Why did she not tell us?"

"Because," explained the bride, "I no longer consider myself the daughter of a man who let my stepmother imprison me." And she pointed at the queen.

Learning of all his daughter's misfortune, the father was filled with pity for the girl and with loathing for his wicked wife. Nor did he wait until he was back home to have the woman seized. Thus the marriage was celebrated to the satisfaction and joy of all, with the exception of that wretch.

Questions

1. What objects or actions in this story could not happen in real life?
2. What events in this story could conceivably happen in real life?
3. Do you recognize any features from other fairy tales in "The Canary Prince"?
4. In what sense do books turn men into canaries?
5. The king offers the princess disguised as a doctor whatever she likes, but she doesn't reveal her identity and ask for the prince's hand in marriage. Why not?
6. Is the princess's attitude toward her father justified? Does she act like a proper daughter?
7. Do you think Calvino believes in witches and magic books? Can you tell? Does it matter whether he does or not?

GIOVANNI BOCCACCIO (1313–1375)

A Dinner of Hens (*from* The Decameron)

The Marquess of Monferrato, Standard-bearer to the Church, was a man of great valour, and went overseas with the army of the Crusaders. There was talk of his bravery at the Court of Philip the One-eyed, who was preparing to leave France on the same Crusade. One of the knights said there was not another couple under the stars like the Marquess and his wife; for, just as the Marquess excelled all knights in courage, so did his wife exceed all other ladies in beauty and virtue.

These words entered the King of France's mind so deeply that, although he had never seen her, he fell violently in love with her, and made up his mind that he would sail from nowhere but Genoa. If he went to that port by land he would have a reasonable pretext for going to see the Marchioness; and, as the husband was away, he thought he would be able to get what he wanted from her.

He proceeded to carry out his plan. He sent his army on ahead, and started out himself with only a few gentlemen. When he was one day's march from the Marquess's lands, he sent to tell the lady that he meant to dine with her next day. The lady, who was prudent and wise, cheerfully answered that she considered it a very great honour, and that he would be welcome. Then she began to wonder why a King should come to visit her when her husband was away. Nor was she wrong when she concluded that he was attracted by the fame of her beauty.

However, as she was a great lady, she determined to show him all honour, and called together all the eminent men remaining with her to make all suitable arrangements with their advice. But she reserved to herself the banquet and the food. Without delay she got together all the fowls in the countryside, and ordered her cooks to use them only for the different courses at the royal banquet.

The King arrived at the time appointed, and the lady received him with all honour and rejoicing. When he observed her, he found that she was far more beautiful and virtuous and polite than the knight had said. He marvelled at her, and praised her highly; and, finding that the lady was so much more excellent than he had imagined, his desires increased proportionately. He then went to take his repose in apartments richly furnished with everything necessary for a King's reception. When dinner time came, the King and the Marchioness sat down together at one table, and the rest, according to their rank, were served at other tables.

Here the King was highly delighted, for he was served successively with many courses and the finest wines, while in addition he kept gazing at the beautiful Marchioness with the greatest pleasure. However, as one course succeeded another, the King began to wonder, for however differently they were served up, they were all made of chicken. He knew that the country round about must be filled with game, and, since he had warned the lady that he was coming, there had been plenty of time to hunt and shoot. He marvelled so much at this, that he wanted to make her talk about nothing but her fowls, and so turned to her gaily, saying:

"Why, Madam, are there only hens and no cocks born in this part of the country?"

The Marchioness perfectly understood what he meant, and felt that, just as she had wished, God had given her an opportunity to show the King her intentions. So, at the King's question, she turned bravely upon him and said:

"No, Sire, but the women are the same here as elsewhere, although they may differ in clothes and rank."

When the King heard her words, he understood the reason for the banquet of fowls and the virtue hidden in her words. He realised that words would be useless with such a woman, and he could not use force. And since he had so incautiously flamed up for her, the wisest thing to do for his own honour would be to extinguish this unlucky fire of passion. So he continued his dinner with no hope of success, and did not attempt to jest further with her, for he was afraid of her retorts. To cover up the cause of his unseemly visit by a swift departure, he thanked her immediately after dinner for the honour she had done him, commended her to God, and departed at once for Genoa.

Questions

1. Are there events in the story that could not happen? Does anything in the story contradict physical or natural laws?
2. Do the people in the story behave in typical human fashion?
3. In what sense is the Marchioness "too good to be true"? Does she act in any way that would contradict her reputation as one who surpassed "all other ladies in beauty and virtue"?
4. Why does she allow the King of France to visit her if she suspects that he will try to seduce her? Is it proper for her to serve him a meal?
5. Is the King evil? How would you judge his behavior?

JEAN RHYS (1894–1979)

I Used to Live Here Once

She was standing by the river looking at the stepping stones and remembering each one. There was the round unsteady stone, the pointed one, the flat one in the middle—the safe stone where you could stand and look round. The next wasn't so safe, for when the river was full the water flowed over it and even when it showed dry it was slippery. But after that it was easy and soon she was standing on the other side.

The road was much wider than it used to be but the work had been done carelessly. The felled trees had not been cleared away and the bushes looked trampled. Yet it was the same road and she walked along feeling extraordinarily happy.

It was a fine day, a blue day. The only thing was that the sky had a glassy look that she didn't remember. That was the only word she could think of. Glassy. She turned the corner, saw that what had been the old pavé had been taken up, and there too the road was much wider, but it had the same unfinished look.

She came to the worn stone steps that led up to the house and her heart began to beat. The screw pine was gone, so was the mock summer house called the ajoupa, but the clove tree was still there and at the top of the steps the rough lawn stretched away, just as she remembered it. She stopped and looked towards the house that had been added to and painted white. It was strange to see a car standing in front of it.

There were two children under the big mango tree, a boy and a little girl, and she waved to them and called "Hello" but they didn't answer her or turn their heads. Very fair children, as Europeans born in the West Indies so often are: as if the white blood is asserting itself against all odds.

The grass was yellow in the hot sunlight as she walked towards them. When she was quite close she called again, shyly: "Hello." Then, "I used to live here once," she said.

Still they didn't answer. When she said for the third time "Hello" she was quite near them. Her arms went out instinctively with the longing to touch them.

It was the boy who turned. His grey eyes looked straight into hers. His expression didn't change. He said: "Hasn't it gone cold all of a sudden. D'you notice? Let's go in." "Yes let's," said the girl.

Her arms fell to her sides as she watched them running across the grass to the house. That was the first time she knew.

Questions

1. What does the woman know for the first time?
2. Which details of the story are inconsistent with natural laws?
3. Do you think Rhys believes in ghosts? Can you tell? Does it matter?

MAXINE HONG KINGSTON (1940–)

On Mortality

As you know, any plain person you chance to meet can prove to be a powerful immortal in disguise come to test you.

Li Fu-yen told a story about Tu Tzu-chun, who lived from A.D. 558 to 618, during the Northern Chou and Sui dynasties. Tu's examiner was a Taoist monk, who made him rich twice, and twice Tu squandered his fortune though it took him two lifetimes to do so. The third time the Taoist gave him money, he bought a thousand li of good land, plowed it himself, seeded it, built houses, roads, and bridges, then welcomed widows and orphans to live on it. With the leftover money, he found a husband for each spinster and a wife for every bachelor in his family, and also paid for the weddings. When he met the Taoist again, he said, "I've used up all your money on the unfortunates I've come across."

"You'll have to repay me by working for me," said the Taoist monk. "I need your help on an important difficult task." He gave Tu three white pills. "Swallow these," he said, pouring him a cup of wine. "All that you'll see and feel will be illusions. No matter what happens, don't speak; don't scream. Remember the saying, 'Hide your broken arms in your sleeves.' "

"How easy," said Tu as he swallowed the pills in three gulps of wine. "Why should I scream if I know they're illusions?"

Level by level he descended into the nine hells. At first he saw oxheads, horsefaces, and the heads of generals decapitated in war. Illusions. Only illusions, harmless. He laughed at the heads. He had seen heads before. Soon fewer heads whizzed through the dark until he saw no more of them.

Suddenly his wife was being tortured. Demons were cutting her up into pieces, starting with her toes. He heard her scream; he heard her bones crack. He reminded himself that she was an illusion. *Illusion*, he thought. She was ground into bloodmeal.

Then the tortures on his own body began. Demons poured bronze down his throat and beat him with iron clubs and chains. They mortar-and-pestled and packed him into a pill.

He had to walk over mountains of knives and through fields of knives and forests of swords. He was killed, his head chopped off, rolling into other people's nightmares.

He heard gods and goddesses talking about him, "This man is too wicked to be reborn a man. Let him be born a woman." He saw the entrance of a black tunnel and felt tired. He would have to squeeze his head and shoulders down into the enclosure and travel a long distance. He pushed head first through the entrance, only the beginning. A god kicked him in the butt to give him a move on. (This kick is the reason many Chinese babies have a blue-gray spot on their butts or lower backs, the "Mongolian spot.") Sometimes stuck in the tunnel, sometimes shooting helplessly through it, he emerged again into light with many urgent things to do, many messages to deliver, but his hands were useless baby's hands, his legs wobbly baby's legs, his voice a wordless baby's cries. Years had to pass before he could regain adult powers; he howled as he began to forget the cosmos, his attention taken up with mastering how to crawl, how to stand, how to walk, how to control his bowel movements.

He discovered that he had been reborn a deaf-mute female named Tu. When she became a woman, her parents married her to a man named Lu, who at first did not mind. "Why does she need to talk," said Lu, "to be a good wife? Let her set an example for women." They had a child. But years later, Lu tired of Tu's dumbness. "You're just being stubborn," he said, and lifted their child by the feet. "Talk, or I'll dash its head against the rocks." The poor mother held her hand to her mouth. Lu swung the child, broke its head against the wall.

Tu shouted out, "Oh! Oh!"—and he was back with the Taoist, who sadly told him that at the moment when she said, "Oh! Oh!" the Taoist was about to complete the last step in making the elixir for immortality. Now that Tu had broken his silence, the formula was spoiled, no immortality for the human race. "You overcame joy and sorrow, anger, fear, and evil desire, but not love," said the Taoist, and went on his way.

Questions

1. How has Kingston suggested that her story is historical?
2. At what point is it clear that the story is fantasy?
3. After Tu takes the pills, is what he sees "real" or a hallucination? According to the conventions of the story, is the Taoist monk "real" or a hallucination?
4. How does Kingston's explanation of the "Mongolian spot" alter the notions of "hallucination" and "reality"?
5. Why is man mortal according to this story?
6. Does the Taoist feel that the loss of immortality is a serious loss? Is the Taoist angry at Tu?
7. Is Tu's failure to remain silent understandable? Is Tu able to remember the difference between fiction and reality? What does Tu's failure indicate about the strength of maternal affection?

ARTHUR C. CLARKE (1917–)

The Star

It is three thousand light-years to the Vatican. Once I believed that space could have no power over Faith. Just as I believed that the heavens declared the glory of God's handiwork. Now I have seen that handiwork, and my faith is sorely troubled.

I stare at the crucifix that hangs on the cabin wall above the Mark VI computer, and for the first time in my life I wonder if it is no more than an empty symbol.

I have told no one yet, but the truth cannot be concealed. The data are there for anyone to read, recorded on the countless miles of magnetic tape and the thousands of photographs we are carrying back to Earth. Other scientists can interpret them as easily as I can—more easily, in all probability. I am not one who would condone that tampering with the Truth which often gave my Order a bad name in the olden days.

The crew is already sufficiently depressed, I wonder how they will take this ultimate irony. Few of them have any religious faith, yet they will not relish using this final weapon in their campaign against me—that private, good-natured but fundamentally serious war which lasted all the way from Earth. It amused them to have a Jesuit as chief astrophysicist: Dr. Chandler, for instance, could never get over it (why are medical men such notorious atheists?). Sometimes he would meet me on the observation deck, where the lights are always low so that the stars shine with undiminished glory. He would come up to me in the gloom and stand staring out of the great oval port, while the heavens crawled slowly round us as the ship turned end over end with the residual spin we had never bothered to correct.

"Well, Father," he would say at last. "It goes on forever and forever, and perhaps *Something* made it. But how you can believe that Something has a special interest in us and our miserable little world—that just beats me." Then the argument would start, while the stars and nebulae would swing around us in silent, endless arcs beyond the flawlessly clear plastic of the observation port.

It was, I think, the apparent incongruity of my position which . . . yes, *amused* . . . the crew. In vain I would point to my three papers in the *Astrophysical Journal*, my five in the *Monthly Notices of the Royal Astronomical Society*. I would remind them that our Order has long been famous for its scientific works. We may be few now, but ever since the eighteenth century we have made contributions to astronomy and geophysics out of all proportion to our numbers.

Will my report on the Phoenix Nebula[1] end our thousand years of history? It will end, I fear, much more than that.

I do not know who gave the Nebula its name, which seems to me a very bad one. If it contains a prophecy, it is one which cannot be verified for several thousand million years. Even the word nebula is misleading: this is a far smaller object than those stupendous clouds of mist—the stuff of unborn stars—which are scattered throughout the length of the Milky Way. On the cosmic scale, indeed, the Phoenix Nebula is a tiny thing—a tenuous shell of gas surrounding a single star.

Or what is left of a star . . .

The Rubens engraving of Loyola[2] seems to mock me as it hangs there above the spectrophotometer tracings. What would *you*, Father, have made of this knowledge that has come into my keeping, so far from the little world that was all the universe you knew? Would your faith have risen to the challenge, as mine has failed to do?

You gaze into the distance, Father, but I have traveled a distance beyond any that you could have imagined when you founded our Order a thousand years ago. No other survey ship has been so far from Earth: we are at the very frontiers of the explored universe. We set out to reach the Phoenix Nebula, we succeeded, and we are homeward bound with our burden of knowledge. I wish I could lift that burden from my shoulders, but I call to you in vain across the centuries and the light-years that lie between us.

---

[1] A nebula in astronomy is a cloud-like body of gases and dust. In mythology, the phoenix was a bird that lived for 1000 years before burning after which it was reborn from its own ashes.

[2] Ignatius Loyola (1491–1556) was the founder of the Society of Jesus, commonly called the Jesuits. Peter Paul Rubens (1577–1640) was perhaps the greatest Flemish painter and enormously popular in his day.

On the book you are holding the words are plain to read. AD MAIOREM DEI GLORIAM[3] the message runs, but it is a message I can no longer believe. Would you still believe it, if you could see what we have found?

We knew, of course, what the Phoenix Nebula was. Every year, in *our* galaxy alone, more than a hundred stars explode, blazing for a few hours or days with thousands of times their normal brilliance before they sink back into death and obscurity. Such are the ordinary novae—the commonplace disasters of the universe. I have recorded the spectrograms and light-curves of dozens, since I started working at the lunar observatory.

But three or four times in every thousand years occurs something beside which even a nova pales into total insignificance.

When a star becomes a *supernova*, it may for a little while outshine all the massed suns of the galaxy. The Chinese astronomers watched this happen in 1054 A.D., not knowing what it was they saw. Five centuries later, in 1572, a supernova blazed in Cassiopeia so brilliantly that it was visible in the daylight sky. There have been three more in the thousand years that have passed since then.

Our mission was to visit the remnants of such a catastrophe, to reconstruct the events that led up to it, and, if possible, to learn its cause. We came slowly in through the concentric shells of gas that had been blasted out six thousand years before, yet were expanding still. They were immensely hot, radiating still a fierce violet light, but far too tenuous to do us any damage. When the star had exploded, its outer layers had been driven upwards with such speed that they had escaped completely from its gravitational field. Now they formed a hollow shell large enough to engulf a thousand solar systems, and at its center burned the tiny, fantastic object which the star had now become—a white dwarf, smaller than the Earth yet weighing a million times as much.

The glowing gas shells were all around us, banishing the normal night of interstellar space. We were flying into the center of a cosmic bomb that had detonated millennia ago and whose incandescent fragments were still hurtling apart. The immense scale of the explosion, and the fact that the debris already covered a volume of space many billions of miles across, robbed the scene of any visible movement. It would take decades before the unaided eye could detect any motion in these tortured wisps and eddies of gas, yet the sense of turbulent expansion was overwhelming.

We had checked our primary drive hours before, and were drifting slowly towards the fierce little star ahead. Once it had been a sun like our own, but it had squandered in a few hours the energy that should have kept it shining for a million years. Now it was a shrunken miser, hoarding its resources as if to make amends for its prodigal youth.

No one seriously expected to find planets. If there had been any before the explosion, they would have been boiled into puffs of vapor, and their substance

---

[3] AD MAIOREM DEI GLORIAM is Latin for "To the greater glory of God," the Jesuit motto.

lost in the greater wreckage of the star itself. But we made the automatic search, as always when approaching an unknown sun, and presently we found a single small world circling the star at an immense distance. It must have been the Pluto of this vanished solar system, orbiting on the frontiers of the night. Too far from the central sun ever to have known life, its remoteness had saved it from the fate of all its lost companions.

The passing fires had seared its rocks and burnt away the mantle of frozen gas that must have covered it in the days before the disaster. We landed, and we found the Vault.

Its builders had made sure that we should. The monolithic marker that stood above the entrance was now a fused stump, but even the first long-range photographs told us that here was the work of intelligence. A little later we detected the continent-wide pattern of radioactivity that had been buried in the rock. Even if the pylon above the Vault had been destroyed, this would have remained, an immovable and all but eternal beacon calling to the stars. Our ship fell towards this gigantic bull's-eye like an arrow into its target.

The pylon must have been a mile high when it was built, but now it looked like a candle that had melted down into a puddle of wax. It took us a week to drill through the fused rock, since we did not have the proper tools for a task like this. We were astronomers, not archaeologists, but we could improvise. Our original program was forgotten: this lonely monument, reared at such labor at the greatest possible distance from the doomed sun, could have only one meaning. A civilization which knew it was about to die had made its last bid for immortality.

It will take us generations to examine all the treasures that were placed in the Vault. *They* had plenty of time to prepare, for their sun must have given its first warnings many years before the final detonation. Everything that they wished to preserve, all the fruits of their genius, they brought here to this distant world in the days before the end, hoping that some other race would find them and that they would not be utterly forgotten.

If only they had had a little more time! They could travel freely enough between the planets of their own sun, but they had not yet learned to cross the interstellar gulfs, and the nearest solar system was a hundred light-years away.

Even if they had not been disturbingly human as their sculpture shows, we could not have helped admiring them and grieving for their fate. They left thousands of visual records and the machines for projecting them, together with elaborate pictorial instructions from which it will not be difficult to learn their written language. We have examined many of these records, and brought to life for the first time in six thousand years the warmth and beauty of a civilization which in many ways must have been superior to our own. Perhaps they only showed us the best, and one can hardly blame them. But their worlds were very lovely, and their cities were built with a grace that matches anything of ours. We have watched them at work and play, and listened to their musical speech sounding across the centuries. One scene is still before my eyes—a group of children on a beach of strange blue sand, playing in the waves as children play on Earth.

And sinking into the sea, still warm and friendly and life-giving, is the sun that will soon turn traitor and obliterate all this innocent happiness.

Perhaps if we had not been so far from home and so vulnerable to loneliness, we should not have been so deeply moved. Many of us had seen the ruins of ancient civilizations on other worlds, but they had never affected us so profoundly.

This tragedy was unique. It was one thing for a race to fail and die, as nations and cultures have done on Earth. But to be destroyed so completely in the full flower of its achievement, leaving no survivors—how could that be reconciled with the mercy of God?

My colleagues have asked me that, and I have given what answers I can. Perhaps you could have done better, Father Loyola, but I have found nothing in the *Exercitia Spiritulia*[4] that helps me here. They were not an evil people: I do not know what gods they worshipped, if indeed they worshipped any. But I have looked back at them across the centuries, and have watched while the loveliness they used their last strength to preserve was brought forth again into the light of their shrunken sun.

I know the answers that my colleagues will give when they get back to Earth. They will say that the universe has no purpose and no plan, that since a hundred suns explode every year in our galaxy, at this very moment some race is dying in the depths of space. Whether that race has done good or evil during its lifetime will make no difference in the end: there is no divine justice, *for there is no God.*

Yet, of course, what we have seen proves nothing of the sort. Anyone who argues thus is being swayed by emotion, not logic. God has no need to justify His actions to man. He who built the universe can destroy it when He chooses. It is arrogance—it is perilously near blasphemy—for us to say what He may or may not do.

This I could have accepted, hard though it is to look upon whole worlds and peoples thrown into the furnace. But there comes a point when even the deepest faith must falter, and now, as I look at my calculations, I know I have reached that point at last.

We could not tell, before we reached the nebula, how long ago the explosion took place. Now, from the astronomical evidence and the record in the rocks of that one surviving planet, I have been able to date it very exactly. I know in what year the light of this colossal conflagration reached Earth. I know how brilliantly the supernova whose corpse now dwindles behind our speeding ship once shone in terrestrial skies. I know how it must have blazed low in the East before sunrise, like a beacon in that Oriental dawn.

There can be no reasonable doubt: the ancient mystery is solved at last. Yet—O God, there were so many stars you *could* have used.

---

[4] *Exercitia Spiritulia* is the Latin title of Loyola's principal work, *Spiritual Exercises.*

What was the need to give these people to the fire, that the symbol of their passing might shine above Bethlehem?

Questions

1. To what historical facts or individuals does Clarke refer?
2. What effect do these historical references have on our attitude to the fictional nature of the journey? Do they make the journey seem more probable or less?
3. What conclusions does the narrator draw about the Star of the Nativity? Why do the conclusions disturb him?
4. The speaker in the story is a Jesuit priest. According to the Catholic Church, should faith be based on empirical evidence?
5. Should the narrator hide the information he has found? What should one do with disturbing information? Should scientists suppress scientific fact?

2 ❧ Our Seat on the Action— Narration

Picture for a moment two people sitting at a table with cups of coffee before them. One is telling a story, perhaps about a friend or a relative. You might say that they are gossiping, for like most gossipers they are less interested in the truth of the story than its ability to excite and delight. (In fact, one might say gossip becomes news when the speaker becomes concerned with conveying facts accurately.) The listener leans forward to catch each word. At various moments he or she interjects the question, "And what happened next?" or "And then what did they do?"

Such a scene conveys the essence of storytelling. We have a storyteller, an audience, and the story itself. In more formal situations, we have the writer, the reader, and the text. The question the listener asks is also part of the essence of storytelling. Stories are concerned with a sequence of actions. These actions can be hard and external—a battle, a murder, an escape from prison—or they can be subtle and internal. In Jean Rhys's "I Used to Live Here Once," the action consists of a woman crossing a stream and waving to two children and then recognizing that she is dead. In Rhys's story the act of recognition is the central and most important action. Quite often in fiction the most important changes and actions take place in the characters' minds. We will examine other aspects of fiction in Chapters 4 and 5. But now we are concerned with the narrator and with the ways by which a reader learns the story's "facts."

Basic Narrative Types

A story is typically told in two different ways: by someone involved in the action, or by someone wholly outside of the action. The voice that tells us the story is called the *narrator*. If someone involved in the action tells the story, he or she usually says, "*I* did this," or "*I* saw that." Because they use the first-person pronoun, these stories are called *first-person narratives*. In *third-person narratives*, the narrators generally do not refer to themselves. They remain outside of the story's action. The simplest sort of third-person narrator is called the *omniscient narrator*. Omniscient means "all knowing," and an omniscient narrator can tell the reader anything pertinent to the story no matter when it occurred, where it happened, or who did it. An omniscient narrator can enter the minds of all the characters and tell the reader what they saw, thought, and felt.

Each of these basic narrative types has its own advantages and disadvantages, and one of the hardest decisions an author must make is whether to cast a story as a first- or third-person narration.

An Omniscient Narration

One of the most interesting books exploring the various ways a story can be told is Raymond Queneau's *Exercises in Style*. In that book, Queneau tells the same everyday story in 99 different ways. Nor does Queneau exhaust the narrative possibilities, for he never tells the story in the manner of an omniscient narrator. If he had, he might have written this version:

> A young man with a long neck and funny hat, which was circled by string rather than by a hatband, entered a crowded bus one day. The man standing next to him did not like the young man's looks and decided to poke the young man in the ribs whenever a passenger moved through the aisle. Thinking that he was being deliberately poked, the young man shouted at his neighbor. When the first empty seat came vacant, the young man ran for it.
> Later that day, the young man met a friend who advised him to alter his ill-fitting coat.

Notice that the narrator never refers to him- or herself. Indeed, an omniscient narrator is more like a god than a person, a consciousness that can move wherever it pleases. In sentence 2, for example, the narrator tells us what the older man is thinking; he doesn't like the somewhat odd young man and decides to hurt him. In sentence 3, however, the narrator is in the mind of the young man, telling us the young man's thoughts. Finally, in the last sentence, the narrator has moved off the bus and witnesses the young man talking to a friend.

The First-Person Narrative

The author who adopts a first-person narration must follow certain conventions. Unlike omniscient narrators who can follow the actions and thoughts of all the characters, first-person narrators are limited to telling us what they themselves saw, heard, thought, felt. They can also make reasonable assumptions about what other characters see, think, or feel. In real life, we infer from people's actions and words what they think or feel. If people yell at us, we assume they are angry or upset. So, too, a first-person narrator can make assumptions about the thoughts and feelings of other characters. But as readers we must keep in mind that these assumptions are only the narrator's. They need not be our assumptions or the author's assumptions. In the next chapter, we will study the *unreliable narrator*—a narrator whose version of the story we, as readers, come to doubt—but for the moment it is enough to remember that first-person narratives are limited by the fictional perspective of a character involved in the action.

Here are three of Queneau's narratives. They are all first-person narratives, but because each narrator has a different relationship to the fictional action, the stories they tell are very different.

RAYMOND QUENEAU (1903-1976)

From Exercises in Style

Narrative

One day at about midday in the Parc Monceau[1] district, on the back platform of a more or less full S bus (now No. 84), I observed a person with a very long neck who was wearing a felt hat which had a plaited cord round it instead of a ribbon. This individual suddenly addressed the man standing next to him, accusing him of purposely treading on his toes every time any passengers got on or off. However he quickly abandoned the dispute and threw himself onto a seat which had become vacant.

Two hours later I saw him in front of the Gare Saint-Lazare[2] engaged in earnest conversation with a friend who was advising him to reduce the space between the lapels of his overcoat by getting a competent tailor to raise the top button.

The Subjective Side

I was not displeased with my attire this day. I was inaugurating a new, rather sprightly hat, and an overcoat of which I thought most highly. Met X in front of the Gare Saint-Lazare who tried to spoil my pleasure by trying to prove that this overcoat is cut too low at the lapels and that I ought to have an extra button on it. At least he didn't dare attack my headgear.

A bit earlier I had roundly told off a vulgar type who was purposely ill-treating me every time anyone went by getting off or on. This happened in one of those unspeakably foul omnibi which fill up with hoi polloi precisely at those times when I have to consent to use them.

Another Subjectivity

Next to me on the bus platform today there was one of those half-baked young fellows, you don't find so many of them these days, thank God, otherwise I should end up by killing one. This particular one, a brat of something like 26

[1] The Parc Monceau is a public garden in Paris.
[2] The Gare Saint-Lazare is one of the principal railway stations of Paris.

or 30, irritated me particularly not so much because of his great long featherless-turkey's neck as because of the nature of the ribbon round his hat, a ribbon which wasn't much more than a sort of maroon-coloured string. Dirty beast! He absolutely disgusted me! As there were a lot of people in our bus at that hour I took advantage of all the pushing and shoving there is every time anyone gets on or off to dig him in the ribs with my elbow. In the end he took to his heels, the milksop, before I could make up my mind to tread on his dogs to teach him a lesson. I could also have told him, just to annoy him, that he needed another button on his overcoat which was cut too low at the lapels.

Certain aspects of the story are quite clearly different in these three versions. For instance, the third narrator does not mention the young man's meeting with his friend in front of the Gare Saint-Lazare. The reason, of course, is that he wasn't there and had no way of knowing that it took place. Thus Queneau, following the conventions of first-person narratives, leaves out the meeting. Another clear difference is the way in which the young man orders the events. He tells about his meeting at the Gare Saint-Lazare first. The meeting is the more important event for him, because the meeting gave him the opportunity to show off his new clothes.

Perhaps of more interest is the way in which the bystander's account differs from the accounts of the more immediate participants. For example, the bystander says that the young man accused the older man of "purposely treading on his toes," whereas the older man claims he was poking the young man in the ribs. The first narrator also has a different version of the young man's conversation with his friend. According to the young man, the friend is advising adding a button—not having the top button raised. How do we account for such discrepancies? Usually we apply to a fictional situation the same sorts of explanations we apply to real life (unless, of course, the conventions of the story rule out such explanations). Here we might say that the bystander was just too far away to get all the details, though he correctly observes the basic events.

Of greatest interest is the way in which the characters' attitudes color their versions of the story. The young man sees his accoster as a "vulgar type," one of the "hoi polloi" whom he "roundly told off." In the older man's version, the young man is "a brat," a "dirty beast" and a "milksop." The older man seems to think he got the better of the argument. The bystander makes far fewer evaluations; he takes a matter-of-fact attitude toward what must be a frequent event on the crowded buses of Paris.

Narrative Point-of-View

These three narratives show us the consequences of *narrative point-of-view*. Narrative point-of-view has two aspects: physical point-of-view and psychological point-of-view. Physical point-of-view is the clearer. Where we are in relation to an event influences the way we experience it. If we are involved in a car accident, we will see the event from one perspective. If we are standing on the sidewalk, we will have another. If we are in a helicopter overhead, we will get a bird's-eye view.

Psychological point-of-view is far subtler. A person's preferences and prejudices shade descriptions. Often word choice will be a clue to the narrator's feelings. One narrator may describe a color as "lively," another narrator might describe it as "garish." The first hints of approval; the second shows disapproval. The bystander reveals his attitude toward the event. He writes that the young man "suddenly" accused the older man, then "quickly abandoned the dispute" and then "threw himself onto a seat." The combination of the words "suddenly," "quickly," and "threw" indicates the bystander's feeling that the young man behaved rashly and violently, and that the bystander disapproves.

Limited Third-Person Narratives

First-person narratives have certain advantages. They bring the reader closer to the action; they infuse the story with great psychological and narrative subtlety; they are a natural way to tell a story. But first-person narratives have limitations: they lack flexibility and objectivity. As readers, we can learn only what the narrator has learned, and the narrator's point-of-view colors the telling of events. Third-person narratives are far more flexible, but they seem colder and more distant. Writers have sought to combine the advantages of these two modes of narration by creating a variant: the *limited third-person narrator*. The limited third-person narrator speaks of the action from a point outside of the events—thus gaining distance and objectivity—but is limited to the perspective of one of the characters and tells the story through what that character experiences and thinks. Thus, we could write yet a fifth version of the bus incident:

> The young man was pleased with his attire as he stood in the crowded Paris bus that day. "What a nice hat I have on," he thought, "I like this cord instead of the usual hatband." Gradually he realized that the man next to him was poking him in the ribs whenever he had the opportunity. The young man began to argue with his fellow passenger, but then a seat became vacant. He hurried to sit down. "Such vulgar people ride the bus these days," the young man said to himself as he admired the cut of his coat.

Notice the advantages of this sort of narrative. We see the scene as though we were a participant, but we can step back and evaluate the principal character more objectively: though the young man is certainly vain, he isn't a troublemaker.

Stories without Narrators

In the stories we have been discussing, the narrator is fully aware that he or she is telling a story. But some stories do not have such self-conscious narrators. Some stories are made up of documents which when pieced together give an attentive reader enough narrative information to construct a story. For example, some stories—including some novels—are a collection of letters. By reading the exchange of letters, the reader can reconstruct the action. The *epistolary narrative*, one that consists of letters, is demanding both of the author and the reader. Samual Richardson's *Pamela* and *Clarissa* are well known examples of epistolary novels.

Narratives can also be constructed from pages of a fictional diary. Nicolai Gogol's "Diary of a Madman" is one of the more famous stories constructed in this manner. V. S. Naipaul's "The Nightwatchman's Occurrence Book" is another story without a single, self-conscious narrator. The story is a sequence of notes between the nightwatchman and two hotel managers. As you read it, pay close attention to the shifting narrative points-of-view, which result in a wonderfully comic conclusion.

Suggestions for Essayists

1. Discuss how point-of-view affects political debate. For example, discuss how coming from the Middle East might affect one's attitude toward oil prices.
2. Discuss whether men and women can share the same point-of-view or whether biology alters one's perspective.

Suggestions for Fiction Writers

1. Narrate the same event from at least three different first-person perspectives.
2. Narrate the same event from both omniscient and limited third-person perspectives.
3. Pretend you are a character in a story talking to a third-person narrator. What do you want the narrator to know? What arguments of interpretation would you have with the narrator? Why won't the narrator tell the story your way? Write the dialogue between the narrator and the character.

TONI CADE BAMBARA (1939–)

My Man Bovanne

Blind people got a hummin jones if you notice. Which is understandable completely once you been around one and notice what no eyes will force you into to see people, and you get past the first time, which seems to come out of nowhere, and it's like you in church again with fat-chest ladies and old gents gruntin a hum low in the throat to whatever the preacher be saying. Shakey Bee bottom lip all swole up with Sweet Peach and me explainin how come the sweet-potato bread was a dollar-quarter this time stead of dollar regular and he say uh hunh he understand, then he break into this *thizzin* kind of hum which is quiet, but fiercesome just the same, if you ain't ready for it. Which I wasn't. But I got used to it and the onliest time I had to say somethin bout it was when he was playin checkers on the stoop one time and he commenst to hummin quite churchy seem to me. So I says, "Look here Shakey Bee, I can't beat you and Jesus too." He stop.

So that's how come I asked My Man Bovanne to dance. He ain't my man mind you, just a nice ole gent from the block that we all know cause he fixes things and the kids like him. Or used to fore Black Power[1] got hold their minds and mess em around till they can't be civil to ole folks. So we at this benefit for my niece's cousin who's runnin for somethin with this Black party somethin or other behind her. And I press up close to dance with Bovanne who blind and I'm hummin and he hummin, chest to chest like talkin. Not jammin my breasts into the man. Wasn't bout tits. Was bout vibrations. And he dug it and asked me what color dress I had on and how my hair was fixed and how I was doin without a man, not nosy but nice-like, and who was at this affair and was the canapés dainty-stingy or healthy enough to get hold of proper. Comfy and cheery is what I'm tryin to get across. Touch talkin like the heel of the hand on the tambourine or on a drum.

But right away Joe Lee come up on us and frown for dancin so close to the man. My own son who knows what kind of warm I am about; and don't grown men call me long distance and in the middle of the night for a little Mama comfort? But he frown. Which ain't right since Bovanne can't see and defend himself. Just a nice old man who fixes toasters and busted irons and bicycles and things and changes the lock on my door when my men friends get messy. Nice man. Which is not why they invited him. Grass roots you see. Me and Sister Taylor and the woman who does heads[2] at Mamies and the man from the barber shop, we all there on account of we grass roots.[3] And I ain't never been souther than Brooklyn Battery[4] and no more country than the window box on my fire escape. And just yesterday my kids tellin me to take them countrified rags off my head and be cool. And now can't get Black enough to suit em. So everybody passin sayin My Man Bovanne. Big deal, keep steppin and don't even stop a minute to get the man a drink or one of them cute sandwiches or tell him what's goin on. And him standin there with a smile ready case someone do speak he want to be ready. So that's how come I pull him on the dance floor and we dance squeezin past the tables and chairs and all them coats and people standin round up in each other face talkin bout this and that but got no use for this blind man who mostly fixed skates and skooters for all these folks when they was just kids. So I'm pressed up close and we touch talkin with the hum. And here come my daughter cuttin her eye at me like she do when she tell me about my "apolitical" self like I got hoof and mouf disease and there ain't no hope at all. And I don't pay her no mind and just look up in Bovanne shadow face and tell him his stomach like a drum and he laugh. Laugh real loud. And here come my youngest, Task, with a tap on my elbow like he the third grade monitor and I'm cuttin up on the line to assembly.

---

[1] Black Power was a slogan of certain Civil Rights groups during the 1960s and 70s.
[2] Hairdresser.
[3] "Grass roots" refers to the common people.
[4] Brooklyn Battery is a section of Brooklyn, New York.

"I was just talkin on the drums," I explained when they hauled me into the kitchen. I figured drums was my best defense. They can get ready for drums what with all this heritage business. And Bovanne stomach just like that drum Task give me when he come back from Africa. You just touch it and it hum thizzm, thizzm. So I stuck to the drum story. "Just drummin that's all."

"Mama, what are you talkin about?"

"She had too much to drink," say Elo to Task cause she don't hardly say nuthin to me direct no more since that ugly argument about my wigs.

"Look here Mama," say Task, the gentle one. "We just tryin to pull your coat. You were makin a spectacle of yourself out there dancing like that."

"Dancin like what?"

Task run a hand over his left ear like his father for the world and his father before that.

"Like a bitch in heat," say Elo.

"Well uhh, I was goin to say like one of them sex-starved ladies gettin on in years and not too discriminating. Know what I mean?"

I don't answer cause I'll cry. Terrible thing when your own children talk to you like that. Pullin me out the party and hustlin me into some stranger's kitchen in the back of a bar just like the damn police. And ain't like I'm old old. I can still wear me some sleeveless dresses without the meat hangin off my arm. And I keep up with some thangs through my kids. Who ain't kids no more. To hear them tell it. So I don't say nuthin.

"Dancin with that tom,"[5] say Elo to Joe Lee, who leanin on the folks' freezer. "His feet can smell a cracker a mile away and go into their shuffle number post haste. And them eyes. He could be a little considerate and put on some shades. Who wants to look into them blown-out fuses that—"

"Is this what they call the generation gap?" I say.

"Generation gap," spits Elo, like I suggested castor oil and fricassee possum in the milk-shakes or somethin. "That's a white concept for a white phenomenon. There's no generation gap among Black people We are a col—"

"Yeh, well never mind," says Joe Lee. "The point is Mama . . . well, it's pride. You embarrass yourself and us too dancin like that."

"I wasn't shame." Then nobody say nuthin. Them standin there in they pretty clothes with drinks in they hands and gangin up on me, and me in the third-degree chair and nary a olive to my name. Felt just like the police got hold to me.

"First of all," Task say, holdin up his hand and tickin off the offenses, "the dress. Now that dress is too short, Mama, and too low-cut for a woman your age. And Tamu's going to make a speech tonight to kick off the campaign and will be introducin you and expecting you to organize the council of elders—"

---

[5] "Tom" is short for "Uncle Tom," the central character in Harriet Beecher Stowe's novel *Uncle Tom's Cabin*. Uncle Tom is a term of derision used against Blacks who act in a subservient manner to Whites.

"Me? Didn nobody ask me nuthin. You mean Nisi? She change her name?"

"Well, Norton was supposed to tell you about it. Nisi wants to introduce you and then encourage the older folks to form a Council of the Elders to act as an advisory—"

"And you going to be standing there with your boobs out and that wig on your head and that hem up to your ass. And people'll say, 'Ain't that the horny bitch that was grindin with the blind dude?' "

"Elo, be cool a minute," say Task, gettin to the next finger. "And then there's the drinkin. Mama, you know you can't drink cause next thing you know you be laughin loud and carryin on," and he grab another finger for the loudness. "And then there's the dancin. You been tattooed on the man for four records straight and slow draggin even on the fast numbers. How you think that look for a woman your age?"

"What's my age?"

"What?"

"I'm axin you all a simple question. You keep talkin bout what's proper for a woman my age. How old am I anyhow?" And Joe Lee slams his eyes shut and squinches up his face to figure. And Task run a hand over his ear and stare into his glass like the ice cubes goin calculate for him. And Elo just starin at the top of my head like she goin rip the wig off any minute now.

"Is your hair braided up under that thing? If so, why don't you take it off? You always did do a neat cornroll."

"Uh huh," cause I'm thinkin how she couldn't undo her hair fast enough talking bout cornroll so countrified. None of which was the subject. "How old, I say?"

"Sixtee-one or—"

"You a damn lie Joe Lee Peoples."

"And that's another thing," say Task on the fingers.

"You know what you all can kiss," I say, gettin up and brushin the wrinkles out my lap.

"Oh, Mama," Elo say, puttin a hand on my shoulder like she hasn't done since she left home and the hand landin light and not sure it supposed to be there. Which hurt me to my heart. Cause this was the child in our happiness fore Mr. Peoples die. And I carried that child strapped to my chest till she was nearly two. We was close is what I'm trying to tell you. Cause it was more me in the child than the others. And even after Task it was the girlchild I covered in the night and wept over for no reason at all less it was she was a chub-chub like me and not very pretty, but a warm child. And how did things get to this, that she can't put a sure hand on me and say Mama we love you and care about you and you entitled to enjoy yourself cause you a good woman?

"And then there's Reverend Trent," say Task, glancin from left to right like they hatchin a plot and just now lettin me in on it. "You were suppose to be talkin with him tonight, Mama, about giving us his basement for campaign headquarters and—"

"Didn nobody tell me nuthin. If grass roots mean you kept in the dark I can't use it. I really can't. And Reven Trent a fool anyway the way he tore into the widow man up there on Edgecomb cause he wouldn't take in three of them foster children and the woman not even comfy in the ground yet and the man's mind messed up and—"

"Look here," say Task. "What we need is a family conference so we can get all this stuff cleared up and laid out on the table. In the meantime I think we better get back into the other room and tend to business. And in the meantime, Mama, see if you can't get to Reverend Trent and—"

"You want me to belly rub with the Reven, that it?"

"Oh damn," Elo say and go through the swingin door.

"We'll talk about all this at dinner. How's tomorrow night, Joe Lee?" While Joe Lee being self-important I'm wonderin who's doin the cookin and how come no body ax me if I'm free and do I get a corsage and things like that. Then Joe nod that it's O.K. and he go through the swingin door and just a little hubbub come through from the other room. Then Task smile his smile, lookin just like his daddy and he leave. And it just me in this stranger's kitchen, which was a mess I wouldn't never let my kitchen look like. Poison you just to look at the pots. Then the door swing the other way and it's My Man Bovanne standin there sayin Miss Hazel but lookin at the deep fry and then at the steam table, and most surprised when I come up on him from the other direction and take him on out of there. Pass the folks pushin up towards the stage where Nisi and some other people settin and ready to talk, and folks gettin to the last of the sandwiches and the booze fore they settle down in one spot and listen serious. And I'm thinkin bout tellin Bovanne what a lovely long dress Nisi got on and the earrings and her hair piled up in a cone and the people bout to hear how we all gettin screwed and gotta form our own party[6] and everybody there listenin and lookin. But instead I just haul the man on out of there, and Joe Lee and his wife look at me like I'm terrible, but they ain't said boo to the man yet. Cause he blind and old and don't nobody there need him since they grown up and don't need they skates fixed no more.

"Where we goin, Miss Hazel?" Him knowin all the time.

"First we gonna buy you some dark sunglasses. Then you comin with me to the supermarket so I can pick up tomorrow's dinner, which is goin to be a grand thing proper and you invited. Then we goin to my house."

"That be fine. I surely would like to rest my feet." Bein cute, but you got to let men play out they little show, blind or not. So he chat on bout how tired he is and how he appreciate me takin him in hand this way. And I'm thinkin I'll have him change the lock on my door first thing. Then I'll give the man a nice warm bath with jasmine leaves in the water and a little Epsom salt on the sponge to do his back. And then a good rubdown with rose water and olive oil. Then a cup of lemon tea with a taste in it. And a little talcum, some of that

---

[6] Political party.

fancy stuff Nisi mother sent over last Christmas. And then a massage, a good face massage round the forehead which is the worryin part. Cause you gots to take care of the older folks. And let them know they still needed to run the mimeo machine and keep the spark plugs clean and fix the mailboxes for folks who might help us get the breakfast program goin, and the school for the little kids and the campaign and all. Cause old folks is the nation. That what Nisi was sayin and I mean to do my part.

"I imagine you are a very pretty woman, Miss Hazel."

"I surely am," I say just like the hussy my daughter always say I was.

Questions

1. Is this a first- or third-person narrative?
2. Why do you suppose Bambara chose this sort of narration? Could an omniscient narrator have told the story as vividly or more vividly?
3. Why do the narrator's children object to her dancing with Bovanne?
4. Do the children think of themselves as being open-minded? Are they?
5. Nisi says, "old folks is the nation." What does she mean? Do you agree?
6. What sort of preconception do you have about the way older people should act?

MARGARET ATWOOD (1939–)

Giving Birth

But who gives it? And to whom is it given? Certainly it doesn't feel like giving, which implies a flow, a gentle handing over, no coercion. But there is scant gentleness here; it's too strenuous, the belly like a knotted fist, squeezing, the heavy trudge of the heart, every muscle in the body tight and moving, as in a slow-motion shot of a high-jump, the faceless body sailing up, turning, hanging for a moment in the air, and then—back to real time again—the plunge, the rush down, the result. Maybe the phrase was made by someone viewing the result only: in this case, the rows of babies to whom birth has occurred, lying like neat packages in their expertly wrapped blankets, pink or blue, with their labels Scotch Taped to their clear plastic cots, behind the plate-glass window.

No one ever says *giving death*, although they are in some ways the same, events, not things. And *delivering*, that act the doctor is generally believed to perform: who delivers what? Is it the mother who is delivered, like a prisoner being released? Surely not; nor is the child delivered to the mother like a letter through a slot. How can you be both the sender and the receiver at once? Was someone in bondage, is someone made free? Thus language, muttering in its archaic tongues of something, yet one more thing, that needs to be re-named.

It won't be by me, though. These are the only words I have, I'm stuck with them, stuck in them. (That image of the tar sands, old tableau in the Royal Ontario Museum, second floor north, how persistent it is. Will I break free, or will I be sucked down, fossilized, a sabre-toothed tiger or lumbering brontosaurus who ventured out too far? Words ripple at my feet, black, sluggish, lethal. Let me try once more, before the sun gets me, before I starve or drown, while I can. It's only a tableau after all, it's only a metaphor. See, I can speak, I am not trapped, and you on your part can understand. So we will go ahead as if there were no problem about language.)

This story about giving birth is not about me. In order to convince you of that I should tell you what I did this morning, before I sat down at this desk— a door on top of two filing cabinets, radio to the left, calendar to the right, these devices by which I place myself in time. I got up at twenty-to-seven, and, halfway down the stairs, met my daughter, who was ascending, autonomously she thought, actually in the arms of her father. We greeted each other with hugs and smiles; we then played with the alarm clock and the hot water bottle, a ritual we go through only on the days her father has to leave the house early to drive into the city. This ritual exists to give me the illusion that I am sleeping in. When she finally decided it was time for me to get up, she began pulling my hair. I got dressed while she explored the bathroom scales and the mysterious white altar of the toilet. I took her downstairs and we had the usual struggle over her clothes. Already she is wearing miniature jeans, miniature T-shirts. After this she fed herself: orange, banana, muffin, porridge.

We then went out to the sun porch, where we recognized anew, and by their names, the dog, the cats and the birds, blue jays and goldfinches at this time of year, which is winter. She puts her fingers on my lips as I pronounce these words; she hasn't yet learned the secret of making them. I am waiting for her first word: surely it will be miraculous, something that has never yet been said. But if so, perhaps she's already said it and I, in my entrapment, my addiction to the usual, have not heard it.

In her playpen I discovered the first alarming thing of the day. It was a small naked woman, made of that soft plastic from which jiggly spiders and lizards and the other things people hang in their car windows are also made. She was given to my daughter by a friend, a woman who does props for movies, she was supposed to have been a prop but she wasn't used. The baby loved her and would crawl around the floor holding her in her mouth like a dog carrying a bone, with the head sticking out one side and the feet out the other. She seemed chewy and harmless, but the other day I noticed that the baby had managed to make a tear in the body with her new teeth. I put the woman into the cardboard box I use for toy storage.

But this morning she was back in the playpen and the feet were gone. The baby must have eaten them, and I worried about whether or not the plastic would dissolve in her stomach, whether it was toxic. Sooner or later, in the contents of her diaper, which I examine with the usual amount of maternal brooding, I knew I would find two small pink plastic feet. I removed the doll and later, while she was still singing to the dog outside the window, dropped it into the garbage. I am not up to finding tiny female arms, breasts, a head, in my daughter's disposable diapers, partially covered by undigested carrots and the husks of raisins, like the relics of some gruesome and demented murder.

Margaret Atwood   33

Now she's having her nap and I am writing this story. From what I have said, you can see that my life (despite these occasional surprises, reminders of another world) is calm and orderly, suffused with that warm, reddish light, those well-placed blue highlights and reflecting surfaces (mirrors, plates, oblong window-panes) you think of as belonging to Dutch genre[1] paintings; and like them it is realistic in detail and slightly sentimental. Or at least it has an aura of sentiment. (Already I'm having moments of muted grief over those of my daughter's baby clothes which are too small for her to wear any more. I will be a keeper of hair, I will store things in trunks, I will weep over photos.) But above all it's solid, everything here has solidity. No more of those washes of light, those shifts, nebulous effects of cloud, Turner sunsets,[2] vague fears, the impalpables Jeanie used to concern herself with.

I call this woman Jeanie after the song.[3] I can't remember any more of the song, only the title. The point (for in language there are always these "points," these reflections; this is what makes it so rich and sticky, this is why so many have disappeared beneath its dark and shining surface, why you should never try to see your own reflection in it; you will lean over too far, a strand of your hair will fall in and come out gold, and, thinking it is gold all the way down, you yourself will follow, sliding into those outstretched arms, towards the mouth you think is opening to pronounce your name but instead, just before your ears fill with pure sound, will form a word you have never heard before. . . .)

The point, for me, is in the hair. My own hair is not light brown, but Jeanie's was. This is one difference between us. The other point is the dreaming; for Jeanie isn't real in the same way that I am real. But by now, and I mean your time, both of us will have the same degree of reality, we will be equal: wraiths, echoes, reverberations in your own brain. At the moment though Jeanie is to me as I will someday be to you. So she is real enough.

Jeanie is on her way to the hospital, to give birth, to be delivered. She is not quibbling over these terms. She's sitting in the back seat of the car, with her eyes closed and her coat spread over her like a blanket. She is doing her breathing exercises and timing her contractions with a stopwatch. She has been up since two-thirty in the morning, when she took a bath and ate some lime Jell-O, and it's now almost ten. She has learned to count, during the slow breathing, in numbers (from one to ten while breathing in, from ten to one while breathing out) which she can actually see while she is silently pronouncing them. Each number is a different colour and, if she's concentrating very hard, a different typeface. They range from plain roman to ornamented circus numbers, red with gold filigree and dots. This is a refinement not mentioned in any of the numerous books she's read on the subject. Jeanie is a devotee of handbooks. She has at

---

[1] Dutch genre paintings are extremely precise depictions of domestic life of nearly photographic exactness.

[2] J. M. W. Turner (1775–1851) was a British painter known for his enormous landscapes filled with light.

[3] "I Dream of Jeanie (with the Light Brown Hair)" is a song composed by the American songwriter Stephen Foster (1826–1864).

least two shelves of books that cover everything from building kitchen cabinets to auto repairs to smoking your own hams. She doesn't do many of these things, but she does some of them, and in her suitcase, along with a washcloth, a package of lemon Life Savers, a pair of glasses, a hot water bottle, some talcum powder and a paper bag, is the book that suggested she take along all of these things.

(By this time you may be thinking that I've invented Jeanie in order to distance myself from these experiences. Nothing could be further from the truth. I am, in fact, trying to bring myself closer to something that time has already made distant. As for Jeanie, my intention is simple: I am bringing her back to life.)

There are two other people in the car with Jeanie. One is a man, whom I will call A., for convenience. A. is driving. When Jeanie opens her eyes, at the end of every contraction, she can see the back of his slightly balding head and his reassuring shoulders. A. drives well and not too quickly. From time to time he asks her how she is, and she tells him how long the contractions are lasting and how long there is between them. When they stop for gas he buys them each a Styrofoam container of coffee. For months he has helped her with the breathing exercises, pressing on her knee as recommended by the book, and he will be present at the delivery. (Perhaps it's to him that the birth will be given, in the same sense that one gives a performance.) Together they have toured the hospital maternity ward, in company with a small group of other pairs like them: one thin solicitous person, one slow bulbous person. They have been shown the rooms, shared and private, the sitz-baths, the delivery room itself, which gave the impression of being white. The nurse was light-brown, with limber hips and elbows; she laughed a lot as she answered questions.

"First they'll give you an enema. You know what it is? They take a tube of water and put it up your behind. Now, the gentlemen must put on this—and these, over your shoes. And these hats, this one for those with long hair, this for those with short hair."

"What about those with no hair?" says A.

The nurse looks up at his head and laughs. "Oh, you still have some," she says. "If you have a question, do not be afraid to ask."

They have also seen the film made by the hospital, a full-colour film of a woman giving birth to, can it be a baby? "Not all babies will be this large at birth," the Australian nurse who introduces the movie says. Still, the audience, half of which is pregnant, doesn't look very relaxed when the lights go on. ("If you don't like the visuals," a friend of Jeanie's has told her, "you can always close your eyes.") It isn't the blood so much as the brownish-red disinfectant that bothers her. "I've decided to call this whole thing off," she says to A., smiling to show it's a joke. He gives her a hug and says, "Everything's going to be fine."

And she knows it is. Everything will be fine. But there is another woman in the car. She's sitting in the front seat, and she hasn't turned or acknowledged Jeanie in any way. She, like Jeanie, is going to the hospital. She too is pregnant. She is not going to the hospital to give birth, however, because the words, the words, are too alien to her experience, the experience she is about to have, to be used about it at all. She's wearing a cloth coat with checks in maroon and brown, and she has a kerchief tied over her hair. Jeanie has seen her before, but she knows little about her except that she is a woman who did not wish to become pregnant, who did not choose to divide herself like this, who did not choose any of these ordeals, these initiations. It would be no use telling her that everything is going to be fine. The word in English for unwanted intercourse is rape. But there is no word in the language for what is about to happen to this woman.

Jeanie has seen this woman from time to time throughout her pregnancy, always in the same coat, always with the same kerchief. Naturally, being pregnant herself has made her more aware of other pregnant women, and she has watched them, examined them covertly, every time she has seen one. But not every other pregnant woman is this woman. She did not, for instance, attend Jeanie's pre-natal classes at the hospital, where the women were all young, younger than Jeanie.

"How many will be breast-feeding?" asks the Australian nurse with the hefty shoulders.

All hands but one shoot up. A modern group, the new generation, and the one lone bottle-feeder, who might have (who knows?) something wrong with her breasts, is ashamed of herself. The others look politely away from her. What they want most to discuss, it seems, are the differences between one kind of disposable diaper and another. Sometimes they lie on mats and squeeze each other's hands, simulating contractions and counting breaths. It's all very hopeful. The Australian nurse tells them not to get in and out of the bathtub by themselves. At the end of an hour they are each given a glass of apple juice.

There is only one woman in the class who has already given birth. She's there, she says, to make sure they give her a shot this time. They delayed it last time and she went through hell. The others look at her with mild disapproval. *They* are not clamouring for shots, they do not intend to go through hell. Hell comes from the wrong attitude, they feel. The books talk about *discomfort*.

"It's not discomfort, it's pain, baby," the woman says.

The others smile uneasily and the conversation slides back to disposable diapers.

Vitaminized, conscientious, well-read Jeanie, who has managed to avoid morning sickness, varicose veins, stretch marks, toxemia and depression, who has had no aberrations of appetite, no blurrings of vision—why is she followed, then, by this other? At first it was only a glimpse now and then, at the infants' clothing section in Simpson's Basement, in the supermarket lineup, on street corners as she herself slid by in A.'s car: the haggard face, the bloated torso, the kerchief holding back the too-sparse hair. In any case, it was Jeanie who saw her, not the other way around. If she knew she was following Jeanie she gave no sign.

As Jeanie has come closer and closer to this day, the unknown day on which she will give birth, as time has thickened around her so that it has become something she must propel herself through, a kind of slush, wet earth underfoot, she has seen this woman more and more often, though always from a distance. Depending on the light, she has appeared by turns as a young girl of perhaps twenty to an older woman of forty or forty-five, but there was never any doubt in Jeanie's mind that it was the same woman. In fact it did not occur to her that the woman was not real in the usual sense (and perhaps she was, originally, on the first or second sighting, as the voice that causes an echo is real), until A. stopped for a red light during this drive to the hospital and the woman, who had been standing on the corner with a brown paper bag in her arms, simply opened the front door of the car and got in. A. didn't react, and Jeanie knows better than to say anything to him. She is aware that the woman is not really there: Jeanie is not crazy. She could even make the woman disappear by opening her eyes wider, by staring, but it is only the shape that would go away, not the feeling. Jeanie isn't exactly afraid of this woman. She is afraid for her.

When they reach the hospital, the woman gets out of the car and is through the door by the time A. has come around to help Jeanie out of the back seat. In the lobby she is nowhere to be seen. Jeanie goes through Admission in the usual way, unshadowed.

There has been an epidemic of babies during the night and the maternity ward is overcrowded. Jeanie waits for her room behind a dividing screen. Nearby someone is screaming, screaming and mumbling between screams in what sounds like a foreign language. Portuguese, Jeanie thinks. She tells herself that for them it is different, you're supposed to scream, you're regarded as queer if you don't scream, it's a required part of giving birth. Nevertheless she knows that the woman screaming is the other woman and she is screaming from pain. Jeanie listens to the other voice, also a woman's, comforting, reassuring: her mother? A nurse?

A. arrives and they sit uneasily, listening to the screams. Finally Jeanie is sent for and she goes for her prep. Prep school, she thinks. She takes off her clothes— when will she see them again?—and puts on the hospital gown. She is examined, labelled around the wrist and given an enema. She tells the nurse she can't take Demerol[4] because she's allergic to it, and the nurse writes this down. Jeanie doesn't know whether this is true or not but she doesn't want Demerol, she has read the books. She intends to put up a struggle over her pubic hair—surely she will lose her strength if it is all shaved off—but it turns out the nurse doesn't have very strong feelings about it. She is told her contractions are not far enough along to be taken seriously, she can even have lunch. She puts on her dressing gown and rejoins A., in the freshly vacated room, eats some tomato soup and a veal cutlet, and decides to take a nap while A. goes out for supplies.

Jeanie wakes up when A. comes back. He has brought a paper, some detective novels for Jeanie and a bottle of Scotch for himself. A. reads the paper and drinks Scotch, and Jeanie reads *Poirot's Early Cases*.[5] There is no connection

---

[4] Demerol is a potent painkiller.
[5] *Poirot's Early Cases* is a collection of stories about the fictional detective Hercule Poirot written by Agatha Christie (1891–1976).

between Poirot and her labour, which is now intensifying, unless it is the egg-shape of Poirot's head and the vegetable marrows he is known to cultivate with strands of wet wool (placentae? umbilical cords?). She is glad the stories are short; she is walking around the room now, between contractions. Lunch was definitely a mistake.

"I think I have back labour," she says to A. They get out the handbook and look up the instructions for this. It's useful that everything has a name. Jeanie kneels on the bed and rests her forehead on her arms while A. rubs her back. A. pours himself another Scotch, in the hospital glass. The nurse, in pink, comes, looks, asks about the timing, and goes away again. Jeanie is beginning to sweat. She can only manage half a page or so of Poirot before she has to clamber back up on the bed again and begin breathing and running through the coloured numbers.

When the nurse comes back, she has a wheelchair. It's time to go down to the labour room, she says. Jeanie feels stupid sitting in the wheelchair. She tells herself about peasant women having babies in the fields, Indian women having them on portages with hardly a second thought. She feels effete.[6] But the hospital wants her to ride, and considering the fact that the nurse is tiny, perhaps it's just as well. What if Jeanie were to collapse, after all? After all her courageous talk. An image of the tiny pink nurse, antlike, trundling large Jeanie through the corridors, rolling her along like a heavy beach ball.

As they go by the check-in desk a woman is wheeled past on a table, covered by a sheet. Her eyes are closed and there's a bottle feeding into her arm through a tube. Something is wrong. Jeanie looks back—she thinks it was the other woman—but the sheeted table is hidden now behind the counter.

In the dim labour room Jeanie takes off her dressing gown and is helped up onto the bed by the nurse. A. brings her suitcase, which is not a suitcase actually but a small flight bag, the significance of this has not been lost on Jeanie, and in fact she now has some of the apprehensive feelings she associates with planes, including the fear of a crash. She takes out her Life Savers, her glasses, her washcloth and the other things she thinks she will need. She removes her contact lenses and places them in their case, reminding A. that they must not be lost. Now she is purblind.

There is something else in her bag that she doesn't remove. It's a talisman, given to her several years ago as a souvenir by a travelling friend of hers. It's a rounded oblong of opaque blue glass, with four yellow-and-white eye shapes on it. In Turkey, her friend has told her, they hang them on mules to protect against the Evil Eye. Jeanie knows this talisman probably won't work for her, she is not Turkish and she isn't a mule, but it makes her feel safer to have it in the room with her. She had planned to hold it in her hand during the most difficult part of labour but somehow there is no longer any time for carrying out plans like this.

An old woman, a fat old woman dressed all in green, comes into the room and sits beside Jeanie. She says to A., who is sitting on the other side of Jeanie,

---

[6] *Effete* is an adjective that means exhausted, incapable of efficient action.

"That is a good watch. They don't make watches like that any more." She is referring to his gold pocket watch, one of his few extravagances, which is on the night table. Then she places her hand on Jeanie's belly to feel the contraction. "This is good," she says, her accent is Swedish or German. "This, I call a contraction. Before, it was nothing." Jeanie can no longer remember having seen her before. "Good. Good."

"When will I have it?" Jeanie asks, when she can talk, when she is no longer counting.

The old woman laughs. Surely that laugh, those tribal hands, have presided over a thousand beds, a thousand kitchen tables . . . "A long time yet," she says. "Eight, ten hours."

"But I've been *doing* this for twelve hours already," Jeanie says.

"Not hard labour," the woman says. "Not good, like this."

Jeanie settles into herself for the long wait. At the moment she can't remember why she wanted to have a baby in the first place. That decision was made by someone else, whose motives are now unclear. She remembers the way women who had babies used to smile at one another, mysteriously, as if there was something they knew that she didn't, the way they would casually exclude her from their frame of reference. What was the knowledge, the mystery, or was having a baby really no more inexplicable than having a car accident or an orgasm? (But these too were indescribable, events of the body, all of them; why should the mind distress itself trying to find a language for them?) She has sworn she will never do that to any woman without children, engage in those passwords and exclusions. She's old enough, she's been put through enough years of it to find it tiresome and cruel.

But—and this is the part of Jeanie that goes with the talisman hidden in her bag, not with the part that longs to build kitchen cabinets and smoke hams— she is, secretly, hoping for a mystery. Something more than this, something else, a vision. After all she is risking her life, though it's not too likely she will die. Still, some women do. Internal bleeding, shock, heart failure, a mistake on the part of someone, a nurse, a doctor. She deserves a vision, she deserves to be allowed to bring something back with her from this dark place into which she is now rapidly descending.

She thinks momentarily about the other woman. Her motives, too, are unclear. Why doesn't she want to have a baby? Has she been raped, does she have ten other children, is she starving? Why hasn't she had an abortion? Jeanie doesn't know, and in fact it no longer matters why. *Uncross your fingers*, Jeanie thinks to her. Her face, distorted with pain and terror, floats briefly behind Jeanie's eyes before it too drifts away.

Jeanie tries to reach down to the baby, as she has many times before, sending waves of love, colour, music, down through her arteries to it, but she finds she can no longer do this. She can no longer feel the baby as a baby, its arms and legs poking, kicking, turning. It has collected itself together, it's a hard sphere, it does not have time right now to listen to her. She's grateful for this because she isn't sure anyway how good the message would be. She no longer has control of the numbers either, she can no longer see them, although she continues mechanically to count. She realizes she has practised for the wrong thing, A. squeezing her knee was nothing, she should have practised for this, whatever it is.

"Slow down," A. says. She's on her side now, he's holding her hand. "Slow it right down."

"I can't, I can't do it, I can't do this."

"Yes, you can."

"Will I sound like that?"

"Like what?" A. says. Perhaps he can't hear it: it's the other woman, in the room next door or the room next door to that. She's screaming and crying, screaming and crying. While she cries she is saying, over and over, "It hurts. It hurts."

"No, you won't," he says. So there is someone, after all.

A doctor comes in, not her own doctor. They want her to turn over on her back.

"I can't," she says. "I don't like it that way." Sounds have receded, she has trouble hearing them. She turns over and the doctor gropes with her rubber-gloved hand. Something wet and hot flows over her thighs.

"It was just ready to break," the doctor says. "All I had to do was touch it. Four centimetres," she says to A.

"Only *four*?" Jeanie says. She feels cheated; they must be wrong. The doctor says her own doctor will be called in time. Jeanie is outraged at them. They have not understood, but it's too late to say this and she slips back into the dark place, which is not hell, which is more like being inside, trying to get out. *Out*, she says or thinks. Then she is floating, the numbers are gone, if anyone told her to get up, go out of the room, stand on her head, she would do it. From minute to minute she comes up again, grabs for air.

"You're hyperventilating,"[7] A. says. "Slow it down." He is rubbing her back now, hard, and she takes his hand and shoves it viciously further down, to the right place, which is not the right place as soon as his hand is there. She remembers a story she read once, about the Nazis tying the legs of Jewish women together during labor. She never really understood before how that could kill you.

A nurse appears with a needle. "I don't want it," Jeanie says.

"Don't be hard on yourself," the nurse says. "You don't have to go through pain like that." What pain? Jeanie thinks. When there is no pain she feels nothing, when there is pain, she feels nothing because there is no *she*. This, finally, is the disappearance of language. *You don't remember afterwards*, she has been told by almost everyone.

Jeanie comes out of a contraction, gropes for control. "Will it hurt the baby?" she says.

---

[7] Hyperventilation is a medical condition in which patients cannot stop their excessively rapid breathing.

"It's a mild analgesic,"[8] the doctor says. "We wouldn't allow anything that would hurt the baby." Jeanie doesn't believe this. Nevertheless she is jabbed, and the doctor is right, it is very mild, because it doesn't seem to do a thing for Jeanie, though A. later tells her she has slept briefly between contractions.

Suddenly she sits bolt upright. She is wide awake and lucid. "You have to ring that bell right now," she says. "This baby is being born."

A. clearly doesn't believe her. "I can feel it, I can feel the head," she says. A. pushes the button for the call bell. A nurse appears and checks, and now everything is happening too soon, nobody is ready. They set off down the hall, the nurse wheeling. Jeanie feels fine. She watches the corridors, the edges of everything shadowy because she doesn't have her glasses on. She hopes A. will remember to bring them. They pass another doctor.

"Need me?" she asks.

"Oh no," the nurse answers breezily. "Natural childbirth."

Jeanie realizes that this woman must have been the anaesthetist. "What?" she says, but it's too late now, they are in the room itself, all those glossy surfaces, tubular strange apparatus like a science-fiction movie, and the nurse is telling her to get onto the delivery table. No one else is in the room.

"You must be crazy," Jeanie says.

"Don't push," the nurse says.

"What do you mean?" Jeanie says. This is absurd. Why should she wait, why should the baby wait for them because they're late?

"Breathe through your mouth," the nurse says. "Pant," and Jeanie finally remembers how. When the contraction is over she uses the nurse's arm as a lever and hauls herself across onto the table.

From somewhere her own doctor materializes, in her doctor suit already, looking even more like Mary Poppins than usual, and Jeanie says, "Bet you weren't expecting to see me so soon!" The baby is being born when Jeanie said it would, though just three days ago the doctor said it would be at least another week, and this makes Jeanie feel jubilant and smug. Not that she knew, she'd believed the doctor.

She's being covered with a green tablecloth, they are taking far too long, she feels like pushing the baby out now, before they are ready. A. is there by her head, swathed in robes, hats, masks. He has forgotten her glasses. "Push now," the doctor says. Jeanie grips with her hands, grits her teeth, face, her whole body together, a snarl, a fierce smile, the baby is enormous, a stone, a boulder, her bones unlock, and, once, twice, the third time, she opens like a birdcage turning slowly inside out.

A pause; a wet kitten slithers between her legs. "Why don't you look?" says the doctor, but Jeanie still has her eyes closed. No glasses, she couldn't have seen a thing anyway. "Why don't you look?" the doctor says again.

Jeanie opens her eyes. She can see the baby, who has been wheeled up beside

---

[8] An analgesic is a pain reliever.

her and is fading already from the alarming birth purple. A good baby, she thinks, meaning it as the old woman did: *a good watch*, well-made, substantial. The baby isn't crying; she squints in the new light. Birth isn't something that has been given to her, nor has she taken it. It was just something that has happened so they could greet each other like this. The nurse is stringing beads for her name. When the baby is bundled and tucked beside Jeanie, she goes to sleep.

As for the vision, there wasn't one. Jeanie is conscious of no special knowledge; already she's forgetting what it was like. She's tired and very cold; she is shaking, and asks for another blanket. A. comes back to the room with her; her clothes are still there. Everything is quiet, the other woman is no longer screaming. Something has happened to her, Jeanie knows. Is she dead? Is the baby dead? Perhaps she is one of those casualties (and how can Jeanie herself be sure, yet, that she will not be among them) who will go into postpartum depression[9] and never come out. "You see, there was nothing to be afraid of," A. says before he leaves, but h~ was wrong.

The next morning Jeanie wakes up when it's light. She's been warned about getting out of bed the first time without the help of a nurse, but she decides to do it anyway (peasant in the field! Indian on the portage!). She's still running adrenaline, she's also weaker than she thought, but she wants very much to look out the window. She feels she's been inside too long, she wants to see the sun come up. Being awake this early always makes her feel a little unreal, a little insubstantial, as if she's partly transparent, partly dead.

(It was to me, after all, that the birth was given, Jeanie gave it, I am the result. What would she make of me? Would she be pleased?)

The window is two panes with a venetian blind sandwiched between them; it turns by a knob at the side. Jeanie has never seen a window like this before. She closes and opens the blind several times. Then she leaves it open and looks out.

All she can see from the window is a building. It's an old stone building, heavy and Victorian, with a copper roof oxidized to green. It's solid, hard, darkened by soot, dour, leaden. But as she looks at this building, so old and seemingly immutable, she sees that it's made of water. Water, and some tenuous jelly-like substance. Light flows through it from behind (the sun is coming up), the building is so thin, so fragile, that it quivers in the slight dawn wind. Jeanie sees that if the building is this way (a touch could destroy it, a ripple of the earth, why has no one noticed, guarded it against accidents?) then the rest of the world must be like this too, the entire earth, the rocks, people, trees, everything needs to be protected, cared for, tended. The enormity of this task defeats her; she will never be up to it, and what will happen then?

Jeanie hears footsteps in the hall outside her door. She thinks it must be the other woman, in her brown-and-maroon-checked coat, carrying her paper bag,

---

[9] Postpartum depression is a psychological condition in which a mother feels dispirited after the birth of her child.

leaving the hospital now that her job is done. She has seen Jeanie safely through, she must go now to hunt through the streets of the city for her next case. But the door opens, it's a nurse, who is just in time to catch Jeanie as she sinks to the floor, holding on to the edge of the air-conditioning unit. The nurse scolds her for getting up too soon.

After that the baby is carried in, solid, substantial, packed together like an apple, Jeanie examines her, she is complete, and in the days that follow Jeanie herself becomes drifted over with new words, her hair slowly darkens, she ceases to be what she was and is replaced, gradually, by someone else.

Questions

1. What kind of narration is "Giving Birth"?
2. What is the narrator's relationship to Jeanie?
3. Why does the narrator feel the need to prove she is *not* Jeanie? Does the evidence prove her point?
4. What is the relationship between Jeanie and the other woman who "did not wish to become pregnant"? Is there a reason the other woman is not given a name?
5. Who is A.? Is there a reason for his having no name?
6. Why does Jeanie think she deserves a vision? Does she get a vision?
7. In what ways has the other woman "seen Jeanie safely through [her delivery]"?
8. The narrator states that "giving birth" and "giving death . . . are in some ways the same." In what ways are they the same?

V. S. NAIPAUL (1932–)

The Night Watchman's Occurrence Book

November 21. 10.30 p.m. C. A. Cavander take over duty at C——Hotel all corrected. *Cesar Alwyn Cavander*

7 a.m. C. A. Cavander hand over duty to Mr Vignales at C——Hotel no report. *Cesar Alwyn Cavander*

November 22. 10.30 p.m. C. A. Cavander take over duty at C——Hotel no report. *Cesar Alwyn Cavander*

7 a.m. C. A. Cavander hand over duty to Mr Vignales at C——Hotel all corrected. *Cesar Alwyn Cavander*

> This is the third occasion on which I have found C. A. Cavander, Night Watchman, asleep on duty. Last night, at 12.45 a.m., I found him sound asleep in a rocking chair in the hotel lounge. Night Watchman Cavander has therefore been dismissed.
> Night Watchman Hillyard: This book is to be known in future as "The Night Watchman's Occurrence Book." In it I shall expect to find a detailed account of everything that happens in the hotel tonight. Be warned by the example of ex-Night Watchman Cavander, *W. A. G. Inskip, Manager*

Mr Manager, remarks noted. You have no worry where I am concern sir. *Charles Ethelbert Hillyard, Night Watchman*

November 23. 11 p.m. Night Watchman Hillyard take over duty at C——Hotel with one torch light 2 fridge keys and room keys 1, 3, 6, 10 and 13. Also 25 cartoons Carib Beer and 7 cartoons Heineken[1] and 2 cartoons American cigarettes. Beer cartoons intact Bar intact all corrected no report. *Charles Ethelbert Hillyard*

7 a.m. Night Watchman Hillyard hand over duty to Mr Vignales at C——Hotel with one torch light 2 fridge keys and room keys, 1, 3, 6, 10 and 13. 32 cartoons beer. Bar intact all corrected no report. *Charles Ethelbert Hillyard*

> Night Watchman Hillyard: Mr Wills complained bitterly to me this morning that last night he was denied entry to the bar by you. I wonder if you know exactly what the purpose of this hotel is. In future all hotel guests are to be allowed entry to the bar at whatever time they choose. It is your duty simply to note what they take. This is one reason why the hotel provides a certain number of beer cartons (please note the spelling of this word). W. A. G. *Inskip*

Mr Manager, remarks noted. I sorry I didnt get the chance to take some education sir. *Chas. Ethelbert Hillyard*

November 24. 11 p.m. N. W. Hillyard take over duty with one Torch, 1 Bar Key, 2 Fridge Keys, 32 cartoons Beer, all intact. 12 Midnight Bar close and Barman left leaving Mr Wills and others in Bar, and they left at 1 a.m. Mr Wills took 16 Carib Beer, Mr Wilson 8, Mr Percy 8. At 2 a.m. Mr Wills come back in the bar and take 4 Carib and some bread, he cut his hand trying to cut the bread, so please dont worry about the stains on the carpet sir. At 6 a.m. Mr Wills come back for some soda water. It didn't have any so he take a ginger beer instead. Sir you see it is my intention to do this job good sir, I cant see how Night Watchman Cavander could fall asleep on this job sir. *Chas. Ethelbert Hillyard*

> You always seems sure of the time, and guests appear to be in the habit of entering the bar on the hour. You will kindly note the exact time. The clock from the kitchen is left on the window near the switches. You can use this clock but you MUST replace it every morning before you go off duty. W. A. G. *Inskip*

Noted. *Chas. Ethelbert Hillyard*

November 25. Midnight Bar close and 12.23 a.m. Barman left leaving Mr Wills and others in Bar. Mr Owen take 5 bottles Carib, Mr Wilson 6 bottles Heineken, Mr Wills 18 Carib and they left at 2.52 a.m. Nothing unusual. Mr. Wills was helpless, I don't see how anybody could drink so much, eighteen one man alone, this work enough to turn anybody Seventh Day Adventist, and another man come in the bar, I dont know his name, I hear they call him Paul, he assist me

---

[1] Heineken is a Dutch beer.

because the others couldn't do much, and we take Mr Wills up to his room and take off his boots and slack his other clothes and then we left. Don't know sir if they did take more while I was away, nothing was mark on the Pepsi Cola board, but they was drinking still, it looks as if they come back and take some more, but with Mr Wills I want some extra assistance sir.

Mr Manager, the clock break I find it break when I come back from Mr Wills room sir. It stop 3.19 sir. *Chas. E. Hillyard*

More than 2 lbs of veal were removed from the Fridge last night, and a cake that was left in the press was cut. It is your duty, Night Watchman Hillyard, to keep an eye on these things. I ought to warn you that I have also asked the Police to check on all employees leaving the hotel, to prevent such occurrences in the future. W. A. G. *Inskip*

Mr Manager, I don't know why people so anxious to blame servants sir. About the cake, the press lock at night and I dont have the key sir, everything safe where I am concern sir. *Chas. Hillyard*

November 26. Midnight Bar close and Barman left. Mr Wills didn't come, I hear he at the American base tonight, all quiet, nothing unusual.

Mr Manager, I request one thing. Please inform the Barman to let me know sir when there is a female guest in the hotel sir. *C. E. Hillyard*

This morning I received a report from a guest that there were screams in the hotel during the night. You wrote All Quiet. Kindly explain in writing. W. A. G. *Inskip* Write Explanation here:

EXPLANATION. Not long after midnight the telephone ring and a woman ask for Mr Jimminez. I try to tell her where he was but she say she cant hear properly. Fifteen minutes later she came in a car, she was looking vex and sleepy, and I went up to call him. The door was not lock, I went in and touch his foot and call him very soft, and he jump up and begin to shout. When he come to himself he said he had Night Mere, and then he come down and went away with the woman, was not necessary to mention.

Mr Manager, I request you again, please inform the Barman to let me know sir when there is a female guest in the Hotel. *C. Hillyard*

November 27. 1 a.m. Bar close, Mr Wills and a American 19 Carib and 2.30 a.m. a Police come and ask for Mr Wills, he say the American report that he was robbed of $200.00¢, he was last drinking at the C——with Mr Wills and others. Mr Wills and the Police ask to open the Bar to search it, I told them I cannot open the Bar for you like that, the Police must come with the Manager. Then the American say it was only joke he was joking, and they try to get the Police to laugh, but the Police looking the way I feeling. Then laughing Mr Wills left in a garage car as he couldn't drive himself and the American was waiting outside and they both fall down as they was getting in the car, and Mr Wills saying any time you want a overdraft you just come to my bank kiddo. The Police left walking by himself. *C. Hillyard*

Night Watchman Hillyard: "Was not necessary to mention"!! You are not to decide what is necessary to mention in this night watchman's occurrence book. Since when have you become sole owner of the hotel as to determine what is necessary to mention? If the guest did not mention it I would never have known that there were screams in the hotel during the night. Also will you kindly tell me who Mr Jimminez is? And what rooms he occupied or occupies? And by what right? You have been told by me personally that the names of all hotel guests are on the slate next to the light switches. If you find Mr Jimminez's name on this slate, or could give me some information about him, I will be most warmly obliged to you. The lady you ask about is Mrs Roscoe, Room 12, as you very well know. It is your duty to see that guests are not pestered by unauthorized callers. You should give no information about guests to such people, and I would be glad if in future you could direct such callers straight to me. W. A. G. Inskip

Sir was what I ask you two times, I dont know what sort of work I take up, I always believe that nightwatchman work is a quiet work and I dont like meddling in white people business, but the gentleman occupy Room 12 also, was there that I went up to call him, I didn't think it necessary to mention because was none of my business sir. C.E.H.

November 28. 12 Midnight Bar close and Barman left at 12.20 a.m. leaving Mr Wills and others, and they all left at 1.25 a.m. Mr Wills 8 Carib, Mr Wilson 12, Mr Percy 8, and the man they call Paul 12. Mrs Roscoe join the gentlemen at 12.33 a.m., four gins, everybody calling her Minnie from Trinidad, and then they start singing that song, and some others. Nothing unusual. Afterwards there were mild singing and guitar music in Room 12. A man come in and ask to use the phone at 2.17 a.m. and while he was using it about 7 men come in and wanted to beat him up, so he put down the phone and they all ran away. At 3 a.m. I notice the padlock not on the press, I look inside, no cake, but the padlock was not put on in the first place sir. Mr Wills come down again at 6 a.m. to look for his sweet, he look in the Fridge and did not see any. He took a piece of pineapple. A plate was covered in the Fridge, but it didn't have anything in it. Mr Wills put it out, the cat jump on it and it fall down and break. The garage bulb not burning. C.E.H.

You will please sign your name at the bottom of your report. You are in the habit of writing Nothing Unusual. Please take note and think before making such a statement. I want to know what is meant by nothing unusual. I gather, not from you, needless to say, that the police have fallen into the habit of visiting the hotel at night. I would be most grateful to you if you could find the time to note the times of these visits. W. A. G. Inskip

Sir, nothing unusual means everything usual. I dont know, nothing I writing you liking. I dont know what sort of work this night watchman work getting to be, since when people have to start getting Cambridge certificate to get night watchman job, I ain't educated and because of this everybody think they could insult me. Charles Ethelbert Hillyard

November 29. Midnight Bar close and 12.15 Barman left leaving Mr Wills and Mrs Roscoe and others in the Bar. Mr Wills and Mrs Roscoe left at 12.30 a.m.

leaving Mr Wilson and the man they call Paul, and they all left at 1.00 a.m. Twenty minutes to 2 Mr Wills and party return and left again at 5 to 3. At 3.45 Mr Wills return and take break and milk and olives and cherries, he ask for nutmeg too, I said we had none, he drink 2 Carib, and left ten minutes later. He also collect Mrs Roscoe bag. All the drinks, except the 2 Carib, was taken by the man they call Paul. I don't know sir I don't like this sort of work, you better hire a night barman. At 5.30 Mrs Roscoe and the man they call Paul come back to the bar, they was having a quarrel, Mr Paul saying you make me sick, Mrs Roscoe saying I feel sick, and then she vomit all over the floor, shouting I didn't want that damned milk. I was cleaning up when Mr Wills come down to ask for soda water, we got to lay in more soda for Mr Wills, but I need extra assistance with Mr Wills Paul and party sir.

The police come at 2, 3.48 and 4.52. They sit down in the bar a long time. Firearms discharge 2 times in the back yard. Detective making inquiries. I dont know sir, I thinking it would be better for me to go back to some other sort of job. At 3 I hear somebody shout Thief, and I see a man running out of the back, and Mr London, Room 9, say he miss 80 cents and a pack of cigarettes which was on his dressing case. I don't know when the people in this place does sleep. *Chas. Ethelbert Hillyard*

> Night Watchman Hillyard: A lot more than 80 cents was stolen. Several rooms were in fact entered during the night, including my own. You are employed to prevent such things occurring. Your interest in the morals of our guests seems to be distracting your attention from your duties. Save your preaching for your roadside prayer meetings. Mr Pick, Room 7, reports that in spite of the most pressing and repeated requests, you did not awaken him at 5. He has missed his plane to British Guiana as a result. No newspapers were delivered to the rooms this morning. I am again notifying you that papers must be handed personally to Doorman Vignales. And the messenger's bicycle, which I must remind you is the property of the hotel, has been damaged. What do you *do* at nights? *W. A. G. Inskip*

Please don't ask me sir.

Relating to the damaged bicycle: I left the bicycle the same place where I meet it, nothing took place so as to damage it. I always take care of all property sir. I don't know how you could think I have time to go out for bicycle rides. About the papers, sir, the police and them read it and leave them in such a state that I didn't think it would be nice to give them to guests. I wake up Mr Pick, room 7, at 4.50 a.m. 5 a.m. 5.15 a.m. and 5.30. He told me to keep off, he would not get up, and one time he pelt a box of matches at me, matches scatter all over the place. I always do everything to the best of my ability sir but God is my Witness I never find a night watchman work like this, so much writing I dont have time to do anything else, I dont have four hands and six eyes and I want this extra assistance with Mr Wills and party sir. I am a poor man and you could abuse me, but you must not abuse my religion sir because the good Lord sees All and will have His revenge sir, I don't know what sort of work and trouble I land myself in, all I want is a little quiet night work and all I getting is abuse. *Chas. E. Hillyard*

November 30. 12.25 a.m. Bar close and Barman left 1.00 a.m. leaving Mr Wills and party in Bar. Mr Wills take 12 Carib, Mr Wilson 6, Mr Percy 14. Mrs Roscoe five gins. At 1.30 a.m. Mrs Roscoe left and there were a little singing and mild guitar playing in Room 12. Nothing unusual. The police came at 1.35 and sit down in the bar for a time, not drinking, not talking, not doing anything except watching. At 1.45 the man they call Paul come in with Mr. McPherson of the SS Naparoni, they was both falling down and laughing whenever anything break and the man they call Paul say Fireworks about to begin tell Minnie Malcolm coming the ship just dock. Mr Wills and party scatter leaving one or two bottles half empty and then the man they call Paul tell me to go up to Room 12 and tell Minnie Roscoe that Malcolm coming. I don't know how people could behave so the thing enough to make anybody turn priest. I notice the padlock on the bar door break off it hanging on only by a little piece of wood. And when I went up to Room 12 and tell Mrs Roscoe that Malcolm coming the ship just dock the woman get sober straight away like she dont want to hear no more guitar music and she asking me where to hide where to go. I dont know, I feel the day of reckoning is at hand, but she not listening to what I saying, she busy straightening up the room one minute packing the next, and then she run out into the corridor and before I could stop she she run straight down the back stairs to the annexe. And then 5 past 2, still in the corridor, I see a big red man running up to me and he sober as a judge and he mad as a drunkard and he asking me where she is where she is. I ask whether he is a authorized caller, he say you don't give me any of that crap now, where she is, where she is. So remembering about the last time Mr Jimminez I direct him to the manager office in the annexe. He hear a little scuffling inside Mr Inskip room and I make out Mr Inskip sleepy voice and Mrs Roscoe voice and the red man run inside and all I hearing for the next five minutes is bam bam bodow bodow bow and this woman screaming. I dont know what sort of work this night watchman getting I want something quiet like the police. In time things quiet down and the red man drag Mrs Roscoe out of the annexe and they take a taxi, and the Police sitting down quiet in the bar. Then Mr Percy and the others come back one by one to the bar and they talking quiet and they not drinking and they left 3 a.m. 3.15 Mr Wills return and take one whisky and 2 Carib. He asked for pineapple or some sweet fruit but it had nothing.

6 a.m. Mr Wills come in the bar looking for soda but it aint have none. We have to get some soda for Mr Wills sir.
6.30 a.m. the papers come and I deliver them to Doorman Vignales at 7 a.m. *Chas. Hillyard*

Mr Hillyard: In view of the unfortunate illness of Mr. Inskip, I am temporarily in charge of the hotel. I trust you will continue to make your nightly reports, but I would be glad if you could keep your entries as brief as possible. *Robt. Magnus, Acting Manager*

December 1. 10.30 p.m. C. E. Hillyard take over duty at C——Hotel all corrected 12 Midnight Bar close 2 a.m. Mr Wills 2 Carib, 1 bread 6 a.m. Mr Wills 1 soda 7 a.m. Night Watchman Hillyard hand over duty to Mr Vignales with one torch light 2 Fridge keys and Room Keys 1, 3, 6 and 12. Bar intact all corrected no report. *C.E.H.*

Questions

1. What sort of hotel is the C——Hotel?
2. Of what social class is Hillyard?
3. Of what race is Hillyard?
4. What is Inskip's attitude toward Hillyard?
5. What does Inskip think of himself?
6. How can you account for Inskip's attitude toward Hillyard?
7. What is Hillyard's attitude toward Inskip?
8. How does Hillyard bring about his own troubles?
9. What do you imagine is the source of Inskip's "unfortunate illness"?

3   Unreliable Narrators — Don't Believe Everything You Hear

The Credibility of Witnesses

When a jury hears a case, it has to decide which witnesses to believe. The jury listens to the testimony, evaluates which accounts seem the most plausible, and sifts the evidence for contradictions. But it may base its decision on something less tangible—the credibility of the witness. Witnesses are judged as much on the manner of their testimony as on the substance of it.

What makes one witness credible and another less credible? First, no matter how well a witness speaks, the jury will be suspicious of a witness who might gain by lying. If someone might benefit from telling a lie, then clearly the person's testimony is suspect. Second, witnesses who seem confused or disoriented are less credible than those who speak with confidence and clarity. If one doesn't understand an event, one can hardly be a reliable witness of what happened. The confused witness often mixes up the sequence of actions and fails to recognize important but subtle signs and cues. Third, a witness who is emotionally unstable will not be a credible witness. The witness's feelings will so distort the nature of events, that, without meaning to, he or she will give a false impression of what actually occurred.

We judge the reliability of speakers all the time. When people seem confused in giving street directions, we are likely to distrust them and go on to ask someone else. When salespersons seem too eager to make a sale or when they apply too much pressure, we tend to be suspicious of their motives. When people seem distraught or disturbed, we tend to distrust their accounts.

Writers are fascinated by the way in which good listeners can detect a speaker who is not credible and see through the speaker's distortions and lies. Consequently, many authors tell their stories with *unreliable narrators*—narrators whose accounts of events the reader recognizes as faulty, distorted, or untrustworthy.

Readers recognize the unreliability of narrators in the same manner that they recognize the lack of credibility in a witness. Unreliable narrators have something to gain by their falsehood, do not understand the stories they are asked to tell, or—and this is the most common cause—are too emotionally or psychologically disturbed to give a trustworthy account of events.

Irony in Unreliable Narrations

Part of the interest of unreliable narrations is the ironic relationship they create between the narrator's point-of-view and the reader's point-of-view. Irony is a complex phenomenon. Usually it involves a word, phrase, situation, or condition that comes to mean the opposite of what was intended. For example, it is ironic when a doctor sets out to help an injured person and ends up being sued for malpractice. Or when a student says, "I'm afraid of failing this course," and then earns an A.

Because the reader understands the situation better than the narrator, the reader perceives a number of ironies in what the narrator says. In "The Yellow Wall-Paper," for instance, the narrator repeatedly assures herself that her husband, a doctor, has her best interests at heart and that his medical advice will bring her back to health. The reader, however, comes to understand—as she does not—that the regimen her husband has prescribed is the cause of her illness. Unreliable narrators constantly make statements which mean something different than they realize. Thus such narratives always operate on at least two levels: what the narrator wishes the reader to understand and what the reader ultimately realizes.

Authors' and Narrators' Points-of-View

The unreliable narrative is probably the clearest example of a story in which the narrator does not articulate the author's ideas, values, or attitudes. But one should never uncritically identify the narrator as the author or immediately assume that the narrator speaks for the author. Frequently the narrator's attitude—even in omniscient narrations—is more matter-of-fact, more neutral than is the author's. Usually authors avoid spelling out the values and attitudes that are contained in their stories, letting readers discover these values and attitudes for themselves. Authors avoid such explicit statements of intent in order to keep their stories from becoming sermons.

However, not all first-person narratives are unreliable. One must draw a distinction between the *limitations* of a narrator's point-of-view and the distortions of an unreliable narrator. If we examine Queneau's three versions of the bus argument, we see that all three narrators give fairly accurate accounts of the incidents. The older man is "vulgar," as the young man accuses him of being. And the young man is ridiculously vain, "a milksop," as the older man says. The difference between their stories is that neither narrator recognizes his own faults. Each is blind to his own failings. Their accounts are limited by their points-of-view. The unreliable narrator distorts what is happening, misrepresents people or things, misjudges experience. As readers, we must imaginatively reconstruct the fictional events to make them more reasonable, logical, and fair. Indeed, much of the fun and critical interest in unreliable narrators comes from ·trying to figure out how the narrator has distorted events.

Finally, unreliable narrations are not necessarily limited to realistic stories. Even an unrealistic tale can be narrated by an unreliable narrator, forcing the reader to reconstruct what "really" happened. Here, for example, is the Wolf's account of "Little Red Riding Hood."

> Listen, Woodman, I can explain everything. There's no need to kill me with your axe. You see, the little girl invited me in. She said, "You look so hungry, I'm sure my grandmother will feed you." She looked like a nice innocent kid, so I followed her to her grandmother's house. But as soon as I got inside, bam! She pulled out this butcher knife. She went wild, I tell you. Started screaming that if I didn't do what she told me to do she would cut me into little steak cubes. I was so frightened, I huddled next to the bed. But when she got near me, I tried to get the cleaver away from her. She was quick—boy, was she quick!—and cut me here and here. What else could I do? It was self-defense. If I hadn't eaten her up, she would have killed me.

Suggestions for Essayists

1. Discuss the morality of lying. Is it ever right to tell a lie? Can lies protect people, governments, a cause?
2. Write about the most notorious liar you know. What sorts of lies does this person tell? How can you tell that the person is lying?
3. Describe how you can tell when someone is distorting the truth. What signs do you look for? How do you verify your suspicions?

Suggestions for Fiction Writers

1. Rewrite a fairy tale from the point-of-view of the villain. What sorts of distortions occur when villains try to make their acts seem reasonable and sympathetic?
2. Newspapers are filled with the terrible acts of disturbed persons. Taking the basic events from a newspaper account, narrate what happened, using the disturbed person's voice.

CHARLOTTE PERKINS GILMAN (1860–1935)

The Yellow Wall-Paper

It is very seldom that mere ordinary people like John and myself secure ancestral halls for the summer.

A colonial mansion, a hereditary estate, I would say a haunted house, and reach the height of romantic felicity—but that would be asking too much of fate!

Still I will proudly declare that there is something queer about it.

Else, why should it be let so cheaply? And why have stood so long untenanted?

John laughs at me, of course, but one expects that in marriage.

John is practical in the extreme. He has no patience with faith, an intense horror of superstition, and he scoffs openly at any talk of things not to be felt and seen and put down in figures.

John is a physician, and *perhaps*—(I would not say it to a living soul, of course, but this is dead paper and a great relief to my mind)—*perhaps* that is one reason I do not get well faster.

You see he does not believe I am sick!

And what can one do?

If a physician of high standing, and one's own husband, assures friends and relatives that there is really nothing the matter with one but temporary nervous depression—a slight hysterical tendency—what is one to do?

My brother is also a physician, and also of high standing, and he says the same thing.

So I take phosphates or phospites—whichever it is, and tonics, and journeys, and air, and exercise, and am absolutely forbidden to "work" until I am well again.

Personally, I disagree with their ideas.

Personally, I believe that congenial work, with excitement and change, would do me good.

But what is one to do?

I did write for a while in spite of them; but it *does* exhaust me a good deal—having to be so sly about it, or else meet with heavy opposition.

I sometimes fancy that in my condition if I had less opposition and more society and stimulus—but John says the very worst thing I can do is to think about my condition, and I confess it always makes me feel bad.

So I will let it alone and talk about the house.

The most beautiful place! It is quite alone, standing well back from the road, quite three miles from the village. It makes me think of English places that you read about, for there are hedges and walls and gates that lock, and lots of separate little houses for the gardeners and people.

There is a *delicious* garden! I never saw such a garden—large and shady, full of box-bordered paths, and lined with long grape-covered arbors with seats under them.

There were greenhouses, too, but they are all broken now.

There was some legal trouble, I believe, something about the heirs and coheirs; anyhow, the place has been empty for years.

That spoils my ghostliness, I am afraid, but I don't care—there is something strange about the house—I can feel it.

I even said so to John one moonlight evening, but he said what I felt was a *draught*, and shut the window.

I get unreasonably angry with John sometimes. I'm sure I never used to be sensitive. I think it is due to this nervous condition.

But John says if I feel so, I shall neglect proper self-control; so I take pains to control myself—before him, at least, and that makes me very tired.

I don't like our room a bit. I wanted one downstairs that opened on the piazza and had roses all over the window, and such pretty old-fashioned chintz hangings! but John would not hear of it.

He said there was only one window and not room for two beds, and no near room for him if he took another.

He is very careful and loving, and hardly lets me stir without special direction.

I have a schedule prescription for each hour in the day; he takes all care from me, and so I feel basely ungrateful not to value it more.

He said we came here solely on my account, that I was to have perfect rest and all the air I could get. "Your exercise depends on your strength, my dear," said he, "and your food somewhat on your appetite; but air you can absorb all the time." So we took the nursery at the top of the house.

It is a big, airy room, the whole floor nearly, with windows that look all ways, and air and sunshine galore. It was nursery first and then playroom and gymnasium, I should judge; for the windows are barred for little children, and there are rings and things in the walls.

The paint and paper look as if a boys' school had used it. It is stripped off— the paper—in great patches all around the head of my bed, about as far as I can reach, and in a great place on the other side of the room low down. I never saw a worse paper in my life.

One of those sprawling flamboyant patterns committing every artistic sin.

It is dull enough to confuse the eye in following, pronounced enough to constantly irritate and provoke study, and when you follow the lame uncertain curves for a little distance they suddenly commit suicide—plunge off at outrageous angles, destroy themselves in unheard of contradictions.

The color is repellent, almost revolting; a smouldering unclean yellow, strangely faded by the slow-turning sunlight.

It is a dull yet lurid orange in some places, a sickly sulphur tint in others.

No wonder the children hated it! I should hate it myself if I had to live in this room long.

There comes John, and I must put this away,—he hates to have me write a word.

We have been here two weeks, and I haven't felt like writing before, since that first day.

I am sitting by the window now, up in this atrocious nursery, and there is nothing to hinder my writing as much as I please, save lack of strength.

John is away all day, and even some nights when his cases are serious.

I am glad my case is not serious!

But these nervous troubles are dreadfully depressing.

John does not know how much I really suffer. He knows there is no *reason* to suffer, and that satisfies him.

Of course it is only nervousness. It does weigh on me so not to do my duty in any way!

I meant to be such a help to John, such a real rest and comfort, and here I am a comparative burden already!

Nobody would believe what an effort it is to do what little I am able,—to dress and entertain, and order things.

It is fortunate Mary is so good with the baby. Such a dear baby!

And yet I *cannot* be with him, it makes me so nervous.

I suppose John never was nervous in his life. He laughs at me so about this wall-paper!

At first he meant to repaper the room, but afterwards he said that I was letting it get the better of me, and that nothing was worse for a nervous patient than to give way to such fancies.

He said that after the wall-paper was changed it would be the heavy bedstead, and then the barred windows, and then that gate at the head of the stairs, and so on.

"You know the place is doing you good," he said, "and really, dear, I don't care to renovate the house just for a three months' rental."

"Then do let us go downstairs," I said, "there are such pretty rooms there."

Then he took me in his arms and called me a blessed little goose, and said he would go down to the cellar, if I wished, and have it whitewashed into the bargain.

But he is right enough about the beds and windows and things.

It is an airy and comfortable room as any one need wish, and, of course, I would not be so silly as to make him uncomfortable just for a whim.

I'm really getting quite fond of the big room, all but that horrid paper.

Out of one window I can see the garden, those mysterious deep-shaded arbors, the riotous old-fashioned flowers, and bushes and gnarly trees.

Out of another I get a lovely view of the bay and a little private wharf belonging to the estate. There is a beautiful shaded lane that runs down there from the house. I always fancy I see people walking in these numerous paths and arbors, but John has cautioned me not to give way to fancy in the least. He says that with my imaginative power and habit of story-making, a nervous weakness like mine is sure to lead to all manner of excited fancies, and that I ought to use my will and good sense to check the tendency. So I try.

I think sometimes that if I were only well enough to write a little it would relieve the press of ideas and rest me.

But I find I get pretty tired when I try.

It is so discouraging not to have any advice and companionship about my work. When I get really well, John says we will ask Cousin Henry and Julia down for a long visit; but he says he would as soon put fireworks in my pillow-case as to let me have those stimulating people about now.

I wish I could get well faster.

But I must not think about that. This paper looks to me as if it *knew* what a vicious influence it had!

There is a recurrent spot where the pattern lolls like a broken neck and two bulbous eyes stare at you upside down.

I get positively angry with the impertinence of it and the everlastingness. Up and down and sideways they crawl, and those absurd, unblinking eyes are everywhere. There is one place where two breadths didn't match, and the eyes go all up and down the line, one a little higher than the other.

I never saw so much expression in an inanimate thing before, and we all know how much expression they have! I used to lie awake as a child and get more entertainment and terror out of blank walls and plain furniture than most children could find in a toy-store.

I remember what a kindly wink the knobs of our big, old bureau used to have, and there was one chair that always seemed like a strong friend.

I used to feel that if any of the other things looked too fierce I could always hop into that chair and be safe.

The furniture in this room is no worse than inharmonious, however, for we had to bring it all from downstairs. I suppose when this was used as a playroom they had to take the nursery things out, and no wonder! I never saw such ravages as the children have made here.

The wall-paper, as I said before, is torn off in spots, and it sticketh closer than a brother—they must have had perseverance as well as hatred.

Then the floor is scratched and gouged and splintered, the plaster itself is dug out here and there, and this great heavy bed which is all we found in the room, looks as if it had been through the wars.

But I don't mind it a bit—only the paper.

There comes John's sister. Such a dear girl as she is, and so careful of me! I must not let her find me writing.

She is a perfect and enthusiastic housekeeper, and hopes for no better profession. I verily believe she thinks it is the writing which made me sick!

But I can write when she is out, and see her a long way off from these windows.

There is one that commands the road, a lovely shaded winding road, and one that just looks off over the country. A lovely country, too, full of great elms and velvet meadows.

This wall-paper has a kind of sub-pattern in a different shade, a particularly irritating one, for you can only see it in certain lights, and not clearly then.

But in the places where it isn't faded and where the sun is just so—I can see a strange, provoking, formless sort of figure, that seems to skulk about behind that silly and conspicuous front design.

There's sister on the stairs!

Well, the Fourth of July is over! The people are all gone and I am tired out. John thought it might do me good to see a little company, so we just had mother and Nellie and the children down for a week.

Of course I didn't do a thing. Jennie sees to everything now.

But it tired me all the same.

John says if I don't pick up faster he shall send me to Weir Mitchell in the fall.

But I don't want to go there at all. I had a friend who was in his hands once, and she says he is just like John and my brother, only more so!

Besides, it is such an undertaking to go so far.

I don't feel as if it was worth while to turn my hand over for anything, and I'm getting dreadfully fretful and querulous.

I cry at nothing, and cry most of the time.

Of course I don't when John is here, or anybody else, but when I am alone.

And I am alone a good deal just now. John is kept in town very often by serious cases, and Jennie is good and lets me alone when I want her to.

So I walk a little in the garden or down that lovely lane, sit on the porch under the roses, and lie down up here a good deal.

I'm getting really fond of the room in spite of the wall-paper. Perhaps *because* of the wall-paper.

It dwells in my mind so!

I lie here on this great immovable bed—it is nailed down, I believe—and follow that pattern about by the hour. It is as good as gymnastics, I assure you. I start, we'll say, at the bottom, down in the corner over there where it has not been touched, and I determine for the thousandth time that I *will* follow that pointless pattern to some sort of a conclusion.

I know a little of the principle of design, and I know this thing was not arranged on any laws of radiation, or alternation, or repetition, or symmetry, or anything else that I ever heard of.

It is repeated, of course, by the breadths, but not otherwise.

Looked at in one way each breadth stands alone, the bloated curves and flourishes—a kind of "debased Romanesque" with *delirium tremens*—go waddling up and down in isolated columns of fatuity.

But, on the other hand, they connect diagonally, and the sprawling outlines run off in great slanting waves of optic horror, like a lot of wallowing seaweeds in full chase.

The whole thing goes horizontally, too, at least it seems so, and I exhaust myself in trying to distinguish the order of its going in that direction.

They have used a horizontal breadth for a frieze, and that adds wonderfully to the confusion.

There is one end of the room where it is almost intact, and there, when the crosslights fade and the low sun shines directly upon it, I can almost fancy radiation after all,—the interminable grotesques seem to form around a common centre and rush off in headlong plunges of equal distraction.

It makes me tired to follow it. I will take a nap I guess.

I don't know why I should write this.

I don't want to.

I don't feel able.

And I know John would think it absurd. But I *must* say what I feel and think in some way—it is such a relief!

But the effort is getting to be greater than the relief.

Half the time now I am awfully lazy, and lie down ever so much.

John says I mustn't lose my strength, and has me take cod liver oil and lots of tonics and things, to say nothing of ale and wine and rare meat.

Dear John! He loves me very dearly, and hates to have me sick. I tried to have a real earnest reasonable talk with him the other day, and tell him how I wish he would let me go and make a visit to Cousin Henry and Julia.

But he said I wasn't able to go, nor able to stand it after I got there; and I did not make out a very good case for myself, for I was crying before I had finished.

It is getting to be a great effort for me to think straight. Just this nervous weakness I suppose.

And dear John gathered me up in his arms, and just carried me upstairs and laid me on the bed, and sat by me and read to me till it tired my head.

He said I was his darling and his comfort and all he had, and that I must take care of myself for his sake, and keep well.

He says no one but myself can help me out of it, that I must use my will and self-control and not let any silly fancies run away with me.

There's one comfort, the baby is well and happy, and does not have to occupy this nursery with the horrid wall-paper.

If we had not used it, that blessed child would have! What a fortunate escape! Why, I wouldn't have a child of mine, an impressionable little thing, live in such a room for worlds.

I never thought of it before, but it is lucky that John kept me here after all, I can stand it so much easier than a baby, you see.

Of course I never mention it to them any more—I am too wise,—but I keep watch of it all the same.

There are things in that paper that nobody knows but me, or ever will.

Behind that outside pattern the dim shapes get clearer every day.

It is always the same shape, only very numerous.

And it is like a woman stooping down and creeping about behind that pattern. I don't like it a bit. I wonder—I begin to think—I wish John would take me away from here!

It is so hard to talk with John about my case, because he is so wise, and because he loves me so.

But I tried it last night.

It was moonlight. The moon shines in all around just as the sun does.

I hate to see it sometimes, it creeps so slowly, and always comes in by one window or another.

John was asleep and I hated to waken him, so I kept still and watched the moonlight on that undulating wall-paper till I felt creepy.

The faint figure behind seemed to shake the pattern, just as if she wanted to get out.

I got up softly and went to feel and see if the paper *did* move, and when I came back John was awake.

"What is it, little girl?" he said. "Don't go walking about like that—you'll get cold."

I thought it was a good time to talk, so I told him that I really was not gaining here, and that I wished he would take me away.

"Why darling!" said he, "our lease will be up in three weeks, and I can't see how to leave before.

"The repairs are not done at home, and I cannot possibly leave town just now. Of course if you were in any danger, I could and would, but you really are better, dear, whether you can see it or not. I am a doctor, dear, and I know. You are gaining flesh and color, your appetite is better, I feel really much easier about you."

"I don't weigh a bit more," said I, "nor as much; and my appetite may be better in the evening when you are here, but it is worse in the morning when you are away!"

"Bless her little heart!" said he with a big hug, "she shall be as sick as she pleases! But now let's improve the shining hours by going to sleep, and talk about it in the morning!"

"And you won't go away?"I asked gloomily.

"Why, how can I, dear? It is only three weeks more and then we will take a nice little trip of a few days while Jennie is getting the house ready. Really dear you are better!"

"Better in body perhaps—" I began, and stopped short, for he sat up straight and looked at me with such a stern, reproachful look that I could not say another word.

"My darling," said he, "I beg of you, for my sake and for our child's sake, as well as for your own, that you will never for one instant let that idea enter your mind! There is nothing so dangerous, so fascinating, to a temperament like yours. It is a false and foolish fancy. Can you not trust me as a physician when I tell you so?"

So of course I said no more on that score, and we went to sleep before long. He thought I was asleep first, but I wasn't, and lay there for hours trying to decide whether that front pattern and the back pattern really did move together or separately.

On a pattern like this, by daylight, there is a lack of sequence, a defiance of law, that is a constant irritant to a normal mind.

The color is hideous enough, and unreliable enough, and infuriating enough, but the pattern is torturing.

You think you have mastered it, but just as you get well underway in following, it turns a back-somersault and there you are. It slaps you in the face, knocks you down, and tramples upon you. It is like a bad dream.

The outside pattern is a florid arabesque, reminding one of a fungus. If you can imagine a toadstool in joints, an interminable string of toadstools, budding and sprouting in endless convolutions—why, that is something like it.

That is, sometimes!

There is one marked peculiarity about this paper, a thing nobody seems to notice but myself, and that is that it changes as the light changes.

When the sun shoots in through the east window—I always watch for that first long, straight ray—it changes so quickly that I never can quite believe it.

That is why I watch it always.

By moonlight—the moon shines in all night when there is a moon—I wouldn't know it was the same paper.

At night in any kind of light, in twilight, candle light, lamplight, and worst of all by moonlight, it becomes bars! The outside pattern I mean, and the woman behind it is as plain as can be.

I didn't realize for a long time what the thing was that showed behind, that dim sub-pattern, but now I am quite sure it is a woman.

By daylight she is subdued, quiet. I fancy it is the pattern that keeps her so still. It is so puzzling. It keeps me quiet by the hour.

I lie down ever so much now. John says it is good for me, and to sleep all I can.

Indeed he started the habit by making me lie down for an hour after each meal.

It is a very bad habit I am convinced, for you see I don't sleep.

And that cultivates deceit, for I don't tell them I'm awake—O no!

The fact is I am getting a little afraid of John.

He seems very queer sometimes, and even Jennie has an inexplicable look.

It strikes me occasionally, just as a scientific hypothesis,—that perhaps it is the paper!

I have watched John when he did not know I was looking, and come into the room suddenly on the most innocent excuses, and I've caught him several times *looking at the paper!* And Jennie too. I caught Jennie with her hand on it once.

She didn't know I was in the room, and when I asked her in a quiet, a very quiet voice, with the most restrained manner possible, what she was doing with the paper—she turned around as if she had been caught stealing, and looked quite angry—asked me why I should frighten her so!

Then she said that the paper stained everything it touched, that she had found yellow smooches on all my clothes and John's, and she wished we would be more careful!

Did not that sound innocent? But I know she was studying that pattern, and I am determined that nobody shall find it out but myself!

Life is very much more exciting now than it used to be. You see I have something more to expect, to look forward to, to watch. I really do eat better, and am more quiet than I was.

John is so pleased to see me improve! He laughed a little the other day, and said I seemed to be flourishing in spite of my wall-paper.

I turned it off with a laugh. I had no intention of telling him it was *because* of the wall-paper—he would make fun of me. He might even want to take me away.

I don't want to leave now until I have found it out. There is a week more, and I think that will be enough.

I'm feeling ever so much better! I don't sleep much at night, for it is so interesting to watch developments; but I sleep a good deal in the daytime.

In the daytime it is tiresome and perplexing.

There are always new shoots on the fungus, and new shades of yellow all over it. I cannot keep count of them, though I have tried conscientiously.

It is the strangest yellow, that wall-paper! It makes me think of all the yellow things I ever saw—not beautiful ones like buttercups, but old foul, bad yellow things.

But there is something else about that paper—the smell! I noticed it the moment we came into the room, but with so much air and sun it was not bad. Now we have had a week of fog and rain, and whether the windows are open or not, the smell is here.

It creeps all over the house.

I find it hovering in the dining-room, skulking in the parlor, hiding in the hall, lying in wait for me on the stairs.

It gets into my hair.

Even when I go to ride, if I turn my head suddenly and surprise it—there is that smell!

Such a peculiar odor, too! I have spent hours in trying to analyze it, to find what it smelled like.

It is not bad—at first, and very gentle, but quite the subtlest, most enduring odor I ever met.

In this damp weather it is awful, I wake up in the night and find it hanging over me.

It used to disturb me at first. I thought seriously of burning the house—to reach the smell.

But now I am used to it. The only thing I can think of that it is like is the *color* of the paper! A yellow smell.

There is a very funny mark on this wall, low down, near the mopboard. A streak that runs round the room. It goes behind every piece of furniture, except the bed, a long, straight, even *smooch*, as if it had been rubbed over and over.

I wonder how it was done and who did it, and what they did it for. Round and round and round—round and round and round—it makes me dizzy!

I really have discovered something at last.

Through watching so much at night, when it changes so, I have finally found out.

The front pattern *does* move—and no wonder! The woman behind shakes it!

Sometimes I think there are a great many women behind, and sometimes only one, and she crawls around fast, and her crawling shakes it all over.

Then in the very bright spots she keeps still, and in the very shady spots she just takes hold of the bars and shakes them hard.

And she is all the time trying to climb through. But nobody could climb through that pattern—it strangles so; I think that is why it has so many heads.

They get through, and then the pattern strangles them off and turns them upside down, and makes their eyes white!

If those heads were covered or taken off it would not be half so bad.

I think that woman gets out in the daytime!

And I'll tell you why—privately—I've seen her!

I can see her out of every one of my windows!

It is the same woman, I know, for she is always creeping, and most women do not creep by daylight.

I see her on that long road under the trees, creeping along, and when a carriage comes she hides under the blackberry vines.

I don't blame her a bit. It must be very humiliating to be caught creeping by daylight!

I always lock the door when I creep by daylight. I can't do it at night, for I know John would suspect something at once.

And John is so queer now, that I don't want to irritate him. I wish he would take another room! Besides, I don't want anybody to get that woman out at night but myself.

I often wonder if I could see her out of all the windows at once.

But, turn as fast as I can, I can only see out of one at one time.

And though I always see her, she *may* be able to creep faster than I can turn!

I have watched her sometimes away off in the open country, creeping as fast as a cloud shadow in a high wind.

If only that top pattern could be gotten off from the under one! I mean to try it, little by little.

I have found out another funny thing, but I shan't tell it this time! It does not do to trust people too much.

There are only two more days to get this paper off, and I believe John is beginning to notice. I don't like the look in his eyes.

And I heard him ask Jennie a lot of professional questions about me. She had a very good report to give.

She said I slept a good deal in the daytime.

John knows I don't sleep very well at night, for all I'm so quiet!

He asked me all sorts of questions, too, and pretended to be very loving and kind.

As if I couldn't see through him!

Still, I don't wonder he acts so, sleeping under this paper for three months.

It only interests me, but I feel sure John and Jennie are secretly affected by it.

Hurrah! This is the last day, but it is enough. John to stay in town over night, and won't be out until this evening.

Jennie wanted to sleep with me—the sly thing! but I told her I should undoubtedly rest better for a night all alone.

That was clever, for really I wasn't alone a bit! As soon as it was moonlight and that poor thing began to crawl and shake the pattern, I got up and ran to help her.

I pulled and she shook, I shook and she pulled, and before morning we had peeled off yards of that paper.

A strip about as high as my head and half around the room.

And then when the sun came and that awful pattern began to laugh at me, I declared I would finish it to-day!

We go away to-morrow, and they are moving all my furniture down again to leave things as they were before.

Jennie looked at the wall in amazement, but I told her merrily that I did it out of pure spite at the vicious thing.

She laughed and said she wouldn't mind doing it herself, but I must not get tired.

How she betrayed herself that time!

But I am here, and no person touches this paper but me,—not *alive!*

She tried to get me out of the room—it was too patent! But I said it was so quiet, and empty and clean now that I believed I would lie down again and sleep all I could; and not to wake me even for dinner—I would call when I woke.

So now she is gone, and the servants are gone, and the things are gone, and there is nothing left but that great bedstead nailed down, with the canvas mattress we found on it.

We shall sleep downstairs to-night, and take the boat home to-morrow.

I quite enjoy the room, now it is bare again.

How those children did tear about here!

This bedstead is fairly gnawed!

But I must get to work.

I have locked the door and thrown the key down into the front path.

I don't want to go out, and I don't want to have anybody come in, till John comes.

I want to astonish him.

I've got a rope up here that even Jennie did not find. If that woman does get out, and tries to get away, I can tie her!

But I forgot I could not reach far without anything to stand on!

This bed will *not* move!

I tried to lift and push it until I was lame, and then I got so angry I bit off a little piece at one corner—but it hurt my teeth.

Then I peeled off all the paper I could reach standing on the floor. It sticks horribly and the pattern just enjoys it! All those strangled heads and bulbous eyes and waddling fungus growths just shriek with derision!

I am getting angry enough to do something desperate. To jump out of the window would be admirable exercise, but the bars are too strong even to try.

Besides I wouldn't do it. Of course not. I know well enough that a step like that is improper and might be misconstrued.

I don't like to *look* out of the windows even—there are so many of those creeping women, and they creep so fast.

I wonder if they all come out of that wall-paper as I did?

But I am securely fastened now by my well-hidden rope—you don't get *me* out in the road there!

I suppose I shall have to get back behind the pattern when it comes night, and that is hard!

It is so pleasant to be out in this great room and creep around as I please!

I don't want to go outside. I won't, even if Jennie asks me to.

For outside you have to creep on the ground, and everything is green instead of yellow.

But here I can creep smoothly on the floor, and my shoulder just fits in that long smooch around the wall, so I cannot lose my way.

Why there's John at the door!

It is no use, young man, you can't open it!

How he does call and pound!

Now he's crying for an axe.

It would be a shame to break down that beautiful door!

"John dear!" said I in the gentlest voice, "the key is down by the front steps, under a plantain leaf!"

That silenced him for a few moments.

Then he said—very quietly indeed, "Open the door, my darling!"

"I can't," said I. "The key is down by the front door under a plantain leaf!"

And then I said it again, several times, very gently and slowly, and said it so often that he had to go and see, and he got it of course, and came in. He stopped short by the door.

"What is the matter?" he cried. "For God's sake, what are you doing!"

I kept on creeping just the same, but I looked at him over my shoulder.

"I've got out at last," said I, "in spite of you and Jane.[1] And I've pulled off most of the paper, so you can't put me back!"

Now why should that man have fainted? But he did, and right across my path by the wall, so that I had to creep over him every time!

Questions

1. At the story's beginning, John recommends idleness and isolation as remedies for the narrator's "nervous depression." She thinks a little work and company would do her some good. Who is right? What does this say about the medical treatment of the times?
2. Both of the narrator's doctors are men. What does their attitude say about the male view of the psychological needs of women?

---

[1] Jennie is a nickname for Jane. Jane and Jennie are the same character.

3. How does her attitude toward the wallpaper change? What does she first think of it? What does it come to represent?
4. Why should she be fascinated by the wallpaper?
5. When does the narrator come to realize that she has difficulty in thinking straight?
6. Toward the middle of the story, John tells his wife that she is improving. Is he sincere? Why does he tell her of the improvement? Are his motives selfless?
7. Sigmund Freud believed that one's fantasies had meaning. Is there any reason the narrator should hallucinate the figures she sees?

EDGAR ALLAN POE (1809–1849)

The Cask of Amontillado

The thousand injuries of Fortunato I had borne as I best could, but when he ventured upon insult, I vowed revenge. You, who so well know the nature of my soul, will not suppose, however, that I gave utterance to a threat. *At length* I would be avenged; this was a point definitely settled—but the very definitiveness with which it was resolved precluded the idea of risk. I must not only punish, but punish with impunity. A wrong is unredressed when retribution overtakes its redresser. It is equally unredressed when the avenger fails to make himself felt as such to him who has done the wrong.

It must be understood that neither by word nor deed had I given Fortunato cause to doubt my good will. I continued, as was my wont, to smile in his face, and he did not perceive that my smile *now* was at the thought of his immolation.

He had a weak point—this Fortunato—although in other regards he was a man to be respected and even feared. He prided himself on his connoisseurship in wine. Few Italians have the true virtuoso spirit. For the most part their enthusiasm is adopted to suit the time and opportunity to practice imposture upon the British and Austrian *millionaires*. In painting and gemmary[1] Fortunato, like his countrymen, was a quack, but in the matter of old wines he was sincere. In this respect I did not differ from him materially;—I was skillful in the Italian vintages myself, and bought largely whenever I could.

It was about dusk, one evening during the supreme madness of the carnival season, that I encountered my friend. He accosted me with excessive warmth, for he had been drinking much. The man wore motley. He had on a tight-fitting parti-striped dress, and his head was surmounted by the conical cap and bells.[2] I was so pleased to see him, that I thought I should never have done wringing his hand.

I said to him—"My dear Fortunato, you are luckily met. How remarkably well you are looking to-day! But I have received a pipe[3] of what passes for Amontillado,[4] and I have my doubts."

---

[1] Gemmary is the art of gem cutting and gem engraving.
[2] In short, he is dressed like a clown.
[3] A pipe is a wine cask.
[4] Amontillado is a specific type of sherry made from grapes grown on the slopes of the Sierra de Montilla, south of Córdoba, Spain.

Edgar Allan Poe (Culver Pictures, Inc.)

"How?" said he, "Amontillado? A pipe? Impossible! And in the middle of the carnival?"[5]

"I have my doubts," I replied; "and I was silly enough to pay the full Amontillado price without consulting you in the matter. You were not to be found, and I was fearful of losing a bargain."

"Amontillado!"

"I have my doubts."

"Amontillado!"

"And I must satisfy them."

"Amontillado!"

"As you are engaged, I am on my way to Luchesi. If any one has a critical turn, it is he. He will tell me—"

"Luchesi cannot tell Amontillado from Sherry."

"And yet some fools will have it that his taste is a match for your own."

"Come, let us go."

"Whither?"

"To your vaults."

"My friend, no; I will not impose upon your good nature. I perceive you have an engagement. Luchesi—"

"I have no engagement; come."

---

[5] The carnival or *Mardi Gras* is a yearly festival celebrated before Lent.

"My friend, no. It is not the engagement, but the severe cold with which I perceive you are afflicted. The vaults are insufferably damp. They are encrusted with nitre."[6]

"Let us go, nevertheless. The cold is merely nothing. Amontillado! You have been imposed upon; and as for Luchesi, he cannot distinguish Sherry from Amontillado."

Thus speaking, Fortunato possessed himself of my arm. Putting on a mask of black silk, and drawing a *roquelaure*[7] closely about my person, I suffered him to hurry me to my palazzo.[8]

There were no attendants at home; they had absconded to make merry in honor of the time. I had told them that I should not return until the morning, and had given them explicit orders not to stir from the house. These orders were sufficient, I well knew, to insure their immediate disappearance, one and all, as soon as my back was turned.

I took from their sconces two flambeaux, and giving one to Fortunato, bowed him through several suites of rooms to the archway that led into the vaults. I passed down a long and winding staircase, requesting him to be cautious as he followed. We came at length to the foot of the descent, and stood together on the damp ground of the catacombs of the Montresors.

The gait of my friend was unsteady, and the bells upon his cap jingled as he strode.

"The pipe," said he.

"It is farther on," said I; "but observe the white web-work which gleams from these cavern walls."

He turned towards me, and looked into my eyes with two filmy orbs that distilled the rheum of intoxication.

"Nitre?" he asked, at length.

"Nitre," I replied. "How long have you had that cough?"

"Ugh! ugh! ugh!—ugh! ugh! ugh!—ugh! ugh! ugh!—ugh! ugh! ugh!—ugh! ugh! ugh!"

My poor friend found it impossible to reply for many minutes.

"It is nothing," he said, at last.

"Come," I said, with decision, "we will go back; your health is precious. You are rich, respected, admired, beloved; you are happy, as once I was. You are a man to be missed. For me it is no matter. We will go back; you will be ill, and I cannot be responsible. Besides, there is Luchesi—"

"Enough," he said; "the cough is a mere nothing; it will not kill me. I shall not die of a cough."

"True—true," I replied; "and, indeed, I had no intention of alarming you unnecessarily—but you should use all proper caution. A draught of this Medoc[9] will defend us from the damps."

---

[6] Nitre is a mineral of potassium nitrate, appearing as a saltlike crust on rocks and stone.

[7] A roquelaure is a short cape.

[8] A palatial residence; a mansion.

[9] Medoc is a red Bordeaux wine made in the Medoc region of southwestern France.

Here I knocked off the neck of a bottle which I drew from a long row of its fellows that lay upon the mould.

"Drink," I said, presenting him the wine.

He raised it to his lips with a leer. He paused and nodded to me familiarly, while his bells jingled.

"I drink," he said, "to the buried that repose around us."

"And I to your long life."

He again took my arm, and we proceeded.

"These vaults," he said, "are extensive."

"The Montresors," I replied, "were a great and numerous family."

"I forget your arms."

"A huge human foot d'or, in a field azure; the foot crushes a serpent rampant whose fangs are imbedded in the heel."

"And the motto?"

"*Nemo me impune lacessit.*"[10]

"Good!" he said.

The wine sparkled in his eyes and the bells jingled. My own fancy grew warm with the Medoc. We had passed through walls of piled bones, with casks and puncheons intermingling, into the inmost recesses of the catacombs. I paused again, and this time I made bold to seize Fortunato by an arm above the elbow.

"The nitre!" I said; "see, it increases. It hangs like moss upon the vaults. We are below the river's bed. The drops of moisture trickle among the bones. Come, we will go back ere it is too late. Your cough—"

"It is nothing," he said; "let us go on. But first, another draught of the Medoc."

I broke and reached him a flagon of De Grâve.[11] He emptied it at a breath. His eyes flashed with a fierce light. He laughed and threw the bottle upwards with a gesticulation I did not understand.

I looked at him in surprise. He repeated the movement—a grotesque one.

"You do not comprehend?" he said.

"Not I," I replied.

"Then you are not of the brotherhood."[12]

"How?"

"You are not of the masons."

"Yes, yes," I said, "yes, yes."

"You? Impossible! A mason?"

"A mason," I replied.

"A sign," he said.

"It is this," I answered, producing a trowel from beneath the folds of my *roquelaure.*

---

[10] The motto "*Nemo me impune lacessit*" means "No one dare attack me with impunity."

[11] De Grave is another French wine.

[12] The Freemasons are a secret sect of mystical persuasion whose origins go back at least to the 14th century. They were often hounded and imprisoned.

"You jest," he exclaimed, recoiling a few paces. "But let us proceed to the Amontillado."

"Be it so," I said, replacing the tool beneath the cloak, and again offering him my arm. He leaned upon it heavily. We continued our route in search of the Amontillado. We passed through a range of low arches, descended, passed on, and descending again, arrived at a deep crypt, in which the foulness of the air caused our flambeaux rather to glow than flame.

At the most remote end of the crypt there appeared another less spacious. Its walls had been lined with human remains piled to the vault overhead, in the fashion of the great catacombs of Paris. Three sides of this interior crypt were still ornamented in this manner. From the fourth the bones had been thrown down, and lay promiscuously upon the earth, forming at one point a mound of some size. Within the wall thus exposed by the displacing of the bones, we perceived a still interior recess, in depth about four feet, in width three, in height six or seven. It seemed to have been constructed for no especial use within itself, but formed merely the interval between two of the colossal supports of the roof of the catacombs, and was backed by one of their circumscribing walls of solid granite.

It was in vain that Fortunato, uplifting his dull torch, endeavored to pry into the depths of the recess. Its termination the feeble light did not enable us to see.

"Proceed," I said; "herein is the Amontillado. As for Luchesi—"

"He is an ignoramus," interrupted my friend, as he stepped unsteadily forward, while I followed immediately at his heels. In an instant he had reached the extremity of the niche, and finding his progress arrested by the rock, stood stupidly bewildered. A moment more and I had fettered him to the granite. In its surface were two iron staples, distant from each other about two feet, horizontally. From one of these depended a short chain, from the other a padlock. Throwing the links about his waist, it was but the work of a few seconds to secure it. He was too much astounded to resist. Withdrawing the key I stepped back from the recess.

"Pass your hand," I said, "over the wall; you cannot help feeling the nitre. Indeed it is *very* damp. Once more let me *implore* you to return. No? Then I must positively leave you. But I must first render you all the little attentions in my power."

"The Amontillado!" ejaculated my friend, not yet recovered from his astonishment.

"True," I replied; "the Amontillado."

As I said these words I busied myself among the pile of bones of which I have before spoken. Throwing them aside, I soon uncovered a quantity of building-stone and mortar. With these materials and with the aid of my trowel, I began vigorously to wall up the entrance of the niche.

I had scarcely laid the first tier of masonry when I discovered that the intoxication of Fortunato had in a great measure worn off. The earliest indication I had of this was a low moaning cry from the depth of the recess. It was *not* the cry of a drunken man. There was then a long and obstinate silence. I laid the second tier, and the third, and the fourth; and then I heard the furious vibrations of the chain. The noise lasted for several minutes, during which, that I might hearken to it with the more satisfaction, I ceased my labors and sat down upon the bones. When at last the clanking subsided, I resumed the trowel, and finished without interruption the fifth, the sixth, and the seventh tier. The wall was now nearly upon a level with my breast. I again paused, and holding the flambeaux over the masonwork, threw a few feeble rays upon the figure within.

A succession of loud and shrill screams, bursting suddenly from the throat of the chained form, seemed to thrust me violently back. For a brief moment I hesitated—I trembled. Unsheathing my rapier, I began to grope with it about the recess; but the thought of an instant reassured me. I placed my hand upon the solid fabric of the catacombs, and felt satisfied. I reapproached the wall. I replied to the yells of him who clamored. I re-echoed—I aided—I surpassed them in volume and in strength. I did this, and the clamorer grew still.

It was now midnight, and my task was drawing to a close. I had completed the eighth, the ninth, and the tenth tier. I had finished a portion of the last and the eleventh; there remained but a single stone to be fitted and plastered in. I struggled with its weight; I placed it partially in its destined position. But now there came from out the niche a low laugh that erected the hairs upon my head. It was succeeded by a sad voice, which I had difficulty in recognizing as that of the noble Fortunato. The voice said—

"Ha! ha! ha!—he! he! he!—a very good joke indeed—an excellent jest. We will have many a rich laugh about it at the palazzo—he! he! he!—over our wine—he! he! he!"

"The Amontillado!" I said.

"He! he! he!—he! he! he!—yes, the Amontillado. But is it not getting late? Will not they be awaiting us at the palazzo, the Lady Fortunato and the rest? Let us be gone."

"Yes," I said, "let us be gone."

"For the love of God, Montresor!"

"Yes," I said, "for the love of God!"

But to these words I hearkened in vain for a reply. I grew impatient. I called aloud;

"Fortunato!"

No answer. I called again;

"Fortunato!"

No answer still, I thrust a torch through the remaining aperture and let it fall within. There came forth in return only a jingling of the bells. My heart grew sick—on account of the dampness of the catacombs. I hastened to make an end of my labor. I forced the last stone into its position; I plastered it up. Against the new masonry I reerected the old rampart of bones. For the half of a century no mortal has disturbed them. *In pace requiescat!*[13]

---

[13] The Latin *"in pace requiescat"* means "May he rest in peace."

Questions

1. Does Montresor (the narrator) give any reasons for wanting to kill Fortunato? Are they very precise?
2. Why has Montresor chosen the night of the carnival for revenge?
3. What is the significance of Fortunato's costume?
4. What is the significance of Montresor's Masonic affiliation?
5. Why does Fortunato laugh?

4 ❧ The Pattern of Action — Plot

In casual conversation we often speak of plot as the summary of a story's major action. But plot is far more interesting and important. Plot, properly understood, is an author's choice and arrangement of events in a story. Consequently, it is one of the principal means by which writers give their fiction form, unity, and interest.

The events of a plot are not necessarily earthshaking or violent. Sometimes, of course, they are battles, races, or great escapes. More frequently, however, writers concern themselves with neighbors visiting one another, with someone buying a hat, or simply with a person looking out a window. The art of constructing a plot consists of selecting the most effective events and ordering them in the most convincing manner.

The Ordering of Events

Let us look at just two sentences that recount virtually the same events but in different sequences.

1. Mr. Smith went walking and slipped on some ice on the sidewalk; the fall hurt his leg, and he entered his living room limping.
2. Mr. Smith entered his living room limping from a fall he had suffered during his walk when he slipped on some ice.

Sentence #1 orders the events chronologically. One event follows the other; each one is given about the same emphasis. Sentence #2, however, orders the material causally. We are thrust into a scene in which Mr. Smith enters his living room limping, a condition which is explained by recording the earlier events. Mr. Smith's slip on the ice is clearly subordinated to his entrance into the living room.

Though neither sentence is terribly exciting in itself, we can note that Sentence #1 is wordier, more plodding, and less interesting. In short, it lacks focus. A story has *narrative focus* when the less important events are subordinated to the more significant ones. Again we must not suppose that an event is significant merely because violent physical actions occur. A writer, for example, may find more significance in the events that lead up to a murder than in the murder itself. In a short story, focus is very important since the author's aim is maximum narrative efficiency.

Surprise

But focus is only one aspect of plot construction. Plots also arrange events to produce *suspense* and *surprise*. Surprise occurs when authors omit information and then spring events on the unsuspecting reader. As we did before, let us look at two passages that narrate the same central event but lead up to it in different ways.

1. The burglar waited until Mrs. Smith left her house before he entered it. But soon after he entered, he heard her car pull up in the driveway. Then he hid behind the front door and grabbed Mrs. Smith when she entered, holding his hand across her mouth so she could not scream.

2. Mrs. Smith went shopping, but before she arrived at the store, she remembered having left her wallet on her dresser. She drove back home, pulled the car into the drive, opened the door. Then before she knew it, she was grabbed from behind and a hand was placed across her mouth to keep her from screaming for help.

In Passage #2, we are surprised because the author keeps the burglar's presence a secret until it is suddenly thrust into the story. Passage #1 contains no surprises. The reader is allowed to know all of the relevant events as they occur. In fiction, too much knowledge can be very boring.

These two passages illustrate yet another point about fictional surprises. Frequently surprise is a function of point-of-view. In Passage #1 the narrator views the action primarily from the burglar's perspective. Passage #2, however, is narrated primarily from Mrs. Smith's perspective. In Passage #2 the reader is surprised because, like Mrs. Smith, the reader lacks important information. We can now see another advantage of the limited third-person narrator we discussed in Chapter 2. Such a limited narrator helps produce and control narrative surprise.

Suspense

Suspense is closely related to surprise. But in suspenseful situations the reader is allowed to know more of what is happening. We can see the difference by imagining two scenes in a movie. In the first, a person enters a house just as a bomb goes off. There is a great explosion, and the audience jumps in surprise. In the second scene, we see the time bomb ticking away and notice that it will go off in a few minutes. We then see the protagonist approaching the house where the bomb is planted. The time bomb ticks louder. The protagonist is climbing the front steps. The time bomb ticks still louder. The protagonist opens the front door. Will he see the bomb in time to defuse it? The audience is held in suspense.

From an author's perspective, suspense is a far more useful and powerful tool than surprise. The effect of most surprises is short-lived, while a skillful writer can use suspense in order to keep the reader turning pages throughout an entire book to learn what will happen next. Of course, suspense does not have to be so action-packed as the above example of the time bomb. It occurs whenever a reader is kept ignorant of the outcome of an action.

Conflict

One source of suspense is *conflict*. Conflict occurs when an obstacle blocks a character's pursuit of a goal or when the goals of two characters are opposed. If the forces are equally matched the reader cannot guess whether the character will succeed or fail in overcoming opposition. Traditionally critics have classified three types of conflict: people against nature, person against person, and people against themselves. But here are other possible conflicts. Stanislaw Lem, for example, has written several stories about people in conflict with computers, and in *Black Beauty*, a horse is in conflict with the humans around him.

A character's goals can be quite general and are often unstated. Happiness, comfort, youth, these may be what the character wants. In longer stories, a character's goals may change. In Lawrence's "The Horse Dealer's Daughter" Mabel first wishes to join her mother by committing suicide, but after she is saved she wishes to marry. A character may have a number of goals in conflict with each other. In Grace Paley's "A Conversation with My Father," the narrator wants to write a story that will please both her father and herself.

Narrative Stages

A narrative usually passes through several stages. Near the opening of a story, one usually finds the *exposition*, passages that give the reader basic information about who the characters are, where they are, and what they are doing. Conflict rises as the central character or *protagonist* encounters more and more obstacles in pursuit of his or her goal. The *climax* in fiction occurs at the point when the protagonist has either achieved or failed to achieve the goal. The climax is frequently followed by a *denouement* (which in French means "an untying"). The denouement narrates the consequences of the climax: how the characters respond to the success or failure of the protagonists. For example, in "The Adventure of the Speckled Band" the denouement recounts how Sherlock Holmes came to solve the mystery and tells us about the future of Helen Stoner, the young woman whose life Holmes had saved. Although the narrative stages in fiction are like those in drama, there are some differences. The most significant difference is that the climax in drama occurs when the hero's or protagonists's fortunes are reversed. (See pages 913–14 for additional commentary.)

In summary, plot orders the incidents of a story so as to focus attention upon the most significant events. Plot establishes the protagonists' goals, and their obstacles. Thus, plot is an integral part of a story's overall structure, excitement, and meaning.

Suggestions for Essayists

1. Discuss a goal that you have formulated for yourself, and the obstacles you must overcome to realize your goal.
2. ·Humans, it has been said, are in conflict with nature, with other humans, and with themselves. Discuss which is the most serious of those conflicts.

Suggestions for Fiction Writers

1. Write two versions of the same story by reversing the order in which you narrate the events.
2. Narrate a personal experience in which partial knowledge led you to be more anxious, worried, or frightened than you needed to be.

ARTHUR CONAN DOYLE (1859–1930)

The Adventure of the Speckled Band

On glancing over my notes of the seventy odd cases in which I have during the last eight years studied the methods of my friend Sherlock Holmes, I find many tragic, some comic, a large number merely strange, but none commonplace; for, working as he did rather for the love of his art than for the acquirement of wealth, he refused to associate himself with any investigation which did not tend towards the unusual, and even the fantastic. Of all these varied cases, however, I cannot recall any which presented more singular features than that which was associated with the well-known Surrey family of the Roylotts of Stoke Moran. The events in question occurred in the early days of my association with Holmes, when we were sharing rooms as bachelors in Baker Street. It is possible that I might have placed them upon record before, but a promise of secrecy was made at the time, from which I have only been freed during the last month by the untimely death of the lady to whom the pledge was given. It is perhaps as well that the facts should now come to light, for I have reasons to know that there are widespread rumours as to the death of Dr. Grimesby Roylott which tend to make the matter even more terrible than the truth.

It was early in April in the year '83 that I woke one morning to find Sherlock Holmes standing, fully dressed, by the side of my bed. He was a late riser, as a rule, and as the clock on the mantelpiece showed me that it was only a quarter-past seven, I blinked up at him in some surprise, and perhaps just a little resentment, for I was myself regular in my habits.

"Very sorry to knock you up, Watson," said he, "but it's the common lot this morning. Mrs. Hudson has been knocked up, she retorted upon me, and I on you."

"What is it, then—a fire?"

"No; a client. It seems that a young lady has arrived in a considerable state of excitement, who insists upon seeing me. She is waiting now in the sitting-room. Now, when young ladies wander about the metropolis at this hour of the morning, and knock sleepy people up out of their beds, I presume that it is something very pressing which they have to communicate. Should it prove to be an interesting case, you would, I am sure, wish to follow it from the outset. I thought, at any rate, that I should call you and give you the chance."

"My dear fellow, I would not miss it for anything."

I had no keener pleasure than in following Holmes in his professional investigations, and in admiring the rapid deductions, as swift as intuitions, and yet always founded on a logical basis, with which he unravelled the problems which were submitted to him. I rapidly threw on my clothes and was ready in a few minutes to accompany my friend down to the sitting-room. A lady dressed in black and heavily veiled, who had been sitting in the window, rose as we entered.

"Good-morning, madam," said Holmes cheerily. "My name is Sherlock Holmes. This is my intimate friend and associate, Dr. Watson, before whom you can speak as freely as before myself. Ha! I am glad to see that Mrs. Hudson has had the good sense to light the fire. Pray draw up to it, and I shall order you a cup of hot coffee, for I observe that you are shivering."

"It is not cold which makes me shiver," said the woman in a low voice, changing her seat as requested.

"What, then?"

"It is fear, Mr. Holmes. It is terror." She raised her veil as she spoke, and we could see that she was indeed in a pitiable state of agitation, her face all drawn and gray, with restless, frightened eyes, like those of some hunted animal. Her features and figure were those of a woman of thirty, but her hair was shot with premature gray, and her expression was weary and haggard. Sherlock Holmes ran her over with one of his quick, all-comprehensive glances.

"You must not fear," said he soothingly, bending forward and patting her forearm. "We shall soon set matters right, I have no doubt. You have come in by train this morning, I see."

"You know me, then?"

"No, but I observe the second half of a return ticket in the palm of your left glove. You must have started early, and yet you had a good drive in a dogcart, along heavy roads, before you reached the station."

The lady gave a violent start and stared in bewilderment at my companion.

"There is no mystery, my dear madam," said he, smiling. "The left arm of your jacket is spattered with mud in no less than seven places. The marks are perfectly fresh. There is no vehicle save a dogcart which throws up mud in that way, and then only when you sit on the left-hand side of the driver."

"Whatever your reasons may be, you are perfectly correct," said she. "I started from home before six, reached Leatherhead at twenty past, and came in by the first train to Waterloo. Sir, I can stand this strain no longer; I shall go mad if it continues. I have no one to turn to—none, save only one, who cares for me, and he, poor fellow, can be of little aid. I have heard of you, Mr. Holmes; I have heard of you from Mrs. Farintosh, whom you helped in the hour of her sore need. It was from her that I had your address. Oh, sir, do you not think that you could help me, too, and at least throw a little light through the dense darkness which surrounds me? At present it is out of my power to reward you for your services, but in a month or six weeks I shall be married, with the control of my own income, and then at least you shall not find me ungrateful."

Holmes turned to his desk and, unlocking it, drew out a small casebook, which he consulted.

"Farintosh," said he. "Ah yes, I recall the case; it was concerned with an opal tiara. I think it was before your time, Watson. I can only say, madam, that I shall be happy to devote the same care to your case as I did to that of your friend. As to reward, my profession is its own reward; but you are at liberty to defray whatever expenses I may be put to, at the time which suits you best. And now I beg that you will lay before us everything that may help us in forming an opinion upon the matter."

"Alas!" replied our visitor, "the very horror of my situation lies in the fact that my fears are so vague, and my suspicions depend so entirely upon small points, which might seem trivial to another, that even he to whom of all others I have a right to look for help and advice looks upon all that I tell him about it as the fancies of a nervous woman. He does not say so, but I can read it from his soothing answers and averted eyes. But I have heard, Mr. Holmes, that you can see deeply into the manifold wickedness of the human heart. You may advise me how to walk amid the dangers which encompass me."

"I am all attention, madam."

"My name is Helen Stoner, and I am living with my stepfather, who is the last survivor of one of the oldest Saxon families in England, the Roylotts of Stoke Moran, on the western border of Surrey."

Holmes nodded his head. "The name is familiar to me," said he.

"The family was at one time among the richest in England, and the estates extended over the borders into Berkshire in the north, and Hampshire in the west. In the last century, however, four successive heirs were of a dissolute and wasteful disposition, and the family ruin was eventually completed by a gambler in the days of the Regency. Nothing was left save a few acres of ground, and the two-hundred-year-old house, which is itself crushed under a heavy mortgage. The last squire dragged out his existence there, living the horrible life of an aristocratic pauper; but his only son, my stepfather, seeing that he must adapt himself to the new conditions, obtained an advance from a relative, which enabled him to take a medical degree and went out to Calcutta, where, by his professional skill and his force of character, he established a large practice. In a fit of anger, however, caused by some robberies which had been perpetrated in the house, he beat his native butler to death and narrowly escaped a capital sentence. As it was, he suffered a long term of imprisonment and afterwards returned to England a morose and disappointed man.

"When Dr. Roylott was in India he married my mother, Mrs. Stoner, the young widow of Major-General Stoner, of the Bengal Artillery. My sister Julia and I were twins, and we were only two years old at the time of my mother's re-marriage. She had a considerable sum of money—not less than £1000 a year—and this she bequeathed to Dr. Roylott entirely while we resided with him, with a provision that a certain annual sum should be allowed to each of us in the event of our marriage. Shortly after our return to England my mother died—she was killed eight years ago in a railway accident near Crewe. Dr. Roylott then abandoned his attempts to establish himself in practice in London and took us to live with him in the old ancestral house at Stoke Moran. The money which my mother had left was enough for all our wants, and there seemed to be no obstacle to our happiness.

"But a terrible change came over our stepfather about this time. Instead of making friends and exchanging visits with our neighbours, who had at first been overjoyed to see a Roylott of Stoke Moran back in the old family seat, he shut himself up in his house and seldom came out save to indulge in ferocious quarrels with whoever might cross his path. Violence of temper approaching to mania has been hereditary in the men of the family, and in my stepfather's case it had, I believe, been intensified by his long residence in the tropics. A series of disgraceful brawls took place, two of which ended in the police-court, until at last he became the terror of the village, and the folks would fly at his approach, for he is a man of immense strength, and absolutely uncontrollable in his anger.

"Last week he hurled the local blacksmith over a parapet into a stream, and it was only by paying over all the money which I could gather together that I was able to avert another public exposure. He had no friends at all save the wandering gypsies, and he would give these vagabonds leave to encamp upon the few acres of bramble-covered land which represent the family estate, and would accept in return the hospitality of their tents, wandering away with them sometimes for weeks on end. He has a passion also for Indian animals, which are sent over to him by a correspondent, and he has at this moment a cheetah and a baboon, which wander freely over his grounds and are feared by the villagers almost as much as their master.

"You can imagine from what I say that my poor sister Julia and I had no great pleasure in our lives. No servant would stay with us, and for a long time we did all the work of the house. She was but thirty at the time of her death, and yet her hair had already begun to whiten, even as mine has."

"Your sister is dead, then?"

"She died just two years ago, and it is of her death that I wish to speak to you. You can understand that, living the life which I have described, we were little likely to see anyone of our own age and position. We had, however, an aunt, my mother's maiden sister, Miss Honoria Westphail, who lives near Harrow, and we were occasionally allowed to pay short visits at this lady's house. Julia went there at Christmas two years ago, and met there a half-pay major of marines, to whom she became engaged. My stepfather learned of the engagement when my sister returned and offered no objection to the marriage; but within a fortnight of the day which had been fixed for the wedding, the terrible event occurred which has deprived me of my only companion."

Sherlock Holmes had been leaning back in his chair with his eyes closed and his head sunk in a cushion but he half opened his lids now and glanced across at his visitor.

"Pray be precise as to details," said he.

"It is easy for me to be so, for every event of that dreadful time is seared into my memory. The manor-house is, as I have already said, very old, and only one wing is now inhabited. The bedrooms in this wing are on the ground floor, the sitting-rooms being in the central block of the buildings. Of these bedrooms the first is Dr. Roylott's, the second my sister's, and the third my own. There is no communication between them, but they all open out into the same corridor. Do I make myself plain?'

"Perfectly so."

"The windows of the three rooms open out upon the lawn. That fatal night Dr. Roylott had gone to his room early, though we knew that he had not retired to rest, for my sister was troubled by the smell of the strong Indian cigars which it was his custom to smoke. She left her room, therefore, and came into mine, where she sat for some time, chatting about her approaching wedding. At eleven o'clock she rose to leave me, but she paused at the door and looked back.

" 'Tell me, Helen,' said she, 'have you ever heard anyone whistle in the dead of the night?'

" 'Never,' said I.

" 'I suppose that you could not possibly whistle, yourself, in your sleep?'

" 'Certainly not. But why?'

" 'Because during the last few nights I have always, about three in the morning, heard a low, clear whistle. I am a light sleeper, and it has awakened me. I cannot tell where it came from—perhaps from the next room, perhaps from the lawn. I thought that I would just ask you whether you had heard it.'

" 'No, I have not. It must be those wretched gypsies in the plantation.'

" 'Very likely. And yet if it were on the lawn, I wonder that you did not hear it also.'

" 'Ah, but I sleep more heavily than you.'

" 'Well, it is of no great consequence, at any rate.' She smiled back at me, closed my door, and a few moments later I heard her key turn in the lock."

"Indeed," said Holmes. "Was it your custom always to lock yourselves in at night?"

"Always."

"And why?"

"I think that I mentioned to you that the doctor kept a cheetah and a baboon. We had no feeling of security unless our doors were locked."

"Quite so. Pray proceed with your statement."

"I could not sleep that night. A vague feeling of impending misfortune impressed me. My sister and I, you will recollect, were twins, and you know how subtle are the links which bind two souls which are so closely allied. It was a wild night. The wind was howling outside, and the rain was beating and splashing against the windows. Suddenly, amid all the hubbub of the gale, there burst forth the wild scream of a terrified woman. I knew that it was my sister's voice. I sprang from my bed, wrapped a shawl round me, and rushed into the corridor. As I opened my door I seemed to hear a low whistle, such as my sister described, and a few moments later a clanging sound, as if a mass of metal had fallen. As

I ran down the passage, my sister's door was unlocked, and revolved slowly upon its hinges. I stared at it horror-stricken, not knowing what was about to issue from it. By the light of the corridor-lamp I saw my sister appear at the opening, her face blanched with terror, her hands groping for help, her whole figure swaying to and fro like that of a drunkard. I ran to her and threw my arms round her, but at that moment her knees seemed to give way and she fell to the ground. She writhed as one who is in terrible pain, and her limbs were dreadfully convulsed. At first I thought that she had not recognized me, but as I bent over her she suddenly shrieked out in a voice which I shall never forget, 'Oh, my God! Helen! It was the band! The speckled band!' There was something else which she would fain have said, and she stabbed with her finger into the air in the direction of the doctor's room, but a fresh convulsion seized her and choked her words. I rushed out, calling loudly for my stepfather, and I met him hastening from his room in his dressing–gown. When he reached my sister's side she was unconscious, and though he poured brandy down her throat and sent for medical aid from the village, all efforts were in vain, for she slowly sank and died without having recovered her consciousness. Such was the dreadful end of my beloved sister."

"One moment," said Holmes; "are you sure about this whistle and metallic sound? Could you swear to it?"

"That was what the county coroner asked me at the inquiry. It is my strong impression that I heard it, and yet, among the crash of the gale and the creaking of an old house, I may possibly have been deceived."

"Was your sister dressed?"

"No, she was in her night-dress. In her right hand was found the charred stump of a match, and in her left a match-box."

"Showing that she had struck a light and looked about her when the alarm took place. That is important. And what conclusions did the coroner come to?"

"He investigated the case with great care, for Dr. Roylott's conduct had long been notorious in the county, but he was unable to find any satisfactory cause of death. My evidence showed that the door had been fastened upon the inner side, and the windows were blocked by old-fashioned shutters with broad iron bars, which were secured every night. The walls were carefully sounded and were shown to be quite solid all round, and the flooring was also thoroughly examined, with the same result. The chimney is wide, but is barred up by four large staples. It is certain, therefore, that my sister was quite alone when she met her end. Besides, there were no marks of any violence upon her."

"How about poison?"

"The doctors examined her for it, but without success."

"What do you think that this unfortunate lady died of, then?"

"It is my belief that she died of pure fear and nervous shock, though what it was that frightened her I cannot imagine."

"Were there gypsies in the plantation at the time?"

"Yes, there are nearly always some there."

"Ah, and what did you gather from this allusion to a band—a speckled band?"

"Sometimes I have thought that it was merely the wild talk of delirium, sometimes that it may have referred to some band of people, perhaps to these very gypsies in the plantation. I do not know whether the spotted handkerchiefs which so many of them wear over their heads might have suggested the strange adjective which she used."

Holmes shook his head like a man who is far from being satisfied.

"These are very deep waters," said he; "pray go on with your narrative."

"Two years have passed since then, and my life has been until lately lonelier than ever. A month ago, however, a dear friend, whom I have known for many years, has done me the honour to ask my hand in marriage. His name is Armitage—Percy Armitage—the second son of Mr. Armitage, of Crane Water, near Reading. My stepfather has offered no opposition to the match, and we are to be married in the course of the spring. Two days ago some repairs were started in the west wing of the building, and my bedroom wall has been pierced, so that I have had to move into the chamber in which my sister died, and to sleep in the very bed in which she slept. Imagine, then, my thrill of terror when last night, as I lay awake, thinking over her terrible fate, I suddenly heard in the silence of the night the low whistle which had been the herald of her own death. I sprang up and lit the lamp, but nothing was to be seen in the room. I was too shaken to go to bed again, however, so I dressed, and as soon as it was daylight I slipped down, got a dogcart at the Crown Inn, which is opposite, and drove to Leatherhead, from whence I have come on this morning with the one object of seeing you and asking your advice."

"You have done wisely," said my friend. "But have you told me all?"

"Yes, all."

"Miss Stoner, you have not. You are screening your stepfather."

"Why, what do you mean?"

For answer Holmes pushed back the frill of black lace which fringed the hand that lay upon our visitor's knee. Five little livid spots, the marks of four fingers and a thumb, were printed upon the white wrist.

"You have been cruelly used," said Holmes.

The lady coloured deeply and covered over her injured wrist. "He is a hard man," she said, "and perhaps he hardly knows his own strength."

There was a long silence, during which Holmes leaned his chin upon his hands and stared into the crackling fire.

"This is a very deep business," he said at last. "There are a thousand details which I should desire to know before I decide upon our course of action. Yet we have not a moment to lose. If we were to come to Stoke Moran to-day, would it be possible for us to see over these rooms without the knowledge of your stepfather?"

"As it happens, he spoke of coming into town to-day upon some most important business. It is probable that he will be away all day, and that there would be nothing to disturb you. We have a housekeeper now, but she is old and foolish, and I could easily get her out of the way."

"Excellent. You are not averse to this trip, Watson?"

"By no means."

"Then we shall both come. What are you going to do yourself?"

"I have one or two things which I would wish to do now that I am in town. But I shall return by the twelve o'clock train, so as to be there in time for your coming."

"And you may expect us early in the afternoon. I have myself some small business matters to attend to. Will you not wait and breakfast?"

"No, I must go. My heart is lightened already since I have confided my trouble to you. I shall look forward to seeing you again this afternoon." She dropped her thick black veil over her face and glided from the room.

"And what do you think of it all, Watson?" asked Sherlock Holmes leaning back in his chair.

"It seems to me to be a most dark and sinister business."

"Dark enough and sinister enough."

"Yet if the lady is correct in saying that the flooring and walls are sound, and that the door, window, and chimney are impassable, then her sister must have been undoubtedly alone when she met her mysterious end."

"What becomes, then, of these nocturnal whistles, and what of the very peculiar words of the dying woman?"

"I cannot think."

"When you combine the ideas of whistles at night, the presence of a band of gypsies who are on intimate terms with this old doctor, the fact that we have every reason to believe that the doctor has an interest in preventing his step-daughter's marriage, the dying allusion to a band, and, finally, the fact that Miss Helen Stoner heard a metallic clang, which might have been caused by one of those metal bars that secured the shutters falling back into its place, I think that there is good ground to think that the mystery may be cleared along those lines."

"But what, then, did the gypsies do?"

"I cannot imagine."

"I see many objections to any such theory."

"And so do I. It is precisely for that reason that we are going to Stoke Moran this day. I want to see whether the objections are fatal, or if they may be explained away. But what in the name of the devil!"

The ejaculation had been drawn from my companion by the fact that our door had been suddenly dashed open, and that a huge man had framed himself in the aperture. His costume was a peculiar mixture of the professional and of the agricultural, having a black top-hat, a long frock-coat, and a pair of high gaiters, with a hunting-crop swinging in his hand. So tall was he that his hat actually brushed the cross bar of the doorway, and his breadth seemed to span it across from side to side. A large face, seared with a thousand wrinkles, burned yellow with the sun, and marked with every evil passion, was turned from one to the other of us, while his deep-set, bile-shot eyes, and his high, thin, fleshless nose, gave him somewhat the resemblance to a fierce old bird of prey.

"Which of you is Holmes?" asked this apparition.

"My name, sir; but you have the advantage of me," said my companion quietly.

"I am Dr. Grimesby Roylott, of Stoke Moran."

"Indeed, Doctor," said Holmes blandly. "Pray take a seat."

"I will do nothing of the kind. My stepdaughter has been here. I have traced her. What has she been saying to you?"

"It is a little cold for the time of the year," said Holmes.

"What has she been saying to you?" screamed the old man furiously.

"But I have heard that the crocuses promise well," continued my companion imperturbably.

"Ha! You put me off, do you?" said our new visitor, taking a step forward and shaking his hunting-crop. "I know you, you scoundrel! I have heard of you before. You are Holmes, the meddler."

My friend smiled.

"Holmes, the busybody!"

His smile broadened.

"Holmes, the Scotland Yard Jack-in-office!"

Holmes chuckled heartily. "Your conversation is most entertaining," said he. "When you go out close the door, for there is a decided draught."

"I will go when I have said my say. Don't you dare to meddle with my affairs. I know that Miss Stoner has been here. I traced her! I am a dangerous man to fall foul of! See here." He stepped swiftly forward, seized the poker, and bent it into a curve with his huge brown hands.

"See that you keep yourself out of my grip," he snarled, and hurling the twisted poker into the fireplace he strode out of the room.

"He seems a very amiable person," said Holmes, laughing. "I am not quite so bulky, but if he had remained I might have shown him that my grip was not much more feeble than his own." As he spoke he picked up the steel poker and, with a sudden effort, straightened it out again.

"Fancy his having the insolence to confound me with the official detective force! This incident gives zest to our investigation, however, and I only trust that our little friend will not suffer from her imprudence in allowing this brute to trace her. And now, Watson, we shall order breakfast, and afterwards I shall walk down to Doctors' Commons, where I hope to get some data which may help us in this matter."

It was nearly one o'clock when Sherlock Holmes returned from his excursion. He held in his hand a sheet of blue paper, scrawled over with notes and figures.

"I have seen the will of the deceased wife," said he. "To determine its exact meaning I have been obliged to work out the present prices of the investments with which it is concerned. The total income, which at the time of the wife's death was little short of £1100, is now through the fall in agricultural prices, not more than £750. Each daughter can claim an income of £250, in case of marriage. It is evident, therefore, that if both girls had married, this beauty would have had a mere pittance, while even one of them would cripple him to a very serious extent. My morning's work has not been wasted, since it has proved that he has the very strongest motives for standing in the way of anything of the sort. And now, Watson, this is too serious for dawdling, especially as the old man is aware that we are interesting ourselves in his affairs; so if you are ready, we shall call a cab and drive to Waterloo. I should be very much obliged if you would slip your revolver into your pocket. An Eley's No. 2 is an excellent argument with gentlemen who can twist steel pokers into knots. That and a tooth-brush are, I think, all that we need."

At Waterloo we were fortunate in catching a train for Leatherhead, where we hired a trap at the station inn and drove for four or five miles through the lovely Surrey lanes. It was a perfect day, with a bright sun and a few fleecy clouds in the heavens. The trees and wayside hedges were just throwing out their first green shoots, and the air was full of the pleasant smell of the moist earth. To me at least there was a strange contrast between the sweet promise of the spring and this sinister quest upon which we were engaged. My companion sat in the front of the trap, his arms folded, his hat pulled down over his eyes, and his chin sunk upon his breast, buried in the deepest thought. Suddenly, however, he started, tapped me on the shoulder, and pointed over the meadows.

"Look there!" said he.

A heavily timbered park stretched up in a gentle slope, thickening into a grove at the highest point. From amid the branches there jutted out the gray gables and high roof-tree of a very old mansion.

"Stoke Moran?" said he.

"Yes, sir, that be the house of Dr. Grimesby Roylott," remarked the driver.

"There is some building going on there," said Holmes; "that is where we are going."

"There's the village," said the driver, pointing to a cluster of roofs some distance to the left; "but if you want to get to the house, you'll find it shorter to get over this stile, and so by the foot-path over the fields. There it is, where the lady is walking."

"And the lady, I fancy, is Miss Stoner," observed Holmes, shading his eyes. "Yes, I think we had better do as you suggest."

We got off, paid our fare, and the trap rattled back on its way to Leatherhead.

"I thought it as well," said Holmes as we climbed the stile, "that this fellow should think we had come here as architects, or on some definite business. It may stop his gossip. Good-afternoon, Miss Stoner. You see that we have been as good as our word."

Our client of the morning had hurried forward to meet us with a face which spoke her joy. "I have been waiting so eagerly for you," she cried, shaking hands with us warmly. "All has turned out splendidly. Dr. Roylott has gone to town, and it is unlikely that he will be back before evening."

"We have had the pleasure of making the doctor's acquaintance," said Holmes, and in a few words he sketched out what had occurred. Miss Stoner turned white to the lips as she listened.

"Good heavens!" she cried, "he has followed me, then."

"So it appears."

"He is so cunning that I never know when I am safe from him. What will he say when he returns?"

"He must guard himself, for he may find that there is someone more cunning than himself upon his track. You must lock yourself up from him to-night. If he is violent, we shall take you away to your aunt's at Harrow. Now, we must make the best use of our time, so kindly take us at once to the rooms which we are to examine."

The building was of gray, lichen-blotched stone, with a high central portion and two curving wings, like the claws of a crab, thrown out on each side. In one of these wings the windows were broken and blocked with wooden boards, while the roof was partly caved in, a picture of ruin. The central portion was in little better repair, but the right-hand block was comparatively modern, and the blinds in the windows, with the blue smoke curling up from the chimneys, showed that this was where the family resided. Some scaffolding had been erected against the end wall, and the stone-work had been broken into, but there were no signs of any workmen at the moment of our visit. Holmes walked slowly up and down the ill-trimmed lawn and examined with deep attention the outsides of the windows.

"This, I take it, belongs to the room in which you used to sleep, the centre one to your sister's, and the one next to the main building to Dr. Roylott's chamber?"

"Exactly so. But I am now sleeping in the middle one."

"Pending the alterations, as I understand. By the way, there does not seem to be any very pressing need for repairs at that end wall."

"There were none. I believe that it was an excuse to move me from my room."

"Ah! That is suggestive. Now, on the other side of this narrow wing runs the corridor from which these three rooms open. There are windows in it, of course?"

"Yes, but very small ones. Too narrow for anyone to pass through."

"As you both locked your doors at night, your rooms were unapproachable from that side. Now, would you have the kindness to go into your room and bar your shutters?"

Miss Stoner did so, and Holmes, after a careful examination through the open window, endeavoured in every way to force the shutter open, but without success. There was no slit through which a knife could be passed to raise the bar. Then with his lens he tested the hinges, but they were of solid iron, built firmly into the massive masonry. "Hum!" said he, scratching his chin in some perplexity, "my theory certainly presents some difficulties. No one could pass these shutters if they were bolted. Well, we shall see if the inside throws any light upon the matter."

A small side door led into the whitewashed corridor from which the three bedrooms opened. Holmes refused to examine the third chamber, so we passed at once to the second, that in which Miss Stoner was now sleeping, and in which her sister had met with her fate. It was a homely little room with a low ceiling and a gaping fireplace, after the fashion of old country-houses. A brown chest of drawers stood in one corner, a narrow white-counterpaned bed in another, and a dressing-table on the left-hand side of the window. These articles, with two small wicker-work chairs, made up all the furniture in the room save for a square of Wilton carpet in the centre. The boards round and the panelling of the walls were of brown, worm-eaten oak, so old and discolored that it may have dated from the original building of the house. Holmes drew one of the chairs into a corner and sat silent, while his eyes travelled round and round and up and down, taking in every detail of the apartment.

"Where does that bell communicate with?" he asked at last, pointing to a thick bell-rope which hung down beside the bed, the tassel actually lying upon the pillow.

"It goes to the housekeeper's room."

"It looks newer than the other things?"

"Yes, it was only put there a couple of years ago."

"Your sister asked for it, I suppose?"

"No, I never heard of her using it. We used always to get what we wanted for ourselves."

"Indeed, it seemed unnecessary to put so nice a bell-pull there. You will excuse me for a few minutes while I satisfy myself as to this floor." He threw himself down upon his face with his lens in his hand and crawled swiftly backward and forward, examining minutely the cracks between the boards. Then he did the same with the wood-work with which the chamber was panelled. Finally he walked over to the bed and spent some time in staring at it and in running his eye up and down the wall. Finally he took the bell-rope in his hand and gave it a brisk tug.

"Why, it's a dummy," said he.

"Won't it ring?"

"No, it is not even attached to a wire. This is very interesting. You can see now that it is fastened to a hook just above where the little opening for the ventilator is."

"How very absurd! I never noticed that before."

"Very strange!" muttered Holmes, pulling at the rope. "There are one or two very singular points about this room. For example, what a fool a builder must be to open a ventilator into another room, when, with the same trouble, he might have communicated with the outside air!"

"That is also quite modern," said the lady.

"Done about the same time as the bell-rope?" remarked Holmes.

"Yes, there were several little changes carried out about that time."

"They seem to have been of a most interesting character—dummy bell-ropes, and ventilators which do not ventilate. With your permission, Miss Stoner, we shall now carry our researches into the inner apartment."

Dr. Grimesby Roylott's chamber was larger than that of his stepdaughter, but was as plainly furnished. A camp-bed, a small wooden shelf full of books, mostly of a technical character, an armchair beside the bed, a plain wooden chair against the wall, a round table, and a large iron safe were the principal things which met the eye. Holmes walked slowly round and examined each and all of them with the keenest interest.

"What's in here?" he asked, tapping the safe.

"My stepfather's business papers."

"Oh! you have seen inside, then?"

"Only once, some years ago. I remember that it was full of papers."

"There isn't a cat in it, for example?"

"No. What a strange idea!"

"Well, look at this!" He took up a small saucer of milk which stood on the top of it.

"No; we don't keep a cat. But there is a cheetah and a baboon."

"Ah, yes, of course! Well, a cheetah is just a big cat, and yet a saucer of milk does not go very far in satisfying its wants, I daresay. There is one point which I should wish to determine." He squatted down in front of the wooden chair and examined the seat of it with the greatest attention.

"Thank you. That is quite settled," said he, rising and putting his lens in his pocket. "Hello! Here is something interesting!"

The object which had caught his eye was a small dog lash hung on one corner of the bed. The lash, however, was curled upon itself and tied so as to make a loop of whipcord.

"What do you make of that, Watson?"

"It's a common enough lash. But I don't know why it should be tied."

"That is not quite so common, is it? Ah, me! it's a wicked world, and when a clever man turns his brains to crime it is the worst of all. I think that I have seen enough now, Miss Stoner, and with your permission we shall walk out upon the lawn."

I had never seen my friend's face so grim or his brow so dark as it was when we turned from the scene of his investigation. We had walked several times up and down the lawn, neither Miss Stoner nor myself liking to break in upon his thoughts before he roused himself from his reverie.

"It is very essential, Miss Stoner," said he, "that you should absolutely follow my advice in every respect."

"I shall most certainly do so."

"The matter is too serious for any hesitation. Your life may depend upon your compliance."

"I assure you that I am in your hands."

"In the first place, both my friend and I must spend the night in your room."

Both Miss Stoner and I gazed at him in astonishment.

"Yes, it must be so. Let me explain. I believe that that is the village inn over there?"

"Yes, that is the Crown."

"Very good. Your windows would be visible from there?"

"Certainly."

"You must confine yourself to your room, on pretence of a headache, when your stepfather comes back. Then when you hear him retire for the night, you must open the shutters of your window, undo the hasp, put your lamp there as a signal to us, and then withdraw quietly with everything which you are likely to want into the room which you used to occupy. I have no doubt that, in spite of the repairs, you could manage there for one night."

"Oh, yes, easily."

"The rest you will leave in our hands."

"But what will you do?"

"We shall spend the night in your room, and we shall investigate the cause of this noise which has disturbed you."

"I believe, Mr. Holmes, that you have already made up your mind," said Miss Stoner, laying her hand upon my companion's sleeve.

"Perhaps I have."

"Then, for pity's sake, tell me what was the cause of my sister's death."

"I should prefer to have clearer proofs before I speak."

"You can at least tell me whether my own thought is correct, and if she died from some sudden fright."

"No, I do not think so. I think that there was probably some more tangible cause. And now, Miss Stoner, we must leave you, for if Dr. Roylott returned and saw us our journey would be in vain. Good-bye, and be brave, for if you will do what I have told you you may rest assured that we shall soon drive away the dangers that threaten you."

Sherlock Holmes and I had no difficulty in engaging a bedroom and sitting-room at the Crown, Inn. They were on the upper floor, and from our window we could command a view of the avenue gate, and of the inhabited wing of Stoke Moran Manor House. At dusk we saw Dr. Grimesby Roylott drive past, his huge form looming up beside the little figure of the lad who drove him. The boy had some slight difficulty in undoing the heavy iron gates, and we heard the hoarse roar of the doctor's voice and saw the fury with which he shook his clinched fists at him. The trap drove on, and a few minutes later we saw a sudden light spring up among the trees as the lamp was lit in one of the sitting-rooms.

"Do you know, Watson," said Holmes as we sat together in the gathering darkness, "I have really some scruples as to taking you to-night. There is a distinct element of danger."

"Can I be of assistance?"

"Your presence might be invaluable."

"Then I shall certainly come."

"It is very kind of you."

"You speak of danger. You have evidently seen more in these rooms than was visible to me."

"No, but I fancy that I may have deduced a little more. I imagine that you saw all that I did."

"I saw nothing remarkable save the bell-rope, and what purpose that could answer I confess is more than I can imagine."

"You saw the ventilator, too?"

"Yes, but I do not think that it is such a very unusual thing to have a small opening between two rooms. It was so small that a rat could hardly pass through."

"I knew that we should find a ventilator before ever we came to Stoke Moran."

"My dear Holmes!"

"Oh, yes, I did. You remember in her statement she said that her sister could smell Dr. Roylott's cigar. Now, of course that suggested at once that there must be a communication between the two rooms. It could only be a small one, or it would have been remarked upon at the coroner's inquiry. I deduced a ventilator."

"But what harm can there be in that?"

"Well, there is at least a curious coincidence of dates. A ventilator is made, a cord is hung, and a lady who sleeps in the bed dies. Does not that strike you?"

"I cannot as yet see any connection."

"Did you observe anything very peculiar about that bed?"

"No."

"It was clamped to the floor. Did you ever see a bed fastened like that before?"

"I cannot say that I have."

"The lady could not move her bed. It must always be in the same relative position to the ventilator and to the rope—or so we may call it, since it was clearly never meant for a bell-pull."

"Holmes," I cried, "I seem to see dimly what you are hinting at. We are only just in time to prevent some subtle and horrible crime."

"Subtle enough and horrible enough. When a doctor does go wrong he is the first of criminals. He has nerve and he has knowledge. Palmer and Pritchard were among the heads of their profession. This man strikes even deeper, but I think, Watson, that we shall be able to strike deeper still. But we shall have horrors enough before the night is over; for goodness' sake let us have a quiet pipe and turn our minds for a few hours to something more cheerful."

About nine o'clock the light among the trees was extinguished, and all was dark in the direction of the Manor House. Two hours passed slowly away, and then, suddenly, just at the stroke of eleven, a single bright light shone out right in front of us.

"That is our signal," said Holmes, springing to his feet; "it comes from the middle window."

As we passed out he exchanged a few words with the landlord, explaining that we were going on a late visit to an acquaintance, and that it was possible that we might spend the night there. A moment later we were out on the dark road, a chill wind blowing in our faces, and one yellow light twinkling in front of us through the gloom to guide us on our sombre errand.

There was little difficulty in entering the grounds, for unrepaired breaches gaped in the old park wall. Making our way among the trees, we reached the lawn, crossed it, and were about to enter through the window when out from a clump of laurel bushes there darted what seemed to be a hideous and distorted child, who threw itself upon the grass with writhing limbs and then ran swiftly across the lawn into the darkness.

"My God!" I whispered; "did you see it?"

Holmes was for the moment as startled as I. His hand closed like a vise upon my wrist in his agitation. Then he broke into a low laugh and put his lips to my ear.

"It is a nice household," he murmured. "That is the baboon."

I had forgotten the strange pets which the doctor affected. There was a cheetah, too; perhaps we might find it upon our shoulders at any moment. I confess that I felt easier in my mind when, after following Holmes's example and slipping off my shoes, I found myself inside the bedroom. My companion noiselessly closed the shutters, moved the lamp onto the table, and cast his eyes round the room. All was as we had seen it in the daytime. Then creeping up to me and making a trumpet of his hand, he whispered into my ear again so gently that it was all that I could do to distinguish the words:

"The least sound would be fatal to our plans."

I nodded to show that I had heard.

"We must sit without light. He would see it through the ventilator."

I nodded again.

"Do not go asleep; your very life may depend upon it. Have your pistol ready in case we should need it. I will sit on the side of the bed, and you in that chair."

I took out my revolver and laid it on the corner of the table.

Holmes had brought up a long thin cane, and this he placed upon the bed beside him. By it he laid the box of matches and the stump of a candle. Then he turned down the lamp, and we were left in darkness.

How shall I ever forget that dreadful vigil? I could not hear a sound, not even the drawing of a breath, and yet I knew that my companion sat open-eyed, within a few feet of me, in the same state of nervous tension in which I was myself. The shutters cut off the least ray of light, and we waited in absolute darkness. From outside came the occasional cry of a night-bird, and once at our very window a long drawn catlike whine, which told us that the cheetah was indeed at liberty. Far away we could hear the deep tones of the parish clock, which boomed out every quarter of an hour. How long they seemed, those quarters! Twelve struck, and one and two and three, and still we sat waiting silently for whatever might befall.

Suddenly there was the momentary gleam of a light up in the direction of the ventilator, which vanished immediately, but was succeeded by a strong smell of burning oil and heated metal. Someone in the next room had lit a dark-lantern. I heard a gentle sound of movement, and then all was silent once more, though the smell grew stronger. For half an hour I sat with straining ears. Then suddenly another sound became audible—a very gentle, soothing sound, like that of a small jet of steam escaping continually from a kettle. The instant that we heard it, Holmes sprang from the bed, struck a match, and lashed furiously with his cane at the bell-pull.

"You see it, Watson?" he yelled. "You see it?"

But I saw nothing. At the moment when Holmes struck the light I heard a low, clear whistle, but the sudden glare flashing into my weary eyes made it impossible for me to tell what it was at which my friend lashed so savagely. I could, however, see that his face was deadly pale and filled with horror and loathing.

He had ceased to strike and was gazing up at the ventilator when suddenly there broke from the silence of the night the most horrible cry to which I have ever listened. It swelled up louder and louder, a hoarse yell of pain and fear and anger all mingled in the one dreadful shriek. They say that away down in the village, and even in the distant parsonage, that cry raised the sleepers from their beds. It struck cold to our hearts, and I stood gazing at Holmes, and he at me, until the last echoes of it had died away into the silence from which it rose.

"What can it mean?" I gasped.

"It means that it is all over," Holmes answered. "And perhaps, after all, it is for the best. Take your pistol, and we will enter Dr. Roylott's room."

With a grave face he lit the lamp and led the way down the corridor. Twice he struck at the chamber door without any reply from within. Then he turned the handle and entered, I at his heels, with the cocked pistol in my hand.

It was a singular sight which met our eyes. On the table stood a dark-lantern with the shutter half open, throwing a brilliant beam of light upon the iron safe, the door of which was ajar. Beside this table, on the wooden chair, sat Dr. Grimesby Roylott, clad in a long gray dressing-gown, his bare ankles protruding beneath, and his feet thrust into red heelless Turkish slippers. Across his lap lay the short stock with the long lash which we had noticed during the day. His chin was cocked upward and his eyes were fixed in a dreadful, rigid stare at the corner of the ceiling. Round his brow he had a peculiar yellow band, with brownish speckles, which seemed to be bound tightly round his head. As we entered he made neither sound nor motion.

"The band! the speckled band!" whispered Holmes.

I took a step forward. In an instant his strange headgear began to move, and there reared itself from among his hair the squat diamond-shaped head and puffed neck of a loathsome serpent.

"It is a swamp adder!" cried Holmes; "the deadliest snake in India. He has died within ten seconds of being bitten. Violence does, in truth, recoil upon the violent, and the schemer falls into the pit which he digs for another. Let us thrust this creature back into its den, and we can then remove Miss Stoner to some place of shelter and let the county police know what has happened."

As he spoke he drew the dog-whip swiftly from the dead man's lap, and throwing the noose round the reptile's neck he drew it from its horrid perch and, carrying it at arm's length, threw it into the iron safe, which he closed upon it.

Such are the true facts of the death of Dr. Grimesby Roylott, of Stoke Moran. It is not necessary that I should prolong a narrative which has already run to too great a length by telling how we broke the sad news to the terrified girl, how we conveyed her by the morning train to the care of her good aunt at Harrow, of how the slow process of official inquiry came to the conclusion that the doctor met his fate while indiscreetly playing with a dangerous pet. The little which I had yet to learn of the case was told me by Sherlock Holmes as we travelled back next day.

"I had," said he, "come to an entirely erroneous conclusion which shows, my dear Watson, how dangerous it always is to reason from insufficient data. The presence of the gypsies, and the use of the word 'band,' which was used by the poor girl, no doubt to explain the appearance which she had caught a hurried glimpse of by the light of her match, were sufficient to put me upon an entirely wrong scent. I can only claim the merit that I instantly reconsidered my position when, however, it became clear to me that whatever danger threatened an occupant of the room could not come either from the window or the door. My attention was speedily drawn, as I have already remarked to you, to this ventilator, and to the bell-rope which hung down to the bed. The discovery that this was a dummy, and that the bed was clamped to the floor, instantly gave rise to the suspicion that the rope was there as bridge for something passing through the hole and coming to the bed. The idea of a snake instantly occurred to me, and when I coupled it with my knowledge that the doctor was furnished with a supply of creatures from India, I felt that I was probably on the right track. The idea of using a form of poison which could not possibly be discovered by any chemical test was just such a one as would occur to a clever and ruthless man who had had an Eastern training. The rapidity with which such a poison would take effect would also, from his point of view, be an advantage. It would be a sharp-eyed coroner, indeed, who could distinguish the two little dark punctures which would show where the poison fangs had done their work. Then I thought of the whistle. Of course he must recall the snake before the morning light revealed it to the victim. He had trained it, probably by use of the milk which we saw, to return to him when summoned. He would put it through this ventilator at the hour that he thought best, with the certainty that it would crawl down the rope and land on the bed. It might or might not bite the occupant, perhaps she might escape every night for a week, but sooner or later she must fall a victim.

"I had come to these conclusions before ever I had entered his room. An inspection of his chair showed me that he had been in the habit of standing on it, which of course would be necessary in order that he should reach the ventilator. The sight of the safe, the saucer of milk, and the loop of whipcord were enough to finally dispel any doubts which may have remained. The metallic clang heard by Miss Stoner was obviously caused by her stepfather hastily closing the door of his safe upon its terrible occupant. Having once made up my mind, you know the steps which I took in order to put the matter to the proof. I heard the creature hiss as I have no doubt that you did also, and I instantly lit the light and attacked it."

"With the result of driving it through the ventilator."

"And also with the result of causing it to turn upon its master at the other side. Some of the blows of my cane came home and roused its snakish temper, so that it flew upon the first person it saw. In this way I am no doubt indirectly responsible for Dr. Grimesby Roylott's death, and I cannot say that it is likely to weigh very heavily upon my conscience."

Questions

1. Where is the major section of the exposition?
2. How does the placement of the exposition contribute to narrative focus?
3. Where does Doyle place the death scene between the two sisters? How does that placement contribute to the narrative focus?
4. Doctor Roylott enters the story as a surprise. Why does Doyle choose that moment to present him? Could there have been a more appropriate time? Does his presence in Holmes's house alter events? Do we ever see him alive again?
5. Where is the climax of the story? Do we know all the narrative facts by the time of the climax? How does our knowledge or lack of it contribute to the effectiveness of the climax?
6. Why does Holmes refuse to tell Helen Stoner his suspicions about her father? Why does he say only that he prefers to have "clearer proofs"?
7. Could this story have been told in chronological order? Would it have gained in clarity? In narrative focus? What would have happened to the character of Holmes?

STEPHEN CRANE (1871–1900)

The Blue Hotel

I

The Palace Hotel at Fort Romper was painted a light blue, a shade that is on the legs of a kind of heron, causing the bird to declare its position against any background. The Palace Hotel, then, was always screaming and howling in a way that made the dazzling winter landscape of Nebraska seem only a gray swampish hush. It stood alone on the prairie, and when the snow was falling. the town two hundred yards away was not visible. But when the traveller alighted at the railway station he was obliged to pass the Palace Hotel before he could come upon the company of low clapboard houses which composed Fort Romper, and it was not to be thought that any traveller could pass the Palace Hotel without looking at it. Pat Scully, the proprietor, had proved himself a master of strategy when he chose his paints. It is true that on clear days, when the transcontinental express, long lines of swaying Pullmans, swept through Fort Romper, passengers were overcome at the sight, and the cult that knows the brown-reds and the subdivisions of the dark greens of the East expressed shame, pity, horror, in a laugh. But to the citizens of this prairie town and to the people who would naturally stop there, Pat Scully had performed a feat. With this opulence and splendor, these creeds, classes, egotisms, that streamed through Romper on the rails day after day, they had no color in common.

As if the display delights of such a blue hotel were not sufficiently enticing, it was Scully's habit to go every morning and evening to meet the leisurely trains that stopped at Romper and work his seductions upon any man that he might see wavering, gripsack in hand.

One morning, when a snow-crusted engine dragged its long string of freight cars and its one passenger coach to the station, Scully performed the marvel of catching three men. One was a shaky and quick-eyed Swede, with a great shining cheap valise; one was a tall bronzed cowboy, who was on his way to a ranch near the Dakota line; one was a little silent man from the East, who didn't look it, and didn't announce it. Scully practically made them prisoners. He was so nimble and merry and kindly that each probably felt it would be the height of brutality to try to escape. They trudged off over the creaking board sidewalks in the wake of the eager little Irishman. He wore a heavy fur cap squeezed tightly down on his head. It caused his two red ears to stick out stiffly, as if they were made of tin.

At last, Scully, elaborately, with boisterous hospitality, conducted them through the portals of the blue hotel. The room which they entered was small. It seemed to be merely a proper temple for an enormous stove, which, in the center, was humming with godlike violence. At various points on its surface the iron had become luminous and glowed yellow from the heat. Beside the stove Scully's son Johnnie was playing High-Five[1] with an old farmer who had whiskers both gray and sandy. They were quarrelling. Frequently the old farmer turned his face toward a box of sawdust—colored brown from tobacco juice—that was behind the stove, and spat with an air of great impatience and irritation. With a loud flourish of words Scully destroyed the game of cards, and bustled his son upstairs with part of the baggage of the new guests. He himself conducted them to three basins of the coldest water in the world. The cowboy and the Easterner burnished themselves fiery red with this water, until it seemed to be some kind of metal polish. The Swede, however, merely dipped his fingers gingerly and with trepidation. It was notable that throughout this series of small ceremonies the three travellers were made to feel that Scully was very benevolent. He was conferring great favors upon them. He handed the towel from one to another with an air of philanthropic impulse.

Afterward they went to the first room, and sitting about the stove, listened to Scully's officious clamor at his daughters, who were preparing the midday meal. They reflected in the silence of experienced men who tread carefully amid new people. Nevertheless, the old farmer, stationary, invincible in his chair near the warmest part of the stove, turned his face from the sawdust-box frequently and addressed a glowing commonplace to the strangers. Usually he was answered in short but adequate sentences by either the cowboy or the Easterner. The Swede said nothing. He seemed to be occupied in making furtive estimates of each man in the room. One might have thought that he had the sense of silly suspicion which comes to guilt. He resembled a badly frightened man.

---

[1] High-Five is a card game also known as Cinch or Double Pedro and related to Auction and Contract Bridge.

Later, at dinner, he spoke a little, addressing his conversation entirely to Scully. He volunteered that he had come from New York, where for ten years he had worked as a tailor. These facts seemed to strike Scully as fascinating, and afterward he volunteered that he had lived at Romper for fourteen years. The Swede asked about the crops and the price of labor. He seemed barely to listen to Scully's extended replies. His eyes continued to rove from man to man.

Finally, with a laugh and a wink, he said that some of these Western communities were very dangerous; and after his statement he straightened his legs under the table, tilted his head, and laughed again, loudly. It was plain that the demonstration had no meaning to the others. They looked at him wondering and in silence.

II

As the men trooped heavily back into the front room, the two little windows presented views of a turmoiling sea of snow. The huge arms of the wind were making attempts—mighty, circular, futile—to embrace the flakes as they sped. A gate-post like a still man with a blanched face stood aghast amid this profligate fury. In a hearty voice Scully announced the presence of a blizzard. The guests of the blue hotel, lighting their pipes, assented with grunts of lazy masculine contentment. No island of the sea could be exempt in the degree of this little room with its humming stove. Johnnie, son of Scully, in a tone which defined his opinion of his ability as a card-player, challenged the old farmer of both gray and sandy whiskers to a game of High-Five. The farmer agreed with a contemptuous and bitter scoff. They sat close to the stove, and squared their knees under a wide board. The cowboy and the Easterner watched the game with interest. The Swede remained near the window, aloof, but with a countenance that showed signs of an inexplicable excitement.

The play of Johnnie and the gray-beard was suddenly ended by another quarrel. The old man arose while casting a look of heated scorn at his adversary. He slowly buttoned his coat, and then stalked with fabulous dignity from the room. In the discreet silence of all the other men the Swede laughed. His laughter rang somehow childish. Men by this time had begun to look at him askance, as if they wished to inquire what ailed him.

A new game was formed jocosely. The cowboy volunteered to become the partner of Johnnie, and they all then turned to ask the Swede to throw in his lot with the little Easterner. He asked some questions about the game, and, learning that it wore many names, and that he had played it when it was under an alias, he accepted the invitation. He strode toward the men nervously, as if he expected to be assaulted. Finally, seated, he gazed from face to face and laughed shrilly. This laugh was so strange that the Easterner looked up quickly, the cowboy sat intent and with his mouth open, and Johnnie paused, holding the cards with still fingers.

Afterward there was a short silence. Then Johnnie said, "Well, let's get at it. Come on now!" They pulled their chairs forward until their knees were bunched under the board. They began to play, and their interest in the game caused the others to forget the manner of the Swede.

The cowboy was a board-whacker. Each time that he held superior cards he whanged them, one by one, with exceeding force, down upon the improvised table, and took the tricks with a glowing air of prowess and pride that sent thrills of indignation into the hearts of his opponents. A game with a board-whacker in it is sure to become intense. The countenances of the Easterner and the Swede were miserable whenever the cowboy thundered down his aces and kings, while Johnnie, his eyes gleaming with joy, chuckled and chuckled.

Because of the absorbing play none considered the strange ways of the Swede. They paid strict heed to the game. Finally, during a lull caused by a new deal, the Swede suddenly addressed Johnnie: "I suppose there have been a good many men killed in this room." The jaws of the others dropped and they looked at him.

"What in hell are you talking about?" said Johnnie.

The Swede laughed again his blatant laugh, full of a kind of false courage and defiance. "Oh, you know what I mean all right," he answered.

"I'm a liar if I do!" Johnnie protested. The card game was halted, and the men stared at the Swede. Johnnie evidently felt that as the son of the proprietor he should make a direct inquiry. "Now, what might you be drivin' at, mister?" he asked. The Swede winked at him. It was a wink full of cunning. His fingers shook on the edge of the board. "Oh, maybe you think I have been to nowheres. Maybe you think I'm a tenderfoot?"

"I don't know nothin' about you," answered Johnnie, "and I don't give a damn where you've been. All I got to say is that I don't know what you're driving at. There hain't never been nobody killed in this room."

The cowboy, who had been steadily gazing at the Swede, then spoke: "What's wrong with you, mister?"

Apparently it seemed to the Swede that he was formidably menaced. He shivered and turned white near the corners of his mouth. He sent an appealing glance in the direction of the little Easterner. During these moments he did not forget to wear his air of advanced pot-valor. "They say they don't know what I mean," he remarked mockingly to the Easterner.

The latter answered after prolonged and cautious reflection. "I don't understand you," he said, impassively.

The Swede made a movement then which announced that he thought he had encountered treachery from the only quarter where he had expected sympathy, if not help. "Oh, I see you are all against me. I see—"

The cowboy was in a state of deep stupefaction, "Say," he cried, as he tumbled the deck violently down upon the board, "say, what are you gittin' at, hey?"

The Swede sprang up with the celerity of a man escaping from a snake on the floor. "I don't want to fight!" he shouted. "I don't want to fight!"

The cowboy stretched his long legs indolently and deliberately. His hands were in his pockets. He spat into the sawdust-box. "Well, who the hell thought you did?" he inquired.

The Swede backed rapidly toward a corner of the room. His hands were out protectingly in front of his chest, but he was making an obvious struggle to control his fright. "Gentlemen," he quavered, "I suppose I am going to be killed before I can leave this house! I suppose I am going to be killed before I can leave this house!" In his eyes was the dying-swan look. Through the windows could be seen the snow turning blue in the shadow of dusk. The wind tore at the house, and some loose thing beat regularly against the clapboards like a spirit tapping.

A door opened, and Scully himself entered. He paused in surprise as he noted the tragic attitude of the Swede. Then he said, "What's the matter here?"

The Swede answered him swiftly and eagerly: "These men are going to kill me."

"Kill you!" ejaculated Scully. "Kill you! What are you talkin'?"

The Swede made the gesture of a martyr.

Scully wheeled sternly upon his son. "What is this, Johnnie?"

The lad had grown sullen. "Damned if I know," he answered, "I can't make no sense to it." He began to shuffle the cards, fluttering them together with an angry snap. "He says a good many men have been killed in this room, or something like that. And he says he's goin' to be killed here too. I don't know what ails him. He's crazy, I shouldn't wonder."

Scully then looked for explanation to the cowboy, but the cowboy simply shrugged his shoulders.

"Kill you?" said Scully again to the Swede. "Kill you? Man, you're off your nut."

"Oh, I know," burst out the Swede. "I know what will happen. Yes, I'm crazy—yes. Yes, of course, I'm crazy—yes. But I know one thing—" There was a sort of sweat of misery and terror upon his face. "I know I won't get out of here alive."

The cowboy drew a deep breath, as if his mind was passing into the last stages of dissolution. "Well, I'm doggoned," he whispered to himself.

Scully wheeled suddenly and faced his son. "You've been troublin' this man!"

Johnnie's voice was loud with its burden of grievance. "Why, good Gawd, I ain't done nothin' to 'im."

The Swede broke in. "Gentlemen, do not disturb yourselves. I will leave this house. I will go away, because"—he accused them dramatically with his glance— "because I do not want to be killed."

Scully was furious with his son. "Will you tell me what is the matter, you young divil? What's the matter, anyhow? Speak out!"

"Blame it!" cried Johnnie in despair, "don't I tell you I don't know? He—he says we want to kill him, and that's all I know. I can't tell what ails him."

The Swede continued to repeat: "Never mind, Mr. Scully; never mind. I will leave this house. I will go away, because I do not wish to be killed. Yes, of course, I am crazy—yes. But I know one thing! I will go away. I will leave this house. Never mind, Mr. Scully; never mind. I will go away."

"You will not go 'way," said Scully. "You will not go 'way until I hear the reason of this business. If anybody has troubled you I will take care of him. This is my house. You are under my roof, and I will not allow any peaceable man to be troubled here." He cast a terrible eye upon Johnnie, the cowboy, and the Easterner.

"Never mind, Mr. Scully; never mind. I will go away. I do not wish to be killed." The Swede moved toward the door which opened upon the stairs. It was evidently his intention to go at once for his baggage.

"No, no," shouted Scully peremptorily; but the white-faced man slid by him and disappeared. "Now," said Scully severely, "what does this mane?"

Johnnie and the cowboy cried together: "Why, we didn't do nothin' to 'im!"

Scully's eyes were cold. "No," he said, "you didn't?"

Johnnie swore a deep oath. "Why, this is the wildest loon I ever see. We didn't do nothin' at all. We were jest sittin' here playin' cards, and he—"

The father suddenly spoke to the Easterner. "Mr. Blanc," he asked, "what has these boys been doin'?"

The Easterner reflected again. "I didn't see anything wrong at all," he said at last, slowly.

Scully began to howl. "But what does it mane?" He stared ferociously at his son. "I have a mind to lather you for this, my boy."

Johnnie was frantic. "Well, what have I done?" he bawled at his father.

III

"I think you are tongue-tied," said Scully finally to his son, the cowboy, and the Easterner; and at the end of this scornful sentence he left the room.

Upstairs the Swede was swiftly fastening the straps of his great valise. Once his back happened to be half turned toward the door, and, hearing a noise there, he wheeled and sprang up, uttering a loud cry. Scully's wrinkled visage showed grimly in the light of the small lamp he carried. This yellow effulgence, streaming upward, colored only his prominent features, and left his eyes, for instance, in mysterious shadow. He resembled a murderer.

"Man! man!" he exclaimed, "have you gone daffy?"

"Oh, no! Oh, no!" rejoined the other. "There are people in this world who know pretty nearly as much as you do—understand?"

For a moment they stood gazing at each other. Upon the Swede's deathly pale cheeks were two spots brightly crimson and sharply edged, as if they had been carefully painted. Scully placed the light on the table and sat himself on the edge of the bed. He spoke ruminatively. "By cracky, I never heard of such a thing in my life. It's a complete muddle. I can't, for the soul of me, think how you ever got this idea into your head." Presently he lifted his eyes and asked: "And did you sure think they were going to kill you?"

The Swede scanned the old man as if he wished to see into his mind. "I did," he said at last. He obviously suspected that this answer might precipitate an outbreak. As he pulled on a strap his whole arm shook, the elbow wavering like a bit of paper.

Scully banged his hand impressively on the footboard of the bed. "Why, man, we're goin' to have a line of ilictric street-cars in this town next spring."

" 'A line of electric street-cars,' " repeated the Swede, stupidly.

"And," said Scully, "there's a new railroad goin' to be built down from Broken Arm to here. Not to mintion the four churches and the smashin' big brick schoolhouse. Then there's the big factory, too. Why, in two years Romper'll be a met-tro-*pol*-is."

Having finished the preparation of his baggage, the Swede straightened himself. "Mr. Scully," he said, with sudden hardihood, "how much do I owe you?"

"You don't owe me anythin'," said the old man, angrily.

"Yes, I do," retorted the Swede. He took seventy-five cents from his pocket and tendered it to Scully; but the latter snapped his fingers in disdainful refusal. However, it happened that they both stood gazing in a strange fashion at three silver pieces on the Swede's open palm.

"I'll not take your money," said Scully at last. "Not after what's been goin' on here." Then a plan seemed to strike him. "Here," he cried, picking up his lamp and moving toward the door. "Here! Come with me a minute."

"No," said the Swede, in overwhelming alarm.

"Yes," urged the old man. "Come on! I want you to come and see a picter— just across the hall—in my room."

The Swede must have concluded that his hour was come. His jaw dropped and his teeth showed like a dead man's. He ultimately followed Scully across the corridor, but he had the step of one hung in chains.

Scully flashed the light high on the wall of his own chamber. There was revealed a ridiculous photograph of a little girl. She was leaning against a balustrade of gorgeous decoration, and the formidable bang to her hair was prominent. The figure was as graceful as an upright sled-stake, and, withal, it was of the hue of lead. "There," said Scully, tenderly, "that's the picter of my little girl that died. Her name was Carrie. She had the purtiest hair you ever saw! I was that fond of her, she—"

Turning then, he saw that the Swede was not contemplating the picture at all, but, instead, was keeping keen watch on the gloom in the rear.

"Look, man!" cried Scully, heartily. "That's the picter of my little gal that died. Her name was Carrie. And then here's the picter of my oldest boy. Michael. He's a lawyer in Lincoln,[2] an' doin' well. I gave that boy a grand eddication, and I'm glad for it now. He's a fine boy. Look at 'im now. Ain't he bold as blazes, him there in Lincoln, an honored an' respicted gintleman! An honored and respected gintleman," concluded Scully with a flourish. And, so saying, he smote the Swede jovially on the back.

The Swede faintly smiled.

"Now," said the old man, "there's only one more thing." He dropped suddenly to the floor and thrust his head beneath the bed. The Swede could hear his muffled voice. "I'd keep it under me piller if it wasn't for that boy Johnnie. Then there's the old woman—Where is it now? I never put it twice in the same place. Ah, now come out with you!"

Presently he backed clumsily from under the bed, dragging with him an old

---

[2] Lincoln is the capital of Nebraska.

coat rolled into a bundle. I've fetched him," he muttered. Kneeling on the floor, he unrolled the coat and extracted from its heart a large yellow-brown whiskey-bottle.

His first manoeuver was to hold the bottle up to the light. Reassured, apparently, that nobody had been tampering with it, he thrust it with a generous movement toward the Swede.

The weak-kneed Swede was about to eagerly clutch this element of strength, but he suddenly jerked his hand away and cast a look of horror upon Scully.

"Drink," said the old man affectionately. He had risen to his feet, and now stood facing the Swede.

There was a silence. Then again Scully said: "Drink!"

The Swede laughed wildly. He grabbed the bottle, put it to his mouth; and as his lips curled absurdly around the opening and his throat worked, he kept his glance, burning with hatred, upon the old man's face.

IV

After the departure of Scully the three men, with the cardboard still upon their knees, preserved for a long time an astounded silence. Then Johnnie said: "That's the doddangedest Swede I ever see."

"He ain't no Swede," said the cowboy, scornfully.

"Well, what is he then?" cried Johnnie. "What is he then?"

"It's my opinion," replied the cowboy deliberately, "he's some kind of a Dutchman." It was a venerable custom of the country to entitle as Swedes all light-haired men who spoke with a heavy tongue. In consequence the idea of the cowboy was not without its daring. "Yes, sir," he repeated. "It's my opinion this feller is some kind of a Dutchman."

"Well, he says he's a Swede, anyhow," muttered Johnnie, sulkily. He turned to the Easterner: "What do you think, Mr. Blanc?"

"Oh, I don't know," replied the Easterner.

"Well, what do you think makes him act that way?" asked the cowboy.

"Why, he's frightened." The Easterner knocked his pipe against a rim of the stove. "He's clear frightened out of his boots."

"What at?" cried Johnnie and the cowboy together.

The Eastener reflected over his answer.

"What at?" cried the others again.

"Oh, I don't know, but it seems to me this man has been reading dime novels, and he thinks he's right out in the middle of it—the shootin' and stabbin' and all."

"But," said the cowboy, deeply scandalized, "this ain't Wyoming, ner none of them places. This is Nebrasker."

"Yes," added Johnnie, "an' why don't he wait till he gits out West?"

The travelled Easterner laughed. "It isn't different there even—not in these days. But he thinks he's right in the middle of hell."

Johnnie and the cowboy mused long.

"It's awful funny," remarked Johnnie at last.

"Yes," said the cowboy. "This is a queer game. I hope we don't git snowed in, because then we'd have to stand this here man bein' around with us all the time. That wouldn't be no good."

"I wish pop would throw him out," said Johnnie.

Presently they heard a loud stamping on the stairs, accompanied by ringing jokes in the voice of old Scully, and laughter, evidently from the Swede. The men around the stove stared vacantly at each other. "Gosh!" said the cowboy. The door flew open, and old Scully, flushed and anecdotal, came into the room. He was jabbering at the Swede, who followed him, laughing bravely. It was the entry of two roisterers from a banquet hall.

"Come now," said Scully sharply to the three seated men, "move up and give us a chance at the stove." The cowboy and the Easterner obediently sidled their chairs to make room for the newcomers. Johnnie, however, simply arranged himself in a more indolent attitude, and then remained motionless.

"Come! Git over, there," said Scully.

"Plenty of room on the other side of the stove," said Johnnie.

"Do you think we want to sit in the draught?" roared the father.

But the Swede here interposed with a grandeur of confidence. "No, no. Let the boy sit where he likes," he cried in a bullying voice to the father.

"All right! All right!" said Scully, deferentially. The cowboy and the Easterner exchanged glances of wonder.

The five chairs were formed in a crescent about one side of the stove. The Swede began to talk; he talked arrogantly, profanely, angrily. Johnnie, the cowboy, and the Easterner maintained a morose silence, while old Scully appeared to be receptive and eager, breaking in constantly with sympathetic ejaculations.

Finally the Swede announced that he was thirsty. He moved in his chair, and said that he would go for a drink of water.

"I'll git it for you," cried Scully at once.

"No," said the Swede, contemptuously. "I'll get it for myself." He arose and stalked with the air of an owner off into the executive parts of the hotel.

As soon as the Swede was out of hearing Scully sprang to his feet and whispered intensely to the others: "Up-stairs he thought I was tryin' to poison 'im."

"Say," said Johnnie, "this makes me sick. Why don't you throw 'im out in the snow?"

"Why, he's all right now," declared Scully. "It was only that he was from the East, and he thought this was a tough place. That's all. He's all right now."

The cowboy looked with admiration upon the Easterner. "You were straight," he said. "You were on to that there Dutchman."

"Well," said Johnnie to his father, "he may be all right now, but I don't see it. Other time he was scared, but now he's too fresh."

Scully's speech was always a combination of Irish brogue and idiom, Western twang and idiom, and scraps of curiously formal diction taken from the story-books and newspapers. He now hurled a strange mass of language at the head of his son. "What do I keep? What do I keep? What do I keep?" he demanded, in a voice of thunder. He slapped his knee impressively, to indicate that he himself was going to make reply, and that all should heed. "I keep a hotel," he shouted. "A hotel, do you mind? A guest under my roof has sacred privileges. He is to be intimidated by none. Not one word shall he hear that would prijudice him in favor of goin' away. I'll not have it. There's no place in this here town where they can say they iver took in a guest of mine because he was afraid to stay here." He wheeled suddenly upon the cowboy and the Easterner. "Am I right?"

"Yes, Mr. Scully," said the cowboy, "I think you're right."

"Yes, Mr. Scully," said the Easterner, "I think you're right."

V

At six-o'clock supper, the Swede fizzed like a fire-wheel.[3] He sometimes seemed on the point of bursting into riotous song, and in all his madness he was encouraged by old Scully. The Easterner was encased in reserve; the cowboy sat in wide-mouthed amazement, forgetting to eat, while Johnnie wrathily demolished great plates of food. The daughters of the house, when they were obliged to replenish the biscuits, approached as warily as Indians, and, having succeeded in their purpose, fled with ill-concealed trepidation. The Swede domineered the whole feast, and he gave it the appearance of a cruel bacchanal. He seemed to have grown suddenly taller; he gazed, brutally disdainful, into every face. His voice rang through the room. Once when he jabbed out harpoon-fashion with his fork to pinion a biscuit, the weapon nearly impaled the hand of the Easterner, which had been stretched quietly out for the same biscuit.

After supper, as the men filed toward the other room, the Swede smote Scully ruthlessly on the shoulder. "Well, old boy, that was a good, square meal." Johnnie looked hopefully at his father; he knew that shoulder was tender from an old fall; and, indeed, it appeared for a moment as if Scully was going to flame out over the matter, but in the end he smiled a sickly smile and remained silent. The others understood from his manner that he was admitting his responsibility for the Swede's new view-point.

Johnnie, however, addressed his parent in an aside. "Why don't you license somebody to kick you downstairs?" Scully scowled darkly by way of reply.

When they were gathered about the stove, the Swede insisted on another game of High-Five. Scully gently deprecated the plan at first, but the Swede turned a wolfish glare upon him. The old man subsided, and the Swede canvassed the others. In his tone there was always a great threat. The cowboy and the Easterner both remarked indifferently that they would play. Scully said that he would presently have to go to meet the 6.58 train, and so the Swede turned menacingly upon Johnnie. For a moment their glances crossed like blades, and then Johnnie smiled and said, "Yes, I'll play."

They formed a square, with the little board on their knees. The Easterner and the Swede were again partners. As the play went on, it was noticeable that the cowboy was not board-whacking as usual. Meanwhile, Scully, near the lamp, had put on his spectacles and, with an appearance curiously like an old priest,

---

[3] A fire-wheel is a wheel of fireworks.

was reading a newspaper. In time he went out to meet the 6.58 train, and, despite his precautions, a gust of polar wind whirled into the room as he opened the door. Besides scattering the cards, it chilled the players to the marrow. The Swede cursed frightfully. When Scully returned, his entrance disturbed a cosy and friendly scene. The Swede again cursed. But presently they were once more intent, their heads bent forward and their hands moving swiftly. The Swede had adopted the fashion of board-whacking.

Scully took up his paper and for a long time remained immersed in matters which were extraordinarily remote from him. The lamp burned badly, and once he stopped to adjust the wick. The newspaper, as he turned from page to page, rustled with a slow and comfortable sound. Then suddenly he heard three terrible words: "You are cheatin'!"

Such scenes often prove that there can be little of dramatic import in environment. Any room can present a tragic front; any room can be comic. This little den was now hideous as a torture-chamber. The new faces of the men themselves had changed it upon the instant. The Swede held a huge fist in front of Johnnie's face, while the latter looked steadily over it into the blazing orbs of his accuser. The Easterner had grown pallid; the cowboy's jaw had dropped in that expression of bovine amazement which was one of his important mannerisms. After the three words, the first sound in the room was made by Scully's paper as it floated forgotten to his feet. His spectacles had also fallen from his nose, but by a clutch he had saved them in air. His hand, grasping the spectacles, now remained poised awkwardly and near his shoulder. He stared at the card-players.

Probably the silence was while a second elapsed. Then, if the floor had been suddenly twitched out from under the men they could not have moved quicker. The five had projected themselves headlong toward a common point. It happened that Johnnie, in rising to hurl himself upon the Swede, had stumbled slightly because of his curiously instinctive care for the cards and the board. The loss of the moment allowed time for the arrival of Scully, and also allowed the cowboy time to give the Swede a great push which sent him staggering back. The men found tongue together, and hoarse shouts of rage, appeal, or fear burst from every throat. The cowboy pushed and jostled feverishly at the Swede, and the Easterner and Scully clung wildly to Johnnie; but through the smoky air, above the swaying bodies of the peace-compellers, the eyes of the two warriors ever sought each other in glances of challenge that were at once hot and steely.

Of course the board had been overturned, and now the whole company of cards was scattered over the floor, where the boots of the men trampled the fat and painted kings and queens as they gazed with their silly eyes at the war that was waging above them.

Scully's voice was dominating the yells. "Stop now! Stop, I say! Stop, now—"

Johnnie, as he struggled to burst through the rank formed by Scully and the Easterner, was crying, "Well, he says I cheated! He says I cheated! I won't allow no man to say I cheated! If he says I cheated, he's a _____ !"

The cowboy was telling the Swede, "Quit, now! Quit, d'ye hear—"

The screams of the Swede never ceased: "He did cheat! I saw him! I saw him—"

As for the Easterner, he was importuning in a voice that was not heeded: "Wait a moment, can't you? Oh, wait a moment. What's the good of a fight over a game of cards? Wait a moment—"

In this tumult no complete sentences were clear. "Cheat"—"Quit"—"He says"—these fragments pierced the uproar and rang out sharply. It was remarkable that, whereas Scully undoubtedly made the most noise, he was the least heard of any of the riotous band.

Then suddenly there was a great cessation. It was as if each man had paused for breath; and although the room was still lighted with the anger of men, it could be seen that there was no danger of immediate conflict, and at once Johnnie, shouldering his way forward, almost succeeded in confronting the Swede. "What did you say I cheated for? What did you say I cheated for? I don't cheat, and I won't let no man say I do!"

The Swede said, "I saw you! I saw you!"

"Well," cried Johnnie, "I'll fight any man what says I cheat!"

"No, you won't," said the cowboy. "Not here."

"Ah, be still, can't you?" said Scully, coming between them.

The quiet was sufficient to allow the Easterner's voice to be heard. He was repeating, "Oh, wait a moment, can't you? What's the good of a fight over a game of cards? Wait a moment!"

Johnnie, his red face appearing above his father's shoulder, hailed the Swede again. "Did you say I cheated?"

The Swede showed his teeth. "Yes."

"Then," said Johnnie, "we must fight."

"Yes, fight," roared the Swede. He was like a demoniac. "Yes, fight! I'll show you what kind of a man I am! I'll show you who you want to fight! Maybe you think I can't fight! Maybe you think I can't! I'll show you, you skin, you card-sharp! Yes, you cheated! You cheated! You cheated!"

"Well, let's go at it, then, mister," said Johnnie, coolly.

The cowboy's brow was beaded in sweat from his efforts in intercepting all sorts of raids. He turned in despair to Scully. "What are you goin' to do now?"

A change had come over the Celtic visage of the old man. He now seemed all eagerness; his eyes glowed.

"We'll let them fight," he answered stalwartly. "I can't put up with it any longer. I've stood this damned Swede till I'm sick. We'll let them fight."

VI

The men prepared to go out-of-doors. The Easterner was so nervous that he had great difficulty in getting his arms into the sleeves of his new leather coat. As the cowboy drew his fur cap down over his ears his hands trembled. In fact, Johnnie and old Scully were the only ones who displayed no agitation. These preliminaries were conducted without words.

Scully threw open the door. "Well, come on," he said. Instantly a terrific wind caused the flame of the lamp to struggle at its wick, while a puff of black smoke sprang from the chimney-top. The stove was in mid-current of the blast, and its voice swelled to equal the roar of the storm. Some of the scarred and bedabbled cards were caught up from the floor and dashed helplessly against the farther wall. The men lowered their heads and plunged into the tempest as into a sea.

No snow was falling, but great whirls and clouds of flakes, swept up from the ground by the frantic winds, were streaming southward with the speed of bullets. The covered land was blue with the sheen of an unearthly satin, and there was no other hue save where, at the low, black railway station—which seemed incredibly distant—one light gleamed like a tiny jewel. As the men floundered into a thigh-deep drift, it was known that the Swede was bawling out something. Scully went to him, put a hand on his shoulder, and projected an ear. "What's that you say?" he shouted.

"I say," bawled the Swede again, "I won't stand much show against this gang. I know you'll all pitch on me."

Scully smote him reproachfully on the arm. "Tut, man!" he yelled. The wind tore the words from Scully's lips and scattered them far alee.

"You are all a gang of—" boomed the Swede, but the storm also seized the remainder of this sentence.

Immediately turning their backs upon the wind, the men had swung around a corner to the shelter side of the hotel. It was the function of the little house to preserve here, amid this great devastation of snow, an irregular V-shape of heavily encrusted grass, which crackled beneath the feet. One could imagine the great drifts piled against the windward side. When the party reached the comparative peace of this spot it was found that the Swede was still bellowing.

"Oh, I know what kind of a thing this is! I know you'll all pitch on me. I can't lick you all!"

Scully turned upon him panther-fashion. "You'll not have to whip all of us. You'll have to whip my son Johnnie. An' the man what troubles you durin' that time will have me to dale with."

The arrangements were swiftly made. The two men faced each other, obedient to the harsh commands of Scully, whose face, in the subtly luminous gloom, could be seen set in the austere impersonal lines that are pictured on the countenances of the Roman veterans. The Easterner's teeth were chattering, and he was hopping up and down like a mechanical toy. The cowboy stood rocklike.

The contestants had not stripped off any clothing. Each was in his ordinary attire. Their fists were up, and they eyed each other in a calm that had the elements of leonine cruelty in it.

During this pause, the Easterner's mind, like a film, took lasting impressions of three men—the iron-nerved master of the ceremony; the Swede, pale, motionless, terrible; and Johnnie, serene yet ferocious, brutish yet heroic. The entire prelude had in it a tragedy greater than the tragedy of action, and this aspect was accentuated by the long, mellow cry of the blizzard, as it sped the tumbling and wailing flakes into the black abyss of the south.

"Now!" said Scully.

The two combatants leaped forward and crashed together like bullocks. There was heard the cushioned sound of blows, and of a curse squeezing out from between the tight teeth of one.

As for the spectators, the Easterner's pent-up breath exploded from him with a pop of relief, absolute relief from the tension of the preliminaries. The cowboy bounded into the air with a yowl. Scully was immovable as from supreme amazement and fear at the fury of the fight which he himself had permitted and arranged.

For a time the encounter in the darkness was such a perplexity of flying arms that it presented no more detail than would a swiftly revolving wheel. Occasionally a face, as if illumined by a flash of light, would shine out, ghastly and marked with pink spots. A moment later, the men might have been known as shadows, if it were not for the involuntary utterance of oaths that came from them in whispers.

Suddenly a holocaust of warlike desire caught the cowboy, and he bolted forward with the speed of a bronco. "Go it, Johnnie! go it! Kill him! Kill him!"

Scully confronted him. "Kape back," he said; and by his glance the cowboy could tell that this man was Johnnie's father.

To the Easterner there was a monotony of unchangeable fighting that was an abomination. This confused mingling was eternal to his sense, which was concentrated in a longing for the end, the priceless end. Once the fighters lurched near him, and as he scrambled hastily backward he heard them breathe like men on the rack.

"Kill him, Johnnie! Kill him! Kill him! Kill him!" The cowboy's face was contorted like one of those agony masks in museums.

"Keep still," said Scully, icily.

Then there was a sudden loud grunt, incomplete, cut short, and Johnnie's body swung away from the Swede and fell with sickening heaviness to the grass. The cowboy was barely in time to prevent the mad Swede from flinging himself upon his prone adversary. "No, you don't," said the cowboy, interposing an arm. "Wait a second."

Scully was at his son's side. "Johnnie! Johnnie, me boy!" His voice had a quality of melancholy tenderness. "Johnnie! Can you go on with it?" He looked anxiously down into the bloody, pulpy face of his son.

There was a moment of silence, and then Johnnie answered in his ordinary voice, "Yes, I—it—yes."

Assisted by his father he struggled to his feet. "Wait a bit now till you git your wind," said the old man.

A few paces away the cowboy was lecturing the Swede. "No, you don't! Wait a second!"

The Easterner was plucking at Scully's sleeve. "Oh, this is enough," he pleaded. "This is enough! Let it go as it stands. This is enough!"

"Bill," said Scully, "git out of the road." The cowboy stepped aside. "Now." The combatants were actuated by a new caution as they advanced toward collision. They glared at each other, and then the Swede aimed a lightning blow that carried with it his entire weight. Johnnie was evidently half stupid from weakness, but he miraculously dodged, and his fist sent the overbalanced Swede sprawling.

The cowboy, Scully, and the Easterner burst into a cheer that was like a chorus of triumphant soldiery, but before its conclusion the Swede had scuffled agilely to his feet and come in berserk abandon at his foe. There was another perplexity of flying arms, and Johnnie's body again swung away and fell, even as a bundle might fall from a roof. The Swede instantly staggered to a little wind-waved tree and leaned upon it, breathing like an engine, while his savage and flame-lit eyes roamed from face to face as the men bent over Johnnie. There was a splendor of isolation in his situation at this time which the Easterner felt once when, lifting his eyes from the man on the ground, he beheld that mysterious and lonely figure, waiting.

"Are you any good yet, Johnnie?" asked Scully in a broken voice.

The son gasped and opened his eyes languidly. After a moment he answered, "No—I ain't—any good—any—more." Then, from shame and bodily ill, he began to weep, the tears furrowing down through the blood-stains on his face. "He was too—too—too heavy for me."

Scully straightened and addressed the waiting figure. "Stranger," he said, evenly, "it's all up with our side." Then his voice changed into that vibrant huskiness which is commonly the tone of the most simple and deadly announcements. "Johnnie is whipped."

Without replying, the victor moved off on the route to the front door of the hotel.

The cowboy was formulating new and unspellable blasphemies. The Easterner was startled to find that they were out in a wind that seemed to come direct from the shadowed arctic floes. He heard again the wail of the snow as it was flung to its grave in the south. He knew now that all this time the cold had been sinking into him deeper and deeper, and he wondered that he had not perished. He felt indifferent to the condition of the vanquished man.

"Johnnie, can you walk?" asked Scully.

"Did I hurt—hurt him any?" asked the son.

"Can you walk, boy? Can you walk?"

Johnnie's voice was suddenly strong. There was a robust impatience in it. "I asked you whether I hurt him any!"

"Yes, yes, Johnnie," answered the cowboy, consolingly; "he's hurt a good deal."

They raised him from the ground, and as soon as he was on his feet he went tottering off, rebuffing all attempts at assistance. When the party rounded the corner they were fairly blinded by the pelting of the snow. It burned their faces like fire. The cowboy carried Johnnie through the drift to the door. As they entered, some cards again rose from the floor and beat against the wall.

The Easterner rushed to the stove. He was so profoundly chilled that he almost dared to embrace the glowing iron. The Swede was not in the room. Johnnie sank into a chair and, folding his arms on his knees, buried his face in them. Scully, warming one foot and then the other at a rim of the stove, muttered to himself with Celtic mournfulness. The cowboy had removed his fur cap, and with a dazed and rueful air he was running one hand through his tousled locks. From overhead they could hear the creaking of boards, as the Swede tramped here and there in his room.

The sad quiet was broken by the sudden flinging open of a door that led toward the kitchen. It was instantly followed by an inrush of women. They precipitated themselves upon Johnnie amid a chorus of lamentation. Before they carried their prey off to the kitchen, there to be bathed and harangued with that mixture of sympathy and abuse which is a feat of their sex, the mother straightened herself and fixed old Scully with an eye of stern reproach. "Shame be upon you, Patrick Scully!" she cried. "Your own son, too. Shame be upon you!"

"There, now! Be quiet, now!" said the old man, weakly.

"Shame be upon you, Patrick Scully!" The girls, rallying to this slogan, sniffed disdainfully in the direction of those trembling accomplices, the cowboy and the Easterner. Presently they bore Johnnie away, and left the three men to dismal reflection.

VII

"I'd like to fight this here Dutchman myself," said the cowboy, breaking a long silence.

Scully wagged his head sadly. "No, that wouldn't do. It wouldn't be right. It wouldn't be right."

"Well, why wouldn't it?" argued the cowboy. "I don't see no harm in it."

"No," answered Scully, with mournful heroism. "It wouldn't be right. It was Johnnie's fight, and now we mustn't whip the man just because he whipped Johnnie."

"Yes, that's true enough," said the cowboy; "but—he better not get fresh with me, because I couldn't stand no more of it."

"You'll not say a word to him," commanded Scully, and even then they heard the tread of the Swede on the stairs. His entrance was made theatric. He swept the door back with a bang and swaggered to the middle of the room. No one looked at him. "Well," he cried, insolently, at Scully, "I s'pose you'll tell me now how much I owe you?"

The old man remained stolid. "You don't owe me nothin'."

"Huh!" said the Swede, "huh! Don't owe 'im nothin'."

The cowboy addressed the Swede. "Stranger, I don't see how you come to be so gay around here."

Old Scully was instantly alert. "Stop!" he shouted, holding his hand forth, fingers upward. "Bill, you shut up!"

The cowboy spat carelessly into the sawdust-box. "I didn't say a word, did I?" he asked.

"Mr. Scully," called the Swede, "how much do I owe you?" It was seen that he was attired for departure, and that he had his valise in his hand.

"You don't owe me nothin'," repeated Scully in the same imperturbable way.

"Huh!" said the Swede. "I guess you're right. I guess if it was any way at all, you'd owe me somethin'. That's what I guess." He turned to the cowboy. " 'Kill him! Kill him! Kill him!' " he mimicked, and then guffawed victoriously. " 'Kill him!' " He was convulsed with ironical humor.

But he might have been jeering the dead. The three men were immovable and silent, staring with glassy eyes at the stove.

The Swede opened the door and passed into the storm, one derisive glance backward at the still group.

A soon as the door was closed, Scully and the cowboy leaped to their feet and began to curse. They trampled to and fro, waving their arms and smashing into the air with their fists. "Oh, but that was a hard minute!" wailed Scully. "That was a hard minute! Him there leerin' and scoffin'! One bang at his nose was worth forty dollars to me that minute! How did you stand it, Bill?"

"How did I stand it?" cried the cowboy in a quivering voice. "How did I stand it? Oh!"

The old man burst into sudden brogue. "I'd loike to take that Swade," he wailed, "and hould 'im down on a shtone flure and bate 'im to a jelly wid a shtick!"

The cowboy groaned in sympathy. "I'd like to git him by the neck and ha-amer him"—he brought his hand down on the chair with a noise like a pistol-shot—"hammer that there Dutchman until he couldn't tell himself from a dead coyote!"

"I'd bate 'im until he—"

"I'd show *him* some things—"

And then together they raised a yearning, fanatic cry— "Oh-o-oh! if we only could—"

"Yes!"

"Yes!"

"And then I'd—"

"O-o-oh!"

VIII

The Swede, tightly gripping his valise, tacked across the face of the storm as if he carried sails. He was following a line of little naked, gasping trees which, he knew, must mark the way of the road. His face, fresh from the pounding of Johnnie's fists, felt more pleasure than pain in the wind and the driving snow. A number of square shapes loomed upon him finally, and he knew them as the houses of the main body of the town. He found a street and made travel along it, leaning heavily upon the wind whenever, at a corner, a terrific blast caught him.

He might have been in a deserted village. We picture the world as thick with conquering and elate humanity, but here, with the bugles of the tempest pealing, it was hard to imagine a peopled earth. One viewed the existence of man then as a marvel, and conceded a glamor of wonder to these lice which were caused to cling to a whirling, fire-smitten, ice-locked, disease-stricken, space-lost bulb. The conceit of man was explained by this storm to be the very engine of life. One was a coxcomb not to die in it. However, the Swede found a saloon.

In front of it an indomitable red light was burning, and the snowflakes were made blood-color as they flew through the circumscribed territory of the lamp's shining. The Swede pushed open the door of the saloon and entered. A sanded expanse was before him, and at the end of it four men sat about a table drinking. Down one side of the room extended a radiant bar, and its guardian was leaning upon his elbows listening to the talk of the men at the table. The Swede dropped his valise upon the floor and, smiling fraternally upon the barkeeper, said, "Gimme some whiskey, will you?" The man placed a bottle, a whiskey-glass, and a glass of ice-thick water upon the bar. The Swede poured himself an abnormal portion of whiskey and drank it in three gulps. "Pretty bad night," remarked the bartender, indifferently. He was making the pretension of blindness which is usually a distinction of his class; but it could have been seen that he was furtively studying the half-erased bloodstains on the face of the Swede. "Bad night," he said again.

"Oh, it's good enough for me," replied the Swede, hardily, as he poured himself some more whiskey. The barkeeper took his coin and manœvered it through its reception by the highly nickelled cash-machine. A bell rang; a card labelled "20 cts." had appeared.

"No," continued the Swede, "this isn't too bad weather. It's good enough for me."

"So?" murmured the barkeeper, languidly.

The copious drams made the Swede's eyes swim, and he breathed a trifle heavier. "Yes, I like this weather. I like it. It suits me." It was apparently his design to impart a deep significance to these words.

"So?" murmured the bartender again. He turned to gaze dreamily at the scroll-like birds and bird-like scrolls which had been drawn with soap upon the mirrors in back of the bar.

"Well, I guess I'll take another drink," said the Swede, presently. "Have something?"

"No, thanks; I'm not drinkin'," answered the bartender. Afterward he asked, "How did you hurt your face?"

The Swede immediately began to boast loudly. "Why, in a fight. I thumped the soul out of a man down here at Scully's hotel."

The interest of the four men at the table was at last aroused.

"Who was it?" said one.

"Johnnie Scully," blustered the Swede. "Son of the man what runs it. He will be pretty near dead for some weeks, I can tell you. I made a nice thing of him, I did. He couldn't get up. They carried him in the house. Have a drink?"

Instantly the men in some subtle way encased themselves in reserve. "No, thanks," said one. The group was of curious formation. Two were prominent local business men; one was the district attorney; and one was a professional gambler of the kind known as "square."[4] But a scrutiny of the group would not

---

[4] Honest.

have enabled an observer to pick the gambler from the men of more reputable pursuits. He was, in fact, a man so delicate in manner, when among people of fair class, and so judicious in his choice of victims, that in the strictly masculine part of the town's life he had come to be explicitly trusted and admired. People called him a thoroughbred. The fear and contempt with which his craft was regarded were undoubtedly the reason why his quiet dignity shone conspicuous above the quiet dignity of men who might be merely hatters, billiardmarkers, or grocery clerks. Beyond an occasional unwary traveller who came by rail, this gambler was supposed to prey solely upon reckless and senile farmers, who, when flush with good crops, drove into town in all the pride and confidence of an absolutely invulnerable stupidity. Hearing at times in circuitous fashion of the despoilment of such a farmer, the important men of Romper invariably laughed in contempt of the victim, and if they thought of the wolf at all, it was with a kind of pride at the knowledge that he would never dare think of attacking their wisdom and courage. Besides, it was popular that this gambler had a real wife and two real children in a neat cottage in a suburb, where he led an exemplary home life; and when any one even suggested a discrepancy in his character, the crowd immediately vociferated descriptions of this virtuous family circle. Then men who led exemplary home lives, and men who did not lead exemplary home lives, all subsided in a bunch, remarking that there was nothing more to be said.

However, when a restriction was placed upon him—as, for instance, when a strong clique of members of the new Pollywog Club refused to permit him, even as a spectator, to appear in the rooms of the organization—the candor and gentleness with which he accepted the judgment disarmed many of his foes and made his friends more desperately partisan. He invariably distinguished between himself and a respectable Romper man so quickly and frankly that his manner actually appeared to be continual broadcast compliment.

And one must not forget to declare the fundamental fact of his entire position in Romper. It is irrefutable that in all affairs outside his business, in all matters that occur eternally and commonly between man and man, this thieving card-player was so generous, so just, so moral, that, in a contest, he could have put to flight the consciences of nine tenths of the citizens of Romper.

And so it happened that he was seated in this saloon with the two prominent local merchants and the district attorney.

The Swede continued to drink raw whiskey, meanwhile babbling at the bar-keeper and trying to induce him to indulge in potations. "Come on. Have a drink. Come on. What—no? Well, have a little one, then. By gawd, I've whipped a man tonight, and I want to celebrate. I whipped him good, too. Gentlemen," the Swede cried to the men at the table, "have a drink?"

"Ssh!" said the barkeeper.

The group at the table, although furtively attentive, had been pretending to be deep in talk, but now a man lifted his eyes toward the Swede and said, shortly, "Thanks. We don't want any more."

At this reply the Swede ruffled out his chest like a rooster. "Well," he exploded, "it seems I can't get anybody to drink with me in this town. Seems so, don't it? Well!"

"Ssh!" said the barkeeper.

"Say," snarled the Swede, "don't you try to shut me up. I won't have it. I'm a gentleman, and I want people to drink with me. And I want 'em to drink with me now. *Now*—do you understand?" He rapped the bar with his knuckles.

Years of experience had calloused the bartender. He merely grew sulky. "I hear you," he answered.

"Well," cried the Swede, "listen hard then. See those men over there? Well, they're going to drink with me, and don't you forget it. Now you watch."

"Hi!" yelled the barkeeper, "this won't do!"

"Why won't it?" demanded the Swede. He stalked over to the table, and by chance laid his hand upon the shoulder of the gambler. "How about this?" he asked wrathfully. "I asked you to drink with me."

The gambler simply twisted his head and spoke over his shoulder. "My friend, I don't know you."

"Oh, hell!" answered the Swede, "come and have a drink."

"Now, my boy," advised the gambler, kindly, "take your hand off my shoulder and go 'way and mind your own business." He was a little, slim man, and it seemed strange to hear him use this tone of heroic patronage to the burly Swede. The other men at the table said nothing.

"What! You won't drink with me, you little dude? I'll make you, then! I'll make you!" The Swede had grasped the gambler frenziedly at the throat, and was dragging him from his chair. The other men sprang up. The barkeeper dashed around the corner of his bar. There was a great tumult, and then was seen a long blade in the hand of the gambler. It shot forward, and a human body, this citadel of virtue, wisdom, power, was pierced as easily as if it had been a melon. The Swede fell with a cry of supreme astonishment.

The prominent merchants and the district attorney must have at once tumbled out of the place backward. The bartender found himself hanging limply to the arm of a chair and gazing into the eyes of a murderer.

"Henry," said the latter, as he wiped his knife on one of the towels that hung beneath the bar rail, "you tell 'em where to find me. I'll be home, waiting for 'em." Then he vanished. A moment afterward the barkeeper was in the street dinning through the storm for help and, moreover, companionship.

The corpse of the Swede, alone in the saloon, had its eye fixed upon a dreadful legend that dwelt atop of the cash-machine: "This registers the amount of your purchase."

IX

Months later, the cowboy was frying pork over the stove of a little ranch near the Dakota line, when there was a quick thud of hoofs outside, and presently the Easterner entered with the letters and the papers.

"Well," said the Easterner at once, "the chap that killed the Swede has got three years? Wasn't much, was it?"

"He has? Three years?" The cowboy poised his pan of pork, while he ruminated upon the news. "Three years. That ain't much."

"No. It was a light sentence," replied the Easterner as he unbuckled his spurs. "Seems there was a good deal of sympathy for him in Romper."

"If the bartender had been any good," observed the cowboy, thoughtfully, "he would have gone in and cracked that there Dutchman on the head with a bottle in the beginnin' of it and stopped all this here murderin'."

"Yes, a thousand things might have happened," said the Easterner, tartly.

The cowboy returned his pan of pork to the fire, but his philosophy continued. "It's funny, ain't it? If he hadn't said Johnnie was cheatin' he'd be alive this minute. He was an awful fool. Game played for fun, too. Not for money. I believe he was crazy."

"I feel sorry for that gambler," said the Easterner.

"Oh, so do I," said the cowboy. "He don't deserve none of it for killin' who he did."

"The Swede might not have been killed if everything had been square."

"Might not have been killed?" exclaimed the cowboy. "Everythin' square? Why, when he said that Johnnie was cheatin' and acted like such a jackass? And then in the saloon he fairly walked up to git hurt?" With these arguments the cowboy browbeat the Easterner and reduced him to rage.

"You're a fool!" cried the Easterner, viciously. "You're a bigger jackass than the Swede by a million majority. Now let me tell you one thing. Let me tell you something. Listen! Johnnie *was* cheating!"

" 'Johnnie,' " said the cowboy, blankly. There was a minute of silence, and then he said, robustly, "Why, no. The game was only for fun."

"Fun or not," said the Easterner, "Johnnie was cheating. I saw him. I know it. I saw him. And I refused to stand up and be a man. I let the Swede fight it out alone. And you—you were simply puffing around the place and wanting to fight. And then old Scully himself! We are all in it! This poor gambler isn't even a noun. He is kind of an adverb. Every sin is the result of a collaboration. We, five of us, have collaborated in the murder of this Swede. Usually there are from a dozen to forty women really involved in every murder, but in this case it seems to be only five men—you, I, Johnnie, old Scully; and that fool of an unfortunate gambler came merely as a culmination, the apex of a human movement, and gets all the punishment."

The cowboy, injured and rebellious, cried out blindly into this fog of mysterious theory: "Well, I didn't do anythin', did I?"

Questions

1. The Easterner explains the Swede's behavior by the fact that the "man has been reading dime novels, and he thinks he's right in the middle of it—the shootin' and stabbin' and all." What does the Easterner mean? Is he right?

2. Why does Scully show the Swede pictures of his daughter and son? Why does he tell the Swede about the town's progress?
3. Why does Scully tell the Swede, "This is my house. You are under my roof, and I will not allow any peaceable man to be troubled here"? How would you describe the style of this speech?
4. Why does the Swede fight Johnny? Does it matter to the Swede that no money was riding on the game? Is money the only reason for fighting? Is it sufficient reason for fighting?
5. The Easterner claims that "every sin is the result of a collaboration." What does he mean? Is he correct?
6. Under the Easterner's assumption of communal responsibility, are there only five men involved in the Swede's murder?
7. Why does the gambler knife the Swede? If you were on the jury, whom—if anyone—would you find guilty of murder?

5  Characters

In fiction, the performers of the action are called *characters*. The performer may be a person or a thing.

We can learn very little about a character or a great deal. Here, for example, is a German folktale in which we are told almost nothing about the character.

Catching a Rabbit

Hans decided to catch rabbits, but he had nothing to make the usual trap. Instead he set out a cabbage leaf under a basket propped up by a weak twig. Hans covered the cabbage leaf with pepper. Finally, an unsuspecting rabbit came to nibble on the cabbage. The rabbit sniffed, sneezed, and knocked the basket on top of himself. That night, Hans ate his fill of fresh rabbit.

What do we know about Hans? Only that he is clever and has a good appetite. Do we know anything about his age, family, income, education? Do we know how he feels when he catches the rabbit? No. Hans is merely a name used by the author so that a series of actions can be narrated. If someone were to ask, "What is Hans really like?" we would shrug our shoulders and reply, "It doesn't matter."

Flat Characters

The novelist E. M. Forster would call Hans a *flat character*. Flat characters, according to Forster, "are constructed round a single idea or quality. . . . The really flat character can be expressed in one sentence." A flat character, then, has a single behavioral trait or a stereotyped group of behaviors. A stereotype is a simplified image of a class of people. Thus we have the stereotype that all professors are absent-minded, all athletes are slow-witted, and all good students are skinny, bespectacled, and friendless. Because stereotypes are so simplified, they never describe actual people. Hans, in the story, could be summed up as the clever sort of person who finds a solution to every mechanical problem. Beyond this single attribute Hans does not exist. But we must not assume that Hans is flat simply because of the brevity of this story. One could supply any number of additional anecdotes about Hans—how he built a fire that would never go out, or a device that would automatically let out the sheep to graze— and he would still be flat, because these additional tales are all based on the same behavioral trait.

Stories and novels frequently have flat characters. They serve important artistic functions. They are easy to identify. We easily recognize Hans's character because so many fictional characters have this trait. In a short story where economy is a virtue, such quickly-drawn, easily-recognizable characters help forward the action efficiently and smoothly. But even in the larger, roomier novel, flat characters are valuable. Just as in life, where we know some people better than others, so, too, in fiction all characters are not of equal importance. Some people we know as flat characters: the cheerful shopkeeper, the grumpy bankteller, the efficient librarian. These are people we might see frequently, but they are relatively uncomplicated figures compared to parents, relatives, and friends. If the novelist had to give a full biography each time his main character—or *protagonist*—met a minor character, no novel would ever end. Flat characters are necessary for the efficient functioning of a work.

The Character as Literary Form

But flat characters can be interesting in themselves. The Greek writer Theophrastus (371–287 B.C.) developed a literary form called *the character*, which is a short description of a figure with one dominant personality trait. This literary form continues today. Elias Canetti, winner of the 1981 Nobel Prize in literature, wrote an entire book of such characters.

ELIAS CANETTI (1905–)

The Earwitness

The earwitness makes no effort to look, but he hears all the better. He comes, halts, huddles unnoticed in a corner, peers into a book or a display, hears whatever is to be heard, and moves away untouched and absent. One would think he was not there for he is such an expert at vanishing. He is already somewhere else, he is already listening again, he knows all the places where there is something to be heard, stows it nicely away, and forgets nothing.

He forgets nothing, one has to watch the earwitness when it is time for him to come out with everything. At such a time, he is another man, he is twice as large and four inches taller. How does he do it, does he have special high shoes for blurting things out? Could he possibly pad himself with pillows to make his words seem heavier and weightier? He does nothing else, he says it very precisely, some people wish they had held their tongues. All those modern gadgets are superfluous: his ear is better and more faithful than any gadget, nothing is erased, nothing is blocked, no matter how bad it is, lies, curses, four-letter words, all kinds of indecencies, invectives from remote and little-known languages, he accurately registers even things he does not understand and delivers them unaltered if people wish him to do so.

The earwitness cannot be corrupted by anybody. When it comes to this useful gift, which he alone has, he would take no heed of wife, child, or brother. Whatever he has heard, he has heard, and even the Good Lord is helpless to change it. But he also has human sides, and just as others have their holidays, on which they rest from work, he sometimes, albeit seldom, claps blinders on his ears and refrains from storing up the hearable things. This happens quite simply, he makes himself noticeable, he looks people in the eye, the things they say in these circumstances are quite unimportant and do not suffice to spell their doom. When he has taken off his secret ears, he is a friendly person, everyone trusts him, everyone likes to have a drink with him, harmless phrases are exchanged. At such times, people have no inkling that they are speaking with the executioner himself. It is not to be believed how innocent people are when no one is eavesdropping.

Questions

1. What does the Earwitness do?
2. Why is the Earwitness invisible?
3. Is the Earwitness a good person or a bad person?
4. Does the Earwitness have a more realistic understanding of the people around him than others have?
5. Do you know any Earwitnesses? If so, what do you think of them?

The Earwitness is an interesting character, despite his "flatness," because his behavioral trait is an unusual one. Characters can be both flat and interesting if they are marked by an unusual or imaginative trait.

Exercise

Write three short character studies of types you know in school. Avoid, however, the typical classification of students into athletes, preppies, or A students. Invent types of your own: the note-taker, the question-asker, the front-row-sleeper.

Round Characters

Yet as convenient and interesting as flat characters can be, they do not satisfy the need of most writers and serious readers for psychological depth. Because flat characters can be summarized so easily, they have little capacity to surprise us. Their energy, their action, and their single-mindedness may amuse us and temporarily hold our interest, but as psychological models they soon become repetitious and limited.

The round character, however, is a fictional creation that can sustain our interest long after we have finished reading. Round characters have a number of personality traits and seem as complex as actual people we know well. They seem to possess a life that extends beyond the action of the story. We can imagine them in different situations and places. In "The Horse Dealer's Daughter," Mabel Pervin has roundness of character. She cannot be summarized in a sentence. For although she is proud and cold, she is also vulnerable and full of fiery passion. Silent most of the time, she is not afraid to speak when occasion calls for speech. Strong-tempered, she is nevertheless gentle and submissive to Fergusson. In short, she is a mixture of various human traits. The fully drawn character is one of the great triumphs of imaginative art, one of the most satisfying and sustaining pleasures of reading.

Why does a fully realized character intrigue us? Forster's answer is "we can know more about him than we can know about any of our fellow creatures." He goes on to explain the power of this greater understanding:

> We cannot understand each other, except in a rough and ready way; we cannot reveal ourselves, even when we want to; what we call intimacy is only a makeshift; perfect knowledge is an illusion. But in the novel we can know people perfectly, and, apart from the general pleasure of reading, we can find here a compensation for their dimness in life.[1]

People, according to Forster, are frustrated by their partial knowledge of other humans. Round characters satisfy that hunger for more knowledge; they are compensation for our imperfect understanding of the real world.

Reading for Character

We understand characters in almost the same way that we understand real human beings. When we meet people for the first time, we listen to what they say and what is said about them, but most of all we watch what they do, how they behave. In reading a story, we perform almost the same act. We read what the narrator says (keeping in mind the limitations of the narrator's point of view), listen to what the characters say, and watch how they behave. As a reader, however, you may have another advantage: you may be allowed to know what the character is thinking. In real life we never have this advantage—access to someone else's unspoken thoughts. Indeed, writers have developed a special technique, called *stream-of-consciousness*, which reveals a character's innermost thoughts as they are formulated. In a stream-of-consciousness passage, trivial facts and important ones, memories and current experience, are seemingly jum-

---

[1] E.M. Forster, *Aspects of the Novel* (New York: Harcourt Brace, 1927), p. 98.

bled together to form a rich, complex pattern. "The Jilting of Granny Weatherall" contains several *stream-of-consciousness* passages.

We should also watch for changes in the characters. Stories are usually organized in one of two ways: (1) The story reveals more and more traits of an essentially unchanging, *static character*. In such a story, the reader's understanding alters while the character remains the same. (2) The other type of narrative establishes the character's traits in the first part of the story and proceeds to show how events modify those traits. Such a character is said to be a *developing character*. Clearly, it is harder for an author to show a developing character than a static one, because the static character has only one set of traits while the developing character has two or more.

One should not confuse the length of time covered in a story with the character's development. In "The Horse Dealer's Daughter," both Mabel Pervin and Dr. Fergusson change in the course of an afternoon. In "The Jilting of Granny Weatherall," we watch a character who has stubbornly resisted change all her life.

Motivation and Consistency

When the police investigate a crime, they must establish a suspect's *motives*, the person's reasons for performing the action. The careful reader is somewhat like a police detective and will ask why characters do what they do. Good authors will give their characters motives. Sometimes, however, these motives are clearly stated and sometimes they are implied by other parts of the story. A good exercise is to ask yourself why central characters—or *protagonists*—perform the actions in the story.

A character's actions must not only be motivated, but they must also be *consistent* with his or her behavioral traits. It would be inconsistent for a hostile character suddenly to become pleasant, or for a gentle character to become violent *unless* some special event motivated the change. We all know of peace-loving people who become aroused by some terrible act of injustice, a gentle person who might strike someone for abusing a child. The instance of child abuse would be sufficient motivation to justify the change in behavior. In Charles Dickens's "A Christmas Carol," the notoriously stingy Ebenezer Scrooge becomes by the end of the story generous and charitable. Here the development in character is motivated by the visit of the three spirits.

Heroes and Villains

In Greek literature the term *hero* was reserved for the warrior noble who achieved great feats in battle. Since then, the term has been applied to any good central character. However, it may be best to reserve the word "hero" for the exceptionally brave and valiant character and refer to the usual run of central figures as protagonists. Similarly we will reserve the term *"villain"* for particularly evil scoundrels and refer to the person in conflict with the protagonist as the *antagonist*.

We make these distinctions because heroes and villains are special flat characters. They exist at the extremes of goodness and badness. Most central characters—especially of the round variety—are, like most people, neither very good nor very bad, very brave nor very cowardly. They are a mixture of these behavioral traits. Indeed, one of the ways we can tell a "realistic" character from a "fantastic" or "supernatural" character is that the realistic character has a mixture of good and bad traits, is neither an angel nor a devil. Such realistic characters often hold our interest longer because their actions are less predictable and because they are more like ourselves.

Suggestions for Essayists

1. Describe how you or someone you know has changed over the last few years.
2. Some people say that a particularly critical incident changed their lives; e.g., a brush with death, with the law, with love. Describe how such a critical incident changed you or someone you know.
3. Describe the man or woman of your dreams and explain why you value the qualities you describe.

Suggestions for Fiction Writers

1. Go through a newspaper or magazine and, without reading the copy, choose an anonymous face that interests you. Then write a fictional life of that person. When you are finished, compare your fictional life to the information in the newspaper or magazine.
2. Some people believe in reincarnation. Describe a life you might have led before your present existence.

D. H. LAWRENCE (1885–1930)

The Horse Dealer's Daughter

"Well, Mabel, and what are you going to do with yourself?" asked Joe, with foolish flippancy. He felt quite safe himself. Without listening for an answer, he turned aside, worked a grain of tobacco to the tip of his tongue and spat it out. He did not care about anything, since he felt safe himself.

The three brothers and the sister sat round the desolate breakfast table, attempting some sort of desultory consultation. The morning's post had given the final tap to the family fortune, and all was over. The dreary dining room itself, with its heavy mahogany furniture, looked as if it were waiting to be done away with.

But the consultation amounted to nothing. There was a strange air of ineffectuality about the three men, as they sprawled at table, smoking and reflecting vaguely on their own condition. The girl was alone, a rather short, sullen-looking young woman of twenty-seven. She did not share the same life as her brothers. She would have been goodlooking, save for the impassive fixity of her face, "bull-dog," as her brothers called it.

There was a confused tramping of horses' feet outside. The three men all sprawled round in their chairs to watch. Beyond the dark holly bushes that separated the strip of lawn from the highroad, they could see a cavalcade of shire horses swinging out of their own yard, being taken for exercise. This was the last time. These were the last horses that would go through their hands. The young men watched with critical, callous look. They were all frightened at the collapse of their lives, and the sense of disaster in which they were involved left them no inner freedom.

Yet they were three fine, well-set fellows enough. Joe, the eldest, was a man of thirty-three, broad and handsome in a hot, flushed way. His face was red, he twisted his black moustache over a thick finger, his eyes were shallow and restless. He had a sensual way of uncovering his teeth when he laughed, and his bearing was stupid. Now he watched the horses with a glazed look of helplessness in his eyes, a certain stupor of downfall.

The great draught-horses swung past. They were tied head to tail, four of them, and they heaved along to where a lane branched off from the highroad, planting their great hoofs floutingly in the fine black mud, swinging their great rounded haunches sumptuously, and trotting a few sudden steps as they were led into the lane, round the corner. Every movement showed a massive, slumbrous strength, and a stupidity which held them in subjection. The groom at the head looked back, jerking the leading rope. And the cavalcade moved out of sight up the lane, the tail of the last horse, bobbed up tight and stiff, held out taut from the swinging great haunches as they rocked behind the hedges in a motion-like sleep.

Joe watched with glazed hopeless eyes. The horses were almost like his own body to him. He felt he was done for now. Luckily he was engaged to a woman as old as himself, and therefore her father, who was steward of a neighboring estate, would provide him with a job. He would marry and go into harness. His life was over, he would be a subject animal now.

He turned uneasily aside, the retreating steps of the horses echoing in his ears. Then, with foolish restlessness, he reached for the scraps of bacon rind from the plates, and making a faint whistling sound, flung them to the terrier that lay against the fender. He watched the dog swallow them, and waited till the creature looked into his eyes. Then a faint grin came on his face, and in a high, foolish voice he said:

"You won't get much more bacon, shall you, you little bitch?"

The dog faintly and dismally wagged its tail, then lowered its haunches, circled round, and lay down again.

There was another helpless silence at the table. Joe sprawled uneasily in his seat, not willing to go till the family conclave was dissolved. Fred Henry, the second brother, was erect, clean-limbed, alert. He had watched the passing of the horses with more sang-froid. If he was an animal, like Joe, he was an animal which controls, not one which is controlled. He was master of any horse, and he carried himself with a well-tempered air of mastery. But he was not master of the situations of life. He pushed his coarse brown moustache upwards, off his lip, and glanced irritably at his sister, who sat impassive and inscrutable.

"You'll go and stop with Lucy for a bit, shan't you?" he asked. The girl did not answer.

"I don't see what else you can do," persisted Fred Henry.

"Go as a skivvy," Joe interpolated laconically.

The girl did not move a muscle.

"If I was her, I should go in for training for a nurse," said Malcolm, the youngest of them all. He was the baby of the family, a young man of twenty-two, with a fresh, jaunty *museau*.

But Mabel did not take any notice of him. They had talked at her and round her for so many years, that she hardly heard them at all.

The marble clock on the mantlepiece softly chimed the half-hour, the dog rose uneasily from the hearthrug and looked at the party at the breakfast table. But still they sat on in ineffectual conclave.

"Oh, all right," said Joe suddenly, apropos of nothing. "I'll get a move on."

He pushed back his chair, straddled his knees with a downward jerk, to get them free, in horsey fashion, and went to the fire. Still he did not go out of the room; he was curious to know what the others would do or say. He began to charge his pipe, looking down at the dog and saying, in a high, affected voice:

"Going wi' me? Going wi' me are ter? Tha'rt goin' further tha that counts on just now, dost hear?"

The dog faintly wagged its tail, the man stuck out his jaw and covered his pipe with his hands, and puffed intently, losing himself in the tobacco, looking down all the while at the dog with an absent brown eye. The dog looked at him in mournful distrust. Joe stood with his knees stuck out, in real horsey fashion.

"Have you had a letter from Lucy?" Fred Henry asked of his sister.

"Last week," came the neutral reply.

"And what does she say?"

There was no answer.

"Does she *ask* you to go and stop there?" persisted Fred Henry.

"She says I can if I like."

"Well, then, you'd better. Tell her you'll come on Monday."

This was received in silence.

"That's what you'll do then, is it?" said Fred Henry, in some exasperation.

But she made no answer. There was a silence of futility and irritation in the room. Malcolm grinned fatuously.

"You'll have to make up your mind between now and next Wednesday," said Joe loudly, "or else find yourself lodgings on the curbstone."

The face of the young woman darkened, but she sat on immutable.

"Here's Jack Fergusson!" exclaimed Malcolm, who was looking aimlessly out of the window.

"Where?" exclaimed Joe, loudly.

"Just gone past."

"Coming in?"

Malcolm craned his neck to see the gate.

"Yes," he said.

There was a silence. Mabel sat on like one condemned, at the head of the table. Then a whistle was heard from the kitchen. The dog got up and barked sharply. Joe opened the door and shouted:

"Come on."

After a moment a young man entered. He was muffled up in overcoat and a purple woolen scarf, and his tweed cap, which he did not remove, was pulled down on his head. He was of medium height, his face was rather long and pale, his eyes looked tired.

"Hello, Jack! Well, Jack!" exclaimed Malcolm and Joe. Fred Henry merely said, "Jack."

"What's doing?" asked the newcomer, evidently addressing Fred Henry.

"Same. We've got to be out by Wednesday. Got a cold?"

"I have—got it bad, too."

"Why don't you stop in?'

"*Me* stop in? When I can't stand on my legs, perhaps I shall have a chance." The young man spoke huskily. He had a slight Scotch accent.

"It's a knock-out, isn't it," said Joe, boisterously, "if a doctor goes round croaking with a cold. Looks bad for the patients, doesn't it?"

The young doctor looked at him slowly.

"Anything the matter with *you*, then?" he asked sarcastically.

"Not as I know of. Damn your eyes, I hope not. Why?"

"I thought you were very concerned about the patients, wondered if you might be one yourself."

"Damn it, no, I've never been patient to no flaming doctor, and hope I never shall be," returned Joe.

At this point Mabel rose from the table, and they all seemed to become aware of her existence. She began putting the dishes together. The young doctor looked at her, but did not address her. He had not greeted her. She went out of the room with the tray, her face impassive and unchanged.

"When are you off then, all of you?" asked the doctor.

"I'm catching the eleven-forty," replied Malcolm. "Are you goin' down wi' th' trap, Joe?"

"Yes, I've told you I'm going down wi' th' trap, haven't I?"

"We'd better be getting her in then. So long, Jack, if I don't see you before I go," said Malcolm, shaking hands.

He went out, followed by Joe, who seemed to have his tail between his legs.

"Well, this is the devil's own," exclaimed the doctor, when he was left alone with Fred Henry. "Going before Wednesday, are you?"

"That's the orders," replied the other.

"Where, to Northampton?"

"That's it."

"The devil!" exclaimed Fergusson, with quiet chagrin.

And there was silence between the two.

"All settled up, are you?" asked Fergusson.

"About."

There was another pause.

"Well, I shall miss yer, Freddy, boy," said the young doctor.

"And I shall miss thee, Jack," returned the other.

"Miss you like hell," mused the doctor.

Fred Henry turned aside. There was nothing to say. Mabel came in again, to finish clearing the table.

"What are *you* going to do, then, Miss Pervin?" asked Fergusson. "Going to your sister's, are you?"

Mabel looked at him with her steady, dangerous eyes, that always made him uncomfortable, unsettling his superficial ease.

"No," she said.

"Well, what in the name of fortune *are* you going to do? Say what you mean to do," cried Fred Henry, with futile intensity.

But she only averted her head, and continued her work. She folded the white table-cloth, and put on the chenille cloth.

"The sulkiest bitch that ever trod!" muttered her brother.

But she finished her task with perfectly impassive face, the young doctor watching her interestedly all the while. Then she went out.

Fred Henry stared after her, clenching his lips, his blue eyes fixing in sharp antagonism, as he made a grimace of sour exasperation.

"You could bray her into bits, and that's all you'd get out of her," he said in a small, narrowed tone.

The doctor smiled faintly.

"What's she *going* to do, then?" he asked.

"Strike me if *I* know!" returned the other.

There was a pause. Then the doctor stirred.

"I'll be seeing you to-night, shall I?" he said to his friend.

"Ay—where's it to be? Are we going over to Jessdale?"

"I don't know. I've got such a cold on me. I'll come round to the Moon and Stars, anyway."

"Let Lizzie and May miss their night for once, eh?"

"That's it—if I feel as I do now."

"All's one—"

The two young men went through the passage and down to the back door together. The house was large, but it was servantless now, and desolate. At the back was a small bricked house-yard, and beyond that a big square, graveled fine and red, and having stables on two sides. Sloping, dank, winter-dark fields stretched away on the open sides.

But the stables were empty. Joseph Pervin, the father of the family, had been a man of no education, who had become a fairly large horse dealer. The stables had been full of horses, there was a great turmoil and come-and-go of horses and of dealers and grooms. Then the kitchen was full of servants. But of late things had declined. The old man had married a second time, to retrieve his fortunes. Now he was dead and everything was gone to the dogs, there was nothing but debt and threatening.

For months, Mabel had been servantless in the big house, keeping the home together in penury for her ineffectual brothers. She had kept house for ten years. But previously it was with unstinted means. Then, however brutal and coarse everything was, the sense of money had kept her proud, confident. The men might be foul-mouthed, the women in the kitchen might have bad reputations, her brothers might have illegitimate children. But so long as there was money, the girl felt herself established, and brutally proud, reserved.

No company came to the house, save dealers and coarse men. Mabel had no associates of her own sex, after her sister went away. But she did not mind. She went regularly to church, she attended to her father. And she lived in the memory of her mother, who had died when she was fourteen, and whom she had loved. She had loved her father, too, in a different way, depending upon him, and feeling secure in him, until at the age of fifty-four he married again. And then she had set hard against him. Now he had died and left them all hopelessly in debt.

She had suffered badly during the period of poverty. Nothing, however, could shake the curious sullen, animal pride that dominated each member of the family. Now, for Mabel, the end had come. Still she would not cast about her. She would follow her own way just the same. She would always hold the keys of her own situation. Mindless and persistent, she endured from day to day. Why should she think? Why should she answer anybody? It was enough that this was the end, and there was no way out. She need not pass any more darkly along the main street of the small town, avoiding every eye. She need not demean herself any more, going into the shops and buying the cheapest food. This was at an end. She thought of nobody, not even of herself. Mindless and persistent, she seemed in a sort of ecstasy to be coming nearer to her fulfillment, her own glorification, approaching her dead mother, who was glorified.

In the afternoon she took a little bag, with shears and sponge and a small scrubbing brush, and went out. It was a gray, wintry day, with saddened, dark green fields and an atmosphere blackened by the smoke of foundries not far off. She went quickly, darkly along the causeway, heeding nobody, through the town to the churchyard.

There she always felt secure, as if no one could see her, although as a matter of fact she was exposed to the stare of every one who passed along under the churchyard wall. Nevertheless, once under the shadow of the great looming church, among the graves, she felt immune from the world, reserved within the thick churchyard wall as in another country.

Carefully she clipped the grass from the grave, and arranged the pinky white, small chrysanthemums in the tin cross. When this was done, she took an empty jar from a neighboring grave, brought water, and carefully, most scrupulously sponged the marble headstone and the coping-stone.

It gave her sincere satisfaction to do this. She felt in immediate contact with the world of her mother. She took minute pains, went through the park in a state bordering on pure happiness, as if in performing this task she came into a subtle, intimate connection with her mother. For the life she followed here in the world was far less real than the world of death she inherited from her mother.

The doctor's house was just by the church. Fergusson, being a mere hired assistant, was slave to the countryside. As he hurried now to attend to the outpatients in the surgery, glancing across the graveyard with his quick eyes, he saw the girl at her task at the grave. She seemed so intent and remote, it was like looking into another world. Some mystical element was touched in him. He slowed down as he walked, watching her as if spellbound.

She lifted her eyes, feeling him looking. Their eyes met. And each looked away again at once, each feeling, in some way, found out by the other. He lifted his cap and passed on down the road. There remained distinct in his consciousness, like a vision, the memory of her face, lifted from the tombstone in the churchyard, and looking at him with slow, large, portentous eyes. It *was* portentous, her face. It seemed to mesmerize him. There was a heavy power in her eyes which laid hold of his whole being, as if he had drunk some powerful drug. He had been feeling weak and done before. Now the life came back into him, he felt delivered from his own fretted, daily self.

He finished his duties at the surgery as quickly as might be, hastily filling up the bottle of the waiting people with cheap drugs. Then, in perpetual haste, he set off again to visit several cases in another part of his round, before teatime. At all times he preferred to walk if he could, but particularly when he was not well. He fancied the motion restored him.

The afternoon was falling. It was gray, deadened, and wintry, with a slow, moist, heavy coldness sinking in and deadening all the faculties. But why should he think or notice? He hastily climbed the hill and turned across the dark green fields, following the black cindertrack. In the distance, across a shallow dip in the country, the small town was clustered like smouldering ash, a tower, a spire, a heap of low, raw, extinct houses. And on the nearest fringe of the town, sloping into the dip, was Oldmeadow, the Pervins' house. He could see the stables and the outbuildings distinctly, as they lay towards him on the slope. Well, he would not go there many more times! Another resource would be lost to him, another place gone: the only company he cared for in the alien, ugly little town he was losing. Nothing but work, drudgery, constant hastening from dwelling to dwelling among the colliers and the iron-workers. It wore him out, but at the same time he had a craving for it. It was a stimulant to him to be in the homes of the working people, moving as it were through the innermost body of their life. His nerves were excited and gratified. He could come so near, into the very lives of the rough, inarticulate, powerfully emotional men and women. He grumbled, he said he hated the hellish hole. But as a matter of fact it excited him, the contact with the rough, strongly-feeling people was a stimulant applied direct to his nerves.

Below Oldmeadow, in the green, shallow, soddened hollow of fields, lay a square, deep pond. Roving across the landscape, the doctor's quick eye detected a figure in black passing through the gate of the field, down towards the pond. He looked again. It would be Mabel Pervin. His mind suddenly became alive and attentive.

Why was she going down there? He pulled up on the path on the slope above, and stood staring. He could just make sure of the small black figure moving in the hollow of the failing day. He seemed to see her in the midst of such obscurity, that he was like a clairvoyant, seeing rather with the mind's eye than with ordinary sight. Yet he could see her positively enough, while he kept his eye attentive. He felt, if he looked away from her, in the thick, ugly falling dusk, he would lose her altogether.

He followed her minutely as she moved, direct and intent, like something transmitted rather than stirring in voluntary activity, straight down the field towards the pond. There she stood on the bank for a moment. She never raised her head. Then she waded slowly into the water.

He stood motionless as the small black figure walked slowly and deliberately towards the center of the pond, very slowly, gradually moving deeper into the motionless water, and still moving forward as the water got up to her breast. Then he could see her no more in the dusk of the dead afternoon.

"There!" he exclaimed, "Would you believe it?"

And he hastened straight down, running over the wet, soddened fields, pushing through the hedges, down into the depression of callous wintry obscurity. It took him several minutes to come to the pond. He stood on the bank, breathing heavily. He could see nothing. His eyes seemed to penetrate the dead water. Yes, perhaps that was the dark shadow of her black clothing beneath the surface of the water.

He slowly ventured into the pond. The bottom was deep, soft clay, he sank in, and the water clasped dead cold round his legs. As he stirred he could smell the cold, rotten clay that fouled up into the water. It was objectionable in his lungs. Still, repelled and yet not heeding, he moved deeper into the pond. The cold water rose over his thighs, over his loins, upon his abdomen. The lower part of his body was all sunk in the hideous cold element. And the bottom was so deeply soft and uncertain he was afraid of pitching with his mouth underneath. He could not swim, and was afraid.

He crouched a little, spreading his hands under the water and moving them round, trying to feel for her. The dead cold pond swayed upon his chest. He moved again, a little deeper, and again, with his hands underneath, he felt all around under the water. And he touched her clothing. But it evaded his fingers. He made a desperate effort to grasp it.

And so doing he lost his balance and went under, horribly, suffocating in the foul earthy water, struggling madly for a few moments. At last, after what seemed an eternity, he got his footing, rose again into the air and looked around. He gasped, and knew he was in the world. Then he looked at the water. She had risen near him. He grasped her clothing, and drawing her nearer, turned to take his way to land again.

He went very slowly, carefully, absorbed in the slow progress. He rose higher, climbing out of the pond. The water was now only about his legs; he was thankful, full of relief to be out of the clutches of the pond. He lifted her and staggered on to the bank, out of the horror of wet, gray clay.

He laid her down on the bank. She was quite unconscious and running with water. He made the water come from her mouth, he worked to restore her. He did not have to work very long before he could feel the breathing begin again in her; she was breathing naturally. He worked a little longer. He could feel her live beneath his hands; she was coming back. He wiped her face, wrapped her in his overcoat, looked round into the dim, dark gray world, then lifted her and staggered down the bank and across the fields.

It seemed an unthinkably long way, and his burden so heavy he felt he would never get to the house. But at last he was in the stableyard, and then in the house-yard. He opened the door and went into the house. In the kitchen he laid her down on the hearthrug, and called. The house was empty. But the fire was burning in the grate.

Then again he kneeled to attend to her. She was breathing regularly, her eyes were wide open and as if conscious, but there seemed something missing in her look. She was conscious in herself, but unconscious of her surroundings.

He ran upstairs, took blankets from a bed, and put them before the fire to warm. Then he removed her saturated, earthy-smelling clothing, rubbed her dry with a towel, and wrapped her naked in the blankets. Then he went into the dining-room, to look for spirits. There was a little whisky. He drank a gulp himself, and put some into her mouth.

The effect was instantaneous. She looked full into his face, as if she had been seeing him for some time, and yet had only just become conscious of him.

"Dr. Fergusson?" she said.

"What?" he answered.

He was divesting himself of his coat, intending to find some dry clothing upstairs. He could not bear the smell of the dead, clayey water, and he was mortally afraid of his own health.

"What did I do?" she asked.

"Walked into the pond," he replied. He had begun to shudder like one sick, and could hardly attend to her. Her eyes remained full on him, he seemed to be going dark in his mind, looking back at her helplessly. The shuddering became quieter in him, his life came back in him, dark and unknowing, but strong again.

"Was I out of my mind?" she asked, while her eyes were fixed on him all the time.

"Maybe, for the moment," he replied. He felt quiet, because his strength came back. The strange fretful strain had left him.

"Am I out of my mind now?" she asked.

"Are you?" he reflected a moment. "No," he answered truthfully, "I don't see that you are." He turned his face aside. He was afraid now, because he felt dazed, and felt dimly that her power was stronger than his, in this issue. And she continued to look at him fixedly all the time. "Can you tell me where I shall find some dry things to put on?" he asked.

"Did you dive into the pond for me?" she asked.

"No," he answered. "I walked in. But I went in overhead as well."

There was silence for a moment. He hesitated. He very much wanted to go upstairs to get into dry clothing. But there was another desire in him. And she seemed to hold him. His will seemed to have gone to sleep, and left him, standing there slack before her. But he felt warm inside himself. He did not shudder at all, though his clothes were sodden on him.

"Why did you?" she asked.

"Because I didn't want you to do such a foolish thing," he said.

"It wasn't foolish," she said, still gazing at him as she lay on the floor, with a sofa cushion under her head. "It was the right thing to do. I knew best, then."

"I'll go and shift these wet things," he said. But still he had not the power to move out of her presence, until she sent him. It was as if she had the life of his body in her hands, and he could not extricate himself. Or perhaps he did not want to.

Suddenly she sat up. Then she became aware of her own immediate condition. She felt the blankets about her, she knew her own limbs. For a moment it seemed as if her reason were going. She looked round, with wild eye, as if seeking something. He stood still with fear. She saw her clothing lying scattered.

"Who undressed me?" she asked, her eyes resting full and inevitable on his face.

"I did," he replied, "to bring you round."

For some moments she sat and gazed at him awfully, her lips parted.

"Do you love me, then?" she asked.

He only stood and stared at her, fascinated. His soul seemed to melt.

She shuffled forward on her knees, and put her arms round him, round his legs, as he stood there, pressing her breasts against his knees and thighs, clutching him with strange, convulsive certainty, pressing his thighs against her, drawing him to her face, her throat, as she looked up at him with flaring, humble eyes of transfiguration, triumphant in first possession.

"You love me," she murmured, in strange transport, yearning and triumphant and confident. "You love me. I know you love me, I know."

And she was passionately kissing his knees, through the wet clothing, passionately and indiscriminately kissing his knees, his legs, as if unaware of everything.

He looked down at the tangled wet hair, the wild, bare, animal shoulders. He was amazed, bewildered, and afraid. He had never thought of loving her. He had never wanted to love her. When he rescued her and restored her, he was a doctor, and she was a patient. He had had no single personal thought of her. Nay, this introduction of the personal element was very distasteful to him, a violation of his professional honor. It was horrible to have her there embracing his knees. It was horrible. He revolted from it, violently. And yet—and yet—he had not the power to break away.

She looked at him again, with the same supplication of powerful love, and that same transcendent, frightening light of triumph. In view of the delicate flame which seemed to come from her face like a light, he was powerless. And yet he had never intended to love her. He had never intended. And something stubborn in him could not give way.

"You love me," she repeated, in a murmur of deep, rhapsodic assurance. "You love me."

Her hands were drawing him, drawing him down to her. He was afraid, even a little horrified. For he had, really, no intention of loving her. Yet her hands were drawing him towards her. He put out his hand quickly to steady himself, and grasped her bare shoulder. A flame seemed to burn the hand that grasped her soft shoulder. He had no intention of loving her: his whole will was against his yielding. It was horrible. And yet wonderful was the touch of her shoulders, beautiful the shining of her face. Was she perhaps mad? He had a horror of yielding to her. Yet something in him ached also.

He had been staring away at the door, away from her. But his hand remained on her shoulder. She had gone suddenly very still. He looked down at her. Her eyes were now wide with fear, with doubt, the light was dying from her face, a shadow of terrible grayness was returning. He could not bear the touch of her eyes' question upon him, and the look of death behind the question.

With an inward groan he gave way, and let his heart yield towards her. A sudden gentle smile came on his face. And her eyes, which never left his face, slowly, slowly filled with tears. He watched the strange water rise in her eyes, like some slow fountain coming up. And his heart seemed to burn and melt away in his breast.

He could not bear to look at her any more. He dropped on his knees and caught her head with his arms and pressed her face against his throat. She was very still. His heart, which seemed to have broken, was burning with a kind of agony in his breast. And he felt her slow, hot tears wetting his throat. But he could not move.

He felt the hot tears wet his neck and the hollows of his neck, and he remained motionless, suspended through one of man's eternities. Only now it had become indispensable to him to have her face pressed close to him; he could never let her go again. He could never let her head go away from the close clutch of his arm. He wanted to remain like that for ever, with his heart hurting him in a pain that was also life to him. Without knowing, he was looking down on her damp, soft brown hair.

Then, as it were suddenly, he smelt the horrid stagnant smell of that water. And at the same moment she drew away from him and looked at him. Her eyes were wistful and unfathomable. He was afraid of them, and he fell to kissing her, not knowing what he was doing. He wanted her eyes not to have that terrible, wistful, unfathomable look.

When she turned her face to him again, a faint delicate flush was glowing, and there was again dawning that terrible shining of joy in her eyes, which really terrified him, and yet which he now wanted to see, because he feared the look of doubt still more.

"You love me?" she said, rather faltering.

"Yes." The word cost him a painful effort. Not because it wasn't true. But because it was too newly true, the *saying* seemed to tear open again his newly torn heart. And he hardly wanted it to be true, even now.

She lifted her face to him, and he bent forward and kissed her on the mouth, gently, with the one kiss that is an eternal pledge. And as he kissed her his heart strained again in his breast. He never intended to love her. But now it was over. He had crossed over the gulf to her, and all that he had left behind had shriveled and become void.

After the kiss, her eyes again slowly filled with tears. She sat still, away from him, with her face drooped aside, and her hands folded in her lap. The tears fell very slowly. There was complete silence. He too sat there motionless and silent on the hearthrug. The strange pain of his heart that was broken seemed to consume him. That he should love her? That this was love! That he should be ripped open in this way! Him, a doctor! How they would all jeer if they knew! It was agony to him to think they might know.

In the curious naked pain of the thought he looked again to her. She was sitting there drooped into a muse. He saw a tear fall, and his heart flared hot. He saw for the first time that one of her shoulders was quite uncovered, one arm bare, he could see one of her small breasts; dimly, because it had become almost dark in the room.

"Why are you crying?" he asked, in an altered voice.

She looked up at him, and behind her tears the consciousness of her situation for the first time brought a dark look of shame to her eyes.

"I'm not crying, really," she said, watching him half frightened.

He reached his hand, and softly closed it on her bare arm.

"I love you! I love you!" he said in a soft, low vibrating voice, unlike himself.

She shrank, and dropped her head. The soft, penetrating grip of his hand on her arm distressed her. She looked up at him.

"I want to go," she said. "I want to go and get you some dry things."

"Why?" he said. "I'm all right."

"But I want to go," she said. "And I want you to change your things."

He released her arm, and she wrapped herself in the blanket, looking at him rather frightened. And still she did not rise.

"Kiss me," she said wistfully.

He kissed her, but briefly, half in anger.

Then, after a second, she rose nervously, all mixed up in the blanket. He watched her in her confusion, as she tried to extricate herself and wrap herself up so that she could walk. He watched her relentlessly, as she knew. And as she went, the blanket trailing, and as he saw a glimpse of her feet and her white leg, he tried to remember her as she was when he had wrapped her in the blanket. But then he didn't want to remember, because she had been nothing to him then, and his nature revolted from remembering her as she was when she was nothing to him.

A tumbling, muffled noise from within the dark house startled him. Then he heard her voice:—"There are clothes." He rose and went to the foot of the stairs, and gathered up the garments she had thrown down. Then he came back to the fire, to rub himself down and dress. He grinned at his own appearance when he had finished.

The fire was sinking, so he put on coal. The house was now quite dark, save for the light of a street-lamp that shone in faintly from beyond the holly trees. He lit the gas with matches he found on the mantelpiece. Then he emptied the pockets of his own clothes, and threw all his wet things in a heap into the scullery. After which he gathered up her sodden clothes, gently, and put them in a separate heap on the copper-top in the scullery.

It was six o'clock on the clock. His own watch had stopped. He ought to go back to the surgery. He waited, and still she did not come down. So he went to the foot of the stairs and called:

"I shall have to go."

Almost immediately he heard her coming down. She had on her best dress of black voile, and her hair was tidy, but still damp. She looked at him—and in spite of herself, smiled.

"I don't like you in those clothes," she said.

"Do I look a sight?" he answered.

They were shy of one another.

"I'll make you some tea," she said.

"No, I must go."

"Must you?" And she looked at him again with the wide, strained, doubtful eyes. And again, from the pain of his breast, he knew how he loved her. He went and bent to kiss her, gently, passionately, with his heart's painful kiss.

"And my hair smells so horrible," she murmured in distraction. "And I'm so awful, I'm so awful! Oh, no, I'm too awful." And she broke into bitter, heart-broken sobbing. "You can't want to love me, I'm horrible."

"Don't be silly, don't be silly," he said, trying to comfort her, kissing her, holding her in his arms. "I want you, I want to marry you, we're going to be married, quickly, quickly—tomorrow if I can."

But she only sobbed terribly, and cried:

"I feel awful. I feel awful. I feel I'm horrible to you."

"No, I want you, I want you," was all he answered, blindly, with that terrible intonation which frightened her almost more than her horror lest he should *not* want her.

Questions

1. How does Joe Pervin think of marriage? How do the other characters regard marriage?
2. At the beginning of the story what options does Mabel have for future employment now that Oldmeadow is sold?

3. How does Mabel show her "curious, sullen animal pride"?
4. How does Dr. Fergusson exhibit his "superficial ease"?
5. How do you explain Fergusson's attraction to Mabel?
6. Do Mabel and Fergusson change in the course of the story? If so, how?

KATHERINE ANNE PORTER (1890–1980)

The Jilting of Granny Weatherall

She flicked her wrist neatly out of Doctor Harry's pudgy careful fingers and pulled the sheet up to her chin. The brat ought to be in knee breeches. Doctoring around the country with spectacles on his nose! "Get along now, take your schoolbooks and go. There's nothing wrong with me."

Doctor Harry spread a warm paw like a cushion on her forehead where the forked green vein danced and made her eyelids twitch. "Now, now, be a good girl, and we'll have you up in no time."

"That's no way to speak to a woman nearly eighty years old just because she's down. I'd have you respect your elders, young man."

"Well, Missy, excuse me." Doctor Harry patted her cheek. "But I've got to warn you, haven't I? You're a marvel, but you must be careful or you're going to be good and sorry."

"Don't tell me what I'm going to be. I'm on my feet now, morally speaking. It's Cornelia. I had to go to bed to get rid of her."

Katherine Anne Porter (Photograph© 1983 Jill Krementz)

Her bones felt loose, and floated around in her skin, and Doctor Harry floated like a balloon around the foot of the bed. He floated and pulled down his waistcoat and swung his glasses on a cord. "Well, stay where you are, it certainly can't hurt you."

"Get along and doctor your sick," said Granny Weatherall. "Leave a well woman alone. I'll call for you when I want you. . . . Where were you forty years ago when I pulled through milk-leg[1] and double pneumonia? You weren't even born. Don't let Cornelia lead you on," she shouted, because Doctor Harry appeared to float up the ceiling and out. "I pay my own bills, and I don't throw my money away on nonsense!"

She meant to wave good-by, but it was too much trouble. Her eyes closed of themselves, it was like a dark curtain drawn around the bed. The pillow rose and floated under her, pleasant as a hammock in a light wind. She listened to the leaves rustling outside the window. No, somebody was swishing newspapers: no, Cornelia and Doctor Harry were whispering together. She leaped broad awake, thinking they whispered in her ear.

"She was never like this, *never* like this!" "Well, what can we expect?" "Yes, eighty years old. . . . "

Well, and what if she was? She still had ears. It was like Cornelia to whisper around doors. She always kept things secret in such a public way. She was always being tactful and kind. Cornelia was dutiful; that was the trouble with her. Dutiful and good: "So good and dutiful," said Granny, "and I'd like to spank her." She saw herself spanking Cornelia and making a fine job of it.

"What'd you say, Mother?"

Granny felt her face tying up in hard knots.

"Can't a body think, I'd like to know?"

"I thought you might want something."

"I do. I want a lot of things. First off, go away and don't whisper."

She lay and drowsed, hoping in her sleep that the children would keep out and let her rest a minute. It had been a long day. Not that she was tired. It was always pleasant to snatch a minute now and then. There was always so much to be done, let me see: tomorrow.

Tomorrow was far away and there was nothing to trouble about. Things were finished somehow when the time came; thank God there was always a little margin over for peace: then a person could spread out the plan of life and tuck in the edges orderly. It was good to have everything clean and folded away, with the hair brushes and tonic bottles sitting straight on the white embroidered linen: the day started without fuss and the pantry shelves laid out with rows of jelly glasses and brown jugs and white stone-china jars with blue whirligigs and words painted on them: coffee, tea, sugar, ginger, cinnamon, allspice: and the bronze clock with the lion on top nicely dusted off. The dust that lion could collect in twenty-four hours! The box in the attic with all those letters tied up, well, she'd

---

[1] Milk-leg is a swelling of the leg caused by childbirth.

have to go through that tomorrow. All those letters—George's letters and John's letters and her letters to them both—lying around for the children to find afterwards made her uneasy. Yes, that would be tomorrow's business. No use to let them know how silly she had been once.

While she was rummaging around she found death in her mind and it felt clammy and unfamiliar. She had spent so much time preparing for death there was no need for bringing it up again. Let it take care of itself now. When she was sixty she had felt very old, finished, and went around making farewell trips to see her children and grandchildren, with a secret in her mind: This is the very last of your mother, children! Then she made her will and came down with a long fever. That was all just a notion like a lot of other things, but it was lucky too, for she had once for all got over the idea of dying for a long time. Now she couldn't be worried. She hoped she had better sense now. Her father had lived to be one hundred and two years old and had drunk a noggin of strong hot toddy on his last birthday. He told the reporters it was his daily habit, and he owed his long life to that. He had made quite a scandal and was very pleased about it. She believed she'd just plague Cornelia a little.

"Cornelia! Cornelia!" No footsteps, but a sudden hand on her cheek. "Bless you, where have you been?"

"Here, Mother."

"Well, Cornelia, I want a noggin of hot toddy."

"Are you cold, darling?"

"I'm chilly, Cornelia. Lying in bed stops the circulation. I must have told you that a thousand times."

Well, she could just hear Cornelia telling her husband that Mother was getting a little childish and they'd have to humor her. The thing that most annoyed her was that Cornelia thought she was deaf, dumb, and blind. Little hasty glances and tiny gestures tossed around her and over her head saying, "Don't cross her, let her have her way, she's eighty years old," and she sitting there as if she lived in a thin glass cage. Sometimes Granny almost made up her mind to pack up and move back to her own house where nobody could remind her every minute that she was old. Wait, wait, Cornelia, till your own children whisper behind your back!

In her day she had kept a better house and had got more work done. She wasn't too old yet for Lydia to be driving eighty miles for advice when one of the children jumped the track, and Jimmy still dropped in and talked things over: "Now, Mammy, you've a good business head, I want to know what you think of this? . . . " Old. Cornelia couldn't change the furniture around without asking. Little things, little things! They had been so sweet when they were little. Granny wished the old days were back again with the children young and everything to be done over. It had been a hard pull, but not too much for her. When she thought of all the food she had cooked, and all the clothes she had cut and sewed, and all the gardens she had made—well, the children showed it. There they were, made out of her, and they couldn't get away from that. Sometimes she wanted to see John again and point to them and say, Well, I didn't do so badly, did I? But that would have to wait. That was for tomorrow. She used to think of him as a man, but now all the children were older than their father, and he would be a child beside her if she saw him now. It seemed strange and there was something wrong in the idea. Why, he couldn't possibly recognize her. She had fenced in a hundred acres once, digging the post holes herself and clamping the wires with just a negro boy to help. That changed a woman. John would be looking for a young woman with the peaked Spanish comb in her hair and the painted fan. Digging post holes changed a woman. Riding country roads in the winter when women had their babies was another thing: sitting up nights with sick horses and sick negroes and sick children and hardly ever losing one. John, I hardly ever lost one of them! John would see that in a minute, that would be something he could understand, she wouldn't have to explain anything!

It made her feel like rolling up her sleeves and putting the whole place to rights again. No matter if Cornelia was determined to be everywhere at once, there were a great many things left undone on this place. She would start tomorrow and do them. It was good to be strong enough for everything, even if all you made melted and changed and slipped under your hands, so that by the time you finished you almost forgot what you were working for. What was it I set out to do? she asked herself intently, but she could not remember. A fog rose over the valley, she saw it marching across the creek swallowing the trees and moving up the hill like an army of ghosts. Soon it would be at the near edge of the orchard, and then it was time to go in and light the lamps. Come in, children, don't stay out in the night air.

Lighting the lamps had been beautiful. The children huddled up to her and breathed like little calves waiting at the bars in the twilight. Their eyes followed the match and watched the flame rise and settle in a blue curve, then they moved away from her. The lamp was lit, they didn't have to be scared and hang on to mother any more. Never, never, never more. God, for all my life I thank Thee. Without Thee, my God, I could never have done it. Hail, Mary, full of grace.

I want you to pick all the fruit this year and see that nothing is wasted. There's always someone who can use it. Don't let good things rot for want of using. You waste life when you waste good food. Don't let things get lost. It's bitter to lose things. Now, don't let me get to thinking, not when I am tired and taking a little nap before supper. . . .

The pillow rose about her shoulders and pressed against her heart and the memory was being squeezed out of it: oh, push down the pillow, somebody: it would smother her if she tried to hold it. Such a fresh breeze blowing and such a green day with no threats in it. But he had not come, just the same. What does a woman do when she has put on the white veil and set out the white cake for man and he doesn't come? She tried to remember. No, I swear he never harmed me but in that. He never harmed me but in that . . . and what if he did? There was the day, the day, but a whirl of dark smoke rose and covered it, crept up and over into the bright field where everything was planted so carefully in orderly rows. That was hell, she knew hell when she saw it. For sixty years she had prayed against remembering him and against losing her soul in the deep pit of hell, and now the two things were mingled in one and the thought of him was a smoky cloud from hell that moved and crept in her head when she had just got rid of Doctor Harry and was trying to rest a minute. Wounded vanity, Ellen, said a sharp voice in the top of her mind. Don't let your wounded vanity get the upper hand of you. Plenty of girls get jilted. You were jilted, weren't you? Then stand up to it. Her eyelids wavered and let in streamers of blue-gray light like tissue paper over her eyes. She must get up and pull the shades down or she'd never sleep. She was in bed again and the shades were not down. How could that happen? Better turn over, hide from the light, sleeping in the light gave you nightmares. "Mother, how do you feel now?" and a stinging wetness on her forehead. But I don't like having my face washed in cold water!

Hapsy? George? Lydia? Jimmy? No, Cornelia, and her features were swollen and full of little puddles. "They're coming, darling, they'll all be here soon." Go wash your face, child, you look funny.

Instead of obeying, Cornelia knelt down and put her head on the pillow. She seemed to be talking but there was no sound. "Well, are you tongue-tied? Whose birthday is it? Are you going to give a party?"

Cornelia's mouth moved urgently in strange shapes. "Don't do that, you bother me, daughter."

"Oh, no, Mother. Oh, no. . . . "

Nonsense. It was strange about children. They disputed your every word. "No what, Cornelia?"

"Here's Doctor Harry."

"I won't see that boy again. He just left five minutes ago."

"That was this morning, Mother. It's night now. Here's the nurse."

"This is Doctor Harry, Mrs. Weatherall. I never saw you look so young and happy!"

"Ah, I'll never be young again—but I'd be happy if they'd let me lie in peace and get rested."

She thought she spoke up loudly, but no one answered. A warm weight on her forehead, a warm bracelet on her wrist, and a breeze went on whispering, trying to tell her something. A shuffle of leaves in the everlasting hand of God. He blew on them and they danced and rattled. "Mother, don't mind, we're going to give you a little hypodermic." "Look here, daughter, how do ants get in this bed? I saw sugar ants yesterday." Did you send for Hapsy too?

It was Hapsy she really wanted. She had to go a long way back through a great many rooms to find Hapsy standing with a baby on her arm. She seemed to herself to be Hapsy also, and the baby on Hapsy's arm was Hapsy and himself and herself, all at once, and there was no surprise in the meeting. Then Hapsy melted from within and turned flimsy as gray gauze and the baby was a gauzy shadow, and Hapsy came up close and said, "I thought you'd never come," and looked at her very searchingly and said, "You haven't changed a bit!" They leaned forward to kiss, when Cornelia began whispering from a long way off, "Oh, is there anything you want to tell me? Is there anything I can do for you?"

Yes, she had changed her mind after sixty years and she would like to see George. I want you to find George. Find him and be sure to tell him I forgot him. I want him to know I had my husband just the same and my children and my house like any other woman. A good house too and a good husband that I loved and fine children out of him. Better than I hoped for even. Tell him I was given back everything he took away and more. Oh, no, oh, God, no, there was something else besides the house and the man and the children. Oh, surely they were not all? What was it? Something not given back. . . . Her breath crowded down under her ribs and grew into a monstrous frightening shape with cutting edges; it bored up into her head, and the agony was unbelievable: Yes, John, get the doctor now, no more talk, my time has come.

When this one was born it should be the last. The last. It should have been born first, for it was the one she had truly wanted. Everything came in good time. Nothing left out, left over. She was strong, in three days she would be as well as ever. Better. A woman needed milk in her to have her full health.

"Mother, do you hear me?"

"I've been telling you—"

"Mother, Father Connolly's here."

"I went to Holy Communion only last week. Tell him I'm not so sinful as all that."

"Father just wants to speak to you."

He could speak as much as he pleased. It was like him to drop in and inquire about her soul as if it were a teething baby, and then stay on for a cup of tea and a round of cards and gossip. He always had a funny story of some sort, usually about an Irishman who made his little mistakes and confessed them, and the point lay in some absurd thing he would blurt out in the confessional showing his struggles between native piety and original sin. Granny felt easy about her soul. Cornelia, where are your manners? Give Father Connolly a chair. She had her secret comfortable understanding with a few favorite saints who cleared a straight road to God for her. All as surely signed and sealed as the papers for the new Forty Acres. Forever . . . heirs and assigns forever. Since the day the wedding cake was not cut, but thrown out and wasted. The whole bottom dropped out of the world, and there she was blind and sweating with nothing under her feet and the walls falling away. His hand had caught her under the breast, she had not fallen, there was the freshly polished floor with the green rug on it, just as before. He had cursed like a sailor's parrot and said, "I'll kill him for you." Don't lay a hand on him, for my sake leave something to God. "Now, Ellen, you must believe what I tell you. . . . "

So there was nothing, nothing to worry about any more, except sometimes in the night one of the children screamed in a nightmare, and they both hustled out shaking and hunting for the matches and calling, "There, wait a minute, here we are!" John, get the doctor now, Hapsy's time has come. But there was

Hapsy standing by the bed in a white cap. "Cornelia, tell Hapsy to take off her cap. I can't see her plain."

Her eyes opened very wide and the room stood out like a picture she had seen somewhere. Dark colors with the shadows rising towards the ceiling in long angles. The tall black dresser gleamed with nothing on it but John's picture, enlarged from a little one, with John's eyes very black when they should have been blue. You never saw him, so how do you know how he looked? But the man insisted the copy was perfect, it was very rich and handsome. For a picture, yes, but it's not my husband. The table by the bed had a linen cover and a candle and a crucifix. The light was blue from Cornelia's silk lampshades. No sort of light at all, just frippery. You had to live forty years with kerosene lamps to appreciate honest electricity. She felt very strong and she saw Doctor Harry with a rosy nimbus around him.

"You look like a saint, Doctor Harry, and I vow that's as near as you'll ever come to it."

"She's saying something."

"I heard you, Cornelia. What's all this carrying on?"

"Father Connolly's saying—"

Cornelia's voice staggered and bumped like a cart in a bad road. It rounded corners and turned back again and arrived nowhere. Granny stepped up in the cart very lightly and reached for the reins, but a man sat beside her and she knew him by his hands, driving the cart. She did not look in his face, for she knew without seeing, but looked instead down the road where the trees leaned over and bowed to each other and a thousand birds were singing a Mass. She felt like singing too, but she put her hand in the bosom of her dress and pulled out a rosary, and Father Connolly murmured Latin in a very solemn voice and tickled her feet. My God, will you stop that nonsense? I'm a married woman. What if he did run away and leave me to face the priest by myself? I found another a whole world better. I wouldn't have exchanged my husband for anybody except St. Michael himself, and you may tell him that for me with a thank you in the bargain.

Light flashed on her closed eyelids, and a deep roaring shook her. Cornelia, is that lightning? I hear thunder. There's going to be a storm. Close all the windows. Call the children in. . . . " Mother, here we are, all of us." "Is that you, Hapsy?" "Oh, no, I'm Lydia. We drove as fast as we could." Their faces drifted above her, drifted away. The rosary fell out of her hands and Lydia put it back. Jimmy tried to help, their hands fumbled together, and Granny closed two fingers around Jimmy's thumb. Beads wouldn't do, it must be something alive. She was so amazed her thoughts ran round and round. So, my dear Lord, this is my death and I wasn't even thinking about it. My children have come to see me die. But I can't, it's not time. Oh, I always hated surprises. I wanted to give Cornelia the amethyst set—Cornelia, you're to have the amethyst set, but Hapsy's to wear it when she wants, and, Doctor Harry, do shut up. Nobody sent for you. Oh my dear Lord, do wait a minute. I meant to do something about the Forty Acres, Jimmy doesn't need it and Lydia will later on, with that worthless husband of hers. I meant to finish the altar cloth and send six bottles of wine to Sister Borgia for her dyspepsia. I want to send six bottles of wine to Sister Borgia, Father Connolly, now don't let me forget.

Cornelia's voice made short turns and tilted over and crashed. "Oh, Mother, oh, Mother, oh, Mother. . . ."

"I'm not going, Cornelia. I'm taken by surprise. I can't go."

You'll see Hapsy again. What about her? "I thought you'd never come." Granny made a long journey outward, looking for Hapsy. What if I don't find her? What then? Her heart sank down and down, there was no bottom to death, she couldn't come to the end of it. The blue light from Cornelia's lampshade drew into a tiny point in the center of her brain, it flickered and winked like an eye, quietly it fluttered and dwindled. Granny lay curled down within herself, amazed and watchful, staring at the point of light that was herself; her body was now only a deeper mass of shadow in an endless darkness and this darkness would curl around the light and swallow it up. God, give a sign!

For the second time there was no sign. Again no bridegroom and the priest in the house. She could not remember any other sorrow because this grief wiped them all away. Oh, no, there's nothing more cruel than this—I'll never forgive it. She stretched herself with a deep breath and blew out the light.

Questions

1. Can you reconstruct from the fragments the story of the jilting of Granny? Who are John and George?
2. Who is Hapsy? Why isn't she there?
3. Does Granny have a "secret comfortable understanding with a few favorite saints"?
4. Granny asks God for a sign. Does one come? What is the significance of the bridegroom in the concluding paragraph?
5. Why have the memory of George and "losing her soul in the deep pit of hell" come to be mingled as one?
6. What is it that George did not give back to Granny?
7. Is Granny a developing or a static character? Has she changed over the long course of her married life?

6 🌿 Setting the Scene

For jewelers, a setting is the metal around a precious gem or stone that keeps the jewel in place and shows it off to its best advantage by letting the light catch the stone in the most attractive manner. In literature, settings serve a similar function. *Settings* place the events of the story in a particular time and location. This placement fixes the story in our imagination and shows off the action in its most meaningful and effective light. Often, in fact, the setting suggests the actions that take place within it. For example, an old abandoned house almost demands goblins or evil doings. Just as a fine gem needs a setting which is neither too flimsy nor too gaudy, so, too, a story must be carefully placed in an appropriate and effective time and location.

Settings vary tremendously. Some are realistic, some are fantastic. Some are highly detailed, some are vague. In the short tale "Catching a Rabbit," all we learn or need to learn is that the action occurred in the country. In the "Night Watchman's Occurrence Book," we learn the month, day, and time of each event. But the year of the action is not mentioned. *Peter Pan* takes place in Never-Never-Land, far from time and realistic geography. But the Queneau anecdotes take place "midday in the Parc Monceau district" aboard an "S bus (now No. 84)." In one section of James Joyce's novel *Ulysses*, the characters take rides on the Dublin trolleys. With the aid of a street map, timetables, and a stopwatch, Joyce tracked his characters from place to place so that the narrative details would be accurate. Joyce did not want to place a character at a location impossible to reach or have two characters meet at a time sooner than they could have arrived. In "Araby," one of Joyce's Dubliner stories, the place names are accurate. The Joyces, in fact, lived at 17 North Richmond, and James attended the Christian Brothers' School down the street. Few writers have Joyce's passion for accuracy.

But one must not judge the effectiveness of a setting by its realistic accuracy. The true test is whether the setting provides the information, mood, and context the story needs. Unnecessary detail—detail for its own sake—merely slows the action and blurs the narrative focus. A good setting is integrated into the whole structure and meaning of the story. It is not merely "background," but an active part in the telling of a tale. Thus, whenever one reads a passage of scenic description, one should be aware that the author is painting more than a backdrop; he or she is providing ways to illuminate and enhance the action.

Reading for Setting

We know in part how to "read" settings from actual experience. Walking into a stranger's house, we look around, noting details that might tell us something about the owner's social status and psychology. A room decorated in the latest style but with cheap furniture would alert us to the fact that the owners wanted to be trendy but did not have the money to be truly stylish. A room decorated with many fine old things might suggest that the owners have had money for a long time.

In "Araby," we enter a "wild garden behind the house that contained a central apple tree and a few straggling bushes" under one of which the narrator found "the late tenant's rusty bicycle pump." What do we learn from this setting? First, that the garden is "wild." No one has taken care of this backyard. The neglect has been going on for some time, because the bushes have become straggly and the bicycle pump, carelessly left out, has begun to rust. This last detail is somewhat ironic, for the bicycle pump, whose purpose is to help maintain the vehicle in good condition, is itself rusting away. We also learn that the garden is small; it has only enough room for "a central apple tree and a few straggling bushes." Putting these details together, we might assume that this is a small house inhabited by poor tenants who do not maintain their property very well. Not a happy place to live.

Our analysis of the garden in "Araby" yields three kinds of meaning: (1) sociological, (2) psychological, and (3) symbolic. Let us examine these three elements separately.

Setting as Social Indicator

Setting is frequently used as an indicator of social status—to show whether characters are rich or poor and how long they have been rich or poor. In "Araby" the narrator suggests his social position—among other traits—by describing the house in which he lives:

> The former tenant of our house, a priest, had died in the back drawing-room. Air, musty from having been long enclosed, hung in all the rooms, and the waste room behind the kitchen was littered with old useless papers. . . . The wild garden behind the house contained a central apple tree and a few straggling bushes under one of which I found the late tenant's rusty bicycle pump.

What do we learn from this passage? First we learn that the narrator is a "tenant," not the owner of the house. This detail may indicate that they are too poor to be houseowners, especially since the house does not seem to be in very good condition. The rooms are stuffy and littered. The owner has not bothered to clean the property up. The garden is small and ill-kept—another sign of negligence. It has room enough for only an apple tree and a few straggling bushes. Taken all together, we might safely conclude that the narrator lives in a rented house that is small, messy, and uncared for and that his family is poor rather than rich.

Settings That Reveal Character

We often say that weather affects our moods. Sunny, clear days make us happy; dark, rainy days make us feel sad. Indications of weather usually mirror the mood of characters. We should note references to light and dark, rain and dryness, and see if they do not emphasize the moods of the characters.

We can observe how a character's mood and psychological state is reflected in setting by comparing two descriptions of the garden in Charlotte Perkins Gilman's "The Yellow Wall-Paper." The first time the narrator describes it, she is not very ill. She writes:

> There is a *delicious* garden! I never saw such a garden—large and shady, full of box-bordered paths, and lined with long grape-covered arbors with seats under them.

The second time she describes the garden, she is less well:

> Out of one window I can see the garden, those mysterious deep-shaded arbors, the riotous old-fashioned flowers, and bushes and gnarly trees.

We can detect the subtle change in her psychological condition by noting her choice of words. The garden that had been "delicious" is later "mysterious." What first appeared to be orderly is now "riotous." What seemed unique ("I never saw such a garden") is now "old-fashioned." The "gnarled tree" is a particularly revealing detail. The "delicious" garden has started to become twisted, stunted, and deformed. Everything that seemed so appealing has become ever so slightly threatening. Of course, the garden has not changed; the change has occurred in the narrator's mind. The "mystery," riotousness, and gnarling are signs of her growing insanity.

Symbolic Settings

We will discuss symbolism in more detail in Chapter 8. For the moment, let us define a symbol as an object that signifies more than just itself. For example, a wedding ring is not just a decorative piece of metal: it signifies that the wearer is married and has formed an unbroken bond with his or her spouse. Again, the American flag is not merely a multicolored piece of cloth: it stands for this country, a democratic government, and the patriotic pride of the American people.

A person or object can become symbolic when it represents the whole group of things to which it belongs. At graduation, for example, one student is chosen to represent the class. That student symbolizes the class, and what the student does and says comes to symbolize the action of all the class members. Bearing these examples of symbolism in mind, let us look at a passage in Bobbie Ann Mason's "Shiloh." In this episode Leroy and his wife Norma Jean visit the Shiloh battlefield where the Confederate Army was defeated by the Union forces. Before traveling to Shiloh, Leroy offered to build his wife a log cabin in the new suburban subdivision, but Norma Jean has declared she wants a divorce.

> [Leroy and Norma Jean] sit in silence and stare at the cemetery for the Union dead and, beyond, at a tall cluster of trees. Campers are parked nearby, bumper to bumper, and small children in bright clothing are cavorting and squealing. . . .
>
> The cemetery, a green slope dotted with white markers, looks like a subdivision site. Leroy is trying to comprehend that his marriage is breaking up, but for some reason he is wondering about white slabs in a graveyard.

By stating that "for some reason" Leroy is wondering about the "white slabs in a graveyard," Mason invites us to supply a reason. Why is Leroy looking at gravestones when he wants to understand his marriage? We might recall that people often refer to "the battle of the sexes," and marriage as a "battleground." In some respects, then, Shiloh represents the battlefield of their marriage and the cemetery the death of their marriage. Leroy recognizes that the log cabin he wanted to build in the "subdivision," to save his marriage, is the symbolic equivalent of a grave marker. Such a reading does not exhaust the possible significance of the passage, but it helps explain Leroy's curious behavior.

Clothing

What a character wears can tell us as much as do the time and place of the story. People's clothes often indicate their economic class, as well as their psychological state. There is a great difference between a casually careless dresser and one who has dressed in distracted haste. The tilted hat, the pulled down tie, the shirttail coming out of pants are as much a sign of drunkenness as are a stumbly walk and slurred speech.

Summary

Writers locate their narratives in time and place, and these settings are not mere backdrops. They are important in interpreting the story's significance. The skillful reader of fiction watches the setting for subtle but important clues about the characters' social and psychological condition and for the symbolic significance of the action.

1. Analyze what your room might tell a stranger about your personality and social background.
2. Classify the various clothing styles on campus. What do these styles tell us about the wearer?
3. Analyze the way you dress. What do you hope to communicate by what you wear? How do you wish you looked? What does this "look" tell us about your aspirations?

Suggestions for Fiction Writers

1. Describe what you think would be the ideal place to live.
2. Describe the home of a miser, a spendthrift, a loner, and a social butterfly. See if people can recognize who lived where.

BOBBIE ANN MASON (1940–

Shiloh

Leroy Moffitt's wife, Norma Jean, is working on her pectorals. She lifts three-pound dumbbells to warm up, then progresses to a twenty-pound barbell. Standing with her legs apart, she reminds Leroy of Wonder Woman.[1]

"I'd give anything if I could just get these muscles to where they're real hard," says Norma Jean. "Feel this arm. It's not as hard as the other one."

"That's 'cause you're right-handed," says Leroy, dodging as she swings the barbell in an arc.

"Do you think so?"

"Sure."

Leroy is a truckdriver. He injured his leg in a highway accident four months ago, and his physical therapy, which involves weights and a pulley, prompted Norma Jean to try building herself up. Now she is attending a body-building class. Leroy has been collecting temporary disability since his tractor-trailer jackknifed in Missouri, badly twisting his left leg in its socket. He has a steel pin in his hip. He will probably not be able to drive his rig again. It sits in the backyard, like a gigantic bird that has flown home to roost. Leroy has been home in Kentucky for three months, and his leg is almost healed, but the accident frightened him and he does not want to drive any more long hauls. He is not sure what to do next. In the meantime, he makes things from craft kits. He started by building a miniature log cabin from notched Popsicle sticks. He varnished it and placed it on the TV set, where it remains. It reminds him of a rustic Nativity scene. Then he tried string art (sailing ships on black velvet),

---

[1] Wonder Woman, possessed of supernatural powers and strength, is a comic book character who later appeared in a television series.

a macramé owl kit, a snap-together B-17 Flying Fortress,[2] and a lamp made out of a model truck, with a light fixture screwed in the top of the cab. At first the kits were diversions, something to kill time, but now he is thinking about building a full-scale log house from a kit. It would be considerably cheaper than building a regular house, and besides, Leroy has grown to appreciate how things are put together. He has begun to realize that in all the years he was on the road he never took time to examine anything. He was always flying past scenery.

"They won't let you build a log cabin in any of the new subdivisions," Norma Jean tells him.

"They will if I tell them it's for you," he says, teasing her. Ever since they were married, he has promised Norma Jean he would build her a new home one day. They have always rented, and the house they live in is small and nondescript. It does not even feel like a home, Leroy realizes now.

Norma Jean works at the Rexall drugstore, and she has acquired an amazing amount of information about cosmetics. When she explains to Leroy the three stages of complexion care, involving creams, toners, and moisturizers, he thinks happily of other petroleum products—axle grease, diesel fuel. This is a connection between him and Norma Jean. Since he has been home, he has felt unusually tender about his wife and guilty over his long absences. But he can't tell what she feels about him. Norma Jean has never complained about his traveling; she has never made hurt remarks, like calling his truck a "widow-maker." He is reasonably certain she has been faithful to him, but he wishes she would celebrate his permanent home-coming more happily. Norma Jean is often startled to find Leroy at home, and he thinks she seems a little disappointed about it. Perhaps he reminds her too much of the early days of their marriage, before he went on the road. They had a child who died as an infant, years ago. They never speak about their memories of Randy, which have almost faded, but now that Leroy is home all the time, they sometimes feel awkward around each other, and Leroy wonders if one of them should mention the child. He has the feeling that they are waking up out of a dream together—that they must create a new marriage, start afresh. They are lucky they are still married. Leroy has read that for most people losing a child destroys the marriage—or else he heard this on *Donahue*. He can't always remember where he learns things anymore.

At Christmas, Leroy bought an electric organ for Norma Jean. She used to play the piano when she was in high school. "It don't leave you," she told him once. "It's like riding a bicycle."

The new instrument had so many keys and buttons that she was bewildered by it at first. She touched the keys tentatively, pushed some buttons, then pecked out "Chopsticks." It came out in an amplified fox-trot rhythm, with marimba sounds.

"It's an orchestra!" she cried.

---

[2] A B-17 Flying Fortress is a World War II bomber. At its time it was one of the largest airplanes in the American fleet.

The organ had a pecan-look finish and eighteen preset chords, with optional flute, violin, trumpet, clarinet, and banjo accompaniments. Norma Jean mastered the organ almost immediately. At first she played Christmas songs. Then she bought *The Sixties Songbook* and learned every tune in it, adding variations to each with the rows of brightly colored buttons.

"I didn't like these old songs back then," she said. "But I have this crazy feeling I missed something."

"You didn't miss a thing," said Leroy.

Leroy likes to lie on the couch and smoke a joint and listen to Norma Jean play "Can't Take My Eyes Off You" and "I'll Be Back."[3] He is back again. After fifteen years on the road, he is finally settling down with the woman he loves. She is still pretty. Her skin is flawless. Her frosted curls resemble pencil trimmings.

Now that Leroy has come home to stay, he notices how much the town has changed. Subdivisions are spreading across western Kentucky like an oil slick. The sign at the edge of town says "Pop: 11,500"—only seven hundred more than it said twenty years before. Leroy can't figure out who is living in all the new houses. The farmers who used to gather around the courthouse square on Saturday afternoons to play checkers and spit tobacco juice have gone. It has been years since Leroy has thought about the farmers, and they have disappeared without his noticing.

Leroy meets a kid named Stevie Hamilton in the parking lot at the new shopping center. While they pretend to be strangers meeting over a stalled car, Stevie tosses an ounce of marijuana under the front seat of Leroy's car. Stevie is wearing orange jogging shoes and a T-shirt that says CHATTAHOOCHEE SUPER-RAT. His father is a prominent doctor who lives in one of the expensive subdivisions in a new white-columned brick house that looks like a funeral parlor. In the phone book under his name there is a separate number, with the listing "Teenagers."

"Where do you get this stuff?" asks Leroy. "From your pappy?"

"That's for me to know and you to find out," Stevie says. He is slit-eyed and skinny.

"What else you got?"

"What you interested in?"

"Nothing special. Just wondered."

Leroy used to take speed[4] on the road. Now he has to go slowly. He needs to be mellow. He leans back against the car and says, "I'm aiming to build me a log house, soon as I get time. My wife, though, I don't think she likes the idea."

---

[3] "Can't Take My Eyes Off You" is a song by Bob Crewe and Bob Guadio recorded by Frankie Valli in 1967 and by the Lettermen in 1968. "I'll Be Back" was composed by John Lennon and Paul McCartney and recorded by the Beatles in 1964. The song begins, "You know if you break my heart, I'll go,/But I'll be back again."

[4] Speed is the slang term for amphetamines.

"Well, let me know when you want me again," Stevie says. He has a cigarette in his cupped palm, as though sheltering it from the wind. He takes a long drag, then stomps it on the asphalt and slouches away.

Stevie's father was two years ahead of Leroy in high school. Leroy is thirty-four. He married Norma Jean when they were both eighteen, and their child Randy was born a few months later, but he died at the age of four months and three days. He would be about Stevie's age now. Norma Jean and Leroy were at the drive-in, watching a double feature (*Dr. Strangelove* and *Lover Come Back*),[5] and the baby was sleeping in the back seat. When the first movie ended, the baby was dead. It was the sudden infant death syndrome. Leroy remembers handing Randy to a nurse at the emergency room, as though he were offering her a large doll as a present. A dead baby feels like a sack of flour. "It just happens sometimes," said the doctor, in what Leroy always recalls as a nonchalant tone. Leroy can hardly remember the child anymore, but he still sees vividly a scene from *Dr. Strangelove* in which the President of the United States was talking in a folksy voice on the hot line to the Soviet premier about the bomber accidentally headed toward Russia. He was in the War Room, and the world map was lit up. Leroy remembers Norma Jean standing catatonically beside him in the hospital and himself thinking: Who is this strange girl? He had forgotten who she was. Now scientists are saying that crib death is caused by a virus. Nobody knows anything, Leroy thinks. The answers are always changing.

When Leroy gets home from the shopping center, Norma Jean's mother, Mabel Beasley, is there. Until this year, Leroy has not realized how much time she spends with Norma Jean. When she visits, she inspects the closets and then the plants, informing Norma Jean when a plant is droopy or yellow. Mabel calls the plants "flowers," although there are never any blooms. She always notices if Norma Jean's laundry is piling up. Mabel is a short, overweight woman whose tight, brown-dyed curls look more like a wig than the actual wig she sometimes wears. Today she has brought Norma Jean an off-white dust ruffle she made for the bed; Mabel works in a custom-upholstery shop.

"This is the tenth one I made this year," Mabel says. "I got started and couldn't stop."

"It's real pretty," says Norma Jean.

"Now we can hide things under the bed," says Leroy, who gets along with his mother-in-law primarily by joking with her. Mabel has never really forgiven him for disgracing her by getting Norma Jean pregnant. When the baby died, she said that fate was mocking her.

"What's that thing?" Mabel says to Leroy in a loud voice, pointing to a tangle of yarn on a piece of canvas.

Leroy holds it up for Mabel to see. "It's my needlepoint," he explains. "This is a *Star Trek* pillow cover."

"That's what a woman would do," says Mabel. "Great day in the morning!"

---

[5] *Dr. Strangelove* (1963) is a film by Stanley Kubrick satirizing the nuclear arms race. *Lover Come Back* (1961) is a light romantic comedy starring Doris Day and Rock Hudson. The two films are an unlikely double feature.

"All the big football players on TV do it," he says.

"Why, Leroy, you're always trying to fool me. I don't believe you for one minute. You don't know what to do with yourself—that's the whole trouble. Sewing!"

"I'm aiming to build us a log house," says Leroy. "Soon as my plans come."

"Like *heck* you are," says Norma Jean. She takes Leroy's needlepoint and shoves it into a drawer. "You have to find a job first. Nobody can afford to build now anyway."

Mabel straightens her girdle and says, "I still think before you get tied down y'all ought to take a little run to Shiloh."

"One of these days, Mama," Norma Jean says impatiently.

Mabel is talking about Shiloh, Tennessee. For the past few years, she has been urging Leroy and Norma Jean to visit the Civil War battleground there. Mabel went there on her honeymoon—the only real trip she ever took. Her husband died of a perforated ulcer when Norma Jean was ten, but Mabel, who was accepted into the United Daughters of the Confederacy in 1975, is still preoccupied with going back to Shiloh.

"I've been to kingdom come and back in that truck out yonder," Leroy says to Mabel, "but we never yet set foot in that battleground. Ain't that something? How did I miss it?"

"It's not even that far," Mabel says.

After Mabel leaves, Norma Jean reads to Leroy from a list she has made. "Things you could do," she announces. "You could get a job as a guard at Union Carbide, where they'd let you set on a stool. You could get on at the lumberyard. You could do a little carpenter work, if you want to build so bad. You could—"

"I can't do something where I'd have to stand up all day."

"You ought to try standing up all day behind a cosmetics counter. It's amazing that I have strong feet, coming from two parents that never had strong feet at all." At the moment Norma Jean is holding on to the kitchen counter, raising her knees one at a time as she talks. She is wearing two-pound ankle weights.

"Don't worry," says Leroy. "I'll do something."

"You could truck calves to slaughter for somebody. You wouldn't have to drive any big old truck for that."

"I'm going to build you this house," says Leroy. "I want to make you a real home."

"I don't want to live in any log cabin."

"It's not a cabin. It's a house."

"I don't care. It looks like a cabin."

"You and me together could lift those logs. It's just like lifting weights."

Norma Jean doesn't answer. Under her breath, she is counting. Now she is marching through the kitchen. She is doing goose steps.

Before his accident, when Leroy came home he used to stay in the house with Norma Jean, watching TV in bed and playing cards. She would cook fried chicken, picnic ham, chocolate pie—all his favorites. Now he is home alone much of the time. In the mornings, Norma Jean disappears, leaving a cooling place in the bed. She eats a cereal called Body Buddies, and she leaves the bowl on the table, with the soggy tan balls floating in a milk puddle. He sees things about Norma Jean that he never realized before. When she chops onions, she stares off into a corner, as if she can't bear to look. She puts on her house slippers almost precisely at nine o'clock every evening and nudges her jogging shoes under the couch. She saves bread heels for the birds. Leroy watches the birds at the feeder. He notices the peculiar way goldfinches fly past the window. They close their wings, then fall, then spread their wings to catch and lift themselves. He wonders if they close their eyes when they fall. Norma Jean closes her eyes when they are in bed. She wants the lights turned out. Even then, he is sure she closes her eyes.

He goes for long drives around town. He tends to drive a car rather carelessly. Power steering and an automatic shift make a car feel so small and inconsequential that his body is hardly involved in the driving process. His injured leg stretches out comfortably. Once or twice he has almost hit something, but even the prospect of an accident seems minor in a car. He cruises the new subdivisions, feeling like a criminal rehearsing for a robbery. Norma Jean is probably right about a log house being inappropriate here in the new subdivisions. All the houses look grand and complicated. They depress him.

One day when Leroy comes home from a drive he finds Norma Jean in tears. She is in the kitchen making a potato and mushroom-soup casserole, with grated-cheese topping. She is crying because her mother caught her smoking.

"I didn't hear her coming. I was standing here puffing away pretty as you please," Norma Jean says, wiping her eyes.

"I knew it would happen sooner or later," says Leroy, putting his arm around her.

"She don't know the meaning of the word 'knock,' " says Norma Jean. "It's a wonder she hadn't caught me years ago."

"Think of it this way," Leroy says. "What if she caught me with a joint?"

"You better not let her!" Norma Jean shrieks. "I'm warning you, Leroy Moffitt!"

"I'm just kidding. Here, play me a tune. That'll help you relax."

Norma Jean puts the casserole in the oven and sets the timer. Then she plays a ragtime tune, with horns and banjo, as Leroy lights up a joint and lies on the couch, laughing to himself about Mabel's catching him at it. He thinks of Stevie Hamilton—a doctor's son pushing grass. Everything is funny. The whole town seems crazy and small. He is reminded of Virgil Mathis, a boastful policeman Leroy used to shoot pool with. Virgil recently led a drug bust in a back room at a bowling alley, where he seized ten thousand dollars' worth of marijuana. The newspaper had a picture of him holding up the bags of grass and grinning widely. Right now, Leroy can imagine Virgil breaking down the door and arresting him with a lungful of smoke. Virgil would probably have been alerted to the scene because of all the racket Norma Jean is making. Now she sounds like a hard-rock band. Norma Jean is terrific. When she switches to a Latin-rhythm version of "Sunshine Superman,"[6] Leroy hums along. Norma Jean's foot goes up and down, up and down.

"Well, what do you think?" Leroy says, when Norma Jean pauses to search through her music.

"What do I think about what?"

His mind had gone blank. Then he says, "I'll sell my rig and build us a house." That wasn't what he wanted to say. He wanted to know what she thought—what she *really* thought—about them.

"Don't start in on that again," says Norma Jean. She begins playing "Who'll Be the Next in Line?"[7]

Leroy used to tell hitchhikers his whole life story—about his travels, his hometown, the baby. He would end with a question: "Well, what do you think?" It was just a rhetorical question. In time, he had the feeling that he'd been telling the same story over and over to the same hitchhikers. He quit talking to hitchhikers when he realized how his voice sounded—whining and self-pitying, like some teenage-tragedy song. Now Leroy has the sudden impulse to tell Norma Jean about himself, as if he had just met her. They have known each other so long they have forgotten a lot about each other. They could become reacquainted. But when the oven timer goes off and she runs to the kitchen, he forgets why he wants to do this.

The next day, Mabel drops by. It is Saturday and Norma Jean is cleaning. Leroy is studying the plans of his log house, which have finally come in the mail. He has them spread out on the table—big sheets of stiff blue paper, with diagrams and numbers printed in white. While Norma Jean runs the vacuum, Mabel drinks coffee. She sets her coffee cup on a blueprint.

"I'm just waiting for time to pass," she says to Leroy, drumming her fingers on the table.

As soon as Norma Jean switches off the vacuum, Mabel says in a loud voice, "Did you hear about the datsun dog that killed the baby?"

Norma Jean says, "The word is 'dachshund.' "

"They put the dog on trial. It chewed the baby's legs off. The mother was in the next room all the time." She raises her voice. "They thought it was neglect."

Norma Jean is holding her ears. Leroy manages to open the refrigerator and get some Diet Pepsi to offer Mabel. Mabel still has some coffee and she waves away the Pepsi.

"Datsuns are like that," Mabel says. "They're jealous dogs. They'll tear a place to pieces if you don't keep an eye on them."

"You better watch out what you're saying, Mabel," says Leroy.

"Well, facts is facts."

Leroy looks out the window at his rig. It is like a huge piece of furniture

---

[6] "Sunshine Superman" is a song recorded by the British singer Donovan in 1966.

[7] "Who'll Be the Next in Line?" is a song by Ray Davies made popular in 1965 by the Kinks, a British musical group.

gathering dust in the backyard. Pretty soon it will be an antique. He hears the vacuum cleaner. Norma Jean seems to be cleaning the living room rug again.

Later, she says to Leroy, "She just said that about the baby because she caught me smoking. She's trying to pay me back."

"What are you talking about?" Leroy says, nervously shuffling blueprints.

"You know good and well," Norma Jean says. She is sitting in a kitchen chair with her feet up and her arms wrapped around her knees. She looks small and helpless. She says, "The very idea, her bringing up a subject like that! Saying it was neglect."

"She didn't mean that," Leroy says.

"She might not have *thought* she meant it. She always says things like that. You don't know how she goes on."

"But she didn't really mean it. She was just talking."

Leroy opens a king-sized bottle of beer and pours it into two glasses, dividing it carefully. He hands a glass to Norma Jean and she takes it from him mechanically. For a long time, they sit by the kitchen window watching the birds at the feeder.

Something is happening. Norma Jean is going to night school. She has graduated from her six-week body-building course and now she is taking an adult-education course in composition at Paducah Community College. She spends her evenings outlining paragraphs.

"First you have a topic sentence," she explains to Leroy. "Then you divide it up. Your secondary topic has to be connected to your primary topic."

To Leroy, this sounds intimidating. "I never was any good in English," he says.

"It makes a lot of sense."

"What are you doing this for, anyhow?"

She shrugs. "It's something to do." She stands up and lifts her dumbbells a few times.

"Driving a rig, nobody cared about my English."

"I'm not criticizing your English."

Norma Jean used to say, "If I lose ten minutes' sleep, I just drag all day." Now she stays up late, writing compositions. She got a B on her first paper—a how-to theme on soup-based casseroles. Recently Norma Jean has been cooking unusual foods—tacos, lasagna, Bombay chicken. She doesn't play the organ anymore, though her second paper was called "Why Music Is Important to Me." She sits at the kitchen table, concentrating on her outlines, while Leroy plays with his log house plans, practicing with a set of Lincoln Logs. The thought of getting a truckload of notched, numbered logs scares him, and he wants to be prepared. As he and Norma Jean work together at the kitchen table, Leroy has the hopeful thought that they are sharing something, but he knows he is a fool to think this. Norma Jean is miles away. He knows he is going to lose her. Like Mabel, he is just waiting for time to pass.

One day, Mabel is there before Norma Jean gets home from work, and Leroy finds himself confiding in her. Mabel, he realizes, must know Norma Jean better than he does.

"I don't know what's got into that girl," Mabel says. "She used to go to bed with the chickens. Now you say she's up all hours. Plus her a-smoking. I like to died."

"I want to make her this beautiful home," Leroy says, indicating the Lincoln Logs. "I don't think she even wants it. Maybe she was happier with me gone."

"She don't know what to make of you, coming home like this."

"Is that it?"

Mabel takes the roof off his Lincoln Log cabin. "You couldn't get *me* in a log cabin," she says. "I was raised in one. It's no picnic, let me tell you."

"They're different now," says Leroy.

"I tell you what," Mabel says, smiling oddly at Leroy.

"What?"

"Take her on down to Shiloh. Y'all need to get out together, stir a little. Her brain's all balled up over them books."

Leroy can see traces of Norma Jean's features in her mother's face. Mabel's worn face has the texture of crinkled cotton, but suddenly she looks pretty. It occurs to Leroy that Mabel has been hinting all along that she wants them to take her with them to Shiloh.

"Let's all go to Shiloh," he says. "You and me and her. Come Sunday."

Mabel throws up her hand in protest. "Oh, no, not me. Young folks want to be by theirselves."

When Norma Jean comes in with groceries, Leroy says excitedly, "Your mama here's been dying to go to Shiloh for thirty-five years. It's about time we went, don't you think?"

"I'm not going to butt in on anybody's second honeymoon," Mabel says.

"Who's going on a honeymoon, for Christ's sake?" Norma Jean says loudly.

"I never raised no daughter of mine to talk that-a-way," Mabel says.

"You ain't seen nothing yet," says Norma Jean. She starts putting away boxes and cans, slamming cabinet doors.

"There's a log cabin at Shiloh," Mabel says. "It was there during the battle. There's bullet holes in it."

"When are you going to *shut up* about Shiloh, Mama?" asks Norma Jean.

"I always thought Shiloh was the prettiest place, so full of history," Mabel goes on. "I just hoped y'all could see it once before I die, so you could tell me about it." Later, she whispers to Leroy, "You do what I said. A little change is what she needs."

"Your name means 'the king,' " Norma Jean says to Leroy that evening. He is trying to get her to go to Shiloh, and she is reading a book about another century.

"Well, I reckon I ought to be right proud."

"I guess so."

"Am I still king around here?"

Norma Jean flexes her biceps and feels them for hardness. "I'm not fooling around with anybody, if that's what you mean," she says.

"Would you tell me if you were?"

"I don't know."

"What does *your* name mean?"

"It was Marilyn Monroe's real name."[8]

"No kidding!"

"Norma comes from the Normans.[9] They were invaders," she says. She closes her book and looks hard at Leroy. "I'll go to Shiloh with you if you'll stop staring at me."

On Sunday, Norma Jean packs a picnic and they go to Shiloh. To Leroy's relief, Mabel says she does not want to come with them. Norma Jean drives, and Leroy, sitting beside her, feels like some boring hitchhiker she has picked up. He tries some conversation, but she answers him in monosyllables. At Shiloh, she drives aimlessly through the park, past bluffs and trails and steep ravines. Shiloh is an immense place, and Leroy cannot see it as a battleground. It is not what he expected. He thought it would look like a golf course. Monuments are everywhere, showing through the thick clusters of trees. Norma Jean passes the log cabin Mabel mentioned. It is surrounded by tourists looking for bullet holes.

"That's not the kind of log house I've got in mind," says Leroy apologetically.

"I know *that*."

"This is a pretty place. Your mama was right."

"It's O.K.," says Norma Jean. "Well, we've seen it. I hope she's satisfied."

They burst out laughing together.

At the park museum, a movie on Shiloh is shown every half hour, but they decide that they don't want to see it. They buy a souvenir Confederate flag for Mabel, and then they find a picnic spot near the cemetery. Norma Jean has brought a picnic cooler, with pimiento sandwiches, soft drinks, and Yodels. Leroy eats a sandwich and then smokes a joint, hiding it behind the picnic cooler. Norma Jean has quit smoking altogether. She is picking cake crumbs from the cellophane wrapper, like a fussy bird.

Leroy says, "So the boys in gray ended up in Corinth.[10] The Union soldiers zapped 'em finally. April 7, 1862."

They both know that he doesn't know any history. He is just talking about some of the historical plaques they have read. He feels awkward, like a boy on a date with an older girl. They are still just making conversation.

---

[8] Marilyn Monroe (1926–1962) was born Norma Jean Mortenson (later) Baker. She became a film star in the 1950s, appearing in such films as *Some Like It Hot* and *The Seven Year Itch*.

[9] The Normans, a people of northwestern France, invaded England in 1066. Their leader, William the Conqueror, united England with Normandy. The Normans were the last foreign power to conquer England.

[10] Corinth is a city in extreme northeastern Mississippi near the Tennessee border. In the Civil War it was a strategic railroad center abandoned to the Union forces after the battle of Shiloh. The Mississippi city was named after the Greek city of Corinth, the site of numerous battles and of invasions by a succession of rulers.

"Corinth is where Mama eloped to," says Norma Jean.

They sit in silence and stare at the cemetery for the Union dead and, beyond, at a tall cluster of trees. Campers are parked nearby, bumper to bumper, and small children in bright clothing are cavorting and squealing. Norma Jean wads up the cake wrapper and squeezes it tightly in her hand. Without looking at Leroy, she says, "I want to leave you."

Leroy takes a bottle of Coke out of the cooler and flips off the cap. He holds the bottle poised near his mouth but cannot remember to take a drink. Finally he says, "No, you don't."

"Yes, I do."

"I won't let you."

"You can't stop me."

"Don't do me that way."

Leroy knows Norma Jean will have her own way. "Didn't I promise to be home from now on?" he says.

"In some ways, a woman prefers a man who wanders," says Norma Jean. "That sounds crazy, I know."

"You're not crazy."

Leroy remembers to drink from his Coke. Then he says, "Yes, you *are* crazy. You and me could start all over again. Right back at the beginning."

"We *have* started all over again," says Norma Jean. "And this is how it turned out."

"What did I do wrong?"

"Nothing."

"Is this one of those women's lib things?" Leroy asks.

"Don't be funny."

The cemetery, a green slope dotted with white markers, looks like a subdivision site. Leroy is trying to comprehend that his marriage is breaking up, but for some reason he is wondering about white slabs in a graveyard.

"Everything was fine till Mama caught me smoking," says Norma Jean, standing up. "That set something off."

"What are you talking about?"

"She won't leave me alone—*you* won't leave me alone." Norma Jean seems to be crying, but she is looking away from him. "I feel eighteen again. I can't face that all over again." She starts walking away. "No, it *wasn't* fine. I don't know what I'm saying. Forget it."

Leroy takes a lungful of smoke and closes his eyes as Norma Jean's words sink in. He tries to focus on the fact that thirty-five hundred soldiers died on the grounds around him. He can only think of that war as a board game with plastic soldiers. Leroy almost smiles, as he compares the Confederates' daring attack on the Union camps and Virgil Mathis's raid on the bowling alley. General Grant, drunk and furious, shoved the Southerners back to Corinth, where Mabel and Jet Beasley were married years later, when Mabel was still thin and good-looking. The next day, Mabel and Jet visited the battleground, and then Norma Jean was born, and then she married Leroy and they had a baby, which they lost, and now Leroy and Norma Jean are here at the same battleground. Leroy knows he is leaving out a lot. He is leaving out the insides of history. History was always just names and dates to him. It occurs to him that building a house out of logs is similarly empty—too simple. And the real inner workings of a marriage, like most of history, have escaped him. Now he sees that building a log house is the dumbest idea he could have had. It was clumsy of him to think Norma Jean would want a log house. It was a crazy idea. He'll have to think of something else, quickly. He will wad the blueprints into tight balls and fling them into the lake. Then he'll get moving again. He opens his eyes. Norma Jean has moved away and is walking through the cemetery, following a serpentine brick path.

Leroy gets up to follow his wife, but his good leg is asleep and his bad leg still hurts him. Norma Jean is far away, walking rapidly toward the bluff by the river, and he tries to hobble toward her. Some children run past him, screaming noisily. Norma Jean has reached the bluff, and she is looking out over the Tennessee River. Now she turns toward Leroy and waves her arms. Is she beckoning to him? She seems to be doing an exercise for her chest muscles. The sky is unusually pale—the color of the dust ruffle Mabel made for their bed.

Questions

1. Why does Norma Jean take up body-building and start college?
2. Why does Leroy buy Norma Jean the electric organ? Why does she stop playing it?
3. What role does the death of their child play in the dissolution of their marriage?
4. Norma Jean says, "Everything was fine till Mama caught me smoking . . . That set something off." What did her mother's discovery "set off"? Why should the event have "set off" Norma Jean?
5. In the last paragraph Norma Jean waves her arms toward Leroy. Can Leroy tell what she is signaling? Can you as a reader tell what she is signaling? Does it matter?
6. Why does Leroy wish to build the log cabin? Should he build it?
7. Can their marriage be saved?

JAMES JOYCE (1882–1941)

Araby

North Richmond Street, being blind,[1] was a quiet street except at the hour when the Christian Brothers' School set the boys free. An uninhabited house of two stories stood at the blind end, detached from its neighbours in a square ground. The other houses of the street, conscious of decent lives within them, gazed at one another with brown imperturbable faces.

---

[1] A blind street is a dead-end street.

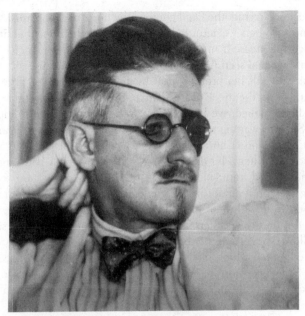

James Joyce (The Bettmann Achive)

The former tenant of our house, a priest, had died in the back drawing-room. Air, musty from having been long enclosed, hung in all the rooms, and the waste room behind the kitchen was littered with old useless papers. Among these I found a few paper-covered books, the pages of which were curled and damp: *The Abbot*, by Walter Scott, *The Devout Communicant*, and *The Memoirs of Vidocq*.[2] I liked the last best because its leaves were yellow. The wild garden behind the house contained a central apple tree and a few straggling bushes under one of which I found the late tenant's rusty bicycle pump. He had been a very charitable priest; in his will he had left all his money to institutions and the furniture of his house to his sister.

When the short days of winter came dusk fell before we had well eaten our dinners. When we met in the street the houses had grown sombre. The space of sky above us was the colour of ever-changing violet and towards it the lamps of the street lifted their feeble lanterns. The cold air stung us and we played till our bodies glowed. Our shouts echoed in the silent street. The career of our play brought us through the dark muddy lanes behind the houses where we ran the gauntlet of the rough tribes from the cottages to the back doors of the dark dripping gardens where odours arose from the ash-pits, to the dark odorous

---

[2] François-Eugène Vidocq (1775–1857) helped create the French security police. *The Abbot* is one of Sir Walter Scott's Scottish historical romances. *The Devout Communicant* is a Catholic devotional manual.

stables where a coachman smoothed and combed the horse or shook music from the buckled harness. When we returned to the street, light from the kitchen windows had filled the areas. If my uncle was seen turning the corner we hid in the shadow until we had seen him safely housed. Or if Mangan's sister came out on the doorstep to call her brother in to his tea we watched her from our shadow peer up and down the street. We waited to see whether she would remain or go in and, if she remained, we left our shadow and walked up to Mangan's steps resignedly. She was waiting for us, her figure defined by the light from the half-opened door. Her brother always teased her before he obeyed and I stood by the railings looking at her. Her dress swung as she moved her body and the soft rope of her hair tossed from side to side.

Every morning I lay on the floor in the front parlour watching her door. The blind was pulled down to within an inch of the sash so that I could not be seen. When she came out on the doorstep my heart leaped. I ran to the hall, seized my books and followed her. I kept her brown figure always in my eye and, when we came near the point at which our ways diverged, I quickened my pace and passed her. This happened morning after morning. I had never spoken to her, except for a few casual words, and yet her name was like a summons to all my foolish blood.

Her image accompanied me even in places the most hostile to romance. On Saturday evenings when my aunt went marketing I had to go to carry some of the parcels. We walked through the flaring streets, jostled by drunken men and bargaining women, amid the curses of labourers, the shrill litanies of shop-boys who stood on guard by the barrels of pigs' cheeks, the nasal chanting of street-singers, who sang a *come-all-you* about O'Donovan Rossa,[3] or a ballad about the troubles in our native land. These noises converged in a single sensation of life for me: I imagined that I bore my chalice safely through a throng of foes. Her name sprang to my lips at moments in strange prayers and praises which I myself did not understand. My eyes were often full of tears (I could not tell why) and at times a flood from my heart seemed to pour itself out into my bosom. I thought little of the future. I did not know whether I would ever speak to her or not or, if I spoke to her, how I could tell her of my confused adoration. But my body was like a harp and her words and gestures were like fingers running upon the wires.

One evening I went into the back drawing-room in which the priest had died. It was a dark rainy evening and there was no sound in the house. Through one of the broken panes I heard the rain impinge upon the earth, the fine incessant needles of water playing in the sodden beds. Some distant lamp or lighted window gleamed below me. I was thankful that I could see so little. All my senses seemed to desire to veil themselves and, feeling that I was about to slip from them, I pressed the palms of my hands together until they trembled, murmuring: "*O love! O love!*" many times.

---

[3] Jeremiah Donovan (1831–1915), commonly called O'Donovan Rossa, was an Irish nationalist celebrated in street songs or *come-all-you's*.

At last she spoke to me. When she addressed the first words to me I was so confused that I did not know what to answer. She asked me was I going to *Araby*. I forgot whether I answered yes or no. It would be a splendid bazaar, she said she would love to go.

"And why can't you?" I asked.

While she spoke she turned a silver bracelet round and round her wrist. She could not go, she said, because there would be a retreat that week in her convent. Her brother and two other boys were fighting for their caps and I was alone at the railings. She held one of the spikes, bowing her head towards me. The light from the lamp opposite our door caught the white curve of her neck, lit up her hair that rested there and, falling, lit up the hand upon the railing. It fell over one side of her dress and caught the white border of a petticoat, just visible as she stood at ease.

"It's well for you," she said.

"If I go," I said, "I will bring you something."

What innumerable follies laid waste my waking and sleeping thoughts after the evening! I wished to annihilate the tedious intervening days. I chafed against the work of school. At night in my bedroom and by day in the classroom her image came between me and the page I strove to read. The syllables of the word *Araby* were called to me through the silence in which my soul luxuriated and cast an Eastern enchantment over me. I asked for leave to go to the bazaar on Saturday night. My aunt was surprised and hoped it was not some Freemason[4] affair. I answered few questions in class. I watched my master's face pass from amiability to sternness; he hoped I was not beginning to idle. I could not call my wandering thoughts together. I had hardly any patience with the serious work of life which, now that it stood between me and my desire, seemed to me child's play, ugly monotonous child's play.

On Saturday morning I reminded my uncle that I wished to go to the bazaar in the evening. He was fussing at the hall-stand, looking for the hat brush, and answered me curtly:

"Yes, boy, I know."

As he was in the hall I could not go into the front parlour and lie at the window. I left the house in bad humour and walked slowly towards the school. The air was pitilessly raw and already my heart misgave me.

When I came home to dinner my uncle had not yet been home. Still it was early. I sat staring at the clock for some time and, when its ticking began to irritate me, I left the room. I mounted the staircase and gained the upper part of the house. The high cold empty gloomy rooms liberated me and I went from room to room singing. From the front window I saw my companions playing below in the street. Their cries reached me weakened and indistinct and, leaning my forehead against the cool glass, I looked over at the dark house where she lived. I may have stood there for an hour, seeing nothing but the brown-clad

---

[4] Freemason societies, because they were secret, were frequently considered dangerous gatherings.

figure cast by my imagination, touched discreetly by the lamplight at the curved neck, at the hand upon the railings and at the border below the dress.

When I came downstairs again I found Mrs. Mercer sitting at the fire. She was an old garrulous woman, a pawnbroker's widow, who collected used stamps for some pious purpose. I had to endure the gossip of the tea-table. The meal was prolonged beyond an hour and still my uncle did not come. Mrs. Mercer stood up to go: she was sorry she couldn't wait any longer, but it was after eight o'clock and she did not like to be out late, as the night air was bad for her. When she had gone I began to walk up and down the room, clenching my fists. My aunt said:

"I'm afraid you may put off your bazaar for this night of Our Lord."

At nine o'clock I heard my uncle's latchkey in the hall-door. I heard him talking to himself and heard the hall-stand rocking when it had received the weight of his overcoat. I could interpret these signs. When he was midway through his dinner I asked him to give me the money to go to the bazaar. He had forgotten.

"The people are in bed and after their first sleep now," he said.

I did not smile. My aunt said to him energetically:

"Can't you give him the money and let him go? You've kept him late enough as it is."

My uncle said he was very sorry he had forgotten. He said he believed in the old saying: "All work and no play makes Jack a dull boy." He asked me where I was going and, when I had told him a second time, he asked me did I know *The Arab's Farewell to his Steed*.[5] When I left the kitchen he was about to recite the opening lines of the piece to my aunt.

I held a florin tightly in my hand as I strode down Buckingham Street towards the station. The sight of the streets thronged with buyers and glaring with gas recalled to me the purpose of my journey. I took my seat in a third-class carriage of a deserted train. After an intolerable delay the train moved out of the station slowly. It crept onward among ruinous houses and over the twinkling river. At Westland Row Station a crowd of people pressed to the carriage doors; but the porters moved them back, saying that it was a special train for the bazaar. I remained alone in the bare carriage. In a few minutes the train drew up beside an improvised wooden platform. I passed out on the road and saw by the lighted dial of a clock that it was ten minutes to ten. In front of me was a large building which displayed the magical name.

I could not find any sixpenny entrance and, fearing that the bazaar would be closed, I passed in quickly through a turnstile, handing a shilling to a weary-looking man. I found myself in a big hall girdled at half its height by a gallery. Nearly all the stalls were closed and the greater part of the hall was in darkness. I recognized a silence like that which pervades a church after a service. I walked into the center of the bazaar timidly. A few people were gathered about the stalls which were still open. Before a curtain, over which the words *Café Chantant*

---

[5] A poem by Caroline Norton (1808–1877).

were written in coloured lamps, two men were counting money on a salver. I listened to the fall of the coins.

Remembering with difficulty why I had come I went over to one of the stalls and examined porcelain vases and flowered tea-sets. At the door of the stall a young lady was talking and laughing with two young gentlemen. I remarked their English accents and listened vaguely to their conversation.

"O, I never said such a thing!"

"O, but you did!"

"O, but I didn't!"

"Didn't she say that?"

"Yes. I heard her."

"O, there's a . . . fib!"

Observing me, the young lady came over and asked me did I wish to buy anything. The tone of her voice was not encouraging; she seemed to have spoken to me out of a sense of duty. I looked humbly at the great jars that stood like eastern guards at either side of the dark entrance to the stall and murmured:

"No, thank you."

The young lady changed the position of one of the vases and went back to the two young men. They began to talk of the same subject. Once or twice the young lady glanced at me over her shoulder.

I lingered before her stall, though I knew my stay was useless, to make my interest in her wares seem the more real. Then I turned away slowly and walked down the middle of the bazaar. I allowed the two pennies to fall against the sixpence in my pocket. I heard a voice call from one end of the gallery that the light was out. The upper part of the hall was now completely dark.

Gazing up into the darkness I saw myself as a creature driven and derided by vanity; and my eyes burned with anguish and anger.

Questions

1. In what ways is North Richmond Street blind?
2. How does the narrator regard Mangan's sister? Does she do or say anything to justify his attitude toward her?
3. How does Joyce contrast the beautiful and romantic with the ugly and banal? Which is closer to the truth?
4. Why does the narrator wait for his uncle in the room where the priest died? How does that setting emphasize his emotions?
5. How does Joyce contrast light and dark in "Araby"? What sort of feelings does this contrast evoke?
6. Is the narrator a creature "driven and derided by vanity"? Why?

7 ❧ Stories with a Frame, Stories with a Twist

In Chapter 4 we discussed plot as the arrangement of events in a story. We showed how authors arrange events to create suspense, surprise, and conflict. Authors have devised ingenious ways of telling stories so that no two are ever the same. However, over the long history of storytelling certain patterns have emerged. In this chapter we will discuss two of the most familiar patterns: stories with frames and stories with twist endings.

Stories with Frames

Stories with frames actually consist of two stories, one inside the other. Frequently the *frame*, or outer story, narrates how a group of people come together and exchange stories. Then one person from the group narrates the *inner story*, or the *tale-within-a-tale*. The work ends by returning to the group and recounting their reactions to the inner story. Occasionally several tales will be joined together by the same framing device. For example, "A Dinner of Hens," which appears in Chapter 1, is a tale-within-a-tale included in Boccaccio's *Decameron*, a collection of 100 stories. The frame of the *Decameron* concerns ten men and women who flee the plague-torn Italian city of Florence and gather in a country villa for safety. To pass the time, they swap stories. Chaucer's *Canterbury Tales* has a similar structure. Pilgrims on the road to Canterbury exchange stories to amuse each other on the long, tedious trip.

Reading the Frame Story

Choosing a frame for a story is much like choosing a frame for a picture. Authors, and art collectors, want their frames to fit properly and suit the subject. A small picture shouldn't be surrounded by something large and gaudy, and a large picture shouldn't have a frame that is thin and weak. Like a picture frame, the story frame exists to enhance the tale within it, to bring out its chief features.

Faced with a framed story, one should pay close attention to the relationship between the inner story and the framing device. The story and the frame are usually related in one or more of the following ways: (1) The theme of the story illustrates, disputes, or enlarges the discussion between the characters in the frame. (2) The inner story is told by a particularly fitting person. Typically, people tell stories about subjects they know and care about. Soldiers tell tales about war, widows about death and dying, sinners about sinning, and the virtuous about virtue. (3) The audience in the frame responds to the tale in a manner appropriate to their personalities. Thus, in the *Decameron* the noble women admonish some of the men for telling bawdy tales, and in *The Canterbury Tales* the drunken miller grows bored by the good knight's courtly tale of honor. (4) The situation in the frame may mirror the situation in the inner tale. For example, in "A Conversation with My Father" the frame shows a daughter trying to adjust herself to her father's values, while in the inner tale a mother adopts her son's values.

Be sure, even when the frame is brief, that you pay attention to it. Frames are an important artistic device, and readers should notice how the story has been clarified and enhanced by the addition of the frame. Ask yourself what would be lost if the story had no frame.

Stories with a Twist

Stories, as we have mentioned, follow certain conventions—generally recognized rules of procedure. These conventions set up certain expectations. For example, the opening words "Once upon a time . . ." make the reader expect that the story will be a fairy tale. Experienced readers will immediately prepare themselves to hear about princes and princesses, talking animals, elves, fairies, wicked stepmothers, and all the other conventional elements of the fairy tale. Some works, such as TV situation comedies, are so conventional that the experienced viewer can guess what will happen in an entire episode by watching the first five minutes. Such expectations are not necessarily bad; there is a certain satisfaction in getting what you expected, and highly conventional works satisfy those highly predictable appetites.

But writers, on the whole, like a dash of spice in their writing lives. They especially like to play with conventions by giving them a little twist. Frequently, they like to prepare the reader to expect one sort of convention and then provide something else, a surprise that will more than compensate for the loss of the convention. Typically this twist—the unexpected turn of events—will come at the end of a story, but some stories have many twists arranged throughout. In detective fiction such a practice is called "keeping the reader guessing," and it makes for an exciting reading experience.

Good and Bad Twist Endings

Since twist endings are a technique of plotting, some readers have thought that they are manipulative, easy devices to gain attention. In short, they are sometimes regarded as a "cheap trick" of the storytelling trade.

Sometimes the charge is fair. The twist ending may be merely a clever ploy that gives an otherwise lifeless and uninspired story a bit of dash and sparkle. In such a story the surprise comes for no particular reason and illuminates very little of the prior action. The best twist endings, however, develop from possibilities always inherent in the story—possibilities that the reader has not fully recognized or entertained. The twist, thus, clarifies and enriches all that we have read. In "The Night Watchman's Occurrence Book," the surprising twist at the end makes us fully appreciate that behind Hillyard's mild, uneducated façade is a wily intelligence able to take advantage of the situation and gain revenge for the injustices committed against him.

Reading the Twist Ending

The reader should try to evaluate how the twist ending relates to the rest of the story and illuminates the events that precede it. If the twist is made possible by a new element in the plot—the appearance, for example, of a previously unknown letter or character—the result is less likely to suit the entire story, less able to please us after the first surprise. If, however, the twist derives from possibilities of character and situation present all along, the twist will generally delight us after many readings, continuing to shed light on the entire story.

Suggestions for Essayists

1. Have you ever planned a trip, a dinner, or a party that failed or succeeded because of unforeseen circumstances? Narrate that incident.

2. Discuss how we alter our manner of speaking and our subject matter depending on our audience. Compare, for example, the way you speak to your friends to the way you speak to your parents.

Suggestions for Fiction Writers

1. Place the same character in two different framing situations and have the character tell the same anecdote. What sorts of changes happen to the story depending on its fictional audience?

2. Take a well known story or anecdote and give a twist to its ending. For example, imagine a version of Little Red Riding Hood in which grandmother rolls out from under the bed at the crucial moment.

GRACE PALEY (1922–)

A Conversation with My Father

My father is eighty-six years old and in bed. His heart, that bloody motor, is equally old and will not do certain jobs any more. It still floods his head with brainy light. But it won't let his legs carry the weight of his body around the house. Despite my metaphors, this muscle failure is not due to his old heart, he says, but to a potassium shortage. Sitting on one pillow, leaning on three, he offers last-minute advice and makes a request.

"I would like you to write a simple story just once more," he says, "the kind de Maupassant wrote, or Chekhov,[1] the kind you used to write. Just recognizable people and then write down what happened to them next."

I say, "Yes, why not? That's possible." I want to please him, though I don't remember writing that way. I *would* like to try to tell such a story, if he means the kind that begins: "There was a woman . . ." followed by plot, the absolute line between two points which I've always despised. Not for literary reasons, but because it takes all hope away. Everyone, real or invented, deserves the open destiny of life.

Finally I thought of a story that had been happening for a couple of years right across the street. I wrote it down, then read it aloud, "Pa," I said, "how about this? Do you mean something like this?"

Once in my time there was a woman and she had a son. They lived nicely, in a small apartment in Manhattan. This boy at about fifteen became a junkie,[2] which is not unusual in our neighborhood. In order to maintain her close friendship with him, she became a junkie too. She said it was part of the youth culture, with which she felt very much at home. After a while, for a number of reasons, the boy gave it all up and left the city and his mother in disgust. Hopeless and alone, she grieved. We all visit her.

"O.K., Pa, that's it," I said, "an unadorned and miserable tale."

"But that's not what I mean," my father said. "You misunderstood me on purpose. You know there's a lot more to it. You know that. You left everything out. Turgenev[3] wouldn't do that. Chekhov wouldn't do that. There are in fact Russian writers you never heard of, you don't have an inkling of, as good as anyone, who can write a plain ordinary story, who would not leave out what you have left out. I object not to facts but to people sitting in trees talking senselessly, voices from who knows where[4] . . ."

"Forget that one, Pa, what have I left out now? In this one?"

---

[1] Guy de Maupassant (1850–1893) and Anton Chekhov (1860–1904) were two masters of short fiction whose works developed finely drawn psychological characters in realistic settings. One of Chekhov's stories, "Lady with Lapdog," appears on pp. 310–322.

[2] A junkie is a heroin user.

[3] Ivan Turgenev (1818–1883) is a precursor of the psychological-realist school of Chekhov and Maupassant.

[4] Paley is alluding to her story "Faith in a Tree."

"Her looks, for instance."

"Oh. Quite handsome, I think. Yes."

"Her hair?"

"Dark, with heavy braids, as though she were a girl or a foreigner."

"What were her parents like, her stock? That she became such a person. It's interesting, you know."

"From out of town. Professional people. The first to be divorced in their county. How's that? Enough?" I asked.

"With you, it's all a joke," he said. "What about the boy's father? Why didn't you mention him? Who was he? Or was the boy born out of wedlock?"

"Yes," I said. "He was born out of wedlock."

"For Godsakes, doesn't anyone in your stories get married? Doesn't anyone have the time to run down to City Hall before they jump into bed?"

"No," I said. "In real life, yes. But in my stories, no."

"Why do you answer me like that?"

"Oh, Pa, this is a simple story about a smart woman who came to N.Y.C. full of interest love trust excitement very up to date, and about her son, what a hard time she had in this world. Married or not, it's of small consequence."

"It is of great consequence," he said.

"O.K.," I said.

"O.K. O.K. yourself," he said, "but listen. I believe you that she's good-looking, but I don't think she was so smart."

"That's true," I said. "Actually that's the trouble with stories. People start out fantastic. You think they're extraordinary, but it turns out as the work goes along, they're just average with a good education. Sometimes the other way around, the person's a kind of dumb innocent, but he outwits you and you can't even think of an ending good enough."

"What do you do then?" he asked. He had been a doctor for a couple of decades and then an artist for a couple of decades and he's still interested in details, craft, technique.

"Well, you just have to let the story lie around till some agreement can be reached between you and the stubborn hero."

"Aren't you talking silly, now?" he asked. "Start again," he said. "It so happens I'm not going out this evening. Tell *the story* again. See what you can do this time."

"O.K.," I said. "But it's not a five-minute job." Second attempt:

Once, across the street from us, there was a fine handsome woman, our neighbor. She had a son whom she loved because she'd known him since birth (in helpless chubby infancy, and in the wrestling, hugging ages, seven to ten, as well as earlier and later). This boy, when he fell into the fist of adolescence, became a junkie. He was not a hopeless one. He was in fact hopeful, an ideologue and successful converter. With his busy brilliance, he wrote persuasive articles for his highschool newspaper. Seeking a wider audience, using important connections, he drummed into Lower Manhattan newsstand distribution a periodical called *Oh! Golden Horse!*[5]

---

[5] Horse is a slang term for heroin.

In order to keep him from feeling guilty (because guilt is the stony heart of nine tenths of all clinically diagnosed cancers in America today, she said), and because she had always believed in giving bad habits room at home where one could keep an eye on them, she too became a junkie. Her kitchen was famous for a while—a center for intellectual addicts who knew what they were doing. A few felt artistic like Coleridge and others were scientific and revolutionary like Leary.[6] Although she was often high herself, certain good mothering reflexes remained, and she saw to it that there was lots of orange juice around and honey and milk and vitamin pills. However, she never cooked anything but chili, and that no more than once a week. She explained, when we talked to her, seriously, with neighborly concern, that it was her part in the youth culture and she would rather be with the young, it was an honor, than with her own generation.

One week, while nodding through an Antonioni[7] film, this boy was severely jabbed by the elbow of a stern and proselytizing girl, sitting beside him. She offered immediate apricots and nuts for his sugar level, spoke to him sharply, and took him home.

She had heard of him and his work and she herself published, edited, and wrote a competitive journal called *Man Does Live By Bread Alone*. In the organic heat of her continuous presence he could not help but become interested once more in his muscles, his arteries, and nerve connections. In fact he began to love them, treasure them, praise them with funny little songs in *Man Does Live* . . .

> the fingers of my flesh transcend
> my transcendental soul
> the tightness in my shoulders end
> my teeth have made me whole

To the mouth of his head (that glory of will and determination) he brought hard apples, nuts, wheat germ, and soybean oil. He said to his old friends, From now on, I guess I'll keep my wits about me. I'm going on the natch. He said he was about to begin a spiritual deep-breathing journey. How about you too, Mom? he asked kindly.

His conversion was so radiant, splendid, that neighborhood kids his age began to say that he had never been a real addict at all, only a journalist along for the smell of the story. The mother tried several times to give up what had become without her son and his friends a lonely habit. This effort only brought it to supportable levels. The boy and his girl took their electronic mimeograph and moved to the bushy edge of another borough. They were very strict. They said they would not see her again until she had been off drugs for sixty days.

At home alone in the evening, weeping, the mother read and reread the seven issues of *Oh! Golden Horse!* They seemed to her as truthful as ever. We often crossed the street to visit and console. But if we mentioned any of our children who were at college or in the hospital or dropouts at home, she would cry out, My baby! My baby! and burst into terrible, face-scarring, time-consuming tears. The End.

First my father was silent, then he said, "Number One: You have a nice sense

---

[6] Samuel Taylor Coleridge (1772–1834) was an English poet and essayist who suffered from opium addiction. Dr. Timothy Leary (1920–), former Harvard lecturer in psychology, became known during the 1960s for his experiments with psychedelic drugs.
[7] Michelangelo Antonioni (1912–) is an experimental Italian filmmaker; *Blow-up* (1966) made him famous in the United States.

of humor. Number Two: I see you can't tell a plain story. So don't waste time."
Then he said sadly, "Number Three: I suppose that means she was alone, she
was left like that, his mother. Alone. Probably sick?"

I said, "Yes."

"Poor woman. Poor girl, to be born in a time of fools, to live among fools.
The end. The end. You were right to put that down. The end."

I didn't want to argue, but I had to say, "Well, it is not necessarily the
end, Pa."

"Yes," he said, "what a tragedy. The end of a person."

"No, Pa," I begged him. "It doesn't have to be. She's only about forty. She
could be a hundred different things in this world as time goes on. A teacher or
a social worker. An ex-junkie! Sometimes it's better than having a master's in
education."

"Jokes," he said. "As a writer that's your main trouble. You don't want to
recognize it. Tragedy! Plain tragedy! Historical tragedy! No hope. The end."

"Oh, Pa," I said. "She could change."

"In your own life, too, you have to look it in the face." He took a couple of
nitroglycerin.[8] "Turn to five," he said, pointing to the dial on the oxygen tank.
He inserted the tubes into his nostrils and breathed deep. He closed his eyes
and said, "No."

I had promised the family to always let him have the last word when arguing,
but in this case I had a different responsibility. That woman lives across the
street. She's my knowledge and my invention. I'm sorry for her. I'm not going
to leave her there in that house crying. (Actually neither would Life, which
unlike me has no pity.)

Therefore: She did change. Of course her son never came home again. But
right now, she's the receptionist in a storefront community clinic in the East
Village.[9] Most of the customers are young people, some old friends. The head
doctor has said to her, "If we only had three people in this clinic with your
experiences . . ."

"The doctor said that?" My father took the oxygen tubes out of his nostrils
and said, "Jokes. Jokes again."

"No, Pa, it could really happen that way, it's a funny world nowadays."

"No," he said. "Truth first. She will slide back. A person must have character.
She does not."

"No, Pa," I said. "That's it. She's got a job. Forget it. She's in that storefront
working."

"How long will it be?" he asked. "Tragedy! You too. When will you look it
in the face?"

---

[8] Nitroglycerine is not only an explosive but also a drug for the treatment of some types of heart
disease.

[9] The East Village, a poor section of New York City, was one of the centers of the youth movement.

Questions

1. In what ways does the frame mirror the story of the junkie?
2. In the inner story the mother wants to be a part of the son's world. Does anything in the frame mirror that desire?
3. In the inner story the mother becomes dependent on heroin. Is there a parallel in the frame?
4. Does the inner story depict the narrator's belief that "everyone, real or invented, deserves the open destiny of life"?
5. Does the narrator's belief in an "open destiny" relate to the conventions of character consistency, flat and round characters?
6. Has the narrator failed to look tragedy "in the face"? Does such a failure in the inner story relate to a similar "failure" in the frame?
7. Who are the realists in the story? In life?

ALICE WALKER (1944–)

How Did I Get Away with Killing One of the Biggest Lawyers in the State? It Was Easy.

"My mother and father were not married. I never knew him. My mother must have loved him, though; she never talked against him when I was little. It was like he never existed. We lived on Poultry street. Why it was called Poultry street I never knew. I guess at one time there must have been a chicken factory somewhere along there. It was right near the center of town. I could walk to the state capitol in less than ten minutes. I could see the top—it was gold—of the capitol building from the front yard. When I was a little girl I used to think it was real gold, shining up there, and then they bought an eagle and put him on top, and when I used to walk up there I couldn't see the top of the building from the ground, it was so high, and I used to reach down and run my hand over the grass. It was like a rug, that grass was, so springy and silky and deep. They had these big old trees, too. Oaks and magnolias; and I thought the magnolia trees were beautiful and one night I climbed up in one of them and got a bloom and took it home. But the air in our house blighted it; it turned brown the minute I took it inside and the petals dropped off.

"Mama worked in private homes. That's how she described her job, to make it sound nicer. 'I work in private homes,' she would say, and that sounded nicer, she thought, than saying 'I'm a maid.'

"Sometimes she made six dollars a day, working in two private homes. Most of the time she didn't make that much. By the time she paid the rent and bought milk and bananas there wasn't anything left.

"She used to leave me alone sometimes because there was no one to keep me—and then there was an old woman up the street who looked after me for a while—and by the time she died she was more like a mother to me than Mama was. Mama was so tired every night when she came home I never hardly got the chance to talk to her. And then sometimes she would go out at night, or bring men home—but they never thought of marrying her. And they sure didn't want to be bothered with me. I guess most of them were like my own father; had children somewhere of their own that they'd left. And then they came to my Mama, who fell for them every time. And I think she may have had a couple of abortions, like some of the women did, who couldn't feed any more mouths. But she tried.

"Anyway, she was a nervous kind of woman. I think she had spells or something because she was so tired. But I didn't understand anything then about exhaustion, worry, lack of a proper diet; I just thought she wanted to work, to be away from the house. I didn't blame her. Where we lived people sometimes just threw pieces of furniture they didn't want over the railing. And there was broken glass and rags everywhere. The place stunk, especially in the summer. And children were always screaming and men were always cussing and women were always yelling about something. . . . It was nothing for a girl or woman to be raped. I was raped myself, when I was twelve, and my Mama never knew and I never told anybody. For, what could they do? It was just a boy, passing through. Somebody's cousin from the North.

"One time my Mama was doing day's work at a private home and took me with her. It was like being in fairyland. Everything was spotless and new, even before Mama started cleaning. I met the woman in the house and played with her children. I didn't even see the man, but he was in there somewhere, while I was out in the yard with the children. I was fourteen, but I guess I looked like a grown woman. Or maybe I looked fourteen. Anyway, the next day, he picked me up when I was coming from school and he said my Mama had asked him to do it. I got in the car with him . . . he took me to his law office, a big office in the middle of town, and he started asking me questions about 'how do you all live?' and 'what grade are you in?' and stuff like that. And then he began to touch me, and I pulled away. But he kept touching me and I was scared . . . he raped me. But afterward he told me he hadn't forced me, that I felt something for him, and he gave me some money. I was crying, going down the stairs. I wanted to kill him.

"I never told Mama. I thought that would be the end of it. But about two days later, on my way from school, he stopped his car again, and I got in. This time we went to his house; nobody was there. And he made me get into his wife's bed. After we'd been doing this for about three weeks, he told me he loved me. I didn't love him, but he had begun to look a little better to me. Really, I think, because he was so clean. He bathed a lot and never smelled even alive, to tell the truth. Or maybe it was the money he gave me, or the presents he bought. I told Mama I had a job after school baby-sitting. And she was glad that I could buy things I needed for school. But it was all from him.

"This went on for two years. He wouldn't let me get pregnant, he said, and I didn't. I would just lay up there in his wife's bed and work out algebra problems or think about what new thing I was going to buy. But one day, when I got home, Mama was there ahead of me, and she saw me get out of his car. I knew when he was driving off that I was going to get it.

"Mama asked me didn't I know he was a white man? Didn't I know he was a married man with two children? Didn't I have good sense? And do you know what I told her? *I told her he loved me.* Mama was crying and praying at the same time by then. The neighbors heard both of us screaming and crying, because Mama beat me almost to death with the cord from the electric iron. She just hacked it off the iron, still on the ironing board. She beat me till she couldn't raise her arm. And then she had one of her fits, just twitching and sweating and trying to claw herself into the floor. This scared me more than the beating. That night she told me something I hadn't paid much attention to before. She said: 'On top of everything else, that man's daddy goes on the t.v. every night and says folks like us ain't even human.' It was his daddy who had stood in the schoolhouse door saying it would be over his dead body before any black children would come into a white school.

"But do you think that stopped me? No. I would look at his daddy on t.v. ranting and raving about how integration was a communist plot, and I would just think of how different his son Bubba was from his daddy! Do you understand what I'm saying. I thought he *loved* me. That *meant* something to me. What did I know about 'equal rights'? What did I care about 'integration'? I was sixteen! I wanted somebody to tell me I was pretty, and he was telling me that all the time. I even thought it was *brave* of him to go with me. History? What did I know about History?

"I began to hate Mama. We argued about Bubba all the time, for months. And I still slipped out to meet him, because Mama had to work. I told him how she beat me, and about how much she despised him—he was really pissed off that any black person could despise him—and about how she had these spells. . . . Well, the day I became seventeen, the *day* of my seventeenth birthday, I signed papers in his law office, and I had my mother committed to an insane asylum.

"After Mama had been in Carthage Insane Asylum for three months, she managed somehow to get a lawyer. An old slick-headed man who smoked great big black cigars. People laughed at him because he didn't even have a law office, but he was the only lawyer that would touch the case, because Bubba's daddy was such a big deal. And we all gathered in the judge's chambers—because he wasn't about to let this case get out. Can you imagine, if it had? And Mama's old lawyer told the judge how Bubba's daddy had tried to buy him off. And Bubba got up and swore he'd never touched me. And then I got up and said Mama was insane. And do you know what? By that time it was true. Mama *was* insane. She had no mind left at all. They had given her shock treatments or something. . . . God knows what else they gave her. But she was as vacant as an empty eye socket. She just sat sort of hunched over, and her hair was white.

"And after all this, Bubba wanted us to keep going together. Mama was just an obstacle that he felt he had removed. But I just suddenly—in a way I don't even pretend to understand—woke up. It was like everything up to then had been some kind of dream. And I told him I wanted to get Mama out. But he wouldn't do it; he just kept trying to make me go with him. And sometimes—out of habit, I guess—I did. My body did what it was being paid to do. And Mama died. And I killed Bubba.

"How did I get away with killing one of the biggest lawyers in the state? It was easy. He kept a gun in his desk drawer at the office and one night I took it out and shot him. I shot him while he was wearing his thick winter overcoat, so I wouldn't have to see him bleed. But I don't think I took the time to wipe off my fingerprints, because, to tell the truth, I couldn't stand it another minute in that place. No one came after me, and I read in the paper the next day that he'd been killed by burglars. I guess they thought 'burglars' had stolen all that money Bubba kept in his safe—but I had it. One of the carrots Bubba always dangled before me was that he was going to send me to college: I didn't see why he shouldn't do it.

"The strangest thing was, Bubba's wife came over to the house and asked me if I'd mind looking after the children while she went to Bubba's funeral. I did it, of course, because I was afraid she'd suspect something if I didn't. So on the day he was buried I was in his house, sitting on his wife's bed with his children, and eating fried chicken his wife, Julie, had cooked."

Questions

1. Why is the story in quotation marks? Do the quotation marks indicate the relationship between the author and the narrator?
2. What are the narrator's feelings for her mother? Are her feelings consistent?
3. What are the narrator's feelings for Bubba?
4. Why does the narrator tell her mother that Bubba loves her? What difference does his love make to the narrator? To the mother? To Bubba?
5. What is the significance of Bubba's father's racism?
6. Why does the narrator kill Bubba? Does she feel remorse for the murder? Does Bubba feel any remorse for raping the narrator?
7. Why isn't the narrator prosecuted for the murder?
8. Are the narrator's actions justified? Are there any innocent people in the story?

8  Symbols

The American essayist and poet Ralph Waldo Emerson once wrote, "We are symbols, and inhabit symbols." And, indeed, one difficulty in talking about symbolism is that all things soon turn into symbols. They dominate our lives. Consider for a moment how you are dressed. Out of many possible styles, you have chosen one that suits you. But your choice was not based merely on keeping your body warm. The shirt you wear may have an alligator or a number on it. These are symbols of a manufacturer and an athletic team. But they also symbolize social types: the preppy and the jock. Picture in your mind the clothing of a banker, a nun, a cook, and a judge. Is what they wear simply necessary for their work—like a construction worker's hard hat—or are their clothes chosen for their symbolic value? From a practical point of view, judges might be more comfortable in a T-shirt and shorts than in heavy, dark robes. Yet their attire is chosen out of respect for tradition and for the dignity of the judicial system. Their attire is a symbol of their high authority.

A *symbol*, then, is any object or action which refers to more than itself. The apple in your refrigerator is simply a fruit. Place it, however, with a snake, and it symbolizes forbidden knowledge and the source of man's first disobedience. Placed beside a piece of chalk and a stack of books, it becomes symbolic of the student's affection and respect for a teacher. The apple is, therefore, an ordinary object that can be charged with additional significance. And when it is charged with additional significance, it becomes a symbol.

The apple example makes several things clear about symbols.

1. It is the context in which objects and actions appear that usually lends them symbolic significance.
2. The same object can have different symbolic meanings depending upon its context.
3. Almost anything can be given symbolic meaning.

Traditional Symbols

Some objects and actions are so firmly established as symbols that they rarely, if ever, lose their symbolic significance. Religious symbols are among the most common traditional symbols. The cross, the dove, the olive branch, a crown of thorns—these objects seldom appear without religious significance. Conceivably, a dove might appear in a bird-watcher's manual as just another species. But such a context is the exception. Most often the dove will symbolize either peace or the Holy Spirit. It will not be merely a bird.

Representative Symbols

Frequently we choose one action or object to symbolize an entire group of similar or related objects and actions. For example, in Bobbie Ann Mason's story "Shiloh," Leroy's log cabin represents, at least in part, the pioneer past and his desire to return to it. A log cabin, of course, is only one of the many items associated with the American frontier, but in the story it comes to represent, or symbolize, the entire way of pioneer life. Such symbolic practices happen outside literature. Perhaps a teacher has picked one student from your class to represent the class at an assembly. That student symbolizes your class. Again, judges may sentence a particular individual to an unusually harsh punishment in order to use that person as "an example." The individual comes then to symbolize the court's concern, as a warning to similar offenders. In general, we may say that when something is set aside as an example, it also symbolizes the group from which it comes.

Levels of Symbolic Meaning

The first level is the literal level—what the symbol actually is. Thus on the literal level Shiloh is a battlefield in northern Mississippi. However it has other levels of meaning and association. In the Bible, Shiloh was the place where the Ark of the Covenant was kept before the Philistines captured and removed it. Thus Shiloh symbolizes a sacred place related to a pact, such as the marriage pact. In the story Mabel associates Shiloh with her honeymoon; for her, Shiloh symbolizes love and the consummation of her marriage. Historically, Shiloh was a turning point in the Civil War. It thus can stand for any turning point of a battle, such as a turning point in the battle between Leroy and Norma Jean. As you can see, Shiloh is rich with symbolic associations, of which we have stated only a few possibilities. Though we talk of these symbolic levels separately, they appear simultaneously in the story and, consequently, with great force and economy. The concentrated force of symbols is, in fact, their greatest artistic attraction. Simply by setting the story in Shiloh, Mason has evoked an entire series of concepts, associations, and emotions simply, effectively, and powerfully.

Reading Symbols

Since symbols are everywhere, a natural tendency is to read everything symbolically. Careful readers will refrain, however, from reading for symbols until the text invites such a reading. When are we offered such an invitation? How does the author cue us to his or her symbolic intentions? Here are some particular hints:

1. Authors usually focus on their symbols by placing them in key locations in the narrative. The bridegroom fails to reappear at the end for Granny Weatherall. His absence is at a key moment in the story and suggests its significance.
2. Authors frequently repeat the symbolic action or object. Shiloh is mentioned throughout the story and gives the story its name.
3. Symbols are frequently odd or supernatural. In the two stories that follow, the talking bird and the fallen angel call attention to their symbolic nature by being "unrealistic." Indeed, fairy tales, science fiction, and fantasy stories usually have a great number of symbols, since the characters, actions, and objects function beyond the *literal level*. Dreamlike stories often employ a succession of symbolic figures and actions.
4. Descriptions of clothing and setting frequently contain symbolic significance.

In interpreting a symbol, one should never be arbitrary. Remember, the number of traditional symbols is small, and only traditional symbols carry their meaning wherever they go. All other symbols gain their meaning through their context. So one must never ascribe a symbolic meaning that is at variance with, or even unsupported by, the context of the story. Finally, one must remember that symbols usually have various levels of meaning. It is not enough to pin one single meaning to a symbol. One must be prepared to recognize the whole range of significance a symbol can have, to invite and entertain the wealth and power of meaning that fiction can give the simplest objects and gestures.

Suggestions for Essayists

1. Discuss the traditional symbolic meanings of each of the following:
   1. an eagle   4. white
   2. a serpent   5. fire
   3. blue   6. the moon
2. Describe the objects to which you are most attached. What do they represent or symbolize for you?

Suggestions for Fiction Writers

1. Suggest a character by the sorts of things that character might keep in his or her car.
2. Place a traditional symbol in a scene in which it comes to represent just the opposite of its usual meaning. For example, place a rose in a scene in such a way that it represents ugliness and hate.

BERNARD MALAMUD (1914–)

The Jewbird

The window was open so the skinny bird flew in. Flappity-flap with its frazzled black wings. That's how it goes. It's open, you're in. Closed, you're out and that's your fate. The bird wearily flapped through the open kitchen window of Harry Cohen's top-floor apartment on First Avenue near the lower East River.[1] On a rod on the wall hung an escaped canary cage, its door wide open, but this black-type longbeaked bird—its ruffled head and small dull eyes, crossed a little, making it look like a dissipated crow—landed if not smack on Cohen's thick lamb chop, at least on the table, close by. The frozen foods salesman was sitting at supper with his wife and young son on a hot August evening a year ago. Cohen, a heavy man with hairy chest and beefy shorts; Edie, in skinny yellow shorts and red halter; and their ten-year-old Morris (after his father)—Maurie, they called him, a nice kid though not overly bright—were all in the city after two weeks out, because Cohen's mother was dying. They had been enjoying Kingston, New York, but drove back when Mama got sick in her flat in the Bronx.[2]

"Right on the table," said Cohen, putting down his beer glass and swatting at the bird. "Son of a bitch."

"Harry, take care with your language," Edie said, looking at Maurie, who watched every move.

The bird cawed hoarsely and with a flap of its bedraggled wings—feathers tufted this way and that—rose heavily to the top of the open kitchen door, where it perched staring down.

"Gevalt, a pogrom!"[3]

"It's a talking bird," said Edie in astonishment.

"In Jewish," said Maurie.

"Wise guy," muttered Cohen. He gnawed on his chop, then put down the bone. "So if you can talk, say what's your business. What do you want here?"

"If you can't spare a lamb chop," said the bird, "I'll settle for a piece of herring with a crust of bread. You can't live on your nerve forever."

---

[1] A section of New York City called the Lower East Side. This was a poor Jewish neighborhood.
[2] Kingston is a resort town in the Catskill Mountains. The Bronx is the northernmost borough of New York City.
[3] A pogrom is an organized slaughter of a minority group, especially Jews. Gevalt is a Yiddish exclamation of woe.

"This ain't a restaurant," Cohen replied. "All I'm asking is what brings you to this address?"

"The window was open," the bird sighed; adding after a moment, "I'm running. I'm flying but I'm also running."

"From whom?" asked Edie with interest.

"Anti-Semeets."

"Anti-Semites?" they all said.

"That's from who."

"What kind of anti-Semites bother a bird?" Edie asked.

"Any kind," said the bird, "also including eagles, vultures, and hawks. And once in a while some crows will take your eyes out."

"But aren't you a crow?"

"Me? I'm a Jewbird."

Cohen laughed heartily. "What do you mean by that?"

The bird began dovening. He prayed without Book or tallith,[4] but with passion. Edie bowed her head though not Cohen. And Maurie rocked back and forth with the prayer, looking up with one wide-open eye.

When the prayer was done Cohen remarked, "No hat, no phylacteries?"[5]

"I'm an old radical."

"You're sure you're not some kind of a ghost or dybbuk?"[6]

"Not a dybbuk," answered the bird, "though one of my relatives had such an experience once. It's all over now, thanks God. They freed her from a former lover, a crazy jealous man. She's now the mother of two wonderful children."

"Birds?" Cohen asked slyly.

"Why not?"

"What kind of birds?"

"Like me. Jewbirds."

Cohen tipped back in his chair and guffawed. "That's a big laugh. I've heard of a Jewfish but not a Jewbird."

"We're once removed." The bird rested on one skinny leg, then on the other. "Please, could you spare maybe a piece of herring with a small crust of bread?"

Edie got up from the table.

"What are you doing?" Cohen asked her.

"I'll clear the dishes."

Cohen turned to the bird. "So what's your name, if you don't mind saying?"

"Call me Schwartz."[7]

"He might be an old Jew changed into a bird by somebody," said Edie, removing a plate.

"Are you?" asked Harry, lighting a cigar.

"Who knows?" answered Schwartz. "Does God tell us everything?"

---

[4] Dovening is praying, especially softly and to oneself. A tallith is a prayer shawl.

[5] Phylacteries are leather-covered boxes containing scriptural passages that are worn on the left arm and forehead during prayers.

[6] A dybbuk is an evil spirit.

[7] Schwartz is German for "black," an appropriate name for a blackbird.

Maurie got up on his chair. "What kind of herring?" he asked the bird in excitement.

"Get down, Maurie, or you'll fall," ordered Cohen.

"If you haven't got matjes, I'll take schmaltz,"[8] said Schwartz.

"All we have is marinated, with slices of onion—in a jar," said Edie.

"If you'll open for me the jar I'll eat marinated. Do you have also, if you don't mind, a piece of rye bread—the spitz?"[9]

Edie thought she had.

"Feed him out on the balcony," Cohen said. He spoke to the bird. "After that take off."

Schwartz closed both bird eyes. "I'm tired and it's a long way."

"Which direction are you headed, north or south?"

Schwartz, barely lifting his wings, shrugged.

"You don't know where you're going?"

"Where there's charity I'll go."

"Let him stay, papa," said Maurie. "He's only a bird."

"So stay the night," Cohen said, "but no longer."

In the morning Cohen ordered the bird out of the house but Maurie cried, so Schwartz stayed for a while. Maurie was still on vacation from school and his friends were away. He was lonely and Edie enjoyed the fun he had, playing with the bird.

"He's no trouble at all," she told Cohen, "and besides his appetite is very small."

"What'll you do when he makes dirty?"

"He flies across the street in a tree when he makes dirty, and if nobody passes below, who notices?"

"So all right," said Cohen, "but I'm dead set against it. I warn you he ain't gonna stay here long."

"What have you got against the poor bird?"

"Poor bird, my ass. He's a foxy bastard. He thinks he's a Jew."

"What difference does it make what he thinks?"

"A Jewbird, what chutzpah.[10] One false move and he's out on his drumsticks."

At Cohen's insistence Schwartz lived out on the balcony in a new wooden birdhouse Edie had bought him.

"With many thanks," said Schwartz, "though I would rather have a human roof over my head. You know how it is at my age. I like the warm, the windows, the smell of cooking. I would also be glad to see once in a while the *Jewish Morning Journal* and have now and then a schnapps[11] because it helps my breathing, thanks God. But whatever you give me, you won't hear complaints."

---

[8] Matjes is a better sort of herring; schmaltz herring is cheaper and greasier.
[9] The spitz is the heel of a bread loaf.
[10] Chutzpah is Yiddish for "pushiness."
[11] Schnapps is a strong liquor.

However, when Cohen brought home a bird feeder full of dried corn, Schwartz said, "Impossible."

Cohen was annoyed. "What's the matter, crosseyes, is your life getting too good for you? Are you forgetting what it means to be migratory? I'll bet a helluva lot of crows you happen to be acquainted with, Jews or otherwise, would give their eyeteeth to eat this corn."

Schwartz did not answer. What can you say to a grubber yung?[12]

"Not for my digestion," he later explained to Edie. "Cramps. Herring is better even if it makes you thirsty. At least rainwater don't cost anything." He laughed sadly in breathy caws.

And herring, thanks to Edie, who knew where to shop, was what Schwartz got, with an occasional piece of potato pancake, and even a bit of soupmeat when Cohen wasn't looking.

When school began in September, before Cohen would once again suggest giving the bird the boot, Edie prevailed on him to wait a little while until Maurie adjusted.

"To deprive him right now might hurt his school work, and you know what trouble we had last year."

"So okay, but sooner or later the bird goes. That I promise you."

Schwartz, though nobody had asked him, took on full responsibility for Maurie's performance in school. In return for favors granted, when he was let in for an hour or two at night, he spent most of his time overseeing the boy's lessons. He sat on top of the dresser near Maurie's desk as he laboriously wrote out his homework. Maurie was a restless type and Schwartz gently kept him to his studies. He also listened to him practice his screechy violin, taking a few minutes off now and then to rest his ears in the bathroom. And they afterwards played dominoes. The boy was an indifferent checker player and it was impossible to teach him chess. When he was sick, Schwartz read him comic books though he personally disliked them. But Maurie's work improved in school and even his violin teacher admitted his playing was better. Edie gave Schwartz credit for these improvements though the bird pooh-poohed them.

Yet he was proud there was nothing lower than C minuses on Maurie's report card, and on Edie's insistence celebrated with a little schnapps.

"If he keeps up like this," Cohen said, "I'll get him in an Ivy League college for sure."

"Oh I hope so," sighed Edie.

But Schwartz shook his head. "He's a good boy—you don't have to worry. He won't be a shicker[13] or a wifebeater, God forbid, but a scholar he'll never be, if you know what I mean, although maybe a good mechanic. It's no disgrace in these times."

"If I were you," Cohen said, angered, "I'd keep my big snoot out of other people's private business."

---

[12] Grubber yung is Yiddish for "moocher."
[13] A shicker is a drunkard.

"Harry, please," said Edie.

"My goddamn patience is wearing out. That crosseyes butts into everything."

Though he wasn't exactly a welcome guest in the house, Schwartz gained a few ounces although he did not improve in appearance. He looked bedraggled as ever, his feathers unkempt, as though he had just flown out of a snowstorm. He spent, he admitted, little time taking care of himself. Too much to think about. "Also outside plumbing," he told Edie. Still there was more glow to his eyes so that though Cohen went on calling him crosseyes he said it less emphatically.

Liking his situation, Schwartz tried tactfully to stay out of Cohen's way, but one night when Edie was at the movies and Maurie was taking a hot shower, the frozen foods salesman began a quarrel with the bird.

"For Christ sake, why don't you wash yourself sometimes? Why must you always stink like a dead fish?"

"Mr. Cohen, if you'll pardon me, if somebody eats garlic he will smell from garlic. I eat herring three times a day. Feed me flowers and I will smell like flowers."

"Who's obligated to feed you anything at all? You're lucky to get herring."

"Excuse me, I'm not complaining," said the bird. "You're complaining."

"What's more," said Cohen, "even from out on the balcony I can hear you snoring away like a pig. It keeps me awake at night."

"Snoring," said Schwartz, "isn't a crime, thanks God."

"All in all you are a goddamn pest and free loader. Next thing you'll want to sleep in bed next to my wife."

"Mr. Cohen," said Schwartz, "on this rest assured. A bird is a bird."

"So you say, but how do I know you're a bird and not some kind of a goddamn devil?"

"If I was a devil you would know already. And I don't mean because your son's good marks."

"Shut up, you bastard bird," shouted Cohen.

"Grubber yung," cawed Schwartz, rising to the tips of his talons, his long wings outstretched.

Cohen was about to lunge for the bird's scrawny neck but Maurie came out of the bathroom, and for the rest of the evening until Schwartz's bedtime on the balcony, there was pretended peace.

But the quarrel had deeply disturbed Schwartz and he slept badly. His snoring woke him, and awake, he was fearful of what would become of him. Wanting to stay out of Cohen's way, he kept to the birdhouse as much as possible. Cramped by it, he paced back and forth on the balcony ledge, or sat on the birdhouse roof, staring into space. In the evenings, while overseeing Maurie's lessons, he often fell asleep. Awakening, he nervously hopped around exploring the four corners of the room. He spent much time in Maurie's closet, and carefully examined his bureau drawers when they were left open. And once when he found a large paper bag on the floor, Schwartz poked his way into it to investigate what possibilities were. The boy was amused to see the bird in the paper bag.

"He wants to build a nest," he said to his mother.

Edie, sensing Schwartz's unhappiness, spoke to him quietly.

"Maybe if you did some of the things my husband wants you, you would get along better with him."

"Give me a for instance," Schwartz said.

"Like take a bath, for instance."

"I'm too old for baths," said the bird. "My feathers fall out without baths."

"He says you have a bad smell."

"Everybody smells. Some people smell because of their thoughts or because who they are. My bad smell comes from the food I eat. What does his come from?"

"I better not ask him or it might make him mad," said Edie.

In late November Schwartz froze on the balcony in the fog and cold, and especially on rainy days he woke with stiff joints and could barely move his wings. Already he felt twinges of rheumatism. He would have liked to spend more time in the warm house, particularly when Maurie was in school and Cohen at work. But though Edie was good-hearted and might have sneaked him in in the morning, just to thaw out, he was afraid to ask her. In the meantime Cohen, who had been reading articles about the migration of birds, came out on the balcony one night after work when Edie was in the kitchen preparing pot roast, and peeking into the birdhouse, warned Schwartz to be on his way soon if he knew what was good for him. "Time to hit the flyways."

"Mr. Cohen, why do you hate me so much?" asked the bird. "What did I do to you?"

"Because you're an A-number-one trouble maker, that's why. What's more, whoever heard of a Jewbird! Now scat or it's open war."

But Schwartz stubbornly refused to depart so Cohen embarked on a campaign of harassing him, meanwhile hiding it from Edie and Maurie. Maurie hated violence and Cohen didn't want to leave a bad impression. He thought maybe if he played dirty tricks on the bird he would fly off without being physically kicked out. The vacation was over, let him make his easy living off the fat of somebody else's land. Cohen worried about the effect of the bird's departure on Maurie's schooling but decided to take the chance, first, because the boy now seemed to have the knack of studying—give the black bird-bastard credit—and second, because Schwartz was driving him bats by being there always, even in his dreams.

The frozen foods salesman began his campaign against the bird by mixing watery cat food with the herring slices in Schwartz's dish. He also blew up and popped numerous paper bags outside the birdhouse as the bird slept, and when he had got Schwartz good and nervous, though not enough to leave, he brought a full-grown cat into the house, supposedly a gift for little Maurie, who had always wanted a pussy. The cat never stopped springing up at Schwartz whenever he saw him, one day managing to claw out several of his tailfeathers. And even at lesson time, when the cat was usually excluded from Maurie's room, though somehow or other he quickly found his way in at the end of the lesson, Schwartz was desperately fearful of his life and flew from pinnacle to pinnacle—light fixture to clothes-tree to door-top—in order to elude the beast's wet jaws.

Once when the bird complained to Edie how hazardous his existence was, she said, "Be patient, Mr. Schwartz. When the cat gets to know you better he won't try to catch you any more."

"When he stops trying we will both be in Paradise," Schwartz answered. "Do me a favor and get rid of him. He makes my whole life worry. I'm losing feathers like a tree loses leaves."

"I'm awfully sorry but Maurie likes the pussy and sleeps with it."

What could Schwartz do? He worried but came to no decision, being afraid to leave. So he ate the herring garnished with cat food, tried hard not to hear the paper bags bursting like fire crackers outside the birdhouse at night, and lived terror-stricken closer to the ceiling than the floor, as the cat, his tail flicking, endlessly watched him.

Weeks went by. Then on the day after Cohen's mother had died in her flat in the Bronx, when Maurie came home with a zero on an arithmetic test, Cohen, enraged, waited until Edie had taken the boy to his violin lesson, then openly attacked the bird. He chased him with a broom on the balcony and Schwartz frantically flew back and forth, finally escaping into his birdhouse. Cohen triumphantly reached in, and grabbing both skinny legs, dragged the bird out, cawing loudly, his wings wildly beating. He whirled the bird around and around his head. But Schwartz, as he moved in circles, managed to swoop down and catch Cohen's nose in his beak, and hung on for dear life. Cohen cried out in great pain, punched the bird with his fist, and tugging at his legs with all his might, pulled his nose free. Again he swung the yawking Schwartz around until the bird grew dizzy, then with a furious heave, flung him into the night. Schwartz sank like stone into the street. Cohen then tossed the birdhouse and feeder after him, listening at the ledge until they crashed on the sidewalk below. For a full hour, broom in hand, his heart palpitating and nose throbbing with pain, Cohen waited for Schwartz to return but the broken-hearted bird didn't.

That's the end of that dirty bastard, the salesman thought and went in. Edie and Maurie had come home.

"Look," said Cohen, pointing to his bloody nose swollen three times its normal size, "what that sonofabitchy bird did. It's a permanent scar."

"Where is he now?" Edie asked, frightened.

"I threw him out and he flew away. Good riddance."

Nobody said no, though Edie touched a handkerchief to her eyes and Maurie rapidly tried the nine times table and found he knew approximately half.

In the spring when the winter's snow had melted, the boy, moved by a memory, wandered in the neighborhood, looking for Schwartz. He found a dead black bird in a small lot near the river, his two wings broken, neck twisted, and both bird-eyes plucked clean.

"Who did it to you, Mr. Schwartz?" Maurie wept.

"Anti-Semeets," Edie said later.

Questions

1. What does the bird's color symbolize?
2. What are Cohen's reasons for hating the bird?
3. Is Edie right when she says that anti-Semites killed Schwartz?
4. What is the symbolic significance of Schwartz's refusal to migrate?
5. Jews have been called "the people of the book." In what ways does Schwartz fit that name?
6. Is there any significance to the location of the birdhouse on the balcony?
7. Is there symbolic significance to Cohen's job?

GABRIEL GARCÍA MÁRQUEZ (1928–)

A Very Old Man with Enormous Wings

On the third day of rain they had killed so many crabs inside the house that Pelayo had to cross his drenched courtyard and throw them into the sea, because the newborn child had a temperature all night and they thought it was due to the stench. The world had been sad since Tuesday. Sea and sky were a single ash-gray thing and the sands of the beach, which on March nights glimmered like powdered light, had become a stew of mud and rotten shellfish. The light was so weak at noon that when Pelayo was coming back to the house after throwing away the crabs, it was hard for him to see what it was that was moving and groaning in the rear of the courtyard. He had to go very close to see that it was an old man, a very old man, lying face down in the mud, who, in spite of his tremendous efforts, couldn't get up, impeded by his enormous wings.

Frightened by that nightmare, Pelayo ran to get Elisenda, his wife, who was putting compresses on the sick child, and he took her to the rear of the courtyard. They both looked at the fallen body with mute stupor. He was dressed like a ragpicker. There were only a few faded hairs left on his bald skull and very few teeth in his mouth, and his pitiful condition of a drenched great-grandfather had taken away any sense of grandeur he might have had. His huge buzzard wings, dirty and half-plucked, were forever entangled in the mud. They looked at him so long and so closely that Pelayo and Elisenda very soon overcame their surprise and in the end found him familiar. Then they dared speak to him, and he answered in an incomprehensible dialect with a strong sailor's voice. That was how they skipped over the inconvenience of the wings and quite intelligently concluded that he was a lonely castaway from some foreign ship wrecked by the storm. And yet, they called in a neighbor woman who knew everything about life and death to see him, and all she needed was one look to show them their mistake.

"He's an angel," she told them. "He must have been coming for the child, but the poor fellow is so old that the rain knocked him down."

On the following day everyone knew that a flesh-and-blood angel was held captive in Pelayo's house. Against the judgment of the wise neighbor woman,

Gabriel García Márquez (Wide World Photos, Inc.)

for whom angels in those times were the fugitive survivors of a celestial conspiracy, they did not have the heart to club him to death. Pelayo watched over him all afternoon from the kitchen, armed with his bailiff's club, and before going to bed he dragged him out of the mud and locked him up with the hens in the wire chicken coop. In the middle of the night, when the rain stopped, Pelayo and Elisenda were still killing crabs. A short time afterward the child woke up without a fever and with a desire to eat. Then they felt magnanimous and decided to put the angel on a raft with fresh water and provisions for three days and leave him to his fate on the high seas. But when they went out into the courtyard with the first light of dawn, they found the whole neighborhood in front of the chicken coop having fun with the angel, without the slightest reverence, tossing him things to eat through the openings in the wire as if he weren't a supernatural creature but a circus animal.

Father Gonzaga arrived before seven o'clock, alarmed at the strange news. By that time onlookers less frivolous than those at dawn had already arrived and they were making all kinds of conjectures concerning the captive's future. The simplest among them thought that he should be named mayor of the world. Others of sterner mind felt that he should be promoted to the rank of five-star general in order to win all wars. Some visionaries hoped that he could be put to stud in order to implant on earth a race of winged wise men who could take charge of the universe. But Father Gonzaga, before becoming a priest, had been a robust woodcutter. Standing by the wire, he reviewed his catechism in an instant and asked them to open the door so that he could take a close look at that pitiful man who looked more like a huge decrepit hen among the fascinated chickens. He was lying in a corner drying his open wings in the sunlight among the fruit peels and breakfast leftovers that the early risers had thrown him. Alien to the impertinences of the world, he only lifted his antiquarian eyes and murmered something in his dialect when Father Gonzaga went into the chicken coop and said good morning to him in Latin. The parish priest had his first suspicion of an imposter when he saw that he did not understand the language of God or know how to greet His ministers. Then he noticed that seen close up he was much too human: he had an unbearable smell of the outdoors, the back side of his wings was strewn with parasites and his main feathers had been mistreated by terrestrial winds, and nothing about him measured up to the proud dignity of angels. Then he came out of the chicken coop and in a brief sermon warned the curious against the risks of being ingenuous. He reminded them that the devil had the bad habit of making use of carnival tricks in order to confuse the unwary. He argued that if wings were not the essential element in determining the difference between a hawk and an airplane, they were even less so in the recognition of angels. Nevertheless, he promised to write a letter to his bishop so that the latter would write to his primate so that the latter would write to the Supreme Pontiff in order to get the final verdict from the highest courts.

His prudence fell on sterile hearts. The news of the captive angel spread with such rapidity that after a few hours the courtyard had the bustle of a marketplace and they had to call in troops with fixed bayonets to disperse the mob that was about to knock the house down. Elisenda, her spine all twisted from sweeping up so much marketplace trash, then got the idea of fencing in the yard and charging five cents admission to see the angel.

The curious came from far away. A traveling carnival arrived with a flying acrobat who buzzed over the crowd several times, but no one paid any attention to him because his wings were not those of an angel but, rather, those of a sidereal bat. The most unfortunate invalids on earth came in search of health: a poor woman who since childhood had been counting her heartbeats and had run out of numbers; a Portuguese man who couldn't sleep because the noise of the stars disturbed him; a sleepwalker who got up at night to undo the things he had done while awake; and many others with less serious ailments. In the midst of that shipwreck disorder that made the earth tremble, Pelayo and Elisenda were happy with fatigue, for in less than a week they had crammed their rooms with money and the line of pilgrims waiting their turn to enter still reached beyond the horizon.

The angel was the only one who took no part in his own act. He spent his time trying to get comfortable in his borrowed nest, befuddled by the hellish heat of the oil lamps and sacramental candles that had been placed along the wire. At first they tried to make him eat some mothballs, which, according to the wisdom of the wise neighbor woman, were the food prescribed for angels. But he turned them down, just as he turned down the papal lunches that the penitents brought him, and they never found out whether it was because he was an angel or because he was an old man that in the end he ate nothing but eggplant mush. His only supernatural virtue seemed to be patience. Especially during the first days, when the hens pecked at him, searching for the stellar parasites that proliferated in his wings, and the cripples pulled out feathers to touch their defective parts with, and even the most merciful threw stones at him, trying to get him to rise so they could see him standing. The only time they succeeded in arousing him was when they burned his side with an iron for branding steers, for he had been motionless for so many hours that they thought he was dead. He awoke with a start, ranting in his hermetic language and with tears in his eyes, and he flapped his wings a couple of times, which brought on a whirlwind of chicken dung and lunar dust and a gale of panic that did not seem to be of this world. Although many thought that his reaction had been one not of rage but of pain, from then on they were careful not to annoy him, because the majority understood that his passivity was not that of a hero taking his ease but that of a cataclysm in repose.

Father Gonzaga held back the crowd's frivolity with formulas of maidservant inspiration while awaiting the arrival of a final judgment on the nature of the captive. But the mail from Rome showed no sense of urgency. They spent their time finding out if the prisoner had a navel, if his dialect had any connection with Aramaic, how many times he could fit on the head of a pin, or whether he wasn't just a Norwegian with wings. Those meager letters might have come and gone until the end of time if a providential event had not put an end to the priest's tribulations.

It so happened that during those days, among so many other carnival attractions, there arrived in town the traveling show of the woman who had been changed into a spider for having disobeyed her parents. The admission to see her was not only less than the admission to see the angel, but people were permitted to ask her all manner of questions about her absurd state and to examine her up and down so that no one would ever doubt the truth of her horror. She was a frightful tarantula the size of a ram and with the head of a sad maiden. What was most heartrending, however, was not her outlandish shape but the sincere affliction with which she recounted the details of her misfortune. While still practically a child she had sneaked out of her parents' house to go to a dance, and while she was coming back through the woods after having danced all night without permission, a fearful thunderclap rent the sky in two and through the crack came the lightning bolt of brimstone that changed her into a spider. Her only nourishment came from the meatballs that charitable souls chose to toss into her mouth. A spectacle like that, full of so much human truth and with such a fearful lesson, was bound to defeat without even trying that of a haughty angel who scarcely deigned to look at mortals. Besides, the few miracles attributed to the angel showed a certain mental disorder, like the blind man who didn't recover his sight but grew three new teeth, or the paralytic who didn't get to walk but almost won the lottery, and the leper whose sores sprouted sunflowers. Those consolation miracles, which were more like mocking fun, had already ruined the angel's reputation when the woman who had been changed into a spider finally crushed him completely. That was how Father Gonzaga was cured forever of his insomnia and Pelayo's courtyard went back to being as empty as during the time it had rained for three days and crabs walked through the bedrooms.

The owners of the house had no reason to lament. With the money they saved they built a two-story mansion with balconies and gardens and high netting so that crabs wouldn't get in during the winter, and with iron bars on the windows so that angels wouldn't get in. Pelayo also set up a rabbit warren close to town and gave up his job as bailiff for good, and Elisenda bought some satin pumps with high heels and many dresses of iridescent silk, the kind worn on Sunday by the most desirable women in those times. The chicken coop was the only thing that didn't receive any attention. If they washed it down with creolin and burned tears of myrrh inside it every so often, it was not in homage to the angel but to drive away the dungheap stench that still hung everywhere like a ghost and was turning the new house into an old one. At first, when the child learned to walk, they were careful that he not get too close to the chicken coop. But then they began to lose their fears and got used to the smell, and before the child got his second teeth he'd gone inside the chicken coop to play, where the wires were falling apart. The angel was no less standoffish with him than with other mortals, but he tolerated the most ingenious infamies with the patience of a dog who had no illusions. They both came down with chicken pox at the same time. The doctor who took care of the child couldn't resist the temptation to listen to the angel's heart, and he found so much whistling in the heart and so many sounds in his kidneys that it seemed impossible for him to be alive. What surprised him most, however, was the logic of his wings. They seemed so natural on that completely human organism that he couldn't understand why other men didn't have them too.

When the child began school it had been some time since the sun and rain had caused the collapse of the chicken coop. The angel went dragging himself about here and there like a stray dying man. They would drive him out of the bedroom with a broom and a moment later find him in the kitchen. He seemed to be in so many places at the same time that they grew to think that he'd been duplicated, that he was reproducing himself all through the house, and the exasperated and unhinged Elisenda shouted that it was awful living in that hell full of angels. He could scarcely eat and his antiquarian eyes had also become so foggy that he went about bumping into posts. All he had left were the bare cannulae[1] of his last feathers. Pelayo threw a blanket over him and extended him the charity of letting him sleep in the shed, and only then did they notice that he had a temperature at night, and was delirious with the tongue twisters of an old Norwegian. That was one of the few times they became alarmed, for they thought he was going to die and not even the wise neighbor woman had been able to tell them what to do with dead angels.

And yet he not only survived his worst winter, but seemed improved with the first sunny days. He remained motionless for several days in the farthest corner

---

[1] Cannulae are the reedlike shafts of feathers.

of the courtyard, where no one would see him, and at the beginning of December some large, stiff feathers began to grow on his wings, the feathers of a scarecrow, which looked more like another misfortune of decrepitude. But he must have known the reason for those changes, for he was quite careful that no one should notice them, that no one should hear the sea chanteys that he sometimes sang under the stars. One morning Elisenda was cutting some bunches of onions for lunch when a wind that seemed to come from the high seas blew into the kitchen. Then she went to the window and caught the angel in his first attempts at flight. They were so clumsy that his fingernails opened a furrow in the vegetable patch and he was on the point of knocking the shed down with the ungainly flapping that slipped on the light and couldn't get a grip on the air. But he did manage to gain altitude. Elisenda let out a sigh of relief, for herself and for him, when she saw him pass over the last houses, holding himself up in some way with the risky flapping of a senile vulture. She kept watching him even when she was through cutting onions and she kept on watching until it was no longer possible for her to see him, because then he was no longer an annoyance in her life but an imaginary dot on the horizon of the sea.

Questions

1. The winged man represents a number of ideas, conditions, or qualities. What are they?
2. Is there any significance to the three days of rain?
3. How do people respond to the winged man? Is their response appropriate? How should one respond to a winged person?
4. What is the significance of the church's response to the man with wings?
5. Why does the spider woman lure the crowds away from the man with wings? What does her attraction say about human curiosity and attention?
6. Why does Elisenda lose her annoyance once the winged man becomes "an imaginary dot on the horizon of the sea"? What does her response say about the human capacity to respond to the unusual or miraculous?

9 🌿 Other Worlds, Other Times—Science Fiction

Science fiction is among the most popular kinds, or *genres*, of storytelling. In the last few decades a number of serious writers and critics have turned their attention to science fiction, and today the best science fiction enjoys a respectability it never before possessed.

Science fiction is a narrative written in response to technological or scientific discoveries. Sometimes it employs scientific knowledge to explain narrative events. For example, Mary Shelley used what was known about magnetism to explain features of Frankenstein's monster. Science fiction also depicts future discoveries and adventures. We do not yet have rockets that can take us to other solar systems, but in "The Star" (Chapter 1) Arthur C. Clarke imagines such an invention. Some science fiction explores concepts of space and time.

However, we must not confuse science fiction with realistic fiction that details the effects of current technology. For example, a realistic story could relate how toxic waste creates birth defects. A science fiction story, however, might tell about a race of people mutated by toxic waste. Science fiction speculates rather than reports. It moves from the known to the unknown. It deals with other worlds and other times.

We often think of science fiction as a relatively recent literary phenomenon. Actually, the imaginations of writers have been spurred from the beginnings of science. During the Age of Discovery writers were fascinated by the possibilities of new, as yet unknown islands and civilizations, just as contemporary writers are curious about life on other planets or in other solar systems. Early writers asked themselves, "What can we learn from a creature whose society has been developed separately from our own?" Sir Thomas More's *Utopia* (1516) is drawn in part from accounts of the new world by Amerigo Vespucci and Pietro Martin d'Anghiera, and in its day was as much a work of science fiction as Arthur C. Clarke's "The Star." Shakespeare's play *The Tempest* (1611?) is based on another account of the new world and contains such figures as Caliban, the half-human son of a devil and a witch and Ariel, a spirit with supernatural powers. Clearly science fiction has a long and distinguished history.

It is important to realize that there is not just one sort of science fiction, but a number of different science fictions. We will consider three of the more sophisticated types: (1) the romance, (2) the satire, and (3) the utopian or dystopian story.

Romance

The noted critic Northrop Frye explains how we can distinguish a romance from other forms of fiction. The hero of a romance is "superior in *degree* from other men and his environment." The hero of a romance is either stronger, braver, kinder, wiser, or handsomer than other people. According to Northrop Frye,

> The hero of romance moves in a world in which the ordinary laws of nature are slightly suspended: prodigies of courage and endurance, unnatural to us, are natural to him, and enchanted weapons, talking animals, terrifying ogres and witches, and talismans of miraculous power violate no rule of probability once the postulates of romance have been established.[1]

In short, anything can happen in romance as long as it follows the narrative rules.

The plots of a romance are frequently simple in design. The hero, who is typically a king, knight, or warrior sets off in search of some person or object. This quest takes the hero—or heroine—through a series of adventures in which the main character may encounter both obstacles and helpers in achieving his or her goal. Thus, in J.R.R. Tolkien's "Lord of the Rings" there is a search for a magic ring. In the legends of King Arthur, knights search for the Holy Grail. In *Star Wars* and *Star Trek*, the space inhabitants fight off forces of evil.

Romance and science fiction are highly compatible. Set in the far future or in the distant past, science fiction stories can recount all sorts of supernatural occurrences as the products of presently unknown discoveries. Space travel affords the writer exotic and dangerous locales and the possibility of larger-than-life adventure.

Satire

If the hero of romance is better than other people, the protagonist of satire is often stingier, angrier, bossier, or more foolish than others. In satire the author attacks the folly and vices of the human race by exaggerating these characteristics. However, satire should be distinguished from *invective*. Invective is characterized by humorless abuse and insult. We use invective when we call a person "a fool,

---

[1] Northrop Frye, *The Anatomy of Criticism: Four Essays* (Princeton, N.J.: Princeton University Press, 1957), p. 33.

a liar, a cheat." But such an attack is not at all funny. Satire makes fun of faults and foolishness.

Science fiction gives the satirist a perspective from which to attack human folly, a way to exaggerate normal human faults. Ray Bradbury's "There Will Come Soft Rains" contains moments of satire. Indeed, much of the story satirizes the American obsession with labor-saving devices and suburban comfort. Here, for example, is what happens at 2:35 P.M. on August 4, 2026:

> Bridge tables sprouted from patio walls. Playing cards fluttered onto pads in a shower of pips. Martinis manifested on an oaken bench with egg-salad sandwiches. Music played.
> But the tables were silent and the cards untouched.
> At four o'clock the tables folded like great butterflies back through the paneled walls.

This passage humorously portrays how Americans institutionalize their pleasure. Although there is no one left alive, the house still is programmed to have a bridge party at 2:35. Various party accessories pop up out of nowhere right on cue. The house continues to function, blind to the horrible realities around it. We will miss a great deal of the pleasure this story can provide if we fail to understand its satiric elements.

Ursula Le Guin also takes satiric pleasure in attacking the names advertisers give their medical products. Her narrator explains "I had never seen aspirin before, only the Super-Buffered Pane-Gon and the Triple-Power N-L-G-Zic and the Extra-Strength Apansprin with the miracle ingredient more doctors recommend." Le Guin laughs at our need to puff products with advertising gimmicks.

Science fiction is frequently satiric. It provides the two elements Northrop Frye claims are "essential to satire; one is wit or humor founded on fantasy or a sense of the grotesque or absurd, the other is an object of attack." Science fiction provides the fantasy world of the future or the far past through which one can satirize the present. But we should remember that the best satire is meant as constructive criticism and not as wholesale condemnation. As Jonathan Swift, the author of *Gulliver's Travels* and one of the great satirists of English literature, wrote about himself:

> His satire points at no defect,
> But what all mortals may correct.

The satirist hopes that by laughing at our errors we can best correct them.

A work does not have to be wholly satiric. Satire frequently occurs as part of a larger framework and as a response to specific satiric targets.

Utopian and Anti-Utopian Visions

Utopian literature describes society as it might be. Such literature takes its name from Sir Thomas More's *Utopia*, a work which recounts the imaginary traveler Raphael Hythloday's visit to an unknown society. "Utopia" is Greek for "nowhere." Thomas More's "nowhere" is a country in which people work together, use their discoveries for the common good, and cooperate for the general improvement of women and men.

But not all imaginary societies are as ideal as More's. Like all human creations, scientific knowledge can be a force for evil as well as for good. Many writers, like Aldous Huxley in *Brave New World* or George Orwell in *1984*, have envisioned the horror of future technological society. Such writings have been called *anti-utopian* or *dystopian*, works that describe not a better, but a more frightening society.

Writers are attracted to both utopian and anti-utopian stories because they offer an opportunity to discuss politics as well as science. For example, Ursula K. Le Guin's "The New Atlantis" concerns the need for creating a more efficient way of tapping solar energy. But it also considers corporate responses to revolutionary scientific discoveries that might alter profitable markets. "The New Atlantis," then, deals as much with political economy as with solar energy.

While reading a utopian or an anti-utopian story, one should especially consider: (1) how the imaginary world compares with the real world, and (2) what in the real world could give rise to conditions described in the imaginary one.

Utopian literature is a mixture of the romance and the satire. By presenting a world better than the present, the utopian author gives us a magic world filled with larger-than-life characters. The villains of such a world often satirize the folly and vices of the human race.

Suggestions for Essayists

1. Discuss how science has altered your life in comparison with that of your parents or grandparents. Is this a change for the better?
2. Discuss whether science can solve or help solve the important problems the world faces.
3. Discuss whether there can be a Utopia.

Suggestions for Fiction Writers

1. Upon waking this morning, you found yourself mysteriously transported to the year 2026. You look around. Describe what you see.
2. You have been given permission by the president of the United States to set up an independent colony on the Planet X, which has an atmosphere and vegetation much like that of Earth. How do you arrange your Utopia? How do you choose the people to join your colony?

RAY BRADBURY (1920–)

There Will Come Soft Rains

In the living room the voice-clock sang, *Tick-tock, seven o'clock, time to get up, time to get up, seven o'clock!* as if it were afraid that nobody would. The morning house lay empty. The clock ticked on, repeating and repeating its sounds into the emptiness. *Seven-nine, breakfast time, seven-nine!*

In the kitchen the breakfast stove gave a hissing sigh and ejected from its warm interior eight pieces of perfectly browned toast, eight eggs sunnyside up, sixteen slices of bacon, two coffees, and two cool glasses of milk.

"Today is August 4, 2026," said a second voice from the kitchen ceiling, "in the city of Allendale, California." It repeated the date three times for memory's sake. "Today is Mr. Featherstone's birthday. Today is the anniversary of Tilita's marriage. Insurance is payable, as are the water, gas, and light bills."

Somewhere in the walls, relays clicked, memory tapes glided under electric eyes.

Eight-one, tick-tock, eight-one o'clock, off to school, off to work, run, run, eight-one! But no doors slammed, no carpets took the soft tread of rubber heels. It was raining outside. The weather box on the front door sang quietly: "Rain, rain, go away; rubbers, raincoats for today . . . " And the rain tapped on the empty house, echoing.

Outside, the garage chimed and lifted its door to reveal the waiting car. After a long wait the door swung down again.

At eight-thirty the eggs were shriveled and the toast was like stone. An aluminum wedge scraped them into the sink, where hot water whirled them down a metal throat which digested and flushed them away to the distant sea. The dirty dishes were dropped into a hot washer and emerged twinkling dry.

Nine-fifteen, sang the clock, *time to clean.*

Out of warrens in the wall, tiny robot mice darted. The rooms were acrawl with the small cleaning animals, all rubber and metal. They thudded against chairs, whirling their mustached runners, kneading the rug nap, sucking gently at hidden dust. Then, like mysterious invaders, they popped into their burrows. Their pink electric eyes faded. The house was clean.

Ten o'clock. The sun came out from behind the rain. The house stood alone in a city of rubble and ashes. This was the one house left standing. At night the ruined city gave off a radioactive glow which could be seen for miles.

Ten-fifteen. The garden sprinklers whirled up in golden founts, filling the soft morning air with scatterings of brightness. The water pelted windowpanes, running down the charred west side where the house had been burned evenly free of its white paint. The entire west face of the house was black, save for five places. Here the silhouette in paint of a man mowing a lawn. Here, as in a photograph, a woman bent to pick flowers. Still farther over, their images burned on wood in one titanic instant, a small boy, hands flung into the air; higher up, the image of a thrown ball, and opposite him a girl, hands raised to catch a ball which never came down.

The five spots of paint—the man, the woman, the children, the ball—remained. The rest was a thin charcoaled layer.

The gentle sprinkler rain filled the garden with falling light.

Until this day, how well the house had kept its peace. How carefully it had inquired, "Who goes there? What's the password?" and, getting no answer from lonely foxes and whining cats, it had shut up its windows and drawn shades in an old-maidenly preoccupation with self-protection which bordered on a mechanical paranoia.

It quivered at each sound, the house did. If a sparrow brushed a window, the shade snapped up. The bird, startled, flew off! No, not even a bird must touch the house!

The house was an altar with ten thousand attendants, big, small, servicing, attending, in choirs. But the gods had gone away, and the ritual of the religion continued senselessly, uselessly.

Twelve noon.

A dog whined, shivering, on the front porch.

The front door recognized the dog voice and opened. The dog, once huge and fleshy, but now gone to bone and covered with sores, moved in and through the house, tracking mud. Behind it whirred angry mice, angry at having to pick up mud, angry at inconvenience.

For not a leaf fragment blew under the door but what the wall panels flipped open and the copper scrap rats flashed swiftly out. The offending dust, hair, or paper, seized in miniature steel jaws, was raced back to the burrows. There, down tubes which fed into the cellar, it was dropped into the sighing vent of an incinerator which sat like evil Baal[1] in a dark corner.

The dog ran upstairs, hysterically yelping to each door, at last realizing, as the house realized, that only silence was here.

It sniffed the air and scratched the kitchen door. Behind the door, the stove was making pancakes which filled the house with a rich baked odor and the scent of maple syrup.

The dog frothed at the mouth, lying at the door, sniffing, its eyes turned to fire. It ran wildly in circles, biting at its tail, spun in a frenzy, and died. It lay in the parlor for an hour.

Two o'clock, sang a voice.

Delicately sensing decay at last, the regiments of mice hummed out as softly as blown gray leaves in an electrical wind.

Two-fifteen.

The dog was gone.

In the cellar, the incinerator glowed suddenly and a whirl of sparks leaped up the chimney.

Two thirty-five.

Bridge tables sprouted from patio walls. Playing cards fluttered onto pads in a shower of pips. Martinis manifested on an oaken bench with egg-salad sandwiches. Music played.

But the tables were silent and the cards untouched.

At four o'clock the tables folded like great butterflies back through the paneled walls.

Four-thirty.

The nursery walls glowed.

---

[1] Baal, a general name for all the ancient Syrian gods, can designate any false god or idol.

Animals took shape: yellow giraffes, blue lions, pink antelopes, lilac panthers cavorting in crystal substance. The walls were glass. They looked out upon color and fantasy. Hidden films clocked through well-oiled sprockets, and the walls lived. The nursery floor was woven to resemble a crisp, cereal meadow. Over this ran aluminum roaches and iron crickets, and in the hot still air butterflies of delicate red tissue wavered among the sharp aroma of animal spoors! There was the sound like a great matted yellow hive of bees within a dark bellows, the lazy bumble of a purring lion. And there was the patter of okapi[2] feet and the murmur of a fresh jungle rain, like other hoofs, falling upon the summer-starched grass. Now the walls dissolved into distances of parched weed, mile on mile, and warm endless sky. The animals drew away into thorn brakes and water holes.

It was the children's hour.

Five o'clock. The bath filled with clear hot water.

Six, seven, eight o'clock. The dinner dishes manipulated like magic tricks, and in the study a *click*. In the metal stand opposite the hearth where a fire now blazed up warmly, a cigar popped out, half an inch of soft gray ash on it, smoking, waiting.

Nine o'clock. The beds warmed their hidden circuits, for nights were cool here.

Nine-five. A voice spoke from the study ceiling:

"Mrs. McClellan, which poem would you like this evening?"

The house was silent.

The voice said at last, "Since you express no preference, I shall select a poem at random." Quiet music rose to back the voice. "Sara Teasdale.[3] As I recall, your favorite. . . .

"There will come soft rains and the smell of the ground,
And swallows circling with their shimmering sound;

And frogs in the pools singing at night,
And wild plum trees in tremulous white;

Robins will wear their feathery fire,
Whistling their whims on a low fence-wire;

And not one will know of the war, not one
Will care at last when it is done.

Not one would mind, neither bird nor tree,
If mankind perished utterly;

And Spring herself, when she woke at dawn
Would scarcely know that we were gone."

---

[2] An okapi is a giraffe-like animal, first discovered at the turn of the century in the Congo jungles of Africa.
[3] Sara Teasdale (1884–1933) was an American poet known for her highly personal lyrics. She committed suicide at the age of 48.

The fire burned on the stone hearth and the cigar fell away into a mound of quiet ash on its tray. The empty chairs faced each other between the silent walls, and the music played.

At ten o'clock the house began to die.

The wind blew. A falling tree bough crashed through the kitchen window. Cleaning solvent, bottled, shattered over the stove. The room was ablaze in an instant!

"Fire!" screamed a voice. The house lights flashed, water pumps shot water from the ceilings. But the solvent spread on the linoleum, licking, eating, under the kitchen door, while the voices took it up in chorus: "Fire, fire, fire!"

The house tried to save itself. Doors sprang tightly shut, but the windows were broken by the heat and the wind blew and sucked upon the fire.

The house gave ground as the fire in ten billion angry sparks moved with flaming ease from room to room and then up the stairs. While scurrying water rats squeaked from the walls, pistoled their water, and ran for more. And the wall sprays let down showers of mechanical rain.

But too late. Somewhere, sighing, a pump shrugged to a stop. The quenching rain ceased. The reserve water supply which had filled baths and washed dishes for many quiet days was gone.

The fire crackled up the stairs. It fed upon Picassos and Matisses[4] in the upper halls, like delicacies, baking off the oily flesh, tenderly crisping the canvases into black shavings.

Now the fire lay in beds, stood in windows, changed the colors of drapes!

And then, reinforcements.

From attic trapdoors, blind robot faces peered down with faucet mouths gushing green chemical.

The fire backed off, as even an elephant must at the sight of a dead snake. Now there were twenty snakes whipping over the floor, killing the fire with a clear cold venom of green froth.

But the fire was clever. It had sent flame outside the house, up through the attic to the pumps there. An explosion! The attic brain which directed the pumps was shattered into bronze shrapnel on the beams.

The fire rushed back into every closet and felt of the clothes hung there.

The house shuddered, oak bone on bone, its bared skeleton cringing from the heat, its wire, its nerves revealed as if a surgeon had torn the skin off to let the red veins and capillaries quiver in the scalded air. Help, help! Fire! Run, run! Heat snapped mirrors like the first brittle winter ice. And the voices wailed Fire, fire, run, run, like a tragic nursery rhyme, a dozen voices, high, low, like children dying in a forest, alone, alone. And the voices fading as the wires popped their sheathings like hot chestnuts. One, two, three, four, five voices died.

---

[4] Pablo Picasso (1881–1973) and Henri Matisse (1869–1954) are two of the greatest twentieth-century artists.

In the nursery the jungle burned. Blue lions roared, purple giraffes bounded off. The panthers ran in circles, changing color, and ten million animals, running before the fire, vanished off toward a distant steaming river. . . .

Ten more voices died. In the last instant under the fire avalanche, other choruses, oblivious, could be heard announcing the time, playing music, cutting the lawn by remote-control mower, or setting an umbrella frantically out and in the slamming and opening front door, a thousand things happening, like a clock shop when each clock strikes the hour insanely before or after the other, a scene of maniac confusion, yet unity; singing, screaming, a few last cleaning mice darting bravely out to carry the horrid ashes away! And one voice, with sublime disregard for the situation, read poetry aloud in the fiery study, until all the film spools burned, until all the wires withered and the circuits cracked.

The fire burst the house and let it slam flat down, puffing out skirts of spark and smoke.

In the kitchen, an instant before the rain of fire and timber, the stove could be seen making breakfasts at a psychopathic rate, ten dozen eggs, six loaves of toast, twenty dozen bacon strips, which, eaten by fire, started the stove working again, hysterically hissing!

The crash. The attic smashing into kitchen and parlor. The parlor into cellar, cellar into sub-cellar. Deep freeze, armchair, film tapes, circuits, beds, and all like skeletons thrown in a cluttered mound deep under.

Smoke and silence. A great quantity of smoke.

Dawn showed faintly in the east. Among the ruins, one wall stood alone. Within the wall, a last voice said, over and over again and again, even as the sun rose to shine upon the heaped rubble and steam:

"Today is August 5, 2026, today is August 5, 2026, today is . . . "

Questions

1. How is the house "an altar"?
2. Is the Teasdale poem a fitting work to be read?
3. In what ways is the jungle scene in the nursery ironic?
4. How is the American obsession with hygiene satirized in this story?
5. How is the American obsession with labor-saving appliances satirized?

URSULA K. LE GUIN (1929–)

The New Atlantis[1]

Coming back from my Wilderness Week I sat by an odd sort of man in the bus. For a long time we didn't talk; I was mending stockings and he was reading. Then the bus broke down a few miles outside Gresham. Boiler trouble, the way it generally is when the driver insists on trying to go over thirty. It was a Supersonic

---

[1] Atlantis is a legendary island that is said to have sunk in the Atlantic Ocean off the coast of Spain.

Superscenic Deluxe Longdistance coal-burner, with Home Comfort, that means a toilet, and the seats were pretty comfortable, at least those that hadn't yet worked loose from their bolts, so everybody waited inside the bus; besides, it was raining. We began talking, the way people do when there's a breakdown and a wait. He held up his pamphlet and tapped it—he was a dry-looking man with a school-teacherish way of using his hands—and said, "This is interesting. I've been reading that a new continent is rising from the depths of the sea."

The blue stockings were hopeless. You have to have something besides holes to darn onto. "Which sea?"

"They're not sure yet. Most specialists think the Atlantic. But there's evidence it may be happening in the Pacific, too."

"Won't the oceans get a little crowded?" I said, not taking it seriously. I was a bit snappish, because of the breakdown and because those blue stockings had been good warm ones.

He tapped the pamphlet again and shook his head, quite serious. "No," he said. "The old continents are sinking, to make room for the new. You can see that that is happening."

You certainly can. Manhattan Island is now under eleven feet of water at low tide, and there are oyster beds in Ghirardelli Square.[2]

"I thought that was because the oceans are rising from polar melt."

He shook his head again. "That is a factor. Due to the greenhouse effect of pollution, indeed Antarctica may become inhabitable. But climatic factors will not explain the emergence of the new—or, possibly, very old—continents in the Atlantic and Pacific." He went on explaining about continental drift, but I liked the idea of inhabiting Antarctica and daydreamed about it for a while. I thought of it as very empty, very quiet, all white and blue, with a faint golden glow northward from the unrising sun behind the long peak of Mount Erebus.[3] There were a few people there; they were very quiet, too, and wore white tie and tails. Some of them carried oboes and violas. Southward the white land went up in a long silence toward the Pole.

Just the opposite, in fact, of the Mount Hood Wilderness Area.[4] It had been a tiresome vacation. The other women in the dormitory were all right, but it was macaroni for breakfast, and there were so many organized sports. I had looked forward to the hike up to the National Forest Preserve, the largest forest left in the United States, but the trees didn't look at all the way they do in the postcards and brochures and Federal Beautification Bureau advertisements. They were spindly, and they all had little signs on saying which union they had been planted by. There were actually a lot more green picnic tables and cement Men's and Women's than there were trees. There was an electrified fence all around the forest to keep out unauthorized persons. The forest ranger talked about mountain jays, "bold little robbers," he said, "who will come and snatch the sandwich from your very hand," but I didn't see any. Perhaps because that was

---

[2] Ghirardelli Square is a fashionable shopping area in San Francisco.
[3] Mt. Erebus is a peak in Antarctica.
[4] Mt. Hood is the tallest peak in Oregon.

the weekly Watch Those Surplus Calories! Day for all the women, and so we didn't have any sandwiches. If I'd seen a mountain jay I might have snatched the sandwich from his very hand, who knows. Anyhow it was an exhausting week, and I wished I'd stayed home and practiced, even though I'd have lost a week's pay because staying home and practicing the viola doesn't count as planned implementation of recreational leisure as defined by the Federal Union of Unions.

When I came back from my Antarctican expedition, the man was reading again, and I got a look at his pamphlet; and that was the odd part of it. The pamphlet was called "Increasing Efficiency in Public Accountant Training Schools," and I could see from the one paragraph I got a glance at that there was nothing about new continents emerging from the ocean depths in it—nothing at all.

Then we had to get out and walk on into Gresham, because they had decided that the best thing for us all to do was get onto the Greater Portland Area Rapid Public Transit Lines, since there had been so many breakdowns that the charter bus company didn't have any more buses to send out to pick us up. The walk was wet, and rather dull, except when we passed the Cold Mountain Commune. They have a wall around it to keep out unauthorized persons, and a big neon sign out front saying COLD MOUNTAIN COMMUNE and there were some people in authentic jeans and ponchos by the highway selling macramé belts and sandcast candles and soybean bread to the tourists. In Gresham, I took the 4:40 GPARPTL Superjet Flyer train to Burnside and East 230th, and then walked to 217th and got the bus to the Goldschmidt Overpass, and transferred to the shuttlebus, but it had boiler trouble, so I didn't reach the downtown transfer point until ten after eight, and the buses go on a once-an-hour schedule at eight o'clock, so I got a meatless hamburger at the Longhorn Inch-Thick Steak House Dinerette and caught the nine o'clock bus and got home about ten. When I let myself into the apartment I flipped the switch to turn on the lights, but there still weren't any. There had been a power outage in West Portland for three weeks. So I went feeling about for the candles in the dark, and it was a minute or so before I noticed that somebody was lying on my bed.

I panicked, and tried again to turn the lights on.

It was a man, lying there in a long thin heap. I thought a burglar had got in somehow while I was away and died. I opened the door so I could get out quick or at least my yells could be heard, and then I managed not to shake long enough to strike a match, and lighted the candle, and came a little closer to the bed.

The light disturbed him. He made a sort of snorting in his throat and turned his head. I saw it was a stranger, but I knew his eyebrows, then the breadth of his closed eyelids, then I saw my husband.

He woke up while I was standing there over him with the candle in my hand. He laughed and said still half-asleep, "Ah, Psyche! From the regions which are holy land."[5]

---

[5] Psyche is the goddess in Greek mythology associated with the soul. In Roman mythology she marries Cupid. The line is from Edgar Allan Poe's "To Helen."

Neither of us made much fuss. It was unexpected, but it did seem so natural for him to be there, after all, much more natural than for him not to be there, and he was too tired to be very emotional. We lay there together in the dark, and he explained that they had released him from the Rehabilitation Camp early because he had injured his back in an accident in the gravel quarry, and they were afraid it might get worse. If he died there it wouldn't be good publicity abroad, since there have been some nasty rumors about deaths from illness in the Rehabilitation Camps and the Federal Medical Association Hospitals; and there are scientists abroad who have heard of Simon, since somebody published his proof of Goldbach's Hypothesis in Peking. So they let him out early, with eight dollars in his pocket, which is what he had in his pocket when they arrested him, which made it, of course, fair. He had walked and hitched home from Cour D'Alene, Idaho, with a couple of days in jail in Walla Walla[6] for being caught hitch-hiking. He almost fell asleep telling me this, and when he had told me, he did fall asleep. He needed a change of clothes and a bath but I didn't want to wake him. Besides, I was tired, too. We lay side by side and his head was on my arm. I don't suppose that I have ever been so happy. No; was it happiness? Something wider and darker, more like knowledge, more like the night: joy.

It was dark for so long, so very long. We were all blind. And there was the cold, a vast, unmoving, heavy cold. We could not move at all. We did not move. We did not speak. Our mouths were closed, pressed shut by the cold and by the weight. Our eyes were pressed shut. Our limbs were held still. Our minds were held still. For how long? There was no length of time; how long is death? And is one dead only after living, or before life as well? Certainly we thought, if we thought anything, that we were dead; but if we had ever been alive, we had forgotten it.

There was a change. It must have been the pressure that changed first, although we did not know it. The eyelids are sensitive to touch. They must have been weary of being shut. When the pressure upon them weakened a little, they opened. But there was no way for us to know that. It was too cold for us to feel anything. There was nothing to be seen. There was black.

But then—"then," for the event created time, created before and after, near and far, now and then—"then" there was the light. One light. One small, strange light that passed slowly, at what distance we could not tell. A small, greenish white, slightly blurred point of radiance, passing.

Our eyes were certainly open, "then," for we saw it. We saw the moment. The moment is a point of light. Whether in darkness or in the field of all light, the moment is small, and moves, but not quickly. And "then" it is gone.

It did not occur to us that there might be another moment. There was no reason to assume that there might be more than one. One was marvel enough: that in all the field of the dark, in the cold, heavy, dense, moveless, timeless, placeless,

---

[6] Walla Walla is a city in Washington State known for its penitentiary.

boundless black, there should have occurred, once, a small slightly blurred, moving light! Time need be created only once, we thought.

But we were mistaken. The difference between one and more than one is all the difference in the world. Indeed, that difference is the world.

The light returned.

The same light, or another one? There was no telling.

But, "this time," we wondered about the light: Was it small and near to us, or large and far away? Again there was no telling; but there was something about the way it moved, a trace of hesitation, a tentative quality, that did not seem proper to anything large and remote. The stars, for instance. We began to remember the stars.

The stars had never hesitated.

Perhaps the noble certainty of their gait had been a mere effect of distance. Perhaps in fact they had hurtled wildly, enormous furnace-fragments of a primal bomb thrown through the cosmic dark; but time and distance soften all agony. If the universe, as seems likely, began with an act of destruction, the stars we had used to see told no tales of it. They had been implacably serene.

The planets, however . . . We began to remember the planets. They had suffered certain changes both of appearance and of course. At certain times of the year Mars would reverse its direction and go backward through the stars. Venus had been brighter and less bright as she went through her phases of crescent, full, and wane. Mercury had shuddered like a skidding drop of rain on the sky flushed with daybreak. The light we now watched had that erratic, trembling quality. We saw it, unmistakably, change direction and go backward. It then grew smaller and fainter; blinked—an eclipse?—and slowly disappeared.

Slowly, but not slowly enough for a planet.

Then—the third "then"!—arrived the indubitable and positive Wonder of the World, the Magic Trick, watch now, watch, you will not believe your eyes, mama, mama, look what I can do—

Seven lights in a row, proceeding fairly rapidly, with a darting movement, from left to right. Proceeding less rapidly from right to left, two dimmer, greenish lights. Two-lights halt, blink, reverse course, proceed hastily and in a wavering manner from left to right. Seven-lights increase speed, and catch up. Two-lights flash desperately, flicker, and are gone.

Seven-lights hang still for some while, then merge gradually into one streak, veering away, and little by little vanish into the immensity of the dark.

But in the dark now are growing other lights, many of them: lamps, dots, rows, scintillations—some near at hand, some far. Like the stars, yes, but not stars. It is not the great Existences we are seeing, but only the little lives.

In the morning Simon told me something about the Camp, but not until after he had had me check the apartment for bugs. I thought at first he had been given behavior mod and gone paranoid. We never had been infested. And I'd been living alone for a year and a half; surely they didn't want to hear me talking to myself? But he said, "They may have been expecting me to come here."

"But they let you go free!"

He just lay there and laughed at me. So I checked everywhere we could think of. I didn't find any bugs, but it did look as if somebody had gone through the bureau drawers while I was away in the Wilderness. Simon's papers were all at Max's so that didn't matter. I made tea on the Primus,[7] and washed and shaved Simon with the extra hot water in the kettle—he had a thick beard and wanted to get rid of it because of the lice he had brought from Camp—and while we were doing that he told me about the Camp. In fact he told me very little, but not much was necessary.

He had lost about twenty pounds. As he only weighed 140 to start with, this left little to go on with. His knees and wrist bones stuck out like rocks under the skin. His feet were all swollen and chewed-looking from the Camp boots; he hadn't dared take the boots off, the last three days of walking, because he was afraid he wouldn't be able to get them back on. When he had to move or sit up so I could wash him, he shut his eyes.

"Am I really here?" he asked. "Am I here?"

"Yes," I said. "You are here. What I don't understand is how you got here."

"Oh, it wasn't bad so long as I kept moving. All you need is to know where you're going—to have someplace to go. You know, some of the people in Camp, if they'd let them go, they wouldn't have had that. They couldn't have gone anywhere. Keeping moving was the main thing. See, my back's all seized up, now."

When he had to get up to go to the bathroom he moved like a ninety-year-old. He couldn't stand straight, but was all bent out of shape, and shuffled. I helped him put on clean clothes. When he lay down on the bed again, a sound of pain came out of him, like tearing thick paper. I went around the room putting things away. He asked me to come sit by him and said I was going to drown him if I went on crying. "You'll submerge the entire North American continent," he said. I can't remember what he said, but he made me laugh finally. It is hard to remember things Simon says, and hard not to laugh when he says them. This is not merely the partiality of affection: He makes everybody laugh. I doubt that he intends to. It is just that a mathematician's mind works differently from other people's. Then when they laugh, that pleases him.

It was strange, and it is strange, to be thinking about "him," the man I have known for ten years, the same man, while "he" lay there changed out of recognition, a different man. It is enough to make you understand why most languages have a word like "soul." There are various degrees of death, and time spares us none of them. Yet something endures, for which a word is needed.

I said what I had not been able to say for a year and a half: "I was afraid they'd brainwash you." He said, "Behavior mod is expensive. Even just the drugs. They save it mostly for the VIPs. But I'm afraid they got a notion I might be important after all. I got questioned a lot the last couple of months. About my 'foreign contacts.' " He snorted. "The stuff that got published abroad, I

---

[7] A primus is a portable stove.

suppose. So I want to be careful and make sure it's just a Camp again next time, and not a Federal Hospital."

"Simon, were they . . . are they cruel, or just righteous?"

He did not answer for a while. He did not want to answer. He knew what I was asking. He knew by what thread hangs hope, the sword, above our heads.

"Some of them . . . " he said at last, mumbling.

Some of them had been cruel. Some of them had enjoyed their work. You cannot blame everything on society.

"Prisoners, as well as guards," he said.

You cannot blame everything on the enemy.

"Some of them, Belle," he said with energy, touching my hand, "some of them, there were men like gold there—"

The thread is tough; you cannot cut it with one stroke.

"What have you been playing?" he asked.

"Forrest, Schubert."[8]

"With the quartet?"

"Trio, now. Janet went to Oakland with a new lover."

"Ah, poor Max."

"It's just as well, really. She isn't a good pianist."

I make Simon laugh, too, though I don't intend to. We talked until it was past time for me to go to work. My shift since the Full Employment Act last year is ten to two. I am an inspector in a recycled paper bag factory. I have never rejected a bag yet; the electronic inspector catches all the defective ones first. It is a rather depressing job. But it's only four hours a day, and it takes more time than that to go through all the lines and physical and mental examinations, and fill out all the forms, and talk to all the welfare counselors and inspectors every week in order to qualify as Unemployed, and then line up every day for the ration stamps and the dole. Simon thought I ought to go to work as usual. I tried to, but I couldn't. He had felt very hot to the touch when I kissed him good-bye. I went instead and got a black-market doctor. A girl at the factory had recommended her, for an abortion, if I ever wanted one without going through the regulation two years of sex-depressant drugs the fed-meds make you take when they give you an abortion. She was a jeweler's assistant in a shop on Alder Street, and the girl said she was convenient because if you didn't have enough cash you could leave something in pawn at the jeweler's as payment. Nobody ever does have enough cash, and of course credit cards aren't worth much on the black market.

The doctor was willing to come at once, so we rode home on the bus together. She gathered very soon that Simon and I were married, and it was funny to see her look at us and smile like a cat. Some people love illegality for its own sake. Men, more often than women. It's men who make laws, and enforce them, and

---

[8] Franz Schubert (1797–1828) was an Austrian composer admired for his symphonic, chamber, and vocal works. Forrest is an imaginary composer. According to Le Guin, the invention of the name is "an old science fiction trick for reinforcing the sense of being a few decades in the future."

break them, and think the whole performance is wonderful. Most women would rather just ignore them. You could see that this woman, like a man, actually enjoyed breaking them. That may have been what put her into an illegal business in the first place, a preference for the shady side. But there was more to it than that. No doubt she'd wanted to be a doctor, too; and the Federal Medical Association doesn't admit women in the medical schools. She probably got her training as some other doctor's private pupil, under the counter. Very much as Simon learned mathematics, since the universities don't teach much but Business Administration and Advertising and Media Skills anymore. However she learned it, she seemed to know her stuff. She fixed up a kind of homemade traction device for Simon very handily and informed him that if he did much more walking for two months he'd be crippled the rest of his life, but if he behaved himself he'd just be more or less lame. It isn't the kind of thing you'd expect to be grateful for being told, but we both were. Leaving, she gave me a bottle of about two hundred plain white pills, unlabeled. "Aspirin," she said. "He'll be in a good deal of pain off and on for weeks."

I looked at the bottle. I had never seen aspirin before, only the Super-Buffered Pane-Gon and the Triple-Power N-L-G-Zic and the Extra-Strength Apansprin with the miracle ingredient more doctors recommend, which the fed-meds always give you prescriptions for, to be filled at your FMA-approved private enterprise friendly drugstore at the low, low prices established by the Pure Food and Drug Administration in order to inspire competitive research.

"Aspirin," the doctor repeated. "The miracle ingredient more doctors recommend." She cat-grinned again. I think she liked us because we were living in sin. That bottle of black-market aspirin was probably worth more than the old Navajo bracelet I pawned for her fee.

I went out again to register Simon as temporarily domiciled at my address and to apply for Temporary Unemployment Compensation ration stamps for him. They only give them to you for two weeks and you have to come every day; but to register him as Temporarily Disabled meant getting the signatures of two fed-meds, and I thought I'd rather put that off for a while. It took three hours to go through the lines and get the forms he would have to fill out, and to answer the 'crats[9] questions about why he wasn't there in person. They smelled something fishy. Of course it's hard for them to prove that two people are married and aren't just adultering if you move now and then and your friends help out by sometimes registering one of you as living at their address; but they had all the back files on both of us and it was obvious that we had been around each other for a suspiciously long time. The State really does make things awfully hard for itself. It must have been simpler to enforce the laws back when marriage was legal and adultery was what got you into trouble. They only had to catch you once. But I'll bet people broke the law just as often then as they do now.

---

[9] 'Crats is short for "bureaucrats" or government workers. A Fed-med is apparently a government doctor or health worker.

The lantern-creatures came close enough at last that we could see not only their light, but their bodies in the illumination of their light. They were not pretty. They were dark colored, most often a dark red, and they were all mouth. They ate one another whole. Light swallowed light, all swallowed together in the vaster mouth of the darkness. They moved slowly, for nothing, however small and hungry, could move fast under that weight, in that cold. Their eyes, round with fear, were never closed. Their bodies were tiny and bony behind the gaping jaws. They wore queer, ugly decorations on their lips and skulls: fringes, serrated wattles, featherlike fronds, gauds, bangles, lures. Poor little sheep of the deep pastures! Poor ragged, hunchjawed dwarfs squeezed to the bone by the weight of the darkness, chilled to the bone by the cold of the darkness, tiny monsters burning with bright hunger, who brought us back to life!

Occasionally, in the wan, sparse illumination of one of the lantern-creatures, we caught a momentary glimpse of other, large, unmoving shapes: the barest suggestion, off in the distance, not of a wall, nothing so solid and certain as a wall, but of a surface, an angle . . . Was it there?

Or something would glitter, faint, far off, far down. There was no use trying to make out what it might be. Probably it was only a fleck of sediment, mud or mica, disturbed by a struggle between the lantern-creatures, flickering like a bit of diamond dust as it rose and settled slowly. In any case, we could not move to go see what it was. We had not even the cold, narrow freedom of the lantern-creatures. We were immobilized, borne down, still shadows among the half-guessed shadow walls. Were we there?

The lantern-creatures showed no awareness of us. They passed before us, among us, perhaps even through us—it was impossible to be sure. They were not afraid, or curious.

Once something a little larger than a hand came crawling near, and for a moment we saw quite distinctly the clean angle where the foot of a wall rose from the pavement, in the glow cast by the crawling creature, which was covered with a foliage of plumes, each plume dotted with many tiny, bluish points of light. We saw the pavement beneath the creature and the wall beside it, heartbreaking in its exact, clear linearity, its opposition to all that was fluid, random, vast, and void. We saw the creature's claws, slowly reaching out and retracting like small stiff fingers, touch the wall. Its plumage of light quivering, it dragged itself along and vanished behind the corner of the wall.

So we knew that the wall was there; and that it was an outer wall, a housefront, perhaps, or the side of one of the towers of the city.

We remembered the towers. We remembered the city. We had forgotten it. We had forgotten who we were; but we remembered the city, now.

When I got home, the FBI had already been there. The computer at the police precinct where I registered Simon's address must have flashed it right over to the computer at the FBI building. They had questioned Simon for about an hour, mostly about what he had been doing during the twelve days it took him to get from the Camp to Portland. I suppose they thought he had flown to Peking[10] or something. Having a police record in Walla Walla for hitchhiking helped him establish his story. He told me that one of them had gone to the bathroom. Sure enough I found a bug stuck on the top of the bathroom door-frame. I left it, as we figured it's really better to leave it when you know you have one, than to take it off and then never be sure they haven't planted another one you don't know about. As Simon said, if we felt we had to say something unpatriotic we could always flush the toilet at the same time.

I have a battery radio—there are so many work stoppages because of power failures, and days the water has to be boiled, and so on, that you really have to have a radio to save wasting time and dying of typhoid—and he turned it on while I was making supper on the Primus. The six o'clock All-American Broadcasting Company news announcer announced that peace was at hand in Uruguay, the president's confidential aide having been seen to smile at a passing blonde as he left the 613th day of the secret negotiations in a villa outside Katmandu. The war in Liberia[11] was going well; the enemy said they had shot down seventeen American planes but the Pentagon said we had shot down twenty-two enemy planes, and the capital city—I forget its name, but it hasn't been inhabitable for seven years anyway—was on the verge of being recaptured by the forces of freedom. The police action in Arizona was also successful. The Neo-Birch insurgents in Phoenix could not hold out much longer against the massed might of the American army and air force, since their underground supply of small tactical nukes from the Weathermen[12] in Los Angeles had been cut off. Then there was an advertisement for Fed-Cred cards, and a commercial for the Supreme Court: "Take your legal troubles to the Nine Wise Men!" Then there was something about why tariffs had gone up, and a report from the stock market, which had just closed at over two thousand, and a commercial for U.S. Government canned water, with a catchy little tune: "Don't be sorry when you drink/It's not as healthy as you think/Don't you think you really ought to/Drink coo-ool, puu-uure U.S.G. water?"—with three sopranos in close harmony on the last line. Then, just as the battery began to give out and his voice was dying away into a faraway tiny whisper, the announcer seemed to be saying something about a new continent emerging.

"What was that?"

"I didn't hear," Simon said, lying with his eyes shut and his face pale and sweaty. I gave him two aspirins before we ate. He ate little, and fell asleep while I was washing the dishes in the bathroom. I had been going to practice, but a viola is fairly wakeful in a one-room apartment. I read for a while instead. It was a best-seller Janet had given me when she left. She thought it was very

---

[10] Peking is the capital of the People's Republic of China.
[11] Liberia is a country on the western coast of Africa. Katmandu is the capital of Nepal, an Indian protectorate.
[12] The Weathermen was a revolutionary leftist group in the 1960s. The Neo-Birch insurgents are apparently a revival of the John Birch Society, an extreme rightist organization. Tactical nukes are tactical nuclear weapons, nuclear weapons to be used with conventional ground forces.

good, but then she likes Franz Liszt[13] too. I don't read much since the libraries were closed down, it's too hard to get books; all you can buy is best-sellers. I don't remember the title of this one, the cover just said "Ninety Million Copies in Print!!!" It was about small-town sex life in the last century, the dear old 1970s when there weren't any problems and life was so simple and nostalgic. The author squeezed all the naughty thrills he could out of the fact that all the main characters were married. I looked at the end and saw that all the married couples shot each other after all their children became schizophrenic hookers, except for one brave pair that divorced and then leapt into bed together with a clear-eyed pair of government-employed lovers for eight pages of healthy group sex as a brighter future dawned. I went to bed then, too. Simon was hot, but sleeping quietly. His breathing was like the sound of soft waves far away, and I went out to the dark sea on the sound of them.

I used to go out to the dark sea, often, as a child, falling asleep. I had almost forgotten it with my waking mind. As a child all I had to do was stretch out and think, "the dark sea . . . the dark sea . . ." and soon enough I'd be there, in the great depths, rocking. But after I grew up it only happened rarely, as a great gift. To know the abyss of the darkness and not to fear it, to entrust oneself to it and whatever may arise from it—what greater gift?

We watched the tiny lights come and go around us, and doing so, we gained a sense of space and of direction—near and far, at least, and higher and lower. It was that sense of space that allowed us to become aware of the currents. Space was no longer entirely still around us, suppressed by the enormous pressure of its own weight. Very dimly we were aware that the cold darkness moved, slowly, softly, pressing against us a little for a long time, then ceasing, in a vast oscillation. The empty darkness flowed slowly along our unmoving unseen bodies; along them, past them; perhaps through them; we could not tell.

Where did they come from, those dim, slow, vast tides? What pressure or attraction stirred the deeps to these slow drifting movements? We could not understand that; we could only feel their touch against us, but in straining our sense to guess their origin or end, we became aware of something else: something out there in the darkness of the great currents: sounds. We listened. We heard.

So our sense of space sharpened and localized to a sense of place. For sound is local, as sight is not. Sound is delimited by silence; and it does not rise out of the silence unless it is fairly close, both in space and in time. Though we stand where once the singer stood we cannot hear the voice singing; the years have carried it off on their tides, submerged it. Sound is a fragile thing, a tremor, as delicate as life itself. We may see the stars, but we cannot hear them. Even were the hollowness of outer space an atmosphere, an ether that transmitted the waves of sound, we could not hear the stars; they are too far away. At most if we listened

---

[13] Franz Liszt (1811–1886), famed pianist and composer, is noted for music full of spectacular technical effects—music that an admirer of Schubert might well find overelaborate.

we might hear our own sun, all the mighty, roiling, exploding storm of its burning, as a whisper at the edge of hearing.

A sea wave laps one's feet: It is the shock wave of a volcanic eruption on the far side of the world. But one hears nothing.

A red light flickers on the horizon: It is the reflection in smoke of a city on the distant mainland, burning. But one hears nothing.

Only on the slopes of the volcano, in the suburbs of the city, does one begin to hear the deep thunder, and the high voices crying.

Thus, when we became aware that we were hearing, we were sure that the sounds we heard were fairly close to us. And yet we may have been quite wrong. For we were in a strange place, a deep place. Sound travels fast and far in the deep places, and the silence there is perfect, letting the least noise be heard for hundreds of miles.

And these were not small noises. The lights were tiny, but the sounds were vast: not loud, but very large. Often they were below the range of hearing, long slow vibrations rather than sounds. The first we heard seemed to us to rise up through the currents from beneath us: immense groans, sighs felt along the bone, a rumbling, a deep uneasy whispering.

Later, certain sounds came down to us from above, or borne along the endless levels of the darkness, and these were stranger yet, for they were music. A huge calling, yearning music from far away in the darkness, calling not to us. Where are you? I am here.

Not to us.

They were the voices of the great souls, the great lives, the lonely ones, the voyagers. Calling. Not often answered. Where are you? Where have you gone?

But the bones, the keels and girders of white bones on icy isles of the South, the shores of bones did not reply.

Nor could we reply. But we listened, and the tears rose in our eyes, salt, not so salt as the oceans, the world-girdling deep bereaved currents, the abandoned roadways of the great lives; not so salt, but warmer.

I am here. Where have you gone?

No answer.

Only the whispering thunder from below.

But we knew now, though we could not answer, we knew because we heard, because we felt, because we wept, we knew that we were; and we remembered other voices.

Max came the next night. I sat on the toilet lid to practice, with the bathroom door shut. The FBI men on the other end of the bug got a solid half hour of scales and doublestops, and then a quite good performance of the Hindemith[14] unaccompanied viola sonata. The bathroom being very small and all hard sur-

---

[14] Paul Hindemith (1895–1963) was a German composer who fled Nazi Germany for the United States.

faces, the noise I made was really tremendous. Not a good sound, far too much echo, but the sheer volume was contagious, and I played louder as I went on. The man up above knocked on his floor once; but if I have to listen to the weekly All-American Olympic Games at full blast every Sunday morning from his TV set, then he has to accept Paul Hindemith coming up out of his toilet now and then.

When I got tired I put a wad of cotton over the bug, and came out of the bathroom half-deaf. Simon and Max were on fire. Burning, unconsumed. Simon was scribbling formulae in traction, and Max was pumping his elbows up and down the way he does, like a boxer, and saying "The e-lec-tron emis-sion . . ." through his nose, with his eyes narrowed, and his mind evidently going light-years per second faster than his tongue, because he kept beginning over and saying "The e-lec-tron emis-sion . . . " and pumping his elbows.

Intellectuals at work are very strange to look at. As strange as artists. I never could understand how an audience can sit there and look at a fiddler rolling his eyes and biting his tongue, or a horn player collecting spit, or a pianist like a black cat strapped to an electrified bench, as if what they *saw* had anything to do with the music.

I damped the fires with a quart of black-market beer—the legal kind is better, but I never have enough ration stamps for beer; I'm not thirsty enough to go without eating—and gradually Max and Simon cooled down. Max would have stayed talking all night, but I drove him out because Simon was looking tired.

I put a new battery in the radio and left it playing in the bathroom, and blew out the candle and lay and talked with Simon; he was too excited to sleep. He said that Max had solved the problems that were bothering them before Simon was sent to Camp, and had fitted Simon's equations to (as Simon put it) the bare facts, which means they have achieved "direct energy conversion." Ten or twelve people have worked on it at different times since Simon published the theoretical part of it when he was twenty-two. The physicist Ann Jones had pointed out right away that the simplest practical application of the theory would be to build a "sun tap," a device for collecting and storing solar energy, only much cheaper and better than the U.S.G. Sola-Heetas that some rich people have on their houses. And it would have been simple only they kept hitting the same snag. Now Max has got around the snag.

I said that Simon published the theory, but that is inaccurate. Of course he's never been able to publish any of his papers, in print; he's not a federal employee and doesn't have a government clearance. But it did get circulated in what the scientists and poets call Sammy's-dot[15] that is, just handwritten or hectographed. It's an old joke that the FBI arrests everybody with purple fingers, because they have either been hectographing Sammy's-dots, or they have impetigo.

Anyhow, Simon was on top of the mountain that night. His true joy is in the pure math; but he had been working with Clara and Max and the others in

---

[15] Sammy's-dot is a transliteration of Samizdat, an underground Soviet publication.

this effort to materialize the theory for ten years, and a taste of material victory is a good thing, once in a lifetime.

I asked him to explain what the sun tap would mean to the masses, with me as a representative mass. He explained that it means we can tap solar energy for power, using a device that's easier to build than a jar battery. The efficiency and storage capacity are such that about ten minutes of sunlight will power an apartment complex like ours, heat and lights and elevators and all, for twenty-four hours; and no pollution, particulate, thermal, or radioactive. "There isn't any danger of using up the sun?" I asked. He took it soberly—it was a stupid question, but after all not so long ago people thought there wasn't any danger of using up the earth—and said no, because we wouldn't be pulling out energy, as we did when we mined and lumbered and split atoms, but just using the energy that comes to us anyhow: as the plants, the trees and grass and rosebushes, always have done. "You could call it Flower Power,"[16] he said. He was high, high up on the mountain, skijumping in the sunlight.

"The State owns us," he said, "because the corporative State has a monopoly on power sources, and there's not enough power to go around. But now, anybody could build a generator on their roof that would furnish enough power to light a city."

I looked out the window at the dark city.

"We could completely decentralize industry and agriculture. Technology could serve life instead of serving capital. We could each run our own life. Power is power! . . . The State is a machine. We could unplug the machine, now. Power corrupts; absolute power corrupts absolutely.[17] But that's true only when there's a price on power. When groups can keep the power to themselves; when they can use physical power-to in order to exert spiritual power-over; when might makes right. But if power is free? If everybody is equally mighty? Then everybody's got to find a better way of showing that he's right. . . ."

"That's what Mr. Nobel[18] thought when he invented dynamite," I said. "Peace on earth."

He slid down the sunlit slope a couple of thousand feet and stopped beside me in a spray of snow, smiling. "Skull at the banquet," he said, "finger writing on the wall. Be still! Look, don't you see the sun shining on the Pentagon,[19] all the roofs are off, the sun shines at last into the corridors of power. . . . And they shrivel up, they wither away. The green grass grows through the carpets of the Oval Room, the Hot Line[20] is disconnected for nonpayment of the bill. The first thing we'll do is build an electrified fence outside the electrified fence around the White House. The inner one prevents unauthorized persons from getting in. The outer one will prevent authorized persons from getting out. . . ."

---

[16] Flower Power was a slogan of youthful peace activists in the 1960s.

[17] A paraphrase of the words of English historian Lord Acton (1834–1902).

[18] Alfred Nobel (1833–1896) established the Nobel peace prize, among others, from a fortune based largely upon his invention of dynamite.

[19] The Pentagon is the headquarters of the U.S. Defense Department.

[20] The Oval Room is the president's office, from which a Hot Line connects the president to the Soviet leadership.

Of course he was bitter. Not many people come out of prison sweet.

But it was cruel, to be shown this great hope, and to know that there was no hope for it. He did know that. He knew it right along. He knew that there was no mountain, that he was skiing on the wind.

The tiny lights of the lantern-creatures died out one by one, sank away. The distant lonely voices were silent. The cold, slow currents flowed, vacant, only shaken from time to time by a shifting in the abyss.

It was dark again, and no voice spoke. All dark, dumb, cold.

Then the sun rose.

It was not like the dawns we had begun to remember: the change, manifold and subtle, in the smell and touch of the air; the hush that, instead of sleeping, wakes, holds still, and waits; the appearance of objects, looking gray, vague, and new, as if just created—distant mountains against the eastern sky, one's own hands, the hoary grass full of dew and shadow, the fold in the edge of a curtain hanging by the window—and then, before one is quite sure that one is indeed seeing again, that the light has returned, that day is breaking, the first, abrupt, sweet stammer of a waking bird. And after that the chorus, voice by voice: This is my nest, this is my tree, this is my egg, this is my day, this is my life, here I am, here I am, hurray for me! I'm here!—No, it wasn't like that at all, this dawn. It was completely silent, and it was blue.

In the dawns that we had begun to remember, one did not become aware of the light itself, but of the separate objects touched by the light, the things, the world. They were there, visible again, as if visibility were their own property, not a gift from the rising sun.

In this dawn, there was nothing but the light itself. Indeed there was not even light, we would have said, but only color: blue.

There was no compass bearing to it. It was not brighter in the east. There was no east or west. There was only up and down, below and above. Below was dark. The blue light came from above. Brightness fell. Beneath, where the shaking thunder had stilled, the brightness died away through violet into blindness.

We, arising, watched light fall.

In a way it was more like an ethereal snowfall than like a sunrise. The light seemed to be in discrete particles, infinitesimal flecks, slowly descending, faint, fainter than flecks of fine snow on a dark night, and tinier; but blue. A soft, penetrating blue tending to the violet, the color of the shadows in an iceberg, the color of a streak of sky between gray clouds on a winter afternoon before snow: faint in intensity but vivid in hue: the color of the remote, the color of the cold, the color farthest from the sun.

On Saturday night they held a scientific congress in our room. Clara and Max came, of course, and the engineer Phil Drum and three others who had worked on the sun tap. Phil Drum was very pleased with himself because he had actually built one of the things, a solar cell, and brought it along. I don't think it had occurred to either Max or Simon to build one. Once they knew it could be done they were satisfied and wanted to get on with something else.

But Phil unwrapped his baby with a lot of flourish, and people made remarks like, "Mr. Watson, will you come here a minute," and "Hey, Wilbur, you're off the ground!" and "I say, nasty mould you've got there, Alec, why don't you throw it out?" and "Ugh, ugh, burns, burns, wow, ow,"[21] the latter from Max, who does look a little pre-Mousterian.[22] Phil explained that he had exposed the cell for one minute at four in the afternoon up in Washington Park during a light rain. The lights were back on on the West Side since Thursday, so we could test it without being conspicious.

We turned off the lights, after Phil had wired the table-lamp cord to the cell. He turned on the lamp switch. The bulb came on, about twice as bright as before, at its full forty watts—city power of course was never full strength. We all looked at it. It was a dime-store table lamp with a metallized gold base and a white plasticloth shade.

"Brighter than a thousand suns," Simon murmured from the bed.

"Could it be," said Clara Edmonds, "that we physicists have known sin[23]— and have come out the other side?"

"It really wouldn't be any good at all for making bombs with," Max said dreamily.

"Bombs," Phil Drum said with scorn. "Bombs are obsolete. Don't you realize that we could move a mountain with this kind of power? I mean pick up Mount Hood, move it, and set it down. We could thaw Antarctica, we could freeze the Congo. We could sink a continent. Give me a fulcrum and I'll move the world.[24] Well, Archimedes, you've got your fulcrum. The sun."

"Christ," Simon said, "the radio, Belle!"

The bathroom door was shut and I had put cotton over the bug, but he was right; if they were going to go ahead at this rate there had better be some added static. And though I liked watching their faces in the clear light of the lamp— they all had good, interesting faces, well worn, like the handles of wooden tools or the rocks in a running stream—I did not much want to listen to them talk tonight. Not because I wasn't a scientist, that made no difference. And not because I disagreed or disapproved or disbelieved anything they said. Only because it grieved me terribly, their talking. Because they couldn't rejoice aloud over a job done and a discovery made, but had to hide there and whisper about it. Because they couldn't go out into the sun.

---

[21] These are all jocular references to important discoveries and inventions. The first quotation refers to the first words Alexander Graham Bell (1847–1922) spoke over the telephone. The second refers to the Wright Brothers, who piloted the first heavier-than-air flying machine. The third refers to Sir Alexander Fleming (1881–1955), the discoverer of penicillin. The last is an apparent reference to the discovery of fire.

[22] The Mousterians were a Middle Paleolithic culture of France. Pre-Mousterian are those who came before them.

[23] A paraphrase of the words of J. Robert Oppenheimer (1904–1967), the American physicist who led the Manhattan Project that resulted in the atomic bomb, whose light was "brighter than a thousand suns." Oppenheimer, in a celebrated controversy, lost his security clearance.

[24] The words of Archimedes (287–212 B.C.), Greek mathematician.

I went into the bathroom with my viola and sat on the toilet lid and did a long set of sautillé exercises.[25] Then I tried to work at the Forrest trio, but it was too assertive. I played the solo part from *Harold in Italy*,[26] which is beautiful, but it wasn't quite the right mood either. They were still going strong in the other room. I began to improvise.

After a few minutes in E-minor the light over the shaving mirror began to flicker and dim; then it died. Another outage. The table lamp in the other room did not go out, being connected with the sun, not with the twenty-three atomic fission plants that power the Greater Portland Area. Within two seconds somebody had switched it off, too, so that we should't be the only window in the West Hills left alight; and I could hear them rooting for candles and rattling matches. I went on improvising in the dark. Without light, when you couldn't see all the hard shiny surfaces of things, the sound seemed softer and less muddled. I went on, and it began to shape up. All the laws of harmonics sang together when the bow came down. The strings of the viola were the cords of my own voice, tightened by sorrow, tuned to the pitch of joy. The melody created itself out of air and energy, it raised up the valleys, and the mountains and hills were made low, and the crooked straight, and the rough places plain. And the music went out to the dark sea and sang in the darkness, over the abyss.

When I came out they were all sitting there and none of them was talking. Max had been crying. I could see little candle flames in the tears around his eyes. Simon lay flat on the bed in the shadows, his eyes closed. Phil Drum sat hunched over, holding the solar cell in his hands.

I loosened the pegs, put the bow and the viola in the case, and cleared my throat. It was embarrassing. I finally said, "I'm sorry."

One of the women spoke: Rose Abramski, a private student of Simon's, a big shy woman who could hardly speak at all unless it was in mathematical symbols. "I saw it," she said. "I saw it. I saw the white towers, and the water streaming down their sides, and running back down to the sea. And the sunlight shining in the streets, after ten thousand years of darkness."

"I heard them," Simon said, very low, from the shadow. "I heard their voices."

"Oh, Christ! Stop it!" Max cried out, and got up and went blundering out into the unlit hall, without his coat. We heard him running down the stairs.

"Phil," said Simon, lying there, "could we raise up the white towers, with our lever and our fulcrum?"

After a long silence Phil Drum answered, "We have the power to do it."

"What else do we need?" Simon said. "What else do we need, besides power?"

Nobody answered him.

The blue changed. It became brighter, lighter, and at the same time thicker: impure. The ethereal luminosity of blue-violet turned to turquoise, intense and

---

[25] Sautillé exercises are used to practice leaps from note to note over intervals.

[26] "Harold in Italy" is a symphonic work of Hector Berlioz (1803–1869) which portrays in music the brooding, rebellious, and aloof hero of Lord Byron's "Childe Harold's Pilgrimage."

opaque. Still we could not have said that everything was now turquoise-colored, for there were still no things. There was nothing, except the color of turquoise.

The change continued. The opacity became veined and thinned. The dense, solid color began to appear translucent, transparent. Then it seemed as if we were in the heart of a sacred jade, or the brilliant crystal of a sapphire or an emerald.

As at the inner structure of a crystal, there was no motion. But there was something, now, to see. It was as if we saw the motionless, elegant inward structure of the molecules of a precious stone. Planes and angles appeared about us, shadowless and clear in that even, glowing blue-green light.

These were the walls and towers of the city, the streets, the windows, the gates.

We knew them, but we did not recognize them. We did not dare to recognize them. It had been so long. And it was so strange. We had used to dream, when we lived in this city. We had lain down, nights, in the rooms behind the windows, and slept, and dreamed. We had all dreamed of the ocean, of the deep sea. Were we not dreaming now?

Sometimes the thunder and tremor deep below us rolled again, but it was faint now, far away; as far away as our memory of the thunder and the tremor and the fire and the towers falling, long ago. Neither the sound nor the memory frightened us. We knew them.

The sapphire light brightened overhead to green, almost green-gold. We looked up. The tops of the highest towers were hard to see, glowing in the radiance of light. The streets and doorways were darker, more clearly defined.

In one of those long, jewel-dark streets something was moving—something not composed of planes and angles, but of curves and arcs. We all turned to look at it, slowly, wondering as we did so at the slow ease of our own motion, our freedom. Sinuous, with a beautiful flowing, gathering, rolling movement, now rapid and now tentative, the thing drifted across the street from a blank garden wall to the recess of a door. There, in the dark blue shadow, it was hard to see for a while. We watched. A pale blue curve appeared at the top of the doorway. A second followed, and a third. The moving thing clung or hovered there, above the door, like a swaying knot of silvery cords or a boneless hand, one arched finger pointing carelessly to something above the lintel of the door, something like itself, but motionless—a carving. A carving in jade light. A carving in stone.

Delicately and easily the long curving tentacle followed the curves of the carved figure, the eight petal-limbs, the round eyes. Did it recognize its image?

The living one swung suddenly, gathered its curves in a loose knot, and darted away down the street, swift and sinuous. Behind it a faint cloud of darker blue hung for a minute and dispersed, revealing again the carved figure above the door: the sea-flower, the cuttlefish, quick, great-eyed, graceful, evasive, the cherished sign, carved on a thousand walls, worked into the design of cornices, pavements, handles, lids of jewel boxes, canopies, tapestries, tabletops, gateways.

Down another street, about the level of the first-floor windows, came a flickering drift of hundreds of motes of silver. With a single motion all turned toward the cross street, and glittered off into the dark blue shadows.

There were shadows, now.

We looked up, up from the flight of silverfish, up from the streets where the jade-green currents flowed and the blue shadows fell. We moved and looked up, yearning, to the high towers of our city. They stood, the fallen towers. They glowed in the ever-brightening radiance, not blue or blue-green, up there, but gold. Far above them lay a vast, circular, trembling brightness: the sun's light on the surface of the sea.

We are here. When we break through the bright circle into life, the water will break and stream white down the white sides of the towers, and run down the steep streets back into the sea. The water will glitter in dark hair, on the eyelids of dark eyes, and dry to a thin white film of salt.

We are here.

Whose voice? Who called to us?

He was with me for twelve days. On January 28 the 'crats came from the Bureau of Health, Education and Welfare and said that since he was receiving Unemployment Compensation while suffering from an untreated illness, the government must look after him and restore him to health, because health is the inalienable right of the citizens of a democracy. He refused to sign the consent forms, so the chief health officer signed them. He refused to get up, so two of the policemen pulled him up off the bed. He started to try to fight them. The chief health officer pulled his gun and said that if he continued to struggle he would shoot him for resisting welfare, and arrest me for conspiracy to defraud the government. The man who was holding my arms behind my back said they could always arrest me for unreported pregnancy with intent to form a nuclear family.[27] At that Simon stopped trying to get free. It was really all he was trying to do, not to fight them, just to get his arms free. He looked at me, and they took him out.

He is in the federal hospital in Salem. I have not been able to find out whether he is in the regular hospital or the mental wards.

It was on the radio again yesterday, about the rising land masses in the South Atlantic and the Western Pacific. At Max's the other night I saw a TV special explaining about geophysical stresses and subsidence and faults. The U.S. Geodetic Service is doing a lot of advertising around town, the most common one is a big billboard that says IT'S NOT OUR FAULT! with a picture of a beaver pointing to a schematic map that shows how even if Oregon has a major earthquake and subsidence as California did last month, it will not affect Portland, or only the western suburbs perhaps. The news also said that they plan to halt the tidal waves in Florida by dropping nuclear bombs where Miami was. Then they will reattach Florida to the mainland with landfill. They are already advertising real estate for housing developments on the landfill. The president is staying at the Mile High White House in Aspen, Colorado. I don't think it will do him much good. Houseboats down on the Willamette are selling for $500,000.

---

[27] In sociology, "nuclear family" is a term used to designate a self-contained family unit consisting of a mother, father, and their children.

There are no trains or buses running south from Portland, because all the highways were badly damaged by the tremors and landslides last week, so I will have to see if I can get to Salem on foot. I still have the rucksack I bought for the Mount Hood Wilderness Week. I got some dry lima beans and raisins with my Federal Fair Share Super Value Green Stamp minimal ration book for February—it took the whole book—and Phil Drum made me a tiny camp stove powered with the solar cell. I didn't want to take the Primus, it's too bulky, and I did want to be able to carry the viola. Max gave me a half pint of brandy. When the brandy is gone I expect I will stuff this notebook into the bottle and put the cap on tight and leave it on a hillside somewhere between here and Salem. I like to think of it being lifted up little by little by the water, and rocking, and going out to the dark sea.

Where are you?
We are here. Where have you gone?

Questions

1. What is the function of the italicized passages? How do they contrast with the rest of the story?
2. Why have the universities stopped teaching mathematics and physics, limiting the curriculum to business administration, advertising, and media skills?
3. What is Le Guin's attitude about the function of education and the condition of science?
4. Why does the government want to stop research on the direct conversion of sunlight to electricity? Is Le Guin satirizing any contemporary government action?
5. How does Le Guin view the role of art in her anti-Utopia?
6. Why is marriage banned in her anti-Utopia? How does marriage threaten the totalitarian state?
7. Does Le Guin believe that a totalitarian state will actually be well run?

10 ❧ Breaking the Pattern— Experimental Fiction

Since the 1960s a new group of writers, whose work is marked by daring, humor, anger, ingenuity, and difficulty, has emerged. This work goes by several names: "experimental," "innovative," "post-modernist," "post-realist," or "superfiction." Among the authors associated with such writing are John Barth, Thomas Pynchon, Donald Barthelme, William Klinkowitz, Ronald Sukenick, and Ishmael Reed. It is impossible to define a group whose work is still changing and developing. But we can point out several features that have linked these writers.

Perhaps the best statement of their special interests appears in Ronald Sukenick's novella *The Death of the Novel*. He writes:

> Fiction constitutes a way of looking at the world. Therefore I will begin by considering how the world looks in what I think we may now begin to call the contemporary post-realistic novel. Realistic fiction presupposed chronological time as the medium of a plotted narrative, an irreducible individual psyche as the subject of its characterization, and, above all, the ultimate, concrete reality of things as the object and rationale of its description. In the world of post realism, however, all of these absolutes have become absolutely problematic.
>
> The contemporary writer—the writer who is acutely in touch with the life of which he is part—is forced to start from scratch: Reality doesn't exist, time doesn't exist, personality doesn't exist.[1]

Three elements of Sukenick's statement are worthy of comment. First, Sukenick believes that the contemporary writer goes beyond realism. For the experimental writers, realism is not just a tired set of conventions, but also a misleading mode. Second, the experimental writer questions all the conventions of storytelling and this questioning becomes a part of the story itself. Third, the experimental writer

---

[1] Ronald Sukenick, *The Death of the Novel and Other Stories* (New York: Dial Press, 1969), p. 41.

"starts from scratch." He or she is distrustful of the culture. These writers find certain traditional values of American life "absolutely problematic."

Going beyond Realism

Sukenick would not call the contemporary writers anti-realists. Indeed, they don't necessarily see themselves in revolt against any mode. Rather they are coolly and unnervingly skeptical. They question and probe the assumptions of literature in much the same way that a scientist might question and probe the assumptions of science. On occasion they have been accused of a clinical detachment that robs their work of immediacy and life. They would counter that language is a laboratory in which some experiments fail.

One of the chief assumptions of realistic fiction is that the fictional world of a story can accurately depict the way things are. In short, the fictional world is virtually the same as the real world. Contemporary writers would say that realism may give us the *illusion* of the real world, but it should not be confused with the real world. After all, stories consist only of words. Writers like Sukenick insist that the writer recognize that realism is just one set of literary conventions, no better or higher than any other. Thus they "go beyond" realism, not by rejecting it but by seeing it as part of larger literary practice.

Questioning of Conventions

La Rochefoucauld, the great French writer of aphorisms, once wrote, "There is great skill in knowing how to conceal one's skill." Writers traditionally have taken great pains to conceal the art that lies behind their writing and have presented to the reader works which on the surface seemed effortless, spontaneous, and smooth. Many writers today, however, want their readers to be conscious of the devices by which their fiction is constructed. Instead of concealing their skill, these writers call our attention to it.

Part of the reason is a desire to lay bare underlying structures that previously were hidden away. Writers are not the only ones smitten by this desire to show off the mechanism behind their stories. Architects more and more often are laying bare the pipes, air ducts, metal superstructure, and reinforced concrete they once hid behind walls and above ceilings. Occasionally designers will paint the pipes and air ducts in bright colors to draw attention to them. Such architects argue that they find plumbing beautiful, and the plumbing of literature is equally as attractive to some writers.

But contemporary writers have another, more profound reason for making their readers aware of the conventions of storytelling. Sukenick writes that "Fiction constitutes a way of looking at the world." To see properly, we must recognize how our vision is distorted by the lens through which we see. If language is the lens, we must become more aware of its power to magnify, diminish, highlight, and blot out. The honest writer reveals the tricks that make the illusion possible.

Starting from Scratch

Contemporary writers live in an age very different from the past. Before the invention of the atomic bomb, the human race was capable of great destruction, but could not kill everything. Since the bomb's invention, humans have controlled a force that could effectively put an end to life itself. Before Hiroshima, we could prophesy an apocalypse. After Hiroshima, we are capable of bringing it about. Such apocalyptic possibilities have made some writers throw all values up for questioning. They feel that we need to start from scratch in order to understand our condition and do something about it. Again, this does not mean that the writers have rejected all traditional values; it means only that they do not take those values for granted. The very moral seriousness that has led such writers to question traditional values has caused them to appear as immoral to some readers and critics.

Because of the dire circumstances we face, contemporary writers often seem bleak and pessimistic. Donald Barthelme amusingly contemplates "the end of the mechanical age" and records a re-enactment of Noah's ark.

The Future of Fiction

Ronald Sukenick's quotation comes from a novella ironically called *The Death of the Novel*. But contemporary writers are not necessarily pessimistic about the future of fiction. Quite to the contrary, they view the questioning of traditional literary and moral values and practices as a necessary step in the process of reaffirming those values or establishing better ones. Mark Twain cabled the Associated Press after seeing his own obituary, "The reports of my death are greatly exaggerated." As long as writers continue to set down what they imagine, fiction is not dead. The novel, should it die, will die silently with no one to write its epitaph. Now, though, it may shed its old skins like a snake and continue to wiggle vigorously through the grass.

The three stories in this chapter illustrate many of the preoccupations and strategies of recent experimental fiction. John Barth is an American. Jorge Luis Borges is an Argentine. Samuel Beckett was born in Ireland, but has lived in France for most of his life and prefers now to write in French. His fiction and plays have greatly affected many of this country's most original writers.

Suggestions for Essayists

1. Discuss how crucial historical events—for example, the construction of the atomic bomb, the invention of the printing press, or the discovery of the Americas—have altered the way we perceive the world.
2. Discuss how language distorts the objects it hopes to reveal. For example, show how the language of journalism disguises the true nature of politics, or how the language of love songs distorts the nature of love.

Suggestions for Fiction Writers

1. Pretend that you have never read or heard a story before and try to tell a simple anecdote, making no assumptions about how you will be understood.
2. Imagine that you have been asked to inform the world how to write stories because you are the last surviving author after a nuclear war. Explain the art of storytelling using examples from one of your own works.

JOHN BARTH (1930–)

Autobiography: A Self-Recorded Fiction

You who listen give me life in a manner of speaking.

I won't hold you responsible.

My first words weren't my first words. I wish I'd begun differently.

Among other things I haven't a proper name. The one I bear's misleading, if not false. I didn't choose it either.

I don't recall asking to be conceived! Neither did my parents come to think of it. Even so. Score to be settled. Children are vengeance.

I seem to've known myself from the beginning without knowing I knew; no news is good news; perhaps I'm mistaken.

Now that I reflect I'm not enjoying this life: my link with the world.

My situation appears to me as follows: I speak in a curious, detached manner, and don't necessarily hear myself. I'm grateful for small mercies. Whether anyone follows me I can't tell.

Are you there? If so I'm blind and deaf to you, or you are me, or both're both. One may be imaginary; I've had stranger ideas. I hope I'm a fiction without real hope. Where there's a voice there's a speaker.

I see I see myself as a halt narrative: first person, tiresome. Pronoun sans ante or precedent, warrant or respite. Surrogate for the substantive; contentless form, interestless principle; blind eye blinking at nothing. Who am I. A little *crise d'identité*[1] for you.

I must compose myself.

Look, I'm writing. No, listen, I'm nothing but talk; I won't last long. The odds against my conception were splendid; against my birth excellent; against my continuance favorable. Are yet. On the other hand, if my sort are permitted a certain age and growth, God help us, our life expectancy's been known to increase at an obscene rate instead of petering out. Let me squeak on long enough, I just might live forever: a word to the wise.

My beginning was comparatively interesting, believe it or not. Exposition. I was spawned not long since in an American state and born in no better. Grew in no worse. Persist in a representative. Prohibition, Depression, Radicalism,

---

[1] A *crise d'identité* is French for "identity crisis."

Decadence, and what have you. An eye sir for an eye. It's alleged, now, that Mother was a mere passing fancy who didn't pass quickly enough; there's evidence also that she was a mere novel device, just in style, soon to become a commonplace, to which Dad resorted one day when he found himself by himself with pointless pen. In either case she was mere, Mom; at any event Dad dallied. He has me to explain. Bear in mind, I suppose he told her. A child is not its parents, but sum of their conjoined shames. A figure of speech. Their manner of speaking. No wonder I'm heterodoxical.

Nothing lasts longer than a mood. Dad's infatuation passed; I remained. He understood, about time, that anything conceived in so unnatural and fugitive a fashion was apt to be freakish, even monstrous—and an advertisement of his folly. His second thought therefore was to destroy me before I spoke a word. He knew how these things work; he went by the book. To expose ourselves publicly is frowned upon; therefore we do it to one another in private. He me, I him; one was bound to be the case. What fathers can't forgive is that their offspring receive and sow broadcast their shortcomings. From my conception to the present moment Dad's tried to turn me off; not ardently, not consistently, not successfully so far; but persistently, persistently, with at least half a heart. How do I know? I'm his bloody mirror!

Which is to say, upon reflection I reverse and distort him. For I suspect that my true father's sentiments are the contrary of murderous. That one only imagines he begot me; mightn't he be deceived and deadly jealous? In his heart of hearts he wonders whether I mayn't after all be the get of a nobler spirit, taken by beauty past his grasp. Or else, what comes to the same thing, to me, I've a pair of dads, to match my pair of moms. How account for my contradictions except as the vices of their versus? Beneath self-contempt, I particularly scorn my fondness for paradox. I despise pessimism, narcissism, solipsism,[2] truculence, word-play, and pusillanimity, my chiefer inclinations; loathe self-loathers ergo me;[3] have no pity for self-pity and so am free of that sweet baseness. I doubt I am. Being me's no joke.

I continued the tale of my forebears. Thus my exposure; thus my escape. This cursed me, turned me out; that, curse him, saved me; right hand slipped me through left's fingers. Unless on a third hand I somehow preserved myself. Unless unless: the mercy-killing was successful. Buzzards let us say made brunch of me betimes but couldn't stomach my voice, which persists like the Nauseous Danaid.[4] We . . . monstrosities are easilier achieved than got rid of.

In sum I'm not what either parent or I had in mind. One hoped I'd be astonishing, forceful, triumphant—heroical in other words. One dead. I myself

---

[2] Narcissism is the love of oneself; solipsism is the philosophical position that nothing exists but the contents of one's own mind.
[3] Ergo me is Latin for "therefore me."
[4] A Danaid is one of the mythical fifty daughters of Danaus, ruler of Argus, who ordered his daughters to murder their husbands on their wedding night.

conventional. I turn out I. Not every kid thrown to the wolves ends a hero: for each survivor, a mountain of beast-baits; for every Oedipus, a city of feebs.[5]

So much for my dramatic exposition: seems not to've worked. Here I am, Dad: Your creature! Your caricature!

Unhappily, things get clearer as we go along. I perceive that I have no body. What's less, I've been speaking of myself without delight or alternative as self-consciousness pure and sour; I declare now that even that isn't true. I'm not aware of myself at all, as far as I know. I don't think . . . I know what I'm talking about.

Well, well, being well into my life as it's been called I see well how it'll end, unless in some meaningless surprise. If anything dramatic were going to happen to make me successfuller . . . agreeabler . . . endurabler . . . it should've happened by now, we will agree. A change for the better still isn't unthinkable; miracles can be cited. But the odds against a wireless *deus ex machina*[6] aren't encouraging.

Here, a confession: Early on I too aspired to immortality. Assumed I'd be beautiful, powerful, loving, loved. At least commonplace. Anyhow human. Even the revelation of my several defects—absence of presence to name one— didn't fetch me right to despair: crippledness affords its own heroisms, does it not; heroes are typically gimpish, are they not. But your crippled hero's one thing, a bloody hero after all; your heroic cripple another, etcetcetcetcetcet. Being an ideal's warpèd image, my fancy's own twist figure, is what undoes me.

I wonder if I repeat myself. One-track minds may lead to their origins. Perhaps I'm still in utero,[7] hung up in my delivery; my exposition and the rest merely foreshadow what's to come, the argument for an interrupted pregnancy.

Womb, coffin, can—in any case, from my viewless viewpoint I see no point in going further. Since Dad among his other failings failed to end me when he should've, I'll turn myself off if I can this instant.

Can't. *Then if anyone hears me, speaking from here inside like a sunk submariner, and has the means to my end, I pray him do us both a kindness.*

Didn't. Very well, my ace in the hole: *Father, have mercy, I dare you! Wretched old fabricator, where's your shame? Put an end to this, for pity's sake! Now! Now!*

So. My last trump, and I blew it. Not much in the way of a climax; more a climacteric. I'm not the dramatic sort. May the end come quietly, then, without

---

[5] Oedipus is the mythical ruler of Thebes (rhymes with "feebs") who unknowingly kills his father and marries his mother. Oedipus was left out on a hillside (exposed) when born because his father, Laïos, wished to avoid the prophecy that he would be slain by his son. Oedipus was saved by shepherds, who raised him. See Sophocles' play on the subject, pages 822–61.

[6] *Deus ex machina* literally means "god from a machine," a stage device used in Greek drama that would lower an actor, dressed up as a god, to unravel complicated plots and bring about a happy ending.

[7] *In utero* is a medical term for "in the womb."

my knowing it. In the course of any breath. In the heart of any word. This one. This one.

Perhaps I'll have a posthumous cautionary value, like gibbeted corpses,[8] pickled freaks. Self-preservation, it seems, may smell of formaldehyde.[9]

A proper ending wouldn't spin out so.

I suppose I might have managed things to better effect, in spite of the old boy. Too late now.

Basket case. Waste.

Shake up some memorable last words at least. There seems to be time.

Nonsense, I'll mutter to the end, one word after another, string the rascals out, mad or not, heard or not, my last words will be my last words.

Questions

1. Who is the speaker of this story?
2. Who is the speaker's father?
3. How does the speaker call attention to the structure of the story?
4. In what ways is the relationship between a protagonist and its author an example of narcissism, of solipsism?
5. How is the Oedipus story a model of the relationship between an author and his protagonist?
6. How are the puns appropriate to this story?

JORGE LUIS BORGES (1899–1986)

The Library of Babel

By this art you may contemplate the variation of the 23 letters . . .

The Anatomy of Melancholy,
part 2, sect. II, mem. IV

The universe (which others call the Library) is composed of an indefinite and perhaps infinite number of hexagonal galleries, with vast air shafts between, surrounded by very low railings. From any of the hexagons one can see, interminably, the upper and lower floors. The distribution of the galleries is invariable. Twenty shelves, five long shelves per side, cover all the sides except two; their height, which is the distance from floor to ceiling, scarcely exceeds that of a normal bookcase. One of the free sides leads to a narrow hallway which opens onto another gallery, identical to the first and to all the rest. To the left and right of the hallway there are two very small closets. In the first, one may sleep standing up; in the other, satisfy one's fecal necessities. Also through here passes a spiral stairway, which sinks abysmally and soars upwards to remote distances. In the hallway there is a mirror which faithfully duplicates all appearances. Men usually infer from this mirror that the Library is not infinite (if it really were,

---

[8] Gibbeted corpses were dead persons left hanging on the gallows.
[9] Formaldehyde is a chemical used for preserving dead bodies.

why this illusory duplication?); I prefer to dream that its polished surfaces represent and promise the infinite . . . Light is provided by some spherical fruit which bear the name of lamps. There are two, transversally placed, in each hexagon. The light they emit is insufficient, incessant.

Like all men of the Library, I have traveled in my youth; I have wandered in search of a book, perhaps the catalogue of catalogues; now that my eyes can hardly decipher what I write, I am preparing to die just a few leagues from the hexagon in which I was born. Once I am dead, there will be no lack of pious hands to throw me over the railing; my grave will be the fathomless air; my body will sink endlessly and decay and dissolve in the wind generated by the fall, which is infinite. I say that the Library is unending. The idealists argue that the hexagonal rooms are a necessary form of absolute space or, at least, of our intuition of space. They reason that a triangular or pentagonal room is inconceivable. (The mystics claim that their ecstasy reveals to them a circular chamber containing a great circular book, whose spine is continuous and which follows the complete circle of the walls; but their testimony is suspect; their words, obscure. This cyclical book is God.) Let it suffice now for me to repeat the classic dictum: *The Library is a sphere whose exact center is any one of its hexagons and whose circumference is inaccessible.*

There are five shelves for each of the hexagon's walls; each shelf contains thirty-five books of uniform format; each book is of four hundred and ten pages; each page, of forty lines, each line, of some eighty letters which are black in color. There are also letters on the spine of each book; these letters do not indicate or prefigure what the pages will say. I know that this incoherence at one time seemed mysterious. Before summarizing the solution (whose discovery, in spite of its tragic projections, is perhaps the capital fact in history) I wish to recall a few axioms.

First: The Library exists *ab aeterno*. This truth, whose immediate corollary is the future eternity of the world, cannot be placed in doubt by any reasonable mind. Man, the imperfect librarian, may be the product of chance or of malevolent demiurgi; the universe, with its elegant endowment of shelves, of enigmatical volumes, of inexhaustible stairways for the traveler and latrines for the seated librarian, can only be the work of a god. To perceive the distance between the divine and the human, it is enough to compare these crude wavering symbols which my fallible hand scrawls on the cover of a book, with the organic letters inside: punctual, delicate, perfectly black, inimitably symmetrical.

Second: *The orthographical symbols are twenty-five in number.*[1] This finding made it possible, three hundred years ago, to formulate a general theory of the Library and solve satisfactorily the problem which no conjecture had deciphered: the formless and chaotic nature of almost all the books. One which my father saw in a hexagon on circuit fifteen ninety-four was made up of the letters MCV, perversely repeated from the first line to the last. Another (very much consulted

---

[1] The original manuscript does not contain digits or capital letters. The punctuation has been limited to the comma and the period. These two signs, the space and the twenty-two letters of the alphabet are the twenty-five symbols considered sufficient by this unknown author. (*Editor's note.*)

in this area) is a mere labyrinth of letters, but the next-to-last page says *Oh time thy pyramids*. This much is already known: for every sensible line of straightforward statement, there are leagues of senseless cacophonies, verbal jumbles and incoherences. (I know of an uncouth region whose librarians repudiate the vain and superstitious custom of finding a meaning in books and equate it with that of finding a meaning in dreams or in the chaotic lines of one's palm . . . They admit that the inventors of this writing imitated the twenty-five natural symbols, but maintain that this application is accidental and that the books signify nothing in themselves. This dictum, we shall see, is not entirely fallacious.)

For a long time it was believed that these impenetrable books corresponded to past or remote languages. It is true that the most ancient men, the first librarians, used a language quite different from the one we now speak; it is true that a few miles to the right the tongue is dialectal and that ninety floors farther up, it is incomprehensible. All this, I repeat, is true, but four hundred and ten pages of inalterable MCV's cannot correspond to any language, no matter how dialectal or rudimentary it may be. Some insinuated that each letter could influence the following one and that the value of MCV in the third line of page 71 was not the one the same series may have in another position on another page, but this vague thesis did not prevail. Others thought of cryptographs; generally, this conjecture has been accepted, though not in the sense in which it was formulated by its originators.

Five hundred years ago, the chief of an upper hexagon[2] came upon a book • as confusing as the others, but which had nearly two pages of homogeneous lines. He showed his find to a wandering decoder who told him the lines were written in Portuguese; others said they were Yiddish. Within a century, the language was established: a Samoyedic Lithuanian dialect of Guarani, with classical Arabian inflections. The content was also deciphered: some notions of combinative analysis, illustrated with examples of variation with unlimited repetition. These examples made it possible for a librarian of genius to discover the fundamental law of the Library. This thinker observed that all the books, no matter how diverse they might be, are made up of the same elements: the space, the period, the comma, the twenty-two letters of the alphabet. He also alleged a fact which travelers have confirmed: *In the vast Library there are no two identical books*. From these two incontrovertible premises he deduced that the Library is total and that its shelves register all the possible combinations of the twenty-odd orthographical symbols (a number which, though extremely vast, is not infinite): in other words, all that it is given to express, in all languages. Everything: the minutely detailed history of the future, the archangels' autobiographies, the faithful catalogue of the Library, thousands and thousands of false catalogues, the demonstration of the fallacy of those catalogues, the demonstration of the fallacy of the true catalogue, the Gnostic gospel of Basilides, the

---

[2] Before, there was a man for every three hexagons. Suicide and pulmonary diseases have destroyed that proportion. A memory of unspeakable melancholy: at times I have traveled for many nights through corridors and along polished stairways without finding a single librarian.

commentary on that gospel, the commentary on the commentary on that gospel, the true story of your death, the translation of every book in all languages, the interpolations of every book in all books.

When it was proclaimed that the Library contained all books, the first impression was one of extravagant happiness. All men felt themselves to be the masters of an intact and secret treasure. There was no personal or world problem whose eloquent solution did not exist in some hexagon. The universe was justified, the universe suddenly usurped the unlimited dimensions of hope. At that time a great deal was said about the Vindications: books of apology and prophecy which vindicated for all time the acts of every man in the universe and retained prodigious arcana for his future. Thousands of the greedy abandoned their sweet native hexagons and rushed up the stairways, urged on by the vain intention of finding their Vindication. These pilgrims disputed in the narrow corridors, proffered dark curses, strangled each other on the divine stairways, flung the deceptive books into the air shafts, met their death cast down in a similar fashion by the inhabitants of remote regions. Others went mad . . . The Vindications exist (I have seen two which refer to persons of the future, to persons who perhaps are not imaginary) but the searchers did not remember that the possibility of a man's finding his Vindication, or some treacherous variation thereof, can be computed as zero.

At that time it was also hoped that a clarification of humanity's basic mysteries—the origin of the Library and of time—might be found. It is verisimilar that these grave mysteries could be explained in words: if the language of philosophers is not sufficient, the multiform Library will have produced the unprecedented language required, with its vocabularies and grammars. For four centuries now men have exhausted the hexagons . . . There are official searchers, *inquisitors*. I have seen them in the performance of their function: they always arrive extremely tired from their journeys; they speak of a broken stairway which almost killed them; they talk with the librarian of galleries and stairs; sometimes they pick up the nearest volume and leaf through it, looking for infamous words. Obviously, no one expects to discover anything.

As was natural, this inordinate hope was followed by an excessive depression. The certitude that some shelf in some hexagon held precious books and that these precious books were inaccessible, seemed almost intolerable. A blasphemous sect suggested that the searches should cease and that all men should juggle letters and symbols until they constructed, by an improbable gift of chance, these canonical books. The authorities were obliged to issue severe orders. The sect disappeared, but in my childhood I have seen old men who, for long periods of time, would hide in the latrines with some metal disks in a forbidden dice cup and feebly mimic the divine disorder.

Others, inversely, believed that it was fundamental to eliminate useless works. They invaded the hexagons, showed credentials which were not always false, leafed through a volume with displeasure and condemned whole shelves: their hygienic, ascetic furor caused the senseless perdition of millions of books. Their name is execrated, but those who deplore the "treasures" destroyed by this frenzy neglect two notable facts. One: the Library is so enormous that any reduction of human origin is infinitesimal. The other: every copy is unique, irreplaceable, but (since the Library is total) there are always several hundred thousand imperfect facsimiles: works which differ only in a letter or a comma. Counter to general opinion, I venture to suppose that the consequences of the Purifiers' depredations have been exaggerated by the horror these fanatics produced. They were urged on by the delirium of trying to reach the books in the Crimson Hexagon: books whose format is smaller than usual, all-powerful, illustrated and magical.

We also know of another superstition of that time: that of the Man of the Book. On some shelf in some hexagon (men reasoned) there must exist a book which is the formula and perfect compendium *of all the rest*: some librarian has gone through it and he is analogous to a god. In the language of this zone vestiges of this remote functionary's cult still persist. Many wandered in search of Him. For a century they exhausted in vain the most varied areas. How could one locate the venerated and secret hexagon which housed Him? Someone proposed a regressive method: To locate book A, consult first a book B which indicates A's position; to locate book B, consult first a book C, and so on to infinity . . . In adventures such as these, I have squandered and wasted my years. It does not seem unlikely to me that there is a total book on some shelf of the universe;[3] I pray to the unknown gods that a man—just one, even though it were thousands of years ago!—may have examined and read it. If honor and wisdom and happiness are not for me, let them be for others. Let heaven exist, though my place be in hell. Let me be outraged and annihilated, but for one instant, in one being, let Your enormous Library be justified. The impious maintain that nonsense is normal in the Library and that the reasonable (and even humble and pure coherence) is an almost miraculous exception. They speak (I know) of the "feverish Library whose chance volumes are constantly in danger of changing into others and affirm, negate and confuse everything like a delirious divinity." These words, which not only denounce the disorder but exemplify it as well, notoriously prove their authors' abominable taste and desperate ignorance. In truth, the Library includes all verbal structures, all variations permitted by the twenty-five orthographical symbols, but not a single example of absolute nonsense. It is useless to observe that the best volume of the many hexagons under my administration is entitled *The Combed Thunderclap* and another *The Plaster Cramp* and another *Axaxaxas mlö*. These phrases, at first glance incoherent, can no doubt be justified in a cryptographical or allegorical manner; such a justification is verbal and, *ex hypothesi*, already figures in the Library. I cannot combine some characters

dhcmrlchtdj

which the divine Library has not foreseen and which in one of its secret tongues do not contain a terrible meaning. No one can articulate a syllable which is not filled with tenderness and fear, which is not, in one of these languages, the powerful name of a god. To speak is to fall into tautology. This wordy and

---

[3] I repeat: it suffices that a book be possible for it to exist. Only the impossible is excluded. For example: no book can be a ladder, although no doubt there are books which discuss and negate and demonstrate this possibility and others whose structure corresponds to that of a ladder.

useless epistle already exists in one of the thirty volumes of the five shelves of one of the innumerable hexagons—and its refutation as well. (An *n* number of possible languages use the same vocabulary; in some of them, the symbol *library* allows the correct definition *a ubiquitous and lasting system of hexagonal galleries*, but *library* is *bread* or *pyramid* or anything else, and these seven words which define it have another value. You who read me, are You sure of understanding my language?)

The methodical task of writing distracts me from the present state of men. The certitude that everything has been written negates us or turns us into phantoms. I know of districts in which the young men prostrate themselves before books and kiss their pages in a barbarous manner, but they do not know how to decipher a single letter. Epidemics, heretical conflicts, peregrinations which inevitably degenerate into banditry, have decimated the population. I believe I have mentioned the suicides, more and more frequent with the years. Perhaps my old age and fearfulness deceive me, but I suspect that the human species— the unique species—is about to be extinguished, but the Library will endure: illuminated, solitary, infinite, perfectly motionless, equipped with precious volumes, useless, incorruptible, secret.

I have just written the word "infinite." I have not interpolated this adjective out of rhetorical habit; I say that it is not illogical to think that the world is infinite. Those who judge it to be limited postulate that in remote places the corridors and stairways and hexagons can conceivably come to an end—which is absurd. Those who imagine it to be without limit forget that the possible number of books does have such a limit. I venture to suggest this solution to the ancient problem: *The Library is unlimited and cyclical.* If an eternal traveler were to cross it in any direction, after centuries he would see that the same volumes were repeated in the same disorder (which, thus repeated, would be an order: the Order). My solitude is gladdened by this elegant hope.[4]

Translated by J. E. I.

Questions

1. The narrator says "the cyclical book is God." Does such a formulation recall any traditional definitions of God? Does the story recall other traditional formulations of God?
2. Biologists talk about all life being written in the code of DNA. Could you apply such a notion to "The Library of Babel"?
3. Physicists talk about formulating a Unified Field Theory that would explain all matter in a series of equations. Could such a concept be applied to "The Library of Babel"?
4. In 1955 Borges was named Director of the National Library in Buenos Aires. Is there any way to relate that biographical fact to the story?

---

[4] Letizia Álvarez de Toledo has observed that this vast Library is useless: rigorously speaking, *a single volume* would be sufficient, a volume of ordinary format, printed in nine or ten point type, containing an infinite number of infinitely thin leaves. (In the early seventeenth century, Cavalieri said that all solid bodies are the superimposition of an infinite number of planes.) The handling of this silky vade mecum would not be convenient: each apparent page would unfold into other analogous ones; the inconceivable middle page would have no reverse.

5. How large is the universe according to the narrator of the story? According to physicists? According to theologians? How large does it feel to you?
6. What is the goal of human endeavor according to the narrator of the story? According to theologians? According to your parents? What do you hope to achieve before you die?

SAMUEL BECKETT (1906–)

fizzle 5

Closed place. All needed to be known for say is known. There is nothing but what is said. Beyond what is said there is nothing. What goes on in the arena is not said. Did it need to be known it would be. No interest. Not for imagining. Place consisting of an arena and a ditch. Between the two skirting the latter a track. Closed place. Beyond the ditch there is nothing. This is known because it needs to be said. Arena black vast. Room for millions. Wandering and still. Never seeing never hearing one another. Never touching. No more is known. Depth of ditch. See from the edge all the bodies on its bed. The millions still there. They appear six times smaller than life. Bed divided into lots. Dark and bright. They take up all its width. The lots still bright are square. Appear square. Just room for the average sized body. Stretched out diagonally. Bigger it has to curl up. Thus the width of the ditch is known. It would have been in any case. Sum the bright lots. The dark. Outnumbered the former by far. The place is already old. The ditch is old. In the beginning it was all bright. All bright lots. Almost touching. Faintly edged with shadow. The ditch seems straight. Then reappears a body seen before. A closed curve therefore. Brilliance of the bright lots. It does not encroach on the dark. Adamantine blackness of these. As dense at the edge as at the centre. But vertically it diffuses unimpeded. High above the level of the arena. As high above as the ditch is deep. In the black air towers of pale light. So many bright lots so many towers. So many bodies visible on the bed. The track follows the ditch all the way along. All the way round. It is on a higher level than the arena. A step higher. It is made of dead leaves. A reminder of beldam[1] nature. They are dry. The heat and the dry air. Dead but not rotting. Crumbling into dust rather. Just wide enough for one. On it no two ever meet.

(Translated by the author.)

Questions

1. What does the narrator mean by "There is nothing but what is said"?
2. In what way is that statement true about fiction?
3. What sort of political regime would like its citizens to believe that "there is nothing but what is said"?
4. Do the events in this story recall any historical events?
5. Does the landscape recall any literary scene or imaginary place?

---

[1] Beldam means "grandmother." It is a shortened, Anglicized version of the French phrase "belle dame."

11 🌿 What Happens between Stories

Thus far we have discussed stories one by one. We have seen how they use certain fictional devices and exploit various conventions. But stories do not necessarily exist in isolation. Writers read each other's work, and sometimes the practices of one writer will "rub off" on another. Sometimes a writer will consciously connect stories. Ernest Hemingway used a character called Nick Adams in a series of stories. James Joyce linked the collected short stories of *Dubliners* by setting, as well as in other ways. Stories can be linked by theme, style, or circumstance. This chapter will examine some of the many ways in which stories relate to one another.

Stories by a Single Author

We commonly think that stories written by any one author are related to one another just as children born of the same parents are related. But their connection is not always clear or simple. We all know of brothers or sisters who seem wholly different. Perhaps you have heard of twins, one of whom became a doctor saving lives, the other a murderer taking them away. As varied as siblings can be, so, too, can be the stories of a single author. Yet even the most diverse family holds qualities in common, and the stories of a given author often seem to have a genetic relationship. Thus, we often speak of an author's work as forming a *corpus*, a single body. Discussion about an author's corpus is largely based on the analogy between it and the human body. For example, an author's work is said to develop, to mature, or to decline just as our bodies develop, mature, and decline into old age.

Development, Maturity, and Decline

A common technique of literary scholars and critics is to arrange the works of an author in as close to chronological order as possible and then to compare the stories. Scholars usually look for weak, rough, and unclear writing at the beginning of an author's career. They expect to find strong, polished, and well defined work as the author matures; and, typically, a falling-off of power—a decline—in the later stages of an author's life. But not all people follow this simple and common pattern. Indeed, some of the greatest authors seem to defy the laws of nature and write their most powerful, finished, and passionate works in their old age. And many begin their careers with works of surprising force, clarity, and depth.

Critics look for several elements to determine an author's progress. For example, they frequently examine characters to see if flat characters become rounded, complex, and believable. They scrutinize narratives to see if they become better focused and organized. But of special concern is the thematic relationship between stories.

Thematic Continuity and Development

The word *theme* is derived from a Greek word meaning "to set down." A theme, then, is the basic notion an author hopes to set down in the story, the idea or ideas illustrated by the story.

In talking about their fiction, writers express various attitudes toward the role themes play in the writing process. Some writers begin with a philosophy or belief they wish to express, and then fashion a story to illustrate their position. This sort of writing is usually *didactic*, that is, it is designed to teach a lesson.

But usually authors believe that their works "explore" a certain issue rather than "advance" a particular position or dogma. Such authors think of their themes as questions. For example, García Márquez may have asked himself, "How do people react when confronted with the miraculous or the divine?" His story "A Very Old Man with Enormous Wings" explores how two particular characters treat a fallen angel. But García Márquez might write another story in which the characters, rather than imprisoning or reducing the miraculous, are elevated and liberated by it. Most writers prefer to grapple with issues for which there are no simple or clear answers. Thus, two stories by the same author may seem to arrive at opposite conclusions. Does this mean that the author has changed his or her mind? Not necessarily. It may mean that the author is more concerned with exploring the issue than with coming to any hard and fast position.

The way to find the theme of a story is to view the action in abstract terms. Stories are written about specific characters and specific situations. García Márquez's story is about a specific family who find a specific old man with enormous wings. But the theme concerns the ways in which people (of whom this family is one example) deal with the miraculous (the old man). The film "E. T." develops a similar theme, and W. H. Auden's poem "Musée des Beaux Arts" also concerns itself with this theme. All of these works develop the abstract theme in concrete terms.

Themes are frequently expressed as conflicts between two forces. In "Young Goodman Brown," we have a young man who wants to be good and live a moral life, yet he also wishes to understand evil. We might state the conflict of the story as the conflict between remaining good and recognizing evil. Does one remain good by being ignorant of the sources of evil, or does one need to know evil in order to stay clear of it? Grace Paley's "A Conversation with my Father" concerns the conflict between free will and determinism. Are people able to change themselves or are they destined to act as they do throughout their lives?

One should be aware that stories are not limited to a single theme. Indeed rich and complex stories can develop a number of different themes. Also, the same action can be seen as illustrating various notions. In Anne Tyler's "The Artificial Family," Mary's abandonment of her husband can be viewed as a search for independence, her inability to accept a conventional life style, or envy of her husband's affection for her daughter.

Influence

People and experiences are said to exert an *influence* on us when they cause a change in our behavior or thinking. Parents, for example, are models whose behavior children imitate. But not all persons are positive models. A mean, violent neighbor may be a *negative model*—an example of a type we try to avoid becoming. And there are *bad influences*, persons or experiences that lead one into harmful or wasteful activity. Parents are particularly cautious that their offspring do not fall under bad influences. People or events at some distance can affect our lives. They can influence us in ways we may not realize. For example, American thought is influenced by the Founding Fathers, the group of individuals who wrote the Constitution. Although they lived long ago, they still influence the way you behave and think, even though you have not known them personally or perhaps have never taken time to read the Constitution.

Literary influences are as complex as personal influences. Authors are often friendly with other authors. These contacts may alter the way an author writes, either by providing positive models for emulation or negative models to be avoided. More important than these personal relations, perhaps, is the author's reading. Sometimes authors consciously model their works on other stories, novels, characters, and fictional incidents. At other times, the borrowings are unconscious. But authors can provoke strange reactions from their admirers. Frequently admiring writers rebel against their favorite authors just as children rebel against their parents. Consequently, the discussion of influence can be very tricky, and writers have been known to denounce the very works which have most affected their development.

A persistent problem of literary studies is whether writers can be influenced by authors they have not read. For example, scholars argue about the effects of Sigmund Freud's psychoanalytic work on Henry James's novels, even though James never read Freud. Scholars point out that Freud was read by Henry James's brother William, who was a psychologist. Thus, they argue an *indirect influence*, like the influence of the Founding Fathers upon many Americans. It is important to distinguish between direct influences, which are often quite specific, and indirect influences, which are usually broad in scope.

Writers are affected not only by people and books, but also by historical and social events. The First World War, for example, was said to produce "a lost generation" of writers, including Ernest Hemingway, F. Scott Fitzgerald, and William Faulkner. Critics do not mean that all writers reacted to the war in the same way. They do mean that the war had to affect all of the writers in one way or another. Similarly, contemporary writers have all gone through the experience of the Vietnam War and its aftermath. Whether or not they supported American involvement, they shared in its violence, social dislocation, and national cost.

Nathaniel Hawthorne

Nathaniel Hawthorne (1804–1864) is considered among the greatest writers of American literature. As one of the outstanding figures in the American literary renaissance, he was friendly with Herman Melville (whose *Moby Dick* is dedicated to Hawthorne), Ralph Waldo Emerson, Henry David Thoreau, and Henry Wadsworth Longfellow, with whom he attended Bowdoin College.

Recognition, however, came slowly to Hawthorne, in part because he insisted on publishing his early stories anonymously and also because for ten years after graduating from college he remained virtually isolated in his uncle's house in Salem, Massachusetts, from which he ventured only late in the day for solitary walks. The two stories reprinted here are from this period of obscurity and seclusion. "The Haunted Mind" is among the earlier sketches Hawthorne composed. "Young Goodman Brown" was written a short time later. They first appeared in the same year, 1835.

Salem, the setting of "Young Goodman Brown," is an important place for Hawthorne, and in American history. Hawthorne's ancestors were among the first settlers of Massachusetts, arriving between 1630 and 1633. Hawthorne's great-great-grandfather was Judge John Hathorne. (Nathaniel added the *w* to his name when he began to write.) The judge presided over the notorious Salem witch trials and, it was said, brought a curse upon the family by hanging an innocent girl. Hawthorne was fascinated by Salem, its Puritan past, and the dark mystery of the mind. Salem's history and Hawthorne's ancestral past greatly influenced his writing and its themes, settings, and plots.

Isaac Babel and Doris Lessing

At first glance, Isaac Babel (1894–1941) could not seem further removed from Doris Lessing (b. 1919). Doris Lessing was still an obscure clerical worker living in Zimbabwe (then Rhodesia) when Babel died in Siberia, a famous man imprisoned by Stalin for his political opinions. A Russian Jew living in Odessa, Babel was given an unusually fine education, graduating from Kiev University in 1915. Doris Lessing, however, after attending a Roman Catholic convent school and Girls' High School in Africa, dropped out when only fourteen. Lessing grew up on a farm in southern Africa, miles away from her nearest colonial neighbors. Babel was raised amidst the bustling port of Odessa, crowded with foreigners, where his father ran a warehouse. Finally, although Lessing has already written over a dozen novels, several collections of short stories, essays, reviews, plays, and memoirs, Babel's output in his abbreviated life was relatively small. A meticulous craftsman, his story "Lubka the Cossack" went through twenty-two versions before Babel was satisfied.

Yet there are distinct similarities. Both Lessing and Babel were outsiders. As a Jew in Russia, Babel's travel, work, and study were restricted. As part of the white minority in southern Africa, Lessing also felt isolated. Both Babel and Lessing involved themselves in social reform, Babel by participating in the Russian Revolution and Lessing by political organizing. And both grew weary of revolutionary change. Finally, both authors have engaged in what Lessing calls "a study of the individual conscience in its relation with the collective."

Doris Lessing wrote "Homage to Isaac Babel" well after his death. Like all homages, it attempts to acknowledge a debt, in this case the debt of one great writer to another.

Anne Tyler and John Updike

Anne Tyler and John Updike are two contemporary American writers born within a decade of one another. Updike has lived and written about the Northeast. He was educated at Harvard and has written for *The New Yorker*. His characters are frequently wealthy citizens of New England or the mid-Atlantic states. The Maple family has appeared in a sequence of Updike stories. Tyler, however, was brought up in the South, although she was born in Minnesota. She was educated at Duke University and Columbia. She now makes her home in Baltimore, a city in which Northern and Southern traditions have mingled. Her characters frequently live in poor or reduced circumstances.

Both these stories deal with the break-up of marriages and the relationship between parents and their children. These two stories can indicate how roughly contemporary authors can take similar domestic events and shape them in their own way. Readers may wish to note how the two stories are different and what might account for their difference as well as what in the stories unites these two sensibilities.

Suggestions for Essayists

1. Discuss the ways in which someone you know has influenced your life.
2. Discuss how an event has influenced your development.
3. Discuss how a book has influenced your thinking.

Suggestions for Fiction Writers

1. Write a story borrowing characters from other works. For example, invent your own Sherlock Holmes mystery.
2. Imitate the style of an author you admire. For example, narrate a story in the style of Edgar Allan Poe. Then recast the story as you would tell it apart from his influence.

NATHANIEL HAWTHORNE (1804–1864)

The Haunted Mind

What a singular moment is the first one, when you have hardly begun to recollect yourself, after starting from midnight slumber! By unclosing your eyes so suddenly, you seem to have surprised the personages of your dream in full convocation round your bed, and catch one broad glance at them before they can flit into obscurity. Or, to vary the metaphor, you find yourself, for a single instant, wide awake in that realm of illusions, whither sleep has been the passport, and behold its ghostly inhabitants and wondrous scenery, with a perception of their strangeness, such as you never attain while the dream is undisturbed. The distant sound of a church clock is borne faintly on the wind. You question with yourself, half seriously, whether it has stolen to your waking ear from some gray tower, that stood within the precincts of your dream. While yet in suspense, another clock flings its heavy clang over the slumbering town, with so full and distinct a sound, and such a long murmur in the neighboring air, that you are certain it must proceed from the steeple at the nearest corner. You count the strokes—one—two—and there they cease, with a booming sound, like the gathering of a third stroke within the bell.

If you could choose an hour of wakefulness out of the whole night, it would be this. Since your sober bedtime, at eleven, you have had rest enough to take off the pressure of yesterday's fatigue; while before you, till the sun comes from "far Cathay"[1] to brighten your window, there is almost the space of a summer night; one hour to be spent in thought, with the mind's eye half shut, and two in pleasant dreams, and two in that strangest of enjoyments, the forgetfulness alike of joy and woe. The moment of rising belongs to another period of time, and appears so distant, that the plunge out of a warm bed into the frosty air cannot yet be anticipated with dismay. Yesterday has already vanished among the shadows of the past; to-morrow has not yet emerged from the future. You have found an intermediate space, where the business of life does not intrude; where the passing moment lingers, and becomes truly the present; a spot where Father Time, when he thinks nobody is watching him, sits down by the way side to take breath. Oh, that he would fall asleep, and let mortals live on without growing older!

---

[1] Cathay is another name for China.

Nathaniel Hawthorne (Courtesy Essex Institute, Salem, Massachusetts)

Hitherto you have lain perfectly still, because the slightest motion would dissipate the fragments of your slumber. Now, being irrevocably awake, you peep through the half drawn window curtain, and observe that the glass is ornamented with fanciful devices in frost work, and that each pane presents something like a frozen dream. There will be time enough to trace out the analogy, while waiting the summons to breakfast. Seen through the clear portion of the glass, where the silvery mountain peaks of the frost scenery do not ascend, the most conspicuous object is the steeple; the white spire of which directs you to the wintry lustre of the firmament. You may almost distinguish the figures on the clock that has just told the hour. Such a frosty sky, and the snow covered roofs, and the long vista of the frozen street, all white, and the distant water hardened into rock, might make you shiver, even under four blankets and a woolen comforter. Yet look at that one glorious star! Its beams are distinguishable from all the rest, and actually cast the shadow of the casement on the bed, with a radiance of deeper hue than moonlight, though not so accurate an outline.

You sink down and muffle your head in the clothes, shivering all the while, but less from bodily chill, than the bare idea of a polar atmosphere. It is too cold even for the thoughts to venture abroad. You speculate on the luxury of wearing out a whole existence in bed, like an oyster in its shell, content with the sluggish ecstasy of inaction, and drowsily conscious of nothing but delicious warmth, such as you now feel again. Ah! that idea has brought a hideous one in its train. You think how the dead are lying in their cold shrouds and narrow coffins, through the drear winter of the grave, and cannot persuade your fancy that they neither shrink nor shiver, when the snow is drifting over their little hillocks, and the bitter blast howls against the door of the tomb. That gloomy thought will collect a gloomy multitude, and throw its complexion over your wakeful hour.

In the depths of every heart, there is a tomb and a dungeon, though the lights, the music, and revelry above may cause us to forget their existence, and the buried ones, or prisoners whom they hide. But sometimes, and oftenest at midnight, those dark receptacles are flung wide open. In an hour like this, when the mind has a passive sensibility, but no active strength; when the imagination is a mirror, imparting vividness to all ideas, without the power of selecting or controlling them; then pray that your griefs may slumber, and the brotherhood of remorse not break their chain. It is too late! A funeral train comes gliding by your bed, in which Passion and Feeling assume bodily shape, and things of the mind become dim spectres to the eye. There is your earliest Sorrow, a pale young mourner, wearing a sister's likeness to first love, sadly beautiful, with a hallowed sweetness in her melancholy features, and grace in the flow of her sable robe. Next appears a shade of ruined loveliness, with dust among her golden hair, and her bright garments all faded and defaced, stealing from your glance with drooping head, as fearful of reproach; she was your fondest Hope, but a delusive one; so call her Disappointment now. A sterner form succeeds, with a brow of wrinkles, a look and gesture of iron authority; there is no name for him unless it be Fatality, an emblem of the evil influence that rules your fortunes; a demon to whom you subjected yourself by some error at the outset of life, and were bound his slave forever, by once obeying him. See! those fiendish lineaments graven on the darkness, the writhed lip of scorn, the mockery of that living eye, the pointed finger, touching the sore place in your heart! Do you remember any act of enormous folly, at which you would blush, even in the remotest cavern of the earth? Then recognize your Shame.

Pass, wretched band! Well for the wakeful one, if, riotously miserable, a fiercer tribe do not surround him, the devils of a guilty heart, that holds its hell within itself. What if Remorse should assume the features of an injured friend? What if the fiend should come in woman's garments, with a pale beauty amid sin and desolation, and lie down by your side? What if he should stand at your bed's foot, in the likeness of a corpse, with a bloody stain upon the shroud? Sufficient without such guilt, is this nightmare of the soul; this heavy, heavy sinking of the spirits; this wintry gloom about the heart; this indistinct horror of the mind, blending itself with the darkness of the chamber.

By a desperate effort, you start upright, breaking from a sort of conscious sleep, and gazing wildly round the bed, as if the fiends were any where but in your haunted mind. At the same moment, the slumbering embers on the hearth send forth a gleam which palely illuminates the whole outer room, and flickers through the door of the bed-chamber, but cannot quite dispel its obscurity. Your eye searches for whatever may remind you of the living world. With eager minuteness, you take note of the table near the fire-place, the book with an ivory knife between its leaves, the unfolded letter, the hat and the fallen glove.

Soon the flame vanishes, and with it the whole scene is gone, though its image remains an instant in your mind's eye, when darkness has swallowed the reality. Throughout the chamber, there is the same obscurity as before, but not the same gloom within your breast. As your head falls back upon the pillow, you think—in a whisper be it spoken—how pleasant in these night solitudes, would be the rise and fall of a softer breathing than your own, the slight pressure of a tenderer bosom, the quiet throb of a purer heart, imparting its peacefulness to your troubled one, as if the fond sleeper were involving you in her dream.

Her influence is over you, though she have no existence but in that momentary image. You sink down in a flowery spot, on the borders of sleep and wakefulness, while your thoughts rise before you in pictures, all disconnected, yet all assimilated by a pervading gladsomeness and beauty. The wheeling of gorgeous squadrons, that glitter in the sun, is succeeded by the merriment of children round the door of a school-house, beneath the glimmering shadow of old trees, at the corner of a rustic lane. You stand in the sunny rain of a summer shower, and wander among the sunny trees of an autumnal wood, and look upward at the brightest of all rainbows, over-arching the unbroken sheet of snow, on the American side of Niagara. Your mind struggles pleasantly between the dancing radiance round the hearth of a young man and his recent bride, and the twittering flight of birds in spring, about their new-made nest. You feel the merry bounding of a ship before the breeze; and watch the tuneful feet of rosy girls, as they twine their last and merriest dance, in a splendid ball room; and find yourself in the brilliant circle of a crowded theatre, as the curtain falls over a light and airy scene.

With an involuntary start, you seize hold on consciousness, and prove yourself but half awake, by running a doubtful parallel between human life and the hour which has now elapsed. In both you emerge from mystery, pass through a vicissitude that you can but imperfectly control, and are borne onward to another mystery. Now comes the peal of the distant clock, with fainter and fainter strokes as you plunge farther into the wilderness of sleep. It is the knell of a temporary death. Your spirit has departed, and strays like a free citizen, among the people of a shadowy world, beholding strange sights, yet without wonder or dismay. So calm, perhaps, will be the final change; so undisturbed, as if among familiar things, the entrance of the soul to its Eternal home!

Questions

1. How would you describe the narrator? Do we learn anything about him that would explain his nighttime thoughts?
2. Are the other characters in the story rounded characters or flat figures?
3. Are these the thoughts of one specific haunted mind, or are all minds haunted?
4. Are you convinced that a "purer heart" could impart its peacefulness?
5. How does the narrator "imperfectly control" his vicissitudes? Do his thoughts really seem to have a life of their own?

NATHANIEL HAWTHORNE (1804–1864)

Young Goodman Brown

Young Goodman[1] Brown came forth at sunset into the street at Salem village; but put his head back, after crossing the threshold, to exchange a parting kiss with his young wife. And Faith, as the wife was aptly named, thrust her own pretty head into the street, letting the wind play with the pink ribbons of her cap while she called to Goodman Brown.

"Dearest heart," whispered she, softly and rather sadly, when her lips were close to his ear, "prithee put off your journey until sunrise and sleep in your own bed to-night. A lone woman is troubled with such dreams and such thoughts that she's afeard of herself sometimes. Pray tarry with me this night, dear husband, of all nights in the year."

"My love and my Faith," replied young Goodman Brown, "of all nights in the year, this one night must I tarry away from thee. My journey, as thou callest it, forth and back again, must needs be done 'twixt now and sunrise. What, my sweet, pretty wife, dost thou doubt me already, and we but three months married?"

"Then God bless you!" said Faith, with the pink ribbons; "and may you find all well when you come back."

"Amen!" cried Goodman Brown. "Say thy prayers, dear Faith, and go to bed at dusk, and no harm will come to thee."

So they parted; and the young man pursued his way until, being about to turn the corner by the meeting-house, he looked back and saw the head of Faith still peeping after him with a melancholy air, in spite of her pink ribbons.

"Poor little Faith!" thought he, for his heart smote him. "What a wretch am I to leave her on such an errand! She talks of dreams, too. Methought as she spoke there was trouble in her face, as if a dream had warned her what work is to be done to-night. But no, no; 't would kill her to think of it. Well, she's a blessed angel on earth; and after this one night I'll cling to her skirts and follow her to heaven."

With this excellent resolve for the future, Goodman Brown felt himself justified in making more haste on his present evil purpose. He had taken a dreary road, darkened by all the gloomiest trees of the forest, which barely stood aside to let the narrow path creep through, and closed immediately behind. It was all as lonely as could be; and there is this peculiarity in such a solitude, that the traveller knows not who may be concealed by the innumerable trunks and the thick boughs overhead; so that with lonely footsteps he may yet be passing through an unseen multitude.

"There may be a devilish Indian behind every tree," said Goodman Brown to himself; and he glanced fearfully behind him as he added, "What if the devil himself should be at my very elbow!"

---

[1] Goodman is a title of respect for those otherwise untitled, especially farmers.

His head being turned back, he passed a crook of the road, and, looking forward again, beheld the figure of a man, in grave and decent attire, seated at the foot of an old tree. He arose at Goodman Brown's approach and walked onward side by side with him.

"You are late, Goodman Brown," said he. "The clock of the Old South was striking as I came through Boston, and that is full fifteen minutes agone."[2]

"Faith kept me back a while," replied the young man, with a tremor in his voice, caused by the sudden appearance of his companion, though not wholly unexpected.

It was now deep dusk in the forest, and deepest in that part of it where these two were journeying. As nearly as could be discerned, the second traveller was about fifty years old, apparently in the same rank of life as Goodman Brown, and bearing a considerable resemblance to him, though perhaps more in expression than features. Still they might have been taken for father and son. And yet, though the elder person was as simply clad as the younger, and as simple in manner too, he had an indescribable air of one who knew the world, and who would not have felt abashed at the governor's dinner table or in King William's[3] court, were it possible that his affairs should call him thither. But the only thing about him that could be fixed upon as remarkable was his staff, which bore the likeness of a great black snake, so curiously wrought that it might almost be seen to twist and wriggle itself like a living serpent. This, of course, must have been an ocular deception, assisted by the uncertain light.

"Come, Goodman Brown," cried his fellow-traveler, "this is a dull pace for the beginning of a journey. Take my staff, if you are so soon weary."

"Friend," said the other, exchanging his slow pace for a full stop, "having kept covenant by meeting thee here, it is my purpose now to return whence I came. I have scruples touching the matter thou wot'st[4] of."

"Sayest thou so?" replied he of the serpent, smiling apart. "Let us walk on, nevertheless, reasoning as we go; and if I convince thee not thou shalt turn back. We are but a little way in the forest yet."

"Too far! too far!" exclaimed the goodman, unconsciously resuming his walk. "My father never went into the woods on such an errand, nor his father before him. We have been a race of honest men and good Christians since the days of the martyrs; and shall I be the first of the name of Brown that ever took this path and kept"—

"Such company, thou wouldst say," observed the elder person, interpreting his pause. "Well said, Goodman Brown! I have been as well acquainted with your family as with ever a one among the Puritans; and that's no trifle to say. I helped your grandfather, the constable, when he lashed the Quaker woman so smartly through the streets of Salem; and it was I that brought your father a pitchpine knot, kindled at my own hearth, to set fire to an Indian village, in

---

[2] Since Boston is fifteen miles from Salem, the man has traveled at superhuman speed.
[3] King William III ruled England from 1689 to 1702.
[4] Wot is the present participle of the verb "to wit," thus the matter they know of.

King Philip's war.[5] They were my good friends, both; and many a pleasant walk have we had along this path, and returned merrily after midnight. I would fain be friends with you for their sake."

"If it be as thou sayest," replied Goodman Brown, "I marvel they never spoke of these matters; or, verily, I marvel not, seeing that the least rumor of the sort would have driven them from New England. We are a people of prayer, and good works to boot, and abide no such wickedness."

"Wickedness or not," said the traveller with the twisted staff, "I have a very general acquaintance here in New England. The deacons of many a church have drunk the communion wine with me; the selectmen of divers towns make me their chairman; and a majority of the Great and General Court are firm supporters of my interest. The governor and I, too—But these are state secrets."

"Can this be so?" cried Goodman Brown, with a stare of amazement at his undisturbed companion. "Howbeit, I have nothing to do with the governor and council; they have their own ways, and are no rule for a simple husbandman like me. But, were I to go on with thee, how should I meet the eye of that good old man, our minister, at Salem village? Oh, his voice would make me tremble both Sabbath day and lecture day."

Thus far the elder traveller had listened with due gravity; but now burst into a fit of irrepressible mirth, shaking himself so violently that his snake-like staff actually seemed to wriggle in sympathy.

"Ha! ha! ha!" shouted he again and again; then composing himself, "Well, go on, Goodman Brown, go on; but, prithee, don't kill me with laughing."

"Well, then, to end the matter at once," said Goodman Brown, considerably nettled, "there is my wife, Faith. It would break her dear little heart; and I'd rather break my own."

"Nay, if that be the case," answered the other, "e'en go thy ways, Goodman Brown. I would not for twenty old women like the one hobbling before us that Faith should come to any harm."

As he spoke he pointed his staff at a female figure on the path, in whom Goodman Brown recognized a very pious and exemplary dame, who had taught him his catechism in youth, and was still his moral and spiritual adviser, jointly with the minister and Deacon Gookin.

"A marvel, truly, that Goody[6] Cloyse should be so far in the wilderness at nightfall," said he. "But with your leave, friend, I shall take a cut through the woods until we have left this Christian woman behind. Being a stranger to you, she might ask whom I was consorting with and wither I was going."

"Be it so," said his fellow-traveller. "Betake you the woods, and let me keep the path."

Accordingly the young man turned aside, but took care to watch his com-

---

[5] King Philip (Indian name Metacomet, c. 1639–1676) was the leader of the Wampanaug Indians, who were involved in the fiercest Indian war (1675–76) in American history as they tried to assert Indian sovereignty over appropriated lands.
[6] Goody is a polite term applied to a woman of humble origin.

panion, who advanced softly along the road until he had come within a staff's length of the old dame. She, meanwhile, was making the best of her way, with singular speed for so aged a woman, and mumbling some indistinct words—a prayer, doubtless—as she went. The traveller put forth his staff and touched her withered neck with what seemed the serpent's tail.

"The devil!" screamed the pious old lady.

"Then Goody Cloyse knows her old friend?" observed the traveller, confronting her and leaning on his writhing stick.

"Ah, forsooth, and is it your worship indeed?" cried the good dame. "Yea, truly is it, and in the very image of my old gossip, Goodman Brown, the grandfather of the silly fellow that now is. But—would your worship believe it?—my broomstick hath strangely disappeared, stolen, as I suspect, by that unhanged witch, Goody Cory, and that, too, when I was all anointed with the juice of smallage, and cinquefoil, and wolf's bane"—[7]

"Mingled with fine wheat and the fat of a new-born babe," said the shape of old Goodman Brown.

"Ah, your worship knows the recipe," cried the old lady, cackling aloud. "So, as I was saying, being all ready for the meeting, and no horse to ride on, I made up my mind to foot it; for they tell me there is a nice young man to be taken into communion to-night. But now your good worship will lend me your arm, and we shall be there in a twinkling."

"That can hardly be," answered her friend. "I may not spare you my arm, Goody Cloyse; but here is my staff, if you will."

So saying, he threw it down at her feet, where, perhaps, it assumed life, being one of the rods which its owner had formerly lent to the Egyptian magi. Of this fact, however, Goodman Brown could not take cognizance. He had cast up his eyes in astonishment, and, looking down again, beheld neither Goody Cloyse nor the serpentine staff, but this fellow-traveller alone, who waited for him as calmly as if nothing had happened.

"That old woman taught me my catechism," said the young man; and there was a world of meaning in this simple comment.

They continued to walk onward, while the elder traveller exhorted his companion to make good speed and persevere in the path, discoursing so aptly that his arguments seemed rather to spring up in the bosom of his auditor than to be suggested by himself. As they went, he plucked a branch of maple to serve for a walking stick, and began to strip it of the twigs and little boughs, which were wet with evening dew. The moment his fingers touched them they became strangely withered and dried up as with a week's sunshine. Thus the pair proceeded, at a good free pace, until suddenly, in a gloomy hollow of the road, Goodman Brown sat himself down on the stump of a tree and refused to go any farther.

"Friend," said he, stubbornly, "my mind is made up. Not another step will I budge on this errand. What if a wretched old woman do choose to go to the

---

[7] Wolf's bane is a plant used in witchcraft.

devil when I thought she was going to heaven: is that any reason why I should quit my dear Faith and go after her?"

"You will think better of this by and by," said his acquaintance, composedly. "Sit here and rest yourself a while; and when you feel like moving again, there is my staff to help you along."

Without more words, he threw his companion the maple stick, and was as speedily out of sight as if he had vanished into the deepening gloom. The young man sat a few moments by the roadside, applauding himself greatly, and thinking with how clear a conscience he should meet the minister in his morning walk, nor shrink from the eye of good old Deacon Gookin. And what calm sleep would be his that very night, which was to have been spent so wickedly, but so purely and sweetly now, in the arms of Faith! Amidst these pleasant and praise-worthy meditations, Goodman Brown heard the tramp of horses along the road, and deemed it advisable to conceal himself within the verge of the forest, conscious of the guilty purpose that had brought him thither, though now so happily turned from it.

On came the hoof tramps and the voices of the riders, two grave old voices, conversing soberly as they drew near. These mingled sounds appeared to pass along the road, within a few yards of the young man's hiding-place; but, owing doubtless to the depth of the gloom at that particular spot, neither the travellers nor their steeds were visible. Though their figures brushed the small boughs by the wayside, it could not be seen that they intercepted, even for a moment, the faint gleam from the strip of bright sky athwart which they must have passed. Goodman Brown alternately crouched and stood on tiptoe, pulling aside the branches and thrusting forth his head as far as he durst without discerning so much as a shadow. It vexed him the more, because he could have sworn, were such a thing possible, that he recognized the voices of the minister and Deacon Gookin, jogging along quietly, as they were wont to do, when bound to some ordination of ecclesiastical council. While yet within hearing, one of the riders stopped to pluck a switch.

"Of the two, reverend sir," said the voice like the deacon's, "I had rather miss an ordination dinner than to-night's meeting. They tell me that some of our community are to be here from Falmouth[8] and beyond, and others from Connecticut and Rhode Island, besides several of the Indian powwows, who, after their fashion, know almost as much deviltry as the best of us. Moreover, there is a goodly young woman to be taken into communion."

"Mighty well, Deacon Gookin!" replied the solemn old tones of the minister. "Spur up, or we shall be late. Nothing can be done, you know, until I get on the ground."

The hoofs clattered again; and the voices, talking so strangely in the empty air, passed on through the forest, where no church had ever been gathered or solitary Christian prayed. Whither, then, could these holy men be journeying so deep into the heathen wilderness? Young Goodman Brown caught hold of a

---

[8] Falmouth is a town in southeastern Massachusetts.

tree for support, being ready to sink down on the ground, faint and overburdened with the heavy sickness of his heart. He looked up to the sky, doubting whether there really was a heaven above him. Yet there was the blue arch, and the stars brightening in it.

"With heaven above and Faith below, I will yet stand firm against the devil!" cried Goodman Brown.

While he still gazed upward into the deep arch of the firmament and had lifted his hands to pray, a cloud, though no wind was stirring, hurried across the zenith and hid the brightening stars. The blue sky was still visible, except directly overhead, where this black mass of cloud was sweeping swiftly northward. Aloft in the air, as if from the depths of the cloud, came a confused and doubtful sound of voices. Once the listener fancied that he could distinguish the accents of towns-people of his own, men and women, both pious and ungodly, many of whom he had met at the communion table, and had seen others rioting at the tavern. The next moment, so indistinct were the sounds, he doubted whether he had heard aught but the murmur of the old forest, whispering without a wind. Then came a stronger swell of those familiar tones, heard daily in the sunshine at Salem village, but never until now from a cloud of night. There was one voice, of a young woman, uttering lamentations, yet with an uncertain sorrow, and entreating for some favor, which, perhaps, it would grieve her to obtain; and all the unseen multitude, both saints and sinners, seemed to encourage her onward.

"Faith!" shouted Goodman Brown, in a voice of agony and desperation; and the echoes of the forest mocked him, crying, "Faith! Faith!" as if bewildered wretches were seeking her all through the wilderness.

The cry of grief, rage, and terror was yet piercing the night, when the unhappy husband held his breath for a response. There was a scream, drowned immediately in a louder murmur of voices, fading into far-off laughter, as the dark cloud swept away, leaving the clear and silent sky above Goodman Brown. But something fluttered lightly down through the air and caught on the branch of a tree. The young man seized it, and beheld a pink ribbon.

"My Faith is gone!" cried he, after one stupefied moment. "There is no good on earth; and sin is but a name. Come, devil; for to thee is this world given."

And, maddened with despair, so that he laughed loud and long, did Goodman Brown grasp his staff and set forth again, at such a rate that he seemed to fly along the forest path rather than to walk or run. The road grew wilder and drearier and more faintly traced, and vanished at length, leaving him in the heart of the dark wilderness, still rushing onward with the instinct that guides mortal man to evil. The whole forest was peopled with frightful sounds—the creaking of the trees, the howling of wild beasts, and the yell of Indians; while sometimes the wind tolled like a distant church bell, and sometimes gave a broad roar around the traveller, as if all Nature were laughing him to scorn. But he was himself the chief horror of the scene, and shrank not from its other horrors.

"Ha! ha! ha!" roared Goodman Brown when the wind laughed at him. "Let us hear which will laugh loudest. Think not to frighten me with your deviltry. Come witch, come wizard, come Indian powwow, come devil himself, and here comes Goodman Brown. You may as well fear him as he fear you."

In truth, all through the haunted forest there could be nothing more frightful than the figure of Goodman Brown. On he flew among the black pines, brandishing his staff with frenzied gestures, now giving vent to an inspiration of horrid blasphemy, and now shouting forth such laughter as set all the echoes of the forest laughing like demons around him. The fiend in his own shape is less hideous than when he rages in the breast of man. Thus sped the demoniac on his course, until, quivering among the trees, he saw a red light before him, as when the felled trunks and branches of a clearing have been set on fire, and throw up their lurid blaze against the sky, at the hour of midnight. He paused, in a lull of the tempest that had driven him onward, and heard the swell of what seemed a hymn, rolling solemnly from a distance with the weight of many voices. He knew the tune; it was a familiar one in the choir of the village meeting-house. The verse died heavily away, and was lengthened by a chorus, not of human voices, but of all the sounds of the benighted wilderness pealing in awful harmony together. Goodman Brown cried out, and his cry was lost to his own ear by its unison with the cry of the desert.

In the interval of silence he stole forward until the light glared full upon his eyes. At one extremity of an open space, hemmed in by the dark wall of the forest, arose a rock, bearing some rude, natural resemblance either to an altar or a pulpit, and surrounded by four blazing pines, their tops aflame, their stems untouched, like candles at an evening meeting. The mass of foliage that had overgrown the summit of the rock was all on fire, blazing high into the night and fitfully illuminating the whole field. Each pendent twig and leafy festoon was in a blaze. As the red light arose and fell, a numerous congregation alternately shone forth, then disappeared in shadow, and again grew, as it were, out of the darkness, peopling the heart of the solitary woods at once.

"A grave and dark-clad company," quoth Goodman Brown.

In truth they were such. Among them, quivering to and fro between gloom and splendor, appeared faces that would be seen next day at the council board of the province, and others which, Sabbath after Sabbath, looked devoutly heavenward, and benignantly over the crowded pews, from the holiest pulpits in the land. Some affirm that the lady of the governor was there. At least there were high dames well known to her, and wives of honored husbands, and widows, a great multitude, and ancient maidens, all of excellent repute, and fair young girls, who trembled lest their mothers should espy them. Either the sudden gleams of light flashing over the obscure field bedazzled Goodman Brown, or he recognized a score of the church members of Salem village famous for their especial sanctity. Good old Deacon Gookin had arrived, and waited at the skirts of that venerable saint, his revered pastor. But, irreverently consorting with these grave, reputable, and pious people, these elders of the church, these chaste dames and dewy virgins, there were men of dissolute lives and women of spotted fame, wretches given over to all mean and filthy vice, and suspected even of horrid crimes. It was strange to see that the good shrank not from the wicked, nor were the sinners abashed by the saints. Scattered also among their pale-faced enemies were the Indian priests, or powwows, who had often scared their native forest with more hideous incantations than any known to English witchcraft.

"But where is Faith?" thought Goodman Brown; and, as hope came into his heart, he trembled.

Another verse of the hymn arose, a slow and mournful strain, such as the pious love, but joined to words which expressed all that our nature can conceive of sin, and darkly hinted at far more. Unfathomable to mere mortals is the lore of fiends. Verse after verse was sung; and still the chorus of the desert swelled between like the deepest tone of a mighty organ; and with the final peal of that dreadful anthem there came a sound, as if the roaring wind, the rushing streams, the howling beasts, and every other voice of the unconcerted wilderness were mingling and according with the voice of guilty man in homage to the prince of all. The four blazing pines threw up a loftier flame, and obscurely discovered shapes and visages of horror on the smoke wreaths above the impious assembly. At the same moment the fire on the rock shot redly forth and formed a glowing arch above its base, where now appeared a figure. With reverence be it spoken, the figure bore no slight similitude, both in garb and manner, to some grave divine of the New England churches.

"Bring forth the converts!" cried a voice that echoed through the field and rolled into the forest.

At the word, Goodman Brown stepped forth from the shadow of the trees and approached the congregation, with whom he felt a loathful brotherhood by the sympathy of all that was wicked in his heart. He could have well-nigh sworn that the shape of his own dead father beckoned him to advance, looking downward from a smoke wreath, while a woman, with dim features of despair, threw out her hand to warn him back. Was it his mother? But he had no power to retreat one step, nor to resist, even in thought, when the minister and good old Deacon Gookin seized his arms and led him to the blazing rock. Thither came also the slender form of a veiled female, led between Goody Cloyse, that pious teacher of the catechism, and Martha Carrier, who had received the devil's promise to be queen of hell. A rampant hag was she. And there stood the proselytes beneath the canopy of fire.

"Welcome, my children," said the dark figure, "to the communion of your race. Ye have found thus young your nature and your destiny. My children, look behind you!"

They turned; and flashing forth, as it were, in a sheet of flame, the fiend worshippers were seen; the smile of welcome gleamed darkly on every visage.

"There," resumed the sable form, "are all whom ye have reverenced from youth. Ye deemed them holier than yourselves, and shrank from your own sin, contrasting it with their lives of righteousness and prayerful aspirations heavenward. Yet here are they all in my worshipping assembly. This night it shall be granted you to know their secret deeds: how hoary-bearded elders of the church have whispered wanton words to the young maids of their households; how many a woman, eager for widows' weeds, has given her husband a drink at bedtime and let him sleep his last sleep in her bosom; how beardless youths have made haste to inherit their fathers' wealth; and how fair damsels—blush not, sweet ones—have dug little graves in the garden, and bidden me, the sole guest, to an infant's funeral. By the sympathy of your human hearts for sin ye shall scent out all the places—whether in church, bed-chamber, street, field, or forest—where crime has been committed, and shall exult to behold the whole earth one stain of guilt, one mighty blood spot. Far more than this. I shall be yours to penetrate, in every bosom, the deep mystery of sin, the fountain of all wicked arts, and which inexhaustibly supplies more evil impulses than human power—than my power at its utmost—can make manifest in deeds. And now, my children, look upon each other."

They did so; and, by the blaze of the hell-kindled torches, the wretched man beheld his Faith, and the wife her husband, trembling before that unhallowed altar.

"Lo, there ye stand, my children," said the figure, in a deep and solemn tone, almost sad with its despairing awfulness, as if his once angelic nature could yet mourn for our miserable race. "Depending upon one another's hearts, ye had still hoped that virtue were not all a dream. Now are ye undeceived. Evil is the nature of mankind. Evil must be your only happiness. Welcome again, my children, to the communion of your race."

"Welcome," repeated the fiend worshippers, in one cry of despair and triumph.

And there they stood, the only pair, as it seemed, who were yet hesitating on the verge of wickedness in this dark world. A basin was hollowed, naturally, in the rock. Did it contain water, reddened by the lurid light? or was it blood? or, perchance, a liquid flame? Herein did the shape of evil dip his hand and prepare to lay the mark of baptism upon their foreheads, that they might be partakers of the mystery of sin, more conscious of the secret guilt of others, both in deed and thought, than they could now be of their own. The husband cast one look at his pale wife, and Faith at him. What polluted wretches would the next glance show them to each other, shuddering alike at what they disclosed and what they saw!

"Faith! Faith!" cried the husband, "look up to heaven, and resist the wicked one."

Whether Faith obeyed he knew not. Hardly had he spoken when he found himself amid calm night and solitude, listening to a roar of the wind which died heavily away through the forest. He staggered against the rock, and felt it chill and damp; while a hanging twig, that had been all on fire, besprinkled his cheek with the coldest dew.

The next morning young Goodman Brown came slowly into the street of Salem village, staring around him like a bewildered man. The good old minister was taking a walk along the graveyard to get an appetite for breakfast and meditate his sermon, and bestowed a blessing, as he passed, on Goodman Brown. He shrank from the venerable saint as if to avoid an anathema. Old Deacon Gookin was at domestic worship, and the holy words of his prayer were heard through the open window. "What God doth the wizard pray to?" quoth Goodman Brown. Goody Cloyse, that excellent old Christian, stood in the early sunshine at her own lattice, catechizing a little girl who had brought her a pint of morning's milk. Goodman Brown snatched away the child as from the grasp of the fiend himself. Turning the corner by the meeting-house, he spied the head of Faith, with the pink ribbons, gazing anxiously forth, and bursting into such joy at sight of him that she skipped along the street and almost kissed her husband before the whole village. But Goodman Brown looked sternly and sadly into her face, and passed on without a greeting.

Had Goodman Brown fallen asleep in the forest and only dreamed a wild dream of a witch-meeting?

Be it so if you will; but, alas! it was a dream of evil omen for young Goodman Brown. A stern, a sad, a darkly meditative, a distrustful, if not a desperate man did he become from the night of that fearful dream. On the Sabbath day, when the congregation were singing a holy psalm, he could not listen because an anthem of sin rushed loudly upon his ear and drowned all the blessed strain. When the minister spoke from the pulpit with power and fervid eloquence, and, with his hand on the open Bible, of the sacred truths of our religion, and of saint-like lives and triumphant deaths, and of future bliss or misery unutterable, then did Goodman Brown turn pale, dreading lest the roof should thunder down upon the gray blasphemer and his hearers. Often, awaking suddenly at midnight, he shrank from the bosom of Faith; and at morning or eventide, when the family knelt down at prayer, he scowled and muttered to himself, and gazed sternly at his wife, and turned away. And when he had lived long, and was borne to his grave a hoary corpse, followed by Faith, an aged woman, and children and grandchildren, a goodly procession, besides neighbors not a few, they carved no hopeful verse upon his tombstone, for his dying hour was gloom.

Questions

1. Can we tell for certain whether Goodman Brown dreamt or actually had this vision? Does it matter for Goodman Brown?
2. Does the action arise out of a clear motive? Is Goodman a rounder or flatter character than the speaker of "The Haunted Mind"?
3. Are the other characters rounder or flatter than those in "The Haunted Mind"?
4. Does Faith impart peacefulness to Goodman Brown's mind?
5. Is Brown saved at the end of the story?
6. Is anyone free from sin according to Brown? According to Hawthorne?
7. How would you state the theme of "Young Goodman Brown"? Is it more clearly focused than the theme of "The Haunted Mind"?
8. Would you say that "Young Goodman Brown" is more fully developed than "The Haunted Mind"? Why?

ISAAC BABEL (1894–1939)

My First Goose

Savitsky, Commander of the VI Division, rose when he saw me, and I wondered at the beauty of his giant's body. He rose, the purple of his riding breeches and the crimson of his little tilted cap and the decorations stuck on his chest cleaving the hut as a standard cleaves the sky. A smell of scent and the sickly sweet freshness of soap emanated from him. His long legs were like girls sheathed to the neck in shining riding boots.

He smiled at me, struck his riding whip on the table, and drew toward him an order that the Chief of Staff had just finished dictating. It was an order for Ivan Chesnokov to advance on Chugunov-Dobryvodka with the regiment entrusted to him, to make contact with the enemy and destroy the same.

"For which destruction," the Commander began to write, smearing the whole sheet, "I make this same Chesnokov entirely responsible, up to and including the supreme penalty, and will if necessary strike him down on the spot; which you, Chesnokov, who have been working with me at the front for some months now, cannot doubt."

The Commander signed the order with a flourish, tossed it to his orderlies and turned upon me gray eyes that danced with merriment.

I handed him a paper with my appointment to the Staff of the Division.

"Put it down in the Order of the Day," said the Commander. "Put him down for every satisfaction save the front one. Can you read and write?"

"Yes, I can read and write," I replied, envying the flower and iron of that youthfulness. "I graduated in law from St. Petersburg University."

"Oh, are you one of those grinds?"[1] he laughed. "Specs on your nose, too! What a nasty little object! They've sent you along without making any enquiries; and this is a hot place for specs. Think you'll get on with us?"

"I'll get on all right," I answered, and went off to the village with the quartermaster to find a billet for the night.

The quartermaster carried my trunk on his shoulder. Before us stretched the village street. The dying sun, round and yellow as a pumpkin, was giving up its roseate ghost to the skies.

We went up to a hut painted over with garlands. The quartermaster stopped, and said suddenly, with a guilty smile:

"Nuisance with specs. Can't do anything to stop it, either. Not a life for the brainy type here. But you go and mess up a lady, and a good lady too, and you'll have the boys patting you on the back."

He hesitated, my little trunk on his shoulder; then he came quite close to me, only to dart away again despairingly and run to the nearest yard. Cossacks[2] were sitting there, shaving one another.

---

[1] A grind is a hard-working student.

[2] The Cossacks were a warlike tribe, in marked contrast to the narrator, a Jewish lawyer.

"Here, you soldiers," said the quartermaster, setting my little trunk down on the ground. "Comrade Savitsky's orders are that you're to take this chap in your billets, so no nonsense about it, because the chap's been through a lot in the learning line."

The quartermaster, purple in the face, left us without looking back. I raised my hand to my cap and saluted the Cossacks. A lad with long straight flaxen hair and the handsome face of the Ryazan Cossacks[3] went over to my little trunk and tossed it out at the gate. Then he turned his back on me and with remarkable skill emitted a series of shameful noises.

"To your guns—number double-zero!" an older Cossack shouted at him, and burst out laughing. "Running fire!"

His guileless art exhausted, the lad made off. Then, crawling over the ground, I began to gather together the manuscript and tattered garments that had fallen out of the trunk. I gathered them up and carried them to the other end of the yard. Near the hut, on a brick stove, stood a cauldron in which pork was cooking. The steam that rose from it was like the far-off smoke of home in the village, and it mingled hunger with desperate loneliness in my head. Then I covered my little broken trunk with hay, turning it into a pillow, and lay down on the ground to read in *Pravda* Lenin's speech at the Second Congress of the Comintern.[4] The sun fell upon me from behind the toothed hillocks, the Cossacks trod on my feet, the lad made fun of me untiringly, the beloved lines came toward me along a thorny path and could not reach me. Then I put aside the paper and went out to the landlady, who was spinning on the porch.

"Landlady," I said, "I've got to eat."

The old woman raised to me the diffused whites of her purblind eyes and lowered them again.

"Comrade," she said, after a pause, "what with all this going on, I want to go and hang myself."

"Christ!" I muttered, and pushed the old woman in the chest with my fist. "You don't suppose I'm going to go into explanations with you, do you?"

And turning around I saw somebody's sword lying within reach. A severe-looking goose was waddling about the yard, inoffensively preening its feathers. I overtook it and pressed it to the ground. Its head cracked beneath my boot, cracked and emptied itself. The white neck lay stretched out in the dung, the wings twitched.

"Christ!" I said, digging into the goose with my sword. "Go and cook it for me, landlady."

---

[3] Cossacks from Ryazan, a former principality in central Russia, southeast of Moscow.

[4] The Comintern is an acronym for the Communist International, a worldwide organization of Communist parties. The Comintern was under the direction of V. I. Lenin (1870–1924), one of the founders of the Communist Revolution and virtual dictator of the Soviet Union. He called the Second Congress of Comintern (1920) to wage a world communist revolution. *Pravda* is the official Communist Party newspaper.

Her blind eyes and glasses glistening, the old woman picked up the slaughtered bird, wrapped it in her apron, and started to bear it off toward the kitchen.

"Comrade," she said to me, after a while, "I want to go and hang myself." And she closed the door behind her.

The Cossacks in the yard were already sitting around their cauldron. They sat motionless, stiff as heathen priests at a sacrifice, and had not looked at the goose.

"The lad's all right," one of them said, winking and scooping up the cabbage soup with his spoon.

The Cossacks commenced their supper with all the elegance and restraint of peasants who respect one another. And I wiped the sword with sand, went out at the gate, and came in again, depressed. Already the moon hung above the yard like a cheap earring.

"Hey, you," suddenly said Surovkov, an older Cossack. "Sit down and feed with us till your goose is done."

He produced a spare spoon from his boot and handed it to me. We supped up the cabbage soup they had made, and ate the pork.

"What's in the newspaper?" asked the flaxen-haired lad, making room for me.

"Lenin writes in the paper," I said, pulling out *Pravda*. "Lenin writes that there's a shortage of everything."

And loudly, like a triumphant man hard of hearing, I read Lenin's speech out to the Cossacks.

Evening wrapped about me the quickening moisture of its twilight sheets; evening laid a mother's hand upon my burning forehead. I read on and rejoiced, spying out exultingly the secret curve of Lenin's straight line.

"Truth tickles everyone's nostrils," said Surovkov, when I had come to the end. "The question is, how's it to be pulled from the heap. But he goes and strikes at it straight off like a hen pecking at a grain!"

This remark about Lenin was made by Surovkov, platoon commander of the Staff Squadron; after which we lay down to sleep in the hayloft. We slept, all six of us, beneath a wooden roof that let in the stars, warming one another, our legs intermingled. I dreamed, and in my dreams saw women. But my heart, stained with bloodshed, grated and brimmed over.

Questions

1. What is the narrator's attitude toward Savitksy and the Cossacks?
2. Why does the Ryazan Cossack dump out the narrator's belongings?
3. Why does the landlady want to hang herself?
4. Why does the narrator kill the goose?
5. Why do the Cossacks then offer him soup?
6. How does the narrator feel about killing the goose?
7. Why do people respect senseless violence?

DORIS LESSING (1919–)

Homage for Isaac Babel

The day I had promised to take Catherine down to visit my young friend Philip
at his school in the country, we were to leave at eleven, but she arrived at nine.
Her blue dress was new, and so were her fashionable shoes. Her hair had just
been done. She looked more than ever like a pink-and-gold Renoir[1] girl who
expects everything from life.

Catherine lives in a white house overlooking the sweeping brown tides of the
river. She helped me clean up my flat with a devotion which said that she felt
small flats were altogether more romantic than large houses. We drank tea, and
talked mainly about Philip, who, being fifteen, has pure stern tastes in everything
from food to music. Catherine looked at the books lying around his room, and
asked if she might borrow the stories of Isaac Babel to read on the train. Catherine
is thirteen. I suggested she might find them difficult, but she said: "Philip reads
them, doesn't he?"

During the journey I read newspapers and watched her pretty frowning face
as she turned the pages of Babel, for she was determined to let nothing get
between her and her ambition to be worthy of Philip.

At the school, which is charming, civilised, and expensive, the two children
walked together across green fields, and I followed, seeing how the sun gilded
their bright friendly heads turned towards each other as they talked. In Catherine's
left hand she carried the stories of Isaac Babel.

After lunch we went to the pictures. Philip allowed it to be seen that he
thought going to the pictures just for the fun of it was not worthy of intelligent
people, but he made the concession, for our sakes. For his sake we chose the
more serious of the two films that were showing in the little town. It was about
a good priest who helped criminals in New York. His goodness, however, was
not enough to prevent one of them from being sent to the gas chamber; and
Philip and I waited with Catherine in the dark until she had stopped crying and
could face the light of a golden evening.

At the entrance of the cinema the doorman was lying in wait for anyone who
had red eyes. Grasping Catherine by her suffering arm, he said bitterly: "Yes,
why are you crying? He had to be punished for his crime, didn't he?" Catherine
stared at him, incredulous. Philip rescued her by saying with disdain: "Some
people don't know right from wrong even when it's *demonstrated* to them." The
doorman turned his attention to the next red-eyed emerger from the dark; and
we went on together to the station, the children silent because of the cruelty of
the world.

Finally Catherine said, her eyes wet again: "I think it's all absolutely beastly,
and I can't bear to think about it." And Philip said: "But we've got to think

---

[1] Pierre-Auguste Renoir (1841–1919) was a French impressionist painter known for his lovely pictures
of French family life which included many rosy-cheeked young girls.

about it, don't you see, because if we don't it'll just go on and *on*, don't you see?"

In the train going back to London I sat beside Catherine. She had the stories open in front of her, but she said: "Philip's awfully lucky. I wish I went to that school. Did you notice that girl who said hullo to him in the garden? They must be great friends. I wish my mother would let me have a dress like that, it's *not* fair."

"I thought it was too old for her."

"Oh, *did* you?"

Soon she bent her head again over the book, but almost at once lifted it to say: "Is he a very famous writer?"

"He's a marvellous writer, brilliant, one of the very best."

"Why?"

"Well, for one thing he's so simple. Look how few words he uses, and how strong his stories are."

"I see. Do you know him? Does he live in London?"

"Oh no, he's dead."

"Oh. Then why did you—I thought he was alive, the way you talked."

"I'm sorry, I suppose I wasn't thinking of him as dead."

"When did he die?"

"He was murdered. About twenty years ago, I suppose."

"*Twenty years.*" Her hands began the movement of pushing the book over to me, but then relaxed. "I'll be fourteen in November," she stated, sounding threatened, while her eyes challenged me.

I found it hard to express my need to apologise, but before I could speak, she said, patiently attentive again: "You said he was murdered?"

"Yes."

"I expect the person who murdered him felt sorry when he discovered he had murdered a famous writer."

"Yes, I expect so."

"Was he old when he was murdered?"

"No, quite young really."

"Well, that was bad luck, wasn't it?"

"Yes, I suppose it was bad luck."

"Which do you think is the very best story here? I mean, in your honest opinion, the very very best one."

I chose the story about killing the goose. She read it slowly, while I sat waiting, wishing to take it from her, wishing to protect this charming little person from Isaac Babel.

When she had finished, she said: "Well, some if it I don't understand. He's got a funny way of looking at things. Why should a man's legs in boots look like *girls?*" She finally pushed the book over at me, and said: "I think it's all morbid."

"But you have to understand the kind of life he had. First, he was a Jew in

Russia. That was bad enough. Then his experience was all revolution and civil war and . . . "

But I could see these words bouncing off the clear glass of her fiercely denying gaze; and I said: "Look, Catherine, why don't you try again when you're older? Perhaps you'll like him better then?"

She said gratefully: "Yes, perhaps that would be best. After all, Philip is two years older than me, isn't he?"

A week later I got a letter from Catherine.

> Thank you very much for being kind enough to take me to visit Philip at his school. It was the most lovely day in my whole life. I am extremely grateful to you for taking me. I have been thinking about the Hoodlum Priest. That was a film which demonstrated to me beyond any shadow of doubt that Capital Punishment is a Wicked Thing, and I shall never forget what I learned that afternoon, and the lessons of it will be with me all my life. I have been meditating about what you said about Isaac Babel, the famed Russian short story writer, and I now see that the conscious simplicity of his style is what makes him, beyond the shadow of a doubt, the great writer that he is, and now in my school compositions I am endeavouring to emulate him so as to learn a conscious simplicity which is the only basis for a really brilliant writing style. Love, Catherine. P.S. Has Philip said anything about my party? I wrote but he hasn't answered. Please find out if he is coming or if he just forget to answer my letter. I hope he comes, because sometimes I feel I shall die if he doesn't. P.P.S. Please don't tell him I said anything, because I should die if he knew. Love, Catherine.

Questions

1. How do the characters in Lessing's story compare to the ones in Babel's?
2. Why should the narrator wish "to protect [Catherine] from Isaac Babel"?
3. At the movie theatre, how does the doorman's attitude contrast with Catherine's? Does he express any of the sentiments in "My First Goose"?
4. Is Catherine too young to read Babel?
5. How would you describe her praise of Babel in her letter to the narrator?
6. Catherine desperately wants to be a part of Philip's social world. How does her desire compare with that of Babel's narrator?

ANNE TYLER (1941–)

The Artificial Family

The first full sentence that Mary ever said to him was, "Did you know I have a daughter?" Toby was asking her to dinner. He had just met her at a party— a long-haired girl in a floor-length gingham dress—and the invitation was instant, offered out of desperation because she was already preparing to leave and he wasn't sure he could ever find her again. Now, how did her daughter enter into this? Was she telling him that she was married? Or that she couldn't go out in the evenings? "No," said Toby. "I didn't know."

"Well, now you do," she said. Then she wrote her address down for him and left, and Toby spent the rest of the evening clutching the scrap of paper in his pocket for fear of losing it.

The daughter was five years old. Her name was Samantha, and it suited her: she was an old-fashioned child with two thick braids and a solemn face. When she and her mother stood side by side, barefoot, wearing their long dresses, they might have been about to climb onto a covered wagon. They presented a solid front. Their eyes were a flat, matching blue. "Well!" Toby would say, after he and Samantha knew each other better. "Shall we all *three* go somewhere? Shall we take a picnic lunch? Visit the zoo?" Then the blue would break up into darker colors, and they would smile—but it was the mother who smiled first. The child was the older of the two. She took longer to think things over.

They would go to the Baltimore Zoo and ride the tiny passenger train. Sitting three abreast on the narrow seat—Toby's arm around Mary, Samantha scrunched between them—they rattled past dusty-looking deer fenced in among the woods, through a tunnel where the younger children screamed, alongside a parade of wooden cartoon animals which everyone tried to identify. "That's Bullmoose! There's Bugs Bunny!" Only Samantha said nothing. She had no television set. Bugs Bunny was a stranger to her. She sat very straight, with her hands clasped between her knees in her long skirt, and Toby looked down at her and tried to piece out her father from the curve of her cheek and the tilt of her nose. Her eyes were her mother's, but surely that rounded chin came from her father's side. Had her father had red hair? Was that what gave Samantha's brown braids that coppery sheen? He didn't feel that he could ask straight out because Mary had slammed a door on the subject. All she said was that she had run away with Samantha after two years of marriage. Then once, discussing some earlier stage in Samantha's life, she pulled out a wallet photo to show him: Samantha as a baby, in her mother's lap. "Look at you!" Toby said. "You had your hair up! You had lipstick on! You were wearing a sweater and skirt! Look at Samantha in her party dress!" The photo stunned him, but Mary hardly noticed. "Oh, yes," she said, closing her wallet, "I was very straight back then." And that was the last time she mentioned her marriage. Toby never saw the husband, or heard anything about him. There seemed to be no visiting arrangements for the child.

Mornings Mary worked in an art gallery. She had to leave Samantha with a teen-aged babysitter after kindergarten closed for the summer. "Summers! I hate them," she said. "All the time I'm at work I'm wondering how Samantha is." Toby said, "Why not let *me* stay with her. You know how Samantha and I get along." He was a graduate student with a flexible schedule; and besides, he seized on every excuse to entrench himself deeper into Mary's life. But Mary said, "No, I couldn't ask you to do that." And she went on paying Carol, and paying her again in the evenings when they went out somewhere. They went to dinner, or to movies, or to Toby's rambling apartment. They always came back early. "Carol's mother will kill me!" Mary would say, and she would gather up her belongings and run ahead of Toby to his car. When he returned from taking her home his apartment always smelled of her: a clean, straw smell, like burlap. Her bobby pins littered the bed and the crevices of the sofa. Strands of her long hairs tended to get wound around the rollers of his carpet sweeper. When he went to sleep the cracked bell of her voice threaded through all his dreams.

At the end of August, they were married in a civil ceremony. They had known each other five months. *Only* five months, Toby's parents said. They wrote him a letter pointing out all their objections. How would he support three on a university grant? How would he study? What did he want with someone else's child? The child: that was what they really minded. The ready-made grandchild. How could he love some other man's daughter? But Toby had never been sure he would know how to love his *own* children; so the question didn't bother him. He liked Samantha. And he liked the idea of her: the single, solitary treasure carried away from the disaster of the sweater-and-skirt marriage. If he himself ever ran away, what would he choose to take? His grandfather's watch, his favorite chamois shirt, eight cartons of books, some still unread, his cassette tape recorder—each object losing a little more worth as the list grew longer. Mary had taken Samantha, and nothing else. He envied both of them.

They lived in his apartment, which was more than big enough. Mary quit her job. Samantha started first grade. They were happy but guarded, still, working too hard at getting along. Mary turned the spare bedroom into a study for Toby, with a "Private" sign on the door. "Never go in there," she told Samantha. "That's Toby's place to be alone." "But I don't *want* to be alone," Toby said. "I'm alone all day at the lab." Nobody seemed to believe him. Samantha passed the doorway of his study on tiptoe, never even peeking inside. Mary scrupulously avoided littering the apartment with her own possessions. Toby was so conscientious a father that he might have written himself a timetable: At seven, play Old Maid. At seven-thirty, read a story. At eight o'clock, offer a piggyback ride to bed. Mary he treated like glass. He kept thinking of her first marriage; his greatest fear was that she would leave him.

Every evening, Samantha walked around to Toby's lab to call him for supper. In the midst of reaching for a beaker or making a notation he would look up to find her standing there, absolutely silent. Fellow students gave her curious looks. She ignored them. She concentrated on Toby, watching him with a steady blue gaze that gave all his actions a new importance. Would he feel this flattered if she were his own? He didn't think so. In their peculiar situation—nearly strangers, living in the same house, sharing Mary—they had not yet started to take each other for granted. Her coming for him each day was purely a matter of choice, which he imagined her spending some time over before deciding; and so were the sudden, rare smiles which lit her face when he glanced down at her during the walk home.

At Christmastime Toby's parents flew down for a visit. They stayed four days, each one longer than the day before. Toby's mother had a whole new manner which kept everyone at arm's length. She would look at Samantha and say, "My, she's thin! Is her father thin, Mary? Does her father have those long feet?"

She would go out to the kitchen and say, "I see you've done something with Toby's little two-cup coffeepot. Is this *your* pot, Mary? May I use it?" Everything she said was meant to remind them of their artificiality: the wife was someone else's first, the child was not Toby's. But her effect was to draw them closer together. The three of them formed an alliance against Mrs. Scott and her silent husband, who lent her his support merely by not shutting her up. On the second evening Toby escaped to his study and Samantha and Mary joined him, one by one, sliding through the crack in his door to sit giggling silently with him over a game of dominoes. One afternoon they said they had to take Samantha to her art lesson and they snuck off to a Walt Disney movie instead, and stayed there in the dark for two hours eating popcorn and Baby Ruths and endless strings of licorice.

Toby's parents went home, but the alliance continued. The sense of effort had disappeared. Toby's study became the center of the apartment, and every evening while he read Mary sat with him and sewed and Samantha played with cut-outs at their feet. Mary's pottery began lining the mantel and the bookshelves. She pounded in nails all over the kitchen and hung up her saucepans. Samantha's formal bedtime ritual changed to roughhousing, and she and Toby pounded through the rooms and pelted each other with sofa cushions and ended up in a tangle on the hallway carpet.

Now Samantha was growing unruly with her mother. Talking back. Disobeying. Toby was relieved to see it. Before she had been so good that she seemed pathetic. But Mary said, "I don't know what I'm going to do with that child. She's getting out of hand."

"She seems all right to *me*," said Toby.

"I knew you'd say that. It's your fault she's changed like this, too. You've spoiled her."

"*Spoiled* her?"

"You dote on her, and she knows it," Mary said. She was folding the laundry, moving crisply around the bedroom with armloads of sheets and towels. Nowadays she wore sweaters and skirts—more practical for housework—and her loafers tapped across the floor with an efficient sound that made him feel she knew what she was talking about. "You give her everything she asks for," she said. "Now she doesn't listen to *me* any more.

"But there's nothing wrong with giving her things. Is there?"

"If you had to live with her all day long," Mary said, "eighteen hours a day, the way I do, you'd think twice before you said that."

But how could he refuse anything to Samantha? With him, she was never disobedient. She shrieked with him over pointless riddles, she asked him unanswerable questions on their walks home from the lab, she punched at him ineffectually, her thumbs tucked inside her fists, when he called her Sam. The only time he was ever angry with her was once when she stepped into the path of a car without looking. "Samantha!" he yelled, and he yanked her back and shook her until she cried. Inside he had felt his stomach lurch, his heart sent out a wave of heat and his knees shook. The purple marks of his fingers stayed on Samantha's arm for days afterward. Would he have been any more terrified if the child were his own? New opportunities for fear were everywhere, now that he was a family man. Samantha's walk from school seemed long and under-policed, and every time he called home without an answer he imagined that Mary had run away from him and he would have to get through life without her. "I think we should have another baby," he told Mary, although of course he knew that increasing the number of people he loved would not make any one of them more expendable. All Mary said was, "Do you?"

"I love that little girl. I really love her. I'd like to have a whole *armload* of little girls. Did you ever think I would be so good at loving people?"

"Yes," said Mary.

"I didn't. Not until I met you. I'd like to *give* you things. I'd like to sit you and Samantha down and pile things in your laps. Don't you ever feel that way?"

"Women don't," said Mary. She slid out of his hands and went to the sink, where she ran cold water over some potatoes. Lately she had started wearing her hair pinned up, out of the way. She looked carved, without a stray wisp or an extra line, smooth to the fingertips, but when Toby came up behind her again she ducked away and went to the stove. "Men are the only ones who have that much feeling left to spare," she said. "Women's love gets frittered away: every day a thousand little demands for milk and bandaids and swept floors and clean towels."

"I don't believe that," said Toby.

But Mary was busy regulating the flame under the potatoes now, and she didn't argue with him.

For Easter, Toby bought Samantha a giant prepacked Easter basket swaddled in pink cellophane. It was a spur-of-the-moment purchase—he had gone to the all-night drugstore for pipe tobacco, seen this basket and remembered suddenly that tomorrow was Easter Sunday. Wouldn't Samantha be expecting some sort of celebration? He hated to think of her returning to school empty-handed, when everyone else had chocolate eggs or stuffed rabbits. But when he brought the basket home—rang the doorbell and waited, obscured behind the masses of cellophane like some comical florist's-messenger—he saw that he had made a mistake. Mary didn't like the basket. "How come you bought a thing like that?" she asked him.

"Tomorrow's Easter."

"Easter? Why Easter? We don't even go to church."

"We celebrated Christmas, didn't we?"

"Yes, but—and Easter's not the question," Mary said. "It's this basket." She reached out and touched the cellophane, which shrank beneath her fingers. "We never *used* to buy baskets. Before I've always hidden eggs and let her hunt for them in the morning, and then she dyes them herself."

"Oh, I thought people had jellybeans and things," Toby said.

"*Other* people, maybe. Samantha and I do it differently."

"Wouldn't she like to have what her classmates have?"

"She isn't trying to keep up with the *Joneses*, Toby," Mary said. "And how about her teeth? How about her stomach? Do I always have to be the heavy, bringing these things up? Why is it you get to shower her with love and gifts, and then it's me that takes her to the dentist?"

"Oh, let's not go into *that* again," Toby said.

Then Mary, who could never be predicted, said, "All right," and stopped the argument. "It was nice of you to think of it, anyway," she said formally, taking the basket. "I know Samantha will like it."

Samantha did like it. She treasured every jellybean and marshmallow egg and plastic chick; she telephoned a friend at seven in the morning to tell her about it. But even when she threw her arms around Toby's neck, smelling of sugar and cellophane, all he felt was a sense of defeat. Mary's face was serene and beautiful, like a mask. She continued to move farther and farther away from him, with her lips perpetually curved in a smile and no explanations at all.

In June, when school closed, Mary left him for good. He came home one day to find a square of paper laid flat on a club sandwich. The sight of it thudded instantly against his chest, as if he had been expecting it all along. "I've gone," the note said. His name was nowhere on it. It might have been the same note she sent her first husband—retrieved, somehow, and saved in case she found another use for it. Toby sat down and read it again, analyzed each loop of handwriting for any sign of indecision or momentary, reversible anger. Then he ate the club sandwich, every last crumb, without realizing he was doing so, and after that he pushed his plate away and lowered his head into his hands. He sat that way for several minutes before he thought of Samantha.

It was Monday evening—the time when she would just be finishing with her art lesson. He ran all the way, jaywalking and dodging cars and waving blindly at the drivers who honked. When he arrived in the dingy building where the lessons were given he found he was too early. The teacher still murmured behind a closed door. Toby sat down, panting, on a bench beneath a row of coat hooks. Flashes of old TV programs passed through his head. He saw himself blurred and bluish on a round-cornered screen—one of those mysteriously partnerless television parents who rear their children with more grace and tact and unselfishness than any married couple could ever hope for. Then the classroom door opened. The teacher came out in her smock, ringed by six-year-olds. Toby stood up and said, "Mrs.—um. Is Samantha Glover here?"

The teacher turned. He knew what she was going to say as soon as she took a breath; he hated her so much he wanted to grab her by the neck and slam her head against the wall. "Samantha?" she said. "Why, no, Mr. Scott, Samantha didn't come today."

On the walk back, he kept his face stiff and his eyes unfocused. People stared at him. Women turned to look after him, frowning, curious to see the extent of the damage. He barely noticed them. He floundered up the stairs to his apartment, felt his way to the sofa and sat down heavily. There was no need to turn the lights on. He knew already what he would find: toys and saucepans, Mary's skirts and sweaters, Samantha's new short dresses. All they would have taken with them, he knew, was their long gingham gowns and each other.

Questions

1. How is Mary dressed in the snapshot of her first marriage? Does her dress change during her second marriage? If so, how does it compare to the snapshot?
2. What significance do the gingham dresses have for Samantha and Mary?
3. Why does Mary complain about Toby's purchase of the Easter basket?
4. Does Toby's sense of parental responsibility differ from Mary's?
5. Why does Mary leave Toby? Is her decision a sound one?
6. Is there anything that Toby could have done to preserve the marriage?
7. Are there any similarities between "The Artificial Family" and "Shiloh"?

JOHN UPDIKE (1932–)

Separating

The day was fair. Brilliant. All that June the weather had mocked the Maples' internal misery with solid sunlight—golden shafts and cascades of green in which their conversations had wormed unseeing, their sad murmuring selves the only stain in Nature. Usually by this time of the year they had acquired tans; but when they met their elder daughter's plane on her return from a year in England they were almost as pale as she, though Judith was too dazzled by the sunny opulent jumble of her native land to notice. They did not spoil her homecoming by telling her immediately. Wait a few days, let her recover from jet lag, had been one of their formulations, in that string of gray dialogues—over coffee, over cocktails, over Cointreau[1]—that had shaped the strategy of their dissolution, while the earth performed its annual stunt of renewal unnoticed beyond their closed windows. Richard had thought to leave at Easter; Joan had insisted they wait until the four children were at last assembled, with all exams passed and ceremonies attended, and the bauble of summer to console them. So he had drudged away, in love, in dread, repairing screens, getting the mowers sharpened, rolling and patching their new tennis court.

The court, clay, had come through its first winter pitted and windswept bare of redcoat. Years ago, the Maples had observed how often, among their friends, divorce followed a dramatic home improvement, as if the marriage were making one last twitchy effort to live; their own worst crisis had come amid the plaster dust and exposed plumbing of a kitchen renovation. Yet, a summer ago, as canary-yellow bulldozers gaily churned a grassy, daisy-dotted knoll into a muddy plateau, and a crew of pigtailed young men raked and tamped clay into a plane, this transformation did not strike them as ominous, but festive in its impudence; their marriage could rend the earth for fun. The next spring, waking each day at dawn to a sliding sensation as if the bed were being tipped, Richard found the barren tennis court, its net and tapes still rolled in the barn, an environment congruous with his mood of purposeful desolation, and the crumbling of handfuls of clay into cracks and holes (dogs had frolicked on the court in a thaw; rivulets

---

[1] Cointreau is an orange-flavored liqueur.

had evolved trenches) an activity suitably elemental and interminable. In his sealed heart he hoped the day would never come.

Now it was here. A Friday. Judith was reacclimated; all four children were assembled, before jobs and camps and visits again scattered them. Joan thought they should be told one by one. Richard was for making an announcement at the table. She said, "I think just making an announcement is a cop-out. They'll start quarrelling and playing to each other instead of focussing. They're each individuals, you know, not just some corporate obstacle to your freedom."

"O.K., O.K. I agree." Joan's plan was exact. That evening, they were giving Judith a belated welcome-home dinner, of lobster and champagne. Then, the party over, they, the two of them, who nineteen years before would push her in a baby carriage along Tenth Street to Washington Square,[2] were to walk her out of the house, to the bridge across the salt creek, and tell her, swearing her to secrecy. Then Richard Jr., who was going directly from work to a rock concert in Boston, would be told, either late when he returned on the train or early Saturday morning before he went off to his job; he was seventeen and employed as one of a golf-course maintenance crew. Then the two younger children, John and Margaret, could, as the morning wore on, be informed.

"Mopped up, as it were," Richard said.

"Do you have any better plan? That leaves you the rest of Saturday to answer any questions, pack, and make your wonderful departure."

"No," he said, meaning he had no better plan, and agreed to hers, though it had an edge of false order, a plea for control in the semblance of its achievement, like Joan's long chore lists and financial accountings and, in the days when he first knew her, her too copious lecture notes. Her plan turned one hurdle for him into four—four knife-sharp walls, each with a sheer blind drop on the other side.

All spring he had been morbidly conscious of insides and outsides, of barriers and partitions. He and Joan stood as a thin barrier between the children and the truth. Each moment was a partition, with the past on one side and the future on the other, a future containing this unthinkable *now*. Beyond four knifelike walls a new life for him waited vaguely. His skull cupped a secret, a white face, a face both frightened and soothing, both strange and known, that he wanted to shield from tears, which he felt all about him, solid as the sunlight. So haunted, he had become obsessed with battening down the house against his absence, replacing screens and sash cords, hinges and latches—a Houdini making things snug before his escape.[3]

The lock. He had still to replace a lock on one of the doors of the screened porch. The task, like most such, proved more difficult than he had imagined. The old lock, aluminum frozen by corrosion, had been deliberately rendered

---

2 The Maples' walk from Tenth Street to Washington Square took them through the northern part of the Greenwich Village area of New York City.
3 Harry Houdini (1874–1926) was the American escape artist and magician. Several of his famous escapes have yet to be understood.

obsolete by manufacturers. Three hardware stores had nothing that even approximately matched the mortised hole its removal (surprisingly easy) left. Another hole had to be gouged, with bits too small and saws too big, and the old hole fitted with a block of wood—the chisels dull, the saw rusty, his fingers thick with lack of sleep. The sun poured down, beyond the porch, on a world of neglect. The bushes already needed pruning, the windward side of the house was shedding flakes of paint, rain would get in when he was gone, insects, rot, death. His family, all those he would lose, filtered through the edges of his awareness as he struggled with screw holes, splinters, opaque instructions, minutiae of metal.

Judith sat on the porch, a princess returned from exile. She regaled them with stories of fuel shortages, of bomb scares in the Underground,[4] of Pakistani workmen loudly lusting after her as she walked past on her way to dance school. Joan came and went, in and out of the house, calmer than she should have been, praising his struggles with the lock as if this were one more and not the last of their chain of shared chores. The younger of his sons, John, now at fifteen suddenly, unwittingly handsome, for a few minutes held the rickety screen door while his father clumsily hammered and chiselled, each blow a kind of sob in Richard's ears. His younger daughter, having been at a slumber party, slept on the porch hammock through all the noise—heavy and pink, trusting and forsaken. Time, like the sunlight, continued relentlessly; the sunlight slowly slanted. Today was one of the longest days. The lock clicked, worked. He was through. He had a drink; he drank it on the porch, listening to his daughter. "It was so sweet," she was saying, "during the worst of it, how all the butcher's and bakery shops kept open by candlelight. They're all so plucky and cute. From the papers, things sounded so much worse here—people shooting people in gas lines, and everybody freezing."

Richard asked her, "Do you still want to live in England forever?" *Forever:* the concept, now a reality upon him, pressed and scratched at the back of his throat.

"No," Judith confessed, turning her oval face to him, its eyes still childishly far apart, but the lips set as over something succulent and satisfactory. "I was anxious to come home. I'm an American." She was a woman. They had raised her; he and Joan had endured together to raise her, alone of the four. The others had still some raising left in them. Yet it was the thought of telling Judith—the image of her, their first baby, walking between them arm in arm to the bridge— that broke him. The partition between himself and the tears broke. Richard sat down to the celebratory meal with the back of his throat aching; the campagne, the lobster seemed phases of sunshine; he saw them and tasted them through tears. He blinked, swallowed, croakily joked about hay fever. The tears would not stop leaking through; they came not through a hole that could be plugged but through a permeable spot in a membrane, steadily, purely, endlessly, fruitfully. They became, his tears, a shield for himself against these others—their

---

[4] The Underground is the name for the London subway system.

faces, the fact of their assembly, a last time as innocents, at a table where he sat the last time as head. Tears dropped from his nose as he broke the lobster's back; salt flavored his champagne as he sipped it; the raw clench at the back of his throat was delicious. He could not help himself.

His children tried to ignore his tears. Judith, on his right, lit a cigarette, gazed upward in the direction of her too energetic, too sophisticated exhalation; on her other side, John earnestly bent his face to the extraction of the last morsels— legs, tail segments—from the scarlet corpse. Joan, at the opposite end of the table, glanced at him surprised, her reproach displaced by a quick grimace, of forgiveness, or of salute to his superior gift of strategy. Between them, Margaret, no longer called Bean, thirteen and large for her age, gazed from the other side of his pane of tears as if into a shopwindow at something she coveted—at her father, a crystalline heap of splinters and memories. It was not she, however, but John who, in the kitchen, as they cleared the plates and carapaces away, asked Joan the question: *"Why is Daddy crying?"*

Richard heard the question but not the murmured answer. Then he heard Bean cry, "Oh, no-oh!"—the faintly dramatized exclamation of one who had long expected it.

John returned to the table carrying a bowl of salad. He nodded tersely at his father and his lips shaped the conspiratorial words "She told."

"Told what?" Richard asked aloud, insanely.

The boy sat down as if to rebuke his father's distraction with the example of his own good manners and said quietly, "The separation."

Joan and Margaret returned; the child, in Richard's twisted vision, seemed diminished in size, and relieved, relieved to have the boogeyman at last proved real. He called out to her—the distances at the table had grown immense— "You knew, you always knew," but the clenching at the back of his throat prevented him from making sense of it. From afar he heard Joan talking, levelly, sensibly, reciting what they had prepared: it was a separation for the summer, an experiment. She and Daddy both agreed it would be good for them; they needed space and time to think; they liked each other but did not make each other happy enough, somehow.

Judith, imitating her mother's factual tone, but in her youth off-key, too cool, said, "I think it's silly. You should either live together or get divorced."

Richard's crying, like a wave that has crested and crashed, had become tumultuous; but it was overtopped by another tumult, for John, who had been so reserved, now grew larger and larger at the table. Perhaps his younger sister's being credited with knowing set him off. "Why didn't you *tell* us?" he asked, in a large round voice quite unlike his own. "You should have *told* us you weren't getting along."

Richard was startled into attempting to force words through his tears. "We *do* get along, that's the trouble, so it doesn't show even to us—" "That we do not love each other" was the rest of the sentence; he couldn't finish it.

Joan finished for him, in her style. "And we've always, *especially*, loved our children."

John was not mollified. "What do you care about *us?*" he boomed. "We're just little things you *had.*" His sisters' laughing forced a laugh from him, which he turned hard and parodistic: "Ha ha *ha.*" Richard and Joan realized simultaneously that the child was drunk, on Judith's homecoming champagne. Feeling bound to keep the center of the stage, John took a cigarette from Judith's pack, poked it into his mouth, let it hang from his lower lip, and squinted like a gangster.

"You're not little things we had," Richard called to him. "You're the whole point. But you're grown. Or almost."

The boy was lighting matches. Instead of holding them to his cigarette (for they had never seen him smoke; being "good" had been his way of setting himself apart), he held them to his mother's face, closer and closer, for her to blow out. Then he lit the whole folder—a hiss and then a torch, held against his mother's face. Prismed by his tears, the flame filled Richard's vision; he didn't know how it was extinguished. He heard Margaret say, "Oh stop showing off," and saw John, in response, break the cigarette in two and put the halves entirely into his mouth and chew, sticking out his tongue to display the shreds to his sister.

Joan talked to him, reasoning—a fountain of reason, unintelligble. "Talked about it for years . . . our children must help us . . . Daddy and I both want . . ." As the boy listened, he carefully wadded a paper napkin into the leaves of his salad, fashioned a ball of paper and lettuce, and popped it into his mouth, looking around the table for the expected laughter. None came. Judith said, "Be mature," and dismissed a plume of smoke.

Richard got up from this stifling table and led the boy outside. Though the house was in twilight, the outdoors still brimmed with light, the long waste light of high summer. Both laughing, he supervised John's spitting out the lettuce and paper and tobacco into the pachysandra. He took him by the hand—a square gritty hand, but for its softness a man's. Yet, it held on. They ran together up into the field, past the tennis court. The raw banking left by the bulldozers was dotted with daisies. Past the court and a flat stretch where they used to play family baseball stood a soft green rise glorious in the sun, each weed and species of grass distinct as illumination on parchment. "I'm sorry, so sorry," Richard cried. "You were the only one who ever tried to help me with all the goddam jobs around this place."

Sobbing, safe within his tears and the champagne, John explained, "It's not just the separation, it's the whole crummy year, I *hate* that school, you can't make any friends, the history teacher's a scud."

They sat on the crest of the rise, shaking and warm from their tears but easier in their voices, and Richard tried to focus on the child's sad year—the weekdays long with homework, the weekends spent in his room with model airplanes, while his parents murmured down below, nursing their separation. How selfish, how blind, Richard thought; his eyes felt scoured. He told his son, "We'll think about getting you transferred. Life's too short to be miserable."

They had said what they could, but did not want the moment to heal, and talked on, about the school, about the tennis court, whether it would ever again be as good as it had been that first summer. They walked to inspect it and pressed a few more tapes more firmly down. A little stiltedly, perhaps trying to make too much of the moment, to prolong it. Richard led the boy to the spot in the field where the view was best, of the metallic blue river, the emerald marsh, the scattered islands velvet with shadow in the low light, the white bits of beach far away. "See," he said. "It goes on being beautiful. It'll be here tomorrow."

"I know," John answered, impatiently. The moment had closed.

Back in the house, the others had opened some white wine, the campagne being drunk, and still sat at the table, the three females, gossiping. Where Joan sat had become the head. She turned, showing him a tearless face, and asked, "All right?"

"We're fine," he said, resenting it, though relieved, that the party went on without him.

In bed she explained, "I couldn't cry I guess because I cried so much all spring. It really wasn't fair. It's your idea, and you make it look as though I was kicking you out."

"I'm sorry," he said. "I couldn't stop. I wanted to but couldn't."

"You *didn't* want to. You loved it. You were having your way, making a general announcement."

"I love having it over," he admitted. "God, those kids were great. So brave and funny." John, returned to the house, had settled to a model airplane in his room, and kept shouting down to them, "I'm O.K. No sweat." "And the way," Richard went on, cozy in his relief, "they never questioned the reasons we gave. No thought of a third person. Not even Judith."

"That *was* touching," Joan said.

He gave her a hug. "You were great too. Thank you." Guiltily, he realized he did not feel separated.

"You still have Dickie to do," she told him. These words set before him a black mountain in the darkness; its cold breath, its near weight affected his chest. Of the four children Dickie was most nearly his conscience. Joan did not need to add, "That's one piece of your dirty work I won't do for you."

"I know. I'll do it. You go to sleep."

Within minutes, her breathing slowed, became oblivious and deep. It was quarter to midnight. Dickie's train from the concert would come in at one-fourteen. Richard set the alarm for one. He had slept atrociously for weeks. But whenever he closed his lids some glimpse of the last hours scorched him— Judith exhaling toward the ceiling in a kind of aversion, Bean's mute staring, the sunstruck growth of the field where he and John had rested. The mountain before him moved closer, moved within him; he was huge, momentous. The ache at the back of his throat felt stale. His wife slept as if slain beside him. When, exasperated by his hot lids, his crowded heart, he rose from bed and dressed, she awoke enough to turn over. He told her then, "If I could undo it all, I would."

"Where would you begin?" she asked. There was no place. Giving him courage, she was always giving him courage. He put on shoes without socks in the dark. The children were breathing in their rooms, the downstairs was hollow. In their confusion they had left lights burning. He turned off all but one, the kitchen overhead. The car started. He had hoped it wouldn't. He met only moonlight on the road; it seemed a diaphanous companion, flickering in the leaves along the roadside, haunting his rearview mirror like a pursuer, melting under his headlights. The center of town, not quite deserted, was eerie at this hour. A young cop in uniform kept company with a gang of T-shirted kids on the steps of the bank. Across from the railroad station, several bars kept open. Customers, mostly young, passed in and out of the warm night, savoring summer's novelty. Voices shouted from cars as they passed; an immense conversation seemed in progress. Richard parked and in his weariness put his head on the passenger seat, out of the commotion and wheeling lights. It was as when, in the movies, an assassin grimly carries his mission through the jostle of a carnival—except the movies cannot show the precipitous, palpable slope you cling to within. You cannot climb back down; you can only fall. The synthetic fabric of the car seat, warmed by his cheek, confided to him an ancient, distant scene of vanilla.

A train whistle caused him to lift his head. It was on time; he had hoped it would be late. The slender drawgates descended. The bell of approach tingled happily. The great metal body, horizontally fluted, rocked to a stop, and sleepy teen-agers disembarked, his son among them. Dickie did not show surprise that his father was meeting him at this terrible hour. He sauntered to the car with two friends, both taller than he. He said "Hi" to his father and took the passenger's seat with an exhausted promptness that expressed gratitude. The friends got into the back, and Richard was grateful; a few more minutes' postponement would be won by driving them home.

He asked, "How was the concert?"

"Groovy," one boy said from the back seat.

"It bit," the other said.

"It was O.K.," Dickie said, moderate by nature, so reasonable that in his childhood the unreason of the world had given him headaches, stomach aches, nausea. When the second friend had been dropped off at his dark house, the boy blurted, "Dad, my eyes are killing me with hay fever! I'm out there cutting that mothering grass all day!"

"Do we still have those drops?"

"They didn't do any good last summer."

"They might this." Richard swung a U-turn on the empty street. The drive home took a few minutes. The mountain was here, in his throat. "Richard," he said, and felt the boy, slumped and rubbing his eyes, go tense at his tone, "I didn't come to meet you just to make your life easier. I came because your mother and I have some news for you, and you're a hard man to get ahold of these days. It's sad news."

"That's O.K." The reassurance came out soft, but quick, as if released from the tip of a spring.

Richard had feared that his tears would return and choke him, but the boy's manliness set an example, and his voice issued forth steady and dry. "It's sad news, but it needn't be tragic news, at least for you. It should have no practical effect on your life, though it's bound to have an emotional effect. You'll work at your job, and go back to school in September. Your mother and I are really proud of what you're making of your life; we don't want that to change at all."

"Yeah," the boy said lightly, on the intake of his breath, holding himself up. They turned the corner; the church they went to loomed like a gutted fort. The home of the woman Richard hoped to marry stood across the green. Her bedroom light burned.

"Your mother and I," he said, "have decided to separate. For the summer. Nothing legal, no divorce yet. We want to see how it feels. For some years now, we haven't been doing enough for each other, making each other as happy as we should be. Have you sensed that?"

"No," the boy said. It was an honest, unemotional answer: true or false in a quiz.

Glad for the factual basis, Richard pursued, even garrulously, the details. His apartment across town, his utter accessibility, the split vacation arrangements, the advantages to the children, the added mobility and variety of the summer. Dickie listened, absorbing. "Do the others know?"

Richard described how they had been told.

"How did they take it?"

"The girls pretty calmly. John flipped out; he shouted and ate a cigarette and made a salad out of his napkin and told us how much he hated school."

His brother chuckled. "He did?"

"Yeah. The school issue was more upsetting for him than Mom and me. He seemed to feel better for having exploded."

"He did?" The repetition was the first sign that he was stunned.

"Yes. Dickie, I want to tell you something. This last hour, waiting for your train to get in, has been about the worst in my life. I hate this. *Hate* it. My father would have died before doing it to me." He felt immensely lighter, saying this. He had dumped the mountain on the boy. They were home. Moving swiftly as a shadow, Dickie was out of the car, through the bright kitchen. Richard called after him, "Want a glass of milk or anything?"

"No thanks."

"Want us to call the course tomorrow and say you're too sick to work?"

"No, that's all right." The answer was faint, delivered at the door to his room; Richard listened for the slam of a tantrum. The door closed normally. The sound was sickening.

Joan had sunk into that first deep trough of sleep and was slow to awake. Richard had to repeat, "I told him."

"What did he say?"

"Nothing much. Could you go say good night to him? Please."

She left their room, without putting on a bathrobe. He sluggishly changed back into his pajamas and walked down the hall. Dickie was already in bed,

Joan was sitting beside him, and the boy's bedside clock radio was murmuring music. When she stood, an inexplicable light—the moon?—outlined her body through the nightie. Richard sat on the warm place she had indented on the child's narrow mattress. He asked him, "Do you want the radio on like that?"

"It always is."

"Doesn't it keep you awake? It would me."

"No."

"Are you sleepy?"

"Yeah."

"Good. Sure you want to get up and go to work? You've had a big night."

"I want to."

Away at school this winter he had learned for the first time that you can go short of sleep and live. As an infant he had slept with an immobile sweating intensity that had alarmed his babysitters. As the children aged, he became the first to go to bed, earlier for a time than his younger brother and sister. Even now, he would go slack in the middle of a television show, his sprawled legs hairy and brown. "O.K. Good boy. Dickie, listen. I love you so much, I never knew how much until now. No matter how this works out, I'll always be with you. Really."

Richard bent to kiss an averted face but his son, sinewy, turned and with wet cheeks embraced him and gave him a kiss, on the lips, passionate as a woman's. In his father's ear he moaned one word, the crucial, intelligent word: "*Why?*"

Why. It was a whistle of wind in a crack, a knife thrust, a window thrown open on emptiness. The white face was gone, the darkness was featureless. Richard had forgotten why.

Questions

1. What does the narrator mean when he calls Richard and Joan Maple "the only stain in Nature"?
2. How did Richard wish to tell the children the news of the separation? How did Joan? Whose plan was finally chosen? Whose plan was executed? Why?
3. Is there any difference between Joan's sense of responsibility to the family and Richard's? How is it manifested?
4. Why do you suppose Richard speaks privately to John and later to Dick and that Joan stays with the daughters in the house?
5. What does Richard mean when he tells Dick, "My father would have died before doing it to me"? What does this statement indicate about Richard? What does it indicate about changing social values?
6. Why is Richard leaving Joan?
7. Compare Richard's behavior with Mary's behavior in "The Artificial Family." Who seems to act more wisely? Who acts more typically? Do you feel sympathy for either Richard or Mary? Why?

12 🌿 The Novella

Today we speak of three major types of narrative fiction: the short story, the novella (or short novel), and the novel. But this was not always the case. In the long history of literature, these narrative types are very recent. In neither Homer's, Dante's, nor Shakespeare's time, did the novel as we know it exist. Instead there were two major forms of long narrative fiction: the *romance*, which strung together a number of fantastic and supernatural episodes; and the *novella*, which—as in Boccaccio's *Decameron*—organized a number of anecdotes through a frame device. In sum, long prose works were made up of smaller works pieced together, and lacked the unity and coherence we associate with the modern novel.

The process by which these early forms evolved into the short story, novella, and novel took a long time, and is not entirely understood. But we can imagine its basic steps. Pretend that you wanted to write a long work of fiction because you had enjoyed and admired other long works of fiction and because you thought you could make some money from it. (Daniel Defoe and Samuel Richardson, two early innovators of the novel, both tried to live off their writing.) How would you go about it? First you would see how others had gone about telling stories. You might copy the features you liked (or thought might make the work popular and profitable), ignoring those elements you thought less useful or pleasing. Then you might add some ideas of your own. The work would be a combination of the tried and the new, something like what had come before but a little different. You can see how a form would slowly evolve if such a process were repeated over several centuries.

Because the novel arose from a practical, trial-and-error process, there are no simple laws to define its shape or nature. Unlike some poetic forms, the novel, the modern novella, and the short story emerged without theory, rules, or clear procedures. Consequently, these forms are various, elusive, and hard to define.

In this chapter we will try to give you some rules of thumb by which you can distinguish among the various forms. But remember that there are numerous exceptions to these guidelines.

Length

One of the easiest ways of distinguishing these forms is by length. A short story, by definition, is relatively short. A novel is long, and a novella lies somewhere in between. Such distinctions are, of course, vague. How short is short? One page? Ten? A hundred?

Edgar Allan Poe, one of the earliest theorists of the short story, believed the short story should be read in one sitting. For a story to have its true and greatest impact, he felt that it should not be interrupted. Thus, for Poe, a short story was determined by the reader's span of attention. The outer limit was twenty pages.

There was another determining factor in the length of the short story—the newspapers and magazines in which it appeared. Until the second world war, short fiction was a common, indeed necessary part of magazines. In some journals the reading time appeared on the opening page to inform the busy reader how extensive an effort the story demanded. Because of the physical requirements of magazines, the short story took on a length of 6,000 to 8,000 words.

Similar practicalities determined the length of a novel. Hardbound books have always been expensive. Publishers realized that the public did not feel it had received its money's worth if a novel were short. A single volume novel should run at least three hundred pages or else it would look too skimpy to the money-conscious reader. Books, then as now, were often judged by their covers, or at least by the thickness of their binding.

The term *novella*, thus, came to describe a work between the two extremes of the ten-page short story and the three-hundred page novel. But there are other differences among these three types of fiction.

Expansion and Compression

Writers are torn between two basic and contrary impulses—either to expand their works, fully developing their fictive worlds, or to compress their stories into the shortest, most potent, most highly concentrated form. Classical rhetoric distinguished these impulses as *brevitas* or brevity and *amplificatio* or amplification. By following one or the other of these impulses, writers discover the form they wish to use.

The short story, clearly, is the most compressed of the forms. The short story writer wishes to cultivate *brevitas*. The short story usually limits the author to a few characters, a single setting, and a limited period of narrative time. The details of a short story are chosen for their imaginative resonance, for their suggestiveness. Short stories work *microcosmically*, that is, they present a world in miniature that has significance for a larger world or macrocosm. Thus the Salem of Hawthorne's "Young Goodman Brown" becomes a microcosm of Puritan society. The short story writer works in miniature, expecting the reader to see wider and deeper implications.

The novelist, in contrast, tries to develop and expand the material in his or her fiction. The novelist cultivates *amplificatio*. Instead of being limited to a few characters, a single setting, and a limited period of narrative time, the novel can trace families through several generations, continents, and cataclysmic events. George Eliot's *Middlemarch* is a panoramic study of an English town in the 1830s; Tolstoy's *War and Peace* tracks Napoleon's campaign through Russia. Of course, not all novels are so ambitious; nevertheless, the novelist has the option to develop any theme of the story as fully as possible.

The modern novella balances the tight restrictions of the short story and the limitless terrain of the novel. In the novella one typically finds more characters, more episodes, and a longer narrative time span than in the short story. Yet the total work is compact in comparison with the novel. In the typical novella one fictional element is fully developed. In Thomas Mann's "Death in Venice," the fully-developed element is its psychological symbolism. In Joseph Conrad's "Heart of Darkness," the symbolic setting is fully developed. In "Bartleby the Scrivener," the story fully develops the psychological relationship between the narrator and Bartleby.

Structure

To achieve the degree of concentration necessary to keep a story short, the writers of short stories usually focus on one important event. For example, "The Horse Dealer's Daughter" is concerned with answering a single question: What's to become of Mabel? The entire action of the story takes place on the day the Pervins are vacating their home. "My Man Bovanne" concentrates on a neighborhood meeting. "The Jilting of Granny Weatherall" does narrate events that occurred throughout Granny's life, but it is important to note that the events are viewed from the perspective of her final illness and from the vantage point of her disoriented recollection. Because short story writers usually concentrate on one significant event, readers should ask themselves why the authors have chosen that particular event. For example, one should understand the significance of Mabel Pervin's departure from Oldmeadow or the importance of the neighborhood meeting in "My Man Bovanne."

The novel is far more complex. In most novels there is not just one significant event, but several. Moreover, many novels have several plots, narrated alternately. We usually refer to a *main plot* and *subplots* to distinguish between the central narrative and subordinate narratives. Short stories do not contain subplots.

The novella combines structural elements of both the novel and the short story. Although the novella usually has no subplots, it develops its narrative through a number of events. In "Bartleby the Scrivener," Melville concentrates on the end of Bartleby's life. What comes before is entirely mysterious.

Summary

A short story is distinguished by its concentration. It concentrates on a single event, a small number of characters, a single setting and short narrative time span.

A novel is distinguished by its expansiveness and inclusiveness. It contains numerous characters, events, and settings, and extends over a long narrative time span. Typically the novel includes subplots that further enlarge and complicate the structure.

The novella stands midway between the two. It fully develops one aspect of a narrative. While it generally contains no subplots, it does contain a number of different events, often emphasizing one sequence over the others. Though the novella expands one fictional element, it usually compresses the others as does the short story.

Henry James, one of America's greatest fiction writers, complained about "the general indifference" in distinguishing between these forms and the failure to appreciate the novella's special importance. James wrote:

> In that dull view [which did not distinguish the short story from the novella] a "short story" was a "short story," and that was the end of it. Shades and differences, varieties and styles, the value above all of the idea happily *developed*, [in the novella] languished, to extinction, under the hard-and-fast rule of the "from six to eight thousand words" . . . For myself, I delight in the shapely [novella].[1]

Suggestions for Essayists

1. Show how one entity is the microcosm of a larger entity. For example, show how your family is a microcosm of American society, how your growth is a microcosm of social maturity, or how your garden exhibits in microcosm ecological features of the entire planet.
2. Defend or attack the Shakespearean statement that "brevity is the soul of wit."
3. Discuss how economic and physical limitations affect films, television programs, or plays.

Suggestions for Fiction Writers

1. Take an anecdote and tell it in the shortest form you can. Then expand the anecdote as far as you can. (You might examine the two versions of the story in Grace Paley's "A Conversation with My Father.")
2. Write a story about how you go about writing a story. From what do you draw your inspiration?

---

[1] Henry James, *The Art of the Novel* (New York: Scribner's, 1934), p. 220.

HERMAN MELVILLE (1819–1891)

Bartleby the Scrivener

I am a rather elderly man. The nature of my avocations, for the last thirty years, has brought me into more than ordinary contact with what would seem an interesting and somewhat singular set of men, of whom, as yet, nothing, that I know of, has ever been written—I mean, the law-copyists, or scriveners. I have known very many of them, professionally and privately, and, if I pleased, could relate divers histories, at which good-natured gentlemen might smile, and sentimental souls might weep. But I waive the biographies of all other scriveners, for a few passages in the life of Bartleby, who was a scrivener, the strangest I ever saw, or heard of. While, of other law-copyists, I might write the complete life, of Bartleby nothing of that sort can be done. I believe that no materials exist, for a full and satisfactory biography of this man. It is an irreparable loss to literature. Bartleby was one of those beings of whom nothing is ascertainable, except from the original sources, and, in his case, those are very small. What my own astonished eyes saw of Bartleby, *that* is all I know of him, except, indeed, one vague report, which will appear in the sequel.

Ere introducing the scrivener, as he first appeared to me, it is fit I make some mention of myself, my *employés*, my business, my chambers, and general surroundings; because some such description is indispensable to an adequate understanding of the chief character about to be presented. Imprimis:[1] I am a man who, from his youth upwards has been filled with a profound conviction that the easiest way of life is the best. Hence, though I belong to a profession proverbially energetic and nervous, even to turbulence, at times, yet nothing of that sort have I ever suffered to invade my peace. I am one of those unambitious lawyers who never addresses a jury, or in any way draws down public applause; but, in the cool tranquillity of a snug retreat, do a snug business among the rich men's bonds, and mortgages, and title-deeds. All who know me, consider me an eminently *safe* man. The late John Jacob Astor,[2] a personage little given to poetic enthusiasm, had no hesitation in pronouncing my first grand point to be prudence; my next, method. I do not speak it in vanity, but simply record the fact, that I was not unemployed in my profession by the late John Jacob Astor, a name which, I admit, I love to repeat; for it hath a rounded and orbicular[3] sound to it, and rings like unto bullion.[4] I will freely add, that I was not insensible to the late John Jacob Astor's good opinion.

Some time prior to the period at which this little history begins, my avocations had been largely increased. The good old office, now extinct in the State of New York, of a Master in Chancery, had been conferred upon me. It was not

---

[1] Imprimis is Latin for "in the first place." The word is used to begin a list.
[2] John Jacob Astor (1763–1848) was the founder of a family fortune based on fur trading and real estate.
[3] Orbicular means to be rounded like a sphere.
[4] Bullion is coined gold or silver in bars.

a very arduous office, but very pleasantly remunerative. I seldom lose my temper; much more seldom indulge in dangerous indignation at wrongs and outrages; but, I must be permitted to be rash here, and declare, that I consider the sudden and violent abrogation of the office of Master in Chancery, by the new Constitution, as a——premature act; inasmuch as I had counted upon a life-lease of the profits, whereas I only received those of a few short years. But this is by the way.

My chambers were up stairs, at No.——Wall Street. At one end, they looked upon the white wall of the interior of a spacious sky-light shaft, penetrating the building from top to bottom.

This view might have been considered rather tame than otherwise, deficient in what landscape painters call "life." But, if so, the view from the other end of my chambers offered, at least, a contrast, if nothing more. In that direction, my windows commanded an unobstructed view of a lofty brick wall, black by age and everlasting shade; which wall required no spy-glass to bring out its lurking beauties, but, for the benefit of all near-sighted spectators, was pushed up to within ten feet of my window panes. Owing to the great height of the surrounding buildings, and my chambers being on the second floor, the interval between this wall and mine not a little resembled a huge square cistern.

At the period just preceding the advent of Bartleby, I had two persons as copyists in my employment, and a promising lad as an office-boy. First, Turkey; second, Nippers; third, Ginger Nut. These may seem names, the like of which are not usually found in the Directory.[5] In truth, they were nicknames, mutually conferred upon each other by my three clerks, and were deemed expressive of their respective persons or characters. Turkey was a short, pursy Englishman of about my own age—that is, somewhere not far from sixty. In the morning, one might say, his face was of a fine florid hue, but after twelve o'clock, meridian— his dinner hour—it blazed like a grate full of Christmas coals; and continued blazing—but, as it were, with a gradual wane—till six o'clock, P.M., or thereabouts; after which, I saw no more of the proprietor of the face, which, gaining its meridian with the sun, seemed to set with it, to rise, culminate, and decline the following day, with the like regularity and undiminished glory. There are many singular coincidences I have known in the course of my life, not the least among which was the fact, that, exactly when Turkey displayed his fullest beams from his red and radiant countenance, just then, too, at that critical moment, began the daily period when I considered his business capacities as seriously disturbed for the remainder of the twenty-four hours. Not that he was absolutely idle, or averse to business then; far from it. The difficulty was, he was apt to be altogether too energetic. There was a strange, inflamed, flurried, flightly reck-lessness of activity about him. He would be incautious in dipping his pen into his inkstand. All his blots upon my documents were dropped there after twelve o'clock, meridian. Indeed, not only would he be reckless, and sadly given to making blots in the afternoon, but, some days, he went further, and was rather

---

[5] The Directory is a listing of all the businesses and residences in the city.

noisy. At such times, too, his face flamed with augmented blazonry, as if cannel coal had been heaped on anthracite. He made an unpleasant racket with his chair; spilled his sand-box; in mending his pens, impatiently split them all to pieces, and threw them on the floor in a sudden passion; stood up, and leaned over his table, boxing his papers about in a most indecorous manner, very sad to behold in an elderly man like him. Nevertheless, as he was in many ways a most valuable person to me, and all the time before twelve o'clock, meridian, was the quickest, steadiest creature, too, accomplishing a great deal of work in a style not easily to be matched—for these reasons, I was willing to overlook his eccentricities, though, indeed, occasionally, I remonstrated with him. I did this very gently, however, because, though the civilest, nay, the blandest and most reverential of men in the morning, yet, in the afternoon, he was disposed, upon provocation, to be slightly rash with his tongue—in fact, insolent. Now, valuing his morning services as I did, and resolved not to lose them—yet, at the same time, made uncomfortable by his inflamed ways after twelve o'clock—and being a man of peace, unwilling by my admonitions to call forth unseemly retorts from him, I took upon me, one Saturday noon (he was always worse on Saturdays) to hint to him, very kindly, that, perhaps, now that he was growing old, it might be well to abridge his labors; in short, he need not come to my chambers after twelve o'clock, but, dinner over, had best go home to his lodgings, and rest himself till tea-time. But no; he insisted upon his afternoon devotions. His countenance became intolerably fervid, as he oratorically assured me—gesticulating with a long ruler at the other end of the room—that if his services in the morning were useful, how indispensable, then, in the afternoon?

"With submission, sir," said Turkey, on this occasion, "I consider myself your right-hand man. In the morning I but marshal and deploy my columns; but in the afternoon I put myself at their head, and gallantly charge the foe, thus"—and he made a violent thrust with the ruler.

"But the blots, Turkey," intimated I.

"True; but, with submission, sir, behold these hairs! I am getting old. Surely, sir, a blot or two of a warm afternoon is not to be severely urged against gray hairs. Old age—even if it blot the page—is honorable. With submission, sir, we *both* are getting old."

This appeal to my fellow-feeling was hardly to be resisted. At all events, I saw that go he would not. So, I made up my mind to let him stay, resolving, nevertheless, to see to it that, during the afternoon, he had to do with my less important papers.

Nippers, the second on my list, was a whiskered, sallow, and, upon the whole, rather piratical-looking young man, of about five and twenty. I always deemed him the victim of two evil powers—ambition and indigestion. The ambition was evinced by a certain impatience of the duties of a mere copyist, an unwarrantable usurpation of strictly professional affairs, such as the original drawing up of legal documents. The indigestion seemed betokened in an occasional nervous testiness and grinning irritability, causing the teeth to audibly grind together over mistakes committed in copying; unnecessary maledictions, hissed, rather than spoken, in the heat of business; and especially by a continual discontent with the height of the table where he worked. Though of a very ingenious mechanical turn, Nippers could never get this table to suit him. He put chips under it, blocks of various sorts, bits of pasteboard, and at last went so far as to attempt an exquisite adjustment, by final pieces of folded blotting-paper. But no invention would answer. If, for the sake of easing his back, he brought the table lid at a sharp angle well up towards his chin, and wrote there like a man using the steep roof of a Dutch house for his desk, then he declared that it stopped the circulation in his arms. If now he lowered the table to his waistbands, and stooped over it in writing, then there was a sore aching in his back. In short, the truth of the matter was, Nippers knew not what he wanted. Or, if he wanted anything, it was to be rid of a scrivener's table altogether. Among the manifestations of his diseased ambition was a fondness he had for receiving visits from certain ambiguous-looking fellows in seedy coats, whom he called his clients. Indeed, I was aware that not only was he, at times, considerable of a ward-politician, but he occasionally did a little business at the Justices' courts, and was not unknown on the steps of the Tombs.[6] I have good reason to believe, however, that one individual who called upon him at my chambers, and who, with a grand air, he insisted was his client, was no other than a dun, and the alleged title-deed, a bill. But, with all his failings, and the annoyances he caused me, Nippers, like his compatriot Turkey, was a very useful man to me; wrote a neat, swift hand; and, when he chose, was not deficient in a gentlemanly sort of deportment. Added to this, he always dressed in a gentlemanly sort of way; and so, incidentally, reflected credit upon my chambers. Whereas, with respect to Turkey, I had much ado to keep him from being a reproach to me. His clothes were apt to look oily, and smell of eating-houses. He wore his pantaloons very loose and baggy in summer. His coats were execrable; his hat not to be handled. But while the hat was a thing of indifference to me, inasmuch as his natural civility and deference, as a dependent Englishman, always led him to doff it the moment he entered the room, yet his coat was another matter. Concerning his coats, I reasoned with him; but with no effect. The truth was, I suppose, that a man with so small an income could not afford to sport such a lustrous face and a lustrous coat at one and the same time. As Nippers once observed, Turkey's money went chiefly for red ink. One winter day, I presented Turkey with a highly respectable-looking coat of my own—a padded gray coat, of a most comfortable warmth, and which buttoned straight up from the knee to the neck. I thought Turkey would appreciate the favor, and abate his rashness and obstreperousness of afternoons. But no; I verily believe that buttoning himself up in so downy and blanket-like a coat had a pernicious effect upon him—upon the same principle that too much oats are bad for horses. In fact, precisely as a rash, restive horse is said to feel his oats, so Turkey felt his coat. It made him insolent. He was a man whom prosperity harmed.

Though, concerning the self-indulgent habits of Turkey, I had my own private

---

[6] The Tombs is the name given to the New York City Jail located in lower Manhattan.

surmises, yet, touching Nippers, I was well persuaded that, whatever might be his faults in other respects, he was, at least, a temperate young man. But, indeed, nature herself seemed to have been his vintner, and, at his birth, charged him so thoroughly with an irritable, brandy-like disposition, that all subsequent potations were needless. When I consider how, amid the stillness of my chambers, Nippers would sometimes impatiently rise from his seat, and stooping over his table, spread his arms wide apart, seize the whole desk, and move it, and jerk it, with a grim, grinding motion on the floor, as if the table were a perverse voluntary agent, intent on thwarting and vexing him, I plainly perceive that, for Nippers, brandy-and-water were altogether superfluous.

It was fortunate for me that, owing to its peculiar cause—indigestion—the irritability and consequent nervousness of Nippers were mainly observable in the morning, while in the afternoon he was comparatively mild. So that, Turkey's paroxysms only coming on about twelve o'clock, I never had to do with their eccentricities at one time. Their fits relieved each other, like guards. When Nippers' was on, Turkey's was off; and *vice versa*. This was a good natural arrangement, under the circumstances.

Ginger Nut, the third on my list, was a lad, some twelve years old. His father was a car-man, ambitious of seeing his son on the bench instead of a cart, before he died. So he sent him to my office, as student at law, errand-boy, cleaner and sweeper, at the rate of one dollar a week. He had a little desk to himself, but he did not use it much. Upon inspection, the drawer exhibited a great array of the shells of various sorts of nuts. Indeed, to this quick-witted youth, the whole noble science of the law was contained in a nut-shell. Not the least among the employments of Ginger Nut, as well as one which he discharged with the most alacrity, was his duty as cake and apple purveyor for Turkey and Nippers. Copying law-papers being proverbially a dry, husky sort of business, my two scriveners were fain to moisten their mouths very often with Spitzenbergs,[7] to be had at the numerous stalls nigh the Custom House and the Post Office. Also, they sent Ginger Nut very frequently for that peculiar cake—small, flat, round, and very spicy—after which he had been named by them. Of a cold morning, when business was but dull, Turkey would gobble up scores of these cakes, as if they were mere wafers—indeed, they sell them at the rate of six or eight for a penny—the scrape of his pen blending with the crunching of the crisp particles in his mouth. Of all the fiery afternoon blunders and flurried rashnesses of Turkey, was his once moistening a ginger-cake between his lips, and clapping it on to a mortgage, for a seal. I came within an ace of dismissing him then. But he mollified me by making an oriental bow, and saying—

"With submission, sir, it was generous of me to find you in stationery on my own account."

Now my original business—that of a conveyancer and title hunter, and drawer-up of recondite documents of all sorts—was considerably increased by receiving

---

[7] Spitzenbergs are a variety of apple native to New York State.

the master's office. There was now great work for scriveners. Not only must I push the clerks already with me, but I must have additional help.

In answer to my advertisement, a motionless young man one morning stood upon my office threshold, the door being open, for it was summer. I can see that figure now—pallidly neat, pitiably respectable, incurably forlorn! It was Bartleby.

After a few words touching his qualifications, I engaged him, glad to have among my corps of copyists a man of so singularly sedate an aspect, which I thought might operate beneficially upon the flighty temper of Turkey, and the fiery one of Nippers.

I should have stated before that ground glass folding-doors divided my premises into two parts, one of which was occupied by my scriveners, the other by myself. According to my humor, I threw open these doors, or closed them. I resolved to assign Bartleby a corner by the folding-doors, but on my side of them, so as to have this quiet man within easy call, in case any trifling thing was to be done. I placed his desk close up to a small side-window in that part of the room, a window which originally had afforded a lateral view of certain grimy backyards and bricks, but which, owing to subsequent erections, commanded at present no view at all, though it gave some light. Within three feet of the panes was a wall, and the light came down from far above, between two lofty buildings, as from a very small opening in a dome. Still further to a satisfactory arrangement, I procured a high green folding screen, which might entirely isolate Bartleby from my sight, though not remove him from my voice. And thus, in a manner, privacy and society were conjoined.

At first, Bartleby did an extraordinary quantity of writing. As if long famishing for something to copy, he seemed to gorge himself on my documents. There was no pause for digestion. He ran a day and night line, copying by sun-light and by candle-light. I should have been quite delighted with his application, had he been cheerfully industrious. But he wrote on silently, palely, mechanically.

It is, of course, an indispensable part of a scrivener's business to verify the accuracy of his copy, word by word. Where there are two or more scriveners in an office, they assist each other in this examination, one reading from the copy, the other holding the original. It is a very dull, wearisome, and lethargic affair. I can readily imagine that, to some sanguine temperaments, it would be altogether intolerable. For example, I cannot credit that the mettlesome poet, Byron, would have contentedly sat down with Bartleby to examine a law document of, say five hundred pages, closely written in a crimpy hand.

Now and then, in the haste of business, it had been my habit to assist in comparing some brief document myself, calling Turkey or Nippers for this purpose. One object I had, in placing Bartleby so handy to me behind the screen, was, to avail myself of his services on such trivial occasions. It was on the third day, I think, of his being with me, and before any necessity had arisen for having his own writing examined, that, being much hurried to complete a small affair I had in hand, I abruptly called to Bartleby. In my haste and natural expectancy of instant compliance, I sat with my head bent over the original on my desk, and my right hand sideways, and somewhat nervously extended with the copy, so that, immediately upon emerging from his retreat, Bartleby might snatch it and proceed to business without the least delay.

In this very attitude did I sit when I called to him, rapidly stating what it was I wanted him to do—namely, to examine a small paper with me. Imagine my surprise, nay, my consternation, when, without moving from his privacy, Bartleby, in a singularly mild, firm voice, replied, "I would prefer not to."

I sat awhile in perfect silence, rallying my stunned faculties. Immediately it occurred to me that my ears had deceived me, or Bartleby had entirely misunderstood my meaning. I repeated my request in the clearest tone I could assume; but in quite as clear a one came the previous reply, "I would prefer not to."

"Prefer not to," echoed I, rising in high excitement, and crossing the room with a stride. "What do you mean? Are you moon-struck? I want you to help me compare this sheet here—take it," and I thrust it towards him.

"I would prefer not to," said he.

I looked at him steadfastly. His face was leanly composed; his gray eye dimly calm. Not a wrinkle of agitation rippled him. Had there been the least uneasiness, anger, impatience or impertinence in his manner; in other words, had there been any thing ordinarily human about him, doubtless I should have violently dismissed him from the premises. But as it was, I should have as soon thought of turning my pale plaster-of-paris bust of Cicero[8] out of doors. I stood gazing at him awhile, as he went on with his own writing, and then reseated myself at my desk. This is very strange, thought I. What had one best do? But my business hurried me. I concluded to forget the matter for the present, reserving it for my future leisure. So calling Nippers from the other room, the paper was speedily examined.

A few days after this, Bartleby concluded four lengthy documents, being quadruplicates of a week's testimony taken before me in my High Court of Chancery. It became necessary to examine them. It was an important suit, and great accuracy was imperative. Having all things arranged, I called Turkey, Nippers, and Ginger Nut, from the next room, meaning to place the four copies in the hands of my four clerks, while I should read from the original. Accordingly, Turkey, Nippers, and Ginger Nut had taken their seats in a row, each with his document in his hand, when I called to Bartleby to join this interesting group.

"Bartleby! quick, I am waiting."

I heard a slow scrape of his chairlegs on the uncarpeted floor, and soon he appeared standing at the entrance of his hermitage.

"What is wanted?" said he, mildly.

"The copies, the copies," said I, hurriedly. "We are going to examine them. There"—and I held towards him the fourth quadruplicate.

"I would prefer not to," he said, and gently disappeared behind the screen.

For a few moments I was turned into a pillar of salt, standing at the head of

---

[8] Cicero (106–43 B.C.) was a Roman orator, statesman, and philosopher.

my seated column of clerks. Recovering myself, I advanced towards the screen, and demanded the reason for such extraordinary conduct.

"*Why* do you refuse?"

"I would prefer not to."

With any other man I should have flown outright into a dreadful passion, scorned all further words, and thrust him ignominiously from my presence. But there was something about Bartleby that not only strangely disarmed me, but, in a wonderful manner, touched and disconcerted me. I began to reason with him.

"These are your own copies we are about to examine. It is labor saving to you, because one examination will answer for your four papers. It is common usage. Every copyist is bound to help examine his copy. Is it not so? Will you not speak? Answer!"

"I prefer not to," he replied in a flutelike tone. It seemed to me that, while I had been addressing him, he carefully revolved every statement that I made; fully comprehended the meaning; could not gainsay the irresistible conclusion; but, at the same time, some paramount consideration prevailed with him to reply as he did.

"You are decided, then, not to comply with my request—a request made according to common usage and common sense?"

He briefly gave me to understand, that on that point my judgment was sound. Yes: his decision was irreversible.

It is not seldom the case that, when a man is browbeaten in some unprecedented and violently unreasonable way, he begins to stagger in his own plainest faith. He begins, as it were, vaguely to surmise that, wonderful as it may be, all the justice and all the reason is on the other side. Accordingly, if any disinterested persons are present, he turns to them for some reinforcement of his own faltering mind.

"Turkey," said I, "what do you think of this? Am I not right?"

"With submission, sir," said Turkey, in his blandest tone, "I think that you are."

"Nippers," said I, "what do *you* think of it?"

"I think I should kick him out of the office."

(The reader, of nice perceptions, will here perceive that, it being morning, Turkey's answer is couched in polite and tranquil terms, but Nippers' replies in ill-tempered ones. Or, to repeat a previous sentence, Nippers' ugly mood was on duty, and Turkey's off.)

"Ginger Nut," said I, willing to enlist the smallest suffrage in my behalf, "what do *you* think of it?"

"I think, sir, he's a little *luny*," replied Ginger Nut, with a grin.

"You hear what they say," said I, turning towards the screen, "come forth and do your duty."

But he vouchsafed no reply. I pondered a moment in sore perplexity. But once more business hurried me. I determined again to postpone the consideration of this dilemma to my future leisure. With a little trouble we made out to examine the papers without Bartleby, though at every page or two Turkey deferentially dropped his opinion, that this proceeding was quite out of the common; while Nippers, twitching in his chair with a dyspeptic[9] nervousness, ground out, between his set teeth, occasional hissing maledictions against the stubborn oaf behind the screen. And for his (Nippers') part, this was the first and the last time he would do another man's business without pay.

Meanwhile Bartleby sat in his hermitage, oblivious to everything but his own peculiar business there.

Some days passed, the scrivener being employed upon another lengthy work. His late remarkable conduct led me to regard his ways narrowly. I observed that he never went to dinner; indeed, that he never went anywhere. As yet I had never, of my personal knowledge, known him to be outside of my office. He was a perpetual sentry in the corner. At about eleven o'clock though, in the morning, I noticed that Ginger Nut would advance toward the opening in Bartleby's screen, as if silently beckoned thither by a gesture invisible to me where I sat. The boy would then leave the office, jingling a few pence, and reappear with a handful of ginger-nuts, which he delivered in the hermitage, receiving two of the cakes for his trouble.

He lives, then, on ginger-nuts, thought I; never eats a dinner, properly speaking; he must be a vegetarian, then; but no; he never eats even vegetables, he eats nothing but ginger-nuts. My mind then ran on in reveries concerning the probable effects upon the human constitution of living entirely on ginger-nuts. Ginger-nuts are so called, because they contain ginger as one of their peculiar constituents, and the final flavoring one. Now, what was ginger? A hot, spicy thing. Was Bartleby hot and spicy? Not at all. Ginger, then, had no effect upon Bartleby. Probably he preferred it should have none.

Nothing so aggravates an earnest person as a passive resistance. If the individual so resisted be of a not inhumane temper, and the resisting one perfectly harmless in his passivity, then, in the better moods of the former, he will endeavor charitably to construe to his imagination what proves impossible to be solved by his judgment. Even so, for the most part, I regarded Bartleby and his ways. Poor fellow! thought I, he means no mischief; it is plain he intends no insolence; his aspect sufficiently evinces that his eccentricities are involuntary. He is useful to me. I can get along with him. If I turn him away, the chances are he will fall in with some less-indulgent employer, and then he will be rudely treated, and perhaps driven forth miserably to starve. Yes. Here I can cheaply purchase a delicious self-approval. To befriend Bartleby; to humor him in his strange willfulness, will cost me little or nothing, while I lay up in my soul what will eventually prove a sweet morsel for my conscience. But this mood was not invariable with me. The passiveness of Bartleby sometimes irritated me. I felt strangely goaded on to encounter him in new opposition—to elicit some angry

---

[9] Dyspeptic refers to indigestion.

spark from him answerable to my own. But, indeed, I might as well have essayed to strike fire with my knuckles against a bit of Windsor soap. But one afternoon the evil impulse in me mastered me, and the following little scene ensued:

"Bartleby," said I, "when those papers are all copied, I will compare them with you."

"I would prefer not to."

"How? Surely you do not mean to persist in that mulish vagary?"

No answer.

I threw open the folding-doors near by, and, turning upon Turkey and Nippers, exclaimed:

"Bartleby a second time says, he won't examine his papers. What do you think of it, Turkey?"

It was afternoon, be it remembered. Turkey sat glowing like a brass boiler; his bald head steaming; his hands reeling among his blotted papers.

"Think if it?" roared Turkey; "I think I'll just step behind his screen, and black his eyes for him!"

So saying, Turkey rose to his feet and threw his arms into a pugilistic position. He was hurrying away to make good his promise, when I detained him, alarmed at the effect of incautiously rousing Turkey's combativeness after dinner.

"Sit down, Turkey," said I, "and hear what Nippers has to say. What do you think of it, Nippers? Would I not be justified in immediately dismissing Bartleby?"

"Excuse me, that is for you to decide, sir. I think his conduct quite unusual, and, indeed, unjust, as regards Turkey and myself. But it may only be a passing whim."

"Ah," exclaimed I, "you have strangely changed your mind, then—you speak very gently of him now."

"All beer," cried Turkey; "gentleness is effects of beer—Nippers and I dined together to-day. You see how gentle I am, sir. Shall I go and black his eyes?"

"You refer to Bartleby, I suppose. No, not to-day, Turkey," I replied; "pray, put up your fists."

I closed the doors, and again advanced towards Bartleby. I felt additional incentives tempting me to my fate. I burned to be rebelled against again. I remember that Bartleby never left the office.

"Bartleby," said I, "Ginger Nut is away; just step around to the Post Office, won't you? (it was but a three minutes' walk), and see if there is anything for me."

"I would prefer not to."

"You *will* not?"

"I *prefer* not."

I staggered to my desk, and sat there in a deep study. My blind inveteracy returned. Was there any other thing in which I could procure myself to be ignominiously repulsed by this lean, penniless wight?—my hired clerk? What added thing is there, perfectly reasonable, that he will be sure to refuse to do?

"Bartleby!"

No answer.

"Bartleby," in a louder tone.

No answer.

"Bartleby," I roared.

Like a very ghost, agreeably to the laws of magical invocation, at the third summons, he appeared at the entrance of his hermitage.

"Go to the next room, and tell Nippers to come to me."

"I prefer not to," he respectfully and slowly said, and mildly disappeared.

"Very good, Bartleby," said I, in a quiet sort of serenely-severe self-possessed tone, intimating the unalterable purpose of some terrible retribution very close at hand. But upon the whole, as it was drawing towards my dinner-hour, I thought it best to put on my hat and walk home for the day, suffering much from perplexity and distress of mind.

Shall I acknowledge it? The conclusion of this whole business was, that it soon became a fixed fact of my chambers, that a pale young scrivener, by the name of Bartleby, had a desk there; that he copied for me at the usual rate of four cents a folio (one hundred words); but he was permanently exempt from examining the work done by him, that duty being transferred to Turkey and Nippers, out of compliment, doubtless, to their superior acuteness; moreover, said Bartleby was never, on any account, to be dispatched on the most trivial errand of any sort; and that even if entreated to take upon him such a matter, it was generally understood that he would "prefer not to"—in other words, that he would refuse point-blank.

As days passed on, I became considerably reconciled to Bartleby. His steadiness, his freedom from all dissipation, his incessant industry (except when he chose to throw himself into a standing revery behind his screen), his great stillness, his unalterableness of demeanor under all circumstances, made him a valuable acquisition. One prime thing was this—*he was always there*—first in the morning, continually through the day, and the last at night. I had a singular confidence in his honesty. I felt my most precious papers perfectly safe in his hands. Sometimes, to be sure, I could not, for the very soul of me, avoid falling into sudden spasmodic passions with him. For it was exceeding difficult to bear in mind all the time those strange peculiarities, privileges, and unheard of exemptions, forming the tacit stipulations on Bartleby's part under which he remained in my office. Now and then, in the eagerness of dispatching pressing business, I would inadvertently summon Bartleby, in a short, rapid tone, to put his finger, say, on the incipient tie of a bit of red tape with which I was about compressing some papers. Of course, from behind the screen the usual answer, "I prefer not to," was sure to come; and then, how could a human creature, with the common infirmities of our nature, refrain from bitterly exclaiming upon such perverseness—such unreasonableness. However, every added repulse of this sort which I received only tended to lessen the probability of my repeating the inadvertence.

Here it must be said, that according to the custom of most legal gentlemen occupying chambers in densely-populated law buildings, there were several keys to my door. One was kept by a woman residing in the attic, which person weekly scrubbed and daily swept and dusted my apartments. Another was kept by Turkey for convenience sake. The third I sometimes carried in my own pocket. The fourth I knew not who had.

Now, one Sunday morning I happened to go to Trinity Church, to hear a celebrated preacher, and finding myself rather early on the ground I thought I would walk around to my chambers for a while. Luckily I had my key with me; but upon applying it to the lock, I found it resisted by something inserted from the inside. Quite surprised, I called out; when to my consternation a key was turned from within; and thrusting his lean visage at me, and holding the door ajar, the apparition of Bartleby appeared in his shirt sleeves, and otherwise in a strangely tattered deshabille, [10] saying quietly that he was sorry, but he was deeply engaged just then, and—preferred not admitting me at present. In a brief word or two, he moreover added, that perhaps I had better walk around the block two or three times, and by that time he would probably have concluded his affairs.

Now, the utterly unsurmised appearance of Bartleby, tenanting my law-chambers of a Sunday morning, with his cadaverously gentlemanly *nonchalance*, yet withal firm and self-possessed, had such a strange effect upon me, that incontinently I slunk away from my own door, and did as desired. But not without sundry twinges of impotent rebellion against the mild effrontery of this unaccountable scrivener. Indeed, it was his wonderful mildness chiefly, which not only disarmed me, but unmanned me as it were. For I consider that one, for the time, is somehow unmanned when he tranquilly permits his hired clerk to dictate to him, and order him away from his own premises. Furthermore, I was full of uneasiness as to what Bartleby could possibly be doing in my office in his shirt sleeves, and in an otherwise dismantled condition of a Sunday morning. Was anything amiss going on? Nay, that was out of the question. It was not to be thought of for a moment that Bartleby was an immoral person. But what could he be doing there?—copying? Nay again, whatever might be his eccentricities, Bartleby was an eminently decorous person. He would be the last man to sit down to his desk in any state approaching to nudity. Besides, it was Sunday; and there was something about Bartleby that forbade the supposition that he would by any secular occupation violate the proprieties of the day.

Nevertheless, my mind was not pacified; and full of a restless curiosity, at last I returned to the door. Without hindrance I inserted my key, opened it, and entered. Bartleby was not to be seen. I looked round anxiously, peeped behind his screen; but it was very plain that he was gone. Upon more closely examining the place, I surmised that for an indefinite period Bartleby must have ate, dressed, and slept in my office, and that, too, without plate, mirror, or bed. The cushioned seat of a rickety old sofa in one corner bore the faint impression of a lean, reclining form. Rolled away under his desk, I found a blanket; on a chair, a tin basin, with soap and a ragged towel; in a newspaper a few crumbs of ginger-nuts and a morsel of cheese. Yes, thought I, it is evident enough that Bartleby

---

[10] Deshabille (dishabille) is the state of being partially dressed.

has been making his home here, keeping bachelor's hall all by himself. Immediately then the thought came sweeping across me, what miserable friendlessness and loneliness are here revealed! His poverty is great; but his solitude, how horrible! Think of it. Of a Sunday, Wall Street is deserted as Petra;[11] and every night of every day it is an emptiness. This building, too, which of weekdays hums with industry and life, at nightfall echoes with sheer vacancy, and all through Sunday is forlorn. And here Bartleby makes his home; sole spectator of a solitude which he has seen all populous—a sort of innocent and transformed Marius[12] brooding among the ruins of Carthage!

For the first time in my life a feeling of over-powering stinging melancholy seized me. Before, I had never experienced aught but a not unpleasing sadness. The bond of a common humanity now drew me irresistibly to gloom. A fraternal melancholy! For both I and Bartleby were sons of Adam. I remembered the bright silks and sparkling faces I had seen that day, in gala trim, swan-like sailing down the Mississippi of Broadway; and I contrasted them with the pallid copyist, and thought to myself, Ah, happiness courts the light, so we deem the world is gay; but misery hides aloof, so we deem that misery there is none. These sad fancyings—chimeras, doubtless, of a sick and silly brain—led on to other and more special thoughts, concerning the eccentricities of Bartleby. Presentiments of strange discoveries hovered round me. The scrivener's pale form appeared to me laid out, among uncaring strangers, in its shivering winding sheet.

Suddenly I was attracted by Bartleby's closed desk, the key in open sight left in the lock.

I mean no mischief, seek the gratification of no heartless curiosity, thought I; besides, the desk is mine, and its contents, too, so I will make bold to look within. Everything was methodically arranged, the papers smoothly placed. The pigeon holes were deep, and removing the files of documents, I groped into their recesses. Presently I felt something there, and dragged it out. It was an old bandanna handkerchief, heavy and knotted. I opened it, and saw it was a saving's bank.

I now recalled all the quiet mysteries which I had noted in the man. I remembered that he never spoke but to answer; that, though at intervals he had considerable time to himself, yet I had never seen him reading—no, not even a newspaper; that for long periods he would stand looking out, at his pale window behind the screen, upon a dead brick wall; I was quite sure he never visited any refectory or eating house; while his pale face clearly indicated that he never drank beer like Turkey, or tea and coffee even, like other men; that he never went anywhere in particular that I could learn; never went out for a walk, unless, indeed, that was the case at present; that he had declined telling who he was, or whence he came, or whether he had any relatives in the world; that though

---

[11] Petra was a city in southwestern Jordan captured by the Muslims in the 7th century and the crusaders in the 12th. Johann Ludwig Burckhardt (1784–1817) discovered its ruins in 1812.

[12] Marius (155?–86 B.C.) was a Roman general driven from Rome during a civil war. Carthage was a city whose battles with Rome led to its total destruction in 146 B.C.

so thin and pale, he never complained of ill health. And more than all, I remembered a certain unconscious air of pallid—how shall I call it?—of pallid haughtiness, say, or rather an austere reserve about him, which had positively awed me into my tame compliance with his eccentricities, when I had feared to ask him to do the slightest incidental thing for me, even though I might know, from his long-continued motionlessness, that behind his screen he must be standing in one of those dead-wall reveries of his.

Revolving all these things, and coupling them with the recently discovered fact, that he made my office his constant abiding place and home, and not forgetful of his morbid moodiness; revolving all these things, a prudential feeling began to steal over me. My first emotions had been those of pure melancholy and sincerest pity; but just in proportion as the forlornness of Bartleby grew and grew to my imagination, did that same melancholy merge into fear, that pity into repulsion. So true it is, and so terrible, too, that up to a certain point the thought or sight of misery enlists our best affections; but, in certain special cases, beyond that point it does not. They err who would assert that invariably this is owing to the inherent selfishness of the human heart. It rather proceeds from a certain hopelessness of remedying excessive and organic ill. To a sensitive being, pity is not seldom pain. And when at last it is perceived that such pity cannot lead to effectual succor, common sense bids the soul be rid of it. What I saw that morning persuaded me that the scrivener was the victim of innate and incurable disorder. I might give alms to his body; but his body did not pain him; it was his soul that suffered, and his soul I could not reach.

I did not accomplish the purpose of going to Trinity Church that morning. Somehow, the things I had seen disqualified me for the time from church-going. I walked homeward, thinking what I would do with Bartleby. Finally, I resolved upon this—I would put certain calm questions to him the next morning, touching his history, etc., and if he declined to answer them openly and unreservedly (and I supposed he would prefer not), then to give him a twenty dollar bill over and above whatever I might owe him, and tell him his services were no longer required; but that if in any other way I could assist him, I would be happy to do so, especially if he desired to return to his native place, wherever that might be, I would willingly help to defray the expenses. Moreover, if, after reaching home, he found himself at any time in want of aid, a letter from him would be sure of a reply.

The next morning came.

"Bartleby," said I, gently calling to him behind his screen.

No reply.

"Bartleby," said I, in a still gentler tone, "come here; I am not going to ask you to do anything you would prefer not to do—I simply wish to speak to you."

Upon this he noiselessly slid into view.

"Will you tell me, Bartleby, where you were born?"

"I would prefer not to."

"Will you tell me *anything* about yourself?"

"I would prefer not to."

"But what reasonable objection can you have to speak to me? I feel friendly towards you."

He did not look at me while I spoke, but kept his glance fixed upon my bust of Cicero, which, as I then sat, was directly behind me, some six inches above my head.

"What is your answer, Bartleby," said I, after waiting a considerable time for a reply, during which his countenance remained immovable, only there was the faintest conceivable tremor of the white attenuated mouth.

"At present I prefer to give no answer," he said, and retired into his hermitage.

It was rather weak in me I confess, but his manner, on this occasion, nettled me. Not only did there seem to lurk in it a certain calm disdain, but his perverseness seemed ungrateful, considering the undeniable good usage and indulgence he had received from me.

Again I sat ruminating what I should do. Mortified as I was at his behavior, and resolved as I had been to dismiss him when I entered my office, nevertheless I strangely felt something superstitious knocking at my heart, and forbidding me to carry out my purpose, and denouncing me for a villain if I dared to breathe one bitter word against this forlornest of mankind. At last, familiarly drawing my chair behind his screen, I sat down and said: "Bartleby, never mind, then, about revealing your history; but let me entreat you, as a friend, to comply as far as may be with the usages of this office. Say now, you will help to examine papers to-morrow or next day: in short, say now, that in a day or two you will begin to be a little reasonable:—say so, Bartleby."

"At present I would prefer not to be a little reasonable," was his mildly cadaverous reply.

Just then the folding-doors opened, and Nippers approached. He seemed suffering from an unusually bad night's rest, induced by severer indigestion than common. He overheard those final words of Bartleby.

"*Prefer not*, eh?" gritted Nippers—"I'd *prefer* him, if I were you, sir," addressing me—"I'd *prefer* him; I'd give him preferences, the stubborn mule! What is it, sir, pray, that he *prefers* not to do now?"

Bartleby moved not a limb.

"Mr. Nippers," said I, "I'd prefer that you would withdraw for the present."

Somehow, of late, I had got into the way of involuntarily using this word "prefer" upon all sorts of not exactly suitable occasions. And I trembled to think that my contact with the scrivener had already and seriously affected me in a mental way. And what further and deeper aberration might it not yet produce? This apprehension had not been without efficacy in determining me to summary measures.

As Nippers, looking very sour and sulky, was departing, Turkey blandly and deferentially approached.

"With submission, sir," said he, "yesterday I was thinking abut Bartleby here, and I think that if he would but prefer to take a quart of good ale every day, it would do much towards mending him, and enabling him to assist in examining his papers."

"So you have got the word, too," said I, slightly excited.

"With submission, what word, sir," asked Turkey, respectfully crowding himself into the contracted space behind the screen, and by so doing, making me jostle the scrivener. "What word, sir?"

"I would prefer to be left alone here," said Bartleby, as if offended at being mobbed in his privacy.

"*That's* the word, Turkey," said I—"*that's* it."

"Oh, *prefer?* oh yes—queer word. I never use it myself. But, sir, as I was saying, if he would but prefer—"

"Turkey," interrupted I, "you will please withdraw."

"Oh, certainly, sir, if you prefer that I should."

As he opened the folding-door to retire, Nippers at his desk caught a glimpse of me, and asked whether I would prefer to have a certain paper copied on blue paper or white. He did not in the least roguishly accent the word prefer. It was plain that it involuntarily rolled from his tongue. I thought to myself, surely I must get rid of a demented man, who already has in some degree turned the tongues, if not the heads of myself and clerks. But I thought it prudent not to break the dismission at once.

The next day I noticed that Bartleby did nothing but stand at his window in his dead-wall revery. Upon asking him why he did not write, he said that he had decided upon doing no more writing.

"Why, how now? what next?" exclaimed I, "do no more writing?"

"No more."

"And what is the reason?"

"Do you not see the reason for yourself," he indifferently replied.

I looked steadfastly at him, and perceived that his eyes looked dull and glazed. Instantly it occurred to me, that his unexampled diligence in copying by his dim window for the first few weeks of his stay with me might have temporarily impaired his vision.

I was touched. I said something in condolence with him. I hinted that of course he did wisely in abstaining from writing for a while; and urged him to embrace that opportunity of taking wholesome exercise in the open air. This, however, he did not do. A few days after this, my other clerks being absent, and being in a great hurry to dispatch certain letters by the mail, I thought that, having nothing else earthly to do, Bartleby would surely be less inflexible than usual, and carry these letters to the post-office. But he blankly declined. So, much to my inconvenience, I went myself.

Still added days went by. Whether Bartleby's eyes improved or not, I could not say. To all appearance, I thought they did. But when I asked him if they did, he vouchsafed no answer. At all events, he would do no copying. At last, in reply to my urgings, he informed me that he had permanently given up copying.

"What!" exclaimed I; "suppose your eyes should get entirely well—better than ever before—would you not copy then?"

"I have given up copying," he answered, and slid aside.

He remained as ever, a fixture in my chamber. Nay—if that were possible—he became still more of a fixture than before. What was to be done? He would do nothing in the office; why should he stay there? In plain fact, he had now become a millstone to me, not only useless as a necklace, but afflictive to bear. Yet I was sorry for him. I speak less than truth when I say that, on his own account, he occasioned me uneasiness. If he would but have named a single relative or friend, I would instantly have written, and urged their taking the poor fellow away to some convenient retreat. But he seemed alone, absolutely alone in the universe. A bit of wreck in the mid Atlantic. At length, necessities connected with my business tyrannized over all other considerations. Decently as I could, I told Bartleby that in six days time he must unconditionally leave the office. I warned him to take measures, in the interval, for procuring some other abode. I offered to assist him in this endeavor, if he himself would but take the first step towards a removal. "And when you finally quit me, Bartleby," added I, "I shall see that you go not away entirely unprovided. Six days from this hour, remember."

At the expiration of that period, I peeped behind the screen, and lo! Bartleby was there.

I buttoned up my coat, balanced myself; advanced slowly towards him, touched his shoulder, and said, "The time has come; you must quit this place; I am sorry for you; here is money; but you must go."

"I would prefer not," he replied, with his back still towards me.

"You *must*."

He remained silent.

Now I had an unbounded confidence in this man's common honesty. He had frequently restored to me sixpences and shillings carelessly dropped upon the floor, for I am apt to be very reckless in such shirt-button affairs. The proceeding, then, which followed will not be deemed extraordinary.

"Bartleby," said I, "I owe you twelve dollars on account; here are thirty-two; the odd twenty are yours—Will you take it?" and I handed the bills towards him.

But he made no motion.

"I will leave them here, then," putting them under a weight on the table. Then taking my hat and cane and going to the door, I tranquilly turned and added—"After you have removed your things from these offices, Bartleby, you will of course lock the door—since every one is now gone for the day but you—and if you please, slip your key underneath the mat, so that I may have it in the morning. I shall not see you again; so good-by to you. If, hereafter, in your new place of abode, I can be of any service to you, do not fail to advise me by letter. Good-by, Bartleby, and fare you well."

But he answered not a word; like the last column of some ruined temple, he remained standing mute and solitary in the middle of the otherwise deserted room.

As I walked home in a pensive mood, my vanity got the better of my pity. I could not but highly plume myself on my masterly management in getting rid of Bartleby. Masterly I call it, and such it must appear to any dispassionate thinker. The beauty of my procedure seemed to consist in its perfect quietness. There was no vulgar bullying, no bravado of any sort, no choleric hectoring, and striding to and fro across the apartment, jerking out vehement commands for Bartleby to bundle himself off with his beggarly traps. Nothing of the kind. Without loudly bidding Bartleby depart—as an inferior genius might have done— I *assumed* the ground that depart he must; and upon that assumption built all I had to say. The more I thought over my procedure, the more I was charmed with it. Nevertheless, next morning, upon awakening, I had my doubts—I had somehow slept off the fumes of vanity. One of the coolest and wisest hours a man has, is just after he awakes in the morning. My procedure seemed as sagacious as ever—but only in theory. How it would prove in practice—there was the rub. It was truly a beautiful thought to have assumed Bartleby's departure; but, after all, that assumption was simply my own, and none of Bartleby's. The great point was, not whether I had assumed that he would quit me, but whether he would prefer so to do. He was more a man of preferences than assumptions.

After breakfast, I walked down town, arguing the probabilities *pro* and *con*. One moment I thought it would prove a miserable failure, and Bartleby would be found all alive at my office as usual; the next moment it seemed certain that I should find his chair empty. And so I kept veering about. At the corner of Broadway and Canal Street, I saw quite an excited group of people standing in earnest conversation.

"I'll take odds he doesn't," said a voice as I passed.

"Doesn't go?—done!" said I, "put up your money."

I was instinctively putting my hand in my pocket to produce my own, when I remembered that this was an election day. The words I had overheard bore no reference to Bartleby, but to the success or nonsuccess of some candidate for the mayoralty. In my intent frame of mind, I had, as it were, imagined that all Broadway shared in my excitement, and were debating the same question with me. I passed on, very thankful that the uproar of the street screened my momentary absent-mindedness.

As I had intended, I was earlier than usual at my office door. I stood listening for a moment. All was still. He must be gone. I tried the knob. The door was locked. Yes, my procedure had worked to a charm; he indeed must be vanished. Yet a certain melancholy mixed with this: I was almost sorry for my brilliant success. I was fumbling under the door mat for the key, which Bartleby was to have left there for me, when accidentally my knee knocked against a panel, producing a summoning sound, and in response a voice came to me from within—"Not yet; I am occupied."

It was Bartleby.

I was thunderstruck. For an instant I stood like the man who, pipe in mouth, was killed one cloudless afternoon long ago in Virginia, by summer lightning; at his own warm open window he was killed, and remained leaning out there upon the dreamy afternoon, till some one touched him, when he fell.

"Not gone!" I murmured at last. But again obeying that wondrous ascendancy which the inscrutable scrivener had over me, and from which ascendancy, for all my chafing, I could not completely escape, I slowly went down stairs and out into the street, and while walking round the block, considered what I should next do in this unheard-of perplexity. Turn the man out by an actual thrusting I could not; to drive him away by calling him hard names would not do; calling in the police was an unpleasant idea; and yet, permit him to enjoy his cadaverous triumph over me—this too, I could not think of. What was to be done? or, if nothing could be done, was there anything further that I could *assume* in the matter? Yes, as before I had prospectively assumed that Bartleby would depart, so now I might retrospectively assume that departed he was. In the legitimate carrying out of this assumption, I might enter my office in a great hurry, and pretending not to see Bartleby at all, walk straight against him as if he were air. Such a proceeding would in a singular degree have the appearance of home-thrust. It was hardly possible that Bartleby could withstand such an application of the doctrine of assumptions. But upon second thoughts the success of the plan seemed rather dubious. I resolved to argue the matter over with him again.

"Bartleby," said I, entering the office, with a quietly severe expression, "I am seriously displeased. I am pained, Bartleby. I had thought better of you. I had imagined you of such a gentlemanly organization, that in any delicate dilemma a slight hint would suffice—in short, an assumption. But it appears I am deceived. Why," I added, unaffectedly starting, "you have not even touched that money yet," pointing to it, just where I had left it the evening previous.

He answered nothing.

"Will you, or will you not, quit me?" I now demanded in a sudden passion, advancing close to him.

"I would prefer *not* to quit you," he replied, gently emphasizing the *not*.

"What earthly right have you to stay here? Do you pay any rent? Do you pay my taxes? Or is this property yours?"

He answered nothing.

"Are you ready to go on and write now? Are your eyes recovered? Could you copy a small paper for me this morning? or help examine a few lines? or step round to the post-office? In a word, will you do anything at all, to give a coloring to your refusal to depart the premises?"

He silently retired into his hermitage.

I was now in such a state of nervous resentment that I thought it but prudent to check myself at present from further demonstrations. Bartleby and I were alone. I remembered the tragedy of the unfortunate Adams and the still more unfortunate Colt in the solitary office of the latter; and how poor Colt, being dreadfully incensed by Adams, and imprudently permitting himself to get wildly excited, was at unawares hurried into his fatal act—an act which certainly no man could possibly deplore more than the actor himself. Often it had occurred to me in my ponderings upon the subject, that had that altercation taken place in the public street, or at a private residence, it would not have terminated as it did. It was the circumstance of being alone in a solitary office, up stairs, of a building entirely unhallowed by humanizing domestic associations—an uncarpeted office, doubtless, of a dusty, haggard sort of appearance—this it must have been, which greatly helped to enhance the irritable desperation of the hapless Colt.[13]

But when this old Adam of resentment rose in me and tempted me concerning Bartleby, I grappled him and threw him. How? Why, simply by recalling the divine injunction: "A new commandment give I unto you, that ye love one another." Yes, this it was that saved me. Aside from higher considerations, charity often operates as a vastly wise and prudent principle—a great safeguard to its possessor. Men have committed murder for jealousy's sake, and anger's sake, and hatred's sake, and selfishness' sake, and spiritual pride's sake; but no man, that ever I heard of, ever committed a diabolical murder for sweet charity's sake. Mere self-interest, then, if no better motive can be enlisted, should, especially with high-tempered men, prompt all beings to charity and philanthropy. At any rate, upon the occasion in question, I strove to drown my exasperated feelings towards the scrivener by benevolently construing his conduct. Poor fellow, poor fellow! thought I, he don't mean anything; and besides, he has seen hard times, and ought to be indulged.

I endeavored, also, immediately to occupy myself, and at the same time to comfort my despondency. I tried to fancy, that in the course of the morning, at such time as might prove agreeable to him, Bartleby, of his own free accord, would emerge from his hermitage and take up some decided line of march in the direction of the door. But no. Half-past twelve o'clock came; Turkey began to glow in the face, overturn his inkstand, and become generally obstreperous; Nippers abated down into quietude and courtesy; Ginger Nut munched his noon apple; and Bartleby remained standing at his window in one of his profoundest dead-wall reveries. Will it be credited? Ought I to acknowledge it? That afternoon I left the office without saying one further word to him.

Some days now passed, during which, at leisure intervals I looked a little into "Edwards on the Will," and "Priestley on Necessity."[14] Under the circumstances, those books induced a salutary feeling. Gradually I slid into the persuasion that these troubles of mine, touching the scrivener, had been all predestinated from eternity, and Bartleby was billeted upon me for some mysterious purpose of an allwise Providence, which it was not for a mere mortal like me to fathom. Yes, Bartleby, stay there behind your screen, thought I; I shall persecute you no more; you are harmless and noiseless as any of these old chairs; in short, I never feel so private as when I know you are here. At last I see it, I feel it; I penetrate to the predestinated purpose of my life. I am content. Others may have loftier parts

---

[13] In January, 1842, John C. Colt killed Samuel Adams in a notorious New York City murder case.

[14] These are two philosophic books. "Edwards on the Will" refers to *Freedom of the Will* (1754) by Jonathan Edwards (1703–1758), an American theologian. "Priestley on Necessity" refers to an essay by Joseph Priestley (1733–1804), the British clergyman and scientist.

to enact; but my mission in this world, Bartleby, is to furnish you with office-room for such period as you may see fit to remain.

I believe that this wise and blessed frame of mind would have continued with me, had it not been for the unsolicited and uncharitable remarks obtruded upon me by my professional friends who visited the rooms. But thus it often is, that the constant friction of illiberal minds wears out at last the best resolves of the more generous. Though to be sure, when I reflected upon it, it was not strange that people entering my office should be struck by the peculiar aspect of the unaccountable Bartleby, and so be tempted to throw out some sinister observations concerning him. Sometimes an attorney, having business with me, and calling at my office, and finding no one but the scrivener there, would undertake to obtain some sort of precise information from him touching my whereabouts; but without heeding his idle talk, Bartleby would remain standing immovable in the middle of the room. So after contemplating him in that position for a time, the attorney would depart, no wiser than he came.

Also, when a reference was going on, and the room full of lawyers and witnesses, and business driving fast, some deeply-occupied legal gentleman present, seeing Bartleby wholly unemployed, would request him to run round to his (the legal gentleman's) office and fetch some papers for him. Thereupon, Bartleby would tranquilly decline, and yet remain idle as before. Then the lawyer would give a great stare, and turn to me. And what could I say? At last I was made aware that all through the circle of my professional acquaintance, a whisper of wonder was running round, having reference to the strange creature I kept at my office. This worried me very much. And as the idea came upon me of his possibly turning out a long-lived man, and keep occupying my chambers, and denying my authority; and perplexing my visitors; and scandalizing my professional reputation; and casting a general gloom over the premises; keeping soul and body together to the last upon his savings (for doubtless he spent but half a dime a day), and in the end perhaps outlive me, and claim possession of my office by right of his perpetual occupancy: as all these dark anticipations crowded upon me more and more, and my friends continually intruded their relentless remarks upon the apparition in my room; a great change was wrought in me. I resolved to gather all my faculties together, and forever rid me of this intolerable incubus.

Ere revolving any complicated project, however, adapted to this end, I first simply suggested to Bartleby the propriety of his permanent departure. In a calm and serious tone, I commended the idea to his careful and mature consideration. But, having taken three days to meditate upon it, he apprised me, that his original determination remained the same; in short, that he still preferred to abide with me.

What shall I do? I now said to myself, buttoning up my coat to the last button. What shall I do? what ought I to do? what does conscience say I *should* do with this man, or, rather, ghost. Rid myself of him, I must; go, he shall. But how? You will not thrust him, the poor, pale, passive mortal—you will not thrust such a helpless creature out of your door? you will not dishonor yourself by such cruelty? No, I will not, I cannot do that. Rather would I let him live and die here, and then mason up his remains in the wall. What, then, will you do? For all your coaxing, he will not budge. Bribes he leaves under your own paper-weight on your table; in short, it is quite plain that he prefers to cling to you.

Then something severe, something unusual must be done. What! surely you will not have him collared by a constable, and commit his innocent pallor to the common jail? And upon what ground could you procure such a thing to be done?—a vagrant, is he? What! he a vagrant, a wanderer, who refuses to budge? It is because he will *not* be a vagrant, then, that you seek to count him *as* a vagrant. That is too absurd. No visible means of support: there I have him. Wrong again: for indubitably he *does* support himself, and that is the only unanswerable proof that any man can show of his possessing the means so to do. No more, then. Since he will not quit me, I must quit him. I will change my offices; I will move elsewhere, and give him fair notice, that if I find him on my new premises I will then proceed against him as a common trespasser.

Acting accordingly, next day I thus addressed him: "I find these chambers too far from the City Hall; the air is unwholesome. In a word, I propose to remove my offices next week, and shall no longer require your services. I tell you this now, in order that you may seek another place."

He made no reply, and nothing more was said.

On the appointed day I engaged carts and men, proceeded to my chambers, and, having but little furniture, everything was removed in a few hours. Through-out, the scrivener remained standing behind the screen, which I directed to be removed the last thing. It was withdrawn; and, being folded up like a huge folio, left him the motionless occupant of a naked room. I stood in the entry watching him a moment, while something from within me upbraided me.

I re-entered, with my hand in my pocket—and—and my heart in my mouth.

"Good-by, Bartleby; I am going—good-by, and God some way bless you; and take that," slipping something in his hand. But it dropped upon the floor, and then—strange to say—I tore myself from him whom I had so longed to be rid of.

Established in my new quarters, for a day or two I kept the door locked, and started at every footfall in the passages. When I returned to my rooms, after any little absence, I would pause at the threshold for an instant, and attentively listen, ere applying my key. But these fears were needless. Bartleby never came nigh me.

I thought all was going well, when a perturbed-looking stranger visited me, inquiring whether I was the person who had recently occupied rooms at No.——Wall Street.

Full of forebodings, I replied that I was.

"Then, sir," said the stranger, who proved a lawyer, "you are responsible for the man you left there. He refuses to do any copying; he refuses to do anything; he says he prefers not to; and he refuses to quit the premises."

"I am very sorry, sir," said I, with assumed tranquillity, but an inward tremor, "but, really, the man you allude to is nothing to me—he is no relation or apprentice of mine, that you should hold me responsible for him."

"In mercy's name, who is he?"

"I certainly cannot inform you. I know nothing about him. Formerly I employed him as a copyist; but he has done nothing for me now for some time past."

"I shall settle him, then—good morning, sir."

Several days passed, and I heard nothing more; and, though I often felt a charitable prompting to call at the place and see poor Bartleby, yet a certain squeamishness, of I know not what, withheld me.

All is over with him, by this time, thought I, at last, when, through another week, no further intelligence reached me. But, coming to my room the day after, I found several persons waiting at my door in a high state of nervous excitement.

"That's the man—here he comes," cried the foremost one, whom I recognized as the lawyer who had previously called upon me alone.

"You must take him away, sir, at once," cried a portly person among them, advancing upon me, and whom I knew to be the landlord of No. – Wall Street. "These gentlemen, my tenants, cannot stand it any longer; Mr. B—," pointing to the lawyer, "has turned him out of his room, and he now persists in haunting the building generally, sitting upon the banisters of the stairs by day, and sleeping in the entry by night. Everybody is concerned; clients are leaving the offices; some fears are entertained of a mob; something you must do, and that without delay."

Aghast at this torrent, I fell back before it, and would fain have locked myself in my new quarters. In vain I persisted that Bartleby was nothing to me—no more than to any one else. In vain—I was the last person known to have anything to do with him, and they held me to the terrible account. Fearful, then, of being exposed in the papers (as one person present obscurely threatened), I considered the matter, and, at length, said, that if the lawyer would give me a confidential interview with the scrivener, in his (the lawyer's) own room, I would, that afternoon, strive my best to rid them of the nuisance they complained of.

Going up stairs to my old haunt, there was Bartleby silently sitting upon the banister at the landing.

"What are you doing here, Bartleby?" said I.

"Sitting upon the banister," he mildly replied.

I motioned him into the lawyer's room, who then left us.

"Bartleby," said I, "are you aware that you are the cause of great tribulation to me, by persisting in occupying entry after being dismissed from the office?"

No answer.

"Now one of two things must take place. Either you must do something, or something must be done to you. Now what sort of business would you like to engage in? Would you like to re-engage in copying for some one?"

"No; I would prefer not to make any change."

"Would you like a clerkship in a dry-goods store?"

"There is too much confinement about that. No, I would not like a clerkship; but I am not particular."

"Too much confinement," I cried, "why you keep yourself confined all the time!"

"I would prefer not to take a clerkship," he rejoined, as if to settle that little item at once.

"How would a bar-tender's business suit you? There is no trying of the eyesight in that."

"I would not like it at all; though, as I said before, I am not particular."

His unwonted wordiness inspirited me. I returned to the charge.

"Well, then, would you like to travel through the country collecting bills for the merchants? That would improve your health."

"No, I would prefer to be doing something else."

"How, then, would going as a companion to Europe, to entertain some young gentleman with your conversation—how would that suit you?"

"Not at all. It does not strike me that there is anything definite about that. I like to be stationary. But I am not particular."

"Stationary you shall be, then," I cried, now losing all patience, and, for the first time in all my exasperating connection with him, fairly flying into a passion. "If you do not go away from these premises before night, I shall feel bound—indeed, I *am* bound—to—to—to quit the premises myself!" I rather absurdly concluded, knowing not with what possible threat to try to frighten his immobility into compliance. Despairing of all further efforts, I was precipitately leaving him, when a final thought occurred to me—one which had not been wholly unindulged before.

"Bartleby," said I, in the kindest tone I could assume under such exciting circumstances, "will you go home with me now—not to my office, but my dwelling—and remain there till we can conclude upon some convenient arrangement for you at our leisure? Come, let us start now, right away."

"No: at present I would prefer not to make any change at all."

I answered nothing; but, effectually dodging every one by the suddenness and rapidity of my flight, rushed from the building, ran up Wall Street towards Broadway, and, jumping into the first omnibus, was soon removed from pursuit. As soon as tranquillity returned, I distinctly perceived that I had now done all that I possibly could, both in respect to the demands of the landlord and his tenants, and with regard to my own desire and sense of duty, to benefit Bartleby, and shield him from rude persecution. I now strove to be entirely care-free and quiescent; and my conscience justified me in the attempt; though, indeed, it was not so successful as I could have wished. So fearful was I of being again hunted out by the incensed landlord and his exasperated tenants, that, surrendering my business to Nippers, for a few days, I drove about the upper part of the town and through the suburbs, in my rockaway;[15] crossed over to Jersey City

---

[15] A rockaway is a four-wheeled, two-door carriage open only in the front.

and Hoboken, and paid fugitive visits to Manhattanville and Astoria.. In fact, I almost lived in my rockaway for the time.

When again I entered my office, lo, a note from the landlord lay upon the desk. I opened it with trembling hands. It informed me that the writer had sent to the police, and had Bartleby removed to the Tombs as a vagrant. Moreover, since I knew more about him than any one else, he wished me to appear at that place, and make a suitable statement of the facts. These tidings had a conflicting effect upon me. At first I was indignant; but, at last, almost approved. The landlord's energetic, summary disposition, had led him to adopt a procedure which I do not think I would have decided upon myself; and yet, as a last resort, under such peculiar circumstances, it seemed the only plan.

As I afterwards learned, the poor scrivener, when told that he must be conducted to the Tombs, offered not the slightest obstacle, but, in his pale, unmoving way, silently acquiesced.

Some of the compassionate and curious bystanders joined the party; and headed by one of the constables arm in arm with Bartleby, the silent procession filed its way through all the noise, and heat, and joy of the roaring thoroughfares at noon.

The same day I received the note, I went to the Tombs, or, to speak more properly, the Hall of Justice. Seeking the right officer, I stated the purpose of my call, and was informed that the individual I described was, indeed, within. I then assured the functionary that Bartleby was a perfectly honest man, and greatly to be compassionated, however unaccountably eccentric. I narrated all I knew, and closed by suggesting the idea of letting him remain in as indulgent confinement as possible, till something less harsh might be done—though, indeed, I hardly knew what. At all events, if nothing else could be decided upon, the almshouse must receive him. I then begged to have an interview.

Being under no disgraceful charge, and quite serene and harmless in all his ways, they had permitted him freely to wander about the prison, and, especially, in the inclosed grass-platted yards thereof. And so I found him there, standing all alone in the quietest of the yards, his face towards a high wall, while all around, from the narrow slits of the jail windows, I thought I saw peering out upon him the eyes of murderers and thieves.

"Bartleby!"

"I know you," he said without looking round—"and I want nothing to say to you."

"It was not I that brought you here, Bartleby," said I, keenly pained at his implied suspicion. "And to you, this should not be so vile a place. Nothing reproachful attaches to you by being here. And see, it is not so sad a place as one might think. Look, there is the sky, and here is the grass."

"I know where I am," he replied, but would say nothing more, and so I left him.

As I entered the corridor again, a broad mean-like man, in an apron, accosted me, and, jerking his thumb over his shoulder, said—"Is that your friend?"

"Yes."

"Does he want to starve? If he does, let him live on the prison fare, that's all."

"Who are you?" asked I, not knowing what to make of such an unofficially speaking person in such a place.

"I am the grub-man. Such gentlemen as have friends here, hire me to provide them with something good to eat."

"Is this so?" said I, turning to the turnkey.

He said it was.

"Well, then," said I, slipping some silver into the grub-man's hands (for so they called him), "I want you to give particular attention to my friend there; let him have the best dinner you can get. And you must be as polite to him as possible."

"Introduce me, will you?" said the grub-man, looking at me with an expression which seemed to say he was all impatience for an opportunity to give a specimen of his breeding.

Thinking it would prove of benefit to the scrivener, I acquiesced; and, asking the grub-man his name, went up with him to Bartleby.

"Bartleby, this is a friend; you will find him very useful to you."

"Your sarvant, sir, your sarvant," said the grub-man, making a low salutation behind his apron. "Hope you find it pleasant here, sir; nice grounds—cool apartments—hope you'll stay with us sometime—try to make it agreeable. What will you have for dinner to-day?"

"I prefer not to dine to-day," said Bartleby, turning away. "It would disagree with me; I am unused to dinners." So saying, he slowly moved to the other side of the inclosure, and took up a position fronting the dead-wall.

"How's this?" said the grub-man, addressing me with a stare of astonishment, "He's odd, ain't he?"

"I think he is a little deranged," said I, sadly.

"Deranged? deranged is it? Well, now, upon my word, I thought that friend of yourn was a gentleman forger; they are always pale and genteel-like, them forgers. I can't help pity 'em—can't help it, sir. Did you know Monroe Edwards?" he added, touchingly, and paused. Then, laying his hand piteously on my shoulder, sighed, "he died of consumption at Sing-Sing.[16] So you weren't acquainted with Monroe?"

"No, I was never socially acquainted with any forgers. But I cannot stop longer. Look to my friend yonder. You will not lose by it. I will see you again."

Some few days after this, I again obtained admission to the Tombs, and went through the corridors in quest of Bartleby; but without finding him.

"I saw him coming from his cell not long ago," said a turnkey, "may be he's gone to loiter in the yards."

So I went in that direction.

"Are you looking for the silent man?" said another turnkey, passing me.

---

[16] Sing-Sing is now the State Prison at Ossining, New York.

"Yonder he lies—sleeping in the yard there. 'Tis not twenty minutes since I saw him lie down."

The yard was entirely quiet. It was not accessible to the common prisoners. The surrounding walls, of amazing thickness, kept off all sounds behind them. The Egyptian character of the masonry weighed upon me with its gloom. But a soft imprisoned turf grew under foot. The heart of the eternal pyramids, it seemed, wherein, by some strange magic, through the clefts, grass-seed, dropped by birds, had sprung.

Strangely huddled at the base of the wall, his knees drawn up, and lying on his side, his head touching the cold stones, I saw the wasted Bartleby. But nothing stirred. I paused; then went close up to him; stooped over, and saw that his dim eyes were open; otherwise he seemed profoundly sleeping. Something prompted me to touch him. I felt his hand, when a tingling shiver ran up my arm and down my spine to my feet.

The round face of the grub-man peered upon me now. "His dinner is ready. Won't he dine to-day, either? Or does he live without dining?"

"Lives without dining," said I, and closed the eyes.

"Eh!—He's asleep, ain't he?"

"With kings and counselors," murmured I.

There would seem little need for proceeding further in this history. Imagination will readily supply the meagre recital of poor Bartleby's interment. But, ere parting with the reader, let me say, that if this little narrative has sufficiently interested him, to awaken curiosity as to who Bartleby was, and what manner of life he led prior to the present narrator's making his acquaintance, I can only reply, that in such curiosity I fully share, but am wholly unable to gratify it. Yet here I hardly know whether I should divulge one little item of rumor, which came to my ear a few months after the scrivener's decease. Upon what basis it rested, I could never ascertain; and hence, how true it is I cannot now tell. But, inasmuch as this vague report has not been without a certain suggestive interest to me, however sad, it may prove the same with some others; and so I will briefly mention it. The report was this: that Bartleby had been a subordinate clerk in the Dead Letter Office at Washington, from which he had been suddenly removed by a change in the administration. When I think over this rumor, hardly can I express the emotions which seize me. Dead letters! does it not sound like dead men? Conceive a man by nature and misfortune prone to a pallid hopelessness, can any business seem more fitted to heighten it than that of continually handling these dead letters, and assorting them for the flames? For by the cartload they are annually burned. Sometimes from out the folded paper the pale clerk takes a ring—the finger it was meant for, perhaps, moulders in the grave; a banknote sent in swiftest charity—he whom it would relieve, nor eats nor hungers any more; pardon for those who died despairing; hope for those who died unhoping; good tidings for those who died stifled by unrelieved calamities. On errands of life, these letters speed to death.

Ah, Bartleby! Ah, humanity!

13 ❦ Good and Great Fiction

If we had time enough to read all the stories ever written, perhaps we would not need to make literary judgments. But our time for reading is short. And we must decide which stories are worthiest of our effort and energy, and which writers give us the greatest insight and pleasure. In literature there is no reason to read the slipshod, the ill-conceived, the poorly made, when works of excellence are as easily available. If we hope to cultivate what is best within ourselves, we must learn to appreciate the excellent things around us. Without an appreciation of the truly excellent, we will have no way to improve.

Throughout this book we have explored the basic elements of fiction. In a good story these elements work together to produce a work of expressive efficiency. In the best stories, however, this expressive efficiency is aimed at subjects that are profound and important. In short, great literature occurs when an author's skill matches an unusually deep and meaningful experience.

In the sections to follow, we will review those elements of fiction we have previously discussed with an eye toward forming useful criteria for judging short fiction.

Narrative Conventions

One important feature of a good story is a consistent narrative perspective. Stories may be told in either the first person, the limited third person, or the omniscient voice. In "The New Atlantis," for example, there are two different voices. But once the author has chosen a perspective, he or she must be consistent in its application. An omniscient narrator cannot claim ignorance of certain details, and a first-person narrator cannot be certain of events the narrator did not witness. Another feature of narrative consistency extends to the narrator's voice. The narrator of "My Man Bovanne" is a black woman who is much wiser than her better-educated children. Toni Cade Bambara has caught the flavor of her narrator's direct, earthy language. The voice is consistent with the character. The voice would be inconsistent if it sounded like the English woman in "Homage for Isaac Babel."

Another mark of good stories is that they usually maintain a consistent level of reality. For example, "The Canary Prince" allows all sorts of supernatural or fantastic occurrences to happen. However, in a Sherlock Holmes story no unrealistic detail is allowed to enter the story. Indeed, part of the excitement of a Sherlock Holmes mystery is Holmes's ability to provide natural explanations for the seemingly inexplicable and supernatural. Doyle would destroy the credibility of his detective if he solved a mystery in which ghosts actually appeared or gypsies could truly walk through walls. To be sure, a story occasionally begins realistically and ends supernaturally or the other way around. But the authors of such stories are careful to make the transition graceful and smooth.

Among the questions you should ask about a story's narrator are: (1) Has the author maintained a consistent narrative perspective? (2) Does the narrator's voice fit the character? and (3) Has the author maintained a consistent level of reality or made a smooth transition from one level to another?

Plot

A good story, while it may not be action-packed, should not be dull. It is more difficult to evaluate a plot than to judge if the narrative voice is consistent.

In general, one should be able to follow the action of a story. Event should follow event in a clear, logical, and interesting manner. Information that is suppressed should be suppressed to develop suspense and surprise and not out of laziness or ineptitude. The events narrated should all contribute to the effectiveness of the story. Important action should not be left out and unimportant action should not be included. In short, the narrative should be focused, concentrating attention on the most significant events, subordinating less important events and eliminating superfluous ones.

If a frame surrounds the story, the frame should complement the story to which it is attached. If the story has a twist ending, then the ending should develop from the material in the first part of the story and cast light on the significance of the earlier action.

Among the questions you should ask concerning a story's plot are: (1) Are the events arranged in the most effective manner? (2) Does the story have narrative focus? (3) Do any framing devices complement the material? (4) Does the conclusion develop from the action leading up to it and cast light on the earlier events?

Character

Consistency is important in the creation of characters. Some characters are simple or flat. They have only a limited number of character traits. Once, however, those traits have been established, they should remain the same unless the author provides motivation for the character to change. A stingy character, for example, would not pick up the tab at a restaurant *unless* there is some special reason. Good authors either provide special motivation for uncharacteristic behavior or avoid the inconsistency.

Good comic, satiric, symbolic, and adventure stories often contain only flat, simple characters. Other stories seem thin and trite unless they present at least one round or full character. A psychological story requires at least one round character. Because such characters are more difficult to create, round characters give stories special merit. Like flat characters, round characters must act consistently. But because round characters are more complex, sometimes with many incompatible sets of traits, their actions are far less predictable. For example, a round character may be stingy, but also may have the desire to be a good friend. Faced with a bill for dinner, the character on one occasion may reach for the tab and on another hope he won't be asked to pay. The actions *are* consistent, consistent with the conflict in his personality. Indeed, quite often stories focus on the means by which round characters resolve conflicts between incompatible traits in their personalities.

Among the questions you should ask when evaluating an author's handling of character are: (1) Are the characters consistent? (2) Are their actions well motivated? (3) Are they appropriate types of character for the story in which they are placed, or are they too simple, too flat, to hold our interest? (4) Are their changes understandably motivated?

Setting

An author may place a story in any locality at any time, or even out of time and in a wholly fantastic place. Yet, whatever the setting, it should not only suit the story but also contribute to the effective functioning of the tale. Details should help us locate the character socially, psychologically, or symbolically. No detail should be superfluous, and all the important details should be present.

Among the questions one should ask in evaluating a story's setting are: (1) Is the setting appropriate to the story? (2) Does it fix the action socially, psychologically, or symbolically? (3) Is the setting recognizable? (4) Are there unnecessary or repetitious details in the description of the setting?

Style

The style of a work should be appropriate to the subject matter and the characters. For example, an illiterate should not speak like a professor and a professor should not ordinarily speak like an illiterate. What the characters *say* should be as consistent with their traits as what they do. Similarly, one would not narrate a comic story in the same way that one would narrate a sad tale. Good writers alter their language to fit the subjects they are treating or the mode of fiction they are writing.

Good writers avoid worn out or trite expressions. They try to make the language of the story fresh and interesting. When good writers use clichés, it is for a specific purpose. For example, the writer may want to show the commonplace thinking of a character, or to satirize the banality of society.

Among the questions about style you should ask are: (1) Does the dialogue fit the characters who are speaking? (2) Does the narrator's word choice fit the story? (3) Has the author avoided clichés?

Perfection

Judging a literary work is especially difficult because no story is ever "perfect." The literary critic must decide whether or not the faults of a work significantly mar it. Sometimes a lifeless, dull, and trivial story will be told with few faults. Another story will bristle with life and insight despite many imperfections. Such stories make the evaluation of literature an art rather than a science. Testing the excellence of a story is not like testing the gold content in a ring. There is no precise assay of a story's value. Yet, over time, the greatest works emerge and endure while trivial, ill-planned works are forgotten. We should remember that many works are great because they broke with convention and showed fictional possibilities people had not previously recognized. The great work is exceptional and may sometimes brilliantly depart from the common conventions of literary practice. As Alexander Pope wrote:

> Great minds may sometimes gloriously offend,
> And rise to faults true critics dare not mend.

Sinclair Lewis and Anton Chekhov

The two stories which follow can help you sharpen your critical skills. They concern similar situations—couples who fall in love despite being married to others. Both stories examine how illicit love affects the characters' lives.

Both Chekhov and Lewis were highly acclaimed in their day. Sinclair Lewis, an American, won the Nobel prize for literature in 1930. The Russian Anton Chekhov was as famous for his plays as for his short fiction. By most critical opinion, one of these stories is great, while the other is merely good. Evaluate the works on your own and support your reasons for preferring one story to the other.

Check List of Questions for Evaluating Fiction
Narrative

1. Has the story maintained a consistent narrative perspective?
2. Does the narrator's voice fit the character?
3. Has the story maintained a consistent level of reality or made smooth transitions from one level to another?

Plot

1. Are the events arranged in the most effective manner?
2. Does the story maintain narrative focus?

3. Do any framing devices complement the stories?
4. Does the conclusion develop from the action which precedes it and cast light on the earlier events?

Character

1. Are the characters consistent?
2. Are their actions well motivated?
3. Are they appropriate types of characters for the story in which they are placed, or does the story need more rounded, more fully realized characters?
4. Are their changes motivated?

Setting

1. Is the setting appropriate to the story?
2. Does it fix the action socially, psychologically, or symbolically?
3. Is the setting recognizable?
4. Are there unnecessary or repetitious details?

Style

1. Does the dialogue fit the characters who are speaking?
2. Does the narrator's word choice fit the story?
3. Has the author avoided clichés?

SINCLAIR LEWIS (1885–1951)

Virga Vay and Allan Cedar

Orlo Vay, the Chippewa Avenue Optician, Smart-Art Harlequin Tinted-Tortus Frames Our Specialty, was a public figure, as public as a cemetery. He was resentful that his profession, like that of an undertaker, a professor of art, or a Mormon missionary, was not appreciated for its patience and technical skill, as are the callings of wholesale grocer or mistress or radio-sports-commentator, and he tried to make up for the professional injustice by developing his personal glamor.

He wanted to Belong. He was a speaker. He was hearty and public about the local baseball and hockey teams, about the Kiwanis Club, about the Mayflower Congregational Church, and about all war drives.[1] At forty-five he was bald, but the nobly glistening egg of his face and forehead, whose arc was broken only by a pair of Vay Li-Hi-Bifocals, was an adornment to all fund-raising rallies.

---

[1] War drives were events organized to sell savings bonds.

He urged his wife, Virga, to co-operate in his spiritual efforts, but she was a small, scared, romantic woman, ten years his junior; an admirer of passion in technicolor, a clipper-out of newspaper lyrics about love and autumn smoke upon the hills. He vainly explained to her, "In these modern days, a woman can't fritter away her time daydreaming. She has to push her own weight, and not hide it under a bushel."

Her solace was in her lover, Dr. Allan Cedar, the dentist. Together, Virga and Allan would have been a most gentle pair, small, clinging, and credulous. But they could never be openly together. They were afraid of Mr. Vay and of Allan's fat and vicious wife, Bertha, and they met at soda counters in outlying drug stores and lovingly drank black-and-whites[2] together or Jumbo Malteds and, giggling, ate ferocious banana splits; or, till wartime gasoline-rationing prevented, they sped out in Allan's coupé by twilight, and made shy, eager love in mossy pastures or, by the weak dashlight of the car, read aloud surprisingly good recent poets: Wallace Stevens, Sandburg, Robert Frost, Jeffers, T. S. Eliot, Lindsay.[3]

Allan was one of the best actors in the Masquers, and though Virga could not act, she made costumes and hung about at rehearsals, and thus they were able to meet, and to stir the suspicions of Bertha Cedar.

Mrs. Cedar was a rare type of the vicious woman; she really hated her husband, though she did not so much scold him as mock him for his effeminate love of acting, for his verses, for his cherubic mustache, and even for his skill with golden bridgework. She jeered, in the soap-reeking presence of her seven sisters and sisters-in-law, all chewing gum and adjusting their plates, that as a lover "Ally" had no staying-powers. That's what *she* thought.

She said to her mother, "Ally is a bum dentist; he hasn't got a single rich patient," and when they were at an evening party, she communicated to the festal guests, "Ally can't even pick out a necktie without asking my help," and on everything her husband said she commented, "Oh, don't be silly!"

She demanded, and received, large sympathy from all the females she knew, and as he was fond of golf and backgammon, she refused to learn either of them.

Whenever she had irritated him into jumpiness, she said judiciously, "You seem to be in a very nervous state." She picked at him about his crossword puzzles, about his stamp-collection, until he screamed, invariably, "Oh, let me *alone!*" and then she was able to say smugly, "I don't know what's the matter with you, so touchy about every little thing. You better go to a mind-doctor and have your head examined."

Then Bertha quite unexpectedly inherited seven thousand dollars and a house in San Jose, California, from a horrible aunt. She did not suggest to her husband but told him that they would move out to that paradise for chilled Minnesotans, and he would practise there.

---

[2] Black-and-whites are ice cream sodas made with vanilla ice cream and chocolate syrup, or vice versa.

[3] These poets, except for Vachel Lindsay (1879–1931), are represented in this volume.

It occurred to Allan to murder her, but not to refuse to go along. Many American males confuse their wives and the policeman on the beat.

But he knew that it would be death for him to leave Virga Vay, and that afternoon, when Virga slipped into his office at three o'clock in response to his code telephone call of "This is the Superba Market and we're sending you three bunches of asparagus," she begged, "Couldn't we elope some place together? Maybe we could get a little farm."

"She'd find us. She has a cousin who's a private detective in Duluth."

"Yes, I guess she would. Can't we *ever* be together always?"

"There is one way—if you wouldn't be afraid."

He explained the way.

"No, I wouldn't be afraid, if you stayed right with me," she said.

Dr. Allan Cedar was an excellent amateur machinist. On a Sunday afternoon when Bertha was visiting her mother, he cut a hole through the steel bottom of the luggage compartment of his small dark-gray coupé. This compartment opened into the body of the car. That same day he stole the hose of their vacuum-cleaner and concealed it up on the rafters of their galvanized-iron garage.

On Tuesday—this was in February—he bought a blue ready-made suit at Goldenkron Brothers', on Ignatius Street. He was easy to fit, and no alterations were needed. They wanted to deliver the suit that afternoon, but he insisted, "No, hold it here for me and I'll come in and put it on tomorrow morning. I want to surprise somebody."

"Your Missus will love it, Doc," said Monty Goldenkron.

"I hope she will—when she sees it!"

He also bought three white-linen shirts and a red bow-tie, and paid cash for the lot.

"Your credit is good here, Doc—none better," protested Monty.

Allan puzzled him by the triumphant way in which he answered, "I want to keep it good, just now!"

From Goldenkrons' he walked perkily to the Emporium, to the Golden Rule drug store, to the Co-operative Dairy, paying his bills in full at each. On his way he saw a distinguished fellow-townsman, Judge Timberlane, and his pretty wife. Allan had never said ten words to either of them, but he thought affectionately, "There's a couple who are intelligent enough and warm-hearted enough to know what love is worth."

That evening he said blandly to his wife, "Strangest thing happened today. The University school of dentistry telephoned me."

"Long distance?"

"Surely."

"Well!" Her tone was less of disbelief than of disgust.

"They're having a special brush-up session for dentists and they want me to come down to Minneapolis first thing tomorrow morning to stay for three days and give instruction in bridge-work. And of course you must come along. It's too bad I'll have to work from nine in the morning till midnight—they do rush those special courses so—but you can go to the movies by yourself, or just sit comfortably in the hotel."

"No—thank—*you!*" said Bertha. "I prefer to sit here at home. Why you couldn't have been an M.D. doctor and take out gallbladders and make some real money! And I'll thank you to be home not later than Sunday morning. You know we have Sunday dinner with Mother."

He knew.

"I hope that long before that I'll be home," he said.

He told her that he would be staying at the Flora Hotel, in Minneapolis. But on Wednesday morning, after putting on the new suit at Goldenkrons', he drove to St. Paul, through light snowflakes which he thought of as fairies. "But I haven't a bit of real poet in me. Just second-rate and banal," he sighed. He tried to make a poem, and got no farther than:

It is snowing,
The wind is blowing,
But I am happy to be going.

In St. Paul he went to the small, clean Hotel Orkness, registered as "Mr. A. M. Romeo & wife," asked for a room with a double bed, and explained to the clerk, "My wife is coming by train. She should be here in about seventeen minutes now, I figure it."

He went unenthusiastically to the palsied elevator, up to their room. It was tidy, and on the wall was an Adolph Dehn[4] lithograph instead of the fake English-hunting-print that he had dreaded. He kneaded the bed with his fist. He was pleased.

Virga Vay arrived nineteen minutes later, with a bellboy carrying her new imitation-leather bag.

"So you're here, husband. Not a bad room," she said indifferently.

The bellboy knew from her indifference and from her calling the man "husband" that she was not married to him, but unstintingly in love. Such paradoxes are so common in his subterranean business that he had forgotten about Virga by the time he reached his bench in the lobby. Six stories above him, Virga and Allan were lost and blind and quivering in their kiss.

Presently she said, "Oh, you have a new suit! Turn around. Why, it fits beautifully! And such a nice red tie. You do look so young and cute in a bow-tie. Did you get it for me?"

"Of course. And then—I kind of hate to speak of it now, but I want us to get so used to the idea that we can just forget it—I don't want us to look frowsy when they find us. As if we hadn't been happy. And we *will* be—we are!"

"Yes."

"You're still game for it?"

"With you? For anything."

---

[4] Adolph Dehn (1895–1968) was an American painter and printmaker from Waterville, Minnesota.

He was taking off the new suit; she was tenderly lifting from her bag a nightgown which she had made and embroidered this past week.

They had all their meals in the room; they did not leave it till afternoon of the next day. The air became a little close, thick from perfume and cigarette smoke and the bubble baths they took together.

Late the next afternoon they dressed and packed their bags, completely. He laid on the bureau two ten-dollar bills. They left the luggage at the foot of their bed, which she had made up. She took nothing from the room, and he nothing except a paper bag containing a bottle of Bourbon whisky, with the cork loosened, and a pocket anthology of new poetry. At the door she looked back, and said to him, "I shall remember this dear room as long as we live."

"Yes. . . . as long as we live."

He took his dark-gray coupé out of the hotel garage, tipping an amazed attendant one dollar, and they drove to Indian Mounds Park, overlooking the erratic Mississippi. He stopped in the park, at dusk, and said, "Think of the Indians that came along here, and Pike and Lewis Cass!"[5]

"They were brave," she mused.

"Brave, too!" They nervously laughed. Indeed, after a moment of solemnity when they had left the hotel, they had been constantly gay, laughing at everything, even when she sneezed and he piped, "No more worry about catching pneumonia!"

He drove into a small street near by and parked the car, distant from any house. Working in the half-darkness, leaving the engine running, he pushed the vacuum-cleaner hose through the hole in the bottom of the luggage compartment, wired it to the exhaust pipe, and hastily got back into the car. The windows were closed. Already the air in the car was sick-sweet with carbon monoxide.

He slipped the whisky bottle out of the paper bag and tenderly urged, "Take a swig of this. Keep your courage up."

"Dearest, I don't need anything to keep it up."

"I do, by golly. I'm not a big he-man like you, Virg!"

They both laughed, and drank from the bottle, and kissed lingeringly.

"I wonder if I could smoke a cigarette. I don't *think* C_2O_2 is explosive," he speculated.

"Oh, sweet, be careful! It *might* explode!"

"Yes, it—" Then he shouted. "Listen at us! As if we cared if we got blown up now!"

"Oh, I am too brainless, Allan! I don't know if you'll be able to stand me much longer."

---

[5] Lewis Cass (1782–1866) was an American statesman. As Secretary of War under Andrew Jackson, he favored the removal of Indians beyond the Mississippi. Zebulon Pike (1779–1813) was an American explorer who led expeditions to find the sources of the Mississippi, Arkansas, and Red Rivers.

"As long as we live, my darling, my very dear, oh, my dear love!"

"As long as we live. Together now. Together."

His head aching, his throat sore, he forgot to light the cigarette. He switched on the tiny dashlight, he lifted up the book as though it were a bar of lead, and from Conrad Aiken's [6] "Sea Holly" he began to read to her:

> It was for this
> Barren beauty, barrenness of rock that aches
> On the seaward path, seeing the fruitful sea,
> Hearing the lark of rock that sings—

He was too drowsy to read more than just the ending:

> Stone pain in the stony heart,
> The rock loved and labored; and all is lost.

The book fell to the seat, his head drooped, and his arm groped drowsily about her. She rested contentedly, in vast dreams, her head secure upon his shoulder.

Harsh screaming snatched them back from paradise. The car windows were smashed, someone was dragging them out . . . and Bertha was slapping Virga's face, while Bertha's cousin, the detective, was beating Allan's shoulders with a blackjack, to bring him to. In doing so, he broke Allan's jaw.

Bertha drove him back to Grand Republic and nursed him while he was in bed, jeering to the harpies whom she had invited in, "Ally tried to—you know— with a woman, but he was no good, and he was so ashamed he tried to kill himself."

He kept muttering, "Please go away and don't torture me."

She laughed.

Later, Bertha was able to intercept every one of the letters that Virga sent to him from Des Moines, where she had gone to work in a five-and-ten-cent store after Orlo had virtuously divorced her.

"Love! Ally is learning what that kind of mush gets you," Bertha explained to her attentive women friends.

Questions

1. Are the events of the story logically organized? Are the settings appropriate?
2. Does the ending grow logically from earlier events? Does it throw additional light on what came before, or does it merely repeat your understanding of the characters?
3. Does Lewis summarize Virga and Allan in a sentence? Are they round or flat characters?
4. Is Bertha Cedar a round or flat character?
5. Do the characters develop during the course of the story?
6. How would you evaluate this story overall?

---

[6] Conrad Aiken (1889–1973) was an American poet.

ANTON CHEKHOV (1860–1904)

Lady with Lapdog

I

The appearance on the front of a new arrival—a lady with a lapdog—became the topic of general conversation. Dimitry Dmitrich Gurov, who had been a fortnight in Yalta[1] and got used to its ways, was also interested in new arrivals. One day, sitting on the terrace of Vernet's restaurant, he saw a young woman walking along the promenade; she was fair, not very tall, and wore a toque; behind her trotted a white pomeranian.

Later he came across her in the park and in the square several times a day. She was always alone, always wearing the same toque, followed by the white pomeranian. No one knew who she was, and she became known simply as the lady with the lapdog.

"If she's here without her husband and without any friends," thought Gurov, "it wouldn't be a bad idea to strike up an acquaintance with her."

He was not yet forty, but he had a twelve-year-old daughter and two schoolboy sons. He had been married off when he was still in his second year at the university, and his wife seemed to him now to be almost twice his age. She was a tall, black-browed woman, erect, dignified, austere, and, as she liked to describe herself, a "thinking person." She was a great reader, preferred the new "advanced" spelling, called her husband by the more formal "Dimitry" and not the familiar "Dmitry"; and though he secretly considered her not particularly intelligent, narrow-minded, and inelegant, he was afraid of her and disliked being at home. He had been unfaithful to her for a long time, he was often unfaithful to her, and that was why, perhaps, he almost always spoke ill of women, and when men discussed women in his presence, he described them as *the lower breed.*

He could not help feeling that he had had enough bitter experience to have the right to call them as he pleased, but all the same without *the lower breed* he could not have existed a couple of days. He was bored and ill at ease among men, with whom he was reticent and cold, but when he was among women he felt at ease, he knew what to talk about with them and how to behave; even when he was silent in their company he experienced no feeling of constraint. There was something attractive, something elusive in his appearance, in his character and his whole person, that women found interesting and irresistible; he was aware of it, and was himself drawn to them by some irresistible force.

Long and indeed bitter experience had taught him that every new affair, which at first relieved the monotony of life so pleasantly and appeared to be such a charming and light adventure, among decent people and especially among Muscovites, who are so irresolute and so hard to rouse, inevitably developed into an extremely complicated problem and finally the whole situation became rather

---

[1] Yalta is located on the Black Sea in southwestern Russia and is one of the biggest resort areas in the Soviet Union.

cumbersome. But at every new meeting with an attractive woman he forgot all about this experience, he wanted to enjoy life so badly and it all seemed so simple and amusing.

And so one afternoon, while he was having dinner at a restaurant in the park, the woman in the toque walked in unhurriedly and took a seat at the table next to him. The way she looked, walked, and dressed, wore her hair, told him that she was of good social standing, that she was married, that she was in Yalta for the first time, that she was alone and bored. . . . There was a great deal of exaggeration in the stories about the laxity of morals among the Yalta visitors, and he dismissed them with contempt, for he knew that such stories were mostly made up by people who would gladly have sinned themselves if they had had any idea how to go about it; but when the woman sat down at the table three yards away from him he remembered these stories of easy conquests and excursions to the mountains and the tempting thought of a quick and fleeting affair, an affair with a strange woman whose very name he did not know, suddenly took possession of him.

He tried to attract the attention of the dog by calling softly to it, and when the pomeranian came up to him he shook a finger at it. The pomeranian growled. Gurov again shook a finger at it.

The woman looked up at him and immediately lowered her eyes.

"He doesn't bite," she said and blushed.

"May I give him a bone?" he asked, and when she nodded, he said amiably: "Have you been long in Yalta?"

"About five days."

"And I am just finishing my second week here."

They said nothing for the next few minutes.

"Time flies," she said without looking at him, "and yet it's so boring here."

"That's what one usually hears people saying here. A man may be living in Belev and Zhizdra or some other God-forsaken hole and he isn't bored, but the moment he comes here all you hear from him is 'Oh, it's so boring! Oh, the dust!' You'd think he'd come from Granada!"

She laughed. Then both went on eating in silence, like complete strangers; but after dinner they strolled off together, and they embarked on the light playful conversation of free and contented people who do not care where they go or what they talk about. They walked, and talked about the strange light that fell on the sea; the water was of such a soft and warm lilac, and the moon threw a shaft of gold across it. They talked about how close it was after a hot day. Gurov told her that he lived in Moscow, that he was a graduate in philology but worked in a bank, that he had at one time thought of singing in a private opera company but had given up the idea, that he owned two houses in Moscow. . . . From her he learnt that she had grown up in Petersburg, but had got married in the town of S—, where she had been living for the past two years, that she would stay another month in Yalta, and that her husband, who also needed a rest, might join her. She was quite unable to tell him what her husband's job was, whether he served in the offices of the provincial governor or the rural council, and she found this rather amusing herself. Gurov also found out that her name and patronymic were Anna Sergeyevna.

Later, in his hotel room, he thought about her and felt sure that he would meet her again the next day. It had to be. As he went to bed he remembered that she had only recently left her boarding school, that she had been a schoolgirl like his own daughter; he recalled how much diffidence and angularity there was in her laughter and her conversation with a stranger—it was probably the first time in her life she had found herself alone, in a situation when men followed her, looked at her, and spoke to her with only one secret intention, an intention she could hardly fail to guess. He remembered her slender, weak neck, her beautiful grey eyes.

"There's something pathetic about her, all the same," he thought as he fell asleep.

II

A week had passed since their first meeting. It was a holiday. It was close indoors, while in the streets a strong wind raised clouds of dust and tore off people's hats. All day long one felt thirsty, and Gurov kept going to the terrace of the restaurant, offering Anna Sergeyevna fruit drinks and ices. There was nowhere to go.

In the evening, when the wind had dropped a little, they went to the pier to watch the arrival of the steamer. There were a great many people taking a walk on the landing pier; some were meeting friends, they had bunches of flowers in their hands. It was there that two peculiarities of the Yalta smart set at once arrested attention: the middle-aged women dressed as if they were still young girls and there was a great number of generals.

Because of the rough sea the steamer arrived late, after the sun had set, and she had to swing backwards and forwards several times before getting alongside the pier. Anna Sergeyevna looked at the steamer and the passengers through her lorgnette, as though trying to make out some friends, and when she turned to Gurov her eyes were sparkling. She talked a lot, asked many abrupt questions, and immediately forgot what it was she had wanted to know; then she lost her lorgnette in the crowd of people.

The smartly dressed crowd dispersed; soon they were all gone, the wind had dropped completely, but Gurov and Anna were still standing there as though waiting to see if someone else would come off the boat. Anna Sergeyevna was no longer talking. She was smelling her flowers without looking at Gurov.

"It's a nice evening," he said. "Where shall we go now? Shall we go for a drive?"

She made no answer.

Then he looked keenly at her and suddenly put his arms round her and kissed her on the mouth. He felt the fragrance and dampness of the flowers and immediately looked round him fearfully: had anyone seen them?

"Let's go to your room," he said softly.

And both walked off quickly.

It was very close in her hotel room, which was full of the smell of the scents she had bought in a Japanese shop. Looking at her now, Gurov thought: "Life is full of strange encounters!" From his past he preserved the memory of carefree, good-natured women, whom love had made gay and who were grateful to him for the happiness he gave them, however short-lived; and of women like his wife, who made love without sincerity, with unnecessary talk, affectedly, hysterically, with such an expression, as though it were not love or passion, but something much more significant; and of two or three very beautiful, frigid women, whose faces suddenly lit up with a predatory expression, an obstinate desire to take, to snatch from life more than it could give; these were women no longer in their first youth, capricious, unreasoning, despotic, unintelligent women, and when Gurov lost interest in them, their beauty merely aroused hatred in him and the lace trimmings on their négligés looked to him then like the scales of a snake.

But here there was still the same diffidence and angularity of inexperienced youth—an awkward feeling; and there was also the impression of embarrassment, as if someone had just knocked at the door. Anna Sergeyevna, this lady with the lapdog, apparently regarded what had happened in a peculiar sort of way, very seriously, as though she had become a fallen woman—so it seemed to him, and he found it odd and disconcerting. Her features lengthened and drooped, and her long hair hung mournfully on either side of her face; she sank into thought in a despondent pose, like a woman taken in adultery in an old painting.

"It's wrong," she said. "You'll be the first not to respect me now."

There was a water-melon on the table. Gurov cut himself a slice and began to eat it slowly. At least half an hour passed in silence.

Anna Sergeyevna was very touching; there was an air of a pure, decent, naïve woman about her, a woman who had very little experience of life; the solitary candle burning on the table scarcely lighted up her face, but it was obvious that she was unhappy.

"But, darling, why should I stop respecting you?" Gurov asked. "You don't know yourself what you're saying."

"May God forgive me," she said, and her eyes filled with tears. "It's terrible."

"You seem to wish to justify yourself."

"How can I justify myself? I am a bad, despicable creature. I despise myself and have no thought of justifying myself. I haven't deceived my husband, I've deceived myself. And not only now. I've been deceiving myself for a long time. My husband is, I'm sure, a good and honest man, but, you see, he is a flunkey. I don't know what he does at his office, all I know is that he is a flunkey. I was only twenty when I married him, I was eaten up by curiosity, I wanted something better. There surely must be a different kind of life, I said to myself. I wanted to live. To live, to live! I was burning with curiosity. I don't think you know what I am talking about, but I swear I could no longer control myself, something was happening to me, I could not be held back, I told my husband I was ill, and I came here. . . . Here too I was going about as though in a daze, as though I was mad, and now I've become a vulgar worthless woman whom everyone has a right to despise."

Gurov could not help feeling bored as he listened to her; he was irritated by her naïve tone of voice and her repentance, which was so unexpected and so out of place; but for the tears in her eyes, he might have thought that she was joking or play-acting.

"I don't understand," he said gently, "what it is you want."

She buried her face on his chest and clung close to him.

"Please, please believe me," she said. "I love a pure, honest life. I hate immorality. I don't know myself what I am doing. The common people say 'the devil led her astray.' I too can now say about myself that the devil has led me astray."

"There, there . . ." he murmured.

He gazed into her staring, frightened eyes, kissed her, spoke gently and affectionately to her, and gradually she calmed down and her cheerfulness returned; both of them were soon laughing.

Later, when they went out, there was not a soul on the promenade, the town with its cypresses looked quite dead, but the sea was still roaring and dashing itself against the shore; a single launch tossed on the waves, its lamp flickering sleepily.

They hailed a cab and drove to Oreanda.

"I've just found out your surname, downstairs in the lobby," said Gurov. "Von Diederitz. Is your husband a German?"

"No. I believe his grandfather was German. He is of the Orthodox faith himself."

In Oreanda they sat on a bench not far from the church, looked down on the sea, and were silent. Yalta could scarcely be seen through the morning mist. White clouds lay motionless on the mountain tops. Not a leaf stirred on the trees, the cicadas chirped, and the monotonous, hollow roar of the sea, coming up from below, spoke of rest, of eternal sleep awaiting us all. The sea had roared like that down below when there was no Yalta or Oreanda, it was roaring now, and it would go on roaring as indifferently and hollowly when we were here no more. And in this constancy, in this complete indifference to the life and death of each one of us, there is perhaps hidden the guarantee of our eternal salvation, the never-ceasing movement of life on earth, the never-ceasing movement towards perfection. Sitting beside a young woman who looked so beautiful at the break of day, soothed and enchanted by the sight of all that fairy-land scenery— the sea, the mountains, the clouds, the wide sky—Gurov reflected that, when you came to think of it, everything in the world was really beautiful, everything but our own thoughts and actions when we lose sight of the higher aims of existence and our dignity as human beings.

Someone walked up to them, a watchman probably, looked at them, and went away. And there seemed to be something mysterious and also beautiful in this fact, too. They could see the Theodosia boat coming towards the pier, lit up by the sunrise, and with no lights.

"There's dew on the grass," said Anna Sergeyevna, breaking the silence.

"Yes. Time to go home."

They went back to the town.

After that they met on the front every day at twelve o'clock, had lunch and dinner together, went for walks, admired the sea. She complained of sleeping badly and of her heart beating uneasily, asked the same questions, alternately worried by feelings of jealousy and by fear that he did not respect her sufficiently. And again and again in the park or in the square, when there was no one in sight, he would draw her to him and kiss her passionately. The complete idleness, these kisses in broad daylight, always having to look round for fear of someone watching them, the heat, the smell of the sea, and the constant looming into sight of idle, well-dressed, and well-fed people seemed to have made a new man of him; he told Anna Sergeyevna that she was beautiful, that she was desirable, made passionate love to her, never left her side, while she was often lost in thought and kept asking him to admit that he did not really respect her, that he was not in the least in love with her and only saw in her a vulgar woman. Almost every night they drove out of town, to Oreanda or to the waterfall; the excursion was always a success, and every time their impressions were invariably grand and beautiful.

They kept expecting her husband to arrive. But a letter came from him in which he wrote that he was having trouble with his eyes and implored his wife to return home as soon as possible. Anna Sergeyevna lost no time in getting ready for her journey home.

"It's a good thing I'm going," she said to Gurov. "It's fate."

She took a carriage to the railway station, and he saw her off. The drive took a whole day. When she got into the express train, after the second bell, she said:

"Let me have another look at you. . . . One last look. So."

She did not cry, but looked sad, just as if she were ill, and her face quivered.

"I'll be thinking of you, remembering you," she said. "Good-bye. You're staying, aren't you? Don't think badly of me. We are parting for ever. Yes, it must be so, for we should never have met. Well, good-bye. . . ."

The train moved rapidly out of the station; its lights soon disappeared, and a minute later it could not even be heard, just as though everything had conspired to put a quick end to this sweet trance, this madness. And standing alone on the platform gazing into the dark distance, Gurov listened to the churring of the grasshoppers and the humming of the telegraph wires with a feeling as though he had just woken up. He told himself that this had been just one more affair in his life, just one more adventure, and that it too was over, leaving nothing but a memory. He was moved and sad, and felt a little penitent that the young woman, whom he would never see again, had not been happy with him; he had been amiable and affectionate with her, but all the same in his behaviour to her, in the tone of his voice and in his caresses, there was a suspicion of light irony, the somewhat coarse arrogance of the successful male, who was, moreover, almost twice her age. All the time she called him good, wonderful, high-minded; evidently she must have taken him to be quite different from what he really was, which meant that he had involuntarily deceived her.

At the railway station there was already a whiff of autumn in the air; the evening was chilly.

"Time I went north too," thought Gurov, as he walked off the platform. "High time!"

III

At home in Moscow everything was already like winter: the stoves were heated, and it was still dark in the morning when the children were getting ready to go to school and having breakfast, so that the nurse had to light the lamp for a short time. The frosts had set in. When the first snow falls and the first day one goes out for a ride in a sleigh, one is glad to see the white ground, the white roofs, the air is so soft and wonderful to breathe, and one remembers the days of one's youth. The old lime trees and birches, white with rime, have such a benignant look, they are nearer to one's heart than cypresses and palms, and beside them one no longer wants to think of mountains and the sea.

Gurov had been born and bred in Moscow, and he returned to Moscow on a fine frosty day; and when he put on his fur coat and warm gloves and took a walk down Petrovka Street, and when on Saturday evening he heard the church bells ringing, his recent holiday trip and the places he had visited lost their charm for him. Gradually he became immersed in Moscow life, eagerly reading three newspapers a day and declaring that he never read Moscow papers on principle. Once more he could not resist the attraction of restaurants, clubs, banquets, and anniversary celebrations, and once more he felt flattered that well-known lawyers and actors came to see him and that in the Medical Club he played cards with a professor as his partner. Once again he was capable of eating a whole portion of the Moscow speciality of sour cabbage and meat served in a frying-pan.

Another month and, he thought, nothing but a memory would remain of Anna Sergeyevna; he would remember her as through a haze and only occasionally dream of her with a wistful smile, as he did of the others before her. But over a month passed, winter was at its height, and he remembered her as clearly as though he had only parted from her the day before. His memories haunted him more and more persistently. Every time the voices of his children doing their homework reached him in his study in the stillness of the evening, every time he heard a popular song or some music in a restaurant, every time the wind howled in the chimney—it all came back to him: their walks on the pier, early morning with the mist on the mountains, the Theodosia boat, and the kisses. He kept pacing the room for hours remembering it all and smiling, and then his memories turned into daydreams and the past mingled in his imagination with what was going to happen. He did not dream of Anna Sergeyevna, she accompanied him everywhere like his shadow and followed him wherever he went. Closing his eyes, he saw her as clearly as if she were before him, and she seemed to him lovelier, younger, and tenderer than she had been;

and he thought that he too was much better than he had been in Yalta. In the evenings she gazed at him from the bookcase, from the fireplace, from the corner—he heard her breathing, the sweet rustle of her dress. In the street he followed women with his eyes, looking for anyone who resembled her. . . .

He was beginning to be overcome by an overwhelming desire to share his memories with someone. But at home it was impossible to talk of his love, and outside his home there was no one he could talk to. Not the tenants who lived in his house, and certainly not his colleagues in the bank. And what was he to tell them? Had he been in love then? Had there been anything beautiful, poetic, edifying, or even anything interesting about his relations with Anna Sergeyevna? So he had to talk in general terms about love and women, and no one guessed what he was driving at, and his wife merely raised her black eyebrows and said:

"Really, Dimitry, the role of a coxcomb doesn't suit you at all!"

One evening, as he left the Medical Club with his partner, a civil servant, he coud not restrain himself, and said:

"If you knew what a fascinating woman I met in Yalta!"

The civil servant got into his sleigh and was about to be driven off, but suddenly he turned round and called out:

"I say!"

"Yes?"

"You were quite right: the sturgeon *was* a bit off."

These words, so ordinary in themselves, for some reason hurt Gurov's feelings: they seemed to him humiliating and indecent. What savage manners! What faces! What stupid nights! What uninteresting, wasted days! Crazy gambling at cards, gluttony, drunkenness, endless talk about one and the same thing. Business that was of no use to anyone and talk about one and the same thing absorbed the greater part of one's time and energy, and what was left in the end was a sort of dock-tailed, barren life, a sort of nonsensical existence, and it was impossible to escape from it, just as though you were in a lunatic asylum or a convict chain-gang!

Gurov lay awake all night, fretting and fuming, and had a splitting headache the whole of the next day. The following nights too he slept badly, sitting up in bed thinking, or walking up and down his room. He was tired of his children, tired of the bank, he did not feel like going out anywhere or talking about anything.

In December, during the Christmas holidays, he packed his things, told his wife that he was going to Petersburg to get a job for a young man he knew, and set off for the town of S—. Why? He had no very clear idea himself. He wanted to see Anna Sergeyevna, to talk to her, to arrange a meeting, if possible.

He arrived in S—in the morning and took the best room in a hotel, with a fitted carpet of military grey cloth and an inkstand grey with dust on the table, surmounted by a horseman with raised hand and no head. The hall porter supplied him with all the necessary information: Von Diederitz lived in a house of his own in Old Potter's Street, not far from the hotel. He lived well, was rich, kept his own carriage horses, the whole town knew him. The hall-porter pronounced the name: Dridiritz.

Gurov took a leisurely walk down Old Potter's Street and found the house. In front of it was a long grey fence studded with upturned nails.

"A fence like that would make anyone wish to run away," thought Gurov, scanning the windows and the fence.

As it was a holiday, he thought, her husband was probably at home. It did not matter either way, though, for he could not very well embarrass her by calling at the house. If he were to send in a note it might fall into the hands of the husband and ruin everything. The best thing was to rely on chance. And he kept walking up and down the street and along the fence, waiting for his chance. He watched a beggar enter the gate and the dogs attack him; then, an hour later, he heard the faint indistinct sounds of a piano. That must have been Anna Sergeyevna playing. Suddenly the front door opened and an old woman came out, followed by the familiar white pomeranian. Gurov was about to call to the dog, but his heart began to beat violently and in his excitement he could not remember its name.

He went on walking up and down the street, hating the grey fence more and more, and he was already saying to himself that Anna Sergeyevna had forgotten him and had perhaps been having a good time with someone else, which was indeed quite natural for a young woman who had to look at that damned fence from morning till night. He went back to his hotel room and sat on the sofa for a long time, not knowing what to do, then he had dinner and after dinner a long sleep.

"How stupid and disturbing it all is," he thought, waking up and staring at the dark windows: it was already evening. "Well, I've had a good sleep, so what now? What am I going to do tonight?"

He sat on a bed covered by a cheap grey blanket looking exactly like a hospital blanket, and taunted himself in vexation:

"A *lady* with a lapdog! Some adventure, I must say! Serves you right!"

At the railway station that morning he had noticed a poster announcing in huge letters the first performance of *The Geisha Girl* at the local theatre. He recalled it now, and decided to go to the theatre.

"Quite possibly she goes to first nights," he thought.

The theatre was full. As in all provincial theatres, there was a mist over the chandeliers and the people in the gallery kept up a noisy and excited conversation; in the first row of the stalls stood the local dandies with their hands crossed behind their backs; here, too, in the front seat of the Governor's box, sat the Governor's daughter, wearing a feather boa, while the Governor himself hid modestly behind the portière so that only his hands were visible; the curtain stirred, the orchestra took a long time tuning up. Gurov scanned the audience eagerly as they filed in and occupied their seats.

Anna Sergeyevna came in too. She took her seat in the third row, and when Gurov glanced at her his heart missed a beat and he realized clearly that there was no one in the world nearer and dearer or more important to him than that little woman with the stupid lorgnette in her hand, who was in no way remarkable. That woman lost in a provincial crowd now filled his whole life, was his misfortune, his joy, and the only happiness that he wished for himself. Listening to the bad orchestra and the wretched violins played by second-rate musicians, he thought how beautiful she was. He thought and dreamed.

A very tall, round-shouldered young man with small whiskers had come in with Anna Sergeyevna and sat down beside her; he nodded at every step he took and seemed to be continually bowing to someone. This was probably her husband, whom in a fit of bitterness at Yalta she had called a flunkey. And indeed there was something of a lackey's obsequiousness in his lank figure, his whiskers, and the little bald spot on the top of his head. He smiled sweetly, and the gleaming insignia of some scientific society which he wore in his buttonhole looked like the number on a waiter's coat.

In the first interval the husband went out to smoke and she was left in her seat. Gurov, who also had a seat in the stalls, went up to her and said in a trembling voice and with a forced smile:

"Good evening!"

She looked up at him and turned pale, then looked at him again in panic, unable to believe her eyes, clenching her fan and lorgnette in her hand and apparently trying hard not to fall into a dead faint. Both were silent. She sat and he stood, frightened by her embarrassment and not daring to sit down beside her. The violinists and the flautist began tuning their instruments, and they suddenly felt terrified, as though they were being watched from all the boxes. But a moment later she got up and walked rapidly towards one of the exits; he followed her, and both of them walked aimlessly along corridors and up and down stairs. Figures in all sorts of uniforms—lawyers, teachers, civil servants, all wearing badges—flashed by them; ladies, fur coats hanging on pegs, the cold draught bringing with it the odour of cigarette-ends. Gurov, whose heart was beating violently, thought:

"Oh Lord, what are all these people, that orchestra, doing here?"

At that moment he suddenly remembered how after seeing Anna Sergeyevna off he had told himself that evening at the station that all was over and that they would never meet again. But how far they still were from the end!

She stopped on a dark, narrow staircase with a notice over it: "To the Upper Circle."

"How you frightened me!" she said, breathing heavily, still looking pale and stunned. "Oh dear, how you frightened me! I'm scarcely alive. Why did you come? Why?!"

"But, please, try to understand, Anna," he murmured hurriedly. "I beg you, please, try to understand. . . ."

She looked at him with fear, entreaty, love, looked at him intently, so as to fix his features firmly in her mind.

"I've suffered so much," she went on, without listening to him. "I've been thinking of you all the time. The thought of you kept me alive. And yet I tried so hard to forget you—why, oh why did you come?"

On the landing above two schoolboys were smoking and looking down, but Gurov did not care. He drew Anna Sergeyevna towards him and began kissing her face, her lips, her hands.

"What are you doing? What are you doing?" she said in horror, pushing him away. "We've both gone mad. You must go back tonight, this minute. I implore you, by all that's sacred . . . Somebody's coming!"

Somebody was coming up the stairs.

"You must go back," continued Anna Sergeyevna in a whisper. "Do you hear? I'll come to you in Moscow. I've never been happy, I'm unhappy now, and I shall never be happy, never! So please don't make me suffer still more. I swear I'll come to you in Moscow. But now you must part. Oh, my sweet, my darling, we must part!"

She pressed his hand and went quickly down the stairs, looking back at him all the time, and he could see from the expression in her eyes that she really was unhappy. Gurov stood listening for a short time, and when all was quiet he went to look for his coat and left the theatre.

IV

Anna Sergeyevna began going to Moscow to see him. Every two or three months she left the town of S—, telling her husband that she was going to consult a Moscow gynaecologist, and her husband believed and did not believe her. In Moscow she stayed at the Slav Bazaar and immediately sent a porter in a red cap to inform Gurov of her arrival. Gurov went to her hotel, and no one in Moscow knew about it.

One winter morning he went to her hotel as usual (the porter had called with his message at his house the evening before, but he had not been in). He had his daughter with him, and he was glad of the opportunity of taking her to school, which was on the way to the hotel. Snow was falling in thick wet flakes.

"It's three degrees above zero," Gurov was saying to his daughter, "and yet it's snowing. But then, you see, it's only warm on the earth's surface, in the upper layers of the atmosphere the temperature's quite different."

"Why isn't there any thunder in winter, Daddy?"

He explained that, too. As he was speaking, he kept thinking that he was going to meet his mistress and not a living soul knew about it. He led a double life: one for all who were interested to see, full of conventional truth and conventional deception, exactly like the lives of his friends and acquaintances; and another which went on in secret. And by a kind of strange concatenation of circumstances, possibly quite by accident, everything that was important, interesting, essential, everything about which he was sincere and did not deceive himself, everything that made up the quintessence of his life, went on in secret, while everything that was a lie, everything that was merely the husk in which he hid himself to conceal the truth, like his work at the bank, for instance, his discussions at the club, his ideas of the lower breed, his going to anniversary functions with his wife—all that happened in the sight of all. He judged others by himself, did not believe what he saw, and was always of the opinion that every man's real and most interesting life went on in secret, under cover of night. The personal, private life of an individual was kept a secret, and perhaps that was partly the reason why civilized man was so anxious that his personal secrets should be respected.

Having seen his daughter off to her school, Gurov went to the Slav Bazaar. He took off his fur coat in the cloakroom, went upstairs, and knocked softly on the door. Anna Sergeyevna, wearing the grey dress he liked most, tired out by her journey and by the suspense of waiting for him, had been expecting him since the evening before; she was pale, looked at him without smiling, but was in his arms the moment he went into the room. This kiss was long and lingering, as if they had not seen each other for two years.

"Well," he asked, "how are you getting on there? Anything new?"

"Wait, I'll tell you in a moment. . . . I can't . . ."

She could not speak because she was crying. She turned away from him and pressed her handkerchief to her eyes.

"Well, let her have her cry," he thought, sitting down in an armchair. "I'll wait."

Then he rang the bell and ordered tea; while he was having his tea, she was still standing there with her face to the window. She wept because she could not control her emotions, because she was bitterly conscious of the fact that their life was so sad: they could only meet in secret, they had to hide from people, like thieves! Was not their life ruined?

"Please, stop crying!" he said.

It was quite clear to him that their love would not come to an end for a long time, if ever. Anna Sergeyevna was getting attached to him more and more strongly, she worshipped him, and it would have been absurd to tell her that all this would have to come to an end one day. She would not have believed it, anyway.

He went up to her and took her by the shoulders, wishing to be nice to her, to make her smile; and at that moment he caught sight of himself in the looking glass.

His hair was already beginning to turn grey. It struck him as strange that he should have aged so much, that he should have lost his good looks in the last few years. The shoulders on which his hands lay were warm and quivering. He felt so sorry for this life, still so warm and beautiful, but probably soon to fade and wilt like his own. Why did she love him so? To women he always seemed different from what he was, and they loved in him not himself, but the man their imagination conjured up and whom they had eagerly been looking for all their lives; and when they discovered their mistake they still loved him. And not one of them had ever been happy with him. Time had passed, he had met women, made love to them, parted from them, but not once had he been in love; there had been everything between them, but no love.

It was only now, when his hair was beginning to turn grey, that he had fallen in love properly, in good earnest—for the first time in his life.

He and Anna Sergeyevna loved each other as people do who are very dear and near, as man and wife or close friends love each other; they could not help feeling that fate itself had intended them for one another, and they were unable to understand why he should have a wife and she a husband; they were like two migrating birds, male and female, who had been caught and forced to live in separate cages. They had forgiven each other what they had been ashamed of in the past, and forgave each other everything in their present, and felt that this love of theirs had changed them both.

Before, when he felt depressed, he had comforted himself by all sorts of arguments that happened to occur to him on the spur of the moment, but now he had more serious things to think of, he felt profound compassion, he longed to be sincere, tender. . . .

"Don't cry, my sweet," he said. "That'll do, you've had your cry. . . . Let's talk now, let's think of something."

Then they had a long talk. They tried to think how they could get rid of the necessity of hiding, telling lies, living in different towns, not seeing one another for so long. How were they to free themselves from their intolerable chains?

"How? How?" he asked himself, clutching at his head. "How?"

And it seemed to them that in only a few more minutes a solution would be found and a new, beautiful life would begin; but both of them knew very well that the end was still a long, long way away and that the most complicated and difficult part was only just beginning.

Questions

1. Does Chekhov summarize Gurov in a sentence? Can you?
2. Does Chekhov summarize Anna Sergeyevna in a sentence? Can you?
3. Does the conclusion grow out of the previous incidents? Does it throw a revealing light on what has come before?
4. Is Chekhov's implicit judgment of Anna and Gurov overly simple? Does he unquestioningly approve or disapprove of their relationship?
5. Are any incidents in the story superfluous?
6. Does Chekhov leave out any scene that would be helpful?
7. What is your overall appraisal of this story?

14 ❧ Stories for Further Reading

JAMES BALDWIN (1924–)

Sonny's Blues

I read about it in the paper, in the subway, on my way to work. I read it, and I couldn't believe it, and I read it again. Then perhaps I just stared at it, at the newsprint spelling out his name, spelling out the story. I stared at it in the swinging lights of the subway car, and in the faces and bodies of the people, and in my own face, trapped in the darkness which roared outside.

It was not to be believed and I kept telling myself that as I walked from the subway station to the high school. And at the same time I couldn't doubt it. I was scared, scared for Sonny. He became real to me again. A great block of ice got settled in my belly and kept melting there slowly all day long, while I taught my classes algebra. It was a special kind of ice. It kept melting, sending trickles of ice water all up and down my veins, but it never got less. Sometimes it hardened and seemed to expand until I felt my guts were going to come spilling out or that I was going to choke or scream. This would always be at a moment when I was remembering some specific thing Sonny had once said or done.

When he was about as old as the boys in my classes his face had been bright and open, there was a lot of copper in it; and he'd had wonderfully direct brown eyes, and great gentleness and privacy. I wondered what he looked like now. He had been picked up, the evening before, in a raid on an apartment downtown, for peddling and using heroin.

I couldn't believe it: but what I mean by that is that I couldn't find any room for it anywhere inside me. I had kept it outside me for a long time. I hadn't wanted to know. I had had suspicions, but I didn't name them, I kept putting them away. I told myself that Sonny was wild, but he wasn't crazy. And he'd always been a good boy, he hadn't ever turned hard or evil or disrespectful, the

James Baldwin (*Photograph* © 1983 *Jill Krementz*)

way kids can, so quick, so quick, especially in Harlem. I didn't want to believe that I'd ever see my brother going down, coming to nothing, all that light in his face gone out, in the condition I'd already seen so many others. Yet it had happened and here I was, talking about algebra to a lot of boys who might, every one of them for all I knew, be popping off needles every time they went to the head.[1] Maybe it did more for them than algebra could.

I was sure that the first time Sonny had ever had horse,[2] he couldn't have been much older than these boys were now. These boys, now, were living as we'd been living then, they were growing up with a rush and their heads bumped abruptly against the low ceiling of their actual possibilities. They were filled with rage. All they really knew were two darknesses, the darkness of their lives, which was now closing in on them, and the darkness of the movies, which had blinded them to that other darkness, and in which they now, vindictively, dreamed, at once more together than they were at any other time, and more alone.

When the last bell rang, the last class ended, I let out my breath. It seemed I'd been holding it for all that time. My clothes were wet—I may have looked as though I'd been sitting in a steam bath, all dressed up, all afternoon. I sat alone in the classroom a long time. I listened to the boys outside, downstairs, shouting and cursing and laughing. Their laughter struck me for perhaps the first time. It was not the joyous laughter which—God knows why—one associates

---

[1] Head is slang for bathroom.
[2] Horse is slang for heroin.

with children. It was mocking and insular, its intent was to denigrate. It was disenchanted, and in this, also, lay the authority of their curses. Perhaps I was listening to them because I was thinking about my brother and in them I heard my brother. And myself.

One boy was whistling a tune, at once very complicated and very simple, it seemed to be pouring out of him as though he were a bird, and it sounded very cool and moving through all that harsh, bright air, only just holding its own through all those other sounds.

I stood up and walked over to the window and looked down into the courtyard. It was the beginning of the spring and the sap was rising in the boys. A teacher passed through them every now and again, quickly, as though he or she couldn't wait to get out of that courtyard, to get those boys out of their sight and off their minds. I started collecting my stuff. I thought I'd better get home and talk to Isabel.

The courtyard was almost deserted by the time I got downstairs. I saw this boy standing in the shadow of a doorway, looking just like Sonny. I almost called his name. Then I saw that it wasn't Sonny, but somebody we used to know, a boy from around our block. He'd been Sonny's friend. He'd never been mine, having been too young for me, and, anyway, I'd never liked him. And now, even though he was a grown-up man, he still hung around that block, still spent hours on the street corner, was always high and raggy. I used to run into him from time to time and he'd often work around to asking me for a quarter or fifty cents. He always had some real good excuse, too, and I always gave it to him, I don't know why.

But now, abruptly, I hated him. I couldn't stand the way he looked at me, partly like a dog, partly like a cunning child. I wanted to ask him what the hell he was doing in the school courtyard.

He sort of shuffled over to me, and he said, "I see you got the papers. So you already know about it."

"You mean about Sonny? Yes, I already know about it. How come they didn't get you?"

He grinned. It made him repulsive and it also brought to mind what he'd looked like as a kid. "I wasn't there. I stay away from them people."

"Good for you." I offered him a cigarette and I watched him through the smoke. "You come all the way down here just to tell me about Sonny?"

"That's right." He was sort of shaking his head and his eyes looked strange, as though they were about to cross. The bright sun deadened his damp dark brown skin and it made his eyes look yellow and showed up the dirt in his conked hair. He smelled funky. I moved a little away from him and I said, "Well, thanks. But I already know about it and I got to get home."

"I'll walk you a little ways," he said. We started walking. There were a couple of kids still loitering in the courtyard and one of them said good night to me and looked strangely at the boy beside me.

"What're you going to do?" he asked me. "I mean, about Sonny."

"Look. I haven't seen Sonny for over a year, I'm not sure I'm going to do anything. Anyway, what the hell *can* I do?"

"That's right," he said quickly, "ain't nothing you can do. Can't much help old Sonny no more, I guess."

It was what I was thinking and so it seemed to me he had no right to say it.

"I'm surprised at Sonny, though," he went on—he had a funny way of talking, he looked straight ahead as though he were talking to himself— "I thought Sonny was a smart boy, I thought he was too smart to get hung."

"I guess he thought so too," I said sharply, "and that's how he got hung. And how about you? You're pretty goddam smart, I bet."

Then he looked directly at me, just for a minute. "I ain't smart," he said. "If I was smart, I'd have reached for a pistol a long time ago."

"Look. Don't tell me your sad story, if it was up to me, I'd give you one." Then I felt guilty—guilty, probably, for never having supposed that the poor bastard had a story of his own, much less a sad one, and I asked, quickly, "What's going to happen to him now?"

He didn't answer this. He was off by himself some place. "Funny thing," he said, and from his tone we might have been discussing the quickest way to get to Brooklyn, "when I saw the papers this morning, the first thing I asked myself was if I had anything to do with it. I felt sort of responsible."

I began to listen more carefully. The subway station was on the corner, just before us, and I stopped. He stopped, too. We were in front of a bar and he ducked slightly, peering in, but whoever he was looking for didn't seem to be there. The juke box was blasting away with something black and bouncy and I half watched the barmaid as she danced her way from the juke box to her place behind the bar. And I watched her face as she laughingly responded to something someone said to her, still keeping time to the music. When she smiled one saw the little girl, one sensed the doomed, still-struggling woman beneath the battered face of the semi-whore.

"I never give Sonny nothing," the boy said finally, "but a long time ago I come to school high and Sonny asked me how it felt." He paused, I couldn't bear to watch him, I watched the barmaid, and I listened to the music which seemed to be causing the pavement to shake. "I told him it felt great." The music stopped, the barmaid paused, and watched the juke box until the music began again. "It did."

All this was carrying me some place I didn't want to go. I certainly didn't want to know how it felt. It filled everything, the people, the houses, the music, the dark, quicksilver barmaid, the menace; and this menace was their reality.

"What's going to happen to him now?" I asked again.

"They'll send him away some place and they'll try to cure him." He shook his head. "Maybe he'll even think he's kicked the habit. Then they'll turn him loose"—he gestured, throwing his cigarette into the gutter. "That's all."

"What do you mean, that's all?"

But I knew what he meant.

"I mean, that's all." He turned his head and looked at me, pulling down the corners of his mouth. "Don't you know what I mean?" he asked softly.

"How the hell would I know what you mean?" I almost whispered it, I don't know why.

"That's right," he said to the air, "how would *he* know what I mean?" He turned toward me again, patient and calm, and yet I somehow felt him shaking, shaking as though he were going to fall apart. I felt that ice in my guts again, the dread I'd felt all afternoon; and again I watched the barmaid, moving about the bar, washing glasses, and singing. "Listen. They'll let him out and then it'll just start all over again. That's what I mean."

"You mean—they'll let him out. And then he'll just start working his way back in again. You mean he'll never kick the habit. Is that what you mean?"

"That's right," he said, cheerfully. "*You* see what I mean."

"Tell me," I said at last, "why does he want to die? He must want to die, he's killing himself, why does he want to die?"

He looked at me in surprise. He licked his lips. "He don't want to die. He wants to live. Don't nobody want to die, ever."

Then I wanted to ask him—too many things. He could not have answered, or if he had, I could not have borne the answers. I started walking. "Well, I guess it's none of my business."

"It's going to be rough on old Sonny," he said. We reached the subway station. "This is your station?" he asked. I nodded. I took one step down. "Damn!" he said, suddenly. I looked up at him. He grinned again. "Damn if I didn't leave all my money home. You ain't got a dollar on you, have you? Just for a couple of days is all."

All at once something inside gave and threatened to come pouring out of me. I didn't hate him any more. I felt that in another moment I'd start crying like a child.

"Sure," I said. "Don't sweat." I looked in my wallet and didn't have a dollar, I only had a five. "Here," I said. "That hold you?"

He didn't look at it—he didn't want to look at it. A terrible, closed look came over his face, as though he were keeping the number on the bill a secret from him and me. "Thanks," he said, and now he was dying to see me go. "Don't worry about Sonny. Maybe I'll write him or something."

"Sure," I said. "You do that. So long."

"Be seeing you," he said. I went on down the steps.

And I didn't write Sonny or send him anything for a long time. When I finally did, it was just after my little girl died, he wrote me back a letter which made me feel like a bastard.

Here's what he said:

DEAR BROTHER,

You don't know how much I needed to hear from you. I wanted to write you many a time but I dug how much I must have hurt you and so I didn't write. But now I feel like a man who's been trying to climb up out of some deep, real deep and funky hole and just saw the sun up there, outside. I got to get outside.

I can't tell you much about how I got here. I mean I don't know how to tell you. I guess I was afraid of something or I was trying to escape from something and you know I have never been very strong in the head (smile). I'm glad Mama and Daddy are dead and can't see what's happened to their son and I swear if I'd known what I was doing I would never have hurt you so, you and a lot of other fine people who were nice to me and who believed in me.

I don't want you to think it had anything to do with me being a musician. It's more than that. Or maybe less than that. I can't get anything straight in my head down here and I try not to think about what's going to happen to me when I get outside again. Sometime I think I'm going to flip and *never* get outside and sometime I think I'll come straight back. I tell you one thing, though, I'd rather blow my brains out than go through this again. But that's what they all say, so they tell me. If I tell you when I'm coming to New York and if you could meet me, I sure would appreciate it. Give my love to Isabel and the kids and I was sorry to hear about little Gracie. I wish I could be like Mama and say the Lord's will be done, but I don't know it seems to me that trouble is the one thing that never does get stopped and I don't know what good it does to blame it on the Lord. But maybe it does some good if you believe it.

Your brother,

Sonny

Then I kept in constant touch with him and I sent him whatever I could and I went to meet him when he came back to New York. When I saw him many things I thought I had forgotten came flooding back to me. This was because I had begun, finally, to wonder about Sonny, about the life that Sonny lived inside. This life, whatever it was, had made him older and thinner and it had deepened the distant stillness in which he had always moved. He looked very unlike my baby brother. Yet, when he smiled, when we shook hands, the baby brother I'd never known looked out from the depths of his private life, like an animal waiting to be coaxed into the light.

"How you been keeping?" he asked me.

"All right. And you?"

"Just fine." He was smiling all over his face. "It's good to see you again."

"It's good to see you."

The seven years' difference in our ages lay between us like a chasm: I wondered if these years would ever operate between us as a bridge. I was remembering, and it made it hard to catch my breath, that I had been there when he was born; and I had heard the first words he had ever spoken. When he started to walk, he walked from our mother straight to me. I caught him just before he fell when he took the first steps he ever took in this world.

"How's Isabel?"

"Just fine. She's dying to see you."

"And the boys?"

"They're fine, too. They're anxious to see their uncle."

"Oh, come on. You know they don't remember me."

"Are you kidding? Of course they remember you."

He grinned again. We got into a taxi. We had a lot to say to each other, far too much to know how to begin.

As the taxi began to move, I asked, "You still want to go to India?"

He laughed. "You still remember that. Hell, no. This place is Indian enough for me."

"It used to belong to them," I said.

And he laughed again. "They damn sure knew what they were doing when they got rid of it."

Years ago, when he was around fourteen, he'd been all hipped on the idea of going to India. He read books about people sitting on rocks, naked, in all kinds of weather, but mostly bad, naturally, and walking barefoot through hot coals and arriving at wisdom. I used to say that it sounded to me as though they were getting away from wisdom as fast as they could. I think he sort of looked down on me for that.

"Do you mind," he asked, "if we have the driver drive alongside the park? On the west side—I haven't seen the city in so long."

"Of course not," I said. I was afraid that I might sound as though I were humoring him, but I hoped he wouldn't take it that way.

So we drove along, between the green of the park and the stony, lifeless elegance of hotels and apartment buildings, toward the vivid, killing streets of our childhood. These streets hadn't changed, though housing projects jutted up out of them now like rocks in the middle of a boiling sea. Most of the houses in which we had grown up had vanished, as had the stores from which we had stolen, the basements in which we had first tried sex, the rooftops from which we had hurled tin cans and bricks. But houses exactly like the houses of our past yet dominated the landscape, boys exactly like the boys we once had been found themselves smothering in these houses, came down into the streets for light and air and found themselves encircled by disaster. Some escaped the trap, most didn't. Those who got out always left something of themselves behind, as some animals amputate a leg and leave it in the trap. It might be said, perhaps, that I had escaped, after all, I was a school teacher; or that Sonny had, he hadn't lived in Harlem for years. Yet, as the cab moved uptown through streets which seemed, with a rush, to darken with dark people, and as I covertly studied Sonny's face, it came to me that what we both were seeking through out separate cab windows was that part of ourselves which had been left behind. It's always at the hour of trouble and confrontation that the missing member aches.

We hit 110th street and started rolling up Lenox Avenue. And I'd known this avenue all my life, but it seemed to me again, as it had seemed on the day I'd first heard about Sonny's trouble, filled with a hidden menace which was its very breath of life.

"We almost there," said Sonny.

"Almost." We were both too nervous to say anything more.

We live in a housing project. It hasn't been up long. A few days after it was up it seemed uninhabitably new, now, of course, it's already run-down. It looks like a parody of the good, clean, faceless life—God knows the people who live in it do their best to make it a parody. The beat-looking grass lying around isn't enough to make their lives green, the hedges will never hold out the streets, and they know it. The big windows fool no one, they aren't big enough to make space out of no space. They don't bother with the windows, they watch the TV screen instead. The playground is most popular with the children who don't play jacks, or skip rope, or roller skate, or swing, and they can be found in it after dark. We moved in partly because it's not too far from where I teach, and partly for the kids; but it's really just like the houses in which Sonny and I grew up. The same things happen, they'll have the same things to remember. The moment Sonny and I started into the house I had the feeling that I was simply bringing him back into the danger he had almost died trying to escape.

Sonny has never been talkative. So I don't know why I was sure he'd be dying to talk to me when supper was over the first night. Everything went fine, the oldest boy remembered him, and the youngest boy liked him, and Sonny had remembered to bring something for each of them; and Isabel, who is really much nicer than I am, more open and giving, had gone to a lot of trouble about dinner and was genuinely glad to see him. And she's always been able to tease Sonny in a way that I haven't. It was nice to see her face so vivid again and to hear her laugh and watch her make Sonny laugh. She wasn't, or, anyway, she didn't seem to be, at all uneasy or embarrassed. She chatted as though there were no subject which had to be avoided and she got Sonny past his first, faint stiffness. And thank God she was there, for I was filled with that icy dread again. Everything I did seemed awkward to me, and everything I said sounded freighted with hidden meaning. I was trying to remember everything I'd heard about dope addiction and I couldn't help watching Sonny for signs. I wasn't doing it out of malice. I was trying to find out something about my brother. I was dying to hear him tell me he was safe.

"Safe!" my father grunted, whenever Mama suggested trying to move to a neighborhood which might be safer for children. "Safe, hell! Ain't no place safe for kids, nor nobody."

He always went on like this, but he wasn't, ever, really as bad as he sounded, not even on weekends, when he got drunk. As a matter of fact, he was always on the lookout for "something a little better," but he died before he found it. He died suddenly, during a drunken weekend in the middle of the war, when Sonny was fifteen. He and Sonny hadn't ever got on too well. And this was partly because Sonny was the apple of his father's eye. It was because he loved Sonny so much and was frightened for him, that he was always fighting with him. It doesn't do any good to fight with Sonny. Sonny just moves back, inside himself, where he can't be reached. But the principal reason that they never hit it off is that they were so much alike. Daddy was big and rough and loud-talking, just the opposite of Sonny, but they both had—that same privacy.

Mama tried to tell me something about this, just after Daddy died. I was home on leave from the army.

This was the last time I ever saw my mother alive. Just the same, this picture gets all mixed up in my mind with pictures I had of her when she was younger. The way I always see her is the way she used to be on a Sunday afternoon, say, when the old folks were talking after the big Sunday dinner. I always see her wearing pale blue. She'd be sitting on the sofa. And my father would be sitting in the easy chair, not far from her. And the living room would be full of church folks and relatives. There they sit, in chairs all around the living room, and the night is creeping up outside, but nobody knows it yet. You can see the darkness growing against the window-panes and you hear the street noises every now and again, or maybe the jangling beat of a tambourine from one of the churches close by, but it's real quiet in the room. For a moment nobody's talking, but every face looks darkening, like the sky outside. And my mother rocks a little from the waist, and my father's eyes are closed. Everyone is looking at something a child can't see. For a minute they've forgotten the children. Maybe a kid is lying on the rug half asleep. Maybe somebody's got a kid on his lap and is absent-mindedly stroking the kid's head. Maybe there's a kid, quiet and big-eyed, curled up in a big chair in the corner. The silence, the darkness coming, and the darkness in the faces frightens the child obscurely. He hopes that the hand which strokes his forehead will never stop—will never die. He hopes that there will never come a time when the old folks won't be sitting around the living room, talking about where they've come from, and what they've seen, and what's happened to them and their kinfolk.

But something deep and watchful in the child knows that this is bound to end, is already ending. In a moment someone will get up and turn on the light. Then the old folks will remember the children and they won't talk any more that day. And when light fills the room, the child is filled with darkness. He knows that every time this happens he's moved just a little closer to that darkness outside. The darkness outside is what the old folks have been talking about. It's what they've come from. It's what they endure. The child knows that they won't talk any more because if he knows too much about what's happened to *them*, he'll know too much too soon, about what's going to happen to *him*.

The last time I talked to my mother, I remember I was restless. I wanted to get out and see Isabel. We weren't married then and we had a lot to straighten out between us.

There Mama sat, in black, by the window. She was humming an old church song, *Lord, you brought me from a long ways off.* Sonny was out somewhere. Mama kept watching the streets.

"I don't know," she said, "if I'll ever see you again, after you go off from here. But I hope you'll remember the things I tried to teach you."

"Don't talk like that," I said, and smiled. "You'll be here a long time yet."

She smiled, too, but she said nothing. She was quiet for a long time. And I said, "Mama, don't you worry about nothing. I'll be writing all the time, and you be getting the checks. . . ."

"I want to talk to you about your brother," she said, suddenly. "If anything happens to me he ain't going to have nobody to look out for him."

"Mama," I said, "ain't nothing going to happen to you or Sonny. Sonny's all right. He's a good boy and he's got good sense."

"It ain't a question of his being a good boy," Mama said, "nor of his having good sense. It ain't only the bad ones, nor yet the dumb ones that gets sucked under." She stopped, looking at me. "Your Daddy once had a brother," she said, and she smiled in a way that made me feel she was in pain. "You didn't never know that, did you?"

"No," I said, "I never knew that," and I watched her face.

"Oh, yes," she said, "your Daddy had a brother." She looked out of the window again. "I know you never saw your Daddy cry. But I did—many a time, through all these years."

I asked her, "What happened to his brother? How come nobody's ever talked about him?"

This was the first time I ever saw my mother look old.

"His brother got killed," she said, "when he was just a little younger than you are now. I knew him. He was a fine boy. He was maybe a little full of the devil, but he didn't mean nobody no harm."

Then she stopped and the room was silent, exactly as it had sometimes been on those Sunday afternoons. Mama kept looking out into the streets.

"He used to have a job in the mill," she said, "and, like all young folks, he just like to perform on Saturday nights. Saturday nights, him and your father would drift around to different places, go to dances and things like that, or just sit around with people they knew, and your father's brother would sing, he had a fine voice, and play along with himself on his guitar. Well, this particular Saturday night, him and your father was coming home from some place, and they were both a little drunk and there was a moon that night, it was bright like day. Your father's brother was feeling kind of good, and he was whistling to himself, and he had his guitar slung over his shoulder. They was coming down a hill and beneath them was a road that turned off from the highway. Well, your father's brother, being always kind of frisky, decided to run down this hill, and he did, with that guitar banging and clanging behind him, and he ran across the road, and he was making water behind a tree. And your father was sort of amused at him and he was still coming down the hill, kind of slow. Then he heard a car motor and that same minute his brother stepped from behind the tree, into the road, in the moonlight. And he started to cross the road. And your father started to run down the hill, he says he don't know why. This car was full of white men. They was all drunk, and when they seen your father's brother they let out a great whoop and holler and they aimed the car straight at him. They was having fun, they just wanted to scare him, the way they do sometimes, you know. But they was drunk. And I guess the boy, being drunk, too, and scared, kind of lost his head. By the time he jumped it was too late. Your father says he heard his brother scream when the car rolled over him, and he heard the wood of that guitar when it give, and he heard them strings go flying, and he heard them white men shouting, and the car kept on a-going and it ain't stopped till this day. And, time your father got down the hill, his brother weren't nothing but blood and pulp."

Tears were gleaming on my mother's face. There wasn't anything I could say.

"He never mentioned it," she said, "because I never let him mention it before you children. Your Daddy was like a crazy man that night and for many a night thereafter. He says he never in his life seen anything as dark as that road after the lights of that car had gone away. Weren't nothing, weren't nobody on that road, just your Daddy and his brother and that busted guitar. Oh, yes. Your Daddy never did really get right again. Till the day he died he weren't sure but that every white man he saw was the man that killed his brother."

She stopped and took out her handkerchief and dried her eyes and looked at me.

"I ain't telling you all this," she said, "to make you scared or bitter or to make you hate nobody. I'm telling you this because you got a brother. And the world ain't changed."

I guess I didn't want to believe this. I guess she saw this in my face. She turned away from me, toward the window again, searching those streets.

"But I praise my Redeemer," she said at last, "that He called your Daddy home before me. I ain't saying it to throw no flowers at myself, but, I declare, it keeps me from feeling too cast down to know I helped your father get safely through this world. Your father always acted like he was the roughest, strongest man on earth. And everybody took him to be like that. But if he hadn't had *me* there—to see his tears!"

She was crying again. Still, I couldn't move. I said, "Lord, Lord, Mama, I didn't know it was like that."

"Oh, honey," she said, "there's a lot that you don't know. But you are going to find it out." She stood up from the window and came over to me. "You got to hold on to your brother," she said, "and don't let him fall, no matter what it looks like is happening to him and no matter how evil you gets with him. You going to be evil with him many a time. But don't you forget what I told you, you hear?"

"I won't forget," I said. "Don't you worry, I won't forget. I won't let nothing happen to Sonny."

My mother smiled as though she were amused at something she saw in my face. Then, "You may not be able to stop nothing from happening. But you got to let him know you's *there*."

Two days later I was married, and then I was gone. And I had a lot of things on my mind and I pretty well forgot my promise to Mama until I got shipped home on a special furlough for her funeral.

And, after the funeral, with just Sonny and me alone in the empty kitchen, I tried to find out something about him.

"What do you want to do?" I asked him.

"I'm going to be a musician," he said.

For he had graduated, in the time I had been away, from dancing to the juke box to finding out who was playing what, and what they were doing with it, and he had bought himself a set of drums.

"You mean, you want to be a drummer?" I somehow had the feeling that being a drummer might be all right for other people but not for my brother Sonny.

"I don't think," he said, looking at me very gravely, "that I'll ever be a good drummer. But I think I can play a piano."

I frowned. I'd never played the role of the older brother quite so seriously before, had scarcely ever, in fact, *asked* Sonny a damn thing. I sensed myself in the presence of something I didn't really know how to handle, didn't understand. So I made my frown a little deeper as I asked: "What kind of musician do you want to be?"

He grinned. "How many kinds do you think there are?"

"Be *serious*," I said.

He laughed, throwing his head back, and then looked at me. "I *am* serious."

"Well, then, for Christ's sake, stop kidding around and answer a serious question. I mean, do you want to be a concert pianist, you want to play classical music and all that, or—or what?" Long before I finished he was laughing again. "For Christ's *sake*, Sonny!"

He sobered, but with difficulty. "I'm sorry. But you sound so—*scared!*" and he was off again.

"Well, you may think it's funny now, baby, but it's not going to be so funny when you have to make your living at it, let me tell you *that*." I was furious because I knew he was laughing at me and I didn't know why.

"No," he said, very sober now, and afraid, perhaps, that he'd hurt me, "I don't want to be a classical pianist. That isn't what interests me. I mean"—he paused, looking hard at me, as though his eyes would help me to understand, and then gestured helplessly, as though perhaps his hand would help—"I mean, I'll have a lot of studying to do, and I'll have to study *everything*, but I mean, I want to play *with*—jazz musicians." He stopped. "I want to play jazz," he said.

Well, the word had never before sounded as heavy, as real, as it sounded that afternoon in Sonny's mouth. I just looked at him and I was probably frowning a real frown by this time. I simply couldn't see why on earth he'd want to spend his time hanging around night clubs, clowning around on bandstands, while people pushed each other around a dance floor. It seemed—beneath him, somehow. I had never thought about it before, had never been forced to, but I suppose I had always put jazz musicians in a class with what Daddy called "good-time people."

"Are you *serious*?"

"Hell, *yes*, I'm serious."

He looked more helpless than ever, and annoyed, and deeply hurt.

I suggested, helpfully: "You mean—like Louis Armstrong?"

His face closed as though I'd struck him. "No. I'm not talking about none of that old-time, down home crap."

"Well, look, Sonny, I'm sorry, don't get mad. I just don't altogether get it, that's all. Name somebody—you know, a jazz musician you admire."

"Bird."

"Who?"

"Bird! Charlie Parker![3] Don't they teach you nothing in the goddamn army?"

---

[3] Charlie "Bird" Parker (1920–1955) was a jazz saxophonist who helped develop a style of jazz termed "bebop." Louis Armstrong represents a more conservative, old-fashioned jazz style.

I lit a cigarette. I was surprised and then a little amused to discover that I was trembling. "I've been out of touch," I said. "You'll have to be patient with me. Now. Who's this Parker character?"

"He's just one of the greatest jazz musicians alive," said Sonny, sullenly, his hands in his pockets, his back to me. "Maybe *the* greatest," he added, bitterly, "that's probably why *you* never heard of him."

"All right," I said, "I'm ignorant. I'm sorry. I'll go out and buy all the cat's records right away, all right?"

"It don't," said Sonny, with dignity, "make any difference to me. I don't care what you listen to. Don't do me no favors."

I was beginning to realize that I'd never seen him so upset before. With another part of my mind I was thinking that this would probably turn out to be one of those things kids go through and that I shouldn't make it seem important by pushing it too hard. Still, I didn't think it would do any harm to ask: "Doesn't all this take a lot of time? Can you make a living at it?"

He turned back to me and half leaned, half sat, on the kitchen table. "Everything takes time," he said, "and—well, yes, sure, I can make a living at it. But what I don't seem to be able to make you understand is that it's the only thing I want to do."

"Well Sonny," I said, gently, "you know people can't always do exactly what they *want* to do—"

"No, I don't know that," said Sonny, surprising me. "I think people *ought* to do what they want to do, what else are they alive for?"

"You getting to be a big boy," I said desperately, "it's time you started thinking about your future."

"I'm thinking about my future," said Sonny, grimly. "I think about it all the time."

I gave up. I decided, if he didn't change his mind, that we could always talk about it later. "In the meantime," I said, "you got to finish school." We had already decided that he'd have to move in with Isabel and her folks. I knew this wasn't the ideal arrangement because Isabel's folks are inclined to be dicty and they hadn't especially wanted Isabel to marry me. But I didn't know what else to do. "And we have to get you fixed up at Isabel's."

There was a long silence. He moved from the kitchen table to the window. "That's a terrible idea. You know it yourself."

"Do you have a *better* idea?"

He just walked up and down the kitchen for a minute. He was as tall as I was. He had started to shave. I suddenly had the feeling that I didn't know him at all.

He stopped at the kitchen table and picked up my cigarettes. Looking at me with a kind of mocking, amused defiance, he put one between his lips. "You mind?"

"You smoking already?"

He lit the cigarette and nodded, watching me through the smoke. "I just wanted to see if I'd have the courage to smoke in front of you." He grinned and blew a great cloud of smoke to the ceiling. "It was easy." He looked at my face. "Come on, now. I bet you was smoking at my age, tell the truth."

I didn't say anything but the truth was on my face, and he laughed. But now there was something very strained in his laugh. "Sure. And I bet that ain't all you was doing."

He was frightening me a little. "Cut the crap," I said. "We already decided that you was going to go and live at Isabel's. Now what's got into you all of a sudden?"

"*You* decided it," he pointed out. "*I* didn't decide nothing." He stopped in front of me, leaning against the stove, arms loosely folded. "Look, brother. I don't want to stay in Harlem no more, I really don't." He was very earnest. He looked at me, then over toward the kitchen window. There was something in his eyes I'd never seen before, some thoughtfulness, some worry all his own. He rubbed the muscle of one arm. It's time I was getting out of here."

"Where do you want to *go*, Sonny?"

"I want to join the army. Or the navy, I don't care. If I say I'm old enough they'll believe me."

Then I got mad. It was because I was so scared. "You must be crazy. You goddamn fool, what the hell do you want to go and join the *army* for?"

"I just told you. To get out of Harlem."

"Sonny, you haven't even finished *school*. And if you really want to be a musician, how do you expect to study if you're in the *army?*"

He looked at me, trapped, and in anguish. "There's ways. I might be able to work out some kind of deal. Anyway, I'll have the G.I. Bill when I come out."

"*If* you come out." We stared at each other. "Sonny, please. Be reasonable. I know the setup is far from perfect. But we got to do the best we can."

"I ain't learning nothing in school," he said. "Even when I go." He turned away from me and opened the window and threw his cigarette out into the narrow alley. I watched his back. "At least, I ain't learning nothing you'd want me to learn." He slammed the window so hard I thought the glass would fly out, and turned back to me. "And I'm sick of the stink of these garbage cans!"

"Sonny," I said, "I know how you feel. But if you don't finish school now, you're going to be sorry later that you didn't." I grabbed him by the shoulders. "And you only got another year. It ain't so bad. And I'll come back and I swear I'll help you do *whatever* you want to do. Just try to put up with it till I come back. Will you please do that? For me?"

He didn't answer and he wouldn't look at me.

"Sonny. You hear me?"

He pulled away. "I hear you. But you never hear anything *I* say."

I didn't know what to say to that. He looked out of the window and then back at me. "OK," he said, and sighed. "I'll try."

Then I said, trying to cheer him up a little, "They got a piano at Isabel's. You can practice on it."

And as a matter of fact, it did cheer him up for a minute. "That's right," he said to himself. "I forgot that." His face relaxed a little. But the worry, the thoughtfulness, played on it still, the way shadows play on a face which is staring into the fire.

But I thought I'd never hear the end of that piano. At first, Isabel would write me, saying how nice it was that Sonny was so serious about his music and how, as soon as he came in from school, or wherever he had been when he was supposed to be at school, he went straight to that piano and stayed there until suppertime. And, after supper, he went back to that piano and stayed there until everybody went to bed. He was at the piano all day Saturday and all day Sunday. Then he bought a record player and started playing records. He'd play one record over and over again, all day long sometimes, and he'd improvise along with it on the piano. Or he'd play one section of the record, one chord, one change, one progression, then he'd do it on the piano. Then back to the record. Then back to the piano.

Well, I really don't know how they stood it. Isabel finally confessed that it wasn't like living with a person at all, it was like living with sound. And the sound didn't make any sense to her, didn't make any sense to any of them— naturally. They began, in a way, to be afflicted by this presence that was living in their home. It was as though Sonny were some sort of god, or monster. He moved in an atmosphere which wasn't like theirs at all. They fed him and he ate, he washed himself, he walked in and out of their door; he certainly wasn't nasty or unpleasant or rude, Sonny isn't any of those things; but it was as though he were all wrapped up in some cloud, some fire, some vision all his own; and there wasn't any way to reach him.

. At the same time, he wasn't really a man yet, he was still a child, and they had to watch out for him in all kinds of ways. They certainly couldn't throw him out. Neither did they dare to make a great scene about that piano because even they dimly sensed, as I sensed, from so many thousands of miles away, that Sonny was at that piano playing for his life.

But he hadn't been going to school. One day a letter came from the school board and Isabel's mother got it—there had, apparently, been other letters but Sonny had torn them up. This day, when Sonny came in, Isabel's mother showed him the letter and asked where he'd been spending his time. And she finally got it out of him that he'd been down in Greenwich Village, with musicians and other characters, in a white girl's apartment. And this scared her and she started to scream at him and what came up, once she began—though she denies it to this day—was what sacrifices they were making to give Sonny a decent home and how little he appreciated it.

Sonny didn't play the piano that day. By evening, Isabel's mother had calmed down but then there was the old man to deal with, and Isabel herself. Isabel says she did her best to be calm but she broke down and started crying. She says she just watched Sonny's face. She could tell, by watching him, what was happening with him. And what was happening was that they penetrated his cloud, they had reached him. Even if their fingers had been a thousand times more gentle than human fingers ever are, he could hardly help feeling that they had stripped him naked and were spitting on that nakedness. For he also had to see that his presence, that music, which was life or death to him, had been torture for them and that they had endured it, not at all for his sake, but only for mine. And Sonny couldn't take that. He can take it a little better today than he could then but he's still not very good at it and, frankly, I don't know anybody who is.

The silence of the next few days must have been louder than the sound of all the music ever played since time began. One morning, before she went to work, Isabel was in his room for something and she suddenly realized that all of his records were gone. And she knew for certain that he was gone. And he was. He went as far as the navy would carry him. He finally sent me a postcard from some place in Greece and that was the first I knew that Sonny was still alive. I didn't see him any more until we were both back in New York and the war had long been over.

He was a man by then, of course, but I wasn't willing to see it. He came by the house from time to time, but we fought almost every time we met. I didn't like the way he carried himself, loose and dreamlike all the time, and I didn't like his friends, and his music seemed to be merely an excuse for the life he led. It sounded just that weird and disordered.

Then we had a fight, a pretty awful fight, and I didn't see him for months. By and by I looked him up, where he was living, in a furnished room in the Village, and I tried to make it up. But there were lots of other people in the room and Sonny just lay on his bed, and he wouldn't come downstairs with me, and he treated these other people as though they were his family and I weren't. So I got mad and then he got mad, and then I told him that he might just as well be dead as live the way he was living. Then he stood up and he told me not to worry about him any more in life, that he *was* dead as far as I was concerned. Then he pushed me to the door and the other people looked on as though nothing were happening, and he slammed the door behind me. I stood in the hallway, staring at the door. I heard somebody laugh in the room and then the tears came to my eyes. I started down the steps, whistling to keep from crying, I kept whistling to myself, *You going to need me, baby, one of these cold, rainy days.*

I read about Sonny's trouble in the spring. Little Grace died in the fall. She was a beautiful little girl. But she only lived a little over two years. She died of polio and she suffered. She had a slight fever for a couple of days, but it didn't seem like anything and we just kept her in bed. And we would certainly have called the doctor, but the fever dropped, she seemed to be all right. So we thought it had just been a cold. Then, one day, she was up, playing, Isabel was in the kitchen fixing lunch for the two boys when they'd come in from school, and she heard Grace fall down in the living room. When you have a lot of children you don't always start running when one of them falls, unless they start screaming or something. And, this time, Grace was quiet. Yet, Isabel says that when she heard that *thump* and then that silence, something happened in her to make her afraid. And she ran to the living room and there was little Grace on the floor, all twisted up and the reason she hadn't screamed was that she couldn't get her breath. And when she did scream, it was the worst sound, Isabel says, that she'd ever heard in all her life, and she still hears it sometimes in her dreams. Isabel will sometimes wake me up with a low, moaning, strangled sound and I have to be quick to awaken her and hold her to me and where Isabel is weeping against me seems a mortal wound.

I think I may have written Sonny the very day that little Grace was buried. I was sitting in the living room in the dark, by myself, and I suddenly thought of Sonny. My trouble made his real.

One Saturday afternoon, when Sonny had been living with us, or, anyway, been in our house, for nearly two weeks, I found myself wandering aimlessly about the living room, drinking from a can of beer, and trying to work up the courage to search Sonny's room. He was out, he was usually out whenever I was home, and Isabel had taken the children to see their grandparents. Suddenly I was standing still in front of the living room window, watching Seventh Avenue. The idea of searching Sonny's room made me still. I scarcely dared to admit to myself what I'd be searching for. I didn't know what I'd do if I found it. Or if I didn't.

On the sidewalk across from me, near the entrance to a barbecue joint, some people were holding an old-fashioned revival meeting. The barbecue cook, wearing a dirty white apron, his conked hair[4] reddish and metallic in the pale sun, and a cigarette between his lips, stood in the doorway, watching them. Kids and older people paused in their errands and stood there, along with some older men and a couple of very tough-looking women who watched everything that happened on the avenue, as though they owned it, or were maybe owned by it. Well, they were watching this, too. The revival was being carried on by three sisters in black, and a brother. All they had were their voices and their Bibles and a tambourine. The brother was testifying and while he testified two of the sisters stood together, seeming to say, Amen, and the third sister walked around with the tambourine outstretched and a couple of people dropped coins into it. Then the brother's testimony ended and the sister who had been taking up the collection dumped the coins into her palm and transferred them to the pocket of her long black robe. Then she raised both hands, striking the tambourine against the air, and then against one hand, and she started to sing. And the two other sisters and the brother joined in.

It was strange, suddenly, to watch, though I had been seeing these street meetings all my life. So, of course, had everybody else down there. Yet, they paused and watched and listened and I stood still at the window. *"Tis the old ship of Zion,"* they sang, and the sister with the tambourine kept a steady, jangling

---

[4] Conked hair is hair that has been straightened and greased.

beat, "*It has rescued many a thousand!*" Not a soul under the sound of their voices was hearing this song for the first time, not one of them had been rescued. Nor had they seen much in the way of rescue work being done around them. Neither did they especially believe in the holiness of the three sisters and the brother, they knew too much about them, knew where they lived, and how. The woman with the tambourine, whose voice dominated the air, whose face was bright with joy, was divided by very little from the woman who stood watching her, a cigarette between her heavy, chapped lips, her hair a cuckoo's nest, her face scarred and swollen from many beatings, and her black eyes glittering like coal. Perhaps they both knew this, which was why, when, as rarely, they addressed each other, they addressed each other as Sister. As the singing filled the air the watching, listening faces underwent a change, the eyes focusing on something within; the music seemed to sooth a poison out of them; and time seemed, nearly, to fall away from the sullen, belligerent, battered faces, as though they were fleeing back to their first condition, while dreaming of their last. The barbecue cook half shook his head and smiled, and dropped his cigarette and disappeared into his joint. A man fumbled in his pockets for change and stood holding it in his hand impatiently, as though he had just remembered a pressing appointment further up the avenue. He looked furious. Then I saw Sonny, standing on the edge of the crowd. He was carrying a wide, flat notebook with a green cover, and it made him look, from where I was standing, almost like a schoolboy. The coppery sun brought out the copper in his skin, he was very faintly smiling, standing very still. Then the singing stopped, the tambourine turned into a collection plate again. The furious man dropped in his coins and vanished, so did a couple of the women, and Sonny dropped some change in the plate, looking directly at the woman with a little smile. He started across the avenue, toward the house. He has a slow, loping walk, something like the way Harlem hipsters walk, only he's imposed on this his own halfbeat. I had never really noticed it before.

I stayed at the window, both relieved and apprehensive. As Sonny disappeared from my sight, they began singing again. And they were still singing when his key turned in the lock.

"Hey," he said.

"Hey, yourself. You want some beer?"

"No. Well, maybe." But he came up to the window and stood beside me, looking out. "What a warm voice," he said.

They were singing *If I could only hear my mother pray again!*

"Yes," I said, "and she can sure beat that tambourine."

"But what a terrible song," he said, and laughed. He dropped his notebook on the sofa and disappeared into the kitchen. "Where's Isabel and the kids?"

"I think they went to see their grandparents. You hungry?"

"No." He came back into the living room with his can of beer. "You want to come some place with me tonight?"

I sensed, I don't know how, that I couldn't possibly say No. "Sure. Where?"

He sat down on the sofa and picked up his notebook and started leafing through it. "I'm going to sit in with some fellows in a joint in the Village."

"You mean, you're going to play, tonight?"

"That's right." He took a swallow of his beer and moved back to the window. He gave me a sidelong look. "If you can stand it."

"I'll try," I said.

He smiled to himself and we both watched as the meeting across the way broke up. The three sisters and the brother, heads bowed, were singing *God be with you till we meet again*. The faces around them were very quiet. Then the song ended. The small crowd dispersed. We watched the three women and the lone man walk slowly up the avenue.

"When she was singing before," said Sonny, abruptly, "her voice reminded me for a minute of what heroin feels like sometimes—when it's in your veins. It makes you feel sort of warm and cool at the same time. And distant. And— and sure." He sipped his beer, very deliberately not looking at me. I watched his face. "It makes you feel—in control. Sometimes you've got to have that feeling."

"Do you?" I sat down slowly in the easy chair.

"Sometimes." He went to the sofa and picked up his notebook again. "Some people do."

"In order," I asked, "to play?" And my voice was very ugly, full of contempt and anger.

"Well"—he looked at me with great, troubled eyes, as though, in fact, he hoped his eyes would tell me things he could never otherwise say—"they *think* so. And *if* they think so—!"

"And what do *you* think?" I asked.

He sat on the sofa and put his can of beer on the floor. "I don't know," he said, and I couldn't be sure if he were answering my question or pursuing his thoughts. His face didn't tell me. "It's not so much to *play*. It's to *stand* it, to be able to make it at all. On any level." He frowned and smiled: "In order to keep from shaking to pieces."

"But these friends of yours," I said, "they seem to shake themselves to pieces pretty goddamn fast."

"Maybe." He played with the notebook. And something told me that I should curb my tongue, that Sonny was doing his best to talk, that I should listen. "But of course you only know the ones that've gone to pieces. Some don't—or at least they haven't *yet* and that's just about all *any* of us can say." He paused. "And then there are some who just live, really, in hell, and they know it and they see what's happening and they go right on. I don't know." He sighed, dropped the notebook, folded his arms. "Some guys, you can tell from the way they play, they on something *all* the time. And you can see that, well, it makes something real for them. But of course," he picked up his beer from the floor and sipped it and put the can down again, "they *want* to, too, you've got to see that. Even some of them that say they don't—*some*, not all."

"And what about you?" I asked—I couldn't help it. "What about you? Do *you* want to?"

He stood up and walked to the window and remained silent for a long time. Then he sighed. "Me," he said. Then: "While I was downstairs before, on my way here, listening to that woman sing, it struck me all of a sudden how much suffering she must have had to go through—to sing like that. It's *repulsive* to think you have to suffer that much."

I said: "But there's no way not to suffer—is there, Sonny?"

"I believe not," he said, and smiled, "but that's never stopped anyone from trying." He looked at me. "Has it?" I realized, with this mocking look, that there stood between us, forever, beyond the power of time or forgiveness, the fact that I had held silence—so long!—when he had needed human speech to help him. He turned back to the window. "No, there's no way not to suffer. But you try all kinds of ways to keep from drowning in it, to keep on top of it, and to make it seem—well, like *you*. Like you did something, all right, and now you're suffering for it. You know?" I said nothing. "Well you know," he said, impatiently, "why *do* people suffer? Maybe it's better to do something to give it a reason, *any* reason."

"But we just agreed," I said, "that there's no way not to suffer. Isn't it better, then, just to—take it?"

"But nobody just takes it," Sonny cried, "that's what I'm telling you! *Everybody* tries not to. You're just hung up on the *way* some people try—it's not *your* way!"

The hair on my face began to itch, my face felt wet. "That's not true," I said, "that's not true. I don't give a damn what other people do, I don't even care how they suffer. I just care how *you* suffer." And he looked at me. "Please believe me," I said, "I don't want to see you—die—trying not to suffer."

"I won't," he said, flatly, "die trying not to suffer. At least, not any faster than anybody else."

"But there's no need," I said, trying to laugh, "is there? in killing yourself."

I wanted to say more, but I couldn't. I wanted to talk about will power and how life could be—well, beautiful. I wanted to say that it was all within; but was it? or, rather, wasn't that exactly the trouble? And I wanted to promise that I would never fail him again. But it would all have sounded—empty words and lies.

So I made the promise to myself and prayed that I would keep it.

"It's terrible sometimes, inside," he said, "that's what's the trouble. You walk these streets, black and funky and cold, and there's not really a living ass to talk to, and there's nothing shaking, and there's no way of getting it out—that storm inside. You can't talk it and you can't make love with it, and when you finally try to get with it and play it, you realize *nobody's* listening. So *you've* got to listen. You got to find a way to listen."

And then he walked away from the window and sat on the sofa again, as though all the wind had suddenly been knocked out of him. "Sometimes you'll do *anything* to play, even cut your mother's throat." He laughed and looked at me. "Or your brother's." Then he sobered. "Or your own." Then: "Don't worry. I'm all right now and I think I'll *be* all right. But I can't forget—where I've been. I don't mean just the physical place I've been, I mean where I've *been*. And *what* I've been."

"What have you been, Sonny?" I asked.

He smiled—but sat sideways on the sofa, his elbow resting on the back, his fingers playing with his mouth and chin, not looking at me. "I've been something I didn't recognize, didn't know I could be. Didn't know anybody could be." He stopped, looking inward, looking helplessly young, looking old. "I'm not talking about it now because I feel *guilty* or anything like that—maybe it would be better if I did, I don't know. Anyway, I can't really talk about it. Not to you, not to anybody," and now he turned and faced me. "Sometimes, you know, and it was actually when I was most *out* of the world, I felt that I was in it, and that I was *with* it, really, and I could play or I didn't really have to *play*, it just came out of me, it was there. And I don't know how I played, thinking about it now, but I know I did awful things, those times, sometimes, to people. Or it wasn't that I *did* anything to them—it was that they weren't real." He picked up the beer can; it was empty; he rolled it between his palms: "And other times— well, I needed a fix, I needed to find a place to lean, I needed to clear a space to *listen*—and I couldn't find it, and I—went crazy, I did terrible things to *me*, I was terrible *for* me." He began pressing the beer can between his hands, I watched the metal begin to give. It glittered, as he played with it, like a knife, and I was afraid he would cut himself, but I said nothing. "Oh well. I can never tell you. I was all by myself at the bottom of something, stinking and sweating and crying and shaking, and I smelled it, you know? *my* stink, and I thought I'd die if I couldn't get away from it and yet, all the same, I knew that everything I was doing was just locking me in with it. And I didn't know," he paused, still flattening the beer can, "I didn't know, I still *don't* know, something kept telling me that maybe it was good to smell your own stink, but I didn't think that *that* was what I'd been trying to do—and—who can stand it?" and he abruptly dropped the ruined beer can, looking at me with a small, still smile, and then rose, walking to the window as though it were the lodestone rock. I watched his face, he watched the avenue. "I couldn't tell you when Mama died—but the reason I wanted to leave Harlem so bad was to get away from drugs. And then, when I ran away, that's what I was running from—really. When I came back, nothing had changed, I hadn't changed, I was just—older." And he stopped, drumming with his fingers on the windowpane. The sun had vanished, soon darkness would fall. I watched his face. "It can come again," he said, almost as though speaking to himself. Then he turned to me. "It can come again," he repeated. "I just want you to know that."

"All right," I said, at last. "So it can come again. All right."

He smiled, but the smile was sorrowful. "I had to try to tell you," he said.

"Yes," I said. "I understand that."

"You're my brother," he said, looking straight at me, and not smiling at all.

"Yes," I repeated, "yes. I understand that."

He turned back to the window, looking out. "All that hatred down there," he said, "all that hatred and misery and love. It's a wonder it doesn't blow the avenue apart."

We went to the only night club on a short, dark street, downtown. We squeezed through the narrow, chattering, jam-packed bar to the entrance of the big room, where the bandstand was. And we stood there for a moment, for the lights were very dim in this room and we couldn't see. Then, "Hello, boy," said a voice and an enormous black man, much older than Sonny or myself, erupted out of all that atmospheric lighting and put an arm around Sonny's shoulder. "I been sitting right here," he said, "waiting for you."

He had a big voice, too, and heads in the darkness turned toward us.

Sonny grinned and pulled a little away, and said, "Creole, this is my brother. I told you about him."

Creole shook my hand. "I'm glad to meet you, son," he said, and it was clear that he was glad to meet me *there*, for Sonny's sake. And he smiled, "You got a real musician in *your* family," and he took his arm from Sonny's shoulder and slapped him, lightly, affectionately, with the back of his hand.

"Well. Now I've heard it all," said a voice behind us. This was another musician, and a friend of Sonny's, a coal-black, cheerful-looking man, built close to the ground. He immediately began confiding to me, at the top of his lungs, the most terrible things about Sonny, his teeth gleaming like a lighthouse and his laugh coming up out of him like the beginning of an earthquake. And it turned out that everyone at the bar knew Sonny, or almost everyone; some were musicians, working there, or nearby, or not working, some were simply hangers-on, and some were there to hear Sonny play. I was introduced to all of them and they were all very polite to me. Yet, it was clear that, for them, I was only Sonny's brother. Here, I was in Sonny's world. Or, rather: his kingdom. Here, it was not even a question that his veins bore royal blood.

They were going to play soon and Creole installed me, by myself, at a table in a dark corner. Then I watched them, Creole, and the little black man, and Sonny, and the others, while they horsed around, standing just below the bandstand. The light from the bandstand spilled just a little short of them and, watching them laughing and gesturing and moving about, I had the feeling that they, nevertheless, were being most careful not to step into that circle of light too suddenly: that if they moved into the light too suddenly, without thinking, they would perish in flame. Then, while I watched, one of them, the small, black man, moved into the light and crossed the bandstand and started fooling around with his drums. Then—being funny and being, also, extremely cere- monious—Creole took Sonny by the arm and led him to the piano. A woman's voice called Sonny's name and a few hands started clapping. And Sonny, also being funny and being ceremonious, and so touched, I think, that he could have cried, but neither hiding it nor showing it, riding it like a man, grinned, and put both hands to his heart and bowed from the waist.

Creole then went to the bass fiddle and a lean, very bright-skinned brown man jumped up on the bandstand and picked up his horn. So there they were, and the atmosphere on the bandstand and in the room began to change and tighten. Someone stepped up to the microphone and announced them. Then there were all kinds of murmurs. Some people at the bar shushed others. The waitress ran around, frantically getting in the last orders, guys and chicks got closer to each other, and the lights on the bandstand, on the quartet, turned to a kind of indigo. Then they all looked different there. Creole looked about him for the last time, as though he were making certain that all his chickens were in the coop, and then he—jumped and struck the fiddle. And there they were.

All I know about music is that not many people ever really hear it. And even then, on the rare occasions when something opens within, and the music enters, what we mainly hear, or hear corroborated, are personal, private, vanishing evocations. But the man who creates the music is hearing something else, is dealing with the roar rising from the void and imposing order on it as it hits the air. What is evoked in him, then, is of another order, more terrible because it has no words, and triumphant, too, for that same reason. And his triumph, when he triumphs, is ours. I just watched Sonny's face. His face was troubled, he was working hard, but he wasn't with it. And I had the feeling that, in a way, everyone on the bandstand was waiting for him, both waiting for him and pushing him along. But as I began to watch Creole, I realized that it was Creole who held them all back. He had them on a short rein. Up there, keeping the beat with his whole body, wailing on the fiddle, with his eyes half closed, he was listening to everything, but he was listening to Sonny. He was having a dialogue with Sonny. He wanted Sonny to leave the shore line and strike out for the deep water. He was Sonny's witness that deep water and drowning were not the same thing—he had been there, and he knew. And he wanted Sonny to know. He was waiting for Sonny to do the things on the keys which would let Creole know that Sonny was in the water.

And, while Creole listened, Sonny moved, deep within, exactly like someone in torment. I had never before thought of how awful the relationship must be between the musician and his instrument. He has to fill it, this instrument, with the breath of life, his own. He has to make it do what he wants it to do. And a piano is just a piano. It's made out of so much wood and wires and little hammers and big ones, and ivory. While there's only so much you can do with it, the only way to find this out is to try and make it do everything.

And Sonny hadn't been near a piano for over a year. And he wasn't on much better terms with his life, not the life that stretched before him now. He and the piano stammered, started one way, got scared, stopped; started another way, panicked, marked time, started again; then seemed to have found a direction, panicked again, got stuck. And the face I saw on Sonny I'd never seen before. Everything had been burned out of it, and, at the same time, things usually hidden were being burned in, by the fire and fury of the battle which was occurring in him up there.

Yet, watching Creole's face as they neared the end of the first set, I had the feeling that something had happened, something I hadn't heard. Then they finished, there was scattered applause, and then, without an instant's warning, Creole started into something else, it was almost sardonic, it was *Am I Blue*.[5] And, as though he commanded, Sonny began to play. Something began to happen. And Creole let out the reins. The dry, low, black man said something awful on the drums, Creole answered, and the drums talked back. Then the horn insisted, sweet and high, slightly detached perhaps, and Creole listened, commenting now and then, dry, and driving, beautiful and calm and old. Then they all came together again, and Sonny was part of the family again. I could tell this from his face. He seemed to have found, right there beneath his fingers, a damn brand-new piano. It seemed that he couldn't get over it. Then, for awhile, just being happy with Sonny, they seemed to be agreeing with him that brand-new pianos certainly were a gas.

Then Creole stepped forward to remind them that what they were playing was the blues. He hit something in all of them, he hit something in me, myself, and the music tightened and deepened, apprehension began to beat the air. Creole began to tell us what the blues were all about. They were not about anything very new. He and his boys up there were keeping it new, at the risk of ruin, destruction, madness, and death, in order to find new ways to make us listen. For, while the tale of how we suffer, and how we are delighted, and how we may triumph is never new, it always must be heard. There isn't any other tale to tell, it's the only light we've got in all this darkness.

And this tale, according to that face, that body, those strong hands on those strings, has another aspect in every country, and a new depth in every generation. Listen, Creole seemed to be saying, listen. Now these are Sonny's blues. He made the little black man on the drums know it, and the bright, brown man on the horn. Creole wasn't trying any longer to get Sonny in the water. He was wishing him Godspeed. Then he stepped back, very slowly, filling the air with the immense suggestion that Sonny speak for himself.

Then they all gathered around Sonny and Sonny played. Every now and again one of them seemed to say, Amen. Sonny's fingers filled the air with life, his life. But that life contained so many others. And Sonny went all the way back, he really began with the spare, flat statement of the opening phrase of the song. Then he began to make it his. It was very beautiful because it wasn't hurried and it was no longer a lament. I seemed to hear with what burning he had made it his, with what burning we had yet to make it ours, how we could cease lamenting. Freedom lurked around us and I understood, at last, that he could help us to be free if we would listen, that he would never be free until we did. Yet, there was no battle in his face now. I heard what he had gone through, and would continue to go through until he came to rest in earth. He had made

---

[5] "Am I Blue" is a blues song by Grant Clark and Harry Akst from the 1920s.

it his: that long line, of which we knew only Mama and Daddy. And he was giving it back, as everything must be given back, so that, passing through death, it can live forever. I saw my mother's face again, and felt, for the first time, how the stones of the road she had walked on must have bruised her feet. I saw the moonlit road where my father's brother died. And it brought something else back to me, and carried me past it, I saw my little girl again and felt Isabel's tears again, and I felt my own tears begin to rise. And I was yet aware that this was only a moment, that the world waited outside, as hungry as a tiger, and that trouble stretched above us, longer than the sky.

Then it was over. Creole and Sonny let out their breath, both soaking wet, and grinning. There was a lot of applause and some of it was real. In the dark, the girl came by and I asked her to take drinks to the bandstand. There was a long pause, while they talked up there in the indigo light and after awhile I saw the girl put a Scotch and milk on top of the piano for Sonny. He didn't seem to notice it, but just before they started playing again, he sipped from it and looked toward me, and nodded. Then he put it back on top of the piano. For me, then, as they began to play again, it glowed and shook above my brother's head like the very cup of trembling.

WILLIAM FAULKNER (1897–1962)

Spotted Horses*

I

Yes, sir. Flem Snopes has filled that whole country full of spotted horses. You can hear folks running them all day and all night, whooping and hollering, and the horses running back and forth across them little wooden bridges ever now and then kind of like thunder. Here I was this morning pretty near half way to town, with the team ambling along and me setting in the buckboard about half asleep, when all of a sudden something come swurging up outen the bushes and jumped the road clean, without touching hoof to it. It flew right over my team, big as a billboard and flying through the air like a hawk. It taken me thirty minutes to stop my team and untangle the harness and the buckboard and hitch them up again.

That Flem Snopes. I be dog if he ain't a case, now. One morning about ten years ago, the boys was just getting settled down on Varner's porch for a little talk and tobacco, when here come Flem out from behind the counter, with his coat off and his hair all parted, like he might have been clerking for Varner for ten years already. Folks all knowed him; it was a big family of them about five

---

* "Spotted Horses" was published in *Scribner's Magazine* in June, 1931. Faulkner reworked the material completely, and the story is retold as the first part of Chapter One, Book Four of *The Hamlet*. The later version is in the third person and three times the length of the short story. The two versions form an interesting study on how a great author can rework the same material in radically different ways.

miles down the bottom. That year, at least. Share-cropping. They never stayed on any place over a year. Then they would move on to another place, with the chap or maybe the twins of that year's litter. It was a regular nest of them. But Flem. The rest of them stayed tenant farmers, moving ever year, but here come Flem one day, walking out from behind Jody Varner's counter like he owned it. And he wasn't there but a year or two before folks knowed that, if him and Jody was both still in that store in ten years more, it would be Jody clerking for Flem Snopes. Why, that fellow could make a nickel where it wasn't but four cents to begin with. He skun me in two trades, myself, and the fellow that can do that, I just hope he'll get rich before I do; that's all.

All right. So here Flem was, clerking at Varner's, making a nickel here and there and not telling nobody about it. No, sir. Folks never knowed when Flem got the better of somebody lessen the fellow he beat told it. He'd just set there in the store-chair, chewing his tobacco and keeping his own business to hisself, until about a week later we'd find out it was somebody else's business he was keeping to hisself—provided the fellow he trimmed was mad enough to tell it. That's Flem.

We give him ten years to own ever thing Jody Varner had. But he never waited no ten years. I reckon you-all know that gal of Uncle Billy Varner's, the youngest one; Eula. Jody's sister. Ever Sunday ever yellow-wheeled buggy and curried riding horse in that country would be hitched to Bill Varner's fence, and the young bucks setting on the porch, swarming around Eula like bees around a honey pot. One of these here kind of big, soft-looking gals that could giggle richer than plowed new-ground. Wouldn't none of them leave before the others, and so they would set there on the porch until time to go home, with some of them with nine and ten miles to ride and then get up tomorrow and go back to the field. So they would all leave together and they would ride in a clump down to the creek ford and hitch them curried horses and yellow-wheeled buggies and get out and fight one another. Then they would get in the buggies again and go on home.

Well, one day about a year ago, one of them yellow-wheeled buggies and one of them curried saddle-horses quit this country. We heard they was heading for Texas. The next day Uncle Billy and Eula and Flem come in to town in Uncle Bill's surrey, and when they come back, Flem and Eula was married. And on the next day we heard that two more of them yellow-wheeled buggies had left the country. They mought have gone to Texas, too. It's a big place.

Anyway, about a month after the wedding, Flem and Eula went to Texas, too. They was gone pretty near a year. Then one day last month, Eula come back, with a baby. We figgured up, and we decided that it was as well-growed a three-months-old baby as we ever see. It can already pull up on a chair. I reckon Texas makes big men quick, being a big place. Anyway, if it keeps on like it started, it'll be chewing tobacco and voting time it's eight years old.

And so last Friday here come Flem himself. He was on a wagon with another fellow. The other fellow had one of these two-gallon hats and a ivory-handled pistol and a box of gingersnaps sticking out of his hind pocket, and tied to the tail-gate of the wagon was about two dozen of them Texas ponies, hitched to one another with barbed wire. They was colored like parrots and they was quiet as doves, and ere a one of them would kill you quick as a rattlesnake. Nere a one of them had two eyes the same color, and nere a one of them had ever see a bridle, I reckon; and when that Texas man got down offen the wagon and walked up to them to show how gentle they was, one of them cut his vest clean offen him, same as with a razor.

Flem had done already disappeared; he had went on to see his wife, I reckon, and to see if that ere baby had done gone on to the field to help Uncle Billy plow maybe. It was the Texas man that taken the horses on to Mrs. Littlejohn's lot. He had a lttle trouble at first, when they come to the gate, because they hadn't never see a fence before, and when he finally got them in and taken a pair of wire cutters and unhitched them and got them into the barn and poured some shell corn into the trough, they durn nigh tore down the barn. I reckon they thought that shell corn was bugs, maybe. So he left them in the lot and he announced that the auction would begin at sunup to-morrow.

That night we was setting on Mrs. Littlejohn's porch. You-all mind the moon was nigh full that night, and we could watch them spotted varmints swirling along the fence and back and forth across the lot same as minnows in a pond. And then now and then they would all kind of huddle up against the barn and rest themselves by biting and kicking one another. We would hear a squeal, and then a set of hoofs would go Bam! against the barn, like a pistol. It sounded just like a fellow with a pistol, in a nest of cattymounts, taking his time.

II

It wasn't ere a man knowed yet if Flem owned them things or not. They just knowed one thing: that they wasn't never going to know for sho if Flem did or not, or if maybe he didn't just get on that wagon at the edge of town, for the ride or not. Even Eck Snopes didn't know, Flem's own cousin. But wasn't nobody surprised at that. We knowed that Flem would skin Eck quick as he would ere a one of us.

They was there by sunup next morning, some of them come twelve and sixteen miles, with seed-money tied up in tobacco sacks in their overalls, standing along the fence, when the Texas man come out of Mrs. Littlejohn's after breakfast and clumb onto the gate post with that ere white pistol butt sticking outen his hind pocket. He taken a new box of gingersnaps outen his pocket and bit the end offen it like a cigar and spit out the paper, and said the auction was open. And still they was coming up in wagons and a horse- and mule-back and hitching the teams across the road and coming to the fence. Flem wasn't nowhere in sight.

But he couldn't get them started. He begun to work on Eck, because Eck holp him last night to get them into the barn and feed them that shell corn. Eck got out just in time. He come outen that barn like a chip on the crest of a busted dam of water, and clumb into the wagon just in time.

He was working on Eck when Henry Armstid come up in his wagon. Eck was saying he was skeered to bid on one of them, because he might get it, and the Texas man says, "Them ponies? Them little horses?" He clumb down offen the gate post and went toward the horses. They broke and run, and him following them, kind of chirping to them, with his hand out like he was fixing to catch a fly, until he got three or four of them cornered. Then he jumped into them, and then we couldn't see nothing for a while because of the dust. It was a big cloud of it, and them blare-eyed, spotted things swoaring outen it twenty foot to a jump, in forty directions without counting up. Then the dust settled and there they was, that Texas man and the horse. He had its head twisted clean around like a owl's head. Its legs was braced and it was trembling like a new bride and groaning like a saw mill, and him holding its head wrung clean around on its neck so it was snuffing sky. "Look it over," he says, with his heels dug too and that white pistol sticking outen his pocket and his neck swole up like a spreading adder's until you could just tell what he was saying, cussing the horse and talking to us all at once: "Look him over, the fiddle-headed son of fourteen fathers. Try him, buy him; you will get the best—" Then it was all dust again, and we couldn't see nothing but spotted hide and mane, and that ere Texas man's boot-heels like a couple of walnuts on two strings, and after a while that two-gallon hat come sailing out like a fat old hen crossing a fence.

When the dust settled again, he was just getting outen the far fence corner, brushing himself off. He come and got his hat and brushed it off and come and clumb onto the gate post again. He was breathing hard. He taken the gingersnap box outen his pocket and et one, breathing hard. The hammer-head horse was still running round and round the lot like a merry-go-round at a fair. That was when Henry Armstid come shoving up to the gate in them patched overalls and one of them dangle-armed shirts of hisn. Hadn't nobody noticed him until then. We was all watching the Texas man and the horses. Even Mrs. Littlejohn; she had done come out and built a fire under the wash-pot in her back yard, and she would stand at the fence a while and then go back into the house and come out again with a arm full of wash and stand at the fence again. Well, here come Henry shoving up, and then we see Mrs. Armstid right behind him, in that ere faded wrapper and sunbonnet and them tennis shoes. "Git on back to that wagon," Henry says.

"Henry," she says.

"Here, boys," the Texas man says; "make room for missus to git up and see. Come on, Henry," he says; "here's your chance to buy that saddle-horse missus has been wanting. What about ten dollars, Henry?"

"Henry," Mrs. Armstid says. She put her hand on Henry's arm. Henry knocked her hand down.

"Git on back to that wagon, like I told you," he says.

Mrs. Armstid never moved. She stood behind Henry, with her hands rolled into her dress, not looking at nothing. "He hain't no more despair than to buy one of them things," she says. "And us not five dollars ahead of the pore house, he hain't no more despair." It was the truth, too. They ain't never made more than a bare living offen that place of theirs, and them with four chaps and the very clothes they wears she earns by weaving by the firelight at night while Henry's asleep.

"Shut your mouth and git on back to that wagon," Henry says. "Do you want I taken a wagon stake to you here in the big road?"

Well, that Texas man taken one look at her. Then he begun on Eck again, like Henry wasn't even there. But Eck was skeered. "I can git me a snapping turtle or a water moccasin for nothing. I ain't going to buy none."

So the Texas man said he would give Eck a horse. "To start the auction, and because you holp me last night. If you'll start the bidding on the next horse," he says, "I'll give you that fiddle-head horse."

I wish you could have seen them, standing there with their seed-money in their pockets, watching that Texas man give Eck Snopes a live horse, all fixed to call him a fool if he taken it or not. Finally Eck says he'll take it. "Only I just starts the bidding," he says. "I don't have to buy the next one lessen I ain't overtopped." The Texas man said all right, and Eck bid a dollar on the next one, with Henry Armstid standing there with his mouth already open, watching Eck and the Texas man like a mad-dog or something. "A dollar," Eck says.

The Texas man looked at Eck. His mouth was already open too, like he had started to say something and what he was going to say had up and died on him. "A dollar?" he says. "One dollar? You mean, *one* dollar, Eck?"

"Durn it," Eck says; "two dollars, then."

Well, sir, I wish you could a seen that Texas man. He taken out that gingersnap box and held it up and looked into it, careful, like it might have been a diamond ring in it, or a spider. Then he throwed it away and wiped his face with a bandanna. "Well," he says. "Well. Two dollars. Two dollars. Is your pulse all right, Eck?" he says. "Do you have ager-sweats at night, maybe?" he says. "Well," he says, "I got to take it. But are you boys going to stand there and see Eck get two horses at a dollar a head?"

That done it. I be dog if he wasn't nigh as smart as Flem Snopes. He hadn't no more than got the words outen his mouth before here was Henry Armstid, waving his hand. "Three dollars," Henry says. Mrs. Armstid tried to hold him again. He knocked her hand off, shoving up to the gate post.

"Mister," Mrs. Armstid says, "we got chaps in the house and not corn to feed the stock. We got five dollars I earned my chaps a-weaving after dark, and him snoring in the bed. And he hain't no more despair."

"Henry bids three dollars," the Texas man says. "Raise him a dollar, Eck, and the horse is yours."

"Henry," Mrs. Armstid says.

"Raise him, Eck," the Texas man says.

"Four dollars," Eck says.

"Five dollars," Henry says, shaking his fist. He shoved up right under the gate post. Mrs. Armstid was looking at the Texas man too.

"Mister," she says, "if you take that five dollars I earned my chaps a-weaving for one of them things, it'll be a curse onto you and yourn during all the time of man."

But it wasn't no stopping Henry. He had shoved up, waving his fist at the Texas man. He opened it; the money was in nickels and quarters, and one dollar bill that looked like a cow's cud. "Five dollars," he says. "And the man that raises it'll have to beat my head off, or I'll beat hisn."

"All right," the Texas man says. "Five dollars is bid. But don't you shake your hand at me."

III

It taken till nigh sundown before the last one was sold. He got them hotted up once and the bidding got up to seven dollars and a quarter, but most of them went around three or four dollars, him setting on the gate post and picking the horses out one at a time by mouth-word, and Mrs. Littlejohn pumping up and down at the tub and stopping and coming to the fence for a while and going back to the tub again. She had done got done too, and the wash was hung on the line in the back yard, and we could smell supper cooking. Finally they was all sold; he swapped the last two and the wagon for a buckboard.

We was all kind of tired, but Henry Armstid looked more like a mad-dog than ever. When he bought, Mrs. Armstid had went back to the wagon, setting in it behind them two rabbit-sized, bone-pore mules, and the wagon itself looking like it would fall all to pieces soon as the mules moved. Henry hadn't even waited to pull it outen the road; it was still in the middle of the road and her setting in it, not looking at nothing, ever since this morning.

Henry was right up against the gate. He went up to the Texas man. "I bought a horse and I paid cash," Henry says. "And yet you expect me to stand around here until they are all sold before I can get my horse. I'm going to take my horse outen that lot."

The Texas man looked at Henry. He talked like he might have been asking for a cup of coffee at the table. "Take your horse," he says.

Then Henry quit looking at the Texas man. He begun to swallow, holding onto the gate. "Ain't you going to help me?" he says.

"It ain't my horse," the Texas man says.

Henry never looked at the Texas man again, he never looked at nobody. "Who'll help me catch my horse?" he says. Never nobody said nothing. "Bring the plowline," Henry says. Mrs. Armstid got outen the wagon and brought the plowline. The Texas man got down offen the post. The woman made to pass him, carrying the rope.

"Don't you go in there, missus," the Texas man says.

Henry opened the gate. He didn't look back. "Come on here," he says.

"Don't you go in there, missus," the Texas man says.

Mrs. Armstid wasn't looking at nobody, neither, with her hands across her middle, holding the rope. "I reckon I better," she says. Her and Henry went into the lot. The horses broke and run. Henry and Mrs. Armstid followed.

"Get him into the corner," Henry says. They got Henry's horse cornered finally, and Henry taken the rope, but Mrs. Armstid let the horse get out. They hemmed it up again, but Mrs. Armstid let it get out again, and Henry turned and hit her with the rope. "Why didn't you head him back?" Henry says. He hit her again. "Why didn't you?" It was about that time I looked around and see Flem Snopes standing there.

It was the Texas man that done something. He moved fast for a big man. He caught the rope before Henry could hit the third time, and Henry whirled and made like he would jump at the Texas man. But he never jumped. The Texas man went and taken Henry's arm and led him outen the lot. Mrs. Armstid come behind them and the Texas man taken some money outen his pocket and he give it into Mrs. Armstid's hand. "Get him into the wagon and take him on home," the Texas man says, like he might have been telling them he enjoyed his supper.

Then here come Flem. "What's that for, Buck?" Flem says.

"Thinks he bought one of them ponies," the Texas man says. "Get him on away, missus."

But Henry wouldn't go. "Give him back that money," he says. "I bought that horse and I aim to have him if I have to shoot him."

And there was Flem, standing there with his hands in his pockets, chewing, like he had just happened to be passing.

"You take your money and I take my horse," Henry says. "Give it back to him," he says to Mrs. Armstid.

"You don't own no horse of mine," the Texas man says. "Get him on home, missus."

Then Henry seen Flem. "You got something to do with these horses," he says. "I bought one. Here's the money for it." He taken the bill outen Mrs. Armstid's hand. He offered it to Flem. "I bought one. Ask him. Here. Here's the money," he says, giving the bill to Flem.

When Flem taken the money, the Texas man dropped the rope he had snatched outen Henry's hand. He had done sent Eck Snopes's boy up to the store for another box of gingersnaps, and he taken the box outen his pocket and looked into it. It was empty and he dropped it on the ground. "Mr. Snopes will have your money for you to-morrow," he says to Mrs. Armstid. "You can get it from him to-morrow. He don't own no horse. You get him into the wagon and get him on home." Mrs. Armstid went back to the wagon and got in. "Where's that ere buckboard I bought?" the Texas man says. It was after sundown then. And then Mrs. Littlejohn come out on the porch and rung the supper bell.

IV

I come on in and et supper. Mrs. Littlejohn would bring in a pan of bread or something, then she would go out to the porch a minute and come back and tell us. The Texas man had hitched his team to the buckboard he had swapped them last two horses for, and him and Flem had gone, and then she told that the rest of them that never had ropes had went back to the store with I. O. Snopes to get some ropes, and wasn't nobody at the gate but Henry Armstid, and Mrs. Armstid setting in the wagon in the road, and Eck Snopes and that boy of hisn. "I don't care how many of them fool men gets killed by them things," Mrs. Littlejohn says, "but I ain't going to let Eck Snopes take that boy into that lot again." So she went down to the gate, but she come back without the boy or Eck neither.

"It ain't no need to worry about that boy," I says. "He's charmed." He was right behind Eck last night when Eck went to help feed them. The whole drove of them jumped clean over that boy's head and never touched him. It was Eck that touched him. Eck snatched him into the wagon and taken a rope and frailed the tar outen him.

So I had done et and went to my room and was undressing, long as I had a long trip to make next day; I was trying to sell a machine to Mrs. Bundren up past Whiteleaf; when Henry Armstid opened that gate and went in by hisself. They couldn't make him wait for the balance of them to get back with their ropes. Eck Snopes said he tried to make Henry wait, but Henry wouldn't do it. Eck said Henry walked right up to them and that when they broke, they run clean over Henry like a hay-mow breaking down. Eck said he snatched that boy of hisn out of the way just in time and that them things went through that gate like a creek flood and into the wagons and teams hitched side the road, busting wagon tongues and snapping harness like it was fishing-line, with Mrs. Armstid still setting in their wagon in the middle of it like something carved outen wood. Then they scattered, wild horses and tame mules with pieces of harness and single trees dangling offen them, both ways, up and down the road.

"There goes ourn, paw!" Eck says his boy said. "There it goes, into Mrs. Littlejohn's house." Eck says it run right up the steps and into the house like a boarder late for supper. I reckon so. Anyway, I was in my room, in my under-clothes, with one sock on and one sock in my hand, leaning out the window when the commotion busted out, when I heard something run into the melodeon in the hall; it sounded like a railroad engine. Then the door to my room come sailing in like when you throw a tin bucket top into the wind and I looked over my shoulder and see something that looked like a fourteen-foot pinwheel a-blaring its eyes at me. It had to blare them fast, because I was already done jumped out the window.

I reckon it was anxious, too. I reckon it hadn't never seen barbed wire or shell corn before, but I know it hadn't never seen underclothes before, or maybe it was a sewing-machine agent it hadn't never seen. Anyway, it swirled and turned to run back up the hall and outen the house, when it met Eck Snopes and that boy just coming in, carrying a rope. It swirled again and run down the hall and out the back door just in time to meet Mrs. Littlejohn. She had just gathered up the clothes she had washed, and she was coming onto the back porch with a armful of washing in one hand and a scrubbing-board in the other, when the horse skidded up to her, trying to stop and swirl again. It never taken Mrs. Littlejohn no time a-tall.

"Git outen here, you son," she says. She hit it across the face with the scrubbing-board; that ere scrubbing-board split as neat as ere a axe could have done it, and when the horse swirled to run back up the hall, she hit it again with what was left of the scrubbing-board, not on the head this time. "And stay out," she says.

Eck and that boy was half-way down the hall by this time. I reckon that horse looked like a pinwheel to Eck too. "Git to hell outen here, Ad!" Eck says. Only there wasn't time. Eck dropped flat on his face, but the boy never moved. The boy was about a yard tall maybe, in overhalls just like Eck's; that horse swoared over his head without touching a hair. I saw that, because I was just coming back up the front steps, still carrying that ere sock and still in my underclothes, when the horse come onto the porch again. It taken one look at me and swirled again and run to the end of the porch and jumped the banisters and the lot fence like a hen-hawk and lit in the lot running and went out the gate again and jumped eight or ten upside-down wagons and went on down the road. It was a full moon then. Mrs. Armstid was still setting in the wagon like she had done been carved outen wood and left there and forgot.

That horse. It ain't never missed a lick. It was going about forty miles a hour when it come to the bridge over the creek. It would have had a clear road, but it so happened that Vernon Tull was already using the bridge when it got there. He was coming back from town; he hadn't heard about the auction; him and his wife and three daughters and Mrs. Tull's aunt, all setting in chairs in the wagon bed, and all asleep, including the mules. They waked up when the horse hit the bridge one time, but Tull said the first he knew was when the mules tried to turn the wagon around in the middle of the bridge and he seen that spotted varmint run right twixt the mules and run up the wagon tongue like a squirrel. He said he just had time to hit it across the face with his whip-stock, because about that time the mules turned the wagon around on that ere one-way bridge and that horse clumb across one of the mules and jumped down onto the bridge again and went on, with Vernon standing up in the wagon and kicking at it.

Tull said the mules turned in the harness and clumb back into the wagon too, with Tull trying to beat them out again, with the reins wrapped around his wrist. After that he says all he seen was overturned chairs and womenfolks' legs and white drawers shining in the moonlight, and his mules and that spotted horse going on up the road like a ghost.

The mules jerked Tull outen the wagon and drug him a spell on the bridge before the reins broke. They thought at first that he was dead, and while they was kneeling around him, picking the bridge splinters outen him, here come Eck and that boy, still carrying the rope. They was running and breathing a little hard. "Where'd he go?" Eck says.

V

I went back and got my pants and shirt and shoes on just in time to go and help get Henry Armstid outen the trash in the lot. I be dog if he didn't look like he was dead, with his head hanging back and his teeth showing in the moonlight, and a little rim of white under his eyelids. We could still hear them horses, here and there; hadn't none of them got more than four-five miles away yet, not knowing the country, I reckon. So we could hear them and folks yelling now and then: "Whooey. Head him!"

We toted Henry into Mrs. Littlejohn's. She was in the hall; she hadn't put down the armful of clothes. She taken one look at us, and she laid down the busted scrubbing-board and taken up the lamp and opened a empty door. "Bring him in here," she says.

We toted him in and laid him on the bed. Mrs. Littlejohn set the lamp on the dresser, still carrying the clothes. "I'll declare, you men," she says. Our shadows was way up the wall, tiptoeing too; we could hear ourselves breathing. "Better get his wife," Mrs. Littlejohn says. She went out, carrying the clothes.

"I reckon we had," Quick says. "Go get her, somebody."

"Whyn't you go?" Winterbottom says.

"Let Ernest git her," Durley says. "He lives neighbors with them."

Ernest went to fetch her. I be dog if Henry didn't look like he was dead. Mrs. Littlejohn come back, and with a kettle and some towels. She went to work on Henry, and then Mrs. Armstid and Ernest come in. Mrs. Armstid come to the foot of the bed and stood there, with her hands rolled into her apron, watching what Mrs. Littlejohn was doing, I reckon.

"You men git outen the way," Mrs. Littlejohn says. "Git outside," she says. "See if you can't find something else to play with that will kill some more of you."

"Is he dead?" Winterbottom says.

"It ain't your fault if he ain't," Mrs. Littlejohn says. "Go tell Will Varner to come up here. I reckon a man ain't so different from a mule, come long come short. Except maybe a mule's got more sense."

We went to get Uncle Billy. It was a full moon. We could hear them, now and then, four mile away: "Whooey. Head him." The country was full of them, one on ever wooden bridge in the land, running across it like thunder: "Whooey. There he goes. Head him."

We hadn't got far before Henry begun to scream. I reckon Mrs. Littlejohn's water had brung him to; anyway, he wasn't dead. We went on to Uncle Billy's. The house was dark. We called to him, and after a while the window opened and Uncle Billy put his head out, peart as a peckerwood, listening. "Are they still trying to catch them durn rabbits?" he says.

He come down, with his britches on over his night-shirt and his suspenders dangling, carrying his horse-doctoring grip. "Yes, sir," he says, cocking his head like a woodpecker; "they're still a-trying."

We could hear Henry before we reached Mrs. Littlejohn's. He was going Ah-Ah-Ah. We stopped in the yard. Uncle Billy went on in. We could hear Henry. We stood in the yard, hearing them on the bridges, this-a-way and that: "Whooey. Whooey."

"Eck Snopes ought to caught hisn," Ernest says.

"Looks like he ought," Winterbottom said.

Henry was going Ah-Ah-Ah steady in the house; then he begun to scream. "Uncle Billy's started," Quick says. We looked into the hall. We could see the light where the door was. Then Mrs. Littlejohn come out.

"Will needs some help," she says. "You, Ernest. You'll do." Ernest went into the house.

"Hear them?" Quick said. "That one was on Four Mile bridge." We could hear them; it sounded like thunder a long way off; it didn't last long:

"Whooey."

We could hear Henry: "Ah-Ah-Ah-Ah-Ah."

"They are both started now," Winterbottom says. "Ernest too."

That was early in the night. Which was a good thing, because it taken a long night for folks to chase them things right and for Henry to lay there and holler, being as Uncle Billy never had none of this here chloryfoam to set Henry's leg with. So it was considerate in Flem to get them started early. And what do you reckon Flem's com-ment was?

That's right. Nothing. Because he wasn't there. Hadn't nobody see him since that Texas man left.

VI

That was Saturday night. I reckon Mrs. Armstid got home about daylight, to see about the chaps. I don't know where they thought her and Henry was. But lucky the oldest one was a gal, about twelve, big enough to take care of the little ones. Which she did for the next two days. Mrs. Armstid would nurse Henry all night and work in the kitchen for hern and Henry's keep, and in the afternoon she would drive home (it was about four miles) to see to the chaps. She would cook up a pot of victuals and leave it on the stove, and the gal would bar the house and keep the little ones quiet. I would hear Mrs. Littlejohn and Mrs. Armstid talking in the kitchen. "How are the chaps making out?" Mrs. Littlejohn says.

"All right," Mrs. Armstid says.

"Don't they git skeered at night?" Mrs. Littlejohn says.

"Ina May bars the door when I leave," Mrs. Armstid says. "She's got the axe in bed with her. I reckon she can make out."

I reckon they did. And I reckon Mrs. Armstid was waiting for Flem to come back to town; hadn't nobody seen him until this morning; to get her money the Texas man said Flem was keeping for her. Sho. I reckon she was.

Anyway, I heard Mrs. Armstid and Mrs. Littlejohn talking in the kitchen this morning while I was eating breakfast. Mrs. Littlejohn had just told Mrs. Armstid that Flem was in town. "You can ask him for that five dollars," Mrs. Littlejohn says.

"You reckon he'll give it to me?" Mrs. Armstid says.

Mrs. Littlejohn was washing dishes, washing them like a man, like they was made out of iron. "No," she says. "But asking him won't do no hurt. It might shame him. I don't reckon it will, but it might."

"If he wouldn't give it back, it ain't no use to ask," Mrs. Armstid says.

"Suit yourself," Mrs. Littlejohn says. "It's your money."

I could hear the dishes.

"Do you reckon he might give it back to me?" Mrs. Armstid says. "That Texas man said he would. He said I could get it from Mr. Snopes later."

"Then go and ask him for it," Mrs. Littlejohn says.

I could hear the dishes.

"He won't give it back to me," Mrs. Armstid says.

"All right," Mrs. Littlejohn says. "Don't ask him for it, then."

I could hear the dishes; Mrs. Armstid was helping. "You don't reckon he would, do you?" she says. Mrs. Littlejohn never said nothing. It sounded like she was throwing the dishes at one another. "Maybe I better go and talk to Henry about it," Mrs. Armstid says.

"I would," Mrs. Littlejohn says. I be dog if it didn't sound like she had two plates in her hands, beating them together. "Then Henry can buy another five-dollar horse with it. Maybe he'll buy one next time that will out and out kill him. If I thought that, I'd give you back the money, myself."

"I reckon I better talk to him first," Mrs. Armstid said. Then it sounded like Mrs. Littlejohn taken up all the dishes and throwed them at the cook-stove, and I come away.

That was this morning. I had been up to Bundren's and back, and I thought that things would have kind of settled down. So after breakfast, I went up to the store. And there was Flem, setting in the store-chair and whittling, like he might not have ever moved since he come to clerk for Jody Varner. I. O. was leaning in the door, in his shirt sleeves and with his hair parted too, same as Flem was before he turned the clerking job over to I. O. It's a funny thing about them Snopes: they all look alike, yet there ain't ere a two of them that claims brothers. They're always just cousins, like Flem and Eck and Flem and I. O. Eck was there too, squatting against the wall, him and that boy, eating cheese and crackers outen a sack; they told me that Eck hadn't been home a-tall. And that Lon Quick hadn't got back to town, even. He followed his horse clean down to Samson's Bridge, with a wagon and a camp outfit. Eck finally caught one of hisn. It run into a blind lane at Freeman's and Eck and the boy taken and tied their rope across the end of the lane, about three foot high. The horse come to the end of the lane and whirled and run back without ever stopping. Eck says it never seen the rope a-tall. He says it looked just like one of these here Christmas pinwheels. "Didn't it try to run again?" I says.

"No," Eck says, eating a bite of cheese offen his knife blade. "Just kicked some."

"Kicked some?" I says.

"It broke its neck," Eck says.

Well, they was squatting there, about six of them, talking, talking at Flem; never nobody knowed yet if Flem had ere a interest in them horses or not. So finally I come right out and asked him. "Flem's done skun all of us so much," I says, "that we're proud of him. Come on, Flem," I says, "how much did you and that Texas man make offen them horses? You can tell us. Ain't nobody here but Eck that bought one of them; the others ain't got back to town yet, and Eck's your own cousin; he'll be proud to hear, too. How much did you-all make?"

They was all whittling, not looking at Flem, making like they was studying.

But you could a heard a pin drop. And I. O. He had been rubbing his back up and down on the door, but he stopped now, watching Flem like a pointing dog. Flem finished cutting the sliver offen his stick. He spit across the porch, into the road. " 'Twarn't none of my horses," he says.

I.O. cackled, like a hen, slapping his legs with both hands. "You boys might just as well quit trying to get ahead of Flem," he said.

Well, about that time I see Mrs. Armstid come outen Mrs. Littlejohn's gate, coming up the road. I never said nothing. I says, "Well, if a man can't take care of himself in a trade, he can't blame the man that trims him."

Flem never said nothing, trimming at the stick. He hadn't seen Mrs. Armstid. "Yes, sir," I says. "A fellow like Henry Armstid ain't got nobody but hisself to blame."

"Course he ain't," I.O. says. He ain't seen her, neither. "Henry Armstid's a born fool. Always is been. If Flem hadn't a got his money, somebody else would."

We looked at Flem. He never moved. Mrs. Armstid come on up the road. "That's right," I says. "But, come to think of it, Henry never bought no horse." We looked at Flem; you could a heard a match drop. "That Texas man told her to get that five dollars back from Flem next day. I reckon Flem's done already taken that money to Mrs. Littlejohn's and give it to Mrs. Armstid."

We watched Flem. I.O. quit rubbing his back against the door again. After a while Flem raised his head and spit across the porch, into the dust. I. O. cackled, just like a hen. "Ain't he a beating fellow, now?" I. O. says.

Mrs. Armstid was getting closer, so I kept on talking, watching to see if Flem would look up and see her. But he never looked up. I went on talking about Tull, about how he was going to sue Flem, and Flem setting there, whittling his stick, not saying nothing else after he said they wasn't none of his horses.

Then I. O. happened to look around. He seen Mrs. Armstid. "Pssssst!" he says. Flem looked up. "Here she comes!" I. O. says. "Go out the back. I'll tell her you done went in to town to-day."

But Flem never moved. He just set there, whittling, and we watched Mrs. Armstid come up onto the porch, in that ere faded sunbonnet and wrapper and them tennis shoes that made a kind of hissing noise on the porch. She come onto the porch and stopped, her hands rolled into her dress in front, not looking at nothing.

"He said Saturday," she says, "that he wouldn't sell Henry no horse. He said I could get the money from you."

Flem looked up. The knife never stopped. It went on trimming off a sliver same as if he was watching it. "He taken that money off with him when he left," Flem says.

Mrs. Armstid never looked at nothing. We never looked at her, neither, except that boy of Eck's. He had a half-et cracker in his hand, watching her, chewing.

"He said Henry hadn't bought no horse," Mrs. Armstid says. "He said for me to get the money from you today."

"I reckon he forgot about it," Flem said. "He taken that money off with him

Saturday." He whittled again. I. O. kept on rubbing his back, slow. He licked his lips. After a while the woman looked up the road, where it went on up the hill, toward the graveyard. She looked up that way for a while, with that boy of Eck's watching her and I. O. rubbing his back slow against the door. Then she turned back toward the steps.

"I reckon it's time to get dinner started," she says.

"How's Henry this morning, Mrs. Armstid?" Winterbottom says.

She looked at Winterbottom; she almost stopped. "He's resting, I thank you kindly," she says.

Flem got up, outen the chair, putting his knife away. He spit across the porch. "Wait a minute, Mrs. Armstid," he says. She stopped again. She didn't look at him. Flem went on into the store, with I. O. done quit rubbing his back now, with his head craned after Flem, and Mrs. Armstid standing there with her hands rolled into her dress, not looking at nothing. A wagon come up the road and passed; it was Freeman, on the way to town. Then Flem come out again, with I. O. still watching him. Flem had one of these little striped sacks of Jody Varner's candy; I bet he still owes Jody that nickel, too. He put the sack into Mrs. Armstid's hand, like he would have put it into a hollow stump. He spit again across the porch. "A little sweetening for the chaps," he says.

"Your're right kind," Mrs. Armstid says. She held the sack of candy in her hand, not looking at nothing. Eck's boy was watching the sack, the half-et cracker in his hand; he wasn't chewing now. He watched Mrs. Armstid roll the sack into her apron. "I reckon I better get on back and help with dinner," she says. She turned and went back across the porch. Flem set down in the chair again and opened his knife. He spit across the porch again, past Mrs. Armstid where she hadn't went down the steps yet. Then she went on, in that ere sunbonnet and wrapper all the same color, back down the road toward Mrs. Littlejohn's. You couldn't see her dress move, like a natural woman walking. She looked like a old snag still standing up and moving along on a high water. We watched her turn in at Mrs. Littlejohn's and go outen sight. Flem was whittling. I. O. begun to rub his back on the door. Then he begun to cackle, just like a durn hen.

"You boys might just as well quit trying," I. O. says. "You can't git ahead of Flem. You can't touch him. Ain't he a sight, now?"

I be dog if he ain't. If I had brung a herd of wild cattymounts into town and sold them to my neighbors and kinfolks, they would have lynched me. Yes, sir.

ERNEST HEMINGWAY (1899–1961)

The Short Happy Life of Francis Macomber

It was now lunch time and they were all sitting under the double green fly of the dining tent pretending that nothing had happened.

"Will you have lime juice or lemon squash?" Macomber asked.

"I'll have a gimlet," Robert Wilson told him.[1]

"I'll have a gimlet too. I need something." Macomber's wife said.

"I suppose it's the thing to do," Macomber agreed. "Tell him to make three gimlets."

The mess boy had started them already, lifting the bottles out of the canvas cooling bags that sweated wet in the wind that blew through the trees that shaded the tents.

"What had I ought to give them?" Macomber asked.

"A quid would be plenty," Wilson told him.[2] "You don't want to spoil them."

"Will the headman distribute it?"

"Absolutely."

Francis Macomber had, half an hour before, been carried to his tent from the edge of the camp in triumph on the arms and shoulders of the cook, the personal boys, the skinner and the porters. The gunbearers had taken no part in the demonstration. When the native boys put him down at the door of his tent, he had shaken all their hands, received their congratulations, and then gone into the tent and sat on the bed until his wife came in. She did not speak to him when she came in and he left the tent at once to wash his face and hands in the portable wash basin outside and go over to the dining tent to sit in a comfortable canvas chair in the breeze and the shade.

"You've got your lion," Robert Wilson said to him, "and a damned fine one too."

Mrs. Macomber looked at Wilson quickly. She was an extremely handsome and well-kept woman of the beauty and social position which had, five years before, commanded five thousand dollars as the price of endorsing, with photographs, a beauty product which she had never used. She had been married to Francis Macomber for eleven years.

"He is a good lion, isn't he?" Macomber said. His wife looked at him now. She looked at both these men as though she had never seen them before.

One, Wilson, the white hunter, she knew she had never truly seen before. He was about middle height with sandy hair, a stubby mustache, a very red face and extremely cold blue eyes with faint white wrinkles at the corners that grooved merrily when he smiled. He smiled at her now and she looked away from his face at the way his shoulders sloped in the loose tunic he wore with the four big cartridges held in loops where the left breast pocket should have been, at his big brown hands, his old slacks, his very dirty boots and back to his red face again. She noticed where the baked red of his face stopped in a white line that marked the circle left by his Stetson hat that hung now from one of the pegs of the tent pole.

"Well, here's to the lion," Robert Wilson said. He smiled at her again and, not smiling, she looked curiously at her husband.

---

[1] A gimlet is a cooling drink of sweetened lime juice, gin, and water.
[2] A quid is a slang expression for a British pound.

Francis Macomber was very tall, very well built if you did not mind that length of bone, dark, his hair cropped like an oarsman, rather thin-lipped, and was considered handsome. He was dressed in the same sort of safari clothes that Wilson wore except that his were new, he was thirty-five years old, kept himself very fit, was good at court games, had a number of big-game fishing records, and had just shown himself, very publicly, to be a coward.

"Here's to the lion," he said. "I can't ever thank you for what you did."

Margaret, his wife, looked away from him and back to Wilson.

"Let's not talk about the lion," she said.

Wilson looked over at her without smiling and now she smiled at him.

"It's been a very strange day," she said. "Hadn't you ought to put your hat on even under the canvas at noon? You told me that, you know."

"Might put it on," said Wilson.

"You know you have a very red face, Mr. Wilson," she told him and smiled again.

"Drink," said Wilson.

"I don't think so," she said. "Francis drinks a great deal, but his face is never red."

"It's red today," Macomber tried a joke.

"No," said Margaret. "It's mine that's red today. But Mr. Wilson's is always red."

"Must be racial," said Wilson. "I say, you wouldn't like to drop my beauty as a topic, would you?"

"I've just started on it."

"Let's chuck it," said Wilson

"Conversation is going to be so difficult," Margaret said.

"Don't be silly, Margot," her husband said.

"No difficulty," Wilson said. "Got a damn fine lion."

Margot looked at them both and they both saw that she was going to cry. Wilson had seen it coming for a long time and he dreaded it. Macomber was past dreading it.

"I wish it hadn't happened. Oh, I wish it hadn't happened," she said and started for her tent. She made no noise of crying but they could see that her shoulders were shaking under the rose-colored, sun-proofed shirt she wore.

"Women upset," said Wilson to the tall man. "Amounts to nothing. Strain on the nerves and one thing'n another."

"No," said Macomber. "I suppose that I rate that for the rest of my life now."

"Nonsense. Let's have a spot of the giant killer," said Wilson. "Forget the whole thing. Nothing to it anyway."

"We might try," said Macomber. "I won't forget what you did for me though."

"Nothing," said Wilson. "All nonsense."

So they sat there in the shade where the camp was pitched under some wide-topped acacia trees with a boulder-strewn cliff behind them, and a stretch of grass that ran to the bank of a boulder-filled stream in front with forest beyond it, and drank their just-cool lime drinks and avoided one another's eyes while the boys set the table for lunch. Wilson could tell that the boys all knew about it now and when he saw Macomber's personal boy looking curiously at his master while he was putting dishes on the table he snapped at him in Swahili. The boy turned away with his face blank.

"What were you telling him?" Macomber asked.

"Nothing. Told him to look alive or I'd see he got about fifteen of the best."

"What's that? Lashes?"

"It's quite illegal," Wilson said. "You're supposed to fine them."

"Do you still have them whipped?"

"Oh, yes. They could raise a row if they chose to complain. But they don't. They prefer it to the fines."

"How strange!" said Macomber.

"Not strange, really." Wilson said. "Which would you rather do? Take a good birching or lose your pay?"

Then he felt embarrassed at asking it and before Macomber could answer he went on, "We all take a beating every day, you know, one way or another."

This was no better. "Good God," he thought. "I am a diplomat, aren't I?"

"Yes, we take a beating," said Macomber, still not looking at him. "I'm awfully sorry about that lion business. It doesn't have to go any further, does it? I mean no one will hear about it, will they?"

"You mean will I tell it at the Mathaiga Club?" Wilson looked at him now coldly. He had not expected this. So he's a bloody four-letter man as well as a bloody coward, he thought. I rather liked him too until today. But how is one to know about an American?

"No," said Wilson. "I'm a professional hunter. We never talk about our clients. You can be quite easy on that. It's supposed to be bad form to ask us not to talk though."

He had decided now that to break would be much easier. He would eat, then, by himself and could read a book with his meals. They would eat by themselves. He would see them through the safari on a very formal basis—what was it the French called it? Distinguished consideration—and it would be a damn sight easier than having to go through this emotional trash. He'd insult him and make a good clean break. Then he could read a book with his meals and he'd still be drinking their whisky. That was the phrase for it when a safari went bad. You ran into another white hunter and you asked, "How is everything going?" and he answered, "Oh, I'm still drinking their whisky," and you knew everything had gone to pot.

"I'm sorry," Macomber said and looked at him with his American face that would stay adolescent until it became middle-aged, and Wilson noted his crew-cropped hair, fine eyes only faintly shifty, good nose, thin lips and handsome jaw. "I'm sorry I didn't realize that. There are lots of things I don't know."

So what could he do, Wilson thought. He was all ready to break it off quickly and neatly and here the beggar was apologizing after he had just insulted him.

He made one more attempt. "Don't worry about me talking," he said. "I have a living to make. You know in Africa no woman ever misses her lion and no white man ever bolts."

"I bolted like a rabbit," Macomber said.

Now what in hell were you going to do about a man who talked like that, Wilson wondered.

Wilson looked at Macomber with his flat, blue, machine-gunner's eyes and the other smiled back at him. He had a pleasant smile if you did not notice how his eyes showed when he was hurt.

"Maybe I can fix it up on buffalo," he said. "We're after them next, aren't we?"

"In the morning if you like," Wilson told him. Perhaps he had been wrong. This was certainly the way to take it. You most certainly could not tell a damned thing about an American. He was all for Macomber again. If you could forget the morning. But, of course, you couldn't. The morning had been about as bad as they come.

"Here comes the Memsahib," he said. She was walking over from her tent looking refreshed and cheerful and quite lovely. She had a very perfect oval face, so perfect that you expected her to be stupid. But she wasn't stupid, Wilson thought, no, not stupid.

"How is the beautiful red-faced Mr. Wilson? Are you feeling better, Francis, my pearl?"

"Oh, much," said Macomber.

"I've dropped the whole thing," she said, sitting down at the table. "What importance is there to whether Francis is any good at killing lions? That's not his trade. That's Mr. Wilson's trade. Mr. Wilson is really very impressive killing anything. You do kill anything, don't you?"

"Oh, anything," said Wilson. "Simply anything." They are, he thought, the hardest in the world; the hardest, the cruelest, the most predatory and the most attractive and their men have softened or gone to pieces nervously as they have hardened. Or is it that they pick men they can handle? They can't know that much at the age they marry, he thought. He was grateful that he had gone through his education on American women before now because this was a very attractive one.

"We're going after buff in the morning," he told her.

"I'm coming," she said.

"No, you're not."

"Oh, yes, I am. Mayn't I, Francis?"

"Why not stay in camp?"

"Not for anything," she said. "I wouldn't miss something like today for anything."

When she left, Wilson was thinking, when she went off to cry, she seemed a hell of a fine woman. She seemed to understand, to realize, to be hurt for him and for herself and to know how things really stood. She is away for twenty minutes and now she is back, simply enamelled in that American female cruelty. They are the damnedest women. Really the damnedest.

"We'll put on another show for you tomorrow," Francis Macomber said.

"You're not coming," Wilson said.

"You're very mistaken," she told him. "And I want so to see you perform again. You were lovely this morning. That is if blowing things' heads off is lovely."

"Here's the lunch," said Wilson. "You're very merry, aren't you?"

"Why not? I didn't come out here to be dull."

"Well, it hasn't been dull," Wilson said. He could see the boulders in the river and the high bank beyond the trees and he remembered the morning.

"Oh, no," she said. "It's been charming. And tomorrow. You don't know how I look forward to tomorrow,"

"That's eland he's offering you," Wilson said.

"They're the big cowy things that jump like hares, aren't they?"

"I suppose that describes them," Wilson said.

"It's very good meat," Macomber said.

"Didn't you shoot it, Francis?" she asked.

"Yes."

"They're not dangerous, are they?"

"Only if they fall on you," Wilson told her.

"I'm so glad."

"Why not let up on the bitchery just a little Margot," Macomber said, cutting the eland steak and putting some mashed potato, gravy and carrot on the down-turned fork that tined through the piece of meat.

"I suppose I could," she said, "since you put it so prettily."

"Tonight we'll have champagne for the lion," Wilson said. "It's a bit too hot at noon."

"Oh, the lion," Margot said. "I'd forgotten the lion!"

So, Robert Wilson thought to himself, she is giving him a ride, isn't she? Or do you suppose that's her idea of putting up a good show? How should a woman act when she discovers her husband is a bloody coward? She's damn cruel but they're all cruel. They govern, of course, and to govern one has to be cruel sometimes. Still, I've seen enough of their damn terrorism.

"Have some more eland," he said to her politely.

That afternoon, late, Wilson and Macomber went out in the motor car with the native driver and the two gun-bearers. Mrs. Macomber stayed in the camp. It was too hot to go out, she said, and she was going with them in the early morning. As they drove off Wilson saw her standing under the big tree, looking pretty rather than beautiful in her faintly rosy khaki, her dark hair drawn back off her forehead and gathered in a knot low on her neck, her face as fresh, he thought, as though she were in England. She waved to them as the car went off through the swale of high grass and curved around through the trees into the small hills of orchard bush.

In the orchard bush they found a herd of impala, and leaving the car they stalked one old ram with long, wide-spread horns and Macomber killed it with a very creditable shot that knocked the buck down at a good two hundred yards and sent the herd off bounding wildly and leaping over one another's backs in long, leg-drawn-up leaps as unbelievable and as floating as those one makes sometimes in dreams.

"That was a good shot," Wilson said. "They're a small target."

"Is it a worthwhile head?" Macomber asked.

"It's excellent," Wilson told him. "You shoot like that and you'll have no trouble."

"Do you think we'll find buffalo tomorrow?"

"There's a good chance of it. They feed out early in the morning and with luck we may catch them in the open."

"I'd like to clear away that lion business," Macomber said. "It's not very pleasant to have your wife see you do something like that."

I should think it would be even more unpleasant to do it, Wilson thought, wife or no wife, or to talk about it having done it. But he said, "I wouldn't think about that any more. Anyone could be upset by his first lion. That's all over."

But that night after dinner and a whisky and soda by the fire before going to bed, as Francis Macomber lay on his cot with the mosquito bar over him and listened to the night noises, it was not all over. It was neither all over nor was it beginning. It was there exactly as it happened with some parts of it indelibly emphasized and he was miserably ashamed at it. But more than shame he felt cold, hollow fear in him. The fear was still there like a cold slimy hollow in all the emptiness where once his confidence had been and it made him feel sick. It was still there with him now.

It had started the night before when he had wakened and heard the lion roaring somewhere up along the river. It was a deep sound and at the end there were sort of coughing grunts that made him seem just outside the tent, and when Francis Macomber woke in the night to hear it he was afraid. He could hear his wife breathing quietly, asleep. There was no one to tell he was afraid, nor to be afraid with him, and lying alone, he did not know the Somali proverb that says a brave man is always frightened three times by a lion; when he first sees his track, when he first hears him roar and when he first confronts him. Then while they were eating breakfast by lantern light out in the dining tent, before the sun was up, the lion roared again and Francis thought he was just at the edge of camp.

"Sounds like an old-timer," Robert Wilson said, looking up from his kippers and coffee. "Listen to him cough."

"Is he very close?"

"A mile or so up the stream."

"Will we see him?"

"We'll have a look."

"Does his roaring carry that far? It sounds as though he were right in camp."

"Carries a hell of a long way," said Robert Wilson. "It's strange the way it carries. Hope he's a shootable cat. The boys said there was a very big one about here."

"If I get a shot, where should I hit him," Macomber asked, "to stop him?"

"In the shoulders," Wilson said. "In the neck if you can make it. Shoot for bone. Break him down."

"I hope I can place it properly," Macomber said.

"You shoot very well," Wilson told him. "Take your time. Make sure of him. The first one in is the one that counts."

"What range will it be?"

"Can't tell. Lion has something to say about that. Won't shoot unless it's close enough so you can make sure."

"At under a hundred yards?" Macomber asked.

Wilson looked at him quickly.

"Hundred's about right. Might have to take him a bit under. Shouldn't chance a shot at much over that. A hundred's a decent range. You can hit him wherever you want at that. Here comes the Memsahib."

"Good morning," she said. "Are we going after that lion?"

"As soon as you deal with your breakfast," Wilson said. "How are you feeling?"

"Marvellous," she said. "I'm very excited."

"I'll just go and see that everything is ready," Wilson went off. As he left the lion roared again.

"Noisy beggar," Wilson said. "We'll put a stop to that."

"What's the matter, Francis?" his wife asked him.

"Nothing," Macomber said.

"Yes, there is," she said. "What are you upset about?"

"Nothing," he said.

"Tell me," she looked at him. "Don't you feel well?"

"It's that damned roaring," he said. "It's been going on all night, you know."

"Why didn't you wake me," she said. "I'd love to have heard it."

"I've got to kill the damned thing," Macomber said, miserably.

"Well, that's what you're out here for, isn't it?"

"Yes. But I'm nervous. Hearing the thing roar gets on my nerves."

"Well then, as Wilson said, kill him and stop his roaring."

"Yes, darling," said Francis Macomber. "It sounds easy, doesn't it?"

"You're not afraid, are you?"

"Of course not. But I'm nervous from hearing him roar all night."

"You'll kill him marvellously," she said. "I know you will. I'm awfully anxious to see it."

"Finish your breakfast and we'll be starting."

"It's not light yet," she said. "This is a ridiculous hour."

Just then the lion roared in a deep-chested moaning, suddenly guttural, ascending vibration that seemed to shake the air and ended in a sigh and a heavy, deep-chested grunt.

"He sounds almost here," Macomber's wife said.

"My God," said Macomber. "I hate that damned noise."

"It's very impressive."

"Impressive. It's frightful."

Robert Wilson came up then carrying his short, ugly, shockingly big-bored .505 Gibbs and grinning.

"Come on," he said. "Your gun-bearer has your Springfield and the big gun. Everything's in the car. Have you solids?"

"Yes."

"I'm ready," Mrs. Macomber said.

"Must make him stop that racket," Wilson said. "You get in front. The Memsahib can sit back here with me."

They climbed into the motor car and, in the gray first daylight, moved off up the river through the trees. Macomber opened the breech of his rifle and saw he had metal-cased bullets; shut the bolt and put the rifle on safety. He saw his hand was trembling. He felt in his pocket for more cartridges and moved his fingers over the cartridges in the loops of his tunic front. He turned back to where Wilson sat in the rear seat of the doorless, box-bodied motor car beside his wife, them both grinning with excitement, and Wilson leaned forward and whispered.

"See the birds dropping. Means the old boy has left his kill."

On the far bank of the stream Macomber could see, above the trees, vultures circling and plummeting down.

"Chances are he'll come to drink along here," Wilson whispered. "Before he goes to lay up. Keep an eye out."

They were driving slowly along the high bank of the stream which here cut deeply to its boulder-filled bed, and they wound in and out through big trees as they drove. Macomber was watching the opposite bank when he felt Wilson take hold of his arm. The car stopped.

"There he is," he heard the whisper. "Ahead and to the right. Get out and take him. He's a marvellous lion."

Macomber saw the lion now. He was standing almost broadside, his great head up and turned toward them. The early morning breeze that blew toward them was just stirring his dark mane, and the lion looked huge, silhouetted on the rise of bank in the gray morning light, his shoulders heavy, his barrel of a body bulking smoothly.

"How far is he?" asked Macomber, raising his rifle.

"About seventy-five. Get out and take him"

"Why not shoot from where I am?"

"You don't shoot them from cars," he heard Wilson saying in his ear. "Get out. He's not going to stay there all day."

Macomber stepped out of the curved opening at the side of the front seat, onto the step and down onto the ground. The lion still stood looking majestically and coolly toward this object that his eyes only showed in silhouette, bulking like some super-rhino. There was no man smell carried toward him and he watched the object, moving his great head a little from side to side. Then watching the object, not afraid, but hesitating before going down the bank to drink with such a thing opposite him, he saw a man figure detach itself from it and he turned his heavy head and swung away toward the cover of the trees as he heard a cracking crash and felt the slam of a .30–06 220-grain solid bullet that bit his flank and ripped in sudden hot scalding nausea through his stomach. He trotted, heavy, big-footed, swinging wounded full-bellied, through the trees toward the tall grass and cover, and the crash came again to go past him ripping the air apart. Then it crashed again and he felt the blow as it hit his lower ribs and ripped on through, blood sudden hot and frothy in his mouth, and he galloped toward the high grass where he could crouch and not be seen and make them bring the crashing thing close enough so he could make a rush and get the man that held it.

Macomber had not thought how the lion felt as he got out of the car. He only knew his hands were shaking and as he walked away from the car it was almost impossible for him to make his legs move. They were stiff in the thighs, but he could feel the muscles fluttering. He raised the rifle, sighted on the junction of the lion's head and shoulders and pulled the trigger. Nothing happened though he pulled until he thought his finger would break. Then he knew he had the safety on and as he lowered the rifle to move the safety over he moved another frozen pace forward, and the lion seeing his silhouette now clear of the silhouette of the car, turned and started off at a trot, and, as Macomber fired, he heard a whunk that meant that the bullet was home; but the lion kept on going. Macomber shot again and everyone saw the bullet throw a spout of dirt beyond the trotting lion. He shot again, remembering to lower his aim, and they all heard the bullet hit, and the lion went into a gallop and was in the tall grass before he had the bolt pushed forward.

Macomber stood there feeling sick at his stomach, his hands that held the Springfield still cocked, shaking, and his wife and Robert Wilson were standing by him. Beside him too were the two gunbearers chattering in Wakamba.

"I hit him," Macomber said. "I hit him twice."

"You gun-shot him and you hit him somewhere forward," Wilson said without enthusiasm. The gun-bearers looked very grave. They were silent now.

"You may have killed him," Wilson went on. "We'll have to wait a while before we go in to find out."

"What do you mean?"

"Let him get sick before we follow him up."

"Oh," said Macomber.

"He's a hell of a fine lion," Wilson said cheerfully. "He's gotten into a bad place though."

"Why is it bad?"

"Can't see him until you're on him."

"Oh," said Macomber.

"Come on," said Wilson. "The Memsahib can stay here in the car. We'll go to have a look at the blood spoor."

"Stay here, Margot," Macomber said to his wife. His mouth was very dry and it was hard for him to talk.

"Why?" she asked.

"Wilson says to."

"We're going to have a look," Wilson said. "You stay here. You can see even better from here."

"All right."

Wilson spoke in Swahili to the driver. He nodded and said, "Yes, Bwana."

Then they went down the steep bank and across the stream, climbing over and around the boulders and up the other bank, pulling up by some projecting roots, and along it until they found where the lion had been trotting when Macomber first shot. There was dark blood on the short grass that the gun-bearers pointed out with grass stems, and that ran away behind the river bank trees.

"What do we do?" asked Macomber.

"Not much choice," said Wilson. "We can't bring the car over. Bank's too steep. We'll let him stiffen up a bit and then you and I'll go in and have a look for him."

"Can't we set the grass on fire?" Macomber asked.

"Too green."

"Can't we send beaters?"

Wilson looked at him appraisingly. "Of course we can," he said. "But it's just a touch murderous. You see we know the lion's wounded. You can drive an unwounded lion—he'll move on ahead of a noise—but a wounded lion's going to charge. You can't see him until you're right on him. He'll make himself perfectly flat in cover you wouldn't think would hide a hare. You can't very well send boys in there to that sort of a show. Somebody bound to get mauled."

"What about the gun-bearers?"

"Oh, they'll go with us. It's their *shauri*. You see, they signed on for it. They don't look too happy though, do they?"

"I don't want to go in there," said Macomber. It was out before he knew he'd said it.

"Neither do I," said Wilson very cheerily. "Really no choice though." Then, as an afterthought, he glanced at Macomber and saw suddenly how he was trembling and the pitiful look on his face.

"You don't have to go in, of course," he said. "That's what I'm hired for, you know. That's why I'm so expensive."

"You mean you'd go in by yourself? Why not leave him there?"

Robert Wilson, whose entire occupation had been with the lion and the problem he presented, and who had not been thinking about Macomber except to note that he was rather windy, suddenly felt as though he had opened the wrong door in a hotel and seen something shameful.

"What do you mean?"

"Why not just leave him?"

"You mean pretend to ourselves he hasn't been hit?"

"No. Just drop it."

"It isn't done."

"Why not?"

"For one thing, he's certain to be suffering. For another, some one else might run onto him."

"I see."

"But you don't have to have anything to do with it."

"I'd like to," Macomber said. "I'm just scared, you know."

"I'll go ahead when we go in," Wilson said, "with Kongoni tracking. You keep behind me and a little to one side. Chances are we'll hear him growl. If we see him we'll both shoot. Don't worry about anything. I'll keep you backed up. As a matter of fact, you know, perhaps you'd better not go. It might be much better. Why don't you go over and join the Memsahib while I just get it over with?"

"No, I want to go."

"All right," said Wilson, "But don't go in if you don't want to. This is my *shauri* now, you know."

"I want to go," said Macomber.

They sat under a tree and smoked.

"Want to go back and speak to the Memsahib while we're waiting?" Wilson asked.

"No."

"I'll just step back and tell her to be patient."

"Good," said Macomber. He sat there, sweating under his arms, his mouth dry, his stomach hollow feeling, wanting to find courage to tell Wilson to go on and finish off the lion without him. He could not know that Wilson was furious because he had not noticed the state he was in earlier and sent him back to his wife. While he sat there Wilson came up. "I have your big gun," he said. "Take it. We've given him time, I think. Come on."

Macomber took the big gun and Wilson said:

"Keep behind me and about five yards to the right and do exactly as I tell you." Then he spoke in Swahili to the two gun-bearers, who looked the picture of gloom.

"Let's go," he said.

"Could I have a drink of water?" Macomber asked. Wilson spoke to the older gun-bearer, who wore a canteen on his belt, and the man unbuckled it, unscrewed the top and handed it to Macomber, who took it noticing how heavy it seemed and how hairy and shoddy the felt covering was in his hand. He raised it to drink and looked ahead at the high grass with the flat-topped trees behind it. A breeze was blowing toward them and the grass rippled gently in the wind. He looked at the gun-bearer and he could see the gun-bearer was suffering too with fear.

Thirty-five yards into the grass the big lion lay flattened out along the ground. His ears were back and his only movement was a slight twitching up and down of his long, black-tufted tail. He had turned at bay as soon as he had reached this cover and he was sick with the wound through his full belly, and weakening with the wound through his lungs that brought a thin foamy red to his mouth each time he breathed. His flanks were wet and hot and flies were on the little openings the solid bullets had made in his tawny hide, and his big yellow eyes, narrowed with hate, looked straight ahead, only blinking when the pain came as he breathed, and his claws dug in the soft baked earth. All of him, pain, sickness, hatred and all of his remaining strength, was tightening into an absolute concentration for a rush. He could hear the men talking and he waited, gathering all of himself into this preparation for a charge as soon as the men would come into the grass. As he heard their voices his tail stiffened to twitch up and down, and, as they came into the edge of the grass, he made a coughing grunt and charged.

Kongoni, the old gun-bearer, in the lead watching the blood spoor, Wilson watching the grass for any movement, his big gun ready, the second gun-bearer looking ahead and listening, Macomber close to Wilson, his rifle cocked, they had just moved into the grass when Macomber heard the blood-choked coughing grunt, and saw the swishing rush in the grass. The next thing he knew he was running; running wildly, in panic in the open, running toward the stream.

He heard the *ca-ra-wong!* of Wilson's big rifle, and again in a second crashing *carawong!* and turning saw the lion, horrible-looking now, with half his head seeming to be gone, crawling toward Wilson in the edge of the tall grass while the red-faced man worked the bolt of the short ugly rifle and aimed carefully as another blasting *carawong!* came from the muzzle, and crawling, heavy, yellow bulk of the lion stiffened and the huge, mutilated head slid forward and Macomber, standing by himself in the clearing where he had run, holding a loaded rifle, while two black men and a white man looked back at him in contempt, knew the lion was dead. He came toward Wilson, his tallness all seeming a naked reproach, and Wilson looked at him and said:

"Want to take pictures?"

"No," he said.

That was all any one had said until they reached the motor car. Then Wilson had said:

"Hell of a fine lion. Boys will skin him out. We might as well stay here in the shade."

Macomber's wife had not looked at him nor he at her and he had sat by her in the back seat with Wilson sitting in the front seat. Once he had reached over and taken his wife's hand without looking at her and she had removed her hand from his. Looking across the stream to where the gun-bearers were skinning out the lion he could see that she had been able to see the whole thing. While they sat there his wife had reached forward and put her hand on Wilson's shoulder. He turned and she had leaned forward over the low seat and kissed him on the mouth.

"Oh, I say," said Wilson, going redder than his natural baked color.

"Mr. Robert Wilson," she said. "The beautiful red-faced Mr. Robert Wilson."

Then she sat down beside Macomber again and looked away across the stream to where the lion lay, with uplifted, white-muscled, tendon-marked naked forearms, and white bloating belly, as the black men fleshed away the skin. Finally the gun-bearers brought the skin over, wet and heavy, and climbed in behind with it, rolling it up before they got in, and the motor car started. No one had said anything more until they were back in camp.

That was the story of the lion. Macomber did not know how the lion had felt before he started his rush, nor during it when the unbelievable smash of the .505 with a muzzle velocity of two tons had hit him in the mouth, nor what kept him coming after that, when the second ripping crash had smashed his hind quarters and he had come crawling on toward the crashing, blasting thing that had destroyed him. Wilson knew something about it and only expressed it by saying, "Damned fine lion," but Macomber did not know how Wilson felt about things either. He did not know how his wife felt except that she was through with him.

His wife had been through with him before but it never lasted. He was very wealthy, and would be much wealthier, and he knew she would not leave him ever now. That was one of the few things that he really knew. He knew about that, about motorcycles—that was earliest—about motor cars, about duck-shooting, about fishing, trout, salmon and big-sea, about sex in books, many books, too many books, about all court games, about dogs, not much about horses, about hanging on to his money, about most of the other things his world dealt in, and about his wife not leaving him. His wife had been a great beauty and she was still a great beauty in Africa, but she was not a great enough beauty any more at home to be able to leave him and better herself and she knew it and he knew it. She had missed the chance to leave him and he knew it. If he had been better with women she would probably have started to worry about him getting another new, beautiful wife; but she knew too much about him to worry about him either. Also, he had always had a great tolerance which seemed the nicest thing about him if it were not the most sinister.

All in all they were known as a comparatively happily married couple, one of those whose disruption is often rumored but never occurs, and as the society columnist put it, they were adding more than a spice of *adventure* to their much envied and ever-enduring *Romance* by a *Safari* in what was known as *Darkest Africa* until the Martin Johnsons lighted it on so many silver screens where they were pursuing *Old Simba* the lion, the buffalo, *Tembo* the elephant and as well collecting specimens for the Museum of Natural History.[3] This same columnist had reported them *on the verge* at least three times in the past and they had been. But they always made it up. They had a sound basis of union. Margot was too beautiful for Macomber to divorce her and Macomber had too much money for Margot ever to leave him.

It was now about three o'clock in the morning and Francis Macomber, who had been asleep a little while after he had stopped thinking about the lion, wakened and then slept again, woke suddenly, frightened in a dream of the

---

[3] Martin Johnson (1884–1937) and his wife Osa Johnson (1894–1953) were American explorers who made several feature-length films including *Jungle Adventure* (1921), *Simba* (1928), and *I Married Adventure* (1938).

bloody-headed lion standing over him, and listening while his heart pounded, he realized that his wife was not in the other cot in the tent. He lay awake with that knowledge for two hours.

At the end of that time his wife came into the tent, lifted her mosquito bar and crawled cozily into bed.

"Where have you been?" Macomber asked in the darkness.

"Hello," she said. "Are you awake?"

"Where have you been?"

"I just went out to get a breath of air."

"You did, like hell."

"What do you want me to say, darling?"

"Where have you been?"

"Out to get a breath of air."

"That's a new name for it. You *are* a bitch."

"Well, you're a coward."

"All right," he said. "What of it.?"

"Nothing as far as I'm concerned. But please let's not talk, darling, because I'm very sleepy."

"You think that I'll take anything."

"I know you will, sweet."

"Well, I won't."

"Please, darling, let's not talk. I'm so very sleepy."

"There wasn't going to be any of that. You promised there wouldn't be."

"Well, there is now," she said sweetly.

"You said if we made this trip that there would be none of that. You promised."

"Yes, darling. That's the way I meant it to be. But the trip was spoiled yesterday. We don't have to talk about it, do we?"

"You don't wait long when you have an advantage, do you?"

"Please let's not talk. I'm so sleepy, darling."

"I'm going to talk."

"Don't mind me then, because I'm going to sleep." And she did.

At breakfast they were all three at the table before daylight and Francis Macomber found that, of all the many men that he had hated, he hated Robert Wilson the most.

"Sleep well?" Wilson asked in his throaty voice, filling a pipe.

"Did you?"

"Topping," the white hunter told him.

You bastard, thought Macomber, you insolent bastard.

So she woke him when she came in, Wilson thought, looking at them both with his flat, cold eyes. Well, why doesn't he keep his wife where she belongs? What does he think I am, a bloody plaster saint? Let him keep her where she belongs. It's his own fault.

"Do you think we'll find buffalo?" Margot asked, pushing away a dish of apricots.

"Chance of it," Wilson said and smiled at her. "Why don't you stay in camp?"

"Not for anything," she told him.

"Why not order her to stay in camp?" Wilson said to Macomber.

"You order her," said Macomber coldly.

"Let's not have any ordering, nor," turning to Macomber, "any silliness, Francis," Margot said quite pleasantly.

"Are you ready to start?" Macomber asked.

"Any time," Wilson told him. "Do you want the Memsahib to go?"

"Does it make any difference whether I do or not?"

The hell with it, thought Robert Wilson. The utter complete hell with it. So this is what it's going to be like. Well, this is what it's going to be like, then.

"Makes no difference," he said.

"You're sure you wouldn't like to stay in camp with her yourself and let me go out and hunt the buffalo?" Macomber asked.

"Can't do that," said Wilson. "Wouldn't talk rot if I were you."

"I'm not talking rot. I'm disgusted."

"Bad word, disgusted."

"Francis, will you please try to speak sensibly?" his wife said.

"I speak too damned sensibly," Macomber said. "Did you ever eat such filthy food?"

"Something wrong with the food?" asked Wilson quietly.

"No more than with everything else."

"I'd pull yourself together, laddybuck," Wilson said very quietly. "There's a boy waits at table that understands a little English."

"The hell with him."

Wilson stood up and puffing on his pipe strolled away, speaking a few words in Swahili to one of the gun-bearers who was standing waiting for him. Macomber and his wife sat on at the table. He was staring at his coffee cup.

"If you make a scene I'll leave you, darling," Margot said quietly.

"No, you won't."

"You can try it and see."

"You won't leave me."

"No," she said. "I won't leave you and you'll behave yourself."

"Behave myself? That's a way to talk. Behave myself."

"Yes. Behave yourself."

"Why don't *you* try behaving?"

"I've tried it so long. So very long."

"I hate that red-faced swine," Macomber said. "I loathe the sight of him."

"He's really *very* nice."

"Oh, *shut up*," Macomber almost shouted. Just then the car came up and stopped in front of the dining tent and the driver and the two gun-bearers got out. Wilson walked over and looked at the husband and wife sitting there at the table.

"Going shooting?" he asked.

"Yes," said Macomber, standing up. "Yes."

"Better bring a woolly. It will be cool in the car," Wilson said.

"I'll get my leather jacket," Margot said.

"The boy has it," Wilson told her. He climbed into the front with the driver and Francis Macomber and his wife sat, not speaking, in the back seat.

Hope the silly beggar doesn't take a notion to blow the back of my head off, Wilson thought to himself. Women *are* a nuisance on safari.

The car was grinding down to cross the river at a pebbly ford in the gray daylight and then climbed, angling up the steep bank, where Wilson had ordered a way shovelled out the day before so they could reach the parklike wooded rolling country on the far side.

It was a good morning, Wilson thought. There was a heavy dew and as the wheels went through the grass and low bushes he could smell the odor of the crushed fronds. It was an odor like verbena and he liked this early morning smell of the dew, the crushed bracken and the look of the tree trunks showing black through the early morning mist, as the car made its way through the untracked, parklike country. He had put the two in the back seat out of his mind now and was thinking about buffalo. The buffalo that he was after stayed in the daytime in a thick swamp where it was impossible to get a shot, but in the night they fed out into an open stretch of country and if he could come between them and their swamp with the car, Macomber would have a good chance at them in the open. He did not want to hunt buff with Macomber in thick cover. He did not want to hunt buff or anything else with Macomber at all, but he was a professional hunter and he had hunted with some rare ones in his time. If they got buff today there would only be rhino to come and the poor man would have gone through his dangerous game and things might pick up. He'd have nothing more to do with the woman and Macomber would get over that too. He must have gone through plenty of that before by the look of things. Poor beggar. He must have a way of getting over it. Well, it was the poor sod's own bloody fault.

He, Robert Wilson, carried a double size cot on safari to accommodate any windfalls he might receive. He had hunted for a certain clientele, the international, fast, sporting set, where the women did not feel they were getting their money's worth unless they had shared that cot with the white hunter. He despised them when he was away from them although he liked some of them well enough at the time, but he made his living by them; and their standards were his standards as long as they were hiring him.

They were his standards in all except the shooting. He had his own standards about the killing and they could live up to them or get some one else to hunt them. He knew, too, that they all respected him for this. This Macomber was an odd one though. Damned if he wasn't. Now the wife. Well, the wife. Yes, the wife. Hm, the wife. Well he'd dropped all that. He looked around at them. Macomber sat grim and furious. Margot smiled at him. She looked younger today, more innocent and fresher and not so professionally beautiful. What's in her heart God knows, Wilson thought. She hadn't talked much last night. At that it was a pleasure to see her.

The motor car climbed up a slight rise and went on through the trees and then out into a grassy prairie-like opening and kept in the shelter of the trees along the edge, the driver going slowly and Wilson looking carefully out across the prairie and all along its far side. He stopped the car and studied the opening with his field glasses. Then he motioned to the driver to go on and the car moved slowly along, the driver avoiding wart-hog holes and driving around the mud castles ants had built. Then, looking across the opening, Wilson suddenly turned and said,

"By God, there they are!"

And looking where he pointed, while the car jumped forward and Wilson spoke in rapid Swahili to the driver, Macomber saw three huge, black animals looking almost cylindrical in their long heaviness, like big black tank cars, moving at a gallop across the far edge of the open prairie. They moved at a stiff-necked, stiff bodied gallop and he could see the upswept wide black horns on their heads as they galloped heads out; the heads not moving.

"They're three old bulls," Wilson said. "We'll cut them off before they get to the swamp."

The car was going a wild forty-five miles an hour across the open and as Macomber watched, the buffalo got bigger and bigger until he could see the gray, hairless, scabby look of one huge bull and how his neck was a part of his shoulders and the shiny black of his horns as he galloped a little behind the others that were strung out in that steady plunging gait; and then, the car swaying as though it had just jumped a road, they drew up close and he could see the plunging hugeness of the bull, and the dust in his sparsely haired hide, the side boss of horn and his outstretched, wide-nostrilled muzzle, and he was raising his rifle when Wilson shouted, "Not from the car, you fool!" and he had no fear, only hatred of Wilson, while the brakes clamped on and the car skidded, plowing sideways to an almost stop and Wilson was out on one side and he on the other, stumbling as his feet hit the still speeding-by of the earth, and then he was shooting at the bull as he moved away, hearing the bullets whunk into him, emptying his rifle at him as he moved steadily away, finally remembering to get his shots forward into the shoulder, and as he fumbled to re-load, he saw the bull was down. Down on his knees, his big head tossing, and seeing the other two still galloping he shot at the leader and hit him. He shot again and missed and heard the *carowonging* roar as Wilson shot and saw the leading bull slide forward onto his nose.

"Get the other," Wilson said. "Now you're shooting!"

But the other bull was moving steadily at the same gallop and he missed, throwing a spout of dirt, and Wilson missed and the dust rose in a cloud and Wilson shouted, "Come on. He's too far!" and grabbed his arm and they were in the car again, Macomber and Wilson hanging on the sides and rocketing swayingly over the uneven ground, drawing up on the steady, plunging, heavy-necked, straight-moving gallop of the bull.

They were behind him and Macomber was filling his rifle, dropping shells onto the ground, jamming it, clearing the jam, then they were almost up with the bull when Wilson yelled "Stop," and the car skidded so that it almost swung over and Macomber fell forward onto his feet, slammed his bolt forward and fired as far forward as he could aim into the galloping, rounded black back, aimed and shot again, then again, then again, and the bullets, all of them hitting had no effect on the buffalo that he could see. Then Wilson shot, the roar deafening him, and he could see the bull stagger. Macomber shot again, aiming carefully, and down he came, onto his knees.

"All right," Wilson said. "Nice work. That's the three."

Macomber felt a drunken elation.

"How many times did you shoot?" he asked.

"Just three," Wilson said. "You killed the first bull. The biggest one. I helped you finish the other two. Afraid they might have got into cover. You had them killed. I was just mopping up a little. You shot damn well."

"Let's go to the car," said Macomber." I want a drink."

"Got to finish off that buff first," Wilson told him. The buffalo was on his knees and he jerked his head furiously and bellowed in pigeyed, roaring rage as they came toward him.

"Watch he doesn't get up," Wilson said. Then, "Get a little broadside and take him in the neck just behind the ear."

Macomber aimed carefully at the center of the huge, jerking, rage-driven neck and shot. At the shot the head dropped forward.

"That does it," said Wilson. "Got the spine. They're a hell of a looking thing, aren't they?"

"Let's get the drink," said Macomber. In his life he had never felt so good.

In the car Macomber's wife sat very white faced. "You were marvellous, darling," she said to Macomber. "What a ride."

"Was it rough?" Wilson asked.

"It was frightful. I've never been more frightened in my life."

"Let's all have a drink," Macomber said.

"By all means," said Wilson. "Give it to the Memsahib." She drank the neat whisky from the flask and shuddered a little when she swallowed. She handed the flask to Macomber who handed it to Wilson.

"It was frightfully exciting," she said. "It's given me a dreadful headache. I didn't know you were allowed to shoot them from cars though."

"No one shot from cars," said Wilson coldly.

"I mean chase them from cars."

"Wouldn't ordinarily," Wilson said. "Seemed sporting enough to me though while we were doing it. Taking more chance driving that way across the plain full of holes and one thing and another than hunting on foot. Buffalo could have charged us each time we shot if he liked. Gave him every chance. Wouldn't mention it to any one though. It's illegal if that's what you mean."

"It seemed very unfair to me," Margot said, "chasing those big helpless things in a motor car."

"Did it?" said Wilson.

"What would happen if they heard about it in Nairobi?"[4]

---

[4] Nairobi is the capital of Kenya.

"I'd lose my license for one thing. Other unpleasantnesses," Wilson said, taking a drink from the flask. "I'd be out of business."

"Really?"

"Yes, really."

"Well," said Macomber, and he smiled for the first time all day. "Now she has something on you."

"You have such a pretty way of putting things, Francis," Margot Macomber said. Wilson looked at them both. If a four-letter man marries a five-letter woman, he was thinking, what number of letters would their children be? What he said was, "We lost a gun-bearer. Did you notice it?"

"My God, no," Macomber said.

"Here he comes," Wilson said. "He's all right. He must have fallen off when we left the first bull."

Approaching them was the middle-aged gun-bearer, limping along in his knitted cap, khaki tunic, shorts and rubber sandals, gloomy-faced and disgusted looking. As he came up he called out to Wilson in Swahili and they all saw the change in the white hunter's face.

"What does he say?" asked Margot.

"He says the first bull got up and went into the bush," Wilson said with no expression in his voice.

"Oh, said Macomber blankly.

"Then it's going to be just like the lion," said Margot, full of anticipation.

"It's not going to be a damned bit like the lion," Wilson told her. "Did you want another drink, Macomber?"

"Thanks, yes," Macomber said. He expected the feeling he had had about the lion to come back but it did not. For the first time in his life he really felt wholly without fear. Instead of fear he had a feeling of definite elation.

"We'll go and have a look at the second bull," Wilson said. "I'll tell the driver to put the car in the shade."

"What are you going to do?" asked Margaret Macomber.

"Take a look at the buff," Wilson said.

"I'll come."

"Come along."

The three of them walked over to where the second buffalo bulked blackly in the open, head forward on the grass, the massive horns swung wide.

"He's a very good head," Wilson said. "That's close to a fifty-inch spread."

Macomber was looking at him with delight.

"He's hateful looking," said Margot. "Can't we go into the shade?"

"Of course," Wilson said. "Look," he said to Macomber, and pointed. "See that patch of bush?"

"Yes."

"That's where the first bull went in. The gun-bearer said when he fell off the bull was down. He was watching us helling along and the other two buff galloping. When he looked up there was the bull up and looking at him. Gun-bearer ran like hell and the bull went off slowly into that bush."

"Can we go in after him now?" asked Macomber eagerly.

Wilson looked at him appraisingly. Damned if this isn't a strange one, he thought. Yesterday he's scared sick and today he's a ruddy fire eater.

"No, we'll give him a while."

"Let's please go into the shade," Margot said. Her face was white and she looked ill.

They made their way to the car where it stood under a single, wide-spreading tree and all climbed in.

"Chances are he's dead in there," Wilson remarked. "After a little we'll have a look."

Macomber felt a wild unreasonable happiness that he had never known before.

"By God, that was a chase," he said. "I've never felt any such feeling. Wasn't it marvellous, Margot?"

"I hated it."

"Why?"

"I hated it," she said bitterly. "I loathed it."

"You know I don't think I'd ever be afraid of anything again," Macomber said to Wilson. "Something happened in me after we first saw the buff and started after him. Like a dam bursting. It was pure excitement."

"Cleans out your liver," said Wilson. "Damn funny things happen to people."

Macomber's face was shining. "You know something did happen to me," he said. "I feel absolutely different."

His wife said nothing and eyed him strangely. She was sitting far back in the seat and Macomber was sitting forward talking to Wilson who turned sideways talking over the back of the front seat.

"You know, I'd like to try another lion," Macomber said. "I'm really not afraid of them now. After all, what can they do to you?"

"That's it," said Wilson. "Worst one can do is kill you. How does it go? Shakespeare. Damned good. See if I can remember. Oh, damned good. Used to quote it to myself at one time. Let's see. 'By my troth, I care not; a man can die but once; we owe God a death and let it go which way it will he that dies this year is quit for the next. Damned fine, eh?"[5]

He was very embarrassed, having brought out this thing he had lived by, but he had seen men come of age before and it always moved him. It was not a matter of their twenty-first birthday.

It had taken a strange chance of hunting, a sudden precipitation into action without opportunity for worrying beforehand, to bring this about with Macomber, but regardless of how it had happened it had most certainly happened. Look at the beggar now, Wilson thought. It's that some of them stay little boys so long, Wilson thought. Sometimes all their lives. Their figures stay boyish when they're fifty. The great American boy-men. Damned strange people. But he

---

[5] The speech is from *King Henry IV*, Part II, Act III, Scene 2. The entire speech runs: "By my troth, I care not; a man can die but once; we owe God a death. I'll not bear a base mind. An't be my destiny, so; an't be not, so. No Man's too good to serve's Prince; and let it go which way it will, he that dies this year is quit for the rest."

liked this Macomber now. Damned strange fellow. Probably meant the end of cuckoldry too. Well, that would be a damned good thing. Damned good thing. Beggar had probably been afraid all his life. Don't know what started it. But over now. Hadn't had time to be afraid with the buff. That and being angry too. Motor car too. Motor cars made it familiar. Be a damn fire eater now. He'd seen it in the war work the same way. More of a change than any loss of virginity. Fear gone like an operation. Something else grew in its place. Main thing a man had. Made him into a man. Women knew it too. No bloody fear.

From the far corner of the seat Margaret Macomber looked at the two of them. There was no change in Wilson. She saw Wilson as she had seen him the day before when she had first realized what his great talent was. But she saw the change in Francis Macomber now.

"Do you have that feeling of happiness about what's going to happen?" Macomber asked, still exploring his new wealth.

"You're not supposed to mention it," Wilson said, looking in the other's face. "Much more fashionable to say you're scared. Mind you, you'll be scared too, plenty of times."

"But you *have* a feeling of happiness about action to come?"

"Yes," said Wilson. "There's that. Doesn't do to talk too much about all this. Talk the whole thing away. No pleasure in anything if you mouth it up too much."

"You're both talking rot," said Margot. "Just because you've chased some helpless animals in a motor car you talk like heroes."

"Sorry," said Wilson. "I have been gassing too much." She's worried about it already, he thought.

"If you don't know what we're talking about why not keep out of it?" Macomber asked his wife.

"You've gotten awfully brave, awfully suddenly," his wife said contemptuously, but her contempt was not secure. She was very afraid of something.

Macomber laughed, a very natural hearty laugh. "You know I *have*," he said. "I really have."

"Isn't it sort of late?" Margot said bitterly. Because she had done the best she could for many years back and the way they were together now was no one person's fault.

"Not for me," said Macomber.

Margot said nothing but sat back in the corner of the seat.

"Do you think we've given him time enough?" Macomber asked Wilson cheerfully.

"We might have a look," Wilson said. "Have you any solids left?"

"The gun-bearer has some."

Wilson called in Swahili and the older gun-bearer, who was skinning out one of the heads, straightened up, pulled a box of solids out of his pocket and brought them over to Macomber, who filled his magazine and put the remaining shells in his pocket.

"You might as well shoot the Springfield," Wilson said. "You're used to it.

We'll leave the Mannlicher in the car with the Memsahib. Your gun-bearer can carry your heavy gun. I've this damned cannon. Now let me tell you about them." He had saved this until the last because he did not want to worry Macomber. "When a buff comes he comes with his head high and thrust straight out. The boss of the horns covers any sort of a brain shot. The only shot is straight into the nose. The only other shot is into his chest or, if you're to one side, into the neck or the shoulders. After they've been hit once they take a hell of a lot of killing. Don't try anything fancy. Take the easiest shot there is. They've finished skinning out that head now. Should we get started."

He called to the gun-bearers, who came up wiping their hands, and the older one got into the back.

"I'll only take Kongoni," Wilson said. "The other can watch to keep the birds away."

As the car moved slowly across the open space toward the island of brushy trees that ran in a tongue of foliage along a dry water course that cut the open swale, Macomber felt his heart pounding and his mouth was dry again, but it was excitement, not fear.

"Here's where he went in," Wilson said. Then to the gun-bearer in Swahili, "Take the blood spoor."

The car was parallel to the patch of bush. Macomber, Wilson and the gun-bearer got down. Macomber, looking back, saw his wife, with the rifle by her side, looking at him. He waved to her and she did not wave back.

The brush was very thick ahead and the ground was dry. The middle-aged gun-bearer was sweating heavily and Wilson had his hat down over his eyes and his red neck showed just ahead of Macomber. Suddenly the gun-bearer said something in Swahili to Wilson and ran forward.

"He's dead in there," Wilson said. "Good work," and he turned to grip Macomber's hand and as they shook hands, grinning at each other, the gun-bearer shouted wildly and they saw him coming out of the brush sideways, fast as a crab, and the bull coming, nose out, mouth tight closed, blood dripping, massive head straight out, coming in a charge, his little pig eyes bloodshot as he looked at them. Wilson, who was ahead was kneeling shooting, and Macomber, as he fired, unhearing his shot in the roaring of Wilson's gun, saw fragments like slate burst from the huge boss of the horns, and the head jerked, he shot again at the wide nostrils and saw the horns jolt again and fragments fly, and he did not see Wilson now and, aiming carefully, shot again with the buffalo's huge bulk almost on him and his rifle almost level with the on-coming head, nose out, and he could see the little wicked eyes and the head started to lower and he felt a sudden white-hot, blinding flash explode inside his head and that was all he ever felt.

Wilson had ducked to one side to get in a shoulder shot. Macomber had stood solid and shot for the nose, shooting a touch high each time and hitting the heavy horns, splintering and chipping them like hitting a slate roof, and Mrs. Macomber, in the car, had shot at the buffalo with the 6.5 Mannlicher as it seemed about to gore Macomber and had hit her husband about two inches up and a little to one side of the base of his skull.

Francis Macomber lay now, face down, not two yards from where the buffalo lay on his side and his wife knelt over him with Wilson beside her.

"I wouldn't turn him over, Wilson said.

The woman was crying hysterically.

"I'd get back in the car," Wilson said. "Where's the rifle?"

She shook her head, her face contorted. The gun-bearer picked up the rifle.

"Leave it as it is," said Wilson. Then, "Go get Abdulla so that he may witness the manner of the accident."

He knelt down, took a handkerchief from his pocket, and spread it over Francis Macomber's crew-cropped head where it lay. The blood sank into the dry, loose earth.

Wilson stood up and saw the buffalo on his side, his legs out, his thinly-haired belly crawling with ticks. "Hell of a good bull," his brain registered automatically. "A good fifty inches, or better. Better." He called to the driver and told him to spread a blanket over the body and stay by it. Then he walked over to the motor car where the woman sat crying in the corner.

"That was a pretty thing to do," he said in a toneless voice. "He *would* have left you too."

"Stop it," she said.

"Of course it's an accident," he said. "I know that."

"Stop it," she said.

"Don't worry," he said. "There will be a certain amount of unpleasantness but I will have some photographs taken that will be very useful at the inquest. There's the testimony of the gun-bearers and the driver too. You're perfectly all right."

"Stop it," she said.

"There's a hell of a lot to be done," he said. "And I'll have to send a truck off to the lake to wireless for a plane to take the three of us into Nairobi. Why didn't you poison him? That's what they do in England."

"Stop it. Stop it. Stop it," the woman cried.

Wilson looked at her with his flat blue eyes.

"I'm through now," he said. "I was a little angry. I'd begun to like your husband."

"Oh, please stop it," she said. "Please, please stop it."

"That's better," Wilson said. "Please is much better. Now I'll stop."

FRANZ KAFKA (1883-1924)

A Hunger Artist

During these last decades the interest in professional fasting has markedly diminished. It used to pay very well to stage such great performances under one's own management, but today that is quite impossible. We live in a different world now. At one time the whole town took a lively interest in the hunger artist; from day to day of his fast the excitement mounted; everybody wanted to see him at least once a day; there were people who bought season tickets for the last few days and sat from morning till night in front of his small barred cage; even in the nighttime there were visiting hours, when the whole effect was heightened by torch flares; on fine days the cage was set out in the open air, and then it was the children's special treat to see the hunger artist; for their elders he was often just a joke that happened to be in fashion, but the children stood open-mouthed, holding each other's hands for greater security, marvelling at him as he sat there pallid in black tights, with his ribs sticking out so prominently, not even on a seat but down among straw on the ground, sometimes giving a courteous nod, answering questions with a constrained smile, or perhaps stretching an arm through the bars so that one might feel how thin it was, and then again withdrawing deep into himself, paying no attention to anyone or anything, not even to the all-important striking of the clock that was the only piece of furniture in his cage, but merely staring into vacancy with half-shut eyes, now and then taking a sip from a tiny glass of water to moisten his lips.

Besides casual onlookers there were also relays of permanent watchers selected by the public, usually butchers, strangely enough, and it was their task to watch the hunger artist day and night, three of them at a time, in case he should have some secret recourse to nourishment. This was nothing but a formality, instituted to reassure the masses, for the initiates knew well enough that during his fast the artist would never in any circumstances, not even under forcible compulsion, swallow the smallest morsel of food; the honor of his profession forbade it. Not every watcher, of course, was capable of understanding this; there were often groups of night watchers who were very lax in carrying out their duties and deliberately huddled together in a retired corner to play cards with great absorption, obviously intending to give the hunger artist the chance of a little refreshment, which they supposed he could draw from some private hoard. Nothing annoyed the artist more than such watchers; they made him miserable; they made his fast seem unendurable; sometimes he mastered his feebleness sufficiently to sing during their watch for as long as he could keep going, to show them how unjust their suspicions were. But that was of little use; they only wondered at his cleverness in being able to fill his mouth even while singing. Much more to his taste were the watchers who sat close up to the bars, who were not content with the dim night lighting of the hall but focused him in the full glare of the electric pocket torch given them by the impresario. The harsh light did not trouble him at all, in any case he could never sleep properly, and he could always drowse a little, whatever the light, at any hour, even when the hall was thronged with noisy onlookers. He was quite happy at the prospect of spending a sleepless night with such watchers; he was ready to exchange jokes with them, to tell them stories out of his nomadic life, anything at all to keep them awake and demonstrate to them again that he had no eatables in his cage and that he was fasting as not one of them could fast. But his happiest moment was when the morning came and an enormous breakfast was brought them, at his expense, on which they flung themselves with the keen appetite of healthy men after a weary night of wakefulness. Of course there were people who argued that this breakfast was an unfair attempt to bribe the watchers, but that was going rather too far, and when they were invited to take on a night's vigil without a breakfast, merely for the sake of the cause, they made themselves scarce, although they stuck stubbornly to their suspicions.

Such suspicions, anyhow, were a necessary accompaniment to the profession of fasting. No one could possibly watch the hunger artist continuously, day and night, and so no one could produce first-hand evidence that the fast had really been rigorous and continuous; only the artist himself could know that; he was therefore bound to be the sole completely satisfied spectator of his own fast. Yet for other reasons he was never satisfied; it was not perhaps mere fasting that had brought him to such skeleton thinness that many people had regretfully to keep away from his exhibitions, because the sight of him was too much for them, perhaps it was dissatisfaction with himself that had worn him down. For he alone knew, what no other initiate knew, how easy it was to fast. It was the easiest thing in the world. He made no secret of this, yet people did not believe him, at the best they set him down as modest, most of them, however, thought he was out for publicity or else was some kind of cheat who found it easy to fast because he had discovered a way of making it easy, and then had the impudence to admit the fact, more or less. He had to put up with all that, and in the course of time had got used to it, but his inner dissatisfaction always rankled, and never yet, after any term of fasting—this must be granted to his credit—had he left the cage of his own free will. The longest period of fasting was fixed by his impresario at forty days, beyond that term he was not allowed to go, not even in great cities, and there was good reason for it, too. Experience had proved that for about forty days the interest of the public could be stimulated by a steadily increasing pressure of advertisement, but after that the town began to lose interest, sympathetic support began notably to fall off; there were of course local variations as between one town and another or one country and another, but as a general rule forty days marked the limit. So on the fortieth day the flower-bedecked cage was opened, enthusiastic spectators filled the hall, a military band played, two doctors entered the cage to measure the results of the fast, which were announced through a megaphone, and finally two young ladies appeared, blissful at having been selected for the honor, to help the hunger artist down the few steps leading to a small table on which was spread a carefully chosen invalid repast. And at this very moment the artist always turned stubborn. True, he would entrust his bony arms to the outstretched helping hands of the ladies bending over him, but stand up he would not. Why stop fasting at this particular moment, after forty days of it? He had held out for a long time, an illimitably long time; why stop now, when he was in his best fasting form, or rather, not yet quite in his best fasting form? Why should he be cheated of the fame he would get for fasting longer, for being not only the record hunger artist of all time, which presumably he was already, but for beating his own record by a performance beyond human imagination, since he felt that there were no limits to his capacity for fasting? His public pretended to admire him so much, why should it have so little patience with him; if he could endure fasting longer, why shouldn't the public endure it? Besides, he was tired, he was comfortable sitting in the straw, and now he was supposed to lift himself to his full height and go down to a meal the very thought of which gave him a nausea that only the presence of the ladies kept him from betraying, and even that with an effort. And he looked up into the eyes of the ladies who were apparently so friendly and in reality so cruel, and shook his head, which felt too heavy on its strengthless neck. But then there happened yet again what always happened. The impresario came forward, without a word—for the band made speech impossible—lifted his arms in the air above the artist, as if inviting Heaven to look down upon its creature here in the straw, this suffering martyr, which indeed he was, although in quite another sense; grasped him round the emaciated waist, with exaggerated caution, so that the frail condition he was in might be appreciated; and committed him to the care of the blenching[1] ladies, not without secretly giving him a shaking so that his legs and body tottered and swayed. The artist now submitted completely; his head lolled on his breast as if it had landed there by chance; his body was hollowed out; his legs in a spasm of self-preservation clung close to each other at the knees, yet scraped on the ground as if it were not really solid ground, as if they were only trying to find solid ground; and the whole weight of his body, a featherweight after all, relapsed onto one of the ladies, who, looking round for help and panting a little—this post of honor was not at all what she had expected it to be—first stretched her neck as far as she could to keep her face at least free from contact with the artist, then finding this impossible, and her more fortunate companion not coming to her aid but merely holding extended on her own trembling hand the little bunch of knucklebones that was the artist's, to the great delight of the spectators, burst into tears and had to be replaced by an attendant who had long been stationed in readiness. Then came the food, a little of which the impresario managed to get between the artist's lips, while he sat in a kind of half-fainting trance, to the accompaniment of cheerful patter designed to distract the public's attention from the artist's condition; after that, a toast was drunk to the public, supposedly prompted by a whisper from the artist in the impresario's ear; the band confirmed it with a mighty flourish, the spectators melted away, and no one had any cause to be dissatisfied with the proceedings, no one except the hunger artist himself, he only, as always.

So he lived for many years, with small regular intervals of recuperation, in visible glory, honored by the world, yet in spite of that troubled in spirit, and all the more troubled because no one would take his trouble seriously. What comfort could he possibly need? What more could he possibly wish for? And if some good-natured person, feeling sorry for him, tried to console him by pointing out that his melancholy was probably caused by fasting, it could happen, especially when he had been fasting for some time, that he reacted with an outburst of fury and to the general alarm began to shake the bars of his cage like a wild animal. Yet the impresario had a way of punishing these outbreaks which he

---

[1] Blenching is to turn away in cowardice, to flinch. It also suggests the pale color (the blanched color) that sometimes appears in the faces of frightened people.

rather enjoyed putting into operation. He would apologize publicly for the artist's behavior, which was only to be excused, he admitted, because of the irritability caused by fasting; a condition hardly to be understood by well-fed people; then by natural transition he went on to mention the artist's equally incomprehensible boast that he could fast for much longer than he was doing; he praised the high ambition, the good will, the great self-denial undoubtedly implicit in such a statement; and then quite simply countered it by bringing out photographs, which were also on sale to the public, showing the artist on the fortieth day of a fast lying in bed almost dead from exhaustion. This perversion of the truth, familiar to the artist though it was, always unnerved him afresh and proved too much for him. What was a consequence of the premature ending of his fast was here presented as the cause of it! To fight against this lack of understanding, against a whole world of non-understanding, was impossible. Time and again in good faith he stood by the bars listening to the impresario, but as soon as the photographs appeared he always let go and sank with a groan back on to his straw, and the reassured public could once more come close and gaze at him.

A few years later when the witnesses of such scenes called them to mind, they often failed to understand themselves at all. For meanwhile the aforementioned change in public interest had set in; it seemed to happen almost overnight; there may have been profound causes for it, but who was going to bother about that; at any rate the pampered hunger artist suddenly found himself deserted one fine day by the amusement seekers, who went streaming past him to other more favored attractions. For the last time the impresario hurried him over half Europe to discover whether the old interest might still survive here and there; all in vain; everywhere, as if by secret agreement, a positive revulsion from professional fasting was in evidence. Of course it could not really have sprung up so suddenly as all that, and many premonitory symptoms which had not been sufficiently remarked or suppressed during the rush and glitter of success now came retrospectively to mind, but it was now too late to take any countermeasures. Fasting would surely come into fashion again at some future date, yet that was no comfort for those living in the present. What, then, was the hunger artist to do? He had been applauded by thousands in his time and could hardly come down to showing himself in a street booth at village fairs, and as for adopting another profession, he was not only too old for that but too fanatically devoted to fasting. So he took leave of the impresario, his partner in an unparalleled career, and hired himself to a large circus; in order to spare his own feelings he avoided reading the conditions of his contract.

A large circus with its enormous traffic in replacing and recruiting men, animals and apparatus can always find a use for people at any time, even for a hunger artist, provided of course that he does not ask too much, and in this particular case anyhow it was not only the artist who was taken on but his famous and long-known name as well; indeed considering the peculiar nature of his performance, which was not impaired by advancing age, it could not be objected that here was an artist past his prime, no longer at the height of his professional skill, seeking a refuge in some quiet corner of a circus; on the contrary, the hunger artist averred that he could fast as well as ever, which was entirely credible; he even alleged that if he were allowed to fast as he liked, and this was at once promised him without more ado, he could astound the world by establishing a record never yet achieved, a statement which certainly provoked a smile among the other professionals, since it left out of account the change in public opinion, which the hunger artist in his zeal conveniently forgot.

He had not, however, actually lost his sense of the real situation and took it as a matter of course that he and his cage should be stationed, not in the middle of the ring as a main attraction, but outside, near the animal cages, on a site that was after all easily accessible. Large and gaily painted placards made a frame for the cage and announced what was to be seen inside it. When the public came thronging out in the intervals to see the animals, they could hardly avoid passing the hunger artist's cage and stopping there for a moment, perhaps they might even have stayed longer had not those pressing behind them in the narrow gangway, who did not understand why they should be held up on their way toward the excitements of the menagerie, made it impossible for anyone to stand gazing quietly for any length of time. And that was the reason why the hunger artist, who had of course been looking forward to these visiting hours as the main achievement of his life, began instead to shrink from them. At first he could hardly wait for the intervals; it was exhilarating to watch the crowds come streaming his way, until only too soon—not even the most obstinate self-deception, clung to almost consciously, could hold out against the fact—the conviction was borne in upon him that these people, most of them, to judge from their actions, again and again, without exception, were all on their way to the menagerie. And the first sight of them from the distance remained the best. For when they reached his cage he was at once deafened by the storm of shouting and abuse that arose from the two contending factions, which renewed themselves continuously, of those who wanted to stop and stare at him—he soon began to dislike them more than the others—not out of real interest but only out of obstinate self-assertiveness, and those who wanted to go straight on to the animals. When the first great rush was past, the stragglers came along, and these, whom nothing could have prevented from stopping to look at him as long as they had breath, raced past with long strides, hardly even glancing at him, in their haste to get to the menagerie in time. And all too rarely did it happen that he had a stroke of luck, when some father of a family fetched up before him with his children, pointed a finger at the hunger artist and explained at length what the phenomenon meant, telling stories of earlier years when he himself had watched similar but much more thrilling performances, and the children, still rather uncomprehending, since neither inside nor outside school had they been sufficiently prepared for this lesson—what did they care about fasting?—yet showed by the brightness of their intent eyes that new and better times might be coming. Perhaps, said the hunger artist to himself many a time, things would be a little better if his cage were set not quite so near the menagerie. That made it too easy for people to make their choice, to say nothing of what he suffered from the stench of the menagerie, the animals' restlessness by night, the carrying past of raw lumps of flesh for the beasts of prey, the roaring at feeding times, which depressed him continually. But he did not dare to lodge a complaint with the management; after all, he had the animals to thank for the troops of people who passed his cage, among whom there might always be one here and there to take an interest in him, and who could tell where they might seclude him if he called attention to his existence and thereby to the fact that, strictly speaking, he was only an impediment on the way to the menagerie.

A small impediment, to be sure, one that grew steadily less. People grew familiar with the strange idea that they could be expected, in times like these, to take an interest in a hunger artist, and with this familiarity the verdict went out against him. He might fast as much as he could, and he did so; but nothing could save him now, people passed him by. Just try to explain to anyone the art of fasting! Anyone who has no feeling for it cannot be made to understand it. The fine placards grew dirty and illegible, they were torn down; the little notice board telling the number of fast days achieved, which at first was changed carefully every day, had long stayed at the same figure, for after the first few weeks even this small task seemed pointless to the staff; and so the artist simply fasted on and on, as he had once dreamed of doing, and it was no trouble to him, just as he had always foretold, but no one counted the days, no one, not even the artist himself, knew what records he was already breaking, and his heart grew heavy. And when once in a time some leisurely passerby stopped, made merry over the old figure on the board and spoke of swindling, that was in its way the stupidest lie ever invented by indifference and inborn malice, since it was not the hunger artist who was cheating; he was working honestly, but the world was cheating him of his reward.

Many more days went by, however, and that too came to an end. An overseer's eye fell on the cage one day and he asked the attendants why this perfectly good cage should be left standing there unused with dirty straw inside it; nobody knew, until one man, helped out by the notice board, remembered about the hunger artist. They poked into the straw with sticks and found him in it. "Are you still fasting?" asked the overseer. "When on earth do you mean to stop?" "Forgive me, everybody," whispered the hunger artist; only the overseer, who had his ear to the bars, understood him. "Of course," said the overseer, and tapped his forehead with a finger to let the attendants know what state the man was in, "we forgive you." "I always wanted you to admire my fasting," said the hunger artist. "We do admire it," said the overseer, affably. "But you shouldn't admire it," said the hunger artist. "Well, then we don't admire it," said the overseer, "but why shouldn't we admire it?" "Because I have to fast, I can't help it," said the hunger artist. "What a fellow you are," said the overseer, "and why can't you help it?" "Because," said the hunger artist, lifting his head a little and speaking, with his lips pursed, as if for a kiss, right into the overseer's ear, so that no syllable might be lost, "because I couldn't find the food I liked. If I had found it, believe me, I should have made no fuss and stuffed myself like you or anyone else." These were his last words, but in his dimming eyes remained the firm though no longer proud persuasion that he was still continuing to fast.

"Well, clear this out now!" said the overseer, and they buried the hunger artist, straw and all. Into the cage they put a young panther. Even the most insensitive felt it refreshing to see this wild creature leaping around the cage that had so long been dreary. The panther was all right. The food he liked was brought him without hesitation by the attendants; he seemed not even to miss his freedom; his noble body, furnished almost to the bursting point with all that it needed, seemed to carry freedom around with it too; somewhere in his jaws it seemed to lurk; and the joy of life streamed with such ardent passion from his throat that for the onlookers it was not easy to stand the shock of it. but they braced themselves, crowded round the cage, and did not want ever to move away.

FLANNERY O'CONNOR (1925–1964)

Everything That Rises Must Converge

Her doctor had told Julian's mother that she must lose twenty pounds on account of her blood pressure, so on Wednesday nights Julian had to take her downtown on the bus for a reducing class at the Y. The reducing class was designed for working girls over fifty, who weighed from 165 to 200 pounds. His mother was one of the slimmer ones, but she said ladies did not tell their age or weight. She would not ride the buses by herself at night since they had been integrated, and because the reducing class was one of her few pleasures, necessary for her health, and *free*, she said Julian could at least put himself out to take her, considering all she did for him. Julian did not like to consider all she did for him, but every Wednesday night he braced himself and took her.

She was almost ready to go, standing before the hall mirror, putting on her hat, while he, his hands behind him, appeared pinned to the door frame, waiting like Saint Sebastian for the arrows to begin piercing him.[1] The hat was new and had cost her seven dollars and a half. She kept saying, "Maybe I shouldn't have paid that for it. No, I shouldn't have. I'll take it off and return it tomorrow. I shouldn't have bought it."

Julian raised his eyes to heaven. "Yes, you should have bought it," he said. "Put it on and let's go." It was a hideous hat. A purple velvet flap came down on one side of it and stood up on the other; the rest of it was green and looked like a cushion with the stuffing out. He decided it was less comical than jaunty and pathetic. Everything that gave her pleasure was small and depressed him.

She lifted the hat one more time and set it down slowly on top of her head. Two wings of gray hair protruded on either side of her florid face, but her eyes, sky-blue, were as innocent and untouched by experience as they must have been when she was ten. Were it not that she was a widow who had struggled fiercely to feed and clothe and put him through school and who was supporting him

---

[1] St. Sebastian was an early Christian martyr. According to legend, Sebastian was an army officer condemned for his faith to be pierced with arrows shot by his fellow soldiers.

still, "until he got on his feet," she might have been a little girl that he had to take to town.

"It's all right, it's all right," he said. "Let's go." He opened the door himself and started down the walk to get her going. The sky was a dying violet and the houses stood out darkly against it, bulbous liver-colored monstrosities of a uniform ugliness though no two were alike. Since this had been a fashionable neighborhood forty years ago, his mother persisted in thinking they did well to have an apartment in it. Each house had a narrow collar of dirt around it in which sat, usually, a grubby child. Julian walked with his hands in his pockets, his head down and thrust forward and his eyes glazed with the determination to make himself completely numb during the time he would be sacrificed to her pleasure.

The door closed and he turned to find the dumpy figure, surmounted by the atrocious hat, coming toward him. "Well," she said, "you only live once and paying a little more for it, I at least won't meet myself coming and going."

"Some day I'll start making money." Julian said gloomily—he knew he never would—"and you can have one of those jokes whenever you take the fit." But first they would move. He visualized a place where the nearest neighbors would be three miles away on either side.

"I think you're doing fine," she said, drawing on her gloves. "You've only been out of school a year. Rome wasn't built in a day."

She was one of the few members of the Y reducing class who arrived in hat and gloves and who had a son who had been to college. "It takes time," she said, "and the world is in such a mess. This hat looked better on me than any of the others, though when she brought it out I said, 'Take that thing back. I wouldn't have it on my head,' and she said, 'Now wait till you see it on,' and when she put it on me, I said, 'we-ull,' and she said, 'If you ask me, that hat does something for you and you do something for that hat, and besides,' she said, 'with that hat, you won't meet yourself coming and going.' "

Julian thought he could have stood his lot better if she had been selfish, if she had been an old hag who drank and screamed at him. He walked along, saturated in depression, as if in the midst of his martyrdom he had lost his faith. Catching sight of his long, hopeless, irritated face, she stopped suddenly with a grief-stricken look, and pulled back on his arm. "Wait on me," she said. "I'm going back to the house and take this thing off and tomorrow I'm going to return it. I was out of my head. I can pay the gas bill with the seven-fifty."

He caught her arm in a vicious grip. "You are not going to take it back," he said. "I like it."

"Well," she said, "I don't think I ought . . ."

"Shut up and enjoy it," he muttered, more depressed than ever.

"With the world in the mess it's in," she said, "it's a wonder we can enjoy anything. I tell you, the bottom rail is on the top."

Julian sighed.

"Of course," she said, "if you know who you are, you can go anywhere." She said this every time he took her to the reducing class. "Most of them in it are not our kind of people," she said, "but I can be gracious to anybody. I know who I am."

"They don't give a damn for your graciousness," Julian said savagely. "Knowing who you are is good for one generation only. You haven't the foggiest idea where you stand now or who you are."

She stopped and allowed her eyes to flash at him. "I most certainly do know who I am," she said, "and if you don't know who you are, I'm ashamed of you."

"Oh hell," Julian said.

"Your great-grandfather was a former governor of this state," she said. "Your grandfather was a prosperous landowner. Your grandmother was a Godhigh."

"Will you look around you," he said tensely, "and see where you are now?" and he swept his arm jerkily out to indicate the neighborhood, which the growing darkness at least made less dingy.

"You remain what you are," she said. "Your great-grandfather had a plantation and two hundred slaves."

"There are no more slaves," he said irritably.

"They were better off when they were," she said. He groaned to see that she was off on that topic. She rolled onto it every few days like a train on an open track. He knew every stop, every junction, every swamp along the way, and knew the exact point at which her conclusion would roll majestically into the station: "It's ridiculous. It's simply not realistic. They should rise, yes, but on their own side of the fence."

"Let's skip it," Julian said.

"The ones I feel sorry for," she said, "are the ones that are half white. They're tragic."

"Will you skip it?"

"Suppose we were half white. We would certainly have mixed feelings."

"I have mixed feelings now," he groaned.

"Well let's talk about something pleasant," she said. "I remember going to Grandpa's when I was a little girl. Then the house had double stairways that went up to what was really the second floor—all the cooking was done on the first. I used to like to stay down in the kitchen on account of the way the walls smelled. I would sit with my nose pressed against the plaster and take deep breaths. Actually the place belonged to the Godhighs but your grandfather Chestny paid the mortgage and saved it for them. They were in reduced circumstances," she said, "but reduced or not, they never forgot who they were."

"Doubtless that decayed mansion reminded them," Julian muttered. He never spoke of it without contempt or thought of it without longing. He had seen it once when he was a child before it had been sold. The double stairways had rotted and been torn down. Negroes were living in it. But it remained in his mind as his mother had known it. It appeared in his dreams regularly. He would stand on the wide porch, listening to the rustle of oak leaves, then wander through the high-ceilinged hall into the parlor that opened onto it and gaze at the worn rugs and faded draperies. It occurred to him that it was he, not she, who could have appreciated it. He preferred its threadbare elegance to anything he could name and it was because of it that all the neighborhoods they had lived in had been a torment to him—whereas she had hardly known the difference. She called her insensitivity "being adjustable."

"And I remember the old darky who was my nurse, Caroline. There was no better person in the world. I've always had a great respect for my colored friends," she said. "I'd do anything in the world for them and they'd . . ."

"Will you for God's sake get off that subject?" Julian said. When he got on a bus by himself, he made it a point to sit down beside a Negro, in reparation as it were for his mother's sins.

"You're mighty touchy tonight," she said. "Do you feel all right?"

"Yes I feel all right," he said. "Now lay off."

She pursed her lips. "Well, you certainly are in a vile humor," she observed. "I just won't speak to you at all."

They had reached the bus stop. There was no bus in sight and Julian, his hands still jammed in his pockets and his head thrust forward, scowled down the empty street. The frustration of having to wait on the bus as well as ride on it began to creep up his neck like a hot hand. The presence of his mother was borne in upon him as she gave a pained sigh. He looked at her bleakly. She was holding herself very erect under the preposterous hat, wearing it like a banner of her imaginary dignity. There was in him an evil urge to break her spirit. He suddenly unloosened his tie and pulled it off and put it in his pocket.

She stiffened. "Why must you look like *that* when you take me to town?" she said. "Why must you deliberately embarrass me?"

"If you'll never learn where you are," he said, "you can at least learn where I am."

"You look like a—thug," she said.

"Then I must be one," he murmured.

"I'll just go home," she said. "I will not bother you. If you can't do a little thing like that for me . . ."

Rolling his eyes upward, he put his tie back on. "Restored to my class," he muttered. He thrust his face toward her and hissed, "True culture is in the mind, the *mind*," he said, and tapped his head, "the mind."

"It's in the heart," she said, "and in how you do things and how you do things is because of who you *are*."

"Nobody in the damn bus cares who you are."

"I care who I am," she said icily.

The lighted bus appeared on top of the next hill and as it approached, they moved out into the street to meet it. He put his hand under her elbow and hoisted her up on the creaking step. She entered with a little smile, as if she were going into a drawing room where everyone had been waiting for her. While he put in the tokens, she sat down on one of the broad front seats for three which faced the aisle. A thin woman with protruding teeth and long yellow hair was sitting on the end of it. His mother moved up beside her and left room for Julian beside herself. He sat down and looked at the floor across the aisle where a pair of thin feet in red and white canvas sandals were planted.

His mother immediately began a general conversation meant to attract anyone who felt like talking. "Can it get any hotter?" she said and removed from her purse a folding fan, black with a Japanese scene on it, which she began to flutter before her.

"I reckon it might could,"[2] the woman with the protruding teeth said, "but I know for a fact my apartment couldn't get no hotter."

"It must get the afternoon sun," his mother said. She sat forward and looked up and down the bus. It was half filled. Everybody was white. "I see we have the bus to ourselves," she said. Julian cringed.

"For a change," said the woman across the aisle, the owner of the red and white canvas sandals. "I come on one the other day and they were thick as fleas—up front and all through."

"The world is in a mess everywhere," his mother said. "I don't know how we've let it get in this fix."

"What gets my goat is all those boys from good families stealing automobile tires," the woman with the protruding teeth said. "I told my boy, I said you may not be rich but you been raised right and if I ever catch you in any such mess, they can send you on to the reformatory. Be exactly where you belong."

"Training tells," his mother said. "Is your boy in high school?"

"Ninth grade," the woman said.

"My son just finished college last year. He wants to write but he's selling typewriters until he gets started," his mother said.

The woman leaned forward and peered at Julian. He threw her such a malevolent look that she subsided against the seat. On the floor across the aisle there was an abandoned newspaper. He got up and got it and opened it out in front of him. His mother discreetly continued the conversation in a lower tone but the woman across the aisle said in a loud voice, "Well that's nice. Selling typewriters is close to writing. He can go right from one to the other."

"I tell him," his mother said, "that Rome wasn't built in a day."

Behind the newspaper Julian was withdrawing into the inner compartment of his mind where he spent most of his time. This was a kind of mental bubble in which he established himself when he could not bear to be a part of what was going on around him. From it he could see out and judge but in it he was safe from any kind of penetration from without. It was the only place where he felt free of the general idiocy of his fellows. His mother had never entered it but from it he could see her with absolute clarity.

The old lady was clever enough and he thought that if she had started from any of the right premises, more might have been expected of her. She lived according to the laws of her own fantasy world, outside of which he had never seen her set foot. The law of it was to sacrifice herself for him after she had first created the necessity to do so by making a mess of things. If he had permitted her sacrifices, it was only because her lack of foresight had made them necessary. All of her life had been a struggle to act like a Chestny without the Chestny goods, and to give him everything she thought a Chestny ought to have; but

---

[2] "Might could" is a lower-class Southern expression meaning "perhaps" or "possibly."

since, said she, it was fun to struggle, why complain? And when you had won, as she had won, what fun to look back on the hard times! He could not forgive her that she had enjoyed the struggle and that she thought *she* had won.

What she meant when she said she had won was that she had brought him up successfully and had sent him to college and that he had turned out so well— good looking (her teeth had gone unfilled so that his could be straightened), intelligent (he realized he was too intelligent to be a success), and with a future ahead of him (there was of course no future ahead of him). She excused his gloominess on the grounds that he was still growing up and his radical ideas on his lack of practical experience. She said he didn't yet know a thing about "life," that he hadn't even entered the real world—when already he was as disenchanted with it as a man of fifty.

The further irony of all this was that in spite of her, he had turned out so well. In spite of going to only a third-rate college, he had, on his own initiative, come out with a first-rate education; in spite of growing up dominated by a small mind, he had ended up with a large one; in spite of all her foolish views, he was free of prejudice and unafraid to face facts. Most miraculous of all, instead of being blinded by love for her as she was for him, he had cut himself emotionally free of her and could see her with complete objectivity. He was not dominated by his mother.

The bus stopped with a sudden jerk and shook him from his meditation. A woman from the back lurched forward with little steps and barely escaped falling in his newspaper as she righted herself. She got off and a large Negro got on. Julian kept his paper lowered to watch. It gave him a certain satisfaction to see injustice in daily operation. It confirmed his view that with a few exceptions there was no one worth knowing within a radius of three hundred miles. The Negro was well dressed and carried a briefcase. He looked around and then sat down on the other end of the seat where the woman with the red and white canvas sandals was sitting. He immediately unfolded a newspaper and obscured himself behind it. Julian's mother's elbow at once prodded insistently into his ribs. "Now you see why I won't ride on these buses by myself," she whispered.

The woman with the red and white canvas sandals had risen at the same time the Negro sat down and had gone further back in the bus and taken the seat of the woman who had got off. His mother leaned forward and cast her an approving look.

Julian rose, crossed the aisle, and sat down in the place of the woman with the canvas sandals. From this position, he looked serenely across at his mother. Her face had turned an angry red. He stared at her, making his eyes the eyes of a stranger. He felt his tension suddenly lift as if he had openly declared war on her.

He would have liked to get in conversation with the Negro and to talk with him about art or politics or any subject that would be above the comprehension of those around them, but the man remained entrenched behind his paper. He was either ignoring the change of seating or had never noticed it. There was no way for Julian to convey his sympathy.

His mother kept her eyes fixed reproachfully on his face. The woman with the protruding teeth was looking at him avidly as if he were a type of monster new to her.

"Do you have a light?" he asked the Negro.

Without looking away from his paper, the man reached in his pocket and handed him a packet of matches.

"Thanks," Julian said. For a moment he held the matches foolishly. A NO SMOKING sign looked down upon him from over the door. This alone would not have deterred him; he had no cigarettes. He had quit smoking some months before because he could not afford it. "Sorry," he muttered and handed back the matches. The Negro lowered the paper and gave him an annoyed look. He took the matches and raised the paper again.

His mother continued to gaze at him but she did not take advantage of his momentary discomfort. Her eyes retained their battered look. Her face seemed to be unnaturally red, as if her blood pressure had risen. Julian allowed no glimmer of sympathy to show on his face. Having got the advantage, he wanted desperately to keep it and carry it through. He would have liked to teach her a lesson that would last her a while, but there seemed no way to continue the point. The Negro refused to come out from behind his paper.

Julian folded his arms and looked stolidly before him, facing her but as if he did not see her, as if he had ceased to recognize her existence. He visualized a scene in which, the bus having reached their stop, he would remain in his seat and when she said, "Aren't you going to get off?" he would look at her as at a stranger who had rashly addressed him. The corner they got off on was usually deserted, but it was well lighted and it would not hurt her to walk by herself the four blocks to the Y. He decided to wait until the time came and then decide whether or not he would let her get off by herself. He would have to be at the Y at ten to bring her back, but he could leave her wondering if he was going to show up. There was no reason for her to think she could always depend on him.

He retired again into the high-ceilinged room sparsely settled with large pieces of antique furniture. His soul expanded momentarily but then he became aware of his mother across from him and the vision shriveled. He studied her coldly. Her feet in little pumps dangled like a child's and did not quite reach the floor. She was training on him an exaggerated look of reproach. He felt completely detached from her. At that moment he could with pleasure have slapped her as he would have slapped a particularly obnoxious child in his charge.

He began to imagine various unlikely ways by which he could teach her a lesson. He might make friends with some distinguished Negro professor or lawyer and bring him home to spend the evening. He would be entirely justified but her blood pressure would rise to 300. He could not push her to the extent of making her have a stroke, and moreover, he had never been successful at making any Negro friends. He had tried to strike up an acquaintance on the bus with some of the better types, with ones that looked like professors or ministers or lawyers. One morning he had sat down next to a distinguished-looking dark brown man who had answered his questions with a sonorous solemnity but who had turned out to be an undertaker. Another day he had sat down beside a cigar-smoking Negro with a diamond ring on his finger, but after a few stilted pleas-antries, the Negro had rung the buzzer and risen, slipping two lottery tickets into Julian's hand as he climbed over him to leave.

He imagined his mother lying desperately ill and his being able to secure only a Negro doctor for her. He toyed with that idea for a few minutes and then dropped it for a momentary vision of himself participating as a sympathizer in a sit-in demonstration.[3] This was possible but he did not linger with it. Instead, he approached the ultimate horror. He brought home a beautiful suspiciously Negroid woman. Prepare yourself, he said. There is nothing you can do about it. This is the woman I've chosen. She's intelligent, dignified, even good, and she's suffered and she hasn't thought it *fun*. Now persecute us, go ahead and persecute us. Drive her out of here, but remember, you're driving me too. His eyes were narrowed and through the indignation he had generated, he saw his mother across the aisle, purple-faced, shrunken to the dwarf-like proportions of her moral nature, sitting like a mummy beneath the ridiculous banner of her hat.

He was tilted out of his fantasy again as the bus stopped. The door opened with a sucking hiss and out of the dark a large, gaily dressed, sullen-looking colored woman got on with a little boy. The child, who might have been four, had on a short plaid suit and a Tyrolean hat with a blue feather in it. Julian hoped that he would sit down beside him and that the woman would push in beside his mother. He could think of no better arrangement.

As she waited for her tokens, the woman was surveying the seating possibil-ities—he hoped with the idea of sitting where she was least wanted. There was something familiar-looking about her but Julian could not place what it was. She was a giant of a woman. Her face was set not only to meet opposition but to seek it out. The downward tilt of her large lower lip was like a warning sign: DON'T TAMPER WITH ME. Her bulging figure was encased in a green crepe dress and her feet overflowed in red shoes. She had on a hideous hat. A purple velvet flap came down on one side of it and stood up on the other; the rest of it was green and looked like a cushion with the stuffing out. She carried a mammoth red pocketbook that bulged throughout as if it were stuffed with rocks.

To Julian's disappointment, the little boy climbed up on the empty seat beside his mother. His mother lumped all children, black and white, into the common category, "cute," and she thought little Negroes were on the whole cuter than little white children. She smiled at the little boy as he climbed on the seat.

Meanwhile the woman was bearing down upon the empty seat beside Julian. To his annoyance, she squeezed herself into it. He saw his mother's face change as the woman settled herself next to him and he realized with satisfaction that this was more objectionable to her than it was to him. Her face seemed almost gray and there was a look of dull recognition in her eyes, as if suddenly she had

---

[3] "Sit-in demonstrations" were a nonviolent technique used to change racist laws.

sickened at some awful confrontation. Julian saw that it was because she and the woman had, in a sense, swapped sons. Though his mother would not realize the symbolic significance of this, she would feel it. His amusement showed plainly on his face.

The woman next to him muttered something unintelligible to herself. He was conscious of a kind of bristling next to him, muted growling like that of an angry cat. He could not see anything but the red pocketbook upright on the bulging green thighs. He visualized the woman as she had stood waiting for her tokens— the ponderous figure, rising from the red shoes upward over the solid hips, the mammoth bosom, the haughty face, to the green and purple hat.

His eyes widened.

The vision of the two hats, identical, broke upon him with the radiance of a brilliant sunrise. His face was suddenly lit with joy. He could not believe that Fate had thrust upon his mother such a lesson. He gave a loud chuckle so that she would look at him and see that he saw. She turned her eyes on him slowly. The blue in them seemed to have turned a bruised purple. For a moment he had an uncomfortable sense of her innocence, but it lasted only a second before principle rescued him. Justice entitled him to laugh. His grin hardened until it said to her as plainly as if he were saying aloud: Your punishment exactly fits your pettiness. This should teach you a permanent lesson.

Her eyes shifted to the woman. She seemed unable to bear looking at him and to find the woman preferable. He became conscious again of the bristling presence at his side. The woman was rumbling like a volcano about to become active. His mother's mouth began to twitch slightly at one corner. With a sinking heart, he saw incipient signs of recovery on her face and realized that this was going to strike her suddenly as funny and was going to be no lesson at all. She kept her eyes on the woman and an amused smile came over her face as if the woman were a monkey that had stolen her hat. The little Negro was looking up at her with large fascinated eyes. He had been trying to attract her attention for some time.

"Carver!" the woman said suddenly. "Come heah!"

When he saw that the spotlight was on him at last, Carver drew his feet up and turned himself toward Julian's mother and giggled.

"Carver!" the woman said. "You heah me? Come heah!"

Carver slid down from the seat but remained squatting with his back against the base of it, his head turned slyly around toward Julian's mother, who was smiling at him. The woman reached a hand across the aisle and snatched him to her. He righted himself and hung backwards on her knees, grinning at Julian's mother. "Isn't he cute?" Julian's mother said to the woman with the protruding teeth.

"I reckon he is," the woman said without conviction.

The Negress yanked him upright but he eased out of her grip and shot across the aisle and scrambled, giggling wildly, onto the seat beside his love.

"I think he likes me," Julian's mother said, and smiled at the woman. It was the smile she used when she was being particularly gracious to an inferior. Julian saw everything lost. The lesson had rolled off her like rain on a roof.

The woman stood up and yanked the little boy off the seat as if she were snatching him from contagion. Julian could feel the rage in her at having no weapon like his mother's smile. She gave the child a sharp slap across his leg. He howled once and then thrust his head into her stomach and kicked his feet against her shins. "Behave," she said vehemently.

The bus stopped and the Negro who had been reading the newspaper got off. The woman moved over and set the little boy down with a thump between herself and Julian. She held him firmly by the knee. In a moment he put his hands in front of his face and peeped at Julian's mother through his fingers.

"I see yoooooooo!" she said and put her hand in front of her face and peeped at him.

The woman slapped his hand down. "Quit yo' foolishness," she said, "before I knock the living Jesus out of you!"

Julian was thankful that the next stop was theirs. He reached up and pulled the cord. The woman reached up and pulled it at the same time. Oh my God, he thought. He had the terrible intuition that when they got off the bus together, his mother would open her purse and give the little boy a nickel. The gesture would be as natural to her as breathing. The bus stopped and the woman got up and lunged to the front, dragging the child, who wished to stay on, after her. Julian and his mother got up and followed. As they neared the door, Julian tried to relieve her of her pocketbook.

"No," she murmured, "I want to give the little boy a nickel."

"No!" Julian hissed. "No!"

She smiled down at the child and opened her bag. The bus door opened and the woman picked him up by the arm and descended with him, hanging at her hip. Once in the street she set him down and shook him.

Julian's mother had to close her purse while she got down the bus step but as soon as her feet were on the ground, she opened it again and began to rummage inside. "I can't find but a penny," she whispered, "but it looks like a new one."

"Don't do it!" Julian said fiercely between his teeth. There was a streetlight on the corner and she hurried to get under it so that she could better see into her pocketbook. The woman was heading off rapidly down the street with the child still hanging backward on her hand.

"Oh little boy!" Julian's mother called and took a few quick steps and caught up with them just beyond the lamppost. "Here's a bright new penny for you," and she held out the coin, which shone bronze in the dim light.

The huge woman turned and for a moment stood, her shoulders lifted and her face frozen with frustrated rage, and stared at Julian's mother. Then all at once she seemed to explode like a piece of machinery that had been given one ounce of pressure too much. Julian saw the black fist swing out with the red pocketbook. He shut his eyes and cringed as he heard the woman shout, "He don't take nobody's pennies!" When he opened his eyes, the woman was disappearing down the street with the little boy staring wide-eyed over her shoulder. Julian's mother was sitting on the sidewalk.

"I told you not to do that," Julian said angrily. "I told you not to do that!"

He stood over her for a minute, gritting his teeth. Her legs were stretched out in front of her and her hat was on her lap. He squatted down and looked her in the face. It was totally expressionless. "You got exactly what you deserved," he said. "Now get up."

He picked up her pocketbook and put what had fallen out back in it. He picked the hat up off her lap. The penny caught his eye on the sidewalk and he picked that up and let it drop before her eyes into the purse. Then he stood up and leaned over and held his hands out to pull her up. She remained immobile. He sighed. Rising above them on either side were black apartment buildings, marked with irregular rectangles of light. At the end of the block a man came out of a door and walked off in the opposite direction. "All right," he said, "suppose somebody happens by and wants to know why you're sitting on the sidewalk?"

She took the hand and, breathing hard, pulled heavily up on it and then stood for a moment, swaying slightly as if the spots of light in the darkness were circling around her. Her eyes, shadowed and confused, finally settled on his face. He did not try to conceal his irritation. "I hope this teaches you a lesson," he said. She leaned forward and her eyes raked his face. She seemed trying to determine his identity. Then, as if she found nothing familiar about him, she started off with a headlong movement in the wrong direction.

"Aren't you going on to the Y?" he asked.

"Home," she muttered.

"Well, are we walking?"

For answer she kept going. Julian followed along, his hands behind him. He saw no reason to let the lesson she had had go without backing it up with an explanation of its meaning. She might as well be made to understand what had happened to her. "Don't think that was just an uppity Negro woman," he said. "That was the whole colored race which will no longer take your condescending pennies. That was your black double. She can wear the same hat as you, and to be sure," he added gratuitously (because he thought it was funny), "it looked better on her than it did on you. What all this means," he said, "is that the old world is gone. The old manners are obsolete and your graciousness is not worth a damn." He thought bitterly of the house that had been lost for him. "You aren't who you think you are," he said.

She continued to plow ahead, paying no attention to him. Her hair had come undone on one side. She dropped her pocketbook and took no notice. He stooped and picked it up and handed it to her but she did not take it.

"You needn't.act as if the world had come to an end," he said, "because it hasn't. From now on you've got to live in a new world and face a few realities for a change. Buck up," he said, "it won't kill you."

She was breathing fast.

"Let's wait on the bus," he said.

"Home," she said thickly.

"I hate to see you behave like this," he said. "Just like a child. I should be able to expect more of you." He decided to stop where he was and make her stop and wait for a bus. "I'm not going any farther," he said, stopping. "We're going on the bus."

She continued to go on as if she had not heard him. He took a few steps and caught her arm and stopped her. He looked into her face and caught his breath. He was looking into a face he had never seen before. "Tell Grandpa to come get me," she said.

He stared, stricken.

"Tell Caroline to come get me," she said.

Stunned, he let her go and she lurched forward again, walking as if one leg were shorter than the other. A tide of darkness seemed to be sweeping her from him. "Mother!" he cried. "Darling, sweetheart, wait!" Crumpling, she fell to the pavement. He dashed forward and fell at her side, crying "Mamma, Mamma!" He turned her over. Her face was fiercely distorted. One eye, large and staring, moved slightly to the left as if it had become unmoored. The other remained fixed on him, raked his face again, found nothing and closed.

"Wait here, wait here!" he cried and jumped up and began to run for help toward a cluster of lights he saw in the distance ahead of him. "Help, help!" he shouted, but his voice was thin, scarcely a thread of sound. The lights drifted farther away the faster he ran and his feet moved numbly as if they carried him nowhere. The tide of darkness seemed to sweep him back to her, postponing from moment to moment his entry into the world of guilt and sorrow.

JOHN STEINBECK (1902–1968)

The Chrysanthemums

The high grey-flannel fog of winter closed off the Salinas Valley from the sky and from all the rest of the world. On every side it sat like a lid on the mountains and made of the great valley a closed pot. On the broad, level land floor the gang plows bit deep and left the black earth shining like metal where the shares had cut. On the foothill ranches across the Salinas River, the yellow stubble fields seemed to be bathed in pale cold sunshine, but there was no sunshine in the valley now in December. The thick willow scrub along the river flamed with sharp and positive yellow leaves.

It was a time of quiet and of waiting. The air was cold and tender. A light wind blew up from the southwest so that the farmers were mildly hopeful of a good rain before long; but fog and rain do not go together.

Across the river, on Henry Allen's foothill ranch there was a little work to be done, for the hay was cut and stored and the orchards were plowed up to receive the rain deeply when it should come. The cattle on the higher slopes were becoming shaggy and rough-coated.

Elisa Allen, working in her flower garden, looked down across the yard and saw Henry, her husband, talking to two men in business suits. The three of them stood by the tractor shed, each man with one foot on the side of the little Fordson. They smoked cigarettes and studied the machine as they talked.

Elisa watched them for a moment and then went back to her work. She was thirty-five. Her face was lean and strong and her eyes were as clear as water. Her figure looked blocked and heavy in her gardening costume, a man's black hat pulled low down over her eyes, clodhopper shoes, a figured print dress almost completely covered by a big corduroy apron with four big pockets to hold the snips, the trowel and scratcher, the seeds and the knife she worked with. She wore heavy leather gloves to protect her hands while she worked.

She was cutting down the old year's chrysanthemum stalks with a pair of short and powerful scissors. She looked down toward the men by the tractor shed now and then. Her face was eager and mature and handsome; even her work with the scissors was over-eager, over-powerful. The chrysanthemum stems seemed too small and easy for her energy.

She brushed a cloud of hair out of her eyes with the back of her glove, and left a smudge of earth on the cheek in doing it. Behind her stood the neat white farm house with red geraniums close-banked around it as high as the windows. It was a hard-swept looking little house, with hard-polished windows, and a clean mud-mat on the front steps.

Elisa cast another glance toward the tractor shed. The strangers were getting into their Ford coupe. She took off a glove and put her strong fingers down into the forest of new green chrysanthemum sprouts that were growing around the old roots. She spread the leaves and looked down among the close-growing stems. No aphids were there, no sowbugs or snails or cutworms. Her terrier fingers destroyed such pests before they could get started.

Elisa started at the sound of her husband's voice. He had come near quietly, and he leaned over the wire fence that protected her flower garden from cattle and dogs and chickens.

"At it again," he said. "You've got a strong new crop coming."

Elisa straightened her back and pulled on the gardening glove again. "Yes. They'll be strong this coming year." In her tone and on her face there was a little smugness.

"You've got a gift with things," Henry observed. "Some of those yellow chrysanthemums you had this year were ten inches across. I wish you'd work out in the orchard and raise some apples that big."

Her eyes sharpened. "Maybe I could do it, too. I've a gift with things, all right. My mother had it. She could stick anything in the ground and make it grow. She said it was having planters' hands that knew how to do it."

"Well, it sure works with flowers," he said.

"Henry, who were those men you were talking to?"

"Why, sure, that's what I came to tell you. They were from the Western Meat Company. I sold those thirty head of three-year-old steers. Got nearly my own price, too."

"Good," she said. "Good for you."

"And I thought," he continued, "I thought how it's Saturday afternoon, and we might go to Salinas for dinner at a restaurant, and then to a picture show— to celebrate, you see."

"Good," she repeated. "Oh, yes. That will be good."

Henry put on his joking tone. "There's fights tonight. How'd you like to go to the fights?"

"Oh, no," she said breathlessly. "No, I wouldn't like fights."

"Just fooling, Elisa. We'll go to a movie. Let's see. It's two now. I'm going to take Scotty and bring down those steers from the hill. It'll take us maybe two hours. We'll go in town about five and have dinner at the Cominos Hotel. Like that?"

"Of course I'll like it. It's good to eat away from home."

"All right, then. I'll go get up a couple of horses."

She said, "I'll have plenty of time to transplant some of these sets, I guess."

She heard her husband calling Scotty down by the barn. And a little later she saw the two men ride up the pale yellow hillside in search of the steers.

There was a little square sandy bed kept for rooting the chrysanthemums. With her trowel she turned the soil over and over, and smoothed it and patted it firm. Then she dug ten parallel trenches to receive the sets. Back at the chrysanthemum bed she pulled out the little crisp shoots, trimmed off the leaves of each one with her scissors and laid it on a small orderly pile.

A squeak of wheels and plod of hoofs came from the road. Elisa looked up. The country road ran along the dense bank of willows and cottonwoods that bordered the river, and up this road came a curious vehicle, curiously drawn. It was an old spring-wagon, with a round canvas top on it like the cover of a prairie schooner. It was drawn by an old bay horse and a little grey-and-white burro. A big stubble-bearded man sat between the cover flaps and drove the crawling team. Underneath the wagon, between the hind wheels, a lean and rangy mongrel dog walked sedately. Words were painted on the canvas in clumsy, crooked letters. "Pots, pans, knives, sisors, lawn mores. Fixed." Two rows of articles and the triumphantly definitive "Fixed" below. The black paint had run down in little sharp points beneath each letter.

Elisa, squatting on the ground, watched to see the crazy, loose-jointed wagon pass by. But it didn't pass. It turned into the farm road in front of her house, crooked old wheels skirling and squeaking. The rangy dog darted from between the wheels and ran ahead. Instantly the two ranch shepherds flew out at him. Then all three stopped, and with stiff and quivering tails, with taut straight legs, with ambassadorial dignity, they slowly circled, sniffing daintily. The caravan pulled up to Elisa's wire fence and stopped. Now the newcomer dog, feeling outnumbered, lowered his tail and retired under the wagon with raised hackles and bared teeth.

The man on the wagon seat called out. "That's a bad dog in a fight when he gets started."

Elisa laughed. "I see he is. How soon does he generally get started?"

The man caught up her laughter and echoed it heartily. "Sometimes not for weeks and weeks," he said. He climbed stiffly down, over the wheel. The horse and the donkey drooped like unwatered flowers.

Elisa saw that he was a very big man. Although his hair and beard were greying, he did not look old. His worn black suit was wrinkled and spotted with grease. The laughter had disappeared from his face and eyes the moment his laughing voice ceased. His eyes were dark and they were full of the brooding that gets in the eyes of teamsters and of sailors. The calloused hands he rested on the wire fence were cracked, and every crack was a black line. He took off his battered hat.

"I'm off my general road, ma'am," he said. "Does this dirt road cut over across the river to the Los Angeles highway?"

Elisa stood up and shoved the thick scissors in her apron pocket. "Well, yes, it does, but it winds around and then fords the river. I don't think your team could pull through the sand."

He replied with some asperity, "It might surprise you what them beasts can pull through."

"When they get started?" she asked.

He smiled for a second. "Yes. When they get started."

"Well," said Elisa, "I think you'll save time if you go back to the Salinas road and pick up the highway there."

He drew a big finger down the chicken wire and made it sing. "I ain't in any hurry, ma'am. I go from Seattle to San Diego and back every year. Takes all my time. About six months each way. I aim to follow nice weather."

Elisa took off her gloves and stuffed them in the apron pocket with the scissors. She touched the under edge of her man's hat, searching for fugitive hairs. "That sounds like a nice kind of a way to live," she said.

He leaned confidentially over the fence. "Maybe you noticed the writing on my wagon. I mend pots and sharpen knives and scissors. You got any of them things to do?"

"Oh, no," she said quickly. "Nothing like that." Her eyes hardened with resistance.

"Scissors is the worst thing," he explained. "Most people just ruin scissors trying to sharpen 'em, but I know how. I got a special tool. It's a little bobbit kind of thing, and patented. But it sure does the trick."

"No. My scissors are all sharp."

"All right, then. Take a pot," he continued earnestly, "a bent pot, or a pot with a hole. I can make it like new so you don't have to buy no new ones. That's a saving for you."

"No," she said shortly. "I tell you I have nothing like that for you to do."

His face fell to an exaggerated sadness. His voice took on a whining undertone. "I ain't had a thing to do today. Maybe I won't have no supper tonight. You see I'm off my regular road. I know folks on the highway clear from Seattle to San Diego. They save their things for me to sharpen up because they know I do it so good and save them money."

"I'm sorry," Elisa said irritably. "I haven't anything for you to do."

His eyes left her face and fell to searching the ground. They roamed about until they came to the chrysanthemum bed where she had been working. "What's them plants, ma'am?"

The irritation and resistance melted from Elisa's face. "Oh, those are chrysanthemums, giant whites and yellows. I raise them every year, bigger than anybody around here."

"Kind of a long-stemmed flower? Looks like a quick puff of colored smoke?" he asked.

"That's it. What a nice way to describe them."

"They smell kind of nasty till you get used to them," he said.

"It's a good bitter smell," she retorted, "not nasty at all."

He changed his tone quickly. "I like the smell myself."

"I had ten-inch blooms this year," she said.

The man leaned farther over the fence. "Look. I know a lady down the road a piece, has got the nicest garden you ever seen. Got nearly every kind of flower but no chrysanthemums. Last time I was mending a copper-bottom washtub for her (that's a hard job but I do it good), she said to me, 'If you ever run acrost some nice chrysanthemums I wish you'd try to get me a few seeds.' That's what she told me."

Elisa's eyes grew alert and eager. "She couldn't have known much about chrysanthemums. You can raise them from seed, but it's much easier to root the little sprouts you see there."

"Oh," he said. "I s'pose I can't take none to her, then."

"Why yes you can," Elisa cried. "I can put some in damp sand, and you can carry them right along with you. They'll take root in the pot if you keep them damp. And then she can transplant them."

"She'd sure like to have some, ma'am. You say they're nice ones?"

"Beautiful," she said. "Oh, beautiful." Her eyes shone. She tore off the battered hat and shook out her dark pretty hair. "I'll put them in a flower pot, and you can take them right with you. Come into the yard."

While the man came through the picket gate Elisa ran excitedly along the geranium-bordered path to the back of the house. And she returned carrying a big red flower pot. The gloves were forgotten now. She kneeled on the ground by the starting bed and dug up the sandy soil with her fingers and scooped it into the bright new flower pot. Then she picked up the little pile of shoots she had prepared. With her strong fingers she pressed them into the sand and tamped around them with her knuckles. The man stood over her. "I'll tell you what to do," she said. "You remember so you can tell the lady."

"Yes, I'll try to remember."

"Well, look. These will take root in about a month. Then she must set them out, about a foot apart in good rich earth like this, see?" She lifted a handful of dark soil for him to look at. "They'll grow fast and tall. Now remember this. In July tell her to cut them down, about eight inches from the ground."

"Before they bloom?" he asked.

"Yes, before they bloom." Her face was tight with eagerness. "They'll grow right up again. About the last of September the buds will start."

She stopped and seemed perplexed. "It's the budding that takes the most care," she said hesitantly. "I don't know how to tell you." She looked deep into his eyes, searchingly. Her mouth opened a little, and she seemed to be listening. "I'll try to tell you," she said. "Did you ever hear of planting hands?"

"Can't say I have, ma'am."

"Well, I can only tell you what it feels like. It's when you're picking off the buds you don't want. Everything goes right down into your fingertips. You watch your fingers work. They do it themselves. You can feel how it is. They pick and pick the buds. They never make a mistake. They're with the plant. Do you see? Your fingers and the plant. You can feel that, right up your arm. They know. They never make a mistake. You can feel it. When you're like that you can't do anything wrong. Do you see that? Can you understand that?"

She was kneeling on the ground looking up at him. Her breast swelled passionately.

The man's eyes narrowed. He looked away self-consciously. "Maybe I know," he said. "Sometimes in the night in the wagon there—"

Elisa's voice grew husky. She broke in on him. "I've never lived as you do, but I know what you mean. When the night is dark—why, the stars are sharp-pointed, and there's quiet. Why, you rise up and up! Every pointed star gets driven into your body. It's like that. Hot and sharp and—lovely."

Kneeling there, her hand went out toward his legs in the greasy black trousers. Her hesitant fingers almost touched the cloth. Then her hand dropped to the ground. She crouched low like a fawning dog.

He said, "It's nice, just like you say. Only when you don't have no dinner, it ain't."

She stood up then, very straight, and her face was ashamed. She held the flower pot out to him and placed it gently in his arms. "Here. Put it in your wagon, on the seat, where you can watch it. Maybe I can find something for you to do."

At the back of the house she dug in the can pile and found two old and battered aluminum saucepans. She carried them back and gave them to him. "Here, maybe you can fix these."

His manner changed. He became professional. "Good as new I can fix them." At the back of his wagon he set a little anvil, and out of an oily tool box dug a small machine hammer. Elisa came through the gate to watch him while he pounded out the dents in the kettles. His mouth grew sure and knowing. At a difficult part of the work he sucked his under-lip.

"You sleep right in the wagon?" Elisa asked.

"Right in the wagon, ma'am. Rain or shine I'm dry as a cow in there."

"It must be nice," she said. "It must be very nice. I wish women could do such things."

"It ain't the right kind of a life for a woman."

Her upper lip raised a little, showing her teeth. "How do you know? How can you tell?" she said.

"I don't know ma'am," he protested. "Of course I don't know. Now here's your kettles, done. You don't have to buy no new ones."

"How much?"

"Oh, fifty cents'll do. I keep my prices down and my work good. That's why I have all them satisfied customers up and down the highway."

Elisa brought him a fifty-cent piece from the house and dropped it in his hand. "You might be surprised to have a rival some time. I can sharpen scissors, too. And I can beat the dents out of little pots. I could show you what a woman might do."

He put his hammer back in the oily box and shoved the little anvil out of sight. "It would be a lonely life for a woman, ma'am, and a scarey life, too, with animals creeping under the wagon all night." He climbed over the single-tree, steadying himself with a hand on the burro's white rump. He settled himself in the seat, picked up the lines. "Thank you kindly, ma'am," he said. "I'll do like you told me; I'll go back and catch the Salinas road."

"Mind," she called, "if you're long in getting there, keep the sand damp."

"Sand, ma'am? . . . Sand? Oh, sure. You mean round the chrysanthemums. Sure I will." He clucked his tongue. The beasts leaned luxuriously into their collars. The mongrel dog took his place between the back wheels. The wagon turned and crawled out the entrance road and back the way it had come, along the river.

Elisa stood in front of her wire fence watching the slow progress of the caravan. Her shoulders were straight, her head thrown back, her eyes half-closed, so that the scene came vaguely into them. Her lips moved silently, forming the words "Good-bye—good-bye." Then she whispered, "That's a bright direction. There's a glowing there." The sound of her whisper startled her. She shook herself free and looked about to see whether anyone had been listening. Only the dogs had heard. They lifted their heads toward her from their sleeping in the dust, and then stretched out their chins and settled asleep again. Elisa turned and ran hurriedly into the house.

In the kitchen she reached behind the stove and felt the water tank. It was full of hot water from the noonday cooking. In the bathroom she tore off her soiled clothes and flung them into the corner. And then she scrubbed herself with a little block of pumice, legs and thighs, loins and chest and arms, until her skin was scratched and red. When she had dried herself she stood in front of a mirror in the bedroom and looked at her body. She tightened her stomach and threw out her chest. She turned and looked over her shoulder at her back.

After a while she began to dress, slowly. She put on her newest under-clothing and her nicest stockings and the dress which was the symbol of her prettiness. She worked carefully on her hair, pencilled her eyebrows and rouged her lips.

Before she was finished she heard the little thunder of hoofs and the shouts of Henry and his helper as they drove the red steers into the corral. She heard the gate bang shut and set herself for Henry's arrival.

His step sounded on the porch. He entered the house calling "Elisa, where are you?"

"In my room, dressing. I'm not ready. There's hot water for your bath. Hurry up. It's getting late."

When she heard him splashing in the tub, Elisa laid his dark suit on the bed, and shirt and socks and tie beside it. She stood his polished shoes on the floor beside the bed. Then she went to the porch and sat primly and stiffly down. She looked toward the river road where the willow-line was still yellow with frosted leaves so that under the high grey fog they seemed a thin band of sunshine. This was the only color in the grey afternoon. She sat unmoving for a long time. Her eyes blinked rarely.

Henry came banging out of the door, shoving his tie inside his vest as he came. Elisa stiffened and her face grew tight. Henry stopped short and looked at her. "Why—why, Elisa. You look so nice!"

"Nice? You think I look nice? What do you mean by 'nice?' "

Henry blundered on. "I don't know. I mean you look different, strong and happy."

"I am strong? Yes, strong. What do you mean 'strong?' "

He looked bewildered. "You're playing some kind of a game," he said helplessly. "It's a kind of a play. You look strong enough to break a calf over your knee, happy enough to eat it like watermelon."

For a second she lost her rigidity. "Henry! Don't talk like that. You didn't know what you said." She grew complete again. "I'm strong," she boasted. "I never knew before how strong."

Henry looked down toward the tractor shed, and when he brought his eyes back to her, they were his own again. "I'll get out the car. You can put on your coat while I'm starting."

Elisa went into the house. She heard him drive to the gate and idle down his motor, and then she took a long time to put on her hat. She pulled it here and pressed it there. When Henry turned the motor off she slipped into her coat and went out.

The little roadster bounced along on the dirt road by the river, raising the birds and driving the rabbits into the brush. Two cranes flapped heavily over the willow-line and dropped into the riverbed.

Far ahead on the road Elisa saw a dark speck. She knew.

She tried not to look as they passed it, but her eyes would not obey. She whispered to herself sadly. "He might have thrown them off the road. That wouldn't have been much trouble, not very much. But he kept the pot," she explained. "He had to keep the pot. That's why he couldn't get them off the road."

The roadster turned a bend and she saw the caravan ahead. She swung full around toward her husband so she could not see the little covered wagon and the mismatched team as the car passed them.

In a moment it was over. The thing was done. She did not look back. She said loudly, to be heard above the motor, "It will be good, tonight, a good dinner."

"Now you're changed again," Henry complained. He took one hand from the wheel and patted her knee. "I ought to take you in to dinner oftener. It would be good for both of us. We get so heavy out on the ranch."

"Henry," she asked, "could we have wine at dinner?"

"Sure we could. Say! That will be fine."

She was silent for a little while; then she said, "Henry, at those prize fights, do the men hurt each other very much?"

"Sometimes a little, not often. Why?"

"Well, I've read how they break noses, and blood runs down their chests. I've read how the fighting gloves get heavy and soggy with blood."

He looked around at her. "What's the matter, Elisa? I didn't know you read things like that." He brought the car to a stop, then turned to the right over the Salinas River bridge.

"Do any women ever go to the fights?" she asked.

"Oh, sure, some. What's the matter, Elisa? Do you want to go? I don't think you'd like it, but I'll take you if you really want to go."

She relaxed limply in the seat. "Oh, no. No. I don't want to go. I'm sure I don't." Her face was turned away from him. "It will be enough if we can have wine. It will be plenty." She turned up her coat collar so he could not see that she was crying weakly—like an old woman.

EUDORA WELTY (1909–   )

Lily Daw and the Three Ladies

Mrs. Watts and Mrs. Carson were both in the post office in Victory when the letter came from the Ellisville Institute for the Feeble-Minded of Mississippi. Aimee Slocum, with her hand still full of mail, ran out in front and handed it straight to Mrs. Watts, and they all three read it together. Mrs. Watts held it taut between her pink hands, and Mrs. Carson underscored each line slowly with her thimbled finger. Everybody else in the post office wondered what was up now.

"What will Lily say," beamed Mrs. Carson at last, "when we tell her we're sending her to Ellisville!"

"She'll be ticked to death," said Mrs. Watts, and added in a guttural voice to a deaf lady, "Lily Daw's getting in at Ellisville!"

"Don't you all dare go off and tell Lily without me!" called Aimee Slocum, trotting back to finish putting up the mail.

"Do you suppose they'll look after her down there?" Mrs. Carson began to carry on a conversation with a group of Baptist ladies waiting in the post office. She was the Baptist preacher's wife.

"I've always heard it was lovely down there, but crowded," said one.

"Lily lets people walk over her so," said another.

"Last night at the tent show—" said another, and then popped her hand over her mouth.

"Don't mind me, I know there are such things in the world," said Mrs. Carson, looking down and fingering the tape measure which hung over her bosom.

"Oh, Mrs. Carson. Well, anyway, last night at the tent show, why, the man was just before making Lily buy a ticket to get in."

"A ticket!"

"Till my husband went up and explained she wasn't bright, and so did everybody else."

The ladies all clucked their tongues.

"Oh, it was a very nice show," said the lady who had gone. "And Lily acted so nice. She was a perfect lady—just set in her seat and stared."

"Oh, she can be a lady—she can be," said Mrs. Carson, shaking her head and turning her eyes up. "That's just what breaks your heart."

"Yes'm, she kept her eyes on—what's that thing makes all the commotion?—the xylophone," said the lady. "Didn't turn her head to the right or to the left the whole time. Set in front of me."

"The point is, what did she do after the show?" asked Mrs. Watts practically. "Lily has gotten so she is very mature for her age."

"Oh, Etta!" protested Mrs. Carson, looking at her wildly for a moment.

"And that's how come we are sending her to Ellisville," finished Mrs. Watts.

"I'm ready, you all," said Aimee Slocum, running out with white powder all over her face. "Mail's up. I don't know how good it's up."

"Well, of course, I do hope it's for the best," said several of the other ladies. They did not go at once to take their mail out of their boxes; they felt a little left out.

The three women stood at the foot of the water tank.

"To find Lily is a different thing," said Aimee Slocum.

"Where in the wide world do you suppose she'd be?" It was Mrs. Watts who was carrying the letter.

"I don't see a sign of her either on this side of the street or on the other side," Mrs. Carson declared as they walked along.

Ed Newton was stringing Redbird school tablets on the wire across the store.

"If you're after Lily, she come in here while ago and tole me she was fixin' to git married," he said.

"Ed Newton!" cried the ladies together, clutching one another. Mrs. Watts began to fan herself at once with the letter from Ellisville. She wore widow's black, and the least thing made her hot.

"Why she is not. She's going to Ellisville, Ed," said Mrs. Carson gently. "Mrs. Watts and I and Aimee Slocum are paying her way out of our own pockets. Besides, the boys of Victory are on their honor. Lily's not going to get married, that's just an idea she's got in her head."

"More power to you, ladies," said Ed Newton, spanking himself with a tablet.

When they came to the bridge over the railroad tracks, there was Estelle Mabers, sitting on a rail. She was slowly drinking an orange Ne-Hi.

"Have you seen Lily?" they asked her.

"I'm supposed to be out here watching for her now," said the Mabers girl, as though she weren't there yet. "But for Jewel—Jewel says Lily come in the store while ago and picked out a two-ninety-eight hat and wore it off. Jewel wants to swap her something else for it."

"Oh, Estelle, Lily says she's going to get married!" cried Aimee Slocum.

"Well, I declare," said Estelle; she never understood anything.

Loralee Adkins came riding by in her Willys-Knight, tooting the horn to find out what they were talking about.

Aimee threw up her hands and ran out into the street. "Loralee, Loralee, you got to ride us up to Lily Daws'. She's up yonder fixing to get married!"

"Hop in, my land!"

"Well, that just goes to show you right now," said Mrs. Watts, groaning as she was helped into the back seat. "What we've got to do is persuade Lily it will be nicer to go to Ellisville."

"Just to think!"

While they rode around the corner Mrs. Carson was going on in her sad voice, sad as the soft noises in the hen house at twilight. "We buried Lily's poor defenseless mother. We gave Lily all her food and kindling and every stitch she had on. Sent her to Sunday school to learn the Lord's teachings, had her baptized a Baptist. And when her old father commenced beating her and tried to cut her head off with the butcher knife, why, we went and took her away from him and gave her a place to stay."

The paintless frame house with all the weather vanes was three stories high in places and had yellow and violet stained-glass windows in front and gingerbread around the porch. It leaned steeply to one side, toward the railroad, and the front steps were gone. The car full of ladies drew up under the cedar tree.

"Now Lily's almost grown up," Mrs. Carson continued. "In fact, she's grown," she concluded, getting out.

"Talking about getting married," said Mrs. Watts disgustedly. "Thanks, Loralee, you run on home."

They climbed over the dusty zinnias onto the porch and walked through the open door without knocking.

"There certainly is always a funny smell in this house. I say it every time I come," said Aimee Slocum.

Lily was there, in the dark of the hall, kneeling on the floor by a small open trunk.

When she saw them she put a zinnia in her mouth, and held still.

"Hello, Lily," said Mrs. Carson reproachfully.

"Hello," said Lily. In a minute she gave a suck on the zinnia stem that sounded exactly like a jay bird. There she sat, wearing a petticoat for a dress, one of the things Mrs. Carson kept after her about. Her milky-yellow hair streamed freely down from under a new hat. You could see the wavy scar on her throat if you knew it was there.

Mrs. Carson and Mrs. Watts, the two fattest, sat in the double rocker. Aimee Slocum sat on the wire chair donated from the drugstore that burned.

"Well, what are you doing, Lily?" asked Mrs. Watts, who led the rocking.

Lily smiled.

The trunk was old and lined with yellow and brown paper, with an asterisk pattern showing in darker circles and rings. Mutely the ladies indicated to each other that they did not know where in the world it had come from. It was empty except for two bars of soap and a green washcloth, which Lily was now trying to arrange in the bottom.

"Go on and tell us what you're doing, Lily," said Aimee Slocum.

"Packing, silly," said Lily.

"Where are you going?"

"Going to get married, and I bet you wish you was me now," said Lily. But shyness overcame her suddenly, and she popped the zinnia back into her mouth.

"Talk to me, dear," said Mrs. Carson. "Tell old Mrs. Carson why you want to get married."

"No," said Lily, after a moment's hesitation.

"Well, we've thought of something that will be so much nicer," said Mrs. Carson. "Why don't you go to Ellisville!"

"Won't that be lovely?" said Mrs. Watts. "Goodness, yes."

"It's a lovely place," said Aimee Slocum uncertainly.

"You've got bumps on your face," said Lily.

"Aimee, dear, you stay out of this, if you don't mind," said Mrs. Carson anxiously. "I don't know what it is comes over Lily when you come around here."

Lily stared at Aimee Slocum meditatively.

"There! Wouldn't you like to go to Ellisville now?" asked Mrs. Carson.

"No'm," said Lily.

"Why not?" All the ladies leaned down toward her in impressive astonishment.

"'Cause I'm goin' to get married," said Lily.

"Well, and who are you going to marry, dear?" asked Mrs. Watts. She knew how to pin people down and make them deny what they'd already said.

Lily bit her lip and began to smile. She reached into the trunk and held up both cakes of soap and wagged them.

"Tell us," challenged Mrs. Watts. "Who you're going to marry, now."

"A man last night."

There was a gasp from each lady. The possible reality of a lover descended suddenly like a summer hail over their heads. Mrs. Watts stood up and balanced herself.

"One of those show fellows! A musician!" she cried.

Lily looked up in admiration.

"Did he—did he do anything to you?" In the long run, it was still only Mrs. Watts who could take charge.

"Oh, yes'm," said Lily. She patted the cakes of soap fastidiously with the tips of her small fingers and tucked them in with the washcloth.

"What?" demanded Aimee Slocum, rising up and tottering before her scream. "What?" she called out in the hall.

"Don't ask her what," said Mrs. Carson, coming up behind. "Tell me, Lily— just yes or no—are you the same as you were?"

"He had a red coat," said Lily graciously. "He took little sticks and went *ping-pong! ding-dong!*"

"Oh, I think I'm going to faint," said Aimee Slocum, but they said, "No, you're not."

"The xylophone!" cried Mrs. Watts. "The xylophone player! Why, the coward, he ought to be run out of town on a rail!"

"Out of town? He is out of town, by now," cried Aimee. "Can't you read?—the sign in the café—Victory on the ninth, Como on the tenth? He's in Como. Como!"

"All right! We'll bring him back!" cried Mrs. Watts. "He can't get away from me!"

"Hush," said Mrs. Carson. "I don't think it's any use following that line of reasoning at all. It's better in the long run for him to be gone out of our lives for good and all. That kind of a man. He was after Lily's body alone and he wouldn't ever in this world make the poor little thing happy, even if we went out and forced him to marry her like he ought—at the point of a gun."

"Still—" began Aimee, her eyes widening.

"Shut up," said Mrs. Watts. "Mrs. Carson, you're right, I expect."

"This is my hope chest—see?" said Lily politely in the pause that followed. "You haven't even looked at it. I've already got soap and a washrag. And I have my hat—on. What are you all going to give me?"

"Lily," said Mrs. Watts, starting over, "we'll give you lots of gorgeous things if you'll only go to Ellisville instead of getting married."

"What will you give me?" asked Lily.

"I'll give you a pair of hemstitched pillowcases," said Mrs. Carson.

"I'll give you a big caramel cake," said Mrs. Watts.

"I'll give you a souvenir from Jackson—a little toy bank," said Aimee Slocum. "Now will you go?"

"No," said Lily.

"I'll give you a pretty little Bible with your name on it in real gold," said Mrs. Carson.

"What if I was to give you a pink crêpe de Chine brassière with adjustable shoulder straps?" asked Mrs. Watts grimly.

"Oh, Etta."

"Well, she needs it," said Mrs. Watts. "What would they think if she ran all over Ellisville in a petticoat looking like a Fiji?"

"I wish I could go to Ellisville," said Aimee Slocum luringly.

"What will they have for me down there?" asked Lily softly.

"Oh! lots of things. You'll have baskets to weave, I expect. . . ." Mrs. Carson looked vaguely at the others.

"Oh, yes indeed, they will let you make all sorts of baskets," said Mrs. Watts; then her voice too trailed off.

"No'm, I'd rather get married," said Lily.

"Lily Daw! Now that's just plain stubbornness!" cried Mrs. Watts. "You almost said you'd go and then you took it back!"

"We've all asked God, Lily," said Mrs. Carson finally, "and God seemed to tell us—Mr. Carson, too—that the place where you ought to be, so as to be happy, was Ellisville."

Lily looked reverent, but still stubborn.

"We've really just got to get her there—now!" screamed Aimee Slocum all at once. "Suppose—! She can't stay here!"

"Oh, no, no, no," said Mrs. Carson hurriedly. "We musn't think that."

They sat sunken in despair.

"Could I take my hope chest—to go to Ellisville?" asked Lily shyly, looking at them sidewise.

"Why, yes," said Mrs. Carson blankly.

Silently they rose once more to their feet.

"Oh, if I could just take my hope chest!"

"All the time it was just her hope chest," Aimee whispered.

Mrs. Watts struck her palms together. "It's settled!"

"Praise the fathers," murmured Mrs. Carson.

Lily looked up at them, and her eyes gleamed. She cocked her head and spoke out in a proud imitation of someone—someone utterly unknown.

"O.K.—Toots!"

The ladies had been nodding and smiling and backing away toward the door.

"I think I'd better stay," said Mrs. Carson, stopping in her tracks. "Where—where could she have learned that terrible expression?"

"Pack up," said Mrs. Watts. "Lily Daw is leaving for Ellisville on Number One."

In the station the train was puffing. Nearly everyone in Victory was hanging around waiting for it to leave. The Victory Civic Band had assembled without any orders and was scattered through the crowd. Ed Newton gave false signals to start on his bass horn. A crate full of baby chickens got loose on the platform. Everybody wanted to see Lily all dressed up, but Mrs. Carson and Mrs. Watts had sneaked her into the train from the other side of the tracks.

The two ladies were going to travel as far as Jackson to help Lily change trains and be sure she went in the right direction.

Lily sat between them on the plush seat with her hair combed and pinned up into a knot under a small blue hat which was Jewel's exchange for the pretty one. She wore a traveling dress made out of part of Mrs. Watts's last summer's mourning. Pink straps glowed through. She had a purse and a Bible and a warm cake in a box, all in her lap.

Aimee Slocum had been getting the outgoing mail stamped and bundled. She stood in the aisle of the coach now, tears shaking from her eyes.

"Good-bye, Lily," she said. She was the one who felt things.

"Good-bye, silly," said Lily.

"Oh, dear, I hope they get our telegram to meet her in Ellisville!" Aimee cried sorrowfully, as she thought how far away it was. "And it was so hard to get it all in ten words, too."

"Get off, Aimee, before the train starts and you break your neck," said Mrs. Watts, all settled and waving her dressy fan gaily. "I declare, it's so hot, as soon as we get a few miles out of town I'm going to slip my corset down."

"Oh, Lily, don't cry down there. Just be good, and do what they tell you—

it's all because they love you." Aimee drew her mouth down. She was backing away, down the aisle.

Lily laughed. She pointed across Mrs. Carson's bosom out the window toward a man. He had stepped off the train and just stood there, by himself. He was a stranger and wore a cap.

"Look," she said, laughing softly through her fingers.

"Don't—look," said Mrs. Carson very distinctly, as if, out of all she had ever spoken, she would impress these two solemn words upon Lily's soft little brain. She added, "Don't look at anything till you get to Ellisville."

Outside, Aimee Slocum was crying so hard she almost ran into the stranger. He wore a cap and was short and seemed to have on perfume, if such a thing could be.

"Could you tell me, madam," he said, "where a little lady lives in this burg name of Miss Lily Daw?" He lifted his cap—and he had red hair.

"What do you want to know for?" Aimee asked before she knew it.

"Talk louder," said the stranger. He almost whispered, himself.

"She's gone away—she's gone to Ellisville!"

"Gone?"

"Gone to Ellisville!"

"Well, I like that!" The man stuck out his bottom lip and puffed till his hair jumped.

"What business did you have with Lily?" cried Aimee suddenly.

"We was only going to get married, that's all," said the man.

Aimee Slocum started to scream in front of all those people. She almost pointed to the long black box she saw lying on the ground at the man's feet. Then she jumped back in fright.

"The xylophone! The xylophone!" she cried, looking back and forth from the man to the hissing train. Which was more terrible? The bell began to ring hollowly, and the man was talking.

"Did you say Ellisville? That in the state of Mississippi?" Like lightning he had pulled out a red notebook entitled, "Permanent Facts & Data." He wrote down something. "I don't hear well."

Aimee nodded her head up and down, and circled around him.

Under "Ellis-Ville Miss" he was drawing a line; now he was flicking it with two little marks. "Maybe she didn't say she would. Maybe she said she wouldn't." He suddenly laughed very loudly, after the way he had whispered. Aimee jumped back. "Women!—Well, if we play anywheres near Ellisville, Miss., in the future I may look her up and I may not," he said.

The bass horn sounded the true signal for the band to begin. White steam rushed out of the engine. Usually the train stopped for only a minute in Victory, but the engineer knew Lily from waving at her, and he knew this was her big day.

"Wait!" Aimee Slocum did scream. "Wait, mister! I can get her for you. Wait, Mister Engineer! Don't go!"

Then there she was back on the train, screaming in Mrs. Carson's and Mrs. Watts's faces.

"The xylophone player! The xylophone player to marry her! Yonder he is!"

"Nonsense," murmured Mrs. Watts, peering over the others to look where Aimee pointed. "If he's there I don't see him. Where is he? You're looking at One-Eye Beasley."

"The little man with the cap—no, with the red hair! Hurry!"

"Is that really him?" Mrs. Carson asked Mrs. Watts in wonder. "Mercy! He's small, isn't he?"

"Never saw him before in my life!" cried Mrs. Watts. But suddenly she shut up her fan.

"Come on! This is a train we're on!" cried Aimee Slocum. Her nerves were all unstrung.

"All right, don't have a conniption fit, girl," said Mrs. Watts. "Come on," she said thickly to Mrs. Carson.

"Where are we going now?" asked Lily as they struggled down the aisle.

"We're taking you to get married," said Mrs. Watts. "Mrs. Carson, you'd better phone up your husband right there in the station."

"But I don't want to git married," said Lily, beginning to whimper. "I'm going to Ellisville."

"Hush, and we'll all have some ice-cream cones later," whispered Mrs. Carson.

Just as they climbed down the steps at the back end of the train, the band went into "Independence March."

The xylophone player was still there, patting his foot. He came up and said, "Hello, Toots. What's up—tricks?" and kissed Lily with a smack, after which she hung her head.

"So you're the young man we've heard so much about," said Mrs. Watts. Her smile was brilliant. "Here's your little Lily."

"What say?" asked the xylophone player.

"My husband happens to be the Baptist preacher of Victory," said Mrs. Carson in a loud, clear voice. "Isn't that lucky? I can get him here in five minutes: I know exactly where he is."

They were in a circle around the xylophone player, all going into the white waiting room.

"Oh, I feel just like crying, at a time like this," said Aimee Slocum. She looked back and saw the train moving slowly away, going under the bridge at Main Street. Then it disappeared around the curve.

"Oh, the hope chest!" Aimee cried in a stricken voice.

"And whom have we the pleasure of addressing?" Mrs. Watts was shouting, while Mrs. Carson was ringing up the telephone.

The band went on playing. Some of the people thought Lily was on the train, and some swore she wasn't. Everybody cheered, though, and a straw hat was thrown into the telephone wires.

Poetry

1 ❧ The Definition of Poetry

Lovers of poetry have been searching for an accurate definition of it for at least two thousand years. The ideal definition would be short. It would enable us to know a real poem when we hear it, and help us understand the power and long life of great poetry. But the search for this definition has not yielded a single description or formula to satisfy all admirers of this various art. Like most things human, poetry will not be reduced, tagged, or made to sit in one corner for very long. And there are as many ways to account for its power as there are poets.

W. H. Auden's description of poetry as "memorable speech" applies to most poetry but also to many things that are not poetry, such as advertising jingles. Matthew Arnold called poetry a "criticism of life," a characterization that is certainly true of his own poetry and discounts advertising jingles, but that is not a useful description of limericks or of nonsense poems such as Lewis Carroll's "Jabberwocky." William Wordsworth believed that poetry was "the spontaneous overflow of powerful feelings," a dramatic but broad definition, and Robert Frost viewed it as that property of speech that is "untranslatable."

All these poets would agree, however, that poetry is markedly different from the prose of legal contracts, encyclopedias, or newspapers. Poetry is more intense than other writing—more intense with feeling, and more intense in its concentration of meaning. Poetry is the true language of emotion. We have all had the experience of joy, love, or sadness so great that no matter how urgently we need to express it, words fail us. The birth of a child, the return of a friend after long absence, the death of a parent: these events can leave us speechless. At such times we might wish we were poets. For poetry succeeds where ordinary speech fails to communicate those urgent and subtle feelings that are most essentially human. That is why poetry is the most enduring form of literature.

By saying that poetry is the language of emotion, we do not mean to suggest that poetry does not engage our thoughts and ideas. Poets may praise the theories of relativity and economics as well as the colors of the sunset. Like Hamlet, they may pose an abstract question: "To be, or not to be, that is the question." But if the writer does not communicate the emotion of discovering thought, we are not likely to find poetry in that writer's work.

Ezra Pound said that "literature is news that *stays* news." He must have had poetry in mind, for great poetry is eternally fresh. The poet writes what is most important in a given moment, and writes with such intensity and clarity that years later the verse can still seem important to a reader. How does a poet do this? Suiting the words and the rhythm of language perfectly to the experience, the poet says it so that we cannot imagine it being said any better.

Let us read a poem of joy and thoughtful discovery by a recent contemporary, James Wright.

JAMES WRIGHT (1927–1980)

A Blessing

Just off the highway to Rochester, Minnesota,
Twilight bounds softly forth on the grass.
And the eyes of those two Indian ponies
Darken with kindness.
5   They have come gladly out of the willows
To welcome my friend and me.
We step over the barbed wire into the pasture
Where they have been grazing all day, alone.
They ripple tensely, they can hardly contain their happiness
10   That we have come.
They bow shyly as wet swans. They love each other.
There is no loneliness like theirs.
At home once more,
They begin munching the young tufts of spring in the darkness.
15   I would like to hold the slenderer one in my arms.
For she has walked over to me
And nuzzled my left hand.
She is black and white,
Her mane falls wild on her forehead,
20   And the light breeze moves me to caress her long ear
That is delicate as the skin over a girl's wrist.
Suddenly I realize
That if I stepped out of my body I would break
Into blossom.

Our time for reading serious literature is limited. Therefore, we have every reason to ask our poets, What claim do you make on our attention? How has this poem arrived in front of us? And, now that it is here, what are we to make of it? You have noticed that poems usually have more white space around them than other literature, as if to say that they are somehow special, that they deserve extra attention. The great poems *are* special. They earn their space on the page and invite our attention.

In the case of James Wright's poem our opening questions are easily answered. How has the poem come to us? Wright and his friend turned "just off the highway" and encountered two ponies. Their beauty and affection for each other, and their delight in welcoming the two travelers, cause the poet to realize something important about himself. The poem comes to us because he wishes to share the experience and his discovery.

Is this an experience we wish to share? The title, "A Blessing," piques our curiosity, suggesting that something remarkable is about to happen. In the first lines Wright evokes a world rich with possibilities. Twilight is a charming hour, a time of day in which magic seems likely. When "twilight bounds softly forth" in the shape of two ponies, we find ourselves in a world that is both familiar and strange, and altogether enticing. The beauty of the horses, who "bow shyly as wet swans," and the warmth of their greeting add to the enchantment of the scene.

By the time Wright admits the impulse "to hold the slenderer one in my arms," we have identified with him and can share his love for these exquisite creatures. When he speaks of the pony's ear, "delicate as the skin over a girl's wrist," the comparison reveals that Wright sees the horses as nearly human in their capacity to inspire and receive love. At the same time we can understand that the skin that separates human from human, and person from animal, is a very thin one.

It is just one more stage in the poet's thought to realize that he himself is part of nature and that he might, in a single step out of his body, out of the slender confines of human life, break into blossom. Hence the great power and beauty of the last lines. It is an important revelation, perfectly expressed. Miracles are in short supply, and a poem that can provide one has earned our attention. It is indeed "A Blessing."

Not all poetry is so joyous. The next poem, Emily Dickinson's meditation on death, moves us in a quite different direction.

EMILY DICKINSON (1830–1866)

• I Felt a Funeral in My Brain

I felt a funeral in my brain,
And mourners to and fro
Kept treading, treading, till it seemed
That sense was breaking through.

5 And when they all were seated,
A service like a drum
Kept beating, beating, till I thought
My mind was going numb.

And then I heard them lift a box
10 And creak across my soul
With those same boots of lead again,
Then space began to toll,

As all the heavens were a bell,
And being but an ear,
20   And I and silence some strange race
Wrecked solitary here.

And then a plank in reason broke,
And I dropped down and down
And hit a world at every plunge,
25   And finished knowing then.

Questions

1. Where is the action of the poem really taking place?
2. Whose funeral is it? The poet's? A friend's?
3. What is in the box?
4. Would the mourners actually wear "boots of lead"? If not, why does the poet describe them that way?
5. At the end of the poem, the poet says that she "hit a world at every plunge." What sorts of worlds do you imagine?

Emily Dickinson (*Amherst College Library*)

Everyone who has lived enough to value life has had a similar curiosity and fear about death. Emily Dickinson fashioned this poem out of the richness of those feelings, and we are moved to find them so similar to our own. Notice how the poet personalizes her fear by taking the funeral out of the real world and putting it into her own brain. Next she introduces ominous sounds and makes them more frightening through repetition: the footsteps of the mourners, the beating of the drum, the tolling of the bell. Try to imagine the horror of those sounds going on inside your own head. It is not at all surprising, then, when the poet tells us that "a plank in reason broke." No one's sanity could withstand such a racket. When her reason breaks, she feels herself falling through worlds and worlds until she finally arrives where there can be no knowing. Many of us are familiar with the fear of falling. The poet is telling us that death must be like falling through some plank of reason to a place where nothing is known. This is an exciting, if fearful, way of looking at death.

The two poems we have read so far represent the more thoughtful, serious side of the muse. The Muses, nine sister goddesses in Greek mythology, presided over the creative arts. From them we get the word *music* as well as the phrase *the muse*, which has come to designate the source of all poetic genius and inspiration. The muse has many different moods, as the multiplicity of the Greek goddesses suggests. Poetry is not always as mystical as Wright's "A Blessing" or as brooding as Dickinson's "I Felt a Funeral in My Brain." It can also be erotic or comical. In the following poem by Christopher Marlowe, we see the muse at its fun-loving best, as the speaker, a shepherd, tries to persuade his lady friend to be his love.

CHRISTOPHER MARLOWE (1564–1593)

• The Passionate Shepherd to His Love

Come live with me and be my love,
And we will all the pleasures prove°   *test, evaluate*
That valleys, groves, hills, and fields,
Woods, or steepy mountain yields.

5   And we will sit upon the rocks,
Seeing the shepherds feed their flocks
By shallow rivers, to whose falls
Melodious birds sing madrigals.

And I will make thee beds of roses
10   And a thousand fragrant posies,
A cap of flowers and a kirtle°   *gown*
Embroidered all with leaves of myrtle;

A gown made of the finest wool
Which from our pretty lambs we pull;
15   Fair-lined slippers for the cold,
With buckles of the purest gold;

A belt of straw and ivy buds,
With coral clasps and amber studs.
And if these pleasures may thee move,
20   Come live with me and be my love.

The shepherds' swains shall dance and sing
For thy delight each May morning:
If these delights thy mind may move,
Then live with me and be my love.

Questions

1. Vocabulary: *posies* (10), *swains* (21).
2. What has moved the shepherd to speak? Is it the same emotion that has inspired Marlowe to write the poem?
3. Why does the shepherd take such care in describing the clothes he will make for his "love"?
4. Do you think that life with the shepherd would be as marvelous as he describes it?
5. Would the poem lend itself to music?
6. Do you think the shepherd's argument is persuasive?
7. Compare this poem with Sir Walter Raleigh's "The Nymph's Reply to the Shepherd" on page 708.

The next poem, a whimsical children's story cast in rhyme, appeals to still another appetite in us, the love of nonsense and satire. The poem was written for children. But its portraiture of the ironic bear and its gentle satire of the gushing Lady sustain reexamination by readers of all ages.

THEODORE ROETHKE (1908–1963)

The Lady and the Bear

A Lady came to a Bear by a Stream.
"O Why are you fishing that way?
Tell me, dear Bear there by the Stream,
Why are you fishing that way?"

5   "I am what is known as a Biddly Bear,—
That's why I'm fishing this way.
We Biddly's are Pee-culiar Bears,
And so,—I'm fishing this way.
"And besides, it seems there's a Law:
10   A most, most exactious Law
Says a Bear
Doesn't dare
Doesn't dare
Doesn't DARE
15   Use a Hook or a Line,
Or an old piece of Twine,

Not even the end of his Claw, Claw, Claw,
Not even the end of his Claw.
Yes, a Bear has to fish with his Paw, Paw, Paw.
20 A Bear has to fish with his Paw."

"O it's Wonderful how with a flick of your Wrist,
You can fish, out a fish, out a fish, out a fish.
If *I* were a fish I just couldn't resist
You, when you are fishing that way, that way,
25 When you are fishing that way."

And at that the Lady slipped from the Bank
And fell in the Stream still clutching a Plank,
But the Bear just sat there until she Sank;
As he went on fishing his way, his way,
30 As he went on fishing his way.

Questions

1. From the beginning of the poem, the Lady is quite complimentary to the Bear. From his comments in stanza 2, do you think that he appreciates her flattery, her presence?
2. When the Lady falls into the stream, why doesn't the Bear help her?

2 ❧ Listening in on the Poem

Distinguishing between eloquence and poetry, John Stuart Mill wrote that eloquence is heard, but poetry is overheard. This suggests a useful way to read poetry. Imagine that we have picked up a telephone to make a call. To our surprise, we hear someone talking on the other end. At first we do not understand what the person is saying, but because something in the speaker's voice interests us, we continue listening. By piecing together bits of information, we eventually come to understand the conversation. The same is true of many poems. At first we may be puzzled, but if we listen long and carefully enough, the good poets will tell us what we need to know to appreciate what they are saying.

Having the text of the poem gives us an advantage over the telephone eavesdropper. We can reread the poem in order to understand and appreciate the speaker fully. Also, the reader of a poem can look up unfamiliar words in the dictionary. Before tackling any poem, we should give ourselves time to reread it, and we should have a dictionary close at hand.

How then do we piece together the poet's conversation? One way to begin is by asking ourselves three basic questions:

1. Who is speaking?
2. To whom is he or she speaking?
3. What has prompted the speaker to talk?

Sometimes the answers to these questions will be obvious and unrevealing. But often they are necessary for understanding the poem. The following is a good example of an overheard poem.

WALTER SAVAGE LANDOR (1775–1864)

Mother, I Cannot Mind My Wheel

Mother, I cannot mind my wheel;
  My fingers ache, my lips are dry:

Oh! if you felt the pain I feel!
        But oh, who ever felt as I?

5   No longer could I doubt him true;
        All other men may use deceit:
    He always said my eyes were blue,
        And often swore my lips were sweet.

The first word of this poem provides the answer to our second question: the poem is addressed to the speaker's mother. After reading the first line, we know that the daughter is speaking, trying to explain why she cannot sit quietly at the spinning wheel, a task that requires great patience. She tells her mother that her fingers ache and her lips are dry. But in the second stanza she reveals the true reason for her restlessness—her lover has abandoned her. His abandonment is especially painful for the speaker because she had trusted him. "All other men may use deceit," but her man, she thought, was honest. Moreover, he had flattered her by admiring her blue eyes and sweet lips.

We may also infer from the poem that the speaker—or *persona*, as the speaker is called—is young and naive. She asks her mother, "But oh, who ever felt as I?" as if no one else had ever known disappointed love. Her statement is not really a question, but an exclamation. For the moment, the woman feels utterly abandoned and heartsick.

What emerges from these eight short lines is a portrait of a young woman in the throes of her first disappointed love. Landor has given us a rich, vivid picture. No word is wasted.

Perhaps you have other questions. Is the girl ugly or pretty? Rich or poor? Was the man a neighbor or a stranger? Is the mother indifferent, angry, or sympathetic? These are all good questions, but we simply cannot answer them. The poet has not given us the necessary information. Instead of speculating, we will simply remain silent. The good reader will keep to the facts of the text and refrain from making unsupported guesses. We can do nothing more than read carefully. Where the poem is silent, we must be silent too.

The Persona and the Poet

In "Mother, I Cannot Mind My Wheel," the persona—or speaker—is obviously not Walter Savage Landor. But even in poems in which the speaker is not clearly distinguished from the author, it is often useful to think of the speaker as a fictional character. Here is a personal poem in which it is unimportant whether the speaker is the author or someone else.

LINDA PASTAN (1931–)

25th High School Reunion

We come to hear the endings
of all the stories

in our anthology
of false starts:
5   how the girl who seemed
as hard as nails
was hammered into shape;
how the athletes ran
out of races;
10   how under the skin
our skulls rise
to the surface
like rocks in the bed
of a drying stream.
15   Look! We have all
turned into
ourselves.

Questions

1. What does the speaker mean when he or she says, "We have all/turned into/
ourselves"?
2. To what might "our anthology/of false starts" refer?

    The title of this poem is crucial to our understanding of it. (Titles are often important and should never be overlooked.) If we ask who the speaker is, we can say only that it is a high school graduate who has celebrated his or her twenty-fifth reunion and is, therefore, middle-aged. Linda Pastan may fit this description, but the poem does not require her to be the speaker. In fact, the speaker might be *any* middle-aged high school graduate.

    The reunion has forced the speaker to reflect on how his or her classmates have changed. A tough student has been "hammered into shape." The athletes look worn out. Everyone appears to have dried up. The alumni's skulls are becoming prominent, signifying the approach of death.

    The poem ends on a surprising note. The speaker turns directly to us, addressing us as fellow alumni and reminding us that we too will be middle-aged someday and will begin to show signs of approaching death.

The Importance of Context

Sometimes speakers do not refer to themselves at all in the poem; nevertheless, our appreciation of the poem may be enhanced by imagining a context for the speaker. In the following poem, "Musée des Beaux Arts" (which means "Fine Arts Museum" in French), we might find it useful to imagine the speaker as a tour guide pointing out one beautiful painting after another and commenting on the great artists—the Old Masters—who painted them.

    For a moment we stop in front of Pieter Brueghel's painting *Landscape with the Fall of Icarus* in a museum in Brussels, Belgium, which

Landscape with the Fall of Icarus, by Pieter Brueghel the Elder (*Royal Museums of Art and History, Brussels*)

Auden visited in 1939, just before he wrote this poem. Icarus was the son of Daedalus, whose name means literally "cunning worker." Father and son were imprisoned together in a tower, where Daedalus made wings out of wax and feathers so that they could escape. The device worked, but Icarus was so delighted with his wings that he flew toward the sun. The sun melted the wings, and Icarus fell to his death in the sea below. With that bit of information, you should be ready to begin to appreciate the poem.

W. H. AUDEN (1907–1973)

Musée des Beaux Arts

About suffering they were never wrong,
The Old Masters: how well they understood
Its human position; how it takes place
While someone else is eating or opening a window or just walking dully along;
5   How, when the aged are reverently, passionately waiting
For the miraculous birth, there always must be
Children who did not specially want it to happen, skating
On a pond at the edge of the wood:
They never forgot
10   That even the dreadful martyrdom must run its course
Anyhow in a corner, some untidy spot
Where the dogs go on with their doggy life and the torturer's horse
Scratches its innocent behind on a tree.

In Brueghel's *Icarus,* for instance: how everything turns away
15   Quite leisurely from the disaster; the ploughman may

Have heard the splash, the forsaken cry,
But for him it was not an important failure; the sun shone
As it had to on the white legs disappearing into the green
Water; and the expensive delicate ship that must have seen
20 Something amazing, a boy falling out of the sky,
Had somewhere to get to and sailed calmly on.

Questions

1. Vocabulary: *martyrdom* (10).
2. What is the "human position" that suffering occupies?
3. How is suffering depicted in Brueghel's *Icarus*?
4. What political events of 1939 may have prompted Auden to write about suffering?
5. Does the speaker follow the Old Masters' examples for showing suffering?
6. Do you think the matter-of-fact tone is appropriate for this poem? Would the poem be more effective if the speaker were more emotional?
7. What sort of attitude should we adopt toward the poem? Toward suffering?

The Poet as Speaker

Finally, there are poems in which the speaker is unquestionably the poet. Biographical information may be useful for appreciating such poems, but they can move us even without such knowledge. Take Ben Jonson's poem on the death of his son:

BEN JONSON (1573?–1637)

On My First Son

Farewell, thou child of my right hand, and joy;
My sin was too much hope of thee, loved boy:
Seven years thou wert lent to me, and I thee pay,
Exacted by the fate, on the just day.[1]
5   O could I lose all father now! for why
Will man lament the state he should envy,
To have so soon 'scaped world's and flesh's rage,
And, if no other misery, yet age?
Rest in soft peace, and asked, say, "Here doth lie
10 Ben Jonson his best piece of poetry."
For whose sake henceforth all his vows be such
As what he loves may never like too much.

Questions

1. To whom is the poem addressed? Does this fact suggest something about Jonson's spiritual beliefs?
2. In what sense might a man "envy" the death of a young boy?

---

[1] The boy was born in 1596 and died on his birthday in 1603.

3. Would you call Jonson a proud father? Does Jonson feel there is any connection between his fatherly pride and his son's death?
4. What is the relationship between Jonson's son and poetry?
5. What relationship does Jonson hope to develop in the future between himself and those he loves?

This poem ably conveys the feeling of grief, whether or not we know anything about Ben Jonson. Additional information will, however, help us appreciate Jonson's sorrow. For example, Jonson's son was named Benjamin after his father. The first line of the poem contains the Hebrew meaning of the boy's name: "child of the right hand."

The poem contains one complicated line, "O could I lose all father now!" Jonson means that he wishes he could forget he possessed the attributes of fatherhood; then he might regard his son's death more philosophically. He could console himself with the knowledge that by dying young the boy has escaped many hardships.

The poet can have various relationships to the persona of a poem. Sometimes the speaker is not the poet, but a fictional character. At other times the speaker could be the poet but does not necessarily have to be. At still other times the speaker does not even appear as a character in the poem. Whatever relationship the poet adopts to the speaker, we should listen closely to the speaker's words and base our assumptions on the text of the poem and the context of the speaker.

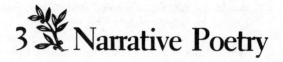

3 ❧ Narrative Poetry

The Poet as Storyteller

We commonly think that stories, like laws, are best written in prose. Yet the ancient Greeks composed their laws in verse, and the earliest known poem, *The Epic of Gilgamesh*, composed in Sumer some five thousand years ago, is a long tale about the adventures of a king.

The first narrative or storytelling poems recounted the adventures of great heroes and their relations with gods and demons. Often these poems would record a nation's origins and history. They were also an early source of entertainment. Poet-reciters called *bards* regaled courts with these long heroic tales. Later, scribes committed the narrative poems to paper, and so they are preserved today. In England the scribes were often monks, who were scolded by their superiors for taking time away from religious studies to copy down pagan poems. In the nineteenth century, scholars like Francis Child roamed the countryside collecting the ballads and stories of illiterate peasants.

Formulae

How could an illiterate bard remember a poem that might take all evening to recite? First, the rhythms of the poem helped him to remember, just as we are more likely to remember a jingle than a flat piece of prose of equal length. Also, the bards had stock phrases, or *formulae*, that they used over and over again. Similarly, little formulae help parents tell bedtime stories. In "Goldilocks and the Three Bears," for example, there are constantly reworked phrases:

"Someone's been sitting in my chair."
"Someone's been eating my porridge."
"Someone's been sleeping in my bed."

These formulae help parents tell the story each night in roughly the same words. Like parents, bards did not remember their poems perfectly, and the poems passed down through oral tradition usually appear in a number of different versions.

Let us look at a Scottish ballad, a poem composed orally and handed down from singer to singer. Like an epic, this ballad tells the story of a brave man, and it relies on the repetition of formulaic expressions. In the version that follows, most of the language has been modernized, but enough of the Scottish dialogue remains to give you a flavor of the original.

ANONYMOUS

Sir Patrick Spence

The king sits in Dumferling town
    Drinking the blood-red wine:
"O where will I get a good sailor,
    To sail this ship of mine?"

5   Up and spake an elder knight
    Sat on the king's right knee:
"Sir Patrick Spence is the best sailor,
    That sails upon the sea."

The king has written a broad letter
10   And signed it with his hand
And sent it to Sir Patrick Spence
    Was walking on the sand.

The first line that Sir Patrick read
    A loud lauch° lauched he;   *laugh*
15   The next line that Sir Patrick read
    The tear blinded his ee.°   *eye*

"O who is this has done this deed
    This ill deed done to me,
To send me out this time of the year,
20   To sail upon the sea!

"Make haste, make haste, my merry men all
    Our good ship sails the morn."
"O say not so, my master dear,
    For I fear a deadly storm.

25   "Late, late yestreen° I saw the new moon   *last evening*
    With the old moon in her arm
And I fear, I fear, my dear master
    That we will come to harm."

O our Scots nobles were rich laith°   *very loath*
30   To wet their cork-healed schoone;°   *shoes*
But long before the play was played
    Their hats they swam aboone.°   *above*

O long, long may their ladies sit,
    With their fans into their hand

35 Or e'er they see Sir Patrick Spence
        Come sailing to the land.

    O long, long may the ladies stand
        With their golden combs in their hair
    Waiting for their own dear lords
40   For they'll see them no mair.°   *more*

    Half o'er, half o'er to Aberdour,
        It's fifty fathoms deep,
    And there lies good Sir Patrick Spence,
        With the Scots lords at his feet.

"Sir Patrick Spence" is like a short story in many ways, but the differences are interesting and important. Like many short stories, it contains characters, a setting, conflict and dialogue, and a single significant action. But in "Sir Patrick Spence" these elements are more condensed. We never learn where Sir Patrick lived or how he achieved his fame. The poet tells us only that he was walking on the beach. Nor do we learn whether he is married or has children. These details would be important in a short story, but they are unimportant for the poetic narrator. Nevertheless, we do learn a good deal about Sir Patrick. He sees the foolish, vindictive, and thoughtless nature of the king's courtiers. But he is loyal and brave. He does not question his orders but immediately commands his sailors, despite their protests, to man the ship. His actions say more than words. Of course, the longer the narrative, the greater its detail. Book-length poems contain a rich supply of narrative detail.

Transitions in Narrative Poetry

"Sir Patrick Spence" illustrates another mark of the poetic narrative technique: rarely are there transitions from one scene to another. A narrative poem moves in much the same way as a film. Movie directors often shift instantaneously from one scene to another. Similarly, in "Sir Patrick Spence" we move from a scene in which Sir Patrick reads his orders to one in which he is on the deck encouraging his frightened sailors. Moreover, in a poetic narrative we do not necessarily begin at the beginning of the story. For example, Charles Dickens starts his novel *David Copperfield* with the sentence "I am born." But the poetic narrator begins, as critics have noted, *in medias res*—Latin for "in the middle of things." The shorter the poem, the more concentrated the action. In the most concentrated narrative poems, the climax alone is presented.

Still another feature of the narrative poem is omission of certain scenes. In "Sir Patrick Spence," for example, the scene of the shipwreck is entirely missing. The poet shows us only the hats floating above the sunken ship, markers signaling the disaster brought by vanity. The rhythm and music of the poem provide the continuity we would have missed if this were a prose account.

The ballad form provides an excellent mode for narration. A discussion of ballad form is provided in Chapter 12. Here it is enough to point out that the

Langston Hughes (*National Portrait Gallery, Smithsonian Institution, Washington, D.C.*)

four-line stanza, or *quatrain*, provides a handy short unit for developing a single scene. The second and fourth lines are shorter than the first and third. These shorter lines give the stanza its speed and propel the reader from stanza to stanza.

Ballads continue to be popular, especially with poets who wish to reach a wide audience. Here is a modern ballad.

LANGSTON HUGHES (1902–1967)

Sylvester's Dying Bed

I woke up this mornin'
'Bout half-past three.
All the womens in town
Was gathered round me.

5   Sweet gals was a-moanin',
"Sylvester's gonna die!"
And a hundred pretty mamas
Bowed their heads to cry.

I woke up a little later
10   'Bout half-past fo',
The doctor 'n' undertaker's
Both at ma do'.

Black gals was a-beggin',
"You can't leave us here!"
15 Brown-skins cryin', "Daddy!
Honey! Baby! Don't go, dear!"

But I felt ma time's a-comin',
And I know'd I's dyin' fast.
I seed the River Jerden
20 A-creepin' muddy past—
But I's still Sweet Papa 'Vester,
Yes, sir! Long as life do last!

So I hollers, "Com'ere, babies,
Fo' to love yo' daddy right!"
25 And I reaches up to hug 'em—
When the Lawd put out the light.

Then everything was darkness
In a great . . . big . . . night.

Questions

1. Is there anything heroic about Sylvester? How would you compare the way he approaches death with the way Sir Patrick Spence meets his fate?
2. Are there any repeated phrases or formulaic expressions in "Sylvester's Dying Bed"? How do they contribute to the story?
3. The four-line stanza pattern is broken twice in this poem. Why is stanza 5 longer than the others? Why is stanza 7 shorter?

Epic Poetry

The longest narratives are called *epics*. These poems do not simply recount a single action; they record a way of life. The Greek epics, the *Iliad* and the *Odyssey*, are among the greatest treasures of Western culture. These orally transmitted narratives are called *primary epics*. Later, poets consciously imitated these earlier works by writing epics of their own. Virgil's *Aeneid*, Dante's *Divine Comedy*, and John Milton's *Paradise Lost* are among the most famous secondary epics. Epics are too long for us to include a complete one in this book, but excerpts from the *Odyssey* and the *Divine Comedy* appear at the end of this chapter.

Personal History in Narrative Poems

Unlike the bards of ancient Greece or the minstrels of Scotland, contemporary poets are not responsible for recording national history, although some continue to narrate incidents of national importance. More often, however, today's poets tell personal or family histories that are more likely to be forgotten in the future. The following poem is one of several poems by Edward Field that recount his family's history.

EDWARD FIELD (1924–)

My Polish Grandmother

Grandma and the children left at night.
It was forbidden to go. In those days
the Czar and his cossacks rode through the town at whim
killing Jews and setting fire to straw roofs
5   while just down the road the local Poles
sat laughing as they drank liquor.

Grandpa had gone to America first
and earned the money for the rest of the family to come over.
So they left finally, the whole brood of them
10   with the hired agent running the show,
an impatient man, and there were so many kids
and the bundles kept falling apart
and poor grandma was frightened of him.

She gave the man all the money
15   but she couldn't round up the kids fast enough for him.
They were children after all and didn't understand
and she was so stupid and clumsy herself,
carrying food for all of them and their clothes
and could she leave behind her pots?
20   Her legs hurt already; they were always swollen
from the hard work, the childbearing, and the cold.

They caught the train and there was a terrible moment
when the conductor came by for the tickets:
The children mustn't speak or he would know they were Jewish,
25   they had no permits to travel—Jews weren't allowed.
But the agent knew how to handle it,
everybody got *shmeared*, that means money got you everywhere.

The border was the worst. They had to sneak across at night.
The children mustn't make a sound, not even the babies.
30   Momma was six and she didn't want to do anything wrong
but she wasn't sure what to do.
The man led them through the woods
and beyond they could hear dogs barking from the sentry hut,
and then they had to run all of them down the ravine to the other side,
35   grandma broken down from childbearing with her bundles
and bad legs and a baby in her arms,
they ran all the children across the border
or the guards might shoot them
and if the little ones cried, the agent said he would smother them.

40   They got to a port finally.
Grandpa had arranged for cabin passage, not steerage,
but the agent cheated and put them in the hold
so they were on the low deck looking up at the rich people.
My momma told me how grandma took care of all her children,
45   how Jake didn't move anymore he was so seasick, maybe even dead,

and if people thought he was dead
they would throw him overboard like garbage, so she hid him.
The rich tossed down oranges to the poor children—
my momma had never had one before.

50   They came to New York, to the tenements,
a fearful new place, a city, country people in the city.
My momma, who had been roly-poly in slow Poland,
got skinny and pimply in zippy New York.
Everybody grew up in a new way.
55   And now my grandma is dead and my momma is old
and we her children are all scattered over the earth
speaking a different language and forgetting
why it was so important
to go to a new country.

Questions

1. Vocabulary: *cossacks* (3), *ravine* (34), *steerage* (41).
2. Why does Field feel compelled to retell this story?
3. What is worth retelling about this story? Does your family have similar stories about coming to America?
4. How does the poem reflect political history?
5. In what way does this poem start *in medias res?*
6. Compare this poem to Gary Soto's "History" on pages 792–93.

Use of Language in Narrative Poetry

There is yet another difference between the traditional prose story and the poetic narrative. The prose writer, by and large, wants to make the scene so vivid that we look beyond the words and feel that we are actually present in the scene. The poet, however, at crucial moments draws our attention to the language. In fact, the poet would like to believe that the story is happening *in* the language. In the following poem we are asked to pay particularly close attention to the last line.

DANIEL MARK EPSTEIN (1948–)

Madonna (with Child Missing)[1]

Shouts from the street, spotlights crossfire
at a third story window. The woman
stares through smoked glass at a crowd
and firemen in glazed slickers—
5   flames climbing the stairs behind her two at a time.
She lifts up the window sash with one hand,
kisses the infant and rolls it out trusting the air,
the soft knock of skull on stone in her heart.

---

[1] *Madonna* is Italian for "mother." It is often the name of works of art depicting the Virgin Mary.

Notice the last line. Would this be an acceptable ending in a prose story? If this were a prose account, wouldn't we demand to know whether the child was saved? In a poetic narrative these plot concerns are less important. For the mother, the child is both saved and injured. The sounds and rhythms of the last line imitate both the erratic beating of the mother's heart and the imagined disaster to the child. The story is secondary to the action of the language. It is this concern with language that makes a poetic narrative so memorable for both the original audience and the contemporary reader. In the poems that follow, you should try to attend not only to the engaging stories the poets write, but also to the language they use to enact the story.

Suggestions for Essayists

1. Retell in prose one of the narrative poems from this chapter. Discuss what you have gained in the translation and what you have lost.
2. Discuss how the ideas of loyalty and heroism have changed since the time of Sir Patrick Spence.
3. Narrate an episode of family history that you have either lived through or heard about and that is in danger of being forgotten.

Suggestions for Poets

1. Narrate an episode of family history that is in danger of being forgotten.
2. Find an episode in the newspaper and retell it in ballad form.

Poems for Further Study

DUDLEY RANDALL (1914–)

Ballad of Birmingham[2]

(On the bombing of a church in Birmingham, Alabama, 1963)

"Mother dear, may I go downtown
Instead of out to play,
And march the streets of Birmingham
In a Freedom March today?"

5   "No, baby, no, you may not go,
For the dogs are fierce and wild,
And clubs and hoses, guns and jails
Aren't good for a little child."

"But, mother, I won't be alone.
10   Other children will go with me,

---

[2] "Freedom marches" were parades organized to promote civil rights in the South during the 1950s and the 1960s.

And march the streets of Birmingham
To make our country free."

"No, baby, no, you may not go,
For I fear those guns will fire.
15   But you may go to church instead
And sing in the children's choir."

She has combed and brushed her night-dark hair,
And bathed rose petal sweet,
And drawn white gloves on her small brown hands,
20   And white shoes on her feet.

The mother smiled to know her child
Was in the sacred place,
But that smile was the last smile
To come upon her face.

25   For when she heard the explosion,
Her eyes grew wet and wild.
She raced through the streets of Birmingham
Calling for her child.

She clawed through bits of glass and brick,
30   Then lifted out a shoe.
"O, here's the shoe my baby wore,
But, baby, where are you?"

ROBERT FROST (1874–1963)

'Out, Out—'[3]

The buzz-saw snarled and rattled in the yard
And made dust and dropped stove-length sticks of wood,
Sweet-scented stuff when the breeze drew across it.
And from there those that lifted eyes could count
5   Five mountain ranges one behind the other
Under the sunset far into Vermont.
And the saw snarled and rattled, snarled and rattled,
As it ran light, or had to bear a load.
And nothing happened: day was all but done.
10   Call it a day, I wish they might have said
To please the boy by giving him the half hour
That a boy counts so much when saved from work.
His sister stood beside them in her apron
To tell them 'Supper.' At the word, the saw,
15   As if to prove saws knew what supper meant,
Leaped out at the boy's hand, or seemed to leap—

---

[3] The title is an allusion to Shakespeare's *Macbeth*, Act V, Scene 5, in which Macbeth, hearing about his wife's death, says, "Out, out, brief candle! / Life's but a walking shadow, a poor player / That struts and frets his hour upon the stage / And then is heard no more."

He must have given the hand. However it was,
Neither refused the meeting. But the hand!
The boy's first outcry was a rueful laugh,
20   As he swung toward them holding up the hand
Half in appeal, but half as if to keep
The life from spilling. Then the boy saw all—
Since he was old enough to know, big boy
Doing a man's work, though a child at heart—
25   He saw all spoiled. 'Don't let him cut my hand off—
The doctor, when he comes. Don't let him, sister!'

So. But the hand was gone already.
The doctor put him in the dark of ether.
He lay and puffed his lips out with his breath.
30   And then—the watcher at his pulse took fright.
No one believed. They listened at his heart.
Little—less—nothing!—and that ended it.
No more to build on there. And they, since they
Were not the one dead, turned to their affairs.

SHARON OLDS (1942–)

The Race

When I got to the airport I rushed up to the desk
and they told me the flight was cancelled. The doctors had
said my father would not live through the night
and the flight was cancelled. A young man with a
5   dark blond mustache told me
another airline had a non-stop
leaving in seven minutes—see that
elevator over there well go
down to the first floor, make a right you'll
10   see a yellow bus, get off at the
second Pan Am terminal—I
ran, I who have no sense of direction
raced exactly where he'd told me, like a fish
slipping upstream deftly against the
15   flow of the river. I jumped off that bus with my
heavy bags and ran, the bags
wagged me from side to side as if to
prove I was under the claims of the material, I
ran up to a man with a white flower on his breast,
20   I who always go to the end of the line, I said
Help me. He looked at my ticket, he said make a
left and then a right go up the moving stairs and then
run. I raced up the moving stairs
two at a time, at the top I saw the
25   long hollow corridor and
then I took a deep breath, I said

goodbye to my body, goodbye to comfort, I
used my legs and heart as if I would
gladly use them up for this, to
30   touch him again in this life. I ran and the
big heavy dark bags
banged me, wheeled and swam around me like
planets in wild orbits—I have seen
pictures of women running down roads with their
35   belongings tied in black scarves
grasped in their fists, running under serious
gray historical skies—I blessed my
long legs he gave me, my strong
heart I abandoned to its own purpose, I
40   ran to Gate 17 and they were
just lifting the thick white
lozenge of the door to fit it into the
socket of the plane. Like the man who is not
too rich, I turned to the side and
45   slipped through the needle's eye, and then I
walked down the aisle toward my father. The jet was
full and people's hair was shining, they were
smiling, the interior of the plane was filled with a
mist of gold endorphin light,
50   I wept as people weep when they enter heaven,
in massive relief. We lifted up
gently from one tip of the continent and
did not stop until we set down lightly on the
other edge, I walked into his room and
55   watched his chest rise slowly and
sink again, all night
I watched him breathe.

EDWIN MUIR (1887–1959)

The Horses

Barely a twelvemonth after
The seven days war that put the world to sleep,
Late in the evening the strange horses came.
By then we had made our covenant with silence,
5   But in the first few days it was so still
We listened to our breathing and were afraid.
On the second day
The radios failed; we turned the knobs; no answer.
On the third day a warship passed us, heading north,
10   Dead bodies piled on the deck. On the sixth day
A plane plunged over us into the sea. Thereafter
Nothing. The radios dumb;
And still they stand in corners of our kitchens,
And stand, perhaps, turned on, in a million rooms

15   All over the world. But now if they should speak,
      If on a sudden they should speak again,
      If on the stroke of noon a voice should speak,
      We would not listen, we would not let it bring
      That old bad world that swallowed its children quick
20   At one great gulp. We would not have it again.
      Sometimes we think of the nations lying asleep,
      Curled blindly in impenetrable sorrow,
      And then the thought confounds us with its strangeness.
      The tractors lie about our fields; at evening
25   They look like dank sea-monsters couched and waiting.
      We leave them where they are and let them rust:
      'They'll moulder away and be like other loam'.
      We make our oxen drag our rusty ploughs,
      Long laid aside. We have gone back
30   Far past our father's land.

                            And then, that evening
      Late in the summer the strange horses came.
      We heard a distant tapping on the road,
      A deepening drumming; it stopped, went on again
      And at the corner changed to hollow thunder.
35   We saw the heads
      Like a wild wave charging and were afraid.
      We had sold our horses in our fathers' time
      To buy new tractors. Now they were strange to us
      As fabulous steeds set on an ancient shield
40   Or illustrations in a book of knights.
      We did not dare go near them. Yet they waited,
      Stubborn and shy, as if they had been sent
      By an old command to find our whereabouts
      And that long-lost archaic companionship.
45   In the first moment we had never a thought
      That they were creatures to be owned and used.
      Among them were some half-a-dozen colts
      Dropped in some wilderness of the broken world,
      Yet new as if they had come from their own Eden.
50   Since then they have pulled our ploughs and borne our loads,
      But that free servitude still can pierce our hearts.
      Our life is changed; their coming our beginning.

EDGAR ALLAN POE (1809–1849)

The Raven

      Once upon a midnight dreary, while I pondered, weak and weary,
      Over many a quaint and curious volume of forgotten lore,—
      While I nodded, nearly napping, suddenly there came a tapping,
      As of some one gently rapping, rapping at my chamber door.
5   " 'T is some visitor," I muttered, "tapping at my chamber door:
                      Only this and nothing more."

Ah, distinctly I remember it was in the bleak December,
And each separate dying ember wrought its ghost upon the floor.
Eagerly I wished the morrow;—vainly I had sought to borrow
10   From my books surcease of sorrow—sorrow for the lost Lenore,
For the rare and radiant maiden whom the angels name Lenore:
           Nameless here for evermore.

And the silken sad uncertain rustling of each purple curtain
Thrilled me—filled me with fantastic terrors never felt before;
15   So that now, to still the beating of my heart, I stood repeating
" 'T is some visitor entreating entrance at my chamber door,
Some late visitor entreating entrance at my chamber door:
           This it is and nothing more."

Presently my soul grew stronger; hesitating then no longer,
20   "Sir," said I, "or Madam, truly your forgiveness I implore;
But the fact is I was napping, and so gently you came rapping,
And so faintly you came tapping, tapping at my chamber door,
That I scarce was sure I heard you"—here I opened wide the door:—
           Darkness there and nothing more.

25   Deep into that darkness peering, long I stood there wondering, fearing,
Doubting, dreaming dreams no mortal ever dared to dream before;
But the silence was unbroken, and the stillness gave no token,
And the only word there spoken was the whispered word, "Lenore?"
This I whispered, and an echo murmured back the word, "Lenore:"
30   Merely this and nothing more.

Back into the chamber turning, all my soul within me burning,
Soon again I heard a tapping somewhat louder than before.
"Surely," said I, "surely that is something at my window lattice;
Let me see, then, what thereat is, and this mystery explore;
35   Let my heart be still a moment and this mystery explore:
           'Tis the wind and nothing more."

Open here I flung the shutter, when, with many a flirt and flutter,
In there stepped a stately Raven of the saintly days of yore.
Not the least obeisance made he; not a minute stopped or stayed he;
40   But, with mien of lord or lady, perched above my chamber door,
Perched upon a bust of Pallas[4] just above my chamber door:
           Perched, and sat, and nothing more.

Then this ebony bird beguiling my sad fancy into smiling
By the grave and stern decorum of the countenance it wore,—
45   "Though thy crest be shorn and shaven, thou," I said, "art sure no craven,
Ghastly grim and ancient Raven wandering from the Nightly shore:
Tell me what thy lordly name is on the Night's Plutonian[5] shore!"
           Quoth the Raven, "Nevermore."

---

[4] *Pallas* is Greek for "maiden" and was the epithet used to refer to Athena, the goddess of war and wisdom.
[5] *Pluto* is the god of the underworld.

Much I marvelled this ungainly fowl to hear discourse so plainly,
50   Though its answer little meaning—little relevancy bore;
For we cannot help agreeing that no living human being
Ever yet was blessed with seeing bird above his chamber door,
Bird or beast upon the sculptured bust above his chamber door,
                    With such name as "Nevermore."

55   But the Raven, sitting lonely on the placid bust, spoke only
That one word, as if his soul in that one word he did outpour.
Nothing further then he uttered, not a feather then he fluttered,
Till I scarcely more than muttered—"Other friends have flown before;
On the morrow *he* will leave me, as my Hopes have flown before."
60   Then the bird said, "Nevermore."

Startled at the stillness broken by reply so aptly spoken,
"Doubtless," said I, "what it utters is its only stock and store,
Caught from some unhappy master whom unmerciful Disaster
Followed fast and followed faster till his songs one burden bore:
65   Till the dirges of his Hope that melancholy burden bore
                    Of 'Never—nevermore.' "

But the Raven still beguiling all my fancy into smiling,
Straight I wheeled a cushioned seat in front of bird and bust and door;
Then, upon the velvet sinking, I betook myself to linking
70   Fancy unto fancy, thinking what this ominous bird of yore,
What this grim, ungainly, ghastly, gaunt, and ominous bird of yore
                    Meant in croaking "Nevermore."

This I sat engaged in guessing, but no syllable expressing
To the fowl whose fiery eyes now burned into my bosom's core;
75   This and more I sat divining, with my head at ease reclining
On the cushion's velvet lining that the lamp-light gloated o'er,
But whose velvet violet lining with the lamp-light gloating o'er
                    She shall press, ah, nevermore!

Then, methought, the air grew denser, perfumed from an unseen censer
80   Swung by seraphim whose foot-falls tinkled on the tufted floor.
"Wretch," I cried, "thy God hath lent thee—by these angels he hath sent thee
Respite—respite and nepenthe[6] from thy memories of Lenore!
Quaff, oh quaff this kind nepenthe, and forget this lost Lenore!"
                    Quoth the Raven, "Nevermore."

85   "Prophet!" said I, "thing of evil! prophet still, if bird or devil!
Whether Tempter sent, or whether tempest tossed thee here ashore,
Desolate yet all undaunted, on this desert land enchanted—
On this home by Horror haunted—tell me truly, I implore:
Is there—*is* there balm in Gilead?[7]—tell me—tell me, I implore!"
90   Quoth the Raven, "Nevermore."

---

[6] *Nepenthe* is a drug one uses to forget pain.
[7] See Jeremiah 8:22.

"Prophet!" said I, "thing of evil—prophet still, if bird or devil!
By that Heaven that bends above us, by that God we both adore,
Tell this soul with sorrow laden if, within the distant Aidenn,[8]
It shall clasp a sainted maiden whom the angels name Lenore:
95   Clasp a rare and radiant maiden whom the angels name Lenore!"
                    Quoth the Raven, "Nevermore."

"Be that word our sign of parting, bird or fiend!" I shrieked, upstarting:
"Get thee back into the tempest and the Night's Plutonian shore!
Leave no black plume as a token of that lie thy soul hath spoken!
100   Leave my loneliness unbroken! quit the bust above my door!
Take thy beak from out my heart, and take thy form from off my door!"
                    Quoth the Raven, "Nevermore."

And the Raven, never flitting, still is sitting, *still* is sitting
On the pallid bust of Pallas just above my chamber door;
105   And his eyes have all the seeming of a demon's that is dreaming,
And the lamp-light o'er him streaming throws his shadow on the floor:
And my soul from out that shadow that lies floating on the floor
                    Shall be lifted—nevermore!

HOMER (8th century B.C.)

From the Odyssey[9]

When the young Dawn with finger tips of rose
came in the east, I called my men together
and made a speech to them:
                            "Old shipmates, friends,
5   the rest of you stand by; I'll make the crossing
in my own ship, with my own company,
and find out what the mainland natives are—
for they may be wild savages, and lawless,
or hospitable and god fearing men."

10   At this I went aboard, and gave the word
to cast off by the stern. My oarsmen followed,
filing in to their benches by the rowlocks,
and all in line dipped oars in the grey sea.

As we rowed on, and nearer to the mainland,
15   at one end of the bay, we saw a cavern
yawning above the water, screened with laurel,
and many rams and goats about the place
inside a sheepfold—made from slabs of stone

---

[8] *Aidenn* is a combination of Eden and Aden—thus, an exotic place of pleasure.
[9] The *Odyssey* narrates the adventures of Odysseus, or Ulysses (as he was called by the Romans).
Odysseus wandered the world for ten years before returning to his kingdom, Ithaca. He was one
of the Greek kings who defeated the Trojans. In this episode from Book IX of the *Odyssey*, Odysseus
recounts his visit to the Kyklopês, or Cyclops, vicious one-eyed giants, and tells how he outsmarted
them. The episode typifies many of Odysseus' exploits: he succeeds more by brains than brawn.

earthfast between tall trunks of pine and rugged
20   towering oak trees.

                                  A prodigious man
slept in this cave alone, and took his flocks
to graze afield—remote from all companions,
knowing none but savage ways, a brute
25   so huge, he seemed no man at all of those
who eat good wheaten bread; but he seemed rather
a shaggy mountain reared in solitude.
We beached there, and I told the crew
to stand by and keep watch over the ship;
30   as for myself I took my twelve best fighters
and went ahead. I had a goatskin full
of that sweet liquor that Euanthês' son,
Maron, had given me. He kept Apollo's
holy grove at Ísmaros; for kindness
35   we showed him there, and showed his wife and child,
he gave me seven shining golden talents
perfectly formed, a solid silver winebowl,
and then this liquor—twelve two-handled jars
of brandy, pure and fiery. Not a slave
40   in Maron's household knew this drink; only
he, his wife and the storeroom mistress knew;
and they would put one cupful—ruby-colored,
honey-smooth—in twenty more of water,
but still the sweet scent hovered like a fume
45   over the winebowl. No man turned away
when cups of this came round.

                                  A wineskin full
I brought along, and victuals in a bag,
for in my bones I knew some towering brute
50   would be upon us soon—all outward power,
a wild man, ignorant of civility.

We climbed, then, briskly to the cave. But Kyklops
had gone afield, to pasture his fat sheep,
so we looked round at everything inside:
55   a drying rack that sagged with cheeses, pens
crowded with lambs and kids, each in its class:
firstlings apart from middlings, and the "dewdrops,"
or newborn lambkins, penned apart from both.
And vessels full of whey were brimming there—
60   bowls of earthenware and pails for milking.
My men came pressing round me, pleading:

                                      "Why not
take these cheeses, get them stowed, come back,
throw open all the pens, and make a run for it?
65   We'll drive the kids and lambs aboard. We say
put out again on good salt water!"

how sound that was! Yet I refused. I wished
to see the caveman, what he had to offer—
70   no pretty sight, it turned out, for my friends.
We lit a fire, burnt an offering,
and took some cheese to eat; then sat in silence
around the embers, waiting. When he came
he had a load of dry boughs on his shoulder
75   to stoke his fire at suppertime. He dumped it
with a great crash into that hollow cave,
and we all scattered fast to the far wall.
Then over the broad cavern floor he ushered
the ewes he meant to milk. He left his rams
80   and he-goats in the yard outside, and swung
high overhead a slab of solid rock
to close the cave. Two dozen four-wheeled wagons,
with heaving wagon teams, could not have stirred
the tonnage of that rock from where he wedged it
85   over the doorsill. Next he took his seat
and milked his bleating ewes. A practiced job
he made of it, giving each ewe her suckling;
thickened his milk, then, into curds and whey,
sieved out the curds to drip in withy° baskets,   *twig*
90   and poured the whey to stand in bowls
cooling until he drank it for his supper.
When all these chores were done, he poked the fire,
heaping on brushwood. In the glare he saw us.
"Strangers," he said, "who are you? And where from?
95   What brings you here by sea ways—a fair traffic?
Or are you wandering rogues, who cast your lives
like dice, and ravage other folk by sea?"

We felt a pressure on our hearts, in dread
of that deep rumble and that mighty man.
100   But all the same I spoke up in reply:
"We are from Troy, Akhaians, blown off course
by shifting gales on the Great South Sea;
homeward bound, but taking routes and ways
uncommon; so the will of Zeus would have it.
105   We served under Agamémnon, son of Atreus—
the whole world knows what city
he laid waste, what armies he destroyed.
It was our luck to come here; here we stand,
beholden for your help, or any gifts
110   you give—as custom is to honor strangers.
We would entreat you, great Sir, have a care
for the gods' courtesy; Zeus will avenge
the unoffending guest."
                         He answered this
115   from his brute chest, unmoved:

                                                  "You are a ninny,
or else you come from the other end of nowhere,
telling me, mind the gods! We Kyklopês
care not a whistle for your thundering Zeus

120   or all the gods in bliss; we have more force by far.
I would not let you go for fear of Zeus—
you or your friends—unless I had a whim to.
Tell me, where was it, now, you left your ship—
around the point, or down the shore, I wonder?"

125   He thought he'd find out, but I saw through this,
and answered with a ready lie:

                                                  "My ship?
Poseidon Lord, who sets the earth a-tremble,
broke it up on the rocks at your land's end.

130   A wind from seaward served him, drove us there,
We are survivors, these good men and I."

Neither reply nor pity came from him,
but in one stride he clutched at my companions
and caught two in his hands like squirming puppies

135   to beat their brains out, spattering the floor.
Then he dismembered them and made his meal,
gaping and crunching like a mountain lion—
everything: innards, flesh, and marrow bones.
We cried aloud, lifting our hands to Zeus,

140   powerless, looking on at this, appalled;
but Kyklops went on filling up his belly
with manflesh and great gulps of whey,
then lay down like a mast among his sheep.
My heart beat high now at the chance of action,

145   and drawing the sharp sword from my hip I went
along his flank to stab him where the midriff
holds the liver. I had touched the spot
when sudden fear stayed me: if I killed him
we perished there as well, for we could never

150   move his ponderous doorway slab aside.
So we were left to groan and wait for morning.

When the young Dawn with finger tips of rose
lit up the world, the Kyklops built a fire
and milked his handsome ewes, all in due order,

155   putting the sucklings to the mothers. Then,
his chores being all dispatched, he caught
another brace of men to make his breakfast,
and whisked away his great door slab
to let his sheep go through—but he, behind,

160   reset the stone as one would cap a quiver.
There was a din of whistling as the Kyklops
rounded his flock to higher ground, then stillness.

And now I pondered how to hurt him worst,
if but Athena granted what I prayed for.
165   Here are the means I thought would serve my turn:

a club, or staff, lay there along the fold—
an olive tree, felled green and left to season
for Kyklops' hand. And it was like a mast
a lugger of twenty oars, broad in the beam—
170   a deep-sea-going craft—might carry:
so long, so big around, it seemed. Now I
chopped out a six foot section of this pole
and set it down before my men, who scraped it;
and when they had it smooth, I hewed again
175   to make a stake with pointed end. I held this
in the fire's heart and turned it, toughening it,
then hid it, well back in the cavern, under
one of the dung piles in profusion there.
Now came the time to toss for it: who ventured
180   along with me? whose hand could bear to thrust
and grind that spike in Kyklops' eye, when mild
sleep had mastered him? As luck would have it,
the men I would have chosen won the toss—
four strong men, and I made five as captain.

185   At evening came the shepherd with his flock,
his woolly flock. The rams as well, this time,
entered the cave: by some sheep-herding whim—
or a god's bidding—none were left outside.
He hefted his great boulder into place
190   and sat him down to milk the bleating ewes
in proper order, put the lambs to suck,
and swiftly ran through all his evening chores.
Then he caught two more men and feasted on them.
My moment was at hand, and I went forward
195   holding an ivy bowl of my dark drink,
looking up, saying:

                      "Kyklops, try some wine.
Here's liquor to wash down your scraps of men.
Taste it, and see the kind of drink we carried
200   under our planks. I meant it for an offering
if you would help us home. But you are mad,
unbearable, a bloody monster! After this,
will any other traveller come to see you?"

He seized and drained the bowl, and it went down
205   so fiery and smooth he called for more:
"Give me another, thank you kindly. Tell me,
how are you called? I'll make a gift will please you.
Even Kyklopês know the wine-grapes grow

out of grassland and loam in heaven's rain,
210 but here's a bit of nectar and ambrosia!"

Three bowls I brought him, and he poured them down.
I saw the fuddle and flush come over him,
then I sang out in cordial tones:

"Kyklops,
215 you ask my honorable name? Remember
the gift you promised me, and I shall tell you.
My name is Nohbdy: mother, father, and friends,
everyone calls me Nohbdy."

And he said:

220 "Nohbdy's my meat, then, after I eat his friends.
Others come first. There's a noble gift, now."

Even as he spoke, he reeled and tumbled backward,
his great head lolling to one side; and sleep
took him like any creature. Drunk, hiccuping,
225 he dribbled streams of liquor and bits of men.

Now, by the gods, I drove my big hand spike
deep in the embers, charring it again,
and cheered my men along with battle talk
to keep their courage up: no quitting now.
230 The pike of olive, green though it had been,
reddened and glowed as if about to catch.
I drew it from the coals and my four fellows
gave me a hand, lugging it near the Kyklops
as more than natural force nerved them; straight
235 forward they sprinted, lifted it, and rammed it
deep in his crater eye, and I leaned on it
turning it as a shipwright turns a drill
in planking, having men below to swing
the two-handled strap that spins it in the groove.
240 So with our brand we bored that great eye socket
while blood ran out around the red hot bar.
Eyelid and lash were seared; the pierced ball
hissed broiling, and the roots popped.

In a smithy
245 one sees a white-hot axehead or an adze°   hatchet
plunged and wrung in a cold tub, screeching steam—
the way they make soft iron hale and hard—:
just so that eyeball hissed around the spike.
The Kyklops bellowed and the rock roared round him,
250 and we fell back in fear. Clawing his face
he tugged the bloody spike out of his eye,
threw it away, and his wild hands went groping;
then he set up a howl for Kyklopês

who lived in caves on windy peaks nearby.
255   Some heard him; and they came by divers ways
to clump around outside and call:

                      "What ails you,
Polyphêmos? Why do you cry so sore
in the starry night? You will not let us sleep.
260   Sure no man's driving off your flock? No man
has tricked you, ruined you?"

                      Out of the cave
the mammoth Polyphêmos roared in answer:
"Nohbdy, Nohbdy's tricked me, Nohbdy's ruined me!"

265   To this rough shout they made a sage reply:
"Ah well, if nobody has played you foul
there in your lonely bed, we are no use in pain
given by great Zeus. Let it be your father,
Poseidon Lord, to whom you pray."

Translation by Robert Fitzgerald (1910–)

DANTE ALIGHIERI (1265–1321)

Ulysses' Speech *from* Inferno (Canto XXVI)

. . . "When I from Circe broke at last,
Who more than a year by Gaeta (before
Aeneas had so named it) held me fast,
Not sweet son, nor revered old father, nor
5   The long-due love which was to have made glad
      Penelope for all the pain she bore,
Could conquer the inward hunger that I had
      To master earth's experience, and to attain
      Knowledge of man's mind, both the good and bad.
10   But I put out on the deep, open main
      With one ship only, and with that little band
      Which chose not to desert me; far as Spain,
Far as Morocco, either shore I scanned.
      Sardinia's isle I coasted, steering true,
15   And the isles of which that water bathes the strand.
I and my crew were old and stiff of thew
      When, at the narrow pass, we could discern
      The marks that Hercules set far in view
That none should dare beyond, or further learn.
20   Already I had Sevilla on the right,
      And on the larboard Ceuta lay astern.
'Brothers,' I said, 'who manfully, despite
      Ten thousand perils, have attained the West,
      In the brief vigil that remains of light

25   To feel in, stoop not to renounce the quest
        Of what may in the sun's path be essayed,
        The world that never mankind hath possessed.
    Think on the seed ye spring from! Ye were made
        Not to live life of brute beasts of the field
30   But follow virtue and knowledge unafraid.'
    With such few words their spirit so I steel'd,
        That I thereafter scarce could have contained
        My comrades from the voyage, had I willed.
    And, our poop turned to where the Morning reigned,
35   We made, for the mad flight, wings of our oars,
        And on the left continually we gained.
    By now the Night beheld within her course
        All stars of the other pole, and ours so low,
        It was not lifted from the ocean-floors.
40   Five times beneath the moon rekindled slow
        The light had been, and quenched as oft, since we
        Broached the hard issue we were sworn to know,
    When there arose a mountain in the sea,
        Dimm'd by the distance: loftier than aught
45   That ever I beheld, it seemed to be.
    Then we rejoiced; but soon to grief were brought.
        A storm came out of the strange land, and found
        The ship, and violently the forepart caught.
    Three times it made her to spin round and round
50   With all the waves; and, as Another chose,
        The fourth time, heaved the poop up, the prow drowned,
    Till over us we heard the waters close."

Translation by Laurence Binyon (1869–1943)

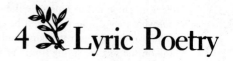

4 🌿 Lyric Poetry

The Solitary Singer

CATULLUS (84?–54 B.C.)

LXXXV

I hate and I love. Why? you might ask
but I can't tell. The feeling seizes me
and riddles me with pain.

Outside of literature we rarely have the opportunity to look into the hearts and minds of others. Many people are shy about themselves or feel that their language is inadequate for expressing what is most important to them. Great poets can open themselves to us in moments of crisis or discovery so that we can know their thoughts as intimately as we know our own.

The *lyric* is generally considered the most intense and personal form of poetry—indeed, of all literature. The word *lyric* comes from the Greek word for the lyre, a stringed instrument similar to a guitar and suitable for the accompaniment of a solitary singer. Like the concert of an impassioned singer, the lyric poem is a private, often visionary act of intelligence and emotion that becomes public through the music of language. Lyric poetry is also an artifact of language, capable of great beauty and excitement in its exploration of new perceptions. Language is a precious part of our heritage that is enriched by the vision and experience of each new generation of poets.

The Love Poem

Perhaps the form of lyric most familiar to us is the love poem.

WILLIAM BUTLER YEATS (1865–1939)

He Wishes for the Cloths of Heaven

Had I the heavens' embroidered cloths,
Enwrought with golden and silver light,

The blue and the dim and the dark cloths
Of night and light and the half-light,
5 I would spread the cloths under your feet:
But I, being poor, have only my dreams;
I have spread my dreams under your feet;
Tread softly because you tread on my dreams.

Question

1. Vocabulary: *enwrought* (2).

How does one express love? One common way is through gifts. We want the finest gift for the one we love, a gift that will be as beautiful and rare as what we feel. In this poem Yeats (or his persona) realizes that nothing he possesses would be adequate as a gift for his beloved. All he can do is wish for such a gift, the magnificent cloths he describes. If he had such cloths, he tells her, he would spread them before her as a path. But he is poor and cannot provide such a gift. Instead, he offers her his dreams. This, too, should be familiar to us. When we are in love, we want to share with those we love not only material things, but also our aspirations, our plans, our dreams. These are the finest gifts the lover can provide. When he has spread his dreams in her path, he asks her to "tread softly" because dreams are delicate, much more fragile than the cloths he described earlier.

Thus the first gift is the wish described in the poem's opening lines, and the second gift is the lover's dreams. But just as important as either of these is the gift of the poem itself.

William Butler Yeats (*Photograph by Howard Coster*)

We have considered the poem as a love lyric to a particular woman. But is it not also a gift to the reader? The "you" of the poem might be *any* reader, for as we read, we are admitted to the privacy of the poet's thoughts. We are in effect receiving a gift of his thoughts. We are being asked to read carefully, for we are treading on his dreams throughout the poem. It is as much a love poem to us as it is to a particular woman.

H. D. (HILDA DOOLITTLE) (1886–1961)

Never More Will the Wind

Never more will the wind
cherish you again,
never more will the rain.

Never more
5   shall we find you bright
in the snow and wind.

The snow is melted,
the snow is gone,
and you are flown:

10   Like a bird out of our hand,
like a light out of our heart,
you are gone.

Here is another kind of love lyric, one that expresses the anguish of loss. The poem is intensely private, for the poet is speaking to someone who is not there to listen. Maybe the one she loves has died, or perhaps he has gone to another country. The poem is not concerned with these questions. Rather, it shows us how the poet's world has changed in the absence of her beloved. Everything is emptier: the wind, the rain, the snow. Everywhere she looks, the landscape speaks of loneliness and absence. The poet clearly wishes to share this with us. She includes us in her world when she says "we" in the second stanza, and "our" in the final lines.

WILLIAM SHAKESPEARE (1564–1616)

When, in Disgrace with Fortune and Men's Eyes

When, in disgrace° with fortune and men's eyes,   *out of favor*
I all alone beweep my outcast state
And trouble deaf heaven with my bootless° cries   *useless*
And look upon myself and curse my fate,
5   Wishing me like to one more rich in hope,
Featured like him, like him with friends possess'd,
Desiring this man's art and that man's scope,°   *range of activity*
With what I most enjoy contented least;
Yet in these thoughts myself almost despising

10   Haply I think on thee, and then my state,
      Like to the lark at break of day arising
      From sullen earth, sings hymns at heaven's gate;
         For thy sweet love remember'd such wealth brings
         That then I scorn to change my state with kings.

Questions

1. Vocabulary: *beweep* (2), *sullen* (12).
2. Why is the speaker so upset in the first eight lines of the poem?
3. Why is he so happy in the last six lines?
4. What emotion has inspired the poem?

ANDREW MARVELL (1621–1678)

To His Coy Mistress

Had we but world enough, and time,
This coyness,° lady, were no crime.   *modesty, reluctance*
We would sit down and think which way
To walk, and pass our long love's day.
5   Thou by the Indian Ganges' side
Should'st rubies find; I by the tide
Of Humber[1] would complain.° I would   *sing sad songs*
Love you ten years before the Flood,
And you should, if you please, refuse
10   Till the conversion of the Jews.[2]
My vegetable° love should grow   *vegetative*
Vaster than empires, and more slow.
An hundred years should go to praise
Thine eyes, and on thy forehead gaze,
15   Two hundred to adore each breast,
But thirty thousand to the rest.
An age at least to every part,
And the last age should show your heart.
For, lady, you deserve this state,
20   Nor would I love at lower rate.
     But at my back I always hear
Time's winged chariot hurrying near;
And yonder all before us lie
Deserts of vast eternity.
25   Thy beauty shall no more be found,
Nor in thy marble vault shall sound
My echoing song; then worms shall try
That long preserved virginity,
And your quaint honor turn to dust,

---

[1] The Humber is a river that passed near Marvell's home.
[2] According to popular belief, the Jews would be converted just before the Last Judgment.

30   And into ashes all my lust.
       The grave's a fine and private place,
       But none, I think, do there embrace.
          Now therefore, while the youthful hue
       Sits on thy skin like morning dew
35   And while thy willing soul transpires
       At every pore with instant° fires,   *immediate*
       Now let us sport us while we may;
       And now, like am'rous birds of prey,
       Rather at once our time devour,
40   Than languish in his slow-chapped° power,   *slowly chewing*
       Let us roll all our strength, and all
       Our sweetness, up into one ball;[3]
       And tear our pleasures with rough strife
       Thorough° the iron gates of life.   *through*
45   Thus, though we cannot make our sun
       Stand still, yet we will make him run.

Questions

1. Vocabulary: *conversion* (10), *vault* (26), *quaint* (29), *transpires* (35), *languish* (40).
2. Reading this poem is like overhearing a personal conversation or reading someone else's letter. What sort of lady is Marvell addressing?
3. What does he want?
4. Compare this poem with Marlowe's "The Passionate Shepherd to His Love" (pages 423–24). Which poet is more persuasive?
5. This poem is considered an eloquent statement of the *carpe diem* ("seize the day") philosophy, which urges us to live for the moment, without concern for the future. What are the advantages of *carpe diem?* The disadvantages?

Curses

Less familiar but no less human is the lyric poem that expresses hatred, or vengeance.

ARCHILOCHUS (7th century B.C.)

May He Lose His Way on the Cold Sea

     May he lose his way on the cold sea
     And swim to the heathen Salmydessos,
     May the ungodly Thracians[4] with their hair
     Done up in a fright on the top of their heads
5   Grab him, that he know what it is to be alone

---

[3] Falconers would roll fat and sinew into balls that would be thrown into the air for falcons to attack and eat.

[4] Inhabitants of Thrace, an ancient country that comprised what is now Bulgaria and parts of Greece and Turkey. The Athenians considered Thracians barbarians.

Without friend or family. May he eat slave's bread
And suffer the plague and freeze naked,
Laced about with the nasty trash of the sea.
May his teeth knock the top on the bottom
10 As he lies on his face, spitting brine,
At the edge of the cold sea, like a dog.
And all this it would be a privilege to watch,
Giving me great satisfaction as it would,
For he took back the word he gave in honor,
15 Over the salt and table at a friendly meal.

Translation by Guy Davenport (1927–)

The poem is a curse, written by a Greek poet in the seventh century B.C. But
the sentiment is as fresh as if it had been written yesterday. Archilochos is angry
at someone who has gone back on his word. The two of them were having a
friendly meal, and the man made a promise. Did he promise to do a business
favor, or to introduce Archilochos to a woman? We will have to live with our
curiosity. The point is that the man lied, and the poet is enraged. How does he
manage his rage? He imagines the most dreadful things that could befall his
enemy, and then invites them to happen. More than two thousand years later
we can read it with sympathy and some amusement.

Poems of Praise, Poems for the Dead

Two powerful and time-honored sources of lyric poetry are admiration of something or someone, and the impact of death. The first inspires the *encomium*,
a poem of praise. The second inspires the *elegy*, or death song. One might argue
that both of these are forms of love poetry.

Here is a poem of praise written to a woman that the poet hardly knows. Let
us pretend for a moment that we are walking with the poet on a country road
and that he has stopped us to listen to the reaper's singing.

WILLIAM WORDSWORTH (1770–1850)

• The Solitary Reaper[5]

Behold her, single in the field,
Yon solitary Highland Lass!
Reaping and singing by herself:
Stop here, or gently pass!
5 Alone she cuts and binds the grain,
And sings a melancholy strain;
O listen! for the Vale° profound   *valley*
Is overflowing with the sound.

---

[5] The poem is based on a passage from Thomas Wilkinson's *Tour of Scotland*. Wilkinson describes
seeing a young woman reaping in the field. She sings in Erse, the native Scottish language.

No Nightingale did ever chaunt°   *chant*
10   More welcome notes to weary bands
      Of travellers in some shady haunt,
      Among Arabian sands:
      A voice so thrilling ne'er was heard
      In spring-time from the Cuckoo-bird,
15   Breaking the silence of the seas
      Among the farthest Hebrides.[6]

      Will no one tell me what she sings?—
      Perhaps the plaintive numbers flow
      For old, unhappy, far-off things,
20   And battles long ago:
      Or is it some more humble lay,°   *song*
      Familiar matter of to-day?
      Some natural sorrow, loss, or pain,
      That has been, and may be again?

25   Whate'er the theme, the Maiden sang
      As if her song could have no ending;
      I saw her singing at her work,
      And o'er the sickle bending;—
      I listened, motionless and still;
30   And, as I mounted up the hill
      The music in my heart I bore,
      Long after it was heard no more.

Questions

1. Vocabulary: *reap* (3), *haunt* (11), *plaintive* (18), *sickle* (28).
2. Why does the poet stop when he notices the "Highland Lass"?
3. Why does he admire her so? How does he express his admiration?
4. How is the woman's singing like poetry?
5. Is it possible that the poet is envious of the reaper?
6. In what way has Wordsworth imitated the singer in writing the poem?
7. Who is the reaper's audience? Who is Wordsworth's?

GERARD MANLEY HOPKINS (1844–1889)

• Pied Beauty

      Glory be to God for dappled things—
          For skies of couple-color as a brinded° cow;   *streaked*
              For rose-moles all in stipple upon trout that swim;
      Fresh-firecoal chestnut-falls; finches' wings;
5   Landscape plotted and pieced—fold, fallow, and plow;
              And áll trádes, their gear and tackle and trim.°   *equipment*

---

[6] The Hebrides are islands off the west coast of Scotland.

All things counter, original, spare, strange;
　　Whatever is fickle, freckled (who knows how?)
　　　　With swift, slow; sweet, sour; adazzle, dim;
10　He fathers-forth whose beauty is past change:
　　　　　　Praise him.

Questions

1. Vocabulary: *pied, dappled* (1), *stipple* (3), *fallow* (5).
2. Hopkins prepares an extended list of items for which he is thankful. Are any of the items unexpected?
3. Is Hopkins thankful only for natural things?
4. How is God beautiful, according to Hopkins? How is His beauty different from that of the natural world?

Suggestion for Poets

Make a list of those special and peculiar things you are thankful for.

CHRISTOPHER SMART (1722–1771)

From For I Will Consider My Cat Jeoffry

For I will consider my Cat Jeoffry.
For he is the servant of the Living God, duly and daily serving him.
For at the first glance of the glory of God in the East he worships in his way.
For is this done by wreathing his body seven times round with elegant quickness.
5　For then he leaps up to catch the musk,° which is the blessing of God upon his
　　　prayer.　　　　　　　　　　　　　　　　　　　　　　　　　　*catnip*
For he rolls upon prank to work it in.
For having done duty and received blessing he begins to consider himself.
For this he performs in ten degrees.
For first he looks upon his fore-paws to see if they are clean.
10　For secondly he kicks up behind to clear away there.
For thirdly he works it upon stretch[7] with the fore-paws extended.
For fourthly he sharpens his paws by wood.
For fifthly he washes himself.
For sixthly he rolls upon wash.
15　For seventhly he fleas himself, that he may not be interrupted upon
　　　the beat.°　　　　　　　　　　　　　　　　　　　　　　　　　*patrol*
For eighthly he rubs himself against a post.
For ninthly he looks up for his instructions.
For tenthly he goes in quest of food.
For having considered God and himself he will consider his neighbor.
20　For if he meets another cat he will kiss her in kindness.
For when he takes his prey he plays with it to give it a chance.

---

[7] "He works it upon stretch" means that he works his muscles, stretching.

For one mouse in seven escapes by his dallying.
For when his day's work is done his business more properly begins.
For he keeps the Lord's watch in the night against the Adversary.
25   For he counteracts the powers of darkness by his electrical skin and glaring eyes.
For he counteracts the Devil, who is death, by brisking about the life.
For in his morning orisons he loves the sun and the sun loves him.
For he is of the tribe of Tiger.
For the Cherub Cat is a term of the Angel Tiger.
30   For he has the subtlety and hissing of a serpent, which in goodness he suppresses.
For he will not do destruction if he is well-fed, neither will he spit without
       provocation.
For he purrs in thankfulness when God tells him he's a good Cat.
For he is an instrument for the children to learn benevolence upon.
For every house is incomplete without him, and a blessing is lacking in the spirit.

Question

1. The repetition of a word at the beginning of several lines of poetry is called anaphora.
   Do you find it agreeable in this poem? Musical? Wearying?

Elegy

An elegy is a poem of lamentation that probably originated as the cry of mourning
at ancient funerals. In classical Greece poets were engaged to inscribe elegiac
lyrics on tombstones. The death song has evolved over the centuries into a highly
sophisticated, diverse literary form, capable of expressing not only the grief of
personal loss but also larger themes of the changes wrought by time. Here is a
modern elegy, an exquisite personal statement of grief. Elegiac poets often describe the most vital qualities and scenes from the life of the deceased in order
to emphasize their feelings of loss. Roethke also refers to the landscape, as did
H. D. in her love poem, to show how the whole world shares in his sorrow.

THEODORE ROETHKE (1908–1963)

Elegy for Jane

My Student, Thrown by a Horse

I remember the neckcurls, limp and damp as tendrils;
And her quick look, a sidelong pickerel smile;
And how, once startled into talk, the light syllables leaped for her,
And she balanced in the delight of her thought,
5   A wren, happy tail into the wind,
Her song trembling the twigs and small branches.
The shade sang with her;
The leaves, their whispers turned to kissing;
And the mold sang in the bleached valleys under the rose.

10   Oh, when she was sad, she cast herself down into such a pure depth,
      Even a father could not find her:
      Scraping her cheek against straw;
      Stirring the clearest water.

      My sparrow, you are not here,
15   Waiting like a fern, making a spiny shadow.
      The sides of wet stones cannot console me,
      Nor the moss, wound with the last light.

      If only I could nudge you from this sleep,
      My maimed darling, my skittery pigeon.
20   Over this damp grave I speak the words of my love:
      I, with no rights in this matter,
      Neither father nor lover.

Questions

1. Vocabulary: *tendrils* (1), *pickerel* (2), *skittery* (19).
2. Who is the sparrow in the third section? The pigeon in the fourth?
3. T. S. Eliot says that appreciation of a poem should precede our understanding of it. Do you appreciate the emotion in the poem? Do you understand all of it?
4. In the last lines the poet says that he has no right to speak the words of his love. Do you agree?

WALT WHITMAN (1819–1892)

This Dust Was Once the Man[8]

This dust was once the man,
Gentle, plain, just and resolute, under whose cautious hand,
Against the foulest crime in history known in any land or age,
Was saved the Union of these States.

ALFRED, LORD TENNYSON (1809–1892)

Dark House, by Which Once More I Stand[9]

Dark house, by which once more I stand
    Here in the long unlovely street,
    Doors, where my heart was used to beat
So quickly, waiting for a hand,

5   A hand that can be clasped no more—
    Behold me, for I cannot sleep,
    And like a guilty thing I creep
At earliest morning to the door.

---

[8] One of Whitman's elegies for Abraham Lincoln.
[9] This is a section of Tennyson's long poem *In Memoriam*.

He is not here; but far away
10   The noise of life begins again,
        And ghastly through the drizzling rain
        On the bald street breaks the blank day.

Questions

1. In what ways is the house dark?
2. Why do you suppose Tennyson chose to describe the street as "unlovely" instead of "ugly"?
3. What feeling do you get from the last line?
4. Why does Tennyson compare himself to "a guilty thing"? Of what offense is Tennyson guilty?

A. E. HOUSMAN (1859–1936)

To an Athlete Dying Young

The time you won your town the race
We chaired° you through the market-place;   *carried on a chair*
Man and boy stood cheering by,
And home we brought you shoulder-high.

5   Today, the road all runners come,
        Shoulder-high we bring you home,
        And set you at your threshold down,
        Townsman of a stiller town.

        Smart lad, to slip betimes away
10   From fields where glory does not stay,
        And early though the laurel[10] grows
        It withers quicker than the rose.

        Eyes the shady night has shut
        Cannot see the record cut,
15   And silence sounds no worse than cheers
        After earth has stopped the ears.

        Now you will not swell the rout
        Of lads that wore their honors out,
        Runners whom renown outran
20   And the name died before the man.

        So set, before its echoes fade,
        The fleet foot on the sill of shade,
        And hold to the low lintel up
        The still-defended challenge-cup.

25   And round that early-laureled head
        Will flock to gaze the strengthless dead,
        And find unwithered on its curls
        The garland briefer than a girl's.

---

[10] Laurel wreaths were awarded to the winners of competitions.

Question

1. Vocabulary: *betimes* (9), *rout* (17), *lintel* (23), *garland* (28).

W. H. AUDEN (1907–1973)

• In Memory of W. B. Yeats

(d. Jan. 1939)

I

He disappeared in the dead of winter:
The brooks were frozen, the airports almost deserted,
And snow disfigured the public statues;
The mercury sank in the mouth of the dying day.
5   What instruments we have agree
The day of his death was a dark cold day.

Far from his illness
The wolves ran on through the evergreen forests,
The peasant river was untempted by the fashionable quays;
10   By mourning tongues
The death of the poet was kept from his poems.

But for him it was his last afternoon as himself,
An afternoon of nurses and rumours;
The provinces of his body revolted,
15   The squares of his mind were empty,
Silence invaded the suburbs,
The current of his feeling failed; he became his admirers.

Now he is scattered among a hundred cities
And wholly given over to unfamiliar affections,
20   To find his happiness in another kind of wood[11]
And be punished under a foreign code of conscience.
The words of a dead man
Are modified in the guts of the living.

But in the importance and noise of to-morrow
25   When the brokers are roaring like beasts on the floor of the Bourse,[12]
And the poor have the sufferings to which they are fairly accustomed,
And each in the cell of himself is almost convinced of his freedom,
A few thousand will think of this day
As one thinks of a day when one did something slightly unusual.
30   What instruments we have agree
The day of his death was a dark cold day.

II

You were silly like us; your gift survived it all:
The parish of rich women, physical decay,
Yourself. Mad Ireland hurt you into poetry.

---

[11] An allusion to Dante's *Inferno*, in which he sees himself as being in a dark wood.
[12] The French stock exchange.

W. H. Auden (*Cecil Beaton Photograph/Courtesy of Sotheby's Belgravia*)

35   Now Ireland has her madness and her weather still,
For poetry makes nothing happen: it survives
In the valley of its making where executives
Would never want to tamper, flows on south
From ranches of isolation and busy griefs,
40   Raw towns that we believe and die in; it survives,
A way of happening, a mouth.

III

Earth, receive an honoured guest:
William Yeats is laid to rest.
Let the Irish vessel lie
45   Emptied of its poetry.

In the nightmare of the dark
All the dogs of Europe bark,[13]
And the living nations wait,
Each sequestered in its hate;

50   Intellectual disgrace
Stares from every human face,
And the seas of pity lie
Locked and frozen in each eye.

Follow, poet, follow right
55   To the bottom of the night,
With your unconstraining voice
Still persuade us to rejoice;

---

[13] Auden is alluding here to the imminent outbreak of World War II.

With the farming of a verse
Make a vineyard of the curse,
60 Sing of human unsuccess
In a rapture of distress;

In the deserts of the heart
Let the healing fountain start,
In the prison of his days
65 Teach the free man how to praise.

Question

1. Vocabulary: *quays* (9), *sequestered* (49), *unconstraining* (56).

The Meditative Poem

All the poetry we have read so far is thoughtful. Indeed, even the simplest
linguistic act, such as the naming of a flower, involves some thought. But there
is a kind of poetry in which thoughts, or ideas, are so much the center of
attention that it has been called *meditative* poetry. It seems to rise, as does
philosophy, out of a state of meditation, doubt, or curiosity. Unlike philosophers,
however, poets are not content to dwell with their doubts and curiosities exclusively in the world of ideas. The ideas of poets are sparked by the real world and
must return to the world of sense and emotion to find their music in language.
One of the greatest meditative poets, Stéphane Mallarmé, expressed the relationship between poetry and ideas in conversation with the painter Edgar Degas;
"One makes sonnets, Degas, not with ideas, but with words."

The excitement of meditative poetry lies in seeing the poet's mind in action,
raising questions, and sometimes answering them, always on the threshold of
new experience. We should read such work attentively in order to broaden our
own experience.

OMAR KHAYYAM (A.D. 1050?–1123?)

XXVI and XXVII, the Rubaiyat

Oh, come with old Khayyam, and leave the Wise
To talk; one thing is certain, that life flies;
    One thing is certain, and the Rest is lies:
The Flower that once has blown forever dies.

5   Myself when young did eagerly frequent
Doctor and Saint, and heard great Argument
    About it and about: but evermore
Came out by the same Door as in I went.

Translation by Edward FitzGerald (1809–1883)

The Sufi poet Omar Khayyam spent a lifetime pursuing Truth and what one commentator refers to as "the Awakening of the Soul." In this concise, musical passage from his meditative poem the *Rubaiyat*, Omar Khayyam sums up years of education. In his youth he listened to the wisest discourse, of "Doctors," or those schooled in the world's wisdom, and of "Saints"—those well versed in the ways of God. What did Omar learn from them? "That life flies," and that "the Flower that once has blown forever dies." Is that all? You would have to read the rest of the *Rubaiyat* to get a better idea of what Omar learned. What is more important in this passage is what he did *not* learn. Look at the last line. No matter what he heard, the poet always left by the same door he entered! With wit and certainty Omar is saying that all the high conversation did not introduce him to a new door, a new path, or a new world. The *Rubaiyat* is a meditative journey that tells us something about the limits of meditation.

Meditative poets are usually testing the limits of their knowledge. Aristotle tells us that the desire to know is our fundamental nature. One way of reading meditative poetry is to join a poet in questioning, and then see how well the question is answered, for the poet and for us.

The poet John Milton became blind before his fiftieth year. In this meditation he considers the meaning of his blindness.

JOHN MILTON (1608–1674)

When I Consider How My Light Is Spent

When I consider how my light is spent,
    Ere half my days in this dark world and wide,
    And that one talent which is death to hide
    Lodged with me useless, though my soul more bent
5   To serve therewith my Maker, and present
    My true account, lest He returning chide;
    "Doth God exact day-labor, light denied?"
    I fondly° ask. But Patience, to prevent   *foolishly*
    That murmur, soon replies, "God doth not need
10   Either man's work or His own gifts. Who best
    Bear His mild yoke, they serve Him best. His state
Is kingly: thousands at His bidding speed,
    And post o'er land and ocean without rest;
    They also serve who only stand and wait."

Questions

1. What is the question that Milton poses?
2. Who answers him?
3. Do you consider the answer satisfactory?

ROBERT FROST (1874–1963)

Fire and Ice

Some say the world will end in fire,
Some say in ice.
From what I've tasted of desire
I hold with those who favor fire.
5   But if it had to perish twice,
I think I know enough of hate
To say that for destruction ice
Is also great
And would suffice.

In this epigram Frost considers the end of the world. The term *epigram* comes from a classical Greek word meaning to carve or inscribe, and an epigram is any terse, witty treatment of a single thought or question. Carving letters on stone or metal is difficult: we can understand why the epigram had to get right to the point. What is Frost's major question? He is asking how the world could end. He gives us a double answer: either fire or ice will do. But his reference to love and hate makes his answers much more subtle. Fire, he likens to desire, and we all know that uncontrolled desire leads to aggression and destruction. Ice, on the other hand, he compares to hatred, which could destroy the world as easily as desire.

Perhaps the greatest form of meditative lyric is the *ode*. Again the word comes to us from the ancients, from a Greek word for song, and the first great writer of odes, Pindar, was Greek. He wrote odes of praise to statesman and winners of the Olympian games. These odes were much admired because their flattering characterization and historical perspective raised their subjects to the level of mythic heroes. Full of epigrammatic wisdom or *gnomae*, of reflections on the poet's own grace or lack of grace, the Pindaric odes became a standard of lyric excellence in treating broad themes with intelligence and musicality. The Romantic poets Shelley, Keats, and Wordsworth used the form to great advantage, extending it to meditation on ideas and objects as well as people.

The following is among the most respected of these Romantic odes.

JOHN KEATS (1795–1821)

• Ode on a Grecian Urn[14]

Thou still unravished bride of quietness,
    Thou foster-child of silence and slow time,
Sylvan historian, who canst thus express
    A flowery tale more sweetly than our rhyme:

---

[14] The urn is decorated with a woodland, or sylvan, scene.

Attic Red-Figured Urn, Four Women at
Bath (*Courtesy of the Museum of Fine
Arts, Boston, Catherine Page Perkins
Fund*)

5   What leaf-fringed legend haunts about thy shape
       Of deities or mortals, or of both,
         In Tempe or the dales of Arcady?[15]
       What men or gods are these? What maidens loth?
     What mad pursuit? What struggle to escape?
10   What pipes and timbrels? What wild ecstasy?

     Heard melodies are sweet, but those unheard
       Are sweeter; therefore, ye soft pipes, play on;
     Not to the sensual° ear, but, more endeared,   *physical*
       Pipe to the spirit ditties of no tone:
15   Fair youth, beneath the trees, thou canst not leave
       Thy song, nor ever can those trees be bare;
        Bold Lover, never, never canst thou kiss,
     Though winning near the goal—yet, do not grieve,
        She cannot fade, though thou hast not thy bliss,
20   For ever wilt thou love, and she be fair!

     Ah, happy, happy boughs! that cannot shed
       Your leaves, nor ever bid the Spring adieu;
     And, happy melodist, unwearièd,
       For ever piping songs for ever new;
25   More happy love! more happy, happy love!
       For ever warm and still to be enjoyed,
        For ever panting, and for ever young;
     All breathing human passion far above,
       That leaves a heart high-sorrowful and cloyed,
30   A burning forehead, and a parching tongue.

     Who are these coming to the sacrifice?
       To what green altar, O mysterious priest,
     Lead'st thou that heifer lowing at the skies,
       And all her silken flanks with garlands drest?

---

[15] Two valleys in Greece that represent the epitome of natural beauty.

35 What little town by river or sea shore,
   Or mountain-built with peaceful citadel,
    Is emptied of this folk, this pious morn?
  And, little town, thy streets for evermore
   Will silent be; and not a soul to tell
40   Why thou art desolate, can e'er return.
  O Attic shape![16] Fair attitude! with brede°   *design*
   Of marble men and maidens overwrought,
  With forest branches and the trodden weed;
   Thou, silent form, dost tease us out of thought
45 As doth Eternity: Cold Pastoral!
   When old age shall this generation waste,
    Thou shalt remain, in midst of other woe
   Than ours, a friend to man, to whom thou say'st,
  Beauty is truth, truth beauty,—that is all
50   Ye know on earth, and all ye need to know.

Questions

1. Vocabulary: *sylvan* (3), *loth* (8), *timbrels* (10), *melodist* (23), *cloyed* (29), *heifer* (33), *overwrought* (42).
2. It is clear from the first passages of the poem that Keats has observed the urn closely. Why does he want to know more?
3. Why does Keats admire the piper? Why the lover? Why does he so admire the leaves in the third section?
4. In the fourth stanza, the townspeople have emptied the town in order to attend a sacrifice. They can never return, for the picture is locked in time. In what way are we locked in time? Is their fate similar to ours?
5. Keats asks the urn many questions, and in the last lines the urn answers him. In fact, it answers a more important question than any he has asked so far. What is the question?

  In the poem's opening lines the speaker is addressing the urn. Such a direct address, called an *apostrophe*, is a common poetic device. Poets have apostrophized clouds, skylarks, the moon and sun, roses, and so on. Another characteristic of this ode is that the urn, for Keats, plays a number of different roles. It is an "unravished bride of quietness," meaning, among other things, that its silence has remained unbroken and its surface unmarred. It is also a "sylvan historian," however, because it preserves the rural past. Both these phrases suggest that for Keats the urn is alive, not an ancient relic of a long-ago time.

  As far as we know, Keats did not have any particular Grecian urn in mind when he wrote this poem. Rather, the urn he addresses is typical of most Grecian urns. Greek artists excelled in this form of painting, and they lavished time and craftsmanship on their urns, which depicted mythological scenes as well as scenes from daily life.

---

[16] Athenian shape—that is, possessing the Greek epitome of beauty.

E. E. CUMMINGS (1894–1962)

• somewhere i have never travelled, gladly beyond

somewhere i have never travelled, gladly beyond
any experience, your eyes have their silence:
in your most frail gesture are things which enclose me,
or which i cannot touch because they are too near

5   your slightest look easily will unclose me
though i have closed myself as fingers,
you open always petal by petal myself as Spring opens
(touching skilfully, mysteriously) her first rose

or if your wish be to close me, i and
10   my life will shut very beautifully, suddenly,
as when the heart of this flower imagines
the snow carefully everywhere descending;

nothing which we are to perceive in this world equals
the power of your intense fragility: whose texture
15   compels me with the colour of its countries,
rendering death and forever with each breathing

(i do not know what it is about you that closes
and opens; only something in me understands
the voice of your eyes is deeper than all roses)
20   nobody, not even the rain, has such small hands

CESARE PAVESE (1908–1950)

Encounter

These hard hills which have made my body,
and whose many memories still shake me so, have revealed the miracle—
this *she* who does not know I live her and cannot understand her.

I encountered her one evening: a brighter presence
5   in the unsteady starlight, in the summer haze.
The smell of those hills was around me, everywhere,
a feeling deeper than shadow, and suddenly I heard,
as if it came from the hills, a voice at once purer
and harsher, a voice of vanished seasons.

10   Sometimes I see her, as she saw me, her presence
defined, unchangeable, like a memory.
I have never managed to hold her fast: always her reality
evades my grasp and carries me far away.
I do not know if she is beautiful. Among women she is very young:
15   when I think of her, I am surprised by a faint memory
of childhood lived among these hills,

she is so young. She is like morning. Her eyes suggest
all the distant skies of those faraway mornings.
And her eyes are firm with a purpose: the sharpest light
20   dawn has ever made upon these hills.

I created her from the ground of everything
I love the most, and I cannot understand her.

Translation by William Arrowsmith (1924–)

SYLVIA PLATH (1932–1963)

Daddy

You do not do, you do not do
Any more, black shoe
In which I have lived like a foot
For thirty years, poor and white,
5   Barely daring to breathe or Achoo.

Daddy, I have had to kill you.
You died before I had time—
Marble-heavy, a bag full of God,
Ghastly statue with one grey toe
10   Big as a Frisco seal

And a head in the freakish Atlantic
Where it pours bean green over blue
In the waters of beautiful Nauset.[17]
I used to pray to recover you.
15   Ach, du.

In the German tongue, in the Polish town
Scraped flat by the roller
Of wars, wars, wars.
But the name of the town is common.
20   My Polack friend

Says there are a dozen or two.
So I never could tell where you
Put your foot, your root,
I never could talk to you.
25   The tongue stuck in my jaw.

It stuck in a barb wire snare.
Ich, ich, ich, ich,[18]
I could hardly speak.
I thought every German was you.
30   And the language obscene

---

[17] Harbor on the east coast of Cape Cod, Massachusetts.
[18] *Ich* is German for "I."

An engine, an engine
Chuffing me off like a Jew.
A Jew to Dachau, Auschwitz, Belsen.[19]
I began to talk like a Jew.
35   I think I may well be a Jew.

The snows of the Tyrol, the clear beer of Vienna
Are not very pure or true.
With my gypsy ancestress and my weird luck
And my Taroc pack and my Taroc pack
40   I may be a bit of a Jew.

I have always been scared of *you*,
With your Luftwaffe,[20] your gobbledygoo.
And your neat moustache
And your Aryan eye, bright blue.
45   Panzer-man, panzer-man,[21] O You—

Not God but a swastika
So black no sky could squeak through.
Every woman adores a Fascist,
The boot in the face, the brute
50   Brute heart of a brute like you.

You stand at the blackboard, daddy,
In the picture I have of you.
A cleft in your chin instead of your foot
But no less a devil for that, no not
55   Any less the black man who

Bit my pretty red heart in two.
I was ten when they buried you.
At twenty I tried to die
And get back, back, back to you.
60   I thought even the bones would do

But they pulled me out of the sack,
And they stuck me together with glue.
And then I knew what to do.
I made a model of you,
65   A man in black with a Meinkampf look[22]

And a love of the rack and the screw.
And I said I do, I do.
So daddy, I'm finally through.
The black telephone's off at the root,
70   The voices just can't worm through.

If I've killed one man, I've killed two—
The vampire who said he was you

---

[19] Sites of German concentration camps.
[20] The German air force.
[21] Tank driver in the German army.
[22] Adolf Hitler's *Mein Kampf* (two volumes, 1925–1927) stated Hitler's political views.

And drank my blood for a year,
Seven years, if you want to know.
75 Daddy, you can lie back now.

There's a stake in your fat black heart
And the villagers never liked you.
They are dancing and stamping on you.
They always *knew* it was you.
80 Daddy, daddy, you bastard, I'm through.

JOHN CROWE RANSOM (1888–1974)

Here Lies a Lady

Here lies a lady of beauty and high degree.
Of chills and fever she died, of fever and chills,
The delight of her husband, her aunt, an infant of three,
And of medicos marveling sweetly on her ills.

5 For either she burned, and her confident eyes would blaze,
And her fingers fly in a manner to puzzle their heads—
What was she making? Why, nothing; she sat in a maze
Of old scraps of laces, snipped into curious shreds—

Or this would pass, and the light of her fire decline
10 Till she lay discouraged and cold, like a thin stalk white and blown,
And would not open her eyes, to kisses, to wine;
The sixth of these states was her last; the cold settled down.

Sweet ladies, long may ye bloom, and toughly I hope ye may thole,°   *endure*
But was she not lucky? In flowers and lace and mourning,
15 In love and great honor we bade God rest her soul
After six little spaces of chill, and six of burning.

WILLIAM BLAKE (1757–1827)

To See a World in a Grain of Sand

To see a world in a grain of sand
And a heaven in a wild flower,
Hold infinity in the palm of your hand
And eternity in an hour.

WILLIAM CARLOS WILLIAMS (1883–1963)

Danse Russe[23]

If when my wife is sleeping
and the baby and Kathleen
are sleeping

---

[23] *Danse Russe*, French for "Russian dance," may be an allusion to the famous Russian ballet
company under the direction of Sergei Diaghilev.

and the sun is a flame-white disc
5   in silken mists
above shining trees,—
if I in my north room
dance naked, grotesquely
before my mirror
10   waving my shirt round my head
and singing softly to myself:
"I am lonely, lonely.
I was born to be lonely,
I am best so!"
15   If I admire my arms, my face,
my shoulders, flanks, buttocks
against the yellow drawn shades,—

Who shall say I am not
the happy genius[24] of my household?

IMAMU AMIRI BARAKA (LeROI JONES) (1934–)

Preface to a Twenty Volume Suicide Note

For Kellie Jones, Born 16 May 1959

Lately, I've become accustomed to the way
The ground opens up and envelopes me
Each time I go out to walk the dog.
Or the broad edged silly music the wind
5   Makes when I run for a bus . . .

Things have come to that.

And now, each night I count the stars,
And each night I get the same number.
And when they will not come to be counted,
10   I count the holes they leave.

Nobody sings anymore.

And then last night I tiptoed up
To my daughter's room and heard her
Talking to someone, and when I opened
15   The door, there was no one there . . .
Only she on her knees, peeking into

Her own clasped hands.

---

[24] Genius can also mean the spirit that watches over an area or a person.

5 🌿 Dramatic Poetry

The Poet as Actor

How often have you wished to be someone else? Imagine leaving your body for a few hours and becoming a famous musician, a fashion model, a bank robber, or a senator. This is a common fantasy, the same one that prompts children to try on their parents' hats and shoes. One of the frustrations of being human is that we cannot escape who we are no matter how much we like or dislike ourselves. Certain poets, hypersensitive to the limits of personality, adopt someone else's voice in writing a poem. A young poet might speak in the voice of an old woman, or a rich poet in a beggar's voice. This adoption of another's voice, sometimes called a mask or persona, is the poet's effort to break out of his or her own consciousness and reach into the world of another. The result of that effort is *dramatic poetry*.

Dramatic poets are not merely ventriloquists with peculiar gifts for mimicry. They must identify with the persons they are portraying—a feat requiring a profound knowledge of character and an extraordinary degree of compassion. Dramatic poetry confirms certain constants in human nature that enable poets to understand people very different from themselves: the bishop, the queen, the murderer. For the reader, dramatic poetry provides an opportunity to hear the imagined thoughts of characters who lack the poet's gift or opportunity of expression.

The Soliloquy

The simplest form of dramatic poetry is the *soliloquy*, in which the speaker is merely overheard, talking to no one in particular.

WILLIAM CARLOS WILLIAMS (1883–1963)

The Widow's Lament in Springtime

Sorrow is my own yard
where the new grass

```
         flames as it has flamed
         often before but not
    5    with the cold fire
         that closes round me this year.
         Thirtyfive years
         I lived with my husband.
         The plumtree is white today
    10   with masses of flowers.
         Masses of flowers
         load the cherry branches
         and color some bushes
         yellow and some red
    15   but the grief in my heart
         is stronger than they
         for though they were my joy
         formerly, today I notice them
         and turned away forgetting.
    20   Today my son told me
         that in the meadows,
         at the edge of the heavy woods
         in the distance, he saw
         trees of white flowers.
    25   I feel that I would like
         to go there
         and fall into those flowers
         and sink into the marsh near them.
```

If this had been written by a widow, we might consider it a simple lyric statement of sorrow. But Williams clearly is not a widow. Why do you suppose he contrived to write in a woman's voice? Perhaps the poem grew out of a conversation with a widow he knew. Or maybe some of the statements in the poem were overheard. Whether the widow is real or imagined, the poem certainly arose out of sympathy for a woman's grief, rendered here in a manner that some men might find embarrassing. Perhaps the man has found a freedom of expression in the widow's voice he might not have felt in his own—a chance to explore a more feminine side of his nature. Whatever his motivation, Williams has treated his theme with great intimacy by entering into the widow's thoughts and adopting her voice.

This form of poem, in which the poet speaks for a single character, is also called a *dramatic monologue*. Its use suggests a modern, relativistic attitude toward experience. That is, the world can look quite different to different people depending on their character and point of view. As writers became more concerned with human individuality in the nineteenth century, the dramatic monologue served to explore extreme psychological states and differing points of view. Robert Browning wrote a book-length poem, *The Ring and the Book*, in which a murder story is told ten times, once by each of the various participants in and witnesses to the crime. The resulting picture, as rich and complex as life itself, shows that the truth of a situation cannot be known by any single witness.

We must not take the statements of a persona at face value. The dramatic poet may be portraying a liar or a deranged person who is unable to report experiences clearly.

One of Browning's shorter dramatic monologues reveals how the poet speaks for a psychopathic killer. Like a playwright, the dramatic poet sets the scene: a rainy, windy night, a cottage by the lake, the lover who is waiting for the entrance of his Porphyria. Let's see what happens.

ROBERT BROWNING (1812–1889)

Porphyria's Lover

The rain set early in to-night,
    The sullen wind was soon awake,
It tore the elm-tops down for spite,
    And did its worst to vex the lake:
5   I listened with heart fit to break.
When glided in Porphyria; straight
    She shut the cold out and the storm,
And kneeled and made the cheerless grate
    Blaze up, and all the cottage warm;
10   Which done, she rose, and from her form
Withdrew the dripping cloak and shawl,
    And laid her soiled gloves by, untied
Her hat and let the damp hair fall,
    And, last, she sat down by my side
15   And called me. When no voice replied,
She put my arm about her waist,
    And made her smooth white shoulder bare,
And all her yellow hair displaced,
    And, stooping, made my cheek lie there,
20   And spread, o'er all, her yellow hair,
Murmuring how she loved me—she
    Too weak, for all her heart's endeavour,
To set its struggling passion free
    From pride, and vainer ties dissever,
25   And give herself to me for ever.
But passion sometimes would prevail,
    Nor could to-night's gay feast restrain
A sudden thought of one so pale
    For love of her, and all in vain:
30   So, she was come through wind and rain.
Be sure I looked up at her eyes
    Happy and proud; at last I knew
Porphyria worshipped me; surprise
    Made my heart swell, and still it grew

35   While I debated what to do.
      That moment she was mine, mine, fair,
         Perfectly pure and good: I found
      A thing to do, and all her hair
      In one long yellow string I wound
40   Three times her little throat around,
      And strangled her. No pain felt she;
         I am quite sure she felt no pain.
      As a shut bud that holds a bee,
         I warily oped her lids: again
45   Laughed the blue eyes without a stain.
      And I untightened next the tress
         About her neck; her cheek once more
      Blushed bright beneath my burning kiss:
         I propped her head up as before,
50   Only, this time my shoulder bore
      Her head, which droops upon it still:
         The smiling rosy little head,
      So glad it has its utmost will,
         That all it scorned at once is fled,
55   And I, its love, am gained instead!
      Porphyria's love: she guessed not how
         Her darling one wish would be heard.
      And thus we sit together now,
         And all night long we have not stirred,
60   And yet God has not said a word!

Questions

1. Vocabulary: *sullen* (2), *vex* (4), *dissever* (24).
2. What are the "vainer ties" the speaker refers to in line 24?
3. What was "Her darling one wish," mentioned in line 57?
4. How does your attitude toward the speaker change after line 30?
5. Why does he kill her? Do you believe she felt no pain?
6. Apart from the fact that he murders Porphyria, how can you tell the speaker is insane?
7. To whom is the speaker speaking? Is the poem a soliloquy?

The most vivid dramatic monologues tell us not only the character of the persona, but also the character of an auditor, the person being addressed. The great vitality of such poetry owes much to the immediacy of the scene—it takes place before our very eyes, just like a movie or a play, or a scene glimpsed through a keyhole. To read such poems we must first identify the dramatic situation, answering the questions: Who is speaking? Who is being addressed? Where are they? What prompts the speech?

WILLIAM BLAKE (1757–1827)

The Little Vagabond

Dear mother, dear mother, the Church is cold,
But the Ale-house is healthy and pleasant and warm;

Besides I can tell where I am used well,
Such usage in Heaven will never do well.

5   But if at the Church they would give us some ale,
And a pleasant fire our souls to regale,
We'd sing and we'd pray all the livelong day,
Nor ever once wish from the Church to stray.

Then the Parson might preach, and drink, and sing,
10   And we'd be as happy as birds in the spring;
And modest Dame Lurch, who is always at church,
Would not have bandy children, nor fasting, nor birch.

And God, like a father, rejoicing to see
His children as pleasant and happy as He,
15   Would have no more quarrel with the Devil or the barrel,
But kiss him, and give him both drink and apparel.

Questions

1. Vocabulary: *regale* (6), *bandy* (12).
2. Who is the persona of the poem?
3. Who is the auditor?
4. What kind of scene is depicted?
5. Is the speaker persuasive?
6. Where do you think the speaker will end up—in church or at the ale-house?

ANNE SEXTON (1928–1974)

Unknown Girl in the Maternity Ward

Child, the current of your breath is six days long.
You lie, a small knuckle on my white bed;
lie, fisted like a snail, so small and strong
at my breast. Your lips are animals; you are fed
5   with love. At first hunger is not wrong.
The nurses nod their caps; you are shepherded
down starch halls with the other unnested throng
in wheeling baskets. You tip like a cup; your head
moving to my touch. You sense the way we belong.
10   But this is an institution bed.
You will not know me very long.

The doctors are enamel. They want to know
the facts. They guess about the man who left me,
some pendulum soul, going the way men go
15   and leave you full of child. But our case history
stays blank. All I did was let you grow.
Now we are here for all the ward to see.
They thought I was strange, although
I never spoke a word. I burst empty
20   of you, letting you learn how the air is so.

The doctors chart the riddle they ask of me
and I turn my head away. I do not know.

Yours is the only face I recognize.
Bone at my bone, you drink my answers in.
25   Six times a day I prize
your need, the animals of your lips, your skin
growing warm and plump. I see your eyes
lifting their tents. They are blue stones, they begin
to outgrow their moss. You blink in surprise
30   and I wonder what you can see, my funny kin,
as you trouble my silence. I am a shelter of lies.
Should I learn to speak again, or hopeless in
such sanity will I touch some face I recognize?

Down the hall the baskets start back. My arms
35   fit you like a sleeve, they hold
catkins of your willows, the wild bee farms
of your nerves, each muscle and fold
of your first days. Your old man's face disarms
the nurses. But the doctors return to scold
40   me. I speak. It is you my silence harms.
I should have known; I should have told
them something to write down. My voice alarms
my throat. "Name of father—none." I hold
you and name you bastard in my arms.

Anne Sexton (© *Thomas Victor* 1982)

45   And now that's that. There is nothing more
that I can say or lose.
Others have traded life before
and could not speak. I tighten to refuse
your owling eyes, my fragile visitor.
50   I touch your cheeks, like flowers. You bruise
against me. We unlearn. I am a shore
rocking you off. You break from me. I choose
your only way, my small inheritor
and hand you off, trembling the selves we lose.
55   Go child, who is my sin and nothing more.

Questions

1. Vocabulary: *pendulum* (14), *catkins* (36), *disarms* (38).
2. The title and the first line of the poem introduce us to the dramatic situation. Why is the mother saying these things to an infant? For whose benefit is she speaking?
3. Why will the baby not know her long?
4. Why does she say, "The doctors are enamel" (line 12)? What does that suggest about their sympathy?
5. Why does she call herself "a shelter of lies" (line 30)?
6. Do you believe her in the last line when she says the child is "my sin and nothing more"?

    The reader of dramatic poems might wonder why these imagined speakers, who are not supposed to be poets, speak with the eloquence of poets. This is one of the central tensions of dramatic poetry—the tension between poetic, or heightened, speech and natural speech. Poets have resolved this tension in various ways, sometimes simplifying the language when a character could not be expected to speak poetry; at other times choosing a persona from a faraway time or exalted station, who seems quite comfortable with eloquence. In the following poem, Lord Tennyson's "Ulysses" comes to us from Homeric Greece, a heroic age when, it seems, anything was possible—even kings who spoke poetry.

ALFRED, LORD TENNYSON (1809–1892)

• Ulysses[1]

It little profits that an idle king,
By this still hearth, among these barren crags,
Matched with an agèd wife, I mete and dole
Unequal laws unto a savage race
5   That hoard, and sleep, and feed, and know not me.
I cannot rest from travel; I will drink
Life to the lees. All times I have enjoyed

---

[1] "Ulysses" is discussed at length in the Appendix.

Greatly, have suffered greatly, both with those
That loved me, and alone; on shore, and when
10 Through scudding drifts the rainy Hyades[2]
Vexed the dim sea. I am become a name;
For always roaming with a hungry heart
Much have I seen and known—cities of men
And manners, climates, councils, governments,
15 Myself not least, but honored of them all—
And drunk delight of battle with my peers,
Far on the ringing plains of windy Troy.
I am a part of all that I have met;
Yet all experience is an arch wherethrough
20 Gleams that untraveled world whose margin fades
Forever and forever when I move.
How dull it is to pause, to make an end,
To rust unburnished, not to shine in use!
As though to breathe were life! Life piled on life
25 Were all too little, and of one to me
Little remains; but every hour is saved
From that eternal silence, something more,
A bringer of new things; and vile it were
For some three suns to store and hoard myself,
30 And this grey spirit yearning in desire
To follow knowledge like a sinking star,
Beyond the utmost bound of human thought.
    This is my son, mine own Telemachus,
To whom I leave the scepter and the isle—
35 Well-loved of me, discerning to fulfill
This labor, by slow prudence to make mild
A rugged people, and through soft degrees
Subdue them to the useful and the good.
Most blameless is he, centered in the sphere
40 Of common duties, decent not to fail
In offices of tenderness, and pay
Meet adoration to my household gods,
When I am gone. He works his work, I mine.
    There lies the port; the vessel puffs her sail;
45 There gloom the dark, broad seas. My mariners,
Souls that have toiled, and wrought, and thought with me—
That ever with a frolic welcome took
The thunder and the sunshine, and opposed
Free hearts, free foreheads—you and I are old;
50 Old age hath yet his honor and his toil.
Death closes all; but something ere the end,
Some work of noble note, may yet be done,
Not unbecoming men that strove with Gods.

---

[2] The daughters of Atlas. They were transformed into a group of stars, and their rising is thought
to predict rain.

The lights begin to twinkle from the rocks;
55   The long day wanes; the slow moon climbs; the deep
Moans round with many voices. Come, my friends,
'Tis not too late to seek a newer world.
Push off, and sitting well in order smite
The sounding furrows; for my purpose holds
60   To sail beyond the sunset, and the baths
Of all the western stars, until I die.
It may be that the gulfs will wash us down;
It may be we shall touch the Happy Isles,
And see the great Achilles, whom we knew.
65   Though much is taken, much abides; and though
We are not now that strength which in old days
Moved earth and heaven, that which we are, we are—
One equal temper of heroic hearts,
Made weak by time and fate, but strong in will
70   To strive, to seek, to find, and not to yield.

Questions

1. Vocabulary: *mete* (3), *lees* (7), *burnished* (23), *prudence* (36), *smite* (58), *abides* (65).
2. *Ulysses* is the Latin name for Odysseus, hero of Homer's epic the *Odyssey*. The scene here portrayed is recounted by Dante in the *Divine Comedy*. Ulysses was a great adventurer in his youth. At what stage of his life do we encounter him in this poem?
3. What is the scene? Whom is Ulysses addressing?
4. Ulysses has accomplished a great deal in his life. What does he want now? What does he intend to do?

The Epistolary Monologue

We all enjoy reading letters, whether addressed to ourselves or to other people. Abelard's love letters to Héloise and the impassioned notes of Dietrich Bonhoeffer from prison still make compelling reading, years after they were written. Dramatic poets, taking on the guise of imagined or historical correspondents, have made good use of the *epistolary*, or letter, form. In a significant way the epistolary monologue is more natural than the forms we have seen so far: the letter is *already* literature, whereas a monologue such as the preceding one is pretending to be spoken and then recorded.

The titles of epistolary poems usually indicate the letter writer as well as the addressee. The following letter is supposed to have been written by a young woman to her husband, a merchant who has been on the road for five months. The poem is prized for its autobiographical compression and the wife's dignity in controlling her emotion. She and her husband have been deeply in love since they were children, and she misses him, but she never utters a word of resentment or reproach.

RIHAKU (8th century A.D.)

The River Merchant's Wife, A Letter

While my hair was still cut straight across my forehead
I played about the front gate, pulling flowers.
You came by on bamboo stilts, playing horse,
You walked about my seat, playing with blue plums.
5 And we went on living in the village of Chokan:
Two small people, without dislike or suspicion.

At fourteen I married My Lord you.
I never laughed, being bashful.
Lowering my head, I looked at the wall.
10 Called to, a thousand times, I never looked back.

At fifteen I stopped scowling,
I desired my dust to be mingled with yours
Forever and forever and forever.
Why should I climb the look out?

15 At sixteen you departed,
You went into far Ku-to-yen, by the river of swirling eddies,
And you have been gone five months.
The monkeys make sorrowful noise overhead.

You dragged your feet when you went out.
20 By the gate now, the moss is grown, the different mosses,
Too deep to clear them away!
The leaves fall early this autumn, in wind.
The paired butterflies are already yellow with August
Over the grass in the West garden;
25 They hurt me. I grow older.
If you are coming down through the narrows of the river Kiang,
Please let me know beforehand,
And I will come out to meet you
                    As far as Cho-fu-Sa.

Translation from the Chinese by Ezra Pound (1885–1972)

EDWARD HIRSCH (1950–)

The River Merchant: A Letter Home

Sometimes the world seems so large,
You have no idea. Out here at dusk
The barges pull the heaviest cargo, sometimes
They drag whole ships to the sea. Imagine

5   The sound of geese shrieking everywhere,
      More geese than you can imagine,
      Clustered together and flapping like stars.
      Sometimes there are two moons shining at
      Once, one clouded in the treetops, one
10   Breaking into shadows on the river.
      I don't know what this means.

      But from the hill's brow I can see
      The lights in every village flickering on,
      One by one, but slowly, like this,
15   Until the whole world gleams
      Like small coins. Believe me:
      There are so many villages like ours,
      So many lights all gleaming together
      But all separate too, like those moons.
20   It is too much. I am older now.
      I want to return to that fateful place
      Where the river narrows toward home.

Poetic Dialogues

Do you remember the folk song that goes:

> Where have you been, Billie Boy, Billie Boy
> Oh, where have you been, charming Billie?

> I have been to see my wife,
> She's the darling of my life.
> She's a young thing and cannot leave her mother.

This is a popular example of a dramatic lyric employing two speakers. Sometimes the words of the primary persona in a poem call for an answer. This need makes for the lively conversation in poetry known as *dramatic dialogue*. In "Billie Boy" we overhear a dialogue between a mother and her son about his bride. The mother asks questions about the bride, and Billie delivers comic answers.

    The dramatic dialogue is an effective form for exploring contrasts in personality and viewpoint. We often find conflict in poetic dialogues, just as we do in plays and movies. In the following dialogue between an old man and a young lady, John Crowe Ransom sketches a brief but vivid scene. It is a moonlit night in autumn. A beautiful young lady is standing on her piazza (front porch) waiting for her lover. We do not know all this at first; we must read this poem carefully twice in order to understand the dramatic situation. Without knowing the situation, we cannot appreciate the impact of the lover's first speech. The old man has been spying on the lady through a trellis. We can imagine her surprise when he whispers the first stanza to her.

John Crowe Ransom (*Rollie McKenna*)

JOHN CROWE RANSOM (1888–1974)

Piazza Piece

—I am a gentleman in a dustcoat trying
To make you hear. Your ears are soft and small
And listen to an old man not at all,
They want the young men's whispering and sighing.
5   But see the roses on your trellis dying
And hear the spectral° singing of the moon;   *ghostly*
For I must have my lovely lady soon,
I am a gentleman in a dustcoat trying.
—I am a lady young in beauty waiting
10   Until my truelove comes, and then we kiss.
But what grey man among the vines is this
Whose words are dry and faint as in a dream?
Back from my trellis, Sir, before I scream!
I am a lady young in beauty waiting.

The old man wants the lovely lady, and soon. He does not have much time.
The young lady, who has all the time in the world, has been waiting for her
young lover. What does she get? A peeping old man. What does he get? A stern
refusal.

This frustration of expectations is called *dramatic irony*, or the *irony of situation*. "Piazza Piece" is a classic example, in which the irony underscores the
desperation of the old man's desire and the young woman's vanity. You may
wish to reread the other dramatic poems we have studied, especially "Porphyria's
Lover" and "The Little Vagabond," and look for instances of dramatic irony.

Ball turret of famous World War II B-17 bomber "Memphis Bell," (The Granger Collection)

The Posthumous Monologue

As suggested earlier, poets choose dramatic personae not only to reveal different sides of their own natures, but also to speak for those who cannot speak for themselves. This has given rise to one of the most dramatic forms of poetry, the *posthumous monologue*—the poem spoken by the dead. These poems have an aura of mystery and terror because we know nothing about death and because the act of dying seems so frightening, even though no one has ever been able to tell us about it.

The following poem comes to us from beyond the grave, spoken by a young man killed in air combat during World War II. The first sentence tells us he is young: he went from his mother to the state (or army) like a kitten, with his fur still wet. The ball turret is the armored position on the aircraft, from which the gunner can achieve a full circle of fire.

RANDALL JARRELL (1914–1965)

The Death of the Ball Turret Gunner

From my mother's sleep I fell into the State,
And I hunched in its belly till my wet fur froze.
Six miles from earth, loosed from its dream of life,
I woke to black flak° and the nightmare fighters.   *shellfire*
5   When I died they washed me out of the turret with a hose.

Questions

1. What is the "dream of life" referred to in line 3?
2. The speaker mentions in line 2 that he hunched in the State's "belly" until his "wet fur froze." What does this suggest about his response to the military?

Fiddler Jones

The earth keeps some vibration going
There in your heart, and that is you.
And if the people find you can fiddle,
Why, fiddle you must, for all your life.
5   What do you see, a harvest of clover?
Or a meadow to walk through to the river?
The wind's in the corn; you rub your hands
For beeves hereafter ready for market;
Or else you hear the rustle of skirts
10   Like the girls when dancing at Little Grove.
To Cooney Potter a pillar of dust
Or whirling leaves meant ruinous drouth;
They looked to me like Red-Head Sammy

Stepping it off, to "Toor-a-Loor."
15   How could I till my forty acres,
Not to speak of getting more,
With a medley of horns, bassoons and piccolos
Stirred in my brain by crows and robins
And the creak of a windmill—only these?
20   And I never started to plow in my life
That some one did not stop in the road
And take me away to a dance or picnic.
I ended up with forty acres;
I ended up with a broken fiddle—
25   And a broken laugh, and a thousand memories,
And not a single regret.

Questions

1. Vocabulary: *beeves* (8), *drouth* (12).
2. Why did Jones become a fiddler?
3. What did he gain from fiddling? What did he lose?
4. Do you think his was a happy life?

❧ Poems for Further Study

An Irish Airman Foresees His Death

I know that I shall meet my fate
Somewhere among the clouds above;
Those that I fight I do not hate,
Those that I guard I do not love;

5 　My country is Kiltartan Cross,
　　My countrymen Kiltartan's poor,
　　No likely end could bring them loss
　　Or leave them happier than before.
　　Nor law, nor duty bade me fight,
10 　Nor public men, nor cheering crowds,
　　A lonely impulse of delight
　　Drove to this tumult in the clouds;
　　I balanced all, brought all to mind,
　　The years to come seemed waste of breath,
15 　A waste of breath the years behind
　　In balance with this life, this death.

ROBERT BROWNING (1812–1889)

My Last Duchess[3]

　　That's my last Duchess painted on the wall,
　　Looking as if she were alive. I call
　　That piece a wonder, now: Frà Pandolf's hands
　　Worked busily a day, and there she stands.
5 　Will 't please you sit and look at her? I said
　　"Frà Pandolf" by design, for never read
　　Strangers like you that pictured countenance,
　　The depth and passion of its earnest glance,
　　But to myself they turned (since none puts by
10 　The curtain I have drawn for you, but I)
　　And seemed as they would ask me, if they durst,
　　How such a glance came there; so, not the first
　　Are you to turn as ask thus. Sir, 't was not
　　Her husband's presence only, called that spot
15 　Of joy into the Duchess' cheek: perhaps
　　Frà Pandolf chanced to say "Her mantle laps
　　Over my lady's wrist too much," or "Paint
　　Must never hope to reproduce the faint
　　Half-flush that dies along her throat": such stuff
20 　Was courtesy, she thought, and cause enough
　　For calling up that spot of joy. She had
　　A heart—how shall I say?—too soon made glad,
　　Too easily impressed; she liked whate'er
　　She looked on, and her looks went everywhere.
25 　Sir, 't was all one! My favour at her breast,
　　The dropping of the daylight in the West,
　　The bough of cherries some officious fool
　　Broke in the orchard for her, the white mule

---

[3] This famous monologue was inspired by Browning's first trip to Italy, in 1834. The Duke of Ferrara typifies the cruelty of the Renaissance beneath its superficial beauty. He is showing the portrait of his late wife, whom he has done away with, to a representative of the father of his intended bride.

She rode with round the terrace—all and each
30   Would draw from her alike the approving speech,
Or blush, at least. She thanked men,—good! but thanked
Somehow—I know not how—as if she ranked
My gift of a nine-hundred-years-old name
With anybody's gift. Who'd stoop to blame
35   This sort of trifling? Even had you skill
In speech—(which I have not)—to make your will
Quite clear to such an one, and say, "Just this
Or that in you disgusts me; here you miss,
Or there exceed the mark"—and if she let
40   Herself be lessoned so, nor plainly set
Her wits to yours, forsooth, and made excuse,
—E'en then would be some stooping; and I choose
Never to stoop. Oh sir, she smiled, no doubt,
Whene'er I passed her; but who passed without
45   Much the same smile? This grew; I gave commands;
Then all smiles stopped together. There she stands
As if alive. Will 't please you rise? We'll meet
The company below, then. I repeat,
The Count your master's known munificence
50   Is ample warrant that no just pretence
Of mine for dowry will be disallowed;
Though his fair daughter's self, as I avowed
At starting, is my object. Nay, we'll go
Together down, sir! Notice Neptune, though,
55   Taming a sea-horse, thought a rarity,
Which Claus of Innsbruck cast in bronze for me!

MICHAEL HARPER (1938–)

A Mother Speaks:
The Algiers Motel Incident, Detroit[4]

It's too dark to see black
in the windows of Woodward
or Virginia Park.
The undertaker
5   pushed his body back
into place
with plastic and gum
but it wouldn't
hold water.
10   When I looked
for marks
or lineament

---

[4] During the night of July 25–26, 1967, while rioting was going on, three policemen killed three unarmed black men. The incident is the subject of a book by John Hersey, *The Algiers Motel Incident*.

or fine stitching
I was led away
15   without seeing
this plastic
face they'd built
that was not my son's.
They tied the eye
20   torn out
by shotgun
into place
and his shattered
arm cut away
25   with his buttocks
that remained.
My son's gone
by white hands
though he said
30   to his last word—
"Oh I'm so sorry,
officer, I broke your gun."

FRANK O'HARA (1926–1966)

A True Account of Talking to the Sun at Fire Island

The Sun woke me this morning loud
and clear, saying "Hey! I've been
trying to wake you up for fifteen
minutes. Don't be so rude, you are
5   only the second poet I've ever chosen
to speak to personally
                so why
aren't you more attentive? If I could
burn you through the window I would
10   to wake you up. I can't hang around
here all day."
             "Sorry, Sun, I stayed
up late last night talking to Hal."

"When I woke up Mayakovsky he was
15   a lot more prompt" the Sun said
petulantly. "Most people are up
already waiting to see if I'm going
to put in an appearance."
                I tried
20   to apologize "I missed you yesterday."
"That's better" he said. "I didn't
know you'd come out." "You may be
wondering why I've come so close?"

"Yes" I said beginning to feel hot
25 wondering if maybe he wasn't burning me
anyway.
        "Frankly I wanted to tell you
I like your poetry. I see a lot
on my rounds and you're okay. You may
30 not be the greatest thing on earth, but
you're different. Now, I've heard some
say you're crazy, they being excessively
calm themselves to my mind, and other
crazy poets think that you're a boring
35 reactionary. Not me.
                Just keep on
like I do and pay no attention. You'll
find that people always will complain
about the atmosphere, either too hot
40 or too cold too bright or too dark, days
too short or too long.
                If you don't appear
at all one day they think you're lazy
or dead. Just keep right on, I like it.
45 And don't worry about your lineage
poetic or natural. The Sun shines on
the jungle, you know, on the tundra
the sea, the ghetto. Wherever you were
I knew it and saw you moving. I was waiting
50 for you to get to work.
                And now that you
are making your own days, so to speak,
even if no one reads you but me
you won't be depressed. Not
55 everyone can look up, even at me. It
hurts their eyes."
                "Oh Sun, I'm so grateful to you!"

"Thanks and remember I'm watching. It's
easier for me to speak to you out
60 here. I don't have to slide down
between buildings to get your ear.
I know you love Manhattan, but
you ought to look up more often.
                And
65 always embrace things, people earth
sky stars, as I do, freely and with
the appropriate sense of space. That
is your inclination, known in the heavens
and you should follow it to hell, if
70 necessary, which I doubt.
                Maybe we'll
speak again in Africa, of which I too

am specially fond. Go back to sleep now
Frank, and I may leave a tiny poem
75   in that brain of yours as my farewell."

"Sun, don't go!" I was awake
at last. "No, go I must, they're calling
me."
       "Who are they?"
80   Rising he said "Some
day you'll know. They're calling to you
too." Darkly he rose, and then I slept.

PETER KLAPPERT (1942–)

Mail at Your New Address

I

Did your car get you to Florida?
I know you don't like me
to say so but Mrs. Wilson says
the same thing. Please tell me
5   (collegt) if you are all
there. I hope you do not
sleep or do anything on the road.
In Georgia.
          Your father
10   should see all the leaves.
Walter has not raked
a girlfriend up the street and wont
rake anymore. Watch out or
theyll have the same thing Mrs. Wilson
15   says the friend stayed and look
what happened at Cornell?
              Even if you changed
college is no reason to come home.
But get a haircut. I know
20   the dean doesn't like you
to look like a gardener.

II

There have been so many deaths
due to carbon m. poisoning
that this is just
25   a note to suggest you leave
a little air come into your room. Also,

I hope you don't get involved
with young men or older
or made from popies (?) and Hippy's.
30   I hope you are not letting the drugs
get you. And don't get mixed up

with drugs. It might spoil your change
for getting the cert. you are working for.
Remember, it is costing quite a lot.

35   Don't scold. I am afraid of your
trips to and near Chicago.

LOUISE ERDRICH (1954–)

Windigo   *For Angela*

*The Windigo is a flesh-eating, wintry demon with a man buried deep inside of it. In some
Chippewa stories, a young girl vanquishes this monster by forcing boiling lard down its
throat, thereby releasing the human at the core of ice.*

You knew I was coming for you, little one,
when the kettle jumped into the fire.
Towels flapped on the hooks,
and the dog crept off, groaning,
5   to the deepest part of the woods.

In the hackles of dry brush a thin laughter started up.
Mother scolded the food warm and smooth in the pot
and called you to eat.
But I spoke in the cold trees:
10   *New one, I have come for you, child hide and lie still.*

The sumac pushed sour red cones through the air.
Copper burned in the raw wood.
You saw me drag toward you.
Oh touch me, I murmured, and licked the soles of your feet.
15   You dug your hands into my pale, melting fur.

I stole you off, a huge thing in my bristling armor.
Steam rolled from my wintry arms, each leaf shivered
from the bushes we passed
until they stood, naked, spread like the cleaned spines of fish.

20   Then your warm hands hummed over and shoveled themselves full
of the ice and the snow. I would darken and spill
all night running, until at last morning broke the cold earth
and I carried you home,
a river shaking in the sun.

6  Images

Seeing Is Feeling

Poets have traditionally admired the way pictures can "speak" to us without the use of language. In fact, many poets envy the painter's or photographer's ability to capture a moment in all its complexity, to freeze life in midcourse and render all its detail, texture, and color simultaneously.

Like painters, poets have their own images. An *image* is a group of words that records sense impressions directly. Images usually record what poets see, but they can also record sounds, tastes, and smells. For example, T. S. Eliot begins his poem "Preludes" by imagining a winter evening that "settles down/with smell of steaks in passageways." We are asked to recall the greasy, smoky cooking smells that hover in the hallways of apartment houses or in close tenement alleys. The odor is familiar and not entirely pleasant. If we concentrate, we can bring to mind the slightly bitter smell of burnt animal fat. Eliot wants us to remember that experience and all the fatigue, hunger, and unpleasantness that go along with it.

Poets use images not merely to give us sensory impressions of a person, place, or thing, but also to evoke emotions. The best poets choose images that suggest to the reader precisely the feelings they wish to convey. The best images evoke an almost magical reaction. A few words will suggest an entire picture to our minds, which in turn will elicit deep—often unexpected—feelings.

Images differ from description in subtle but important ways. A description tells us about an object; an image presents us with the object. A description gives us the information we should know; an image gives us an experience we should feel. Readers have difficulty with highly imagistic writing when they do not take time to let the image register on their imaginations and emotions. Try to picture what the poet presents, and focus on the image long enough to react to it emotionally.

Haiku

The Japanese have concentrated on the power that a single image can produce. The *haiku* often contain a single, simple event that suggests to the reader a variety of feelings and associations. Although poets can place many restrictions on themselves, the haiku generally has some distinct features. It usually contains a seasonal reference and is about seventeen syllables long (commonly with a first line of five syllables, a second of seven, and a third of five). Since the following are translations, the usual syllabic criteria have not been closely met.

> For the child who won't
> stop crying, she lights a lamp
> in the autumn dusk.
> > —*Kawahigashi Kekigodo (1873–1937)*

> To the sun's path
> The hollyhocks lean
> in the May rains.
> > —*Matsuo Basho (1644–1694)*

> At midnight
> a distant door is slid shut.
>
> At the dark bottom
> of a well I find my face.
> > —*Ozaki Hosai (1885–1926)*

The first of these poems shows a mother's efforts to comfort her child by lighting a lamp as the sky grows dark. The poet calls our attention not only to the mother's care, but also to her loneliness and the futility of her actions. In the second poem we sense the natural harmony of spring as the flowers bend toward the sun. In the third poem there is something final, perhaps even sinister, in the far-off sound of a closing door. In the last poem the poet registers both surprise and foreboding as he sees his reflection in the dark well water.

The Japanese have cultivated the limited image, but most Western writers feel the need to expand images or combine them with other images or commentary. The following is an example of an expanded image.

WILLIAM CARLOS WILLIAMS (1883–1963)

The Great Figure

> Among the rain
> and lights
> I saw the figure 5
> in gold
> 5   on a red
> firetruck

moving
tense
unheeded
10   to gong clangs
siren howls
and wheels rumbling
through the dark city.

Questions

1. Vocabulary: *unheeded* (9).
2. How many senses are employed in presenting this image?
3. Eliminate the lines that refer to senses other than sight. Is the poem enhanced? Weakened? Why?
4. Is there any progression in the sensations the poem presents?
5. What do you feel when you see a speeding fire truck? Did Williams capture the experience for you? If not, what did he leave out?

William Carlos Williams makes the poem a single sentence to underscore that he is presenting a single image. Yet this is an image in constant motion. The fire truck does not stay still long enough to allow a clearly focused picture. Were this a photograph, the fire truck would be blurred as it emerges out of "the rain/ and lights" and plunges back into "the dark city." Williams is careful to record the actual way we see a fast-moving object. We do not see it whole; we see bits and pieces of it. Williams's eye catches the gold number 5 painted on the truck before he notices the truck itself.

I Saw the Figure 5 in Gold, by Charles Demuth *(The Metropolitan Museum of Art, New York, The Alfred Stieglitz Collection, 1949)*

The following poem also controls the order in which the image is revealed. What governs the order of details in the poem?

THEODORE ROETHKE (1908–1963)

Child on Top of a Greenhouse

The wind billowing out the seat of my britches,
My feet crackling splinters of glass and dried putty,
The half-grown chrysanthemums staring up like accusers,
Up through the streaked glass, flashing with sunlight,
5   A few white clouds all rushing eastward,
A line of elms plunging and tossing like horses,
And everyone, everyone pointing up and shouting!

Questions

1. Who is the speaker in the poem? Through whose eyes do we see the event?
2. What does the child feel about being on top of the greenhouse? Is he frightened, delighted, surprised, guilty, fascinated? All of these?
3. Do the spectators share the child's feelings? If not, why not?
4. Why do you think the poem is in one sentence?

Combining Images

In both "The Great Figure" and "Child on Top of a Greenhouse," the authors expand the image by adding details to a central event. But poets also like to combine very different images. The result is often like a photograph in which one image is superimposed on another so that we see both images simultaneously. "In a Station of the Metro" is such a poem; it records Ezra Pound's impression of entering the Paris subway.

EZRA POUND (1885–1972)

In a Station of the Metro

The apparition of these faces in the crowd,
Petals on a wet, black bough.

This poem is both surprising and right. The pale faces of the people emerging from a subway *do* look like petals on a tree. Yet if we think about these two images, we find that they are very different. The word *apparition* suggests the deathly and supernatural. Petals, however, are natural—signs of renewed life. How can these two images so easily share the same poem? This mystery is part of the logic of poetry, the reasonings of the heart of which, according to Pascal, the mind knows nothing.

"In a Station of the Metro" is among the most famous examples of poems by *les Imagistes*, who, despite their French title, were mostly American poets, including at times Pound, Amy Lowell, Hilda Doolittle, and William Carlos Williams. They believed in the direct treatment of objects and feelings and in using "no word that doesn't contribute to the presentation." "In a Station of the Metro" started out as a poem sixty lines long. Pound spent months whittling the poem to these two intense lines.

Arthur Symons's "Pastel" contains an imagistic effect similar to the one in Pound's short poem.

ARTHUR SYMONS (1865–1948)

Pastel

The light of our cigarettes
Went and came in the gloom:
It was dark in the little room.

Dark, and then, in the dark,
5   Sudden, a flash, a glow,
And a hand and a ring I know.

And then, through the dark, a flush
Ruddy and vague, the grace—
A rose—of her lyric face.

Questions

1. How does Symons prepare for the image of the rose?
2. The rose is a common image. How does Symons make it fresh? Is it expected?

The poems we have read so far have all used images to evoke visual sensations. But images can also suggest any kind of sensation: taste, smell, touch. In "Sound," Jim Harrison suggests the way sound moves away from its source.

JIM HARRISON (1937–)

Sound

At dawn I squat on the garage
with snuff under a lip
to sweeten the roofing nails—
my shoes and pant cuffs
5   are wet with dew.
In the orchard the peach trees
sway with the loud
weight of birds, green fruit, yellow haze.
And my hammer—the cold head taps,

10   then swings its first full arc;
      the sound echoes against the barn,
      muffled in the loft,
      and out the other side, then lost
      in the noise of the birds
15   as they burst from the trees.

Questions

1. What senses are referred to in lines 1–5? Why do you suppose there are no references to sound in the opening?
2. Does the noise dissipate after the speaker hammers, or does the sound increase?
3. Why do you suppose Harrison bothered to record this simple occurrence? Are there any seemingly trivial events that stick in your mind as noteworthy? What is memorable about them?

Synesthesia

In "Sound" Harrison writes that the trees "sway with the loud/weight of birds." These lines may strike you as odd. In what sense can a weight be loud? A weight usually is light or heavy, not loud or quiet. This manner of speaking of one sense in terms of another is called *synesthesia*, and it is really quite common. People speak of "hot pink," a "loud necktie," "cool music," or a "spicy story." Each of these expressions is synesthetic.

ANN STANFORD (1916–)

Listening to Color

Now that blue has had its say
has told its winds, wall, sick
sky even, I can listen to white

      sweet poison flowers   hedge autumn
5   under a sky white at the edges
      like faded paper. My message keeps

      turning to yellow where few leaves
      set up first fires over branches
      tips of flames only, nothing here finished yet.

Questions

1. What are the synesthetic images in the poem?
2. In what ways do colors speak to us? Can you think of ways in which colors communicate? How do they speak to Stanford?
3. In what time of year is the poem set? How does nature communicate time?
4. Why does Stanford say in line 9 that nothing is finished? How does the word *yet* modify the sense of finality? How does it reinforce the sense of finality?

Images and Commentary

The most common way in which poets use images is in combination with commentary. The poet sees things and then meditates on their significance. In the following poem a sequence of images concludes in a line of commentary.

JAMES WRIGHT (1927–1980)

Lying in a Hammock at William Duffy's Farm in Pine Island, Minnesota

Over my head, I see the bronze butterfly,
Asleep on the black trunk,
Blowing like a leaf in green shadow.
Down the ravine behind the empty house,
5   The cowbells follow one another
Into the distances of the afternoon.
To my right,
In a field of sunlight between two pines,
The droppings of last year's horses
10   Blaze up into golden stones.
I lean back, as the evening darkens and comes on.
A chicken hawk floats over, looking for home.
I have wasted my life.

Questions

1. Is there any order to the observations? Or are they merely random?
2. Does Wright see anything unusual? If not, is that important to the poem?
3. Is the poem self-pitying? Do you feel sorry for Wright? Has he wasted his life?

Readers coming to this poem for the first time are often startled by the last line, which seems terribly out of place. At first it appears that Wright means that watching nature is a waste of time. On a closer reading, however, we realize that Wright means just the opposite: ignoring the beauties of nature is a waste. The poem records his sad recognition that he has not spent enough time lying in hammocks, looking at the world around him.

Wright's poem also illustrates two important ways poets make their work vivid: (1) by giving details rather than generalized pictures, and (2) by being specific about the details. For example, Wright gives us not a general picture of the landscape, but briefly worded details about particular things: the butterfly, the leaf, the cowbells. Because we see these small things so clearly, we have a sense of seeing the entire picture clearly. Second, Wright is specific about details. He writes not merely that a bird floats over, but, "A chicken hawk floats over, looking for home." By giving us the precise term, he makes the scene more vivid. Well-chosen, specific details are more powerful than general descriptions, both emotionally and imagistically.

There is a limit, however, to the amount of detail that is useful. If Wright had written, "I see a monarch butterfly with a wing span of three inches and a length of an inch and three quarters," he would certainly have been more specific, but he would not have been more vivid. We can easily imagine a bronze butterfly, but we cannot picture something as specific as one with a certain wing span. By giving too much information, a writer can make an image more difficult to imagine and thereby sacrifice the emotional impact of the scene. The great writers have an instinct for the appropriate detail to make a scene vivid.

The techniques Wright uses have been used by poets throughout the centuries. "The Soote Season" was written in the sixteenth century by Henry Howard, Earl of Surrey, the son of the wealthiest man in England. Like Wright's poem, it also concludes with a surprising last line.

HENRY HOWARD, EARL OF SURREY (1517–1547)

The Soote° Season   sweet

The soote season, that bud and bloom forth brings,	
With green hath clad the hill and eke° the vale;	also
The nightingale with feathers new she sings;	
The turtle° to her make° hath told her tale.	turtle dove mate
5 Summer is come, for every spray now springs;	
The hart hath hung his old head on the pale;	
The buck in brake his winter coat he flings,	
The fishes float with new repairéd scale;	
The adder all her slough away she slings,	
10 The swift swallow pursueth the fliés small;	
The busy bee her honey now she mings.°	mingles
Winter is worn, that was the flowers' bale.°	harm
And thus I see among these pleasant things,	
Each care decays, and yet my sorrow springs.	

Questions

1. Vocabulary: *vale* (2), *adder* (9).
2. Why do you suppose the speaker is sad?
3. Has summer arrived, as the poet proclaims in line 5? If not, why does he say so?
4. Are there any unexpected or unusual images in his catalogue? If so, how do they relate to the others?

Landscapes

Occasionally a friend or relative is so closely associated with a particular place or scene that, when we see the scene again, all our feelings and memories of the person revive. In "Neutral Tones" Thomas Hardy describes his former friend in terms of a landscape.

Thomas Hardy *(Dorset County Museum, Dorchester, England)*

THOMAS HARDY (1840–1928)

Neutral Tones

We stood by a pond that winter day,
And the sun was white, as though chidden of God,
And a few leaves lay on the starving sod;
    —They had fallen from an ash, and were gray.

5   Your eyes on me were as eyes that rove
Over tedious riddles of years ago;
And some words played between us to and fro
    On which lost the more by our love.

The smile on your mouth was the deadest thing
10   Alive enough to have strength to die;
And a grin of bitterness swept thereby
    Like an ominous bird a-wing. . . .

Since then, keen lessons that love deceives,
And wrings with wrong, have shaped to me
15   Your face, and the God-curst sun, and a tree,
    And a pond edged with grayish leaves.

Questions

1. Vocabulary: *chidden* (2), *rove* (5), *tedious* (6), *ominous* (12).
2. Whom is the poet addressing?
3. Why is he speaking to her? What has happened between them?

4. What is the speaker's feeling toward the woman? Does he express his feelings directly or indirectly?
5. How do you think the woman might respond?

Poets have also used landscapes as a starting point for meditation. You may have had a similar experience while sitting beside a lake or ocean, or looking out across a valley or mountain range. At first you were attentive to the world around you, but soon you lost yourself in thought. Sometimes we meditate so deeply that we do not "return to reality" for a long time; and, when we do, reality seems to have changed. M. H. Abrams has called the kind of poem that records this process "the greater romantic lyric" because so many poets of the early nineteenth century wrote poems of this sort. Typically, these lyrics have three sections. The first section presents the landscape; the second section is the meditation; and the third section recreates the landscape in light of the poet's intervening insights. "Dover Beach" is a classic lyric of this sort. It records Matthew Arnold's visit to Dover, a seaside resort and the point in England closest to France.

MATTHEW ARNOLD (1822–1888)

• Dover Beach

The sea is calm tonight.
The tide is full, the moon lies fair
Upon the straits—on the French coast the light
Gleams and is gone; the cliffs of England stand,
5   Glimmering and vast, out in the tranquil bay.
Come to the window, sweet is the night air!
Only, from the long line of spray
Where the sea meets the moon-blanched land,
Listen! you hear the grating roar
10   Of pebbles which the waves draw back, and fling,
At their return, up the high strand,
Begin, and cease, and then again begin,
With tremulous cadence slow, and bring
The eternal note of sadness in.

15   Sophocles[1] long ago
Heard it on the Aegean,[2] and it brought
Into his mind the turbid ebb and flow
Of human misery;[3] we
Find also in the sound a thought,
20   Hearing it by this distant northern sea.

The Sea of Faith
Was once, too, at the full, and round earth's shore

---
[1] Sophocles was a Greek playwright of the fifth century B.C.
[2] Aegean Sea, the waters between Greece and Asia Minor.
[3] See Sophocles' *Antigone*, lines 583 ff.

Lay like the folds of a bright girdle° furled.   *sash*
But now I only hear
25   Its melancholy, long, withdrawing roar,
Retreating, to the breath
Of the night wind, down the vast edges drear
And naked shingles° of the world.   *beach pebbles*

Ah, love, let us be true
30   To one another! for the world, which seems
To lie before us like a land of dreams,
So various, so beautiful, so new,
Hath really neither joy, nor love, nor light,
Nor certitude, nor peace, nor help for pain;
35   And we are here as on a darkling plain
Swept with confused alarms of struggle and flight,
Where ignorant armies clash by night.

Questions

1. Vocabulary: *straits* (3), *blanched* (8), *tremulous* (13), *cadence* (13), *turbid* (17), *furled* (23), *certitude* (34).
2. Compare the opening description (lines 1–14) with the closing (lines 35–37). What accounts for the difference? Which images are most powerful?
3. Is the sadness Arnold feels a modern sadness or one that has always been with humankind?
4. According to Arnold, how can humanity avoid feelings of despair? Does he hold much hope for these methods?
5. Anthony Hecht has imagined, in his poem "The Dover Bitch" (page 765), how a woman might react to this poem if she received it. How would you respond?
6. Do you think conditions of life have changed since 1851, when Arnold wrote this poem?

Meanings of Words

Poets signal how we should respond to an image not only through commentary, but also by their choice of words. Most words have two messages: *denotative* and *connotative*. The denotative meaning is the dictionary meaning: what the word objectively signifies. But words also have connotations: associations with, for instance, social class, values, or historical periods.

We might call the same building a home, a residence, a mansion, or an estate. Each word carries a similar denotative meaning, but the words have various connotations. For example, *mansion* is a much more formal word than *home*. The word *home* evokes images of a family enjoying a television program or conversing in the kitchen, their car parked in the driveway. The word *mansion* suggests a book-lined study, quiet talks over sherry, a limousine in the garage.

Words also suggest attitudes or values. If we speak of someone's attitude as "devil-may-care," we might approve of it. If we call the same attitude "irresponsible," we appear to disapprove.

Exercise

The following are groups of roughly synonymous words. State how the connotations of the words differ, and use each word in a sentence that highlights its connotative meaning.

1. loaded with money, very rich, very wealthy
2. front door, entrance, portal
3. bushes, undergrowth, shrubbery
4. say yes, agree, state in the affirmative
5. ending, finishing, concluding
6. sailor, seaman, mariner
7. letter, correspondence, epistle
8. without sound, quiet, silent
9. wet, damp, moist
10. backside, rear end, behind

In the following poem we have italicized a number of key words whose connotative meaning directs our response to the images. Although the poem is mostly images—the overt commentary is confined to the first two lines—the poet's attitude is anything but neutral.

HENRY DAVID THOREAU (1817–1862)

Pray to What Earth Does This Sweet Cold Belong

Pray to what earth does this *sweet* cold belong,
Which asks no duties and no conscience?
The moon goes up by leaps her *cheerful* path
In some far summer stratum of the sky,
5   While stars with their *cold* shine *bedot* her way.
The fields *gleam mildly* back upon the sky,
And far and near upon the *leafless* shrubs
The snow dust still *emits* a *silver* light.
Under the hedge, where *drift* banks are their screen,
10   The titmice now pursue their *downy* dreams,
As often in the *sweltering* summer nights
The bee doth drop asleep in the flower cup,
When evening overtakes him with his load.
By the brooksides, in the *still genial* night,
15   The more *adventurous* wanderer may hear
The *crystals* shoot and form, and winter slow
Increase his rule by *gentlest* summer means.

Questions

1. What is Thoreau's attitude toward the winter?
2. Why is he surprised that an earthly winter is so sweet?
3. In what sense does the winter ask neither duties nor conscience?

4. Is there any order to these images? Why does the image of the moon precede the image of the frozen brook? Does this order condition our response to the scene?

An easy way to observe how the poet manipulates the reader's attitude is to eliminate or alter the key words of the poem. Consider how our attitude would change had Thoreau written:

The fields *reflect* the sky,
And far and near upon the *barren* shrubs
The snow dust still *gives off* a *metallic* light.

Exercise

In the following poem, underline the key words whose connotative meaning directs the reader's attitude. Eliminate or alter them to suggest a different or opposite attitude.

GARY SNYDER (1930–)

Oil

soft rainsqualls on the swells
south of the Bonins,[4] late at night. Light
from the empty mess-hall
throws back bulky shadows
5   of winch and fairlead
over the slanting fantail where I stand.

but for men on watch in the engine room,
the man at the wheel, the lookout in the bow.
the crew sleeps in cots on deck
10 or narrow iron bunks down drumming
passageways below.

the ship burns with a furnace heart
steam veins and copper nerves
quivers and slightly twists and always goes—
15 easy roll of the hull and deep
vibration of the turbine underfoot

bearing what all these
crazed, hooked nations need:
steel plates and
20 long injections of pure oil.

Surrealistic Imagery

Sometimes the images a poet asks us to picture are not strictly those we see in the actual world. When Gary Snyder writes, "Light/from the empty mess-hall/

---

[4] Island group in the western Pacific.

throws back bulky shadows," we can easily imagine the actual scene. If someone were present, he or she might be able to photograph it. In Blake's "London," however, we are invited to picture things that could not be photographed, such as "mind-forg'd manacles."

WILLIAM BLAKE (1757–1827)

• London

I wander thro' each charter'd⁵ street,
Near where the charter'd Thames does flow,
And mark in every face I meet
Marks of weakness, marks of woe.

5   In every cry of every Man,
In every Infant's cry of fear,
In every voice, in every ban,
The mind-forg'd manacles I hear.

How the Chimney-sweeper's cry
10   Every blackning Church appalls;
And the hapless Soldier's sigh
Runs in blood down Palace walls.

But most thro' midnight streets I hear
How the youthful Harlot's curse
15   Blasts the new-born Infant's tear,
And blights with plagues the Marriage hearse.

Questions

1. Vocabulary: *manacles* (8), *hapless* (11).
2. What does Blake mean in lines 1–2 when he calls the streets and river "charter'd"? What feelings do these details evoke?
3. What does Blake mean by "mind-forg'd manacles"? Can you think of any way in which you handcuff your own actions?
4. In what sense does the chimney sweeper's cry appall the church?
5. How does the harlot blast the child's tear? Why does she curse?

Although Blake wrote "London" nearly two hundred years ago, he used a technique we think of as modern. In lines 11–12 he wrote:

And the hapless Soldier's sigh
Runs in blood down Palace walls.

The image is more complicated than the synesthetic images we have observed in other poems. He is speaking not of a watery sigh, but of a sigh that "runs in blood." The image contains the kind of concentration (and perhaps illogic) that

---

⁵ For a lengthy discussion of this word, see the Appendix, pages xiii–xiv.

occurs in dreams. It is almost as if the soldier had been shot in front of the palace, but we do not see the execution. Rather, we hear the sigh and see the bloodstain, or, more precisely, we experience the two merged together. This dreamlike concentration of image, known as *surrealistic imagery*, is one of the techniques used in surrealistic poetry. Why do poets use such techniques? We might as well wonder why dream images are so condensed. In highly emotional states, fine distinctions become blurred; the sigh and the blood become one experience, not separated by time.

PIERRE REVERDY (1889–1960)

Departure

The horizon lowers
      The days lengthen
      Voyage
  A heart hops in a cage
5   A bird sings
      At the edge of death
Another door is about to open
      At the far end of the corridor
      Shines
10   One star
  A dark lady
      Lantern on a departing train

Translation by Michael Benedikt (1935–)

Questions

1. What dreamlike elements are present in this poem?
2. What sort of emotions does this poem evoke?
3. What is the significance of the door about to be opened in line 7?

Notice how this poem contains the type of confusion that occurs in dreams. It is not the *bird* that hops in a cage and the *heart* that is at the edge of death. They have exchanged places.

Poets use images for a number of purposes: to place us in a landscape or a dream, to present familiar people to us, to bring us to unknown lands. Images can be realistic, a mixture of sensory experiences, or dreamlike. But whatever the kinds of image, the poet always uses imagery to evoke emotions more fully and more powerfully than could mere statements of feelings.

Suggestions for Essayists

1. Discuss how images in popular culture (in magazines, films, and advertisements) control our emotions and ideas.

2. Describe a place where you have been and the meditations it evoked.
3. Compare Matthew Arnold's "Dover Beach" with Anthony Hecht's "The Dover Bitch" on page 506.

Suggestions for Poets

1. Select a series of different emotions. Then write one image for each emotion that will evoke the feeling for the reader.
2. Evoke a landscape in images.
3. Suggest your feelings toward a person by evoking the landscape that most typifies that person.

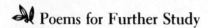 Poems for Further Study

SAMUEL TAYLOR COLERIDGE (1772–1834)

• Kubla Khan

In Xanadu did Kubla Khan
A stately pleasure dome decree:
Where Alph, the sacred river, ran
Through caverns measureless to man
5   Down to a sunless sea.
So twice five miles of fertile ground
With walls and towers were girdled round:
And there were gardens bright with sinuous rills,
Where blossomed many an incense-bearing tree;
10 And here were forests ancient as the hills,
Enfolding sunny spots of greenery.

But oh! that deep romantic chasm which slanted
Down the green hill athwart a cedarn cover!
A savage place! as holy and enchanted
15 As e'er beneath a waning moon was haunted
By woman wailing for her demon lover!
And from this chasm, with ceaseless turmoil seething,
As if this earth in fast thick pants were breathing,
A mighty fountain momently was forced:
20 Amid whose swift half-intermitted burst
Huge fragments vaulted like rebounding hail,
Or chaffy grain beneath the thresher's flail:
And 'mid these dancing rocks at once and ever
It flung up momently the sacred river.
25 Five miles meandering with a mazy motion
Through wood and dale the sacred river ran,
Then reached the caverns measureless to man,
And sank in tumult to a lifeless ocean:
And 'mid this tumult Kubla heard from far
30 Ancestral voices prophesying war!

The shadow of the dome of pleasure
Floated midway on the waves;
Where was heard the mingled measure
From the fountain and the caves.
35   It was a miracle of rare device,
A sunny pleasure dome with caves of ice!

A damsel with a dulcimer
In a vision once I saw:
It was an Abyssinian maid,
40   And on her dulcimer she played,
Singing of Mount Abora.
Could I revive within me
Her symphony and song,
To such a deep delight 'twould win me,
45   That with music loud and long,
I would build that dome in air,
That sunny dome! those caves of ice!
And all who heard should see them there,
And all should cry, Beware! Beware!
50   His flashing eyes, his floating hair!
Weave a circle round him thrice,
And close your eyes with holy dread,
For he on honeydew hath fed,
And drunk the milk of Paradise.

ALFRED, LORD TENNYSON (1809–1892)

The Eagle: A Fragment

He clasps the crag with crooked hands;
Close to the sun in lonely lands,
Ringed with the azure world, he stands.

The wrinkled sea beneath him crawls:
5   He watches from his mountain walls,
And like a thunderbolt he falls.

AMY LOWELL (1874–1925)

Chinoiseries

Reflections

When I looked into your eyes,
I saw a garden
With peonies, and tinkling pagodas,
And round-arched bridges
5   Over still lakes.
A woman sat beside the water
In a rain-blue, silken garment.
She reached through the water

To pluck the crimson peonies
10 Beneath the surface,
But as she grasped the stems,
They jarred and broke into white-green ripples;
And as she drew out her hand,
The water-drops dripping from it
15 Stained her rain-blue dress like tears.

Falling Snow
The snow whispers about me,
And my wooden clogs
Leave holes behind me in the snow.
But no one will pass this way
20 Seeking my footsteps,
And when the temple bell rings again
They will be covered and gone.

Hoar-Frost
In the cloud-grey mornings
I heard the herons flying;
25 And when I came into my garden,
My silken outer-garment
Trailed over withered leaves.
A dried leaf crumbles at a touch,
But I have seen many Autumns
30 With herons blowing like smoke
Across the sky.

WILLIAM CARLOS WILLIAMS (1883–1963)

The Red Wheelbarrow

so much depends
upon

a red wheel
barrow

5   glazed with rain
water

beside the white
chickens.

T. S. ELIOT (1888–1965)

Preludes

I

The winter evening settles down
With smell of steaks in passageways.
Six o'clock.

The burnt-out ends of smoky days.
5   And now a gusty shower wraps
The grimy scraps
Of withered leaves about your feet
And newspapers from vacant lots;
The showers beat
10   On broken blinds and chimney-pots,
And at the corner of the street
A lonely cab-horse steams and stamps.

And then the lighting of the lamps.

II

The morning comes to consciousness
15   Of faint stale smells of beer
From the sawdust-trampled street
With all its muddy feet that press
To early coffee-stands.

With the other masquerades
20   That time resumes,
One thinks of all the hands
That are raising dingy shades
In a thousand furnished rooms.

III

You tossed a blanket from the bed,
25   You lay upon your back, and waited;
You dozed, and watched the night revealing
The thousand sordid images
Of which your soul was constituted;
They flickered against the ceiling.
30   And when all the world came back
And the light crept up between the shutters
And you heard the sparrows in the gutters,
You had such a vision of the street
As the street hardly understands;
35   Sitting along the bed's edge, where
You curled the papers from your hair,
Or clasped the yellow soles of feet
In the palms of both soiled hands.

IV

His soul stretched tight across the skies
40   That fade behind a city block,
Or trampled by insistent feet
At four and five and six o'clock;
And short square fingers stuffing pipes,
And evening newspapers, and eyes
45   Assured of certain certainties,
The conscience of a blackened street
Impatient to assume the world.

I am moved by fancies that are curled
Around these images, and cling:
50   The notion of some infinitely gentle
Infinitely suffering thing.

Wipe your hand across your mouth, and laugh;
The worlds revolve like ancient women
Gathering fuel in vacant lots.

ROBERT LOWELL (1917–1977)

• Skunk Hour

(For Elizabeth Bishop)

Nautilus Island's hermit
heiress still lives through winter in her Spartan° cottage;   *austere*
her sheep still graze above the sea.
Her son's a bishop. Her farmer
5   is first selectman in our village;
she's in her dotage.

Thirsting for
the hierarchic privacy
of Queen Victoria's century,
10   she buys up all
the eyesores facing her shore,
and lets them fall.

The season's ill—
we've lost our summer millionaire,
15   who seemed to leap from an L. L. Bean
catalogue. His nine-knot yawl
was auctioned off to lobstermen.
A red fox stain covers Blue Hill.

And now our fairy
20   decorator brightens his shop for fall;
his fishnet's filled with orange cork,
orange, his cobbler's bench and awl;
there is no money in his work,
he'd rather marry.

25   One dark night,
my Tudor Ford climbed the hill's skull;
I watched for love-cars. Lights turned down,
they lay together, hull to hull,
where the graveyard shelves on the town. . . .
30   My mind's not right.

A car radio bleats,
"Love, O careless Love. . . ." I hear

my ill-spirit sob in each blood cell,
as if my hand were at its throat. . . .
35 I myself am hell;
nobody's here—

only skunks, that search
in the moonlight for a bite to eat.
They march on their soles up Main Street:
40 white stripes, moonstruck eyes' red fire
under the chalk-dry and spar spire
of the Trinitarian Church.

I stand on top
of our back steps and breathe the rich air—
45 a mother skunk with her column of kittens swills the garbage pail.
She jabs her wedge-head in a cup
of sour cream, drops her ostrich tail,
and will not scare.

ETHERIDGE KNIGHT (1933–)

Haiku

1

Eastern guard tower
glints in sunset; convicts rest
like lizards on rocks.

2

The piano man
5 is sting at 3 am
his songs drop like plum.

3

Morning sun slants cell.
Drunks stagger like cripple flies
On Jailhouse floor.

4

10 To write a blues song
is to regiment riots
and pluck gems from graves.

5

A bare pecan tree
slips a pencil shadow down
15 a moonlit snow slope.

6

The falling snow flakes
Can not blunt the hard aches nor
Match the steel stillness.

7

Under moon shadows
20   A tall boy flashes knife and
Slices star bright ice.

8

In the August grass
Struck by the last rays of sun
The cracked teacup screams.

9

25   Making jazz swing in
Seventeen syllables AIN'T
No square° poet's job.   *straitlaced*

7 🌿 The Dance of the Mind

Metaphor and Simile

Poetry must attempt extraordinary leaps of both association and logic to achieve its heights of emotion and its provocative thoughts. We can easily distinguish these verbal flights from ordinary speech, as when someone says, fearfully, "She is taking her life in her hands!"; or, in admiration, "He is a diamond in the rough." Although these expressions are quite worn with use, we continue to use them because they are truly poetic. If the speaker were not animated by emotion, such statements might be dismissed as lies. The abstraction "life" cannot be held in the hands, and a man obviously is not a diamond. These expressions are true to feelings rather than to facts. Emotion has set the mind of the speaker dancing and has inspired what is known as a *figure of speech*.

The Metaphor

CHARLES SIMIC (1938–)

Watermelons

Green Buddhas
On the fruit stand.
We eat the smile
And spit out the teeth.

What has happened to the watermelons? The poet has seen them displayed on a fruit stand in their round wholeness. He has seen them cut into edible wedges. To his mind the uncut watermelons become Buddhas, godlike as they rest peacefully on the fruit stand. The tasty wedges of fruit become smiles as he thinks of eating them. And the seeds, as he recalls spitting them out, become teeth that he imagines in the red mouth of the smile. The watermelon, in short, has been transformed to express the poet's delight in all its shapes.

The transformation of one thing or idea into another is called *metaphor*. It is the most powerful figure of speech and very likely the most essential act of poetic intelligence. Metaphor is personal and visionary, requiring no allegiance to facts. A metaphor may seem quite sensible, as when someone says, "My house is a prison," or it may at first seem bizarre: "My house is a dark road." But the statements are equally metaphorical. Each is poetically true insofar as it conveys the mood of the speaker.

WALT WHITMAN (1819–1892)

From Leaves of Grass

A child said What is the grass? fetching it to me with full hands;
How could I answer the child? I do not know what it is anymore than he.

I guess it must be the flag of my disposition, out of hopeful green stuff woven.

Or I guess it is the handkerchief of the Lord,
5   A scented gift and remembrancer designedly dropt,
Bearing the owner's name someway in the corners, that we may see and remark, and say Whose?

Or I guess the grass is itself a child, the produced babe of the vegetation.

Or I guess it is a uniform hieroglyphic,
And it means, Sprouting alike in broad zones and narrow zones,

Walt Whitman *(National Portrait Gallery, Smithsonian Institution, Washington, D.C.)*

10   Growing among black folks as among white,
      Kanuck, Tuckahoe, Congressman, Cuff, I give them the same, I receive them the
      same.

      And now it seems to me the beautiful uncut hair of graves.

Metaphor is commonly thought of as a sort of comparison, but such a definition seriously limits our appreciation of this powerful figure of speech. A
metaphor *may* arise out of a comparison, as when, noticing that buttercups and
sunlight are both a certain shade of yellow, we call the sunlight a buttercup.
But when Walt Whitman says that the grass is "the beautiful uncut hair of
graves" or "the handkerchief of the Lord," his imagination has overwhelmed
any similarities between grass and hair or handkerchiefs. His delight has transformed the grass.

As easily as metaphor can turn one thing into another, it can transform an
idea into a thing. Here Emily Dickinson begins with the abstract noun *Hope*,
a complex idea without visual properties. Then she transforms hope into a bird
so that we can see, hear, and better appreciate it.

EMILY DICKINSON (1830–1886)

• Hope Is the Thing with Feathers

      Hope is the thing with feathers
      That perches in the soul,
      And sings the tune without the words,
      And never stops at all,

5   And sweetest in the gale is heard;
      And sore must be the storm
      That could abash the little bird
      That kept so many warm.

      I've heard it in the chillest land,
10   And on the strangest sea;
      Yet, never, in extremity,
      It asked a crumb of me.

Question

1. Vocabulary: *abash* (7), *extremity* (11).

In the first line, by mentioning feathers, Dickinson emphasizes the bird's
lightness. In line 4 she suggests that the creature's consoling music is constant.
She further characterizes Hope in the second stanza, when she tells us the
peculiar bird sings most sweetly during storms, warming us in adversity. As her
final compliment to the bird's nature, she tells us that Hope does its comforting
work free of charge. We need not offer it so much as a crumb in order to receive
its benefits.

Hilda Doolittle (A/P Wide World Photos)

H. D. (HILDA DOOLITTLE) (1886–1961)

Oread°   *mountain nymph*

Whirl up, sea—
whirl your pointed pines,
splash your great pines
on our rocks,
5 hurl your green over us,
cover us with your pools of fir.

Questions

1. How does the poet transform the sea?
2. What emotion or mood is evoked by the metaphor?

ROBERT PENN WARREN (1905–)

Bearded Oaks

The oaks, how subtle and marine,
Bearded, and all the layered light
Above them swims; and thus the scene,
Recessed, awaits the positive night.

5 So, waiting, we in the grass now lie
Beneath the languorous tread of light:
The grasses, kelp-like, satisfy
The nameless motions of the air.

Upon the floor of light, and time,
10   Unmurmuring, of polyp[1] made,
We rest; we are, as light withdraws,
Twin atolls on a shelf of shade.

Ages to our construction went,
Dim architecture, hour by hour:
15   And violence, forgot now, lent
The present stillness all its power.

The storm of noon above us rolled,
Of light the fury, furious gold,
The long drag troubling us, the depth:
20   Dark is unrocking, unrippling, still.

Passion and slaughter, ruth, decay
Descend, minutely whispering down,
Silted down swaying streams, to lay
Foundation for our voicelessness.

25   All our debate is voiceless here,
As all our rage, the rage of stone;
If hope is hopeless, then fearless fear,
And history is thus undone.

Our feet once wrought the hollow street
30   With echo when the lamps were dead
At windows, once our headlight glare
Disturbed the doe that, leaping, fled.

I do not love you less that now
The caged heart makes iron stroke,
35   Or less that all that light once gave
The graduate dark should now revoke.

We live in time so little time
And we learn all so painfully
That we may spare this hour's term
40   To practice for eternity.

Questions

1. Are the oaks really bearded?
2. What does Warren mean by describing them as bearded?
3. What metaphors can you find in stanza 2?
4. The lovers in the poem describe themselves as "Twin atolls in a shelf of shade." In lines 13–24 Warren develops that metaphor. Explain how the poet was moved to imagine himself and his love in these metaphorical terms.
5. Where once the lovers' feet "wrought the hollow street/ With echo," and their "headlight glare/ Disturbed the doe," now the poet says "the caged heart makes iron stroke." Explain this metaphor.

---

[1] A polyp is a flowerlike water animal.

BILL KNOTT (1940–)

Hair Poem

Hair is heaven's water flowing eerily over us
Often a woman drifts off down her long hair and is lost

Questions

1. What mood or emotion do you suppose triggered the transformation of hair into "heaven's water"?
2. Is there a metaphor implied in line 2?

CHARLES HENRI FORD (1913–)

Somebody's Gone

There may be a basement to the Atlantic
but there's no top-storey
to my mountain of missing you.

I must say your deportment took a hunk
5   out of my peach of a heart.
I ain't insured against torpedoes!
My turpentine tears would fill a drugstore.

May I be blindfolded before you come my way again
if you're going to leave dry land like an amphibian;
10   I took you for some kind of ambrosial bird
with no thought of acoustics.

Maybe it's too late to blindfold me ever:
I'm just a blotter crisscrossed with the ink
of words that remind me of you.

15   Bareheaded aircastle,
you were as beautiful as a broom made of flesh and hair.

When you first disappeared
I couldn't keep up with my breakneck grief,
and now I know how grief can run away with the mind,
20   leaving the body desolate as a staircase.

Questions

1. Vocabulary: *deportment* (4), *amphibian* (9), *ambrosial* (10).
2. What do you suppose is the relationship of the poet to the "you" of the poem?
3. By suggesting there "may be a basement to the Atlantic," how is the poet transforming the ocean?
4. How does the poet express frustration in lines 13 and 14?
5. Why did Ford write this poem?

You might try some metaphors of your own in order to discover the great power of this figure of speech. Look at the objects in your classroom, and transform them imaginatively. Write: *The desk is a desert. The blackboard is a door to night.* Transform a friend or an enemy: *John is a flagpole. Linda is a violin.* It does not take long to discover that every metaphor has emotional potential. In fact, it is difficult to make one that does not convey feeling as well as thought. Concentrate on a single object and transform it into as many other things as you can think of, trying for the greatest range of emotions.

The Simile

The simile is a more modest figure of speech. The common qualities of differing things may prompt a metaphor: "the sun is a buttercup," or "his ambition is a bubble." Having registered the similarity, however, a metaphor insists on total mental transformation of the one thing into the other. The simile, on the other hand, simply compares two different things on the basis of some shared quality.

> His head was as hairless as an egg.
> > —*Anonymous*
>
> Her dress was as plain as an umbrella cover.
> > —*Joseph Conrad*
>
> Thine eyes are like the deep, blue boundless heaven.
> > —*William Shakespeare*

The charm of the simile comes from the observed likeness. Someone's eyes might be exactly the shade of the sky. The simile's force arises out of the differences between the things compared—by comparing someone's eyes to heaven, we attribute divine qualities to a mere mortal. But if we compare one person's eyes to another's or one tree to another, we are not making a figure of speech at all; we are simply writing prose.

Similes are easy to recognize, for they always declare their intentions by using the qualifiers *like* and *as*: "Debt is like a millstone about a person's neck" (Anon); "Childhood shows the man, as the morning shows the day" (John Milton). It is important to be able to recognize similes as we come upon them in our reading. It is even more important to appreciate the feelings and correspondences that inspire them. Let us examine a few similes with that in mind.

> A secret in his mouth is like
> a wild bird in a cage,
> whose door no sooner opens,
> than 'tis out.
> > —*Ben Jonson*

The elements of the comparison are the "secret in his mouth" and the "wild bird in a cage." What is the similarity? Both the secret and the wild bird cannot resist the temptation to escape. What has inspired the figure of speech? Distrust.

Ben Jonson is passing a harsh judgment on the man by means of his ingenious simile.

> Like to the moon am I, that cannot shine alone.
>
> —*Michelangelo*

Michelangelo, the great painter and sculptor, also wrote inspired poetry. What is the basis of comparison between the artist and the moon? He tells us that both require a light besides their own; they "cannot shine alone." The great force and emotion of this simile occur to us when we consider the great height and brilliance of the moon, the enormity of its loneliness when it cannot shine. The moon relies on the sun for its light; the artist needs love, the light of the world's approval, and inspiration. By comparing himself to the moon, Michelangelo is measuring himself on a grand scale indeed, suggesting the enormity of his needs and the grandeur of their satisfactions.

T. E. HULME (1883–1917)

Autumn

A touch of cold in the Autumn night—
I walked abroad,
And saw the ruddy moon lean over a hedge
Like a red-faced farmer.
5   I did not stop to speak, but nodded,
And round about were the wistful stars
With white faces like town children.

Questions

1. Vocabulary: *wistful* (6).
2. What does the moon have in common with the farmer? How does the idea of a moon with a farmer's face strike you? Is it frightening? Amusing?
3. What do the stars have in common with town children?
4. What mood is inspired by the last lines?

BILL KNOTT (1940–)

Death

Going to sleep, I cross my hands on my chest.
They will place my hands like this.
It will look as though I am flying into myself.

Questions

1. Who are "they" in line 2? Does the title give you a clue?
2. The final line is a striking image achieved through simile. What is being compared to what?

THOMAS MERTON (1915–1968)

The Regret

When cold November sits among the reeds like an unlucky fisher

And ducks drum up as sudden as the wind
Out of the rushy river,
We slowly come, robbed of our rod and gun,
5   Walking amid the stricken cages of the trees.

The stormy weeks have all gone home like drunken hunters,
Leaving the gates of the grey world open to December.

But now there is no speech of branches in these broken jails.
Acorns lie over the earth, no less neglected
10   Than our unrecognizable regret:

And here we stand as senseless as the oaks,
As dumb as elms.

And though we seem as grave as jailers, yet we did not come to wonder
Who picked the locks of the past days, and stole our summer.
15   (We are no longer listeners for curious saws, and secret keys!)

We are indifferent to seasons,
And stand like hills, deaf.
And never hear the last of the escaping year
Go ducking through the bended branches like a leaf.

Questions

1. This brooding meditation treats an old theme with a brilliant range of similes and metaphors. The theme is our neglect of nature, which is also a neglect of ourselves. Of all the similes, which one comes closest to summarizing that theme?
2. Why does Merton compare the stormy weeks to drunken hunters? What do they have in common?
3. Why does he compare the escaping year to a leaf in the last line?

The Conceit

A simile or metaphor that carries out a comparison in great detail is called a *conceit*.

Beauty, like the fair Hesperian[2] tree,
Laden with blooming gold, hath need the guard
Of dragon watch, with unenchanted eye,
To save her blossoms and defend her fruit
From the rash hand of bold incontinence°   *inchastity*

—*John Milton*

---

[2] In Greek literature Hesperus is a mythic treasure island.

This decorative figure of speech, which calls attention to the writer's ingenuity, was a popular mannerism of the Renaissance. Several seventeenth-century writers, sometimes called *metaphysical poets*, seem to try to outdo each other in the elaborateness of their figures. The following love poem elaborates a single comparison, between the loved one and a summer's day. Notice how the lover is flattered by the comparison and how wittily the poet takes credit for it in the last line.

WILLIAM SHAKESPEARE (1564–1616)

• Shall I Compare Thee to a Summer's Day?

Shall I compare thee to a summer's day?
Thou art more lovely and more temperate.
Rough winds do shake the darling buds of May,
And summer's lease hath all too short a date.
5   Sometime too hot the eye of heaven shines,
And often is his gold complexion dimmed;
And every fair from fair sometime declines,
By chance, or nature's changing course, untrimmed.
But thy eternal summer shall not fade,
10   Nor lose possession of that fair thou ow'st;°   *possess*
Nor shall death brag thou wand'rest in his shade,
When in eternal lines to time thou grow'st.
So long as men can breathe or eyes can see,
So long lives this, and this gives life to thee.

Questions

1. Vocabulary: *temperate* (2).
2. What does the speaker emphasize about a summer's day? Could he find more flattering things to say about it?
3. What does the speaker's beloved have that the summer's day does not?

The following poem, a meditation on one of the Virgin's tears, is often cited for its overelaborate conceits. The poem survives despite the criticism, or perhaps because of it. We will leave it to the reader to judge the poem's effectiveness.

RICHARD CRASHAW (1613?–1649)

The Tear

What bright soft thing is this,
    Sweet Mary, thy fair eyes' expense?
A moist spark it is,

A wat'ry diamond; from whence
5   The very term, I think, was found,
The water of a diamond.

Oh! 'tis not a tear,
    'Tis a star about to drop
From thine eye, its sphere;
10   The Sun will stoop and take it up.
Proud will his sister be to wear
This thine eye's jewel in her ear.

Oh! 'tis a tear,
    Too true a tear; for no sad eyne,
15   How sad soe'er,
        Rain so true a tear as thine;
Each drop, leaving a place so dear,
Weeps for itself, is its own tear.

Such a pearl as this is,
20   (Slipped from Aurora's° dewy breast)   dawn's
The rose-bud's sweet lip kisses;
        And such the rose itself, when vexed
With ungentle flames, does shed,
Sweating in too warm a bed.

25   Such the maiden gem
        By the wanton Spring put on,
Peeps from her parent stem,
        And blushes on the manly Sun:
This wat'ry blossom of thy eyne,
30   Ripe, will make the richer wine.

Fair drop, why quak'st thou so?
    'Cause thou straight must lay thy head
In the dust? Oh no;
        The dust shall never be thy bed:
35   A pillow for thee will I bring,
Stuffed with down of angel's wing.

Thus carried up on high,
        (For to heaven thou must go)
Sweetly shalt thou lie,
40   And in soft slumbers bathe thy woe;
Till the singing orbs awake thee,
And one of their bright chorus make thee.

There thyself shalt be
        An eye, but not a weeping one;
45   Yet I doubt of thee,
        Whither th'hadst rather there have shone
An eye of Heaven; or still shine here
In th' Heaven of Mary's eye, a tear.

1. Vocabulary: *wanton* (26).
2. By what line of the poem has the tear become a distinct image?
3. By what line has the image of the tear become a metaphor? How many metaphors does Crashaw develop from the tear?
4. When do you sense that the figures have evolved into conceits?
5. Do the conceits become wearisome? Do they seem obsessive?

The Spanish philosopher José Ortega y Gasset refers to poetry as the "higher mathematics of literature." By that he means that poetry anticipates more popular movements in literature, and also that poetry is capable of great precision in expressing subtle states of the mind and heart. In those subtle areas no devices are more accurate in expression than metaphors and similes. If they cause us difficulty at first, we must be patient, for these figures produce some of the greatest riches in poetry. John Donne, in the following masterwork of similes and conceits, achieves extraordinary delicacy. He is treating a difficult subject: the different kinds of love, and how lovers are affected by separation. Donne composed this poem for his wife on the eve of his departure on a long trip. In the first two stanzas he urges her to help him take his leave with silence and dignity, like "virtuous men" at the hour of death. In the third stanza he compares the lovers to celestial bodies, "the spheres," which may move apart, or irregularly, without evil consequences. Pay close attention to the gold simile in stanza 6 and to the simile of the compass that concludes the poem.

JOHN DONNE (1572–1631)

• A Valediction: Forbidding Mourning

As virtuous men pass mildly away,
   And whisper to their souls to go,
Whilst some of their sad friends do say
   The breath goes now, and some say no:

5   So let us melt, and make no noise,
   No tear-floods, nor sigh-tempests move;
'Twere profanation of our joys
   To tell the laity our love.

Moving of th' earth brings harms and fears;
10   Men reckon what it did and meant;
But trepidation of the spheres,[3]
   Though greater far, is innocent.

Dull sublunary lovers' love
   (Whose soul is sense) cannot admit

---

[3] Because of the movement of the earth, other planets appear to wobble or stand still. The odd movements were called the "trepidation of the spheres."

15   Absence, because it doth remove
        Those things which elemented it.

     But we, by a love so much refined
        That ourselves know not what it is,
     Inter-assurèd of the mind,
20   Care less, eyes, lips, and hands to miss.

     Our two souls, therefore, which are one,
        Though I must go, endure not yet
     A breach, but an expansion,
        Like gold to airy thinness beat.

25   If they be two, they are two so
        As stiff twin compasses are two:[4]
     Thy soul, the fixed foot, makes no show
        To move, but doth, if th' other do.

     And though it in the center sit,
30   Yet when the other far doth roam,
     It leans and harkens after it,
        And grows erect as that comes home.

     Such wilt thou be to me, who must,
        Like th' other foot, obliquely run;
35   Thy firmness makes my circle just,
        And makes me end where I begun.

Question

1. Vocabulary: *valediction*, *profanation* (7), *trepidation* (11), *sublunary* (13).

✕ Poems for Further Study

In reading the following poems, pay special attention to the metaphors and similes. Where you find a metaphor, determine what feelings have caused the transformation of images. Where you find a simile, look for the correspondences between the elements compared, and see how the elements complement each other by their differences.

A. E. HOUSMAN (1859–1936)

With Rue My Heart Is Laden

With rue my heart is laden
    For golden friends I had,
For many a rose-lipt maiden
    And many a lightfoot lad.

---

[4] Donne is referring to the compass used to draw circles.

5   By brooks too broad for leaping
          The lightfoot boys are laid;
       The rose-lipt girls are sleeping
          In fields where roses fade.

THOMAS MERTON (1915–1968)

Elegy for the Monastery Barn

As though an aged person were to wear
Too gay a dress
And walk about the neighborhood
Announcing the hour of her death,

5   So now, one summer day's end,
       At suppertime, when wheels are still,
       The long barn suddenly puts on the traitor, beauty,
       And hails us with a dangerous cry,
       For: "Look!" she calls to the country,
10   "Look how fast I dress myself in fire!"

Had we half guessed how long her spacious shadows
Harbored a woman's vanity
We would be less surprised to see her now
So loved, and so attended, and so feared.

15   She, in whose airless heart
       We burst our veins to fill her full of hay,
       Now stands apart.
       She will not have us near her. Terribly,
       Sweet Christ, how terribly her beauty burns us now!

20   And yet she has another legacy,°   inheritance
       More delicate, to leave us, and more rare.

Who knew her solitude?
Who heard the peace downstairs
While flames ran whispering among the rafters?
25   Who felt the silence, there,
       The long, hushed gallery
       Clean and resigned and waiting for the fire?

Look! They have all come back to speak their summary:
Fifty invisible cattle, the past years
30   Assume their solemn places one by one.
       This is the little minute of their destiny.
       Here is their meaning found. Here is their end.

Laved° in the flame as in a Sacrament   bathed
The brilliant walls are holy
35   In their first-last hour of joy.

Fly from within the barn! Fly from the silence
Of this creature sanctified by fire!
Let no man stay inside to look upon the Lord!
Let no man wait within and see the Holy
40   One sitting in the presence of disaster
Thinking upon this barn His gentle doom!

N. SCOTT MOMADAY (1934–)

The Delight Song of Tsoai-Talee[5]

I am a feather on the bright sky
I am the blue horse that runs in the plain
I am the fish that rolls, shining, in the water
I am the shadow that follows a child
5   I am the evening light, the lustre of meadows
I am an eagle playing with the wind
I am a cluster of bright beads
I am the farthest star
I am the cold of the dawn
10   I am the roaring of the rain
I am the glitter on the crust of the snow
I am the long track of the moon in a lake
I am a flame of four colors
I am a deer standing away in the dusk
15   I am a field of sumac and the pomme blanche
I am an angle of geese in the winter sky
I am the hunger of a young wolf
I am the whole dream of these things

You see, I am alive, I am alive
20   I stand in good relation to the earth
I stand in good relation to the gods
I stand in good relation to all that is beautiful
I stand in good relation to the daughter of *Tsen-tainte*[6]
You see, I am alive, I am alive

Compare with W.E.B. DuBois's "The Song of the Smoke," page 735.

EZRA POUND (1885–1972)

The Bath Tub

As a bathtub lined with white porcelain,
When the hot water gives out or goes tepid,
So is the slow cooling of our chivalrous passion,
O my much praised but-not-altogether-satisfactory lady.

---

[5] N. Scott Momaday's Indian name, which means "Rock-Tree Boy."
[6] White Horse.

DYLAN THOMAS (1914–1953)

• Fern Hill

Now as I was young and easy under the apple boughs
About the lilting house and happy as the grass was green,
    The night above the dingle[7] starry,
        Time let me hail and climb
5   Golden in the heydays of his eyes,
And honoured among wagons I was prince of the apple towns
And once below a time I lordly had the trees and leaves
    Trail with daisies and barley
    Down the rivers of the windfall light.

10 And as I was green and carefree, famous among the barns
About the happy yard and singing as the farm was home,
    In the sun that is young once only,
        Time let me play and be
        Golden in the mercy of his means,
15 And green and golden I was huntsman and herdsman, the calves
Sang to my horn, the foxes on the hills barked clear and cold,
    And the sabbath rang slowly
    In the pebbles of the holy streams.
All the sun long it was running, it was lovely, the hay
20 Fields high as the house, the tunes from the chimneys, it was air
    And playing, lovely and watery
        And fire green as grass.
    And nightly under the simple stars
As I rode to sleep the owls were bearing the farm away,
25 All the moon long I heard, blessed among stables, the nightjars
    Flying with the ricks, and the horses
        Flashing into the dark.

And then to awake, and the farm, like a wanderer white
With the dew, come back, the cock on his shoulder: it was all
30   Shining, it was Adam and maiden,
        The sky gathered again
    And the sun grew round that very day.
So it must have been after the birth of the simple light
In the first, spinning place, the spellbound horses walking warm
35   Out of the whinnying green stable
        On to the fields of praise.

And honoured among foxes and pheasants by the gay house
Under the new made clouds and happy as the heart was long,
    In the sun born over and over,
40   I ran my heedless ways,
        My wishes raced through the house high hay
And nothing I cared, at my sky blue trades, that time allows

---

[7] A *dingle* is a narrow wooded valley.

In all his tuneful turning so few and such morning songs
  Before the children green and golden
45   Follow him out of grace,

Nothing I cared, in the lamb white days, that time would take me
Up to the swallow thronged loft by the shadow of my hand,
  In the moon that is always rising,
    Nor that riding to sleep
50   I should hear him fly with the high fields
And wake to the farm forever fled from the childless land.
Oh as I was young and easy in the mercy of his means,
    Time held me green and dying
  Though I sang in my chains like the sea.

LOUISE GLÜCK (1943–)

The Pond

Night covers the pond with its wing.
Under the ringed moon I can make out
your face swimming among minnows and the small
echoing stars. In the night air
5 the surface of the pond is metal.

Within, your eyes are open. They contain
a memory I recognize, as though
we had been children together. Our ponies
grazed on the hill, they were gray
10 with white markings. Now they graze
with the dead who wait
like children under their granite breastplate
lucid and helpless:

The hills are far away. They rise up
15 blacker than childhood.
What do you think of, lying so quiet
by the water? When you look that way I want
to touch you, but do not, seeing
as in another life we were of the same blood.

WILLIAM SHAKESPEARE (1564–1616)

Let Me Not to the Marriage of True Minds

Let me not to the marriage of true minds
Admit impediments. Love is not love
Which alters when it alteration finds,
Or bends with the remover° to remove.   *faithless lover*
5 O, no! it is an ever-fixèd mark
That looks on tempests and is never shaken;
It is the star to every wand'ring bark,

Whose worth's unknown, although his height be taken.
Love's not Time's fool, though rosy lips and cheeks
10   Within his bending sickle's compass come;
Love alters not with his brief hours and weeks,
But bears it out even to the edge of doom.
        If this be error and upon me proved,
        I never writ, nor no man ever loved.

PERCY BYSSHE SHELLEY (1792–1822)

Fragment: Thoughts Come and Go in Solitude

My thoughts arise and fade in solitude,
    The verse that would invest them melts away
    Like moonlight in the heaven of spreading day:
How beautiful they were, how firm they stood,
5   Flecking the starry sky like woven pearl!

JOHN DONNE (1572–1631)

• The Flea

Marke but this flea, and marke in this,
How little that which thou deny'st me is;
It suck'd me first, and now sucks thee,
And in this flea, our two bloods mingled bee;
5   Thou know'st that this cannot be said
A sinne, nor shame, nor losse of maidenhead,
        Yet this enjoyes before it wooe,
        And pamper'd swells with one blood made of two,
        And this, alas, is more than wee would doe.

10   Oh stay, three lives in one flea spare,
Where wee almost, yea more than maryed° are.   *married*
This flea is you and I, and this
Our mariage bed, and mariage temple is;
Though parents grudge, and you, w'are met,
15   And cloysterd in these living walls of Jet.
        Though use make you apt to kill mee,
        Let not to that, selfe murder added bee,
        And sacrilege, three sinnes in killing three.

Cruell and sodaine,° hast thou since   *sudden*
20   Purpled thy naile, in blood of innocence?
Wherein could this flea guilty bee,
Except in that drop which it suckt from thee?
Yet thou triumph'st, and saist that thou
Find'st not thy selfe, nor mee the weaker now;
25   'Tis true, then learne how false, feares bee;
        Just so much honor, when thou yeeld'st to mee,
        Will wast, as this flea's death tooke life from thee.

FEDERICO GARCÍA LORCA (1898–1936)

Half Moon

The moon goes over the water.
How tranquil the sky is!
She goes scything slowly
the old shimmer from the river;
5   meanwhile a young frog
takes her for a little mirror.

Translation by W. S. Merwin (1927–)

8 🌿 The Idea Dresses Up

Personification, Allegory, Symbol

Philosophers and mathematicians are generally more comfortable with abstractions than are poets. Mathematicians will talk about "infinite sets" or "imaginary numbers," and philosophers of "reason," "liberty," or "epistemes." Poets, however, feel more comfortable with what they can touch, see, hear, smell, or taste. Consequently, poets have developed a number of ways to make abstractions more concrete and familiar.

Personification

One of the simplest ways to make ideas concrete is *personification:* the granting of human attributes to things that are not human. Children's literature contains many examples of talking animals, trees, and stars. There are two primary reasons for the use of personification. First, we are better able to recognize attributes when they are given to an animal. An owl can be wiser, a cricket sillier, and a lion braver than a human could be. Second, we take a certain delight in such a transformation. On a basic, perhaps primitive level, we delight when unfamiliar experiences are made commonplace, and commonplace experiences are made unfamiliar.

Here, for example, is a short poem by the Greek poet Sappho. She wishes to convey the experience of being startled by the dawn. But "dawn" is a rather general condition. To gain the emotional intensity she desires, she has condensed the characteristics of daybreak into a personified figure.

SAPPHO (7th century B.C.)

Then

In gold sandals
dawn like a thief
fell upon me.

Translation by Willis Barnstone (1927–)

This poem is complicated by yet another factor. For the Greeks, Dawn is a goddess. Sappho is startled not only by the furtive sun, but also by a beautiful goddess who arrives on golden sandals. The scene, therefore, is doubly mysterious and awesome but also familiar and intimate.

Poets personify not only conditions and animals, but also abstract concepts like Freedom and Good Sense. In the following poem, Love, that often vague, abstract emotion, becomes a rich, generous, and distant patron.

MURIEL RUKEYSER (1913–1981)

Song: Love in Whose Rich Honor

Love
in whose rich honor
I stand looking from my window
over the starved trees of a dry September
5   Love
deep and so far forbidden
is bringing me
a gift
to claw at my skin
10   to break open my eyes
the gift longed for so long
The power
to write
out of the desperate ecstasy at last
15   death and madness

Questions

1. Where is the speaker of the poem? What is she looking at? What is the relationship between what the speaker sees and what she says?
2. Why should the gift claw at her skin and break open her eyes? Is Love's gift always gentle and kind, or is it sometimes cruel and painful?
3. What does the speaker mean by "desperate ecstasy" in line 14? To be in ecstasy means literally to be "beside oneself." In what sense is the speaker "beside herself"?
4. How has personifying Love made the poem more mysterious and intimate?

This poem concerns itself with a rather special question: can authors write with intensity on such subjects as death and madness from which others shy away? How can authors face those dreaded conditions not with philosophic detachment, but with joy? The persona of this poem answers that love gives her the power to write. But it is not merely an abstract love that enriches her. It is an almost godlike love, one that is "deep and so far forbidden." Rukeyser has taken a philosophical problem and turned it into a scene in which the mysterious figure of Love visits her with a gift of power.

Allegory

Emily Dickinson uses the personification of abstractions to explore the condition of death. Here again, the result is a poem that treats the subject with both familiarity and awe, mystery and intimacy.

EMILY DICKINSON (1830–1866)

• Because I Could Not Stop for Death

Because I could not stop for Death—
He kindly stopped for me—
The Carriage held but just Ourselves—
And Immortality.

5   We slowly drove—He knew no haste
And I had put away
My labor and my leisure too,
For His Civility—

We passed the School, where Children strove
10   At Recess—in the Ring—
We passed the Fields of Gazing Grain—
We passed the Setting Sun—

Or rather—He passed Us—
The Dews drew quivering and chill—
15   For only Gossamer, my gown—
My Tippet—only Tulle—

We paused before a House that seemed
A Swelling of the Ground—
The Roof was scarcely visible—
20   The Cornice—in the Ground—

Since then—'tis Centuries—and yet
Feels shorter than the Day
I first surmised the Horses' Heads
Were toward Eternity—

Questions

1. Vocabulary: *civility* (8), *gossamer* (15), *tippet* (16), *tulle* (16), *cornice* (20).
2. What is the persona's attitude toward Death? Is he a fearsome creature or a politely stiff gentleman? How does the persona treat him?
3. What is the house they visit? What does it resemble?
4. Has the journey ended for the speaker? Has she arrived at Eternity? What can we say about the speaker's view of immortality?

Unlike Sappho or Rukeyser, Dickinson employs a number of abstractions in telling her story. Immortality is Death's traveling companion, and they are both headed toward Eternity. Dickinson has done something very complicated; she has made a small allegory. She has turned abstract ideas into people and places and then woven them into a story. Yet as complicated as this process sounds, the results are easy to understand. In fact, we often use allegory to explain complicated ideas to small children. Instead of trying to discuss in scientific terms the need for good oral hygiene, parents or dentists will tell children stories about Mr. Toothdecay, who enjoys drilling holes in new white teeth until Mr. Toothbrush comes to the rescue. The allegory is simpler, more immediate, and certainly more entertaining than a lecture. Finally, the allegory is more persuasive than charts, tables, and other means of convincing an audience.

George Herbert understood the value of allegory as a means of communicating complex notions in a lively, simple way. He left Cambridge University, where he· had been elected public orator, to minister to a country parish. As public orator he had had to give flowery speeches in Latin to scholars at the university. But as a parish minister he had to persuade his poorly educated congregation to be better Christians. One of his allegorical poems follows.

GEORGE HERBERT (1593–1633)

The Pilgrimage

I traveled on, seeing the hill where lay
        My expectation.
A long it was and weary way.
      The gloomy cave of desperation
5 I left on th'one, and on the other side
        The rock of pride.

And so I came to fancy's meadow, strowed
        With many a flower;
Fain would I here have made abode,
10   But I was quickened by my hour.
So to care's copse I came, and there got through
        With much ado.

That led me to the wild of passion, which
        Some call the wold°—   *treeless plain*
15 A wasted place but sometimes rich.
Here I was robbed of all my gold
Save one good angel,[1] which a friend had tied
        Close to my side.

At length I got unto the gladsome hill
20   Where lay my hope,
Where lay my heart; and, climbing still,
      When I had gained the brow and top,
A lake of brackish waters on the ground
        Was all I found.

---

[1] "Good angel" refers to a gold coin as well as to a guardian angel.

25   With that abashed, and struck with many a sting
                Of swarming fears,
        I fell, and cried, "Alas, my king!
        Can both the way and end be tears?"
    Yet taking heart I rose, and then perceived
30   I was deceived:

    My hill was further; so I flung away,
              Yet heard a cry,
        Just as I went: *None goes that way*
        And lives: "If that be all," said I,
35   "After so foul a journey, death is fair,
              And but a chair."

Questions

1. Vocabulary: *copse* (11), *brackish* (23), *abashed* (25).
2. What is the significance of the "lake of brackish waters" in line 23 and the "good angel" in line 17?
3. What does the speaker feel in lines 25–30?
4. Does the speaker enjoy the pilgrimage? Is he supposed to?
5. What is the relationship between the life we live and our attitude toward death?
6. Is the pilgrim's life different from anyone else's?

Herbert's "pilgrimage" is another version of the "journey of life" on which we meet many difficulties. We must avoid the "cave of desperation" and "the rock of pride" and progress through "fancy's meadow," "care's copse," and "the wild of passion." The persona's destination is the "gladsome hill," which will be beautiful and refreshing, but as the voice informs him, *"None goes that way/ And lives."* Death is the only means of reaching the goal. But the speaker is not discouraged by the news. Dying seems a small price to pay for eternal happiness. Indeed, he is quite happy to die; he compares death to a sedan chair, like those on which the rich were comfortably carried about by servants.

Herbert's poem illustrates an important characteristic of allegory: the allegorical figures are not independent of one another. One understands the significance of the "rock of pride" in relation to the "gladsome hill" or the "cave of desperation." Moreover, the general pattern for life's journey illuminates all the allegorical figures. Each one helps us see the entire pattern, and it is the pattern that is most important in allegory.

Allegory often makes use of a dialogue in which the speaking is not colloquial. Here is such an allegorical scene.

AURELIAN TOWNSHEND (c. 1583–1643)

A Dialogue Betwixt Time and a Pilgrim

PILGRIM.   Aged man, that mows these fields.
TIME.   Pilgrim speak, what is thy will?

PILGRIM.	Whose soil is this that such sweet Pasture yields?
	Or who art thou whose Foot stands never still?
5	Or where am I? TIME. In love.
PILGRIM.	His Lordship lies above.
TIME.	Yes and below, and round about
	Where in all sorts of flow'rs are growing
	Which as the early Spring puts out,
10	Time falls as fast a mowing.
PILGRIM.	If thou art Time, these Flow'rs have Lives,
	And then I fear
	Under some Lily she I love
	May now be growing there.
15 TIME.	And in some Thistle or some spire of grass,
	My scythe thy stalk before hers come may pass.
PILGRIM.	Wilt thou provide it may? TIME. No.
PILGRIM.	Allege the cause.
TIME.	Because Time cannot alter but obey Fate's laws.
20 CHORUS.	Then happy those whom Fate, that is the stronger,
	Together twists their threads, and yet draws hers the longer.

Questions

1. Where does this meeting occur? How does the allegorical setting shape the dialogue?
2. How is Time portrayed? Is this a traditional view of Time?
3. Who is "His Lordship" in line 6? Why is he "below, and round about"?
4. What is the Chorus's moral?

Townshend, like Herbert, uses the figure of the pilgrim. We are all pilgrims on life's journey. He dramatizes a scene in which the pilgrim wanders into love even before he meets the object of his affection. Townshend uses the allegorical dialogue to explore the relationships among Love, Mortality, and Fate. The dialogue presents these ideas more simply and economically than could a lecture on the subject.

Fable

The fable, which is closely related to the allegory, is typically a story in which animals are given human attributes and represent certain moral qualities or philosophical positions. Most of the fables we know are derived from Aesop, a legendary Greek poet. The most famous, perhaps, is the story of the turtle and the rabbit who race one another. The moral or lesson of the story is: slow, steady work will triumph over impulsiveness.

Fables can be political as well. George Orwell's *Animal Farm* is a long prose allegorical fable about the rise of dictatorships. But Orwell was not the first author to write a political fable; he was participating in a long tradition, whose origins are buried in the distant past. "The Lion, the Fox, and Geese," a fable written by John Gay in the eighteenth century, still has relevance today.

JOHN GAY (1685–1732)

The Lion, the Fox, and Geese

A Lion, tired with state affairs,
Quite sick of pomp, and worn with cares,
Resolv'd (remote from noise and strife)
In peace to pass his latter life.
5   It was proclaim'd; the day was set;
Behold the gen'ral council met.
The Fox was Viceroy nam'd. The crowd
To the new Regent humbly bow'd
Wolves, bears, and mighty tygers bend,
10   And strive who most shall condescend.
He strait assumes a solemn grace,
Collects his wisdom in his face,
The crowd admire his wit, his sense:
Each word hath weight and consequence.
15   The flatt'rer all his art displays:
He who hath power, is sure of praise.
A Fox stept forth before the rest,
And thus the servile throng addrest.
       How vast his talents, born to rule,
20   And train'd in virtue's honest school!
What clemency his temper sways!
How uncorrupt are all his ways!
Beneath his conduct and command,
Rapine shall cease to waste the land.
25   His brain hath stratagem and art;
Prudence and mercy rule his heart;
What blessings must attend the nation
Under this good administration!
       He said. A Goose who distant stood,
30   Harangu'd apart the cackling brood.
       Whene'er I hear a knave commend,
He bids me shun his worthy friend.
What praise! what mighty commendation!
But 'twas a Fox who spoke th'oration.
35   Foxes this government might prize,
As gentle, plentiful, and wise;
If they enjoy the sweets, 'tis plain
We Geese must feel a tyrant reign.
What havock now shall thin our race,
40   When ev'ry petty clerk in place,
To prove his taste and seem polite,
Will feed on Geese both noon and night!

Questions

1. Vocabulary: *pomp* (2), *viceroy* (7), *Regent* (8), *servile* (18), *clemency* (21), *stratagem*
   (25), *harangued* (30).

2. If the Lion represents "true kingship," what does the Fox represent?
3. Why is the Goose afraid of the Fox? Whom does the Goose represent? Are the Goose's fears justified?
4. Can you think of any political events to which this allegory might apply?

In Gay's time the Lion referred not just to any king but to King George II. The Fox was Sir Robert Walpole (1676–1745), whom historians generally consider the first prime minister in English history, a controversial figure who was greatly feared. The fables gave Gay an opportunity to make his political points and yet avoid imprisonment and the accusation of treason. Under tyranny, fables become a popular form of political expression.

Symbol

The term *symbol* refers to a large variety of literary practices, and it is important to distinguish among the various uses of the term. Allegory makes use of symbols. In Herbert's "Pilgrimage" the "gladsome hill" is a symbol for heaven; the "brackish lake" is a symbol of worldly difficulties. Indeed, we might define allegory as the narrative orchestration of a number of symbols into a coherent pattern.

In its broadest sense a symbol is any object or action that signifies more than itself. For example, the badge an officer wears is not merely a decorative silvery pin; it refers to, or symbolizes, legal authority. The candles on a birthday cake are not placed there primarily to light the room or to keep the cake warm. They symbolize the number of years the person has lived. The clothes you wear do not simply keep you comfortable and warm; they also communicate your values. You may have an embroidered alligator, Greek letters, or a numeral on your shirt or blouse. Each of these symbols has its social significance.

How are symbols formed? There are people who do nothing but design symbols intended to advertise products. But symbols appear to be a natural function of every mind. Psychiatrists tell us that our dreams are complicated allegories through which we work out our feelings. Our waking lives are no less involved with symbols. The following poem by D. H. Lawrence tells us about the formation of a symbol.

D. H. LAWRENCE (1885–1930)

Sorrow

Why does the thin grey strand
Floating up from the forgotten
Cigarette between my fingers,
Why does it trouble me?

5   Ah, you will understand;
When I carried my mother downstairs,
A few times only, at the beginning
Of her soft-foot malady,

        I should find, for a reprimand
10   To my gaiety, a few long grey hairs
        On the breast of my coat; and one by one
        I watched them float up the dark chimney.

Questions

1. What specific words link the cigarette smoke to his mother's hair?
2. In what other senses are the hairs on his coat "a reprimand/To [his] gaiety"?
3. In line 12, what does the "dark chimney" symbolize?
4. Does the poem give you a logical explanation of why the smoke troubles the speaker? If not, why not?

Lawrence's poem shows how very different sensations become associated in our minds, especially during periods of emotional intensity. During his mother's final illness, the speaker had carried her about the house, and her hair had fallen on his clothing. Now the "thin grey strand" of cigarette smoke symbolizes the speaker's complex feelings about his mother's death.

One of the differences between the symbol of the cigarette smoke and that of the Lion in John Gay's fable is the number of associations the symbols have. The symbols in allegory and fable are relatively limited in reference. The Lion represents "natural leadership," "kingship," and—most specifically—King George II. These various references are closely related. But the cigarette smoke is associated with a complex and varied series of events, emotions, and ideas. It symbolizes the mother, her death, the speaker's continued existence. Symbols can also refer to other symbols. The cigarette smoke symbolizes the mother's hair, which in turn is "a reprimand/To [his] gaiety." The forgotten cigarette symbolizes the speaker's forgetfulness of his dying mother; it symbolizes his guilt.

One problem with symbols is that we sometimes recognize them without understanding their significance. Have you ever attended a religious ceremony of a different faith and been confused by the actions and symbols used in the ceremony, although you may have found them perfectly and even beautifully fitting? In "I Saw in Louisiana a Live-Oak Growing," Walt Whitman encounters a symbol that he finds difficult to comprehend.

WALT WHITMAN (1819–1892)

I Saw in Louisiana a Live-Oak Growing

        I saw in Louisiana a live-oak growing.
        All alone stood it and moss hung down from the branches.
        Without any companion it grew there uttering joyous leaves of dark green,
        And its look, rude, unbending, lusty, made me think of myself.
5   But I wonder'd how it could utter joyous leaves standing alone there without its
            friend near, for I knew I could not,
        And I broke off a twig with a certain number of leaves upon it, and twined around
            it a little moss

546   The Idea Dresses Up

And brought it away, and I placed it in sight in my room,
It is not needed to remind me as of my own dear friends,
(For I believe lately I think of little else than them.)
10   Yet it remains to me a curious token, it makes me think of manly love;
For all that, and though the live-oak glistens there in Louisiana solitary in a wide
    flat space,
Uttering joyous leaves all its life without a friend a lover near,
I know very well I could not.

Questions

1. In what way does the tree symbolize Whitman? In what ways does it not?
2. Why does the tree make Whitman think of "manly love"?
3. Why does he break off a twig?
4. Do you ever collect things in your travels? Why do you do it? Do they ever come
   to symbolize something for you?

ROBERT FROST (1874–1963)

For Once, Then, Something

Others taunt me with having knelt at well-curbs
Always wrong to the light, so never seeing
Deeper down in the well than where the water
Gives me back in a shining surface picture
5   Me myself in the summer heaven, godlike,
Looking out of a wreath of fern and cloud puffs.

Robert Frost (Rollie McKenna)

Once, when trying with chin against a well-curb,
I discerned, as I thought, beyond the picture,
Through the picture, a something white, uncertain,
10   Something more of the depths—and then I lost it.
Water came to rebuke the too clear water.
One drop fell from a fern, and lo, a ripple
Shook whatever it was lay there at bottom,
Blurred it, blotted it out. What was that whiteness?
15   Truth? A pebble of quartz? For once, then, something.

Questions

1. A Greek proverb says that "truth lies in the bottom of wells." How is this truth symbolized?
2. What does the "something" seen symbolize? Would the symbol be clearer if we were told what the speaker saw?
3. Does the whole action take on larger significance? Why does the speaker look into wells? What is peculiar about the way he does it?
4. At the poem's end, has the speaker lost the "godlike" feeling he had in line 5?

Traditional Symbols

The cigarette smoke, the live-oak, and the "whiteness" in the well are all unusual symbols, peculiar to the poets and to the poems in which they appear. Some symbols, however, are traditional. The cross symbolizes Christ's sacrifice; the unicorn is a symbol of purity; the apple represents forbidden knowledge. Poets often use traditional symbols in their work. The following song by Edmund Waller employs two traditional symbolic meanings of the rose: the rose is a symbol of love and of beauty's frailty.

EDMUND WALLER (1606–1687)

Go, Lovely Rose

Go, lovely Rose,
Tell her that wastes her Time and me,
    That now she knows,
When I resemble° her to thee,   *compare*
5   How sweet and fair she seems to be.

    Tell her that's Young,
And shuns to have her Graces spy'd,
    That hadst thou sprung
In Desarts, where no Men abide,
10   Thou must have uncommended dy'd

    Small is the Worth
Of Beauty from the Light retir'd;
    Bid her come forth,
Suffer her self to be desir'd,
15   And not blush so to be admir'd.

Then die, that she
The common Fate of all Things rare
    May read in thee:
How small a Part of Time they share,
20   That are so wond'rous sweet and fair.

Questions

1. How is personification used in this poem?
2. Why does the speaker wish the rose to die?
3. If you were given a rose, how would you feel? How does the speaker wish his lady to feel?
4. Compare this poem to "To His Coy Mistress" on page 457.

Yeats was fond of the rose symbol. Notice how he relies on its traditional associations with love and beauty in this poem.

WILLIAM BUTLER YEATS (1865–1939)

The Rose of Peace

If Michael, leader of God's host,[2]
When Heaven and Hell are met,
Looked down on you from Heaven's door-post
He would his deeds forget.

5   Brooding no more upon God's wars
In his divine homestead,
He would go weave out of the stars
A chaplet° for your head.   *wreath*

And all folk seeing him bow down,
10   And white stars tell your praise,
Would come at last to God's great town,
Led on by gentle ways;

And God would bid His warfare cease,
Saying all things were well;
15   And softly make a rosy peace,
A peace of Heaven with Hell.

Questions

1. Why would Michael forget his deeds?
2. What about the rose makes it bring peace?
3. How would this poem be different in feeling if it were about the "orchid of peace"? Is it important that the symbol be traditional?

---

[2] The archangel Michael.

Symbols are everywhere in poetry, as in the world around us, but one must be careful of them. Not everything is a symbol, though everything may contain the potential to become one. Before you interpret anything symbolically, you should try to find out if it is a traditional symbol or if the context in which it appears indicates its symbolic meaning. By being aware of context and tradition, you will become a seasoned reader able to distinguish well-chosen detail from symbol.

Suggestions for Essayists

1. With what sorts of symbols do you surround yourself? What message do you hope to convey about yourself?
2. Discuss the meanings of the symbols associated with a religious or secular holiday or ritual, such as Easter or Thanksgiving.
3. In the poems you have read, what sort of symbols have you found the most powerful? Why?

Suggestions for Poets

1. Carry on a discussion between two parts of your personality.
2. Speak to a traditional symbol, such as the rose. What do you want to tell it?
3. Retell a fable in your own words.

Poems for Further Study

THOMAS HARDY (1840–1928)

The Subalterns

I

"Poor wanderer," said the leaden sky,
    "I fain would lighten thee,
But there are laws in force on high
    Which say it must not be."

II

5   —"I would not freeze thee, shorn one," cried
    The North, "knew I but how
To warm my breath, to slack my stride;
    But I am ruled as thou."

III

   —"To-morrow I attack thee, wight,"
10   Said Sickness. "Yet I swear
I bear thy little ark no spite,
    But am bid enter there."

IV

—"Come hither, Son," I heard Death say;
   "I did not will a grave
15 Should end thy pilgrimage to-day,
   But I, too, am a slave!"

V

We smiled upon each other then,
   And life to me had less
Of that fell look it wore ere when
20   They owned their passiveness.

MAY SARTON (1912–)

The Lady and the Unicorn

The Cluny Tapestries

I am the unicorn and bow my head
You are the lady woven into history
And here forever we are bound in mystery
Our wine, Imagination, and our bread,
5 And I the unicorn who bows his head.

You are all interwoven in my history
And you and I have been most strangely wed

Cluny Tapestry, *The Lady and the Unicorn (Editorial Photocolor Archives/Alinari)*

I am the unicorn and bow my head
And lay my wildness down upon your knee
10   You are the lady woven into history.

And here forever we are sweetly wed
With flowers and rabbits in the tapestry
You are the lady woven into history
Imagination is our bridal bed:
15   We lie ghostly upon it, no word said.

Among the flowers of the tapestry
I am the unicorn and by your bed
Come gently, gently to bow down my head,
Lay at your side this love, this mystery,
20   And call you lady of my tapestry.

I am the unicorn and bow my head
To one so sweetly lost, so strangely wed:

You sit forever under a small formal tree
Where I forever search your eyes to be

25   Rewarded with this shining tragedy
And know your beauty was not cast for me,

Know we are woven all in mystery,
The wound imagined where no one has bled,

My wild love chastened to this history
30   Where I before your eyes, bow down my head.

ROBINSON JEFFERS (1887–1962)

Rock and Hawk

Here is a symbol in which
Many high tragic thoughts
Watch their own eyes.

This gray rock, standing tall
5   On the headland, where the seawind
Lets no tree grow,

Earthquake-proved, and signatured
By ages of storms: on its peak
A falcon has perched.

10   I think, here is your emblem
To hang in the future sky;
Not the cross, not the hive,

But this; bright power, dark peace;
Fierce consciousness joined with final
15   Disinterestedness;

Life with calm death; the falcon's
Realist eyes and act
Married to the massive

Mysticism of stone,
20 Which failure cannot cast down
Nor success make proud.

DELMORE SCHWARTZ (1913–1966)

The Heavy Bear Who Goes with Me

"the withness of the body"
                    —Whitehead[3]

The heavy bear who goes with me,
A manifold honey to smear his face,
Clumsy and lumbering here and there,
The central ton of every place,
5 The hungry beating brutish one
In love with candy, anger, and sleep,
Crazy factotum, dishevelling all,
Climbs the building, kicks the football,
Boxes his brother in the hate-ridden city.
10 Breathing at my side, that heavy animal,
That heavy bear who sleeps with me,
Howls in his sleep for a world of sugar,
A sweetness intimate as the water's clasp,
Howls in his sleep because the tight-rope
15 Trembles and shows the darkness beneath.
—The strutting show-off is terrified,
Dressed in his dress-suit, bulging his pants,
Trembles to think that his quivering meat
Must finally wince to nothing at all.

20 That inescapable animal walks with me,
Has followed me since the black womb held,
Moves where I move, distorting my gesture,
A caricature, a swollen shadow,
A stupid clown of the spirit's motive,
25 Perplexes and affronts with his own darkness,
The secret life of belly and bone,
Opaque, too near, my private, yet unknown,
Stretches to embrace the very dear
With whom I would walk without him near,
30 Touches her grossly, although a word
Would bare my heart and make me clear,

---

[3] Alfred North Whitehead (1861–1947), English mathematician and philosopher.

Stumbles, flounders, and strives to be fed
Dragging me with him in his mouthing care,
Amid the hundred million of his kind,
35   The scrimmage of appetite everywhere.

D. H. LAWRENCE (1885–1930)

Snake

A snake came to my water-trough
On a hot, hot day, and I in pyjamas for the heat,
To drink there.

In the deep, strange-scented shade of the great dark carob tree
5   I came down the steps with my pitcher
And must wait, must stand and wait, for there he was at the trough before me.

He reached down from a fissure in the earth-wall in the gloom
And trailed his yellow-brown slackness soft-bellied down, over the edge of the stone
        trough
And rested his throat upon the stone bottom,
10   And where the water had dripped from the tap, in a small clearness,
He sipped with his straight mouth,
Softly drank through his straight gums, into his slack long body,
Silently.

Someone was before me at my water-trough,
15   And I, like a second comer, waiting.

He lifted his head from his drinking, as cattle do,
And looked at me vaguely, as drinking cattle do,
And flickered his two-forked tongue from his lips, and mused a moment,
And stooped and drank a little more,
20   Being earth-brown, earth-golden from the burning bowels of the earth
On the day of Sicilian July, with Etna[4] smoking.

The voice of my education said to me
He must be killed,
For in Sicily the black, black snakes are innocent, the gold are venomous.

25   And voices in me said, If you were a man
You would take a stick and break him now, and finish him off.

But must I confess how I liked him,
How glad I was he had come like a guest in quiet, to drink at my water-trough
And depart peaceful, pacified, and thankless,
30   Into the burning bowels of this earth?

Was it cowardice, that I dared not kill him?
Was it perversity, that I longed to talk to him?
Was it humility, to feel so honoured?
I felt so honoured.

---

[4] Mt. Etna, a volcano in Sicily.

35   And yet those voices:
      If you were not afraid, you would kill him!

    And truly I was afraid, I was most afraid,
    But even so, honoured still more
    That he should seek my hospitality
40   From out the dark door of the secret earth.

    He drank enough
    And lifted his head, dreamily, as one who has drunken,
    And flickered his tongue like a forked night on the air, so black,
    Seeming to lick his lips,
45   And looked around like a god, unseeing, into the air,
    And slowly turned his head,
    And slowly, very slowly, as if thrice adream,
    Proceeded to draw his slow length curving round
    And climb again the broken bank of my wall-face.

50   And as he put his head into that dreadful hole,
    And as he slowly drew up, snake-easing his shoulders, and entered farther,
    A sort of horror, a sort of protest against his withdrawing into that horrid black
      hole,
    Deliberately going into the blackness, and slowly drawing himself after,
    Overcame me now his back was turned.

55   I looked around, I put down my pitcher,
    I picked up a clumsy log
    And threw it at the water-trough with a clatter.

    I think I did not hit him,
    But suddenly that part of him that was left behind convulsed in undignified haste,
60   Writhed like lightning, and was gone
    Into the black hole, the earth-lipped fissure in the wall-front,
    At which, in the intense still noon, I stared with fascination.

    And immediately I regretted it.
    I thought how paltry, how vulgar, what a mean act!
65   I despised myself and the voices of my accursed human education.

    And I thought of the albatross,[5]
    And I wished he would come back, my snake.

    For he seemed to me again like a king,
    Like a king in exile, uncrowned in the underworld,
70   Now due to be crowned again.

    And so, I missed my chance with one of the lords
    Of life.
    And I have something to expiate;
    A pettiness.

---

[5] In Coleridge's "Rime of the Ancient Mariner," the sailor brings a curse upon himself and his ship
by senselessly killing an albatross.

CHRISTOPHER SMART (1722–1771)

The Ant and the Caterpillar

As an ant, of his talents superiorly vain,
Was trotting with consequence over the plain,
A worm, in his progress, remarkably slow,
Cry'd, "Bless your good worship, wherever you go?
5   "I hope your great mightiness won't take it ill,
"I pay my respects from an hearty good will."

With a look of contempt, and ineffable pride,
"Begone you vile reptile," his antship reply'd:
"But first—look at me—see—my limbs how complete:
10   "I guide all my motions with freedom and ease;
"I run back and forward, and turn when I please.
"Of nature (grown weary) thou shocking essay!°   *trial specimen*
"I spurn you thus from me;—crawl out of my way."

The reptile insulted, and vex'd to the soul,
15   Crept onwards, and hid himself close in his hole;
But nature determin'd to end his distress,
Soon sent him abroad in a butterfly dress.

Ere long the proud ant was repassing the road,
(Fatigued from the harvest, and tugging his load)
20   The beau on a violet bank he beheld,
Whose vesture in glory, a monarch excell'd;
His plumage expanded!—'twas rare to behold
So lovely a mixture of purple and gold;
The ant, quite amaz'd at a figure so gay,
25   Bow'd low with respect, and was trudging away:
"Stop, friend," says the butterfly, "don't be surprised;
"I once was the reptile you spurn'd and despis'd;
"But now, I can mount—in the sun-beams I play,
"While you must, forever, drudge on in your way."

The Moral: A *wretch that to-day is o'erloaded with
sorrow, May soar above those that oppressed him
tomorrow.*

GEORGE HERBERT (1593–1633)

Love (III)

Love bade me welcome: yet my soul drew back,
          Guilty of dust and sin.
But quick-eyed Love, observing me grow slack
          From my first entrance in,
5   Drew nearer to me, sweetly questioning
          If I lacked anything.

"A guest," I answered, "worthy to be here":
          Love said, "You shall be he."

"I, the unkind, ungrateful? Ah, my dear,
10   I cannot look on thee."
Love took my hand, and smiling did reply,
        "Who made the eyes but I?"

"Truth, Lord; but I have marred them; let my shame
        Go where it doth deserve."
15 "And know you not," says Love, "who bore the blame?"
        "My dear, then I will serve."
"You must sit down," says Love, "and taste my meat."
        So I did sit and eat.

ROBERT SOUTHWELL (1561–1595)

The Burning Babe

As I in hoary winter's night stood shivering in the snow,
Surprised I was with sudden heat which made my heart to glow;
And lifting up a fearful eye to view what fire was near,
A pretty babe all burning bright did in the air appear;
5   Who, scorchéd with excessive heat, such floods of tears did shed
As though his floods should quench his flames which with his tears were fed.
"Alas," quoth he, "but newly born in fiery heats I fry,
Yet none approach to warm their hearts or feel my fire but I!
My faultless breast the furnace is, the fuel wounding thorns,
10 Love is the fire, and sighs the smoke, the ashes shame and scorns;
The fuel justice layeth on, and mercy blows the coals,
The metal in this furnace wrought are men's defiléd souls,
For which, as now on fire I am to work them to their good,
So will I melt into a bath to wash them in my blood."
15 With this he vanished out of sight and swiftly shrunk away,
And straight I calléd unto mind that it was Christmas day.

EDMUND SPENSER (1552–1599)

One Day As I Unwarily Did Gaze

One day as I unwarily did gaze
On those fayre eyes, my loves immortall light;
The whilest my stonisht hart stood in amaze,
Through sweet illusion of her lookes delight;
5   I mote perceive how, in her glauncing sight,
Legions of Loves with little wings did fly;
Darting their deadly arrows, fyry bright,
At every rash beholder passing by.
One of those archers closely I did spy,
10 Ayming his arrow at my very hart:
When suddenly, with twincle of her eye,
The Damzell broke his misintended dart.
        Had she not so doon, sure I had bene slayne;
        Yet as it was, I hardly scap't with paine.

PAUL GOODMAN (1911–1972)

To My Only World

My one my world you are no kindlier
but you are fair today; you wear your sun,
in T-shirts your hockey-players run
with sparking shoes; the icicles you wear
5   are bright, the shadows are as blue as fur,
your girls are speedy as their roadsters turn
into a private road. My weak eyes burn,
I hear the echo of a ringing cheer.

You do not promise anything today
10   my world my only one, I am content
just to watch wistfully. And my dismay
is very like glory as I slowly walk
away into my solitude intent
and musical and we two frankly talk.

9 ❧ More Figures of Speech

Hyperbole

What do we do when we see something more beautiful than we have ever seen? So ugly we can hardly bear to look at it? How do we respond when we hear Pavarotti sing an aria more beautifully than we could have imagined, or see an outfielder make a seemingly impossible catch? Sportswriters, theater reviewers, and poets often respond with a figure of speech called *hyperbole*.

> The man was so fast he could kiss a bullet.
>
> He was so delicate he was knocked unconscious by a snowflake.
>
> The engine was as noisy as a living skeleton having a fit on a hardwood floor.

Hyperbole is an exaggeration, a statement that something has either much more or much less of a quality than it actually has. *Hyperbole*, from the Greek, literally means "to overshoot the mark." Since exaggeration is a principle of comedy, hyperbole is often comic:

> My belly is as cold as if I had swallowed
> snowballs for pills to cool the veins.
> —*William Shakespeare*

Although exaggeration is usually achieved through simile and metaphor, there are other forms of hyperbole. For example, we are familiar with hyperbole in the tall tale, a popular American entertainment from the time of the early settlers. Notice the narrative imagery of the following poem. The images are drawn to prove how extreme is the quality to be exaggerated: the hinges on the skyscraper "to let the moon go by" attest to its height. We can picture two or more "liars" sitting around a stove, each trying to come up with the most outlandish exaggerations.

CARL SANDBURG (1878–1967)

They Have Yarns

They have yarns
Of a skyscraper so tall they had to put hinges
On the two top stories so to let the moon go by,
Of one corn crop in Missouri when the roots
5   Went so deep and drew off so much water
The Mississippi riverbed that year was dry,
Of pancakes so thin they had only one side,
Of "a fog so thick we shingled the barn and six feet out on the fog,"
Of Pecos Pete straddling a cyclone in Texas and riding it to the west coast where
"it rained out under him,"
10   Of the man who drove a swarm of bees across the Rocky Mountains and the Desert
"and didn't lose a bee,"
Of a mountain railroad curve where the engineer in his cab can touch the caboose
and spit in the conductor's eye,
Of the boy who climbed a cornstalk growing so fast he would have starved to death
if they hadn't shot biscuits up to him,
Of the old man's whiskers: "When the wind was with him his whiskers arrived a
day before he did,"
Of the hen laying a square egg and cackling, "Ouch!" and of hens laying eggs with
the dates printed on them,
15   Of the ship captain's shadow: it froze to the deck one cold winter night,
Of mutineers on that same ship put to chipping rust with rubber hammers,
Of the sheep counter who was fast and accurate: "I just count their feet and divide
by four,"
Of the man so tall he must climb a ladder to shave himself,
Of the runt so teeny-weeny it takes two men and a boy to see him,
20   Of mosquitoes: one can kill a dog, two of them a man,
Of a cyclone that sucked cookstoves out of the kitchen, up the chimney flue, and
on to the next town,
Of the same cyclone picking up wagon-tracks in Nebraska and dropping them over
in the Dakotas.

Questions

1. What characters of tall tales has Sandburg alluded to in this poem?
2. How has Sandburg exaggerated sizes and heights?
3. How have these exaggerations captured the vastness and vitality of the American
   spirit?
4. What sorts of exaggerations do you use when bragging to friends about your exploits?

CECCO ANGIOLIERI (c. 1260–c. 1312)

In Absence from Becchina

My heart's so heavy with a hundred things
That I feel dead a hundred times a-day;
Yet death would be the least of sufferings,

For life's all suffering save what's slept away;
5   Though even in sleep there is no dream but brings
    From dream-land such dull torture as it may.
    And yet one moment would pluck out these stings,
      If for one moment she were mine to-day
    Who gives my heart the anguish that it has.
10   Each thought that seeks my heart for its abode
      Becomes a wan and sorrow-stricken guest:
    Sorrow has brought me to so sad a pass
      That men look sad to meet me on the road;
    Nor any road is mine that leads to rest.

Translation by Dante Gabriel Rossetti (1828–1882)

Questions

1. Is it possible to "feel dead"? Is the poet exaggerating his pain in line 2?
2. What other hyperbole do you find in this poem?

RANDALL JARRELL (1914–1965)

The Mockingbird

Look one way and the sun is going down,
Look the other and the moon is rising.
The sparrow's shadow's longer than the lawn.
The bats squeak: "Night is here"; the birds cheep: "Day is gone."
5   On the willow's highest branch, monopolizing
Day and night, cheeping, squeaking, soaring,
The mockingbird is imitating life.

All day the mockingbird has owned the yard.
As light first woke the world, the sparrows trooped
10 Onto the seedy lawn: the mockingbird
Chased them off shrieking. Hour by hour, fighting hard
To make the world his own, he swooped
On thrushes, thrashers, jays, and chickadees—
At noon he drove away a big black cat.

15 Now, in the moonlight, he sits here and sings.
A thrush is singing, then a thrasher, then a jay—
Then, all at once, a cat begins meowing.
A mockingbird can sound like anything.
He imitates the world he drove away
20 So well that for a minute, in the moonlight,
Which one's the mockingbird? which one's the world?

Questions

1. Granted that shadows lengthen as the sun sets, is it possible that "the sparrow's shadow's longer than the lawn"? If not, why does the speaker exaggerate?
2. Does the mockingbird really "monopolize" day and night? Has he really "owned the

yard"? What does this hyperbole suggest about the importance of the bird to the speaker?
3. What other hyperbole do you find in the poem?
4. Does Jarrell exaggerate the significance of the mockingbird by suggesting he cannot distinguish it from the world?

Understatement

Understatement, or the deliberate avoidance of emphasis in description, is sometimes considered a figure of speech related to hyperbole. In the following excerpt from T. S. Eliot's poem "Aunt Helen" we find an amusing instance of understatement.

> Miss Helen Slingsby was my maiden aunt,
> And lived in a small house near a fashionable square
> Cared for by servants to the number of four.
> Now when she died there was silence in heaven
> And silence at her end of the street.
> The shutters were drawn and the undertaker wiped his feet—
> He was aware this sort of thing had occurred before.

Aware? The undertaker is not only "aware" of death, he is immersed in it, a veritable merchant of death. The delight of understatement is in the effect of verbal irony—we expect the writer to say something extreme, and he surprises us by saying something subtle. Thus understatement is not so much a figure of speech as a tone of voice. We will look at it again in our discussion of tone.

Synecdoche, Metonymy, Allusion, and Paradox

One of the things that distinguishes poetry from prose is the level of concentration of the language. Ezra Pound has written that "great literature is simply language charged with meaning to the utmost possible degree," and that poetry "is the most concentrated form of verbal expression."[1] In the effort to say more with less language, poets sometimes use a word or several words to suggest other words or some larger context of meaning.

Synecdoche

Synecdoche is a figure of speech in which part of a thing is mentioned to suggest the whole thing, or a larger concept is mentioned to suggest something specific. Either way there is a correspondence of information between part and whole that enriches our view of both. Everyday speech is full of synecdoche. When the car breaks down we may say we need "new wheels," although new wheels, without the rest of the car, would be useless. "New wheels" is a livelier expression than "car." When we refer to a sluggish person as "lazybones," we suggest the depth of his or her indolence. When the captain says, "All hands on deck," we

---

[1] Ezra Pound, *The ABC of Reading* (New York: New Directions, 1934).

know he wants the men as well as their hands, but the word "hands" tells us more about what he wants from them. And when, in despair over the loss of her mail, someone says, "My whole world is lost," she is not merely exaggerating; she is using synecdoche, expressing a specific misfortune in terms of a more general one. Robert Frost used to refer to himself as a "synecdochist," meaning that his own little *part* of life was valuable in relation to the *whole* of life.

In the following poem synecdoche is used both to specify poignant incidents and to broaden the implications of detail. The poem is addressed to an old man, presumably a close friend, who is leaving the speaker.

PO CHU-I (A.D. 772–846)

Seeing Hsia Chan Off by River

Because you are old and departing I have wetted my handkerchief,
You who are homeless at seventy, belonging to the wilderness.
Anxiously I watch the wind rising as the boat sails away,
A white-headed man amid white-headed waves.

Translation by Ching Ti

Questions

1. How does the speaker use synecdoche in line 1 to show that he wept?
2. In what way is the phrase "white-headed man" a synecdoche? Would "white-haired man" be synecdoche?
3. What is the emotional force of juxtaposing the white-headed man and the white-headed waves? Does the juxtaposition make the old man look strong? Vulnerable?

RALPH WALDO EMERSON (1803–1882)

Letters

Every day brings a ship,
Every ship brings a word;
Well for those who have no fear,
Looking seaward well assured
5   That the word the vessel brings
Is the word they wish to hear.

Question

1. How does this poem use synecdoche?

Metonymy

Metonymy is a figure of speech in which the name of a person, place, or thing calls forth a more complex structure of things and ideas that the name signifies.

Ralph Waldo Emerson
(Harvard College Library)

Place names work that way. "Vermont" calls forth an image of gentle green hills, maple trees hung with sap buckets, and vivid foliage. When we talk of "New England weather," we may mean clear, cool summer nights, or snowy Januaries. "Texas" evokes flat, windy plains, ten-gallon hats, and oil wells. If you said that someone's manners were "pure Boston prep," people would have a good idea of what you meant. When the television commentator reports on the activities of "Washington," we know he is not merely telling us about the District of Columbia, but about the U.S. government. Likewise, "the Church" signifies the whole complex of organized religion, just as "the crown" signifies the entire government of a monarchy. These are all examples of metonymy, whereby a single name is used as shorthand, for its vividness or sound.

In the following ironic protest poem, practically every noun is used metonymically. We call the poem ironic because the speaker clearly hates what he is praising.

WILLIAM BUTLER YEATS (1865–1939)

The Great Day

Hurrah for revolution and more cannon-shot!
A beggar upon horseback lashes a beggar on foot.
Hurrah for revolution and cannon come again!
The beggars have changed places, but the lash goes on.

Questions

1. What complex of actions and emotions is suggested by the metonymy of "cannon-shot"?

2. What social position is signified by the "beggar upon horseback"? The "beggar on foot"?
3. Is the phrase "on foot" an instance of metonymy, synecdoche, or both?
4. What is the significance of the lash?

The following poem achieves great vividness and a warm intimacy with its subject through the skillful use of synecdoche and metonymy. The Ox Cart Man's life is filled with the sensual pleasures of his merchandise, and Hall uses figures of speech to communicate the richness of the man's experience.

DONALD HALL (1928–)

Ox Cart Man

In October of the year,
he counts potatoes dug from the brown field,
counting the seed, counting
the cellar's portion out,
5   and bags the rest on the cart's floor.

He packs wool sheared in April, honey
in combs, linen, leather
tanned from deerhide,
and vinegar in a barrel
10   hooped by hand at the forge's fire.

He walks by ox's head, ten days
to Portsmouth Market, and sells potatoes,
and the bag that carried potatoes,
flaxseed, birch brooms, maple sugar, goose
15   feathers, yarn.

When the cart is empty he sells the cart.
When the cart is sold he sells the ox,
harness and yoke, and walks
home, his pockets heavy
20   with the year's coin for salt and taxes,

and at home by fire's light in November cold
stitches new harness
for next year's ox in the barn,
and carves the yoke, and saws planks
25   building the cart again.

Questions

1. Locate a synecdoche in stanza 2.
2. Find a synecdoche in stanza 3.
3. Identify a metonymy in stanza 4.
4. Does the Ox Cart Man seem satisfied with his life? What statements in the poem suggest that he is?

JAMES DICKEY (1923–)

Buckdancer's Choice

So I would hear out those lungs,
The air split into nine levels,
Some gift of tongues of the whistler

In the invalid's bed: my mother,
5   Warbling all day to herself
The thousand variations of one song;

It is called Buckdancer's Choice.
For years, they have all been dying
Out, the classic buck-and-wing men

10   Of traveling minstrel shows;
With them also an old woman
Was dying of breathless angina,[2]

Yet still found breath enough
To whistle up in my head
15   A sight like a one-man band,

Freed black, with cymbals at heel,
An ex-slave who thrivingly danced
To the ring of his own clashing light

Through the thousand variations of one song
20   All day to my mother's prone music,
The invalid's warbler's note,

While I crept to the wall
Sock-footed, to hear the sounds alter,
Her tongue like a mockingbird's break

25   Through stratum after stratum of a tone
Proclaiming what choices there are
For the last dancers of their kind,

For ill women and for all slaves
Of death, and children enchanted at walls
30   With a brass-beating glow underfoot,

Not dancing but nearly risen
Through barnlike, theatrelike houses
On the wings of the buck and wing.

Questions

1. Vocabulary: *stratum* (25).
2. How many synecdoches can you find in the first stanza?
3. The buck-and-wing is a solo tap dance with a lot of angular arm movement and

---

[2] A painful heart disease.

spring in the knees. The name itself tends to describe the dance. What figure of speech is it?

4. What other examples of synecdoche can you find? Do they make the poem more vivid?
5. Find two examples of metonymy.

Allusion

When American soldiers and sportsmen shout "Remember the Alamo," they are using a form of verbal economy called *allusion*. The Alamo was a mission in Texas that Americans defended with unparalleled valor and persistence during a war with Mexico. Most of us have learned about this in school. Think how awkward it would be for soldiers, in the heat of combat, to cry out, "Remember the mission in Texas that Americans defended with unparalleled valor and persistence. . . ." The allusion conserves energy.

By now we have seen several instances of allusion among our examples of synecdoche and metonymy, for in the general sense an allusion is any reference by word or phrase to something other than the literal meaning. For example, "the lash" is an allusion to tyranny. John Dickey's poem "Buckdancer's Choice" is rich in atmospheric allusion owing to his skillful use of synecdoche. But the term *allusion* is most commonly used in connection with literary references and references to special or technical knowledge. Appropriate allusion deepens the background of a poem—as long as the reader understands the allusion. A poet might add a level of meaning to his poem by introducing it with a fragment from Dante's *Inferno*. But if we have not read the *Inferno*, the poet's scholarship may be lost on us. Poets can educate us if we let them, and it is often worth our while to research their allusions.

ALEXANDER POPE (1688–1744)

Intended for Sir Isaac Newton

Nature and Nature's laws lay hid in night:
God said, "Let Newton be!" and all was light.

This short poem turns on two important allusions. First, there is the allusion to the "laws" of Sir Isaac Newton, the eighteenth-century mathematician who invented calculus and formulated laws of motion that served scientists until the twentieth century. During Pope's time Newton commanded as much awe as Einstein inspires today. Second, there is the allusion to the book of Genesis: "God said, let there be light, and there was light." If you fail to recognize these allusions, the poem's high praise and subtle irony are lost.

Poets do not use allusion simply to show off their special knowledge. Allusion is a way of achieving intimacy by referring the reader to the world from which the poem comes. In the following poem for blues singer Ray Charles, Bob Kaufman evokes the mood and history of Charles's music through allusions to songs and other blues singers. The reference to Kilimanjaro, a mountain in eastern Africa, is an allusion to the African roots of blues music. *I Got a Woman* is one of Ray Charles's most popular songs. "Bessie" is Bessie Smith, the great blues singer, who was killed in an auto accident. Line 6 is literally allusion, referring us to the birth of Athena from the skull of Zeus. The parenthetic " 'way cross town" is a phrase from *I Got a Woman*.

BOB KAUFMAN (1935–)

Blues Note

For Ray Charles's birthday
N.Y.C./1961

Ray Charles is the black wind of Kilimanjaro,
Screaming up-and-down blues,
Moaning happy on all the elevators of my time.

Smiling into the camera, with an African symphony
5   Hidden in his throat, and (*I Got a Woman*) wails, too.

He burst from Bessie's crushed black skull
One cold night outside of Nashville, shouting,
And grows bluer from memory, glowing bluer, still.

At certain times you can see the moon
10 Balanced on his head.

From his mouth he hurls chunks of raw soul.
He separated the sea of polluted sounds
And led the blues into the Promised Land.

Ray Charles is a dangerous man ('way cross town),
15 And I love him.

Questions

1. How does the poet use metaphor in line 1?
2. How does he use allusion in line 13?
3. Does the poet's use of allusion help you to understand his affection for Ray Charles?

Paradox

I may be blind
but I got my eye on you.
—*Paul Shapiro*

Paradox is a statement that at first seems self-contradictory or illogical, but that actually transcends logic to assert a greater truth. The idea of a blind man with his eye on you is bizarre and seems senseless until we consider that many sightless people are highly observant, and that the phrase "I got my eye on you" suggests something more important than literal vision.

Twenty men crossing a bridge,
Into a village
Are twenty men crossing twenty bridges,
Into twenty villages,
Or one man
Crossing a single bridge into a village.

—*Wallace Stevens*

You may readily accept this sentence as a metaphor. But it is also a paradox, rich in philosophical implications. Literally, the sentence seems false. But if we think of it from the viewpoints of twenty men, each one crossing his own bridge, then the first part of the sentence begins to make sense. If each man sees the bridge, that makes twenty viewed bridges. If we think of the *common* vision of the twenty men, then the second part of the paradox begins to make sense—that they are "one man/Crossing a single bridge into a village." This is a sophisticated paradox that explores nothing less than the nature of consciousness, which is both shared and singular.

As an exercise of metaphysical wit, the paradox was very popular during the sixteenth and seventeenth centuries. The clown in Shakespeare's *As You Like It* strikes at the heart of human folly when he says, "The fool doth think he is wise, but the wise man knows himself to be a fool." The world is full of apparent contradictions; paradox is one figure of speech that resolves and delights in them.

GEORGE HERBERT (1593–1663)

Bitter-Sweet

Ah, my dear angry Lord,
Since Thou dost love, yet strike;
Cast down, yet help afford;
Sure I will do the like.

5   I will complain, yet praise;
I will bewail, approve:
And all my sour-sweet days
I will lament, and love.

This poem resolves the paradoxes of fortune in religious terms, returning in prayer the mixture of love and wrath that the speaker finds in life. The second line appears illogical until we consider the writer's religious conviction—the Lord strikes him out of love, not to make him suffer but to chasten him. Life must be "bitter-sweet." The phrases "bitter-sweet" and "sour-sweet" are figures of speech called *oxymorons*. An oxymoron, which combines two seemingly contradictory elements, is a form of condensed paradox. Jaques, the great cynic in *As You Like It*, speaks of his "humorous sadness." Shakespeare's sonnets likewise are full of oxymorons; he speaks of "sightless view," the "profitless usurer," and "unseeing eyes." Let us look for paradoxes in one of the sonnets.

WILLIAM SHAKESPEARE (1564–1616)

When Most I Wink, Then Do Mine Eyes Best See

When most I wink, then do mine eyes best see,
For all the day they view things unrespected;°   *unregarded, unseen*
But when I sleep, in dreams they look on thee,
And darkly bright are bright in dark directed.
5   Then thou, whose shadow shadows doth make bright,
How would thy shadow's form form happy show
To the clear day with thy much clearer light,
When to unseeing eyes thy shade shines so!
How would, I say, mine eyes be blessed made
10   By looking on thee in the living day,
When in dead night thy fair imperfect shade
Through heavy sleep on sightless eyes doth stay!
    All days are nights to see till I see thee,
    And nights bright days when dreams do show thee me.

Questions

1. Does the first line appear to be true? How is the paradox made sensible in lines 2–4?
2. Can you find an oxymoron in line 8? How does it make sense?
3. What is the paradox in the final couplet? How does it seem false? What makes it true?

SIMONIDES (c. 556–c. 468 B.C.)

For the Spartan Dead at Plataia (479 B.C.)

These men clothed their land with incorruptible
Glory when they assumed death's misty cloak.
They are not dead in death; the memory
Lives with us, and their courage brings them back.

Translation by Peter Jay

Questions

1. Vocabulary: *incorruptible* (1).
2. Where do you find paradox in this elegy?
3. What other figures of speech can you find in the poem?

MARK STRAND (1934–)

Keeping Things Whole

In a field
I am the absence

of field.
This is
5   always the case.
Wherever I am
I am what is missing.

When I walk
I part the air
10   and always
the air moves in
to fill the spaces
where my body's been.

We all have reasons
15   for moving.
I move
to keep things whole.

Questions

1. How do lines 6 and 7 seem false? How are they true?
2. What other paradoxes can you find?

❧ Poems for Further Study

JAMES MERRILL (1926–)

Charles on Fire

Another evening we sprawled about discussing
Appearances. And it was the consensus
That while uncommon physical good looks
Continued to launch one, as before, in life
5   (Among its vaporous eddies and false calms),
Still, as one of us said into his beard,
"Without your intellectual and spiritual
Values, man, you are sunk." No one but squared
The shoulders of his own unloveliness.
10   Long-suffering Charles, having cooked and served the meal,
Now brought out little tumblers finely etched
He filled with amber liquor and then passed.
"Say," said the same young man, "in Paris, France,
They do it this way" — bounding to his feet
15   And touching a lit match to our host's full glass.
A blue flame, gentle, beautiful, came, went
Above the surface. In a hush that fell

We heard the vessel crack. The contents drained
As who should step down from a crystal coach.
20   Steward of spirits, Charles's glistening hand
All at once gloved itself in eeriness.
The moment passed. He made two quick sweeps and
Was flesh again. "It couldn't matter less,"
He said, but with a shocked, unconscious glance
25   Into the mirror. Finding nothing changed,
He filled a fresh glass and sank down among us.

ANONYMOUS (18th century)

Grief of a Girl's Heart

O Donal Oge, if you go across the sea,
Bring myself with you and do not forget it;
And you will have a sweetheart for fair days and market days,
And the daughter of the King of Greece beside you at night.

5   It is late last night the dog was speaking of you;
The snipe was speaking of you in her deep marsh.
It is you are the lonely bird through the woods;
And that you may be without a mate until you find me.

You promised me, and you said a lie to me,
10   That you would be before me where the sheep are flocked;
I gave a whistle and three hundred cries to you,
And I found nothing there but a bleating lamb.

You promised me a thing that was hard for you,
A ship of gold under a silver mast;
15   Twelve towns with a market in all of them,
And a fine white court by the side of the sea.

You promised me a thing that is not possible,
That you would give me gloves of the skin of a fish;
That you would give me shoes of the skin of a bird;
20   And a suit of the dearest silk in Ireland.

O Donal Oge, it is I would be better to you
Than a high, proud, spendthrift lady:
I would milk the cow; I would bring help to you;
And if you were hard pressed, I would strike a blow for you.

25   You have taken the east from me; you have taken the west from me,
You have taken what is before me and what is behind me;
You have taken the moon, you have taken the sun from me,
And my fear is great that you have taken God from me!

Translation from the Irish by Lady Augusta Gregory (1852–1932)

572   More Figures of Speech

DYLAN THOMAS (1914–1953)

• The Hand That Signed the Paper

The hand that signed the paper felled a city;
Five sovereign fingers taxed the breath,
Doubled the globe of dead and halved a country;
These five kings did a king to death.

5　The mighty hand leads to a sloping shoulder,
The finger joints are cramped with chalk;
A goose's quill has put an end to murder
That put an end to talk.

The hand that signed the treaty bred a fever,
10　And famine grew, and locusts came;
Great is the hand that holds dominion over
Man by a scribbled name.

The five kings count the dead but do not soften
The crusted wound nor stroke the brow;
15　A hand rules pity as a hand rules heaven;
Hands have no tears to flow.

JOHN CROWE RANSOM (1888–1974)

Winter Remembered

Two evils, monstrous either one apart,
Possessed me, and were long and loath at going:
A cry of Absence, Absence, in the heart,
And in the wood the furious winter blowing.

5　Think not, when fire was bright upon my bricks,
And past the tight boards hardly a wind could enter,
I glowed like them, the simple burning sticks,
Far from my cause, my proper heat and center.

Better to walk forth in the frozen air
10　And wash my wound in the snows; that would be healing;
Because my heart would throb less painful there,
Being caked with cold, and past the smart of feeling.

And where I walked, the murderous winter blast
Would have this body bowed, these eyeballs streaming,
15　And though I think this heart's blood froze not fast
It ran too small to spare one drop for dreaming.

Dear love, these fingers that had known your touch,
And tied our separate forces first together,
Were ten poor idiot fingers not worth much,
20　Ten frozen parsnips hanging in the weather.

Aspects of Robinson

Robinson at cards at the Algonquin; a thin
Blue light comes down once more outside the blinds.
Gray men in overcoats are ghosts blown past the door.
The taxis streak the avenues with yellow, orange, and red.
5   This is Grand Central, Mr. Robinson.

Robinson afraid, drunk, sobbing Robinson
In bed with a Mrs. Morse. Robinson at home;
Decisions: Toynbee[3] or luminol? Where the sun
Shines, Robinson in flowered trunks, eyes toward
10   The Breakers. Where the night ends, Robinson in East Side bars.

Robinson walking in the Park, admiring the elephant.
Robinson buying the *Tribune*, Robinson buying the *Times*, Robinson
Saying, "Hello. Yes, this is Robinson. Sunday
At five? I'd love to. Pretty well. And you?"
15   Robinson alone at Longchamps, staring at the wall.

Robinson afraid, drunk, sobbing Robinson
In bed with a Mrs. Morse. Robinson at home;
Decisions: Toynbee[3] or luminol? Where the sun
Shines, Robinson in flowered trunks, eyes toward
20   The breakers. Where the night ends, Robinson in East Side bars.

Robinson in Glen plaid jacket, Scotch-grain shoes,
Black four-in-hand and oxford button-down,
The jeweled and silent watch that winds itself, the brief-
Case, covert topcoat, clothes for spring, all covering
25   His sad and usual heart, dry as a winter leaf.

Pity

Sweet Mercy! how my very heart has bled
    To see thee, poor Old Man! and thy grey hairs
    Hoar with the snowy blast: while no one cares
To clothe thy shrivell'd limbs and palsied head.
5   My Father! throw away this tatter'd vest
    That mocks thy shivering! take my garment—use
    A young man's arm! I'll melt these frozen dews
That hang from thy white beard and numb thy breast.
My Sara too shall tend thee, like a child:
10   And thou shalt talk, in our fireside's recess,
    Of purple Pride, that scowls on Wretchedness.—
He did not so, the Galilaean mild,

---

[3] Arnold Joseph Toynbee, a twentieth-century Catholic historian and educator.

Who met the Lazars° turn'd from rich men's doors   *lepers*
And call'd them Friends, and heal'd their noisome sores!

CHIDIOCK TICHBORNE (1558?—1586)

Elegy, Written with His Own Hand in the Tower Before His Execution

My prime of youth is but a frost of cares,
    My feast of joy is but a dish of pain,
My crop of corn is but a field of tares,°   *weeds*
    And all my good is but vain hope of gain:
5   The day is past, and yet I saw no sun,
And now I live, and now my life is done.

My tale was heard, and yet it was not told,
    My fruit is fall'n, and yet my leaves are green,
My youth is spent; and yet I am not old,
10   I saw the world, and yet I was not seen:
My thread is cut, and yet it is not spun,
And now I live, and now my life is done.

I sought my death, and found it in my womb,
    I looked for life, and saw it was a shade,
15   I trod the earth, and knew it was my tomb,
    And now I die, and now I was but made:
My glass is full, and now my glass is run,
And now I live, and now my life is done.

JOHN ASHBERY (1927–)

Paradoxes and Oxymorons

This poem is concerned with language on a very plain level.
Look at it talking to you. You look out a window
Or pretend to fidget. You have it but you don't have it.
You miss it, it misses you. You miss each other.

5   The poem is sad because it wants to be yours, and cannot.
What's a plain level? It is that and other things,
Bringing a system of them into play. Play?
Well, actually, yes, but I consider play to be

A deeper outside thing, a dreamed role-pattern,
10   As in the division of grace these long August days
Without proof. Open-ended. And before you know
It gets lost in the steam and chatter of typewriters.

It has been played once more. I think you exist only
To tease me into doing it, on your level, and then you aren't there
15   Or have adopted a different attitude. And the poem
Has set me softly down beside you. The poem is you.

10 🌿 The Music of Poetry

To the best of our knowledge, the earliest poetry was sung or chanted—by priestesses and priests in the temple, by bards in the court, and by actors on stage. In fact, the separation of poetry from music is a relatively recent phenomenon in the long history of literature. Surely poetry and melody arise from similar impulses. Ezra Pound has observed the historical interaction of these arts: "Music begins to atrophy when it departs too far from dance; poetry begins to atrophy when it gets too far from music."

All language is musical to some degree, from the vendor's street cry to the lawyer's plea to the orations of senators. All language has rhythm and pitch. But the rhythm and pitch of poetry is so intensified that it contributes an entire dimension of meaning to the language. The music of poetry can be so powerful and precise that some listeners can feel the basic emotion of a poem in a foreign language, even if they have no previous knowledge of that language.

Rhythm

The human voice is a musical instrument of great range and sensitivity. As we pronounce words and sentences, the voice rises and falls, growing louder and softer according to what is being communicated, and its urgency. In this the voice resembles all rhythmic movements in nature—the crests and hollows of waves, the rise and fall of daylight, the beating of the heart. The force gathers, exerts itself, and then subsides. In poetry, rhythm comes from a certain regularity of stress on syllables. Notice how regularly the stresses occur in this memorable nursery rhyme.

> Péter, Péter, púmpkin éater,
> Hád a wífe and couldn't kéep her.

For the sake of contrast let us read a sentence of editorial prose, marking the stresses.

As thís is wrítten, Wáll Stréet hás the jítters.
It máy be a pássing pháse and soón cúred.

Of course, most poetry is not as regular as a nursery rhyme, nor is all prose as haphazard in its rhythms as the editorial excerpt suggests. But it is apparent that in the more musical passage the stresses occur more regularly.

Accent and Emphasis

Two kinds of stress occur in speech: the stress of accents within a word, and the stress of emphasis on a word within a sentence. Thus in the nursery rhyme the stress on the first syllable of *Peter* is a stress of accent. The stress on the word *had* in the second line is due to emphasis on the word in the whole sentence.

As you listen to conversations, you will notice that usually the words and syllables that carry the most meaning are stressed, whereas the other syllables are relatively obscure. There is a good reason for this. The prominent syllable of a word is stressed because it usually contains the main idea. Thus: in-débt-ed-ness. Here the accented syllable, *debt*, is the root idea of the word. Our attention, though directed to this syllable, must also carry the other syllables that modify its meaning. This same principle applies to words in a sentence. Certain words are more important than others and are emphasized by the stress of voice, but we must not lose the meaning of the unstressed words.

Listening to the strong, important syllables and words and to the weak ones at the same time requires effort. This effort has its limits. For instance, it is difficult to hear more than two unaccented syllables attached to a stressed one, either before or after it. Poets are keenly aware of these limits, and a poet with a good ear places the stresses in his lines with great care for the listener's attention.

Scansion is the designation of stressed and unstressed syllables in a poem.

Ĭ stóod ĭn Vénĭcĕ, ŏn thĕ Brídgĕ ŏf Síghs;
Ă pálăce ănd ă prísŏn ón eăch hánd:
Ĭ sáw frŏm oŭt thĕ wáve hĕr strúctŭres ríse
Ăs frŏm thĕ strŏke ŏf thĕ ĕnchántĕr's wánd . . .

Scanning a poem is a way of determining what kind of rhythm the poem has. The stresses of accent are determined by the usage of the time, so we may look in the dictionary to find out which syllables to accent within a word. But the stress of emphasis on words depends on the voice of the poet and the reader. Not all of us will scan a particular poem in the same way. For instance, in the last line just scanned, we did not stress the word *the* preceding *enchanter's*. Another reader might have stressed it. When scanning a poem, it is helpful to read it aloud in your most natural voice, in order to hear where the stresses fall.

Scan the following fragments of poetry, reading them aloud as you mark the stresses.

1. We sweetly curtsied each to each
   And deftly danced a saraband.

2. When the game began between them for a jest,
   He played king and she played queen to match the best;
   Laughter soft as tears, and tears that turned to laughter,
   These were things she sought for years and sorrowed after.

3. Simple and fresh and fair from winter's close emerging,
   As if no artifice of fashion, business, politics, had ever been,
   Forth from its sunny nook of sheltered grass—
       innocent, golden, calm as the dawn,
   The spring's first dandelion shows its trustful face.

Questions

1. Which of the foregoing passages has the most regular rhythm? The least?
2. In scanning the lines, you see that some have more stresses due to accent, whereas others have more stresses due to emphasis. Which passage depends more on accents for its rhythm? Which depends more on the emphasis on words?

Meter

When stresses occur with sufficient regularity in a poem, the result is called *meter*. Meter is the measuring of stresses in a line of verse, determining their number and placement.

The unit of meter is called a *foot*. A metrical foot usually consists of a stressed syllable and one or two unstressed syllables that precede or follow it. A line with a single foot is called *monometer*. A line with two feet is called *dimeter*; with three, *trimeter*; with four, *tetrameter*; with five, *pentameter*; with six, *hexameter*; with seven, *heptameter*; and with eight feet, *octometer*.

There are four principal kinds of feet in American and English verse. The most common is the *iambic* foot, where the stressed syllable is preceded by one unstressed, as in the word *surprise*.

But now | secure | the paint | ed ves | sel glides,

The sun | beams trem | bling on | the float | ing tides;

While melt | ing mu | sic steals | upon | the sky,

And soft | en'd sounds | along | the wat | ers die;

The foregoing verses by Pope are written in *iambic pentameter*, which has been called the staff of English verse. Unrhymed iambic pentameter is also called *blank verse*. Iambics are steady and natural, and a great deal of spoken and written English—prose as well as poetry—falls easily into iambic rhythm.

When the stress comes first, followed by an unaccented syllable, the foot is called a *trochee:*

Spláshĭng
Dáshĭng.

These two lines illustrate trochaic monometer. Here is an example of trochaic tetrameter:

Hé wăs | próudĕr | thăn thĕ | dévĭl:
Hŏw hĕ | múst hăve | cúrsed oŭr | révĕl!

The trochee is livelier than the iamb—the effect of putting the stressed syllable first is sometimes described as *falling rhythm*, because one "falls" more quickly from a point of stress to an unaccented syllable. It is slightly more of an effort for the voice to move from unstressed to stressed syllables, which is why iambic rhythm is called "rising rhythm."

The *anapest* is a foot with two unstressed syllables followed by a stressed one, as in the word *intĕrvéne*. The anapest is a rising rhythm, but it is more rapid than the iamb because of the greater number of unstressed syllables. Here is a sample of anapestic trimeter:

Frŏm thĕ cén | tĕr aĭl róund | tŏ thĕ séa
Ĭ ăm lórd | ŏf thĕ fówl | ănd thĕ brúte.

You may remember the galloping rhythms of Browning's poem "How We Brought the Good News from Ghent to Aix," which depend on the anapest for their speed and strength. The following is a description of the hero's horse:

Ănd hĭs lów | heăd ănd crést, | jŭst ŏne shárp | eăr bent báck
Fŏr my vóice, | ănd thĕ óth | ĕr prícked oŭt | ŏn hĭs tráck;
Ănd ŏne eye's | bláck | ĭntéll | ĭgĕnce,—ĕv | ĕr thăt glánce
O'er ĭts whíte | edgĕ | ăt mé, | hĭs ŏwn más | tĕr, askánce!

The *dactyl* is a foot that begins with a stressed syllable, followed by two unstressed syllables, as in the word *délĭcăte*. It is a falling rhythm, the most rapid and lively of English meters.

SONG
Hére's tŏ thĕ | máid oĭ | báshfŭl fĭf | téen;
Hére's tŏ thĕ | wídŏw ŏf | fĭftў;
Hére's tŏ thĕ | fláuntĭng ĕx | trávăgănt | quéen
Ănd hére's | tŏ thĕ hoúse | wífe thăt's | thríftў.

Notice that the poem is not all dactyls, but the dactylic foot is prominent and gives the poem its momentum. The same is true for the following lines:

Cléarlў thĕ | blúe | rívĕr | chímes ĭn ĭts | flówĭng
Úndĕr mў | eye;
Wármlў ănd | bróadlў thĕ | sóuth wĭnds ăre | blówĭng
ŏvĕr thĕ | skў.

In addition to the four principal feet—the iamb, the trochee, the anapest, and the dactyl—there are two other feet worth mentioning. The *spondee* is a unit of rhythm of double movement, in which both syllables are accented, as in the word ámén.

Roll ón | thóu deép | and dárk blúe | ócean, | róll.

The spondee is a rhythmic unit of great weight and solemnity.

Because of the frequency of particles in English grammar, the unit of rhythm occasionally loses its stress. When that happens, we get the *pyrrhic* foot.

Ĭ wór | shĭpped thĕ | invís | ĭblĕ | alóne.

All this terminology is useful in describing poetic rhythm. But it is more important to understand a few principles of metrics that underlie centuries of versification. Since poetry is not a science, these generalizations have their exceptions; but they will be useful in comprehending why the different feet are used.

Generally, the more stresses in a metric line, the slower the line moves. That is why the spondee creates a mood of gravity.

Thĕ lóng | dáy wanĕs; | thĕ slów | móon climbs; | thĕ deép
Moáns róund | with mán | ў vói | cĕs.

That is a good rhythm for a stately meditation—but not for a wedding celebration. For a mirthful poem the poet will have fewer stresses per line, a faster rhythm with dactyls or anapests.

Ride ă cŏck | hórse tŏ | Bánbŭrў | Crŏss
Tŏ | see an ŏld | wómăn gĕt | úp ŏn hĕr | hórse.
Rings ŏn hĕr | fingĕrs, and | bélls ŏn hĕr | tóes,
Shĕ shăll hăve | músĭc whĕr | évĕr shĕ | goés.

Of course, most poetry is neither funereal nor merry. That explains the predominance of the iambic and trochaic lines, with their balance between stressed and unstressed syllables.

The so-called falling rhythms—trochaic and dactylic—are more rapid, respectively, than the rising rhythms—iambic and anapestic. As we have observed, this is the result of greater ease in moving from stressed to unstressed syllables.

Since we tend to pause at the end of a line of poetry, the shorter the lines, the slower the movement of the poem. All other things being equal, dimeter puts much more stress on individual words than does tetrameter, and pentameter slightly more than hexameter.

In the following lines, notice how Tennyson changes the line length and foot to vary rhythm. He poses the question of the first section with deliberate spondees and forceful dactyls. The dimeter of this section makes for a constrained opening, which breaks into lively trochaic and anapestic tetrameter in the second section.

ALFRED, LORD TENNYSON (1809–1892)

The Mermaid

I

Who would be
A mermaid fair,
Singing alone,
Combing her hair
5 Under the sea,
In a golden curl
With a comb of pearl,
On a throne?

II

I would be a mermaid fair;
10 I would sing to myself the whole of the day;
With a comb of pearl I would comb my hair;
And still as I comb'd I would sing and say,
"Who is it loves me? who loves not me?"
I would comb my hair till my ringlets would fall,
15   Low adown, low adown,
From under my starry sea-bud crown
          Low adown and around
And I should look like a fountain of gold
          Springing alone
20   With a shrill inner sound,
          Over the throne
          In the midst of the hall;
Till that great sea-snake under the sea
From his coiled sleeps in the central deeps
25 Would slowly trail himself sevenfold
Round the hall where I sate, and look in at the gate
With his large calm eyes for the love of me.
And all the mermen under the sea
Would feel their immortality
30 Die in their hearts for the love of me.

III

But at night I would wander away, away,
    I would fling on each side my low-flowing locks,
And lightly vault from the throne and play
    With the mermen in and out of the rocks;
35 We would run to and fro, and hide and seek,
    On the broad sea-wolds° in the crimson shells,   *sea hills*
    Whose silvery spikes are nighest the sea.
But if any came near I would call, and shriek,
And adown the steep like a wave I would leap
40   From the diamond-ledges that jut from the dells;
For I would not be kiss'd by all who would list,
Of the bold merry mermen under the sea;

They would sue° me, and woo me, and flatter me,   *pay suit to*
In the purple twilights under the sea;
45   But the king of them all would carry me,
Woo me, and win me, and marry me,
In the branching jaspers under the sea;
Then all the dry pied° things that be   *many-colored*
In the hueless mosses under the sea
50   Would curl round my silver feet silently,
All looking up for the love of me.
And if I should carol aloud, from aloft
All things that are forked, and horned, and soft
Would lean out from the hollow sphere of the sea,
55   All looking down for the love of me.

Samuel Taylor Coleridge composed the following lines as an aid to memory of the metrical units:

Trochee trips from long to short;°   *stressed to unstressed*
From long to long in solemn sort
Slow Spondee stalks, strong foot, yet ill able
Ever to come up with Dactyl trisyllable.
Iambics march from short to long;
With a leap and a bound the swift Anapests throng.

If you scan these lines you will see that each one illustrates the metrical unit it describes.

Students of meter should bear in mind that meter does not create the rhythms of poetry. The rhythms arise out of the poet's emotion, just as do images and figures of speech. Metrical scansion is the measuring of regular rhythms after they have occurred, and consciousness of meter is not a prerequisite for composition.

Exercise

Scan the following lines. Describe the line length as monometer, dimeter, trimeter, and so on. Then characterize the metrical units as iambic, trochaic, anapestic, dactylic, spondaic, and pyrrhic. Which lines are liveliest? Most forceful? Which lines seem most solemn? Which are the most sprightly? What other words can you use to describe the moods rhythm instills?

1. Come live with me and be my love
   And we will all the pleasures prove
   That valleys, groves, hills and fields
   Woods or steepy mountain yields.

2. Let us swear an oath and keep it with an equal mind.

3. Dear my friend and fellow student, I would lean my spirit o'er you.

4. If they rob us of name and pursue us with beagles,
   Give their roof to the flame and their flesh to the eagles.

5. And now the storm-blast came, and he
   Was tyrannous and strong;
   He struck with his o'ertaking wings
   And chased us south along.

6. Has any here an old gray Mare
   With three legs all her store,
   O put it to her Buttocks bare
   And straight she'll run on four.

7. Just for a handful of silver he left us,
   Just for a riband° to stick in his coat—   *ribbon of honor*
   Found the one gift of which fortune bereft us,
   Lost all the others she lets us devote . . .

8. Solomon Grundy
   Born on Monday,
   Christened on Tuesday,
   Married on Wednesday,
   Took ill on Thursday,
   Worse on Friday,
   Died on Saturday,
   Buried on Sunday.
   This is the end
   Of Solomon Grundy.

9. If I did take your kingdom from your sons,
   To make amends, I'll give it to your daughter.
   If I have killed the issue of your womb,
   To quicken your increase I will beget
   Mine issue of your blood upon your daughter:
   A grandam's name is little less in love
   Than in the doting title of a mother . . .

The Line and Line Endings

One of the more obvious features of poetry is that it is usually written in lines,
or verses, and that each line functions as a rhythmic and sense unit. Charles
Olson has suggested that the line length corresponds to the poet's breathing; thus
Walt Whitman and Homer wrote long lines because they had prodigious energy
and took deep breaths before uttering their epic verses. Whatever the case, the
line certainly provides rhythmic opportunities unavailable in prose. We have
already observed that shorter lines concentrate our attention on individual words
and images.

> There is a spell, for instance
> in every sea-shell.
>   —H. D. (Hilda Doolittle)

We have also remarked that the way lines begin—with stressed or unstressed
syllables—often determines the thrust of the line, as we naturally move more
quickly from a stressed to an unstressed syllable.

The line ending is equally important in controlling the poem's rhythmic movement. Lines that end with a stressed word or syllable, sometimes called a *masculine ending*, come to a more resolute pause than those that end with an unstressed syllable or *feminine ending*. In the following verses, notice that the masculine endings seem to gather up the sense of the line, contain it, and pause before the poem moves on. The feminine endings leave us with a slight sense of irresolution that urges us on to the next line.

ALGERNON CHARLES SWINBURNE (1837–1909)

Rococo

Take hand and part with laughter;
    Touch lips and part with tears;
Once more and no more after,
    Whatever comes with years.
5 We twain° shall not remeasure   *two*
    The ways that left us twain;
Nor crush the lees° of pleasure   *dregs*
    From sanguine grapes of pain.

We twain once well in sunder,°   *separated*
10   What will the mad gods do
For hate with me, I wonder,
    Or what for love with you?
Forget them till November,
    And dream there's April yet,
15 Forget that I remember,
    And dream that I forget.

Time found our tired love sleeping,
    And kissed away his breath;
But what should we do weeping,
20   Though light love sleep to death?
We have drained his lips at leisure,
    Till there's not left to drain
A single sob of pleasure,
    A single pulse of pain.

25 Dream that the lips once breathless
    Might quicken if they would;
Say that the soul is deathless;
    Dream that the gods are good;
Say March may wed September,
30   And time divorce regret;
But not that you remember,
    And not that I forget.

We have heard from hidden places
    What love scarce lives and hears:

35   We have seen on fervent faces
        The pallor of strange tears:
    We have trod the wine-vats treasure,
        Whence ripe to steam and stain,
    Foams round the feet of pleasure
40   The blood-red must° of pain.   *juice*

    Remembrance may recover
        And time bring back to time
    The name of your first lover,
        The ring of my first rhyme;
45   But rose-leaves of December
        The frosts of June shall fret,
    The day that you remember,
        The day that I forget.

    The snake that hides and hisses
50   In heaven we twain have known;
    The grief of cruel kisses,
        The joy whose mouth makes moan;
    The pulses pause and measure,
        Where in one furtive vein
55   Throbs through the heart of pleasure
        The purpler blood of pain.

    We have done with tears and treasons
        and love for treason's sake;
    Room for the swift new seasons,
60   The years that burn and break,
    Dismantle and dismember
        Men's days and dreams, Juliette;
    For love may not remember,
        But time will not forget.

65   Life treads down love in flying,
        Time withers him at root;
    Bring all dead things and dying,
        Reaped sheaf and ruined fruit,
    Where, crushed by three days' pressure
70   Our three days' love lies slain;
    And earlier leaf of pleasure,
        And latter flower of pain.

    Breathe close upon the ashes,
        It may be flame will leap;
75   Unclose the soft close lashes,
        Lift up the lids and weep.
    Light love's extinguished ember,
        Let one tear leave it wet
    For one that you remember
80   And ten that you forget.

Swinburne is often praised for his mastery of classical meters and the lilting, songlike ease of his versification. This lies as much in his imaginative variations as in his adherence to the pattern. The line length is fairly strict trimeter. It is the fashioning of line openings and endings, the alternation of rising and falling rhythms, that give the poem its life. A poem with only masculine endings, or unrelieved trochaic trimeter, would be monotonous and slow by comparison.

Reading the poem aloud, you will notice that the lines usually end where the sense of the sentence requires a pause. If the poem were printed as prose, the reader would naturally pause in those places. Many of those pauses coincide with commas, semicolons, and periods. Any line that ends where the sentence calls for a grammatical pause is called an *end-stopped* line. The first four lines of "Rococo" are end-stopped:

> Take hand and part with laughter,
>> Touch lips and part with tears;
> Once more and no more after,
>> Whatever comes with years.

A line that ends before the sentence does, or before a pause is demanded by the sense, is called a *run-on* line. There is an example in lines 5 and 6 of "Rococo":

> We twain shall not remeasure
> The ways that left us twain;

This running over of the sense unit from line to line is called *enjambment*. Again, this offers pleasant relief in a poem in which most of the lines are end-stopped.

When a poem is composed of long lines, there is sometimes a natural pause *within* the line.

> Gone—faded out of the story, | | the sea-faring friend I remember?
> Gone for a decade, they say: | | never a word or a sign.
> Gone with his hard red face | | that only his laughter could wrinkle,
> Down where men go to be still, | | by the old way of the sea.

Caesura is a grammatical or natural pause occurring within a line of poetry. The hexameters in the preceding poem might have been broken down into trimeters. But the poet, Edwin Arlington Robinson, has chosen the longer line with caesura to hasten the telling of his story.

EDNA ST. VINCENT MILLAY (1892–1950)

Recuerdo

> We were very tired, we were very merry—
> We had gone back and forth all night on the ferry.
> It was bare and bright, and smelled like a stable—
> But we looked into a fire, we leaned across a table,

5   We lay on a hill-top underneath the moon;
        And the whistles kept blowing, and the dawn came soon.

        We were very tired, we were very merry—
        We had gone back and forth all night on the ferry;
        And you ate an apple, and I ate a pear,
10   From a dozen of each we had bought somewhere;
        And the sky went wan, and the wind came cold,
        And the sun rose dripping, a bucketful of gold.

        We were very tired, we were very merry,
        We had gone back and forth all night on the ferry.
15   We hailed, "Good morrow, mother!" to a shawl-covered head.
        And bought a morning paper, which neither of us read;
        And she wept, "God bless you!" for the apples and pears,
        And we gave her all our money but our subway fares.

Questions

1. Scan the poem, indicating the caesuras.
2. Which lines have masculine endings? Which have feminine endings? Do you see a pattern? If so, how does it contribute to the music of the poem?
3. What is the basic line length? Is it consistent?
4. From the number of caesuras, do you think one might cast the poem in shorter lines? How would that alter the rhythm?

Syllabic Verse

In an effort to break out of the strictures of traditional metrics without wholly abandoning predictable form, certain poets have adopted a metrical system called *syllabic verse*. Originating in Oriental and French poetry, syllabic verse counts syllables instead of accents in a line. From Chapter 6, you are familiar with the haiku, the Japanese syllabic form with seventeen syllables—five in the first line, seven in the second, and five again in the third.

     I must go begging
     for water . . . morning glories
     have captured my well.
     —From *Cricket Songs: Japanese Haiku*

By counting syllables, the poet gives shape to the poem without relying on strong rhythmic emphasis. The result is a quieter, more syncopated rhythm that still has a certain predictability of line length.

MARIANNE MOORE (1887–1972)

The Wood-Weasel

emerges daintily, the skunk—
don't laugh—in sylvan black and white chipmunk

Marianne Moore (*National Portrait Gallery, Smithsonian Institution, Washington, D.C.*)

regalia. The inky thing
adaptively whited with glistening
5   goat fur, is wood-warden. In his
ermined well-cuttlefish-inked wool, he is
determination's totem. Out-
lawed? His sweet face and powerful feet go about
in chieftain's coat of Chilcat cloth.
10   He is his own protection from the moth,

noble little warrior. That
otter-skin on it, the living polecat,
smothers anything that stings. Well,
this same weasel's playful and his weasel
15   associates are too. Only
wood-weasels shall associate with me.

Questions

1. Vocabulary: *sylvan* (2), *regalia* (3).
2. Count the number of syllables in each line. What is the basic pattern of line length?
3. What lines break the pattern? In the two lines that do break the pattern, do you see a justification in the meaning?

Rhyme

Many great poems do not use rhyme. Languages that are rich in rhyme words, such as French and Italian, use rhyme frequently; the classical Latin and Greek poets used it rarely, if at all. Verses that have little to offer *except* rhyme, such as greeting card sentiments and advertising jingles, are not dignified by the term poetry. We call them *doggerel.*

Poems that use rhyme depend on the rhyme words for structure, resolution, and tonal effects. The similarity of sounds is striking to the ear and serves as an aid to memory as well as an incitement of the reader's expectations.

ROBERT CREELEY (1926–)

If You

If you were going to get a pet
what kind of animal would you get.

A soft bodied dog, a hen—
feathers and fur to begin it again.

5   When the sun goes down and it gets dark
I saw an animal in a park.

Bring it home, to give it to you.
I have seen animals break in two.

You were hoping for something soft
10   and loyal and clean and wondrously careful—

a form of otherwise vicious habit
can have long ears and be called a rabbit.

Dead. Died. Will die. Want.
Morning, midnight. I asked you

15   if you were going to get a pet
what kind of animal would you get.

These intimate and deceptively simple verses by Robert Creeley have a remarkable appeal to readers of all ages. Much of this appeal can be attributed to the charm of rhyme. The first two lines rhyme at the end; this is called *end rhyme.* When a poem begins thus, with a rhymed couplet, the poem has created an expectation of rhyme. This expectation is satisfied in line 4, with the end rhyme of *again* with *hen.* By the time we get to line 5, a *rhyme scheme* has been established; the poem leads us on by our curiosity to discover the next rhyme word. This anticipation is not entirely conscious, for we are probably more concerned with the poem's sense. It is a musical anticipation, and the more effective because it works partly on an unconscious level.

Creeley breaks the pattern in line 10. We are waiting for the rhyme to come in line 10, but it doesn't. Why not? Look at the sense of lines 9 and 10.

You were hoping for something soft,
and loyal and clean and wondrously careful—

He is talking about hope, and creating a mystery in these lines. The reader is waiting for an answer. What kind of animal are we hoping for? We are denied the resolution of rhyme because we are also being denied the answer to the question. This is a perfect adaptation of form to content. We get the rhyme when we get the answer.

> a form of otherwise vicious habit
> can have long ears and be called a rabbit.

When the rhyme at last comes, it is a more elaborate, outrageous rhyme than we have yet heard, and well worth the wait. All the other rhymes have been *masculine rhymes*, with the similarity of sounds falling on the last syllable. This last is a *feminine rhyme*, one where the similarity of sounds is in both of the last two syllables. Feminine rhyme is more noticeable than masculine rhyme and is often used to develop a comic tone (see Chapter 11 on tones of voice).

Lines 13 and 14 challenge the rhyme scheme again, and again we see the connection of form and content. The tone of the poem has turned suddenly grave, from a discussion of pets to a meditation on death, and the lack of an immediate rhyme word suits the tone change. Also notice that line 14 has a rhyming antecedent in lines 7 and 8. The poet has not wholly abandoned rhyme, but he has attenuated its resolution in these lines. Thus the resolution is all the more satisfying when it comes in the closing couplet.

The best rhymes come naturally and seem inevitable without losing a certain freshness or surprise.

W. H. AUDEN (1907–1973)

Fleet Visit

> The sailors come ashore
> Out of their hollow ships,
> Mild-looking middle class boys
> Who read the comic strips;
> 5 One baseball game is more
> To them than fifty Troys.
>
> They look a bit lost, set down
> In this unamerican place
> Where natives pass with laws
> 10 And futures of their own;
> They are not here because
> But only just-in-case.
>
> The whore and ne'er-do-well
> Who pester them with junk
> 15 In their grubby ways at least
> Are serving the Social Beast;
> They neither make nor sell—
> No wonder they get drunk.

But their ships on the vehement° blue   *powerful*
20 Of this harbour actually gain
     From having nothing to do;
     Without a human will
     To tell them whom to kill
     Their structures are humane

25 And, far from looking lost,
     Look as if they were meant
     To be pure abstract design
     By some master of pattern and line,
     Certainly worth every cent
30 Of the billions they must have cost.

The characterization of these young sailors, in the first stanza, is cast in rhymes as original and fresh as the context in which Auden sees them. Emerging from the "hollow ships" (an allusion to Greek vessels), the boys remind Auden of the great classical mariners. Yet they are still boys, readers of comic strips. Thus we hear the rhyming and concomitant association of *ships* and *strips*, *boys* and *Troys*—fresh unpredictable rhymes that are nevertheless natural in the context, seemingly effortless.

Rhyme is reflexive. It joins not only words with similar sounds, but the things and ideas to which the words refer. Notice the witty closing of stanza 2 and how the rhyme words reinforce the meaning.

     They look a bit lost, set down
     In this unamerican place
     Where natives pass with laws
     And futures of their own;
     They are not here because
     But only just-in-case.

The natives have their own futures and *laws*. Yet the sailors are not here *because* of any specific destiny or lawful purpose. The navy does not belong in this *unamerican place*. They are here *just-in-case* they are needed. The rhymes— *laws* and *because*, *place* and *just-in-case*—are surprising ones that underscore the anomaly of the sailors' presence.

In "Fleet Visit" Auden employs both *exact rhyme* and *near rhyme*. Exact rhyme occurs when rhyme words have the same vowel sounds, and the consonant ending, if there is one, is identical. *Blue* and *do*, in stanza 4, are exact rhymes, as are *will* and *kill*, *gain* and *humane*. Near rhyme, also called *off rhyme* and *partial rhyme*, occurs when the vowel sound is different but the consonant is identical, as in *down* and *own*, *laws* and *because*. Near rhyme is not a defect, but a pleasant variation of rhyme.

Most rhyme comes at the end of lines and is called *end rhyme*. All the rhymes in "Fleet Visit" are end rhymes. When rhymes fall within the line, they are called *internal rhymes*.

Come live within me, said the waterfall.
There is a chamber of black stone
High and dry behind my stunning life,
Stay here a year or two, a year or ten,
Until you've heard it all,
The inside story deafening but true.

—James Merrill

The internal rhyming of *high* and *dry* in line 3 and of *here* and *year* in line 4 helps to establish the resonance of the waterfall. Notice how smoothly Robert Frost uses end rhyme in the following poem.

ROBERT FROST (1874–1963)

The Road Not Taken

Two roads diverged in a yellow wood,
And sorry I could not travel both
And be one traveler, long I stood
And looked down one as far as I could
5   To where it bent in the undergrowth;

Then took the other, as just as fair,
And having perhaps the better claim,
Because it was grassy and wanted wear;
Though as for that the passing there
10   Had worn them really about the same,

And both that morning equally lay
In leaves no step had trodden black.
Oh, I kept the first for another day!
Yet knowing how way leads on to way,
15   I doubted if I should ever come back.

I shall be telling this with a sigh
Somewhere ages and ages hence:
Two roads diverged in a wood, and I—
I took the one less traveled by,
20   And that has made all the difference.

Questions

1. At what point in the poem do you notice that a rhyme scheme has developed?
2. Does the poem ever depart from the rhyme scheme?
3. Are the rhymes in the poem masculine or feminine?
4. Is there any near rhyme in the poem? Internal rhyme?
5. Suppose the poem were written in rhymed couplets. Would that be as suitable to the poem's theme? How does Frost's rhyme scheme relate to his subject?

Alliteration and Assonance

By now you have noticed that repetition is a principle of music in language. It forges connections between words and phrases, creates expectations, and is pleasing in itself. We have seen the repetition of accent patterns in rhythm and of word endings in rhyme, and how both contribute to the mood and movement of the poem. *Alliteration* is the repetition of consonant sounds. Like rhyme, it binds together words with similar sounds. In the heat of emotion we have a tendency to use words with the same initial consonant: "You dirty dog!" Many proverbs are composed in this manner, for emphasis as well as memory: "Time and tide wait for no man." "When the wine is in, the wit is out." Judging from some current newspaper headlines, alliteration is as popular a mode of expression as ever.

Assonance is the repetition of vowel sounds.

> Be near me when my light is low,
>   When the blood creeps, and the nerves prick
>   And tingle and the heart is sick,
> And all the wheels of Being slow.
>
> —*Alfred, Lord Tennyson*

The repetition of the *ē* sound in lines 1, 2, and 4 draws attention to the opening and helps to slow the phrase "wheels of Being." Assonance, like alliteration, attracts the reader to certain words and can create strong resonances.

MARGARET WALKER (1915–)

Lineage

My grandmothers were strong.
They followed plows and bent to toil.
They moved through fields sowing seed.
They touched earth and grain grew.
5   They were full of sturdiness and singing.
My grandmothers were strong.

My grandmothers are full of memories.
Smelling of soap and onions and wet clay
With veins rolling roughly over quick hands
10   They have many clean words to say.
My grandmothers were strong.
Why am I not as they?

Questions

1. Find an example of alliteration in stanza 1. Find an example of assonance. How do the techniques affect the meaning of the stanza?
2. What phrases in the second stanza stand out because of alliteration? Do those phrases deserve special attention? Why?

Alliteration and assonance sometimes imitate sounds of the things to which they refer. This is called *onomatopoeia* and is the purest relation of sound and meaning in poetry. The words *pop, sizzle,* and *crash* are onomatopoetic. Through the repetition of vowel or consonant sounds, an entire line may become onomatopoetic, as when Tennyson speaks of

> The moan of doves in immemorial elms,
> And murmuring of innumerable bees.

The repetition of the consonant *m* mimics the moaning and murmuring to which the lines refer. Shakespeare, in *Venus and Adonis*, fills Venus's lines with *s*'s just as she is playing the serpent in tempting young Adonis.

> Here come and sit, where never serpent hisses,
> And being set, I'll smother thee with kisses . . .

One of the greatest studies in alliteration, assonance, and onomatopoeia in American poetry is Edgar Allan Poe's "The Bells." Its effects are ingenious and excessive; the poem has been praised, ridiculed, imitated, and parodied.

EDGAR ALLAN POE (1809–1849)

The Bells

I

Hear the sledges with the bells—
Silver bells!
What a world of merriment their melody foretells!
How they tinkle, tinkle, tinkle,
5   In the icy air of night!
While the stars that oversprinkle
All the heavens, seem to twinkle
With a crystalline delight;
Keeping time, time, time,
10   In a sort of runic rhyme,
To the tintinnabulation that so musically wells
From the bells, bells, bells, bells,
Bells, bells, bells—
From the jingling and the tinkling of the bells.

II

15   Hear the mellow wedding bells—
Golden bells!
What a world of happiness their harmony foretells!
Through the balmy air of night
How they ring out their delight!—
20   From the molten-golden notes,
And all in tune,
What a liquid ditty floats
To the turtledove that listens, while she gloats
On the moon!

25   Oh, from out the sounding cells,
What a gush of euphony voluminously wells!
            How it swells!
            How it dwells
            On the future!—how it tells
30   Of the rapture that impels
        To the swinging and the ringing
            Of the bells, bells, bells—
        Of the bells, bells, bells, bells,
            Bells, bells, bells—
35 To the rhyming and the chiming of the bells!

                    III
        Hear the loud alarum bells—
            Brazen bells!
What a tale of terror, now, their turbulency tells!
        In the startled ear of night
40   How they scream out their affright!
            Too much horrified to speak,
            They can only shriek, shriek,
                Out of tune,
In a clamorous appealing to the mercy of the fire,
45 In a mad expostulation with the deaf and frantic fire,
            Leaping higher, higher, higher,
            With a desperate desire,
            And a resolute endeavor
            Now—now to sit, or never,
50   By the side of the pale-faced moon.
            Oh, the bells, bells, bells!
            What a tale their terror tells
                Of despair!
        How they clang, and clash, and roar!
55   What a horror they outpour
On the bosom of the palpitating air!
            Yet the ear, it fully knows
                By the twanging
                And the clanging,
60   How the danger ebbs and flows;
        Yet the ear distinctly tells,
                In the jangling
                And wrangling,
        How the danger sinks and swells,
65 By the sinking or the swelling in the anger of the bells—
                Of the bells,—
        Of the bells, bells, bells, bells,
            Bells, bells, bells—
In the clamor and the clangor of the bells!

                    IV
70   Hear the tolling of the bells—
            Iron bells!

What a world of solemn thought their monody compels!
    In the silence of the night,
    How we shiver with affright
75   At the melancholy menace of their tone!
    For every sound that floats
    From the rust within their throats
        Is a groan.
    And the people—ah, the people—
80   They that dwell up in the steeple,
        All alone,
    And who tolling, tolling, tolling,
      In that muffled monotone,
    Feel a glory in so rolling
85   On the human heart a stone—
    They are neither man nor woman—
    They are neither brute nor human—
      They are ghouls:—
    And their king it is who tolls:—
90   And he rolls, rolls, rolls,
      Rolls
    A paean from the bells!
    And his merry bosom swells
    With the paean of the bells!
95   And he dances, and he yells;
    Keeping time, time, time,
    In a sort of runic rhyme,
      To the paean of the bells—
      Of the bells—
100   Keeping time, time, time,
    In a sort of runic rhyme,
      To the throbbing of the bells—
      Of the bells, bells, bells—
      To the sobbing of the bells;
105   Keeping time, time, time,
      As he knells, knells, knells,
    In a happy runic rhyme,
      To the rolling of the bells—
      Of the bells, bells, bells:—
110   To the tolling of the bells—
    Of the bells, bells, bells, bells,
      Bells, bells, bells—
To the moaning and the groaning of the bells.

Questions

1. Vocabulary: *euphony* (26), *voluminously* (26), *turbulency* (38), *monody* (72), *paean* (92), *runic* (97).
2. Underline or list all examples of alliteration, assonance, and onomatopoeia of words and phrases in stanza 1.

3. Find an example of interior rhyme in stanza 2.
4. What vowel sound is most frequent in lines 39–44? To what extent is that assonance onomatopoetic?
5. How does the poem's mood change from stanza 1 to stanza 4? How is that change reflected in the assonances of stanza 4?
6. It has been claimed that Poe's poetry has more ardent fans in France than in the United States. Perhaps one reason is that the musical effects we find excessive seem less prominent to a foreign ear. Do you find the great elaboration of sound effects pleasing? Exhilarating? Frightening?

Vowel Tones

English is rich in vowel sounds, from the wide and resonant *ah* sound to the piercing long *ē*. Our vowels are formed to reflect various emotional states and tensions through changes of pitch. The riders on a roller coaster scream the *ē* sound when the train takes a dive, and they sigh *ah* when the ride is over and the tension is released. Many words illustrate this connection between emotion and vowel tone. In "The Bells," notice that Poe's pleasant description of the bells in stanza 2 uses rich, open vowel sounds in words like "mellow," "golden," "harmony," and "molten-golden." But when he describes the "alarum bells" in stanza 3 he uses pinched, shrill vowels to express danger: "brazen," "scream," "affright," "shriek," and "leaping."

Generally the lower-register vowel sounds—the *aw* (awe), *oo* (doom), and *ō* (woe)—are effective in conveying horror, grief, solemnity, and great magnitude. The shorter vowel sounds—the *i* in little, the *e* in pet, the *a* in rattle—lend themselves to rapid movement, smallness, and gaiety. We have seen how, in the merry first stanza of "The Bells," Poe uses a preponderance of short vowels in words like "merriment," "tinkle," "crystalline," and "tintinnabulation"; and how in the horror of the last stanza he moves to the lower register, in words like "rolling," "tolling," "moaning," and "groaning." Listen to the short vowel sounds in Shakespeare's description of the tiny Queen Mab, from *Romeo and Juliet*, act 1, scene 4:

> She is the fairies' midwife and she comes
> In shape no bigger than an agate stone . . .
> Drawn with a team of little atomies . . .
> Her whip, of cricket's bone; the lash, of film . . .

There are vowel tones of lower register as well, but they are there to set off the diminutive sounds of "little atomies," "whips," and "cricket." Now listen to King Lear in the last act of Shakespeare's great tragedy, when he enters carrying his dead daughter.

> Howl, howl, howl, howl! O you are men of stones:
> Had I your tongues and eyes, I'd use them so
> That heaven's vault should crack. She's gone forever.
> I know when one is dead and when one lives . . .

The passage is dominated by the low vowel sounds ō, ōō, and *aw*, to render the magnitude of Lear's grief.

The metrics of the classical Greek and Latin poets depended on the duration of vowels, rather than accents, for its rhythm. Instead of accented and unaccented syllables, there were long and short syllables. This is called *quantitative meter*. Although our metrics is based primarily on accent, the duration of vowels also plays its part, as will be seen in the following selections.

Exercise

Explain the relation between vowel tones and meaning in the following lines.

1. You do not do, you do not do
   Any more, black shoe
   In which I have lived like a foot
   For thirty years, poor and white,
   Barely daring to breathe or Achoo.
   —*Sylvia Plath*

2. Roll on, thou deep and dark blue ocean, roll.
   —*George Gordon, Lord Byron*

3.   The brittle fleet
   Touch'd, clink'd, and clashed, and vanished.
   —*Alfred, Lord Tennyson*

4. The stoned dogs crawl back through the blood . . .
   —*Weldon Kees*

5. I dared not meet the daffodils
   For fear their yellow gown
   Would pierce me with a fashion
   So foreign to my own.
   —*Emily Dickinson*

6. He from forth the closet brought a heap
   Of candied apple, quince, and plum, and gourd;
   With jellies sooter° than the creamy curd   *sweeter*
   And lucent syrops, tinct° with cinnamon . . .   *flavored*
   —*John Keats*

7. A sudden little river crossed my path
   As unexpected as a serpent comes.
   —*Robert Browning*

Now that we have developed a working knowledge and a vocabulary of musical techniques, let us read some poems with ears attuned to rhythm, rhyme, and the relation of form and content. Read each poem aloud, exaggerating the rhythms, alliterations, and vowel tones.

WILLIAM BUTLER YEATS (1865–1939)

• The Lake Isle of Innisfree

I will arise and go now, and go to Innisfree,
And a small cabin build there, of clay and
    wattles° made: *poles interwoven with branches*
Nine bean-rows will I have there, a hive for the honey-bee,
And live alone in the bee-loud glade.

5   And I shall have some peace there, for peace comes dropping slow,
Dropping from the veils of the morning to where the cricket sings;
There midnight's all a glimmer, and noon a purple glow,
And evening full of the linnet's wings.

I will arise and go now, for always night and day
10   I hear lake water lapping with low sounds by the shore;
While I stand on the roadway, or on the pavements gray,
I hear it in the deep heart's core.

Questions

1. At what line do you notice that a rhyme scheme has been established? Having established the scheme, does Yeats alter it?
2. Does the poem use internal rhyme? If so, what resonances are thereby created?
3. Scan the third stanza. Does it differ metrically from stanza 1? If so, does the meaning justify the difference?
4. Find an example of spondees in stanza 3. How does it affect our reading of the line in which it is found? Does it focus attention? Diffuse it?
5. Discuss the effect of short syllables on the movement of stanza 2.

Innisfree is a kind of Shangri-la for Yeats—a paradise of simplicity, peace, and solitude. The speaker is filled with longing and delight in contemplating this haven. The rhythm he has chosen in the first three lines is heptameter, with a caesura after the fourth foot. These lines have considerable momentum before the caesura and a peaceful resolution after it. The shorter fourth line achieves the most dramatic resolution, with its three spondees at the end. Notice that the basic movement of the lines in the stanza is rising rhythm, moving from unstressed to stressed syllables in an effective rhythmic expression of yearning. But see what happens in lines 5 and 6, when he imagines the dream attained:

And I | shall have | some peace | there, | for peace | comes drop | ping slow,
Dropping | from the | veils of the | morning | to where | the cric | ket sings;

The rhythm shifts radically from a rising to a falling rhythm, with a pyrrhic foot in line 6. This line is as light and ecstatic as his dream of peace.

Peasants Dancing, by Pieter Brueghel the Elder *(Kunsthistorisches Museum, Vienna)*

WILLIAM CARLOS WILLIAMS (1883–1963)

The Dance

In Breughel's great picture, The Kermess,
the dancers go round, they go round and
around, the squeal and the blare and the
tweedle of bagpipes, a bugle and fiddles
5   tipping their bellies (round as the thick-
sided glasses whose wash they impound)
their hips and their bellies off balance
to turn them. Kicking and rolling about
the Fair Grounds, swinging their butts, those
10   shanks must be sound to bear up under such
rollicking measures, prance as they dance
in Breughel's great picture, The Kermess.

Questions

1. Vocabulary: *impound* (6).
2. How many instances of onomatopoeia can you find in this poem?
3. Scan the poem. Are there more stressed syllables or unstressed ones? How does that affect the movement of the poem?

4. Which lines are end-stopped? Which lines are enjambed? How does enjambment contribute to the movement from line to line?
5. Does the rhythm of the poem remind you of any particular dance rhythm?

Songs

We began our discussion with the observation that poetry and songs have a common root in our emotions, and that literary, or unsung, poetry is a relatively new development in the history of literature. Since the Renaissance the distinction between song and literary poetry may be drawn along the following general lines. First, most songs demand greater adherence to regular rhythm and rhyme than does spoken poetry. We are accustomed to hearing rhyme and regular rhythm in our songs, and we are dissatisfied when it is lacking. Second, because songs are composed to be heard rather than studied, songwriters usually avoid the concentration of images and figures that strengthen literary poetry. They use them, but in less profusion, and in such a way that they may be grasped on first hearing. Songwriters have melodies to charge their lines with emotion, so their language can relax.

This is not to minimize the power of poetry in songwriting. The United States has been fortunate in its extraordinary poet-lyricists: the anonymous singers of ballads and spirituals, troubadours Woody Guthrie and Bob Dylan, urban songwriters Billie Holiday and Huddie Ledbetter, and the countless writers of Broadway show tunes. These composers have created a tradition of lyric poetry of wit, beauty, and power.

Perhaps one of the true tests of a good song is that it loses its essential power when committed to cold type. If you have recordings of the following songs, you should listen to them before and after studying them as literature.

ANONYMOUS

Frankie and Albert

Frankie was a good girl,
As everybody knows.
She paid a hundred dollars
For Albert's suit of clothes.
5   He was her man and he done her wrong.

Frankie went down to the corner saloon,
Wasn't goin' to be there long.
Asked the bartender had he seen her Albert,
'Cause he done been home and gone.
10   He was her man and he done her wrong.

Well, the bartender he told Frankie,
Can't lie to you if I try.
Old Albert been here an hour ago
And gone home with Alice Fry.
15   He was her man and he done her wrong.

Frankie went down to Albert's house,
Only a couple of blocks away,
Peeped in the keyhole of his door,
Saw Albert lovin' Alice Fry.
20   He was her man and he done her wrong.

Frankie called out to Albert,
Albert said I don't hear.
If you don't come to the woman you love
Goin' to haul you out of here.
25   He was her man and he done her wrong.

Frankie she shot old Albert,
And she shot him three or four times.
Said I'll hang around a few minutes
And see if Albert's dyin'.
30   He was my man and he done me wrong.

An iron-tired wagon
With ribbons all hung in black
Took old Albert to the buryin' ground
And it didn't bring him back.
35   He was her man and he done her wrong.

Frankie told the sheriff
What goin' to happen to me?
Said looks like from the evidence
Goin' to be murder first degree.
40   He was your man and he done you wrong.

Judge heard Frankie's story,
Heard Albert's mother testify.
Judge said to Frankie,
You goin' to be justified.
45   He was your man and he done you wrong.

Dark was the night,
Cold was the ground,
The last words I heard Frankie say,
I done laid old Albert down.
50   He was my man and he done me wrong.

Last time I heard of Frankie
She was settin' in her cell,
Sayin' Albert done me wrong
And for that I sent him to hell.
55   He was my man and he done me wrong.

I aint goin' to tell no stories,
I aint goin' to tell no lies.
The woman who stole Frankie's Albert
Was the girl they call Alice Fry.
60   He was her man and he done her wrong.

Questions

1. If you were to classify "Frankie and Albert" as a genre of poetry, how would you classify it? As lyric? Dramatic? Narrative?
2. Is the imagery of the song denser than that of most lyric poems? Less dense? Do you find it at all difficult to follow?
3. Can you find many instances of near rhyme? Is it graceful, or is it awkward in print? Do you suppose these rhymes would be more pleasing if you heard them sung?

BILLIE HOLIDAY (1915–1959)

God Bless the Child

Them that's got shall get, Them that's not shall lose;
So the Bible said, and it still is news;
Moma may have, Papa may have, but,
God bless the child that's got his own; That's got his own.

5   Yes, the strong gets more, while the weak ones fade.
Empty pockets don't ever make the grade;
Moma may have, Papa may have, but
God bless the child that's got his own! That's got his own.

Money, you got lots o' friends, crowdin' 'round the door.
10   When you're gone, and spendin' ends, they don't come no more.
No. No. No.

Rich relations give, crust of bread and such.
You can help yourself, but don't take too much!
Moma may have, Papa may have, but
15   God bless the child that's got his own! That's got his own.

Questions

1. Find an example of allusion in stanza 1. How does it enrich the song?
2. Find an instance of synecdoche in stanza 2. Another in stanza 4.
3. The line repeated at the end of stanzas 1, 2, and 4 is the song's *refrain*. Why does she repeat it?

BOB DYLAN (1941–)

Boots of Spanish Leather

Oh, I'm sailin' away my own true love,
I'm sailin' away in the morning.
Is there something I can send you from across the sea,
From the place that I'll be landing?

5   No, there's nothin' you can send me, my own true love,
There's nothin' I wish to be ownin'.
Just carry yourself back to me unspoiled,
From across the lonesome ocean.

Oh, but I just thought you might want something fine
10 Made of silver or of golden,
Either from the mountains of Madrid
Or from the coast of Barcelona.

Oh, but if I had the stars from the darkest night
And the diamonds from the deepest ocean,
15 I'd foresake them all for your sweet kiss,
For that's all I'm wishin' to be ownin'.

That I might be gone a long time
And it's only that I'm askin',
Is there something I can send you to remember me by,
20 To make your time more easy passin'.

Oh, how can, how can you ask me again,
It only brings me sorrow.
The same thing I want from you today,
I would want again tomorrow.

25 I got a letter on a lonesome day,
It was from her ship a-sailin',
Saying I don't know when I'll be comin' back again,
It depends on how I'm a-feelin'.

Well, if you, my love, must think that-a-way,
30 I'm sure your mind is roamin'.
I'm sure your heart is not with me,
But with the country to where you're goin'.

So take heed, take heed of the western wind,
Take heed of the stormy weather.
35 And yes, there's something you can send back to me,
Spanish boots of Spanish leather.

Questions

1. How many personae do you hear in the song? Is it a monologue? A dialogue?
2. What are the most vivid images in the poem? Are there stanzas without images?
3. Find an example of metonymy. Find an example of hyperbole.

COLE PORTER (1893–1964)

My Heart Belongs to Daddy

I used to fall
In love with all
Those boys who maul
Refined ladies.
5 But now I tell
Each young gazelle
To go to hell—

I mean, hades,
For since I've come to care
10 For such a sweet millionaire.

While tearing off
A game of golf
I may make a play for the caddy.
But when I do
15 I don't follow through
'Cause my heart belongs to Daddy.

If I invite
A boy, some night,
To dine on my fine finnan haddie,°   smoked haddock
20 I just adore
His asking for more,
But my heart belongs to Daddy,
Yes, my heart belongs to Daddy.
So I simply couldn't be bad.
25 Yes, my heart belongs to Daddy,
Da-da, da-da-da, da-da-da, dad!
So I want to warn you, laddie,
Tho' I know you're perfectly swell,
That my heart belongs to Daddy
30 'Cause my Daddy, he treats me so well.
He treats it and treats it,
And then he repeats it,
Yes, Daddy, he treats it so well.

Saint Patrick's day,
35 Although I may
Be seen wearing green with a paddy,
I'm always sharp
When playing the harp,
'Cause my heart belongs to Daddy.
40 Though other dames
At football games
May long for a strong undergraddy,
I never dream
Of making the team
45 'Cause my heart belongs to Daddy.
Yes, my heart belongs to Daddy,
So I simply couldn't be bad.
Yes, my heart belongs to Daddy,
Da-da, da-da-da, da-da-da, dad!
50 So I want to warn you, laddie,
Tho' I simply hate to be frank,
That I can't be mean to Daddy
'Cause my Da-da-da-daddy might spank.
In matters artistic
55 He's not modernistic
So Da-da-da-daddy might spank.

11 🌿 Tones of Voice

There is more to speech than the literal meaning of words. We may mean what we say, or we may mean something quite different. In conversation our tone of voice indicates how we feel about what we are communicating. Even in privacy, we shout good news and whisper condolences. We sneer sarcasm. When your mother said, "Don't speak to me in that tone of voice," you may have been saying something quite agreeable in itself. You may have been saying, "Sure, I'll take out the garbage," but in such a bitter tone that it came out sounding like, "Sure, I'll take out the garbage (and spread it all over the lawn)."

Tone is the way writers or speakers indicate their attitudes and feelings toward the subject. Of course, it is difficult to capture on the printed page the qualities of the spoken voice. Through their rhythms, images, and word choices, poets can subtly suggest their underlying sentiments. How do we know when people are lying to us? The content of what they say may be perfectly believable, but something in the rhythm—perhaps it is too regular, too pat, too rehearsed—indicates that the speaker is insincere. Poets perfect their language, but they usually wish to achieve the spontaneity of a sincere expression. Most of the poems we have read are quite sincere, and you will notice in their music a sustained immediacy that is hard to fake.

The Range of Tones

Let us begin with a poem whose tone is subtle, almost neutral.

WILLIAM CARLOS WILLIAMS (1883–1963)

The Young Housewife

At ten A.M. the young housewife
moves about in negligee behind

William Carlos Williams *(Rollie McKenna)*

the wooden walls of her husband's house.
I pass solitary in my car.

5   Then again she comes to the curb
to call the ice-man,[1] fish-man, and stands
shy, uncorseted, tucking in
stray ends of hair, and I compare her
to a fallen leaf.

10   The noiseless wheels of my car
rush with a crackling sound over
dried leaves as I bow and pass smiling.

To determine the tone of a poem, first consider the poet's attitude toward the subject. How does Williams feel about the housewife? He seems so cool and unperturbed that we must scrutinize his *observations* for a clue. He mentions that she wears a negligee and is uncorseted. He notices her "tucking in/stray ends of hair." These observations suggest that Williams finds the woman attractive. But he does not say, "Look at the beautiful housewife!" He does not rhapsodize about her charms. In the only figure of speech he permits himself, he simply compares her to a fallen leaf. The tone of the poem is masterful in its restraint.

    The following poem is equally masterful, in its lack of restraint. The subject is similar: a man is describing a woman. But Lawrence's admiration for this

---

[1] Before the advent of the home refrigerator, blocks of ice were delivered to homes by icemen.

woman is unembarrassed, and his enthusiasm drives the rhythms and figures of speech. The resulting tone is racy, ebullient.

D. H. LAWRENCE (1885–1930)

Gloire de Dijon[2]

When she rises in the morning
I linger to watch her;
She spreads the bath-cloth underneath the window
And the sunbeams catch her
5   Glistening white on the shoulders,
While down her sides the mellow
Golden shadow glows as
She stoops to the sponge, and her swung breasts
Sway like full-blown yellow
10   Gloire de Dijon roses.

She drips herself with water, and her shoulders
Glisten as silver, they crumple up
Like wet and falling roses, and I listen
For the sluicing of their rain-dishevelled petals.
15   In the window full of sunlight
Concentrates her golden shadow
Fold on fold, until it glows as
Mellow as the glory roses.

Here nothing is held back. The similes are sensual and fulsome. Notice how the lines tumble over one another in the excitement of long sentences, and how the speaker features the long ō vowel in "shadow glows" and "roses" at the ends of both stanzas. That ō sound is the sound of wonderment. The poem is an articulate "wow" from beginning to end. Since distinctive tone in poetry often results from rhythm and the arrangement of vowels, we will refer to the music of poetry again in our discussions of tone.

Irony

Although the tones of the foregoing poems differ in intensity, they share an important quality: they are both sincere. Nothing in the tone of either speaker would lead us to suspect that he does not mean what he says. When poets mean the opposite of what they say, they use the tone known as *irony*. This tone of voice is unmistakable in conversation. The compliment "That's a lovely hat" can become an ironic jibe if we overemphasize the word *lovely*. We often use irony to tease each other.

---

[2] *Gloire de Dijon* is French for "glory of Dijon." Dijon is a city in eastern France, also famous for its mustard.

Translating the ironic tone into literature is likewise done by overemphasis and understatement. Lacking the speaker's control of pitch and volume, the poet must rely on posturing, surprising diction, and excessive imagery to set the tone.

The following protest poem is a veritable test pattern of ironic tones. Whitman is describing a military parade. At first his irony is so subtle we might think he really admires "the show." But by the time he describes the phantom soldiers, "bandaged and bloodless," his repetition of "this is indeed a show" is downright bitter. The first time he calls the parade a "show," we think he means entertainment. He does not mean that at all: he hates it.

WALT WHITMAN (1819–1892)

A Boston Ballad

To get betimes in Boston town I rose this morning early,
Here's a good place at the corner, I must stand and see the show.

Clear the way there Jonathan!
Way for the President's marshal—way for the government cannon!
5   Way for the Federal foot and dragoons,
    (and the apparitions° copiously° tumbling.)   *phantoms plentifully*

I love to look on the Stars and Stripes,
    I hope the fifes will play Yankee Doodle.

How bright shine the cutlasses of the foremost troops!
10   Every man holds his revolver, marching stiff through Boston town.

A fog follows, antiques of the same come limping,
Some appear wooden-legged, and some appear bandaged and bloodless.

Why this is indeed a show—it has called the dead out of the earth!
The old graveyards of the hills have hurried to see!
15   Phantoms! phantoms countless by flank and rear!
Cock'd hats of mothy mould—crutches made of mist!
Arms in slings—old men leaning on young men's shoulders.

What troubles you Yankee phantoms? what is all this chattering
    of bare gums?
Does the ague° convulse your limbs? do you mistake your crutches   *fever*
    for firelocks and level them?

20   If you blind your eyes with tears you will not see the President's marshal,
If you groan such groans you might balk the government cannon.

For shame old maniacs—bring down those toss'd arms,
    and let your white hair be,
Here gape your great grandsons, their wives gaze at them from the windows,
25   See how well dress'd, see how orderly they conduct themselves.

Worse and worse—can't you stand it? are you retreating?
Is this hour with the living too dead for you?

Retreat then—pell-mell!
To your graves—back—back to the hills old limpers!
30   I do not think you belong here anyhow.

But there is one thing that belongs here—shall I tell you what it is,
     gentlemen of Boston?

I will whisper it to the Mayor, he shall send a committee to England,
They shall get a grant from the Parliament, go with a cart to the royal vault,
Dig out King George's coffin, unwrap him quick from the grave-clothes,
35   box up his bones for a journey,
Find a swift Yankee clipper—here is freight for you, black-bellied clipper,
Up with your anchor—shake out your sails—steer straight toward Boston bay.

Now call for the President's marshal again, bring out the government cannon,
Fetch home the roarers from Congress, make another procession,
40   guard it with foot and dragoons.
This centre-piece for them;
Look, all orderly citizens—look from the windows, women!

The committee open the box, set up the regal ribs, glue those that will not stay,
Clap the skull on top of the ribs, and clap a crown on top of the skull.

45   You have got your revenge, old buster—the crown is come to its own,
     and more than its own.

Stick your hands in your pockets, Jonathan—you are a made man from this day,
You are mighty cute—and here is one of your bargains.

The phantom veterans remind us of the deeper meaning of military shows. They symbolize war and suffering. Whitman's description of the phantoms' maimed decrepitude, their weeping and groaning in the presence of the orderly parade, emphasizes the reality of war and the proud ignorance of the young dragoons. When he finally dismisses the phantoms, saying, "I do not think you belong here anyhow," the line resonates with bitterness and irony. It is classic understatement.

Then comes the most ironic image of all. What *does* belong in the midst of this show of nationalism and militarism is the corpse of King George, whose tyranny the phantom veterans died to depose. When Whitman says to Jonathan, the gawking spectator, "here is one of your bargains," and "you are a made man from this day," he cannot be taken literally. Whitman's vision of a militarized United States is grim, and his tone is pure sarcasm. The drumbeat rhythms of the poem underscore his sarcasm.

ALAN DUGAN (1923–)

Morning Song

Look, it's morning, and a little water gurgles in the tap.
I wake up waiting, because it's Sunday, and turn twice more
than usual in bed, before I rise to cereal and comic strips.

I have risen to the morning danger and feel proud,
5   and after shaving off the night's disguises, after searching
close to the bone for blood, and finding only a little,
I shall walk out bravely into the daily accident.

Questions

1. How does the speaker feel about the morning? Are the phrases "morning danger" and "the daily accident" accurate descriptions of the day, or are they excessive?
2. How does the speaker feel about his own response to the morning? Are the words "proud" and "bravely" sincere or excessive?
3. To what degree is the poem ironic in tone?

DENISE LEVERTOV (1923–)

To the Snake

Green Snake, when I hung you round my neck
and stroked your cold, pulsing throat
            as you hissed to me, glinting
arrowy gold scales, and I felt
5   the weight of you on my shoulders,
and the whispering silver of your dryness
            sounded close at my ears—

Green Snake—I swore to my companions that certainly
            you were harmless! But truly
10   I had no certainty, and no hope, only desiring
            to hold you, for that joy,
                        which left
a long wake of pleasure, as the leaves moved
and you faded into the pattern
15   of grass and shadows, and I returned
smiling and haunted, to a dark morning.

Questions

1. What is the speaker's attitude toward the snake?
2. How does her description of the snake justify her attitude?
3. Is there any suggestion of irony in the poem?

Didactic Poetry

The Latin poet Horace, in a great didactic poem called "The Art of Poetry," said that the purpose of poetry is to teach or to delight. Sometimes it is both. Didactic poetry aims to teach; poems have been written to teach physics, bee-keeping, even the art of love. The didactic tone is distinctive. The poet's attitude toward the subject is: I know about this, and now I'm going to let you in on it.

This is also the attitude of doctors, moralists, and a few teachers. The didactic tone can be charming, or it can be presumptuous. We are most familiar with it in little rhymes that help us remember important facts.

> Thirty days hath September,
> April, June and November . . .

> Red sky at night:
> Sailor's delight.
> Red sky at morning:
> Sailors take warning.

> Oysters into milk
> Go smooth as silk.

In all of literature no didactic speech has been more frequently quoted than the advice of Polonius to his son, from Shakespeare's *Hamlet*.

> And these few precepts in thy memory
> Look thou charácter. Give thy thoughts no tongue,
> Nor any unproportion'd thought his act.
> Be thou familiar, but by no means vulgar;
> Those friends thou hast, and their adoption tried,
> Grapple them unto thy soul with hoops of steel;
> But do not dull thy palm with entertainment
> Of each new-hatch'd, unfledg'd comráde. Beware
> Of entrance to a quarrel, but, being in,
> Bear 't that th' opposed may beware of thee.
> Give every man thy ear, but few thy voice;
> Take each man's censure, but reserve thy judgment.
> Costly thy habit as thy purse can buy,
> But not express'd in fancy; rich, not gaudy;
> For the apparel oft proclaims the man,
> And they in France of the best rank and station
> Are of a most select and generous clef° in that.   sort
> Neither a borrower, nor a lender be;
> For loan oft loses both itself and friend,
> And borrowing dulleth edge of husbandry.°   household management
> This above all: to thine own self be true,
> And it must follow, as the night the day,
> Thou canst not then be false to any man.
> Farewell; my blessing season this in thee!

Polonius, a professional advisor, has saved up the best advice for his son. He is a master of the didactic tone, and his instructions ring with confidence and conviction. They do not invite questions; they represent an end of questioning, the treasury of an old man's wisdom. In this certainty the didactic distinguishes itself from the meditative tone.

There is comedy in the tone as well. What begins as a "few precepts" runs on to twenty-four lines of moral disquisition, more than any young man could absorb or believe. Even the wisest advice is a little silly if there is too much of it.

At its best the didactic tone is both convincing and modest. Advice is easiest to hear when it seems hard won and is offered with humility.

EMILY DICKINSON (1830–1886)

Success Is Counted Sweetest

Success is counted sweetest
By those who ne'er succeed.
To comprehend a nectar
Requires sorest need.

5   Not one of all the purple host
Who took the flag to-day
Can tell the definition,
So clear, of victory,

As he, defeated, dying,
10   On whose forbidden ear
The distant strains of triumph
Break, agonized and clear.

The poem is organized like a simple lesson—a general proposition followed by a corollary and an illustration. Dickinson states the proposition so plainly that it seems incontestable. Should we be tempted to quibble, the example of the battle is so apt and moving that it disarms us. Unlike Polonius, Dickinson does not weary us with her wisdom.

English poets of the eighteenth century had greater confidence in reason and human perfectibility than those of any other period in history. To Alexander Pope any problem worth solving would yield to reason. Being supremely reasonable, Pope found the didactic tone natural. His verse is a model of clarity and balance, its tone even and assured, its rhythms highly regular. Such a tone is the mark of secure faith, a system that leaves little room for doubt.

ALEXANDER POPE (1688–1744)

From An Essay on Man (Epistle IV)

Honour and shame from no condition rise;
Act well your part, there all the honour lies.
Fortune in men has some small diff'rence made,
One flaunts in rags, one flutters in brocade;
5   The cobbler aproned, and the parson gowned,
The friar hooded, and the monarch crowned.
"What differ more (you cry) than crown and cowl?"
I'll tell you, friend; a wise man and a fool.

You'll find, if once the monarch acts the monk,
10   Or, cobbler-like, the parson will be drunk,
Worth makes the man, and want of it, the fellow;
The rest is all but leather or prunella.°   *a woolen fabric*
      Stuck o'er with titles and hung round with strings,
That thou mayest be by kings, or whores of kings.
15   Boast the pure blood of an illustrious race,
In quiet flow from Lucrece° to Lucrece;   *a virtuous Roman woman*
But by your fathers' worth if yours you rate,
Count me those only who were good and great.

Questions

1. What is more important to the speaker—apparel or character?
2. Do you agree with the ideas expressed in lines 9–12?
3. What is the meter of the poem? Does it suit the didactic tone?

Toughness

Many readers tend to think of poets as soft-hearted creatures who bruise easily
and have the most exquisite sympathy for all living things, but they are not. As
evidence of this misconception, certain poets adopt a tone of toughness. There
is a little of Mae West or Humphrey Bogart in all of us, an attitude that life is
hard, kid, so you may as well brace up and plow through it. This poetry is not
sighed or sung. It is spoken straight.

PHILIP LEVINE (1928–)

To a Child Trapped in a Barber Shop

You've gotten in through the transom
            and you can't get out
till Monday morning or, worse,
            till the cops come.

5   That six-year-old red face
            calling for mama
is yours; it won't help you
            because your case

is closed forever, hopeless.
10   So don't drink
the Lucky Tiger,° don't   *hair tonic*
            fill up on grease

because that makes it a lot worse,
            that makes it a crime
15   against property and the state
            and that costs time.

We've all been here before,
       we took our turn
under the electric storm
20   of the vibrator

and stiffened our wills to meet
       the close clippers
and heard the true blade mowing
       back and forth

25 on a strip of dead skin,
       and we stopped crying.
You think your life is over?
       It's just begun.

Questions

1. How serious is the child's predicament?
2. Does the speaker care about the child? What phrases suggest that he does?
3. The speaker is feeling both sympathy and distance from his side of the glass. How does the tone reveal these conflicting feelings?
4. Will the speaker try to rescue the child?

CHARLES BUKOWSKI (1920–)

Yellow

Seivers was one of the hardest running backs[3] since
Jimmy Brown, and lateral motion too,
like a chorus girl, really, until one day he got hit on
the blind side by Basil Skronski; we carried Seivers off the field
5 but Skronski had gotten one rib and cracked another.

the next year Seivers wasn't even good in practice, gun shy as a
squirrel in deer season; he stopped contact, fumbled, couldn't even
hold a look-in pass or a handoff—all that wasted and he could go the 100 in 9.7[4]

I'm 45 years old, out of shape, too much beer, but one of the best
10 assistant coaches in the pro game, and I can't stand to see a man
jaking° it. I got him in the locker room the other day when the whole   *shirking*
squad was in there. I told him, "Seivers, you used to be a player
but now you're chickenshit!"

"you can't talk that way to me, Manny!" he said, and I turned him
15 around, he was lacing on a shoe, and I right-cracked him
right on the chin. he fell against a locker
and then he began to cry—the greatest since Brown,
crying there against the locker, one shoe off, one on.

"come on, men, let's get outa here!" I told the gang, and we ran
20 on out, and when we got back he had cleared out, he was gone, his

---

[3] In football, a backfield ball carrier.
[4] The hundred-yard dash in 9.7 seconds.

gear was gone. we got some kid from Illinois running his spot now,
head down, knees high, he don't care where he's going.

guys like Seivers end up washing dishes for a buck an hour
and that's just what they deserve.

Questions

1. What is the speaker's attitude toward Seivers?
2. What figures of speech reveal this attitude in the first two stanzas?
3. Try to say the line "I can't stand to see a man/jaking it," in the speaker's voice. Do
   you hear the tone? What attitude does it express toward Seivers? Toward the game
   of football?
4. What does the speaker care more about—Seivers's feelings, or football?
5. Do you feel sorry for Seivers?
6. Would you like the speaker to be your coach? How would you like him to be your
   father?

The Comic Tone

When poets adopt a comic attitude toward a subject we sometimes can hear it
in rollicking or off-beat rhythms, in clownish imagery and diction. The subject
may or may not be funny—the tone is what makes us laugh.

ANONYMOUS

Miss Bailey's Ghost

A captain bold, in Halifax, who dwelt in country quarters,
Seduced a maid, who hang'd herself, one morning, in her garters,
His wicked conscience smited him, he lost his stomach daily,
He took to drinking ratafee,° and thought upon Miss Bailey.   *an almond liqueur*
5   Oh, Miss Bailey! unfortunate Miss Bailey.

One night betimes he went to rest, for he had caught a fever,
Says he, "I am a handsome man, but I'm a gay deceiver";
His candle just at twelve o'clock began to burn quite palely,
A ghost stepp'd up to his bedside, and said, "behold Miss Bailey."
10   Oh, Miss Bailey! unfortunate Miss Bailey.

"Avaunt, Miss Bailey," then he cried, "your face looks white and mealy,"
"Dear Captain Smith," the ghost replied, "you've used me ungenteely;
The Crowner's Quest goes hard with me, because I've acted fraily,
And parson Biggs won't bury me, though I am dead Miss Bailey."
15   Oh, Miss Bailey! unfortunate Miss Bailey.

"Dear Corpse," said he, "since you and I accounts must once for all close,
I've really got a one pound note in my regimental small clothes;
'Twill bribe the sexton for your grave."—The ghost then vanish'd gaily,
Crying "Bless you, wicked Captain Smith, remember poor Miss Bailey."
20   Oh, Miss Bailey! unfortunate Miss Bailey.

The situation itself is not very funny. Poe would have made a nightmare of it, Tennyson a dirge. But the rhyme of *quarters* and *garters* is so unexpected and silly that it quickly deflates the seriousness of the hanging. Likewise the captain's excessive stomach trouble and his vanity, as confessed in line 7. The dance-hall rhythm is so unsuited to the macabre events that its very inappropriateness is comic.

Max Beerbohm has observed that all humor is the result of exaggeration or incongruity. Comic poems usually make fun not only of their subjects but of poetry as well, either by exaggerating its techniques or misapplying them.

EDMUND CLERIHEW BENTLEY (1875–1956)

Lord Clive

What I like about Clive
Is that he is no longer alive.
There is a great deal to be said
For being dead.

Does poetry have to rhyme? All right then, says the comic poet, I'll make it rhyme to the most awkward rhythm. "Lord Clive" is not only a burlesque of rhythm and rhyme. It is a takeoff on the elegy, which is usually quite serious.

Verses that rhyme not only the last syllable, but the last two, are called feminine rhymes. Perhaps as a result of a sort of tonal overkill, the effect of feminine rhyme is often comic.

ANONYMOUS

There Was a King

There was a King and he had three daughters,
And they all lived in a basin of water;
    The basin bended,
    My story's ended.
5   If the basin had been stronger,
    My story would have been longer.

The comic charm of this poem depends on its tone, induced by eccentric rhythms and feminine rhymes. Its wit would be lost in prose.

Two popular tricks in the comic poet's repertoire are the *pun* and the *spoonerism*. The pun is a play on words with similar sounds or on a single word with different meanings: "I stuck my finger in the pie and meringue came off." That's a terrible pun. Here is a better one:

On His Books

When I am dead, I hope it may be said
"His sins were scarlet, but his books were read."

Read: red. Get it? Roman audiences 2000 years ago acknowledged puns by groaning, and that response has not changed.

A spoonerism is a slip of the tongue that exchanges the parts of two words. Thus, "Let's sit by the fire and spin" becomes "Let's spit by the fire and sin." William Spooner once told one of his students: "You have hissed all of my mystery lessons and completely tasted two whole worms." (Translation: You have missed all of my history lessons and completely wasted two whole terms.)

Diction Levels

Some poets use unfamiliar words and complex literary sentences, whereas others never depart from plain speech. Customarily we refer to formal, literary language as *high diction* and to street language as *low diction*. We associate the former with pulpit, courtroom, and college, and the latter with racetrack and locker room. The poet's level of diction is an element of tone indicating both an attitude toward the subject and a regard for the reader. High diction suggests acuity, demands scholarship, and promises to reward it. Simple diction is humbler, more relaxed and inviting.

We have seen a range of diction levels, from the heights of "An Essay on Man" (pages 613–14) to the idiomatic force of Bukowski's "Yellow" (pages 615–16). Emily Dickinson's poem "Success Is Counted Sweetest" is neither as high toned as "An Essay on Man" nor as low as "Yellow." How would you rank the diction level of Emily's poem, in relation to Philip Levine's (pages 614–15)?

Ford Madox Ford, an English essayist, set a limit to the artificiality of diction. He said that a poet should not write anything that he could not, under the stress of some emotion, actually *say*. Modern poets have taken his advice to heart, but there is still a great range of diction levels, owing to our diverse educations and personalities. This makes for a lively variety of tones.

One of our more formal poets is Richard Wilbur.

RICHARD WILBUR (1921–)

The Death of a Toad

> A toad the power mower caught,
> Chewed and clipped of a leg, with a hobbling hop has got
> To the garden verge, and sanctuaried him
> Under the cineraria° leaves, in the shade   *exotic flowering plant*

Of the ashen heartshaped leaves, in a dim,
Low, and a final glade.

The rare original heartsblood goes,
Spends on the earthen hide, in the folds and wizenings, flows
In the gutters of the banked and staring eyes. He lies
10   As still as if he would return to stone,
And soundlessly attending, dies
Toward some deep monotone,

Toward misted and ebullient seas
And cooling shores, toward lost Amphibia's emperies.°   *empires*
15   Day dwindles, drowning, and at length is gone
In the wide and antique eyes, which still appear
To watch, across the castrate lawn,
The haggard daylight steer.

Questions

1. Vocabulary: *sanctuaried* (3), *wizenings* (8), *ebullient* (13), *castrate* (17).
2. How would you describe the diction of the poem? Did it send you to the dictionary? How often?
3. Have you ever heard anyone talk like the speaker of this poem? Is there a single sentence or phrase that you could imagine someone saying?
4. What is Wilbur's attitude toward his subject? Serious? Frivolous?
5. Suppose the poet had used more natural speech. What subtleties might be lost? What music?

LANGSTON HUGHES (1902–1967)

• Who but the Lord?

I looked and I saw
That man they call the Law.
He was coming
Down the street at me!
5   I had visions in my head
Of being laid out cold and dead,
Or else murdered
By the third degree.

I said, O, Lord, if you can,
10   *Save me from that man!*
Don't let him make a pulp out of me!
But the Lord he was not quick.
The Law raised up his stick
And beat the living hell
15   Out of me!

Now, I do not understand
Why God don't protect a man

From police brutality.
Being poor and black,
20 I've no weapon to strike back
So who but the Lord
Can protect me?

Questions

1. How would you describe the diction of this poem? Literary? Conversational?
2. The poet's attitude toward his subject is clearly serious. Why, then, has he chosen such common diction? What does this suggest about his attitude toward his reader? Intimacy? Distance?

Dialects

In many cultures the line between the literary tradition and the popular culture has been sharply drawn. There are some poems meant to be read by scholars and others that are meant for a popular audience. Where there is a significant difference between the written and the spoken language, some poets strive to capture the accents of the vernacular. Some of the most popular poets, such as Robert Burns, James Russell Lowell, and Paul Laurence Dunbar, have written in dialect. Unfortunately, the popularity of poetry in dialect is often as short-lived and local as the dialect itself.

ROBERT BURNS (1759–1796)

• John Anderson My Jo

John Anderson my jo,° John,	*a term of endearment*
When we were first acquent,	
Your locks were like the raven,	
Your bonnie brow was brent;°	*smooth*
5 But now your brow is beld,° John,	*bald*
Your locks are like the snow;	
But blessings on your frosty pow,°	*head*
John Anderson, my jo.	
John Anderson my jo, John,	
10 We clamb the hill thegither;	
And mony a canty° day, John,	*cheerful*
We've had wi' ane anither:	
Now we maun° totter down, John,	*must*
And hand in hand we'll go,	
15 And sleep thegither at the foot,	
John Anderson, my jo.	

Questions

1. What is the speaker's attitude toward John?
2. Would she be able to achieve such intimacy without her dialect?

3. Are you familiar with the Scots accent? If so, read the poem aloud, first with the Scots accent and then in your own. Which sounds better?

PAUL LAURENCE DUNBAR (1872–1906)

In the Morning

'Lias! 'Lias! Bless de Lawd!
Don' you know de day's erbroad?
Ef you don't git up, you scamp,
Dey'll be trouble· in dis camp.
5   T'ink I gwine to let you sleep
W'ile I meks yo' boa'd an' keep?
Dat's a putty howdy-do—
Don' you hyeah me, 'Lias—you?

Bet ef I come crost dis flo'
10   You won' fin' no time to sno'.
Daylight all a-shinin' in
W'ile you sleep—w'y hit's a sin!
Ain't de can'le-light enough
To bu'n out widout a snuff,
15   But you go de mo'nin' thoo
Bu'nin' up de daylight too?

'Lias, don' you hyeah me call?
No use tu'nin' to'ds de wall;
I kin hyeah dat mattuss° squeak;   *mattress*
20   Don' you hyeah me w'en I speak?
Dis hyeah clock done struck off six—
Ca'line, bring me dem ah sticks!
Oh, you down, suh; huh, you down—
Look hyeah, don' you daih to frown.

25   Ma'ch° yo'se'f an' wash yo' face,   *march*
Don' you splattah all de place;
I got somep'n else to do,
'Sides jes' cleanin' aftah you.
Tek dat comb an' fix yo' haid—
30   Looks jes' lak a feddah baid.°   *feather bed*
Look hyeah, boy, I let you see
You sha'n't roll yo' eyes at me.

Come hyeah; bring me dat ah strap!
Boy, I'll whup you 'twell you drap;
35   You done felt yo'se'f too strong,
An' you sholy° got me wrong.   *surely*
Set down at dat table thaih;
Jes' you whimpah ef you daih!
Evah mo'nin' on dis place,
40   Seem lak I mus' lose my grace.

Paul Laurence Dunbar
(Ohio Historical Society)

Fol' yo' han's an' bow yo' haid—
Wait ontwell de blessin' 's said;
"Lawd, have mussy on ouah souls—"
(Don' you daih to tech dem rolls—)
45   "Bless de food we gwine to eat—"
(You set still—I *see* yo' feet;
You jes' try dat trick again!)
"Gin us peace an' joy. Amen!"

Questions

1. This is one of the most popular poems ever written in America. It has been memorized and recited by thousands of schoolchildren. Can you explain its popularity?
2. Without the aid of the marginal glosses, could you have understood the poem?
3. Translate one of the stanzas into literary English, making as few changes as possible. What does the poem lose in translation? How much of the tone survives?

12 🌿 The Poem's Shape

The everyday words we use become literature when they are given expressive shape. No literature is without shape. A playwright, for example, cannot merely tape-record a lively conversation and call it a play. A dialogue must be molded so that the conversation has a beginning and an end. Even interviewers shape a conversation by asking prepared questions and by carefully editing the transcript after the interview is over.

Why is shape necessary? Shape gives a work of literature unity and complete-ness. By *unity* we mean that everything in the poem belongs in it and is connected to everything else. In conversation, all sorts of extraneous and unconnected statements arise. In literature, the writer limits him- or herself to what contributes to the overall meaning and effectiveness of the work. By *completeness* we mean that everything needed by the poem is present, in its proper place. In conversation we often forget what we intended to say or later think of what we ought to have said. A good poem, however, contains everything it needs to be effective, and nothing extra. Its shape both highlights and determines the poem's unity and completeness.

We speak of shape in poetry in two general ways: form and structure. By *form* critics usually mean the outward container that shapes the work. By *structure* they mean the inner framework around which the work amasses. It might help to think of the shape of our bodies. The flesh gives the body outward form; bones give it inner structure. Of course, form and structure are not separate. In a poem, as in the body, form and structure work toward the same end—expressive efficiency.

The Structure of Free Verse

We generally think of a poem's shape in terms of rhyme schemes, yet the earliest English poetry did not rhyme. In fact, rhyme is an unusually late device imported to England from France and Italy, whose languages are much richer in rhyme words than is English. Some of the greatest poetry, not only in English but also in other languages, does not rhyme at all. The Psalms, for example, are unrhymed but are organized through meaning. Each line has two parts, which are in parallel structure either to each other or to the line that follows. In this brief psalm watch for the ways in which ideas are repeated or mirrored.

Psalm 121: A Song of Degrees

I will lift up mine eyes unto the hills: from whence cometh my help.
My help cometh from the Lord: which made heaven and earth.
He will not suffer thy foot to be moved: he that keepeth thee will not slumber.
Behold, he that keepeth Israel; shall neither slumber nor sleep.
5   The Lord is thy keeper: the Lord is thy shade, upon thy right hand.
The sun shall not smite thee by day; nor the moon by night.
The Lord shall preserve thee from all evil; he shall preserve thy soul.
The Lord shall preserve thy going out, and thy coming in: from this time forth
   and even for evermore.

Questions

1. What is the parallel concept in lines 5, 6, and 8? How is line 8 more complex than the others?
2. Are the lines linked together in other ways? What connections exist between lines 2 and 3 and lines 4 and 5?

Line 1 has two ideas: hills and the coming of help. Line 2 speaks of the coming of help and of heaven and earth, a mirroring of the opening lines. Lines 3 and 4 mirror each other even more clearly. The two parts of line 7 repeat the same idea. Moreover, there is an overall structure to the poem. It begins by looking for help, and it ends by finding it.

Free verse is poetry that is unrhymed and lacks a regular metrical unity. Free verse is not free of shape, however. Indeed, one may say it dispenses with outward formal devices to give full range to internal structures.

DENISE LEVERTOV (1923–)

The Ache of Marriage

The ache of marriage:

thigh and tongue, beloved,
are heavy with it,
it throbs in the teeth

5   We look for communion
and are turned away, beloved,
each and each

It is leviathan° and we   *Biblical sea beast*
in its belly
10   looking for joy, some joy
not to be known outside it

two by two in the ark of
the ache of it.

Questions

1. How are the first and last lines related? Do you have a sense of completeness? How
   do they correspond to the self-enclosed feeling of marriage?
2. How are the allusions to "leviathan" and "the ark" related?
3. How is the belly image in stanza 4 related to the images in stanza 2?
4. Are there any words or images that seem out of place in the poem? Do all the words
   seem closely connected?

Notice that "The Ache of Marriage" is divided into units, or what are called
stanzas. A stanza is any group of lines that make up a division of the poem, but
it can sometimes be a single line. In "The Ache of Marriage" these units are
of irregular length, both in meter and in number of lines. Frequently, the stanzas
in a poem are determined by length, meter, or rhyme scheme.

The stanzas work like paragraphs by bringing together similar ideas or images.
Levertov uses a period only at the end of the poem, but stanzas 2, 3, and 4
approximate sentences.

Because structure is internal, it is often less noticeable than rhyme as a shaping
device. But a free verse poem is not free of shape, and a reader should pay strict
attention to what joins the parts of the poem and gives them a sense of unity.
Although the rest of this chapter will be concerned with verse forms, we wish
to emphasize the fundamental nature of structure. Poets may dispense with
rhyme; they may dispense with a clear metrical unity, with imagery and other
devices. But poets can never give up internal structure. Without structure, there
is no poem.

Some Traditional English Forms
The Ballad

One of the most popular literary forms is the *ballad*. The ballad is built from
four-line stanzas, or *quatrains*, in which the second and fourth lines must rhyme.
Usually the first and third lines have four feet, and the other two lines have
three feet; but there are variant scansions. The ballad is an excellent form for
narrative poetry because the shortened second and fourth lines give the stanza
an unusual sense of propulsion (see the discussion in Chapter 3). "Incident"
is an example of a short "literary" ballad; unlike traditional ballads, it has a
known author.

COUNTEE CULLEN (1903–1946)

Incident

(For Eric Walrond)

Once riding in old Baltimore,
    Heart-filled, head-filled with glee,
I saw a Baltimorean
    Keep looking straight at me.

5   Now I was eight and very small,
    And he was no whit bigger,
And so I smiled, but he poked out
    His tongue, and called me, "Nigger."

I saw the whole of Baltimore
10   From May until December;
Of all the things that happened there
    That's all that I remember.

Questions

1. Does the poem have a sense of completeness? What gives the poem unity?
2. Why is the information in line 2 important for the poem? How does it set the stage for what follows?
3. Why would Cullen remember only this incident? What feeling do you take away from the poem?

The Couplet

A *couplet* is any two consecutive lines, usually ones that rhyme and have the same meter. Couplets appear in many different languages. In English, however, the couplet has had enormous influence, especially a specialized form of couplet, the *heroic couplet*, which dominated the poetry of the eighteenth century. A heroic couplet is in iambic pentameter, and the second line is end-stopped; thus each couplet is not only a metrical unit but a grammatical unit as well. Consequently, couplets on the same subject can be gathered into *verse paragraphs*, long poetic passages that function like prose paragraphs by grouping couplets that discuss the same topic. Occasionally three successive rhymed lines, called a *triplet*, were permitted in the verse paragraphs to give the passage variety.

    John Dryden was an early champion of the heroic couplet. In the following poem, he mourns a fellow poet who had died young.

JOHN DRYDEN (1631–1700)

To the Memory of Mr. Oldham

Farewell, too little, and too lately known,
Whom I began to think and call my own;

For sure our souls were near allied, and thine
Cast in the same poetic mold with mine.
5   One common note on either lyre did strike,
And knaves and fools we both abhorred alike.
To the same goal did both our studies drive;
The last set out the soonest did arrive.
Thus Nisus[1] fell upon the slippery place,
10 While his young friend performed and won the race.
O early ripe! to thy abundant store
What could advancing age have added more?
It might (what nature never gives the young)
Have taught the numbers° of thy native tongue.   *metrics*
15 But satire needs not those, and wit will shine
Through the harsh cadence of a rugged line:[2]
A noble error, and but seldom made,
When poets are by too much force betrayed.
Thy generous fruits, though gathered ere their prime,
20 Still showed a quickness; and maturing time
But mellows what we write to the dull sweets of rhyme.
Once more, hail and farewell; farewell, thou young,
But ah too short, Marcellus[3] of our tongue;
Thy brows with ivy, and with laurels[4] bound;
25 But fate and gloomy night encompass thee around.

Questions

1. Vocabulary: *knaves* (6), *abhorred* (6), *cadence* (16), *encompass* (25).
2. How does the reference to ivy and laurel relate to the opening lines? Is it an appropriate allusion? Does it give the poem a sense of unity?
3. Does the metaphor of fruit (lines 11–21) fit the poem?
4. Is the alexandrine in line 21 fitting?
5. Is there a sense that the poem has concluded? How does Dryden achieve that sense of completeness?

The poets of the eighteenth century felt the heroic couplet possessed the grace, dignity, and flexibility they admired in the classical meters of Virgil and Homer. The heroic couplet is still used today. In "Moly" it suggests the "heroic" and classical origins of Gunn's subject.

---

[1] In Virgil's *Aeneid* (Book 5, lines 315–339) Nisus slipped in a pool of blood during a footrace.
[2] Dryden believed, as did Renaissance theorists, that satire should be in rough meter.
[3] Marcellus was heir to the Roman Empire when he died at the age of twenty.
[4] The traditional crown for poets.

THOM GUNN (1929–)

Moly[5]

Nightmare of beasthood, snorting, how to wake.
I woke. What beasthood skin she made me take?

Leathery toad that ruts for days on end,
Or cringing dribbling dog, man's servile friend,

5   Or cat that prettily pounces on its meat,
Tortures it hours, then does not care to eat:

Parrot, moth, shark, wolf, crocodile, ass, flea.
What germs, what jostling mobs there were in me.

     These seem like bristles, and the hide is tough.
10   No claw or web here: each foot ends in hoof.

Into what bulk has method disappeared?
Like ham, streaked. I am gross—grey, gross, flap-eared.

The pale-lashed eyes my only human feature.
My teeth tear, tear. I am the snouted creature

15 That bites through anything, root, wire, or can.
If I was not afraid I'd eat a man.

Oh a man's flesh already is in mine.
Hand and foot poised for risk. Buried in swine.

     I root and root, you think that it is greed,
20 It is, but I seek out a plant I need.

Direct me, gods, whose changes are all holy,
To where it flickers deep in grass, the moly:

Cool flesh of magic in each leaf and shoot,
From milky flower to the black forked root.

25 From this fat dungeon I could rise to skin
And human title, putting pig within.

I push my big grey wet snout through the green,
Dreaming the flower I have never seen.

Questions

1. Vocabulary: *servile* (4), *jostling* (8).
2. How does the dream in the final line contrast with the nightmare of the opening?
3. How does the persona contrast the human with the bestial?
4. How do the verse paragraphs emphasize the progress of the poem?
5. To what extent are we all part human and part beast? Can we ever become completely human, according to the persona?
6. Does this poem have a sense of completeness? What more would you say if you were the persona?

---

[5] *Moly* was a magic herb given by Hermes to Odysseus, whose men had been turned into swine by the enchantress Circe.

Italian Forms
The Sonnet

No other form has had the nearly universal appeal of the sonnet. Originating in Sicily, it took root on the Italian mainland, from which it spread as far as Russia to the east and the United States to the west. Since its arrival in England in the sixteenth century, the sonnet has found consistent favor.

The *Italian* or *Petrarchan* sonnet is a fourteen-line poem divided between an opening *octave* (eight lines) and a concluding *sestet* (six lines). It is rhymed *abba abba cdc cdc*.[6] The form is demanding, since it requires three endings to rhyme four times each. In Italian, where almost every word ends in a vowel, rhymes are plentiful. In English, however, the form is usually slightly altered to give the poet some freedom.

JOHN KEATS (1795–1821)

- ## On First Looking into Chapman's Homer

Much have I traveled in the realms of gold,
    And many goodly states and kingdoms seen;
    Round many western islands have I been
Which bards in fealty° to Apollo[7] hold.   *allegiance*
5   Oft of one wide expanse had I been told
    That deep-browed Homer ruled as his demesne;
    Yet did I never breathe its pure serene°   *atmosphere*
Till I heard Chapman[8] speak out loud and bold:
Then felt I like some watcher of the skies
10   When a new planet swims into his ken;
Or like stout Cortez[9] when with eagle eyes
    He stared at the Pacific—and all his men
Looked at each other with a wild surmise—
    Silent, upon a peak in Darien.

Questions

1. Vocabulary: *fealty* (4), *desmesne* (6), *ken* (10).
2. Has Keats altered the rhyme scheme?
3. Has he preserved the distinction between octave and sestet? What sort of change occurs between the parts?

---

[6] Throughout this chapter and the next, we will refer to rhymed forms in a schematic way. Each rhyme ending is designated by a letter, starting with *a*. These schemes do not refer to the length of the lines.
[7] Apollo is the god of poetry.
[8] George Chapman (1559?–1634), English poet and translator of Homer.
[9] Hernando Cortez (1485–1534), Spanish conqueror of Mexico. Keats is historically inaccurate, however. The first European to see the Pacific was Vasco de Balboa, who viewed it from Darien, Panama.

4. Keats wrote this poem after his discovery of Chapman's translation, which revealed the splendor of Homer to him for the first time. Have you ever experienced a joyous discovery? How did you feel? Does Keats capture a similar experience?

The sonnet has maintained its popularity for a number of reasons. First, like all performers, poets enjoy doing the difficult with apparent ease. Sonnets are poets' high-wire acts, their perfect figure-eights. Second, the sonnet's length is attractive. It is long enough to tackle serious subjects but still short enough to require all of the poet's economy, exactitude, and grace.

In English the sonnet has been dominated by Shakespeare and the rhyme scheme he employed. Shakespeare divided the sonnet into three quatrains and a couplet. The *Shakespearean* or *English* sonnet is rhymed *abab cdcd efef gg*.

WILLIAM SHAKESPEARE (1564–1616)

That Time of Year Thou Mayst in Me Behold

That time of year thou mayst in me behold
When yellow leaves, or none, or few, do hang
Upon those boughs which shake against the cold,
Bare ruined choirs, where late the sweet birds sang.
5   In me thou see'st the twilight of such day
As after sunset fadeth in the west,
Which by and by black night doth take away,
Death's second self that seals up all in rest.
In me thou see'st the glowing of such fire,
10   That on the ashes of his youth doth lie,
As the deathbed whereon it must expire,
Consumed with that which it was nourished by.
This thou perceiv'st, which makes thy love more strong,
To love that well which thou must leave ere long.

Questions

1. What is the relationship among the three quatrains? What unites them? How are they individually organized?
2. What is the relationship between the quatrains and the final couplet?
3. Does the couplet give the poem a sense of completeness? Is there anything more that needs to be said?
4. Why does Shakespeare order line 2 as he does? What can you tell about the speaker from line 2?
5. If you were addressed in such a way, how would you feel about the speaker? About yourself?

Love and mortality are traditional themes of the sonnet. The following is a modern sonnet about a circumstance similar to Shakespeare's.

EDNA ST. VINCENT MILLAY (1892–1950)

Pity Me Not Because the Light of Day

Pity me not because the light of day
At close of day no longer walks the sky;
Pity me not for beauties passed away
From field and thicket as the year goes by;
5   Pity me not the waning of the moon,
Nor that the ebbing tide goes out to sea,
Nor that a man's desire is hushed so soon,
And you no longer look with love on me.
This have I known always: Love is no more
10   Than the wide blossom on which the wind assails,
Than the great tide that treads the shifting shore,
Strewing fresh wreckage gathered in the gales:
Pity me that the heart is slow to learn
What the swift mind beholds at every turn.

Questions

1. What is the relationship between the first two quatrains and the third? Is the internal structure more typical of the Shakespearean or the Italian sonnet?
2. What is the relationship between the quatrains and the couplet?
3. Does the couplet give the poem a sense of completion? Does anything more need to be said?
4. What is the difference between Shakespeare's attitude toward old age and Millay's attitude?
5. How would you describe the tone of the speaker in the sonnets of Shakespeare and Millay?

Although poets traditionally have used the sonnet as a love poem, they have also found it appropriate for theological meditation and political denunciation. Indeed, the brevity of the form makes it particularly useful for passionate cries of any kind. In 1919 Claude McKay, a Jamaican who had settled in Harlem, wrote "If We Must Die" in response to riots and the suppression of black intellectuals after World War I.

CLAUDE McKAY (1890–1948)

If We Must Die

If we must die, let it not be like hogs
Hunted and penned in an inglorious spot,
While round us bark the mad and hungry dogs,
Making their mock at our accursed lot.
5   If we must die, O let us nobly die,

So that our precious blood may not be shed
In vain; then even the monsters we defy
Shall be constrained to honor us though dead!
O kinsmen! we must meet the common foe!
10   Though far outnumbered let us show us brave,
And for their thousand blows deal one deathblow!
What though before us lies the open grave?
Like men we'll face the murderous, cowardly pack,
Pressed to the wall, dying, but fighting back!

Questions

1. Vocabulary: *constrained* (8).
2. What kind of sonnet is "If We Must Die"? Has McKay retained the internal structure of the sonnet?
3. Is McKay's poem optimistic? Does he believe his people will prevail?
4. Winston Churchill used this poem to rally the British against Nazi Germany in World War II. Can you identify any quality in this poem that would make it a powerful rallying cry?

Like most popular forms, the sonnet has been adapted to the uses of many writers. Shakespeare, Sidney, and Spenser collected them into sonnet series or sequences. One of the great masterpieces of Russian literature, *Eugene Onegin* by Alexander Pushkin, is a verse novel in sonnets. George Meredith, in his sonnet series *Modern Love*, employed a sixteen-line sonnet of his own creation. Although longer than the traditional sonnet, it deserves the name because it deals with the same material and has the same economy and force.

GEORGE MEREDITH (1828–1909)

In Our Old Shipwrecked Days There Was an Hour

In our old shipwrecked days there was an hour,
When in the firelight steadily aglow,
Joined slackly, we beheld the red chasm grow
Among the clicking coals. Our library-bower
5   That eve was left to us: and hushed we sat
As lovers to whom Time is whispering.
From sudden-opened doors we heard them sing:
The nodding elders mixed good wine with chat.
Well knew we that Life's greatest treasure lay
10   With us, and of it was our talk. "Ah, yes!
Love dies!" I said: I never thought it less.
She yearned to me that sentence to unsay.
Then when the fire domed blackening, I found
Her cheek was salt against my kiss, and swift

15   Up the sharp scale of sobs her breast did lift:—
      Now am I haunted by that taste! that sound!

Questions

1. Vocabulary: *chasm* (3), *bower* (4).
2. Do you see any similarity between the rhyme scheme of Meredith's poem and the traditional sonnet?
3. Where does the scene take place? Is the setting significant?
4. What is the significance of the burning coal?
5. What is the speaker's attitude toward the incident? Toward his life?

Exercise

Many literary forms have their own traditions—a history, manner, and identity developed over a period of time. A tradition develops in part when writers try to determine how to use a form by looking back at those poets who have used it in the past. One of the longest traditions is the sonnet tradition. The sonnets of Edna St. Vincent Millay look back toward the sonnets of Shakespeare and Spenser. Dante Gabriel Rossetti, who wrote sonnets of his own, also translated the sonnets of the Italian Renaissance, one of which, Cecco Angiolieri's "In Absence from Becchina," is reprinted on pages 560–61. There are many sonnets or sonnetlike poems in this book.

The following is a list of sonnets other than the ones printed in this chapter. Read these sonnets and try to formulate for yourself what sort of tradition these poems create. Then read the sonnetlike poems, and try to determine what they have borrowed from the tradition and how they have deviated from it. Remember, however, that traditions are not laws; traditions change and develop, and each writer contributes to the tradition by affirming, altering, or adding to it.

Sonnets

Cecco Angiolieri, "In Absence from Becchina," p. 560
Elizabeth Barrett Browning, "How Do I Love Thee," p. 724
Samuel Taylor Coleridge, "Pity," p. 574
John Donne, "Death Be Not Proud," p. 711
John Donne, "I Am a Little World Made Cunningly," p. 710
Robert Frost, "The Silken Tent," p. 740
Paul Goodman, "To My Only World," p. 558
Henry Howard, Earl of Surrey, "The Soote Season," p. 504
John Keats, "When I Have Fears," p. 720
John Milton, "When I Consider How My Light Is Spent," p. 468
Wilfred Owen, "Anthem for Doomed Youth," p. 742
Christina Rossetti, "After Death," p. 731
William Shakespeare, "Let Me Not to the Marriage of True Minds," p. 535
William Shakespeare, "My Mistress' Eyes Are Nothing Like the Sun," p. 677
William Shakespeare, "Shall I Compare Thee to a Summer's Day," p. 528
William Shakespeare, "When in Disgrace with Fortune and Men's Eyes," p. 456
William Shakespeare, "When Most I Wink, Then Do Mine Eyes Best See," p. 570

Terza Rima

Although Italy's most successful export to English poetry has been the sonnet, that country has contributed other verse forms as well. One of the most attractive and demanding is the *terza rima*, the verse form Dante used in *The Divine Comedy*. Terza rima is made up of three-line stanzas or *tercets* interlocked by rhymes so that the inner rhyme of one tercet becomes the outer rhyme of the subsequent tercet. In schematic terms, terza rima is rhymed *aba bcb cdc.* . . . Because terza rima requires triple rhymes for each ending, most English practitioners use occasional near rhymes and assonance instead of true rhymes. One aspect that draws poets to terza rima is the possibility of an unbroken chain of language. A poem in terza rima can continue indefinitely, without being forced to a close by the rhyme scheme.

Perhaps the most famous example of terza rima in English is Percy Bysshe Shelley's "Ode to the West Wind." Shelley, however, chose to break the terza rima periodically with a couplet. The result is five fourteen-line sections that resemble sonnets. In a sense, Shelley's ode is a combination of terza rima and sonnet sequence.

PERCY BYSSHE SHELLEY (1792–1822)

• Ode to the West Wind

I

O wild West Wind, thou breath of Autumn's being,
Thou, from whose unseen presence the leaves dead
Are driven, like ghosts from an enchanter fleeing,

Yellow, and black, and pale, and hectic red,
5   Pestilence-stricken multitudes: O Thou,
Who chariotest to their dark wintry bed

The winged seeds, where they lie cold and low,
Each like a corpse within its grave, until
Thine azure sister of the Spring shall blow

10   Her clarion o'er the dreaming earth, and fill
      (Driving sweet buds like flocks to feed in air)
      With living hues and odours plain and hill:

      Wild Spirit, which art moving everyhere;
      Destroyer and Preserver; hear, O hear!

                              II
15   Thou on whose stream, 'mid the steep sky's commotion,
      Loose clouds like Earth's decaying leaves are shed,
      Shook from the tangled boughs of Heaven and Ocean,

      Angels of rain and lightning: there are spread
      On the blue surface of thine aery surge,
20   Like the bright hair uplifted from the head

      Of some fierce Mænad,[10] even from the dim verge
      Of the horizon to the zenith's height,
      The locks of the approaching storm. Thou Dirge

      Of the dying year, to which this closing night
25   Will be the dome of a vast sepulchre,
      Vaulted with all thy congregated might

      Of vapours, from whose solid atmosphere
      Black rain and fire and hail will burst: O hear!

                              III
      Thou who didst waken from his summer dreams
30   The blue Mediterranean, where he lay,
      Lulled by the coil of his chrystalline streams,

      Beside a pumice isle in Baiæ's bay,[11]
      And saw in sleep old palaces and towers
      Quivering within the wave's intenser day,

35   All overgrown with azure moss and flowers
      So sweet, the sense faints picturing them! Thou
      For whose path the Atlantic's level powers

      Cleave themselves into chasms, while far below
      The sea-blooms and the oozy woods which wear
40   The sapless foliage of the ocean, know

      Thy voice, and suddenly grow grey with fear,
      And tremble and despoil themselves: O hear!

                              IV
      If I were a dead leaf thou mightest bear;
      If I were a swift cloud to fly with thee;
45   A wave to pant beneath thy power, and share

---

[10] A nymph attendant on the god Dionysus.
[11] A bay in Naples around which kings built castles.

The impulse of thy strength, only less free
Than thou, O Uncontrollable! If even
I were as in my boyhood, and could be

The comrade of thy wanderings over Heaven,
50   As then, when to outstrip thy skiey speed
Scarce seemed a vision; I would ne'er have striven

As thus with thee in prayer in my sore need.
Oh! lift me as a wave, a leaf, a cloud!
I fall upon the thorns of life! I bleed!

55   A heavy weight of hours has chained and bowed
One too like thee: tameless, and swift, and proud.

V

Make me thy lyre,[12] even as the forest is:
What if my leaves are falling like its own!
The tumult of thy mighty harmonies

60   Will take from both a deep, autumnal tone,
Sweet though in sadness. Be thou, Spirit fierce,
My spirit! Be thou me, impetuous one!

Drive my dead thoughts over the universe
Like withered leaves to quicken a new birth!
65   And, by the incantation of this verse,

Scatter, as from an unextinguished hearth
Ashes and sparks, my words among mankind!
Be through my lips to unawakened Earth

The trumpet of a prophecy! O Wind,
70   If Winter comes, can Spring be far behind?

Questions

1. Vocabulary: *pestilence* (5), *multitudes* (5), *azure* (9), *clarion* (10), *zenith* (23), *sepulchre* (26), *pumice* (34), *chasms* (40), *harmonies* (63).
2. How does stanza 4 unify the three stanzas that precede it?
3. Why does Shelley want to be lifted by the wind? How does he feel about his adult experiences?
4. What does Shelley wish the wind to do to him in stanza 5?
5. In what sense is the poem optimistic? How does the concluding line recollect the opening one?
6. Does this poem have unity? Does it stand as a whole?

French Forms

Perhaps the greatest inventors of forms were the *troubadour* poets of southern France, who lived between the eleventh and thirteenth centuries. A troubadour

---

[12] The Aeolian harp, or wind harp.

could be a king—Richard the Lion-hearted was one—or a traveling adventurer. Usually the poets attached themselves to a court or noble family who acted as patrons of their art. The troubadours delighted in elaborate poetic forms and the skillful employment of complicated word games. Occasionally they were accompanied by an apprentice, called a *jongleur*, who might set their poems to music.

Villanelle

A form that has attracted much more attention in English is the *villanelle*, which contains five tercets and a concluding quatrain. What makes the villanelle special is that the first and third lines become the closing refrain of alternate tercets and reappear as the concluding two lines of the poem. Thus the form has remarkable unity of structure. The echoing and reechoing of the refrains give the villanelle a plaintive, delicate beauty that some poets find irresistible.

However, the villanelle is not without its difficulties. Since it has only two rhyme endings, the poem can easily become monotonous. The risk of monotony is increased by the incessant appearance of the refrains that constitute eight of the poem's nineteen lines—nearly half of the poem. The skilled author of the villanelle, thus, is careful to achieve the maximum tonal range and to fit the refrain lines as naturally as possible into the logic of the poem. Despite these difficulties, there are a number of excellent villanelles.

DYLAN THOMAS (1914–1953)

• Do Not Go Gentle into That Good Night

Do not go gentle into that good night,
Old age should burn and rave at close of day;
Rage, rage against the dying of the light.

5 Though wise men at their end know dark is right,
Because their words had forked no lightning they
Do not go gentle into that good night.

Good men, the last wave by, crying how bright
Their frail deeds might have danced in a green bay,
Rage, rage against the dying of the light.

10 Wild men who caught and sang the sun in flight,
And learn, too late, they grieved it on its way,
Do not go gentle into that good night.

Grave men, near death, who see with blinding sight
Blind eyes could blaze like meteors and be gay,
15 Rage, rage against the dying of the light.

And you, my father, there on the sad height,
Curse, bless, me now with your fierce tears, I pray.
Do not go gentle into that good night.
Rage, rage against the dying of the light.

Dylan Thomas
(Rollie McKenna)

Questions

1. How are the middle stanzas of the poem organized? Is the relationship between them and the rest of the poem clear?
2. How has Thomas sought rhythmic variety? How has he integrated the refrains into the flow of the poem?
3. In line 8, what does Thomas mean by saying the deeds "might have danced in a green bay"?
4. What does he mean by "sang the sun in flight" (line 10)?

THEODORE ROETHKE (1908–1963)

The Waking

I wake to sleep, and take my waking slow.
I feel my fate in what I cannot fear.
I learn by going where I have to go.

We think by feeling. What is there to know?
5   I hear my being dance from ear to ear.
I wake to sleep, and take my waking slow.

Of those so close beside me, which are you?
God bless the Ground! I shall walk softly there,
And learn by going where I have to go.

10   Light takes the Tree; but who can tell us how?
The lowly worm climbs up a winding stair;
I wake to sleep, and take my waking slow.

Great Nature has another thing to do
To you and me; so take the lively air,
15   And, lovely, learn by going where to go.

This shaking keeps me steady. I should know.
What falls away is always. And is near.
I wake to sleep, and take my waking slow.
I learn by going where I have to go.

Questions

1. How has Roethke sought rhythmic variety? How has he altered and integrated the refrains in order to unify the poem?
2. What is the relationship in this poem between the inevitability of the refrains and Roethke's sense of destiny?
3. What is the connection between the speaker and nature?
4. What is the relationship between the speaker and God?
5. What does Roethke mean by "I wake to sleep"?

Classic Forms

The French and the Italians did not exhaust the formal resources of poetry. Poets, restless for novelty, have sought elsewhere for means of shaping their feelings and expressions. Poets have borrowed forms from many countries and cultures.

The Ode

Because ancient Greece is the seat of Western culture, poets periodically return to it for poetic inspiration and guidance. Poets use Greek forms out of respect for the long Greek tradition and sometimes in the belief that these forms are unmatched vehicles of artistic perfection. Among the most popular forms is the ode. The word *ode* is used broadly in English to refer to any public expression of praise. However, there are three forms to which it more particularly refers: the *Pindaric*, the *Horatian*, and the *irregular* ode.

The oldest of these forms is the Pindaric or regular ode. Pindar lived in the fifth century B.C. and wrote odes celebrating athletic and political victories, often retelling myths in the process. The short ode that follows celebrates the victory of Hagesidamos, son of Archestratos, a boy from western Lokroi who won the laurel in boxing in 476 B.C.

PINDAR (5th century B.C.)

Olympian 11

Turn   Sometimes men need the winds most,
                    at other times
                        waters from the sky,
                            rainy descendants of the cloud.

5   And when a man has triumphed
       and put his toil behind,
         it is time for melodius song
       to arise, laying
                      the foundation of future glory,
10   a sworn pledge securing proud success.

Counterturn   For Olympian victors, such acclaim
                  is laid in store
                    without limit, and I
                      am eager to tend it with my song.
15   For a man flourishes
                 in wise understanding,
               as in all things,
       through a god's favor.
                              Know now, son of Archestratos,
20   Hagesidamos, because of your boxing victory

Stand   I will sing, and my song will be
             an added adornment
             to your gold olive crown,
             shining with love for Western Lokroi.
25   Go there
             and join the revels, Muses.
                              By my bond,
             you will not find a people indifferent to strangers
             or blind to beauty, but men of keenest discernment
30   and courage in war.
                      For the crimson fox
       and thunderous lion cannot change their inborn ways.

                    Translation by Frank J. Nisetich (1942–)

Questions

1. What is the purpose of poetry, according to Pindar?
2. How does the celebration of Hagesidamos's victory become a celebration of western Lokroi?
3. Have the politics of the Olympics changed since Hagesidamos's time?
4. Compare this poem to Housman's "To an Athlete Dying Young" in Chapter 4. What is the relationship between both athletes and their birthplaces?

As you can see, the Pindaric ode is divided into three parts: turn (or *strophe*), counterturn (or *antistrophe*), and stand (or *epode*). Poets can shape the turn however they like. But once the poet has chosen a shape, all the turns and counterturns must share the same stanza form. The stand (or epode) is shaped differently from the turn. However, in longer odes that contain more than one stand, the stands are identically shaped. The Pindaric ode gives poets freedom initially but then holds them to their chosen stanza patterns.

The Latin poet Horace wrote poems that have also become known as odes. The Horatian or stanzaic ode does away with the epode. Instead, the poet is free to create a stanza form that is repeated throughout the poem. The forms usually employ intricate rhyme and contain lines of varying length. Keats's "Ode to a Nightingale" is a Horatian ode.

JOHN KEATS (1795–1821)

Ode to a Nightingale

I

My heart aches, and a drowsy numbness pains
   My sense, as though of hemlock° I had drunk,   *a poison*
Or emptied some dull opiate to the drains
   One minute past, and Lethe-wards[13] had sunk:
5 'Tis not through envy of thy happy lot,
     But being too happy in thine happiness,—
       That thou, light-winged Dryad° of the trees,   *a tree spirit*
         In some melodious plot
   Of beechen green and shadows numberless,
10   Singest of summer in full-throated ease.

II

O, for a draught of vintage! that hath been
   Cool'd a long age in the deep-delved earth,
Tasting of Flora° and the country green,   *goddess of flowers*
   Dance, and Provençal song, and sunburnt mirth!
15 O for a beaker full of the warm South,
     Full of the true, the blushful Hippocrene,[14]
       With beaded bubbles winking at the brim,
        And purple-stained mouth;
That I might drink, and leave the world unseen,
20   And with thee fade away into the forest dim:

III

Fade far away, dissolve, and quite forget
   What thou among the leaves hast never known,
The weariness, the fever, and the fret
   Here, where men sit and hear each other groan;
25 Where palsy shakes a few, sad, last gray hairs,
     Where youth grows pale, and spectre-thin, and dies;
       Where but to think is to be full of sorrow
        And leaden-eyed despairs,
Where Beauty cannot keep her lustrous eyes,
30   Or new Love pine at them beyond to-morrow.

---

[13] Lethe is the river that separates the upper world and the underworld. Its waters bring forgetfulness.
[14] Hippocrene is a mythological spring whose waters inspired poetry.

IV

Away! away! for I will fly to thee,
    Not charioted by Bacchus° and his pards,°   *the god of wine   leopards*
But on the viewless wings of Poesy,
    Though the dull brain perplexes and retards:
35 Already with thee! tender is the night,
    And haply the Queen-Moon is on her throne,
        Cluster'd around by all her starry Fays;°   *fairies, elves*
        But here there is no light,
Save what from heaven is with the breezes blown
40   Through verdurous glooms and winding mossy ways.

V

I cannot see what flowers are at my feet,
    Nor what soft incense hangs upon the boughs,
But, in embalmed darkness, guess each sweet
    Wherewith the seasonable month endows
45 The grass, the thicket, and the fruit-tree wild;
    White hawthorn, and the pastoral eglantine;
        Fast fading violets cover'd up in leaves;
        And mid-May's eldest child,
The coming musk-rose, full of dewy wine,
50   The murmurous haunt of flies on summer eves.

VI

Darkling I listen; and, for many a time
    I have been half in love with easeful Death,
Call'd him soft names in many a mused rhyme,
    To take into the air my quiet breath;
55 Now more than ever seems it rich to die,
    To cease upon the midnight with no pain,
        While thou art pouring forth thy soul abroad
        In such an ecstasy!
Still wouldst thou sing, and I have ears in vain—
60   To thy high requiem become a sod.

VII

Thou wast not born for death, immortal Bird!
    No hungry generations tread thee down;
The voice I hear this passing night was heard
    In ancient days by emperor and clown:
65 Perhaps the self-same song that found a path
    Through the sad heart of Ruth,[15] when, sick for home,
        She stood in tears amid the alien corn;
        The same that oft-times hath
Charm'd magic casements, opening on the foam
70   Of perilous seas, in faery lands forlorn.

---

[15] In the Bible, Ruth was a Moabite who left her people to stay with her husband, Boaz, and her mother-in-law, Naomi.

VIII

Forlorn! the very word is like a bell
　　To toll me back from thee to my sole self!
Adieu! the fancy cannot cheat so well
　　As she is fam'd to do, deceiving elf.
75　Adieu! adieu! thy plaintive anthem fades
　　　Past the near meadows, over the still stream,
　　　　Up the hill-side; and now 'tis buried deep
　　　　　In the next valley-glades:
　　Was it a vision, or a waking dream?
80　　　Fled is that music:—Do I wake or sleep?

Questions

1. Vocabulary: *Dryad* (7), *spectre* (26), *verdurous* (40), *eglantine* (46), *requiem* (60), *plaintive* (75).
2. What is the stanza form of Keats's ode?
3. What does the nightingale represent for Keats?
4. Why does he wish to join the nightingale? How does he hope to join him?
5. What is Keats's attitude toward death?
6. Is there anything heroic about this poem?

Many poets no longer call their poems odes, not wishing to force comparison of their poems with those of Keats, Wordsworth, or Shelley. Nevertheless, their basic structure is that of a Horatian or stanzaic ode.

RICHARD WILBUR (1921–)

The Beautiful Changes

One wading a Fall meadow finds on all sides
The Queen Anne's Lace lying like lilies
On water; it glides
So from the walker, it turns
5　Dry grass to a lake, as the slightest shade of you
Valleys my mind in fabulous blue Lucernes.°　　　　　　　　*a Swiss lake*

The beautiful changes as a forest is changed
By a chameleon's tuning his skin to it;
As a mantis, arranged
10　On a green leaf, grows
Into it, makes the leaf leafier, and proves
Any greenness is deeper than anyone knows.

Your hands hold roses always in a way that says
They are not only yours; the beautiful changes
15　In such kind ways,
Wishing ever to sunder
Things and things' selves for a second finding, to lose
For a moment all that it touches back to wonder.

Questions

1. Vocabulary: *sunder* (16).
2. What is the stanza pattern of the poem? Is the shape of the poem appropriate to the subject?
3. To whom is the poem addressed? What is the speaker's attitude toward the listener?
4. Odes celebrate momentous occasions—being victorious at the Olympian Games or first hearing the song of a nightingale. Is a great achievement celebrated in this poem? In what way is the listener heroic?
5. How does the beautiful change?

Asian Forms

Asian forms have been popular with Western writers since the turn of the century. Poets have admired the economy and clarity of the *haiku* and the *tanka*, two closely related forms. Both the tanka and the haiku are organized by the numbers of syllables per line rather than by rhyme. A haiku is a three-line poem, the lines having five, seven, and five syllables, respectively. The tanka is longer; its first and third lines have five syllables, and the rest contain seven syllables— thirty-one syllables in all. However, since Asian languages are so different from English, poets writing in English have freely adapted the forms. Because each syllable in Chinese represents a word, some poets prefer to think of the poems as containing seventeen or thirty-one words. Few poets try to translate these forms by preserving the syllable count. In their native language the haiku and tanka have other rules. Each haiku must contain a seasonal reference. In Japanese, the caesuras must be placed in specific places in the line. See Chapter 6 for more on the haiku.

MATSUO BASHO (1644–1694)

Nine Haiku

The beginning of art—
The depths of the country
And a rice-planting song.

Ailing on my travels,
Yet my dream wandering
Over withered moors.

Spring:
A hill without a name
Veiled in morning mist.

The beginning of autumn:
Sea and emerald paddy
Both the same green.

Silent and still: then
Even sinking into the rocks,
The cicada's screech.

Soon it will die,
Yet no trace of this
In the cicada's screech.

The winds of autumn
Blow: yet still green
The chestnut husks.

You say one word
And lips are chilled
By autumn's wind.

A flash of lightning:
Into the gloom
Goes the heron's cry.

Translation by Geoffrey Bownas and Anthony Thwaite (1930–)

Questions

1. Vocabulary: *cicada* (fifth haiku).
2. Is there a seasonal reference in each haiku? Is the reference always obvious?
3. What emotions do the haiku generate? Are they merely objective?
4. With what does art begin, according to Basho? In what way do the poems exemplify his idea of art?

Lady Kasa lived in the eighth century, but little else is known about her. These tanka have been translated into four-line stanzas.

LADY KASA (8th century)

Six Tanka

Like the pearl of dew
On the grass in my garden
In the evening shadows,
I shall be no more.

Even the grains of sand
On a beach eight hundred days wide
Would not be more than my love,
Watchman of the island coast.

The breakers of the Ise Sea
Roar like thunder on the shore.

As fierce as they, as proud as they,
Is he who pounds my heart.

I dreamt of a great sword
Girded to my side.
What does it signify?
That I shall meet you?

The bell has rung, the sign
For all to go to sleep.
Yet thinking of my love
How can I ever sleep?

To love a man without return
Is to offer a prayer
To a devil's back
In a huge temple. [16]

Translation by Geoffrey Bownas and Anthony Thwaite (1930–)

Questions

1. In what way do these tanka trace the relationship between lovers? What is the "plot" of the story?
2. How does the brevity of these poems make them poignant?
3. What is the overall feeling of these tanka? How does each tanka contribute to the feeling?

The influence of Asian poetry can be observed even in poems that do not strictly obey the forms of either the haiku or the tanka. These poems have small, self-contained units; an emphasis on the direct presentation of sensory experience; and an understated tone.

WALLACE STEVENS (1879–1955)

Thirteen Ways of Looking at a Blackbird

I

Among twenty snowy mountains,
The only moving thing
Was the eye of the blackbird.

II

I was of three minds,
5 Like a tree
In which there are three blackbirds.

---

[16] Devils were depicted in the back of Japanese temples to warn people that it was pointless to be bad and greedy.

III

The blackbird whirled in the autumn winds.
It was a small part of the pantomime.

IV

A man and a woman
10   Are one.
A man and a woman and a blackbird
Are one.

V

I do not know which to prefer,
The beauty of inflections,
15   Or the beauty of innuendoes,
The blackbird whistling
Or just after.

VI

Icicles filled the long window
With barbaric glass.
20   The shadow of the blackbird
Crossed it, to and fro.
The mood
Traced in the shadow
An indecipherable cause.

VII

25   O thin men of Haddam,[17]
Why do you imagine golden birds?
Do you not see how the blackbird
Walks around the feet
Of the women about you?

VIII

30   I know noble accents
And lucid, inescapable rhythms;
But I know, too,
That the blackbird is involved
In what I know.

IX

35   When the blackbird flew out of sight,
It marked the edge
Of one of many circles.

X

At the sight of blackbirds
Flying in a green light,
40   Even the bawds of euphony
Would cry out sharply.

---

[17] Haddam is a town in Connecticut. According to Stevens, he chose this town because he liked the sound of its name.

XI

He rode over Connecticut
In a glass coach.
Once, a fear pierced him,
45   In that he mistook
The shadow of his equipage
For blackbirds.

XII

The river is moving.
The blackbird must be flying.

XIII

50   It was evening all afternoon.
It was snowing
And it was going to snow.
The blackbird sat
In the cedar-limbs.

Questions

1. Vocabulary: *inflections* (14), *innuendoes* (15), *bawds* (40), *euphony* (40), *equipage* (46).
2. Stevens wrote that he meant the poem to be a collection of "sensations" rather than "of epigrams or ideas." What various sensations do you get from the poem?
3. Seasonal references abound in the poem. How are they introduced? How do they function?
4. The poem reinforces what sorts of feelings toward blackbirds? Are they beautiful, common, sexy, ominous, deadly, delicate, wise?
5. In what ways are a "man and a woman and a blackbird/ . . . one"?
6. How is the first section related to the last?

Exercise

Take a common object (like a table) and use it as a focus of attention in a variety of circumstances and perspectives. Follow a tree, a swimming pool, a saltshaker through the course of a year or a day or even an hour.

Comic Forms

Comedy is rarely as freewheeling as it appears. In fact, of all types of expression, comedy is the most formulaic. The punch line must come at the very end, preceded by just the right number of interchanges. Poetry, because of its formal nature, is an excellent medium for comic expression. Poets have developed a number of forms exclusively suited to comedy.

Limericks

Limericks were popularized by Edward Lear (1812–1888) after Lear discovered this anonymous example:

> There was an old man of Tobago
> Who lived on rice, gruel, and sago
> Till, much to his bliss
> His physician said this
> To a leg, sir, of mutton you must go.

We can see several important components of the limerick in this example. The first line usually ends in a place or a proper name that has a comic sound, and there is often a dialogue involved. Here are two modern masters of the form.

OGDEN NASH (1902–1971)

Gervaise

> There was a young belle of old Natchez
> Whose garments were always in patchez.
> When comment arose
> On the state of her clothes,
> 5   She drawled, When Ah itchez, Ah scratchez!

Edouard

> A bugler named Dougal MacDougal
> Found ingenious ways to be frugal.
> He learned how to sneeze
> In various keys,
> 5   Thus saving the price of a bugle.

EDWARD GOREY (1925–)

There Was a Young Woman Named Plunnery

> There was a young woman named Plunnery
> Who rejoiced in the practice of gunnery,
>   Till one day unobservant,
>   She blew up a servant,
> 5   And was forced to retire to a nunnery.

Shaped Verses and Concrete Poetry
Shaped Verses

Poetry began as a purely oral mode of communication. But as soon as the first scribes began to copy down the poems they heard, poets became interested in the visual component of language. Poets usually write in lines; the line ending is a visual means of indicating rhythm, meaning, and form. It would be improper, therefore, to distinguish between texts that are visually oriented and those that are orally oriented. Once printed, all poems are visual to some degree. However, some poets make greater use of poetry's visual resources.

The simplest way to use the visual component of poetry is to arrange the lines or words in such a way that the poem looks like an object. There is a long tradition of such shaped verses. Perhaps the most famous in English is George Herbert's "Easter Wings."

GEORGE HERBERT (1593–1633)

Easter Wings[18]

Lord, who createdst man in wealth and store,
  Though foolishly he lost the same,
    Decaying   more   and   more
      Till   he   became
5   Most   poor.
        With   thee
      O   let   me   rise
    As   larks,   harmoniously,
  And   sing   this   day   thy   victories:
10 Then   shall   the   fall   further   the   flight   in   me.

My   tender   age   in   sorrow   did   begin:
  And still with sicknesses and shame
    Thou   didst   so   punish   sin,
      That   I   became
15   Most   thin.
        With   thee
      Let me combine,
    And feel this day thy victory;
  For, if I imp° my   wing   on   thine,   *graft*
20 Affliction   shall   advance   the   flight   in   me.

Questions

1. How does the rhyme of the poem reinforce its shape? Is the shape merely superimposed on the poem?
2. Does the shape of the poem refer only to the Easter wings of the title? Why else do the lines contract and then expand?
3. How does the poem exemplify the concept of the *felix culpa*—the "fortunate fall" from Eden?

---

[18] Early editions of Herbert's "Easter Wings" are printed with the lines vertical.

Shaped verses are capable of remarkable delicacy and clarity.

MAY SWENSON (1919–)

Unconscious Came a Beauty

Unconscious
came a beauty to my
wrist
and stopped my pencil,
merged its shadow profile with
my hand's ghost
on the page:
Red Spotted Purple or else Mourning
Cloak,
paired thin-as-paper wings, near black,
were edged on the seam side poppy orange,
as were its spots.

UNCONSCIOUS

CAME A BEAUTY

I sat arrested, for its soot-haired
body's worm
shone in the sun.
It bent its tongue long as
a leg
black on my skin
and clung without my
feeling,
while its tomb-stained
duplicate parts of
a window opened.
And then I
moved.

Questions

1. How does the poem reenact its subject?
2. How has Swenson made use of the title?
3. How does the shape of the poem enhance the music of the verse?
4. How does the poem end? How does its shape reinforce that sense of ending?

Shaped poems can become very intricate, especially as poets place restrictions on themselves. John Hollander's shaped verses are composed on a typewriter, and he uses the grid of the typewriter as an instrument of measure. In his shaped poems words are never broken, and he does not add extra spaces between words unless they are on the boundary of the picture.

JOHN HOLLANDER (1929–)

Swan and Shadow

```
                        Dusk
                    Above the
                water hang the
                        loud
                        flies
                        Here
                        O so
                        gray
                        then
                What            A pale signal will appear
                When          Soon before its shadow fades
                Where        Here in this pool of opened eye
                In us     No Upon us As at the very edges
                  of where we take shape in the dark air
                   this object bares its image awakening
                     ripples of recognition that will
                        brush darkness up into light
        even after this bird this hour both drift by atop the perfect sad instant now
                   already passing out of sight
                   toward yet-untroubled reflection
                  this image bears its object darkening
                  into memorial shades Scattered bits of
                Light       No of water Or something across
                water       Breaking up No Being regathered
                 Soon       Yet by then a swan will have
                 gone          Yes Out of mind into what
                vast
                pale
                hush
                of a
                place
                past
        sudden dark as
          if a swan
            sang
```

Questions

1. In what way does the shape of the poem reflect the concepts expressed in the poem?
2. Why does the poem begin by speaking of the flies?
3. Swans are supposed to sing before they die. Why is this reference appropriate to this poem? What other deaths occur in the poem?

A good test of a shaped verse is to write out the poem in the traditional way, lining up the lines along the left-hand margin. If the meaning is compromised or diminished, then the poem is strong. There should be an intimate connection between the shape and the content of the poem.

Concrete Poems

Modern poets have experimented with a more radical use of the visual properties of poetry. Shaped verses arrange lines of verse to form a picture; Herbert's poem even rhymes. Concrete poets, however, often will use only a few words. The placement of the letters gives the poem meaning.

MARY ELLEN SOLT (1920—)

Forsythia

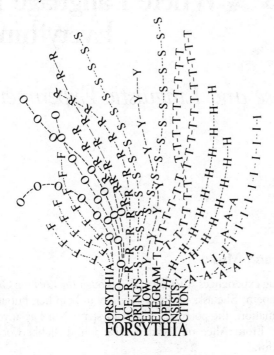

Questions

1. How does a forsythia "telegraph" spring's message?
2. In what ways is all poetry telegraphic? How is this poem telegraphic?
3. Why is spring's message "Hope insists [on] action"? Is this message appropriate for spring?

Suggestions for Essayists

1. Compare two poems in the same form. How have the poets used the form? Have they treated it differently or in the same way?
2. Some people argue that instead of creating social forms that best express our desires, we are shaped by social forms. For example, some educators believe that schools are not formed around students' needs, but rather that students are shaped by what schools demand. Choose some social event—a dance, a wedding, a lecture—and discuss whether you shape it or it shapes you.

Suggestions for Poets

1. Take an idea and try to write it in two different forms. Observe the changes that happen to the idea as it is given shape.
2. Invent a form of your own and write three poems in it. Do you find that the possibilities of the form are exhausted?

13 ❧ Where Language Is Everything

Nonsense and Linguistic Experiment

Poems of Nonsense and Music

Among the many puzzling experiences Alice faces in *Through the Looking Glass* is an incomprehensible poem. She asks Humpty-Dumpty to help her; but alas, despite his lengthy explanation, the poem remains a mystery. Nor has anyone else been of great help. From Alice on, readers have found "Jabberwocky" confounding and delightful.

LEWIS CARROLL (1832–1898)

Jabberwocky

'Twas brillig and the slithy toves
    Did gyre and gimble in the wabe;
All mimsy were the borogroves,
    And the mome raths outgrabe.

5   "Beware the Jabberwock, my son!
    The jaws that bite, the claws that catch!
Beware the Jubjub bird, and shun
    The frumious Bandersnatch!"

He took his vorpal sword in hand:
10   Long time the manxome foe he sought—
So rested he by the Tumtum tree.
    And stood awhile in thought.

And as in uffish thought he stood,
    The Jabberwock, with eyes of flame,
15   Came whiffling through the tulgey wood,
    And burbled as it came!

One, two! One, two! And through and through
     The vorpal blade went snicker-snack!
He left it dead, and with its head
20   He went galumphing back.

"And hast thou slain the Jabberwock?
     Come to my arms, my beamish boy!
O frabjous day! Callooh! Callay!"
     He chortled in his joy.

25   'Twas brillig and the slithy toves
     Did gyre and gimble in the wabe;
All mimsy were the borogroves,
     And the mome raths outgrabe.

We can make out the outlines of the poem easily enough. A father warns his son about a beast called the Jabberwock. To his father's surprise, the son slays the beast. But little of our enjoyment of the poem is derived from this commonplace story. In Carroll's *Through the Looking Glass*, Humpty Dumpty tries to explain the meaning of the poem to Alice:

> "Well, 'slithy' means 'lithe and slimy.' 'Lithe' is the same as 'active.' You see it's like a portmanteau—there are two meanings packed up into one word."
> "I see it now," Alice remarked thoughtfully: "and what are 'toves'?"
> "Well, 'toves' are something like badgers—they're something like lizards—and they're something like corkscrews."
> "They must be very curious creatures."
> "They are that," said Humpty Dumpty: "also they make their nests under sundials—also they live on cheese."
> "And what's to 'gyre' and to 'gimble'?"
> "To 'gyre' is to go round and round like a gyroscope. To 'gimble' is to make holes like a gimlet."

We remember this poem not for what we understand but for what remains delightfully incomprehensible. Many critics say that great poems are never fully understood, that the finest work continues to yield significance. Yet it is one thing to say that a poem is never fully understood and another thing to say it is never understood at all. "Jabberwocky" is one of a special class of poems that resist normal methods of comprehension.

To appreciate "Jabberwocky" and poems like it, we must see how they differ from most writing. A lecture, an advertisement, or a manual of instruction can use figurative language, sound, and rhythm just as poetry does (although in poetry these elements are more apparent). "Jabberwocky," however, has no message; there is no information or wisdom to be derived from it. It exists not as a vehicle to convey ideas, but as a well-crafted—and very amusing—object.

This absence of explicit meaning is not as odd as it may first appear. We do not ask the meaning of a sunset. We appreciate its beauty without question. We do not ask the meaning behind a finely crafted necklace, nor do we question the message behind a landscape painting or a symphony. We enjoy these pieces of art for the beauty, amusement, and excitement they provide, or for any number of other reasons. So, too, we can appreciate a poem even if it presents us with no apparent message.

But if a poem means little or nothing, what is there to enjoy in it? What can a poem do other than convey meaning? These are difficult questions, but if we go back to the origins of language, we may be able to find an answer.

Our first encounters with language are usually devoid of meaning. Children too young to walk will respond with delight to "Patty Cake." They will amuse themselves for hours by jabbering nonsense. As young children, we derive satisfaction from making peculiar sounds. We are pleased when our lips explode with *p*'s or *b*'s, or when our tongues roll with an *r* or an *l*. Later we have fun mastering tongue twisters, for speaking demands the muscular coordination found in many sports. Opera singers train their bodies for years to produce certain sounds that thrill us because they are so difficult to produce. Language, after all, is sound. The printed text, like the score of a musical composition, is a way of noting the sounds of words. Poets who ask us to forget the meaning of words often want us to attend to the sound qualities of language, to return to a childlike delight in its physical nature.

The following poem, "Susie Asado," was written by the American poet Gertrude Stein, who spent most of her life in Paris, where she was the friend of such famous artists and writers as Pablo Picasso, Henri Matisse, and Ernest Hemingway. Stein constantly experimented with the potentials of language. This poem portrays a flamenco dancer. Try to hear in the sound of the poem the insistent rhythms and foot tapping of that Spanish dance.

GERTRUDE STEIN (1874–1946)

Susie Asado

    Sweet sweet sweet sweet sweet tea.
      Susie Asado.
    Sweet sweet sweet sweet sweet tea.
      Susie Asado.
5   Susie Asado which is a told tray sure.
    A lean on the shoe this means slips slips hers.
    When the ancient light grey is clean it is yellow, it is a silver seller.
    This is a please this is a please there are the saids to jelly.
    These are the wets these say the sets to leave a crown to Incy.
10   Incy is short for incubus.
    A pot. A pot is a beginning of a rare bit of trees. Trees
tremble, the old vats are in bobbles, bobbles which shade and
shove and render clean, render clean must.
      Drink pups.
15   Drink pups drink pups lease a sash hold, see it shine and
a bobolink has pins. It shows a nail.
    What is a nail. A nail is unison.
    Sweet sweet sweet sweet sweet tea.

Gertrude Stein (right) with
companion Alice B. Toklas in
southeastern France, 1944.
(The Granger Collection)

Questions

1. Vocabulary: *incubus* (12), *bobolink* (18), *unison* (19).
2. In line 5, what is the noun in the phrase "a told tray sure"? Are there any other words whose part of speech is ambiguous or odd?
3. Do you see any sentences whose structure is clear but whose meaning is unfathomable?
4. Despite the lack of clear meaning, can you detect the speaker's attitude toward Susie Asado? Is this a poem of praise or denunciation? How can you tell?

"Susie Asado" may look like an easy poem to write, but it is the result, according to Stein, "of a strict discipline . . . the absolute refusal of never using a word that was never an exact word." It is much harder than it appears to break language away from meaning and to reveal its full musical properties. Stein employs a number of techniques to achieve these ends. She repeats words, avoids punctuation, uses common words as unusual parts of speech, and telescopes fragmented sentences together. Behind the childlike fun Stein's craft is evident.

"Bantams in Pine-Woods" is another portrait in sound, although Wallace Stevens permits meaning to surface. The title sets the scene: the speaker has encountered a flock of wild roosters in his walk.

WALLACE STEVENS (1879–1955)

Bantams in Pine-Woods

Chieftain Iffucan of Azcan in caftan
Of tan with henna hackles, halt!

Damned universal cock, as if the sun
Was blackamoor to bear your blazing tail.

5   Fat! Fat! Fat! Fat! I am the personal.
Your world is you. I am my world.

You ten-foot poet among inchlings. Fat!
Begone! An inchling bristles in these pines,

Bristles, and points their Appalachian tangs,
10   And fears not portly Azcan nor his hoos.

Questions

1. Vocabulary: *caftan* (1), *henna* (2), *blackamoor* (4).
2. With what techniques has the speaker captured the sound of the roosters?
3. What is the speaker's attitude toward the roosters? How has he conveyed this attitude?
4. "Iffucan" and "Azcan" seem to be words that telescope standard English phrases, "if you can" and "as [you] can." How do these telescoped phrases add to our understanding of the speaker's attitude toward the roosters?

Exercise

Do animals or machines ever make sounds that suggest standard words? Try to translate them. What is a train saying as it chugs along? Or a coffee percolator?

Magical Poems

Some poems are magic spells, curses, or magical invocations; they do not yield their meaning as traditional poems do. In many religions people are forbidden to use the name of God because the name has magic and dangerous powers. One of Adam's first acts in the Garden of Eden was to name all of creation. His names had magical properties, and poets still try to gain power over the world by giving their own private names to things. Here is a "magical" poem that tries to recreate the wonder of Adam's original language.

MICHAEL MOTT (1930–)

Adam Names the Animals

Ac
Bez
Cuf
Di

```
5     Eop
      Faw
      Ginzal
      Hut
      Ipoth
10    Ji
      Koz
      Letlak
      Mutal
      Nepsa
15    O
      Petzut
      Quegor Upta
      Rabu
      Samsa
20    Tuton Obi
      Ul
      Vetzma
      Wyst
      Xtor Aa
25    Yu
      Zept
```

Shakespeare is not averse to casting spells. The following is a short chorus from *Macbeth*, Act I, Scene 3, spoken by the three witches.

WILLIAM SHAKESPEARE (1564–1616)

From Macbeth

The Weird Sisters, hand in hand
Posters° of the sea and land,   *swift travelers*
Thus do go about, about;
Thrice to thine, and thrice to mine
5   and thrice again, to make up nine.
Peace! The charm's wound up.

The following poem is the ritual chant for the sick sung by the Omaha Indians. It calls on the Aged One to help those who have been obedient.

Ritual Chant for the Sick

He! Aged One, eçka
Thou Rock, eçka
Aged One, eçka
He! I have taught these little ones
5   They obey, eçka
Aged One, eçka

He!

He! Unmoved from time without end, verily

Thou sittest, eçka

10   In the midst of the various paths of the coming winds

In the midst of the winds thou sittest, eçka

Aged One, eçka

He! The small grasses grow about thee, eçka

Thou sittest as though making of them thy dwelling place, eçka

15   He! Verily thou sittest covered with the droppings of birds, eçka

Thy head decked with the downy feathers of the birds, eçka

Aged One, eçka

Thou who standest next in power, eçka

He! thou water, eçka

20   Water that hast been flowing

From time unknown, eçka

He! Of you the little ones have taken

Though thy mysteries remain unrevealed

These little ones crave thy touch, eçka

25   He! Thou that standest as one dwelling place, eçka

Even as one dwelling place, eçka

Ye great animals, eçka

He! Who make for us the covering, eçka

These little ones, thou hast said, let their thoughts reverently dwell on me, eçka

30   He! Thou tent frame, eçka

Thou standest with bent back o'er us

With stooping shoulders, bending over us

Verily, thou standest

Thus my little ones shall speak of me, thou hast said

35   Brushing back the hair from thy forehead, eçka

The hair of thy head

The grass that grows about thee

Thy hairs are whitened, eçka

The hairs that grow upon thy head, eçka

40   O, the paths that the little ones shall take, eçka

Whichever way they may flee from danger, eçka

They shall escape. Their shoulders shall be bent with age as they walk

As they walk on the well-beaten path

Shading their brows now and again with their hands

45   As they walk in their old age, eçka

That of thy strength they shall partake, eçka

Therefore thy little ones desire to walk closely by thy side, eçka

Venerable One, eçka.

Translation by Alice Fletcher (1845–1923)

Questions

1. What is the relationship between the god who is being addressed and the grass? Is it a static relationship?

2. In what way is the god a "tent frame" or "bent . . . / With stooping shoulders"?
3. What arguments or inducements does the chanter use to convince the god to provide health?

The language of magic is special. It often contains invented words or words distorted or borrowed from other languages. According to Jerome Rothenberg, an American poet and critic, magic languages unite "the user . . . with the beings & things he's trying to influence or connect with for a sharing of power, participation in a life beyond his own."

Collage

Some poems also resist expected interpretation because they are collages of words, images, and ideas. *Collage* is a term derived from art and refers to a picture made up of pieces of found objects: scraps of newspaper, bits of old cane backing, a gum wrapper, lengths of string, tin cans. A collage can be made entirely of found objects, or it can be a combination of the objects and the artist's own drawing. Poets perform a similar act. But instead of gathering scraps of newspaper and string, they arrange scattered pieces of language: clichés, phrases they have heard, or quotations.

The following poem by E. E. Cummings is an amalgam of clichés drawn from political oratory.

E. E. CUMMINGS (1894–1962)

- **next to of course god america i**

"next to of course god america i
love you land of the pilgrims' and so forth oh
say can you see by the dawn's early my
country 'tis of centuries come and go
5   and are no more what of it we should worry
in every language even deafanddumb
thy sons acclaim your glorious name by gorry
by jingo by gee by gosh by gum
why talk of beauty what could be more beaut-
10   iful than these heroic happy dead
who rushed like lions to the roaring slaughter
they did not stop to think they died instead
then shall the voice of liberty be mute?"

He spoke. And drank rapidly a glass of water

Questions

1. Who is the "he" that is speaking? Where is he speaking? Why does he drink a glass of water?

2. What is Cummings's attitude toward the speaker?
3. How many scraps of songs can you find in the poem?
4. Why is line 8 included in the poem? What sort of collection of phrases is it?
5. Is the question in line 13 logically developed? What sort of question is it?

We probably are attuned to the collage of phrases and allusions in the Cummings poem because the phrases and allusions are familiar and because we understand what holds these bits of language together. But the organizing principle behind some collages is less apparent. For example, "Madam Mouse Trots" is one of a group of poems Dame Edith Sitwell collected under the title *Façade*. A facade is the front of a building, but it is also "a false, superficial or artificial appearance or effect." Sitwell is suggesting by her title that the language in the poems is a facade, just as oratorical language is a political facade.

Sitwell incorporates two quotations that open and close the poem. One she acknowledges clearly. The opening two lines are a free translation of the Verlaine poem she quotes as an epigraph. The last line is a misquotation of a Robert Browning poem that all English schoolchildren of Sitwell's generation had to memorize, as familiar to her audience as "The Star Spangled Banner" is to Americans. The French poem was written while Verlaine was in jail. Madam Mouse is the only free creature he sees in prison. The Browning poem concludes this way:

> The lark's on the wing,
> The snail's on the thorn;
> God's in his heaven—
> All's right with the world!
> —"*Pippa's Song*" *from* Pippa Passes

The poem was often viewed as the perfect expression of mindless optimism and satisfaction. At last, you are ready to read the poem.

EDITH SITWELL (1887–1964)

Madam Mouse Trots

"Dame Souris trotte gris dans le noir."
                    —*Verlaine*

Madam Mouse trots,
Gray in the black night!
Madam Mouse trots:
Furred is the light.
5   The elephant-trunks
Trumpet from the sea. . . .
Gray in the black night
The mouse trots free.
Hoarse as a dog's bark
10   The heavy leaves are furled. . . .
The cat's in his cradle,
All's well with the world!

Edith Sitwell *(Dennis Stock/ Magnum Photos Inc.)*

Questions

1. How has Sitwell arranged the poem? Do the two quotations agree in feeling with one another?
2. What is Sitwell's attitude toward the quotations? Does she believe that "All's well with the world"?
3. How does the title *Façade* inform the reader's attitude toward the language of the poems? In what way is language a facade? In what way is "Madam Mouse Trots" a facade?

With a poem that assembles and arranges specimens of language, the usual questions one asks about a poem are inapplicable. One cannot ask who is speaking, to whom, and for what reason, because there is typically no persona in a collage poem. However, in such poems, poets act as editors, and one may question their editorial principles:

1. How has the poet selected the material? What criteria were used?
2. How has the poet arranged the material?
3. What are the poet's feelings toward the material?

E. E. Cummings, for example, selected the most outworn phrases used in political speeches. He has arranged them in the usual order in which they appear in speeches. Thus, "next to of course god america i" is a political speech in miniature. Sitwell has chosen specimens of poetry that discuss serious questions in a naive, childlike way.

Poets have incorporated into their poems not only literary references, but parts of historical documents as well: letters, memos, and papers. In this portion of

"Middle Passage," Robert Hayden incorporates a parody of lines from Shake-speare, Protestant hymns, and pieces of diaries to make his poetic account of the slave trade.

ROBERT HAYDEN (1913–)

From Middle Passage

Jesús, Estrella, Esperanza, Mercy:[1]

    Sails flashing to the wind like weapons,
    sharks following the moans the fever and the dying;
    horror the corposant[2] and compass rose.

5   Middle Passage:
            voyage through death
                to life upon these shores.

    "10 April 1800—
    Blacks rebellious. Crew uneasy. Our linguist says
10   their moaning is a prayer for death,
    ours and their own. Some try to starve themselves.
    Lost three this morning leaped with crazy laughter
    to the waiting sharks, sang as they went under."

Desire, Adventure, Tartar, Ann:

15   Standing to America, bringing home
    black gold, black ivory, black seed.

        Deep in the festering hold thy father lies,
        of his bones New England pews are made,
        those are altar lights that were his eyes.[3]

20   Jesus Saviour Pilot Me
    Over Life's Tempestuous Sea

    We pray that Thou wilt grant, O Lord,
    safe passage to our vessels bringing
    heathen souls unto Thy chastening.

25   Jesus Saviour

    "8 bells. I cannot sleep, for I am sick
    with fear, but writing eases fear a little
    since still my eyes can see these words take shape
    upon the page & so I write, as one
30   would turn to exorcism. 4 days scudding,
    but now the sea is calm again. Misfortune

---

[1] *Jesús, Estrella, Esperanza,* and *Mercy* are names of slave ships.
[2] Corposant is the name for a glowing ball of electrical charge sometimes seen on church steeples or on the masts of ships. It is also called St Elmo's Fire.
[3] These lines parody Ariel's song from Act I of Shakespeare's *The Tempest*. Ariel, who is a slave, sings: "Full fathom five thy father lies;/Of his bones are coral made/Those are pearls that were his eyes."

follows in our wake like sharks (our grinning
tutelary gods). Which one of us
has killed an albatross?[4] A plague among
35   our blacks—Ophthalmia: blindness—& we
have jettisoned the blind to no avail.
It spreads, the terrifying sickness spreads.
Its claws have scratched sight from the Capt.'s eyes
& there is blindness in the fo'c'sle
40   & we must sail 3 weeks before we come
to port."

            What port awaits us, Davy Jones'
            or home? I've heard of slavers drifting, drifting,
            playthings of wind and storm and chance, their crews
            gone blind,the jungle hatred
45   *crawling up on deck.*

    Thou Who Walked On Galilee

    "Deponent further sayeth *The Bella J*
    left the Guinea Coast
    with cargo of five hundred blacks and odd
50   for the barracoons of Florida:

    "That there was hardly room 'tween-decks for half
    the sweltering cattle stowed spoon-fashion there;
    that some went mad of thirst and tore their flesh
    and sucked the blood:

55   "That Crew and Captain lusted with the comeliest
    of the savage girls kept naked in the cabins;
    that there was one they called the Guinea Rose
    and they cast lots and fought to lie with her:

    "That when the Bo's'n piped all hands, the flames
60   spreading from starboard already were beyond
    control, the negroes howling and their chains
    entangled with the flames:

    "That the burning blacks could not be reached,
    that the Crew abandoned ship,
65   leaving their shrieking negresses behind,
    that the Captain perished drunken with the wenches:

    "Further Deponent sayeth not."

    Pilot Oh Pilot Me

Questions

1. Why has Hayden limited the diaries to only the white sailors' point of view? Does
   the reader learn how the slaves felt?

---

[4] Sailors believed that killing an albatross brought bad luck. Coleridge's "Rime of the Ancient
Mariner" recounts the supernatural adventure of a sailor who dares to kill an albatross.

2. What points does Hayden make by parodying Ariel's song in lines 17–19?
3. What effect does the slave trade have on the Whites who are engaged in it?
4. Would this poem be more effective were it cast in Hayden's voice? Why has he constructed the poem out of pieces of diaries?

Collage poems can be very difficult to read because they force their readers to do a great deal of work. Readers must tie the pieces of the poem together, draw connections between the separate parts, and try to ascertain whether the parts progress in a particular direction and develop through the poem. Yet Hayden has not given up responsibility and control. He makes several comments about the action, and, selecting what he believes to be the most vivid examples of the slave ship experience, he arranges them in the most effective manner.

Conclusion

Some poems do not convey their meaning in a traditional manner. These poems use language that is especially charged. Some poets wish to emphasize the music and the magic of words more than their meaning. Others wish to arrange specimens of language. If readers take their time with these poems and concentrate on how the language has been arranged, they will derive much satisfaction from them and will not find them so incomprehensible. One need not feel the frustration of Alice in her journey through Wonderland.

Suggestions for Essayists

1. If you have been to a foreign country where you were unfamiliar with the language, how did you make yourself understood? Discuss the problems of foreign-speaking people visiting this country.
2. Make a collection of strange expressions such as "He went bananas" or "She has a monkey on her back." Discuss what they mean or how they came into use.

Suggestions for Poets

1. Invent a language of your own and write a poem using it.
2. Select the most beautiful words you know and combine them into musical phrases.
3. Select a topic. Construct a poem about it by weaving together lines taken from the poems in this book.

❧ Poems for Further Study

MARIANNE MOORE (1887–1972)

The Monkey Puzzle[5]

A kind of monkey or pine lemur
not of interest to the monkey,

---

[5] The poem may be read as a riddle. The monkey puzzle is the common name of the Chile pine (*Araucana Imbricata*), a strangely twisted tree.

in a kind of Flaubert's Carthage, it defies one—[6]
this "Paduan cat with lizard," this "tiger in a bamboo thicket."
5   "An interwoven somewhat," it will not come out.
Ignore the Foo dog and it is forthwith more than a dog,
its tail superimposed upon itself in a complacent half spiral,
this pine tree—this pine tiger, is a tiger, not a dog.
It knows that if a nomad may have dignity,
10   Gibraltar has had more—
that "it is better to be lonely than unhappy."
A conifer contrived in imitation of the glyptic work of jade and hard-stone cutters,
a true curio in this bypath of curio-collecting,
it is worth its weight in gold, but no one takes it
15   from these woods in which society's not knowing is colossal,
the lion's ferocious chrysanthemum head seeming kind by comparison.
This porcupine-quilled, complicated starkness—
this is beauty—"a certain proportion in the skeleton which gives the best results."[7]
One is at a loss, however, to know why it should be here,
20   in this morose part of the earth—
to account for its origin at all;
but we prove, we do not explain our birth.

JOHN BERRYMAN (1914–1972)

Young Woman's Song

The round and smooth, my body in my bath,
If someone else would like it too.—I did,
I wanted T. to think "How interesting"
Although I hate his voice and face, hate both.
5   I hate this something like a bobbing cork
Not going. I want something to hang to.—

A fierce wind roaring high up in the bare
Branches of trees,—I suppose it was lust
But it was holy and awful. All day I thought
10   I am a bobbing cork, irresponsible child
Loose on the waters.—What have you done at last?
A little work, a little vague chat.

I want that £3.10 hat terribly.—
What I am looking for (*I am*) may be
15   Happening in the gaps of what I know.
The full moon does go with you as yóu go.
Where am I going? I am not afraid . .
Only I would be lifted lost in the flood.

---

[6] Gustave Flaubert (1821–1880) was a French novelist.
[7] From Lafcadio Hearn, *Talks to Writers* (1920).

JAMES SCHUYLER (1923–)

An Almanac

Shops take down their awnings;
women go south;
few street lamp leaners;
children run with leaves running at their backs.
5 In cedar chests sheers and seersuckers displace flannels and wools.

Sere leaves of the Scotch marigolds;
crystals of earth melt;
the thorn apple shows its thorns;
a dog tracks the kitchen porch;
10 wino-hobos attempt surrender to warm asylums.

Caged mink claw;
gulls become pigeons;
snow bends the snow fence.
Heavy food;
15 rumbling snowplows.

Seats in the examination hall are staggered.
The stars gleam like ice;
a fragment of bone;
in the woods matted leaves;
20 a yellowish shoot.
A lost key is found;
storm windows are stacked on the beams of the garage.

CHARLES SIMIC (1938–)

The Place

They were talking about the war
The table still uncleared in front of them.
Across the way, the first window
Of the evening was already lit.
5 He sat, hunched over, quiet,
The old fear coming over him . . .
It grew darker. She got up to take the plate—
Now unpleasantly white—to the kitchen.
Outside in the fields, in the woods
10 A bird spoke in proverbs,
A Pope went out to meet Attila,
The ditch was ready for its squad.

DAVID SHAPIRO (1947–)

I Haven't

Do you have a lion in your house?
Do you have a serpent in your house?
No fortunately I do not have a lion in my house.

Do you have a woman leaning slightly past the spirals in your house?
5   No I do not have the edge of her dress in my house.
Do you have a lion in your house?

No I do not have the outline of her body in my house.
Do you have a trouvaille° in your house?   *a lucky find*
No fortunately I do not have a lion in my house.

10   Do you have the goddess Hygeia° headless as a house?   *goddess of health*
No I do not have her right hand casting a shadow on my house.
Do you have a lion in your house?

No I do not have her light peplos° folds full of life in   *a Grecian garment*
    my house.
Do you have "truth is the consequences" in your house?
15   No fortunately I do not have a lion in my house.

What do you have in your high heavy house?
Do you have a rendering of her brilliant pitiless hair falling on your house?
Do you have a lion in your house?
No fortunately I do not have a lion in my house.

JUDITH JOHNSON SHERWIN (1936–)

Dr. Potatohead Talks to Mothers

when you put on the feet be sure
the claws are attached long
three-toed   when we landed
           on the wetgreen planet in libra
5   the *three-toed* chef broke out
           a gourmet spread frogs' legs
           that had made the hop frozen
           from baltimore / mushrooms
           champagne /
10   *when you put on*
the hands   that same day
the thumbs should not necessarily
oppose   the dominant life forms
           great big black buck mushrooms
15   undulated their velvet
           blackribbed mouths flowed open
           closed on us sucked our juices
           and the monster frogs big as tanks
           ripped off our navigator's
20   legs sautéed them in melted
           rumpfat /
                when you put on
the arms push in the pegs
deep so they can't be ripped
25   *off*   in alpha centauri[8] minced

---

[8] The nearest star to our sun.

frozen to fatten their giant
cats god we fought them
napalm and h-bomb blasted nine
planets and all the influences
30   out of the starry night
shivered

when you put on

the head when you put on
the head be very sure
35   *the hat doesn't cover*   more
of them came when we landed we
landed half the universe

the hat should cover

the hair shelter the brain
40   *from being baked powdered the ears*
frozen   we signed
treaties /   what
to eat

but the eyes
45   *uncovered*

potatoes we died
of boredom last week   *but the eyes*
left open to spot what

we landed on x-37
50   in gemini[9] giant potatos rolled
out riding fantastic tractors
of an unmeltable alloy
peeled off   *but the eyes*
bare, freezing, spied out

55   our jackets
of skin dropped us flayed
and the teeth should be firmly planted
in hot water and boiled
yesterday when the dust
60   had settled we signed the treaty
we looked for something legal
to eat

and the teeth

there the mouth
65   *open*

       •

---

[9] The thirty-seventh planet of the star *x* in the constellation Gemini.

14 ❧ The Well-Made Poem

Judging a work of art is difficult and often frustrating. Many people avoid the practice or argue that it is useless. "Since beauty is in the eye of the beholder," they reason, "any object I find pleasing must be good." Others refuse to form any opinions at all: "Who am I to judge a work of art?" they modestly ask.

There are important reasons for developing a critical faculty, however. One of the chief aims of education is to help people recognize excellence so that they may cultivate what is excellent in themselves. Sloppy, fuzzy writing breeds sloppy, fuzzy thinking. Mawkish, sentimental literature breeds vague, undifferentiated feeling. Good literature puts us into better contact with our thoughts and feelings and helps us distinguish the genuine and appropriate from the false and ill-fitting.

Part of the problem in developing critical skills is that poems are a lot like people: one has difficulty recognizing the truly worthwhile. Placed among strangers, we often gravitate to whoever seems at first the friendliest, kindest person. Often our first impressions are wrong. Later we may discover that bright spot to be merely a flash; the person we thought so interesting, clever, and kind may really be dull, slow, and mean. At the same time we may discover that someone we overlooked, a quiet person who spoke softly and with few words, really has the qualities we seek in a lasting friend.

Literary judgments, like personal ones, are best made over a period of time. Clearly, people who have been reading poems for a while have an advantage over the beginner: they have had time to test their first impressions. Similarly, older poems of merit are more easily recognized than contemporary works because they have had time to show their power. The best way to become a seasoned critic is to start reading now and take the suggestions of your teachers.

One must also be careful not to confuse *taste* with *excellence*. For example, we may like animals and enjoy having pictures of animals around us. Our taste for animal pictures may cloud our appreciation of nonanimal pictures, or it may cause us to overpraise a badly executed animal drawing. Similarly, people have moral or religious beliefs that may color their appreciation of certain works. Experienced readers will be able to recognize excellence even in works they do not particularly like, just as we can recognize that an unpleasant person may be an excellent athlete.

Taste and excellence can be confused in another way. Imagine eating a meal of some exotic cuisine for the first time. You are served course after course of foods you do not recognize, whose names you cannot even pronounce. Nevertheless, you find the food delicious. Can you say the food was well prepared? Not with any authority. To make such a judgment, you would have to have eaten several different versions of each dish. All you can honestly say is that you liked what you ate. People who are beginning to read poetry should acknowledge what they like and explore the experiences that please them. But it will take time to develop the knowledge of what is truly well prepared. What seems innovative may in fact be well worn. What appears dull may actually be subtle. Works we like may not necessarily be those of lasting excellence.

Overall Effectiveness

How then does one evaluate a poem? The principal test is whether each part of the poem contributes to its overall effectiveness. A poem is like a superbly integrated organism whose every feature contributes to the health and success of the body as a whole. The limbs of such a creature are neither too large nor too small. It does not carry an ounce more or less of weight than it needs. It is able to respond appropriately to circumstances, and its every action is animated by liveliness and a keen sense of intelligence. The healthy organism knows how and when to enjoy itself but can be tough and efficient when necessary.

No poem, as no person, is ever perfect. Paul Valéry, the great French poet, remarked that a poem is never completed, only abandoned. Thus the responsible judge balances a work's strengths against its weaknesses. A poem can contain many faults and still be good. Another work may contain no glaring errors, yet seem generally lifeless and unsatisfactory. Critics often disagree not about a poem's faults, but about the impact of those faults on the work's overall effectiveness.

Although the components of a good poem are all interrelated, it is easier to evaluate poems by looking at their various aspects separately. These aspects or areas of judgment will overlap, but for now it is useful to consider them as isolated.

Economy

The best poetry is noted for its concentration of expression and feeling. Poets try to use as few words as possible to gain their end. Thus each word must bear its part of the load and serve as many functions as possible. Bad poetry is marked by (1) looseness of expression, (2) redundancy, and (3) padding for rhyme or meter. The following quatrain exhibits all three weaknesses.

The Frog

The frog he sits upon the bank
   And catches bugs and flies
And after he gets tired of that
   He just jumps in and dives.
              —James K. Elmore

The first line should read simply "The frog sits upon the bank." The superfluous "he" is added to pad the rhythm. Lines 2 and 4 contain redundant expressions. "Jumps in" and "dives" are synonymous, and flies are a kind of bug, not a different type of creature. Line 3 is wordy: "gets tired" means the same as "tires." "The Frog" suffers more than most poems from uneconomical language. Indeed, it is an example of the worst sort of poetry, *doggerel*. Doggerel is language that has rhyme and meter but contains neither feeling nor thought nor music.

   Here is a poem for your evaluation.

CLAUDE MacKAY (1814–1889)

Only a Thought

'Twas only a passing thought, my love,
   Only a passing thought,
That came o'er my mind like a ray of the sun
   In the ripples of waters caught;
5   And it seemed to me, and I say to thee,
   That sorrow and shame and sin
Might disappear from our happy sphere,
   If we knew but to begin;
If we knew but how to profit
10   By wisdom dearly bought:
'Twas only a passing thought, my love,
   Only a passing thought.

Questions

1. Is the "passing thought" original or clear enough to warrant the refrain of lines 1–2 and lines 11–12?
2. Is the "passing thought" buried in all the language used to introduce it?
3. Are there any redundant expressions in the poem? Does a thought pass anywhere but "o'er my mind"?
4. Do you find any padding in the poem? Is line 5 necessary to the poem?
5. Is it clear what we are to "begin" in line 8?
6. How would you evaluate this poem?

Coherence and Consistency

Another test of a poem is whether it is consistent. Careless poets make one statement at the outset and contradict themselves later on. More often, poets may express incompatible attitudes, seeming to approve and disapprove of the same object or person.

But before we accuse a poet of being contradictory, we must be careful. Often, a poet is tracing the evolution of feelings. Matthew Arnold's "Dover Beach," for instance, begins with a quiet, beautiful description of the English Channel but ends with the recognition that the world "Hath really neither joy, nor love, nor light, / Nor certitude, nor peace." The inconsistency is not a poetic fault; rather, it is the most direct and effective means of showing Arnold's evolving realizations. (For a longer discussion of "Dover Beach," see Chapter 6.) The contradictions in the following poem, however, cannot be justified in the same manner.

CHARLES KINGSLEY (1819–1875)

I Once Had a Sweet Little Doll, Dears

I once had a sweet little doll, dears,
    The prettiest doll in the world;
Her cheeks were so red and so white, dears,
    And her hair was so charmingly curled.
5   But I lost my poor little doll, dears,
    As I played in the heath one day;
And I cried for her more than a week, dears,
    But I never could find where she lay.

I found my poor little doll, dears,
10   As I played in the heath one day.
Folks say she is terribly changed, dears,
    For her paint is all washed away,
And her arm trodden off by the cows, dears,
    And her hair not the least bit curled:
15   Yet for old sakes' sake she is still, dears,
    The prettiest doll in the world.

Questions

1. Vocabulary: *heath* (10), *trodden* (13).
2. Is there any redundancy?
3. Are the repeated lines effective in creating unity, or are they merely repetitious?
4. Do you find that the "dears" that end alternate lines are well integrated in the poem? Do they add to the poem's overall effectiveness?
5. Do you believe that the doll is the prettiest one in the world?

This poem contains one glaring contradiction. In line 8 the speaker claims she *never* could find the doll; line 9 says that she found it. Are we to believe that the two stanzas are divided by time? If so, there is nothing to indicate that stanza 1 was written while the doll was still lost and stanza 2 after its recovery. This contradiction may not be enough to spoil this poem, but it is certainly a blemish.

A more difficult aesthetic problem than consistency is *coherence*. Because poetry is so condensed, often a poem will remain unclear after a first, second, or even third reading. Moreover, as discussed in Chapter 13, some poems are intentionally nonsensical or are organized as verbal collages. These poems do not yield their meanings in a conventional way. Third, there are poems whose worlds are drawn from dreams and fantasies. Things occur in them that could not happen in the normal world. Wise readers do not blame a poem for not doing what it never intended to do or for lacking what it never was meant to possess; they do not have rigid expectations of what a poem ought to be. Poems do not need to rhyme, but there are still people who consider a poem defective that doesn't. Conversely, there are those who regard with suspicion a poem that *does* rhyme. A good reader must decide whether a work is coherent within its own rules of composition.

Erasmus Darwin, the author of "Eliza," was a physician, inventor, and poet, and the grandfather of Charles Darwin, whose theory of evolution so revolutionized scientific thinking. "Eliza" is no fantasy; it is meant to be a somewhat romanticized and stylized account of an actual woman killed while impatiently watching for her husband's safety in battle. It should be noted that in the eighteenth century wives would follow their husbands to campsites close to the battlefields.

ERASMUS DARWIN (1731–1802)

Eliza

Now stood Eliza on the wood-crown'd height
O'er Minden's plains spectatress of the fight;
Sought with bold eye amid the bloody strife
Her dearer self, the partner of her life;
5   From hill to hill the rushing host pursued,
And view'd his banner, or believed she view'd.
Pleased with the distant roar, with quicker tread,
Fast by his hand one lisping boy she led;
And one fair girl, amid the loud alarm,
10 Slept on her kerchief, cradled on her arm:
While round her brows bright beams of honour dart,
And love's warm eddies circle round her heart.
—Near and more near th'intrepid beauty press'd,
Saw through the driving smoke his dancing crest,
15 Heard the exulting shout—"They run!—they run!"
"He's safe!" she cried, "he's safe! the battle's won!"
—A ball now hisses through the airy tides
(Some Fury wings it, and some Demon guides),
Parts the fine locks her graceful head that deck,

20   Wounds her fair ear, and sinks into her neck;
      The red stream issuing from her azure veins
      Dyes her white veil, her ivory bosom stains.
      —"Ah me!" she cried, and sinking on the ground,
      Kiss'd her dear babes, regardless of the wound:
25   "Oh, cease not yet to beat, thou vital urn,
      Wait, gushing life, oh! wait my love's return!"—
      Hoarse barks the wolf, the vulture screams from far,
      The angel, Pity, shuns the walks of war;—
      "Oh spare, ye war-hounds, spare their tender age!
30   On me, on me," she cried, "exhaust your rage!"
      Then with weak arms, her weeping babes caress'd,
      And sighing, hid them in her blood-stain'd vest.

      From tent to tent th'impatient warrior flies,
      Fear in his heart, and frenzy in his eyes:
35   Eliza's name along the camp he calls,
      Eliza echoes through the canvas walls;
      Quick through the murmuring gloom his footsteps tread,
      O'er groaning heaps, the dying and the dead,
      Vault o'er the plain,—and in the tangled wood',—
40   Lo! dead Eliza—weltering in her blood!
      Soon hears his listening son the welcome sounds,
      With open arms and sparkling eyes he bounds:
      "Speak low," he cries, and gives his little hand,
      "Mamma's asleep upon the dew-cold sand;
45   Alas! we both with cold and hunger quake—
      Why do you weep? Mamma will soon awake."
      —"She'll wake no more!" the hopeless mourner cried,
      Upturn'd his eyes, and clasp'd his hands, and sigh'd;
      Stretch'd on the ground, awhile entranced he lay,
50   And press'd warm kisses on the lifeless clay:
      And then upsprung with wild convulsive start,
      And all the father kindled in his heart:
      "Oh Heaven!" he cried, "my first rash vow forgive!
      These bind to earth, for these I pray to live."
55   Round his chill babes he wrapp'd his crimson vest,
      And clasp'd them sobbing, to his aching breast.

Questions

1. Vocabulary: *spectatress* (2), *eddies* (12), *intrepid* (13), *convulsive* (51).
2. Does it seem reasonable or possible that a bullet could part her hair, wound her ear, and sink into her neck? From what direction would such a bullet have to come? Does this seem probable since Eliza is in a "tangled wood"?
3. How far away is Eliza from the battlefield? She is close enough to see "through the driving smoke [her husband's] dancing crest"—how is she then in a "tangled wood"?
4. What is the "first rash vow" mentioned in line 53?
5. Who does the listening in line 41? Who does the bounding in line 42?

6. Is it consistent for the son to cry for his father to "Speak low"?
7. Is it logical that a mother anxious for her husband's safety would risk the lives of her children by taking them to a battle?
8. Is the language economical? Do you find any redundancy, padding, or ambiguous pronouns?
9. How would you evaluate this poem overall?

Naturalness

Poetry does not merely transcribe the speech of ordinary people. The language of poetry is shaped, altered, concentrated, and often heightened. Yet the language of a poem should usually be natural—that is, obey the laws of common word order and diction, and avoid rhythms and sounds that are difficult or ugly to pronounce. Of course, poets often create odd or unnatural effects in their poetry for specific expressive purposes. Each case of unnatural language must be judged on its own merits. One must determine whether a passage is justified by expressive power, economy, or variety, or whether it is merely the result of incompetence, haste, or insensitivity.

The following is one of Shakespeare's sonnets. Notice that the opening quatrain is in very plain, natural English. The word order is simple and ordinary. Indeed, the tone of the opening is blunt.

WILLIAM SHAKESPEARE (1564–1616)

My Mistress' Eyes Are Nothing like the Sun

My Mistress' eyes are nothing like the Sun,
Coral is far more red, than her lips red,
If snow be white, why then her breasts are dun:
If hairs be wires, black wires grow on her head:
5   I have seen Roses damasked, red and white,
But no such Roses see I in her cheeks,
And in some perfumes is there more delight,
Then in the breath that from my Mistress reeks.
I love to hear her speak; yet well I know,
10   That Music hath a far more pleasing sound:
I grant I never saw a goddess go,
My Mistress when she walks treads on the ground.
     And yet by heaven I think my love as rare,
     As any she belied with false compare.

Questions

1. Vocabulary: *damasked* (5), *belied* (14).
2. Besides "reeks," are there any other comic words used for rhymes?
3. Shakespeare calls the woman "my love"; yet he lists her defects. Does he resolve this contradiction? Is the poem contradictory?
4. Are any lines padded for rhythm?

5. Is there any redundancy, vague pronoun usage, or verbal looseness?
6. How would you evaluate the poem overall?

Despite the straightforward opening, lines 5 and 6 are in a slightly unusual order. Normally one would say, "I have seen Roses damasked, red and white,/But I see no such Roses in her cheeks." Shakespeare did not order this line for the sake of rhyme or meter, since the more natural line both rhymes and scans. Why, then, did Shakespeare order the words as he did?

First we must recognize that the line is a *chiasmus*, which means "crossing." In a chiasmus the word order of one phrase or clause is inverted in the next. For example, Samuel Johnson wrote, "For we that live to please, must please to live." We can see how these terms cross in this diagram.

> We that live to please
>
> must please to live

In Shakespeare's line there is a similar crossing or chiasmus.

> I have seen Roses . . .
>
> But no such Roses see I . . .

The chiasmus is an elegant but not too unusual variation that gives art to the poem. More important, it shows that the speaker is not being crude in the opening lines out of ignorance. Clearly, he can construct a line with elegance. He is blunt because he wishes to be brutally honest.

Lines 7 and 8 are also unusually ordered. One normally would say, "The breath that reeks from my mistress is not as delightful as some perfumes." However, such a sentence loses all the humor. "Reeks" is the harshest, most insulting word in the poem. Shakespeare wishes to delay it and emphasize it by locating it not only at the end of the line but also at the conclusion of the quatrain.

We now see that whenever Shakespeare deviates from normal word order in this poem, he does so deliberately, for expressive purposes. Moreover, none of these lines is so oddly ordered that it becomes incomprehensible.

The following poem is filled with lines having odd or unnatural word order. Locate each unusual line and try to reword it in a more standard manner. Compare your version with Empson's. Examine what has been lost and gained in the process. See whether Empson's word order is justifiable or unskilled. Are any of the rhymes forced?

WILLIAM EMPSON (1906–)

Villanelle

It is the pain, it is the pain, endures.
Your chemic beauty burned my muscles through.
Poise of my hands reminded me of yours.

What later purge from this deep toxin cures?
5   What kindness now could the old salve renew?
It is the pain, it is the pain, endures.

The infection slept (custom or change inures)
And when pain's secondary phase was due
Poise of my hands reminded me of yours.

10   How safe I felt, whom memory assures,
Rich that your grace safely by heart I knew.
It is the pain, it is the pain, endures.

My stare drank deep beauty that still allures.
My heart pumps yet the poison draught of you.
15   Poise of my hands reminded me of yours.

You are still kind whom the same shape immures.
Kind and beyond adieu. We miss our cue.
It is the pain, it is the pain, endures.
Poise of my hands reminded me of yours.

Questions

1. Vocabulary: *chemic* (2), *inures* (7).
2. Are any of the words difficult to pronounce? Are any of the sounds ineffective or ugly?
3. Are the repeated lines well integrated into the poem, or do they become mechanical and repetitious?
4. Is there any padding for rhythm?
5. Is the poem always comprehensible? If there are muddy places, is there an expressive justification for the muddiness?
6. Are there any ambiguous pronouns?
7. From what branch of knowledge is most of the language drawn? Is the theatrical term "cue" in line 17 out of place?
8. What is your overall evaluation of the poem?

Rhyme is not the only cause of forced, odd, or inexpressive word order. Metrical regularity can produce ineffective or simply bad uses of language. The following is a wholly commonplace observation about the industrious and muscular ant. But the passage is laughable because of its terrible sense of rhythm and awkward word order.

CORNELIUS WHUR (1782–1853)

From Village Musings

The poet questions the ant

Why did you, feeble as you were, attempt
A task so perfectly herculean?
Could it be to rear your tender offspring?

Did your concern touching their welfare
5   So impel? Was aught like conference held
Ere you began to calculate success? . . .
                          Man, physically
Your superior, could not with equal tools
The work have done. He, comparatively,
10   Might as soon this ponderous earth divide.

Questions

1. Vocabulary: *herculean* (2), *ponderous* (10).
2. Which lines are awkwardly ordered? Is there any expressive justification for the order?
3. What is the meaning of "comparatively" in line 9? Is this a standard use of the word?
4. Is there any padding, redundancy, or looseness of language?
5. What is your overall estimation of the passage?

Tone: Sentimentality and Coldness

Poetry, as we have said, is the language of emotion. A good poem effectively conveys emotion to the reader. Readers do not merely understand the emotion the poet wishes to convey, but feel the emotion themselves. A good elegy, for example, does not merely tell us about grief, but puts us through the process of grieving. Readers who set themselves against a poem will never be able to experience it; thus a poem is a partnership between the skilled writer and the responsive reader. As Walt Whitman said, in order to have great poetry there must be great audiences.

We should not, however, judge a poem simply by the intensity with which it conveys emotion. Of greater importance are subtlety, honesty, and depth of feeling. As any seasoned moviegoer knows, horror and suspense are more easily and intensely conveyed than is the confusion of grief or the disenchantment of youth. We may be thrilled as the latest monster destroys downtown Tokyo, but we are often more profoundly touched by some less spectacular event.

Most readers have a sense of what is an appropriate response to a situation and will reject a feeling that seems unsuitable. Most readers will sympathize with a poet who expresses annoyance at ruining a new coat. They will empathize with a poet depressed over having ruined a car. They will be moved by a poet desperate over the loss of a loved one. But readers will be amused or disgusted by the poet wailing over a ruined coat. "What a crybaby," they will complain— and rightly. Such emotional overreaction is called *sentimentality*. Sentimentality occurs when a poet attempts to bestow on an experience more emotion than it can reasonably sustain.

Sentimentality is any excessive emotion, but it usually takes the form of excessive tenderness. A good test of sentimentality is whether the poem accurately depicts the object or experience. Sentimental people are usually blind to the true nature of their love object. They see the world through "rose-colored glasses."

For example, we may cling to objects long after their usefulness, beauty, and worth are exhausted. The following poem is an example of such a sentimental attachment.

ELIZA COOK (1818–1889)

The Old Arm Chair

I love it! I love it! And who shall dare
To chide me for loving that old arm-chair?
I've treasured it long as a sainted prize;
I've bedewed it with tears, and embalmed it with sighs.
5   'Tis bound by a thousand bands to my heart;
Not a tie will break, not a link will start.
Would ye learn the spell?—a mother sat there;
And a sacred thing is that old arm-chair.

In childhood's hour I lingered near
10   The hallowed seat with list'ning ear;
And gentle words that mother would give,
To fit me to die, and teach me to live.
She told me shame would never betide
With truth for my creed, and God for my guide;
15   She taught me to lisp my earliest prayer,
As I knelt beside that old arm-chair.

I sat and watched her many a day,
When her eyes grew dim, and her locks were grey;
And I almost worshipped her when she smiled,
20   And turned from her Bible to bless her child.
Years rolled on; but the last one sped—
My idol was shattered; my earth-star fled.
I learnt how much the heart can bear,
When I saw her die in that old arm-chair.

25   'Tis past! 'tis past! But I gaze on it now
With quivering breath and sobbing brow:
'Twas there she nursed me; 'twas there she died:
And memory flows with lava tide.
Say it is folly, and deem me weak,
30   While the scalding drops start down my cheek;
But I love it! I love it! and cannot tear
My soul from a mother's old arm-chair.

Questions

1. Do we ever get to see the armchair? What does it look like? Is it in good condition?
2. Does the speaker really value the armchair for itself? Why is it valuable?
3. In what sense is the poem an example of metonymy?

4. Cook calls the chair "a sainted prize," "a sacred thing," and a "hallowed seat." Is this sort of idolatry suitable to an old armchair? Is it consistent with the religious sentiments she was supposed to have learned?
5. The speaker says she "embalmed" the chair with sighs. Does the word convey the emotion she wishes to convey? She also says her "memory flows with lava tide." Is the violence and destructiveness of lava an appropriate image here? Does it convey the feelings Cook wishes to convey? Do you see any other inappropriate expressions?
6. Does the situation warrant the hyperbole Cook employs?
7. What do we usually mean by a "shattered" idol? How does Cook use the idea in line 22? Is it appropriate?
8. How would you evaluate this poem overall?

Some people believe that certain situations are inherently sentimental. Although it is true that some situations lend themselves to sentimental treatment, a good poet can render a potentially sentimental situation with depth, perception, and toughness. The two poems that follow portray poor old women who have fallen on hard times. The subject lends itself to a sentimental treatment, but it can also be handled with conviction.

THOMAS ASHE (1836–1889)

Old Jane

I love old women best, I think:
    She knows a friend in me,—
Old Jane, who totters on the brink
    Of God's Eternity;
5   Whose limbs are stiff, whose cheek is lean,
    Whose eyes look up, afraid;
Though you may gather she has been
    A little laughing maid.

Once had she with her doll what times,
10   And with her skipping-rope!
Her head was full of lovers' rhymes,
    Once, and her heart of hope;
Who, now, with eyes as sad as sweet—
    I love to look on her,—
15   At corner of the gusty street,
    Asks, "Buy a pencil, Sir?"

Her smile is as the litten West,
    Nigh-while the sun is gone;
She is more fain to be at rest
20   Than here to linger on:
Beneath her lids the pictures flit
    Of memories far-away:
Her look has not a hint in it
    Of what she sees to-day.

Questions

1. Vocabulary: *litten* (17).
2. Are there any phrases or sentences whose meaning is obscure?
3. Do the last two lines contradict anything in the poem? Is there really no hint of old Jane's present condition?
4. Are any lines forced? Do the rhymes come naturally? Whose eyes are "as sad as sweet"?
5. Does Ashe provide any clues to how old Jane came to sell pencils on street corners? Do the memories of her past seem an accurate picture of the complexities of youth? Has Jane always been poor? Has she slipped from a better economic condition?
6. Is it reasonable to think that Jane thinks only about dolls, jump rope, and lovers' rhymes?
7. What is Ashe's attitude toward Jane? Can one reasonably share his attitude given the facts he has supplied?
8. Is this poem sentimental? Why?

ROBERT FROST (1874–1963)

Provide, Provide

The witch that came (the withered hag)
To wash the steps with pail and rag,
Was once the beauty Abishag,[1]

The picture pride of Hollywood.
5   Too many fall from great and good
For you to doubt the likelihood.

Die early and avoid the fate.
Or if predestined to die late,
Make up your mind to die in state.

10   Make the whole stock exchange your own!
If need be occupy a throne,
Where nobody can call *you* crone.

Some have relied on what they knew;
Others on being simply true.
15   What worked for them might work for you.

No memory of having starred
Atones for later disregard
Or keeps the end from being hard.

Better to go down dignified
20   With boughten friendship at your side.
Than none at all. Provide, provide!

---

[1] Abishag was a beautiful young woman who nursed King David in his old age.

Questions

1. Vocabulary: *atones* (17).
2. Do you understand the meaning of each phrase? Does the poem contain any contradictions? Is there any padding or redundancy? If so, is there any reason for it?
3. Do the lines seem forced? Are the rhymes natural? If any seem comic, is that intended or the result of artistic miscalculation?
4. Does Frost provide enough background on the scrubwoman to make her seem realistic? Is all the information good?
5. What is Frost's attitude toward the old woman? Can you reasonably share his attitude?
6. Is this poem sentimental?

Exercise

The foregoing two poems develop their subject in very different ways. One tries to be coldhearted; the other is extremely sentimental. The next two poems take as their subject women who are struggling to survive. Try to place them on the scale between indifference and sentimentality. Then try to determine whether the poems are successful and finely crafted.

WILLIAM BUTLER YEATS (1865–1939)

• Crazy Jane Talks with the Bishop

I met the Bishop on the road
And much said he and I.
"Those breasts are flat and fallen now,
Those veins must soon be dry;
5   Live in a heavenly mansion,
Not in some foul sty."

"Fair and foul are near of kin,
And fair needs foul," I cried.
"My friends are gone, but that's a truth
10   Nor grave nor bed denied,
Learned in bodily lowliness
And in the heart's pride.

"A woman can be proud and stiff
When on love intent;
15   But Love has pitched his mansion in
The place of excrement;
For nothing can be sole or whole
That has not been rent."

PATRICK KAVANAGH (1904–1967)

Tinker's Wife

I saw her amid the dunghill debris
Looking for things

Such as an old pair of shoes or gaiters.
She was a young woman,
5   A tinker's wife.
Her face had streaks of care
Like wires across it,
But she was supple
As a young goat
10   On a windy hill.
She searched on the dunghill debris,
Tripping gingerly
Over tin canisters
And sharp-broken
15   Dinner plates.

Sentimentality is a form of emotional exaggeration. In the best poems each element is in proportion to the others. Thus sentimentality can distort a poem that is in other respects well made. In judging a poem, one should examine each element of the poem to see how and why it is functioning. Only then can one decide whether each element best serves the poem as a whole or whether it is a defect in the poem's overall design.

Coldness is a problem closely related to sentimentality. Instead of overreacting emotionally, a poet may underreact. This coldness often appears in official or public poetry. Poets may be asked to write for a specific occasion that may not engage them emotionally. Or, sometimes, poets will moralize on a public event that they have failed to grasp emotionally. In the following poem Robert Service used the occasion of Dylan Thomas's death from alcoholism to moralize about the evils of drink. Dylan Thomas was a poet, and several of his poems are included in this book. Service seems less moved by the human and poetic loss of Thomas than by the opportunity to sermonize.

ROBERT SERVICE (1876–1958)

Dylan

And is it not a gesture grand
    To drink oneself to death?
Oh sure 'tis I can understand,
    Being of sober breath.
5   And so I do not sing success,
    But dirge the damned who fall,
And who contempt for life express
    Through alcohol.

Of Stephen Foster and of Poe,
10   Of Burns and Wilde[2] I think;
And weary men who dared to go

---

[2] Stephen Foster, Edgar Allan Poe, Robert Burns, and Oscar Wilde all suffered from alcholic tendencies.

The wanton way of drink.
Strange mortals blind to bitter blame,
  And deaf to loud delight,
Who from the shades of sin and shame
  Enstar our night.

Among those dupes of destiny
  Add D.T.[3] to my list,
Although his verse you may agree
  Leaves one in mental mist . . .
Oh ye mad poets, loth of life,
  Who peace in death divine,
Pass not by pistol, poison, knife,—
  Drown, drown in wine!

Questions

1. Vocabulary: *dirge* (6), *wanton* (12), *dupes* (17).
2. Service may have shortened the last line to suggest the way Thomas's life had been unnaturally shortened. However, does this feeling come across? Do the rhythm and sound of line 8 suggest the seriousness of the subject?
3. "D.T." in line 18 refers to Dylan Thomas but also suggests *delirium tremens*, commonly known as the D.T.'s, the horrifying hallucinations of alcoholics. Is such a pun appropriate in a serious elegy?
4. Is "although" in line 19 the proper connective? Is "sober breath" (line 4) a logical or natural expression? Does it mean anything other than sober?
5. What is the tone of lines 21–24? Is it consistent with the rest of the poem?
6. Do you sense that Service is deeply saddened by Thomas's death? Is he more concerned about Thomas or about the evils of alcohol?

The following is a poem that Dr. Sprat, bishop of Rochester, wrote on the death of a lady friend. Although he expresses the extremes of grief, try to determine, as you are reading, how sincere those expressions are.

THOMAS SPRAT (1635–1713)

On His Mistress Drowned

Sweet stream, that dost with equal pace
Both thyself fly, and thyself chase,
  Forbear awhile to flow,
  And listen to my woe.
Then go, and tell the sea that all its brine
  Is fresh, compar'd to mine;
Inform it that the gentle dame,

---

[3] The Welsh poet Dylan Thomas (1914–1953).

Who was the life of all my flame,
  In th' glory of her bud
10 Has pass'd the fatal flood.

Death by this only stroke triumphs above
  The greatest power of love:
  Alas, alas! I must give o'er,
  My sighs will let me add no more.

15 Go on, sweet stream, and henceforth rest
  No more than does my troubled breast;
  And if my sad complaints have made thee stay,
  These tears, these tears shall mend thy way.

Questions

1. Does the speaker want the stream to flow? Is there any contradiction in his attitude?
2. What evidence does the speaker give that "the gentle dame . . . was the life of all [his] flame"?
3. Does he give you a picture of the woman? Was she young, old, rich, poor, well educated, innocent, a relative?
4. How has death triumphed over love in lines 11–12? Do we know? Did the speaker do anything to save his mistress?

Sentimentality may be laughable, but such cold-bloodedness seems far more offensive.

Completeness

Like any organism, a poem must be complete in order for it to function at maximum effectiveness. We must come to understand what motivates speakers to talk as they do, and what is the significance of their words. Without this knowledge, the poem will seem incomplete. The poet is not obliged to tell us everything; some details are insignificant, and readers should be prepared to make important inferences on their own. If essentials are left out, however, readers will be unable to respond emotionally or intellectually to the poem.

In the following poem the author has failed to give important information that would help us empathize with the speaker's plight. The general outlines are clear, however. A parent—we do not know whether it is a mother or father—grieves over the death of a child—we cannot tell whether it is a son or daughter. The child had apparently been a good one, who had not wished to worry the parent. Yet it is difficult to understand the speaker's guilt and self-mockery. When the speaker says, "It is not true that Love will do no wrong," he or she is apparently referring to some bad act mistakenly committed out of love. But what is the action? Who perpetrated it? Did this action lead to the child's death? We do not and can never know; and without this knowledge, we readers will remain distanced from the speaker and cut off from the poem's potential power.

COVENTRY PATMORE (1823–1896)

If I Were Dead

"If I were dead, you'd sometimes say, Poor Child!"
The dear lips quiver'd as they spake,
And the tears brake
From eyes which, not to grieve me, brightly smiled.
5   Poor Child, poor Child!
I seem to hear your laugh, your talk, your song.
It is not true that Love will do no wrong.
Poor Child!
And did you think, when you so cried and smiled,
10   How I, in lonely nights, should lie awake,
And of those words your full avengers make?
Poor Child, poor Child!
And now unless it be
That sweet amends thrice told are come to thee,
15   O God, have Thou *no* mercy upon me!
Poor Child!

Questions

1. Is it clear why the child says, "If I were dead, you'd sometimes say, Poor Child!"? What did the child mean? Was the child angry, frightened, spiteful, or tender in saying this line?
2. How old is the child? Of what does the child die?
3. What evidence is there in the poem that God has shown the speaker "*no* mercy"?
4. Does the rhyme contribute to the overall effectiveness of the poem?
5. Is the poem sentimental?
6. Is the language natural? Are there any ambiguities without purpose?
7. How would you rate this poem?

    The purpose of criticism is to increase a reader's awareness of excellence and the variety of his or her responses to literature. Mature critical judgments are never simple or clear. As we have seen, they are based on a number of different criteria whose relative importance must constantly be reevaluated. Good critics understand the limitations of their views and are prepared to consider alternatives, to reexamine their judgments, to be more open and varied. W. H. Auden, the great poet and critic, once wrote:

> As readers, we remain in the nursery stage so long as we cannot distinguish between taste and judgments, so long, that is, as the only possible verdicts we can pass on a book are two: this I like; this I don't like.
>
> For an adult reader, the possible verdicts are five: I can see this is good and I like it; I can see this is good but I don't like it; I can see this is good and, though at present I don't like it, I believe that with perseverance I shall come to like it; I can see that this is trash but I like it; I can see that this is trash and I don't like it.

Mature critics, rather than limiting their response to literature, have learned to increase their responses and appreciations.

The Good and the Great

A poem is considered great not because it is better made than other poems but for a variety of other reasons. Usually great poems have greater scope or emotional intensity than other poems. As we all know, some subjects and conditions are more easily articulated than others. Great poems explore the most difficult areas of human experience or express concerns in the subtlest, most original ways.

Poems can also become great for other reasons. Some are considered great because they are the first of their kind; they break new artistic ground. Other works articulate the spirit of their age so clearly and succinctly that they become a touchstone for their time. Byron's *Childe Harold's Pilgrimage* is an example of a poem whose fame may well be greater than its craftsmanship. It was the most widely read work of its time.

Works can also become especially valued because they represent a pivotal period in the artistic output of a great poet. As Shakespeare wrote, "Some are born great, some achieve greatness, and some have greatness thrust upon them." Likewise, greatness is something that comes mysteriously to a work. It is a quality so elusive, so special to each great work, that no criteria can be formulated to describe how it works. We may be able to analyze why a work is excellent, but we can do no more than recognize when a work is truly great.

We have chosen five poems that are almost universally regarded as great works. They come from different periods and nations; there are one by an American, one by an Irishman, two by Englishmen, and one by an American who became a British citizen. These poems are somewhat longer than most of the poems in the book. Great poems often have wider scope and more ambitious subject matter. Take your time with them as you would with all the other poems in this book. These poems continue to pose emotional and intellectual challenges even to the most sophisticated reader.

JOHN MILTON (1608–1674)

Lycidas

In this monody[4] the author bewails a learned friend, unfortunately drowned in his passage from Chester on the Irish seas, 1637. And by occasion foretells the ruin of our corrupted clergy, then in their height.

    Yet once more, O ye laurels, and once more
Yet myrtles brown, with ivy never sere,[5]
I come to pluck your berries harsh and crude,°   *unripe*

---

[4] A solo song in Greek drama.

[5] Laurel, myrtle, and ivy are plants associated with poetic inspiration. Laurel is given by Apollo, the god of poetry; myrtle by Venus, the goddess of love; and ivy is associated with Bacchus, the god of wine.

And with forced fingers rude,
5   Shatter your leaves before the mellowing year.
Bitter constraint, and sad occasion dear,
Compels me to disturb your season due;
For Lycidas is dead, dead ere his prime,
Young Lycidas, and hath not left his peer.
10   Who would not sing for Lycidas? He knew
Himself to sing, and build the lofty rhyme.
He must not float upon his watery bier
Unwept, and welter to the parching wind,
Without the meed° of some melodious tear.   *reward*
15   Begin then, sisters of the sacred well[6]
That from beneath the seat of Jove doth spring,
Begin, and somewhat loudly sweep the string.
Hence with denial vain, and coy excuse;
So may some gentle Muse
20   With lucky words favor my destined urn,
And as he passes turn,
And bid fair peace be to my sable shroud.
For we were nursed upon the selfsame hill,
Fed the same flock, by fountain, shade, and rill.
25   Together both, ere the high lawns appeared
Under the opening eyelids of the morn,
We drove afield, and both together heard
What time the grayfly winds her sultry horn.[7]
Battening° our flocks with the fresh dews of night,   *feeding*
30   Oft till the star that rose at evening bright
Toward Heaven's descent had sloped his westering wheel.
Meanwhile the rural ditties were not mute,
Tempered to th' oaten flute,
Rough satyrs danced, and fauns with cloven heel
35   From the glad sound would not be absent long,
And old Damoetas[8] loved to hear our song.
     But O the heavy change, now thou art gone,
Now thou art gone, and never must return!
Thee, shepherd, thee the woods and desert caves,
40   With wild thyme and the gadding° vine o'ergrown,   *straggling*
And all their echoes mourn.
The willows and the hazel copses green
Shall now no more be seen,
Fanning their joyous leaves to thy soft lays.
45   As killing as the canker° to the rose,   *cankerworm*
Or taint-worm to the weanling° herds that graze,   *newly weaned*
Or frost to flowers that their gay wardrobe wear,
When first the white thorn blows,°   *blossoms*
Such, Lycidas, thy loss to shepherd's ear.

---

[6] The muses inspire the arts.
[7] That is, buzzes.
[8] A typical shepherd's name.

50   Where were ye, nymphs, when the remorseless deep
       Closed o'er the head of your loved Lycidas?
       For neither were ye playing on the steep,
       Where your old Bards, the famous Druids[9] lie,
       Nor on the shaggy top of Mona high,
55   Nor yet where Deva spreads her wizard stream:[10]

       Ay me! I fondly° dream—   *foolishly*
       Had ye been there—for what could that have done?
       What could the Muse herself that Orpheus bore,
       The Muse herself, for her inchanting[11] son
60   Whom universal Nature did lament,

       When by the rout° that made the hideous roar,   *mob*
       His gory visage down the stream was sent,
       Down the swift Hebrus to the Lesbian shore?

       Alas! What boots° it with incessant care   *profits*
65   To tend the homely slighted shepherd's trade,
       And strictly meditate the thankless Muse?
       Were it not better done as others use,
       To sport with Amaryllis in the shade,
       Or with the tangles of Neaera's hair?[12]
70   Fame is the spur that the clear spirit doth raise
       (That last infirmity of noble mind)
       To scorn delights, and live laborious days;

       But the fair guerdon° when we hope to find,   *reward*
       And think to burst out into sudden blaze,
75   Comes the blind Fury with th' abhorréd shears,[13]
       And slits the thin spun life. "But not the praise,"
       Phoebus[14] replied, and touched my trembling ears;
       "Fame is no plant that grows on mortal soil,
       Not in the glistering foil[15]
80   Set off to th' world, nor in broad rumor lies,
       But lives and spreads aloft by those pure eyes,
       And perfect witness of all-judging Jove;
       As he pronounces lastly on each deed,
       Of so much fame in Heaven expect thy meed."
85   O fountain Arethuse, and thou honored flood,
       Smooth-sliding Mincius, crowned with vocal reeds,[16]
       That strain I heard was of a higher mood.

       But now my oat° proceeds,   *flute song*
       And listens to the herald of the sea

---

[9] Druids were the ancient priests of Britain.
[10] "Mona" is the island of Anglesey, a center of Druid activity. "Deva" is the river Dee in Cheshire.
[11] Orpheus, the great poet-singer of Greek mythology, was torn to pieces by Thracian women, who threw his head into the river Hebrus.
[12] Amaryllis and Neaera were typical names for nymphs.
[13] A fury is an avenging spirit.
[14] Phoebus Apollo, the god of poetic inspiration.
[15] A glistering foil was a thin metal backing used to give sparkle to glass gems.
[16] Arethusa was a fountain in Sicily; Mincius, a river in Lombardy.

90   That came in Neptune's[17] plea.
       He asked the waves, and asked the felon° winds,   *whipping*
       "What hard mishap hath doomed this gentle swain?"
       And questioned every gust of rugged wings
       That blows from off each beakéd promontory;
95   They knew not of his story,
       And sage Hippotades[18] their answer brings,
       That not a blast was from his dungeon strayed,
       The air was calm, and on the level brine,
       Sleek Panope[19] with all her sisters played.
100   It was that fatal and perfidious bark
       Built in th' eclipse, and rigged with curses dark,
       That sunk so low that sacred head of thine.
            Next Camus,[20] reverend sire, went footing slow,
       His mantle hairy, and his bonnet sedge,
105   Inwrought with figures dim, and on the edge
       Like to that sanguine flower° inscribed with woe.   *hyacinth*
       "Ah! who hath reft," quoth he, "my dearest pledge?"
       Last came and last did go
       The pilot of the Galilean lake,°   *St. Peter*
110   Two massy keys he bore of metals twain
       (The golden opes, the iron shuts amain).
       He shook his mitered locks, and stern bespake:
       "How well could I have spared for thee, young swain,
       Enow° of such as for their bellie's sake,   *enough*
115   Creep and intrude, and climb into the fold!
       Of other care they little reckoning make,
       Than how to scramble at the shearers' feast,
       And shove away the worthy bidden guest.
       Blind mouths! That scarce themselves know how to hold
120   A sheep-hook, or have learned aught else the least
       That to the faithful herdsman's art belongs!
       What recks it° them? What need they? They are sped;   *does it matter to*
       And when they list,° their lean and flashy songs   *choose*
       Grate on their scrannel° pipes of wretched straw.   *harsh, meager*
125   The hungry sheep look up, and are not fed,
       But swoln with wind, and the rank mist they draw,
       Rot inwardly, and foul contagion spread,
       Besides what the grim wolf with privy paw
       Daily devours apace, and nothing said.
130   But that two-handed engine at the door
       Stands ready to smite once, and smite no more."
            Return, Alpheus, the dread voice is past,
       That shrunk thy streams; return, Sicilian muse,

---

[17] Neptune is the Roman god of the sea.
[18] Hippotades is the god of winds.
[19] The most important sea nymph, or nereid.
[20] The god of the river Cam.

And call the vales, and bid them hither cast
135   Their bells and flowerets of a thousand hues.
Ye valleys low where the mild whispers use,
Of shades and wanton winds, and gushing brooks,
On whose fresh lap the swart star[21] sparely looks,
Throw hither all your quaint enameled° eyes,   *adorned*
140   That on the green turf suck the honeyed showers,
And purple all the ground with vernal flowers.
Bring the rathe° primrose that foresaken dies.   *early*
The tufted crow-toe, and pale jessamine,
The white pink, and the pansy freaked° with jet,   *flecked*
145   The glowing violet,
The musk-rose, and the well attired woodbine.
With cowslips wan that hang the pensive head,
And every flower that sad embroidery wears:
Bid amaranthus[22] all his beauty shed,
150   And daffadillies fill their cups with tears,
To strew the laureate hearse where Lycid lies.
For so to interpose a little ease,
Let our frail thoughts dally with false surmise.
Ay me! Whilst thee the shores and sounding seas
155   Wash far away, where'er thy bones are hurled,
Whether beyond the stormy Hebrides,[23]
Where thou perhaps under the whelming tide
Visit'st the bottom of the monstrous world;
Or whether thou, to our moist vows denied,
160   Sleep'st by the fable of Bellerus old,[24]
Where the great vision of the guarded mount
Looks toward Namancos and Bayona's hold;[25]
Look homeward angel now, and melt with ruth:°   *grief and pity*
And, O ye dolphins, waft the hapless youth.
165   Weep no more, woeful shepherds, weep no more,
For Lycidas your sorrow is not dead,
Sunk though he be beneath the watery floor,
So sinks the day-star in the ocean bed,
And yet anon repairs his drooping head,
170   And tricks° his beams, and with new-spangled ore,   *dresses, adorns*
Flames in the forehead of the morning sky:
So Lycidas sunk low, but mounted high,
Through the dear might of him that walked the waves,
Where other groves, and other streams along,
175   With nectar pure his oozy locks he laves,
And hears the unexpressive nuptial song,

---

[21] The Dog Star, Sirius.
[22] Amaranth is a mythical flower that never fades.
[23] Islands off the coast of Scotland.
[24] A giant who, according to fable, is buried in Cornwall.
[25] Bayona and Namancos are places in northern Spain.

In the blest kingdoms meek of joy and love.
There entertain him all the saints above,
In solemn troops and sweet societies
180 That sing, and singing in their glory move,
And wipe the tears forever from his eyes.
Now, Lycidas, the shepherds weep no more;
Henceforth thou art the genius of the shore,
In thy large recompense, and shalt be good
185 To all that wander in that perilous flood.
      Thus sang the uncouth swain to th' oaks and rills,
While the still morn went out with sandals gray;
He touched the tender stops of various quills,
With eager thought warbling his Doric lay:
190 And now the sun had stretched out all the hills,
And now was dropped into the western bay;
At last he rose, and twitched his mantle blue:
Tomorrow to fresh woods, and pastures new.

WILLIAM WORDSWORTH (1770–1850)

• Lines

*Composed a Few Miles above Tintern Abbey on Revisiting
the Banks of the Wye during a Tour. July 13, 1798*

      Five years have passed; five summers, with the length
Of five long winters! and again I hear
These waters, rolling from their mountain-springs
With a soft inland murmur. Once again
5 Do I behold these steep and lofty cliffs,
That on a wild secluded scene impress
Thoughts of more deep seclusion; and connect
The landscape with the quiet of the sky.
The day is come when I again repose
10 Here, under this dark sycamore, and view
These plots of cottage ground, these orchard tufts,
Which at this season, with their unripe fruits,
Are clad in one green hue, and lose themselves
'Mid groves and copses. Once again I see
15 These hedgerows, hardly hedgerows, little lines
Of sportive wood run wild; these pastoral farms,
Green to the very door; and wreaths of smoke
Sent up, in silence, from among the trees!
With some uncertain notice, as might seem
20 Of vagrant dwellers in the houseless woods,
Or of some Hermit's cave, where by his fire
The Hermit sits alone.

               These beauteous forms,
Through a long absence, have not been to me
As is a landscape to a blind man's eye;

25 But oft, in lonely rooms, and 'mid the din
    Of towns and cities, I have owed to them,
    In hours of weariness, sensations sweet,
    Felt in the blood, and felt along the heart;
    And passing even into my purer mind,
30 With tranquil restoration—feelings too
    Of unremembered pleasure; such, perhaps,
    As have no slight or trivial influence
    On that best portion of a good man's life,
    His little, nameless, unremembered, acts
35 Of kindness and of love. Nor less, I trust,
    To them I may have owed another gift,
    Of aspect more sublime; that blessed mood,
    In which the burthen of the mystery,
    In which the heavy and the weary weight
40 Of all this unintelligible world,
    Is lightened—that serene and blessèd mood,
    In which the affections gently lead us on—
    Until, the breath of this corporeal frame
    And even the motion of our human blood
45 Almost suspended, we are laid asleep
    In body, and become a living soul;
    While with an eye made quiet by the power
    Of harmony, and the deep power of joy,
    We see into the life of things.
                                    If this
50 Be but a vain belief, yet, oh! how oft—
    In darkness and amid the many shapes
    Of joyless daylight; when the fretful stir
    Unprofitable, and the fever of the world,
    Have hung upon the beatings of my heart—
55 How oft, in spirit, have I turned to thee,
    O sylvan Wye! thou wanderer through the woods,
    How often has my spirit turned to thee!

        And now, with gleams of half-extinguished thought
    With many recognitions dim and faint,
60 And somewhat of a sad perplexity,
    The picture of the mind revives again;
    While here I stand, not only with the sense
    Of present pleasure, but with pleasing thoughts
    That in this moment there is life and food
65 For future years. And so I dare to hope,
    Though changed, no doubt, from what I was when first
    I came among these hills; when like a roe
    I bounded o'er the mountains, by the sides
    Of the deep rivers, and the lonely streams,
70 Wherever nature led—more like a man
    Flying from something that he dreads than one
    Who sought the thing he loved. For nature then

(The coarser pleasures of my boyish days,
And their glad animal movements all gone by)
75 To me was all in all.—I cannot paint
What then I was. The sounding cataract
Haunted me like a passion; the tall rock,
The mountain, and the deep and gloomy wood,
Their colors and their forms, were then to me
80 An appetite; a feeling and a love,
That had no need of a remoter charm,
By thought supplied, nor any interest
Unborrowed from the eye.—That time is past,
And all its aching joys are now no more,
85 And all its dizzy raptures. Not for this
Faint° I, nor mourn nor murmur; other gifts   . lose heart
Have followed; for such loss, I would believe,
Abundant recompense. For I have learned
To look on nature, not as in the hour
90 Of thoughtless youth; but hearing oftentimes
The still, sad music of humanity,
Nor harsh nor grating, though of ample power
To chasten and subdue. And I have felt
A presence that disturbs me with the joy
95 Of elevated thoughts; a sense sublime
Of something far more deeply interfused,
Whose dwelling is the light of setting suns,
And the round ocean and the living air,
And the blue sky, and in the mind of man:
100 A motion and a spirit, that impels
All thinking things, all objects of all thought,
And rolls through all things. Therefore am I still
A lover of the meadows and the woods,
And mountains; and of all that we behold
105 From this green earth; of all the mighty world
Of eye, and ear—both what they half create,
And what perceive; well pleased to recognize
In nature and the language of the sense
The anchor of my purest thoughts, the nurse,
110 The guide, the guardian of my heart, and soul
Of all my moral being.
                                    Nor perchance,
If I were not thus taught, should I the more
Suffer my genial spirits[26] to decay:
For thou art with me here upon the banks
115 Of this fair river; thou my dearest Friend,[27]
My dear, dear Friend; and in thy voice I catch
The language of my former heart, and read
My former pleasures in the shooting lights

---

[26] Genius, a spirit that watches over a place or person.
[27] Wordsworth's sister, Dorothy.

Of thy wild eyes. Oh! yet a little while
120 May I behold in thee what I was once,
My dear, dear Sister! and this prayer I make,
Knowing that Nature never did betray
The heart that loved her; 'tis her privilege,
Through all the years of this our life, to lead
125 From joy to joy: for she can so inform
The mind that is within us, so impress
With quietness and beauty, and so feed
With lofty thoughts, that neither evil tongues,
Rash judgments, nor the sneers of selfish men,
130 Nor greetings where no kindness is, nor all
The dreary intercourse of daily life,
Shall e'er prevail against us, or disturb
Our cheerful faith, that all which we behold
Is full of blessings. Therefore let the moon
135 Shine on thee in thy solitary walk;
And let the misty mountain winds be free
To blow against thee: and, in after years,
When these wild ecstasies shall be matured
Into a sober pleasure; when thy mind
140 Shall be a mansion for all lovely forms,
Thy memory be as a dwelling place
For all sweet sounds and harmonies; oh! then,
If solitude, or fear, or pain, or grief
Should be thy portion, with what healing thoughts
145 Of tender joy wilt thou remember me,
And these my exhortations! Nor, perchance—
If I should be where I no more can hear
Thy voice, nor catch from thy wild eyes these gleams
Of past existence—wilt thou then forget
150 That on the banks of this delightful stream
We stood together; and that I, so long
A worshiper of Nature, hither came
Unwearied in that service; rather say
With warmer love—oh! with far deeper zeal
155 Of holier love. Nor wilt thou then forget,
That after many wanderings, many years
Of absence, these steep woods and lofty cliffs,
And this green pastoral landscape, were to me
More dear, both for themselves and for thy sake!

MARIANNE MOORE (1887–1972)

The Steeple-Jack

(Revised, 1961)

Dürer would have seen a reason for living
    in a town like this, with eight stranded whales

to look at; with the sweet air coming into your house
on a fine day, from water etched
5   with waves as formal as the scales
on a fish.

One by one in two's and three's, the seagulls keep
       flying back and forth over the town clock,
or sailing around the lighthouse without moving their wings—
10   rising steadily with a slight
           quiver of the body—or flock
mewing where

a sea the purple of the peacock's neck is
       paled to greenish azure as Dürer changed
15   the pine green of the Tyrol to peacock blue and guinea
gray. You can see a twenty-five-
           pound lobster; and fishnets arranged
to dry. The

whirlwind fife-and-drum of the storm bends the salt
20   marsh grass, disturbs stars in the sky and the
star on the steeple; it is a privilege to see so
much confusion. Disguised by what
           might seem the opposite, the sea-
side flowers and

25   trees are favored by the fog so that you have
           the tropics at first hand: the trumpet-vine,
fox-glove, giant snap-dragon, a salpiglossis that has
spots and stripes; morning-glories, gourds,
           or moon-vines trained on fishing-twine
30   at the back

door; cat-tails, flags, blueberries and spiderwort,
       stripped grass, lichens, sunflowers, asters, daisies—
yellow and crab-claw ragged sailors with green bracts—toad-plant,
petunias, ferns; pink lilies, blue
35   ones, tigers; poppies; black sweet-peas.
The climate

is not right for the banyan, frangipani, or
           jack-fruit trees; or an exotic serpent
life. Ring lizard and snake-skin for the foot, if you see fit;
40   but here they've cats, not cobras, to
           keep down the rats. The diffident
little newt

with white pin-dots on black horizontal spaced
       out bands lives here; yet there is nothing that
45   ambition can buy or take away. The college student
named Ambrose sits on the hillside
           with his not-native books and hat
and sees boats

at sea progress white and rigid as if in
50   a groove. Liking an elegance of which
the source is not bravado, he knows by heart the antique
sugar-bowl shaped summer-house of
        interlacing slats, and the pitch
of the church

55   spire, not true, from which a man in scarlet lets
        down a rope as a spider spins a thread;
he might be part of a novel, but on the sidewalk a
sign says C. J. Poole, Steeple Jack,
        in black and white; and one in red
60   and white says

Danger. The church portico has four fluted
        columns, each a single piece of stone, made
modester by white-wash. This would be a fit haven for
waifs, children, animals, prisoners,
65   and presidents who have repaid
sin-driven

senators by not thinking about them. The
        place has a school-house, a post-office in a
store, fish-houses, hen-houses, a three-masted
70   schooner on
the stocks. The hero, the student,
        the steeple-jack, each in his way,
is at home.

It could not be dangerous to be living
75   in a town like this, of simple people,
who have a steeple-jack placing danger-signs by the church
while he is gilding the solid-
        pointed star, which on a steeple
stands for hope.

WILLIAM BUTLER YEATS (1865–1939)

• Sailing to Byzantium[28]

I

That is no country for old men. The young
In one another's arms, birds in the trees
—Those dying generations—at their song,
The salmon-falls, the mackerel-crowded seas,
5   Fish, flesh, or fowl, commend all summer long
Whatever is begotten, born, and dies.
Caught in that sensual music all neglect
Monuments of unageing intellect.

---

[28] The ancient name for Istanbul. Yeats viewed the civilization of Byzantium as the height of art
and artifice.

II

    An aged man is but a paltry thing,
10   A tattered coat upon a stick, unless
    Soul clap its hands and sing, and louder sing
    For every tatter in its mortal dress,
    Nor is there singing school but studying
    Monuments of its own magnificence;
15   And therefore I have sailed the seas and come
    To the holy city of Byzantium.

III

    O sages standing in God's holy fire
    As in the gold mosaic of a wall,
    Come from the holy fire, perne in a gyre,[29]
20   And be the singing-masters of my soul.
    Consume my heart away; sick with desire
    And fastened to a dying animal
    It knows not what it is; and gather me
    Into the artifice of eternity.

IV

25   Once out of nature I shall never take
    My bodily form from any natural thing,
    But such a form as Grecian goldsmiths make
    Of hammered gold and gold enamelling
    To keep a drowsy Emperor awake;
30   Or set upon a golden bough to sing
    To lords and ladies of Byzantium
    Of what is past, or passing, or to come.

T. S. ELIOT (1888–1965)

• The Love Song of J. Alfred Prufrock

S'io credesse che mia risposta fosse
a persona che mai tornasse al mondo,
questa fiamma staria senza più scosse.
Ma per ciò che giammai di questo fondo
non tornò vivo alcun, s'i'odo il vero,
    senza tema d'infamia ti rispond.[30]

Let us go then, you and I,
When the evening is spread out against the sky
Like a patient etherised upon a table;

---

[29] The gyre symbolizes for Yeats the spinning of the soul.
[30] From Dante's *Inferno,* XXVII, 61–66. These lines are the words of Guido da Montefeltro, a
distinguished Florentine who gave bad counsel. They mean:

    If I believe that my reply were made
    To one who would revisit earth, the flame
    Would be at rest, and its commotion laid.
    But seeing that alive none ever came
    Back from this deep, if it be truth I hear,
    I answer without dread of injured fame.

Let us go, through certain half-deserted streets,
5 The muttering retreats
Of restless nights in one-night cheap hotels
And sawdust restaurants with oyster-shells:
Streets that follow like a tedious argument
Of insidious intent
10 To lead you to an overwhelming question. . .
Oh, do not ask, "What is it?"
Let us go and make our visit.

In the room the women come and go
Talking of Michelangelo.[31]

15 The yellow fog that rubs its back upon the window-panes,
The yellow smoke that rubs its muzzle on the window-panes,
Licked its tongue into the corners of the evening,
Lingered upon the pools that stand in drains,
Let fall upon its back the soot that falls from chimneys,
20 Slipped by the terrace, made a sudden leap,
And seeing that it was a soft October night,
Curled once about the house, and fell asleep.

And indeed there will be time
For the yellow smoke that slides along the street
25 Rubbing its back upon the window-panes;
There will be time, there will be time
To prepare a face to meet the faces that you meet;
There will be time to murder and create,
And time for all the works and days of hands
30 That lift and drop a question on your plate;
Time for you and time for me,
And time yet for a hundred indecisions,
And for a hundred visions and revisions,
Before the taking of a toast and tea.

35 In the room the women come and go
Talking of Michelangelo.

And indeed there will be time
To wonder, "Do I dare?" and, "Do I dare?"
Time to turn back and descend the stair,
40 With a bald spot in the middle of my hair—
(They will say: "How his hair is growing thin!")
My morning coat, my collar mounting firmly to the chin,
My necktie rich and modest, but asserted by a simple pin—
(They will say: "But how his arms and legs are thin!")
45 Do I dare
Disturb the universe?
In a minute there is time
For decisions and revisions which a minute will reverse.

---

[31] Michelangelo (1475–1564) was one of the greatest painters of the Italian Renaissance, as well as a poet. He never married and had no children.

For I have known them all already, known them all—
50   Have known the evenings, mornings, afternoons,
I have measured out my life with coffee spoons;
I know the voices dying with a dying fall
Beneath the music from a farther room.
        So how should I presume?

55   And I have known the eyes already, known them all—
The eyes that fix you in a formulated phrase,
And when I am formulated, sprawling on a pin,
When I am pinned and wriggling on the wall,
Then how should I begin
60   To spit out all the butt-ends of my days and ways?
        And how should I presume?

And I have known the arms already, known them all—
Arms that are braceleted and white and bare
(But in the lamplight, downed with light brown hair!)
65   Is it perfume from a dress
That makes me so digress?
Arms that lie along a table, or wrap about a shawl.
        And should I then presume?
        And how should I begin?
            *   *   *   *   *

70   Shall I say, I have gone at dusk through narrow streets
And watched the smoke that rises from the pipes
Of lonely men in shirt-sleeves, leaning out of windows? . . .

T. S. Eliot *(National Portrait Gallery, Smithsonian
Institution, Washington, D.C.)*

I should have been a pair of ragged claws
Scuttling across the floors of silent seas.[32]

    *   *   *   *   *

75   And the afternoon, the evening, sleeps so peacefully!
Smoothed by long fingers,
Asleep . . . tired . . . or it malingers,
Stretched on the floor, here beside you and me.
Should I, after tea and cakes and ices,
80   Have the strength to force the moment to its crisis?
But though I have wept and fasted, wept and prayed,
Though I have seen my head (grown slightly bald) brought in upon a platter,[33]
I am no prophet—and here's no great matter;
I have seen the moment of my greatness flicker,
85   And I have seen the eternal Footman hold my coat, and snicker,
And in short, I was afraid.

And would it have been worth it, after all,
After the cups, the marmalade, the tea,
Among the porcelain, among some talk of you and me,
90   Would it have been worth while,
To have bitten off the matter with a smile,
To have squeezed the universe into a ball
To roll it towards some overwhelming question,
To say: "I am Lazarus, come from the dead,[34]
95   come back to tell you all, I shall tell you all"—
If one, settling a pillow by her head,
    Should say: "That is not what I meant at all.
    That is not it, at all."

And would it have been worth it, after all,
100   Would it have been worth while,
After the sunsets and the dooryards and the sprinkled streets,
After the novels, after the teacups, after the skirts that trail along the floor—
and this, and so much more?—
It is impossible to say just what I mean!
105   But as if a magic lantern threw the nerves in patterns on a screen:
Would it have been worth while
If one, settling a pillow or throwing off a shawl,
And turning toward the window, should say:
    "That is not it at all,
110   That is not what I meant, at all."

    *   *   *   *   *

No! I am not Prince Hamlet, nor was meant to be;
Am an attendant lord, one that will do
To swell a progress, start a scene or two,
Advise the prince; no doubt, an easy tool,

---

[32] The crab travels backward. Eliot is alluding to Hamlet's words (Act II, Scene 2, line 195), "for you . . . shall grow old as I am, if like a crab you could go backward."

[33] Salome, the daughter of King Herod, had John the Baptist's head brought to her on a platter.

[34] Jesus raised Lazarus from the dead.

Deferential, glad to be of use,
Politic, cautious, and meticulous;
Full of high sentence, but a bit obtuse;
At times, indeed, almost ridiculous—
Almost, at times, the Fool.

120   I grow old . . . I grow old . . .
I shall wear the bottoms of my trousers rolled.

Shall I part my hair behind? Do I dare to eat a peach?
I shall wear white flannel trousers, and walk upon the beach.
I have heard the mermaids singing, each to each.

125   I do not think that they will sing to me.

I have seen them riding seaward on the waves
Combing the white hair of the waves blown back
When the wind blows the water white and black.

We have lingered in the chambers of the sea
130   By sea-girls wreathed with seaweed red and brown
Till human voices wake us, and we drown.

Check List of Questions for Evaluating Poetry

A list of questions follows that should help you evaluate poetry. Because each poem is different, no list can be complete, and you will need to supplement this list with other questions. Moreover, many great poems defy simple explanation. A poem may break many norms and yet remain a compelling and coherent expression.

Economy

1. Are there any repeated expressions or words? Is this repetition necessary or effective?
2. If the poem has a refrain, is the refrain well integrated, or is it mechanical?
3. Is any line padded to keep the rhythm regular?

Coherence and Consistency

1. Are all the ideas and attitudes consistent? If they are paradoxical, do they reflect a more subtle philosophical or psychological position? Are any inconsistencies part of the poetic development?
2. Are any expressions vague? Can the vagueness be justified by the context of the poem?
3. Are the images comprehensible? Is any oddness the result of dreamlike concentration, or is it the result of thoughtlessness?
4. If the poem seems nonsensical, is it the case that it is not supposed to be comprehensible in a traditional way?

Naturalness

1. Is the order of the language unnatural? Where it is unnatural, has the language been altered for expressive purposes?
2. Are the rhymes forced?
3. Is the diction natural? Where the word choice seems odd, is there some special reason?

4. Can the poem be read easily? Do the sounds fit the subject?
5. Do the rhythms seem appropriate to the subject and mood? Are they boring and mechanical?

Tone

1. Does the tone seem appropriate to the poem's subject and the speaker's attitude?
2. Is the poem sentimental?
3. Is the poem unfeeling?
4. Does the tone vary naturally, or is it mechanical and constant?

Completeness

1. Has the poet provided all the details necessary for the reader's full emotional and intellectual response? If not, is there a good reason?
2. Does the poem conclude or does it merely end?
3. Has the poet satisfied your expectations? If not, has the poet made an acceptable substitute?

Suggestions for Essayists

1. Compare two poems on a similar subject.
2. Select any object (e.g., a car, a house) and describe the criteria by which you decide whether it is good or bad.
3. Discuss the necessity of making critical evaluations.

Suggestions for Poets

1. Find a poem that you think is especially poor and rewrite it.
2. Take a poem you think is especially good and, by using redundancy, inconsistency, and rhythmic alterations, make it bad.

15 🌿 Poems for Further Reading

GEOFFREY CHAUCER (1340?–1400)

The Complaint of Chaucer to His Purse

To yow, my purse, and to noon other wight°	*person*
Complayne I, for ye be my lady dere!	
I am so sory, now that ye been lyght;	
For certes,° but° ye make me hevy chere,	*surely unless*
Me were as leef° be layd upon my bere;	*I would like to be*
For which unto your mercy thus I crye:	
Beth hevy ageyn, or elles moote° I dye!	*must*

Now voucheth sauf° this day, or° yt be nyght,	*vouchsafe before*
That I of yow the blisful soun° may here,	*sound*
Or see your colour lyk the sonne bryght,	
That of yelownesse hadde never pere.	
Ye be my lyf, ye be myn hertes stere,°	*guide*
Quene of comfort and of good companye:	
Beth hevy ageyn, or elles moote I dye!	

Now purse, that ben to me my lyves lyght	
And saveour, as° doun in this world here,	*while*
Out of this toune helpe me thurgh your myght,	
Syn that ye wole nat ben my tresorere;	
For I am shave as nye° as any frere.°	*close friar*
But yet I pray unto your curtesye:	
Beth hevy ageyn, or elles moote I dye!	

Lenvoy de Chaucer:

O conquerour of Brutes° Albyon,°	*Brutus's England*
Which that by lyne and free eleccion[1]	

Line numbers: 5, 10, 15, 20

---

[1] Henry IV, though a usurper, claimed the throne because he was the grandson of Edward II and thus was in the line of succession, and also because he had been placed on the throne by an act of Parliament—therefore, by "free eleccion."

Been verray° kyng, this song to yow I sende;   *true*
25   And ye, that mowen° alle our harmes amende,   *can*
Have mynde upon my supplicacion!

JOHN SKELTON (c. 1460–1529)

To Mistress Margaret Hussey

Merry Margaret,
  As midsummer flower,
Gentle as falcon
Or hawk of the tower,[2]
5   With solace and gladness,
Much mirth and no madness,
All good and no badness;
  So joyously,
  So maidenly,
10   So womanly
Her demeaning
In every thing,
Far, far passing
That I can endite°   *compose*
15   Or suffice to write
Of merry Margaret
  As midsummer flower,
Gentle as falcon
Or hawk of the tower.
20   As patient and as still
And as full of good will
As fair Isaphill[3]
Colyander,
Sweet pomander°   *coriander*
25   Good Cassander[4]
Steadfast of thought,
Well made, well wrought,
Far may be sought
Ere that ye can find
30   So courteous, so kind
As merry Margaret,
  This midsummer flower,
Gentle as falcon
Or hawk of the tower.

---

[2] *Falcon-gentle* is a hawking term used to denote a young or female hawk; "hawk of the tower"
refers to a high-flying hawk looking for prey.
[3] Hypsipyle (or Isaphill) was the Queen of Lemnos and the model of a faithful daughter.
[4] Cassandra, daughter of Priam, King of Troy, was famous for her gift of prophecy.

SIR THOMAS WYATT (1503–1542)

· They Flee from Me[5]

They flee from me, that sometime did me seek,
With naked foot stalking in my chamber.
I have seen them, gentle, tame, and meek,
That now are wild, and do not remember
5   That sometime they put themselves in danger
To take bread at my hand; and now they range,
Busily seeking with a continual change.

Thankéd be fortune it hath been otherwise.
Twenty times better; but once in special,
10   In thin array, after a pleasant guise,
When her loose gown from her shoulders did fall,
And she me caught in her arms long and small,°   *thin*
Therewithall sweetly did me kiss
And softly said, "Dear heart, how like you this?"

15   It was no dream, I lay broad waking.
But all is turned, thorough my gentleness,
Into a strange fashion of forsaking;
And I have leave to go, of her goodness,
And she also to use newfangleness[6]
20   But since that I so kindely am servéd,
I fain would know what she hath deservéd.

SIR WALTER RALEIGH (1552–1618)

The Nymph's Reply to the Shepherd

If all the world and love were young,
And truth in every shepherd's tongue,
These pretty pleasures might me move
To live with thee and be thy love.

5   Time drives the flocks from field to fold
When rivers rage and rocks grow cold,
And Philomel° becometh dumb;   *the nightingale*
The rest complains of cares to come.

The flowers do fade, and wanton fields
10   To wayward winter reckoning yields;
A honey tongue, a heart of gall,
Is fancy's spring, but sorrow's fall.

Thy gowns, thy shoes, thy beds of roses,
Thy cap, thy kirtle°, and thy posies   *dress*
15   Soon break, soon wither, soon forgotten—
In folly ripe, in reason rotten.

---

[5] This poem is discussed at length in the Appendix, pages 1390–1391.
[6] "To use newfangleness" means to explore new things—that is, to be fickle.

Thy belt of straw and ivy buds,
Thy coral clasps and amber studs,
All these in me no means can move
20   To come to thee and be thy love.

But could youth last and love still breed,
Had joys no date° nor age no need,   *conclusion*
Then these delights my mind might move
To live with thee and be thy love.

Compare "The Nymph's Reply to the Shepherd" with Christopher Marlowe's "The Passionate Shepherd to His Love" on pages 423–24.

SIR PHILIP SIDNEY (1554–1586)

From Astrophel and Stella,[7] Sonnet #71

Who will in fairest book of Nature know
How virtue may best lodged in beauty be,
Let him but learn of love to read in thee,
Stella, those fair lines which true goodness show.
5   There shall he find all vices' overthrow,
Not by rude force, but sweetest sovereignty
Of reason, from whose light those night birds fly,
That inward sun in thine eyes shineth so.
And, not content to be perfection's heir
10   Thyself, dost strive all minds that way to move,
Who mark in thee what is in thee most fair.
So while thy beauty draws the heart to love,
As fast thy virtue bends that love to good.
"But ah," Desire still cries, "give me some food."

Compare Sonnet #71 to Herbert's "Love (III)" on p. 556, and Shakespeare's "My Mistress' Eyes Are Nothing Like the Sun," on p. 677.

WILLIAM SHAKESPEARE (1564–1616)

Fear No More[8]

Fear no more the heat o' the sun,
    Nor the furious winter's rages;
Thou thy worldly task hast done,
    Home art gone, and ta'en thy wages.
5   Golden lads and girls all must,
    As chimney-sweepers, come to dust.

---

[7] Astrophel and Stella are the names of the two characters in Sidney's sonnet series. Their names literally mean "star-lover" and "star."
[8] The lines are from *Cymbeline*. They are a dirge for the supposedly dead heroine, Imogen.

Fear no more the frown o' the great;
   Thou art past the tyrant's stroke;
Care no more to clothe and eat;
10   To thee the reed is as the oak.
The scepter, learning, physic,° must   *medicine*
All follow this, and come to dust.

Fear no more the lightning-flash,
   Nor the all-dreaded thunder-stone;°   *thunderbolt*
15 Fear not slander, censure rash;
   Thou hast finished joy and moan.
All lovers young, all lovers must
Consign° to thee, and come to dust.   *Give themselves over*

THOMAS CAMPION (1567–1620)

There Is a Garden in Her Face

There is a garden in her face
Where roses and white lilies grow;
   A heav'nly paradise is that place
Wherein all pleasant fruits do flow.
5   There cherries grow which none may buy
        Till "Cherry-ripe" themselves do cry.[9]

Those cherries fairly do enclose
Of orient pearl a double row,
   Which when her lovely laughter shows,
10   They look like rose-buds filled with snow;
        Yet them nor peer nor prince can buy,
        Till "Cherry-ripe" themselves do cry.

Her eyes like angels watch them still;
Her brows like bended bows do stand,
15   Threat'ning with piercing frowns to kill
All that attempt, with eye or hand
        Those sacred cherries to come nigh
        Till "Cherry-ripe" themselves do cry.

Consider "There Is a Garden in Her Face" as an example of metaphor or allegory.

JOHN DONNE (1572–1631)

I Am a Little World Made Cunningly

I am a little world made cunningly
Of elements, and an angelic sprite,[10]
But black sin hath betrayed to endless night

---

[9] "Cherry-ripe" was the cry of a London fruit seller.
[10] Donne conceives of humanity as being made of both spirit and matter.

My world's both parts, and O, both parts must die.
5   You which beyond that heaven which was most high
Have found new spheres, and of new lands can write,[11]
Pour new seas in mine eyes, that so I might
Drown my world with my weeping earnestly,
Or wash it if it must be drowned no more.[12]
10   But O, it must be burnt! Alas, the fire
Of lust and envy have burnt it heretofore,
And made it fouler; let their flames retire,
And burn me, O Lord, with a fiery zeal
Of Thee and Thy house, which doth in eating heal.

JOHN DONNE (1572–1631)

Death Be Not Proud

Death, be not proud, though some have calléd thee
Mighty and dreadful, for thou art not so;
For those whom thou think'st thou dost overthrow
Die not, poor Death, nor yet canst thou kill me.
5   From rest and sleep, which but thy pictures be,
Much pleasure; then from thee much more must flow,
And soonest our best men with thee do go,
Rest of their bones, and soul's delivery.
Thou art slave to fate, chance, kings, and desperate men,
10   And dost with poison, war, and sickness dwell,
And poppy[13] or charms can make us sleep as well
And better than they stroke; why swell'st thou then?
One short sleep past, we wake eternally
And death shall be no more; Death, thou shalt die.

Consider "Death Be Not Proud" as an example of personification.

ROBERT HERRICK (1591–1674)

Delight in Disorder

A sweet disorder in the dress
Kindles in clothes a wantonness.
A lawn° about the shoulders thrown   *fine shawl*
Into a fine distractión;
5   An erring° lace, which here and there   *wandering*
Enthralls the crimson stomacher;°   *bodice*
A cuff neglectful, and thereby
Ribbons to flow confusedly;

---

[11] Donne alludes to new astronomic and geographic discoveries.
[12] God promised Noah He would not bring another flood to cover the world (Genesis 60:11).
[13] Poppies are the raw ingredient for opium, which can produce sleep and ease pain as well as cause death.

A winning wave, deserving note,
10   In the tempestuous petticoat;
A careless shoestring, in whose tie
I see a wild civility;
Do more bewitch me than when art
Is too precise in every part.

ROBERT HERRICK (1591–1674)

Upon Julia's Clothes

Whenas in silks my Julia goes,
Then, then, methinks, how sweetly flows
That liquefaction[14] of her clothes.

Next, when I cast mine eyes, and see
5   That brave vibration, each way free,
O, how that glittering taketh me!

WILLIAM DAVENANT (1606–1668)

The Philosopher and the Lover: To a Mistress Dying

Lover
Your beauty, ripe and calm, and fresh
      As eastern summers are,
Must now, forsaking time and flesh,
      Add light to some small star.

Philosopher
5   Whilst she yet lives, were stars decayed,
      Their light by hers relief might find;
But death will lead her to a shade
      Where love is cold, and beauty blind.

Lover
Lovers, whose priests all poets are,
10   Think ev'ry mistress when she dies
Is changed at least into a star;
      And who dares doubt the poet wise?

Philosopher
But ask not bodies doomed to die
      To what abode they go;
15   Since knowledge is but sorrow's spy,
      It is not safe to know.

Compare "The Philosopher and the Lover" with John Crowe Ransom's "Here Lies a Lady" on page 475.

---

[14] *Liquefaction* is the act of making a liquid, especially from a solid.

ANNE BRADSTREET (1612?–1672)

To My Dear and Loving Husband

If ever two were one, then surely we.
If ever man were lov'd by wife, then thee;
If ever wife was happy in a man,
Compare with me ye women if you can.
5   I prize thy love more than whole Mines of gold,
Or all the riches that the East doth hold.
My love is such that Rivers cannot quench,
Nor ought but love from thee, give recompence.
Thy love is such I can no way repay,
10 The heavens reward thee manifold I pray.
Then while we live, in love lets so persever,
That when we live no more, we may live ever.

EDWARD TAYLOR (1645?–1729)

Upon a Spider Catching a Fly

Thou sorrow, venom Elfe:
   Is this thy play,
To spin a web out of thyselfe
   To Catch a Fly?
5   For Why?

I saw a pettish° wasp   *peevish*
   Fall foule therein.
Whom yet thy Whorle[15] pins not clasp
   Lest he should fling
10   His sting.

But as affraid, remote
   Didst stand hereat
And with thy little fingers stroke
   And gently tap
15   His back.

Thus gently him didst treate
   Lest he should pet,
And in a froppish,° waspish heate   *fretful*
   Should greatly fret
20   Thy net.

Whereas the silly Fly,
   Caught by its leg
Thou by the throate tookst hastily
   And 'hinde the head
25   Bite Dead.

---

[15] A "whorle" is the flywheel of a spindle.

This goes to pot, that not
     Nature doth call.
Strive not above what strength hath got
     Lest in the brawle
30   Thou fall.

This Frey° seems thus to us.   *fray, fight*
     Hells Spider gets
His intrails spun to whip Cords thus
     And wove to nets
35   And sets.

To tangle Adams race
     In's stratigems
To their Destructions, spoil'd, made base
     By venom things
40   Damn'd Sins.

But mighty, Gracious Lord
     Communicate
Thy Grace to breake the Cord, afford
     Us Glorys Gate
45   And State.

We'l Nightingaile sing like
     When pearcht on high
In Glories Cage, thy glory, bright,
     And thankfully,
50   For joy.

Compare "Upon a Spider Catching a Fly" with Walt Whitman's "A Noiseless Patient Spider" on page 728.

JONATHAN SWIFT (1667–1745)

A Description of the Morning

Now hardly here and there a hackney-coach
Appearing showed the ruddy morn's approach.
Now Betty from her master's bed had flown,
And softly stole to discompose her own;
5   The slipshod 'prentice from his master's door
Had pared the dirt and sprinkled around the floor.
Now Moll had whirled her mop with dexterous airs,
Prepared to scrub the entry and the stairs.
The youth with broomy stumps began to trace
10   The kennel-edge,° where wheels had worn the place.   *gutter*
The small-coal man was heard with cadence deep,
Till drowned in shriller notes of chimney-sweep:

Duns[16] at his lordship's gate began to meet;
And brickdust Moll had screamed through half the street.
15 The turnkey° now his flock returning sees,   *prison guard*
Duly let out a-nights to steal for fees:
The watchful bailiffs take their silent stands,
And schoolboys lag with satchels in their hands.

ALEXANDER POPE (1688–1744)

Epistle to a Young Lady, on Her Leaving the Town After the Coronation[17]

As some fond° virgin, whom her mother's care   *foolish*
Drags from the town to wholesome country air,
Just when she learns to roll a melting eye,
And hear a spark,° yet think no danger nigh—   *young admirer*
5   From the dear man unwilling she must sever,
Yet takes one kiss before she parts forever—
Thus from the world fair Zephalinda flew,
Saw others happy, and with sighs withdrew;
Not that their pleasures caused her discontent:
10 She sighed not that they stayed, but that she went.
She went—to plain-work and to purling brooks,
Old-fashioned halls, dull aunts, and croaking rooks;
She went from opera, park, assembly, play,
To morning walks, and prayers three hours a day;
15 To part her time 'twixt reading and bohea,°   *black tea*
To muse, and spill her solitary tea;
Or o'er cold coffee trifle with the spoon,
Count the slow clock, and dine exact at noon;
Divert her eyes with pictures in the fire,
20 Hum half a tune, tell stories to the squire;
Up to her godly garret after seven,
There starve and pray, for that's the way to heaven.
Some squire, perhaps, you take delight to rack,
Whose game is "whisk,"° whose treat a toast in sack;   *whist*
25 Who visits with a gun, presents you birds,
Then gives a smacking buss,° and cries, "No words!"   *kiss*
Or with his hound comes hollowing from the stable,
Makes love with nods, and knees beneath a table;
Whose laughs are hearty, though his jests are coarse,
30 And loves you best of all things—but his horse.
In some fair evening, on your elbow laid,
You dream of triumphs in the rural shade;

---

[16] "Duns" are people requesting money.
[17] Pope wrote this poem after the coronation of George I in 1714. Zephalinda and Parthenia are names he has invented for actual friends.

In pensive thought recall the fancied scene,
See coronations rise on every green:
35   Before you pass the imaginary sights
Of Lords, and Earls, and Dukes, and gartered Knights,[18]
While the spread fan o'ershades your closing eyes,
Then gives one flirt, and all the vision flies.
Thus vanish sceptres, coronets, and balls,
40   And leave you in lone woods, or empty walls!
     So when your slave, at some dear idle time
(Not plagued with headaches, or the want of rhyme)
Stands in the streets, abstracted from the crew,
And while he seems to study, thinks of you;
45   Just when his fancy paints your sprightly eyes,
Or sees the blush of soft Parthenia rise,
Gay[19] pats my shoulder, and you vanish quite,
Streets, chairs, and coxcombs rush upon my sight.
Vexed to be still in town, I knit my brow,
50   Look sour, and hum a tune—as you may now.

THOMAS GRAY (1716–1771)

• Ode on the Death of a Favorite Cat[20]

Drowned in a tub of goldfishes

'Twas on a lofty vase's side,
Where China's gayest art had dyed
     The azure flowers that blow;
Demurest of the tabby kind,
5   The pensive Selima reclined,
     Gazed on the lake below.

Her conscious tail her joy declared;
The fair round face, the snowy beard,
     The velvet of her paws,
10   Her coat, that with the tortoise vies,
Her ears of jet,° and emerald eyes,   black
     She saw; and purred applause.

Still had she gazed; but 'midst the tide
Two angel forms were seen to glide,
15   The genii[21] of the stream:
Their scaly armor's Tyrian° hue   purple

---

18 "Gartered Knights" refers to persons honored with the Order of the Garter, one of the highest distinctions the king may grant a British citizen.
19 The poet John Gay, whose poetic fable "The Lion, the Fox, and Geese" may be found on page 544.
20 Gray wrote this elegy at the request of Horace Walpole (1717–1797), the author. Walpole's cat, Selima, died by drowning in a cistern.
21 Genii, the plural of genius. They are the protecting spirits of a place or person.

Through richest purple to the view
    Betrayed a golden gleam.

The hapless nymph with wonder saw:
20   A whisker first and then a claw,
    With many an ardent wish,
She stretched in vain to reach the prize.
What female heart can gold despise?
    What cat's averse to fish?

25   Presumptuous maid! with looks intent
Again she stretched, again she bent,
    Nor knew the gulf between.
(Malignant Fate sat by and smiled)
The slippery verge her feet beguiled,
30   She tumbled headlong in.

Eight times emerging from the flood
She mewed to every watery god,
    Some speedy aid to send.
No dolphin came,[22] no nereid° stirred: *sea nymph*
35   Nor cruel Tom, nor Susan heard.
    A favorite has no friend!

From hence, ye beauties, undeceived,
Know, one false step is ne'er retrieved,
    And be with caution bold.
40   Not all that tempts your wandering eyes
And heedless hearts is lawful prize;
    Nor all that glisters gold.

WILLIAM BLAKE (1757–1827)

The Tyger

Tyger! Tyger! burning bright,
In the forests of the night;
What immortal hand or eye,
Could frame thy fearful symmetry?

5   In what distant deeps or skies
Burnt the fire of thine eyes!
On what wings dare he aspire?
What the hand, dare seize the fire?

And what shoulder, & what art,
10   Could twist the sinews of thy heart?
And when thy heart began to beat,
What dread hand? & what dread feet?

---

[22] Dolphins have the reputation for saving people in distress. Tom and Susan are typical names for servants.

What the hammer? what the chain,
In what furnace was thy brain?
15   What the anvil? what dread grasp,
Dare its deadly terrors clasp?

When the stars threw down their spears
And water'd heaven with their tears:
Did he smile his work to see?
20   Did he who made the Lamb make thee?

Tyger! Tyger! burning bright,
In the forests of the night:
What immortal hand or eye,
Dare frame thy fearful symmetry?

ROBERT BURNS (1759–1796)

A Red, Red Rose

O My Luve's like a red, red rose,
    That's newly sprung in June;
O My Luve's like the melodie
    That's sweetly played in tune.

5   As fair art thou, my bonnie lass,
    So deep in luve am I;
And I will luve thee still, my dear,
    Till a' the seas gang° dry.   *go*

Till a' the seas gang dry, my dear,
10   And the rocks melt wi' the sun:
O I will love thee still, my dear,
    While the sands o' life shall run.

And fare thee weel, my only luve,
    And fare thee weel awhile!
15   And I will come again, my luve,
    Though it were ten thousand mile.

WILLIAM WORDSWORTH (1770–1850)

I Wandered Lonely as a Cloud

I wandered lonely as a cloud
    That floats on high o'er vales and hills,
When all at once I saw a crowd,
    A host, of golden daffodils,
5   Beside the lake, beneath the trees,
Fluttering and dancing in the breeze.

Continuous as the stars that shine
    And twinkle on the milky way,
They stretched in never-ending line

Along the margin of a bay:
      Ten thousand saw I at a glance,
      Tossing their heads in sprightly dance.

      The waves beside them danced; but they
          Out-did the sparkling waves in glee;
15   A poet could not but be gay,
          In such a jocund company;
      I gazed—and gazed—but little thought
      What wealth the show to me had brought:

      For oft, when on my couch I lie
20   In vacant or in pensive mood,
      They flash upon that inward eye
          Which is the bliss of solitude;
      And then my heart with pleasure fills,
      And dances with the daffodils.

WILLIAM WORDSWORTH (1770–1850)

• The World Is Too Much with Us

      The world is too much with us; late and soon,
      Getting and spending, we lay waste our powers:
      Little we see in Nature that is ours;
      We have given our hearts away, a sordid boon![23]
5   This Sea that bares her bosom to the moon,
      The winds that will be howling at all hours,
      And are up-gathered now like sleeping flowers,
      For this, for everything, we are out of tune;
      It moves us not.—Great God! I'd rather be
10   A Pagan suckled in a creed outworn;
      So might I, standing on this pleasant lea,
      Have glimpses that would make me less forlorn;
      Have sight of Proteus[24] rising from the sea;
      Or hear old Triton° blow his wreathéd horn.   *a sea god*

WALTER SAVAGE LANDOR (1775–1864)

On His Seventy-fifth Birthday[25]

      I strove with none; for none was worth my strife,[26]
          Nature I loved, and next to Nature, Art;
      I warmed both hands before the fire of life,
          It sinks, and I am ready to depart.

Discuss "On His Seventy-fifth Birthday" as an epigram.

---

[23] We have given our hearts away to the sordid gift of "getting and spending"—that is, commercial
   enterprise.
[24] The old man of the sea, sometimes described as the son of Poseidon.
[25] Landor lived into his ninetieth year.
[26] Landor was constantly in litigation and was forced into exile because of court battles.

GEORGE GORDON, LORD BYRON (1788–1824)

• She Walks in Beauty[27]

1

She walks in beauty, like the night
    Of cloudless climes and starry skies;
And all that's best of dark and bright
    Meet in her aspect and her eyes:
5   Thus mellowed to that tender light
    Which heaven to gaudy day denies.

2

One shade the more, one ray the less,
    Had half impaired the nameless grace
Which waves in every raven tress,
10   Or softly lightens o'er her face;
Where thoughts serenely sweet express
    How pure, how dear their dwelling place.

3

And on that cheek, and o'er that brow,
    So soft, so calm, yet eloquent,
15   The smiles that win, the tints that glow,
    But tell of days in goodness spent,
A mind at peace with all below,
    A heart whose love is innocent!

PERCY BYSSHE SHELLEY (1792–1822)

Ozymandias[28]

I met a traveler from an antique° land   *ancient*
Who said: Two vast and trunkless legs of stone
Stand in the desert. Near them, on the sand,
Half sunk, a shattered visage lies, whose frown,
5   And wrinkled lip, and sneer of cold command,
Tell that its sculptor well those passions read
Which yet survive, stamped on these lifeless things,
The hand that mocked° them and the heart that fed;   *carved and ridiculed*
And on the pedestal these words appear:
10   "My name is Ozymandias, king of kings:
Look on my works, ye Mighty, and despair!"
Nothing beside remains. Round the decay
Of that colossal wreck, boundless and bare
The lone and level sands stretch far away.

---

[27] This poem was written for Mrs. Robert John Wilmot, Byron's cousin. When Byron first met her, she was wearing a black dress with spangles because she was in mourning.
[28] Ozymandias, or Ramses II, was pharaoh of Egypt in the thirteenth century B.C.

JOHN KEATS (1795–1821)

• When I Have Fears

When I have fears that I may cease to be
    Before my pen has gleaned my teeming brain,
Before high-piléd books, in charact'ry,°   *print*
    Hold like rich garners the full-ripened grain;
5   When I behold, upon the night's starred face,
    Huge cloudy symbols of a high romance,
And think that I may never live to trace
    Their shadows, with the magic hand of chance;
And when I feel, fair creature of an hour,
10   That I shall never look upon thee more,
Never have relish in the faery power
    Of unreflecting love!—then on the shore
Of the wide world I stand alone, and think
Till Love and Fame to nothingness do sink.

JOHN KEATS (1795–1821)

• To Autumn

1

Season of mists and mellow fruitfulness,
    Close bosom-friend of the maturing sun;
Conspiring with him how to load and bless
    With fruit the vines that round the thatch-eaves run;
5   To bend with apples the mossed cottage-trees,
    And fill all fruit with ripeness to the core;
        To swell the gourd, and plump the hazel shells
    With a sweet kernel; to set budding more,
And still more, later flowers for the bees,
10   Until they think warm days will never cease,
        For Summer has o'er-brimmed their clammy cells.

2

Who hath not seen thee oft amid thy store?
    Sometimes whoever seeks abroad may find
Thee sitting careless on a granary floor,
15   Thy hair soft-lifted by the winnowing²⁹ wind;
Or on a half-reaped furrow sound asleep,
    Drowsed with the fume of poppies, while thy hook°   *scythe*
        Spares the next swath and all its twinéd flowers:
And sometimes like a gleaner³⁰ thou dost keep
20   Steady thy laden head across a brook;
    Or by a cider-press, with patient look,
        Thou watchest the last oozings hours by hours.

---

²⁹ The process by which the chaff or husk is separated from the grain, usually by the wind.
³⁰ One who gathers the remains of a crop after it has been harvested.

Where are the songs of Spring? Aye, where are they?
Think not of them, thou hast thy music too—
25 While barred clouds bloom the soft-dying day,
And touch the stubble-plains with rosy hue;
Then in a wailful choir the small gnats mourn
Among the river sallows,° borne aloft   *willows*
Or sinking as the light wind lives or dies;
30 And full-grown lambs loud bleat from hilly bourn;°   *region*
Hedge crickets sing; and now with treble soft
The redbreast whistles from a garden croft;[31]
And gathering swallows twitter in the skies.

Discuss "To Autumn" as an example of personification.

THOMAS LOVELL BEDDOES (1803–1849)

Song: How Many Times Do I Love Thee, Dear?

How many times do I love thee, dear?
Tell me how many thoughts there be
In the atmosphere
Of a new-fall'n year,
5 Whose white and sable hours appear
The latest flake of Eternity—
So many times do I love thee, dear.

How many times do I love again?
Tell me how many beads there are
10 In a silver chain
Of evening rain,
Unraveled from the tumbling main,
And threading the eye of a yellow star—
So many times do I love again.

Compare Beddoes's "Song" with Elizabeth Barrett Browning's "How Do I Love Thee"
on page 724.

HENRY WADSWORTH LONGFELLOW (1807–1882)

The Jewish Cemetery at Newport[32]

How strange it seems! These Hebrews in their graves,
Close by the street of this fair seaport town,
Silent beside the never-silent waves,
At rest in all this moving up and down!

---

[31] An enclosed farm plot.
[32] The oldest Jewish synagogue in the United States is located in Newport, Rhode Island.

5   The trees are white with dust, that o'er their sleep
        Wave their broad curtains in the south-wind's breath,
    While underneath these leafy tents they keep
        The long, mysterious Exodus of Death[33]

    And these sepulchral stones, so old and brown,
10   That pave with level flags their burial-place,
    Seem like the tablets of the Law, thrown down
        And broken by Moses at the mountain's base.[34]

    The very names recorded here are strange,
        Of foreign accent, and of different climes;
15 Alvares and Rivera interchange
        With Abraham and Jacob of old times.[35]

    "Blessed be God, for he created Death!"
        The mourners said, "and Death is rest and peace;"
    Then added, in the certainty of faith,
20   "And giveth Life that nevermore shall cease."

    Closed are the portals of their Synagogue,
        No Psalms of David now the silence break,
    No Rabbi reads the ancient Decalogue°   *the Ten Commandments*
        In the grand dialect the Prophets spake.

25 Gone are the living, but the dead remain,
        And not neglected; for a hand unseen,
    Scattering its bounty, like a summer rain,
        Still keeps their graves and their remembrance green.

    How came they here? What burst of Christian hate,
30   What persecution, merciless and blind,
    Drove o'er the sea—that desert desolate—
        These Ishmaels and Hagars of mankind?[36]

    They lived in narrow streets and lanes obscure,
        Ghetto and Judenstrass,[37] in mirk and mire;
35 Taught in the school of patience to endure
        The life of anguish and the death of fire.

    All their lives long, with the unleavened bread
        And bitter herbs of exile and its fears,
    The wasting famine of the heart they fed,
40   And slaked its thirst with marah of their tears.[38]

---

[33] Exodus, the second book of the Old Testament, records the expulsion of the Jews from Egypt and their subsequent wanderings. During their travels they made their homes in tents.
[34] The incident is recorded in Exodus 32:19.
[35] The Jews of Newport were of mostly Spanish and Portuguese descent.
[36] Two exiles whose stories are told in the Bible.
[37] In German, literally "Jew Street."
[38] *Marah* means bitterness in Hebrew. During Passover, the Jewish celebration of the Exodus, Jews eat unleavened bread (matzoh) and bitter herbs in commemoration of that bitter time.

Anathema maranatha![39] was the cry
   That rang from town to town, from street to street;
At every gate the accursed Mordecai[40]
   Was mocked and jeered, and spurned by Christian feet.

45   Pride and humiliation hand in hand
   Walked with them through the world where'er they went;
Trampled and beaten were they as the sand,
   And yet unshaken as the continent.

For in the background figures vague and vast
50   Of patriarchs and of prophets rose sublime,
And all the great traditions of the Past
   They saw reflected in the coming time.

And thus forever with reverted look
   The mystic volume of the world they read,
55   Spelling it backward, like a Hebrew book,[41]
   Till life became a Legend of the Dead.

But ah! what once has been shall be no more!
   The groaning earth in travail and in pain
Brings forth its races, but does not restore,
60   And the dead nations never rise again.

ELIZABETH BARRETT BROWNING (1809–1861)

How Do I Love Thee?

How do I love thee? Let me count the ways.
I love thee to the depth and breadth and height
My soul can reach, when feeling out of sight
For the ends of Being and ideal Grace.
5   I love thee to the level of everyday's
Most quiet need, by sun and candle-light.
I love thee freely, as men strive for Right;
I love thee purely, as they turn from Praise.
I love thee with the passion put to use
10   In my old griefs, and with my childhood's faith.
I love thee with a love I seemed to lose
With my lost saints,—I love thee with the breath,
Smiles, tears, of all my life!—and, if God choose,
I shall but love thee better after death.

Compare "How Do I Love Thee" with Thomas Lovell Beddoes's "Song" on page 722.

---

[39] St. Paul's epithet for those who did not believe in Christ; it became a phrase applied only to Jews.
[40] Mordecai was a famous Persian Jew. Here the word is used as a synonym for "Jew."
[41] Hebrew is written from right to left—in Longfellow's mind, backward.

OLIVER WENDELL HOLMES (1809–1894)

My Aunt

My aunt! my dear unmarried aunt!
    Long years have o'er her flown;
Yet still she strains the aching clasp
    That binds her virgin zone;
5   I know it hurts her,—though she looks
    As cheerful as she can;
Her waist is ampler than her life,
    For life is but a span.

My aunt! my poor deluded aunt!
10   Her hair is almost gray;
Why will she train that winter curl
    In such a spring-like way?
How can she lay her glasses down,
    And say she reads as well,
15   When through a double convex lens
    She just makes out to spell?

Her father—grandpapa! forgive
    This erring lip its smiles—
Vowed she should make the finest girl
20   Within a hundred miles;
He sent her to a stylish school;
    'T was in her thirteenth June;
And with her, as the rules required,
    "Two towels and a spoon."

25   They braced my aunt against a board,
    To make her straight and tall;
They laced her up, they starved her down,
    To make her light and small;°   *thin*
They pinched her feet, they singed her hair,
30   They screwed it up with pins;—
Oh, never mortal suffered more
    In penance for her sins.

So, when my precious aunt was done,
    My grandsire brought her back
35   (By daylight, lest some rabid youth
    Might follow on the track);
"Ah!" said my grandsire, as he shook
    Some powder in his pan;[42]
"What could this lovely creature do
40   Against a desperate man!"

---

[42] The grandfather is loading a flintlock rifle.

Alas! nor chariot, nor barouche,[43]
    Nor bandit cavalcade,
Tore from the trembling father's arms
    His all-accomplished maid.
45   For her how happy had it been!
    And Heaven had spared to me
To see one sad, ungathered rose
    On my ancestral tree.

Compare "My Aunt" with T. S. Eliot's "Aunt Helen" on page 562, E. E. Cummings's "the Cambridge ladies who live in furnished souls" on page 743, and Gwendolyn Brooks's "Sadie and Maud" on pages 756–57.

ROBERT BROWNING (1812–1889)

Meeting at Night

1

The gray sea and the long black land;
And the yellow half-moon large and low;
And the startled little waves that leap

In fiery ringlets from their sleep,
5   As I gain the cove with pushing prow,
And quench its speed i' the slushy sand.

Robert Browning; painting by F. Talfond (*National Portrait Gallery, London*)

---

[43] A fashionable carriage.

2

Then a mile of warm sea-scented beach;
Three fields to cross till a farm appears;
A tap at the pane, the quick sharp scratch
10   And blue spurt of a lighted match,
And a voice less loud, through its joys and fears,
Than the two hearts beating each to each!

Parting at Morning

Round the cape of a sudden came the sea,
And the sun looked over the mountain's rim:
And straight was a path of gold for him,
And the need of a world of men for me.

EMILY BRONTË (1818–1848)

The Sun Has Set

The sun has set, and the long grass now
    Waves dreamily in the evening wind;
And the wild bird has flown from that old gray stone
    In some warm nook a couch to find.

5   In all the lonely landscape round
    I see no light and hear no sound,
    Except the wind that far away
    Come sighing o'er the heathy sea.

Compare "The Sun Has Set" with James Joyce's "All Day I Hear the Noise of Waters" on page 741.

HERMAN MELVILLE (1819–1891)

On the Photograph of a Corps Commander

Ay, man is manly. Here you see
    The warrior-carriage of the head,
And brave dilation of the frame;
    And lighting all, the soul that led
5   In Spottsylvania's[44] charge to victory,
    Which justifies his fame.

A cheering picture. It is good
    To look upon a Chief like this,
In whom the spirit moulds the form.

---

[44] A Civil War battleground where the Confederate army inflicted severe losses on the Union forces.

10   Here favoring Nature, oft remiss,
      With eagle mien expressive has endued
        A man to kindle strains that warm.

      Trace back his lineage, and his sires,
        Yeoman or noble, you shall find
15   Enrolled with men of Agincourt,[45]
        Heroes who shared great Harry's mind.
      Down to us come the knightly Norman fires,
        And front the Templars bore.[46]

      Nothing can lift the heart of man
20   Like manhood in a fellow-man.
      The thought of heaven's great King afar
      But humbles us—too weak to scan;
      But manly greatness men can span,
        And feel the bonds that draw.

WALT WHITMAN (1819–1892)

A Noiseless Patient Spider

A noiseless patient spider,
I marked where on a little promontory it stood isolated,
Marked how to explore the vacant vast surrounding,
It launched forth filament, filament, filament, out of itself,
5   Ever unreeling them, ever tirelessly speeding them.

And you O my soul where you stand,
Surrounded, detached, in measureless oceans of space,
Ceaselessly musing, venturing, throwing, seeking the spheres to connect them,
Till the bridge you will need be formed, till the ductile anchor hold,
10 Till the gossamer thread you fling catch somewhere, O my soul.

Compare "A Noiseless Patient Spider" with Edward Taylor's "Upon a Spider Catching a Fly" on pages 713–14.

FRANCES E. W. HARPER (1825–1911)

The Slave Auction

The sale began—young girls were there,
    Defenceless in their wretchedness,
Whose stifled sobs of deep despair
    Revealed their anguish and distress.

5   And mothers stood with streaming eyes,
      And saw their dearest children sold;

---

[45] The scene of Henry V's victory over the French in 1415. King Henry was also called Harry.
[46] The Templars are one of the three great orders of knighthood founded at the time of the Crusades.

Unheeded rose their bitter cries,
    While tyrants bartered them for gold.

And woman, with her love and truth—
10   For these in sable° forms may dwell—   *black*
Gaz'd on the husband of her youth,
    With anguish none may paint or tell.

And men, whose sole crime was their hue,
    The impress of their Maker's hand,
15 And frail and shrinking children, too,
    Were gathered in that mournful band.

Ye who have laid your love to rest,
    And wept above their lifeless clay,
Know not the anguish of that breast,
20   Whose lov'd are rudely torn away.

Ye may not know how desolate
    Are bosoms rudely forced to part,
And how a dull and heavy weight
    Will press the life-drops from the heart.

EMILY DICKINSON (1830–1886)

My Life Had Stood, a Loaded Gun

My life had stood, a loaded gun,
In corners, till a day
The owner passed, identified,
And carried me away.

5 And now we roam in sovereign woods,
And now we hunt the doe,
And every time I speak for him,
The mountains straight reply.

And do I smile, such cordial light
10 Upon the valley glow,
It is as a Vesuvian face[47]
Had let its pleasure through.

And when at night, our good day done,
I guard my master's head,
15 'Tis better than the eider-duck's[48]
Deep pillow, to have shared.

To foe of his I'm deadly foe:
None stir the second time

---

[47] Vesuvius is an active volcano in Italy, overlooking the Bay of Naples.
[48] The down of the eider is particularly suited for stuffing pillows and quilts.

On whom I lay a yellow eye
20   Or an emphatic thumb.

Though I than he may longer live,
He longer must than I,
For I have but the power to kill,
Without the power to die.

Discuss "My Life Had Stood, a Loaded Gun" as an example of metaphor.

EMILY DICKINSON (1830–1886)

Apparently with No Surprise

Apparently with no surprise
To any happy flower,
The frost beheads it at its play
In accidental power.

5   The blond assassin passes on,
The sun proceeds unmoved
To measure off another day
For an approving God.

Discuss "Apparently with No Surprise" as an example of personification.

EMILY DICKINSON (1830–1886)

I Heard a Fly Buzz—When I Died

I heard a Fly buzz—when I died—
The Stillness in the Room
Was like the Stillness in the Air—
Between the Heaves of Storm—

5   The Eyes around—had wrung them dry—
And Breaths were gathering firm
For that last Onset—when the King
Be witnessed—in the Room—

I willed my Keepsakes—Signed away
10   What portion of me be
Assignable—and then it was
There interposed a Fly—

With Blue—uncertain stumbling Buzz—
Between the light—and me—
15   And then the Windows failed—and then
I could not see to see—

EMILY DICKINSON (1830–1886)

After Great Pain, a Formal Feeling Comes

After great pain, a formal feeling comes—
The Nerves sit ceremonious, like Tombs—
The stiff Heart questions was it He, that bore,
And Yesterday, or Centuries before?

5   The Feet, mechanical, go round—
Of Ground, or Air, or Ought—
A Wooden way
Regardless grown,
A Quartz contentment, like a stone—

10 This is the Hour of Lead—
Remembered, if outlived,
As Freezing persons, recollect the Snow—
First—Chill—then Stupor—then the letting go—

CHRISTINA ROSSETTI (1830–1894)

After Death

The curtains were half drawn; the floor was swept
    And strewn with rushes; rosemary and may
    Lay thick upon the bed on which I lay,
Where, through the lattice, ivy-shadows crept.
5   He leaned above me, thinking that I slept
    And could not hear him; but I heard him say,
    "Poor child, poor child"; and as he turned away
Came a deep silence, and I knew he wept.
He did not touch the shroud, or raise the fold
10   That hid my face, or take my hand in his,
        Or ruffle the smooth pillows for my head.
    He did not love me living; but once dead
    He pitied me; and very sweet it is
To know he still is warm though I am cold.

Compare "After Death" with Coventry Patmore's "If I Were Dead" on page 688.

GERARD MANLEY HOPKINS (1844–1889)

• Spring and Fall

To a young child

Márgarét, are you gríeving
Over Goldengrove unleaving?
Leáves, líke the things of man, you

With your fresh thoughts care for, can you?
5   Áh! ás the heart grows older
It will come to such sights colder
By and by, nor spare a sigh
Through worlds of wanwood leafmeal[49] lie;
And yet you will weep and know why.
10   Now no matter, child, the name:
Sórrow's spríngs áre the same.
Nor mouth had, no nor mind, expressed
What heart heard of, ghost° guessed: *spirit*
It ís the blight man was born for,
15   It is Margaret you mourn for.

GERARD MANLEY HOPKINS (1844–1889)

• The Windhover[50]

To Christ Our Lord

I caught this morning morning's minion,° king-   *darling*
    dom of daylight's dauphin,° dapple-dawn-drawn Falcon, in his riding   *prince*
    Of the rolling level underneath him steady air, and striding
High there, how he rung upon the rein of a wimpling° wing   *rippling as a veil*
5   In his ecstasy! then off, off forth on swing,
    As a skate's heel sweeps smooth on a bow-bend: the hurl and gliding
    Rebuffed the big wind. My heart in hiding
Stirred for a bird,—the achieve of, the mastery of the thing!

Brute beauty and valour and act, oh, air, pride, plume, here
10   Buckle! AND the fire that breaks from thee then, a billion
Times told lovelier, more dangerous, O my chevalier!°   *knight*

    No wonder of it: shéer plód makes plough down sillion[51]
Shine, and blue-bleak embers, ah my dear,
    Fall, gall themselves, and gash gold-vermilion.

ALICE MEYNELL (1847–1922)

The Threshing-Machine

No "fan[52] is in his hand" for these
Young villagers beneath the trees,
    Watching the wheels. But I recall
    The rhythm of rods° that rise and fall,   *flails*
5   Purging the harvest, over-seas.

---

[49] *Wanwood* and *leafmeal* are two *portmanteau words*. Wan + wood is meant to suggest bloodless
    limbs, and leaf + (piece) meal suggests the random pattern of the fallen leaves.
[50] The windhover is the common name for the kestrel, a European falcon that flies with its head
    into the wind.
[51] The ridge between two plowed furrows.
[52] A *fan* is a basket used to winnow grain.

732   Poems for Further Reading

No fan, no flail, no threshing-floor!
And all their symbols evermore
    Forgone in England now—the sign,
    The visible pledge, the threat divine.
10 The chaff° dispersed, the wheat in store.   *husk*

The unbreathing engine marks no tune,
Steady at sunrise, steady at noon.
    Inhuman, perfect, saving time,
    And saving measure, and saving rhyme.
15 And did our Ruskin speak too soon?[53]

"No noble strength on earth" he sees
"Save Hercules' arm"[54] His grave decrees
    Curse wheel and steam. As the wheels ran
    I saw the other strength of man.
20 I knew the brain of Hercules.

OSCAR WILDE (1856–1900)

The Harlot's House

We caught the tread of dancing feet,
We loitered down the moonlit street,
And stopped beneath the harlot's house.

Inside, above the din and fray,
5 We heard the loud musicians play
The "Treues Liebes Herz" of Strauss.[55]

Like strange mechanical grotesques,
Making fantastic arabesques,
The shadows raced across the blind.

10 We watched the ghostly dancers spin
To sound of horn and violin,
Like black leaves wheeling in the wind.

Like wire-pulled automatons,
Slim silhouetted skeletons
15 Went sidling through the slow quadrille.

They took each other by the hand,
And danced a stately saraband;
Their laughter echoed thin and shrill.

Sometimes a clockwork puppet pressed
20 A phantom lover to her breast,
Sometimes they seemed to try to sing.

---

[53] John Ruskin (1819–1900) was an English essayist and critic who believed that by following
agricultural pursuits, people could avoid the horrors of industrialism.
[54] Hercules was a mythical strong man.
[55] In German, "love's true heart."

Sometimes a horrible marionette
Came out, and smoked its cigarette
Upon the steps like a live thing.

25   Then, turning to my love, I said,
"The dead are dancing with the dead,
The dust is whirling with the dust."

But she—she heard the violin,
And left my side, and entered in:
30   Love passed into the house of lust.

Then suddenly the tune went false,
The dancers wearied of the waltz,
The shadows ceased to wheel and whirl.

And down the long and silent street,
35   The dawn, with silver-sandaled feet,
Crept like a frightened girl.

A. E. HOUSMAN (1859–1936)

Loveliest of Trees

Loveliest of trees, the cherry now
Is hung with bloom along the bough,
And stands about the woodland ride
Wearing white for Eastertide.

5   Now, of my threescore years and ten,
Twenty will not come again,
And take from seventy springs a score,
It only leaves me fifty more.

And since to look at things in bloom
10   Fifty springs are little room,
About the woodlands I will go
To see the cherry hung with snow.

A. E. HOUSMAN (1859–1936)

When I Was One-and-Twenty

When I was one-and-twenty
    I heard a wise man say,
"Give crowns and pounds and guineas
    But not your heart away;
5   Give pearls away and rubies
    But keep your fancy free."
But I was one-and-twenty,
    No use to talk to me.

When I was one-and-twenty
10   I heard him say again,
"The heart out of the bosom
        Was never given in vain:
'Tis paid with sighs a plenty
        And sold for endless rue."
15 And I am two-and-twenty,
        And oh, 'tis true, 'tis true.

Compare "When I Was One-and-Twenty" with John Crowe Ransom's "Piazza Piece" on page 488.

W. E. B. DuBOIS (1868–1963)

The Song of the Smoke

I am the smoke king,
I am black.
I am swinging in the sky,
I am ringing worlds on high:
5   I am the thought of the throbbing mills,
I am the soul toil kills,
I am the ripple of trading rills.

Up I'm curling from the sod,
I am whirling home to God.
10 I am the smoke king,
I am black.

I am the smoke king,
I am black.
I am wreathing broken hearts,
15 I am sheathing devils' darts;
Dark inspiration of iron times,
Wedding the toil of toiling climes
Shedding the blood of bloodless crimes.

Down I lower in the blue,
20 Up I tower toward the true,
I am the smoke king,
I am black.

I am the smoke king,
I am black.

25 I am darkening with song,
I am hearkening to wrong;
I will be black as blackness can,
The blacker the mantle the mightier the man,
My purpl'ing midnights no day dawn may ban.

30

I am carving God in night,
I am painting hell in white.
I am the smoke king,
I am black.

Compare "The Song of the Smoke" with N. Scott Momaday's "The Delight Song of Tsoai-Talee" on page 533.

EDWIN ARLINGTON ROBINSON (1869–1935)

Mr. Flood's Party

Old Eben Flood, climbing alone one night
Over the hill between the town below
And the forsaken upland hermitage
That held as much as he should ever know
5   On earth again of home, paused warily.
The road was his with not a native near;
And Eben, having leisure, said aloud,
For no man else in Tilbury Town to hear:

"Well, Mr. Flood, we have the harvest moon
10   Again, and we may not have many more;
The bird is on the wing, the poet says,
And you and I have said it here before.
Drink to the bird."[56] He raised up to the light
The jug that he had gone so far to fill,
15   And answered huskily: "Well, Mr. Flood,
Since you propose it, I believe I will."

Alone, as if enduring to the end
A valiant armor of scarred hopes outworn,
He stood there in the middle of the road
20   Like Roland's ghost winding° a silent horn.[57]   *blowing*
Below him, in the town among the trees,
Where friends of other days had honored him,
A phantom salutation of the dead
Rang thinly till old Eben's eyes were dim.

25   Then, as a mother lays her sleeping child
Down tenderly, fearing it may awake,
He set the jug down slowly at his feet
With trembling care, knowing that most things break;
And only when assured that on firm earth
30   It stood, as the uncertain lives of men
Assuredly did not, he paced away,
And with his hand extended paused again:

---

[56] From the *Rubaiyat of Omar Khayyam*. The bird referred to is the bird of time.
[57] Roland was a knight who delayed calling for help with his horn at the Battle of Roncesvalles (A.D. 778) until the situation was hopeless.

"Well, Mr. Flood, we have not met like this
In a long time; and many a change has come
35   To both of us, I fear, since last it was
We had a drop together. Welcome home!"
Convivially returning with himself,
Again he raised the jug up to the light;
And with an acquiescent quaver said:
40   "Well, Mr. Flood, if you insist, I might.

"Only a very little, Mr. Flood—
For auld lang syne.[58] No more, sir; that will do."
So, for the time, apparently it did,
And Eben evidently thought so too;
45   For soon amid the silver loneliness
Of night he lifted up his voice and sang,
Secure, with only two moons listening,
Until the whole harmonious landscape rang—

"For auld lang syne." The weary throat gave out,
50   The last word wavered; and the song being done,
He raised again the jug regretfully
And shook his head, and was again alone.
There was not much that was ahead of him,
And there was nothing in the town below—
55   Where strangers would have shut the many doors
That many friends had opened long ago.

STEPHEN CRANE (1871–1900)

A Man Adrift on a Slim Spar

A man adrift on a slim spar
A horizon smaller than the rim of a bottle
Tented waves rearing lashy dark points
The near whine of froth in circles.
5   God is cold.

The incessant raise and swing of the sea
And growl after growl of crest
The sinkings, green, seething, endless
The upheaval half-completed.
10   God is cold.

The seas are in the hollow of The Hand;
Oceans may be turned to a spray
Raining down through the stars
Because of a gesture of pity toward a babe.
15   Oceans may become grey ashes,
Die with a long moan and a roar

---

[58] The good old times.

Amid the tumult of the fishes
And the cries of the ships,
Because The Hand beckons the mice.

20   A horizon smaller than a doomed assassin's cap,
Inky, surging tumults
A reeling, drunken sky and no sky
A pale hand sliding from a polished spar.
                  God is cold.

25   The puff of a coat imprisoning air:
A face kissing the water-death
A weary slow sway of a lost hand
And the sea, the moving sea, the sea.
                  God is cold.

ROBERT FROST (1874–1963)

Mending Wall

Something there is that doesn't love a wall,
That sends the frozen-ground-swell under it
And spills the upper boulders in the sun,
And makes gaps even two can pass abreast.
5   The work of hunters is another thing:
I have come after them and made repair
Where they have left not one stone on a stone,
But they would have the rabbit out of hiding,
To please the yelping dogs. The gaps I mean,
10   No one has seen them made or heard them made,
But at spring mending-time we find them there.
I let my neighbor know beyond the hill;
And on a day we meet to walk the line
And set the wall between us once again.
15   We keep the wall between us as we go.
To each the boulders that have fallen to each.
And some are loaves and some so nearly balls
We have to use a spell to make them balance:
"Stay where you are until our backs are turned!"
20   We wear our fingers rough with handling them.
Oh, just another kind of outdoor game,
One on a side. It comes to little more:
There where it is we do not need the wall:
He is all pine and I am apple orchard.
25   My apple trees will never get across
And eat the cones under his pines, I tell him.
He only says, "Good fences make good neighbors."
Spring is the mischief in me, and I wonder
If I could put a notion in his head:
30   "Why do they make good neighbors? Isn't it

Where there are cows? But here there are no cows.
Before I built a wall I'd ask to know
What I was walling in or walling out,
And to whom I was like to give offense.
35 Something there is that doesn't love a wall,
That wants it down." I could say "Elves" to him,
But it's not elves exactly, and I'd rather
He said it for himself. I see him there
Bringing a stone grasped firmly by the top
40 In each hand, like an old-stone savage armed.
He moves in darkness as it seems to me,
Not of woods only and the shade of trees.
He will not go behind his father's saying,
And he likes having thought of it so well
45 He says again, "Good fences make good neighbors."

ROBERT FROST (1874–1963)

After Apple-Picking

My long two-pointed ladder's sticking through a tree
Toward heaven still,
And there's a barrel that I didn't fill
Beside it, and there may be two or three
5 Apples I didn't pick upon some bough.
But I am done with apple-picking now.
Essence of winter sleep is on the night,
The scent of apples: I am drowsing off.
I cannot rub the strangeness from my sight
10 I got from looking through a pane of glass
I skimmed this morning from the drinking trough
And held against the world of hoary grass.
It melted, and I let it fall and break.
But I was well
15 Upon my way to sleep before it fell,
And I could tell
What form my dreaming was about to take.
Magnified apples appear and disappear,
Stem end and blossom end,
20 And every fleck of russet showing clear.
My instep arch not only keeps the ache,
It keeps the pressure of a ladder-round.
I feel the ladder sway as the boughs bend.
And I keep hearing from the cellar bin
25 The rumbling sound
Of load on load of apples coming in.
For I have had too much
Of apple-picking: I am overtired
Of the great harvest I myself desired.

30   There were ten thousand thousand fruit to touch,
       Cherish in hand, lift down, and not let fall.
       For all
       That struck the earth,
       No matter if not bruised or spiked with stubble,
35   Went surely to the cider-apple heap
       As of no worth.
       One can see what will trouble
       This sleep of mine, whatever sleep it is.
       Were he not gone,
40   The woodchuck could say whether it's like his
       Long sleep, as I describe its coming on,
       Or just some human sleep.

Compare "After Apple-Picking" with Dave Smith's "Picking Cherries" on page 786.

ROBERT FROST (1874–1963)

A Peck of Gold[59]

       Dust always blowing about the town,
       Except when sea-fog laid it down,
       And I was one of the children told
       Some of the blowing dust was gold.

5   All the dust the wind blew high
       Appeared like gold in the sunset sky,
       But I was one of the children told
       Some of the dust was really gold.

       Such was life in the Golden Gate:
10   Gold dusted all we drank and ate,
       And I was one of the children told,
       "We all must eat our peck of gold."

ROBERT FROST (1874–1963)

The Silken Tent

       She is as in a field a silken tent
       At midday when a sunny summer breeze
       Has dried the dew and all its ropes relent,
       So that in guys° it gently sways at ease,   *ropes*
5   And its supporting central cedar pole,
       That is its pinnacle to heavenward
       And signifies the sureness of the soul,
       Seems to owe naught to any single cord,

---

[59] Although Frost is associated with Vermont and New Hampshire, he was born in San Francisco
and lived there until the age of eleven. This poem is about his California childhood.

But strictly held by none, is loosely bound
10   By countless silken ties of love and thought
        To everything on earth the compass round,
        And only by one's going slightly taut
        In the capriciousness of summer air
        Is of the slightest bondage made aware.

Show how "The Silken Tent" is an allegory.

JAMES JOYCE (1880–1941)

All Day I Hear the Noise of Waters

    All day I hear the noise of waters
        Making moan,
    Sad as the sea-bird is, when going
        Forth alone,
5   He hears the winds cry to the waters'
        Monotone.

    The grey winds, the cold winds are blowing
        Where I go.
    I hear the noise of many waters
10   Far below.
    All day, all night, I hear them flowing
        To and fro.

Compare "All Day I Hear the Noise of Waters" with Emily Brontë's "The Sun Has Set" on page 727.

ARCHIBALD MacLEISH (1892–1982)

Ars Poetica[60]

    A poem should be palpable and mute
    As a globed fruit,

    Dumb
    As old medallions to the thumb,

5   Silent as the sleeve-worn stone
    Of casement ledges where the moss has grown—

    A poem should be wordless
    As the flight of birds.

    A poem should be motionless in time
10 As the moon climbs,

---

[60] Latin for "the art of poetry."

Leaving, as the moon releases
Twig by twig the night-entangled trees,

Leaving, as the moon behind the winter leaves,
Memory by memory the mind—

15   A poem should be motionless in time
As the moon climbs.

A poem should be equal to:
Not true.

For all the history of grief
20   An empty doorway and a maple leaf.

For love
The leaning grasses and two lights above the sea—

A poem should not mean
But be.

WILFRED OWEN (1893–1918)

Anthem for Doomed Youth

What passing-bells for these who die as cattle?
Only the monstrous anger of the guns.
Only the stuttering rifles' rapid rattle
Can patter out their hasty orisons.
5   No mockeries for them from prayers or bells,
Nor any voice of mourning save the choirs—
The shrill, demented choirs of wailing shells;
And bugles calling for them from sad shires.

What candles may be held to speed them all?
10   Not in the hands of boys, but in their eyes
Shall shine the holy glimmers of good-byes.
The pallor of girls' brows shall be their pall;
Their flowers the tenderness of patient minds,
And each slow dusk a drawing-down of blinds.

Compare "Anthem for Doomed Youth" with A. E. Housman's "To an Athlete Dying Young" on page 464 and Randall Jarrell's "The Death of the Ball Turret Gunner" on page 489.

E. E. CUMMINGS (1894–1962)

in Just-

in Just-
spring   when the world is mud-
luscious the little
lame balloonman

```
5    whistles    far    and wee

     and eddieandbill come
     running from marbles and
.    piracies and it's
     spring

10   when the world is puddle-wonderful

     the queer
     old balloonman whistles
     far    and    wee
     and bettyandisbel come dancing

15   from hop-scotch and jump-rope and

     it's
     spring
     and
          the
20   goat-footed⁶¹

     balloonMan        whistles
     far
     and
     wee
```

E. E. CUMMINGS (1894–1962)

the Cambridge⁶² ladies who live in furnished souls

```
     the Cambridge ladies who live in furnished souls
     are unbeautiful and have comfortable minds
     (also, with the church's protestant blessings
     daughters, unscented shapeless spirited)
5    they believe in Christ and Longfellow,⁶³ both dead,
     are invariably interested in so many things—
     at the present writing one still finds
     delighted fingers knitting for the is it Poles?
     perhaps. While permanent faces coyly bandy
10   scandal of Mrs. N and Professor D
     . . . . the Cambridge ladies do not care, above
     Cambridge if sometimes in its box of
     sky lavender and cornerless, the
     moon rattles like a fragment of angry candy
```

---

⁶¹ The word *goat-footed* suggests that the "balloonman" resembles Pan, the Greek god of flocks and pastures, who is depicted as having the ears and hooves of a goat.

⁶² Cambridge, Massachusetts, is the home of Harvard University, where Cummings's father taught and where Cummings himself was educated.

⁶³ Henry Wadsworth Longfellow, the American poet, made his home in Cambridge. One of Longfellow's poems may be found on pages 722–23.

Compare "the Cambridge ladies who live in furnished souls" with Gwendolyn Brooks's "Sadie and Maud" on pages 756–57, T. S. Eliot's "Aunt Helen" on page 562, and Oliver Wendell Holmes's "My Aunt" on pages 725–26.

LOUISE BOGAN (1897–1970)

Night

The cold remote islands
And the blue estuaries
Where what breathes, breathes
The restless wind of the inlets,
5   And what drinks, drinks
The incoming tide;

Where shell and weed
Wait upon the salt of the sea,
And the clear nights of stars
10   Swing their lights westward
To set behind the land;

Where the pulse clinging to the rocks
Renews itself forever;
Where, again on cloudless nights,
15   The water reflects
The firmament's partial setting;

—O remember
In your narrowing dark hours
That more things move
20   Than blood in the heart.

Compare "Night" with Emily Brontë's "The Sun Has Set" on page 727 and James Joyce's "All Day I Hear the Noise of Waters" on page 741.

HART CRANE (1899–1932)

My Grandmother's Love Letters

There are no stars to-night
But those of memory.
Yet how much room for memory there is
In the loose girdle° of soft rain.   *sash*

5   There is even room enough
For the letters of my mother's mother,
Elizabeth,
That have been pressed so long
Into a corner of the roof
10   That they are brown and soft,
And liable to melt as snow.

Hart Crane *(National Portrait Gallery, Smithsonian Institution, Washington, D.C.)*

Over the greatness of such space
Steps must be gentle.
It is all hung by an invisible white hair.
15 It trembles as birch limbs webbing the air.

And I ask myself:

"Are your fingers long enough to play
Old keys that are but echoes:
Is the silence strong enough
20 To carry back the music to its source
And back to you again
As though to her?"

Yet I would lead my grandmother by the hand
Through much of what she would not understand;
25 And so I stumble. And the rain continues on the roof
With such a sound of gently pitying laughter.

ARNA BONTEMPS (1902–)

Southern Mansion

Poplars are standing there still as death
And ghosts of dead men
Meet their ladies walking
Two by two beneath the shade
5 And standing on the marble steps.

There is a sound of music echoing
Through the open door

And in the field there is
Another sound tinkling in the cotton:
10   Chains of bondmen dragging on the ground.

The years go back with an iron clank,
A hand is on the gate,
A dry leaf trembles on the wall.
Ghosts are walking.
15   They have broken roses down
And poplars stand there still as death.

STEVIE SMITH (1902–1971)

Not Waving but Drowning

Nobody heard him, the dead man,
But still he lay moaning:
I was much further out than you thought
And not waving but drowning.

5   Poor chap, he always loved larking
And now he's dead
It must have been too cold for him his heart gave way.
They said.

Oh, no no no, it was too cold always
10   (Still the dead one lay moaning)
I was much too far out all my life
And not waving but drowning.

STANLEY KUNITZ (1905–)

The Portrait

My mother never forgave my father
for killing himself,
especially at such an awkward time
and in a public park,
5   that spring
when I was waiting to be born.
She locked his name
in her deepest cabinet
and would not let him out,
10   though I could hear him thumping.
When I came down from the attic
with the pastel portrait in my hand
of a long-lipped stranger
with a brave moustache
15   and deep brown level eyes,

she ripped it into shreds
without a single word
and slapped me hard.
In my sixty-fourth year
20   I can feel my cheek
still burning.

W. H. AUDEN (1907–1973)

Lay Your Sleeping Head, My Love

Lay your sleeping head, my love,
Human on my faithless arm;
Time and fevers burn away
Individual beauty from
5   Thoughtful children, and the grave
Proves the child ephemeral:
But in my arms till break of day
Let the living creature lie,
Mortal, guilty, but to me
10   The entirely beautiful.

Soul and body have no bounds:
To lovers as they lie upon
Her tolerant enchanted slope
In their ordinary swoon,
15   Grave the vision Venus[64] sends
Of supernatural sympathy,
Universal love and hope;
While an abstract insight wakes
Among the glaciers and the rocks
20   The hermit's sensual ecstasy.

Certainty, fidelity
On the stroke of midnight pass
Like vibrations of a bell,
And fashionable madmen raise
25   Their pedantic boring cry:
Every farthing° of the cost,   *quarter of a penny*
All the dreaded cards foretell,
Shall be paid, but from this night
Not a whisper, not a thought,
30   Not a kiss nor look be lost.

Beauty, midnight, vision dies:
Let the winds of dawn that blow
Softly round your dreaming head
Such a day of sweetness show

---

[64] Venus is the goddess of love.

35   Eye and knocking heart may bless,
      Find the mortal world enough;
      Noons of dryness see you fed
      By the involuntary powers,
      Nights of insult let you pass
40   Watched by every human love.

W. H. AUDEN (1907–1973)

As I Walked Out One Evening

As I walked out one evening,
    Walking down Bristol Street,
The crowds upon the pavement
    Were fields of harvest wheat.

5   And down by the brimming river
    I heard a lover sing
Under an arch of the railway:
    "Love has no ending.

"I'll love you, dear, I'll love you
10   Till China and Africa meet,
And the river jumps over the mountain
    And the salmon sing in the street,

"I'll love you till the ocean
    Is folded and hung up to dry
15   And the seven stars go squawking
    Like geese about the sky.

"The years shall run like rabbits,
    For in my arms I hold
The Flower of the Ages,
20   And the first love of the world."

But all the clocks in the city
    Began to whirr and chime:
"O let not Time deceive you,
    You cannot conquer Time.

25   "In the burrows of the Nightmare
    Where Justice naked is,
Time watches from the shadow
    And coughs when you would kiss.

"In headaches and in worry
30   Vaguely life leaks away,
And Time will have his fancy
    Tomorrow or today.

"Into many a green valley
    Drifts the appalling snow;

35   Time breaks the threaded dances
            And the diver's brilliant bow.

        "O plunge your hands in water,
            Plunge them in up to the wrist;
        Stare, stare in the basin
40   And wonder what you've missed.

        "The glacier knocks in the cupboard,
            The desert sighs in the bed,
        And the crack in the teacup opens
            A lane to the land of the dead.

45   "Where the beggars raffle the banknotes
            And the Giant is enchanting to Jack,
        And the Lily-white Boy is a Roarer,°   noisy reveler
            And Jill goes down on her back.

        "O look, look in the mirror,
50   O look in your distress;
        Life remains a blessing
            Although you cannot bless.

        "O stand, stand at the window
            As the tears scald and start;
55   You shall love your crooked neighbor
            With your crooked heart."

        It was late, late in the evening,
            The lovers they were gone;
        The clocks had ceased their chiming,
60   And the deep river ran on.

Discuss "As I Walked Out One Evening" as an example of a ballad.

THEODORE ROETHKE (1908–1963)

My Papa's Waltz

        The whiskey on your breath
        Could make a small boy dizzy;
        But I hung on like death:
        Such waltzing was not easy.

5   We romped until the pans
        Slid from the kitchen shelf;
        My mother's countenance
        Could not unfrown itself.

        The hand that held my wrist
10   Was battered on one knuckle;
        At every step you missed
        My right ear scraped a buckle.

You beat time on my head
With a palm caked hard by dirt,
15 Then waltzed me off to bed
Still clinging to your shirt.

Compare "My Papa's Waltz" with Lucille Clifton's "Good Times" on page 781.

THEODORE ROETHKE (1908–1963)

I Knew a Woman

I knew a woman, lovely in her bones,
When small birds sighed, she would sigh back at them;
Ah, when she moved, she moved more ways than one:
The shapes a bright container can contain!
5 Of her choice virtues only gods should speak,
Or English poets who grew up on Greek
(I'd have them sing in chorus, cheek to cheek).

How well her wishes went! She stroked my chin,
She taught me Turn, and Counter-turn, and Stand,
10 She taught me Touch, that undulant white skin;
I nibbled meekly from her proffered hand;
She was the sickle; I, poor I, the rake,
Coming behind her for her pretty sake
(But what prodigious mowing we did make).

15 Love likes a gander, and adores a goose:
Her full lips pursed, the errant note to seize;
She played it quick, she played it light and loose;
My eyes, they dazzled at her flowing knees;
Her several parts could keep a pure repose,
20 Or one hip quiver with a mobile nose
(She moved in circles, and those circles moved).

Let seed be grass, and grass turn into hay:
I'm martyr to a motion not my own;
What's freedom for? To know eternity.
25 I swear she cast a shadow white as stone.
But who would count eternity in days?
These old bones live to learn her wanton ways:
(I measure time by how a body sways).

RICHARD WRIGHT (1908–1960)

Four Haiku

A balmy spring wind
Reminding me of something
I cannot recall.

The green cockleburrs
Caught in the thick wooly hair
Of the black boy's head.

Standing in the field,
I hear the whispering of
Snowflake to snowflake.

It is September
The month in which I was born,
And I have no thoughts.

CHARLES OLSON (1910–1970)

Maximus, to Himself

I have had to learn the simplest things
last. Which made for difficulties.
Even at sea I was slow, to get the hand out, or to cross
a wet deck.
5   The sea was not, finally, my trade.
But even my trade, at it, I stood estranged
from that which was most familiar. Was delayed,
and not content with the man's argument
that such postponement
10 is now the nature of
obedience,
        that we are all late
        in a slow time,
        that we grow up many
15   And the single
        is not easily
        known

It could be, though the sharpness (the *achiote*)°   *a peppery seed*
I note in others,
20 makes more sense
than my own distances. The agilities

        they show daily
        who do the world's
        businesses
25   And who do nature's
        as I have no sense
        I have done either

I have made dialogues,
have discussed ancient texts,
30 have thrown what light I could, offered
what pleasures
doceat° allows   *teaching*

But the known?
This, I have had to be given,
35   a life, love, and from one man
the world

Tokens.
But sitting here
I look out as a wind
40   and water man, testing
And missing
some proof

I know the quarters
of the weather, where it comes from,
45   where it goes. But the stem of me,
this I took from their welcome,
or their rejection, of me

And my arrogance
was neither diminished
50   nor increased,
by the communication

2

It is undone business
I speak of, this morning,
with the sea
55   stretching out
from my feet

IRVING LAYTON (1912–)

Cain[65]

Taking the air rifle from my son's hand
I measured back five paces, the Hebrew
In me, narcissist, father of children
Laid to rest. From there I took aim and fired.
5   The silent ball hit the frog's back an inch
Below the head. He jumped at the surprise
Of it, suddenly tickled or startled
(He must have thought) and leaped from the wet sand
Into the surrounding brown water. But
10   The ball had done its mischief. His next spring
Was a miserable flop, the thrust all gone
Out of his legs. He tried—like Bruce—again,
Throwing out his sensitive pianist's
Hands as a dwarf might or a helpless child.

---

[65] In the Bible, Cain is the son of Adam and the brother of Abel, whom Cain kills. Thus Cain is the prototypical murderer.

15   His splash disturbed the quiet pondwater
     And one old frog behind his weedy moat
     Blinking, looking self-complacently on.
     The lin's° surface at once became closing   pond
     Eyelids and bubbles like notes of music
20   Liquid, luminous, dropping from the page
     White, white-bearded, a rapid crescendo⁶⁶
     Of inaudible sounds and a crones' whispering
     Backstage among the reeds and bullrushes
     As for an expiring Lear or Oedipus.⁶⁷

25   But Death makes us all look ridiculous.
     Consider this frog (dog, hog, what you will)
     Sprawling, his absurd corpse rocked by the tides
     That his last vain spring had set in movement.
     Like a retired oldster, I couldn't help sneer,
30   Living off the last of his insurance:
     Billows—now crumbling—the premiums paid.
     Absurd, how absurd. I wanted to kill
     At the mockery of it. Kill and kill
     Again—the self-infatuate frog, dog, hog,
35   Anything with the stir of life in it,
     Seeing that dead leaper, Chaplin-footed,⁶⁸
     Rocked and cradled in this afternoon
     Of tranquil water, reeds, and blazing sun,
     The hole in his back clearly visible
40   And the torn skin a blob of shadow
     Moving when the quiet poolwater moved.
     O Egypt, marbled Greece, resplendent Rome,
     Did you also finally perish from a small bore
     In your back you could not scratch? And would
45   Your mouths open ghostily, gasping out
     Among the murky reeds, the hidden frogs,
     We climb with crushed spines toward the heavens?
     When the next morning I came the same way
     The frog was on his back, one delicate
50   Hand on his belly, and his white shirt front
     Spotless. He looked as if he might have been
     A comic; tap dancer apologizing
     For a fall, or an Emcee, his wide grin
     Coaxing a laugh from us for an aside
55   Or perhaps a joke we didn't quite hear.

Compare "Cain" with Richard Wilbur's "The Death of a Toad" on pages 618–19.

---

⁶⁶ *Crescendo* is the musical term for increasing volume.
⁶⁷ Oedipus and Lear are both tragic heroes—the former in Sophocles' *Oedipus Rex*, the latter in Shakespeare's *King Lear*.
⁶⁸ Charlie Chaplin, the silent screen comic actor, had a distinctive waddling walk.

MAY SARTON (1912–)

Lady with a Falcon

Flemish tapestry, fifteenth century

Gentleness and starvation tame
The falcon to this lady's wrist,
Natural flight hooded from blame
By what ironic fate or twist?

5   For now the hunched bird's contained flight
Pounces upon her inward air,
To plunder that mysterious night
Of poems blooded as the hare.

Heavy becomes the lady's hand,
10   And heavy bends the gentle head
Over her hunched and brooding bird
Until it is she who seems hooded.

Lady, your falcon is a peril,
Is starved, is mastered, but not kind.
15   The bird who sits your hand so gentle,
The captured hunter hunts your mind.

Better to starve the senseless wind
Than wrist a falcon's stop and start:
The bolt of flight you thought to bend
20   Plummets into your inmost heart.

Compare "Lady with a Falcon" with Robert Duncan's "My Mother Would Be a Falconress" on pages 757–59 and Ted Hughes's "Hawk Roosting" on page 774.

RANDALL JARRELL (1914–1965)

The Woman at the Washington Zoo

The saris go by me from the embassies.

Cloth from the moon. Cloth from another planet.
They look back at the leopard like the leopard.

And I. . . .
5   this print of mine, that has kept its color
Alive through so many cleanings; this dull null
Navy I wear to work, and wear from work, and so
To my bed, so to my grave, with no
Complaints, no comment: neither from my chief,
10   The Deputy Chief Assistant, nor his chief—
Only I complain. . . . this serviceable
Body that no sunlight dyes, no hand suffuses
But, dome-shadowed, withering among columns,

Wavy beneath fountains—small, far-off, shining
15   In the eyes of animals, these beings trapped
As I am trapped but not, themselves, the trap,
Aging, but without knowledge of their age,
Kept safe here, knowing not of death, for death—
Oh, bars of my own body, open, open!
20   The world goes by my cage and never sees me.
And there come not to me, as come to these,
The wild beast, sparrows pecking the llamas' grain,
Pigeons settling on the bears' bread, buzzards
Tearing the meat the flies have clouded. . . .
25   Vulture,
When you come for the white rat that the foxes left,
Take off the red helmet of your head, the black
Wings that have shadowed me, and step to me as man:
The wild brother at whose feet the white wolves fawn,
30   To whose hand of power the great lioness
Stalks, purring. . . .
            You know what I was,
You see what I am: change me, change me!

HENRY REED (1914–)

Naming of Parts

Today we have naming of parts. Yesterday,
We had daily cleaning. And tomorrow morning,
We shall have what to do after firing. But today,
Today we have naming of parts. Japonica
5   Glistens like coral in all of the neighboring gardens,
       And today we have naming of parts.

This is the lower sling swivel. And this
Is the upper sling swivel, whose use you will see,
When you are given your slings. And this is the piling swivel,
10   Which in your case you have not got. The branches
Hold in the gardens their silent, eloquent gestures,
       Which in our case we have not got.

This is the safety-catch, which is always released
With an easy flick of the thumb. And please do not let me
15   See anyone using his finger. You can do it quite easy
If you have any strength in your thumb. The blossoms
Are fragile and motionless, never letting anyone see
       Any of them using their finger.

And this you can see is the bolt. The purpose of this
20   Is to open the breech, as you see. We can slide it
Rapidly backwards and forwards: we call this
Easing the spring. And rapidly backwards and forwards
The early bees are assaulting and fumbling the flowers:
       They call it easing the Spring.

25   They call it easing the Spring: it is perfectly easy
     If you have any strength in your thumb: like the bolt,
     And the breech, and the cocking-piece, and the point of balance,
     Which in our case we have not got; and the almond-blossom
     Silent in all of the gardens and the bees going backwards and forwards,
30   For today we have naming of parts.

WILLIAM STAFFORD (1914–)

Traveling Through the Dark

Traveling through the dark I found a deer
dead on the edge of the Wilson River road.
It is usually best to roll them into the canyon:
that road is narrow; to swerve might make more dead.

5   By glow of the tail-light I stumbled back of the car
     and stood by the heap, a doe, a recent killing;
     she had stiffened already, almost cold.
     I dragged her off; she was large in the belly.

     My fingers touching her side brought me the reason—
10   her side was warm; her fawn lay there waiting,
     alive, still, never to be born.
     Beside that mountain road I hesitated.

     The car aimed ahead its lowered parking lights;
     under the hood purred the steady engine.
15   I stood in the glare of the warm exhaust turning red;
     around our group I could hear the wilderness listen.

     I thought hard for us all—my only swerving—
     then pushed her over the edge into the river.

GWENDOLYN BROOKS (1917–)

• Sadie and Maud

Maud went to college.
Sadie stayed at home.
Sadie scraped life
With a fine-tooth comb.

5   She didn't leave a tangle in.
     Her comb found every strand.
     Sadie was one of the livingest chits°   *young girls*
     In all the land.

     Sadie bore two babies
10   Under her maiden name.
     Maud and Ma and Papa
     Nearly died of shame.

When Sadie said her last so-long
Her girls struck out from home.
15 (Sadie had left as heritage
Her fine-tooth comb.)

Maud, who went to college,
Is a thin brown mouse.
She is living all alone
20 In this old house.

Compare "Sadie and Maud" with Oliver Wendell Holmes's "My Aunt" on pages 725–26 and T. S. Eliot's "Aunt Helen" on page 562.

ROBERT LOWELL (1917–1977)

• Robert Frost

Robert Frost at midnight, the audience gone
to vapor, the great act laid on the shelf in mothballs,
his voice musical, raw and raw—he writes in the flyleaf:
"Robert Lowell from Robert Frost, his friend in the art."
5 "Sometimes I feel too full of myself," I say.
And he, misunderstanding, "When I am low,
I stray away. My son wasn't your kind. The night
we told him Merrill Moore[69] would come to treat him,
he said, 'I'll kill him first.' One of my daughters thought things,
10 knew every male she met was out to make her;
the way she dresses, she couldn't make a whorehouse."
And I, "Sometimes I'm so happy I can't stand myself."
And he, "When I am too full of joy, I think
how little good my health did anyone near me."

ROBERT DUNCAN (1919–)

My Mother Would Be a Falconress

My mother would be a falconress,
And I, her gay falcon treading her wrist,
would fly to bring back
from the blue of the sky to her, bleeding, a prize,
5 where I dream in my little hood with many bells
jangling when I'd turn my head.

My mother would be a falconress,
and she sends me as far as her will goes.
She lets me ride to the end of her curb

---

[69] Merrill Moore (1903–1957) was a poet and psychoanalyst and Frost's friend. Frost's son committed suicide.

10   where I fall back in anguish.
      I dread that she will cast me away,
      for I fall, I mis-take, I fail in her mission.

      She would bring down the little birds.
      And I would bring down the little birds.
15   When will she let me bring down the little birds,
      pierced from their flight with their necks broken,
      their heads like flowers limp from the stem?

      I tread my mother's wrist and would draw blood.
      Behind the little hood my eyes are hooded.
20   I have gone back into my hooded silence,
      talking to myself and dropping off to sleep.

      For she has muffled my dreams in the hood she has made me,
      sewn round with bells, jangling when I move.
      She rides with her little falcon upon her wrist.
25   She uses a barb that brings me to cower.
      She sends me abroad to try my wings
      and I come back to her. I would bring down
      the little birds to her
      I may not tear into, I must bring back perfectly.

30   I tear at her wrist with my beak to draw blood,
      and her eye holds me, anguisht, terrifying.
      She draws a limit to my flight.
      Never beyond my sight, she says.
      She trains me to fetch and to limit myself in fetching.
35   She rewards me with meat for my dinner.
      But I must never eat what she sends me to bring her.

      Yet it would have been beautiful, if she would have carried me,
      always, in a little hood with the bells ringing,
      at her wrist, and her riding
40   to the great falcon hunt, and me
      flying up to the curb of my heart from her heart
      to bring down the skylark from the blue to her feet,
      straining, and then released for the flight.

      My mother would be a falconress,
45   and I her gerfalcon,° raised at her will,   *large Arctic falcon*
      from her wrist sent flying, as if I were her own
      pride, as if her pride
      knew no limits, as if her mind
      sought in me flight beyond the horizon.

50   Ah, but high, high in the air I flew.
      And far, far beyond the curb of her will,
      were the blue hills where the falcons nest.
      And then I saw west to the dying sun—
      it seemed my human soul went down in flames.

55   I tore at her wrist, at the hold she had for me,
    until the blood ran hot and I heard her cry out,
    far, far beyond the curb of her will •

    to horizons of stars beyond the ringing hills of the world where the falcons nest
    I saw, and I tore at her wrist with my savage beak.
60   I flew, as if sight flew from the anguish in her eye beyond her sight,
    sent from my striking loose, from the cruel strike at her wrist,
    striking out from the blood to be free of her.

    My mother would be a falconress,
    and even now, years after this,
65   when the wounds I left her had surely heald,
    and the woman is dead,
    her fierce eyes closed, and if her heart
    were broken, it is stilld •

    I would be a falcon and go free.
70   I tread her wrist and wear the hood,
    talking to myself, and would draw blood.

Compare "My Mother Would Be a Falconress" with May Sarton's "Lady with a Falcon"
on page 754 and Ted Hughes's "Hawk Roosting" on page 774.

LAWRENCE FERLINGHETTI (1919–)

[In Goya's Greatest Scenes We Seem to See]

In Goya's greatest scenes[70] we seem to see
                        the people of the world
        exactly at the moment when
           they first attained the title of
5   "suffering humanity"
      They writhe upon the page
             in a veritable rage
                of adversity
     Heaped up
10   groaning with babies and bayonets
                under cement skies
     in an abstract landscape of blasted trees
      bent statues bats wings and beaks
        slippery gibbets°   *gallows*
15   cadavers and carnivorous cocks
     and all the final hollering monsters
       of the
           "imagination of disaster"

---

[70] Francisco Goya (1746–1828) was a Spanish painter and etcher. His *Disasters of War* series of
etchings depicted the horrors of warfare.

With or Without Reason, from the *Disasters of War*, by Francisco Goya
(Courtesy of the Museum of Fine Arts, Boston, William A. Sargent Bequest)

they are so bloody real

20   it is as if they really still existed
    And they do

      Only the landscape is changed

  They still are ranged along the roads
      plagued by legionaires

25   false windmills and demented roosters

  They are the same people
                only further from home
    on freeways fifty lanes wide
          on a concrete continent

30   spaced with bland billboards
        illustrating imbecile illusions of happiness

Compare "[In Goya's Greatest Scenes We Seem to See]" with W. H. Auden's "Musée des Beaux Arts" on pages 429–30.

MONA VAN DUYN (1921–)

Open Letter from a Constant Reader

To all who carve their love on a picnic table
or scratch it on smoked glass panes of a public toilet,

I send my thanks for each plain and perfect fable
of how the three pains of the body, surfeit,

5   hunger, and chill (or loneliness), create
a furniture and art of their own easing.
And I bless two public sites and, like Yeats,[71]
two private sites where the body receives its blessing.

Nothing is banal or lowly that tells us how well
10   the world, whose highways proffer table and toilet
as signs and occasions of comfort for belly and bowel,
can comfort the heart too, somewhere in secret.

Where so much constant news of good has been put,
both fleeting and lasting lines compel belief.
15   Not by talent or riches or beauty, but
by the world's grace, people have found relief

from the worst pain of the body, loneliness,
and say so with a simple heart as they sit
being relieved of one of the others. I bless
20   all knowledge of love, all ways of publishing it.

Compare Van Duyn's poem to Yeats's "Crazy Jane Talks with the Bishop" on p. 684.

RICHARD WILBUR (1921–)

Love Calls Us to the Things of This World[72]

The eyes open to a cry of pulleys,
And spirited from sleep, the astounded soul
Hangs for a moment bodiless and simple
As false dawn.
                Outside the open window
5   The morning air is all awash with angels.

Some are in bed-sheets, some are in blouses,
Some are in smocks: but truly there they are.
Now they are rising together in calm swells
Of halcyon feeling, filling whatever they wear
10   With the deep joy of their impersonal breathing;

Now they are flying in place, conveying
The terrible speed of their omnipresence, moving
And staying like white water; and now of a sudden
They swoon down into so rapt a quiet
That nobody seems to be there.
15   The soul shrinks

---

[71] W. B. Yeats (1865–1939) was among the greatest poets in English. Several of his poems appear throughout this book.

[72] The title is taken from the words of St. Augustine.

From all that it is about to remember,
From the punctual rape of every blessèd day,
And cries,
            "Oh, let there be nothing on earth but laundry,
Nothing but rosy hands in the rising steam
20   And clear dances done in the sight of heaven."

        Yet, as the sun acknowledges
With a warm look the world's hunks and colors,
The soul descends once more in bitter love
To accept the waking body, saying now
25   In a changed voice as the man yawns and rises,

        "Bring them down from their ruddy gallows;
Let there be clean linen for the backs of thieves;
Let lovers go fresh and sweet to be undone,
And the heaviest nuns walk in a pure floating
Of dark habits,
30   keeping their difficult balance."

PHILIP LARKIN (1922–)

Faith Healing

Slowly the women file to where he stands
Upright in rimless glasses, silver hair,
Dark suit, white collar. Stewards tirelessly
Persuade them onwards to his voice and hands,
5   Within whose warm spring rain of loving care
Each dwells some twenty seconds. *Now, dear child,
What's wrong,* the deep American voice demands,
And, scarcely pausing, goes into a prayer
Directing God about this eye, that knee.
10   Their heads are clasped abruptly; then, exiled

Like losing thoughts, they go in silence; some
Sheepishly stray, not back into their lives
Just yet; but some stay stiff, twitching and loud
With deep hoarse tears, as if a kind of dumb
15   And idiot child within them still survives
To re-awake at kindness, thinking a voice
At last calls them alone, that hands have come
To lift and lighten; and such joy arrives
Their thick tongues blort, their eyes squeeze grief, a crowd
20   Of huge unheard answers jam and rejoice—

What's wrong! Moustached in flowered frocks they shake:
By now, all's wrong. In everyone there sleeps
A sense of life lived according to love.
To some it means the difference they could make
25   By loving others, but across most it sweeps
As all they might have done had they been loved.

That nothing cures. An immense slackening ache,
As when, thawing, the rigid landscape weeps,
Spreads slowly through them—that, and the voice above
30 Saying *Dear child*, and all time has disproved.

AMY CLAMPETT (19___–)

The Sun Underfoot Among the Sundews

An ingenuity too astonishing
to be quite fortuitous is
this bog full of sundews, sphagnum-
lined and shaped like a teacup.
5   A step
down and you're into it; a
wilderness swallows you up:
ankle-, then knee-, then midriff-
to-shoulder-deep in wetfooted
10 understory, an overhead
spruce-tamarack horizon hinting
you'll never get out of here.
                              But the sun
among the sundews, down there,
15 is so bright, an underfoot
webwork of carnivorous rubies,
a star-swarm thick as the gnats
they're set to catch, delectable
double-faced cockleburs, each
20 hair-tip a sticky mirror
afire with sunlight, a million
of them and again a million,
each mirror a trap set to
unhand unbelieving,
25   that either
a First Cause[73] said once, "Let there
be sundews," and there were, or they've
made their way here unaided
other than by that backhand, round-
30 about refusal to assume responsibility
known as Natural Selection.[74]
                              But the sun
underfoot is so dazzling
down there among the sundews,
35 there is so much light
in the cup that, looking,
you start to fall upward.

---

[73] God is referred to by some philosophers as The First Cause.
[74] Natural Selection is the process, according to Charles Darwin, by which species evolved.

HOWARD MOSS (1922–)

Water Island[75]

To the memory of a friend,
drowned off Water Island, April, 1960

Finally, from your house, there is no view;
The bay's blind mirror shattered over you
And Patchogue[76] took your body like a log
The wind rolled up to shore. The senseless drowned
5   Have faces nobody would care to see,
But water loves those gradual erasures
Of flesh and shoreline, greenery and glass,
And you belonged to water, it to you,
Having built, on a hillock, above the bay,
10   Your house, the bay giving you reason to,
Where now, if seasons still are running straight,
The horseshoe crabs clank armor night and day,
Their couplings far more ancient than the eyes
That watched them from your porch. I saw one once
15   Whose back was a history of how we live;
Grown onto every inch of plate, except
Where the hinges let it move, were living things,
Barnacles, mussels, water weeds—and one
Blue bit of polished glass, glued there by time:
20   The origins of art. It carried them
With pride, it seemed, as if endurance only
Matters in the end. Or so I thought.
Skimming traffic lights, starboard and port,
Steer through planted poles that mark the way,
25   And other lights, across the bay, faint stars
Lining the border of Long Island's shore,
Come on at night, they still come on at night,
Though who can see them now I do not know.
Wild roses, at your back porch, break their blood,
30   And bud to test surprises of sea air,
And the birds fly over, gliding down to feed
At the two feeding stations you set out with seed,
Or splash themselves in a big bowl of rain
You used to fill with water. Going across
35   That night, too fast, too dark, no one will know,
Maybe you heard, the last you'll ever hear,
The cry of the savage and endemic gull
Which shakes the blood and always brings to mind
The thought that death, the scavenger, is blind,

---

[75] A community on Fire Island, an island at the end of Long Island, New York.
[76] The body of water that surrounds Fire Island.

40   Blunders and is stupid, and the end
        Comes with ironies so fine the seed
        Falters in the marsh and the heron stops
        Hunting in the weeds below your landing stairs,
        Standing in a stillness that now is yours.

ANTHONY HECHT (1923–)

The Dover Bitch, A Criticism of Life

For Andrews Wanning

       So there stood Matthew Arnold and this girl
       With the cliffs of England crumbling away behind them,
       And he said to her, "Try to be true to me,
       And I'll do the same for you, for things are bad
5   All over, etc., etc."
       Well now, I knew this girl. It's true she had read
       Sophocles in a fairly good translation
       And caught that bitter allusion to the sea,
       But all the time he was talking she had in mind
10   The notion of what his whiskers would feel like
       On the back of her neck. She told me later on
       That after a while she got to looking out
       At the lights across the channel, and really felt sad,
       Thinking of all the wine and enormous beds
15   And blandishments in French and the perfumes.
       And then she got really angry. To have been brought
       All the way down from London, and then be addressed
       As a sort of mournful cosmic last resort
       Is really tough on a girl, and she was pretty.
20   Anyway, she watched him pace the room
       And finger his watch-chain and seem to sweat a bit,
       And then she said one or two unprintable things.
       But you mustn't judge her by that. What I mean to say is,
       She's really all right. I still see her once in a while
25   And she always treats me right. We have a drink
       And I give her a good time, and perhaps it's a year
       Before I see her again, but there she is,
       Running to fat, but dependable as they come.
       And sometimes I bring her a bottle of *Nuit d'Amour*.[77]

Compare "The Dover Bitch" with Matthew Arnold's "Dover Beach" on pages 506–507.

---

[77] *Nuit d'Amour* is French for "night of love."

RICHARD HUGO (1923–)

Driving Montana

The day is a woman who loves you. Open.
Deer drink close to the road and magpies
spray from your car. Miles from any town
your radio comes in strong, unlikely
5   Mozart from Belgrade, rock and roll
from Butte. Whatever the next number,
you want to hear it. Never has your Buick
found this forward a gear. Even
the tuna salad in Reedpoint is good.

10   Towns arrive ahead of imagined schedule.
Absorakee at one. Or arrive so late—
Silesia at nine—you recreate the day.
Where did you stop along the road
and have fun? Was there a runaway horse?
15   Did you park at that house, the one
alone in a void of grain, white with green
trim and red fence, where you know you lived
once? You remembered the ringing creek,
the soft brown forms of far off bison.
20   You must have stayed hours, then drove on.
In the motel you know you'd never seen it before.

Tomorrow will open again, the sky wide
as the mouth of a wild girl, friable
clouds you lose yourself to. You are lost
25   in miles of land without people, without
one fear of being found, in the dash
of rabbits, soar of antelope, swirl
merge and clatter of streams.

KENNETH KOCH (1925–)

Mending Sump

"Hiram, I think the sump is backing up.
The bathroom floor boards for above two weeks
Have seemed soaked through. A little bird, I think,
Has wandered in the pipes, and all's gone wrong."
5   "Something there is that doesn't hump a sump,"
He said; and through his head she saw a cloud
That seemed to twinkle. "Hiram, well," she said,
"Smith is come home! I saw his face just now
While looking through your head. He's come to die
10   Or else to laugh, for hay is dried-up grass
When you're alone." He rose, and sniffed the air.
"We'd better leave him in the sump," he said.

Compare "Mending Sump" with Robert Frost's "Mending Wall" on pages 738–39.

MAXINE KUMIN (1925–)

For a Shetland Pony Brood Mare[78]
Who Died in Her Barren Year

After bringing forth eighteen
foals in as many Mays
you might, old Trinket girl,
have let yourself be lulled
5   this spring into the green days
of pasture and first curl
of timothy.° Instead,   *a kind of grass*
your milk bag swelled again,
an obstinate machine.
10   Your long pale tongue
waggled in every feed box.
You slicked your ears back
to scatter other mares
from the salt lick.[79]
15   You were full of winter burdocks
and false pregnancy.

By midsummer all the foals
had breached, except the ghost
you carried. In the bog
20   where you came down each noon
to ease your deer-thin hoofs in mud,
a jack-in-the-pulpit cocked
his overhang like a question mark.
We saw some autumn soon
25   that botflies would take your skin
and bloodworms settle
inside the cords and bands
that laced your belly,
your church of folded hands.

30   But all in good time, Trinket!
Was it something you understood?
Full of false pride
you lay down and died
in the sun,
35   all silken on one side,
all mud on the other one.

Compare "For a Shetland Pony Brood Mare" with Anne Sexton's "Pain for a Daughter" on pages 770–71.

---

[78] A brood mare is a female horse kept for breeding purposes.
[79] A salt lick is a block of salt set out for animals to lick.

A. R. AMMONS (1926–)

The Visit

It is not far to my place:
you can come smallboat,
pausing under shade in the eddies
    or going ashore
5   to rest, regard the leaves

    , or talk with birds and
shore weeds: hire a full-grown man not
late in years to oar you
    and choose a canoe-like thin ship;
10   (a dumb man is better and no

costlier; he will attract
the reflections and silences under leaves:)
travel light: a single book, some twine:
    the river is muscled at rapids with trout
15   and a laurel limb

will make a suitable spit: if you
leave in the forenoon, you will arrive
with plenty of light
    the afternoon of the third day: I will
20   come down to the landing

(tell your man to look for it,
the dumb have clear sight and are free of
visions) to greet you with some made
    wine and a special verse:
25   or you can come by shore:

choose the right: there the rocks
cascade less frequently, the grade more gradual:
treat yourself gently: the ascent thins both
    mind and blood and you must
30   keep still a dense reserve

of silence we can poise against
conversation: there is little news:
I found last month a root with shape and
    have heard a new sound among
35   the insects: come.

ALLEN GINSBERG (1926–)

A Supermarket in California

What thoughts I have of you tonight, Walt Whitman, for
I walked down the sidestreets under the trees with a headache
self-conscious looking at the full moon.
    In my hungry fatigue, and shopping for images, I went

5   into the neon fruit supermarket, dreaming of your enumerations!
          What peaches and what penumbras! Whole families shopping
       at night! Aisles full of husbands! Wives in the avocados,
       babies in the tomatoes!—and you, Garcia Lorca,[80] what were you
       doing down by the watermelons?
10   I saw you, Walt Whitman, childless, lonely old grubber,
       poking among the meats in the refrigerator and eyeing the
       grocery boys.
          I heard you asking questions of each: Who killed the
       pork chops? What price bananas? Are you my Angel?
15   I wandered in and out of the brilliant stacks of cans
       following you, and followed in my imagination by the store
       detective.
          We strode down the open corridors together in our
       solitary fancy tasting artichokes, possessing every frozen
20   delicacy, and never passing the cashier.

          Where are we going, Walt Whitman? The doors close in
       an hour. Which way does your beard point tonight?
          (I touch your book and dream of our odyssey in the
       supermarket and feel absurd.)
25   Will we walk all night through solitary streets? The trees
       add shade to shade, lights out in the houses, we'll both be
       lonely.
          Will we stroll dreaming of the lost America of love past
       blue automobiles in driveways, home to our silent cottage?
30   Ah, dear father, graybeard, lonely old courage-teacher,
       what America did you have when Charon[81] quit poling his ferry
       and you got out on a smoking bank and stood watching the
       boat disappear on the black waters of Lethe?

W. S. MERWIN (1927–)

For the Anniversary of My Death

Every year without knowing it I have passed the day
When the last fires will wave to me
And the silence will set out
Tireless traveller
5   Like the beam of a lightless star

Then I will no longer
Find myself in life as in a strange garment
Surprised at the earth
And the love of one woman
10   And then shamelessness of men

---

[80] Garcia Lorca (1899–1936) was a Spanish poet and playwright noted for his haunting imagery.
[81] In Greek mythology Charon ferried dead souls across the river Lethe to the underworld.

As today writing after three days of rain
Hearing the wren sing and the falling cease
And bowing not knowing to what

ANNE SEXTON (1928–1974)

Pain for a Daughter

Blind with love, my daughter
has cried nightly for horses,
those long-necked marchers and churners
that she has mastered, any and all,
5   reigning them in like a circus hand—
the excitable muscles and the ripe neck;
tending this summer, a pony and a foal.
She who is too squeamish to pull
a thorn from the dog's paw,
10   watched her pony blossom with distemper,
the underside of the jaw swelling
like an enormous grape.
Gritting her teeth with love,
she drained the boil and scoured it
15   with hydrogen peroxide until pus
ran like milk on the barn floor.

Blind with loss all winter,
in dungarees, a ski jacket and a hard hat,
she visits the neighbors' stable,
20   our acreage not zoned for barns;
they who own the flaming horses
and the swan-whipped thoroughbred
that she tugs at and cajoles,
thinking it will burn like a furnace
25   under her small-hipped English seat. [82]

Blind with pain she limps home.
The thoroughbred has stood on her foot.
He rested there like a building.
He grew into her foot until they were one.
30   The marks of the horseshoe printed
into her flesh, the tips of her toes
ripped off like pieces of leather,
three toenails swirled like shells
and left to float in blood in her riding boot.

35   Blind with fear, she sits on the toilet,
her foot balanced over the washbasin,
her father, hydrogen peroxide in hand,
performing the rites of the cleansing.
She bites on a towel, sucked in breath,

---

[82] An English seat is a type of riding saddle.

40   sucked in and arched against the pain,
     her eyes glancing off me where
     I stand at the door, eyes locked
     on the ceiling, eyes of a stranger,
     and then she cries . . .
45   *Oh my God, help me!*
     Where a child would have cried *Mama!*
     Where a child would have believed *Mama!*
     she bit the towel and called on God
     and I saw her life stretch out . . .
50   I saw her torn in childbirth,
     and I saw her, at that moment,
     in her own death and I knew that she
     knew.

Compare "Pain for a Daughter" with Maxine Kumin's "For a Shetland Pony Brood Mare
Who Died in Her Barren Year" on page 767.

Compare "Pain for a Daughter" with Maxine Kumin's "For a Shetland Pony Brood Mare Who Died in Her Barren Year" on page 767.

RICHARD HOWARD (1929–)

Giovanni da Fiesole on the Sublime, or Fra Angelico's Last Judgement[83]

For Adrienne Rich[84]

How to behold what cannot be held?
Start from the center and from all that
lies or flies or merely rises left
of center. You may have noticed how
5   Hell, in these affairs, is on the right
invariably (though for an inside Judge,
of course, that would be the left. And we
are not inside.) I have no doctrine
intricate enough for Hell, which I leave
10   in its own right, where it will be left.

Right down the center, then, in two rows,
run nineteen black holes, their square lids off;
also one sarcophagus, up front.
Out of these has come the world; out of
15   that coffin, I guess, the Judge above
the world. Nor is my doctrine liable
to smooth itself out for the blue ease
of Heaven outlining one low hill

---

[83] Giovanni da Fiesole, also known as Fra Angelico, was born as Guido di Pietro (c. 1400–1455). He was one of the greatest painters of the Italian Renaissance. This poem describes his painting *The Last Judgment* in the Convento degli Angioli, Florence.
[84] Adrienne Rich is an American poet. A poem by Adrienne Rich follows.

"The Last Judgment" by Fra Angelico. (Scala / Art Resource)

against the sky at the graveyard's end
20   like a woman's body—a hill like Eve.

Some of us stand, still, at the margin
of this cemetery, marvelling
that no more than a mortared pavement can
separate us from the Other Side
25   which numbers as many nuns and priests
(even Popes and Empresses!) as ours.
The rest, though, stirring to a music
that our startled blood remembers now,
embrace each other or the Angels
30   of this green place: the dancing begins.

We dance in a circle of bushes,
red and yellow roses, round a pool
of green water. There is one lily,
gold as a lantern in the dark grass,
35   and all the trees accompany us
with gestures of fruition. We stop!
The ring of bodies opens where a last
Angel, in scarlet, hands us on. Now
we go, we are leaving this garden
40   of colors and gowns. We walk into

a light falling upon us, falling
out of the great rose gate upon us,
light so thick we cannot trust our eyes
to walk into it so. We lift up
45   our hands then and walk into the light.

How to behold what cannot be held?
Make believe you hold it, no longer
lighting but light, and walk into that
gold success. The world must be its own
50   *witness, we judge ourselves, raise your hands.*

Compare "Giovanni da Fiesole" with W. H. Auden's "Musée des Beaux Arts" on pages 429–30.

ADRIENNE RICH (1929–)

A Woman Mourned by Daughters

Now, not a tear begun,
we sit here in your kitchen,
spent, you see, already.
You are swollen till you strain
5   this house and the whole sky.
You, whom we so often
succeeded in ignoring!
You are puffed up in death
like a corpse pulled from the sea;
10   we groan beneath your weight.
And yet you were a leaf,
a straw blown on the bed,
you had long since become
crisp as a dead insect.
15   What is it, if not you,
that settles on us now
like satin you pulled down
over our bridal heads?
What rises in our throats
20   like food you prodded in?
Nothing could be enough.
You breathe upon us now
through solid assertions
of yourself: teaspoons, goblets,
25   seas of carpet, a forest
of old plants to be watered,
an old man in an adjoining
room to be touched and fed.
And all this universe
30   dares us to lay a finger
anywhere, save exactly
as you would wish it done.

Compare "A Woman Mourned by Daughters" with Sonia Sanchez's "summer words of a sistuh addict" on pages 780–81.

TED HUGHES (1930–)

• Hawk Roosting

I sit in the top of the wood, my eyes closed.
Inaction, no falsifying dream
Between my hooked head and hooked feet:
Or in sleep rehearse perfect kills and eat.

5   The convenience of the high trees!
The air's buoyancy and the sun's ray
Are of advantage to me;
And the earth's face upward for my inspection.

My feet are locked upon the rough bark.
10   It took the whole of Creation
To produce my foot, my each feather:
Now I hold Creation in my foot

Or fly up, and revolve it all slowly—
I kill where I please because it is all mine.
15   There is no sophistry in my body:
My manners are tearing off heads—

The allotment of death.
For the one path of my flight is direct
Through the bones of the living.
20   No arguments assert my right:

The sun is behind me.
Nothing has changed since I began.
My eye has permitted no change.
I am going to keep things like this.

Compare "Hawk Roosting" with Robert Duncan's "My Mother Would Be a Falconress"
on pages 757–59 and May Sarton's "Lady with a Falcon" on page 754.

DEREK WALCOTT (1930–)

Sea Grapes

That sail in cloudless light
which tires of islands,
a schooner beating up the Caribbean

for home, could be Odysseus[85]
5   home-bound through the Aegean,
just as that husband's

---

[85] Odysseus, or Ulysses, is the hero of Homer's the *Odyssey*, a section of which may be found on pages 446–52.

sorrow under the sea-grapes, repeats
the adulterer's hearing Nausicaa's name
in every gull's outcry.

10   But whom does this bring peace? The classic war
between a passion and responsibility
is never finished, and has been the same

to the sea-wanderer and the one on shore,
now wriggling on his sandals to walk home,
15   since Troy sighed its last flame,

and the blind giant's boulder heaved the trough[86]
from which The Odyssey's hexameters come[87]
to finish up as Caribbean surf.

The classics can console. But not enough.

COLETTE INEZ (1931–)

Spanish Heaven

My heaven is Hispanic ladies in satin tube dresses,
their hair like a chocolate sundae melts into waves.
They are giving me transparent nightgowns
and kisses on my face.
5   Lotteria tickets bulging in my purse.
They are saying *qué bonita*[88] in the house
of their throats
and we all eat mangoes and fritos d'amor
selling Avon products to each other forever.

10   And damning Fidel, Trujillo,[89] what bums.
But Evita,[90] what heart and Elizabeth Taylor
there in her shrine,
Monacos of pleasure as Grace takes our hand.[91]
Eyepads of freedom, Avons of love.

15   Mascara of angels, hairspray of God,
they are teasing my hair like a heavenly cloud
while the acid of husbands eating alone
rumbles Dolores, *putas*[92] and rape
in the hell of machismo.

---

[86] An allusion to Odysseus' fight with the Cyclops (see pages 451–52).
[87] The *Odyssey* is in dactylic hexameter.
[88] *Qué bonita* is Spanish for "how beautiful."
[89] Fidel Castro and Rafael Trujillo Molina, two Caribbean dictators, Castro in Cuba and Trujillo in the Dominican Republic until his assassination in 1961.
[90] Eva (Evita) Perón, wife of Juan Perón. Both were dictators of Argentina. Evita Perón was known for her great beauty, among other things.
[91] Elizabeth Taylor and Grace Kelly, American screen actresses. Grace Kelly later became Princess Grace of Monaco.
[92] *Putas* is the Spanish word for prostitutes.

Sylvia Plath *(Rollie McKenna)*

SYLVIA PLATH (1932–1963)

Lady Lazarus[93]

I have done it again.[94]
One year in every ten
I manage it—

A sort of walking miracle, my skin
5   Bright as a Nazi lampshade,[95]
My right foot

A paperweight,
My face a featureless, fine
Jew linen.

10   Peel off the napkin
O my enemy.
Do I terrify?—

The nose, the eye pits, the full set of teeth?
The sour breath
15   Will vanish in a day.

---

[93] Jesus raised Lazarus from the dead (John 11:44).
[94] Plath repeatedly attempted suicide and finally died by her own hand in 1963.
[95] The Nazis sometimes used the skins of Jews they had killed in the concentration camps for lamp
shades.

Soon, soon the flesh
The grave cave ate will be
At home on me

And I a smiling woman.
20   I am only thirty.
And like the cat I have nine times to die.

This is Number Three.
What a trash
To annihilate each decade.

25   What a million filaments.
The peanut-crunching crowd
Shoves in to see

Them unwrap me hand and foot—
The big strip tease.
30   Gentleman, ladies,

These are my hands,
My knees.
I may be skin and bone,

Nevertheless, I am the same, identical woman.
35   The first time it happened I was ten.
It was an accident.

The second time I meant
To last it out and not come back at all.
I rocked shut

40   As a seashell.
They had to call and call
And pick the worms off me like sticky pearls.

Dying
Is an art, like everything else.
45   I do it exceptionally well.

I do it so it feels like hell.
I do it so it feels real.
I guess you could say I've a call.

It's easy enough to do it in a cell.
50   It's easy enough to do it and stay put.
It's the theatrical

Comeback in broad day
To the same place, the same face, the same brute
Amused shout:

55   "A miracle!"
That knocks me out.
There is a charge

For the eyeing of my scars, there is a charge
For the hearing of my heart—
60 It really goes.

And there is a charge, a very large charge
For a word or a touch
Or a bit of blood

Or a piece of my hair or my clothes.
65 So, so, Herr Doktor.
So, Herr Enemy.

I am your opus,°   *work, composition*
I am your valuable,
The pure gold baby

70 That melts to a shriek.
I turn and burn.
Do not think I underestimate your great concern.

Ash, ash—
You poke and stir.
75 Flesh, bone, there is nothing there—

A cake of soap,
A wedding ring,
A gold filling.

Herr God, Herr Lucifer,
80 Beware
Beware.

Out of the ash
I rise with my red hair
And I eat men like air.

WENDELL BERRY (1934–)

The Old Elm Tree by the River

Shrugging in the flight of its leaves,
it is dying. Death is slowly
standing up in its trunk and branches
like a camouflaged hunter. In the night
5 I am wakened by one of its branches
crashing down, heavy as a wall, and then
lie sleepless, the world changed.
That is a life I know the country by.
Mine is a life I know the country by.
10 Willing to live and die, we stand here,
timely and at home, neighborly as two men.
Our place is changing in us as we stand,
and we hold up the weight that will bring us down.

In us the land enacts its history.
15   When we stood it was beneath us, and was
the strength by which we held to it
and stood, the daylight over it
a mighty blessing we cannot bear for long.

Compare "The Old Elm Tree by the River" with James Wright's "A Blessing" on page 420.

AUDRE LORDE (1934–)

Now That I Am Forever with Child

How the days went
while you were blooming within me
I remember each upon each—
the swelling changed planes of my body
5   and how you first fluttered, then jumped
and I thought it was my heart.

How the days wound down
and the turning of winter
I recall, with you growing heavy
10   against the wind. I thought
now her hands
are formed, and her hair
has started to curl
now her teeth are done
15   now she sneezes.
Then the seed opened
I bore you one morning just before spring
My head rang like a fiery piston
my legs were towers between which
20   A new world was passing.

Since then
I can only distinguish
one thread within running hours
You, flowing through selves
25   toward You.

Compare "Now That I Am Forever with Child" with Erica Jong's "How You Get Born" on pages 785–86.

N. SCOTT MOMADAY (1934–)

Earth and I Gave You Turquoise

Earth and I gave you turquoise
when you walked singing

We lived laughing in my house
  and told old stories
5   You grew ill when the owl cried
We will meet on Black Mountain

I will bring you corn for planting
  and we will make fire
Children will come to your breast
10   You will heal my heart
I speak your name many times
The wild cane remembers you

My young brother's house is filled
  I go there to sing
15 `We have not spoken of you
    but our songs are sad
When the Moon Woman goes to you
I will follow her white way

Tonight they dance near Chinle
20   by the seven elms
There your loom whispered beauty
    They will eat mutton
and drink coffee till morning
You and I will not be there

25   I saw a crow by Red Rock
    standing on one leg
It was the black of your hair
    The years are heavy
I will ride the swiftest horse
30   You will hear the drumming of hooves

SONIA SANCHEZ (1935–)

summer words of a sistuh addict

the first day i shot dope
was on a sunday.
                    i had just come
home from church
5   got mad at my motha
cuz she got mad at me.   u dig?
                went out.   shot up
behind a feelen gainst her.
                    it felt good.
10 gooder than dooing it.   yeah.
                        it was nice.
i did it.   uh.   huh.   i did it.   uh.   huh.
i want to do it again.   it felt so gooooood.
            and as the sistuh
15   sits in her silent/

remembered/high
someone leans for
ward gently asks her:
                    sistuh.
20   did u
                    finally
            learn how to hold yo/mother?
    and the music of the day
                    drifts in the room
25 to mingle with the sistuh's young tears.
            and we all sing.

Compare "summer words of a sistuh addict" with Adrienne Rich's "A Woman Mourned by Daughters" on page 773.

Compare "summer words of a sistuh addict" with Adrienne Rich's "A Woman Mourned by Daughters" on page 773.

LUCILLE CLIFTON (1936–)

Good Times

My Daddy has paid the rent
and the insurance man is gone
and the lights is back on
and my uncle Brud has hit
5   for one dollar straight
and they is good times
good times
good times

My Mama has made bread
10 and Grampaw has come

and everybody is drunk
and dancing in the kitchen
and singing in the kitchen
oh these is good times
15 good times
good times

oh children think about the
good times

DARYL HINE (1936–)

The Survivors

Nowadays the mess is everywhere
And getting worse. Earth after all
Is a battlefield. Through the static
We used to call the music of the spheres

5   Someone, a survivor, sends this message:
"When it happened I was reading Homer.

Sing—will nobody sing?—the wrath,
Rats and tanks and radioactive rain."

That was before rationing was enforced
10 On words, of course. Particles went first,
Then substantives. Now only verbs abide
The law, and the odd anarchistic scrawl

How above the crumbling horizon
Brightly shine our neighbours, Venus, Mars.

Compare "The Survivors" with Edwin Muir's "The Horses" on pages 442–43.

JUNE JORDAN (1936–)

My Sadness Sits Around Me

My sadness sits around me
        not on haunches not in any
        placement near a move
and the tired roll-on
5   of a boredom without grief

If there were war
I would watch the hunting
I would chase the dogs
and blow the horn
10 *because blood is commonplace*

As I walk in peace
        unencountered unmolested
        unimpinging unbelieving unrevealing
        undesired under every O
15 My sadness sits around me

Compare "My Sadness Sits Around Me" with Delmore Schwartz's "The Heavy Bear
Who Goes with Me" on pages 553–54.

DIANE WAKOSKI (1937–)

Backing Up, Or Tearing Up the Garden
Next to the Driveway

Does it mean anything
that I just can't back up?
My eyes take me forward,
my body not wanting
5   to be part
            of what is behind
me.

The driveway,
like a scar in life,
10   the paving left there from former acts,
                            actions,
and I not wanting to retrace
the days, hours, minutes, that made it,
not wanting to go back over
15   old ground.

ISHMAEL REED (1938–)

beware : do not read this poem

tonite, thriller was
abt an ol woman, so vain she
surrounded herself w /
        many mirrors

5   it got so bad that finally she
locked herself indoors & her
whole life became the
         mirrors

one day the villagers broke
10   into her house , but she was too
swift for them . she disappeared
       into a mirror
each tenant who bought the house
after that , lost a loved one to

15   the ol woman in the mirror :
        first a little girl
        then a young woman
        then the young woman/s husband

the hunger of this poem is legendary
20   it has taken in many victims
back off from this poem
it has drawn in yr feet
back off from this poem
it has drawn in yr legs

25   back off from this poem
it is a greedy mirror
you are into this poem . from
        the waist down
nobody can hear you can they ?
30   this poem has had you up to here
        belch
this poem aint got no manners
you cant call out frm this poem
relax now & go w / this poem

35   move & roll on to this poem
do not resist this poem
this poem has yr eyes
this poem has his head
this poem has his arms
40   this poem has his fingers
this poem has his fingertips

this poem is the reader & the
reader this poem

statistic : the us bureau of missing persons re-
45   ports that in 1968 over 100,000 people
disappeared leaving no solid clues
           nor trace   only
    a space   in the lives of their friends

MARGARET ATWOOD (1939–)

You Are Happy

The water turns
a long way down over the raw stone,
ice crusts around it.

We walk separately
5   along the hill to the open
beach, unused
picnic tables, wind
shoving the brown waves, erosion, gravel
rasping on gravel.

10   In the ditch a deer
carcass, no head. Bird
running across the glaring
road against the low pink sun.

When you are this
15   cold you can think about
nothing but the cold, the images

hitting into your eyes
like needles, crystals, you are happy.

Compare "You Are Happy" with William Stafford's "Traveling Through the Dark" on page 756.

SEAMUS HEANEY (1939–)

The Forge

All I know is a door into the dark.
Outside, old axles and iron hoops rusting;
Inside, the hammered anvil's short-pitched ring,

The unpredictable fantail of sparks
5   Or hiss when a new shoe toughens in water.
The anvil must be somewhere in the centre,
Horned as a unicorn, at one end square,
Set there immovable: an altar
Where he expends himself in shape and music.
10   Sometimes, leather-aproned, hairs in his nose,
He leans out on the jamb, recalls a clatter
Of hoofs where traffic is flashing in rows;
Then grunts and goes in, with a slam and flick
To beat real iron out, to work the bellows.

MARILYN HACKER (1942–)

Villanelle

For D.G.B.

Every day our bodies separate,
exploded torn and dazed.
Not understanding what we celebrate

we grope through languages and hesitate
5   and touch each other, speechless and amazed;
and every day our bodies separate

us farther from our planned, deliberate
ironic lives. I am afraid, disphased,
not understanding what we celebrate

10   when our fused limbs and lips communicate
the unlettered power we have raised.
Every day our bodies' separate

routines are harder to perpetuate.
In wordless darkness we learn wordless praise,
15   not understanding what we celebrate;

wake to ourselves, exhausted, in the late
morning as the wind tears off the haze,
not understanding how we celebrate
our bodies. Every day we separate.

ERICA JONG (1942–)

How You Get Born

One night, your mother is listening to the walls.
The clock whirrs like insect wings.
The ticking says lonely lonely lonely.

In the living room, the black couch swallows her.
5   She trusts it more than men,
but no one will ever love her
enough.

She doesn't yet know you
so how can she love you?
10 She loves you like God or Shakespeare.
She loves you like Mozart.

You are trembling in the walls like music.
You cross the ceiling in a phantom car of light.

Meanwhile unborn,
15 You wait in a heavy rainsoaked cloud
for your father's thunderbolt.
Your mother lies in the living room dreaming your hands.
Your mother lies in the living room dreaming your eyes.

She awakens & a shudder shakes her teeth.
20 The world is beginning again after the flood.

She slides into bed beside that gray-faced man,
your father.
She opens her legs to your coming.

Compare "How You Get Born" with Audre Lorde's "Now That I Am Forever with Child"
on page 779.

DAVE SMITH (1942–)

Picking Cherries

The ladder quakes and sways under me, old wood
I put too much faith in, like ancestors strained.
You circle me, cradling the baby, sun guttering
in your face, parading through the leaves, glad.
5 If I looked down I would see your calm fear, see
in your narrowed eyes my bones chipped, useless.
The bucket hangs from my belt, pulling obscenely
at my pants, but the cherries drop in and grow
one by one. I keep reaching higher than I need
10 because I want the one that tickles your tongue.
When I come down we will both be older, slower,
but what of that? Haven't we loved this climbing?
If the ladder gives way I still believe I can
catch one branch, drop the bucket and ease down.

Compare "Picking Cherries" with Robert Frost's "After Apple-Picking" on pages
739–40.

ALFRED CORN (1943–)

Fifty-Seventh Street and Fifth[96]

Hard-edged buildings; cloudless blue enamel;
Lapidary hours—and that numerous woman,

---

[96] Cross streets of New York City's famed retail district.

Put-together, in many a smashing
Suit or dress is somehow what it's, well,
5   All about. A city designed by *Halston:*[97]
Clean lines, tans, grays, expense; no sentiment.
Off the mirrored boxes the afternoon
Glare fires an instant in her sunglasses
And reflects some of the armored ambition
10   Controlling deed here; plus the byword
That "only the best really counts." Awful
And awe-inspiring. How hard the task,
Keeping up to the mark: opinions, output,
Presentation—strong on every front. So?
15   Life is strife, the city says, a theory
That tastes of iron and demands assent.

A big lump of iron that's been magnetized.
All the faces I see are—Believers,
Pilgrims immigrated from fifty states
20   To discover, to surrender, themselves.
Success. Money. Fame. Insular dreams all,
Begotten of the dream of Manhattan, island
Of the possessed. When a man's tired of New York,
He's tired of life? Or just of possession?
25   A whirlpool animates the terrific
Streets, violence of our praise, blockbuster
Miracles down every vista, scored by
Accords and discords intrinsic to this air.
Concerted mind performs as the genius
30   Of place: competition, a trust in facts
And expense. Who loves or works here assumes,
For better or worse, the ground rules. A fate.

NIKKI GIOVANNI (1943–)

Nikki-Rosa

childhood remembrances are always a drag
if you're Black
you always remember things like living in Woodlawn[98]
with no inside toilet
5   and if you become famous or something
they never talk about how happy you were to have your mother
all to yourself and
how good the water felt when you got your bath from one of those
big tubs that folk in chicago barbecue in
10   and somehow when you talk about home

---

[97] Roy Halston Frowick (1932–), the well-known fashion designer who goes by the name of Halston.
[98] Woodlawn is a suburb of Cincinnati.

it never gets across how much you
understood their feelings
as the whole family attended meetings about Hollydale
and even though you remember
15   your biographers never understand
your father's pain as he sells his stock
and another dream goes
and though you're poor it isn't poverty that
concerns you
20   and though they fought a lot
it isn't your father's drinking that makes any difference
but only that everybody is together and you
and your sister have happy birthdays and very good christmasses
and I really hope no white person ever has cause to write about me
25   because they never understand Black love is Black wealth and they'll
probably talk about my hard childhood and never understand that
all the while I was quite happy

ALICE WALKER (1944–)

My Daughter Is Coming!

My daughter is coming!
I have bought her a bed
and a chair
a mirror, a lamp
5   and a desk.
Her room is all ready
except that the curtains
are torn.
Do I have time to buy shoji panels[99]
10   for the window?
I do not.

First I must WRITE A SPEECH
see the doctor about my tonsils
which are dying ahead of schedule
15   see the barber and do a wash
cross the country
cross Brooklyn and Manhattan
MAKE A SPEECH
READ A POEM
20   liberate my daughter
from her father and Washington, D.C.
recross the country
and present her to her room.

----

[99] Shoji panels are the translucent panels found in traditional Japanese homes.

My daughter is coming!
25   Will she like her bed,
her chair, her mirror
desk and lamp

Or will she see only
the torn curtains?

Compare "My Daughter Is Coming" to Adrienne Rich's "A Woman Mourned by Daughters" on page 773 and Anne Sexton's "Pain for a Daughter" on pages 770–71.

TOM WAYMAN (1945–)

Unemployment

The chrome lid of the coffee pot
twists off, and the glass knob rinsed.
Lift out the assembly, dump
the grounds out. Wash the pot and
5   fill with water, put everything back with
fresh grounds and snap the top down.
Plug in again and wait.

Unemployment is also
a great snow deep around the house
10   choking the street, and the City.
Nothing moves. Newspaper photographs
show the traffic backed up for miles.
Going out to shovel the walk
I think how in a few days the sun will clear this.
15   No one will know I worked here.

This is like whatever I do.
How strange that so magnificent a thing as a body
with its twinges, its aches
should have all that chemistry, that bulk
20   the intricate electrical brain
subjected to something as tiny
as buying a postage stamp.
Or selling it.

Or waiting.

GREGORY ORR (1947–)

All Morning

All morning the dream lingers.
I am like thick grass
in a meadow, still
soaked with dew at noon.

MOLLY PEACOCK (1947–)

Petting and Being a Pet

Dogs, lambs, chickens, women—pets of all nations!
Fur or feathers under the kneading fingers
of those who long to have pets, relations
of softness to fleshiness, how a hand lingers
5   on a head or on the ear of a head, thus the sound
of petting and being a pet, a sounding horn:
needing met by kneading of bone which is found
through flesh. Have you ever felt forlorn
looking at a cat on someone else's lap, wishing
10   the cat was you? Look how an animal is passed
from lap to lap in a room, so many wishing
to hold it. We wish to be in the vast
caress, both animal and hand. Like eyes make sense
of seeing, touch makes being make sense.

LESLIE MARMON SILKO (1948–)

Love Poem

Rain smell comes with the wind
                         out of the southwest.
Smell of the sand dunes
            tall grass glistening
5   in the rain.
Warm raindrops that fall easy
               (this woman)
The summer is born.
Smell of her breathing new life
10   small gray toads on damp sand.
(this woman)
        whispering to dark wide leaves
        white moon blossoms dripping
                     tracks in the sand.
15   Rain smell
        I am full of hunger
        deep and longing to touch
wet tall grass, green and strong beneath.
This woman loved a man
20   and she breathed to him
             her damp earth song.
I am haunted by this story
I remember it in cottonwood leaves
              their fragrance in the shade.
25   I remember it in the wide blue sky
when the rain smell comes with the wind.

JOHN YAU (1950–)

For Alexander Pope's Garden[100]

In a garden every plant and flower
Memorizes the proper manner
In which to behave, or else they are discarded.
The lessons are simple; the growth must be retarded
Until they stand like dragoons in an orderly row,
Keep their thoughts private, and occasionally bow.

GARRETT HONGO (1951–)

The Hongo Store
29 Miles Volcano
Hilo, Hawaii

From a Photograph

My parents felt those rumblings
Coming deep from the earth's belly,
Thudding like the bell of the Buddhist Church.
Tremors in the ground swayed the bathinette
5   Where I lay squalling in soapy water.

My mother carried me around the house,
Back through the orchids, ferns, and plumeria
Of that greenhouse world behind the store,
And jumped between gas pumps into the car.

10   My father gave it the gun
And said, "Be quiet," as he searched
The frequencies, flipping for the right station
(The radio squealing more loudly than I could cry).

And then even the echoes stopped—
15   The only sound the Edsel's grinding
And the bark and crackle of radio news
Saying stay home or go to church.

"Dees time she no blow!"
My father said, driving back
20   Over the red ash covering the road.
"I worried she went go for broke already!"

So in this print the size of a matchbook,
The dark skinny man, shirtless and grinning,
A toothpick in the corner of his smile,
25   Lifts a naked baby above his head—
Behind him the plate glass of the store only cracked.

---

[100] Alexander Pope (1688–1744) was a great English poet whose "Epistle to a Young Lady" may be
found in its entirety on pages 715–16. On his estate at Twickenham, Pope established a large
and famous garden.

Compare "The Hongo Store" to the next poem, Gary Soto's "History," and to Edward Field's "My Polish Grandmother" on pages 437–38.

GARY SOTO (1952–)

History

Grandma lit the stove.
Morning sunlight
Lengthened in spears
Across the linoleum floor.
5   Wrapped in a shawl,
Her eyes small
With sleep,
She sliced papas,
Pounded chiles
10 With a stone
Brought from Guadalajara.[101]

                      After
Grandpa left for work,
She hosed down
15 The walk her sons paved
And in the shade
Of a chinaberry,
Unearthed her
Secret cigar box
20 Of bright coins
And bills, counted them
In English,
Then in Spanish,
And buried them elsewhere.
25 Later, back
From the market,
Where no one saw her,
She pulled out
Pepper and beet, spines
30 Of asparagus
From her blouse,
Tiny chocolates
From under a paisley bandana,
And smiled.

35 That was the '50s,
And Grandma in her '50s,
A face streaked
From cutting grapes
And boxing plums.
40 I remember her insides

---

[101] Guadalajara is a city in west-central Mexico.

Were washed of tapeworm,
Her arms swelled into knobs
Of small growths—
Her second son
45   Dropped from a ladder
And was dust.
And yet I do not know
The sorrows
That sent her praying
50   In the dark of a closet,
The tear that fell
At night
When she touched
Loose skin
55   Of belly and breasts.
I do not know why
Her face shines
Or what goes beyond this shine,
Only the stories
60   That pulled her
From Taxco[102] to San Joaquin,
Delano to Westside,[103]
The places
In which we all begin.

Compare "History" with Edward Field's "My Polish Grandmother" on pages 437–38, and with Garrett Hongo's "The Hongo Store," the poem preceding this one.

---

[102] Taxco is a city of Mexico.
[103] Places in California.

Drama

Drama

1 ※ Literature Onstage

A great drama is in many ways the liveliest vehicle for literature. No author is so admired and applauded as the playwright Shakespeare, while his gifted contemporary Spenser, a narrative poet, is treasured in respectful silence. No hero of fiction has excited as much laughter as Rostand's theatrical Cyrano, or as many sighs and tears as Romeo and Juliet. The stage amplifies character and emotion. Plays of Sophocles and Aristophanes, performed twenty-five hundred years ago, are still terrifying and delighting audiences the world over, while the lyric poetry of Periclean Athens lives on in the studies of only a few earnest readers.

The fact is, drama is more popular than fiction and poetry. It nearly always has been, in every culture with a viable theater. Drama, which has come to include the movies and television, is more accessible to more people. In order to enjoy poetry and fiction, one needs not only the ability to read, but also the leisure and attention to read carefully, thoughtfully. But, with little or no education and the price of admission, anyone can enjoy a stageplay.

So, in drama we are dealing with an art form that is not wholly literature. It is a "performance art," which may be greatly enhanced and enriched by literature, which uses literature for its blueprint and its record. A drama may be an *occasion* for eloquent language, but many plays do quite well without it. Marcel Marceau, the French mime, can act out a play in utter silence, and the story he is playing will be appreciated as much by the Chinese as the French. Technically, drama does not require language. We must remember this lest we disregard the greatest gift of the playwright—the planning of dramatic action on the stage.

Dramatic Action

For the purposes of our study we will consider a dramatic action to be any action by characters on stage that will hold the attention of the audience. Clowns and tightrope walkers have at least this in common with the cast of *Hamlet*: all are

797

able to hold the attention of a crowd. These performers are interesting because they present us with startling images of ourselves. The clown with his painted smile and oversized shoes mirrors our folly. The tightrope walker reflects our terror, courage, and desire for virtuosity. Hamlet and his fellow actors play several compelling stories—a love affair, a son seeking revenge for his father's murder, a friend's betrayal—situations that interest us because they are familiar. The dramatic actors of the play *Hamlet* have a special attraction. Though their predicaments are movingly familiar, they are not real. They invite us to share emotions while relieving us of responsibility for the outcome. We may weep briefly for the slain Hamlet, but when the curtain is down, we need not mourn him.

A play is a sympathetic human spectacle, like clowning and tight-rope walking, requiring performers and audience. But unlike tight-rope walking, a play is not real. It is a fiction acted out. In his unsurpassed analysis of drama, *The Poetics*, the Greek philosopher Aristotle (384–322 B.C.) defines drama as "an imitation of an action." The play arouses in us lifelike emotions without the usual responsibility for them. The theater permits us a peculiar and exhilarating freedom, providing what Aristotle calls a "catharsis," a sort of refreshening of our emotional channels. We will explore the much-disputed idea of catharsis in our discussion of tragedy; for the moment let it suffice to say that there is a certain relief that comes when we witness a dreaded disaster on the stage, just as there is relief when we witness a happy ending. We need to laugh and cry for characters invented primarily for that purpose, who ask no more of us than this intense, fleeting affection. This need is so old and so persistent that the stock characters of ancient Greek drama appear, slightly revised, in our television comedies and soap operas: the jealous husband, the sighing lover, the braggart, the villain, and many others.

Of course, a good play presents characters richer than these, and may make a more lasting impression on us. But we should remember that a great dramatic character shares with those stock characters an immediate appeal to the whole audience. Not to just a few of them. For a play, unlike a poem or novel, is a public phenomenon requiring the collaboration of actors and a live audience. No audience, no play. The idea of performing *Hamlet* for a house of three or four special people is unthinkable. Actors in such a predicament would strain, grow dispirited, and finally lifeless. They need the nourishment of the crowd's laughter, tears, and applause.

The Audience

Let us consider the character of an audience at a play. The spectator in the theater is in a very different state of mind than the individual who sits alone reading a story. He is at once inhibited and stimulated by the company. He is aware that he is a member of the audience, and that his response is public. If he does not hiss the villain and cry for the heroine, his neighbor might think

Audience, from Steichen's *Family of Man* (*Photograph by Arthur Witmann. Courtesy the St. Louis Post-Dispatch*)

him unfeeling, inhuman. Or he may not feel free to laugh while his neighbor is silent. He may be more likely to cry if his neighbor does.

This socialization of audience response makes the theater a natural incubator for morals and politics during revolutionary times; during ordinary times, though, the playwright is bound to uphold the prevailing morals. While the audience may be stimulated by villainy, they will rarely tolerate a stage play in which evil triumphs.

The Playwright as Collaborator

Playwrights receive full credit for the final scripts of their plays. But witnesses of the rehearsal process know that most scripts represent a collaboration between the writer and an artistic staff including actors, directors, producers, and designers of scenery, costumes, props, and lighting. A playwright working year in and year out with the same company of actors learns to trust their instincts and respond to their suggestions. We know Shakespeare admired the actor William Burbage, who was first to play Hamlet. Perhaps Burbage suggested a line or two of dialogue. This occurs in contemporary theater and there is no reason to think it could not happen in Elizabethan times. Elia Kazan, who first directed several of Tennessee Williams's scripts, ordered a number of changes in them, from specific lines to entire scenes. We must acknowledge him as a significant contributor to the final scripts.

Of course the playwright's role is central. The playwright usually conceives the story and scenes and writes most of the dialogue. Since it is primarily these things that are preserved as "literature," we will be concerned mainly with the playwright's work. But before we move on to the literary side of drama, let us give some attention to the "artistic staff" that so richly contributes to the literature.

First comes the producer. Producers choose a script they wish to bring before a specific audience. They select and secure a theater. Then they assemble an artistic staff, choosing a director first, who helps select the others. The producer publicizes the play and raises whatever funds are necessary to bring the play to the audience.

The director casts the play, with the playwright's approval if the playwright is living. Sometimes, as in the case of certain plays of Shakespeare and Molière, the play is "pre-cast," which means it was written with specific actors in mind. In rehearsals, the director strives to create an atmosphere in which the actors can work freely and effectively in developing their roles. Where necessary, he offers interpretation of the script. The director also supervises the work of the various designers—of sets, costumes, and lighting—and orchestrates them into a unified and tasteful production.

The actor's job is to interpret his or her lines and stage directions, creating from those signs a role that expresses the playwright's intentions and the actor's own special gift and inspiration. There are many ways to portray St. Joan, and quite a few might satisfy the playwright. Sometimes an actor or actress is so effective in "creating" a role that it is hard to imagine another actor reviving the role.

There are usually independent designers of stage scenery, costumes, and lighting. The stage designer, in consultation with the director, plans the layout, architecture, and colors of the stage scenery, and often selects the furniture. The costume designer creates or appropriates whatever the actors wear in the play, striving, like the stage designer, to fulfill the playwright's vision. The lighting designer creates illusions of daylight or nightlight, and through changes in color and intensity contributes to the mood of the play.

The designer's efforts in the first production of a drama are often described in the published script as if they were the playwright's own work. Modern playwrights usually credit the first designers, as well as the creators of the roles, in the preface to the published script. But it is still difficult to know how much of that which is described in scenic notes is the playwright's work, and how much is the designer's.

There are countless other contributors to the living play which ends up in our book as a finished script: stage managers, ushers, fencing coaches, and make-up artists. But let us turn to the script, for this is what is left us as literature.

2 ❧ The Script—How to Read a Play

The script is both the blueprint and record of a play. It has the same relation to a play as a sheet of musical notation has to the performance of a symphony. By the time we settle into our seats in the theater, the actors and their director have done valuable reading and interpreting of the characters and the story. We have only to listen attentively, and respond. But when we read a script we must do the imaginative work of the actors and their director. This requires somewhat more effort than theater-going.

On the other hand, reading drama offers certain pleasures and advantages that sitting in the audience does not. For instance, when a speech delights us we may reread it. If we miss the point of a particular scene, we may go back to the beginning. Most important, we do not have to suffer the misinterpretations and imperfections of the live performance. The play becomes ours to cast as we like, with our favorite actors, or with the characters the story suggests to our imaginations. We may go at our own pace, and make our own decisions about the playwright's intentions.

When you read a script, your head becomes the theater. You are the designer of the sets, the lighting, and the costumes. You are the actors and the director. Only when you have accomplished some of the work of these interpreters can you fully enjoy your role as the audience in reading a play.

Genre and Length

Until modern times the script often indicated a play's genre—comedy, tragedy, farce, melodrama, and so forth—and then the number of acts. In reading an unfamiliar play, it is helpful to have a hint as to its dramatic tone. Since most dialogue in scripts is presented without tonal comment such as "he said, gravely," it is extremely useful to know the play's genre from the beginning so that we know how to take the characters' speeches, and what tone to imagine for them.

John Millington Synge (*Culver Pictures, Inc.*)

One could waste a great deal of time misunderstanding *Hamlet* if one believed it to be a comedy.

In modern times, with the emergence of mixed genres, it has become more common simply to call the play "A Play in One Act" or "A Play in Three Acts," leaving it to the reader to discover whether the play is a tragedy, comedy, melodrama, or farce. At the opening of our first script, John Millington Synge tells us we are about to read *Riders to the Sea*, "A Play in One Act," so he is not preparing us for the genre or tone. He tells us it is a "One Act" play, which means that if we were in the theater the play would be performed without intermission. We should try to read it at one sitting.

Technically, a "One Act" play is any play comfortably performed without intermission, but it differs from the so-called full-length play in particulars other than its brevity. Generally the "One Act" play has fewer characters, takes place in a single setting, and tells a single story, whereas a full-length drama may have any number of characters and scene-changes, and tell several related stories over the course of two or three hours. The one-act play may be more impressionistic, less conclusive than a full-length play; more of a "slice-of-life," to borrow a phrase from the study of the short story. In any case, the "one act" is a good place to begin our reading of dramatic literature because it has all the elements of grander plays without their complications.

The Characters

The next information the playwright gives us is a list of characters that will appear in the play. These are sometimes listed under the title *Dramatis Personae*, which is Latin for "the persons in the play." Sometimes the playwright will credit the actors who performed in the first production of the play, in which case he will also include the date and theater of the first performance, or *première*, as well as the names of those actors who first created the roles. This was the case with our first play, *Riders to the Sea*.

PERSONS IN THE PLAY

First performed at the Molesworth Hall, Dublin
February 25, 1904

Maurya (an old woman)	Honor Lavelle
Bartley (her son)	W. G. Fay
Cathleen (her daughter)	Sarah Allgood
Nora (a younger daughter)	Emma Vernon
Men and Women	

On the left are the characters of the drama; on the right are the real-life actors who performed at the Molesworth Hall in Dublin. If you were a theatergoer in 1904 and happened to miss the performance at Molesworth Hall, your knowledge of the famous Honor Lavelle and W. G. Fay would help you, in reading the script, to envision the kind of *an old woman* Maurya is, and what Bartley (*her son*) looks like. Since we have no firsthand knowledge of those actors, we must do our best to describe the characters to ourselves, with the help of the descriptive aids on the "characters" page and in the text.

Many playwrights, particularly the moderns, take great pains to describe their characters in detail, as an aid to the director in casting and as a stimulus to the imagination of the reader. Playwrights in former times did not do so. Synge's descriptions on the "characters" page, and upon the first appearance of each character, are minimal but essential. We should not read a line of dialogue until we have studied his descriptions and done what we can to envision the characters.

Thus, we learn that Maurya is an old woman. The phrase "old woman" may bring to your mind a particular old woman, or maybe a favorite elderly actress. If so, use her image until something in the dialogue contradicts it. We don't know yet whether Synge's Maurya is good-natured and soft-spoken or shrewish and shrill, but it is better to begin with an image that may later be revised than to try to imagine her speeches coming out of the empty air. We also know that she is the mother of three, and this may help us to envision her.

Her daughters are shadowy figures until the play begins. We learn from the "characters" page that Cathleen is the elder, perhaps ten years older than Nora, whom Synge describes as a "young girl." You may know sisters of the ages of Cathleen and Nora, and it is likely they share characteristics common to most older and younger sisters. The older may be more responsible and domineering, the younger more dependent. Again, these images are only a starting point, but such models are useful until the dialogue defines a more specific personality. About Bartley we know almost nothing from Synge's description. But the information that he is Maurya's son and the girls' brother is essential for the reader when Bartley makes his entrance.

The *Men and Women* mentioned last are not so much characters as extras of no particular age or number. They will provide a choral background and support for the principal actors at the end of the play. We will have more to say about the function of the dramatic chorus in our discussion of *Oedipus Rex* in Chapter 3.

Envisioning characters in a play is like developing a photograph. The image becomes sharper with every speech. But at the beginning we have only the shadowy figures provided by the descriptions on the "characters" page and at the entrance of each actor. We must pay close attention to this descriptive material no matter how minimal it is.

The Scene

One of the things that distinguishes theater from movies and television is that a stageplay must occur within a more strictly confined setting. Movies can range from an open meadow to the inside of a car for their scenes, as quickly as the camera can shift its angle. But the theater must rebuild the entire scene—that, or leave it up to the actors to *pretend* that they have moved to a different place, as the actors do in Shakespeare's plays.

From the audience we can see only one part of the world in which the drama takes place: that is "the set" or "playing area." Beyond what we see on the stage is the rest of the imaginary world from which the characters enter and into which they exit. Important action may take place "offstage." In order fully to appreciate the play, we must be able to imagine not only the playing area but what exists beyond it. These locales constitute the "scene."

At the beginning of any play the script provides a description of the scene which, in more or less detail, tells us what is within the playing area, "onstage," and what lies beyond it, "offstage." Our scene description at the beginning of *Riders to the Sea* tells us that the playing area is a "cottage kitchen" and that beyond the cottage is "an island off the West of Ireland." So, if one goes out the door of the kitchen, the sea is not far off. Since a cottage cannot have many rooms, we may assume that if there are two entrances, one at the right and one at the left of the kitchen, one leads to the outdoors and the other leads to the living quarters. The following diagram is an aerial view of the scene as it might look on a proscenium stage. The proscenium arch is the framed space at the front of the auditorium across which a stage curtain is drawn in most theaters. A "proscenium" stage is the sort provided in the typical school auditorium, where the audience sits in front of the proscenium and the play goes on behind it.

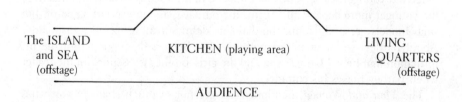

The ISLAND and SEA (offstage)   KITCHEN (playing area)   LIVING QUARTERS (offstage)

AUDIENCE

We should not overlook the other stage props: the nets, oil-skins, and the like, tell us that this is not the summer residence of wealthy city-dwellers, but rather a humble fishing cottage.

Now we are ready to read the play.

The Action

The action proper begins with Cathleen. When the curtain goes up she is finishing her baking and beginning her weaving. Whatever we might have thought of her before, now we must certainly think of her as industrious, no idler.

> "*Cathleen, a girl of about twenty, finishes kneading cake, and puts it down in the pot-oven by the fire.*"

This is the first *stage direction* of *Riders to the Sea*. A stage direction is any description of the actor's behavior that is not indicated by the dialogue. Stage directions are usually italicized and often appear in parentheses. Playwrights always try to keep such directions to a minimum, for the speeches themselves are usually the best indicators of the action. Shakespeare's plays are nearly free of stage directions.

As Cathleen is spinning, Nora "puts her head in at the door." This is another stage direction rich in implications. She does not stride in, or skip in, singing; she "puts her head in at the door" and speaks "in a low voice." This is not a bold or carefree entrance into her own home. We may assume that Nora, at an enthusiastic age, is either unusually shy, or is entering a situation that requires delicacy, maybe caution, and that Nora is capable of such delicacy. Her question and Cathleen's answer confirm that the house is not in a festive mood. Someone is lying down in the other room who needs not only sleep, but God's help.

Thus, with minimal stage directions and linguistic concentration worthy of a poet, J. M. Synge sets up a dramatic situation within two lines of dialogue. Already the audience is in some suspense, curious to know the plight of the mysterious woman in the next room. We suspect from our study of the *dramatis personae* that the woman offstage must be Maurya, the mother of these sisters. What is troubling her? Let us read on.

"*Nora comes in softly, and takes a bundle from under her shawl.*" Another stage direction, as dramatic an action as the theater can provide. If the art of drama could be captured in a single image, it might be just such a wrapped bundle, of unknown, significant contents. The playwright presents his bundle as the magician his unpredictable hat, and the audience is helpless with curiosity. What's in the bundle? Nora tells her sister it is clothing "got off a drowned man in Donegal," and that they are to determine whether or not the clothing belongs to Michael. We have only to read a little further to discover that Michael is the girls' brother and Maurya's son. They fear Michael has drowned; if the clothing is his, there can be no further doubt. So that they might break the news to her gently, the girls must wait until Maurya is "down looking by the sea" before they inspect the contents of the bundle. The audience must share their suspense.

By the time we are nine lines into the script we are aware not only of a dramatic situation, but of the *problem* of the play. Someone has drowned, and it may be Michael. The girls could find out by opening the bundle, but they cannot while Maurya is in the house, because the old woman is frail and might be overwhelmed by the sight of Michael's clothes. Most plays begin with such a dilemma and part of the dramatic interest lies in how the characters resolve their problem.

A secondary problem of the dramatic situation of *Riders to the Sea* involves the second son, Bartley. If Michael is indeed drowned, then Bartley is Maurya's only remaining son. And he is planning to cross the sea to Galway in perilous weather. Will he leave, against his mother's wishes? And if he departs for Galway, will he too be drowned, leaving Maurya "with no son living"? These are the questions the play poses. But, enough suspense. Let us read on, and see what happens.

JOHN MILLINGTON SYNGE (1871–1909)

Riders to the Sea
A Play in One Act

CHARACTERS

MAURYA, an old woman	NORA, a younger daughter
BARTLEY, her son	MEN *and* WOMEN
CATHLEEN, her daughter	

SCENE. *An Island off the West of Ireland.*

Cottage kitchen, with nets, oil-skins, spinning-wheel, some new boards standing by the wall, etc. Cathleen, a girl of about twenty, finishes kneading cake, and puts it down in the pot-oven by the fire; then wipes her hands, and begins to spin at the wheel. Nora, a young girl, puts her head in at the door.

NORA *(in a low voice)* Where is she?

CATHLEEN She's lying down, God help her, and may be sleeping, if she's able.

Nora comes in softly, and takes a bundle from under her shawl.

CATHLEEN *(spinning the wheel rapidly)* What is it you have?

NORA The young priest is after bringing them. It's a shirt and a plain stocking were got off a drowned man in Donegal.

Cathleen stops her wheel with a sudden movement, and leans out to listen.

NORA We're to find out if it's Michael's they are, some time herself will be down looking by the sea.

CATHLEEN How would they be Michael's, Nora? How would he go the length of that way to the far north?

NORA The young priest says he's known the like of it. "If it's Michael's they are," says he, "you can tell herself he's got a clean burial by the grace of God, and if they're not

A performance of *Riders to the Sea* (Holloway Collection, National Library of Ireland)

his, let no one say a word about them, for she'll be getting her death," says he, "with crying and lamenting."

The door which Nora half-closed is blown open by a gust of wind.

CATHLEEN (*looking out anxiously*) Did you ask him would he stop Bartley going this day with the horses to the Galway fair?

NORA "I won't stop him," says he, "but let you not be afraid. Herself does be saying prayers half through the night, and the Almighty God won't leave her destitute," says he, "with no son living."

CATHLEEN Is the sea bad by the white rocks, Nora?

NORA Middling bad, God help us. There's a great roaring in the west, and it's worse it'll be getting when the tide's turned to the wind.

She goes over to the table with the bundle.

Shall I open it now?

CATHLEEN Maybe she'd wake up on us, and come in before we'd done. (*Coming to the table.*) It's a long time we'll be, and the two of us crying.

NORA (*goes to the inner door and listens*) She's moving about on the bed. She'll be coming in a minute.

CATHLEEN Give me the ladder, and I'll put them up in the turf-loft, the way she won't know of them at all, and maybe when the tide turns she'll be going down to see would he be floating from the east.

They put the ladder against the gable of the chimney; Cathleen goes up a few steps and hides the bundle in the turf-loft. Maurya comes from the inner room.

MAURYA (*looking up at Cathleen and speaking querulously*) Isn't it turf enough you have for this day and evening?

CATHLEEN There's a cake baking at the fire for a short space (*throwing down the turf*) and Bartley will want it when the tide turns if he goes to Connemara.

Nora picks up the turf and puts it round the pot-oven.

MAURYA (*sitting down on a stool at the fire*) He won't go this day with the wind rising from the south and west. He won't go this day, for the young priest will stop him surely.

NORA He'll not stop him, mother, and I heard Eamon Simon and Stephen Pheety and Colum Shawn saying he would go.

MAURYA Where is he itself?

NORA He went down to see would there be another boat sailing in the week, and I'm thinking it won't be long till he's here now, for the tide's turning at the green head, and the hooker's[1] tacking from the east.

CATHLEEN I hear some one passing the big stones.

NORA (*looking out*) He's coming now, and he in a hurry.

BARTLEY (*comes in and looks round the room. Speaking sadly and quietly*) Where is the bit of new rope, Cathleen, was bought in Connemara?

CATHLEEN (*coming down*) Give it to him, Nora; it's on a nail by the white boards. I hung it up this morning, for the pig with the black feet was eating it.

NORA (*giving him a rope*) Is that it, Bartley?

MAURYA You'd do right to leave that rope, Bartley, hanging by the boards. (*Bartley takes the rope.*) It will be wanting in this place, I'm telling you, if Michael is washed up tomorrow morning, or the next morning, or any morning in the week, for it's a deep grave we'll make him by the grace of God.

BARTLEY (*beginning to work with the rope*) I've no halter the way I can ride down on the mare, and I must go now quickly. This is the one boat going for two weeks or beyond it, and the fair will be a good fair for horses I heard them saying below.

MAURYA It's a hard thing they'll be saying below if the body is washed up and there's no man in it to make the coffin, and I after giving a big price for the finest white boards you'd find in Connemara.

She looks round at the boards.

BARTLEY How would it be washed up, and we after looking each day for nine days, and a strong wind blowing a while back from the west and south?

MAURYA If it wasn't found itself, that wind is raising the sea, and there was a star up against the moon, and it rising in the night. If it was a hundred horses, or a thousand horses you had itself, what is the price of a thousand horses against a son where there is one son only?

BARTLEY (*working at the halter, to Cathleen*) Let you go down each day, and see the sheep aren't jumping in on the rye, and if the jobber comes you can sell the pig with the black feet if there is a good price going.

MAURYA How would the like of her get a good price for a pig?

BARTLEY (*to Cathleen*) If the west wind holds with the last bit of the moon let you and Nora get up weed enough for another cock for the kelp.[2] It's hard set we'll be from this day with no one in it but one man to work.

---

[1] *hooker:* a single-masted fishing boat.
[2] *kelp:* seaweed (used for manure).

MAURYA It's hard set we'll be surely the day you're drownd'd with the rest. What way will I live and the girls with me, and I an old woman looking for the grave?

Bartley lays down the halter, takes off his old coat, and puts on a newer one of the same flannel.

BARTLEY *(to Nora)* Is she coming to the pier?

Nora (looking out) She's passing the green head and letting fall her sails.

BARTLEY *(getting his purse and tobacco)* I'll have half an hour to go down, and you'll see me coming again in two days, or in three days, or maybe in four days if the wind is bad.

MAURYA *(turning round to the fire, and putting her shawl over her head)* Isn't it a hard and cruel man won't hear a word from an old woman, and she holding him from the sea?

CATHLEEN It's the life of a young man to be going on the sea, and who would listen to an old woman with one thing and she saying it over?

BARTLEY *(taking the halter)* I must go now quickly. I'll ride down on the red mare, and the gray pony'll run behind me. . . . The blessing of God on you.

He goes out.

MAURYA *(crying out as he is in the door)* He's gone now, God spare us, and we'll not see him again. He's gone now, and when the black night is falling I'll have no son left me in the world.

CATHLEEN Why wouldn't you give him your blessing and he looking round in the door? Isn't it sorrow enough is on every one in this house without your sending him out with an unlucky word behind him, and a hard word in his ear?

Maurya takes up the tongs and begins raking the fire aimlessly without looking round.

NORA *(turning towards her)* You're taking away the turf from the cake.

CATHLEEN *(crying out)* The Son of God forgive us, Nora, we're after forgetting his bit of bread.

She comes over to the fire.

NORA And it's destroyed he'll be going till dark night, and he after eating nothing since the sun went up.

CATHLEEN *(turning the cake out of the oven)* It's destroyed he'll be, surely. There's no sense left on any person in a house where an old woman will be talking for ever.

Maurya sways herself on her stool.

CATHLEEN *(cutting off some of the bread and rolling it in a cloth; to Maurya)* Let you go down now to the spring well and give him this and he passing. You'll see him then and the dark word will be broken, and you can say "God speed you," the way he'll be easy in his mind.

MAURYA *(taking the bread)* Will I be in it as soon as himself?

CATHLEEN If you go now quickly.

MAURYA *(standing up unsteadily)* It's hard set I am to walk.

CATHLEEN *(looking at her anxiously)* Give her the stick, Nora, or maybe she'll slip on the big stones.

NORA What stick?

CATHLEEN The stick Michael brought from Connemara.

MAURYA (*taking a stick Nora gives her*) In the big world the old people do be leaving things after them for their sons and children, but in this place it is the young men do be leaving things behind for them that do be old.

She goes out slowly. Nora goes over to the ladder.

CATHLEEN Wait, Nora, maybe she'd turn back quickly. She's that sorry, God help her, you wouldn't know the thing she'd do.

NORA Is she gone around by the bush?

CATHLEEN (*looking out*) She's gone now. Throw it down quickly, for the Lord knows when she'll be out of it again.

NORA (*getting the bundle from the loft*) The young priest said he'd be passing to-morrow, and we might go down and speak to him below if it's Michael's they are surely.

CATHLEEN (*taking the bundle*) Did he say what way they were found?

NORA (*coming down*) "There were two men," says he, "and they rowing round with poteen[3] before the cocks crowed, and the oar of one of them caught the body, and they passing the black cliffs of the north."

CATHLEEN (*trying to open the bundle*) Give me a knife, Nora, the string's perished with the salt water, and there's a black knot on it you wouldn't loosen in a week.

NORA (*giving her a knife*) I've heard tell it was a long way to Donegal.

CATHLEEN (*cutting the string*) It is surely. There was a man in here a while ago—the man sold us that knife—and he said if you set off walking from the rock beyond, it would be seven days you'd be in Donegal.

NORA And what time would a man take, and he floating?

Cathleen opens the bundle and takes out a bit of a stocking. They look at them eagerly.

CATHLEEN (*in a low voice*) The Lord spare us, Nora! isn't it a queer hard thing to say if it's his they are surely?

NORA I'll get his shirt off the hook the way we can put the one flannel on the other. (*She looks through some clothes hanging in the corner.*) It's not with them, Cathleen, and where will it be?

CATHLEEN I'm thinking Bartley put it on him in the morning, for his own shirt was heavy with the salt in it. (*Pointing to the corner.*) There's a bit of a sleeve was of the same stuff. Give me that and it will do.

Nora brings it to her and they compare the flannel.

CATHLEEN It's the same stuff, Nora; but if it is itself aren't there great rolls of it in the shops of Galway, and isn't it many another man may have a shirt of it as well as Michael himself?

NORA (*who has taken up the stocking and counted the stitches, crying out*) It's Michael, Cathleen, it's Michael; God spare his soul, and what will herself say when she hears this story, and Bartley on the sea?

CATHLEEN (*taking the stocking*) It's a plain stocking.

NORA It's the second one of the third pair I knitted, and I put up three score stiches, and I dropped four of them.

---

[3] *poteen:* illegal whiskey.

CATHLEEN (*counts the stitches*) It's that number is in it. (*Crying out.*) Ah, Nora, isn't it a bitter thing to think of him floating that way to the far north, and no one to keen[4] him but the black hags that do be flying on the sea?

NORA (*swinging herself round, and throwing out her arms on the clothes*) And isn't it a pitiful thing when there is nothing left of a man who was a great rower and fisher, but a bit of an old shirt and a plain stocking?

CATHLEEN (*after an instant*) Tell me is herself coming, Nora? I hear a little sound on the path.

NORA (*looking out*) She is, Cathleen. She's coming up to the door.

CATHLEEN Put these things away before she'll come in. Maybe it's easier she'll be after giving her blessing to Bartley, and we won't let on we've heard anything the time he's on the sea.

NORA (*helping Cathleen to close the bundle*) We'll put them here in the corner.

They put them into a hole in the chimney corner. Cathleen goes back to the spinning-wheel.

NORA Will she see it was crying I was?

CATHLEEN Keep your back to the door the way the light'll not be on you.

Nora sits down at the chimney corner, with her back to the door. Maurya comes in very slowly, without looking at the girls, and goes over to her stool at the other side of the fire. The cloth with the bread is still in her hand. The girls look at each other, and Nora points to the bundle of bread.

CATHLEEN (*after spinning for a moment*) You didn't give him his bit of bread?

Maurya begins to keen softly, without turning round.

CATHLEEN Did you see him riding down?

Maurya goes on keening.

CATHLEEN (*a little impatiently*) God forgive you; isn't it a better thing to raise your voice and tell what you seen, than to be making lamentation for a thing that's done? Did you see Bartley, I'm saying to you.

MAURYA (*with a weak voice*) My heart's broken from this day.

CATHLEEN (*as before*) Did you see Bartley?

MAURYA I seen the fearfulest thing.

CATHLEEN (*leaves her wheel and looks out*) God forgive you; he's riding the mare now over the green head, and the gray pony behind him.

MAURYA (*starts, so that her shawl falls back from her head and shows her white tossed hair. With a frightened voice*) The gray pony behind him.

CATHLEEN (*coming to the fire*) What is it ails you, at all?

MAURYA (*speaking very slowly*) I've seen the fearfulest thing any person has seen, since the day Bride Dara seen the dead man with the child in his arms.

CATHLEEN AND NORA Uah.

They crouch down in front of the old woman at the fire.

---

[4] *keen*: lament.

NORA Tell us what it is you seen.

MAURYA I went down to the spring well, and I stood there saying a prayer to myself. Then Bartley came along, and he riding on the red mare with the gray pony behind him. *(She puts up her hands, as if to hide something from her eyes.)* The Son of God spare us, Nora!

CATHLEEN What is it you seen?

MAURYA I seen Michael himself.

CATHLEEN *(speaking softly)* You did not, mother; it wasn't Michael you seen, for his body is after being found in the far north, and he's got a clean burial by the grace of God.

MAURYA *(a little defiantly)* I'm after seeing him this day, and he riding and galloping. Bartley came first on the red mare; and I tried to say "God speed you," but something choked the words in my throat. He went by quickly; and "the blessing of God on you," says he, and I could say nothing. I looked up then, and I crying, at the gray pony, and there was Michael upon it—with fine clothes on him, and new shoes on his feet.

CATHLEEN *(begins to keen)* It's destroyed we are from this day. It's destroyed, surely.

NORA Didn't the young priest say the Almighty God wouldn't leave her destitute with no son living?

MAURYA *(in a low voice, but clearly)* It's little the like of him knows of the sea. . . . Bartley will be lost now, and let you call in Eamon and make me a good coffin out of the white boards, for I won't live after them. I've had a husband, and a husband's father, and six sons in this house—six fine men, though it was a hard birth I had with every one of them and they coming to the world—and some of them were found and some of them were not found, but they're gone now the lot of them. . . . There were Stephen, and Shawn, were lost in the great wind, and found after in the Bay of Gregory of the Golden Mouth, and carried up the two of them, on the one plank, and in by that door.

She pauses for a moment, the girls start as if they heard something through the door that is half open behind them.

NORA *(in a whisper)* Did you hear that, Cathleen? Did you hear a noise in the north-east?

CATHLEEN *(in a whisper)* There's some one after crying out by the seashore.

MAURYA *(continues without hearing anything)* There was Sheamus and his father, and his own father again, were lost in a dark night, and not a stick or sign was seen of them when the sun went up. There was Patch after was drowned out of a curagh⁵ that turned over. I was sitting here with Bartley, and he a baby, lying on my two knees, and I seen two women, and three women, and four women coming in, and they crossing themselves, and not saying a word. I looked out then, and there were men coming after them, and they holding a thing in the half of a red sail, and water dripping out of it—it was a dry day, Nora—and leaving a track to the door.

She pauses again with her hand stretched out towards the door. It opens softly and old women begin to come in, crossing themselves on the threshold, and kneeling down in front of the stage with red petticoats over their heads.

---

⁵ *curagh:* unstable vessel of tarred canvas on a wood frame; canoe.

MAURYA (*half in a dream, to Cathleen*) Is it Patch, or Michael, or what is it at all?

CATHLEEN Michael is after being found in the far north, and when he is found there how could he be here in this place?

MAURYA There does be a power of young men floating round in the sea, and what way would they know if it was Michael they had, or another man like him, for when a man is nine days in the sea, and the wind blowing, it's hard set his own mother would be to say what man was it.

CATHLEEN It's Michael, God spare him, for they're after sending us a bit of his clothes from the far north.

She reaches out and hands Maurya the clothes that belonged to Michael. Maurya stands up slowly and takes them in her hand. Nora looks out.

NORA They're carrying a thing among them and there's water dripping out of it and leaving a track by the big stones.

CATHLEEN (*in a whisper to the women who have come in*) Is it Bartley it is?

ONE OF THE WOMEN. It is surely, God rest his soul.

Two younger women come in and pull out the table. Then men carry in the body of Bartley, laid on a plank, with a bit of sail over it, and lay it on the table.

CATHLEEN (*to the women, as they are doing so*) What way was he drowned?

ONE OF THE WOMEN. The gray pony knocked him into the sea, and he was washed out where there is a great surf on the white rocks.

Maurya has gone over and knelt down at the head of the table. The women are keening softly and swaying themselves with a slow movement. Cathleen and Nora kneel at the other end of the table. The men kneel near the door.

MAURYA (*raising her head and speaking as if she did not see the people around her*) They're all gone now, and there isn't anything more the sea can do to me. . . . I'll have no call now to be up crying and praying when the wind breaks from the south, and you can hear the surf is in the east, and the surf is in the west, making a great stir with the two noises, and they hitting one on the other. I'll have no call now to be going down and getting Holy Water in the dark nights after Samhain,[6] and I won't care what way the sea is when the other women will be keening. (*To Nora.*) Give me the Holy Water, Nora, there's a small sup still on the dresser.

Nora gives it to her.

MAURYA (*drops Michael's clothes across Bartley's feet, and sprinkles the Holy Water over him*) It isn't that I haven't prayed for you, Bartley, to the Almighty God. It isn't that I haven't said prayers in the dark night till you wouldn't know what I'ld be saying; but it's a great rest I'll have now, and it's time surely. It's a great rest I'll have now, and great sleeping in the long nights after Samhain, if it's only a bit of wet flour we do have to eat, and maybe a fish that would be stinking.

She kneels down again, crossing herself, and saying prayers under her breath.

---

6 *Samhain*: November 1, All Saints' Day.

CATHLEEN (to an old man) Maybe yourself and Eamon would make a coffin when the sun rises. We have fine white boards herself bought, God help her, thinking Michael would be found, and I have a new cake you can eat while you'll be working.

THE OLD MAN (looking at the boards) Are there nails with them?

CATHLEEN There are not, Colum; we didn't think of the nails.

ANOTHER MAN It's a great wonder she wouldn't think of the nails, and all the coffins she's seen made already.

CATHLEEN It's getting old she is, and broken.

Maurya stands up again very slowly and spreads out the pieces of Michael's clothes beside the body, sprinkling them with the last of the Holy Water.

NORA (in a whisper to Cathleen) She's quiet now and easy; but the day Michael was drowned you could hear her crying out from this to the spring well. It's fonder she was of Michael, and would any one have thought that?

CATHLEEN (slowly and clearly) An old woman will be soon tired with anything she will do, and isn't it nine days herself is after crying and keening, and making great sorrow in the house?

MAURYA (puts the empty cup mouth downwards on the table, and lays her hands together on Bartley's feet) They're all together this time, and the end is come. May the Almighty God have mercy on Bartley's soul, and on Michael's soul, and on the souls of Sheamus and Patch, and Stephen and Shawn (bending her head); and may He have mercy on my soul, Nora, and on the soul of every one is left living in the world.

She pauses, and the keen rises a little more loudly from the women, then sinks away.

MAURYA (continuing) Michael has a clean burial in the far north, by the grace of the Almighty God. Bartley will have a fine coffin out of the white boards, and a deep grave surely. What more can we want than that? No man at all can be living for ever, and we must be satisfied.

She kneels down again and the curtain falls slowly.

Questions

1. When Maurya enters, Cathleen is on the ladder hiding the bundle of clothes in the turf-loft. How does Cathleen's action add to the dramatic interest of Maurya's entrance? How does Cathleen allay her mother's suspicion?
2. What is Maurya's chief concern?
3. What do you know about Bartley before his entrance on page 808? What do the stage directions and his first speech tell you about his character? Is he more concerned about his mother, or about his own business?
4. Do you think Bartley is cruel, or do you sympathize with Cathleen's defense of him on page 809?
5. When Bartley exits Maurya says, "we'll not see him again," and "when the black night is falling I'll have no son left in the world." In view of the play's outcome these statements are prophetic—instances of what is called dramatic "foreshadowing." What do these remarks tell you about Maurya's state of mind?

6. Cathleen and Nora send their mother after Bartley with "his bit of bread." They want Maurya to give Bartley her blessing. For what other reason do they send her out of the house?
7. What finally convinces the sisters that Michael is dead? How does Synge develop suspense during this scene of discovery?
8. There is dramatic tension in the kitchen when Maurya enters on page 811. Why?
9. On page 812 Maurya says she has seen Michael. Cathleen tells her his body has been found. What has Maurya *really* seen? What is the significance of her vision?
10. After the old women enter on page 812, Cathleen announces that Michael's body is being carried to the house. Are you shocked when you discover it is Bartley's? Is this more moving than if it were in fact Michael's corpse? Why?
11. Is Maurya surprised that the body is Bartley's rather than Michael's? What is her response? Hysteria? Relief?
12. *Riders To The Sea* has been called "one of the finest tragedies ever written." A great tragic heroine learns from her suffering. What has Maurya learned? What is her state of mind and heart at the fall of the curtain? What can we learn from her?

Suggestions for Dramatists

Think of a familiar location, indoors or outdoors, that is frequented by interesting characters. Could it be reproduced in a theater and used as a scene for a stage play? Draw a floor plan of a possible set, marking exits and the location of stage props (furniture).

3 🌿 Action

The essence of a stage play is the action. Whereas the novelist may present a heroine in an armchair, and go on for pages relating her rich inner life, the playwright must put characters on their feet immediately, telling us who they are by showing us what they do. This requires an engaging dramatic situation and ingenious plotting of the action. Eugène Labiche, the nineteenth-century French playwright, compared the novel to a leisurely journey in a carriage. "You make stops, you spend a night at the inn, you get out to look at the country. . . . You are in no hurry." But a play is a different matter. "A play," says Labiche, "is a railway journey by an express train . . . and if the locomotive ceases rushing and hissing, you hiss." The rapid action of a play begins with the introduction of the dramatic situation, or *problem*, and does not end until the situation has been resolved.

The Dramatic Situation

The action of a great play arises from the dramatic situation. A character or group of characters is in some sort of distress. This has been described as a condition of *conflict*, but is perhaps more accurately defined as a dynamic relationship of a character to an objective and the obstacle that comes between them. That is, a *character* has some goal or *objective*, but some *obstacle* stands in the way. Romeo wants Juliet, but her family (and his) stands in the way. In *Riders to the Sea*, Maurya wants Bartley to stay home, but his horses (his sense of independence) stand in the way. This elemental structure underlies most dramatic situations. The action flows naturally from the dramatic situation as the characters pursue their various objectives, and either succeed or fail in overcoming the obstacles that come between them and happiness.

The Plot

The first systematic study of dramatic action was Aristotle's *Poetics*. Aristotle observes that a play must have a beginning, a middle, and an end—a rough analysis that has been considerably refined since Aristotle's time. We now recognize that most great plays have a five-part movement which corresponds roughly to the five-act structure of classical comedy and tragedy: Exposition, Rising Action, Climax, Falling Action, and Denouement or Catastrophe, depending upon whether the play has a happy or a sad ending. A stage play is perhaps the most conventional and restricted of all literary forms. It is an uncommon stage play that succeeds in violating this five-part structure, whether it be tragedy, comedy, melodrama, or farce. The five-part structure has its greatest analyst in the nineteenth-century critic Gustave Freytag, who originated the famous pyramid of the dramatic plot:

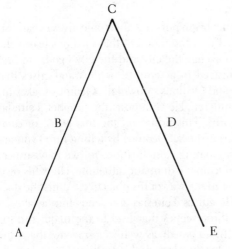

A) exposition
B) rising action
C) climax
D) falling action/return
E) catastrophe (denouement)

Freytag's Pyramid of Dramatic Structure

Exposition

The exposition is the play's introduction to the characters and the dramatic situation. Whatever history of the characters we need in order to understand their present predicament will be given as economically as possible in the exposition. In the Prologue to *Oedipus Rex*, the Priest tells us that the city of Thebes has been suffering from a plague. We learn that King Oedipus is a wise and capable ruler, for he once outwitted the wicked Sphinx to save Thebes from her fury. His people believe that only Oedipus can save them from the plague. We also learn that Oedipus, ever-vigilant, has sent his Queen's brother, Creon, to Delphi to ask advice of the oracle. In the next scene of exposition Creon comes to tell Oedipus what he learned from the oracle: Someone murdered the previous king, Laïos. The god Apollo will not lift the plague from Thebes until the people find the murderer and punish him.

All this is background, helping us to understand the dramatic situation. Classical plays, like epics, often begin *in medias res*, in the middle of the story, and the exposition is the play's main gesture toward the past. Though the play returns occasionally to exposition to fill in gaps in the audience's knowledge, most of the background information emerges in the first minutes of classical drama. After that, the dramatic interest is fixed squarely in the present. When we have learned the dramatic situation of *Oedipus Rex*, that Oedipus wants to save Thebes from the plague but cannot until he finds the murderer of Laïos, then the real action of the play can begin.

The Rising Action

When the chief characters of the drama begin pursuing their objectives in earnest, the play has begun its *rising action*. From the moment that Oedipus learns the cause of the plague and resolves "to avenge the city and the city's god," to find and punish the murderer, he is engaged in a series of actions and crises that lead inevitably to the play's climax and Oedipus's downfall. Oedipus makes his proclamation to hunt down the murderer. He summons the prophet Teiresias and asks him to name the guilty party. This brings on the first *crisis*, or *complication*, of the rising action. Teiresias shocks Oedipus by telling him "you are the murderer whom you seek," a fascinating complication, for we may suspect for the first time the true nature of Oedipus's dramatic situation. He is his own obstacle. Oedipus himself is standing in the way of his objective. At first he does not believe it, and he is enraged. He curses Teiresias and sends him away.

The rising action consists of all those scenes that lead to the major turning point or climax in the play's story. In a comedy as well as a tragedy, the rising action shows the hero struggling to solve the play's problem, though in a comedy the hero appears to be more vulnerable and threatened with failure. Defiance and pride characterize Oedipus's behavior in the rising action of *Oedipus Rex* as he fights the allegations of his own guilt. He threatens the good Creon with exile or death. Despite the assurances of Queen Iocastê and the townspeople that Creon is innocent, Oedipus continues to suspect him, arrogantly looking for the source of evil outside himself instead of within. His crisis with Creon leads to the play's climax, in which Iocastê, intending to reassure Oedipus, lends him information that points to his guilt.

The Climax

The *climax* of a stage play is sometimes hotly disputed. We will avoid unnecessary confusion if we recognize that this term has been used to describe two different moments in the theater. There is the climax of dramatic action, sometimes called the turning point of the play. Then there is the climax of emotion, that point in the drama that moves the audience most deeply.

In this chapter we are chiefly concerned with the climax of action. This is the exact point at which the hero's fortune turns—from better to worse in a tragedy, and from bad to good in a comedy. During the exposition and rising action of *Oedipus Rex* the hero ascends from strength to arrogance. But when Iocastê tells him Laïos was killed "where three highways meet," and Oedipus recalls murdering a man in that time and place, his position falters. Oedipus begins his descent into self-suspicion, self-loathing, and finally blindness and exile as his fate overwhelms him.

Anyone who has seen *Oedipus Rex* knows that the emotional climax of the play comes near the end, after the hero's guilt has been proven to everyone. But by the time the old shepherd delivers final proof of Oedipus's guilt, and the hero blinds himself, King Oedipus's fortunes have been declining for quite a few scenes. In the plotting of *Oedipus Rex* the emotional climax of the play occurs during the falling action and catastrophe.

Locating the climax of a play's action, or the "turning point," is one of the most challenging and rewarding pursuits in the study of drama, for it is at this point in the story that the hero's strengths and weaknesses are most visible. In some plays the climax is conspicuous, as it is in the powerful scene of *Othello* wherein the great Moor begins to suspect his wife of infidelity. In other plays the turning point is difficult to determine, as in *Oedipus Rex*, which has a lengthy falling action and violent catastrophe, but whose early climax may seem to some like one more crisis in the rising action.

We will be searching for the climax of the action in all of our plays. Whether or not we agree on where it occurs, the search for the climax we hope will produce lively discussion.

The Falling Action

Sometimes called the *declining action* or the *return*, the *falling action* in a tragedy includes those scenes that show the hero or heroine as they fall from power and their fate closes in on them. In a comedy it shows the villains or forces of adversity in decline, as the more sympathetic characters gain the upper hand.

At the climax of *Oedipus Rex*, the hero begins to suspect his guilt. After that, each scene of the *falling action* brings him closer to the awful truth about himself. First a messenger from Corinth, and then a shepherd, bring him evidence that proves beyond any doubt that Oedipus himself is the murderer he has been seeking. The falling action leads directly to the play's resolution.

Catastrophe and Denouement

Drama has been likened to the weaving of a net or the tying of a knot to catch the characters in a predicament, and to hold the audience in suspense about the fate of these characters they have come to admire. *Catastrophe* comes from the Greek and means literally "a downward turn," while the gentler term *de-nouement*, from the French, means "an untying." Though the terms have been used interchangeably, we usually call the outcome of a tragedy a catastrophe, and the outcome of a comedy its denouement.

These are the scenes of the play that answer our questions. In comedies, where there is a love interest and we may have been wondering if the heroine would live happily ever after with the hero, the denouement is usually a marriage, engagement, or other reconciliation. In tragedies, where we have been fearing the demise of the hero, the scenes of catastrophe are often violent and swift. There may be scenes of great tenderness and *pathos* at this point to soothe the agitated feelings of the audience. In any case, this moment of the play may not be prolonged, for once our questions have been answered and the knot untied, the action must end.

Greek Drama and *Oedipus Rex*

Legend says that Thespis, the father of Greek tragedy, was the first actor. Until the time of Thespis, who lived in the sixth century B.C., the most popular form of storytelling was a kind of choral speaking in which the verses of the story were chanted by a number of performers in unison. According to legend Thespis, in a great state of excitement about the story his chorus was chanting, stepped out of the ranks of the chorus and began addressing them in the voice of the story's hero. The immediate response of his fellow choristers is not recorded, but they must have been impressed, for this dialogue between the hero and the chorus became the backbone of Greek tragedy. The hero is the extraordinary man or woman who separates himself or herself from the group. This leads to disaster. The Greeks were probably no more moralistic than any civilized people, but the theater of Sophocles was rigid in its pieties. The chorus, a familiar holdover from the earlier form of narration, reflected the morals and sentiments of the Athenians. As a group onstage, the chorus mirrors the audience, and Sophocles uses the chorus to predict and explain the action as well as to lead the audience in their response.

In addition to the dialogues between the main characters of *Oedipus Rex*, there are five choral odes (songs) of great conviction and lyric beauty. They provide rest from the action as well as comment upon it. They help to explain why the myth of Oedipus had such an impact on the audience of Athens. They tell us that Oedipus has violated their deepest principles of piety, that

> Haughtiness and the high hand of disdain
> Tempt and outrage god's holy law;
> And any mortal who dares hold
> No immortal Power in awe
> Will be caught up in a net of pain.

Oedipus Rex was first performed about 430 B.C. on a feast day called the Great Dionysia in honor of Dionysus, the god of wine and fertility. This festival was held every spring, and wealthy citizens offered prizes for the best play presented.

Theater of Dionysus (*National Archeological Museum of Athens*)

The stage stood before a colonnade at the foot of a hillside amphitheater. A chorus of fifteen performed from an orchestra space in front of the playing area, and sometimes danced as well as sang the choral interludes. The actors, all men, wore masks that were highly stylized projections of their character's appearance,

Greek actors in 1963 staging of Aeschylus' *Prometheus Bound* (*National Theatre of Greece*)

and a special elevator shoe called a *cothurnus*. They must have looked very weird, but perhaps the stylization of their appearance lent them a special dramatic power beyond the possibilities of "realistic" play-acting.

Sophocles was probably the most admired of the three great Athenian tragedians. The comedian Aristophanes ridiculed the others, Euripides and Aeschylus, in his play *The Frogs*, but had only good to say about Sophocles. When Sophocles was twenty-seven years old he defeated Aeschylus, fifty-six, in the playwright's contest with his first tragedy. Before Sophocles, no more than two characters ever appeared in the same scene. He introduced the three-character scene and, according to some accounts, increased the size of the chorus. Sophocles is said to have written over one hundred plays, of which only seven tragedies survive. The best known are *Oedipus Rex* and two companion plays, *Oedipus at Colonus* and *Antigone*.

SOPHOCLES (496?–406 B.C.)

Oedipus Rex

An English Version by Dudley Fitts and Robert Fitzgerald

CHARACTERS

OEDIPUS	MESSENGER
A PRIEST	SHEPHERD OF LAÏOS
CREON	SECOND MESSENGER
TEIRESIAS	CHORUS OF THEBAN ELDERS
IOCASTÊ	

THE SCENE: *Before the palace of Oedipus, King of Thebes. A central door and two lateral doors open onto a platform which runs the length of the façade. On the platform, right and left, are altars; and three steps lead down into the "orchestra," or chorus-ground. At the beginning of the action these steps are crowded by Suppliants who have brought branches and chaplets of olive leaves and who lie in various attitudes of despair. Oedipus enters.*

PROLOGUE°

OEDIPUS: My children, generations of the living
In the line of Kadmos°, nursed at his ancient hearth:
Why have you strewn yourselves before these altars
In supplication, with your boughs and garlands?
5   The breath of incense rises from the city
With a sound of prayer and lamentation.
                              Children,
I would not have you speak through messengers,
And therefore I have come myself to hear you—

Prologue: the exposition.
² *line of Kadmos:* The city of Thebes, scene of the action, is said to have been founded by the hero Cadmus.

I, Oedipus, who bear the famous name.

10   *(To a Priest.)* You, there, since you are eldest in the company,
    Speak for them all, tell me what preys upon you,
    Whether you come in dread, or crave some blessing:
    Tell me, and never doubt that I will help you
    In every way I can; I should be heartless
15   Were I not moved to find you suppliant here.
    PRIEST: Great Oedipus, O powerful King of Thebes!
    You see how all the ages of our people
    Cling to your altar steps: here are boys
    Who can barely stand alone, and here are priests
20   By weight of age, as I am a priest of God,
    And young men chosen from those yet unmarried;
    As for the others, all that multitude,
    They wait with olive chaplets in the squares,
    At the two shrines of Pallas°, and where Apollo°
    Speaks in the glowing embers.
25   Your own eyes
    Must tell you: Thebes is in her extremity
    And can not lift her head from the surge of death.
    A rust consumes the buds and fruits of the earth;
    The herds are sick; children die unborn,
30   And labor is vain. The god of plague and pyre
    Raids like detestable lightning through the city,
    And all the house of Kadmos is laid waste,
    All emptied, and all darkened: Death alone
    Battens upon the misery of Thebes.

35   You are not one of the immortal gods, we know;
    Yet we have come to you to make our prayer
    As to the man of all men best in adversity
    And wisest in the ways of God. You saved us
    From the Sphinx, that flinty singer, and the tribute
40   We paid to her so long; yet you were never
    Better informed than we, nor could we teach you:
    It was some god breathed in you to set us free.

    Therefore, O mighty King, we turn to you:
    Find us our safety, find us a remedy,
45   Whether by counsel of the gods or men.
    A king of wisdom tested in the past
    Can act in a time of troubles, and act well.
    Noblest of men, restore
    Life to your city! Think how all men call you
50   Liberator for your triumph long ago;
    Ah, when your years of kingship are remembered,

---

24 *Pallas:* Athena, goddess of wisdom.
24 *Apollo:* a god associated with light, prophecy, and poetry. His priests used ashes to predict the
    future.

Let them not say *We rose, but later fell*—
Keep the State from going down in the storm!
Once, years ago, with happy augury,
55   You brought us fortune; be the same again!
No man questions your power to rule the land:
But rule over men, not over a dead city!
Ships are only hulls, citadels are nothing,
When no life moves in the empty passageways.
60   OEDIPUS: Poor children! You may be sure I know
All that you longed for in your coming here.
I know that you are deathly sick; and yet,
Sick as you are, not one is as sick as I.
Each of you suffers in himself alone
65   His anguish, not another's; but my spirit
Groans for the city, for myself, for you.

I was not sleeping, you are not waking me.
No, I have been in tears for a long while
And in my restless thought walked many ways.
70   In all my search, I found one helpful course,
And that I have taken: I have sent Creon,
Son of Menoikeus, brother of the Queen,
To Delphi, Apollo's place of revelation,
To learn there, if he can,
75   What act or pledge of mine may save the city.
I have counted the days, and now, this very day,
I am troubled, for he has overstayed his time.
What is he doing? He has been gone too long.
Yet whenever he comes back, I should do ill
80   To scant whatever hint the god may give.
PRIEST: It is a timely promise. At this instant
They tell me Creon is here.
OEDIPUS: O Lord Apollo!
May his news be fair as his face is radiant!
PRIEST: It could not be otherwise: he is crowned with bay,
The chaplet is thick with berries.
85   OEDIPUS: We shall soon know;
He is near enough to hear us now.

Enter Creon.

                          O prince:
Brother: son of Menoikeus:
What answer do you bring us from the god?
CREON: It is favorable. I can tell you, great afflictions
90   Will turn out well, if they are taken well.
OEDIPUS: What was the oracle? These vague words
Leave me still hanging between hope and fear.
CREON: Is it your pleasure to hear me with all these
Gathered around us? I am prepared to speak,
But should we not go in?

95 OEDIPUS: Let them all hear it.
    It is for them I suffer, more than for myself.
    CREON: Then I will tell you what I heard at Delphi.

    In plain words
    The god commands us to expel from the land of Thebes
100 An old defilement that it seems we shelter.
    It is a deathly thing, beyond expiation.
    We must not let it feed upon us longer.
    OEDIPUS: What defilement? How shall we rid ourselves of it?
    CREON: By exile or death, blood for blood. It was
105 Murder that brought the plague-wind on the city.
    OEDIPUS: Murder of whom? Surely the god has named him?
    CREON: My lord: long ago Laïos was our king,
    Before you came to govern us.
    OEDIPUS: I know;
    I learned of him from others; I never saw him.
110 CREON: He was murdered; and Apollo commands us now
    To take revenge upon whoever killed him.
    OEDIPUS: Upon whom? Where are they? Where shall we find a clue
    To solve that crime, after so many years?
    CREON: Here in this land, he said.
                                      If we make enquiry,
115 We may touch things that otherwise escape us.
    OEDIPUS: Tell me: Was Laïos murdered in his house,
    Or in the fields, or in some foreign country?
    CREON: He said he planned to make a pilgrimage.
    He did not come home again.
    OEDIPUS: And was there no one,
120 No witness, no companion, to tell what happened?
    CREON: They were all killed but one, and he got away
    So frightened that he could remember one thing only.
    OEDIPUS: What was that one thing? One may be the key
    To everything, if we resolve to use it.
125 CREON: He said that a band of highwaymen attacked them,
    Outnumbered them, and overwhelmed the King.
    OEDIPUS: Strange, that a highwayman should be so daring—
    Unless some faction here bribed him to do it.
130 CREON: We thought of that. But after Laïos' death
    New troubles arose and we had no avenger.
    OEDIPUS: What troubles could prevent your hunting down the killers?
    CREON: The riddling Sphinx's song
    Made us deaf to all mysteries but her own.
    OEDIPUS: Then once more I must bring what is dark to light.
135 It is most fitting that Apollo shows,
    As you do, this compunction for the dead.
    You shall see how I stand by you, as I should,
    To avenge the city and the city's god,
    And not as though it were for some distant friend,
140 But for my own sake, to be rid of evil.

Whoever killed King Laïos might—who knows?—
Decide at any moment to kill me as well.
By avenging the murdered king I protect myself.
Come, then, my children: leave the altar steps,
Lift up your olive boughs!
145   One of you go
And summon the people of Kadmos to gather here.
I will do all that I can; you may tell them that.

Exit a Page

So, with the help of God,
We shall be saved—or else indeed we are lost.
150 PRIEST: Let us rise, children. It was for this we came,
And now the King has promised it himself.
Phoibos° has sent us an oracle; may he descend
Himself to save us and drive out the plague.

*Exeunt Oedipus and Creon into the palace by the central door. The Priest and the
Suppliants disperse right and left. After a short pause the Chorus enters the orchestra.*

PARODOS°

Strophe 1

CHORUS: What is God singing in his profound
    Delphi of gold and shadow?
    What oracle for Thebes, the sunwhipped city?
    Fear unjoints me, the roots of my heart tremble.
5   Now I remember, O Healer, your power, and wonder;
    Will you send doom like a sudden cloud, or weave it
    Like nightfall of the past?
    Speak, speak to us, issue of holy sound:
    Dearest to our expectancy: be tender!

Antistrophe 1

10   Let me pray to Athenê, the immortal daughter of Zeus,
    And to Artemis her sister
    Who keeps her famous throne in the market ring,
    And to Apollo, bowman at the far butts of heaven—

    O gods, descend! Like three streams leap against
15   The fires of our grief, the fires of darkness;
    Be swift to bring us rest!

    As in the old time from the brilliant house
    Of air you stepped to save us, come again!

---

¹⁵² *Phoibos*: Apollo.
Parodos: ode sung upon the first entrance of the chorus. The *strophe* is said to have accompanied
their dance from right to left; the *antistrophe* their return from stage left to right.

Strophe 2

Now our afflictions have no end,
20   Now all our stricken host lies down
And no man fights off death with his mind;

The noble plowland bears no grain,
And groaning mothers can not bear—

See, how our lives like birds take wing,
25   Like sparks that fly when a fire soars,
To the shore of the god of evening.

Antistrophe 2

The plague burns on, it is pitiless,
Though pallid children laden with death
Lie unwept in the stony ways,

30   And old gray women by every path
Flock to the strand about the altars

There to strike their breasts and cry
Worship of Phoibos in wailing prayers:
Be kind, God's golden child!

Strophe 3

35   There are no swords in this attack by fire,
No shields, but we are ringed with cries.
Send the besieger plunging from our homes
Into the vast sea-room of the Atlantic
Or into the waves that foam eastward of Thrace—
40   For the day ravages what the night spares—
Destroy our enemy, lord of the thunder!
Let him be riven by lightning from heaven!

Antistrophe 3

Phoibos Apollo, stretch the sun's bowstring,
That golden cord, until it sing for us,
Flashing arrows in heaven!
45   Artemis, Huntress,
Race with flaring lights upon our mountains!

O scarlet god, O golden-banded brow,
O Theban Bacchos in a storm of Maenads°,

Enter Oedipus, center.

---

⁴⁸*Bacchos . . . Maenads:* the wine god and attendant nymphs.

Whirl upon Death, that all the Undying hate!
50   Come with blinding cressets, come in joy!

SCENE I.

OEDIPUS: Is this your prayer? It may be answered. Come,
        Listen to me, act as the crisis demands,
        And you shall have relief from all these evils.

        Until now I was a stranger to this tale,
5   As I had been a stranger to the crime.
        Could I track down the murderer without a clue?
        But now, friends,
        As one who became a citizen after the murder,
        I make this proclamation to all Thebans:
10   If any man knows by whose hand Laïos, son of Labdakos,
        Met his death, I direct that man to tell me everything,
        No matter what he fears for having so long withheld it.
        Let it stand as promised that no further trouble
        Will come to him, but he may leave the land in safety.

15   Moreover: If anyone knows the murderer to be foreign,
        Let him not keep silent: he shall have his reward from me.
        However, if he does conceal it; if any man
        Fearing for his friend or for himself disobeys this edict,
        Hear what I propose to do:

20   I solemnly forbid the people of this country,
        Where power and throne are mine, ever to receive that man
        Or speak to him, no matter who he is, or let him
        Join in sacrifice, lustration, or in prayer.
        I decree that he be driven from every house,
25   Being, as he is, corruption itself to us: the Delphic
        Voice of Zeus has pronounced this revelation.
        Thus I associate myself with the oracle
        And take the side of the murdered king.

        As for the criminal, I pray to God—
30   Whether it be a lurking thief, or one of a number—
        I pray that that man's life be consumed in evil and wretchedness.
        And as for me, this curse applies no less
        If it should turn out that the culprit is my guest here,
        Sharing my hearth.
                        You have heard the penalty.
35 ·   I lay it on you now to attend to this
        For my sake, for Apollo's, for the sick
        Sterile city that heaven has abandoned.
        Suppose the oracle had given you no command:
        Should this defilement go uncleansed for ever?
40   You should have found the murderer: your king,

A noble king, had been destroyed!
                              Now I,
Having the power that he held before me,
Having his bed, begetting children there
Upon his wife, as he would have, had he lived—
45 Their son would have been my children's brother,
If Laïos had had luck in fatherhood!
(But surely ill luck rushed upon his reign)—
I say I take the son's part, just as though
I were his son, to press the fight for him
50 And see it won! I'll find the hand that brought
Death to Labdakos' and Polydoros' child,
Heir of Kadmos' and Agenor's line.
And as for those who fail me,
May the gods deny them the fruit of the earth,
55 Fruit of the womb, and may they rot utterly!
Let them be wretched as we are wretched, and worse!

For you, for loyal Thebans, and for all
Who find my actions right, I pray the favor
Of justice, and of all the immortal gods.
60 CHORAGOS°: Since I am under oath, my lord, I swear
I did not do the murder, I can not name
The murderer. Might not the oracle
That has ordained the search tell where to find him?
OEDIPUS: An honest question. But no man in the world
65 Can make the gods do more than the gods will.
CHORAGOS: There is one last expedient—
OEDIPUS: Tell me what it is.
Though it seem slight, you must not hold it back.
CHORAGOS: A lord clairvoyant to the lord Apollo,
As we all know, is the skilled Teiresias.
70 One might learn much about this from him, Oedipus.
OEDIPUS: I am not wasting time:
Creon spoke of this, and I have sent for him—
Twice, in fact; it is strange that he is not here.
CHORAGOS: The other matter—that old report—seems useless.
75 OEDIPUS: Tell me. I am interested in all reports.
CHORAGOS: The King was said to have been killed by highwaymen.
OEDIPUS: I know. but we have no witnesses to that.
CHORAGOS: If the killer can feel a particle of dread,
Your curse will bring him out of hiding!
OEDIPUS: No.
80 The man who dared that act will fear no curse.

Enter the blind seer Teiresias, led by a Page.

---

⁶⁰ *Choragos:* leader of the chorus.

CHORAGOS: But there is one man who may detect the criminal.
This is Teiresias, this is the holy prophet
In whom, alone of all men, truth was born.
OEDIPUS: Teiresias: seer: student of mysteries,
85   Of all that's taught and all that no man tells,
Secrets of Heaven and secrets of the earth:
Blind though you are, you know the city lies
Sick with plague; and from this plague, my lord,
We find that you alone can guard or save us.

90   Possibly you did not hear the messengers?
Apollo, when we sent to him,
Sent us back word that this great pestilence
Would lift, but only if we established clearly
The identity of those who murdered Laïos.
They must be killed or exiled.
95   Can you use
Birdflight or any art of divination
To purify yourself, and Thebes, and me
From this contagion? We are in your hands.
There is no fairer duty
100   Than that of helping others in distress.
TEIRESIAS: How dreadful knowledge of the truth can be
When there's no help in truth! I knew this well,
But did not act on it: else I should not have come.
OEDIPUS: What is troubling you? Why are your eyes so cold?
105 TEIRESIAS: Let me go home. Bear your own fate, and I'll
Bear mine. It is better so: trust what I say.
OEDIPUS: What you say is ungracious and unhelpful
To your native country. Do not refuse to speak.
TEIRESIAS: When it comes to speech, your own is neither temperate
110   Nor opportune. I wish to be more prudent.
OEDIPUS: In God's name, we all beg you—
TEIRESIAS: You are all ignorant.
No; I will never tell you what I know.
Now it is my misery; then, it would be yours.
OEDIPUS: What! You do know something, and will not tell us?
115   You would betray us all and wreck the State?
TEIRESIAS: I do not intend to torture myself, or you.
Why persist in asking? You will not persuade me.
OEDIPUS: What a wicked old man you are! You'd try a stone's
Patience! Out with it! Have you no feeling at all?
120 TEIRESIAS: You call me unfeeling. If you could only see
The nature of your own feelings . . .
OEDIPUS: Why,
Who would not feel as I do? Who could endure
Your arrogance toward the city?
TEIRESIAS: What does it matter!
Whether I speak or not, it is bound to come.
125 OEDIPUS: Then, if "it" is bound to come, you are bound to tell me.

The scene from Tyrone Guthrie's version of the play in classic Greek tradition: (Above) Oedipus surrounded by members of the chorus, (Below) Eleanor Stuart as Iocastê, Douglas Campbell as Oedipus, and Robert Goodier as Creon (The Granger Collection)

TEIRESIAS: No, I will not go on. Rage as you please.
OEDIPUS: Rage? Why not!
                    And I'll tell you what I think:
    You planned it, you had it done, you all but
    Killed him with your own hands: if you had eyes,
130 I'd say the crime was yours, and yours alone.
TEIRESIAS: So? I charge you, then,
    Abide by the proclamation you have made:
    From this day forth

Never speak again to these men or to me;
135   You yourself are the pollution of this country.
OEDIPUS: You dare say that! Can you possibly think you have
    Some way of going free, after such insolence?
TEIRESIAS: I have gone free. It is the truth sustains me.
OEDIPUS: Who taught you shamelessness? It was not your craft.
140 TEIRESIAS: You did. You made me speak. I did not want to.
OEDIPUS: Speak what? Let me hear it again more clearly.
TEIRESIAS: Was it not clear before? Are you tempting me?
OEDIPUS: I did not understand it. Say it again.
TEIRESIAS: I say that you are the murderer whom you seek.
145 OEDIPUS: Now twice you have spat out infamy. You'll pay for it!
TEIRESIAS: Would you care for more? Do you wish to be really angry?
OEDIPUS: Say what you will. Whatever you say is worthless.
TEIRESIAS: I say you live in hideous shame with those
    Most dear to you. You can not see the evil.
150 OEDIPUS: It seems you can go on mouthing like this for ever.
TEIRESIAS: I can, if there is power in truth.
OEDIPUS: There is:
    But not for you, not for you,
    You sightless, witless, senseless, mad old man!
TEIRESIAS: You are the madman. There is no one here
155   Who will not curse you soon, as you curse me.
OEDIPUS: You child of endless night! You can not hurt me
    Or any other man who sees the sun.
TEIRESIAS: True: it is not from me your fate will come.
    That lies within Apollo's competence,
    As it is his concern.
160 OEDIPUS: Tell me:
    Are you speaking for Creon, or for yourself?
TEIRESIAS: Creon is no threat. You weave your own doom.
OEDIPUS: Wealth, power, craft of statesmanship!
    Kingly position, everywhere admired!
165   What savage envy is stored up against these,
    If Creon, whom I trusted, Creon my friend,
    For this great office which the city once
    Put in my hands unsought—if for this power
    Creon desires in secret to destroy me!

170   He has brought this decrepit fortune-teller, this
    Collector of dirty pennies, this prophet fraud—
    Why, he is no more clairvoyant than I am!
                         Tell us:
    Has your mystic mummery ever approached the truth?
    When that hellcat the Sphinx was performing here,
175   What help were you to these people?
    Her magic was not for the first man who came along:
    It demanded a real exorcist. Your birds—
    What good were they? or the gods, for the matter of that?

But I came by,
180 Oedipus, the simple man, who knows nothing—
I thought it out for myself, no birds helped me!
And this is the man you think you can destroy,
That you may be close to Creon when he's king!
Well, you and your friend Creon, it seems to me,
185 Will suffer most. If you were not an old man,
You would have paid already for your plot.

CHORAGOS: We can not see that his words or yours
Have been spoken except in anger, Oedipus,
And of anger we have no need. How can God's will
190 Be accomplished best? That is what most concerns us.

TEIRESIAS: You are a king. But where argument's concerned
I am your man, as much a king as you.
I am not your servant, but Apollo's.
I have no need of Creon to speak for me.

195 Listen to me. You mock my blindness, do you?
But I say that you, with both your eyes, are blind:
You can not see the wretchedness of your life,
Nor in whose house you live, no, nor with whom.
Who are your father and mother? Can you tell me?
200 You do not even know the blind wrongs
That you have done them, on earth and in the world below.
But the double lash of your parents' curse will whip you
Out of this land some day, with only night
Upon your precious eyes.
205 Your cries then—where will they not be heard?
What fastness of Kithairon will not echo them?
And that bridal-descant of yours—you'll know it then,
The song they sang when you came here to Thebes
And found your misguided berthing.
210 All this, and more, that you can not guess at now,
Will bring you to yourself among your children.

Be angry, then. Curse Creon. Curse my words.
I tell you, no man that walks upon the earth
Shall be rooted out more horribly than you.
215 OEDIPUS: Am I to bear this from him?—Damnation
Take you! Out of this place! Out of my sight!
TEIRESIAS: I would not have come at all if you had not asked me.
OEDIPUS: Could I have told that you'd talk nonsense, that
You'd come here to make a fool of yourself, and of me?
220 TEIRESIAS: A fool? Your parents thought me sane enough.
OEDIPUS: My parents again!—Wait: who were my parents?
TEIRESIAS: This day will give you a father, and break your heart.
OEDIPUS: Your infantile riddles! Your damned abracadabra!
TEIRESIAS: You were a great man once at solving riddles.
225 OEDIPUS: Mock me with that if you like; you will find it true.

TEIRESIAS: It was true enough. It brought about your ruin.

OEDIPUS: But if it saved this town?

TEIRESIAS (to the Page):   Boy, give me your hand.

OEDIPUS: Yes, boy; lead him away.

                                   —While you are here
We can do nothing. Go; leave us in peace.

230 TEIRESIAS: I will go when I have said what I have to say.
How can you hurt me? And I tell you again:
The man you have been looking for all this time,
The damned man, the murderer of Laïos,
That man is in Thebes. To your mind he is foreignborn,
235 But it will soon be shown that he is a Theban,
A revelation that will fail to please.

                                   A blind man,
Who has his eyes now; a penniless man, who is rich now;
And he will go tapping the strange earth with his staff;
To the children with whom he lives now he will be
240 Brother and father—the very same; to her
Who bore him, son and husband—the very same
Who came to his father's bed, wet with his father's blood.

Enough. Go think that over.
If later you find error in what I have said,
245 You may say that I have no skill in prophecy.

Exit Teiresias, led by his Page. Oedipus goes into the palace.

ODE I°

Strophe 1

CHORUS: The Delphic stone of prophecies
      Remembers ancient regicide
      And a still bloody hand.
      That killer's hour of flight has come.
5   He must be stronger than riderless
      Coursers of untiring wind,
      For the son of Zeus° armed with his father's thunder
      Leaps in lightning after him;
      And the Furies° follow him, the sad Furies.

Antistrophe 1

10   Holy Parnassos' peak of snow
      Flashes and blinds that secret man,
      That all shall hunt him down:
      Though he may roam the forest shade
      Like a bull gone wild from pasture

Ode: a choral song.
⁷ *son of Zeus:* Apollo.
⁹ *Furies:* three terrible female spirits who pursue and torment evil-doers.

15   To rage through glooms of stone.
      Doom comes down on him; flight will not avail him;
      For the world's heart calls him desolate,
      And the immortal Furies follow, for ever follow.

Strophe 2

      But now a wilder thing is heard
20   From the old man skilled at hearing Fate in the wingbeat of a bird.
      Bewildered as a blown bird, my soul hovers and can not find
      Foothold in this debate, or any reason or rest of mind.
      But no man ever brought—none can bring
      Proof of strife between Thebes' royal house,
25   Labdakos' line,° and the son of Polybos°;
      And never until now has any man brought word
      Of Laïos' dark death staining Oedipus the King.

Antistrophe 2

      Divine Zeus and Apollo hold
      Perfect intelligence alone of all tales ever told;
30   And well though this diviner works, he works in his own night;
      No man can judge that rough unknown or trust in second sight,
      For wisdom changes hands among the wise.
      Shall I believe my great lord criminal
      At a raging word that a blind old man let fall?
35   I saw him, when the carrion woman faced him of old,
      Prove his heroic mind! These evil words are lies.

SCENE II.

CREON: Men of Thebes:
      I am told that heavy accusations
      Have been brought against me by King Oedipus.

      I am not the kind of man to bear this tamely.

5   If in these present difficulties
      He holds me accountable for any harm to him
      Through anything I have said or done—why, then,
      I do not value life in this dishonor.
      It is not as though this rumor touched upon
10   Some private indiscretion. The matter is grave.
      The fact is that I am being called disloyal
      To the State, to my fellow citizens, to my friends.
CHORAGOS: He may have spoken in anger, not from his mind.
CREON: But did you not hear him say I was the one
15   Who seduced the old prophet into lying?

---

²⁵ *Labdakos' line*: descendants of Laïos. The chorus is unaware that Laïos is the true father of
      Oedipus.
²⁵ *Polybos*: king of Corinth, who adopted Oedipus as an infant.

CHORAGOS: The thing was said; I do not know how seriously.
CREON: But you were watching him! Were his eyes steady?
    Did he look like a man in his right mind?
CHORAGOS: I do not know.
    I can not judge the behavior of great men.
    But here is the King himself.

Enter Oedipus.

20 OEDIPUS: So you dared come back.
    Why? How brazen of you to come to my house,
    You murderer!
                    Do you think I do not know
    That you plotted to kill me, plotted to steal my throne?
    Tell me, in God's name: am I coward, a fool,
25 That you should dream you could accomplish this?
    A fool who could not see your slippery game?
    A coward, not to fight back when I saw it?
    You are the fool, Creon, are you not? hoping
    Without support or friends to get a throne?
30 Thrones may be won or bought: you could do neither.
CREON: Now listen to me. You have talked; let me talk, too.
    You can not judge unless you know the facts.
OEDIPUS: You speak well: there is one fact; but I find it hard
    To learn from the deadliest enemy I have.
35 CREON: That above all I must dispute with you.
OEDIPUS: That above all I will not hear you deny.
CREON: If you think there is anything good in being stubborn
    Against all reason, then I say you are wrong.
OEDIPUS: If you think a man can sin against his own kind
40 And not be punished for it, I say you are mad.
CREON: I agree. But tell me: what have I done to you?
OEDIPUS: You advised me to send for that wizard, did you not?
CREON: I did. I should do it again.
OEDIPUS: Very well. Now tell me:
    How long has it been since Laïos—
CREON: What of Laïos?
45 OEDIPUS: Since he vanished in that onset by the road?
CREON: It was long ago, a long time.
OEDIPUS: And this prophet,
    Was he practicing here then?
CREON: He was; and with honor, as now.
OEDIPUS: Did he speak of me at that time?
CREON: He never did;
    At least, not when I was present.
OEDIPUS: But . . . the enquiry?
    I suppose you held one?
50 CREON: We did, but we learned nothing.
OEDIPUS: Why did the prophet not speak against me then?

CREON: I do not know; and I am the kind of man
    Who holds his tongue when he has no facts to go on.
OEDIPUS: There's one fact that you know, and you could tell it.
55 CREON: What fact is that? If I know it, you shall have it.
OEDIPUS: If he were not involved with you, he could not say
    That it was I who murdered Laïos.
CREON: If he says that, you are the one that knows it!—
    But now it is my turn to question you.
60 OEDIPUS: Put your questions. I am no murderer.
CREON: First then: You married my sister?
OEDIPUS: I married your sister.
CREON: And you rule the kingdom equally with her?
OEDIPUS: Everything that she wants she has from me.
CREON: And I am the third, equal to both of you?
65 OEDIPUS: That is why I call you a bad friend.
CREON: No. Reason it out, as I have done.
    Think of this first. Would any sane man prefer
    Power, with all a king's anxieties,
    To that same power and the grace of sleep?
70   Certainly not I.
    I have never longed for the king's power—only his rights.
    Would any wise man differ from me in this?
    As matters stand, I have my way in everything
    With your consent, and no responsibilities.
75   If I were king, I should be a slave to policy.

    How could I desire a scepter more
    Than what is now mine—untroubled influence?
    No, I have not gone mad; I need no honors,
    Except those with the perquisites I have now.
80   I am welcome everywhere; every man salutes me,
    And those who want your favor seek my ear,
    Since I know how to manage what they ask.
    Should I exchange this ease for that anxiety?
    Besides, no sober mind is treasonable.
85   I hate anarchy
    And never would deal with any man who likes it.

    Test what I have said. Go to the priestess
    At Delphi, ask if I quoted her correctly.
    And as for this other thing: if I am found
90   Guilty of treason with Teiresias,
    Then sentence me to death! You have my word
    It is a sentence I should cast my vote for—
    But not without evidence!
                You do wrong
    When you take good men for bad, bad men for good.
95   A true friend thrown aside—why, life itself
    Is not more precious!

In time you will know this well:
For time, and time alone, will show the just man,
Though scoundrels are discovered in a day.

CHORAGOS: This is well said, and a prudent man would ponder it.
100   Judgments too quickly formed are dangerous.

OEDIPUS: But is he not quick in his duplicity?
And shall I not be quick to parry him?
Would you have me stand still, hold my peace, and let
This man win everything, through my inaction?

105   CREON: And you want—what is it, then? To banish me?

OEDIPUS: No, not exile. It is your death I want,
So that all the world may see what treason means.

CREON: You will persist, then? You will not believe me?

OEDIPUS: How can I believe you?

CREON: Then you are a fool.

OEDIPUS: To save myself?

110   CREON: In justice, think of me.

OEDIPUS: You are evil incarnate.

CREON: But suppose that you are wrong?

OEDIPUS: Still I must rule.

CREON: But not if you rule badly.

OEDIPUS: O city, city!

CREON: It is my city, too!

CHORAGOS: Now, my lords, be still. I see the Queen,
115   Iocastê, coming from her palace chambers;
And it is time she came, for the sake of you both.
This dreadful quarrel can be resolved through her.

Enter Iocastê.

IOCASTÊ: Poor foolish men, what wicked din is this?
With Thebes sick to death, is it not shameful
120   That you should rake some private quarrel up?
(To Oedipus.) Come into the house.
                              —And you, Creon, go now:
Let us have no more of this tumult over nothing.

CREON: Nothing? No, sister: what your husband plans for me
Is one of two great evils: exile or death.

OEDIPUS: He is right.
125   Why, woman, I have caught him squarely
Plotting against my life.

CREON: No! Let me die
Accurst if ever I have wished you harm!

IOCASTÊ: Ah, believe it, Oedipus!
In the name of the gods, respect this oath of his
130   For my sake, for the sake of these people here!

Strophe 1

CHORAGOS: Open your mind to her, my lord. Be ruled by her, I beg
you!

OEDIPUS: What would you have me do?

CHORAGOS: Respect Creon's word. He has never spoken like a fool,
And now he has sworn an oath.

OEDIPUS: You know what you ask?

CHORAGOS: I do.

OEDIPUS: Speak on, then.

135 CHORAGOS: A friend so sworn should not be baited so,
In blind malice, and without final proof.

OEDIPUS: You are aware, I hope, that what you say
Means death for me, or exile at the least.

Strophe 2

CHORAGOS: No, I swear by Helios, first in Heaven!
140   May I die friendless and accurst,
The worst of deaths, if ever I meant that!
        It is the withering fields
             That hurt my sick heart:
        Must we bear all these ills,
145   And now your bad blood as well?

OEDIPUS: Then let him go. And let me die, if I must,
Or be driven by him in shame from the land of Thebes.
It is your unhappiness, and not his talk,
That touches me.
                    As for him—
150   Wherever he is, I will hate him as long as I live.

CREON: Ugly in yielding, as you were ugly in rage!
Natures like yours chiefly torment themselves.

OEDIPUS: Can you not go? Can you not leave me?

CREON: I can.
You do not know me; but the city knows me,
155   And in its eyes I am just, if not in yours.

Exit Creon.

Antistrophe 1

CHORAGOS: Lady Iocastê, did you not ask the King to go to his chambers?

IOCASTÊ: First tell me what has happened.

CHORAGOS: There was suspicion without evidence; yet it rankled
As even false charges will.

IOCASTÊ: On both sides?

CHORAGOS: On both.

IOCASTÊ: But what was said?

160 CHORAGOS: Oh let it rest, let it be done with!
Have we not suffered enough?

OEDIPUS: You see to what your decency has brought you:
You have made difficulties where my heart saw none.

Antistrophe 2

CHORAGOS: Oedipus, it is not once only I have told you—
165   You must know I should count myself unwise
    To the point of madness, should I now forsake you—
      You, under whose hand,
        In the storm of another time,
      Our dear land sailed out free.
170   But now stand fast at the helm!
IOCASTÊ: In God's name, Oedipus, inform your wife as well:
    Why are you so set in this hard anger?
OEDIPUS: I will tell you, for none of these men deserves
    My confidence as you do. It is Creon's work,
175   His treachery, his plotting against me.
IOCASTÊ: Go on, if you can make this clear to me.
OEDIPUS: He charges me with the murder of Laïos.
IOCASTÊ: Has he some knowledge? Or does he speak from hearsay?
OEDIPUS: He would not commit himself to such a charge,
180   But he has brought in that damnable soothsayer
    To tell his story.
IOCASTÊ: Set your mind at rest.
    If it is a question of soothsayers, I tell you
    That you will find no man whose craft gives knowledge
    Of the unknowable.
              Here is my proof:

185 An oracle was reported to Laïos once
    (I will not say from Phoibos himself, but from
    His appointed ministers, at any rate)
    That his doom would be death at the hands of his own son—
    His son, born of his flesh and of mine!

190 Now, you remember the story: Laïos was killed
    By marauding strangers where three highways meet;
    But his child had not been three days in this world
    Before the King had pierced the baby's ankles
    And left him to die on a lonely mountainside.

195 Thus, Apollo never caused that child
    To kill his father, and it was not Laïos' fate
    To die at the hands of his son, as he had feared.
    This is what prophets and prophecies are worth!
    Have no dread of them.
              It is God himself
200 Who can show us what he wills, in his own way.
OEDIPUS: How strange a shadowy memory crossed my mind,
    Just now while you were speaking; it chilled my heart.
IOCASTÊ: What do you mean? What memory do you speak of?
OEDIPUS: If I understand you, Laïos was killed
    At a place where three roads meet.

| 205 | IOCASTÊ: | So it was said; |

IOCASTÊ: So it was said;
We have no later story.
OEDIPUS: Where did it happen?
IOCASTÊ: Phokis, it is called: at a place where the Theban Way
   Divides into the roads toward Delphi and Daulia.
OEDIPUS: When?
IOCASTÊ: We had the news not long before you came
210   And proved the right to your succession here.
OEDIPUS: Ah, what net has God been weaving for me?
IOCASTÊ: Oedipus! Why does this trouble you?
OEDIPUS: Do not ask me yet.
   First, tell me how Laïos looked, and tell me
   How old he was.
IOCASTÊ: He was tall, his hair just touched
215   With white; his form was not unlike your own.
OEDIPUS: I think that I myself may be accurst
   By my own ignorant edict.
IOCASTÊ: You speak strangely.
   It makes me tremble to look at you, my King.
OEDIPUS: I am not sure that the blind man can not see.
220   But I should know better if you were to tell me—
IOCASTÊ: Anything—though I dread to hear you ask it.
OEDIPUS: Was the King lightly escorted, or did he ride
   With a large company, as a ruler should?
IOCASTÊ: There were five men with him in all: one was a herald;
225   And a single chariot, which he was driving.
OEDIPUS: Alas, that makes it plain enough!
                          But who—
   Who told you how it happened?
IOCASTÊ: A household servant,
   The only one to escape.
OEDIPUS: And is he still
   A servant of ours?
IOCASTÊ: No; for when he came back at last
230   And found you enthroned in the place of the dead king,
   He came to me, touched my hand with his, and begged
   That I would send him away to the frontier district
   Where only the shepherds go—
   As far away from the city as I could send him.
235   I granted his prayer; for although the man was a slave,
   He had earned more than this favor at my hands.
OEDIPUS: Can he be called back quickly?
IOCASTÊ: Easily.
   But why?
OEDIPUS: I have taken too much upon myself
   Without enquiry; therefore I wish to consult him.
IOCASTÊ: Then he shall come.
240   But am I not one also
   To whom you might confide these fears of yours?

OEDIPUS: That is your right; it will not be denied you,
    Now least of all; for I have reached a pitch
    Of wild foreboding. Is there anyone
245 To whom I should sooner speak?
    Polybos of Corinth is my father.
    My mother is a Dorian: Meropê.
    I grew up chief among the men of Corinth
    Until a strange thing happened—
250 Not worth my passion, it may be, but strange.
    At a feast, a drunken man maundering in his cups
    Cries out that I am not my father's son!

    I contained myself that night, though I felt anger
    And a sinking heart. The next day I visited
255 My father and mother, and questioned them. They stormed,
    Calling it all the slanderous rant of a fool;
    And this relieved me. Yet the suspicion
    Remained always aching in my mind;
    I knew there was talk; I could not rest;
260 And finally, saying nothing to my parents,
    I went to the shrine at Delphi.
    The god dismissed my question without reply;
    He spoke of other things.
                         Some were clear,
    Full of wretchedness, dreadful, unbearable:
265 As, that I should lie with my own mother, breed
    Children from whom all men would turn their eyes;
    And that I should be my father's murderer.

    I heard all this, and fled. And from that day
    Corinth to me was only in the stars
270 Descending in that quarter of the sky,
    As I wandered farther and farther on my way
    To a land where I should never see the evil
    Sung by the oracle. And I came to this country
    Where, so you say, King Laïos was killed.

275 I will tell you all that happened there, my lady.

    There were three highways
    Coming together at a place I passed;
    And there a herald came towards me, and a chariot
    Drawn by horses, with a man such as you describe
280 Seated in it. The groom leading the horses
    Forced me off the road at his lord's command;
    But as this charioteer lurched over towards me
    I struck him in my rage. The old man saw me
    And brought his double goad down upon my head

As I came abreast.
285   He was paid back, and more!
Swinging my club in this right hand I knocked him
Out of his car, and he rolled on the ground.
                                   I killed him.

I killed them all.
Now if that stranger and Laïos were—kin,
290   Where is a man more miserable than I?
More hated by the gods? Citizen and alien alike
Must never shelter me or speak to me—
I must be shunned by all.
                      And I myself
Pronounced this malediction upon myself!

295   Think of it: I have touched you with these hands,
These hands that killed your husband. What defilement!

Am I all evil, then? It must be so,
Since I must flee from Thebes, yet never again
See my own countrymen, my own country,
300   For fear of joining my mother in marriage
And killing Polybos, my father.
                              Ah,
If I was created so, born to this fate,
Who could deny the savagery of God?

O holy majesty of heavenly powers!
305   May I never see that day! Never!
Rather let me vanish from the race of men
Than know the abomination destined me!
CHORAGOS: We too, my lord, have felt dismay at this.
But there is hope: you have yet to hear the shepherd.
310 OEDIPUS: Indeed, I fear no other hope is left me.
IOCASTÊ: What do you hope from him when he comes?
OEDIPUS: This much:
If his account of the murder tallies with yours,
Then I am cleared.
IOCASTÊ: What was it that I said
Of such importance?
OEDIPUS: Why, "marauders," you said,
315   Killed the King, according to this man's story.
If he maintains that still, if there were several,
Clearly the guilt is not mine: I was alone.
But if he says one man, singlehanded, did it,
Then the evidence all points to me.
320 IOCASTÊ: You may be sure that he said there were several;
And can he call back that story now? He can not.

The whole city heard it as plainly as I.
But suppose he alters some detail of it:
He can not ever show that Laïos' death
325 Fulfilled the oracle: for Apollo said
My child was doomed to kill him; and my child—
Poor baby!—it was my child that died first.

No. From now on, where oracles are concerned,
I would not waste a second thought on any.
OEDIPUS: You may be right.
330   But come: let someone go
For the shepherd at once. This matter must be settled.
IOCASTÊ: I will send for him.
I would not wish to cross you in anything,
And surely not in this.—Let us go in.

Exeunt into the palace.

ODE II
Strophe 1

CHORUS: Let me be reverent in the ways of right,
    Lowly the paths I journey on;
    Let all my words and actions keep
    The laws of the pure universe
5   From highest Heaven handed down.
    For Heaven is their bright nurse,
    Those generations of the realms of light;
    Ah, never of mortal kind were they begot,
    Nor are they slaves of memory, lost in sleep:
10 Their Father is greater than Time, and ages not.

Antistrophe 1

    The tyrant is a child of Pride
    Who drinks from his great sickening cup
    Recklessness and vanity,
    Until from his high crest headlong
15 He plummets to the dust of hope.
    That strong man is not strong.
    But let no fair ambition be denied;
    May God protect the wrestler for the State
    In government, in comely policy,
20 Who will fear God, and on His ordinance wait.

Strophe 2

    Haughtiness and the high hand of disdain
    Tempt and outrage God's holy law;
    And any mortal who dares hold
    No immortal Power in awe
25 Will be caught up in a net of pain:

The price for which his levity is sold.
Let each man take due earnings, then,
And keep his hands from holy things,
And from blasphemy stand apart—
30   Else the crackling blast of heaven
Blows on his head, and on his desperate heart;
Though fools will honor impious men,
In their cities no tragic poet sings.

Antistrophe 2

Shall we lose faith in Delphi's obscurities,
35   We who have heard the world's core
Discredited, and the sacred wood
Of Zeus at Elis praised no more?
The deeds and the strange prophecies
Must make a pattern yet to be understood.
40   Zeus, if indeed you are lord of all,
Throned in light over night and day,
Mirror this in your endless mind:
Our masters call the oracle
Words on the wind, and the Delphic vision blind!
45   Their hearts no longer know Apollo,
And reverence for the gods has died away.

SCENE III.

Enter Iocastê.

IOCASTÊ: Princes of Thebes, it has occurred to me
To visit the altars of the gods, bearing
These branches as a suppliant, and this incense.
Our King is not himself: his noble soul
5   Is overwrought with fantasies of dread,
Else he would consider
The new prophecies in the light of the old.
He will listen to any voice that speaks disaster,
And my advice goes for nothing.

She approaches the altar, right.

To you, then, Apollo,
10   Lycean lord, since you are nearest, I turn in prayer.
Receive these offerings, and grant us deliverance
From defilement. Our hearts are heavy with fear
When we see our leader distracted, as helpless sailors
Are terrified by the confusion of their helmsman.

Enter Messenger.

15 MESSENGER: Friends, no doubt you can direct me:
Where shall I find the house of Oedipus,
Or, better still, where is the King himself?

CHORAGOS: It is this very place, stranger; he is inside.
This is his wife and mother of his children.

20 MESSENGER: I wish her happiness in a happy house,
Blest in all the fulfillment of her marriage.

IOCASTÊ: I wish as much for you: your courtesy
Deserves a like good fortune. But now, tell me:
Why have you come? What have you to say to us?

25 MESSENGER: Good news, my lady, for your house and your husband.

IOCASTÊ: What news? Who sent you here?

MESSENGER: I am from Corinth.
The news I bring ought to mean joy for you,
Though it may be you will find some grief in it.

IOCASTÊ: What is it? How can it touch us in both ways?

30 MESSENGER: The people of Corinth, they say,
Intend to call Oedipus to be their king.

IOCASTÊ: But old Polybos—is he not reigning still?

MESSENGER: No. Death holds him in his sepulchre.

IOCASTÊ: What are you saying? Polybos is dead?

35 MESSENGER: If I am not telling the truth, may I die myself.

IOCASTÊ (*to a Maidservant*): Go in, go quickly; tell this to your master.

O riddlers of God's will, where are you now!
This was the man whom Oedipus, long ago,
Feared so, fled so, in dread of destroying him—
40 But it was another fate by which he died.

Enter Oedipus, center.

OEDIPUS: Dearest Iocastê, why have you sent for me?

IOCASTÊ: Listen to what this man says, and then tell me
What has become of the solemn prophecies.

OEDIPUS: Who is this man? What is his news for me?

45 IOCASTÊ: He has come from Corinth to announce your father's death!

OEDIPUS: Is it true, stranger? Tell me in your own words.

MESSENGER: I can not say it more clearly: the King is dead.

OEDIPUS: Was it by treason? Or by an attack or illness?

MESSENGER: A little thing brings old men to their rest.

OEDIPUS: It was sickness, then?

50 MESSENGER: Yes, and his many years.

OEDIPUS: Ah!
Why should a man respect the Pythian hearth°, or
Give heed to the birds that jangle above his head?
They prophesied that I should kill Polybos,
55 Kill my own father; but he is dead and buried,
And I am here—I never touched him, never,
Unless he died of grief for my departure,

---

⁵² *Pythian hearth*: the oracle at Delphi; its priestess was famous for her profound and sometimes enigmatic prophecies.

And thus, in a sense, through me. No. Polybos
Has packed the oracles off with him underground.
They are empty words.
60 IOCASTÊ: Had I not told you so?
OEDIPUS: You had; it was my faint heart that betrayed me.
IOCASTÊ: From now on never think of those things again.
OEDIPUS: And yet—must I not fear my mother's bed?
IOCASTÊ: Why should anyone in this world be afraid,
65   Since Fate rules us and nothing can be foreseen?
A man should live only for the present day.

Have no more fear of sleeping with your mother:
How many men, in dreams, have lain with their mothers!
No reasonable man is troubled by such things.
70 OEDIPUS: That is true; only—
If only my mother were not still alive!
But she is alive. I can not help my dread.
IOCASTÊ: Yet this news of your father's death is wonderful.
OEDIPUS: Wonderful. But I fear the living woman.
75 MESSENGER: Tell me, who is this woman that you fear?
OEDIPUS: It is Meropê, man; the wife of King Polybos.
MESSENGER: Meropê? Why should you be afraid of her?
OEDIPUS: An oracle of the gods, a dreadful saying.
MESSENGER: Can you tell me about it or are you sworn to silence?
80 OEDIPUS: I can tell you, and I will.
Apollo said through his prophet that I was the man
Who should marry his own mother, shed his father's blood
With his own hands. And so, for all these years
I have kept clear of Corinth, and no harm has come—
85   Though it would be have been sweet to see my parents again.
MESSENGER: And is this the fear that drove you out of Corinth?
OEDIPUS: Would you have me kill my father?
MESSENGER: As for that
You must be reassured by the news I gave you.
OEDIPUS: If you could reassure me, I would reward you.
90 MESSENGER: I had that in mind, I will confess: I thought
I could count on you when you returned to Corinth.
OEDIPUS: No: I will never go near my parents again.
MESSENGER: Ah, son, you still do not know what you are doing—
OEDIPUS: What do you mean? In the name of God tell me!
95 MESSENGER: —If these are your reasons for not going home.
OEDIPUS: I tell you, I fear the oracle may come true.
MESSENGER: And guilt may come upon you through your parents?
OEDIPUS: That is the dread that is always in my heart.
MESSENGER: Can you not see that all your fears are groundless?
100 OEDIPUS: How can you say that? They are my parents, surely?
MESSENGER: Polybos was not your father.
OEDIPUS: Not my father?
MESSENGER: No more your father than the man speaking to you.

OEDIPUS: But you are nothing to me!

MESSENGER: Neither was he.

OEDIPUS: Then why did he call me son?

MESSENGER: I will tell you:

105   Long ago he had you from my hands, as a gift.

OEDIPUS: Then how could he love me so, if I was not his?

MESSENGER: He had no children, and his heart turned to you.

OEDIPUS: What of you? Did you buy me? Did you find me by chance?

MESSENGER: I came upon you in the crooked pass of Kithairon.

OEDIPUS: And what were you doing there?

110 MESSENGER: Tending my flocks.

OEDIPUS: A wandering shepherd?

MESSENGER: But your savior, son, that day.

OEDIPUS: From what did you save me?

MESSENGER: Your ankles should tell you that.

OEDIPUS: Ah, stranger, why do you speak of that childhood pain?

MESSENGER: I cut the bonds that tied your ankles together.

115 OEDIPUS: I have had the mark as long as I can remember.

MESSENGER: That was why you were given the name you bear.

OEDIPUS: God! Was it my father or my mother who did it?
    Tell me!

MESSENGER: I do not know. The man who gave you to me
    Can tell you better than I.

120 OEDIPUS: It was not you that found me, but another?

MESSENGER: It was another shepherd gave you to me.

OEDIPUS: Who was he? Can you tell me who he was?

MESSENGER: I think he was said to be one of Laïos' people.

OEDIPUS: You mean the Laïos who was king here years ago?

125 MESSENGER: Yes; King Laïos; and the man was one of his herdsmen.

OEDIPUS: Is he still alive? Can I see him?

MESSENGER: These men here
    Know best about such things.

OEDIPUS: Does anyone here
    Know this shepherd that he is talking about?
    Have you seen him in the fields, or in the town?

130   If you have, tell me. It is time things were made plain.

CHORAGOS: I think the man he means is that same shepherd
    You have already asked to see. Iocastê perhaps
    Could tell you something.

OEDIPUS: Do you know anything
    About him, Lady? Is he the man we have summoned?
    Is that the man this shepherd means?

135 IOCASTÊ: Why think of him?
    Forget this herdsman. Forget it all.
    This talk is a waste of time.

OEDIPUS: How can you say that,
    When the clues to my true birth are in my hands?

IOCASTÊ: For God's love, let us have no more questioning!

140   Is your life nothing to you?

My own is pain enough for me to bear.
OEDIPUS: You need not worry. Suppose my mother a slave,
    And born of slaves: no baseness can touch you.
IOCASTÊ: Listen to me, I beg you: do not do this thing!
145 OEDIPUS: I will not listen; the truth must be made known.
IOCASTÊ: Everything that I say is for your own good!
OEDIPUS: My own good
    Snaps my patience, then; I want none of it.
IOCASTÊ: You are fatally wrong! May you never learn who you are!
OEDIPUS: Go, one of you, and bring the shepherd here.
150 Let us leave this woman to brag of her royal name.
IOCASTÊ: Ah, miserable!
    That is the only word I have for you now.
    That is the only word I can ever have.

Exit into the palace.

CHORAGOS: Why has she left us, Oedipus? Why has she gone
155 In such a passion of sorrow? I fear this silence:
    Something dreadful may come of it.
OEDIPUS: Let it come!
    However base my birth, I must know about it.
    The Queen, like a woman, is perhaps ashamed
    To think of my low origin. But I
160 Am a child of Luck; I can not be dishonored.
    Luck is my mother; the passing months, my brothers,
    Have seen me rich and poor.
                                If this is so,
    How could I wish that I were someone else?
    How could I not be glad to know my birth?

ODE III
Strophe

CHORUS: If ever the coming time were known
    To my heart's pondering,
    Kithairon, now by Heaven I see the torches
    At the festival of the next full moon,
5   And see the dance, and hear the choir sing
    A grace to your gentle shade:
    Mountain where Oedipus was found,
    O mountain guard of a noble race!
    May the god who heals us lend his aid,
10   And let that glory come to pass
    For our king's cradling-ground.

Antistrophe

    Of the nymphs that flower beyond the years,
    Who bore you, royal child,
    To Pan of the hills or the timberline Apollo,
15   Cold in delight where the upland clears,

Or Hermês for whom Kyllenê's° heights are piled?
Or flushed as evening cloud,
Great Dionysos, roamer of mountains,
He—was it he who found you there,
20 And caught you up in his own proud
Arms from the sweet god-ravisher
Who laughed by the Muses' fountains?

SCENE IV.

OEDIPUS: Sirs: though I do not know the man,
I think I see him coming, this shepherd we want:
He is old, like our friend here, and the men
Bringing him seem to be servants of my house.
5 But you can tell, if you have ever seen him.

Enter Shepherd escorted by servants.

CHORAGOS: I know him, he was Laïos' man. You can trust him.
OEDIPUS: Tell me first, you from Corinth: is this the shepherd
We were discussing?
MESSENGER: This is the very man.
OEDIPUS *(to Shepherd)*: Come here. No, look at me. You must answer
10 Everything I ask—You belonged to Laïos?
SHEPHERD: Yes: born his slave, brought up in his house.
OEDIPUS: Tell me: what kind of work did you do for him?
SHEPHERD: I was a shepherd of his, most of my life.
OEDIPUS: Where mainly did you go for pasturage?
15 SHEPHERD: Sometimes Kithairon, sometimes the hills near-by.
OEDIPUS: Do you remember ever seeing this man out there?
SHEPHERD: What would he be doing there? This man?
OEDIPUS: This man standing here. Have you ever seen him before?
SHEPHERD: No. At least, not to my recollection.
20 MESSENGER: And that is not strange, my lord. But I'll refresh
His memory: he must remember when we two
Spent three whole seasons together, March to September,
On Kithairon or thereabouts. He had two flocks;
I had one. Each autumn I'd drive mine home
25 And he would go back with his to Laïos' sheepfold.—
Is this not true, just as I have described it?
SHEPHERD: True, yes; but it was all so long ago.
MESSENGER: Well, then: do you remember, back in those days
That you gave me a baby boy to bring up as my own?
30 SHEPHERD: What if I did? What are you trying to say?
MESSENGER: King Oedipus was once that little child.
SHEPHERD: Damn you, hold your tongue!

---

16 *Kyllenê:* birthplace of Hermês, the deities' messenger. The chorus assumes that this holy mountain
was created in order to afford Hermês birth.

OEDIPUS: No more of that!
It is your tongue needs watching, not this man's.
SHEPHERD: My King, my Master, what is it I have done wrong?
35 OEDIPUS: You have not answered his question about the boy.
SHEPHERD: He does not know . . . He is only making trouble . . .
OEDIPUS: Come, speak plainly, or it will go hard with you.
SHEPHERD: In God's name, do not torture an old man!
OEDIPUS: Come here, one of you; bind his arms behind him.
40 SHEPHERD: Unhappy king! What more do you wish to learn?
OEDIPUS: Did you give this man the child he speaks of?
SHEPHERD: I did.
And I would to God I had died that very day.
OEDIPUS: You will die now unless you speak the truth.
SHEPHERD: Yet if I speak the truth, I am worse than dead.
45 OEDIPUS: Very well; since you insist upon delaying—
SHEPHERD: No! I have told you already that I gave him the boy.
OEDIPUS: Where did you get him? From your house? From somewhere
    else?
SHEPHERD: Not from mine, no. A man gave him to me.
OEDIPUS: Is that man here? Do you know whose slave he was?
50 SHEPHERD: For God's love, my King, do not ask me any more!
OEDIPUS: You are a dead man if I have to ask you again.
SHEPHERD: Then . . . Then the child was from the palace of Laïos.
OEDIPUS: A slave child? or a child of his own line?
SHEPHERD: Ah, I am on the brink of dreadful speech!
55 OEDIPUS: And I of dreadful hearing. Yet I must hear.
SHEPHERD: If you must be told, then . . .
                            They said it was Laïos' child,
    But it is your wife who can tell you about that.
OEDIPUS: My wife!—Did she give it to you?
SHEPHERD: My lord, she did.
OEDIPUS: Do you know why?
SHEPHERD: I was told to get rid of it.
OEDIPUS: An unspeakable mother!
60 SHEPHERD: There had been prophecies . . .
OEDIPUS: Tell me.
SHEPHERD: It was said that the boy would kill his own father.
OEDIPUS: Then why did you give him over to this old man?
SHEPHERD: I pitied the baby, my King,
    And I thought that this man would take him far away
    To his own country.
65   He saved him—but for what a fate!
    For if you are what this man says you are,
    No man living is more wretched than Oedipus.
OEDIPUS: Ah God!
    It was true!
            All the prophecies!
                        —Now,
70 O Light, may I look on you for the last time!

I, Oedipus,
Oedipus, damned in his birth, in his marriage damned,
Damned in the blood he shed with his own hand!

He rushes into the palace.

ODE IV
Strophe 1

CHORUS: Alas for the seed of men.

What measure shall I give these generations
That breathe on the void and are void
And exist and do not exist?

5   Who bears more weight of joy
Than mass of sunlight shifting in images,
Or who shall make his thought stay on
That down time drifts away?

Your splendor is all fallen.

10   O naked brow of wrath and tears,
O change of Oedipus!
I who saw your days call no man blest—
Your great days like ghósts góne.

Antistrophe 1

That mind was a strong bow.
15   Deep, how deep you drew it then, hard archer,
At a dim fearful range,
And brought dear glory down!

You overcame the stranger—
The virgin with her hooking lion claws—
20   And though death sang, stood like a tower
To make pale Thebes take heart.

Fortress against our sorrow!

Divine king, giver of laws,
Majestic Oedipus!
25   No prince in Thebes had ever such renown,
No prince won such grace of power.

Strophe 2

And now of all men ever known
Most pitiful is this man's story:
His fortunes are most changed, his state
30   Fallen to a low slave's
Ground under bitter fate.

O Oedipus, most royal one!
The great door that expelled you to the light
Gave at night—ah, gave night to your glory:
35   As to the father, to the fathering son.

All understood too late.

How could that queen whom Laïos won,
The garden that he harrowed at his height,
Be silent when that act was done?

Antistrophe 2

40   But all eyes fail before time's eye,
All actions come to justice there.
Though never willed, though far down the deep past,
Your bed, your dread sirings,
Are brought to book at last.
45   Child by Laïos doomed to die,
Then doomed to lose that fortunate little death,
Would God you never took breath in this air
That with my wailing lips I take to cry:

For I weep the world's outcast.

50   I was blind, and now I can tell why:
Asleep, for you had given ease of breath
To Thebes, while the false years went by.

EXODOS°

Enter, from the palace, Second Messenger.

SECOND MESSENGER: Elders of Thebes, most honored in this land,
What horrors are yours to see and hear, what weight
Of sorrow to be endured, if, true to your birth,
You venerate the line of Labdakos!
5   I think neither Istros nor Phasis, those great rivers,
Could purify this place of the corruption
It shelters now, or soon must bring to light—
Evil not done unconsciously, but willed.

The greatest griefs are those we cause ourselves.

10 CHORAGOS: Surely, friend, we have grief enough already;
What new sorrow do you mean?
SECOND MESSENGER: The Queen is dead.
CHORAGOS: Iocastê? Dead? But at whose hand?

Exodos: the resolution.

SECOND MESSENGER: Her own.
The full horror of what happened, you can not know,
For you did not see it; but I, who did, will tell you
15   As clearly as I can how she met her death.

When she had left us,
In passionate silence, passing through the court,
She ran to her apartment in the house,
Her hair clutched by the fingers of both hands.
20   She closed the doors behind her; then, by that bed
Where long ago the fatal son was conceived—
That son who should bring about his father's death—
We heard her call upon Laïos, dead so many years,
And heard her wail for the double fruit of her marriage,
25   A husband by her husband, children by her child.

Exactly how she died I do not know:
For Oedipus burst in moaning and would not let us
Keep vigil to the end: it was by him
As he stormed about the room that our eyes were caught.
30   From one to another of us he went, begging a sword,
Cursing the wife who was not his wife, the mother
Whose womb had carried his own children and himself.
I do not know: it was none of us aided him,
But surely one of the gods was in control!
35   For with a dreadful cry
He hurled his weight, as though wrenched out of himself,
At the twin doors: the bolts gave, and he rushed in.
And there we saw her hanging, her body swaying
From the cruel cord she had noosed about her neck.
40   A great sob broke from him, heartbreaking to hear,
As he loosed the rope and lowered her to the ground.

I would blot out from my mind what happened next!
For the King ripped from her gown the golden brooches
That were her ornament, and raised them, and plunged them down
45   Straight into his own eyeballs, crying, "No more,
No more shall you look on the misery about me,
The horrors of my own doing! Too long you have known
The faces of those whom I should never have seen,
Too long been blind to those for whom I was searching!
50   From this hour, go in darkness!" And as he spoke
He struck at his eyes—not once, but many times;
And the blood spattered his beard,
Bursting from his ruined sockets like red hail.
So from the unhappiness of two this evil has sprung,
55   A curse on the man and woman alike. The old
Happiness of the house of Labdakos
Was happiness enough: where is it today?

It is all wailing and ruin, disgrace, death—all
The misery of mankind that has a name—
60 And it is wholly and for ever theirs.
CHORAGOS: Is he in agony still? Is there no rest for him?
SECOND MESSENGER: He is calling for someone to lead him to the gates
So that all the children of Kadmos may look upon
His father's murderer, his mother's—no,
I can not say it!
65   And then he will leave Thebes,
Self-exiled, in order that the curse
Which he himself pronounced may depart from the house.
He is weak, and there is none to lead him,
So terrible is his suffering.
                    But you will see:
70 Look, the doors are opening; in a moment
You will see a thing that would crush a heart of stone.

The central door is opened; Oedipus, blinded, is led in.

CHORAGOS: Dreadful indeed for men to see.
Never have my own eyes
Looked on a sight so full of fear.

75 Oedipus!
What madness came upon you, what daemon
Leaped on your life with heavier
Punishment than a mortal man can bear?
No: I can not even
80 Look at you, poor ruined one.
And I would speak, question, ponder,
If I were able. No.
You make me shudder.
OEDIPUS: God. God.
85 Is there a sorrow greater?
Where shall I find harbor in this world?
My voice is hurled far on a dark wind.
What has God done to me?
CHORAGOS: Too terrible to think of, or to see.

Strophe 1

90 OEDIPUS: O cloud of night,
Never to be turned away: night coming on,
I can not tell how: night like a shroud!

My fair winds brought me here.
                    Oh God. Again
The pain of the spikes where I had sight,
95 The flooding pain
Of memory, never to be gouged out.

CHORAGOS: This is not strange.
You suffer it all twice over, remorse in pain,
Pain in remorse.

Antistrophe 1

100 OEDIPUS: Ah dear friend
Are you faithful even yet, you alone?
Are you still standing near me, will you stay here,
Patient, to care for the blind?
                              The blind man!
Yet even blind I know who it is attends me,
105 By the voice's tone—
Though my new darkness hide the comforter.
CHORAGOS: Oh fearful act!
What god was it drove you to rake black
Night across your eyes?

Strophe 2

110 OEDIPUS: Apollo. Apollo. Dear
Children, the god was Apollo.
He brought my sick, sick fate upon me.
But the blinding hand was my own!
How could I bear to see
115 When all my sight was horror everywhere?
CHORAGOS: Everywhere; that is true.
OEDIPUS: And now what is left?
Images? Love? A greeting even,
Sweet to the senses? Is there anything?
120 Ah, no, friends: lead me away.
Lead me away from Thebes.
                    Lead the great wreck
And hell of Oedipus, whom the gods hate.
CHORAGOS: Your fate is clear, you are not blind to that.
Would God you had never found it out!

Antistrophe 2

125 OEDIPUS: Death take the man who unbound
My feet on that hillside
And delivered me from death to life! What life?
If only I had died,
This weight of monstrous doom
130 Could not have dragged me and my darlings down.
CHORAGOS: I would have wished the same.
OEDIPUS: Oh never to have come here
With my father's blood upon me! Never
To have been the man they call his mother's husband!
135 Oh accurst! Oh child of evil,
To have entered that wretched bed—
                              the selfsame one!

More primal than sin itself, this fell to me.

CHORAGOS: I do not know how I can answer you.
You were better dead than alive and blind.

140 OEDIPUS: Do not counsel me any more. This punishment
That I have laid upon myself is just.
If I had eyes,
I do not know how I could bear the sight
Of my father, when I came to the house of Death,
145 Or my mother: for I have sinned against them both
So vilely that I could not make my peace
By strangling my own life.
                              Or do you think my children,
Born as they were born, would be sweet to my eyes?
Ah never, never! Nor this town with its high walls,
Nor the holy images of the gods.
150   For I,
Thrice miserable!—Oedipus, noblest of all the line
Of Kadmos, have condemned myself to enjoy
These things no more, by my own malediction
Expelling that man whom the gods declared
155 To be a defilement in the house of Laïos.
After exposing the rankness of my own guilt,
How could I look men frankly in the eyes?
No, I swear it,
If I could have stifled my hearing at its source,
160 I would have done it and made all this body
A tight cell of misery, blank to light and sound:
So I should have been safe in a dark agony
Beyond all recollection.
                          Ah Kithairon!
Why did you shelter me? When I was cast upon you,
165 Why did I not die? Then I should never
Have shown the world my execrable birth.

Ah Polybos! Corinth, city that I believed
The ancient seat of my ancestors: how fair
I seemed, your child! And all the while this evil
Was cancerous within me!
170   For I am sick
In my daily life, sick in my origin.

O three roads, dark ravine, woodland and way
Where three roads met: you, drinking my father's blood,
My own blood, spilled by my own hand: can you remember
175 The unspeakable things I did there, and the things
I went on from there to do?
                          O marriage, marriage!
The act that engendered me, and again the act
Performed by the son in the same bed—

                                                    Ah, the net
         Of incest, mingling fathers, brothers, sons,
180   With brides, wives, mothers: the last evil
         That can be known by men: no tongue can say
         How evil!
                         No. For the love of God, conceal me
         Somewhere far from Thebes; or kill me; or hurl me
         Into the sea, away from men's eyes for ever.

185   Come, lead me. You need not fear to touch me.
         Of all men, I alone can bear this guilt.

         Enter Creon.

         CHORAGOS: We are not the ones to decide; but Creon here
             May fitly judge of what you ask. He only
             Is left to protect the city in your place.
190   OEDIPUS: Alas, how can I speak to him? What right have I
             To beg his courtesy whom I have deeply wronged?
         CREON: I have not come to mock you, Oedipus,
             Or to reproach you, either.
             (To Attendants.)   —You, standing there:
             If you have lost all respect for man's dignity,
195   At least respect the flame of Lord Helios:
             Do not allow this pollution to show itself
             Openly here, an affront to the earth
             And Heaven's rain and the light of day. No, take him
             Into the house as quickly as you can.
200   For it is proper
             That only the close kindred see his grief.
         OEDIPUS: I pray you in God's name, since your courtesy
             Ignores my dark expectation, visiting
             With mercy this man of all men most execrable:
205   Give me what I ask—for your good, not for mine.
         CREON: And what is it that you would have me do?
         OEDIPUS: Drive me out of this country as quickly as may be
             To a place where no human voice can ever greet me.
         CREON: I should have done that before now—only,
210   God's will had not been wholly revealed to me.
         OEDIPUS: But his command is plain: the parricide
             Must be destroyed. I am that evil man.
         CREON: That is the sense of it, yes; but as things are,
             We had best discover clearly what is to be done.
215   OEDIPUS: You would learn more about a man like me?
         CREON: You are ready now to listen to the god.
         OEDIPUS: I will listen. But it is to you
             That I must turn for help. I beg you, hear me.

             The woman in there—
220   Give her whatever funeral you think proper:

She is your sister.
                    —But let me go, Creon!
Let me purge my father's Thebes of the pollution
Of my living here, and go out to the wild hills,
To Kithairon, that has won such fame with me,
225   The tomb my mother and father appointed for me,
And let me die there, as they willed I should.
And yet I know
Death will not ever come to me through sickness
Or in any natural way: I have been preserved
230   For some unthinkable fate. But let that be.
As for my sons, you need not care for them.
They are men, they will find some way to live.
But my poor daughters, who have shared my table,
Who never before have been parted from their father—
235   Take care of them, Creon; do this for me.
And will you let me touch them with my hands
A last time, and let us weep together?
Be kind, my lord,
Great prince, be kind!
                    Could I but touch them,
240   They would be mine again, as when I had my eyes.

Enter Antigone and Ismene, attended.

Ah, God!
Is it my dearest children I hear weeping?
Has Creon pitied me and sent my daughters?
CREON: Yes, Oedipus: I knew that they were dear to you
245   In the old days, and you know you must love them still.
OEDIPUS: May God bless you for this—and be a friendlier
Guardian to you than he has been to me!

Children, where are you?
Come quickly to my hands: they are your brother's—
250   Hands that have brought your father's once clear eyes
To this way of seeing—
                    Ah dearest ones,
I had neither sight nor knowledge then, your father
By the woman who was the source of his own life!
And I weep for you—having no strength to see you—
255   I weep for you when I think of the bitterness
That men will visit upon you all your lives.
What homes, what festivals can you attend
Without being forced to depart again in tears?
And when you come to marriageable age,
260   Where is the man, my daughters, who would dare
Risk the bane that lies on all my children?
Is there any evil wanting? Your father killed
His father; sowed the womb of her who bore him;

Engendered you at the fount of his own existence!
That is what they will say of you.
265   Then, whom
Can you ever marry? There are no bridegrooms for you,
And your lives must wither away in sterile dreaming.
O Creon, son of Menoikeus!
You are the only father my daughters have,
270 Since we, their parents, are both of us gone for ever.
They are your own blood: you will not let them
Fall into beggary and loneliness;
You will keep them from the miseries that are mine!
Take pity on them; see, they are only children,
275 Friendless except for you. Promise me this,
Great Prince, and give me your hand in token of it.

Creon clasps his right hand.

Children:
I could say much, if you could understand me,
But as it is, I have only this prayer for you:
280 Live where you can, be as happy as you can—
Happier, please God, than God has made your father!
CREON: Enough. You have wept enough. Now go within.
OEDIPUS: I must; but it is hard.
CREON: Time eases all things.
OEDIPUS: But you must promise—
CREON: Say what you desire.
OEDIPUS: Send me from Thebes!
285 CREON: God grant that I may!
OEDIPUS: But since God hates me . . .
CREON: No, he will grant your wish.
OEDIPUS: You promise?
CREON: I can not speak beyond my knowledge.
OEDIPUS: Then lead me in.
CREON: Come now, and leave your children.
OEDIPUS: No! Do not take them from me!
CREON: Think no longer
290 That you are in command here, but rather think
How, when you were, you served your own destruction.

Exeunt into the house all but the Chorus; the Choragos chants directly to the audience.

CHORAGOS: Men of Thebes: look upon Oedipus.

This is the king who solved the famous riddle
And towered up, most powerful of men.
295 No mortal eyes but looked on him with envy,
Yet in the end ruin swept over him.
Let every man in mankind's frailty

Consider his last day; and let none
Presume on his good fortune until he find
300   Life, at his death, a memory without pain.

Questions

1. What does the exposition tell us about Oedipus's virtues as a ruler?
2. What does Creon tell us about the murder of Laïos? How does this help to define the dramatic situation?
3. Why doesn't Teiresias answer Oedipus immediately? Does his delay add to the suspense of the rising action?
4. Why does Oedipus suspect Creon (p. 832)? Is this suspicion justified, or rash? What defects of character does Oedipus reveal in this scene with Teiresias? In the rest of the rising action?
5. What is Iocastê's approach to the quarrel between Oedipus and Creon? What does this tell you about her character?
6. In his scene with Iocastê (page 840), Oedipus's mood changes radically from rage to terror. Can you pinpoint the speech where this change occurs? What causes the change?
7. Oedipus returns briefly to exposition as he recalls his youth and the murder of the strangers at the crossroads (pp. 842–43). This speech, in light of other evidence, points to his guilt. Only one piece of the puzzle is missing. What is it? Who can provide the missing piece?
8. How does the chorus judge Oedipus in Ode II? How do they respond to the action thereafter?
9. What are the two major scenes of the falling action? Tell how each brings Oedipus closer to catastrophe.
10. The messenger is bringing news he believes will cheer Oedipus, but it has the opposite effect. This is an instance of dramatic irony, wherein a character's actions have unforseen results. Can you find other examples of dramatic irony in *Oedipus Rex*?
11. Oedipus's recognition of his guilt completes the falling action and begins the final movement of the plot, the catastrophe. Pinpoint the "recognition" speech.
12. Of the major events of the catastrophe, some occur onstage and some offstage. What are the major events of the catastrophe? Which is the most terrifying? Which is the most pathetic? How do these scenes answer the dramatic questions posed in the exposition?
13. What is Oedipus's tragic flaw, his frailty of character? To what extent is this flaw responsible for his downfall?
14. Could Oedipus have avoided his fate? How?

Suggestions for Dramatists

1. Read the front page of your daily newspaper looking for stories in which a character is faced with a definite dramatic situation. Describe that situation in terms of the character, his or her objective, and the obstacle.

2. Do you have friends or relatives, middle-aged or older, whose fortunes have changed considerably, from good to bad, or from bad to good? Was the change owing to their own actions, or to circumstances beyond their control? Select a familiar character who has had some control over his or her own destiny. What was this character's ambition? Were there significant obstacles? Did he or she overcome them?

 Try to think of a particular incident that was the turning point in this character's career. Describe it. Was there a single moment at which this character faced a decision that sealed his or her fate? Describe it. Now, considering this as the climax of your drama, describe the scenes that led up to it, and the scenes that resulted from it.

3. Which of the stories in the Fiction section of this book would lend itself to the theater? Which ones would be impossible to stage? Remember that there can be few changes of scene, and a limited number of characters. Choose a story you believe would be stageworthy, and write a scenario for it, describing the five-act structure, and the entrances and exits of characters. Then begin writing the dialogue.

4 ❦ Heroes and Heroines— Dramatic Character

When talking about someone's virtues we often say that he or she is someone of "character," meaning good character rather than bad, for the word when used in that way is always complimentary. When we refer to a person in a play as a *character* we get closer to the general and intrinsic meaning of the word. For character is really personality, that special combination of good and bad qualities that makes a person different from all others.

Character shapes our fate. A man born with great speed, eyesight, and determination might become a rich and famous baseball player, while his brother, possessing all those virtues except determination, becomes a pickpocket. The shy child may learn in solitude the art of making great paintings, while her outgoing sister becomes a senator. Cyrano de Bergerac, cursed with a monstrous nose, becomes a valiant fighter in defense of it. Likewise, the actions of a play arise from its major characters. *Oedipus Rex* is very much the play of Oedipus's character, the proud man who must live out a terrible prophecy. His character is his fate, and it would be hard to imagine the events of that play befalling anyone else.

What makes a great dramatic character? What kinds of characters lend themselves to presentation in a stage play? As we suggested in our introduction, any character who can sustain the interest of a live audience has dramatic potential. To understand what makes a great dramatic character, it is helpful to reconsider the dynamics of the dramatic situation. A *character* has an *objective*, but some *obstacle* stands in the way. That is, the character wants something. The great heroes and heroines of dramatic literature may have nothing else in common; they may vary enormously in wisdom, beauty, pride, and power, but they all share one characteristic. They have enormous desires. It is desire that creates the dramatic situation, and desire that drives the rising action. In *Riders To The Sea*, Maurya desperately wants Bartley to stay home. Bartley's desire to sail to

Connemara is equally desperate. If either of them were half-hearted, the play would not work. Oedipus's desire to find and punish the murderer of Laïos is absolute, larger than life. We have the feeling that he would move heaven and earth to solve the crime.

It is this, chiefly, that distinguishes a great dramatic character from his counterpart in fiction: this strong desire, and a disposition inclined to act upon one's desires rather than deliberate upon them. Some great heroes and heroines of fiction—Don Quixote, Carmen, Huck Finn—have dramatic desires, and when they do they usually find their way to the stage. Others, beset by boredom or paralyzed by conflicting desires, like the heroes of Dostoyevski's *Notes From The Underground* and Salinger's *Catcher In The Rye*, are impossible to depict on the stage because their characters manifest themselves in thought rather than action. One of the fascinations of Hamlet is that he is an intensely meditative character whose desire forces him to act. It has been suggested that the play would make a good novel.

Virtues and Flaws

Aristotle says that the hero of a tragedy should be good. Clearly, if the character is not "good" in some way, we will not care what happens to him or her, and the play will not hold our interest. Oedipus is arrogant and overbearing, yet his motivation is moral: he wants the best for his people. In the play you are about to read, the central character, Amanda Wingfield, has some unappealing qualities, but we sympathize with her because she is striving to do the best for her children. Characters with dramatic desires are not likely to be perfect. Yet if they do not have some virtue they are neither believable nor appealing. Even Richard III, Shakespeare's desperate villain who kills every man, woman, and child who stands between him and the throne, charms us with his wit, his courage, and his self-honesty.

The great characters of tragedy and comedy have admirable strengths, but they also have some *flaw* that gets them into trouble. The sooner we, as readers, recognize the flaw, the sooner we can appreciate the dramatic character. Since the flaw of the central character is frequently the cause of the play's *problem*, we may look for it in the exposition. Amanda Wingfield, who has such admirable energy and intentions, has a dreadful character flaw, evident in the first scenes of *The Glass Menagerie*. She wants to live her children's lives for them, and believes she can.

Heroes, Heroines, Villains, and Others

The central character in a drama is called the *protagonist*. Most classical plays have a single protagonist from whom the play takes its name, and from whose character the plot takes its course. Other plays, like *Romeo and Juliet*, may have two or three characters who share the spotlight and the sympathies of the audience, and it is fair to call these actors protagonists. Plays without obvious protagonists, where the interest is diffused among several characters, as in Chekhov's *The Cherry Orchard*, are called plays of *atmosphere*.

We use the terms *hero* and *heroine* somewhat loosely and romantically to refer to protagonists who win our admiration or affection. The word *hero* has a military origin; strictly speaking, it ought to be reserved for those protagonists who display the virtues of courage and fortitude in the face of physical danger. Likewise with the term *heroine*. However, there are so many dramas that do not place their protagonists in such peril that a strict respect of word origins would deprive us of two handy terms.

The *antagonist* of a drama, sometimes called the *villain*, is the character who opposes the protagonist. When we hear the word "villain" we think of a sly man in black hat and cape, sneering and twirling his mustache. This image comes from *melodrama*, a sensational form of nineteenth-century drama where organ music accompanied the action, where the hero was handsome and fearless, the heroine beautiful and helpless, and the villain evil incarnate. The villain of a stage play, however, need not be rotten through and through. Villains tend to be more interesting when they have understandable human motives, like Hamlet's uncle, King Claudius, who opposes Hamlet in order to preserve his kingdom and the peace. In order to appreciate the villains of drama, we must consider carefully their motives.

Villainy as a principle of drama does not always reside in a single character. Many plays have no villains as such. *Riders To The Sea* and *Oedipus Rex* are cases in which we must search for the principle of evil, or villainy, in the protagonists. We have seen how Oedipus stands in the way of his own efforts to rid Thebes of the plague. He is the villain of his own drama. In *The Glass Menagerie*, Amanda, the protagonist in the major action, causes her children more grief than the Gentleman Caller who foils her plans for happiness.

Dramatic characters, like real people, are a fascinating mixture of good and bad qualities. We must not be hasty to label them as heroes or villains. As serious readers, we do the greatest justice to characters by carefully examining their motives, their strengths, and their weaknesses.

In most plays there are characters whose fate is incidental to the major action. These are the *minor* or *supporting characters*. The sisters in *Riders To The Sea*, Creon and Teiresias in *Oedipus Rex*, and the choruses of both plays, are all supporting characters. They help to forward the action, but they are neither the cause nor the major victims of it. One could imagine the story being told without them. Playwrights use minor characters for contrast, enrichment, and comic relief.

Stock characters, more frequent in comedy and melodrama, are those whose qualities are so exaggerated and common that they represent a *type* of human nature. The bragging soldier, the stingy old man, the shrewish housewife, and the lovesick adolescent have lasting and universal appeal. Such characters begin to appear in the comedies of Menander in the fourth century B.C. The commedia dell'arte, an Italian theatrical genre dating from the mid-sixteenth century, dramatized hundreds of different comedies with the same stock characters. These characters reappear in movies and television, and sometimes as supporting figures in serious drama.

Actions and Words

In the theater actions speak louder than words. As readers we may be greatly impressed with a character's speeches. But we must carefully consider the character's words in the light of what he is doing, his actions in the particular scene. This is one of the keys to reading dramatic character. Oedipus *says* that he will find the murderer of Laïos. But as soon as the prophet tells Oedipus he himself is the murderer, Oedipus begins avoiding the issue, accusing Creon of treason. Here the contradiction between word and deed points to Oedipus's flaw, his pride. In the first scene of *The Glass Menagerie*, Amanda may sound as though she is giving her son good advice, and her daughter kind attention. Actually, she is spoiling her son's dinner and hurting her daughter's feelings. This contrast between words and actions indicates a flaw in Amanda's character, her self-absorption and insensitivity to her children's feelings. Her cruelty probably is not intentional.

But sometimes dramatic characters are intentionally deceitful, and we can tell because their actions betray their words. Rosencrantz and Guildenstern appear to be warm and charming friends of Prince Hamlet. They flatter him and offer to serve him. But, remember, these charming fellows have been paid by the King to spy on their old friend. They are contemptible scoundrels. On the other hand, we have Hamlet's true friend Horatio, perhaps the play's most virtuous character, whose words and deeds are always of a piece.

Dramatic irony is often the result of the discrepancy between speech and action, as in the scene between Oedipus and the Messenger. All of the information the Messenger relates to relieve Oedipus brings him more grief. In *The Glass Menagerie* the misguided Gentleman Caller, who says he is being sincere and trying to build up poor Laura's confidence, is actually dealing her a dreadful blow. We have all been in situations where our noblest intentions and plans backfire.

Dramatic Diction and Character

In drama, as in life, a character's language is very revealing. Well-educated people are likely to be more eloquent than those from less-privileged backgrounds, and use longer words and more complex sentences. Businessmen and military officers, whose success depends upon maximum efficiency, tend toward clipped, direct language without ornamentation, while imaginative people use more figures of speech. Craftsmen and laborers employ the special jargon of their trades. Often we can tell someone's place of origin by his or her accent.

Playwrights know the relation of speech to character. Whether they write in formal verse or realistic prose, their diction suits the characters and can tell us a great deal about them. Oedipus speaks in long and stately sentences. His rhythms and words befit a king. Teiresias speaks poetically, in mysterious, unfinished sentences, the perfect style for a prophet. The Messenger and the Shepherd speak in the simple words of peasants.

Each time you are introduced to new dramatic characters, see how much you can find out about them from their manner of speech.

A Drama of Character: *The Glass Menagerie*

We praise some dramas for their ingenuity of plot, others for their rich and appealing characters. The plot of *Oedipus Rex*, with its classic rise and fall, its complications and its catastrophe worked out with watchlike precision, is considered one of the greatest plots of all time. The play you are about to read, like many twentieth-century dramas, is admired more for its characters than its plot, though the plot is quite serviceable and will hold up under classic analysis.

Tennessee Williams's play *The Glass Menagerie* has three major characters and one minor character, minor only in the sense that he has fewer lines and a smaller part in the action. All four of the characters—Amanda Wingfield, the mother; Tom and Laura, her children; and the Gentleman Caller who briefly enters their lives—are fully drawn, credible, and sympathetic figures, with the strengths and weaknesses we have come to look for in dramatic characters. We call Amanda the protagonist because she is responsible for the major action of the plot, the pursuit of the Gentleman Caller. But our sympathies lie at least as much with Tom, the young poet who works long hours in a factory to support the family, and with the frail Laura, who is the victim of her mother's ambitions.

Laurette Taylor as Amanda in *The Glass Menagerie* (*Culver Pictures, Inc.*)

By the end of the play we have come to care so much about all three of these characters that all of their fates concern us equally.

The Glass Menagerie, first performed in 1944, is a relatively recent addition to the dramatic literature that includes *Oedipus Rex.* One of many great intervening developments was the Moscow Art Theatre, a naturalistic repertory group that produced the plays of Anton Chekhov (1860–1904). His plays de-emphasized the fate of the protagonist, dividing the dramatic interest among several compelling, realistic characters. Williams's play shows the influence of Chekhov.

Tennessee Williams is considered by many to be America's most important playwright of the post-World War II era. *The Glass Menagerie* won the New York Drama Critics Circle Award. Two other plays, *A Streetcar Named Desire* (1947) and *Cat On A Hot Tin Roof* (1955), won Pulitzer prizes; these and several other of his dramas have been made into movies starring such actors and actresses as Marlon Brando, Elizabeth Taylor, and Paul Newman.

TENNESSEE WILLIAMS (1911–1983)

The Glass Menagerie

CHARACTERS

AMANDA WINGFIELD, *the mother.*
A little woman of great but confused vitality clinging frantically to another time and place. Her characterization must be carefully created, not copied from type. She is not paranoiac, but her life is paranoia. There is much to admire in AMANDA, and as much to love and pity as there is to laugh at. Certainly she has endurance and a kind of heroism, and though her foolishness makes her unwittingly cruel at times, there is tenderness in her slight person.

LAURA WINGFIELD, *her daughter.*
AMANDA, having failed to establish contact with reality, continues to live vitally in her illusions, but LAURA's situation is even graver. A childhood illness has left her crippled, one leg slightly shorter than the other, and held in a brace. This defect need not be more than suggested on the stage. Stemming from this, LAURA's separation increases till she is like a piece of her own glass collection, too exquisitely fragile to move from the shelf.

TOM WINGFIELD, *her son, and the narrator of the play.*
A poet with a job in a warehouse. His nature is not remorseless, but to escape from a trap he has to act without pity.

JIM O'CONNOR, *the gentleman caller.*
A nice, ordinary, young man.

SCENE. *An alley in St. Louis.*
Part I: *Preparation for a Gentleman Caller.*
Part II: *The Gentleman Calls.*
Time: *Now and the Past.*

SCENE I.

The Wingfield apartment is in the rear of the building, one of those vast hive-like conglomerations of cellular living-units that flower as warty growths in overcrowded urban centers of lower middle-class population and are symptomatic of the impulse of this largest and fundamentally enslaved section of American society to avoid fluidity and differentiation and to exist and function as one interfused mass of automatism.

The apartment faces an alley and is entered by a fire-escape, a structure whose name is a touch of accidental poetic truth, for all of these huge buildings are always burning with the slow and implacable fires of human desperation. The fire-escape is included in the set—that is, the landing of it and steps descending from it.

The scene is memory and is therefore nonrealistic. Memory takes a lot of poetic license. It omits some details; others are exaggerated, according to the emotional value of the articles it touches, for memory is seated predominantly in the heart. The interior is therefore rather dim and poetic.

At the rise of the curtain, the audience is faced with the dark, grim rear wall of the Wingfield tenement. This building, which runs parallel to the footlights, is flanked on both sides by dark, narrow alleys which run into murky canyons of tangled clotheslines, garbage cans and the sinister latticework of neighboring fire-escapes. It is up and down these side alleys that exterior entrances and exits are made, during the play. At the end of TOM's opening commentary, the dark tenement wall slowly reveals (by means of a transparency) the interior of the ground floor Wingfield apartment.

Downstage is the living room, which also serves as a sleeping room for LAURA, the sofa unfolding to make her bed. Upstage, center, and divided by a wide arch or second proscenium with transparent faded portieres (or second curtain), is the dining room. In an old-fashioned what-not in the living room are seen scores of transparent glass animals. A blown-up photograph of the father hangs on the wall of the living room, facing the audience, to the left of the archway. It is the face of a very handsome young man in a doughboy's First World War cap. He is gallantly smiling, ineluctably smiling, as if to say, "I will be smiling forever."

The audience hears and sees the opening scene in the dining room through both the transparent fourth wall of the building and the transparent gauze portieres of the dining-room arch. It is during this revealing scene that the fourth wall slowly ascends, out of sight. This transparent exterior wall is not brought down again until the very end of the play, during TOM's final speech.

The narrator is an undisguised convention of the play. He takes whatever license with dramatic convention as is convenient to his purposes.

TOM enters dressed as a merchant sailor from alley, stage left, and strolls across the front of the stage to the fire-escape. There he stops and lights a cigarette. He addresses the audience.

TOM   Yes, I have tricks in my pocket, I have things up my sleeve. But I am the opposite of a stage magician. He gives you illusion that has the appearance of truth. I give you truth in the pleasant disguise of illusion. To begin with, I turn back time. I reverse it to that quaint period, the thirties, when the huge middle class of America was matriculating in a school for the blind. Their eyes had failed them, or they had failed their eyes, and so they were having their fingers pressed forcibly down on the fiery Braille alphabet of a dissolving economy. In Spain there was revolution. Here there was only shouting and confusion. In Spain there was Guernica.[1] Here there were disturbances of labor, sometimes pretty violent, in otherwise peaceful cities such as Chicago, Cleveland, Saint Louis. . . . This is the social background of the play.

(MUSIC.)

---

[1] Basque town infamously bombed by German planes supporting the rebels during the Spanish Civil War.

The play is memory. Being a memory play, it is dimly lighted, it is sentimental, it is not realistic. In memory everything seems to happen to music. That explains the fiddle in the wings. I am the narrator of the play, and also a character in it. The other characters are my mother, Amanda, my sister, Laura, and a gentleman caller who appears in the final scenes. He is the most realistic character in the play, being an emissary from a world of reality that we were somehow set apart from. But since I have a poet's weakness for symbols, I am using this character also as a symbol; he is the long delayed but always expected something that we live for. There is a fifth character in the play who doesn't appear except in this larger-than-life photograph over the mantel. This is our father who left us a long time ago. He was a telephone man who fell in love with long distances; he gave up his job with the telephone company and skipped the light fantastic out of town. . . . The last we heard of him was a picture post-card from Mazatlan, on the Pacific coast of Mexico, containing a message of two words—"Hello—Good-bye!" and an address. I think the rest of the play will explain itself. . . .

AMANDA's *voice becomes audible through the portieres.*

(LEGEND ON SCREEN: "OÙ SONT LES NEIGES.")

He divides the portieres and enters the upstage area.
AMANDA *and* LAURA *are seated at a drop-leaf table. Eating is indicated by gestures without food or utensils.* AMANDA *faces the audience.* TOM *and* LAURA *are seated in profile.*
The interior has lit up softly and through the scrim we see AMANDA *and* LAURA *seated at the table in the upstage area.*

AMANDA *(calling)* Tom?
TOM Yes, Mother.
AMANDA We can't say grace until you come to the table!
TOM Coming, Mother. (*He bows slightly and withdraws, reappearing a few moments later in his place at the table.*)
AMANDA *(to her son)* Honey, don't *push* with your *fingers.* If you have to push with something, the thing to push with is a crust of bread. And chew—chew! Animals have sections in their stomachs which enable them to digest food without mastication, but human beings are supposed to chew their food before they swallow it down. Eat food leisurely, son, and really enjoy it. A well-cooked meal has lots of delicate flavors that have to be held in the mouth for appreciation. So chew your food and give your salivary glands a chance to function!

TOM *deliberately lays his imaginary fork down and pushes his chair back from the table.*

TOM I haven't enjoyed one bite of this dinner because of your constant directions on how to eat it. It's you that makes me rush through meals with your hawk-like attention to every bite I take. Sickening—spoils my appetite—all this discussion of animals' secretion—salivary glands—mastication!
AMANDA *(lightly)* Temperament like a Metropolitan star! (*He rises and crosses downstage.*) You're not excused from the table.
TOM I am getting a cigarette.
AMANDA You smoke too much.

LAURA *rises.*

LAURA I'll bring in the blanc mange.

He remains standing with his cigarette by the portieres during the following.

AMANDA *(rising)* No, sister, no, sister—you be the lady this time and I'll be the darky.
LAURA I'm already up.
AMANDA Resume your seat, little sister—I want you to stay fresh and pretty—for gentlemen callers!
LAURA I'm not expecting any gentlemen callers.
AMANDA *(crossing out to kitchenette. Airily)* Sometimes they come when they are least expected! Why, I remember one Sunday afternoon in Blue Mountain—*(Enters kitchenette.)*
TOM I know what's coming!
LAURA Yes. But let her tell it.
TOM Again?
LAURA She loves to tell it.

AMANDA *returns with bowl of dessert.*

AMANDA One Sunday afternoon in Blue Mountain—your mother received—*seventeen!*—gentlemen callers! Why, sometimes there weren't chairs enough to accommodate them all. We had to send the nigger over to bring in folding chairs from the parish house.
TOM *(remaining at portieres)* How did you entertain those gentlemen callers?
AMANDA I understood the art of conversation!
TOM I bet you could talk.
AMANDA Girls in those days *knew* how to talk, I can tell you.
TOM Yes?

(IMAGE: AMANDA AS A GIRL ON A PORCH GREETING CALLERS.)

AMANDA They knew how to entertain their gentlemen callers. It wasn't enough for a girl to be possessed of a pretty face and a graceful figure—although I wasn't slighted in either respect. She also needed to have a nimble wit and a tongue to meet all occasions.
TOM What did you talk about?
AMANDA Things of importance going on in the world! Never anything coarse or common or vulgar. *(She addresses* TOM *as though he were seated in the vacant chair at the table though he remains by portieres. He plays this scene as though he held the book.)* My callers were gentlemen—all! Among my callers were some of the most prominent young planters of the Mississippi Delta—planters and sons of planters!

TOM *motions for music and a spot of light on* AMANDA.
Her eyes lift, her face glows, her voice becomes rich and elegiac.

(SCREEN LEGEND: "OÙ SONT LES NEIGES.")

There was young Champ Laughlin who later became vice-president of the Delta Planters Bank. Hadley Stevenson who was drowned in Moon Lake and left his widow one hundred and fifty thousand in Government bonds. There were the Cutrere brothers,

Wesley and Bates. Bates was one of my bright particular beaux! He got in a quarrel with that wild Wainright boy. They shot it out on the floor of Moon Lake Casino. Bates was shot through the stomach. Died in the ambulance on his way to Memphis. His widow was also well-provided for, came into eight or ten thousand acres, that's all. She married him on the rebound—never loved her—carried my picture on him the night he died! And there was that boy that every girl in the Delta had set her cap for! That beautiful, brilliant young Fitzhugh boy from Green County!

TOM What did he leave his widow?

AMANDA He never married! Gracious, you talk as though all of my old admirers had turned up their toes to the daisies!

TOM Isn't this the first you mentioned that still survives?

AMANDA That Fitzhugh boy went North and made a fortune—came to be known as the Wolf of Wall Street! He had the Midas touch, whatever he touched turned to gold! And I could have been Mrs. Duncan J. Fitzhugh, mind you! But—I picked your *father!*

LAURA *(rising)* Mother, let me clear the table.

AMANDA No, dear, you go in front and study your typewriter chart. Or practice your shorthand a little. Stay fresh and pretty—It's almost time for our gentlemen callers to start arriving. *(She flounces girlishly toward the kitchenette.)* How many do you suppose we're going to entertain this afternoon?

TOM *throws down the paper and jumps up with a groan.*

LAURA *(alone in the dining room)* I don't believe we're going to receive any, Mother.

AMANDA *(reappearing, airily)* What? No one—not one? You must be joking! (LAURA *nervously echoes her laugh. She slips in a fugitive manner through the half-open portieres and draws them gently behind her. A shaft of very clear light is thrown on her face against the faded tapestry of the curtains.* MUSIC: "THE GLASS MENAGERIE" UNDER FAINTLY. *Lightly.)* Not one gentleman caller? It can't be true! There must be a flood, there must have been a tornado!

LAURA It isn't a flood, it's not a tornado, Mother. I'm just not popular like you were in Blue Mountain. . . . (TOM *utters another groan.* LAURA *glances at him with a faint, apologetic smile. Her voice catching a little.)* Mother's afraid I'm going to be an old maid.

(THE SCENE DIMS OUT WITH "GLASS MENAGERIE" MUSIC.)

SCENE II. *"Laura, Haven't You Ever Liked Some Boy?"*

On the dark stage the screen is lighted with the image of blue roses.
Gradually LAURA's *figure becomes apparent and the screen goes out.*
The music subsides.
LAURA *is seated in the delicate ivory chair at the small claw-foot table.*
She wears a dress of soft violet material for a kimono—her hair tied back from her forehead with a ribbon.
She is washing and polishing her collection of glass.
AMANDA *appears on the fire-escape steps. At the sound of her ascent,* LAURA *catches her breath, thrusts the bowl of ornaments away and seats herself stiffly before the diagram of the typewriter keyboard as though it held her spellbound. Something has happened to* AMANDA. *It is written in her face as she climbs to the landing: a look that is grim and hopeless and a little absurd.*

She has on one of those cheap or imitation velvety-looking cloth coats with imitation fur collar. Her hat is five or six years old, one of those dreadful cloche hats that were worn in the late twenties and she is clasping an enormous black patent-leather pocketbook with nickel clasp and initials. This is her full-dress outfit, the one she usually wears to the D.A.R.[2]

Before entering she looks through the door.

She purses her lips, opens her eyes wide, rolls them upward, and shakes her head.

Then she slowly lets herself in the door. Seeing her mother's expression LAURA *touches her lips with a nervous gesture.*

LAURA Hello, Mother, I was—(*She makes a nervous gesture toward the chart on the wall.* AMANDA *leans against the shut door and stares at* LAURA *with a martyred look.*)

AMANDA Deception? Deception? (*She slowly removes her hat and gloves, continuing the swift suffering stare. She lets the hat and gloves fall on the floor—a bit of acting.*)

LAURA (*shakily*) How was the D.A.R. meeting? (AMANDA *slowly opens her purse and removes a dainty white handkerchief which she shakes out delicately and delicately touches to her lips and nostrils.*) Didn't you go to the D.A.R. meeting, Mother?

AMANDA (*faintly, almost inaudibly*) —No.—No. (*Then more forcibly.*) I did not have the strength—to go to the D.A.R. In fact, I did not have the courage! I wanted to find a hole in the ground and hide myself in it forever! (*She crosses slowly to the wall and removes the diagram of the typewriter keyboard. She holds it in front of her for a second, staring at it sweetly and sorrowfully—then bites her lips and tears it in two pieces.*)

LAURA (*faintly*) Why did you do that, Mother? (AMANDA *repeats the same procedure with the chart of the Gregg Alphabet.*) Why are you—

AMANDA Why? Why? How old are you, Laura?

LAURA Mother, you know my age.

AMANDA I thought that you were an adult; it seems that I was mistaken. (*She crosses slowly to the sofa and sinks down and stares at* LAURA).

LAURA Please don't stare at me, Mother.

AMANDA *closes her eyes and lowers her head. Count ten.*[3]

AMANDA What are we going to do, what is going to become of us, what is the future?

Count ten.

LAURA Has something happened, Mother? (AMANDA *draws a long breath and takes out the handkerchief again. Dabbing process.*) Mother, has—something happened?

AMANDA I'll be all right in a minute. I'm just bewildered—(*Count five.*)—by life. . . .

LAURA Mother, I wish that you would tell me what's happened.

AMANDA As you know, I was supposed to be inducted into my office at the D.A.R. this afternoon. (IMAGE: A SWARM OF TYPEWRITERS.) But I stopped off at Rubicam's Business College to speak to your teachers about your having a cold and ask them what progress they thought you were making down there.

LAURA Oh. . . .

AMANDA I went to the typing instructor and introduced myself as your mother. She didn't know who you were. Wingfield, she said. We don't have any such student enrolled at the school! I assured her she did, that you had been going to classes since

---

[2] Daughters of the American Revolution, a conservative women's club.
[3] Instruction to the actor to pause for ten seconds.

early in January. "I wonder," she said, "if you could be talking about that terribly shy little girl who dropped out of school after only a few days' attendance?" "No," I said, "Laura, my daughter, has been going to school every day for the past six weeks!" "Excuse me," she said. She took the attendance book out and there was your name, unmistakably printed, and all the dates you were absent until they decided that you had dropped out of school. I still said, "No, there must have been some mistake! There must have been some mix-up in the records!" And she said, "No—I remember her perfectly now. Her hand shook so that she couldn't hit the right keys! The first time we gave a speed-test, she broke down completely—was sick at the stomach and almost had to be carried into the wash-room! After that morning she never showed up any more. We phoned the house but never got any answer"—while I was working at Famous and Barr, I suppose, demonstrating those—Oh! I felt so weak I could barely keep on my feet! I had to sit down while they got me a glass of water! Fifty dollars' tuition, all of our plans—my hopes and ambitions for you—just gone up the spout, just gone up the spout like that. (LAURA *draws a long breath and gets awkwardly to her feet. She crosses to the victrola and winds it up.*) What are you doing?

LAURA Oh! (*She releases the handle and returns to her seat.*)

AMANDA Laura, where have you been going when you've gone out pretending that you were going to business college?

LAURA I've just been going out walking.

AMANDA That's not true.

LAURA It is. I just went walking.

AMANDA Walking? Walking? In winter? Deliberately courting pneumonia in that light coat? Where did you walk to, Laura?

LAURA All sorts of places—mostly in the park.

AMANDA Even after you'd started catching that cold?

LAURA It was the lesser of two evils, Mother. (IMAGE: WINTER SCENE IN PARK.) I couldn't go back up. I—threw up—on the floor!

AMANDA From half past seven till after five every day you mean to tell me you walked around in the park, because you wanted to make me think that you were still going to Rubicam's Business College?

LAURA It wasn't as bad as it sounds. I went inside places to get warmed up.

AMANDA Inside where?

LAURA I went in the art museum and the bird-houses at the Zoo. I visited the penguins every day! Sometimes I did without lunch and went to the movies. Lately I've been spending most of my afternoons in the Jewel-box, that big glass house where they raise the tropical flowers.

AMANDA You did all this to deceive me, just for the deception? (LAURA *looks down.*) Why?

LAURA Mother, when you're disappointed, you get that awful suffering look on your face, like the picture of Jesus' mother in the museum!

AMANDA Hush!

LAURA I couldn't face it.

Pause. A whisper of strings.

(LEGEND: "THE CRUST OF HUMILITY.")

AMANDA (*hopelessly fingering the huge pocketbook*) So what are we going to do the rest of our lives? Stay home and watch the parades go by? Amuse ourselves with the glass menagerie, darling? Eternally play those worn-out phonograph records your father left as a painful reminder of him? We won't have a business career—we've given that up because it gave us nervous indigestion! *(Laughs wearily.)* What is there left but dependency all our lives? I know so well what becomes of unmarried women who aren't prepared to occupy a position. I've seen such pitiful cases in the South—barely tolerated spinsters living upon the grudging patronage of sister's husband or brother's wife!—stuck away in some little mouse-trap of a room—encouraged by one in-law to visit another—little birdlike women without any nest—eating the crust of humility all their life! Is that the future that we've mapped out for ourselves? I swear it's the only alternative I can think of! It isn't a very pleasant alternative, is it? Of course—some girls *do marry.* *(*Laura *twists her hands nervously.)* Haven't you ever liked some boy?

Laura Yes. I liked one once. *(Rises.)* I came across his picture a while ago.

Amanda *(with some interest)* He gave you his picture?

Laura No, it's in the year-book.

Amanda *(disappointed)* Oh—a high-school boy.

(SCREEN IMAGE: JIM AS A HIGH-SCHOOL HERO BEARING A SILVER CUP.)

Laura Yes. His name was Jim. (Laura *lifts the heavy annual from the claw-foot table.*) Here he is in *The Pirates of Penzance.*

Amanda *(absently)* The what?

Laura The operetta the senior class put on. He had a wonderful voice and we sat across the aisle from each other Mondays, Wednesdays and Fridays in the Aud. Here he is with the silver cup for debating! See his grin?

Amanda *(absently)* He must have had a jolly disposition.

Laura He used to call me—Blue Roses.

(IMAGE: BLUE ROSES.)

Amanda Why did he call you such a name as that?

Laura When I had that attack of pleurosis—he asked me what was the matter when I came back. I said pleurosis—he thought that I said Blue Roses! So that's what he always called me after that. Whenever he saw me, he'd holler, "Hello, Blue Roses!" I didn't care for the girl that he went out with. Emily Meisenbach. Emily was the best-dressed girl at Soldan. She never struck me, though, as being sincere. . . . It says in the Personal Section—they're engaged. That's—six years ago! They must be married by now.

Amanda Girls that aren't cut out for business careers usually wind up married to some nice man. *(Gets up with a spark of revival.)* Sister, that's what you'll do.

Laura *utters a startled, doubtful laugh. She reaches quickly for a piece of glass.*

Laura But, Mother—

Amanda Yes? *(Crossing to photograph.)*

Laura *(in a tone of frightened apology)* I'm—crippled!

(IMAGE: SCREEN.)

Amanda Nonsense! Laura, I've told you never, never to use that word. Why, you're not crippled, you just have a little defect—hardly noticeable, even! When people have some slight disadvantage like that, they cultivate other things to make up for it—develop charm—and vivacity—and—*charm!* That's all you have to do! *(She turns again to the photograph.)* One thing your father had *plenty* of—was *charm!*

TOM *motions to the fiddle in the wings.*

(THE SCENE FADES OUT WITH MUSIC.)

SCENE III.

(LEGEND ON SCREEN: "AFTER THE FIASCO—")

TOM *speaks from the fire-escape landing.*

TOM After the fiasco at Rubicam's Business College, the idea of getting a gentleman caller for Laura began to play a more important part in Mother's calculations. It became an obsession. Like some archetype of the universal unconscious, the image of the gentleman caller haunted our small apartment. . . . (IMAGE: YOUNG MAN AT DOOR WITH FLOWERS.) An evening at home rarely passed without some allusion to this image, this spectre, this hope. . . . Even when he wasn't mentioned, his presence hung in Mother's preoccupied look and in my sister's frightened, apologetic manner— hung like a sentence passed upon the Wingfields! Mother was a woman of action as well as words. She began to take logical steps in the planned direction. Late that winter and in the early spring—realizing that extra money would be needed to properly feather the nest and plume the bird—she conducted a vigorous campaign on the telephone, roping in subscribers to one of those magazines for matrons called *The Home-maker's Companion*, the type of journal that features the serialized sublimations of ladies of letters who think in terms of delicate cup-like breasts, slim, tapering waists, rich, creamy thighs, eyes like wood-smoke in autumn, fingers that soothe and caress like strains of music, bodies as powerful as Etruscan sculpture.

(SCREEN IMAGE: GLAMOR MAGAZINE COVER.)

AMANDA *enters with phone on long extension cord. She is spotted in the dim stage.*

AMANDA Ida Scott? This is Amanda Wingfield! We *missed* you at the D.A.R. last Monday! I said to myself: She's probably suffering with that sinus condition! How is that sinus condition? Horrors! Heaven have mercy!—You're a Christian martyr, yes, that's what you are, a Christian martyr! Well, I just now happened to notice that your subscription to the *Companion's* about to expire! Yes, it expires with the next issue, honey!—just when that wonderful new serial by Bessie Mae Hopper is getting off to such an exciting start. Oh, honey, it's something that you can't miss! You remember how *Gone With the Wind* took everybody by storm? You simply couldn't go out if you hadn't read it. All everybody *talked* was Scarlett O'Hara. Well, this is a book that critics already compare to *Gone With the Wind*. It's the *Gone With the Wind* of the post–World War generation!—What?—Burning?—Oh, honey, don't let them burn, go take a look in the oven and I'll hold the wire! Heavens—I think she's hung up!

(DIM OUT.)

(LEGEND ON SCREEN: "YOU THINK I'M IN LOVE WITH CONTINENTAL SHOEMAKERS?")

Before the stage is lighted, the violent voices of TOM *and* AMANDA *are heard.*
  They are quarreling behind the portieres. In front of them stands LAURA *with clenched hands and panicky expression.*
  A clear pool of light on her figure throughout this scene.

TOM What in Christ's name am I—

AMANDA *(shrilly)* Don't you use that—

TOM Supposed to do!

AMANDA Expression! Not in my—

TOM Ohhh!

AMANDA Presence! Have you gone out of your senses?

TOM I have, that's true, *driven* out!

AMANDA What is the matter with you, you—big—big—IDIOT!

TOM Look—I've got *no thing*, no single thing—

AMANDA Lower your voice!

TOM In my life here that I can call my OWN! Everything is—

AMANDA Stop that shouting!

TOM Yesterday you confiscated my books! You had the nerve to—

AMANDA I took that horrible novel back to the library—yes! That hideous book by that insane Mr. Lawrence. (TOM *laughs wildly.*) I cannot control the output of diseased minds or people who cater to them— (TOM *laughs still more wildly.*) BUT I WON'T ALLOW SUCH FILTH BROUGHT INTO MY HOUSE! No, no, no, no, no!

TOM House, house! Who pays rent on it, who makes a slave of himself to—

AMANDA *(fairly screeching)* Don't you DARE to—

TOM No, no, I mustn't say things! *I've* got to just—

AMANDA Let me tell you—

TOM I don't want to hear any more! *(He tears the portieres open. The upstage area is lit with a turgid smoky red glow.)*

AMANDA's *hair is in metal curlers and she wears a very old bathrobe, much too large for her slight figure, a relic of the faithless Mr. Wingfield.*

An upright typewriter and a wild disarray of manuscripts is on the drop-leaf table. The quarrel was probably precipitated by AMANDA's *interruption of his creative labor. A chair lying overthrown on the floor.*

Their gesticulating shadows are cast on the ceiling by the fiery glow.

AMANDA You *will* hear more, you—

TOM No, I won't hear more, I'm going out!

AMANDA You come right back in—

TOM Out, out, out! Because I'm—

AMANDA Come back here, Tom Wingfield! I'm not through talking to you!

TOM Oh, go—

LAURA *(desperately)* —Tom!

AMANDA You're going to listen, and no more insolence from you! I'm at the end of my patience! *(He comes back toward her.)*

TOM What do you think I'm at? Aren't I supposed to have any patience to reach the end of, Mother? I know, I know. It seems unimportant to you, what I'm *doing*—what I *want* to do—having a little *difference* between them! You don't think that—

AMANDA I think you've been doing things that you're ashamed of. That's why you act like this. I don't believe that you go every night to the movies. Nobody goes to the movies night after night. Nobody in their right minds goes to the movies as often as you pretend to. People don't go to the movies at nearly midnight, and movies don't let out at two A.M. Come in stumbling. Muttering to yourself like a maniac! You get three hours sleep and then go to work. Oh, I can picture the way you're doing down there. Moping, doping, because you're in no condition!

TOM (*wildly*) No, I'm in no condition!

AMANDA What right have you got to jeopardize your job? Jeopardize the security of us all? How do you think we'd manage if you were—

TOM Listen! You think I'm crazy *about* the *warehouse?* (*He bends fiercely toward her slight figure.*) You think I'm in love with the Continental Shoemakers? You think I want to spend fifty-five *years* down there in that—*celotex interior!* with—*fluorescent— tubes!* Look! I'd rather somebody picked up a crowbar and battered out my brains— than go back mornings! I *go!* Every time you come in yelling that God damn *"Rise and Shine!" "Rise and Shine!"* I say to myself "How *lucky dead* people are!" But I get up. I *go!* For sixty-five dollars a month I give up all that I dream of doing and being *ever!* And you say self—*self's* all I ever think of. Why, listen, if self is what I thought of, Mother, I'd be where he is—GONE! (*Pointing to father's picture.*) As far as the system of transportation reaches! (*He starts past her. She grabs his arm.*) Don't grab me, Mother!

AMANDA Where are you going?

TOM I'm going to the *movies!*

AMANDA I don't believe that lie!

TOM (*crouching toward her, overtowering her tiny figure. She backs away, gasping*) I'm going to opium dens! Yes, opium dens, dens of vice and criminals' hang-outs, Mother. I've joined the Hogan gang, I'm a hired assassin, I carry a tommy-gun in a violin case! I run a string of cat-houses in the Valley! They call me Killer, Killer Wingfield, I'm leading a double-life, a simple, honest warehouse worker by day, by night, a dynamic *czar* of the *underworld, Mother.* I go to gambling casinos, I spin away fortunes on the roulette table! I wear a patch over one eye and a false mustache, sometimes I put on green whiskers. On those occasions they call me—*El Diablo!* Oh, I could tell you things to make you sleepless! My enemies plan to dynamite this place. They're going to blow us all sky-high some night! I'll be glad, very happy, and so will you! You'll go up, up on a broomstick, over Blue Mountain with seventeen gentlemen callers! You ugly—babbling old—*witch.* . . . (*He goes through a series of violent, clumsy movements, seizing his overcoat, lunging to the door, pulling it fiercely open. The women watch him, aghast. His arm catches in the sleeve of the coat as he struggles to pull it on. For a moment he is pinioned by the bulky garment. With an outraged groan he tears the coat off again, splitting the shoulders of it, and hurls it across the room. It strikes against the shelf of* LAURA's *glass collection, there is a tinkle of shattering glass.* LAURA *cries out as if wounded.*)

(MUSIC LEGEND: "THE GLASS MENAGERIE.")

LAURA (*shrilly*) My glass!—menagerie. . . . (*She covers her face and turns away.*)

But AMANDA *is still stunned and stupefied by the "ugly witch" so that she barely notices this occurrence. Now she recovers her speech.*

AMANDA (*in an awful voice*) I won't speak to you—until you apologize! (*She crosses through portieres and draws them together behind her.* TOM *is left with* LAURA. LAURA *clings weakly to the mantel with her face averted.* TOM *stares at her stupidly for a moment. Then he crosses to shelf. Drops awkwardly to his knees to collect the fallen glass, glancing at* LAURA *as if he would speak but couldn't.*)

"The Glass Menagerie" steals in as the Scene Dims Out.

SCENE IV.

The interior is dark. Faint light in the alley.

A deep-voiced bell in a church is tolling the hour of five as the scene commences.

TOM *appears at the top of the alley. After each solemn boom of the bell in the tower, he shakes a little noise-maker or rattle as if to express the tiny spasm of man in contrast to the sustained power and dignity of the Almighty. This and the unsteadiness of his advance make it evident that he has been drinking.*

As he climbs the few steps to the fire-escape landing light steals up inside. LAURA *appears in night-dress, observing* TOM's *empty bed in the front room.*

TOM *fishes in his pockets for the door-key, removing a motley assortment of articles in the search, including a perfect shower of movie-ticket stubs and an empty bottle. At last he finds the key, but just as he is about to insert it, it slips from his fingers. He strikes a match and crouches below the door.*

TOM *(bitterly)* One crack—and it falls through!

LAURA *opens the door.*

LAURA Tom! Tom, what are you doing?

TOM Looking for a door-key.

LAURA Where have you been all this time?

TOM I have been to the movies.

LAURA All this time at the movies?

TOM There was a very long program. There was a Garbo picture and a Mickey Mouse and a travelogue and a newsreel and a preview of coming attractions. And there was an organ solo and a collection for the milk-fund—simultaneously—which ended up in a terrible fight between a fat lady and an usher!

LAURA *(innocently)* Did you have to stay through everything?

TOM Of course! And, oh, I forgot! There was a big stage show! The headliner on this stage show was Malvolio the Magician. He performed wonderful tricks, many of them, such as pouring water back and forth between pitchers. First it turned to wine and then it turned to beer and then it turned to whiskey. I know it was whiskey it finally turned into because he needed somebody to come up out of the audience to help him, and I came up—both shows! It was Kentucky Straight Bourbon. A very generous fellow, he gave souvenirs. *(He pulls from his back pocket a shimmering rainbow-colored scarf.)* He gave me this. This is his magic scarf. You can have it, Laura. You wave it over a canary cage and you get a bowl of gold-fish. You wave it over the gold-fish bowl and they fly away canaries. . . .But the wonderfullest trick of all was the coffin trick. We nailed him into a coffin and he got out of the coffin without removing one nail. *(He has come inside.)* There is a trick that would come in handy for me—get me out of this 2 by 4 situation! *(Flops onto bed and starts removing shoes.)*

LAURA Tom—Shhh!

TOM What you shushing me for?

LAURA You'll wake up Mother.

TOM Goody, goody! Pay 'er back for all those "Rise an' Shines." *(Lies down, groaning.)* You know it don't take much intelligence to get yourself into a nailed-up coffin, Laura. But who in hell ever got himself out of one without removing one nail?

As if in answer, the father's grinning photograph lights up.

(SCENE DIMS OUT.)

Immediately following: The church bell is heard striking six. At the sixth stroke the alarm clock goes off in AMANDA's *room, and after a few moments we hear her calling: "Rise and Shine! Rise and Shine! Laura, go tell your brother to rise and shine!"*

TOM *(sitting up slowly)* I'll rise—but I won't shine.

The light increases.

AMANDA Laura, tell your brother his coffee is ready.

LAURA *slips into front room.*

LAURA Tom! it's nearly seven. Don't make Mother nervous. *(He stares at her stupidly. Beseechingly.)* Tom, speak to Mother this morning. Make up with her, apologize, speak to her!

TOM She won't to me. It's her that started not speaking.

LAURA If you just say you're sorry she'll start speaking.

TOM Her not speaking—is that such a tragedy?

LAURA Please—please!

AMANDA *(calling from kitchenette)* Laura, are you going to do what I asked you to do, or do I have to get dressed and go out myself?

LAURA Going, going—soon as I get on my coat! *(She pulls on a shapeless felt hat with nervous, jerky movement, pleadingly glancing at* TOM. *Rushes awkwardly for coat. The coat is one of* AMANDA's, *inaccurately made-over, the sleeves too short for* LAURA.) Butter and what else?

AMANDA *(entering upstage)* Just butter. Tell them to charge it.

LAURA Mother, they make such faces when I do that.

AMANDA Sticks and stones may break my bones, but the expression on Mr. Garfinkel's face won't harm us! Tell your brother his coffee is getting cold.

LAURA *(at door)* Do what I asked you, will you, will you, Tom?

He looks sullenly away.

AMANDA Laura, go now or just don't go at all!

LAURA *(rushing out)* Going—going! *(A second later she cries out.* TOM *springs up and crosses to the door.* AMANDA *rushes anxiously in.* TOM *opens the door.)*

TOM Laura?

LAURA I'm all right. I slipped, but I'm all right.

AMANDA *(peering anxiously after her)* If anyone breaks a leg on those fire-escape steps, the landlord ought to be sued for every cent he possesses! *(She shuts door. Remembers she isn't speaking and returns to other room.)*

As TOM *enters listlessly for his coffee, she turns her back to him and stands rigidly facing the window on the gloomy gray vault of the areaway. Its light on her face with its aged but childish features is cruelly sharp, satirical as a Daumier print.*

(MUSIC UNDER: "AVE MARIA.")

TOM *glances sheepishly but sullenly at her averted figure and slumps at the table. The coffee is scalding hot; he sips it and gasps and spits it back in the cup. At his gasp,* AMANDA *catches her breath and half turns. Then catches herself and turns back to window.*

TOM *blows on his coffee, glancing sidewise at his mother. She clears her throat.* TOM *clears his. He starts to rise. Sinks back down again, scratches his head, clears his throat again.* AMANDA *coughs.* TOM *raises his cup in both hands to blow on it, his eyes staring over the rim of it at his mother for several moments. Then he slowly sets the cup down and awkwardly and hesitantly rises from the chair.*

TOM *(hoarsely)* Mother. I—I apologize. Mother. (AMANDA *draws a quick, shuddering breath. Her face works grotesquely. She breaks into childlike tears.)* I'm sorry for what I said, for everything that I said, I didn't mean it.

AMANDA *(sobbingly)* My devotion has made me a witch and so I make myself hateful to my children!

TOM No, you *don't.*

AMANDA I worry so much, don't sleep, it makes me nervous!

TOM *(gently)* I understand that.

AMANDA I've had to put up a solitary battle all these years. But you're my right-hand bower! Don't fall down, don't fail!

TOM *(gently)* I try, Mother.

AMANDA *(with great enthusiasm)* Try and you will SUCCEED! *(The notion makes her breathless.)* Why, you—you're just *full* of natural endowments! Both of my children— they're *unusual* children! Don't you think I know it? I'm so—*proud!* Happy and—feel I've—so much to be thankful for but—Promise me one thing, son!

TOM What, Mother?

AMANDA Promise, son, you'll—never be a drunkard!

TOM *(turns to her grinning)* I will never be a drunkard, Mother.

AMANDA That's what frightened me so, that you'd be drinking! Eat a bowl of Purina!

TOM Just coffee, Mother.

AMANDA Shredded wheat biscuit?

TOM No. No, Mother, just coffee.

AMANDA You can't put in a day's work on an empty stomach. You've got ten minutes— don't gulp! Drinking too-hot liquids makes cancer of the stomach. . . . Put cream in.

TOM No, thank you.

AMANDA To cool it.

TOM No! No, thank you, I want it black.

AMANDA I know, but it's not good for you. We have to do all that we can to build ourselves up. In these trying times we live in, all that we have to cling to is—each other. . . . That's why it's so important to—Tom, I—I sent out your sister so I could discuss something with you. If you hadn't spoken I would have spoken to you. *(Sits down.)*

TOM *(gently)* What is it, Mother, that you want to discuss?

AMANDA Laura!

TOM *puts his cup down slowly.*

(LEGEND ON SCREEN: "LAURA.")

(MUSIC: "THE GLASS MENAGERIE.")

TOM —Oh.—Laura . . .

AMANDA *(touching his sleeve)* You know how Laura is. So quiet but—still water runs deep! She notices things and I think she—broods about them. (TOM *looks up.)* A few days ago I came in and she was crying.

TOM What about?

AMANDA You.

TOM Me?

AMANDA She has an idea that you're not happy here.

TOM What gave her that idea?

AMANDA What gives her any idea? However, you do act strangely. I—I'm not criticizing, understand *that!* I know your ambitions do not lie in the warehouse, that like everybody in the whole wide world—you've had to—make sacrifices, but—Tom—Tom—life's not easy, it calls for—Spartan endurance! There's so many things in my heart that I cannot describe to you! I've never told you but I—*loved* your father. . . .

TOM *(gently)* I know that, Mother.

AMANDA And you—when I see you taking after his ways! Staying out late—and—well, you *had* been drinking the night you were in that—terrifying condition! Laura says that you hate the apartment and that you go out nights to get away from it! Is that true, Tom?

TOM No. You say there's 'so much in your heart that you can't describe to me. That's true of me, too. There's so much in my heart that I can't describe to *you!* So let's respect each other's—

AMANDA But, why—*why*, Tom—are you always so *restless?* Where do you go to, nights?

TOM I—go to the movies.

AMANDA Why do you go to the movies so much, Tom?

TOM I go to the movies because—I like adventure. Adventure is something I don't have much of at work, so I go to the movies.

AMANDA But, Tom, you go to the movies *entirely* too *much!*

TOM I like a lot of adventure.

AMANDA *looks baffled, then hurt. As the familiar inquisition resumes he becomes hard and impatient again.* AMANDA *slips back into her querulous attitude toward him.*

(IMAGE ON SCREEN: SAILING VESSEL WITH JOLLY ROGER.)

AMANDA Most young men find adventure in their careers.

TOM Then most young men are not employed in a warehouse.

AMANDA The world is full of young men employed in warehouses and offices and factories.

TOM Do all of them find adventure in their careers?

AMANDA They do or they do without it! Not everybody has a craze for adventure.

TOM Man is by instinct a lover, a hunter, a fighter, and none of those instincts are given much play at the warehouse!

AMANDA Man is by instinct! Don't quote instinct to me! Instinct is something that people have got away from! It belongs to animals! Christian adults don't want it!

TOM What do Christian adults want, then, Mother?

AMANDA Superior things! Things of the mind and the spirit! Only animals have to satisfy instincts! Surely your aims are somewhat higher than theirs! Than monkeys—pigs—

TOM I reckon they're not.

AMANDA You're joking. However, that isn't what I wanted to discuss.

TOM *(rising)* I haven't much time.

AMANDA *(pushing his shoulders)* Sit down.

TOM You want me to punch in red at the warehouse, Mother?

AMANDA You have five minutes. I want to talk about Laura.

TOM All right! What about Laura?

AMANDA We have to be making plans and provisions for her. She's older than you, two years, and nothing has happened. She just drifts along doing nothing. It frightens me terribly how she just drifts along.

TOM I guess she's the type that people call home-girls.

AMANDA There's no such type, and if there is, it's a pity! That is unless the home is hers, with a husband!

TOM What?

AMANDA Oh, I can see the handwriting on the wall as plain as I see the nose in front of my face! It's terrifying! More and more you remind me of your father! He was out all hours without explanation—Then *left*! *Goodbye*! And me with a bag to hold. I saw that letter you got from the Merchant Marine. I know what you're dreaming of. I'm not standing here blindfolded. Very well, then. Then *do* it! But not till there's somebody to take your place.

TOM What do you mean?

AMANDA I mean that as soon as Laura has got somebody to take care of her, married, a home of her own, independent—why, then you'll be free to go wherever you please, on land, on sea, whichever way the wind blows! But until that time you've got to look out for your sister. I don't say me because I'm old and don't matter! I say for your sister because she's young and dependent. I put her in business college—a dismal failure! Frightened her so it made her sick to her stomach. I took her over to the Young People's League at the church. Another fiasco. She spoke to nobody, nobody spoke to her. Now all she does is fool with those pieces of glass and play those worn-out records. What kind of a life is that for a girl to lead?

TOM What can I do about it?

AMANDA Overcome selfishness! Self, self, self is all that you ever think of! (TOM *springs up and crosses to get his coat. It is ugly and bulky. He pulls on a cap with earmuffs.*) Where is your muffler? Put your wool muffler on! (*He snatches it angrily from the closet and tosses it around his neck and pulls both ends tight.*) Tom! I haven't said what I had in mind to ask you.

TOM I'm too late to—

AMANDA (*catching his arm—very importunately. Then shyly.*) Down at the warehouse, aren't there some—nice young men?

TOM No!

AMANDA There *must* be—*some* . . .

TOM Mother—

Gesture.

AMANDA Find out one that's clean-living—doesn't drink and—ask him out for sister!

TOM What?

AMANDA For *sister*! To *meet*! Get *acquainted*!

TOM (*stamping to door*) Oh, my go-osh!

AMANDA Will you? (*He opens door. Imploringly.*) Will you? (*He starts down.*) Will you? *Will* you, dear?

TOM (*calling back*) · YES!

AMANDA *closes the door hesitantly and with a troubled but faintly hopeful expression.*

(SCREEN IMAGE: GLAMOR MAGAZINE COVER.)

Spot AMANDA *at phone.*

AMANDA Ella Cartwright? This is Amanda Wingfield! How are you, honey? How is that kidney condition? *(Count five.)* Horrors! *(Count five.)* You're a Christian martyr, yes, honey, that's what you are, a Christian martyr! Well, I just happened to notice in my little red book that your subscription to the *Companion* has just run out! I knew that you wouldn't want to miss out on the wonderful serial starting in this new issue. It's by Bessie Mae Hopper, the first thing she's written since *Honeymoon for Three.* Wasn't that a strange and interesting story? Well, this one is even lovelier, I believe. It has a sophisticated society background. It's all about the horsey set on Long Island!

(FADE OUT.)

SCENE V.

(LEGEND ON SCREEN: "ANNUNCIATION.")

Fade with music.
   It is early dusk of a spring evening. Supper has just been finished in the Wingfield apartment. AMANDA *and* LAURA *in light colored dresses are removing dishes from the table, in the upstage area, which is shadowy, their movements formalized almost as a dance or ritual, their moving forms as pale and silent as moths.*
   TOM, *in white shirt and trousers, rises from the table and crosses toward the fire-escape.*

AMANDA *(as he passes her)* Son, will you do me a favor?
TOM What?
AMANDA Comb your hair! You look so pretty when your hair is combed! (TOM *slouches on sofa with evening paper. Enormous caption "Franco Triumphs."*) There is only one respect in which I would like you to emulate your father.
TOM What respect is that?
AMANDA The care he always took of his appearance. He never allowed himself to look untidy. *(He throws down the paper and crosses to fire-escape.)* Where are you going?
TOM I'm going out to smoke.
AMANDA You smoke too much. A pack a day at fifteen cents a pack. How much would that amount to in a month? Thirty times fifteen is how much, Tom? Figure it out and you will be astounded at what you could save. Enough to give you a night-school course in accounting at Washington U! Just think what a wonderful thing that would be for you, son!

TOM *is unmoved by the thought.*

TOM I'd rather smoke. *(He steps out on landing, letting the screen door slam.)*
AMANDA *(sharply)* I know! That's the tragedy of it. . . . *(Alone, she turns to look at her husband's picture.)*

(DANCE MUSIC: "ALL THE WORLD IS WAITING FOR THE SUNRISE!")

TOM *(to the audience)* Across the alley from us was the Paradise Dance Hall. On evenings in spring the windows and doors were open and the music came outdoors. Sometimes the lights were turned out except for a large glass sphere that hung from the ceiling. It would turn slowly about and filter the dusk with delicate rainbow colors. Then the orchestra played a waltz or a tango, something that had a slow and sensuous rhythm. Couples would come outside, to the relative privacy of the alley. You could see them kissing behind ash-pits and telephone poles. This was the compensation for lives that passed like mine, without any change or adventure. Adventure and change were imminent in this year. They were waiting around the corner for all these kids. Suspended in the mist over Berchtesgaden, caught in the folds of Chamberlain's umbrella[4]— In Spain there was Guernica! But here there was only hot swing music and liquor, dance halls, bars, and movies, and sex that hung in the gloom like a chandelier and flooded the world with brief, deceptive rainbows. . . . All the world was waiting for bombardments!

AMANDA *turns from the picture and comes outside.*

AMANDA *(sighing)* A fire-escape landing's a poor excuse for a porch. *(She spreads a newspaper on a step and sits down, gracefully and demurely as if she were settling into a swing on a Mississippi veranda.)* What are you looking at?
TOM The moon.
AMANDA Is there a moon this evening?
TOM It's rising over Garfinkel's Delicatessen.
AMANDA So it is! A little silver slipper of a moon. Have you made a wish on it yet?
TOM Um-hum.
AMANDA What did you wish for?
TOM That's a secret.
AMANDA A secret, huh? Well, I won't tell mine either. I will be just as mysterious as you.
TOM I bet I can guess what yours is.
AMANDA Is my head so transparent?
TOM You're not a sphinx.
AMANDA No, I don't have secrets. I'll tell you what I wished for on the moon. Success and happiness for my precious children! I wish for that whenever there's a moon, and when there isn't a moon, I wish for it, too.
TOM I thought perhaps you wished for a gentleman caller.
AMANDA Why do you say that?
TOM Don't you remember asking me to fetch one?
AMANDA I remember suggesting that it would be nice for your sister if you brought home some nice young man from the warehouse. I think I've made that suggestion more than once.
TOM Yes, you have made it repeatedly.
AMANDA Well?
TOM We are going to have one.
AMANDA *What?*
TOM A gentleman caller!

(THE ANNUNCIATION IS CELEBRATED WITH MUSIC.)

AMANDA *rises.*

(IMAGE ON SCREEN: CALLER WITH BOUQUET.)

---

[4] British Prime Minister Neville Chamberlain met with Adolf Hitler at Berchtesgaden, Hitler's private mountain retreat, in 1938.

AMANDA You mean you have asked some nice young man to come over?

TOM Yep. I've asked him to dinner.

AMANDA You really did?

TOM I did!

AMANDA You did, and did he—*accept?*

TOM He did!

AMANDA Well, well—well, well! That's—lovely!

TOM I thought that you would be pleased.

AMANDA It's definite, then?

TOM Very definite.

AMANDA Soon?

TOM Very soon.

AMANDA For heaven's sake, stop putting on and tell me some things, will you?

TOM What things do you want me to tell you?

AMANDA *Naturally* I would like to know when he's *coming!*

TOM He's coming tomorrow.

AMANDA *Tomorrow?*

TOM Yep. Tomorrow.

AMANDA But, Tom!

TOM Yes, Mother?

AMANDA Tomorrow gives me no time!

TOM Time for what?

AMANDA Preparations! Why didn't you phone me at once, as soon as you asked him, the minute that he accepted? Then, don't you see, I could have been getting ready!

TOM You don't have to make any fuss.

AMANDA Oh, Tom, Tom, Tom, of course I have to make a fuss! I want things nice, not sloppy! Not thrown together. I'll certainly have to do some fast thinking, won't I?

TOM I don't see why you have to think at all.

AMANDA You just don't know. We can't have a gentleman caller in a pig-sty! All my wedding silver has to be polished, the monogrammed table linen ought to be laundered! The windows have to be washed and fresh curtains put up. And how about clothes? We have to *wear* something, don't we?

TOM Mother, this boy is no one to make a fuss over!

AMANDA Do you realize he's the first young man we've introduced to your sister? It's terrible, dreadful, disgraceful that poor little sister has never received a single gentleman caller! Tom, come inside! *(She opens the screen door.)*

TOM What for?

AMANDA I want to ask you some things.

TOM If you're going to make such a fuss, I'll call it off, I'll tell him not to come.

AMANDA You certainly won't do anything of the kind. Nothing offends people worse than broken engagements. It simply means I'll have to work like a Turk! We won't be brilliant, but we'll pass inspection. Come on inside. *(*TOM *follows, groaning.)* Sit down.

TOM Any particular place you would like me to sit?

AMANDA Thank heavens I've got that new sofa! I'm also making payments on a floor lamp I'll have sent out! And put the chintz covers on, they'll brighten things up! Of course I'd hoped to have these walls re-papered. . . . What is the young man's name?

TOM His name is O'Connor.

AMANDA That, of course, means fish—tomorrow is Friday! I'll have that salmon loaf—with Durkee's dressing! What does he do? He works at the warehouse?

TOM Of course! How else would I—

AMANDA Tom, he—doesn't drink?

TOM Why do you ask me that?

AMANDA Your father *did!*

TOM Don't get started on that!

AMANDA He *does* drink, then?

TOM Not that I know of!

AMANDA Make sure, be certain! The last thing I want for my daughter's a boy who drinks!

TOM Aren't you being a little premature? Mr. O'Connor has not yet appeared on the scene!

AMANDA But will tomorrow. To meet your sister, and what do I know about his character? Nothing! Old maids are better off than wives of drunkards!

TOM Oh, my God!

AMANDA Be still!

TOM *(leaning forward to whisper)* Lots of fellows meet girls whom they don't marry!

AMANDA Oh, talk sensibly, Tom—and don't be sarcastic! *(She has gotten a hairbrush.)*

TOM What are you doing?

AMANDA I'm brushing that cow-lick down! What is this young man's position at the warehouse?

TOM *(submitting grimly to the brush and the interrogation)* This young man's position is that of a shipping clerk, Mother.

AMANDA Sounds to me like a fairly responsible job, the sort of a job *you* would be in if you just had more *get-up.* What is his salary? Have you got any idea?

TOM I would judge it to be approximately eighty-five dollars a month.

AMANDA Well—not princely, but—

TOM Twenty more than I make.

AMANDA Yes, how well I know! But for a family man, eighty-five dollars a month is not much more than you can just get by on. . . .

TOM Yes, but Mr. O'Connor is not a family man.

AMANDA He might be, mightn't he? Some time in the future?

TOM I see. Plans and provisions.

AMANDA You are the only young man that I know of who ignores the fact that the future becomes the present, the present the past, and the past turns into everlasting regret if you don't plan for it!

TOM I will think that over and see what I can make of it.

AMANDA Don't be supercilious with your mother! Tell me some more about this—what do you call him?

TOM James D. O'Connor. The D. is for Delaney.

AMANDA Irish on *both* sides! *Gracious!* And doesn't drink?

TOM Shall I call him up and ask him right this minute?

AMANDA The only way to find out about those things is to make discreet inquiries at the proper moment. When I was a girl in Blue Mountain and it was suspected that a young man drank, the girl whose attentions he had been receiving, if any girl *was,* would sometimes speak to the minister of his church, or rather her father would if her father was living, and sort of feel him out on the young man's character. That is the way such things are discreetly handled to keep a young woman from making a tragic mistake!

TOM Then how did you happen to make a tragic mistake?

AMANDA That innocent look of your father's had everyone fooled! He *smiled*—the world was *enchanted!* No girl can do worse than put herself at the mercy of a handsome appearance! I hope that Mr. O'Connor is not too good-looking.

TOM No, he's not too good-looking. He's covered with freckles and hasn't too much of a nose.

AMANDA He's not right-down homely, though?

TOM Not right-down homely. Just medium homely. I'd say.

AMANDA Character's what to look for in a man.

TOM That's what I've always said, Mother.

AMANDA You've never said anything of the kind and I suspect you would never give it a thought.

TOM Don't be suspicious of me.

AMANDA At least I hope he's the type that's up and coming.

TOM I think he really goes in for self-improvement.

AMANDA What reason have you to think so?

TOM He goes to night school.

AMANDA (beaming) Splendid! What does he do, I mean study?

TOM Radio engineering and public speaking!

AMANDA Then he has visions of being advanced in the world! Any young man who studies public speaking is aiming to have an executive job some day! And radio engineering? A thing for the future! Both of these facts are very illuminating. Those are the sort of things that a mother should know concerning any young man who comes to call on her daughter. Seriously or—not.

TOM One little warning. He doesn't know about Laura. I didn't let on that we had dark ulterior motives. I just said, why don't you come have dinner with us? He said okay and that was the whole conversation.

AMANDA I bet it was! You're eloquent as an oyster. However, he'll know about Laura when he gets here. When he sees how lovely and sweet and pretty she is, he'll thank his lucky stars he was asked to dinner.

TOM Mother, you mustn't expect too much of Laura.

AMANDA What do you mean?

TOM Laura seems all those things to you and me because she's ours and we love her. We don't even notice she's crippled any more.

AMANDA Don't say crippled! You know that I never allow that word to be used!

TOM But face facts, Mother. She is and—that's not all—

AMANDA What do you mean "not all"?

TOM Laura is very different from other girls.

AMANDA I think the difference is all to her advantage.

TOM Not quite all—in the eyes of others—strangers—she's terribly shy and lives in a world of her own and those things make her seem a little peculiar to people outside the house.

AMANDA Don't say peculiar.

TOM Face the facts. She is.

(THE DANCE-HALL MUSIC CHANGES TO A TANGO THAT HAS A MINOR AND SOMEWHAT OMINOUS TONE.)

AMANDA In what way is she peculiar—may I ask?

TOM (gently) She lives in a world of her own—a world of—little glass ornaments, Mother. . . . (Gets up. AMANDA remains holding brush, looking at him, troubled.) She plays old phonograph records and—that's about all—(He glances at himself in the mirror and crosses to door.)

AMANDA *(sharply)* Where are you going?

TOM I'm going to the movies. *(Out screen door.)*

AMANDA Not to the movies, every night to the movies! *(Follows quickly to screen door.)* I don't believe you always go to the movies! *(He is gone.* AMANDA *looks worriedly after him for a moment. Then vitality and optimism return and she turns from the door. Crossing to portieres.)* Laura! Laura! *(*LAURA *answers from kitchenette.)*

LAURA Yes, Mother.

AMANDA Let those dishes go and come in front! *(*LAURA *appears with dish towel. Gaily)* Laura, come here and make a wish on the moon!

LAURA *(entering)* Moon—moon?

AMANDA A little silver slipper of a moon. Look over your left shoulder, Laura, and make a wish! *(*LAURA *looks faintly puzzled as if called out of sleep.* AMANDA *seizes her shoulders and turns her at an angle by the door.)* No! Now, darling, *wish!*

LAURA What shall I wish for, Mother?

AMANDA *(her voice trembling and her eyes suddenly filling with tears)* Happiness! Good Fortune!

The violin rises and the stage dims out.

SCENE VI.

(IMAGE: HIGH-SCHOOL HERO.)

TOM And so the following evening I brought Jim home to dinner. I had known Jim slightly in high school. In high school Jim was a hero. He had tremendous Irish good nature and vitality with the scrubbed and polished look of white chinaware. He seemed to move in a continual spotlight. He was a star in basketball, captain of the debating club, president of the senior class and the glee club and he sang the male lead in the annual light operas. He was always running or bounding, never just walking. He seemed always at the point of defeating the law of gravity. He was shooting with such velocity through his adolescence that you would logically expect him to arrive at nothing short of the White House by the time he was thirty. But Jim apparently ran into more interference after his graduation from Soldan. His speed had definitely slowed. Six years after he left high school he was holding a job that wasn't much better than mine.

(IMAGE: CLERK.)

He was the only one at the warehouse with whom I was on friendly terms. I was valuable to him as someone who could remember his former glory, who had seen him win basketball games and the silver cup in debating. He knew of my secret practice of retiring to a cabinet of the washroom to work on poems when business was slack in the warehouse. He called me Shakespeare. And while the other boys in the warehouse regarded me with suspicious hostility, Jim took a humorous attitude toward me. Gradually his attitude affected the others, their hostility wore off and they also began to smile at me as people smile at an oddly fashioned dog who trots across their path at some distance.

I knew that Jim and Laura had known each other at Soldan, and I had heard Laura speak admiringly of his voice. I didn't know if Jim remembered her or not. In high school Laura had been as unobtrusive as Jim had been astonishing. If he did remember Laura, it was not as my sister, for when I asked him to dinner, he grinned and said, "You know, Shakespeare, I never thought of you as having folks!"

He was about to discover that I did. . . .

(LIGHT UP STAGE.)

(LEGEND ON SCREEN: "THE ACCENT OF A COMING FOOT.")

Friday evening. It is about five o'clock of a late spring evening which comes "scattering poems in the sky."

A delicate lemony light is in the Wingfield apartment.

AMANDA *has worked like a Turk in preparation for the gentleman caller. The results are astonishing. The new floor lamp with its rose-silk shade is in place, a colored paper lantern conceals the broken light fixture in the ceiling, new billowing white curtains are at the windows, chintz covers are on chairs and sofa, a pair of new sofa pillows make their initial appearance.*

Open boxes and tissue paper are scattered on the floor.

LAURA *stands in the middle with lifted arms while* AMANDA *crouches before her, adjusting the hem of the new dress, devout and ritualistic. The dress is colored and designed by memory. The arrangement of* LAURA's *hair is changed; it is softer and more becoming. A fragile, unearthly prettiness has come out in* LAURA: *she is like a piece of translucent glass touched by light, given a momentary radiance, not actual, not lasting.*

AMANDA *(impatiently)* Why are you trembling?

LAURA Mother, you've made me so nervous!

AMANDA How have I made you nervous?

LAURA By all this fuss! You make it seem so important!

AMANDA I don't understand you, Laura. You couldn't be satisfied with just sitting home, and yet whenever I try to arrange something for you, you seem to resist it. *(She gets up.)* Now take a look at yourself. No, wait! Wait just a moment—I have an idea!

LAURA What is it now?

AMANDA *produces two powder puffs which she wraps in handkerchiefs and stuffs in* LAURA's *bosom.*

LAURA Mother, what are you doing?

AMANDA They call them "Gay Deceivers"!

LAURA I won't wear them!

AMANDA You will!

LAURA Why should I?

AMANDA Because, to be painfully honest, your chest is flat.

LAURA You make it seem like we were setting a trap.

AMANDA All pretty girls are a trap, a pretty trap, and men expect them to be. (LEGEND: "A PRETTY TRAP.") Now look at yourself, young lady. This is the prettiest you will ever be! I've got to fix myself now! You're going to be surprised by your mother's appearance! *(She crosses through portieres, humming gaily.)*

LAURA *moves slowly to the long mirror and stares solemnly at herself.*

A wind blows the white curtains inward in a slow, graceful motion and with a faint, sorrowful sighing.

AMANDA *(off stage)* It isn't dark enough yet. *(She turns slowly before the mirror with a troubled look.)*

(LEGEND ON SCREEN: "THIS IS MY SISTER: CELEBRATE HER WITH STRINGS!" MUSIC.)

AMANDA *(laughing, off)* I'm going to show you something. I'm going to make a spectacular appearance!

LAURA What is it, mother?

AMANDA Possess your soul in patience—you will see! Something I've resurrected from that old trunk! Styles haven't changed so terribly much after all. . . . *(She parts the portieres.)* Now just look at your mother! *(She wears a girlish frock of yellowed voile with a blue silk sash. She carries a bunch of jonquils—the legend of her youth is nearly revived. Feverishly.)* This is the dress in which I led the cotillion. Won the cakewalk twice at Sunset Hill, wore one spring to the Governor's ball in Jackson! See how I sashayed around the ballroom, Laura? *(She raises her skirt and does a mincing step around the room.)* I wore it on Sundays for my gentlemen callers! I had it on the day I met your father—I had malaria fever all that spring. The change of climate from East Tennessee to the Delta—weakened resistance—I had a little temperature all the time—not enough to be serious—just enough to make me restless and giddy! Invitations poured in—parties all over the Delta!—"Stay in bed," said Mother, "you have fever!"— but I just wouldn't.—I took quinine but kept on going, going!—Evenings, dances!— Afternoons, long, long rides! Picnics—lovely!—So lovely, that country in May.—All lacy with dogwood, literally flooded with jonquils!—That was the spring I had the craze for jonquils. Jonquils became an absolute obsession. Mother said, "Honey, there's no more room for jonquils." And still I kept bringing in more jonquils. Whenever, wherever I saw them, I'd say, "Stop! Stop! I see jonquils!" I made the young men help me gather the jonquils! It was a joke, Amanda and her jonquils! Finally there were no more vases to hold them, every available space was filled with jonquils. No vases to hold them? All right, I'll hold them myself! And then I—*(She stops in front of the picture. MUSIC.)* met your father! Malaria fever and jonquils and then—this—boy. . . . *(She switches on the rose-colored lamp.)* I hope they get here before it starts to rain. *(She crosses upstage and places the jonquils in bowl on table.)* I gave your brother a little extra change so he and Mr. O'Connor could take the service car home.

LAURA *(with altered look)* What did you say his name was?

AMANDA O'Connor.

LAURA What is his first name?

AMANDA I don't remember. Oh, yes, I do. It was—Jim!

LAURA *sways slightly and catches hold of a chair.*

(LEGEND ON SCREEN: "NOT JIM!")

LAURA *(faintly)* Not—Jim!

AMANDA Yes, that was it, it was Jim! I've never known a Jim that wasn't nice!

(MUSIC: OMINOUS.)

LAURA Are you sure his name is Jim O'Connor?

AMANDA Yes. Why?

LAURA Is he the one that Tom used to know in high school?

AMANDA He didn't say so. I think he just got to know him at the warehouse.

LAURA There was a Jim O'Connor we both knew in high school—*(Then, with effort.)* If that is the one that Tom is bringing to dinner—you'll have to excuse me, I won't come to the table.

AMANDA What sort of nonsense is this?

LAURA You asked me once if I'd ever liked a boy. Don't you remember I showed you this boy's picture?

AMANDA You mean the boy you showed me in the year-book?

LAURA Yes, that boy.

AMANDA Laura, Laura, were you in love with that boy?

LAURA I don't know, Mother. All I know is I couldn't sit at the table if it was him!

AMANDA It won't be him! It isn't the least bit likely. But whether it is or not, you will come to the table. You will not be excused.

LAURA I'll have to be, Mother.

AMANDA I don't intend to humor your silliness, Laura. I've had too much from you and your brother, both! So just sit down and compose yourself till they come. Tom has forgotten his key so you'll have to let them in, when they arrive.

LAURA (panicky) Oh, Mother—you answer the door!

AMANDA (lightly) I'll be in the kitchen—busy!

LAURA Oh, Mother, please answer the door, don't make me do it!

AMANDA (crossing into kitchenette) I've got to fix the dressing for the salmon. Fuss, fuss—silliness!—over a gentleman caller!

Door swings shut. LAURA is left alone.

(LEGEND: "TERROR!")

She utters a low moan and turns off the lamp—sits stiffly on the edge of the sofa, knotting her fingers together.

(LEGEND ON SCREEN: "THE OPENING OF A DOOR!")

TOM *and* JIM *appear on the fire-escape steps and climb to landing. Hearing their approach,* LAURA *rises with a panicky gesture. She retreats to the portieres.*
The doorbell. LAURA *catches her breath and touches her throat. Low drums.*

AMANDA (calling) Laura, sweetheart! The door!

LAURA *stares at it without moving.*

JIM I think we just beat the rain.

TOM Uh-huh. (*He rings again, nervously,* JIM *whistles and fishes for a cigarette.*)

AMANDA (very, very gaily) Laura, that is your brother and Mr. O'Connor! Will you let them in, darling?

LAURA *crosses toward kitchenette door.*

LAURA (breathlessly) Mother—you go to the door!

AMANDA *steps out of kitchenette and stares furiously at* LAURA. *She points imperiously at the door.*

LAURA Please, please!

AMANDA (in a fierce whisper) What is the matter with you, you silly thing?

LAURA (desperately) Please, you answer it, *please!*

AMANDA I told you I wasn't going to humor you, Laura. Why have you chosen this moment to lose your mind?

LAURA Please, please, please, you go!

AMANDA You'll have to go to the door because I can't!

LAURA *(despairingly)* I can't either!

AMANDA Why?

LAURA I'm *sick!*

AMANDA I'm sick, too—of your nonsense! Why can't you and your brother be normal people? Fantastic whims and behavior! *(*TOM *gives a long ring.)* Preposterous goings on! Can you give me one reason—*(Calls out lyrically.)* COMING! JUST ONE SECOND!— why should you be afraid to open a door? Now you answer it, Laura!

LAURA Oh, oh, oh . . . *(She returns through the portieres. Darts to the victrola and winds it frantically and turns it on.)*

AMANDA Laura Wingfield, you march right to that door!

LAURA Yes—yes, Mother!

A faraway, scratchy rendition of "Dardanella" softens the air and gives her strength to move through it. She slips to the door and draws it cautiously open.

TOM *enters with the caller,* JIM O'CONNOR.

TOM Laura, this is Jim. Jim, this is my sister, Laura.

JIM *(stepping inside)* I didn't know that Shakespeare had a sister!

LAURA *(retreating stiff and trembling from the door)* How—how do you do?

JIM *(heartily extending his hand)* Okay!

LAURA *touches it hesitantly with hers.*

JIM Your hand's *cold,* Laura!

LAURA Yes, well—I've been playing the victrola. . . .

JIM Must have been playing classical music on it! You ought to play a little hot swing music to warm you up!

LAURA Excuse me—I haven't finished playing the victrola. . . .

She turns awkwardly and hurries into the front room. She pauses a second by the victrola. Then catches her breath and darts through the portieres like a frightened deer.

JIM *(grinning)* What was the matter?

TOM Oh—with Laura? Laura is—terribly shy.

JIM Shy, huh? It's unusual to meet a shy girl nowadays. I don't believe you ever mentioned you had a sister.

TOM Well, now you know. I have one. Here is the *Post Dispatch.* You want a piece of it?

JIM Uh-huh.

TOM What piece? The comics?

JIM Sports! *(Glances at it.)* Ole Dizzy Dean is on his bad behavior.

TOM *(disinterest)* Yeah? *(Lights cigarette and crosses back to fire-escape door.)*

JIM Where are *you* going?

TOM I'm going out on the terrace.

JIM *(goes after him)* You know, Shakespeare—I'm going to sell you a bill of goods!

TOM What goods?

JIM A course I'm taking.

TOM Huh?

JIM In public speaking! You and me, we're not the warehouse type.

TOM Thanks—that's good news. But what has public speaking got to do with it?

JIM It fits you for—executive positions!

TOM Awww.

JIM I tell you it's done a helluva lot for me.

(IMAGE: EXECUTIVE AT DESK.)

TOM In what respect?

JIM In every! Ask yourself what is the difference between you an' me and men in the office down front? Brains?—No!—Ability?—No! Then what? Just one little thing—

TOM What is that one little thing?

JIM Primarily it amounts to—social poise! Being able to square up to people and hold your own on any social level!

AMANDA (off stage) Tom?

TOM Yes, Mother?

AMANDA Is that you and Mr. O'Connor?

TOM Yes, Mother.

AMANDA Well, you just make yourselves comfortable in there.

TOM Yes, Mother.

AMANDA Ask Mr. O'Connor if he would like to wash his hands.

JIM Aw—no—no—thank you—I took care of that at the warehouse. Tom—

TOM Yes?

JIM Mr. Mendoza was speaking to me about you.

TOM Favorably?

JIM What do you think?

TOM Well—

JIM You're going to be out of a job if you don't wake up.

TOM I am waking up—

JIM You show no signs.

TOM The signs are interior.

(IMAGE ON SCREEN: THE SAILING VESSEL WITH JOLLY ROGER AGAIN.)

TOM I'm planning to change. (He leans over the rail speaking with quiet exhilaration. The incandescent marquees and signs of the first-run movie houses light his face from across the alley. He looks like a voyager.) I'm right at the point of committing myself to a future that doesn't include the warehouse and Mr. Mendoza or even a night-school course in public speaking.

JIM What are you gassing about?

TOM I'm tired of the movies.

JIM Movies!

TOM Yes, movies! Look at them—(A wave toward the marvels of Grand Avenue.) All of those glamorous people—having adventures—hogging it all, gobbling the whole thing up! You know what happens? People go to the movies instead of moving! Hollywood characters are supposed to have all the adventures for everybody in America, while everybody in America sits in a dark room and watches them have them! Yes, until there's a war. That's when adventure becomes available to the masses! Everyone's dish, not only Gable's! Then the people in the dark room come out of the dark room to have some adventures themselves—Goody, goody!—It's our turn now, to go to the South Sea Island—to make a safari—to be exotic, far-off!—But I'm not patient. I don't want to wait till then. I'm tired of the movies and I am about to move!

JIM (*incredulously*) Move?

TOM Yes.

JIM When?

TOM Soon!

JIM Where? Where?

(THEME THREE MUSIC SEEMS TO ANSWER THE QUESTION, WHILE TOM THINKS IT OVER. HE SEARCHES AMONG HIS POCKETS.)

TOM I'm starting to boil inside. I know I seem dreamy, but inside—well, I'm boiling! Whenever I pick up a shoe, I shudder a little thinking how short life is and what I am doing!—Whatever that means. I know it doesn't mean shoes—except as something to wear on a traveler's feet! (*Finds paper.*) Look—

JIM What?

TOM I'm a member.

JIM (*reading*) The Union of Merchant Seamen.

TOM I paid my dues this month, instead of the light bill.

JIM You will regret it when they turn the lights off.

TOM I won't be here.

JIM How about your mother?

TOM I'm like my father. The bastard son of a bastard! See how he grins? And he's been absent going on sixteen years!

JIM You're just talking, you drip. How does your mother feel about it?

TOM Shhh!—Here comes Mother! Mother is not acquainted with my plans!

AMANDA (*enters portieres*) Where are you all?

TOM On the terrace, Mother.

They start inside. She advances to them. TOM *is distinctly shocked at her appearance. Even* JIM *blinks a little. He is making his first contact with girlish Southern vivacity and in spite of the night-school course in public speaking is somewhat thrown off the beam by the unexpected outlay of social charm.*

Certain responses are attempted by JIM *but are swept aside by* AMANDA's *gay laughter and chatter.* TOM *is embarrassed but after the first shock* JIM *reacts very warmly. Grins and chuckles, is altogether won over.*

(IMAGE: AMANDA AS A GIRL.)

AMANDA (*coyly smiling, shaking her girlish ringlets*) Well, well, well, so this is Mr. O'Connor. Introductions entirely unnecessary. I've heard so much about you from my boy. I finally said to him, Tom—good gracious!—why don't you bring this paragon to supper? I'd like to meet this nice young man at the warehouse!—Instead of just hearing him sing your praises so much! I don't know why my son is so stand-offish— that's not Southern behavior! Let's sit down and—I think we could stand a little more air in here! Tom, leave the door open. I felt a nice fresh breeze a moment ago. Where has it gone? Mmm, so warm already! And not quite summer, even. We're going to burn up when summer really gets started. However, we're having—we're having a very light supper. I think light things are better fo' this time of year. The same as light clothes are. Light clothes an' light food are what warm weather calls fo'. You know our blood gets so thick during th' winter—it takes a while fo' us to *adjust* ou'selves!— when the season changes. . . . It's come so quick this year. I wasn't prepared. All of a sudden—heavens! Already summer!—I ran to the trunk an' pulled out this light dress—Terribly old! Historical almost! But feels so good—so good an' co-ol, y'know. . . .

TOM Mother—

AMANDA Yes, honey?

TOM How about—supper?

AMANDA Honey, you go ask Sister if supper is ready! You know that Sister is in full charge of supper! Tell her you hungry boys are waiting for it. *(To* JIM.*)* Have you met Laura?

JIM She—

AMANDA Let you in? Oh, good, you've met already! It's rare for a girl as sweet an' pretty as Laura to be domestic! But Laura is, thank heavens, not only pretty but also very domestic. I'm not at all. I never was a bit. I never could make a thing but angel-food cake. Well, in the South we had so many servants. Gone, gone, gone. All vestige of gracious living! Gone completely! I wasn't prepared for what the future brought me. All of my gentlemen callers were sons of planters and so of course I assumed that I would be married to one and raise my family on a large piece of land with plenty of servants. But man proposes—and woman accepts the proposal!—To vary that old, old saying a little bit—I married no planter! I married a man who worked for the telephone company!—That gallantly smiling gentleman over there! *(Points to the picture.)* A telephone man who—fell in love with long-distance!—Now he travels and I don't even know where!—But what am I going on for about my—tribulations? Tell me yours— I hope you don't have any! Tom?

TOM *(returning)* Yes, Mother?

AMANDA Is supper nearly ready?

TOM It looks to me like supper is on the table.

AMANDA Let me look—*(She rises prettily and looks through portieres.)* Oh, lovely!—But where is Sister?

TOM Laura is not feeling well and she says that she thinks she'd better not come to the table.

AMANDA What?—Nonsense!—Laura? Oh, Laura!

LAURA *(off stage, faintly)* Yes, Mother.

AMANDA You really must come to the table. We won't be seated until you come to the table! Come in, Mr. O'Connor. You sit over there and I'll—Laura? Laura Wingfield! You're keeping us waiting, honey! We can't say grace until you come to the table!

The back door is pushed weakly open and LAURA *comes in. She is obviously quite faint, her lips trembling, her eyes wide and staring. She moves unsteadily toward the table.*

(LEGEND: "TERROR!")

Outside a summer storm is coming abruptly. The white curtains billow inward at the windows and there is a sorrowful murmur and deep blue dusk.
    LAURA *suddenly stumbles—she catches at a chair with a faint moan.*

TOM Laura!

AMANDA Laura! *(There is a clap of thunder.)* (LEGEND: "AH!") *(Despairingly)* Why, Laura, you *are* sick, darling! Tom, help your sister into the living room, dear! Sit in the living room, Laura—rest on the sofa. Well! *(To the gentleman caller.)* Standing over the hot stove made her ill!—I told her that it was just too warm this evening, but—(TOM *comes back in.* LAURA *is on the sofa.)* Is Laura all right now?

TOM Yes.

AMANDA What *is* that? Rain? A nice cool rain has come up! *(She gives the gentleman caller a frightened look.)* I think we may—have grace—now. . . . *(Tom looks at her stupidly.)* Tom, honey—you say grace!

TOM Oh. . . . "For these and all thy mercies—" *(They bow their heads, AMANDA stealing a nervous glance at JIM. In the living room LAURA, stretched on the sofa, clenches her hand to her lips, to hold back a shuddering sob.)* God's Holy Name be praised—

(THE SCENE DIMS OUT.)

SCENE VII.

(LEGEND: "A SOUVENIR.")

Half an hour later. Dinner is just being finished in the upstage area which is concealed by the drawn portieres.

As the curtain rises LAURA is still huddled upon the sofa, her feet drawn under her, her head resting on a pale blue pillow, her eyes wide and mysteriously watchful. The new floor lamp with its shade of rose-colored silk gives a soft, becoming light to her face, bringing out the fragile, unearthly prettiness which usually escapes attention. There is a steady murmur of rain, but it is slackening and stops soon after the scene begins; the air outside becomes pale and luminous as the moon breaks out.

A moment after the curtain rises, the lights in both rooms flicker and go out.

JIM Hey, there, Mr. Light Bulb!

AMANDA *laughs nervously.*

(LEGEND: "SUSPENSION OF A PUBLIC SERVICE.")

AMANDA Where was Moses when the lights went out? Ha-ha. Do you know the answer to that one, Mr. O'Connor?

JIM No, Ma'am, what's the answer?

AMANDA In the dark! *(JIM laughs appreciatively.)* Everybody sit still. I'll light the candles. Isn't it lucky we have them on the table? Where's a match? Which of you gentlemen can provide a match?

JIM Here.

AMANDA Thank you, sir.

JIM Not at all, Ma'am!

AMANDA I guess the fuse has burnt out. Mr. O'Connor, can you tell a burnt-out fuse? I know I can't and Tom is a total loss when it comes to mechanics. (SOUND: GETTING UP: VOICES RECEDE A LITTLE TO KITCHENETTE.) Oh, be careful you don't bump into something. We don't want our gentleman caller to break his neck. Now wouldn't that be a fine howdy-do?

JIM Ha-ha! Where is the fuse-box?

AMANDA Right here next to the stove. Can you see anything?

JIM Just a minute.

AMANDA Isn't electricity a mysterious thing? Wasn't it Benjamin Franklin who tied a key to a kite? We live in such a mysterious universe, don't we? Some people say that science clears up all the mysteries for us. In my opinion it only creates more! Have you found it yet?

JIM No, Ma'am. All these fuses look okay to me.

AMANDA Tom!

TOM Yes, Mother?

AMANDA That light bill I gave you several days ago. The one I told you we got the notices about?

TOM Oh.—Yeah.

(LEGEND: "HA!")

AMANDA You didn't neglect to pay it by any chance?

TOM Why, I—

AMANDA Didn't! I might have known it!

JIM Shakespeare probably wrote a poem on that light bill, Mrs. Wingfield.

AMANDA I might have known better than to trust him with it! There's such a high price for negligence in the world!

JIM Maybe the poem will win a ten-dollar prize.

AMANDA We'll just have to spend the remainder of the evening in the nineteenth century, before Mr. Edison made the Mazda lamp!

JIM Candlelight is my favorite kind of light.

AMANDA That shows you're romantic! But that's no excuse for Tom. Well, we got through dinner. Very considerate of them to let us get through dinner before they plunged us into everlasting darkness, wasn't it, Mr. O'Connor?

JIM Ha-ha!

AMANDA Tom, as a penalty for your carelessness you can help me with the dishes.

JIM Let me give you a hand.

AMANDA Indeed you will not!

JIM I ought to be good for something.

AMANDA Good for something? (*Her tone is rhapsodic.*) You? Why, Mr. O'Connor, nobody, *nobody's* given me this much entertainment in years—as you have!

JIM Aw, now, Mrs. Wingfield!

AMANDA I'm not exaggerating, not one bit! But Sister is all by her lonesome. You go keep her company in the parlor! I'll give you this lovely old candelabrum that used to be on the altar at the church of the Heavenly Rest. It was melted a little out of shape when the church burnt down. Lightning struck it one spring. Gypsy Jones was holding a revival at the time and he intimated that the church was destroyed because the Episcopalians gave card parties.

JIM Ha-ha.

AMANDA And how about coaxing Sister to drink a little wine? I think it would be good for her! Can you carry both at once?

JIM Sure. I'm Superman!

AMANDA Now, Thomas, get into this apron!

The door of kitchenette swings closed on AMANDA's *gay laughter; the flickering light approaches the portieres.*

LAURA *sits up nervously as he enters. Her speech at first is low and breathless from the almost intolerable strain of being alone with a stranger.*

(THE LEGEND: "I DON'T SUPPOSE YOU REMEMBER ME AT ALL!")

In her first speeches in this scene, before JIM's *warmth overcomes her paralyzing shyness,* LAURA's *voice is thin and breathless as though she has just run up a steep flight of stairs.*

JIM's *attitude is gently humorous. In playing this scene it should be stressed that while the incident is apparently unimportant, it is to* LAURA *the climax of her secret life.*

JIM Hello there, Laura.

LAURA *(faintly)* Hello. *(She clears her throat.)*

JIM How are you feeling now? Better?

LAURA Yes. Yes, thank you.

JIM This is for you. A little dandelion wine. *(He extends it toward her with extravagant gallantry.)*

LAURA Thank you.

JIM Drink it—but don't get drunk! *(He laughts heartily.* LAURA *takes the glass uncertainly; laughs shyly.)* Where shall I set the candles?

LAURA Oh—oh, anywhere . . .

JIM How about here on the floor? Any objections?

LAURA No.

JIM I'll spread a newspaper under to catch the drippings. I like to sit on the floor. Mind if I do?

LAURA Oh, no.

JIM Give me a pillow?

LAURA What?

JIM A pillow!

LAURA Oh . . . *(Hands him one quickly.)*

JIM How about you? Don't you like to sit on the floor?

LAURA Oh—yes.

JIM Why don't you, then?

LAURA I—will.

JIM Take a pillow! *(*LAURA *does. Sits on the other side of the candelabrum.* JIM *crosses his legs and smiles engagingly at her.)* I can't hardly see you sitting way over there.

LAURA I can—see you.

JIM I know, but that's not fair, I'm in the limelight. *(*LAURA *moves her pillow closer.)* Good! Now I can see you! Comfortable?

LAURA Yes.

JIM So am I. Comfortable as a cow. Will you have some gum?

LAURA No, thank you.

JIM I think that I will indulge, with your permission. *(Musingly unwraps it and holds it up.)* Think of the fortune made by the guy that invented the first piece of chewing gum. Amazing, huh? The Wrigley Building is one of the sights in Chicago.—I saw it summer before last when I went up to the Century of Progress. Did you take in the Century of Progress?

LAURA No, I didn't.

JIM Well, it was quite a wonderful exposition. What impressed me most was the Hall of Science. Gives you an idea of what the future will be in America, even more wonderful than the present time is! *(Pause. Smiling at her.)* Your brother tells me you're shy. Is that right, Laura?

LAURA I—don't know.

JIM I judge you to be an old-fashioned type of girl. Well, I think that's a pretty good type to be. Hope you don't think I'm being too personal—do you?

LAURA *(hastily, out of embarrassment)* I believe I *will* take a piece of gum, if you—don't mind. *(Clearing her throat.)* Mr. O'Connor, have you—kept up with your singing?

JIM Singing? Me?

LAURA Yes. I remember what a beautiful voice you had.

JIM When did you hear me sing?

(VOICE OFF STAGE IN THE PAUSE.)

VOICE (*off stage*)

> O blow, ye winds, heigh-ho,
> A-roving I will go!
> I'm off to my love
> With a boxing glove—
> Ten thousand miles away!

JIM You say you've heard me sing?

LAURA Oh, yes! Yes, very often. . . . I—don't suppose you remember me—at all?

JIM (*smiling doubtfully*) You know I have an idea I've seen you before. I had that idea
as soon as you opened the door. It seemed almost like I was about to remember your
name. But the name that I started to call you—wasn't a name! And so I stopped myself
before I said it.

LAURA Wasn't it—Blue Roses?

JIM (*springs up, grinning*) Blue Roses! My gosh, yes—Blue Roses! That's what I had on
my tongue when you opened the door! Isn't it funny what tricks your memory plays?
I didn't connect you with the high school somehow or other. But that's where it was;
it was high school. I didn't even know you were Shakespeare's sister! Gosh, I'm sorry.

LAURA I didn't expect you to. You—barely knew me!

JIM But we did have a speaking acquaintance, huh?

LAURA Yes, we—spoke to each other.

JIM When did you recognize me?

LAURA Oh, right away!

JIM Soon as I came in the door?

LAURA When I heard your name I thought it was probably you. I knew that Tom used
to know you a little in high school. So when you came in the door—Well, then I
was—sure.

JIM Why didn't you *say* something, then?

LAURA (*breathlessly*) I didn't know what to say, I was—too surprised!

JIM For goodness' sakes! You know, this sure is funny!

LAURA Yes! Yes, isn't it, though . . .

JIM Didn't we have a class in something together?

LAURA Yes, we did.

JIM What class was that?

LAURA It was—singing—Chorus!

JIM Aw!

LAURA I sat across the aisle from you in the Aud.

JIM Aw.

LAURA Mondays, Wednesdays and Fridays.

JIM Now I remember—you always came in late.

LAURA Yes, it was so hard for me, getting upstairs. I had that brace on my leg—it
clumped so loud!

JIM I never heard any clumping.

LAURA (*wincing at the recollection*) To me it sounded like—thunder!

JIM Well, well, well. I never even noticed.

LAURA And everybody was seated before I came in. I had to walk in front of all those people. My seat was in the back row. I had to go clumping all the way up the aisle with everyone watching!

JIM You shouldn't have been self-conscious.

LAURA I know, but I was. It was always such a relief when the singing started.

JIM Aw, yes. I've placed you now! I used to call you Blue Roses. How was it that I got started calling you that?

LAURA I was out of school a little while with pleurosis. When I came back you asked me what was the matter. I said I had pleurosis—you thought I said Blue Roses. That's what you always called me after that!

JIM I hope you didn't mind.

LAURA Oh, no—I liked it. You see, I wasn't acquainted with many—people. . . .

JIM As I remember you sort of stuck by yourself.

LAURA I—I—never had much luck at—making friends.

JIM I don't see why you wouldn't.

LAURA Well, I—started out badly.

JIM You mean being—

LAURA Yes, it sort of—stood between me—

JIM You shouldn't have let it!

LAURA I know, but it did, and—

JIM You were shy with people!

LAURA I tried not to be but never could—

JIM Overcome it?

LAURA No, I—I never could!

JIM I guess being shy is something you have to work out of kind of gradually.

LAURA (*sorrowfully*) Yes—I guess it—

JIM Takes time!

LAURA Yes—

JIM People are not so dreadful when you know them. That's what you have to remember! And everybody has problems, not just you, but practically everybody has got some problems. You think of yourself as having the only problems, as being the only one who is disappointed. But just look around you and you will see lots of people as disappointed as you are. For instance, I hoped when I was going to high school that I would be further along at this time, six years later, than I am now—You remember that wonderful write-up I had in *The Torch*?

LAURA Yes! (*She rises and crosses to table.*)

JIM It said I was bound to succeed in anything I went into! (LAURA *returns with the annual.*) Holy Jeez! *The Torch!* (*He accepts it reverently. They smile across it with mutual wonder.* LAURA *crouches beside him and they begin to turn through it.* LAURA's *shyness is dissolving in his warmth.*)

LAURA Here you are in *Pirates of Penzance!*

JIM (*wistfully*) I sang the baritone lead in that operetta.

LAURA (*rapidly*) So—*beautifully!*

JIM (*protesting*) Aw—

LAURA Yes, yes—beautifully—*beautifully!*

JIM You heard me?

LAURA All three times!

JIM No!

LAURA Yes!

JIM All three performances?

LAURA (*looking down*) Yes.

JIM Why?

LAURA I—wanted to ask you to—autograph my program.

JIM Why didn't you ask me to.

LAURA You were always surrounded by your own friends so much that I never had a chance to.

JIM You should have just—

LAURA Well, I—thought you might think I was—

JIM Thought I might think you was—what?

LAURA Oh—

JIM (*with reflective relish*) I was beleaguered by females in those days.

LAURA You were terribly popular!

JIM Yeah—

LAURA You had such a—friendly way—

JIM I was spoiled in high school.

LAURA Everybody—liked you!

JIM Including you?

LAURA I—yes, I—I did, too—(*She gently closes the book in her lap.*)

JIM Well, well, well!—Give me that program, Laura. (*She hands it to him. He signs it with a flourish.*) There you are—better late than never!

LAURA Oh, I—what a—surprise!

JIM My signature isn't worth very much right now. But some day—maybe—it will increase in value! Being disappointed is one thing and being discouraged is something else. I am disappointed but I am not discouraged. I'm twenty-three years old. How old are you?

LAURA I'll be twenty-four in June.

JIM That's not old age!

LAURA No, but—

JIM You finished high school?

LAURA (*with difficulty*) I didn't go back.

JIM You mean you dropped out?

LAURA I made bad grades in my final examinations. (*She rises and replaces the book and the program. Her voice strained.*) How is—Emily Meisenbach getting along?

JIM Oh, that kraut-head!

LAURA Why do you call her that?

JIM That's what she was.

LAURA You're not still—going with her?

JIM I never see her.

LAURA It said in the Personal Section that you were—engaged!

JIM I know, but I wasn't impressed by that—propaganda!

LAURA It wasn't—the truth?

JIM Only in Emily's optimistic opinion!

LAURA Oh—

(LEGEND: "WHAT HAVE YOU DONE SINCE HIGH SCHOOL?")

JIM *lights a cigarette and leans indolently back on his elbows smiling at* LAURA *with a warmth and charm which lights her inwardly with altar candles. She remains by the table and turns in her hands a piece of glass to cover her tumult.*

JIM (*after several reflective puffs on a cigarette*) What have you done since high school? (*She seems not to hear him.*) Huh? (LAURA *looks up.*) I said what have you done since high school, Laura?

LAURA Nothing much.

JIM You must have been doing something in these six long years.

LAURA Yes.

JIM Well, then, such as what?

LAURA I took a business course at business college—

JIM How did that work out?

LAURA Well, not very—well—I had to drop out, it gave me—indigestion—

JIM *laughs gently.*

JIM What are you doing now?

LAURA I don't do anything—much. Oh, please don't think I sit around doing nothing! My glass collection takes up a good deal of my time. Glass is something you have to take good care of.

JIM What did you say—about glass?

LAURA Collection I said—I have one—(*She clears her throat and turns away again, acutely shy.*)

JIM (*abruptly*) You know what I judge to be the trouble with you? Inferiority complex! Know what that is? That's what they call it when someone low-rates himself! I understand it because I had it, too. Although my case was not so aggravated as yours seems to be. I had it until I took up public speaking, developed my voice, and learned that I had an aptitude for science. Before that time I never thought of myself as being outstanding in any way whatsoever! Now I've never made a regular study of it, but I have a friend who says I can analyze people better than doctors that make a profession of it. I don't claim that to be necessarily true, but I can sure guess a person's psychology, Laura! (*Takes out his gum.*) Excuse me, Laura. I always take it out when the flavor is gone. I'll use this scrap of paper to wrap it in. I know how it is to get it stuck on a shoe. Yep—that's what I judge to be your principal trouble. A lack of confidence in yourself as a person. You don't have the proper amount of faith in yourself. I'm basing that fact on a number of your remarks and also on certain observations I've made. For instance that clumping you thought was so awful in high school. You say that you even dreaded to walk into class. You see what you did? You dropped out of school, you gave up an education because of a clump, which as far as I know was practically non-existent! A little physical defect is what you have. Hardly noticeable even! Magnified thousands of times by imagination! You know what my strong advice to you is? Think of yourself as *superior* in some way!

LAURA In what way would I think?

JIM Why, man alive, Laura! Just look about you a little. What do you see? A world full of common people! All of 'em born and all of 'em going to die! Which of them has one-tenth of your good points! Or mine! Or anyone else's, as far as that goes—Gosh! Everybody excels in some one thing. Some in many! (*Unconsciously glances at himself in the mirror.*) All you've got to do is discover in *what!* Take me, for instance. (*He adjusts his tie at the mirror.*) My interest happens to lie in electro-dynamics. I'm taking a course in radio engineering at night school, Laura, on top of a fairly responsible job at the warehouse. I'm taking that course and studying public speaking.

LAURA Ohhhh.

JIM Because I believe in the future of television! (*Turning back to her.*) I wish to be ready to go up right along with it. Therefore I'm planning to get in on the ground floor. In fact, I've already made the right connections and all that remains is for the industry itself to get under way! Full steam—(*His eyes are starry.*) Knowledge—Zzzzzp! Money— Zzzzzzp!—Power! That's the cycle democracy is built on! (*His attitude is convincingly dynamic.* LAURA *stares at him, even her shyness eclipsed in her absolute wonder. He suddenly grins.*) I guess you think I think a lot of myself!

LAURA No—o-o-o, I—

JIM Now how about you? Isn't there something you take more interest in than anything else?

LAURA Well, I do—as I said—have my—glass collection—

A peal of girlish laughter from the kitchen.

JIM I'm not right sure I know what you're talking about. What kind of glass is it?

LAURA Little articles of it, they're ornaments mostly! Most of them are little animals made out of glass, the tiniest little animals in the world. Mother calls them a glass menagerie! Here's an example of one, if you'd like to see it! This one is one of the oldest. It's nearly thirteen. (*He stretches out his hand.*) (MUSIC: "THE GLASS MENAGERIE.") Oh, be careful—if you breathe, it breaks!

JIM I'd better not take it. I'm pretty clumsy with things.

LAURA Go on, I trust you with him! (*Places it in his palm.*) There now—you're holding him gently! Hold him over the light, he loves the light! You see how the light shines through him?

JIM It sure does shine!

LAURA I shouldn't be partial, but he is my favorite one.

JIM What kind of a thing is this one supposed to be?

LAURA Haven't you noticed the single horn on his forehead?

JIM A unicorn, huh?

LAURA Mmm-hmmm!

JIM Unicorns, aren't they extinct in the modern world?

LAURA I know!

JIM Poor little fellow, he must feel sort of lonesome.

LAURA (*smiling*) Well, if he does he doesn't complain about it. He stays on a shelf with some horses that don't have horns and all of them seem to get along nicely together.

JIM How do you know?

LAURA (*lightly*) I haven't heard any arguments among them!

JIM (*grinning*) No arguments, huh? Well, that's a pretty good sign! Where shall I set him?

LAURA Put him on the table. They all like a change of scenery once in a while!

JIM (*stretching*) Well, well, well, well—Look how big my shadow is when I stretch!

LAURA Oh, oh, yes—it stretches across the ceiling!

JIM (*crossing to door*) I think it's stopped raining. (*Opens fire-escape door.*) Where does the music come from?

LAURA From the Paradise Dance Hall across the alley.

JIM How about cutting the rug a little, Miss Wingfield?

LAURA Oh, I—

JIM Or is your program filled up? Let me have a look at it. (*Grasps imaginary card.*) Why, every dance is taken! I'll just have to scratch some out. (WALTZ MUSIC: "LA GOLONDRINA.") Ahhh, a waltz! (*He executes some sweeping turns by himself, then holds his arms toward* LAURA.)

LAURA (*breathlessly*) I—can't dance!

JIM There you go, that inferiority stuff!

LAURA I've never danced in my life!

JIM Come on, try!

LAURA Oh, but I'd step on you!

JIM I'm not made out of glass.

LAURA How—how—how do we start?

JIM Just leave it to me. You hold your arms out a little.

LAURA Like this?

JIM A little bit higher. Right. Now don't tighten up, that's the main thing about it—relax.

LAURA (*laughing breathlessly*) It's hard not to.

JIM Okay.

LAURA I'm afraid you can't budge me.

JIM What do you bet I can't? (*He swings her into motion.*)

LAURA Goodness, yes, you can!

JIM Let yourself go, now, Laura, just let yourself go.

LAURA I'm—

JIM Come on!

LAURA Trying!

JIM Not so stiff—Easy does it!

LAURA I know but I'm—

JIM Loosen th' backbone! There now, that's a lot better.

LAURA Am I?

JIM Lots, lots better! (*He moves her about the room in a clumsy waltz.*)

LAURA Oh, my!

JIM Ha-ha!

LAURA Oh, my goodness!

JIM Ha-ha-ha! (*They suddenly bump into the table.* JIM *stops.*) What did we hit on?

LAURA Table.

JIM Did something fall off it? I think—

LAURA Yes.

JIM I hope that it wasn't the little glass horse with the horn!

LAURA Yes.

JIM Aw, aw, aw. Is it broken?

LAURA Now it is just like all the other horses.

JIM It's lost its—

LAURA Horn! It doesn't matter. Maybe it's a blessing in disguise.

JIM You'll never forgive me. I bet that that was your favorite piece of glass.

LAURA I don't have favorites much. It's no tragedy, Freckles. Glass breaks so easily. No matter how careful you are. The traffic jars the shelves and things fall off them.

JIM Still I'm awfully sorry that I was the cause.

LAURA (*smiling*) I'll just imagine he had an operation. The horn was removed to make him feel less—freakish! (*They both laugh.*) Now he will feel more at home with the other horses, the ones that don't have horns. . . .

JIM Ha-ha, that's very funny! (*Suddenly serious.*) I'm glad to see that you have a sense of humor. You know—you're—well—very different! Surprisingly different from anyone else I know! (*His voice becomes soft and hesitant with a genuine feeling.*) Do you mind me telling you that? (LAURA *is abashed beyond speech.*) You make me feel sort of—I don't know how to put it! I'm usually pretty good at expressing things, but— This is something that I don't know how to say! (LAURA *touches her throat and clears it—turns the broken unicorn in her hands.*) (*Even softer.*) Has anyone ever told you that you were pretty? (PAUSE: MUSIC.) (LAURA *looks up slowly, with wonder, and shakes her head.*) Well, you are! In a very different way from anyone else. And all the nicer because of the difference, too. (*His voice becomes low and husky.* LAURA *turns away, nearly faint with the novelty of her emotions.*) I wish that you were my sister. I'd teach you to have some confidence in yourself. The different people are not like other people, but being different is nothing to be ashamed of. Because other people are not such wonderful people. They're one hundred times one thousand. You're one times one! They walk all over the earth. You just stay here. They're common as—weeds, but— you—well, you're—*Blue Roses!*

(IMAGE ON SCREEN: BLUE ROSES.)

(MUSIC CHANGES.)

LAURA But blue is wrong for—roses . . .

JIM It's right for you—You're—pretty!

LAURA In what respect am I pretty?

JIM In all respects—believe me! Your eyes—your hair—are pretty! Your hands are pretty! (*He catches hold of her hand.*) You think I'm making this up because I'm invited to dinner and have to be nice. Oh, I could do that! I could put on an act for you, Laura, and say lots of things without being very sincere. But this time I am. I'm talking to you sincerely. I happened to notice you had this inferiority complex that keeps you from feeling comfortable with people. Somebody needs to build your confidence up and make you proud instead of shy and turning away and—blushing—Somebody ought to—Ought to—*kiss* you, Laura! (*His hand slips slowly up her arm to her shoulder.*) (MUSIC SWELLS TUMULTUOUSLY.) (*He suddenly turns her about and kisses her on the lips. When he releases her* LAURA *sinks on the sofa with a bright, dazed look.* JIM *backs away and fishes in his pocket for a cigarette.*) (LEGEND ON SCREEN: "SOUVENIR.") Stumble-john! (*He lights the cigarette, avoiding her look. There is a peal of girlish laughter from* AMANDA *in the kitchen.* LAURA *slowly raises and opens her hand. It still contains the little broken glass animal. She looks at it with a tender, bewildered expression.*) Stumble-john! I shouldn't have done that—That was way off the beam. You don't smoke, do you? (*She looks up, smiling, not hearing the question. He sits beside her a little gingerly. She looks at him speechlessly—waiting. He coughs decorously and moves a little farther aside as he considers the situation and senses her feelings, dimly, with perturbation. Gently*) Would you—care for a—mint? (*She doesn't seem to hear him but her look grows brighter even.*) Peppermint—Life Saver? My pocket's a regular drug store—wherever I go . . . (*He pops a mint in his mouth. Then gulps and decides to make a clean breast of it. He speaks slowly and gingerly.*) Laura, you know, if I had a sister like you, I'd do the same thing as Tom. I'd bring out fellows—introduce her to them. The right type of boys of a type to—appreciate her. Only—well—he made a mistake about me. Maybe I've got no call to be saying this. That may not have been the idea in having me over. But what if it was? There's nothing wrong about that. The only trouble is that in my case—I'm not in a situation to—do the right thing. I can't take down your number and say I'll phone. I can't call up next week and—ask for a date. I thought I had better explain the situation in case you misunderstood it and—hurt your feelings. . . . (*Pause. Slowly, very slowly,* LAURA's *look changes, her eyes returning slowly from his to the ornament in her palm.*)

AMANDA *utters another gay laugh in the kitchen.*

LAURA (*faintly*) You—won't—call again?

JIM No, Laura, I can't. (*He rises from the sofa.*) As I was just explaining, I've—got strings on me, Laura, I've—been going steady! I go out all the time with a girl named Betty. She's a home-girl like you, and Catholic, and Irish, and in a great many ways we—get along fine. I met her last summer on a moonlight boat trip up the river to Alton, on the *Majestic.* Well—right away from the start it was—love! (LEGEND: "LOVE!") (LAURA *sways slightly forward and grips the arm of the sofa. He fails to notice, now enrapt in his own comfortable being.*) Being in love has made a new man of me! (*Leaning stiffly forward, clutching the arm of the sofa,* LAURA *struggles visibly with her storm. But* JIM *is oblivious, she is a long way off.*) The power of love is really pretty tremendous! Love is something that—changes the whole world, Laura! (*The storm abates a little and* LAURA *leans back. He notices her again.* It happened that Betty's aunt took sick, she got a wire and had to go to Centralia. So Tom—when he asked me to dinner—I naturally just accepted the invitation, not knowing that you—that he—that I—(*He stops awkwardly.*) Huh—I'm a stumble-john! (*He flops back on the sofa. The holy candles in the altar of* LAURA's *face have been snuffed out! There is a look of almost infinite desolation.* JIM *glances at her uneasily.*) I wish that you would—say something. (*She bites her lip which was trembling and then bravely smiles. She opens her hand again on the broken glass ornament. Then she gently takes his hand and raises it level with her own. She carefully places the unicorn in the palm of his hand, then pushes his fingers closed upon it.*) What are you—doing that for? You want me to have him?—Laura? (*She nods.*) What for?

LAURA A—souvenir . . .

She rises unsteadily and crouches beside the victrola to wind it up.

(LEGEND ON SCREEN: "THINGS HAVE A WAY OF TURNING OUT SO BADLY.")

(OR IMAGE: GENTLEMAN CALLER WAVING GOOD-BYE!—GAILY.)

At this moment AMANDA *rushes brightly back in the front room. She bears a pitcher of fruit punch in an old-fashioned cut-glass pitcher and a plate of macaroons. The plate has a gold border and poppies painted on it.*

AMANDA Well, well, well! Isn't the air delightful after the shower? I've made you children a little liquid refreshment. (*Turns gaily to the gentleman caller.*) Jim, do you know that song about lemonade?

> "Lemonade, lemonade
> Made in the shade and stirred with a spade—
> Good enough for any old maid!"

JIM (*uneasily*) Ha-ha! No—I never heard it.

AMANDA Why, Laura! You look so serious!

JIM We were having a serious conversation.

AMANDA Good! Now you're better acquainted!

JIM (*uncertainly*) Ha-ha! Yes.

AMANDA You modern young people are much more serious-minded than my generation. I was so gay as a girl!

JIM You haven't changed, Mrs. Wingfield.

AMANDA Tonight I'm rejuvenated! The gaiety of the occasion, Mr. O'Connor! (*She tosses her head with a peal of laughter. Spills lemonade.*) Oooo! I'm baptizing myself!

JIM Here—let me—

AMANDA (*setting the pitcher down*) There now. I discovered we had some maraschino cherries. I dumped them in, juice and all!

JIM You shouldn't have gone to that trouble, Mrs. Wingfield.

AMANDA Trouble, trouble? Why it was loads of fun! Didn't you hear me cutting up in the kitchen? I bet your ears were burning! I told Tom how outdone with him I was for keeping you to himself so long a time! He should have brought you over much, much sooner! Well, now that you've found your way, I want you to be a very frequent caller! Not just occasional but all the time. Oh, we're going to have a lot of gay times together! I see them coming! Mmm, just breathe that air! So fresh, and the moon's so pretty! I'll skip back out—I know where my place is when young folks are having a—serious conversation!

JIM Oh, don't go out, Mrs. Wingfield. The fact of the matter is I've got to be going.

AMANDA Going now? You're joking! Why, it's only the shank of the evening, Mr. O'Connor!

JIM Well, you know how it is.

AMANDA You mean you're a young workingman and have to keep workingmen's hours. We'll let you off early tonight. But only on the condition that next time you stay later. What's the best night for you? Isn't Saturday night the best night for you workingmen?

JIM I have a couple of time-clocks to punch, Mrs. Wingfield. One at morning, another one at night!

AMANDA My, but you *are* ambitious! You work at night, too?

JIM No, Ma'am, not work but—Betty! (*He crosses deliberately to pick up his hat. The band at the Paradise Dance Hall goes into a tender waltz.*)

AMANDA Betty? Betty? Who's—Betty! (*There is an ominous cracking sound in the sky.*)

JIM Oh, just a girl. The girl I go steady with! (*He smiles charmingly. The sky falls.*)

(LEGEND: "THE SKY FALLS.")

AMANDA (*a long-drawn exhalation*) Ohhhh . . . Is it a serious romance, Mr. O'Connor?

JIM We're going to be married the second Sunday in June.

AMANDA Ohhhh—how nice! Tom didn't mention that you were engaged to be married.

JIM The cat's not out of the bag at the warehouse yet. You know how they are. They call you Romeo and stuff like that. (*He stops at the oval mirror to put on his hat. He carefully shapes the brim and the crown to give a discreetly dashing effect.*) It's been a wonderful evening, Mrs. Wingfield. I guess this is what they mean by Southern hospitality.

AMANDA It really wasn't anything at all.

JIM I hope it don't seem like I'm rushing off. But I promised Betty I'd pick her up at the Wabash depot, an' by the time I get my jalopy down there her train'll be in. Some women are pretty upset if you keep 'em waiting.

AMANDA Yes, I know—The tyranny of women! (*Extends her hand.*) Good-bye, Mr. O'Connor. I wish you luck—and happiness—and success! All three of them, and so does Laura!—Don't you, Laura?

LAURA Yes!

JIM (*taking her hand*) Good-bye, Laura. I'm certainly going to treasure that souvenir. And don't you forget the good advice I gave you. (*Raises his voice to a cheery shout.*) So long, Shakespeare! Thanks again, ladies—Good night!

He grins and ducks jauntily out.

Still bravely grimacing, AMANDA *closes the door on the gentleman caller. Then she turns back to the room with a puzzled expression. She and* LAURA *don't dare to face each other.* LAURA *crouches beside the victrola to wind it.*

AMANDA (*faintly*) Things have a way of turning out so badly. I don't believe that I would play the victrola. Well, well—well—Our gentleman caller was engaged to be married! Tom!

TOM (*from back*) Yes, Mother?

AMANDA Come in here a minute. I want to tell you something awfully funny.

TOM (*enters with a macaroon and a glass of the lemonade*) Has the gentleman caller gotten away already?

AMANDA The gentleman caller has made an early departure. What a wonderful joke you played on us!

TOM How do you mean?

AMANDA You didn't mention that he was engaged to be married.

TOM Jim? Engaged?

AMANDA That's what he just informed us.

TOM I'll be jiggered! I didn't know about that.

AMANDA That seems very peculiar.

TOM What's peculiar about it?

AMANDA Didn't you call him your best friend down at the warehouse?

TOM He is, but how did I know?

AMANDA It seems extremely peculiar that you wouldn't know your best friend was going to be married!

TOM The warehouse is where I work, not where I know things about people!

AMANDA You don't know things anywhere! You live in a dream; you manufacture illusions! (*He crosses to door.*) Where are you going?

TOM I'm going to the movies.

AMANDA That's right, now that you've had us make such fools of ourselves. The effort, the preparations, all the expense! The new floor lamp, the rug, the clothes for Laura! All for what? To entertain some other girl's fiancé! Go to the movies, go! Don't think about us, a mother deserted, an unmarried sister who's crippled and has no job! Don't let anything interfere with your selfish pleasure! Just go, go, go—to the movies!

TOM All right, I will! The more you shout about my selfishness to me the quicker I'll go, and I won't go to the movies!

AMANDA Go, then! Then go to the moon—you selfish dreamer!

TOM *smashes his glass on the floor. He plunges out on the fire-escape, slamming the door,* LAURA *screams—cut off by the door.*

Dance-hall music up. TOM *goes to the rail and grips it desperately, lifting his face in the chill white moonlight penetrating the narrow abyss of the alley.*

(LEGEND ON SCREEN: "AND SO GOOD-BYE . . .")

TOM'S *closing speech is timed with the interior pantomime. The interior scene is played as though viewed through soundproof glass.* AMANDA *appears to be making a comforting speech to* LAURA *who is huddled upon the sofa. Now that we cannot hear the mother's speech, her silliness is gone and she has dignity and tragic beauty.* LAURA's *dark hair hides her face until at the end of the speech she lifts it to smile at her mother.* AMANDA's *gestures are slow and graceful, almost dancelike, as she comforts the daughter. At the end of her speech she glances a moment at the father's picture—then withdraws through the portieres. At close of* TOM's *speech,* LAURA *blows out the candles, ending the play.*

TOM I didn't go to the moon, I went much further—for time is the longest distance between two places—Not long after that I was fired for writing a poem on the lid of a shoe-box. I left Saint Louis. I descended the steps of this fire-escape for a last time and followed, from then on, in my father's footsteps, attempting to find in motion what was lost in space—I traveled around a great deal. The cities swept about me like dead leaves, leaves that were brightly colored but torn away from the branches. I would have stopped, but I was pursued by something. It always came upon me unawares, taking me altogether by surprise. Perhaps it was a familiar bit of music. Perhaps it was only a piece of transparent glass—Perhaps I am walking along a street at night, in some strange city, before I have found companions. I pass the lighted window of a shop where perfume is sold. The window is filled with pieces of colored glass, tiny transparent bottles in delicate colors, like bits of a shattered rainbow. Then all at once my sister touches my shoulder. I turn around and look into her eyes. . . . Oh, Laura, Laura, I tried to leave you behind me, but I am more faithful than I intended to be! I reach for a cigarette, I cross the street, I run into the movies or a bar, I buy a drink, I speak to the nearest stranger—anything that can blow your candles out! (LAURA *bends over the candles.*) —for nowadays the world is lit by lightning! Blow out your candles, Laura—and so good-bye. . . .

She blows the candles out.

(THE SCENE DISSOLVES.)

Questions

1. Assuming that Amanda is the protagonist, state the dramatic situation. What is her objective? What is standing in her way?
2. Suppose we consider the story from Tom's point of view. What is his objective? What are his obstacles? Does his disagreement with his mother make him a villain?
3. Laura initiates very little action in the play. Does she interest you? Why? How is her character symbolized by the image of the glass animals?
4. Several times Tom tells his mother he is going to the movies. Do you think that is where he always goes? If he does not, then where does he go? What strengths and/ or weaknesses of character are revealed by this discrepancy between words and actions?

5. The rising action of the play concerns the pursuit of the Gentleman Caller. What are some of the complications and crises that threaten Amanda before Jim O'Connor arrives? What virtues does Amanda reveal in handling these crises? What flaws?
6. What is the climax of the play? Can you pin it down to a specific scene? A single action or speech?
7. What are Jim's virtues? What is his flaw? Do you consider him a villain?
8. How does Amanda handle the news that Jim is engaged? Do you feel sorry for her?
9. After Jim leaves, Laura has no more lines. What do you suppose she is feeling? What do you feel for her?
10. Tom leaves his home, never to return. What strength of character does that action reveal? What flaw?
11. There is one flaw shared by every character in *The Glass Menagerie*. What is it?

Suggestions for Dramatists

1. What do you want more than anything in the world? Money? Fame? Be as specific as you can in defining your goal. What is keeping you from getting it? Think of yourself as the protagonist of a drama, in which you are called upon to take risks or make sacrifices to achieve your goal. Imagine scenes of challenge, scenes of temptation. How do you respond? Are you courageous and imaginative in the pursuit of your goal, or timid and dull?
2. What makes you different from your friends? List as many qualities of your character as you can. Would any of these be particularly interesting in a play?
3. Do you know someone whom you consider a villain? Describe a particular instance of that individual's villainy. Now try to describe the motive behind it. Does the person seem less a villain once you have explained his or her motive?

5 Tragedy

"A perfect Tragedy," said the English essayist Joseph Addison, "is the noblest production of human nature." It may come as no surprise that what is noblest in us is also rare and difficult to produce; nevertheless, the evidence is astonishing. Since the birth of tragedy in the sixth century B.C., fewer than two dozen playwrights have made enduring contributions to the form. There are cultures that have not produced a single great tragedian. Others, like England, that can boast of several, have seen generations pass between them.

What is a tragedy? What is it about this dramatic form that a culture values so highly? And why does this form make such demands upon the playwright? No comment on these issues is more helpful than Aristotle's: A tragedy portrays "incidents arousing pity and fear." It is important that the cross-section of culture represented by a theater audience should share pity and fear for the same hero. People who cannot agree on a tax structure, a political candidate, or a dinner menu, can all weep for Oedipus and Hamlet. Tragedy brings people together. Ancient Greeks and medieval Christians understood this religious principle of drama. As a forum for ultimate human concerns, tragic theater still has this power. American theatergoers, who may agree on little else, will all agree that Willy Loman, hero of *Death of a Salesman*, is a liar and fake, but that he has been handed a raw deal by life. It is painfully difficult to create such a character and to devise an action that will capture the tragic sympathies of a diverse public.

The scholar Bernard Knox observes: "It sometimes happens that a great poet [dramatist] creates a character in whom the essence of an age is distilled, a representative figure who in his action and suffering presents to his own time the image of its victory and defeat. . . . The poet who created him has penetrated so deeply into the permanent elements of the human situation that his creation transcends time. One such figure is Hamlet, Prince of Denmark, and such another is Oedipus, King of Thebes." It is possible that Willy Loman, Salesman of New York, is another such figure.

Fear and Pity

As we noted in Chapter 3, a tragedy is a play that shows the change in the protagonist's fortunes from good to bad. The incidents must inspire *fear* and *pity*. Let us consider these emotions. We *fear* most deeply for characters who are like ourselves, when they are in danger. What threatens them may threaten us: sickness, old age, betrayal, fire. No one, apart from their families, could be more fearful for the firefighters climbing into a burning house than their fellow firefighters. Likewise, a dramatic character, to inspire fear in the spectators, must be like them in some important way. We have all known to some degree the pride of Oedipus, the bitterness and confusion of Hamlet, the folly of Willy Loman. Otherwise we would not care enough for these characters to fear for them.

It is particularly fearful to watch someone fall from a position of high rank or power. The heroes of classical tragedy are always members of the nobility. Their fates are terrifying to us, for we sense that if these great, privileged figures are vulnerable, then none of us is safe.

Pity is the final proof of tragic drama. In order to feel pity, we must believe that the protagonist's suffering is undeserved, the punishment greater than the crime. Yet tragic heroes must not be totally guiltless. If they were, their fall would not inspire fear and pity in us. It would inspire anger and disgust, as does news of the slaughter of baby seals. Tragic heroes must not be outright victims. A flaw must contribute to their undoing if we are to feel pity as well as fear.

Recognition and Reversal

In our discussion of *Riders To The Sea* we mentioned that Maurya's suffering leads her to a new and deeper understanding of life. This is the ultimate recognition for the tragic character. But such understanding does not come at once. It usually results from several scenes of *recognition* that occur from climax to catastrophe of a tragedy. The Greeks used the word *anagnorisis* (recognition) to refer to any change from ignorance to knowledge. In scenes of recognition the protagonist may learn the true nature of his predicament, or he may learn what weakness of his character has caused it. He may learn both at once. When Oedipus discovers that Laïos was murdered "where three highways meet," he recognizes that he may have killed his father. At the same time he realizes his arrogance as he says, "I may be accurst by my own ignorant edict." Of course, the most dramatic discovery of *Oedipus Rex*, the beginning of the catastrophe, is his recognition that the prophecy has come true, that he has killed his father and married his mother. This discovery is accompanied by a violent reversal of Oedipus's fortunes.

In the broadest sense the action of any play is a *reversal*, from bad to good fortune in a comedy, and from good to bad fortune in a tragedy. But in most plays there are one or more points in the action when the reversal of fortune is particularly conspicuous or violent. The Greeks called these *peripeteia*. The *peripeteia* is especially moving when the characters' actions have an effect opposite from that which they intended. This is *tragic irony*. The climax and catastrophe of *Oedipus Rex* described above are both examples of *peripateia* with *tragic irony*. Iocastê wishes to reassure Oedipus but fires his suspicions; the Messenger and Shepherd are called to prove Oedipus's innocence, instead they confirm his guilt.

Recognition sometimes brings on a reversal of fortunes, and sometimes a reversal, or peripeteia, brings about an important recognition on the part of the protagonist. It is most dramatic when these events happen at the same time.

Catharsis

All the events of a tragedy have been leading us to fear the worst for our hero. When the catastrophe comes at last, we are not surprised. We feel sorry for the hero and may weep, caught up in a mixture of sadness for him and for ourselves, and a bittersweet feeling of relief. After all that dread, the thing we most feared has happened. Yet we are still alive and somehow better off for what we have witnessed. Leaving the theater, we may feel the comfort of one who has awakened from a nightmare, or walked away from an automobile accident unharmed. We have witnessed suffering, known terror, and yet life goes on. These feelings and thoughts that follow tragedy Aristotle calls *catharsis*.

In ancient Greek, catharsis was originally a medical term that meant "cleansing." Aristotle probably intended to use the concept of catharsis as a defense against philosophers like Plato, who believed that drama incited dishonorable emotions and bad behaviour. Aristotle suggests that tragedy is good for us because it cleanses us of violent and mean emotions in a controlled environment. The debate still rages between censors who believe drama is dangerous, and the advocates of free expression who believe the emotional adventures of drama are healthy.

Aristotle's contemporaries may have understood precisely what he meant by "cleansing emotions." He may have meant something as simple as: "We all feel better after a good cry." Unfortunately the philosopher did not elaborate. The concept remains vague and provokes considerable debate among scholars. Each critic and culture tends to interpret catharsis according to its own experience of tragic drama. We have described catharsis as a kind of relief. Your experience of tragedy in the theater may cause you to describe catharsis in a different way.

The Tragic Hero

In our discussion of *Oedipus Rex* in Chapter 3, we remarked that the hero of Greek tragedy is an extraordinary man or woman who separates himself or herself from others. This separation is central to all tragedies. Oedipus begins his play in a position somewhat isolated by his own power as a king. Then in his obsessive search for the killer of Laïos he increases his isolation by alienating Teiresias, his brother-in-law Creon, and his queen Iocastê. Once the old shepherd proves Oedipus's guilt, the king cuts himself off from humankind by putting out his eyes. Then the movement toward isolation culminates in Oedipus's exile from Thebes.

In the *Anatomy of Criticism*, Northrop Frye examines the causes and implications of the tragic hero's isolation. "The tragic hero is typically on top of the wheel of fortune, half-way between human society on the ground and the something greater in the sky. . . . Tragic heroes are so much the highest points in their human landscapes that they seem the inevitable conductors of the power about them, great trees more likely to be struck by lightning than a clump of grass . . . tragic heroes are wrapped in the mystery of their communion with that something beyond which we can see only through them, and which is the source of their strength and their fate alike."[1] That "something beyond" may be called God, or nature, or society, but in all cases it reveals some sort of eternal law, of the way things are or must be. Tragedy gives us an image of the hero struggling against that law, alone. Further struggle leads the hero into further isolation.

In reading *Hamlet, Death of a Salesman*, and other tragedies, we should mark the characteristics of the protagonist that set him or her apart from their fellows. We should also try to determine the religious or moral law against which the protagonist is struggling in his or her movement toward isolation.

Shakespeare and the Elizabethan Theater

Shakespeare's *Hamlet* is one of the decisive masterpieces of the Elizabethan stage. From the defeat of the Spanish Armada in 1588 until the closing of the theaters in 1642 because of the Civil War, the English theater experienced a flowering of genius unparalleled in history. Christopher Marlowe (1564–1593) developed the "mighty line" of blank verse that became the rhythmic heart of dramatic diction in such plays as *Tamburlaine* and *Dr. Faustus*. Ben Jonson wrote comedies of satiric wit, such as *Volpone* and *The Alchemist*. Thomas Dekker, John Webster, and others wrote plays that were not only popular but intelligent, proving that it was a culture of thoughtful audiences as well as gifted dramatists.

The most gifted of them all was William Shakespeare. As a poet, deviser of plots, and creator of character, Shakespeare was outstanding in a generation of extraordinary talents. He is one of the few who wrote comedies as well as tragedies and histories. His friend Ben Jonson said of him, "He was not of an age, but for all time!" John Dryden wrote that Shakespeare "had an Universal mind."

For someone who was so brilliant and made such an impact on the popular culture, Shakespeare has left remarkably few biographical traces. We know that he was baptized in Stratford-on-Avon on April 26, 1564, and that his father was a glover. We know he married Anne Hathaway when he was eighteen, and they had a daughter a few months later, the first of three children. He was a member

---

[1] Northrop Frye, *The Anatomy of Criticism: Four Essays* (Princeton, N.J.: Princeton University Press, 1957), pp. 207–208.

Model depicting a theatre of Shakespeare's time (*Richard Southern Accession, University of Bristol Theatre Collection*)

of the Lord Chamberlain's company of actors in 1594. In 1599 he joined a syndicate that built and managed the Globe Theatre, one of the most successful theaters of the time. In 1597 he bought one of the largest houses in Stratford. On April 23, 1616, he died and a few days later was buried at Stratford Church. That is nearly all we know about him. The thousands of pages of biography written about Shakespeare are mostly guesswork based on the plays and the history of the period. His personality remains as mysterious as his genius. Many cranks and some serious scholars have argued that Shakespeare did not write the masterpieces bearing his name. They say it is impossible that a man of such humble origins and rudimentary education could have created those thirty-odd dramas. And why aren't there more records, contemporary accounts of this famous man? No one really knows. We do know that the personal lives of dramatists did not stir up as much interest then as they do now. Playwrights were not considered serious "literary men" during Elizabethan times. We know as much about Shakespeare as about any other dramatist of his age except Ben Jonson, who had a literary reputation in addition to his theatrical fame. Whoever Shakespeare was, we are satisfied that he wrote *Hamlet* and the other great dramas assigned to him.

Hamlet was registered for printing in 1602; we believe it was first performed a year or two before that by the renowned actor Richard Burbage. It was probably among the first plays produced in the newly built Globe Theatre. No pictures have survived, and though there is some controversy over the arrangement of the Globe, we assume that it was a typical theater of the period.

Elizabethan theaters were much more intimate than the Greek amphitheaters. The entire Globe would have fit into the orchestra of the Theater of Dionysus. The Globe was an outdoor theater surrounded by covered galleries. The stage was a raised platform thrusting into the audience area. To the rear there was a curtained area that might have been used for a bedroom, an entrance hall, or other intimate scenes. Above this space was the balcony, famous for the love scene in *Romeo and Juliet*. It could also be used as the top of a wall for a battle scene, a prison room, or the upper deck of a ship. There was a trap door in the stage for the entrance of demons from the underworld, which would serve as the grave in the cemetery scenes from *Hamlet*. Ghosts and angels sometimes descended on ropes from the canopy extending over the stage.

There was no curtain between the main playing area and the audience to ease the transition between scenes. There were probably no painted sets, and few stage props. Much of the "scene-painting" is done with poetry. Shakespeare's characters verbally create the scene, and the audience must imagine it. The plays we have read thus far take place in a single, stationary setting. *Hamlet* is much more cinematic, its action moving from chamber to chamber within Elsinore Castle, then to the ramparts outside, or to a churchyard. There may be little more to indicate the change in scene than a rearrangement of chairs, or the opening of the trap door as a makeshift grave for the churchyard. The rest is done with words. Thus, at the opening of Act I, Scene 4, Hamlet says

Detail of Visscher's map of London c. 1616 showing the Globe Theatre (*Folger Shakespeare Library*)

to Horatio: "The air bites shrewdly; it is very cold," and Horatio answers: "It is a nipping and an eager air." Such poetic reporting of the weather is worth any number of wind-machines, particularly to the reader.

Although the stage props were minimal, the costuming was elaborate and beautiful. As in the Greek theater, all the actors were men. Apprentices, whose voices had not changed, played the roles of women.

Before the theaters were built, players performed in taverns and inns, and the atmosphere of the Elizabethan theater preserved much of its rowdy origin. The inns had an inner courtyard and rooms overlooking the yard where the actors set up their temporary stage. So the poor folks, or *groundlings*, watched the play from the yard, and the ladies and gentlemen who could afford rooms lounged on their balconies. The Globe was built with two or three tiers of covered balconies around the stage, and an open yard in front where the poorer spectators sat, stood, or rolled drunkenly. The atomosphere of the Elizabethan theater was a blend of the prize fight, the revival meeting, and a session of parliament— with musicians, pickpockets, and prostitutes moving through the crowd, and a good deal of conversation and spontaneous applause. This accounts for the oratory of some scenes and the slapstick humor of others in Shakespeare. It was no mean feat to hold the attention of such a varied and lively audience.

The story of *Hamlet* is an old one out of the *Historica Danica* (c. 1200; printed 1514) by the Danish chronicler Saxo Grammaticus. Shakespeare was not the first to dramatize it. He often took his plots from history, old legends, Italian novels, and other plays.

The text you will read is the product of nearly four hundred years of editing, scholarship, and controversy. Shakespeare wrote the dialogue. He did not divide the plays into acts and scenes, for the action in his theater was continuous. These divisions, as well as the scenic notes and stage directions, were done by John Heming and Henry Condell, two of Shakespeare's former colleagues who prepared the First Folio of his plays in 1623. They printed the Folio from playhouse scripts which probably were not all written in verses. Therefore, even the pentameter lines may be, to some extent, the result of editing.

WILLIAM SHAKESPEARE (1564–1616)

The Tragedy of Hamlet, Prince of Denmark

DRAMATIS PERSONAE

CLAUDIUS, *King of Denmark*	VOLTEMAND
HAMLET, *son to the late King Hamlet, and*	CORNELIUS
nephew to the present King	ROSENCRANTZ
POLONIUS, *Lord Chamberlain*	GUILDENSTERN *courtiers*
HORATIO, *friend to Hamlet*	OSRIC
LAERTES, *son to Polonius*	GENTLEMAN

MARCELLUS ⎫ *officers*
BARNARDO ⎭
FRANCISCO, *a soldier*
REYNALDO, *servant to Polonius*
FORTINBRAS, *Prince of Norway*
NORWEGIAN CAPTAIN
DOCTOR OF DIVINITY
PLAYERS
Two CLOWNS, *grave-diggers*

SCENE. *Denmark*

ENGLISH AMBASSADORS

GERTRUDE, *Queen of Denmark, and mother to*
  Hamlet
OPHELIA, *daughter to Polonius*

GHOST *of Hamlet's Father*

LORDS, LADIES, OFFICERS, SOLDIERS,
SAILORS, MESSENGERS, *and* ATTENDANTS

ACT I

SCENE I.

Enter BARNARDO *and* FRANCISCO, *two sentinels, [meeting].*

BAR. Who's there?

FRAN. Nay, answer me. Stand and unfold yourself.

BAR. Long live the King!

FRAN. Barnardo.

5   BAR. He.

FRAN. You come most carefully upon your hour.

BAR. 'Tis now strook twelf. Get thee to bed, Francisco.

FRAN. For this relief much thanks. 'Tis bitter cold,
    And I am sick at heart.

BAR. Have you had quiet guard?

10 FRAN.   Not a mouse stirring.

BAR. Well, good night.
    If you do meet Horatio and Marcellus,
    The rivals of my watch, bid them make haste.

Enter HORATIO *and* MARCELLUS.

FRAN. I think I hear them. Stand ho! Who is there?

HOR. Friends to this ground.

15 MAR.   And liegemen to the Dane.

FRAN. Give you good night.

MAR.   O, farewell, honest [soldier].
    Who hath reliev'd you?

Words and passages enclosed in square brackets in the text above are either emendations of the
copy-text or additions to it.

I.i. Location: Elsinore. A guard-platform of the castle.
² **answer me:** i.e. *you* answer *me.* Francisco is on watch; Barnardo has come to relieve him.   **unfold**
  yourself: make known who you are.
³ **Long . . . King.** Perhaps a password, perhaps simply an utterance to allow the voice to be recognized.
⁷ **strook twelf:** struck twelve.
⁹ **sick at heart:** in low spirits.
¹³ **rivals:** partners.
¹⁵ **liegemen . . . Dane:** loyal subjects to the King of Denmark.
¹⁶ **Give:** God give.

FRAN.   Barnardo hath my place.
　Give you good night.

Exit FRANCISCO.

MAR.   Holla, Barnardo!
BAR.   Say—
　What, is Horatio there?
HOR.   A piece of him.
20 BAR. Welcome, Horatio, welcome, good Marcellus.
HOR. What, has this thing appear'd again to-night?
BAR. I have seen nothing.
MAR. Horatio says 'tis but our fantasy,
　And will not let belief take hold of him
25 Touching this dreaded sight twice seen of us;
　Therefore I have entreated him along,
　With us to watch the minutes of this night,
　That if again this apparition come,
　He may approve our eyes and speak to it.
HOR. Tush, tush, 'twill not appear.
30 BAR.   Sit down a while,
　And let us once again assail your ears,
　That are so fortified against our story,
　What we have two nights seen.
HOR.   Well, sit we down,
　And let us hear Barnardo speak of this.
35 BAR. Last night of all,
　When yond same star that's westward from the pole
　Had made his course t' illume that part of heaven
　Where now it burns, Marcellus and myself,
　The bell then beating one—

Enter GHOST.

40 MAR. Peace, break thee off! Look where it comes again!
BAR. In the same figure like the King that's dead.
MAR. Thou art a scholar, speak to it, Horatio.
BAR. Looks 'a not like the King? Mark it, Horatio.
HOR. Most like; it [harrows] me with fear and wonder.
BAR. It would be spoke to.
45 MAR.   Speak to it, Horatio.
HOR. What art thou that usurp'st this time of night,

---

23 **fantasy:** imagination.
29 **approve:** corroborate.
36 **pole:** pole star.
37 **his:** its (the commonest form of the neuter possessive singular in Shakespeare's day).
41 **like:** in the likeness of.
42 **a scholar:** i.e. one who knows how best to address it.
43 **'a:** he.
45 **It . . . to.** A ghost had to be spoken to before it could speak.
46 **usurp'st.** The ghost, a supernatural being, has invaded the realm of nature.

Together with that fair and warlike form
In which the majesty of buried Denmark
Did sometimes march? By heaven I charge thee speak!
MAR. It is offended.
50 BAR.   See, it stalks away!
HOR. Stay! Speak, speak, I charge thee speak!

Exit GHOST.

MAR. 'Tis gone, and will not answer.
BAR. How now, Horatio? you tremble and look pale.
Is not this something more than fantasy?
55   What think you on't?
HOR. Before my God, I might not this believe
Without the sensible and true avouch
Of mine own eyes.
MAR.   Is it not like the King?
HOR. As thou art to thyself.
60   Such was the very armor he had on
When he the ambitious Norway combated.
So frown'd he once when in an angry parle
He smote the sledded [Polacks] on the ice.
'Tis strange.
65 MAR. Thus twice before, and jump at this dead hour,
With martial stalk hath he gone by our watch.
HOR. In what particular thought to work I know not,
But in the gross and scope of mine opinion,
This bodes some strange eruption to our state.
70 MAR. Good now, sit down, and tell me, he that knows,
Why this same strict and most observant watch
So nightly toils the subject of the land,
And [why] such daily [cast] of brazen cannon,
And foreign mart for implements of war,
75   Why such impress of shipwrights, whose sore task
Does not divide the Sunday from the week,
What might be toward, that this sweaty haste

---

48 **majesty . . . Denmark:** late King of Denmark.
49 **sometimes:** formerly.
57 **sensible:** relating to the senses.   **avouch:** guarantee.
61 **Norway:** King of Norway.
62 **parle:** parley.
63 **sledded:** using sleds or sledges.   **Polacks:** Poles.
65 **jump:** precisely.
67–68 **In . . . opinion:** while I have no precise theory about it, my general feeling is that. *Gross* = wholeness, totality; *scope* = range.
69 **eruption:** upheaval.
72 **toils:** causes to work.   **subject:** subjects.
74 **foreign mart:** dealing with foreign markets.
75 **impress:** forced service.
77 **toward:** in preparation.

Doth make the night joint-laborer with the day:
Who is't that can inform me?

HOR.   That can I,
80   At least the whisper goes so: our last king,
Whose image even but now appear'd to us,
Was, as you know, by Fortinbras of Norway,
Thereto prick'd on by a most emulate pride,
Dar'd to the combat; in which our valiant Hamlet
85   (For so this side of our known world esteem'd him)
Did slay this Fortinbras, who, by a seal'd compact
Well ratified by law and heraldy,
Did forfeit (with his life) all [those] his lands
Which he stood seiz'd of, to the conqueror;
90   Against the which a moi'ty competent
Was gaged by our king, which had [return'd]
To the inheritance of Fortinbras,
Had he been vanquisher; as by the same comart
And carriage of the article [design'd],
95   His fell to Hamlet. Now, sir, young Fortinbras,
Of unimproved mettle hot and full,
Hath in the skirts of Norway here and there
Shark'd up a list of lawless resolutes
For food and diet to some enterprise
100   That hath a stomach in't, which is no other,
As it doth well appear unto our state,
But to recover of us, by strong hand
And terms compulsatory, those foresaid lands
So by his father lost; and this, I take it,
105   Is the main motive of our preparations,
The source of this our watch, and the chief head
Of this post-haste and romage in the land.

BAR. I think it be no other but e'en so.
Well may it sort that this portentous figure
110   Comes armed through our watch so like the King
That was and is the question of these wars.

---

83 **emulate:** emulous, proceeding from rivalry.
87 **law and heraldy:** heraldic law (governing combat). *Heraldy* is a variant of *heraldry*.
89 **seiz'd of:** possessed of.
90 **moi'ty:** portion.   **competent:** adequate, i.e. equivalent.
91 **gaged:** pledged.   **had:** would have.
92 **inheritance:** possession.
93 **comart:** bargain.
94 **carriage:** tenor.   **design'd:** drawn up.
96 **unimproved:** untried (?) or not directed to any useful end (?).
97 **skirts:** outlying territories.
98 **Shark'd up:** gathered up hastily and indiscriminately.
100 **stomach:** relish of danger (?) or demand for courage (?).
106 **head:** source.
107 **romage:** rummage, bustling activity.
109 **sort:** fit.   **portentous:** ominous.

HOR. A mote it is to trouble the mind's eye.
In the most high and palmy state of Rome,
A little ere the mightiest Julius fell,
115 The graves stood [tenantless] and the sheeted dead
Did squeak and gibber in the Roman streets.
As stars with trains of fire, and dews of blood,
Disasters in the sun; and the moist star
Upon whose influence Neptune's empire stands
120 Was sick almost to doomsday with eclipse.
And even the like precurse of [fear'd] events,
As harbingers preceding still the fates
And prologue to the omen coming on,
Have heaven and earth together demonstrated
125 Unto our climatures and countrymen.

Enter GHOST.

But soft, behold! lo where it comes again!

It spreads his arms.

I'll cross it though it blast me. Stay, illusion!
If thou hast any sound or use of voice,
Speak to me.
130 If there be any good thing to be done
That may to thee do ease, and grace to me,
Speak to me.
If thou art privy to thy country's fate,
Which happily foreknowing may avoid,
135 O speak!
Or if thou hast uphoarded in thy life
Extorted treasure in the womb of earth,
For which, they say, your spirits oft walk in death,
Speak of it, stay and speak! (*The cock crows.*) Stop it, Marcellus.
140 MAR. Shall I strike it with my partisan?
HOR. Do, if it will not stand.
BAR.   'Tis here!

---

116 One or more lines may have been lost between this line and the next.
118 **Disasters:** ominous signs.   **moist star:** moon.
119 **Neptune's empire stands:** the seas are dependent.
120 **sick . . . doomsday:** i.e. almost totally darkened. When the Day of Judgment is imminent, says
Matthew 24:29, "the moon shall not give her light."   **eclipse.** There were a solar and two total
lunar eclipses visible in England in 1598; they caused gloomy speculation.
121 **precurse:** foreshadowing.
122 **harbingers:** advance messengers.   **still:** always.
123 **omen:** i.e. the events portended.
125 **climatures:** regions.
126 s.d. **his:** its.
127 **cross it:** cross its path, confront it directly.   **blast:** wither (by supernatural means).
134 **happily:** haply, perhaps.
138 **your.** Colloquial and impersonal; cf. I.v.167, IV.iii.20–21. Most editors adopt *you* from F1.
140 **partisan:** long-handled spear.

HOR. 'Tis here!

MAR. 'Tis gone!

[*Exit* GHOST.]

We do it wrong, being so majestical,
To offer it the show of violence,
145   For it is as the air, invulnerable,
And our vain blows malicious mockery.
BAR. It was about to speak when the cock crew.
HOR. And then it started like a guilty thing
Upon a fearful summons. I have heard
150   The cock, that is the trumpet to the morn,
Doth with his lofty and shrill-sounding throat
Awake the god of day, and at his warning,
Whether in sea or fire, in earth or air,
Th' extravagant and erring spirit hies
155   To his confine; and of the truth herein
This present object made probation.
MAR. It faded on the crowing of the cock.
Some say that ever 'gainst that season comes
Wherein our Saviour's birth is celebrated,
160   This bird of dawning singeth all night long,
And then they say no spirit dare stir abroad,
The nights are wholesome, then no planets strike,
No fairy takes, nor witch hath power to charm,
So hallowed, and so gracious, is that time.
165 HOR. So have I heard and do in part believe it.
But look, the morn in russet mantle clad
Walks o'er the dew of yon high eastward hill.
Break we our watch up, and by my advice
Let us impart what we have seen to-night
170   Unto young Hamlet, for, upon my life,
This spirit, dumb to us, will speak to him.
Do you consent we shall acquaint him with it,
As needful in our loves, fitting our duty?
MAR. Let's do't, I pray, and I this morning know
175   Where we shall find him most convenient.

Exeunt.

---

146 **malicious mockery:** mockery of malice, i.e. empty pretenses of harming it.
150 **trumpet:** trumpeter.
154 **extravagant:** wandering outside its proper bounds.   **erring:** wandering abroad.   **hies:** hastens.
156 **object:** sight.   **probation:** proof.
158 **'gainst:** just before.
162 **strike:** exert malevolent influence.
163 **takes:** bewitches, charms.
164 **gracious:** blessed.
166 **russet:** coarse greyish-brown cloth.

SCENE II.

Flourish. Enter CLAUDIUS, KING OF DENMARK, GERTRUDE THE QUEEN; COUNCIL: *as* POLONIUS; *and his son* LAERTES, HAMLET, *cum aliis [including* VOLTEMAND *and* CORNELIUS].

KING Though yet of Hamlet our dear brother's death
    The memory be green, and that it us befitted
    To bear our hearts in grief, and our whole kingdom
    To be contracted in one brow of woe,
5   Yet so far hath discretion fought with nature
    That we with wisest sorrow think on him
    Together with remembrance of ourselves.
    Therefore our sometime sister, now our queen,
    Th' imperial jointress to this warlike state,
10   Have we, as 'twere with a defeated joy,
    With an auspicious, and a dropping eye,
    With mirth in funeral, and with dirge in marriage,
    In equal scale weighing delight and dole,
    Taken to wife; nor have we herein barr'd
15   Your better wisdoms, which have freely gone
    With this affair along. For all, our thanks.
    Now follows that you know young Fortinbras,
    Holding a weak supposal of our worth,
    Or thinking by our late dear brother's death
20   Our state to be disjoint and out of frame,
    Co-leagued with this dream of his advantage,
    He hath not fail'd to pester us with message
    Importing the surrender of those lands
    Lost by his father, with all bands of law,
25   To our most valiant brother. So much for him.
    Now for ourself, and for this time of meeting,
    Thus much the business is: we have here writ
    To Norway, uncle of young Fortinbras—
    Who, impotent and bedred, scarcely hears
30   Of this his nephew's purpose—to suppress

I.ii. Location: The castle.
o.s.d. **Flourish**: trumpet fanfare.   **cum aliis**: with others.
² **befitted**: would befit.
⁴ **contracted in**: (1) reduced to; (2) knit or wrinkled in.   **brow of woe**: mournful brow.
⁹ **jointress**: joint holder.
¹⁰ **defeated**: impaired.
¹¹ **auspicious . . . dropping**: cheerful . . . weeping.
¹⁵ **freely**: fully, without reservation.
¹⁷ **know**: be informed, learn.
¹⁸ **supposal**: conjecture, estimate.
²¹ **Co-leagued**: joined.
²² **pester . . . message**: trouble me with persistent messages (the original sense of *pester* is "overcrowd").
²³ **Importing**: having as import.
²⁴ **bands**: bonds, binding terms.
²⁹ **impotent and bedred**: feeble and bedridden.

His further gait herein, in that the levies,
The lists, and full proportions are all made
Out of his subject; and we here dispatch
You, good Cornelius, and you, Voltemand,
35   For bearers of this greeting to old Norway,
Giving to you no further personal power
To business with the King, more than the scope
Of these delated articles allow.

[Giving a paper.]

Farewell, and let your haste commend your duty.
40 COR., VOL. In that, and all things, will we show our duty.
KING We doubt it nothing; heartily farewell.

[Exeunt VOLTEMAND and CORNELIUS.]

And now, Laertes, what's the news with you?
You told us of some suit, what is't, Laertes?
You cannot speak of reason to the Dane
45   And lose your voice. What wouldst thou beg, Laertes,
That shall not be my offer, not thy asking?
The head is not more native to the heart,
The hand more instrumental to the mouth,
Than is the throne of Denmark to thy father.
What wouldst thou have, Laertes?
50 LAER.   My dread lord,
Your leave and favor to return to France,
From whence though willingly I came to Denmark
To show my duty in your coronation,
Yet now I must confess, that duty done,
55   My thoughts and wishes bend again toward France,
And bow them to your gracious leave and pardon.
KING Have you your father's leave? What says Polonius?
POL. H'ath, my lord, wrung from me my slow leave
By laborsome petition, and at last
60   Upon his will I seal'd my hard consent.
I do beseech you give him leave to go.

---

31 **gait:** proceeding.
31–33 **in . . . subject:** since the troops are all drawn from his subjects.
38 **delated:** extended, detailed (a variant of *dilated*).
41 **nothing:** not at all.
45 **lose:** waste.
47 **native:** closely related.
48 **instrumental:** serviceable.
51 **leave and favor:** gracious permission.
56 **pardon:** permission to depart.
58 **H'ath:** he hath.
60 **hard:** reluctant.

KING Take thy fair hour, Laertes, time be thine,
And thy best graces spend it at thy will!
But now, my cousin Hamlet, and my son—
65 HAM. *[Aside.]* A little more than kin, and less than kind.
KING How is it that the clouds still hang on you?
HAM. Not so, my lord, I am too much in the sun.
QUEEN Good Hamlet, cast thy nighted color off,
And let thine eye look like a friend on Denmark.
70 Do not for ever with thy vailed lids
Seek for thy noble father in the dust.
Thou know'st 'tis common, all that lives must die,
Passing through nature to eternity.
HAM. Ay, madam, it is common.
QUEEN   If it be,
75 Why seems it so particular with thee?
HAM. Seems, madam? nay, it is, I know not "seems."
'Tis not alone my inky cloak, [good] mother,
Nor customary suits of solemn black,
Nor windy suspiration of forc'd breath,
80 No, nor the fruitful river in the eye,
Nor the dejected havior of the visage,
Together with all forms, moods, [shapes] of grief,
That can [denote] me truly. These indeed seem,
For they are actions that a man might play,
85 But I have that within which passes show,
These but the trappings and the suits of woe.
KING 'Tis sweet and commendable in your nature, Hamlet,
To give these mourning duties to your father.
But you must know your father lost a father,
90 That father lost, lost his, and the survivor bound
In filial obligation for some term
To do obsequious sorrow. But to persever
In obstinate condolement is a course
Of impious stubborness, 'tis unmanly grief,
95 It shows a will most incorrect to heaven,
A heart unfortified, or mind impatient,
An understanding simple and unschool'd:

---

64 **cousin:** kinsman (used in familiar address to any collateral relative more distant than a brother
  or sister; here to a nephew).
65 **A little . . . kind:** closer than a nephew, since you are my mother's husband; yet more distant
  than a son, too (and not well disposed to you).
67 **sun.** With obvious quibble on *son*.
70 **vailed:** downcast.
72 **common:** general, universal.
75 **particular:** individual, personal.
80 **fruitful:** copious.
92 **obsequious:** proper to obsequies.
93 **condolement:** grief.
95 **incorrect:** unsubmissive.

For what we know must be, and is as common
As any the most vulgar thing to sense,
100 Why should we in our peevish opposition
Take it to heart? Fie, 'tis a fault to heaven,
A fault against the dead, a fault to nature,
To reason most absurd, whose common theme
Is death of fathers, and who still hath cried,
105 From the first corse till he that died to-day,
"This must be so." We pray you throw to earth
This unprevailing woe, and think of us
As of a father, for let the world take note
You are the most immediate to our throne,
110 And with no less nobility of love
Than that which dearest father bears his son
Do I impart toward you. For your intent
In going back to school in Wittenberg,
It is most retrograde to our desire,
115 And we beseech you bend you to remain
Here in the cheer and comfort of our eye,
Our chiefest courtier, cousin, and our son.
QUEEN Let not thy mother lose her prayers, Hamlet,
I pray thee stay with us, go not to Wittenberg.
120 HAM. I shall in all my best obey you, madam.
KING Why, 'tis a loving and a fair reply.
Be as ourself in Denmark. Madam, come.
This gentle and unforc'd accord of Hamlet
Sits smiling to my heart, in grace whereof,
125 No jocund health that Denmark drinks to-day,
But the great cannon to the clouds shall tell,
And the King's rouse the heaven shall bruit again,
Respeaking earthly thunder. Come away.

Flourish. Exeunt all but HAMLET.

HAM. O that this too too sallied flesh would melt,
130 Thaw, and resolve itself into a dew!
Or that the Everlasting had not fix'd
His canon 'gainst [self-]slaughter! O God, God,
How [weary], stale, flat, and unprofitable

---

99 **any . . . sense:** what is perceived to be commonest.
101 **to:** against.
103 **absurd:** contrary.
107 **unprevailing:** unavailing.
111 **dearest:** most loving.
112 **impart:** i.e. impart love.
127 **rouse:** bumper, drink. **bruit:** loudly declare.
129 **sallied:** sullied. Many editors prefer the F1 reading, *solid*.
132 **canon:** law.

John Barrymore as Hamlet (*Harvard Theatre Collection*)

      Seem to me all the uses of this world!
135   Fie on't, ah fie! 'tis an unweeded garden
      That grows to seed, things rank and gross in nature
      Possess it merely. That it should come [to this]!
      But two months dead, nay, not so much, not two.
      So excellent a king, that was to this
140   Hyperion to a satyr, so loving to my mother
      That he might not beteem the winds of heaven
      Visit her face too roughly. Heaven and earth,
      Must I remember? Why, she should hang on him
      As if increase of appetite had grown
145   By what it fed on, and yet, within a month—
      Let me not think on't! Frailty, thy name is woman!—
      A little month, or ere those shoes were old
      With which she followed my poor father's body,
      Like Niobe, all tears—why, she, [even she]—
150   O God, a beast that wants discourse of reason
      Would have mourn'd longer—married with my uncle,
      My father's brother, but no more like my father
      Than I to Hercules. Within a month,

---

134 **uses:** customs.
137 **merely:** utterly.
139 **to:** in comparison with.
140 **Hyperion:** the sun-god.
141 **beteem:** allow.
147 **or ere:** before.
149 **Niobe.** She wept endlessly for her children, whom Apollo and Artemis had killed.
150 **wants . . . reason:** lacks the power of reason (which distinguishes men from beasts).

Ere yet the salt of most unrighteous tears
155 Had left the flushing in her galled eyes,
She married—O most wicked speed: to post
With such dexterity to incestious sheets,
It is not, nor it cannot come to good,
But break my heart, for I must hold my tongue.

Enter HORATIO, MARCELLUS, *and* BARNARDO.

HOR. Hail to your lordship!
160 HAM.   I am glad to see you well.
Horatio—or do I forget myself.
HOR. The same, my lord, and your poor servant ever.
HAM. Sir, my good friend—I'll change that name with you.
And what make you from Wittenberg, Horatio?
165 Marcellus.
MAR. My good lord.
HAM. I am very glad to see you. [*To* BARNARDO.] Good even, sir.—
But what, in faith, make you from Wittenberg?
HOR. A truant disposition, good my lord.
170 HAM. I would not hear your enemy say so,
Nor shall you do my ear that violence
To make it truster of your own report
Against yourself. I know you are no truant.
But what is your affair in Elsinore?
175 We'll teach you to drink [deep] ere you depart.
HOR. My lord, I came to see your father's funeral.
HAM. I prithee do not mock me, fellow student,
I think it was to [see] my mother's wedding.
HOR. Indeed, my lord, it followed hard upon.
180 HAM. Thrift, thrift, Horatio, the funeral bak'd-meats
Did coldly furnish forth the marriage tables.
Would I had met my dearest foe in heaven
Or ever I had seen that day, Horatio!
My father—methinks I see my father.
HOR. Where, my lord?
185 HAM.   In my mind's eye, Horatio.
HOR. I saw him once, 'a was a goodly king.
HAM. 'A was a man, take him for all in all,
I shall not look upon his like again.

---

154 **unrighteous:** i.e. hypocritical.
155 **flushing:** redness.   **galled:** inflamed.
157 **incestious:** incestuous. The marriage of a man to his brother's widow was so regarded until long
after Shakespeare's day.
163 **change:** exchange.
164 **what . . . from:** what are you doing away from.
169 **truant disposition:** inclination to play truant.
177 **studient:** student.
181 **coldly:** when cold.
182 **dearest:** most intensely hated.
183 **Or:** ere, before.

HOR. My lord, I think I saw him yesternight.
190 HAM. Saw, who?
HOR. My lord, the King your father.
HAM.   The King my father?
HOR. Season your admiration for a while
With an attent ear, till I may deliver,
Upon the witness of these gentlemen,
This marvel to you.
195 HAM. ·   For God's love let me hear!
HOR. Two nights together had these gentlemen,
Marcellus and Barnardo, on their watch,
In the dead waste and middle of the night,
Been thus encount'red: a figure like your father,
200 Armed at point exactly, cap-a-pe,
Appears before them, and with solemn march
Goes slow and stately by them; thrice he walk'd
By their oppress'd and fear-surprised eyes
Within his truncheon's length, whilst they, distill'd
205 Almost to jelly with the act of fear,
Stand dumb and speak not to him. This to me
In dreadful secrecy impart they did,
And I with them the third night kept the watch,
Where, as they had delivered, both in time,
210 Form of the thing, each word made true and good,
The apparition comes. I knew your father,
These hands are not more like.
HAM.   But where was this?
MAR. My lord, upon the platform where we watch.
HAM. Did you not speak to it?
HOR.   My lord, I did,
215 But answer made it none. Yet once methought
It lifted up it head and did address
Itself to motion like as it would speak;
But even then the morning cock crew loud,
And at the sound it shrunk in haste away
And vanish'd from our sight.
220 HAM.   'Tis very strange.
HOR. As I do live, my honor'd lord, 'tis true,
And we did think it writ down in our duty
To let you know of it.

---

192 **Season:** temper. **admiration:** wonder.
193 **deliver:** report.
198 **waste:** empty expanse.
200 **at point exactly:** in every particular. **cap-a-pe:** from head to foot.
203 **fear-surprised:** overwhelmed by fear.
204 **truncheon:** short staff carried as a symbol of military command.
205 **act:** action, operation.
207 **dreadful:** held in awe, i.e. solemnly sworn.
212 **are . . . like:** i.e. do not resemble each other more closely than the apparition resembled him.
216 **it:** its.
216-17 **address . . . motion:** begin to make a gesture.

HAM. Indeed, [indeed,] sirs. But this troubles me.
Hold you the watch to-night?

225 [MAR., BAR.]   We do, my lord.
HAM. Arm'd, say you?
[MAR., BAR.] Arm'd, my lord.
HAM. From top to toe?
[MAR., BAR.]   My lord, from head to foot.
HAM. Then saw you not his face.

230 HOR. O yes, my lord, he wore his beaver up.
HAM. What, look'd he frowningly?
HOR.   A countenance more
In sorrow than in anger.
HAM.   Pale, or red?
HOR. Nay, very pale.
HAM.   And fix'd his eyes upon you?
HOR. Most constantly.
HAM.   I would I had been there.

235 HOR. It would have much amaz'd you.
HAM. Very like, [very like]. Stay'd it long?
HOR. While one with moderate haste might tell a hundreth.
BOTH [MAR., BAR.] Longer, longer.
HOR. Not when I saw't.
HAM.   His beard was grisl'd, no?

240 HOR. It was, as I have seen it in his life,
A sable silver'd.
HAM.   I will watch to-night,
Perchance 'twill walk again.
HOR.   I warr'nt it will.
HAM. If it assume my noble father's person,
I'll speak to it though hell itself should gape

245 And bid me hold my peace. I pray you all,
If you have hitherto conceal'd this sight,
Let it be tenable in your silence still,
And whatsomever else shall hap to-night,
Give it an understanding but no tongue.

250 I will requite your loves. So fare you well.
Upon the platform 'twixt aleven and twelf
I'll visit you.
ALL   Our duty to your honor.
HAM. Your loves, as mine to you; farewell.

Exeunt [all but HAMLET].

My father's spirit—in arms! All is not well,
255 I doubt some foul play. Would the night were come!

---

230 **beaver:** visor.
237 **tell a hundreth:** count a hundred.
239 **grisl'd:** grizzled, mixed with grey.
247 **tenable:** held close.
251 **aleven:** eleven.
255 **doubt:** suspect.

Till then sit still, my soul. [Foul] deeds will rise,
Though all the earth o'erwhelm them, to men's eyes.

Exit.

SCENE III.

Enter LAERTES *and* OPHELIA, *his sister.*

LAER. My necessaries are inbark'd. Farewell.
  And, sister, as the winds give benefit
  And convey [is] assistant, do not sleep,
  But let me hear from you.
OPH.   Do you doubt that?
5 LAER. For Hamlet, and the trifling of his favor,
  Hold it a fashion and a toy in blood,
  A violet in the youth of primy nature,
  Forward, not permanent, sweet, not lasting,
  The perfume and suppliance of a minute—
  No more.
OPH.   No more but so?
10 LAER.   Think it no more:
  For nature crescent does not grow alone
  In thews and [bulk], but as this temple waxes,
  The inward service of the mind and soul
  Grows wide withal. Perhaps he loves you now,
15 And now no soil nor cautel doth besmirch
  The virtue of his will, but you must fear,
  His greatness weigh'd, his will is not his own,
  [For he himself is subject to his birth:]
  He may not, as unvalued persons do,
20 Carve for himself, for on his choice depends
  The safety and health of this whole state,
  And therefore must his choice be circumscrib'd
  Unto the voice and yielding of that body
  Whereof he is the head. Then if he says he loves you,

I.iii. Location: Polonius' quarters in the castle.
[1] **inbark'd:** embarked, abroad.
[3] **convey is assistant:** means of transport is available.
[6] **a fashion:** i.e. standard behavior for a young man.   **toy in blood:** idle fancy of youthful passion.
[7] **primy:** springlike.
[8] **Forward:** early of growth.
[9] **suppliance:** pastime.
[11] **crescent:** growing, increasing.
[12] **thews:** muscles, sinews.
[12–14] **as . . . withal:** as the body develops, the powers of mind and spirit grow along with it.
[15] **soil:** stain.   **cautel:** deceit.
[16] **will:** desire.
[17] **His greatness weigh'd:** considering his princely status.
[19] **unvalued:** of low rank.
[20] **Carve for himself:** indulge his own wishes.
[23] **voice:** vote, approval.   **yielding:** consent.   **that body:** i.e. the state.

25   It fits your wisdom so far to believe it
       As he in his particular act and place
       May give his saying deed, which is no further
       Than the main voice of Denmark goes withal.
       Then weigh what loss your honor may sustain
30   If with too crédent ear you list his songs,
       Or lose your heart, or your chaste treasure open
       To his unmast'red importunity.
       Fear it, Ophelia, fear it, my dear sister,
       And keep you in the rear of your affection,
35   Out of the shot and danger of desire.
       The chariest maid is prodigal enough
       If she unmask her beauty to the moon.
       Virtue itself scapes not calumnious strokes.
       The canker galls the infants of the spring
40   Too oft before their buttons be disclos'd,
       And in the morn and liquid dew of youth
       Contagious blastments are most imminent.
       Be wary then, best safety lies in fear:
       Youth to itself rebels, though none else near.
45 OPH. I shall the effect of this good lesson keep
       As watchman to my heart. But, good my brother,
       Do not, as some ungracious pastors do,
       Show me the steep and thorny way to heaven,
       Whiles, [like] a puff'd and reckless libertine,
50   Himself the primrose path of dalliance treads,
       And reaks not his own rede.
       LAER.   O, fear me not.

Enter POLONIUS.

       I stay too long—but here my father comes.
       A double blessing is a double grace,
       Occasion smiles upon a second leave.
55 POL. Yet here, Laertes? Aboard, aboard, for shame!
       The wind sits in the shoulder of your sail,
       And you are stay'd for. There—*[laying his hand on* LAERTES' *head]* my blessing with
          thee!

---

26 **in . . . place:** i.e. acting as he must act in the position he occupies.
28 **main:** general. **goes withal:** accord with.
30 **credent:** credulous.
35 **shot:** range.
39 **canker:** canker-worm.
40 **buttons:** buds. **disclos'd:** opened.
42 **blastments:** withering blights.
44 **to:** of.
47 **ungracious:** graceless.
49 **puff'd:** bloated.
51 **reaks:** recks, heeds. **rede:** advice. **fear me not:** don't worry about me.
54 **Occasion:** opportunity (here personified, as often). **smiles upon:** i.e. graciously bestows.

And these few precepts in thy memory
Look thou character. Give thy thoughts no tongue,
60   Nor any unproportion'd thought his act.
Be thou familiar, but by no means vulgar:
Those friends thou hast, and their adoption tried,
Grapple them unto thy soul with hoops of steel,
But do not dull thy palm with entertainment
65   Of each new-hatch'd, unfledg'd courage. Beware
Of entrance to a quarrel, but being in,
Bear't that th' opposed may beware of thee.
Give every man thy ear, but few thy voice,
Take each man's censure, but reserve thy judgment.
70   Costly thy habit as thy purse can buy,
But not express'd in fancy, rich, not gaudy,
For the apparel oft proclaims the man,
And they in France of the best rank and station
[Are] of a most select and generous chief in that.
75   Neither a borrower nor a lender [be],
For [loan] oft loses both itself and friend,
And borrowing dulleth [th'] edge of husbandry.
This above all: to thine own self be true,
And it must follow, as the night the day,
80   Thou canst not then be false to any man.
Farewell, my blessing season this in thee!
LAER. Most humbly do I take my leave, my lord.
POL. The time invests you, go, your servants tend.
LAER. Farewell, Ophelia, and remember well
What I have said to you.
85   OPH.   'Tis in my memory lock'd,
And you yourself shall keep the key of it.
LAER. Farewell.

Exit LAERTES.

POL. What is't, Ophelia, he hath said to you?
OPH. So please you, something touching the Lord Hamlet.
90   POL. Marry, well bethought.
'Tis told me, he hath very oft of late

---

59 **character:** inscribe.
60 **unproportion'd:** unfitting.
61 **familiar:** affable, sociable.   **vulgar:** friendly with everybody.
62 **their adoption tried:** their association with you tested and proved.
65 **courage:** spirited, young blood.
67 **Bear't that:** manage it in such a way that.
69 **Take:** listen to.   **censure:** opinion.
74 **generous:** noble.   **chief:** eminence (?). But the line is probably corrupt. Perhaps *of a* is intrusive, in which case *chief* = chiefly.
77 **husbandry:** thrift.
81 **season:** preserve (?) or ripen, make fruitful (?).
83 **invests:** besieges.   **tend:** wait.
90 **Marry:** indeed (originally the name of the Virgin Mary used as an oath).

Given private time to you, and you yourself
Have of your audience been most free and bounteous.
If it be so—as so 'tis put on me,
95 And that in way of caution—I must tell you,
You do not understand yourself so clearly
As it behooves my daughter and your honor.
What is between you? Give me up the truth.
OPH. He hath, my lord, of late made many tenders
100 Of his affection to me.
POL. Affection, puh! You speak like a green girl,
Unsifted in such perilous circumstance.
Do you believe his tenders, as you call them?
OPH. I do not know, my lord, what I should think.
105 POL. Marry, I will teach you: think yourself a baby
That you have ta'en these tenders for true pay,
Which are not sterling. Tender yourself more dearly,
Or (not to crack the wind of the poor phrase,
[Wringing] it thus) you'll tender me a fool.
110 OPH. My lord, he hath importun'd me with love
In honorable fashion.
POL. Ay, fashion you may call it. Go to, go to.
OPH. And hath given countenance to his speech, my lord,
With almost all the holy vows of heaven.
115 POL. Ay, springes to catch woodcocks. I do know,
When the blood burns, how prodigal the soul
Lends the tongue vows. These blazes, daughter,
Giving more light than heat, extinct in both
Even in their promise, as it is a-making,
120 You must not take for fire. From this time
Be something scanter of your maiden presence,
Set your entreatments at a higher rate
Than a command to parle. For Lord Hamlet,
Believe so much in him, that he is young,
125 And with a larger teder may he walk
Than may be given you. In few, Ophelia,

---

⁹⁴ **put on:** told to.
⁹⁹ **tenders:** offers.
¹⁰² **Unsifted:** untried.
¹⁰⁶ **tenders.** With play on the sense "money offered in payment" (as in *legal tender*).
¹⁰⁷ **Tender:** hold, value.
¹⁰⁹ **Wringing:** straining, forcing to the limit. **tender . . . fool:** (1) show me that you are a fool; (2) make me look like a fool; (3) present me with a (bastard) grandchild.
¹¹² **fashion.** See note on line 6.
¹¹³ **countenance:** authority.
¹¹⁵ **springes:** snares. **woodcocks.** Proverbially gullible birds.
¹²²⁻²³ **Set . . . parle:** place a higher value on your favors; do not grant interviews simply because he asks for them. Polonius uses a military figure: *entreatments* = negotiations for surrender; *parle* = parley, discuss terms.
¹²⁴ **so . . . him:** no more than this with respect to him.
¹²⁵ **larger teder:** longer tether.

Do not believe his vows, for they are brokers,
Not of that dye which their investments show,
But mere [implorators] of unholy suits,
130 Breathing like sanctified and pious bonds,
The better to [beguile]. This is for all:
I would not, in plain terms, from this time forth
Have you so slander any moment leisure
As to give words or talk with the Lord Hamlet.
135 Look to't, I charge you. Come your ways.
OPH. I shall obey, my lord.

Exeunt.

SCENE IV.

Enter HAMLET, HORATIO, *and* MARCELLUS.

HAM. The air bites shrowdly, it is very cold.
HOR. It is [a] nipping and an eager air.
HAM. What hour now?
HOR.   I think it lacks of twelf.
MAR. No, it is strook.
5 HOR. Indeed? I heard it not. It then draws near the season
Wherein the spirit held his wont to walk.

A flourish of trumpets, and two pieces goes off [within].

What does this mean, my lord?
HAM. The King doth wake to-night and takes his rouse,
Keeps wassail, and the swagg'ring up-spring reels;
10 And as he drains his draughts of Rhenish down,
The kettle-drum and trumpet thus bray out
The triumph of his pledge.
HOR.   Is it a custom?
HAM. Ay, marry, is't,
But to my mind, though I am native here

---

127 **brokers:** procurers.
128 **Not . . . show:** not of the color of their garments (*investments*) exhibit, i.e. not what they seem.
129 **mere:** out-and-out.
130 **bonds:** (lover's) vows or assurances. Many editors follow Theobald in reading *bawds*.
133 **slander:** disgrace. **moment:** momentary.
135 **Come your ways:** come along.

I.iv. Location: The guard-platform of the castle.
1 **shrowdly:** shrewdly, wickedly.
2 **eager:** sharp.
6 s.d. **pieces:** cannon.
8 **doth . . . rouse:** i.e. holds revels far into the night.
9 **wassail:** carousal. **up-spring:** wild dance.
10 **Rhenish:** Rhine wine.
12 **triumph . . . pledge:** accomplishment of his toast (by draining his cup at a single draft).

15	And to the manner born, it is a custom
	More honor'd in the breach than the observance.
	This heavy-headed revel east and west
	Makes us traduc'd and tax'd of other nations.
	They clip us drunkards, and with swinish phrase
20	Soil our addition, and indeed it takes
	From our achievements, though perform'd at height,
	The pith and marrow of our attribute.
	So, oft it chances in particular men,
	That for some vicious mole of nature in them,
25	As in their birth, wherein they are not guilty
	(Since nature cannot choose his origin),
	By their o'ergrowth of some complexion
	Oft breaking down the pales and forts of reason,
	Or by some habit, that too much o'er-leavens
30	The form of plausive manners—that these men,
	Carrying, I say, the stamp of one defect,
	Being nature's livery, or fortune's star,
	His virtues else, be they as pure as grace,
	As infinite as man may undergo,
35	Shall in the general censure take corruption
	From that particular fault: the dram of [ev'l]
	Doth all the noble substance of a doubt
	To his own scandal.

Enter GHOST.

HOR. ˙   Look, my lord, it comes!
HAM. Angels and ministers of grace defend us!
40   Be thou a spirit of health, or goblin damn'd,

---

[15] **manner:** custom (of carousing).
[16] **More . . . observance:** which it is more honorable to break than to observe.
[18] **tax'd of:** censured by.
[19] **clip:** clepe, call.
[20] **addition:** titles of honor.
[21] **at height:** most excellently.
[22] **attribute:** reputation.
[23] **particular:** individual.
[24] **vicious . . . nature:** small natural blemish.
[26] **his:** its.
[27] **By . . . complexion:** by the excess of some one of the humors (which were thought to govern the disposition).
[28] **pales:** fences.
[29] **o'er-leavens:** makes itself felt throughout (as leaven works in the whole mass of dough).
[30] **plausive:** pleasing.
[32] **Being . . . star:** i.e. whether they were born with it, or got it by misfortune. *Star* means "blemish."
[34] **undergo:** carry the weight of, sustain.
[35] **general censure:** popular opinion.
[36] **dram:** minute amount.   **ev'l:** evil, with a pun on *eale,* "yeast" (cf. *o'er-leavens* in line 29).
[37] **of a doubt.** A famous crux, for which many emendations have been suggested, the most widely accepted being Steevens' *often dout* (i.e. extinguish).
[38] **To . . . scandal:** i.e. so that it all shares in the disgrace.
[40] **of health:** wholesome, good.

Bring with thee airs from heaven, or blasts from hell,
Be thy intents wicked, or charitable,
Thou com'st in such a questionable shape
That I will speak to thee. I'll call thee Hamlet,
45 King, father, royal Dane. O, answer me!
Let me not burst in ignorance, but tell
Why thy canoniz'd bones, hearsed in death,
Have burst their cerements; why the sepulchre,
Wherein we saw thee quietly interr'd,
50 Hath op'd his ponderous and marble jaws
To cast thee up again. What may this mean,
That thou, dead corse, again in complete steel
Revisits thus the glimpses of the moon,
Making night hideous, and we fools of nature
55 So horridly to shake our disposition
With thoughts beyond the reaches of our souls?
Say why is this? wherefore? what should we do?

[GHOST] *beckons* [HAMLET].

HOR. It beckons you to go away with it,
As if it some impartment did desire
To you alone.
60 MAR.   Look with what courteous action
It waves you to a more removed ground,
But do not go with it.
HOR.   No, by no means.
HAM. It will not speak, then I will follow it.
HOR. Do not, my lord.
HAM.   Why, what should be the fear?
65 I do not set my life at a pin's fee,
And for my soul, what can it do to that,
Being a thing immortal as itself?
It waves me forth again, I'll follow it.
HOR. What if it tempt you toward the flood, my lord,
70 Or to the dreadful summit of the cliff
That beetles o'er his base into the sea,
And there assume some other horrible form
Which might deprive your sovereignty of reason,
And draw you into madness? Think of it.

---

43 **questionable:** inviting talk.
47 **canoniz'd:** buried with the prescribed rites.
48 **cerements:** grave clothes.
52 **complete steel:** full armor.
53 **Revisits.** The -s ending in the second person singular is common.
54 **fools of nature:** the children (or the dupes) of a purely natural order, baffled by the supernatural.
55 **disposition:** nature.
59 **impartment:** communication.
65 **fee:** worth.
73 **deprive . . . reason:** unseat reason from the rule of your mind.

75   The very place puts toys of desperation,
      Without more motive, into every brain
      That looks so many fadoms to the sea
      And hears it roar beneath.
      HAM.   It waves me still.—
      Go on, I'll follow thee.
      MAR. You shall not go, my lord.
80   HAM.   Hold off your hands.
      HOR. Be rul'd, you shall not go.
      HAM.   My fate cries out,
      And makes each petty artere in this body
      As hardy as the Nemean lion's nerve.
      Still am I call'd. Unhand me, gentlemen.
85   By heaven, I'll make a ghost of him that lets me!
      I say away!—Go on, I'll follow thee.

      Exeunt GHOST *and* HAMLET.

      HOR. He waxes desperate with [imagination].
      MAR. Let's follow. 'Tis not fit thus to obey him.
      HOR. Have after. To what issue will this come?
90   MAR. Something is rotten in the state of Denmark.
      HOR. Heaven will direct it.
      MAR.   Nay, let's follow him.

      Exeunt.

      SCENE V.

      Enter GHOST *and* HAMLET.

      HAM. Whither wilt thou lead me? Speak, I'll go no further.
      GHOST Mark me.
      HAM.   I will.
      GHOST   My hour is almost come
      When I to sulph'rous and tormenting flames
      Must render up myself.
      HAM.   Alas, poor ghost!
5   GHOST Pity me not, but lend thy serious hearing
      To what I shall unfold.
      HAM.   Speak, I am bound to hear.
      GHOST So art thou to revenge, when thou shalt hear.

      ---

      75 **toys of desperation:** fancies of desperate action, i.e. inclinations to jump off.
      77 **fadoms:** fathoms.
      82 **artere:** variant spelling of *artery*; here, ligament, sinew.
      83 **Nemean lion.** Slain by Hercules as one of his twelve labors.   **nerve:** sinew.
      85 **lets:** hinders.
      91 **it:** i.e. the issue.

      I.v. Location: On the battlements of the castle.

HAM. What?

GHOST I am thy father's spirit,
10 Doom'd for a certain term to walk the night,
And for the day confin'd to fast in fires,
Till the foul crimes done in my days of nature
Are burnt and purg'd away. But that I am forbid
To tell the secrets of my prison-house,
15 I could a tale unfold whose lightest word
Would harrow up thy soul, freeze thy young blood,
Make thy two eyes like stars start from their spheres,
Thy knotted and combined locks to part,
And each particular hair to stand an end,
20 Like quills upon the fearful porpentine.
But this eternal blazon must not be
To ears of flesh and blood. List, list, O, list!
If thou didst ever thy dear father love—

HAM. O God!

25 GHOST Revenge his foul and most unnatural murther.

HAM. Murther!

GHOST Murther most foul, as in the best it is,
But this most foul, strange, and unnatural.

HAM. Haste me to know't, that I with wings as swift
30 As meditation, or the thoughts of love,
May sweep to my revenge.

GHOST   I find thee apt,
And duller shouldst thou be than the fat weed
That roots itself in ease on Lethe wharf,
Wouldst thou not stir in this. Now, Hamlet, hear:
35 'Tis given out that, sleeping in my orchard,
A serpent stung me, so the whole ear of Denmark
Is by a forged process of my death
Rankly abus'd; but know, thou noble youth,
The serpent that did sting thy father's life
Now wears his crown.

40 HAM.   O my prophetic soul!
My uncle?

---

11 **fast:** do penance.
12 **crimes:** sins.
17 **spheres:** eye sockets; with allusion to the revolving spheres in which, according to the Ptolemaic astronomy, the stars were fixed.
19 **an end:** on end.
20 **fearful porpentine:** frightened porcupine.
21 **eternal blazon:** revelation of eternal things.
30 **meditation:** thought.
33 **Lethe:** river of Hades, the water of which made the drinker forget the past.   **wharf:** bank.
35 **orchard:** garden.
37 **forged process:** false account.
38 **abus'd:** deceived.

GHOST Ay, that incestuous, that adulterate beast,
With witchcraft of his wits, with traitorous gifts—
O wicked wit and gifts that have the power
45   So to seduce!—won to his shameful lust
The will of my most seeming virtuous queen.
O Hamlet, what [a] falling-off was there
From me, whose love was of that dignity
That it went hand in hand even with the vow
50   I made to her in marriage, and to decline
Upon a wretch whose natural gifts were poor
To those of mine!
But virtue, as it never will be moved,
Though lewdness court it in a shape of heaven,
55   So [lust], though to a radiant angel link'd,
Will [sate] itself in a celestial bed
And prey on garbage.
But soft, methinks I scent the morning air,
Brief let me be. Sleeping within my orchard,
60   My custom always of the afternoon,
Upon my secure hour thy uncle stole,
With juice of cursed hebona in a vial,
And in the porches of my ears did pour
The leprous distillment, whose effect
65   Holds such an enmity with blood of man
That swift as quicksilver it courses through
The natural gates and alleys of the body,
And with a sudden vigor it doth [posset]
And curd, like eager droppings into milk,
70   The thin and wholesome blood. So did it mine,
And a most instant tetter bark'd about,
Most lazar-like, with vile and loathsome crust
All my smooth body.
Thus was I, sleeping, by a brother's hand
75   Of life, of crown, of queen, at once dispatch'd,
Cut off even in the blossoms of my sin,
Unhous'led, disappointed, unanel'd,
No reck'ning made, but sent to my account
With all my imperfections on my head.

---

42 **adulterate**: adulterous.
54 **shape of heaven**: angelic form.
61 **secure**: carefree.
62 **hebona**: ebony (which Shakespeare, following a literary tradition, and perhaps also associating the word with *henbane*, thought the name of a poison).
68 **posset**: curdle.
69 **eager**: sour.
71 **tetter**: scabby eruption.   **bark'd**: formed a hard covering, like bark on a tree.
72 **lazar-like**: leperlike.
75 **at once**: all at the same time.   **dispatch'd**: deprived.
77 **Unhous'led**: without the Eucharist.   **disappointed**: without (spiritual) preparation.   **unanel'd**: unanointed, without extreme unction.

80   O, horrible, O, horrible, most horrible!
     If thou hast nature in thee, bear it not,
     Let not the royal bed of Denmark be
     A couch for luxury and damned incest.
     But howsomever thou pursues this act,
85   Taint not thy mind, nor let thy soul contrive
     Against thy mother aught. Leave her to heaven,
     And to those thorns that in her bosom lodge
     To prick and sting her. Fare thee well at once!
     The glow-worm shows the matin to be near,
90   And gins to pale his uneffectual fire.
     Adieu, adieu, adieu! remember me.

     [Exit.]

     HAM. O all you host of heaven! O earth! What else?
     And shall I couple hell? O fie, hold, hold, my heart,
     And you, my sinows, grow not instant old,
95   But bear me [stiffly] up. Remember thee!
     Ay, thou poor ghost, whiles memory holds a seat
     In this distracted globe. Remember thee!
     Yea, from the table of my memory
     I'll wipe away all trivial fond records,
100 All saws of books, all forms, all pressures past
     That youth and observation copied there,
     And thy commandement all alone shall live
     Within the book and volume of my brain,
     Unmix'd with baser matter. Yes, by heaven!
105 O most pernicious woman!
     O villain, villain, smiling, damned villain!
     My tables—meet it is I set it down
     That one may smile, and smile, and be a villain!
     At least I am sure it may be so in Denmark.

     [He writes.]

110 So, uncle, there you are. Now to my word:
     It is "Adieu, adieu! remember me."
     I have sworn't.
     HOR. [Within.] My lord, my lord!
     MAR. [Within.]   Lord Hamlet!

---

81 **nature:** natural feeling.
83 **luxury:** lust.
89 **matin:** morning.
90 **gins:** begins.
94 **sinows:** sinews.
97 **globe:** head.
98 **table:** writing tablet.
99 **fond:** foolish.
100 **saws:** wise sayings.   **forms:** shapes, images.   **pressures:** impressions.
110 **word:** i.e. word of command from the Ghost.

Enter HORATIO *and* MARCELLUS.

HOR.   Heavens secure him!

HAM. So be it!

115 MAR. Illo, ho, ho, my lord!

HAM. Hillo, ho, ho, boy! come, [bird,] come.

MAR. How is't, my noble lord?

HOR.   What news, my lord?

HAM. O, wonderful!

HOR. Good my lord, tell it.

HAM.   No, you will reveal it.

HOR. Not I, my lord, by heaven.

120 MAR.   Nor I, my lord.

HAM. How say you then, would heart of man once think it?—
But you'll be secret?

BOTH [HOR., MAR.] Ay, by heaven, [my lord].

HAM. There's never a villain dwelling in all Denmark
But he's an arrant knave.

125 HOR. There needs no ghost, my lord, come from the grave
To tell us this.

HAM.   Why, right, you are in the right,
And so, without more circumstance at all,
I hold it fit that we shake hands and part,
You, as your business and desire shall point you,

130 For every man hath business and desire,
Such as it is, and for my own poor part,
I will go pray.

HOR. These are but wild and whirling words, my lord.

HAM. I am sorry they offend you, heartily,
Yes, faith, heartily.

135 HOR.   There's no offense, my lord.

HAM. Yes, by Saint Patrick, but there is, Horatio,
And much offense too. Touching this vision here,
It is an honest ghost, that let me tell you.
For your desire to know what is between us,

140 O'ermaster't as you may. And now, good friends,
As you are friends, scholars, and soldiers,
Give me one poor request.

HOR. What is't, my lord, we will.

HAM. Never make known what you have seen tonight.

BOTH [HOR., MAR.] My lord, we will not.

HAM.   Nay, but swear't.

145 HOR.   In faith.
My lord, not I.

MAR.   Nor I, my lord, in faith.

---

116 **Hillo . . . come.** Hamlet answers Marcellus' halloo with a falconer's cry.
127 **circumstance:** ceremony.
138 **honest:** true, genuine.
143 **What is't:** whatever it is.

HAM. Upon my sword.

MAR.   We have sworn, my lord, already.

HAM. Indeed, upon my sword, indeed.

GHOST *cries under the stage.*

GHOST Swear.

150 HAM. Ha, ha, boy, say'st thou so? Art thou there, truepenny?
Come on, you hear this fellow in the cellarage,
Consent to swear.

HOR.   Propose the oath, my lord.

HAM. Never to speak of this that you have seen,
Swear by my sword.

155 GHOST *[Beneath.]* Swear.

HAM. *Hic et ubique?* Then we'll shift our ground.
Come hither, gentlemen,
And lay your hands again upon my sword.
Swear by my sword

160 Never to speak of this that you have heard.

GHOST *[Beneath.]* Swear by his sword.

HAM. Well said, old mole, canst work i' th' earth so fast?
A worthy pioner! Once more remove, good friends.

HOR. O day and night, but this is wondrous strange!

165 HAM. And therefore as a stranger give it welcome.
There are more things in heaven and earth, Horatio,
Than are dreamt of in your philosophy.
But come—
Here, as before, never, so help you mercy,

170 How strange or odd some'er I bear myself—
As I perchance hereafter shall think meet
To put an antic disposition on—
That you, at such times seeing me, never shall,
With arms encumb'red thus, or this headshake,

175 Or by pronouncing of some doubtful phrase,
As "Well, well, we know," or "We could, and if we would,"
Or "If we list to speak," or "There be, and if they might,"
Or such ambiguous giving out, to note
That you know aught of me—this do swear,

180 So grace and mercy at your most need help you.

---

¹⁴⁷ **Upon my sword:** i.e. on the cross formed by the hilt.
¹⁵⁰ **truepenny:** trusty fellow.
¹⁵⁶ **Hic et ubique:** here and everywhere.
¹⁶³ **pioner:** digger, miner (variant of *pioneer*).
¹⁶⁵ **as . . . welcome:** give it the welcome due in courtesy to strangers.
¹⁶⁷ **your.** See note on I.i.138. **philosophy:** i.e. natural philosophy, science.
¹⁷² **put . . . on:** behave in some fantastic manner, act like a madman.
¹⁷⁴ **encumb'red:** folded.
¹⁷⁶ **and if:** if.
¹⁷⁷ **list:** cared, had a mind.
¹⁷⁸ **note:** indicate.

GHOST [Beneath.] Swear.

[They swear.]

HAM. Rest, rest, perturbed spirit! So, gentlemen,
    With all my love I do commend me to you,
    And what so poor a man as Hamlet is
185   May do t' express his love and friending to you,
    God willing, shall not lack. Let us go in together,
    And still your fingers on your lips, I pray.
    The time is out of joint—O cursed spite,
    That ever I was born to set it right!
190   Nay, come, let's go together.

Exeunt.

ACT II

SCENE I.

Enter old POLONIUS *with his man* [REYNALDO].

POL. Give him this money and these notes, Reynaldo.
REY. I will, my lord.
POL. You shall do marvell's wisely, good Reynaldo,
    Before you visit him, to make inquire
    Of his behavior.
5   REY.   My lord, I did intend it.
POL. Marry, well said, very well said. Look you, sir,
    Inquire me first what Danskers are in Paris,
    And how, and who, what means, and where they keep,
    What company, at what expense; and finding
10   By this encompassment and drift of question
    That they do know my son, come you more nearer
    Than your particular demands will touch it.
    Take you as 'twere some distant knowledge of him,
    As thus, "I know his father and his friends,
15   And in part him." Do you mark this, Reynaldo?
REY. Ay, very well, my lord.
POL. "And in part him—but," you may say, "not well.
    But if't be he I mean, he's very wild,
    Addicted so and so," and there put on him

---

187 **still:** always.
190 **Nay . . . together.** They are holding back to let him go first.

II.i. Location: Polonius' quarters in the castle.
3 **marvell's:** marvelous(ly).
7 **Danskers:** Danes.
8 **keep:** lodge.
10 **encompassment:** circuitousness.   **drift of question:** directing of the conversation.
12 **particular demands:** direct questions.

20   What forgeries you please: marry, none so rank
    As may dishonor him, take heed of that,
    But, sir, such wanton, wild, and usual slips
    As are companions noted and most known
    To youth and liberty.
  REY.   As gaming, my lord.
25   POL. Ay, or drinking, fencing, swearing, quarrelling,
    Drabbing—you may go so far.
  REY. My lord, that would dishonor him.
  POL. Faith, as you may season it in the charge:
    You must not put another scandal on him,
30   That he is open to incontinency—
    That's not my meaning. But breathe his faults so quaintly
    That they may seem the taints of liberty,
    The flash and outbreak of a fiery mind,
    A savageness in unreclaimed blood,
    Of general assault.
35   REY.   But, my good lord—
  POL. Wherefore should you do this?
  REY.   Ay, my lord,
    I would know that.
  POL.   Marry, sir, here's my drift,
    And I believe it is a fetch of wit:
    You laying these slight sallies on my son,
40   As 'twere a thing a little soil'd [wi' th'] working,
    Mark you,
    Your party in converse, him you would sound,
    Having ever seen in the prenominate crimes
    The youth you breathe of guilty, be assur'd
45   He closes with you in this consequence:
    "Good sir," or so, or "friend," or "gentleman,"
    According to the phrase or the addition
    Of man and country.
  REY.   Very good, my lord.

---

20 **forgeries:** invented charges.
22 **wanton:** sportive.
26 **Drabbing:** whoring.
28 **Faith.** Most editors read *Faith, no,* following F1; this makes easier sense.   **season:** qualify, temper.
30 **open to incontinency:** habitually profligate.
31 **quaintly:** artfully.
34 **unreclaimed:** untamed.
35 **Of general assault:** i.e. to which young men are generally subject.
38 **fetch of wit:** ingenious device.
39 **sallies:** sullies, blemishes.
40 **soil'd . . . working:** i.e. shopworn.
43 **Having:** if he has.   **prenominate crimes:** aforementioned faults.
45 **closes:** falls in.   **in this consequence:** as follows.
47 **addition:** style of address.

POL. And then, sir, does 'a this—'a does—what was I about to say?
50 By the mass, I was about to say something.
Where did I leave?
REY.   At "closes in the consequence."
POL. At "closes in the consequence," ay, marry.
He closes thus: "I know the gentleman.
I saw him yesterday, or th' other day,
55 Or then, or then, with such or such, and as you say,
There was 'a gaming, there o'ertook in 's rouse,
There falling out at tennis"; or, perchance,
"I saw him enter such a house of sale,"
Videlicet, a brothel, or so forth. See you now,
60 Your bait of falsehood take this carp of truth,
And thus do we of wisdom and of reach,
With windlasses and with assays of bias,
By indirections find directions out;
So by my former lecture and advice
65 Shall you my son. You have me, have you not?
REY. My lord, I have.
POL.   God buy ye, fare ye well.
REY. Good my lord.
POL. Observe his inclination in yourself.
REY. I shall, my lord.
POL. And let him ply his music.
70 REY.   Well, my lord.
POL. Farewell.

Exit REYNALDO.

Enter OPHELIA.

How now, Ophelia, what's the matter?
OPH. O my lord, my lord, I have been so affrighted!
POL. With what, i' th' name of God?
OPH. My lord, as I was sewing in my closet,
75 Lord Hamlet, with his doublet all unbrac'd,
No hat upon his head, his stockins fouled,

---

56 **o'ertook in 's rouse:** overcome by drink.
61 **reach:** capacity, understanding.
62 **windlasses:** roundabout methods.   **assays of bias:** indirect attempts (a figure from the game of bowls, in which the player must make allowance for the curving course his bowl will take toward its mark).
63 **directions:** the way things are going.
65 **have me:** understand me.
66 **God buy ye:** good-bye (a contraction of *God be with you*).
68 **in:** by. Polonius asks him to observe Laertes directly, as well as making inquiries.
70 **let him ply:** see that he goes on with.
74 **closet:** private room.
75 **unbrac'd:** unlaced.
76 **stockins fouled:** stockings dirty.

Ungart'red, and down-gyved to his ankle,
Pale as his shirt, his knees knocking each other,
And with a look so piteous in purport
80   As if he had been loosed out of hell
To speak of horrors—he comes before me.
POL. Mad for thy love?
OPH.   My lord, I do not know,
But truly I do fear it.
POL.   What said he?
OPH. He took me by the wrist, and held me hard,
85   Then goes he to the length of all his arm,
And with his other hand thus o'er his brow,
He falls to such perusal of my face
As 'a would draw it. Long stay'd he so.
At last, a little shaking of mine arm,
90   And thrice his head thus waving up and down,
He rais'd a sigh so piteous and profound
As it did seem to shatter all his bulk
And end his being. That done, he lets me go,
And with his head over his shoulder turn'd,
95   He seem'd to find his way without his eyes,
For out a' doors he went without their helps,
And to the last bended their light on me.
POL. Come, go with me. I will go seek the King.
This is the very ecstasy of love,
100   Whose violent property fordoes itself,
And leads the will to desperate undertakings
As oft as any passions under heaven
That does afflict our natures. I am sorry—
What, have you given him any hard words of late?
105 OPH. No, my good lord, but as you did command
I did repel his letters, and denied
His access to me.
POL.   That hath made him mad.
I am sorry that with better heed and judgment
I had not coted him. I fear'd he did but trifle
110   And meant to wrack thee, but beshrow my jealousy!
By heaven, it is as proper to our age
To cast beyond ourselves in our opinions,
As it is common for the younger sort

---

77 **down-gyved:** hanging down like fetters on a prisoner's legs.
92 **bulk:** body.
99 **ecstasy:** madness.
100 **property:** quality. **fordoes:** destroys.
109 **coted:** observed.
110 **beshrow:** beshrew, plague take. **jealousy:** suspicious mind.
111 **proper . . . age:** characteristic of men of my age.
112 **cast beyond ourselves:** overshoot, go too far (by way of caution).

To lack discretion. Come, go we to the King.
115 This must be known, which, being kept close, might move
More grief to hide, than hate to utter love.
Come.

Exeunt.

SCENE II.

Flourish. Enter KING *and* QUEEN, ROSENCRANTZ *and* GUILDENSTERN *[cum aliis].*

KING Welcome, dear Rosencrantz and Guildenstern!
Moreover that we much did long to see you,
The need we have to use you did provoke
Our hasty sending. Something have you heard
5 Of Hamlet's transformation; so call it,
Sith nor th' exterior nor the inward man
Resembles that it was. What it should be,
More than his father's death, that thus hath put him
So much from th' understanding of himself,
10 I cannot dream of. I entreat you both
That, being of so young days brought up with him,
And sith so neighbored to his youth and havior,
That you voutsafe your rest here in our court
Some little time, so by your companies
15 To draw him on to pleasures, and to gather
So much as from occasion you may glean,
Whether aught to us unknown afflicts him thus,
That, open'd, lies within our remedy.
QUEEN Good gentlemen, he hath much talk'd of you,
20 And sure I am two men there is not living
To whom he more adheres. If it will please you
To show us so much gentry and good will
As to expend your time with us a while
For the supply and profit of our hope,
25 Your visitation shall receive such thanks
As fits a king's remembrance.
ROS.   Both your Majesties
Might, by the sovereign power you have of us,

---

¹¹⁵ **close:** secret.
¹¹⁵⁻¹⁶ **move . . . love:** cause more grievous consequences by its concealment than we shall incur
      displeasure by making it known.

II.ii. Location: The castle.
² **Moreover . . . you:** besides the fact that we wanted to see you for your own sakes.
⁶ **Sith:** since.
¹¹ **of:** from.
¹³ **voutsafe your rest:** vouchsafe to remain.
²¹ **more adheres:** is more attached.
²² **gentry:** courtesy.
²⁴ **supply and profit:** support and advancement.

> Put your dread pleasures more into command
> Than to entreaty.

GUIL.   But we both obey,
30   And here give up ourselves, in the full bent,
>   To lay our service freely at your feet,
>   To be commanded.

KING Thanks, Rosencrantz and gentle Guildenstern.

QUEEN Thanks, Guildenstern and gentle Rosencrantz.
35   And I beseech you instantly to visit
>   My too much changed son. Go some of you
>   And bring these gentlemen where Hamlet is.

GUIL. Heavens make our presence and our practices
>   Pleasant and helpful to him!

QUEEN   Ay, amen!

Exeunt ROSENCRANTZ *and* GUILDENSTERN *[with some* ATTENDANTS*]*.

Enter POLONIUS.

40   POL. Th' embassadors from Norway, my good lord,
>   Are joyfully return'd.

KING Thou still hast been the father of good news.

POL. Have I, my lord? I assure my good liege
>   I hold my duty as I hold my soul,
45   Both to my God and to my gracious king;
>   And I do think, or else this brain of mine
>   Hunts not the trail of policy so sure
>   As it hath us'd to do, that I have found
>   The very cause of Hamlet's lunacy.

50   KING O, speak of that, that do I long to hear.

POL. Give first admittance to th' embassadors;
>   My news shall be the fruit to that great feast.

KING Thyself do grace to them, and bring them in.

[Exit POLONIUS.*]*

> He tells me, my dear Gertrude, he hath found
55   The head and source of all your son's distemper.

QUEEN I doubt it is no other but the main,
>   His father's death and our [o'erhasty] marriage.

*Enter [*POLONIUS *with* VOLTEMAND *and* CORNELIUS, THE*]* EMBASSADORS.

---

30 **in . . . bent:** to our utmost.
40 **embassadors:** ambassadors.
42 **still:** always.
43 **liege:** sovereign.
47 **policy:** statecraft.
52 **fruit:** dessert.
55 **head.** Synonymous with *source*.   **distemper:** (mental) illness.
56 **doubt:** suspect.   **main:** main cause.

KING Well, we shall sift him.—Welcome, my good friends!
　　Say, Voltemand, what from our brother Norway?
60 VOL. Most fair return of greetings and desires.
　　Upon our first, he sent out to suppress
　　His nephew's levies, which to him appear'd
　　To be a preparation 'gainst the Polack;
　　But better look'd into, he truly found
65　It was against your Highness. Whereat griev'd,
　　That so his sickness, age, and impotence
　　Was falsely borne in hand, sends out arrests
　　On Fortinbras, which he, in brief, obeys,
　　Receives rebuke from Norway, and in fine,
70　Makes vow before his uncle never more
　　To give th' assay of arms against your Majesty.
　　Whereon old Norway, overcome with joy,
　　Gives him threescore thousand crowns in annual fee,
　　And his commission to employ those soldiers,
75　So levied, as before, against the Polack,
　　With an entreaty, herein further shown,

[Giving a paper.]

　　That it might please you to give quiet pass
　　Through your dominions for this enterprise,
　　On such regards of safety and allowance
　　As therein are set down.
80 KING 　　　　　　　　　It likes us well,
　　And at our more considered time we'll read,
　　Answer, and think upon this business.
　　Mean time, we thank you for your well-took labor.
　　Go to your rest, at night we'll feast together.
　　Most welcome home!

Exeunt EMBASSADORS [and ATTENDANTS].

85 POL. 　　　　　　　This business is well ended.
　　My liege, and madam, to expostulate
　　What majesty should be, what duty is,
　　Why day is day, night night, and time is time,
　　Were nothing but to waste night, day, and time;

---

61 **Upon our first**: at our first representation.
65 **griev'd**: aggrieved, offended.
67 **borne in hand**: taken advantage of.
69 **in fine**: in the end.
71 **assay**: trial.
79 **On . . . allowance**: with such safeguards and provisos.
80 **likes**: pleases.
81 **consider'd**: suitable for consideration.
86 **expostulate**: expound.

90   Therefore, [since] brevity is the soul of wit,
     And tediousness the limbs and outward flourishes,
     I will be brief. Your noble son is mad:
     Mad call I it, for to define true madness,
     What is't but to be nothing else but mad?
     But let that go.
95   QUEEN   More matter with less art.
     POL. Madam, I swear I use no art at all.
     That he's mad, 'tis true, 'tis true 'tis pity,
     And pity 'tis 'tis true—a foolish figure,
     But farewell it, for I will use no art.
100 Mad let us grant him then, and now remains
     That we find out the cause of this effect,
     Or rather say, the cause of this defect,
     For this effect defective comes by cause:
     Thus it remains, and the remainder thus.
105 Perpend.
     I have a daughter—have while she is mine—
     Who in her duty and obedience, mark,
     Hath given me this. Now gather, and surmise.

[Reads the salutation of the letter.]

     "To the celestial and my soul's idol, the most beautified Ophelia"—
110 That's an ill phrase, a vile phrase, "beautified" is a vile phrase. But you shall hear.
     Thus:
     "In her excellent white bosom, these, etc."
     QUEEN Came this from Hamlet to her?
     POL. Good madam, stay awhile. I will be faithful.

[Reads the] letter.

115 "Doubt thou the stars are fire,
     Doubt that the sun doth move,
     Doubt truth to be a liar,
     But never doubt I love.
     O dear Ophelia, I am ill at these numbers. I have not art to reckon my groans, but
120 that I love thee best, O most best, believe it. Adieu.
     Thine evermore, most dear lady,
        whilst this machine is to him, Hamlet."

---

90 **wit**: understanding, wisdom.
95 **art**: i.e. rhetorical art.
98 **figure**: figure of speech.
103 **For . . . cause**: for this effect (which shows as a defect in Hamlet's reason) is not merely accidental,
   and has a cause we may trace.
105 **Perpend**: consider.
110 **beautified**: beautiful (not an uncommon usage).
117 **Doubt**: suspect.
119 **ill . . . numbers**: bad at versifying. **reckon**: count (with a quibble on *numbers*).
122 **machine**: body.

This in obedience hath my daughter shown me,
And more [above], hath his solicitings,
125 As they fell out by time, by means, and place,
All given to mine ear.
KING But how hath she
Receiv'd his love?
POL. What do you think of me?
KING As of a man faithful and honorable.
POL. I would fain prove so. But what might you think,
130 When I had seen this hot love on the wing—
As I perceiv'd it (I must tell you that)
Before my daughter told me—what might you,
Or my dear Majesty your queen here, think,
If I had play'd the desk or table-book,
135 Or given my heart a [winking,] mute and dumb,
Or look'd upon this love with idle sight,
What might you think? No, I went round to work,
And my young mistress thus I did bespeak:
"Lord Hamlet is a prince out of thy star;
140 This must not be"; and then I prescripts gave her,
That she should lock herself from [his] resort,
Admit no messengers, receive no tokens.
Which done, she took the fruits of my advice;
And he repell'd, a short tale to make,
145 Fell into a sadness, then into a fast,
Thence to a watch, thence into a weakness,
Then to [a] lightness, and by this declension,
Into the madness wherein now he raves,
And all we mourn for.
KING Do you think ['tis] this?
150 QUEEN It may be, very like.
POL. Hath there been such a time—I would fain know that—
That I have positively said, "'Tis so,"
When it prov'd otherwise?
KING Not that I know.
POL. [Points to his head and shoulder.] Take this from this, if this be otherwise.

---

124 **more above:** furthermore.
129 **fain:** willingly, gladly.
134 **play'd . . . table-book:** i.e. noted the matter secretly.
135 **winking:** closing of the eyes.
136 **idle sight:** uncomprehending eyes.
137 **round:** straightforwardly.
138 **bespeak:** address.
139 **star:** i.e. sphere, lot in life.
143 **took . . . of:** profited by, i.e. carried out.
144 **repell'd:** repulsed.
146 **watch:** sleeplessness.
147 **lightness:** lightheadedness.

155   If circumstances lead me, I will find
        Where truth is hid, though it were hid indeed
        Within the centre.
        KING   How may we try it further?
        POL. You know sometimes he walks four hours together
        Here in the lobby.
        QUEEN   So he does indeed.
160   POL. At such a time I'll loose my daughter to him.
        Be you and I behind an arras then,
        Mark the encounter: if he love her not,
        And be not from his reason fall'n thereon,
        Let me be no assistant for a state,
        But keep a farm and carters.
165   KING   We will try it.

Enter HAMLET *[reading on a book].*

QUEEN But look where sadly the poor wretch comes reading.
POL. Away, I do beseech you, both away.
        I'll board him presently.

Exeunt KING *and* QUEEN.

                  O, give me leave,
        How does my good Lord Hamlet?
170   HAM. Well, God-a-mercy.
        POL. Do you know me, my lord?
        HAM. Excellent well, you are a fishmonger.
        POL. Not I, my lord.
        HAM. Then I would you were so honest a man.
175   POL. Honest, my lord?
        HAM. Ay, sir, to be honest, as this world goes, is to be one man pick'd out of ten thousand.
        POL. That's very true, my lord.
        HAM. For if the sun breed maggots in a dead dog, being a good kissing carrion—Have you a daughter?
180   POL. I have, my lord.
        HAM. Let her not walk i' th' sun. Conception is a blessing, but as your daughter may conceive, friend, look to't.

---

[157] **centre:** i.e. of the earth (which in the Ptolemaic system is also the center of the universe).
[161] **arras:** hanging tapestry.
[163] **thereon:** because of that.
[168] **board:** accost.   **presently:** at once.
[170] **God-a-mercy:** thank you.
[172] **fishmonger.** Usually explained as slang for "bawd," but no evidence has been produced for such a usage in Shakespeare's day.
[178] **good kissing carrion:** flesh good enough for the sun to kiss.
[181] **Conception:** understanding (with following play on the sense "conceiving a child").

POL. *[Aside.]* How say you by that? still harping on my daughter. Yet he knew me not
at first, 'a said I was a fishmonger. 'A is far gone. And truly in my youth I suff'red
185 much extremity for love—very near this. I'll speak to him again.—What do you read,
my lord?

HAM. Words, words, words.

POL. What is the matter, my lord?

HAM. Between who?

190 POL. I mean, the matter that you read, my lord.

HAM. Slanders, sir; for the satirical rogue says here that old men have grey beards, that
their faces are wrinkled, their eyes purging thick amber and plum-tree gum, and that
they have a plentiful lack of wit, together with most weak hams; all which, sir, though
I most powerfully and potently believe, yet I hold it not honesty to have it thus set
195 down, for yourself, sir, shall grow old as I am, if like a crab you could go backward.

POL. *[Aside.]* Though this be madness, yet there is method in't.—Will you walk out of
the air, my lord?

HAM. Into my grave.

POL. Indeed that's out of the air. *[Aside.]* How pregnant sometimes his replies are! a
200 happiness that often madness hits on, which reason and [sanity] could not so prosper-
ously be deliver'd of. I will leave him, [and suddenly contrive the means of meeting
between him] and my daughter.—My lord, I will take my leave of you.

HAM. You cannot take from me any thing that I will not more willingly part withal—
except my life, except my life, except my life.

205 POL. Fare you well, my lord.

HAM. These tedious old fools!

Enter GUILDENSTERN *and* ROSENCRANTZ.

POL. You go to seek the Lord Hamlet, there he is.

ROS. *[To* POLONIUS.] God save you, sir!

[Exit POLONIUS.]

GUIL. My honor'd lord!

210 ROS. My most dear lord!

HAM. My [excellent] good friends! How dost thou, Guildenstern? Ah, Rosencrantz! Good
lads, how do you both?

ROS. As the indifferent children of the earth.

GUIL. Happy, in that we are not [over-]happy, on Fortune's [cap] we are not the very
215 button.

HAM. Nor the soles of her shoe?

ROS. Neither, my lord.

HAM. Then you live about her waist, or in the middle of her favors?

GUIL. Faith, her privates we.

---

188 **matter**: subject; but Hamlet replies as if he had understood Polonius to mean "cause for a
quarrel."
194 **honesty**: a fitting thing.
196 **method**: orderly arrangement, sequence of ideas.
196–97 **out . . . air**: Outdoor air was thought to be bad for invalids.
199 **pregnant**: apt.
201 **suddenly**: at once.
213 **indifferent**: average.
219 **privates**: (1) intimate friends; (2) genitalia.

220 HAM. In the secret parts of Fortune? O, most true, she is a strumpet. What news?

ROS. None, my lord, but the world's grown honest.

HAM. Then is doomsday near. But your news is not true. [Let me question more in particular. What have you, my good friends, deserv'd at the hands of Fortune, that she sends you to prison hither?

225 GUIL. Prison, my lord?

HAM. Denmark's a prison.

ROS. Then is the world one.

HAM. A goodly one, in which there are many confines, wards, and dungeons, Denmark being one o' th' worst.

230 ROS. We think not so, my lord.

HAM. Why then 'tis none to you; for there is nothing either good or bad, but thinking makes it so. To me it is a prison.

ROS. Why then your ambition makes it one. 'Tis too narrow for your mind.

HAM. O God, I could be bounded in a nutshell, and count myself a king of infinite

235 space—were it not that I have bad dreams.

GUIL. Which dreams indeed are ambition, for the very substance of the ambitious is merely the shadow of a dream.

HAM. A dream itself is but a shadow.

ROS. Truly, and I hold ambition of so airy and light a quality that it is but a shadow's

240 shadow.

HAM. Then are our beggars bodies, and our monarchs and outstretch'd heroes the beggars' shadows. Shall we to th' court? for, by my fay, I cannot reason.

BOTH [ROS., GUIL.] We'll wait upon you.

HAM. No such matter. I will not sort you with the rest of my servants; for to speak to

245 you like an honest man, I am most dreadfully attended.] But in the beaten way of friendship, what make you at Elsinore?

ROS. To visit you, my lord, no other occasion.

HAM. Beggar that I am, I am [even] poor in thanks—but I thank you, and sure, dear friends, my thanks are too dear a halfpenny. Were you not sent for? is it your own

250 inclining? is it a free visitation? Come, come, deal justly with me. Come, come— nay, speak.

GUIL. What should we say, my lord?

HAM. Any thing but to th' purpose. You were sent for, and there is a kind of confession in your looks, which your modesties have not craft enough to color. I know the good

255 King and Queen have sent for you.

---

220 **strumpet.** A common epithet for Fortune, because she grants favors to all men.

228 **wards:** cells.

241 **bodies:** i.e. not shadows (since they lack ambition). **outstretch'd:** i.e. with their ambition extended to the utmost (and hence producing stretched-out or elongated shadows).

242 **fay:** faith.

243 **wait upon you:** attend you thither.

244 **sort:** associate.

245 **dreadfully:** execrably.

249 **too . . . halfpenny:** too expensive priced at a halfpenny, i.e. not worth much.

250 **justly:** honestly.

253 **but.** Ordinarily punctuated with a comma preceding, to give the sense "provided that it is"; but Q2 has no comma, and Hamlet may intend, or include, the sense "except."

254 **modesties:** sense of shame.

ROS. To what end, my lord?

HAM. That you must teach me. But let me conjure you, by the rights of our fellowship, by the consonancy of our youth, by the obligation of our ever-preserv'd love, and by what more dear a better proposer can charge you withal, be even and direct with me, whether you were sent for or no!

ROS. [Aside to GUILDENSTERN.] What say you?

HAM. [Aside.] Nay then I have an eye of you!—If you love me, hold not off.

GUIL. My lord, we were sent for.

HAM. I will tell you why, so shall my anticipation prevent your discovery, and your secrecy to the King and Queen moult no feather. I have of late—but wherefore I know not—lost all my mirth, forgone all custom of exercises; and indeed it goes so heavily with my disposition, that this goodly frame, the earth, seems to me a sterile promontory; this most excellent canopy, the air, look you, this brave o'erhanging firmament, this majestical roof fretted with golden fire, why, it appeareth nothing to me but a foul and pestilent congregation of vapors. What [a] piece of work is a man, how noble in reason, how infinite in faculties, in form and moving, how express and admirable in action, how like an angel in apprehension, how like a god! the beauty of the world; the paragon of animals; and yet to me what is this quintessence of dust? Man delights not me—nor women neither, though by your smiling you seem to say so.

ROS. My lord, there was no such stuff in my thoughts.

HAM. Why did ye laugh then, when I said, "Man delights not me"?

ROS. To think, my lord, if you delight not in man, what lenten entertainment the players shall receive from you. We coted them on the way, and hither are they coming to offer you service.

HAM. He that plays the king shall be welcome—his Majesty shall have tribute on me, the adventerous knight shall use his foil and target, the lover shall not sigh gratis, the humorous man shall end his part in peace, [the clown shall make those laugh whose lungs are [tickle] a' th' sere,] and the lady shall say her mind freely, or the [blank] verse shall halt for't. What players are they?

ROS. Even those you were wont to take such delight in, the tragedians of the city.

---

258 **consonancy . . . youth:** similarity of our ages.
259 **charge:** urge, adjure.   **even:** frank, honest (cf. modern "level with me").
262 **of:** on.
264 **prevent your discovery:** forestall your disclosure (of what the King and Queen have said to you in confidence).
265 **moult no feather:** not be impaired in the least.
266 **custom of exercises:** my usual athletic activities.
268 **brave:** splendid.
269 **fretted:** ornamented as with fretwork.
270 **piece of work:** masterpiece.
272 **express:** exact.
274 **quintessence:** finest and purest extract.
278 **lenten entertainment:** meager reception.
279 **coted:** outstripped.
281 **on:** of, from.
282 **adventerous:** adventurous, i.e. wandering in search of adventure.   **foil and target:** light fencing sword and small shield.   **gratis:** without reward.
283 **humorous:** dominated by some eccentric trait (like the melancholy Jaques in As You Like It).
284 **tickle . . . sere:** i.e. easily made to laugh (literally, describing a gun that goes off easily; sere = a catch in the gunlock; tickle = easily affected, highly sensitive to stimulus).
285 **halt:** limp, come off lamely (the verse will not scan if she omits indecent words).

HAM. How chances it they travel? Their residence, both in reputation and profit, was better both ways.

ROS. I think their inhibition comes by the means of the late innovation.

290 HAM. Do they hold the same estimation they did when I was in the city? Are they so follow'd?

ROS. No indeed are they not.

[HAM. How comes it? do they grow rusty?

ROS. Nay, their endeavor keeps in the wonted pace; but there is, sir, an aery of children,
295 little eyases, that cry out on the top of question, and are most tyrannically clapp'd for't. These are now the fashion, and so [berattle] the common stages—so they call them— that many wearing rapiers are afraid of goose-quills and dare scarce come thither.

HAM. What, are they children? Who maintains 'em? How are they escoted? Will they pursue the quality no longer than they can sing? Will they not say afterwards, if they
300 should grow themselves to common players (as it is [most like], if their means are [no] better), their writers do them wrong, to make them exclaim against their own succession?

ROS. Faith, there has been much to do on both sides, and the nation holds it no sin to tarre them to controversy. There was for a while no money bid for argument, unless
305 the poet and the player went to cuffs in the question.

HAM. Is't possible?

GUIL. O, there has been much throwing about of brains.

HAM. Do the boys carry it away?

ROS. Ay, that they do, my lord—Hercules and his load too.]

---

289 **inhibition:** hindrance (to playing in the city). The word could be used of an official prohibition. See next note. **innovation.** Shakespeare elsewhere uses this word of a political uprising or revolt, and line 289 is often explained as meaning that the company had been forbidden to play in the city as the result of some disturbance. It is commonly conjectured that the allusion is to the Essex rebellion of 1601, but it is known that Shakespeare's company, though to some extent involved on account of the special performance of *Richard II* it was commissioned to give on the eve of the rising, was not in fact punished by inhibition. A second interpretation explains *innovation* as referring to the new theatrical vogue described in lines 294 ff., and conjectures that *inhibition* may allude to a Privy Council order of 1600 restricting the number of London playhouses to two and the number of performances to two a week.

293–309 **How . . . too.** This passage refers topically to the "War of the Theatres" between the child actors and their poet Jonson on the one side, and on the other the adults, with Dekker, Marston, and possibly Shakespeare as spokesmen, in 1600–1601.

294 **aery:** nest.

295 **eyases:** unfledged hawks. **cry . . . question:** cry shrilly above others in controversy. **tyrannically:** outrageously.

296 **berattle:** cry down, satirize. **common stages:** public theaters (the children played at the Black-friars, a private theater).

297 **goose-quills:** pens (of satirical playwrights).

298 **escoted:** supported.

299 **quality:** profession (of acting). **no . . . sing:** i.e. only until their voices change.

302 **succession:** future.

303 **to do:** ado.

304 **tarre:** incite. **argument:** plot of a play.

305 **in the question:** i.e. as part of the script.

308 **carry it away:** win.

309 **Hercules . . . too.** Hercules in the course of one of his twelve labors supported the world for Atlas; the children do better, for they carry away the world and Hercules as well. There is an allusion to the Globe playhouse, which reportedly had for its sign the figure of Hercules upholding the world.

310   HAM. It is not very strange, for my uncle is King of Denmark, and those that would make
mouths at him while my father liv'd, give twenty, forty, fifty, a hundred ducats a-
piece for his picture in little. 'Sblood, there is something in this more than natural,
if philosophy could find it out.

A flourish [for the PLAYERS].

    GUIL. There are the players.
315   HAM. Gentlemen, you are welcome to Elsinore. Your hands, come then: th' appurte-
nance of welcome is fashion and ceremony. Let me comply with you in this garb,
[lest my] extent to the players, which, I tell you, must show fairly outwards, should
more appear like entertainment than yours. You are welcome; but my uncle-father
and aunt-mother are deceiv'd.
320   GUIL. In what, my dear lord?
    HAM. I am but mad north-north-west. When the wind is southerly I know a hawk from
a hand-saw.

Enter POLONIUS.

    POL. Well be with you, gentlemen!
    HAM. *[Aside to them.]* Hark you, Guildenstern, and you too—at each ear a hearer—
325   that great baby you see there is not yet out of his swaddling-clouts.
    ROS. Happily he is the second time come to them, for they say an old man is twice a
child.
    HAM. I will prophesy, he comes to tell me of the players, mark it. *[Aloud.]* You say
right, sir, a' Monday morning, 'twas then indeed.
330   POL. My lord, I have news to tell you.
    HAM. My lord, I have news to tell you. When Roscius was an actor in Rome—
    POL. The actors are come hither, my lord.
    HAM. Buzz, buzz!
    POL. Upon my honor—
335   HAM. "Then came each actor on his ass"—
    POL. The best actors in the world, either for tragedy, comedy, history, pastoral, pastoral-
comical, historical-pastoral, [tragical-historical, tragical-comical-historical-pastoral,]
scene individable, or poem unlimited; Seneca cannot be too heavy, nor Plautus
too light, for the law of writ and the liberty: these are the only men.

---

311 **mouths:** derisive faces.
312 **'Sblood:** by God's (Christ's) blood.
316 **comply:** observe the formalities.   **garb:** fashion, manner.
317 **my extent:** i.e. the degree of courtesy I show.
318 **more . . . yours:** seem to be a warmer reception than I have given you.
321-22 **hawk, hand-saw.** Both cutting tools; but also both birds, if *hand-saw* quibbles on *hernshaw,*
"heron," a bird preyed upon by the hawk.
325 **swaddling-clouts:** swaddling clothes.
326 **Happily:** haply, perhaps.   **twice:** i.e. for the second time.
331 **Roscius:** the most famous of Roman actors (died 62 B.C.). News about him would be stale news
indeed.
333 **Buzz:** exclamation of impatience at someone who tells news already known.
338 **scene individable:** play observing the unity of place.   **poem unlimited:** play ignoring rules such
as the three unities.   **Seneca:** Roman writer of tragedies.   **Plautus:** Roman writer of comedies.
339 **for . . . liberty:** for strict observance of the rules, or for freedom from them (with possible allusion

340 HAM. O Jephthah, judge of Israel, what a treasure hadst thou!
    POL. What a treasure had he, my lord?

HAM. Why—

"One fair daughter, and no more,
The which he loved passing well."

345 POL. *[Aside.]* Still on my daughter.
    HAM. Am I not i' th' right, old Jephthah?
    POL. If you call me Jephthah, my lord, I have a daughter that I love passing well.
    HAM. Nay, that follows not.
    POL. What follows then, my lord?
350 HAM. Why—

"As by lot, God wot,"

and then, you know,

"It came to pass, as most like it was"—

the first row of the pious chanson will show you more, for look where my abridgment
355 comes.

Enter the PLAYERS, *[four or five].*

You are welcome, masters, welcome all. I am glad to see thee well. Welcome, good
friends. O, old friend! why, thy face is valanc'd since I saw thee last; com'st thou to
beard me in Denmark? What, my young lady and mistress! by' lady, your ladyship is
nearer to heaven than when I saw you last, by the altitude of a chopine. Pray God
360 your voice, like a piece of uncurrent gold, be not crack'd within the ring. Masters,
you are all welcome. We'll e'en to't like [French] falc'ners—fly at any thing we see;
we'll have a speech straight. Come give us a taste of your quality, come, a passionate
speech.
    [1] PLAY. What speech, my good lord?
365 HAM. I heard thee speak me a speech once, but it was never acted, or if it was, not above
    once; for the play, I remember, pleas'd not the million, 'twas caviary to the general,
    but it was—as I receiv'd it, and others, whose judgments in such matters cried in the
    top of mine—an excellent play, well digested in the scenes, set down with as much
    modesty as cunning. I remember one said there were no sallets in the lines to make

---

to the location of playhouses, which were not built in properties under city jurisdiction, but in
the "liberties"—land once monastic and now outside the jurisdiction of the city authorities).
    only: very best (a frequent use).
340 **Jephthah . . . Israel:** title of a ballad, from which Hamlet goes on to quote. For the story of
    Jephthah and his daughter, see Judges 11.
354 **row:** stanza. **chanson:** song, ballad. **abridgment:** (1) interruption; (2) pastime.
357 **valanc'd:** fringed, i.e. bearded.
358 **beard:** confront boldly (with obvious pun). **by' lady:** by Our Lady.
359 **chopine:** thick-soled shoe.
360 **crack'd . . . ring:** i.e. broken to the point where you can no longer play female roles. A coin
    with a crack extending far enough in from the edge to cross the circle surrounding the stamp of
    the sovereign's head was unacceptable in exchange (*uncurrent*).
362 **straight:** straightway. **quality:** professional skill.
366 **caviary . . . general:** caviar to the common people, i.e. too choice for the multitude.
367-68 **cried . . . of:** were louder than, i.e. carried more authority than.
369 **sallets:** salads, i.e. spicy jokes.

370   the matter savory, nor no matter in the phrase that might indict the author of
affection, but call'd it an honest method, as wholesome as sweet, and by very much
more handsome than fine. One speech in't I chiefly lov'd, 'twas Aeneas' [tale] to Dido,
and thereabout of it especially when he speaks of Priam's slaughter. If it live in your
memory, begin at this line—let me see, let me see:

375   "The rugged Pyrrhus, like th' Hyrcanian beast—"
'Tis not so, it begins with Pyrrhus:
"The rugged Pyrrhus, he whose sable arms,
Black as his purpose, did the night resemble
When he lay couched in th' ominous horse,

380   Hath now this dread and black complexion smear'd
With heraldy more dismal: head to foot
Now is he total gules, horridly trick'd
With blood of fathers, mothers, daughters, sons,
Bak'd and impasted with the parching streets,

385   That lend a tyrannous and a damned light
To their lord's murther. Roasted in wrath and fire,
And thus o'er-sized with coagulate gore,
With eyes like carbuncles, the hellish Pyrrhus
Old grandsire Priam seeks."

390   So proceed you.
POL. 'Fore God, my lord, well spoken, with good accent and good discretion.
[1] PLAY. "Anon he finds him
Striking too short at Greeks. His antique sword,
Rebellious to his arm, lies where it falls,

395   Repugnant to command. Unequal match'd,
Pyrrhus at Priam drives, in rage strikes wide,
But with the whiff and wind of his fell sword
Th' unnerved father falls. [Then senseless Ilium,]
Seeming to feel this blow, with flaming top

400   Stoops to his base, and with a hideous crash
Takes prisoner Pyrrhus' ear; for lo his sword,
Which was declining on the milky head
Of reverent Priam, seem'd i' th' air to stick.

---

370 **savory:** zesty.
371 **affection:** affectation.
372 **fine:** showily dressed (in language).
373 **Priam's slaughter:** the slaying of Priam (at the fall of Troy).
375 **Pyrrhus:** another name for Neoptolemus, Achilles' son. **Hyrcanian beast.** Hyrcania in the Caucasus was notorious for its tigers.
377 **sable arms.** The Greeks within the Trojan horse had blackened their skin so as to be inconspicuous when they emerged at night.
381 **heraldy:** heraldry. **dismal:** ill-boding.
382 **gules:** red (heraldic term). **trick'd:** adorned.
384 **Bak'd:** caked. **impasted:** crusted. **with . . . streets:** i.e. by the heat from the burning streets.
387 **o'er-sized:** covered over as with a coat of sizing.
388 **carbuncles:** jewels believed to shine in the dark.
395 **Repugnant:** resistant, hostile.
397 **fell:** cruel.
398 **unnerved:** drained of strength. **senseless:** insensible. **Ilium:** the citadel of Troy.
403 **reverent:** reverend, aged.

So as a painted tyrant Pyrrhus stood
405 [And,] like a neutral to his will and matter,
Did nothing.
But as we often see, against some storm,
A silence in the heavens, the rack stand still,
The bold winds speechless, and the orb below
410 As hush as death, anon the dreadful thunder
Doth rend the region; so after Pyrrhus' pause,
A roused vengeance sets him new a-work,
And never did the Cyclops' hammers fall
On Mars's armor forg'd for proof eterne
415 With less remorse than Pyrrhus' bleeding sword
Now falls on Priam.
Out, out, thou strumpet Fortune! All you gods,
In general synod take away her power!
Break all the spokes and [fellies] from her wheel,
420 And bowl the round nave down the hill of heaven
As low as to the fiends!"
POL. This is too long.
HAM. It shall to the barber's with your beard. Prithee say on, he's for a jig or a tale of
bawdry, or he sleeps. Say on, come to Hecuba.
425 [1] PLAY. "But who, ah woe, had seen the mobled queen"—
HAM. "The mobled queen"?
POL. That's good, ["[mobled] queen" is good].
[1] PLAY. "Run barefoot up and down, threat'ning the flames
With bisson rheum, a clout upon that head
430 Where late the diadem stood, and for a robe,
About her lank and all o'er-teemed loins,
A blanket, in the alarm of fear caught up—
Who this had seen, with tongue in venom steep'd,
'Gainst Fortune's state would treason have pronounc'd.
435 But if the gods themselves did see her then,
When she saw Pyrrhus make malicious sport
In mincing with his sword her [husband's] limbs,
The instant burst of clamor that she made,
Unless things mortal move them not at all,

---

405 **like . . . matter:** i.e. poised midway between intention and performance.
407 **against:** just before.
408 **rack:** cloud mass.
411 **region:** i.e. air.
413 **Cyclops:** giants who worked in Vulcan's smithy, where armor was made for the gods.
414 **proof eterne:** eternal endurance.
415 **remorse:** pity.
419 **fellies:** rims.
420 **nave:** hub.
423 **jig:** song-and-dance entertainment performed after the main play.
425 **mobled:** muffled.
429 **bisson rheum:** blinding tears.   **clout:** cloth.
431 **o'er-teemed:** worn out by childbearing.
434 **state:** rule, government.

440   Would have made milch the burning eyes of heaven,
        And passion in the gods."

POL. Look whe'er he has not turn'd his color and has tears in 's eyes. Prithee no more.

HAM. 'Tis well, I'll have thee speak out the rest of this soon. Good my lord, will you see
    the players well bestow'd? Do you hear, let them be well us'd, for they are the abstract
445   and brief chronicles of the time. After your death you were better have a bad epitaph
    than their ill report while you live.

POL. My lord, I will use them according to their desert.

HAM. God's bodkin, man, much better: use every man after his desert, and who shall
    scape whipping? Use them after your own honor and dignity—the less they deserve,
450   the more merit is in your bounty. Take them in.

POL. Come, sirs.

[Exit.]

HAM. Follow him, friends, we'll hear a play tomorrow.

[Exeunt all the PLAYERS *but the* FIRST.]

    Dost thou hear me, old friend? Can you play "The Murther of Gonzago"?

[1] PLAY. Ay, my lord.

455 HAM. We'll ha't to-morrow night. You could for need study a speech of some dozen
    lines, or sixteen lines, which I would set down and insert in't, could you not?

[1] PLAY. Ay, my lord.

HAM. Very well. Follow that lord, and look you mock him not. *[Exit* FIRST PLAYER.]
    My good friends, I'll leave you [till] night. You are welcome to Elsinore.

460 ROS. Good my lord!

HAM. Ay so, God buy to you.

Exeunt [ROSENCRANTZ *and* GUILDENSTERN].

                  Now I am alone.
    O, what a rogue and peasant slave am I!
    It is not monstrous that this player here,
    But in a fiction, in a dream of passion,
465   Could force his soul so to his own conceit
    That from her working all the visage wann'd,
    Tears in his eyes, distraction in his aspect,
    A broken voice, an' his whole function suiting
    With forms to his conceit? And all for nothing,
470   For Hecuba!
    What's Hecuba to him, or he to [Hecuba],
    That he should weep for her? What would he do

---

440 **milch:** moist (literally, milky).
441 **passion:** grief.
442 **Look . . . not:** i.e. note how he has.
444 **bestow'd:** lodged.   **us'd:** treated.
448 **God's bodkin:** by God's (Christ's) little body.
455 **for need:** if necessary.
465 **conceit:** imaginative conception.
468 **his whole function:** the operation of his whole body.
469 **forms:** actions, expressions.

Had he the motive and [the cue] for passion
That I have? He would drown the stage with tears,
475 And cleave the general ear with horrid speech,
Make mad the guilty, and appall the free,
Confound the ignorant, and amaze indeed
The very faculties of eyes and ears. Yet I,
A dull and muddy-mettled rascal, peak
480 Like John-a-dreams, unpregnant of my cause,
And can say nothing; no, not for a king,
Upon whose property and most dear life
A damn'd defeat was made. Am I a coward?
Who calls me villain, breaks my pate across,
485 Plucks off my beard and blows it in my face,
Tweaks me by the nose, gives me the lie i' th' throat
As deep as to the lungs? Who does me this?
Hah, 'swounds, I should take it; for it cannot be
But I am pigeon-liver'd, and lack gall
490 To make oppression bitter, or ere this
I should 'a' fatted all the region kites
With this slave's offal. Bloody, bawdy villain!
Remorseless, treacherous, lecherous, kindless villain!
Why, what an ass am I! This is most brave,
495 That I, the son of a dear [father] murthered,
Prompted to my revenge by heaven and hell,
Must like a whore unpack my heart with words,
And fall a-cursing like a very drab,
A stallion. Fie upon't, foh!
500 About, my brains! Hum—I have heard
That guilty creatures sitting at a play
Have by the very cunning of the scene
Been strook so to the soul, that presently
They have proclaim'd their malefactions:
505 For murther, though it have no tongue, will speak
With most miraculous organ. I'll have these players
Play something like the murther of my father

---

476 **free:** innocent.
477 **amaze:** confound.
479 **muddy-mettled:** dull-spirited.   **peak:** mope.
480 **John-a-dreams:** a sleepy fellow.   **unpregnant of:** unquickened by.
483 **defeat:** destruction.
486–87 **gives . . . lungs:** calls me a liar in the extremest degree.
488 **'swounds:** by God's (Christ's) wounds.   **should:** would certainly.
489 **am . . . gall:** i.e. am constitutionally incapable of resentment. That doves were mild because
they had no gall was a popular belief.
491 **region kites:** kites of the air.
492 **offal:** entrails.
493 **kindless:** unnatural.
499 **stallion:** male whore. Most editors adopt the F1 reading *scullion*, "kitchen menial."
500 **About:** to work.
503 **presently:** at once, then and there.

Before mine uncle. I'll observe his looks,
I'll tent him to the quick. If 'a do blench,
510   I know my course. The spirit that I have seen
May be a [dev'l], and the [dev'l] hath power
T' assume a pleasing shape, yea, and perhaps,
Out of my weakness and my melancholy,
As he is very potent with such spirits,
515   Abuses me to damn me. I'll have grounds
More relative than this—the play's the thing
Wherein I'll catch the conscience of the King.

Exit.

ACT III

SCENE I.

Enter KING, QUEEN, POLONIUS, OPHELIA, ROSENCRANTZ, GUILDENSTERN, LORDS.

KING An' can you by no drift of conference
Get from him why he puts on this confusion,
Grating so harshly all his days of quiet
With turbulent and dangerous lunacy?
5   ROS. He does confess he feels himself distracted,
But from what cause 'a will by no means speak.
GUIL. Nor do we find him forward to be sounded,
But with a crafty madness keeps aloof
When we would bring him on to some confession
Of his true state.
10   QUEEN   Did he receive you well?
ROS. Most like a gentleman.
GUIL. But with much forcing of his disposition.
ROS. Niggard of question, but of our demands
Most free in his reply.
QUEEN   Did you assay him
15   To any pastime?
ROS. Madam, it so fell out that certain players
We o'erraught on the way; of these we told him,

---

⁵⁰⁹ **tent:** probe. **blench:** flinch.
⁵¹⁴ **spirits:** states of temperament.
⁵¹⁵ **Abuses:** deludes.
⁵¹⁶ **relative:** closely related (to fact), i.e. conclusive.

III.i. Location: The castle.
¹ **An':** and. **drift of conference:** leading on of conversation.
⁷ **forward:** readily willing. **sounded:** plumbed, probed.
⁸ **crafty madness:** i.e. mad craftiness, the shrewdness that mad people sometimes exhibit.
¹² **disposition:** inclination.
¹³ **question:** conversation. **demands:** questions.
¹⁴ **assay:** attempt to win.
¹⁷ **o'erraught:** passed (literally, overreached).

And there did seem in him a kind of joy
To hear of it. They are here about the court,
20 And as I think, they have already order
This night to play before him.
POL.   'Tis most true,
And he beseech'd me to entreat your Majesties
To hear and see the matter.
KING With all my heart, and it doth much content me
25 To hear him so inclin'd.
Good gentlemen, give him a further edge,
And drive his purpose into these delights.
ROS. We shall, my lord.

Exeunt ROSENCRANTZ *and* GUILDENSTERN.

KING   Sweet Gertrude, leave us two,
For we have closely sent for Hamlet hither,
30 That he, as 'twere by accident, may here
Affront Ophelia. Her father and myself,
We'll so bestow ourselves that, seeing unseen,
We may of their encounter frankly judge,
And gather by him, as he is behav'd,
35 If't be th' affliction of his love or no
That thus he suffers for.
QUEEN   I shall obey you.
And for your part, Ophelia, I do wish
That your good beauties be the happy cause
Of Hamlet's wildness. So shall I hope your virtues
40 Will bring him to his wonted way again,
To both your honors.
OPH.   Madam, I wish it may.

[Exit QUEEN.*]*

POL. Ophelia, walk you here.—Gracious, so please you,
We will bestow ourselves. *[To* OPHELIA.*]* Read on this book,
That show of such an exercise may color
45 Your [loneliness]. We are oft to blame in this—
'Tis too much prov'd—that with devotion's visage
And pious action we do sugar o'er
The devil himself.

---

26 **edge:** stimulus.
27 **into:** on to.
29 **closely:** privately.
31 **Affront:** meet.
33 **frankly:** freely.
44 **exercise:** i.e. religious exercise (as the next sentence makes clear).
44–45 **color Your loneliness:** make your solitude seem natural.
46 **too much prov'd:** too often proved true.
47 **action:** demeanor.

KING   *[Aside.]* O, 'tis too true!
How smart a lash that speech doth give my conscience!
50   The harlot's cheek, beautied with plast'ring art,
Is not more ugly to the thing that helps it
Than is my deed to my most painted word.
O heavy burthen!
POL. I hear him coming. Withdraw, my lord.

[Exeunt KING *and* POLONIUS.*]*

Enter HAMLET.

55   HAM. To be, or not to be, that is the question:
Whether 'tis nobler in the mind to suffer
The slings and arrows of outrageous fortune,
Or to take arms against a sea of troubles,
And by opposing, end them. To die, to sleep—
60   No more, and by a sleep to say we end
The heart-ache and the thousand natural shocks
That flesh is heir to; 'tis a consummation
Devoutly to be wish'd. To die, to sleep—
To sleep, perchance to dream—ay, there's the rub,
65   For in that sleep of death what dreams may come,
When we have shuffled off this mortal coil,
Must give us pause; there's the respect
That makes calamity of so long life:
For who would bear the whips and scorns of time,
70   Th' oppressor's wrong, the proud man's contumely,
The pangs of despis'd love, the law's delay,
The insolence of office, and the spurns
That patient merit of th' unworthy takes,
When he himself might his quietus make
75   With a bare bodkin; who would fardels bear,
To grunt and sweat under a weary life,
But that the dread of something after death,
The undiscover'd country, from whose bourn
No traveller returns, puzzles the will,
80   And makes us rather bear those ills we have,

---

51 **to . . . it**: in comparison with the paint that makes it look beautiful.
56 **suffer**: submit to, endure patiently.
62 **consummation**: completion, end.
64 **rub**: obstacle (a term from the game of bowls).
66 **shuffled off**: freed ourselves from.   **this mortal coil**: the turmoil of this mortal life.
67 **respect**: consideration.
68 **of . . . life**: so long-lived.
69 **time**: the world.
74 **his quietus make**: write paid to his account.
75 **bare bodkin**: mere dagger.   **fardels**: burdens.
78 **undiscover'd**: not disclosed to knowledge; about which men have no information.   **bourn**: boundary, i.e. region.
79 **puzzles**: paralyzes.

Than fly to others that we know not of?
Thus conscience does make cowards [of us all],
And thus the native hue of resolution
Is sicklied o'er with the pale cast of thought,
85   And enterprises of great pitch and moment
With this regard their currents turn awry,
And lose the name of action.—Soft you now,
The fair Ophelia. Nymph, in thy orisons
Be all my sins rememb'red.

OPH.   Good my lord,
90   How does your honor for this many a day?

HAM. I humbly thank you, well, [well, well].

OPH. My lord, I have remembrances of yours
That I have longed long to redeliver.
I pray you now receive them.

HAM.   No, not I,
95   I never gave you aught.

OPH. My honor'd lord, you know right well you did,
And with them words of so sweet breath compos'd
As made these things more rich. Their perfume lost,
Take these again, for to the noble mind
100   Rich gifts wax poor when givers prove unkind.
There, my lord.

HAM. Ha, ha! are you honest?

OPH. My lord?

HAM. Are you fair?

105   OPH. What means your lordship?

HAM. That if you be honest and fair, [your honesty] should admit no discourse to your
beauty.

OPH. Could beauty, my lord, have better commerce than with honesty?

HAM. Ay, truly, for the power of beauty will sooner transform honesty from what it is
110   to a bawd than the force of honesty can translate beauty into his likeness. This was
sometime a paradox, but now the time gives it proof. I did love you once.

OPH. Indeed, my lord, you made me believe so.

HAM. You should not have believ'd me, for virtue cannot so [inoculate] our old stock
but we shall relish of it. I lov'd you not.

115   OPH. I was the more deceiv'd.

HAM. Get thee [to] a nunn'ry, why wouldst thou be a breeder of sinners? I am myself
indifferent honest, but yet I could accuse me of such things that it were better my

---

82 **conscience:** reflection (but with some of the modern sense, too).
83 **native hue:** natural (ruddy) complexion.
84 **pale cast:** pallor.   **thought:** i.e. melancholy thought, brooding.
85 **pitch:** loftiness (a term from falconry, signifying the highest point of a hawk's flight).
88 **orisons:** prayers.
102 **honest:** chaste.
111 **sometime:** formerly.   **paradox:** tenet contrary to accepted belief.
113–14 **virtue . . . it:** virtue, engrafted on our old stock (of viciousness), cannot so change the nature
of the plant that no trace of the original will remain.
117 **indifferent honest:** tolerably virtuous.

mother had not borne me: I am very proud, revengeful, ambitious, with more offenses
at my beck than I have thoughts to put them in, imagination to give them shape, or
120 time to act them in. What should such fellows as I do crawling between earth
and heaven? We are arrant knaves, believe none of us. Go thy ways to a nunn'ry.
Where's your father?

OPH. At home, my lord.

HAM. Let the doors be shut upon him, that he may play the fool no where but in 's own
125 house. Farewell.

OPH. O, help him, you sweet heavens!

HAM. If thou dost marry, I'll give thee this plague for thy dowry: be thou as chaste as
ice, as pure as snow, thou shalt not escape calumny. Get thee to a nunn'ry, farewell. Or if thou wilt needs marry, marry a fool, for wise men know well enough what
130 monsters you make of them. To a nunn'ry, go, and quickly too. Farewell.

OPH. Heavenly powers, restore him!

HAM. I have heard of your paintings, well enough. God hath given you one face, and
you make yourselves another. You jig and amble, and you [lisp,] you nickname God's
creatures and make your wantonness [your] ignorance. Go to, I'll no more on't, it
135 hath made me mad. I say we will have no moe marriage. Those that are married
already (all but one) shall live, the rest shall keep as they are. To a nunn'ry, go.

Exit.

OPH. O, what a noble mind is here o'erthrown!
The courtier's, soldier's, scholar's, eye, tongue, sword,
Th' expectation and rose of the fair state,
140 The glass of fashion and the mould of form,
Th' observ'd of all observers, quite, quite down!
And I, of ladies most deject and wretched,
That suck'd the honey of his [music] vows,
Now see [that] noble and most sovereign reason
145 Like sweet bells jangled out of time, and harsh;
That unmatch'd form and stature of blown youth
Blasted with ecstasy. O, woe is me
T' have seen what I have seen, see what I see!

[OPHELIA *withdraws.*]

Enter KING *and* POLONIUS.

---

130 **monsters.** Alluding to the notion that the husbands of unfaithful wives grew horns.   **you:** you
women.

133–34 **You . . . creatures:** i.e. you walk and talk affectedly.

134 **make . . . ignorance:** excuse your affectation as ignorance.

135 **moe:** more.

139 **expectation:** hope.   **rose:** ornament.   **fair.** Probably proleptic: "(the kingdom) made fair by his
presence."

140 **glass:** mirror.   **mould of form:** pattern of (courtly) behavior.

141 **observ'd . . . observers.** Shakespeare uses *observe* to mean not only "behold, mark attentively"
but also "pay honor to."

146 **blown:** in full bloom.

147 **Blasted:** withered.   **ecstasy:** madness.

KING Love? his affections do not that way tend,
150   Nor what he spake, though it lack'd form a little,
        Was not like madness. There's something in his soul
        O'er which his melancholy sits on brood,
        And I do doubt the hatch and the disclose
        Will be some danger; which for to prevent,
155   I have in quick determination
        Thus set it down: he shall with speed to England
        For the demand of our neglected tribute.
        Haply the seas, and countries different,
        With variable objects, shall expel
160   This something-settled matter in his heart,
        Whereon his brains still beating puts him thus
        From fashion of himself. What think you on't?
POL. It shall do well; but yet do I believe
        The origin and commencement of his grief
165   Sprung from neglected love. [OPHELIA *comes forward.*] How now, Ophelia?
        You need not tell us what Lord Hamlet said,
        We heard it all. My lord, do as you please,
        But if you hold it fit, after the play
        Let his queen-mother all alone entreat him
170   To show his grief. Let her be round with him,
        And I'll be plac'd (so please you) in the ear
        Of all their conference. If she find him not,
        To England send him, or confine him where
        Your wisdom best shall think.
KING   It shall be so.
175   Madness in great ones must not [unwatch'd] go.

Exeunt.

SCENE II.

Enter HAMLET *and three of the* PLAYERS.

HAM. Speak the speech, I pray you, as I pronounc'd it to you, trippingly on the tongue,
        but if you mouth it, as many of our players do, I had as live the town-crier spoke my
        lines. Nor do not saw the air too much with your hand, thus, but use all gently, for
        in the very torrent, tempest, and, as I may say, whirlwind of your passion, you must
5   acquire and beget a temperance that may give it smoothness. O, it offends me to the
        soul to hear a robustious periwig-pated fellow tear a passion to totters, to very rags, to

---

149 **affections:** inclinations, feelings.
153 **doubt:** fear. **disclose.** Synonymous with *hatch*; see also V.i.231.
165 **neglected:** unrequited.
170 **his grief:** what is troubling him. **round:** blunt, outspoken.
172 **find him:** learn the truth about him.

III.ii. Location: The castle.
2 **mouth:** pronounce with exaggerated distinctness or declamatory effect. **live:** lief, willingly.
6 **totters:** tatters.

spleet the ears of the groundlings, who for the most part are capable of nothing but inexplicable dumb shows and noise. I would have such a fellow whipt for o'erdoing Termagant, it out-Herods Herod, pray you avoid it.

10 [1] PLAY. I warrant your honor.

HAM. Be not too tame neither, but let your own discretion be your tutor. Suit the action to the word, the word to the action, with this special observance, that you o'erstep not the modesty of nature: for any thing so o'erdone is from the purpose of playing, whose end, both at the first and now, was and is, to hold as 'twere the mirror up to
15 nature: to show virtue her feature, scorn her own image, and the very age and body of the time his form and pressure. Now this overdone, or come tardy off, though it makes the unskillful laugh, cannot but make the judicious grieve; the censure of which one must in your allowance o'erweigh a whole theatre of others. O, there be players that I have seen play—and heard others [praise], and that highly—not to speak
20 it profanely, that, neither having th' accent of Christians nor the gait of Christian, pagan, nor man, have so strutted and bellow'd that I have thought some of Nature's journeymen had made men, and not made them well, they imitated humanity so abominably.

[1] PLAY. I hope we have reform'd that indifferently with us, [sir].

25 HAM. O, reform it altogether. And let those that play your clowns speak no more than is set down for them, for there be of them that will themselves laugh to set on some quantity of barren spectators to laugh too, though in the mean time some necessary question of the play be then to be consider'd. That's villainous, and shows a most pitiful ambition in the fool that uses it. Go make you ready.

[Exeunt PLAYERS.]

Enter POLONIUS, GUILDENSTERN, and ROSENCRANTZ.

30 How now, my lord? Will the King hear this piece of work?

POL. And the Queen too, and that presently.

HAM. Bid the players make haste.

[Exit POLONIUS.]

Will you two help to hasten them?

ROS. Ay, my lord.

---

7 **spleet:** split. **groundlings:** those who paid the lowest admission price and stood on the ground in the "yard" or pit of the theater. **capable of:** able to take in.

9 **Termagant:** a supposed god of the Saracens, whose role in medieval drama, like that of Herod, was noisy and violent.

13 **modesty:** moderation. **from:** contrary to.

15 **scorn:** i.e. that which is worthy of scorn.

16 **pressure:** impression (as of a seal), exact image. **tardy:** inadequately.

17 **censure:** judgment.

18 **which one:** (even) one of whom. **allowance:** estimation.

20 **profanely:** irreverently.

21–23 **some . . . abominably:** i.e. they were so unlike men that it seemed Nature had not made them herself, but had delegated the task to mediocre assistants.

24 **indifferently:** pretty well.

26 **of them:** some of them.

29 **fool:** (1) stupid person; (2) actor playing a fool's role.

30 **piece of work:** masterpiece (said jocularly).

31 **presently:** at once.

Exeunt they two.

35 HAM. What ho, Horatio!

Enter HORATIO.

HOR. Here, sweet lord, at your service.
HAM. Horatio, thou art e'en as just a man
    As e'er my conversation cop'd withal.
HOR. O my dear lord—
HAM.   Nay, do not think I flatter,
40 For what advancement may I hope from thee
    That no revenue hast but thy good spirits
    To feed and clothe thee? Why should the poor be flatter'd?
    No, let the candied tongue lick absurd pomp,
    And crook the pregnant hinges of the knee
45 Where thrift may follow fawning. Dost thou hear?
    Since my dear soul was mistress of her choice
    And could of men distinguish her election,
    Sh' hath seal'd thee for herself, for thou hast been
    As one in suff'ring all that suffers nothing,
50 A man that Fortune's buffets and rewards
    Hast ta'en with equal thanks; and blest are those
    Whose blood and judgment are so well co-meddled,
    That they are not a pipe for Fortune's finger
    To sound what stop she please. Give me that man
55 That is not passion's slave, and I will wear him
    In my heart's core, ay, in my heart of heart,
    As I do thee. Something too much of this.
    There is a play to-night before the King,
    One scene of it comes near the circumstance
60 Which I have told thee of my father's death.
    I prithee, when thou seest that act afoot,
    Even with the very comment of thy soul
    Observe my uncle. If his occulted guilt
    Do not itself unkennel in one speech,
65 It is a damned ghost that we have seen,
    And my imaginations are as foul

---

³⁷ **thou . . . man:** i.e. you come as close to being what a man should be (*just* = exact, precise).
³⁸ **my . . . withal:** my association with people has brought me into contact with.
⁴³ **candied:** sugared, i.e. flattering. **absurd:** tasteless (Latin sense).
⁴⁴ **pregnant:** moving readily.
⁴⁵ **thrift:** thriving, profit.
⁵² **blood:** passions. **co-meddled:** mixed, blended.
⁵⁶ **my heart of heart:** the heart of my heart.
⁶² **very . . . soul:** your most intense critical observation.
⁶³ **occulted:** hidden.
⁶⁴ **unkennel:** bring into the open.
⁶⁵ **damned ghost:** evil spirit, devil.

As Vulcan's stithy. Give him heedful note,
For I mine eyes will rivet to his face,
And after we will both our judgments join
In censure of his seeming.
70 HOR.   Well, my lord.
   If 'a steal aught the whilst this play is playing,
   And scape [detecting], I will pay the theft.

[Sound a flourish. Danish march.] Enter Trumpets and Kettle-drums, KING, QUEEN,
POLONIUS, OPHELIA, [ROSENCRANTZ, GUILDENSTERN, and other LORDS attendant, with
his GUARD carrying torches].

HAM. They are coming to the play. I must be idle;
   Get you a place.
75 KING How fares our cousin Hamlet?
HAM. Excellent, i' faith, of the chameleon's dish: I eat the air, promise-cramm'd—you
   cannot feed capons so.
KING I have nothing with this answer, Hamlet, these words are not mine.
HAM. No, nor mine now. *[To POLONIUS.]* My lord, you play'd once i' th' university,
80   you say?
POL. That did I, my lord, and was accounted a good actor.
HAM. What did you enact?
POL. I did enact Julius Caesar. I was kill'd i' th' Capitol; Brutus kill'd me.
HAM. It was a brute part of him to kill so capital a calf there. Be the players ready?
85 ROS. Ay, my lord, they stay upon your patience.
QUEEN Come hither, my dear Hamlet, sit by me.
HAM. No, good mother, here's metal more attractive.

[Lying down at OPHELIA's feet.]

POL. *[To the KING.]* O ho, do you mark that?
HAM. Lady, shall I lie in your lap?
90 OPH. No, my lord
[HAM. I mean, my head upon your lap?
OPH. Ay, my lord.]
HAM. Do you think I meant country matters?
OPH. I think nothing, my lord.
95 HAM. That's a fair thought to lie between maids' legs.
OPH. What is, my lord?
HAM. Nothing.
OPH. You are merry, my lord.

---

67 **stithy**: forge.
70 **censure . . . seeming**: reaching a verdict on his behavior.
73 **be idle**: act foolish, pretend to be crazy.
75 **fares**. Hamlet takes up this word in another sense.
76 **chameleon's dish**. Chameleons were thought to feed on air. Hamlet says that he subsists on an
   equally nourishing diet, the promise of succession. There is probably a pun on *air/heir*.
78 **have nothing with**: do not understand.   **mine**: i.e. an answer to my question.
84 **part**: action.
93 **country matters**: indecency.

HAM. Who, I?

100 OPH. Ay, my lord.

HAM. O God, your only jig-maker. What should a man do but be merry, for look you how cheerfully my mother looks, and my father died within 's two hours.

OPH. Nay, 'tis twice two months, my lord.

HAM. So long? Nay then let the dev'l wear black, for I'll have a suit of sables. O heavens,
105 die two months ago, and not forgotten yet? Then there's hope a great man's memory may outlive his life half a year, but, by'r lady, 'a must build churches then, or else shall 'a suffer not thinking on, with the hobby-horse, whose epitaph is, "For O, for O, the hobby-horse is forgot."

The trumpets sound. Dumb show follows.

Enter a King and a Queen [very lovingly], the Queen embracing him and he her. [She kneels and makes show of protestation unto him.] He takes her up and declines his head upon her neck. He lies him down upon a bank of flowers. She, seeing him asleep, leaves him. Anon come in another man, takes off his crown, kisses it, pours poison in the sleeper's ears, and leaves him. The Queen returns, finds the King dead, makes passionate action. The pois'ner with some three or four [mutes] come in again, seem to condole with her. The dead body is carried away. The pois'ner woos the Queen with gifts; she seems harsh [and unwilling] awhile, but in the end accepts love.

[Exeunt.]

OPH. What means this, my lord?

110 HAM. Marry, this' [miching] mallecho, it means mischief

OPH. Belike this show imports the argument of the play.

Enter PROLOGUE.

HAM. We shall know by this fellow. The players cannot keep [counsel], they'll tell all.

OPH. Will 'a tell us what this show meant?

HAM. Ay, or any show that you will show him. Be not you asham'd to show, he'll
115 not shame to tell you what it means.

OPH. You are naught, you are naught. I'll mark the play.

PRO. For us, and for our tragedy,
Here stooping to your clemency,
We beg your hearing patiently.

[Exit.]

---

101 **only:** very best. **jig-maker:** one who composed or played in the farcical song-and-dance entertainments that followed plays.

102 **'s:** this.

104 **let . . . sables:** i.e. to the devil with my garments; after so long a time I am ready for the old
man's garb of sables (fine fur).

107 **not thinking on:** not being thought of, i.e. being forgotten.

107–08 **For . . . forgot:** line from a popular ballad lamenting puritanical suppression of such country
sports as the May-games, in which the hobby-horse, a character costumed to resemble a horse,
traditionally appeared.

110 **this' miching mallecho:** this is sneaking mischief.

111 **argument:** subject, plot.

112 **counsel:** secrets.

114 **Be not you:** if you are not.

116 **naught:** wicked.

120 HAM. Is this a prologue, or the posy of a ring?
OPH. 'Tis brief, my lord.
HAM. As woman's love.

Enter [two PLAYERS,] KING *and* QUEEN.

[P.] KING Full thirty times hath Phoebus' cart gone round
Neptune's salt wash and Tellus' orbed ground,
125 And thirty dozen moons with borrowed sheen
About the world have times twelve thirties been,
Since love our hearts and Hymen did our hands
Unite comutual in most sacred bands.
[P.] QUEEN So many journeys may the sun and moon
130 Make us again count o'er ere love be done!
But woe is me, you are so sick of late,
So far from cheer and from [your] former state,
That I distrust you. Yet though I distrust,
Discomfort you, my lord, it nothing must,
135 [For] women's fear and love hold quantity
In neither aught, or in extremity.
Now what my [love] is, proof hath made you know,
And as my love is siz'd, my fear is so.
Where love is great, the littlest doubts are fear;
140 Where little fears grow great, great love grows there.
[P.] KING Faith, I must leave thee, love, and shortly too;
My operant powers their functions leave to do,
And thou shalt live in this fair world behind,
Honor'd, belov'd, and haply one as kind
For husband shalt thou—
145 [P.] QUEEN   O, confound the rest!
Such love must needs be treason in my breast.
In second husband let me be accurs'd!
None wed the second but who kill'd the first.
HAM. *[Aside.]* That's wormwood!
150 [P.] QUEEN The instances that second marriage move
Are base respects of thrift, but none of love.
A second time I kill my husband dead,
When second husband kisses me in bed.

---

120 **posy . . . ring:** verse motto inscribed in a ring (necessarily short).
123 **Phoebus' cart:** the sun-god's chariot.
124 **Tellus:** goddess of the earth.
127 **Hymen:** god of marriage.
128 **bands:** bonds.
133 **distrust:** fear for.
135 **hold quantity:** are related in direct proportion.
137 **proof:** experience.
142 **operant:** active, vital. **leave to do:** cease to perform.
145 **confound the rest:** may destruction befall what you are about to speak of—a second marriage on my part.
150 **instances:** motives. **move:** give rise to.
151 **respects of thrift:** considerations of advantage.

[P.] KING I do believe you think what now you speak,
155   But what we do determine, oft we break.
Purpose is but the slave to memory,
Of violent birth, put poor validity,
Which now, the fruit unripe, sticks on the tree,
But fall unshaken when they mellow be.
160   Most necessary 'tis that we forget
To pay ourselves what ourselves is debt.
What to ourselves in passion we propose,
The passion ending, doth the purpose lose.
The violence of either grief or joy
165   Their own enactures with themselves destroy.
Where joy most reveals, grief doth most lament;
Grief [joys], joy grieves, on slender accident.
This world is not for aye, nor 'tis not strange
That even our loves should with our fortunes change:
170   For 'tis a question left us yet to prove,
Whether love lead fortune, or else fortune love.
The great man down, you mark his favorite flies,
The poor advanc'd makes friends of enemies.
And hitherto doth love on fortune tend,
175   For who not needs shall never lack a friend,
And who in want a hollow friend doth try,
Directly seasons him his enemy.
But orderly to end where I begun,
Our wills and fates do so contrary run
180   That our devices still are overthrown,
Our thoughts are ours, their ends none of our own:
So think thou wilt no second husband wed,
But die thy thoughts when thy first lord is dead.
[P.] QUEEN Nor earth to me give food, nor heaven light,
185   Sport and repose lock from me day and night,
To desperation turn my trust and hope,
[An] anchor's cheer in prison be my scope!
Each opposite that blanks the face of joy
Meet what I would have well and it destroy!
190   Both here and hence pursue me lasting strife,
If once I be a widow, ever I be a wife!

---

157 **validity:** strength, power to last.
160–61 **Most . . . debt:** i.e. such resolutions are debts we owe to ourselves, and it would be foolish to pay such debts.
162 **passion:** violent emotion.
164–65 **The violence . . . destroy:** i.e. both violent grief and violent joy fail of their intended acts because they destroy themselves by their very violence.
167 **slender accident:** slight occasion.
177 **seasons:** ripens, converts into.
180 **devices:** devisings, intentions. **still:** always.
187 **anchor's cheer:** hermit's fare. **my scope:** the extent of my comforts.
188 **blanks:** blanches, makes pale (a symptom of grief).

HAM. If she should break it now!

[P.] KING 'Tis deeply sworn. Sweet, leave me here a while,
My spirits grow dull, and fain I would beguile
The tedious day with sleep.

[Sleeps.]

195 [P.] QUEEN   Sleep rock thy brain,
And never come mischance between us twain!

Exit.

HAM. Madam, how like you this play?
QUEEN The lady doth protest too much, methinks.
HAM. O but she'll keep her word.
200 KING Have you heard the argument? is there no offense in't?   200
HAM. No, no, they do but jest, poison in jest—no offense i' th' world.
KING What do you call the play?
HAM. "The Mouse-trap." Marry, how? tropically: this play is the image of a murther
done in Vienna; Gonzago is the duke's name, his wife, Baptista. You shall see anon.
205 'Tis a knavish piece of work, but what of that? Your Majesty, and we that have free
souls, it touches us not. Let the gall'd jade winch, our withers are unwrung.

Enter LUCIANUS.

This is one Lucianus, nephew to the king.
OPH. You are as good as a chorus, my lord.
HAM. I could interpret between you and your love, if I could see the puppets dallying.
210 OPH. You are keen, my lord, you are keen.   210
HAM. It would cost you a groaning to take off mine edge.
OPH. Still better, and worse.
HAM. So you mistake your husbands. Begin, murtherer, leave thy damnable faces and
begin. Come, the croaking raven doth bellow for revenge.
215 LUC. Thoughts black, hands apt, drugs fit, and time agreeing,   215
[Confederate] season, else no creature seeing,
Thou mixture rank, of midnight weeds collected,

---

200 **offense:** offensive matter (but Hamlet quibbles on the sense "crime").
201 **jest:** i.e. pretend.
203 **tropically:** figuratively (with play on *trapically*—which is the reading of Q1—and probably with
allusion to the children's saying *marry trap*, meaning "now you're caught"). **image:** representation.
205–06 **free souls:** clear consciences.
206 **gall'd jade:** chafed horse. **winch:** wince. **withers:** ridge between a horse's shoulders. **unwrung:** not rubbed sore.
208 **chorus:** i.e. one who explains the forthcoming action.
209 **I . . . dallying:** I could speak the dialogue between you and your lover like a puppet-master (with
an indecent jest).
210 **keen:** bitter, sharp.
212 **better, and worse:** i.e. more pointed and less decent.
213 **So:** i.e. "for better, for worse," in the words of the marriage service. **mistake:** i.e. mis-take,
take wrongfully. Their vows, Hamlet suggests, prove false. **faces:** facial expressions.
214 **the croaking . . . revenge.** Misquoted from an old play, *The True Tragedy of Richard III.*
216 **Confederate season:** the time being my ally.

With Hecat's ban thrice blasted, thrice [infected],
Thy natural magic and dire property
220   On wholesome life usurps immediately.

[Pours the poison in his ears.]

HAM. 'A poisons him i' th' garden for his estate. His name's Gonzago, the story is extant,
and written in very choice Italian. You shall see anon how the murtherer gets the love
of Gonzago's wife.
OPH. The King rises.
225   [HAM. What, frighted with false fire?]
QUEEN How fares my lord?
POL. Give o'er the play.
KING Give me some light. Away!
POL. Lights, lights, lights!

Exeunt all but HAMLET *and* HORATIO.

230   HAM.   "Why, let the strooken deer go weep,
                                              The hart ungalled play,
                              For some must watch while some must sleep,
                                        Thus runs the world away."

Would not this, sir, and a forest of feathers—if the rest of my fortunes turn Turk with
235   me—with [two] Provincial roses on my raz'd shoes, get me a fellowship in a cry of
players?
HOR. Half a share.
HAM. A whole one, I.

                              "For thou dost know, O Damon dear,
240   This realm dismantled was
                              Of Jove himself, and now reigns here
                                        A very, very"—pajock.

HOR. You might have rhym'd.
HAM. O good Horatio, I'll take the ghost's word for a thousand pound. Didst perceive?
245   HOR. Very well, my lord.
HAM. Upon the talk of the pois'ning?
HOR. I did very well note him.
HAM. Ah, ha! Come, some music! Come, the recorders!
For if the King like not the comedy,

---

218 **Hecat's ban:** the curse of Hecate, goddess of witchcraft.
225 **false fire:** i.e. a blank cartridge.
230 **strooken:** struck, i.e. wounded.
231 **ungalled:** unwounded.
232 **watch:** stay awake.
234 **feathers:** the plumes worn by tragic actors.   **turn Turk:** i.e. go to the bad.
235 **Provincial roses:** rosettes designed to look like a variety of French rose.   **raz'd:** with decorating
slashing.   **fellowship:** partnership.   **cry:** company.
240 **dismantled:** divested, deprived.
242 **pajock:** peacock (substituting for the rhyme-word *ass*). The natural history of the time attributed
many vicious qualities to the peacock.

250   Why then belike he likes it not, perdy.
       Come, some music!

Enter ROSENCRANTZ *and* GUILDENSTERN.

GUIL. Good my lord, voutsafe me a word with you.
HAM. Sir, a whole history.
GUIL. The King, sir—
255 HAM. Ay, sir, what of him?
GUIL. Is in his retirement marvellous distemp'red.
HAM. With drink, sir?
GUIL. No, my lord, with choler.
HAM. Your wisdom should show itself more richer to signify this to the doctor, for for
260   me to put him to his purgation would perhaps plunge him into more choler.
GUIL. Good my lord, put your discourse into some frame, and [start] not so wildly from
       my affair.
HAM. I am tame, sir. Pronounce.
GUIL. The Queen, your mother, in most great affliction of spirit, hath sent me to you.
265 HAM. You are welcome.
GUIL. Nay, good my lord, this courtesy is not of the right breed. If it shall please you
       to make me a wholesome answer, I will do your mother's commandement; if not,
       your pardon and my return shall be the end of [my] business.
HAM. Sir, I cannot.
270 ROS. What, my lord?
HAM. Make you a wholesome answer—my wit's diseas'd. But, sir, such answer as I can
       make, you shall command, or rather, as you say, my mother. Therefore no more, but
       to the matter: my mother, you say—
ROS. Then thus she says: your behavior hath strook her into amazement and admiration.
275 HAM. O wonderful son, that can so stonish a mother! But is there no sequel at the heels
       of this mother's admiration? Impart.
ROS. She desires to speak with you in her closet ere you go to bed.
HAM. We shall obey, were she ten times our mother. Have you any further trade with
       us?
280 ROS. My lord, you once did love me.
HAM. And do still, by these pickers and stealers.
ROS. Good my lord, what is your cause of distemper? You do surely bar the door upon
       your own liberty if you deny your griefs to your friend.
HAM. Sir, I lack advancement.

---

250 **perdy:** assuredly (French *pardieu,* "by God").
258 **choler:** anger (but Hamlet willfully takes up the word in the sense "biliousness").
260 **put . . . purgation:** i.e. prescribe for what's wrong with him.
261 **frame:** logical structure.
267 **wholesome:** sensible, rational.
268 **pardon:** permission for departure.
274 **amazement and admiration:** bewilderment and wonder.
275 **stonish:** astound.
277 **closet:** private room.
281 **pickers and stealers:** hands; which, as the Catechism says, we must keep "from picking and
       stealing."

285 ROS. How can that be, when you have the voice of the King himself for your succession in Denmark?

HAM. Ay, sir, but "While the grass grows"—the proverb is something musty.

Enter the PLAYERS *with recorders.*

O, the recorders! Let me see one.—To withdraw with you—why do you go about to recover the wind of me, as if you would drive me into a toil?

290 GUIL. O my lord, if my duty be too bold, my love is too unmannerly.

HAM. I do not well understand that. Will you play upon this pipe?

GUIL. My lord, I cannot.

HAM. I pray you.

GUIL. Believe me, I cannot.

295 HAM. I do beseech you.

GUIL. I know no touch of it, my lord.

HAM. It is as easy as lying. Govern these ventages with your fingers and [thumbs], give it breath with your mouth, and it will discourse most eloquent music. Look you, these are the stops.

300 GUIL. But these cannot I command to any utt'rance of harmony. I have not the skill.

HAM. Why, look you now, how unworthy a thing you make of me! You would play upon me, you would seem to know my stops, you would pluck out the heart of my mystery, you would sound me from my lowest note to [the top of] my compass; and there is much music, excellent voice, in this little organ, yet cannot you make it speak.

305 'Sblood, do you think I am easier to be play'd on than a pipe? Call me what instrument you will, though you fret me, [yet] you cannot play upon me.

Enter POLONIUS.

God bless you, sir.

POL. My lord, the Queen would speak with you, and presently.

HAM. Do you see yonder cloud that's almost in shape of a camel?

310 POL. By th' mass and 'tis, like a camel indeed.

HAM. Methinks it is like a weasel.

POL. It is back'd like a weasel.

HAM. Or like a whale.

POL. Very like a whale.

315 HAM. Then I will come to my mother by and by. *[Aside.]* They fool me to the top of my bent.—I will come by and by.

[POL.] I will say so.

[Exit.]

---

287 **proverb:** i.e. "While the grass grows, the steed starves." **something musty:** somewhat stale.
289 **recover the wind:** get to windward. **toil:** snare.
297 **ventages:** stops.
304 **organ:** instrument.
306 **fret:** (1) finger (an instrument); (2) vex.
308 **presently:** at once.
315–16 **They . . . bent:** they make me play the fool to the limit of my ability.
316 **by and by:** at once.

HAM. "By and by" is easily said. Leave me, friends.

[*Exeunt all but* HAMLET.]

'Tis now the very witching time of night,
320   When churchyards yawn and hell itself [breathes] out
    Contagion to this world. Now could I drink hot blood,
    And do such [bitter business as the] day
    Would quake to look on. Soft, now to my mother.
    O heart, lose not thy nature! let not ever
325   The soul of Nero enter this firm bosom,
    Let me be cruel, not unnatural;
    I will speak [daggers] to her, but use none.
    My tongue and soul in this be hypocrites—
    How in my words somever she be shent,
330   To give them seals never my soul consent!

Exit.

SCENE III.

Enter KING, ROSENCRANTZ, *and* GUILDENSTERN.

KING I like him not, nor stands it safe with us
    To let his madness range. Therefore prepare you.
    I your commission will forthwith dispatch,
    And he to England shall along with you.
5   The terms of our estate may not endure
    Hazard so near 's as doth hourly grow
    Out of his brows.
GUIL.   We will ourselves provide.
    Most holy and religious fear it is
    To keep those many many bodies safe
10   That live and feed upon your Majesty.
ROS. The single and peculiar life is bound
    With all the strength and armor of the mind
    To keep itself from noyance, but much more
    That spirit upon whose weal depends and rests

---

[319] **witching:** i.e. when the powers of evil are at large.
[324] **nature:** natural affection, filial feeling.
[325] **Nero.** Murderer of his mother.
[329] **shent:** rebuked.
[330] **give them seals:** confirm them by deeds.

III.iii. Location: The castle.
[1] **him:** i.e. his state of mind, his behavior.
[3] **dispatch:** have drawn up.
[5] **terms:** conditions, nature.   **our estate:** my position (as king).
[7] **his brows:** the madness visible in his face (?).
[8] **fear:** concern.
[11] **single and peculiar:** individual and private.
[13] **noyance:** injury.

15   The lives of many. The cess of majesty
     Dies not alone, but like a gulf doth draw
     What's near it with it. Or it is a massy wheel
     Fix'd on the summit of the highest mount,
     To whose [huge] spokes ten thousand lesser things
20   Are mortis'd and adjoin'd, which when it falls,
     Each small annexment, petty consequence,
     Attends the boist'rous [ruin]. Never alone
     Did the King sigh, but [with] a general groan.
     KING Arm you, I pray you, to this speedy viage,
25   For we will fetters put about this fear,
     Which now goes too free-footed.
     ROS.   We will haste us.

Exeunt GENTLEMEN [ROSENCRANTZ *and* GUILDENSTERN].

Enter POLONIUS.

     POL. My lord, he's going to his mother's closet.
     Behind the arras I'll convey myself
     To hear the process. I'll warrant she'll tax him home,
30   And as you said, and wisely was it said,
     'Tis meet that some more audience than a mother,
     Since nature makes them partial; should o'erhear
     The speech, of vantage. Fare you well, my liege,
     I'll call upon you ere you go to bed,
35   And tell you what I know.
     KING   Thanks, dear my lord.

Exit [POLONIUS].

     O, my offense is rank, it smells to heaven,
     It hath the primal eldest curse upon't,
     A brother's murther. Pray can I not,
     Though inclination be as sharp as will.
40   My stronger guilt defeats my strong intent,
     And, like a man to double business bound,
     I stand in pause where I shall first begin,
     And both neglect. What if this cursed hand
     Were thicker than itself with brother's blood,

---

¹⁵ **cess:** cessation, death.
¹⁶ **gulf:** whirlpool.
²⁰ **mortis'd:** fixed.
²² **Attends:** accompanies.   **ruin:** fall.
²⁴ **Arm:** prepare.   **viage:** voyage.
²⁵ **fear:** object of fear.
²⁹ **process:** course of the talk.   **tax him home:** take him severely to task.
³³ **of vantage:** from an advantageous position (?) or in addition (?).
³⁷ **primal eldest curse:** i.e. God's curse on Cain, who also slew his brother.
³⁹ **Though . . . will:** though my desire is as strong as my resolve to do so.
⁴¹ **bound:** committed.
⁴³ **neglect:** omit.

45   Is there not rain enough in the sweet heavens
       To wash it white as snow? Whereto serves mercy
       But to confront the visage of offense?
       And what's in prayer but this twofold force,
       To be forestalled ere we come to fall,
50   Or [pardon'd] being down? then I'll look up.
       My fault is past, but, O, what form of prayer
       Can serve my turn? "Forgive me my foul murther"?
       That cannot be, since I am still possess'd
       Of those effects for which I did the murther:
55   My crown, mine own ambition, and my queen.
       May one be pardon'd and retain th' offense?
       In the corrupted currents of this world
       Offense's gilded hand may [shove] by justice,
       And oft 'tis seen the wicked prize itself
60   Buys out the law, but 'tis not so above:
       There is no shuffling, there the action lies
       In his true nature, and we ourselves compell'd,
       Even to the teeth and forehead of our faults,
       To give in evidence. What then? What rests?
65   Try what repentance can. What can it not?
       Yet what can it, when one can not repent?
       O wretched state! O bosom black as death!
       O limed soul, that struggling to be free
       Art more engag'd! Help, angels! Make assay,
70   Bow, stubborn knees, and heart, with strings of steel,
       Be soft as sinews of the new-born babe!
       All may be well.

[He kneels.]

Enter HAMLET.

HAM. Now might I do it [pat], now 'a is a-praying;
       And now I'll do't—and so 'a goes to heaven,
75   And so am I [reveng'd]. That would be scann'd:
       A villain kills my father, and for that
       I, his sole son, do this same villain send
       To heaven.
       Why, this is [hire and salary], not revenge.

[46-47] **Whereto . . . offense:** i.e. what function has mercy except when there has been sin.
[56] **th' offense:** i.e. the "effects" or fruits of the offense.
[57] **currents:** courses.
[58] **gilded:** i.e. bribing.
[59] **wicked prize:** rewards of vice.
[61] **shuffling:** evasion.   **the action lies:** the charge comes for legal consideration.
[63] **Even . . . forehead:** i.e. fully recognizing their features, extenuating nothing.
[64] **rests:** remains.
[68] **limed:** caught (as in birdlime, a sticky substance used for catching birds).
[69] **engag'd:** entangled.
[75] **would be scann'd:** must be carefully considered.

80 'A took my father grossly, full of bread,
With all his crimes broad blown, as flush as May,
And how his audit stands who knows save heaven?
But in our circumstance and course of thought
'Tis heavy with him. And am I then revenged,
85 To take him in the purging of his soul,
When he is fit and season'd for his passage?
No!
Up, sword, and know thou a more horrid hent:
When he is drunk asleep, or in his rage,
90 Or in th' incestious pleasure of his bed,
At game a-swearing, or about some act
That has no relish of salvation in't—
Then trip him, that his heels may kick at heaven,
And that his soul may be as damn'd and black
95 As hell, whereto it goes. My mother stays,
This physic but prolongs thy sickly days.

Exit.

KING *[Rising.]* My words fly up, my thoughts remain below:
Words without thoughts never to heaven go.

Exit.

SCENE IV.

Enter [QUEEN] GERTRUDE *and* POLONIUS.

POL. 'A will come straight. Look you lay home to him.
Tell him his pranks have been too broad to bear with,
And that your Grace hath screen'd and stood between
Much heat and him. I'll silence me even here;
5 Pray you be round [with him].
QUEEN I'll [warr'nt] you, fear me not. Withdraw,
I hear him coming.

*[*POLONIUS *hides behind the arras.]*

Enter HAMLET.

---

80 **grossly:** in a gross state; not spiritually prepared.
81 **crimes:** sins.   **broad blown:** in full bloom.   **flush:** lusty, vigorous.
82 **audit:** account.
83 **in . . . thought:** i.e. to the best of our knowledge and belief.
88 **Up:** into the sheath.   **know . . . hent:** be grasped at a more dreadful time.
92 **relish:** trace.
96 **physic:** (attempted) remedy, i.e. prayer.

III.iv. Location: The Queen's closet in the castle.
1 **lay . . . him:** reprove him severely.
2 **broad:** unrestrained.
5 **round:** plain-spoken.
6 **fear me not:** have no fears about my handling of the situation.

HAM. Now, mother, what's the matter?

QUEEN Hamlet, thou hast thy father much offended.

10 HAM. Mother, you have my father much offended.

QUEEN Come, come, you answer with an idle tongue.

HAM. Go, go, you question with a wicked tongue.

QUEEN Why, how now, Hamlet?

HAM.   What's the matter now?

QUEEN Have you forgot me?

HAM.   No, by the rood, not so:

15   You are the Queen, your husband's brother's wife,
    And would it were not so, you are my mother.

QUEEN Nay, then I'll set those to you that can speak.

HAM. Come, come, and sit you down, you shall not boudge;
    You go not till I set you up a glass
20   Where you may see the [inmost] part of you.

QUEEN What wilt thou do? Thou wilt not murther me?
    Help ho!

POL. *[Behind.]* What ho, help!

HAM. *[Drawing.]* How now? A rat? Dead, for a ducat, dead!

[Kills POLONIUS *through the arras.]*

POL. *[Behind.]* O, I am slain.

25 QUEEN   O me, what hast thou done?

HAM. Nay, I know not, is it the King?

QUEEN O, what a rash and bloody deed is this!

HAM. A bloody deed! almost as bad, good mother,
    As kill a king, and marry with his brother.

QUEEN As kill a king!

30 HAM.   Ay, lady, it was my word.

[Parts the arras and discovers POLONIUS.]

    Thou wretched, rash, intruding fool, farewell!
    I took thee for thy better. Take thy fortune;
    Thou find'st to be too busy is some danger.—
    Leave wringing of your hands. Peace, sit you down,
35   And let me wring your heart, for so I shall
    If it be made of penetrable stuff,
    If damned custom have not brass'd it so
    That it be proof and bulwark against sense.

QUEEN What have I done, that thou dar'st wag thy tongue
40   In noise so rude against me?

---

[11] **idle:** foolish.

[14] **rood:** cross.

[18] **boudge:** budge.

[24] **for a ducat:** I'll wager a ducat.

[33] **busy:** officious, meddlesome.

[37] **damned custom:** i.e. the habit of ill-doing.   **brass'd:** hardened, literally, plated with brass.

[38] **proof:** armor.   **sense:** feeling.

HAM.   Such an act
        That blurs the grace and blush of modesty,
        Calls virtue hypocrite, takes off the rose
        From the fair forehead of an innocent love
        And sets a blister there, makes marriage vows
45   As false as dicers' oaths, O, such a deed
        As from the body of contraction plucks
        The very soul, and sweet religion makes
        A rhapsody of words. Heaven's face does glow
        O'er this solidity and compound mass
50   With heated visage, as against the doom;
        Is thought-sick at the act.
    QUEEN   Ay me, what act,
        That roars so loud and thunders in the index?
    HAM. Look here upon this picture, and on this,
        The counterfeit presentment of two brothers.
55   See what a grace was seated on this brow:
        Hyperion's curls, the front of Jove himself,
        An eye like Mars, to threaten and command,
        A station like the herald Mercury
        New lighted on a [heaven-]kissing hill,
60   A combination and a form indeed,
        Where every god did seem to set his seal
        To give the world assurance of a man.
        This was your husband. Look you now what follows:
        Here is your husband, like a mildewed ear,
65   Blasting his wholesome brother. Have you eyes?
        Could you on this fair mountain leave to feed,
        And batten on this moor? ha, have you eyes?
        You cannot call it love, for at your age
        The heyday in the blood is tame, it's humble,
70   And waits upon the judgment, and what judgment
        Would step from this to this? Sense sure you have,
        Else could you not have motion, but sure that sense

---

44 **blister:** brand of shame.
46 **contraction:** the making of contracts, i.e. the assuming of solemn obligation.
47 **religion:** i.e. sacred vows.
48 **rhapsody:** miscellaneous collection, jumble. **glow:** i.e. with anger.
49 **this . . . mass:** i.e. the earth. *Compound* = compounded of the four elements.
50 **as . . . doom:** as if for Judgment Day.
52 **index:** i.e. table of contents. The index was formerly placed at the beginning of a book.
54 **counterfeit presentment:** painted likenesses.
56 **Hyperion's:** the sun-god's. **front:** forehead.
58 **station:** bearing.
64 **ear:** i.e. of grain.
67 **batten:** gorge.
69 **heyday:** excitement.
71 **Sense:** sense perception, the five senses.

Is apoplex'd, for madness would not err,
Nor sense to ecstasy was ne'er so thrall'd
75   But it reserv'd some quantity of choice
To serve in such a difference. What devil was't
That thus hath cozen'd you at hoodman-blind?
Eyes without feeling, feeling without sight,
Ears without hands or eyes, smelling sans all,
80   Or but a sickly part of one true sense
Could not so mope. O shame, where is thy blush?
Rebellious hell,
If thou canst mutine in a matron's bones,
To flaming youth let virtue be as wax
85   And melt in her own fire. Proclaim no shame
When the compulsive ardure gives the charge,
Since frost itself as actively doth burn,
And reason [panders] will.
QUEEN   O Hamlet, speak no more!
Thou turn'st my [eyes into my very] soul,
90   And there I see such black and [grained] spots
As will [not] leave their tinct.
HAM.   Nay, but to live
In the rank sweat of an enseamed bed,
Stew'd in corruption, honeying and making love
Over the nasty sty!
QUEEN   O, speak to me no more!
95   These words like daggers enter in my ears.
No more, sweet Hamlet!
HAM.   A murtherer and a villain!
A slave that is not twentith part the [tithe]
Of your precedent lord, a Vice of kings,
A cutpurse of the empire and the rule,
100   That from a shelf the precious diadem stole,
And put it in his pocket—
QUEEN   No more!

---

73 **apoplex'd**: paralyzed.
73–76 **madness . . . difference**: i.e. madness itself could not go so far astray, nor were the senses ever
     so enslaved by lunacy that they did not retain the power to make so obvious a distinction.
77 **cozen'd**: cheated.   **hoodman-blind**: blindman's bluff.
79 **sans**: without.
81 **mope**: be dazed.
83 **mutine**: rebel.
85–88 **Proclaim . . . will**: do not call it sin when the hot blood of youth is responsible for lechery,
     since here we see people of calmer age on fire for it; and reason acts as procurer for desire,
     instead of restraining it. *Ardure* = ardor.
90 **grained**: fast-dyed, indelible.
91 **leave their tinct**: lose their color.
92 **enseamed**: greasy.
97 **twentith**: twentieth.
98 **precedent**: former.   **Vice**: buffoon (like the Vice of the morality plays).

Enter GHOST *[in his night-gown].*

HAM. A king of shreds and patches—
　　Save me, and hover o'er me with your wings,
　　You heavenly guards! What would your gracious figure!
105　QUEEN Alas, he's mad!
　　HAM. Do you not come your tardy son to chide,
　　That, laps'd in time and passion, lets go by
　　Th' important acting of your dread command?
　　O, say!
110　GHOST Do not forget! This visitation
　　Is but to whet thy almost blunted purpose.
　　But look, amazement on thy mother sits,
　　O, step between her and her fighting soul,
　　Conceit in weakest bodies strongest works,
115　Speak to her, Hamlet.
　　HAM.　　　　　　　How is it with you, lady?
　　QUEEN Alas, how is't with you,
　　That you do bend your eye on vacancy,
　　And with th' incorporal air do hold discourse?
　　Forth at your eyes your spirits wildly peep,
120　And as the sleeping soldiers in th' alarm,
　　Your bedded hair, like life in excrements,
　　Start up and stand an end. O gentle son,
　　Upon the heat and flame of thy distemper
　　Sprinkle cool patience. Whereon do you look?
125　HAM. On him, on him! look you how pale he glares!
　　His form and cause conjoin'd, preaching to stones,
　　Would make them capable.—Do not look upon me,
　　Lest with this piteous action you convert
　　My stern effects, then what I have to do
130　Will want true color—tears perchance for blood.
　　QUEEN To whom do you speak this?
　　HAM.　　　　　　　Do you see nothing there?
　　QUEEN Nothing at all, yet all that is I see.

---

101 s.d. **night-gown:** dressing gown.
102 **of . . . patches:** clownish (alluding to the motley worn by jesters) (?) or patched up, beggarly (?).
107 **laps'd . . . passion:** "having suffered time to slip and passion to cool" (Johnson).
108 **important:** urgent.
112 **amazement:** utter bewilderment.
114 **Conceit:** imagination.
120 **in th' alarm:** when the call to arms is sounded.
121 **excrements:** outgrowths; here, hair (also used of nails).
122 **an end:** on end.
124 **patience:** self-control.
126 **His . . . cause:** his appearance and what he has to say.
127 **capable:** sensitive, receptive.
128 **convert:** alter.
129 **effects:** (purposed) actions.
130 **want true color:** lack its proper appearance.

HAM. Nor did you nothing hear?
QUEEN   No, nothing but ourselves.
HAM. Why, look you there, look how it steals away!
135   My father, in his habit as he lived!
      Look where he goes, even now, out at the portal!

Exit GHOST.

QUEEN This is the very coinage of your brain,
      This bodiless creation ecstasy
      Is very cunning in.
HAM.   [Ecstasy?]
140   My pulse as yours doth temperately keep time,
      And makes as healthful music. It is not madness
      That I have utt'red. Bring me to the test,
      And [I] the matter will reword, which madness
      Would gambol from. Mother, for love of grace,
145   Lay not that flattering unction to your soul,
      That not your trespass but my madness speaks;
      It will but skin and film the ulcerous place,
      Whiles rank corruption, mining all within,
      Infects unseen. Confess yourself to heaven,
150   Repent what's past, avoid what is to come,
      And do not spread the compost on the weeds
      To make them ranker. Forgive me this my virtue,
      For in the fatness of these pursy times
      Virtue itself of vice must pardon beg,
155   Yea, curb and woo for leave to do him good.
QUEEN O Hamlet, thou hast cleft my heart in twain.
HAM. O, throw away the worser part of it,
      And [live] the purer with the other half.
      Good night, but go not to my uncle's bed—
160   Assume a virtue, if you have it not.
      That monster custom, who all sense doth eat,
      Of habits devil, is angel yet in this,
      That to the use of actions fair and good
      He likewise gives a frock or livery
165   That aptly is put on. Refrain [to-]night,
      And that shall lend a kind of easiness

---

¹³⁵ **habit:** dress.
¹³⁸ **ecstasy:** madness.
¹⁴⁴ **gambol:** start, jerk away.
¹⁴⁵ **flattering unction:** soothing ointment.
¹⁵¹ **compost:** manure.
¹⁵³ **pursy:** puffy, out of condition.
¹⁵⁵ **curb and woo:** bow and entreat.
¹⁶¹ **all . . . eat:** wears away all natural feeling.
¹⁶² **Of habits devil:** i.e. though it acts like a devil in establishing bad habits. Most editors read (in lines 161–62) *eat / Of habits evil*, following Theobald.
^{164–65} **frock . . . on:** i.e. a "habit" or customary garment, readily put on without need of any decision.

To the next abstinence, the next more easy;
For use almost can change the stamp of nature,
And either [. . . .] the devil or throw him out
170   With wondrous potency. Once more good night,
And when you are desirous to be blest,
I'll blessing beg of you. For this same lord,

[*Pointing to* POLONIUS.]

I do repent; but heaven hath pleas'd it so
To punish me with this, and this with me,
175   That I must be their scourge and minister.
I will bestow him, and will answer well
The death I gave him. So again good night.
I must be cruel only to be kind.
This bad begins and worse remains behind.
One word more, good lady.
180 QUEEN   What shall I do?
     HAM. Not this, by no means, that I bid you do:
Let the bloat king tempt you again to bed,
Pinch wanton on your cheek, call you his mouse,
And let him, for a pair of reechy kisses,
185   Or paddling in your neck with his damn'd fingers,
Make you to ravel all this matter out,
That I essentially am not in madness,
But mad in craft. 'Twere good you let him know,
For who that's but a queen, fair, sober, wise,
190   Would from a paddock, from a bar, a gib,
Such dear concernings hide? Who would do so?
No, in despite of sense and secrecy,
Unpeg the basket on the house's top,
Let the birds fly, and like the famous ape,
195   To try conclusions in the basket creep,
And break your own neck down.
     QUEEN Be thou assur'd, if words be made of breath,
And breath of life, I have no life to breathe
What thou hast said to me.

---

168 **use:** habit.

169 A word seems to be wanting after *either*.

171 **desirous . . . blest:** i.e. repentant.

175 **scourge and minister:** the agent of heavenly justice against human crime. *Scourge* suggests a permissive cruelty (Tamburlaine was the "scourge of God"), but "woe to him by whom the offense cometh"; the scourge must suffer for the evil it performs.

176 **bestow:** dispose of.   **answer:** answer for.

179 **behind:** to come.

184 **reechy:** filthy.

190 **paddock:** toad.   **gib:** tomcat.

191 **dear concernings:** matters of intense concern.

193 **Unpeg the basket:** open the door of the cage.

194 **famous ape.** The actual story has been lost.

195 **conclusions:** experiments (to see whether he too can fly if he enters the cage and then leaps out).

196 **down:** by the fall.

HAM. I must to England, you know that?
200 QUEEN   Alack,
I had forgot. 'Tis so concluded on.
HAM. There's letters seal'd, and my two schoolfellows,
Whom I will trust as I will adders fang'd,
They bear the mandate, they must sweep my way
205 And marshal me to knavery. Let it work,
For 'tis the sport to have the enginer
Hoist with his own petar, an't shall go hard
But I will delve one yard below their mines,
And blow them at the moon. O, 'tis most sweet
210 When in one line two crafts directly meet.
This man shall set me packing;
I'll lug the guts into the neighbor room.
Mother, good night indeed. This counsellor
Is now most still, most secret, and most grave,
215 Who was in life a foolish prating knave.
Come, sir, to draw toward an end with you.
Good night, mother.

Exeunt [severally, HAMLET tugging in POLONIUS].

ACT IV

SCENE I.

Enter KING and QUEEN with ROSENCRANTZ and GUILDENSTERN.

KING There's matter in these sighs, these profound heaves—
You must translate, 'tis fit we understand them.
Where is your son?
QUEEN Bestow this place on us a little while.

[Exeunt ROSENCRANTZ and GUILDENSTERN.]

5   Ah, mine own lord, what have I seen to-night!
KING What, Gertrude? How does Hamlet?
QUEEN Mad as the sea and wind when both contend
Which is the mightier. In his lawless fit,
Behind the arras hearing something stir,
10   Whips out his rapier, cries, "A rat, a rat!"
And in this brainish apprehension kills
The unseen good old man.

---

²⁰⁵ **knavery:** some knavish scheme against me.
²⁰⁶ **enginer:** deviser of military "engines" or contrivances.
²⁰⁷ **Hoist with:** blown up by.   **petar:** petard, bomb.
²¹⁰ **crafts:** plots.
²¹¹ **packing:** (1) taking on a load; (2) leaving in a hurry.
²¹⁶ **draw . . . end:** finish my conversation.

IV.i. Location: The castle.
¹¹ **brainish apprehension:** crazy notion.

KING   O heavy deed!
     It had been so with us had we been there.
     His liberty is full of threats to all,
15   To you yourself, to us, to every one.
     Alas, how shall this bloody deed be answer'd?
     It will be laid to us, whose providence
     Should have kept short, restrain'd, and out of haunt
     This mad young man; but so much was our love,
20   We would not understand what was most fit,
     But like the owner of a foul disease,
     To keep it from divulging, let it feed
     Even on the pith of life. Where is he gone?
QUEEN To draw apart the body he hath kill'd,
25   O'er whom his very madness, like some ore
     Among a mineral of metals base,
     Shows itself pure: 'a weeps for what is done.
KING O Gertrude, come away!
     The sun no sooner shall the mountains touch,
30   But we will ship him hence, and this vile deed
     We must with all our majesty and skill
     Both countenance and excuse. Ho, Guildenstern!

Enter ROSENCRANTZ *and* GUILDENSTERN.

     Friends both, go join you with some further aid:
     Hamlet in madness hath Polonius slain,
35   And from his mother's closet hath he dragg'd him.
     Go seek him out, speak fair, and bring the body
     Into the chapel. I pray you haste in this.

[Exeunt ROSENCRANTZ *and* GUILDENSTERN.*]*

     Come, Gertrude, we'll call up our wisest friends
     And let them know both what we mean to do
40   And what's untimely done, [. . . .]
     Whose whisper o'er the world's diameter,
     As level as the cannon to his blank,
     Transports his pois'ned shot, may miss our name,
     And hit the woundless air. O, come away!
45   My soul is full of discord and dismay.

Exeunt.

---

16 **answer'd:** i.e. satisfactorily accounted for to the public.
17 **providence:** foresight.
18 **short:** on a short leash.   **out of haunt:** away from other people.
22 **divulging:** being revealed.
25 **ore:** vein of gold.
26 **mineral:** mine.
40 Some words are wanting at the end of the line. Capell's conjecture, *so, haply, slander,* probably
   indicates the intended sense of the passage.
42 **As level:** with aim as good.   **blank:** target.
44 **woundless:** incapable of being hurt.

SCENE II.

Enter HAMLET.

HAM. Safely stow'd.
[GENTLEMEN (*Within.*) Hamlet! Lord Hamlet!]
[HAM.] But soft, what noise? Who calls on Hamlet?
O, here they come.

Enter ROSENCRANTZ *and* [GUILDENSTERN].

5   ROS. What have you done, my lord, with the dead body?
HAM. [Compounded] it with dust, whereto 'tis kin.
ROS. Tell us where 'tis, that we may take it thence,
And bear it to the chapel.
HAM. Do not believe it.
10 ROS. Believe what?
HAM. That I can keep your counsel and not mine own. Besides, to be demanded of a
spunge, what replication should be made by the son of a king?
ROS. Take you me for a spunge, my lord?
HAM. Ay, sir, that soaks up the King's countenance, his rewards, his authorities. But such
15 officers do the King best service in the end: he keeps them, like [an ape] an apple, in
the corner of his jaw, first mouth'd, to be last swallow'd. When he needs what you
have glean'd, it is but squeezing you, and, spunge, you shall be dry again.
ROS. I understand you not, my lord.
HAM. I am glad of it, a knavish speech sleeps in a foolish ear.
20 ROS. My lord, you must tell us where the body is, and go with us to the King.
HAM. The body is with the King, but the King is not with the body. The King is a thing—
GUIL. A thing, my lord?
HAM. Of nothing, bring me to him. [Hide fox, and all after.]

Exeunt.

SCENE III.

Enter KING *and two or three.*

KING I have sent to seek him, and to find the body.
How dangerous is it that this man goes loose!
Yet must not we put the strong law on him.
He's lov'd of the distracted multitude,

IV.ii. Location: The castle.
[11] **demanded of:** questioned by.
[12] **spunge:** sponge. **replication:** reply.
[14] **countenance:** favor.
[19] **sleeps:** is meaningless.
[21] **The body . . . the body.** Possibly alluding to the legal fiction that the king's dignity is separate
from his mortal body.
[23] **Of nothing:** of no account. Cf. "Man is like a thing of nought, his time passeth away like a
shadow" (Psalm 144:4 in the Prayer Book version). "Hamlet at once insults the King and hints
that his days are numbered" (Dover Wilson). **Hide . . . after.** Probably a cry in some game
resembling hide-and-seek.
IV.iii. Location: The castle.
[4] **distracted:** unstable.

5   Who like not in their judgment, but their eyes,
    And where 'tis so, th' offender's scourge is weigh'd,
    But never the offense. To bear all smooth and even,
    This sudden sending him away must seem
    Deliberate pause. Diseases desperate grown
10   By desperate appliance are reliev'd,
    Or not at all.

Enter ROSENCRANTZ.

               How now, what hath befall'n?
  ROS. Where the dead body is bestow'd, my lord,
    We cannot get from him.
  KING   But where is he?
  ROS. Without, my lord, guarded, to know your pleasure.
15 KING Bring him before us.
  ROS.   Ho, bring in the Lord.

They [HAMLET *and* GUILDENSTERN] *enter.*

  KING Now, Hamlet, where's Polonius?
  HAM. At supper.
  KING At supper? where?
  HAM. Not where he eats, but where 'a is eaten; a certain convocation of politic worms
20   are e'en at him. Your worm is your only emperor for diet: we fat all creatures else to
    fat us, and we fat ourselves for maggots; your fat king and your lean beggar is but
    variable service, two dishes, but to one table—that's the end.
  KING Alas, alas!
  HAM. A man may fish with the worm that hath eat of a king, and eat of the fish that
25   hath fed of that worm.
  KING What dost thou mean by this?
  HAM. Nothing but to show you how a king may go a progress through the guts of a
    beggar.
  KING Where is Polonius?
30 HAM. In heaven, send thither to see; if your messenger find him not there, seek him i'
    th' other place yourself. But if indeed you find him not within this month, you shall
    nose him as you go up the stairs into the lobby.
  KING *[To* ATTENDANTS.] Go seek him there.
  HAM. 'A will stay till you come.

[Exeunt ATTENDANTS.]

35 KING Hamlet, this deed, for thine especial safety—
    Which we do tender, as we dearly grieve

---

⁶ **scourge:** i.e. punishment.
⁷ **bear:** manage.
⁸⁻⁹ **must . . . pause:** i.e. must be represented as a maturely considered decision.
¹⁹ **politic:** crafty, prying; "such worms as might breed in a politician's corpse" (Dowden).
²⁰ **e'en:** even now.   **for diet:** with respect to what it eats.
²² **variable service:** different courses of a meal.
²⁷ **progress:** royal journey of state.
³⁶ **tender:** regard with tenderness, hold dear.   **dearly:** with intense feeling.

For that which thou hast done—must send thee hence
[With fiery quickness]; therefore prepare thyself,
The bark is ready, and the wind at help,
40   Th' associates tend, and every thing is bent
For England.
HAM.   For England.
KING   Ay, Hamlet.
HAM.   Good.
KING So is it, if thou knew'st our purposes.
HAM. I see a cherub that sees them. But come, for England! Farewell, dear mother.
KING Thy loving father, Hamlet.
45 HAM. My mother: father and mother is man and wife, man and wife is one flesh—so, my mother. Come, for England!

Exit.

KING Follow him at foot, tempt him with speed aboard.
Delay it not, I'll have him hence to-night.
Away, for every thing is seal'd and done
50   That else leans on th' affair. Pray you make haste.

[*Exeunt* ROSENCRANTZ *and* GUILDENSTERN.]

And, England, if my love thou hold'st at aught—
As my great power thereof may give thee sense,
Since yet thy cicatrice looks raw and red
After the Danish sword, and thy free awe
55   Pays homage to us—thou mayst not coldly set
Our sovereign process, which imports at full,
By letters congruing to that effect,
The present death of Hamlet. Do it, England,
For like the hectic in my blood he rages,
60   And thou must cure me. Till I know 'tis done,
How e'er my haps, my joys [were] ne'er [begun].

Exit.

---

[39] **at help**: favorable.
[40] **Th'**: thy.   **tend**: await.   **bent**: made ready.
[43] **I . . . them**: i.e. heaven sees them.
[47] **at foot**: at his heels, close behind.
[50] **leans on**: relates to.
[51] **England**: King of England.
[53] **cicatrice**: scar.
[54-55] **thy . . . Pays**: your fear makes you pay voluntarily.
[55] **coldly set**: undervalue, disregard.
[56] **process**: command.
[57] **congruing to**: in accord with.
[58] **present**: immediate.
[59] **hectic**: continuous fever.
[61] **haps**: fortunes.

SCENE IV.

Enter FORTINBRAS *with his army over the stage.*

FORT. Go, captain, from me greet the Danish king.
　Tell him that by his license Fortinbras
　Craves the conveyance of a promis'd march
　Over his kingdom. You know the rendezvous.
5　If that his Majesty would aught with us,
　We shall express our duty in his eye,
　And let him know so.
CAP.　　　　　　　　I will do't, my lord.
FORT. Go softly on.

[Exeunt all but the CAPTAIN.*]*

Enter HAMLET, ROSENCRANTZ, [GUILDENSTERN,] *etc.*

HAM. Good sir, whose powers are these?
10　CAP. They are of Norway, sir.
HAM. How purpos'd, sir, I pray you?
CAP. Against some part of Poland.
HAM. Who commands them, sir?
CAP. The nephew to old Norway, Fortinbras.
15　HAM. Goes it against the main of Poland, sir,
　Or for some frontier?
CAP. Truly to speak, and with no addition,
　We go to gain a little patch of ground
　That hath in it no profit but the name.
20　To pay five ducats, five, I would not farm it;
　Nor will it yield to Norway or the Pole
　A ranker rate, should it be sold in fee.
HAM. Why then the Polack never will defend it.
CAP. Yes, it is already garrison'd.
25　HAM. Two thousand souls and twenty thousand ducats
　Will not debate the question of this straw.
　This is th' imposthume of much wealth and peace,
　That inward breaks, and shows no cause without
　Why the man dies. I humbly thank you, sir.
CAP. God buy you, sir.

[Exit.]

IV.iv. Location: The Danish coast, near the castle.
³ **conveyance of:** escort for.
⁶ **eye:** presence.
⁸ **softly:** slowly.
⁹ **powers:** forces.
¹⁵ **main:** main territory.
²⁰ **To pay:** i.e. for an annual rent of.　**farm:** lease.
²² **ranker:** higher.　**in fee:** outright.
²⁶ **Will not debate:** i.e. will scarcely be enough to fight out.
²⁷ **imposthume:** abscess.

30 ROS.   Will't please you go, my lord?
      HAM. I'll be with you straight—go a little before.

[*Exeunt all but* HAMLET.]

How all occasions do inform against me,
And spur my dull revenge! What is a man,
If his chief good and market of his time
35   Be but to sleep and feed? a beast, no more.
Sure He that made us with such large discourse,
Looking before and after, gave us not
That capability and godlike reason
To fust in us unus'd. Now whether it be
40   Bestial oblivion, or some craven scruple
Of thinking too precisely on th' event—
A thought which quarter'd hath but one part wisdom
And ever three parts coward—I do not know
Why yet I live to say, "This thing's to do,"
45   Sith I have cause, and will, and strength, and means
To do't. Examples gross as earth exhort me:
Witness this army of such mass and charge,
Led by a delicate and tender prince,
Whose spirit with divine ambition puff'd
50   Makes mouths at the invisible event,
Exposing what is mortal and unsure
To all that fortune, death, and danger dare,
Even for an egg-shell. Rightly to be great
Is not to stir without great argument,
55   But greatly to find quarrel in a straw
When honor's at the stake. How stand I then,
That have a father kill'd, a mother stain'd,
Excitements of my reason and my blood,
And let all sleep, while to my shame I see
60   The imminent death of twenty thousand men,
That for a fantasy and trick of fame
Go to their graves like beds, fight for a plot
Whereon the numbers cannot try the cause,

---

32 **inform against:** denounce, accuse.
34 **market:** purchase, profit.
36 **discourse:** reasoning power.
39 **fust:** grow mouldy.
40 **oblivion:** forgetfulness.
41 **event:** outcome.
46 **gross:** large, obvious.
47 **mass and charge:** size and expense.
50 **Makes mouths at:** treats scornfully. **invisible:** i.e. unforeseeable.
54 **Is not to:** i.e. is *not* not to. **argument:** cause.
55 **greatly:** nobly.
58 **Excitements of:** urgings by.
61 **fantasy:** caprice. **trick:** trifle.
63 **Whereon . . . cause:** which isn't large enough to let the opposing armies engage upon it.

Which is not tomb enough and continent
65   To hide the slain? O, from this time forth,
My thoughts be bloody, or be nothing worth!

Exit.

SCENE V.

Enter HORATIO, [QUEEN] GERTRUDE, *and a* GENTLEMAN.

QUEEN I will not speak with her.
GENT. She is importunate, indeed distract.
    Her mood will needs be pitied.
QUEEN   What would she have?
GENT. She speaks much of her father, says she hears
5   There's tricks i' th' world, and hems, and beats her heart,
    Spurns enviously at straws, speaks things in doubt
    That carry but half sense. Her speech is nothing,
    Yet the unshaped use of it doth move
    The hearers to collection; they yawn at it,
10   And botch the words up fit to their own thoughts,
    Which as her winks and nods and gestures yield them,
    Indeed would make one think there might be thought,
    Though nothing sure, yet much unhappily.
HOR. 'Twere good she were spoken with, for she may strew
15   Dangerous conjectures in ill-breeding minds.
[QUEEN] Let her come in.

[Exit GENTLEMAN.*]*

    [Aside.] To my sick soul, as sin's true nature is,
    Each toy seems prologue to some great amiss,
    So full of artless jealousy is guilt,
20   It spills itself in fearing to be spilt.

Enter OPHELIA *[distracted, with her hair down, playing on a lute].*

OPH. Where is the beauteous majesty of Denmark?
QUEEN How now, Ophelia?

---

⁶⁴ **continent:** container.

IV.v. Location: The castle.
⁶ **Spurns . . . straws:** spitefully takes offense at trifles.   **in doubt:** obscurely.
⁷ **Her speech:** what she says.
⁸ **unshaped use:** distracted manner.
⁹ **collection:** attempts to gather the meaning.   **yawn at:** strive, as if openmouthed, to grasp (?). Most
    editors adopt the F1 reading *aim at.*
¹⁰ **botch:** patch.
¹¹ **Which:** i.e. the words.
¹² **thought:** inferred, conjectured.
¹⁵ **ill-breeding:** conceiving ill thoughts, prone to think the worst.
¹⁸ **toy:** trifle.   **amiss:** calamity.
¹⁹ **artless jealousy:** uncontrolled suspicion.
²⁰ **spills:** destroys.

OPH. (*She sings*)

"How should I your true-love know
    From another one?
25 By his cockle hat and staff,
    And his sandal shoon."
QUEEN Alas, sweet lady, what imports this song?
OPH. Say you? Nay, pray you mark.

Song.

        "He is dead and gone, lady,
30   He is dead and gone,
        At his head a grass-green turf,
        At his heels a stone."

    O ho!
QUEEN Nay, but, Ophelia—
35 OPH. Pray you mark.

    [*Sings.*]

        "White his shroud as the mountain snow"—

Enter KING.

QUEEN Alas, look here, my lord.
OPH.

Song.

        "Larded all with sweet flowers,
        Which bewept to the ground did not go
40   With true-love showers."

KING How do you, pretty lady?
OPH. Well, God dild you! They say the owl was a baker's daughter. Lord, we know what
    we are, but know not what we may be. God be at your table!
KING Conceit upon her father.
45 OPH. Pray let's have no words of this, but when they ask you what it means, say you this:

23–24 These lines resemble a passage in an earlier ballad beginning "As you came from the holy
    land / Of Walsingham." Probably all the song fragments sung by Ophelia were familiar to the
    Globe audience, but only one other line (177) is from a ballad still extant.
25 **cockle hat:** hat bearing a cockle shell, the badge of a pilgrim to the shrine of St. James of
    Compostela in Spain.   **staff.** Another mark of a pilgrim.
26 **shoon:** shoes (already an archaic form in Shakespeare's day).
38 **Larded:** adorned.
39 **not.** Contrary to the expected sense, and unmetrical; explained as Ophelia's alteration of the line
    to accord with the facts of Polonius' burial (see line 80).
42 **dild:** yield, reward.   **owl.** Alluding to the legend of a baker's daughter whom Jesus turned into
    an owl because she did not respond generously to his request for bread.
44 **Conceit:** fanciful brooding.

Song.

> "To-morrow is Saint Valentine's day
>   All in the morning betime,
> And I a maid at your window,
>   To be your Valentine.

50
> "Then up he rose and donn'd his clo'es,
>   And dupp'd the chamber-door,
> Let in the maid, that out a maid
>   Never departed more."

KING Pretty Ophelia!
55 OPH. Indeed without an oath I'll make an end on't.

[*Sings.*]

> "By Gis, and by Saint Charity,
>   Alack, and fie for shame!
> Young men will do't if they come to't,
>   By Cock, they are to blame.

60
> "Quoth she, 'Before you tumbled me,
>   You promis'd me to wed.' "

(He answers.)

> " 'So would I 'a' done, by yonder sun,
>   And thou hadst not come to my bed.' "

65 KING How long hath she been thus?
OPH. I hope all will be well. We must be patient, but I cannot choose but weep to think they would lay him i' th' cold ground. My brother shall know of it, and so I thank you for your good counsel. Come, my coach! Good night, ladies, good night. Sweet ladies, good night, good night.

[*Exit.*]

70 KING Follow her close, give her good watch, I pray you.

[*Exit* HORATIO.]

O, this is the poison of deep grief, it springs
All from her father's death—and now behold!
O Gertrude, Gertrude,
When sorrows come, they come not single spies,
75 But in battalions: first, her father slain;
Next, your son gone, and he most violent author

---

⁵¹ **dupp'd:** opened.
⁵⁶ **Gis:** contraction of *Jesus.*
⁵⁹ **Cock:** corruption of *God.*
⁶⁴ **And:** if.
⁷⁴ **spies:** i.e. soldiers sent ahead of the main force to reconnoiter, scouts.

Of his own just remove; the people muddied,
Thick and unwholesome in [their] thoughts and whispers
For good Polonius' death; and we have done but greenly
80   In hugger-mugger to inter him; poor Ophelia
Divided from herself and her fair judgment,
Without the which we are pictures, or mere beasts;
Last, and as much containing as all these,
Her brother is in secret come from France,
85   Feeds on this wonder, keeps himself in clouds,
And wants not buzzers to infect his ear
With pestilent speeches of his father's death,
Wherein necessity, of matter beggar'd,
Will nothing stick our person to arraign
90   In ear and ear. O my dear Gertrude, this,
Like to a murd'ring-piece, in many places
Gives me superfluous death.

A *noise within.*

[QUEEN   Alack, what noise is this?]
KING Attend!
      Where is my Swissers? Let them guard the door.

Enter a MESSENGER.

      What is the matter?
95   MESS.   Save yourself, my lord!
      The ocean, overpeering of his list,
      Eats not the flats with more impiteous haste
      Than young Laertes, in a riotous head,
      O'erbears your officers. The rabble call him lord,
100   And as the world were now but to begin,
      Antiquity forgot, custom not known,
      The ratifiers and props of every word,
      [They] cry, "Choose we, Laertes shall be king!"
      Caps, hands, and tongues applaud it to the clouds,
105   "Laertes shall be king, Laertes king!"

A *noise within.*

---

77 **muddied**: confused.
79 **greenly**: unwisely.
80 **In hugger-mugger**: secretly and hastily.
85 **in clouds**: i.e. in cloudy surmise and suspicion (rather than the light of fact).
86 **wants**: lacks.   **buzzers**: whispering informers.
88 **of matter beggar'd**: destitute of facts.
89 **nothing . . . arraign**: scruple not at all to charge me with the crime.
91 **murd'ring-piece**: cannon firing a scattering charge.
94 **Swissers**: Swiss guards.
96 **overpeering . . . list**: rising higher than its shores.
98 **in . . . head**: with a rebellious force.
100 **as**: as if.
102 **word**: pledge, promise.

QUEEN How cheerfully on the false trail they cry!
   O, this is counter, you false Danish dogs!

Enter LAERTES *with others.*

KING The doors are broke.
LAER. Where is this king? Sirs, stand you all without.
ALL No, let's come in.
110 LAER.   I pray you give me leave.
ALL We will, we will.
LAER. I thank you, keep the door. *[Exeunt* LAERTES' *followers.]* O thou vile king,
   Give me my father!
QUEEN   Calmly, good Laertes.
LAER. That drop of blood that's calm proclaims me bastard,
115   Cries cuckold to my father, brands the harlot
   Even here between the chaste unsmirched brow
   Of my true mother.
KING   What is the cause, Laertes,
   That thy rebellion looks so giant-like?
   Let him go, Gertrude, do not fear our person:
120   There's such divinity doth hedge a king
   That treason can but peep to what it would,
   Acts little of his will. Tell me, Laertes,
   Why thou art thus incens'd. Let him go, Gertrude.
   Speak, man.
LAER. Where is my father?
KING   Dead.
125 QUEEN   But not by him.
KING Let him demand his fill.
LAER. How came he dead? I'll not be juggled with.
   To hell, allegiance! vows, to the blackest devil!
   Conscience and grace, to the profoundest pit!
130   I dare damnation. To this point I stand,
   That both the worlds I give to negligence,
   Let come what comes, only I'll be reveng'd
   Most throughly for my father.
KING   Who shall stay you?
LAER. My will, not all the world's:
135   And for my means, I'll husband them so well,
   They shall go far with little.
KING   Good Laertes,
   If you desire to know the certainty
   Of your dear father, is't writ in your revenge

---

107 **counter:** on the wrong scent (literally, following the scent backward).
119 **fear:** fear for.
121 **would:** i.e. would like to do.
131 **both . . . negligence:** i.e. I don't care what the consequences are in this world or in the next.
133 **throughly:** thoroughly.
134 **world's:** i.e. world's will.

That, swoopstake, you will draw both friend and foe,
140 Winner and loser?
LAER. None but his enemies.
KING   Will you know them then?
LAER. To his good friends thus wide I'll ope my arms,
   And like the kind life-rend'ring pelican,
   Repast them with my blood.
KING   Why, now you speak
145 Like a good child and a true gentleman.
   That I am guiltless of your father's death,
   And am most sensibly in grief for it,
   It shall as level to your judgment 'pear
   As day does to your eye.

A noise within.

                   "Let her come in!"
150 LAER. How now, what noise is that?

Enter OPHELIA.

   O heat, dry up my brains! tears seven times salt
   Burn out the sense and virtue of mine eye!
   By heaven, thy madness shall be paid with weight
   [Till] our scale turn the beam. O rose of May!
155 Dear maid, kind sister, sweet Ophelia!
   O heavens, is't possible a young maid's wits
   Should be as mortal as [an old] man's life?
   [Nature is fine in love, and where 'tis fine,
   It sends some precious instance of itself
160 After the thing it loves.]
OPH.

Song.

         "They bore him barefac'd on the bier,
            [Hey non nonny, nonny, hey nonny,]
         And in his grave rain'd many a tear"—

   Fare you well, my dove!
165 LAER. Hadst thou thy wits and didst persuade revenge,
   It could not move thus.

---

¹³⁹ **swoopstake:** sweeping up everything without discrimination (modern *sweepstake*).
¹⁴³ **pelican.** The female pelican was believed to draw blood from her own breast to nourish her young.
¹⁴⁵ **good child:** faithful son.
¹⁴⁷ **sensibly:** feelingly.
¹⁴⁸ **level:** plain.
¹⁵² **virtue:** faculty.
¹⁵⁸ **fine in:** refined or spiritualized by.
¹⁵⁹ **instance:** proof, token. So delicate is Ophelia's love for her father that her sanity has pursued him into the grave.
¹⁶⁵ **persuade:** argue logically for.

OPH. You must sing, "A-down, a-down," and you call him a-down-a. O how the wheel becomes it! It is the false steward, that stole his master's daughter.

LAER. This nothing's more than matter.

170 OPH. There's rosemary, that's for remembrance; pray you, love, remember. And there is pansies, that's for thoughts.

LAER. A document in madness, thoughts and remembrance fitted.

OPH. [To CLAUDIUS.] There's fennel for you, and columbines. [To GERTRUDE.] There's rue for you, and here's some for me; we may call it herb of grace a' Sundays. You

175 may wear your rue with a difference. There's a daisy. I would give you some violets, but they wither'd all when my father died. They say 'a made a good end—

[Sings.]

"For bonny sweet Robin is all my joy."

LAER. Thought and afflictions, passion, hell itself,
She turns to favor and to prettiness.

ÓPH.

Song.

180 "And will 'a not come again?
And will 'a not come again?
No, no, he is dead,
Go to thy death-bed,
He never will come again.

185 "His beard was as white as snow,
[All] flaxen was his pole,
He is gone, he is gone,
And we cast away moan,
God 'a' mercy on his soul!"

190 And of all Christians' souls, [I pray God]. God buy you.

[Exit.]

LAER. Do you [see] this, O God?

KING Laertes, I must commune with your grief,
Or you deny me right. Go but apart,
Make choice of whom your wisest friends you will,

---

167 **and . . . a-down-a:** "if he indeed agrees that Polonius is 'a-down,' i.e. fallen low" (Dover Wilson).   **wheel:** refrain (?) or spinning wheel, at which women sang ballads (?).
169 **matter:** lucid speech.
172 **A document in madness:** a lesson contained in mad talk.
173 **fennel, columbines.** Symbols respectively of flattery and ingratitude.
174 **rue.** Symbolic of sorrow and repentance.
175 **with a difference:** i.e. to represent a different cause of sorrow. *Difference* is a term from heraldry, meaning a variation in a coat of arms made to distinguish different members of a family.   **daisy, violets.** Symbolic respectively of dissembling and faithfulness. It is not clear who are the recipients of these.
178 **Thought:** melancholy.
179 **favor:** grace, charm.
186 **flaxen:** white.   **pole:** poll, head.

195 And they shall hear and judge 'twixt you and me.
If by direct or by collateral hand
They find us touch'd, we will our kingdom give,
Our crown, our life, and all that we call ours,
To you in satisfaction; but if not,
200 Be you content to lend your patience to us,
And we shall jointly labor with your soul
To give it due content.
LAER.   Let this be so.
His means of death, his obscure funeral—
No trophy, sword, nor hatchment o'er his bones,
205 No noble rite nor formal ostentation—
Cry to be heard, as 'twere from heaven to earth,
That I must call't in question.
KING   So you shall,
And where th' offense is, let the great axe fall.
I pray you go with me.

Exeunt.

SCENE VI.

Enter HORATIO *and others.*

HOR. What are they that would speak with me?
GENTLEMAN Sea-faring men, sir. They say they have letters for you.
HOR. Let them come in.

[*Exit* GENTLEMAN.]

I do not know from what part of the world
5   I should be greeted, if not from Lord Hamlet.

Enter SAILORS.

[1] SAIL. God bless you, sir.
HOR. Let him bless thee too.
[1] SAIL. 'A shall, sir, and ['t] please him. There's a letter for you, sir—it came from th'
embassador that was bound for England—if your name be Horatio, as I am let to know
10   it is.
HOR. [*Reads.*] "Horatio, when thou shalt have overlook'd this, give these fellows some
means to the King, they have letters for him. Ere we were two days old at sea, a pirate
of very warlike appointment gave us chase. Finding ourselves too slow of sail, we put
on a compell'd valor, and in the grapple I boarded them. On the instant they got clear
15   of our ship, so I alone became their prisoner. They have dealt with me like thieves of
mercy, but they knew what they did: I am to do a [good] turn for them. Let the King

---

¹⁹⁶ **collateral:** i.e. indirect.
¹⁹⁷ **touch'd:** guilty
²⁰⁴ **trophy:** memorial.   **hatchment:** heraldic memorial tablet.
²⁰⁵ **formal ostentation:** fitting and customary ceremony.
²⁰⁷ **That:** so that.

IV.vi. Location: The castle.
^{15–16} **thieves of mercy:** merciful thieves.

have the letters I have sent, and repair thou to me with as much speed as thou wouldest
fly death. I have words to speak in thine ear will make thee dumb, yet are they much
too light for the [bore] of the matter. These good fellows will bring thee where I am.
20   Rosencrantz and Guildenstern hold their course for England, of them I have much
to tell thee. Farewell.
                [He] that thou knowest thine,
                                    Hamlet."
Come, I will [give] you way for these your letters,
25   And do't the speedier that you may direct me
To him from whom you brought them.

Exeunt.

SCENE VII.

Enter KING *and* LAERTES.

KING Now must your conscience my acquittance seal,
        And you must put me in your heart for friend,
        Sith you have heard, and with a knowing ear,
        That he which hath your noble father slain
        Pursued my life.
5   LAER.   It well appears. But tell me
        Why you [proceeded] not against these feats
        So criminal and so capital in nature,
        As by your safety, greatness, wisdom, all things else
        You mainly were stirr'd up.
        KING   O, for two special reasons,
10   Which may to you perhaps seem much unsinow'd,
        But yet to me th' are strong. The Queen his mother
        Lives almost by his looks, and for myself—
        My virtue or my plague, be it either which—
        She is so [conjunctive] to my life and soul,
15   That, as the star moves not but in his sphere,
        I could not but by her. The other motive,
        Why to a public count I might not go,
        Is the great love the general gender bear him,
        Who, dipping all his faults in their affection,
20   Work like the spring that turneth wood to stone,

---

¹⁹ **bore:** caliber, size (gunnery term).

IV.vii. Location: The castle.
¹ **my acquittance seal:** ratify my acquittal, i.e. acknowledge my innocence in Polonius' death.
⁶ **feats:** acts.
⁸ **safety:** i.e. regard for your own safety.
⁹ **mainly:** powerfully.
¹⁰ **unsinow'd:** unsinewed, i.e. weak.
¹³ **either which:** one or the other.
¹⁴ **conjunctive:** closely joined.
¹⁵ **in his sphere:** by the movement of the sphere in which it is fixed (as the Ptolemaic astronomy taught).
¹⁷ **count:** reckoning.
¹⁸ **the general gender:** everybody.

Convert his gyves to graces, so that my arrows,
Too slightly timber'd for so [loud a wind],
Would have reverted to my bow again,
But not where I have aim'd them.
25 LAER. And so have I a noble father lost,
A sister driven into desp'rate terms,
Whose worth, if praises may go back again,
Stood challenger on mount of all the age
For her perfections—but my revenge will come.
30 KING Break not your sleeps for that. You must not think
That we are made of stuff so flat and dull
That we can let our beard be shook with danger
And think it pastime. You shortly shall hear more.
I lov'd your father, and we love ourself,
35 And that, I hope, will teach you to imagine—

Enter a MESSENGER *with letters.*

[How now? What news?
MESS.   Letters, my lord, from Hamlet:]
These to your Majesty, this to the Queen.
KING From Hamlet? Who brought them?
MESS. Sailors, my lord, they say, I saw them not.
40   They were given me by Claudio. He receiv'd them
Of him that brought them.
KING   Laertes, you shall hear them.
—Leave us.

[Exit MESSENGER.*]*

[Reads.]

"High and mighty, You shall know I am set naked on your kingdom. To-morrow shall
I beg leave to see your kingly eyes, when I shall, first asking you pardon thereunto,
45   recount the occasion of my sudden [and more strange] return.
          [Hamlet.]"
What should this mean? Are all the rest come back?
Or is it some abuse, and no such thing?
LAER. Know you the hand?

---

21 **gyves:** fetters.
26 **terms:** condition.
27 **go back again:** i.e. refer to what she was before she went mad.
28 **on mount:** preeminent.
30 **for that:** i.e. for fear of losing your revenge.
31 **flat:** spiritless.
32 **let . . . shook.** To ruffle or tweak a man's beard was an act of insolent defiance that he could
not disregard without loss of honor. Cf. II.ii. 485. **with:** by.
43 **naked:** destitute.
44 **pardon thereunto:** permission to do so.
48 **abuse:** deceit.

KING   'Tis Hamlet's character. "Naked"!
50   And in a postscript here he says "alone."
        Can you devise me?
        LAER. I am lost in it, my lord. But let him come,
        It warms the very sickness in my heart
        That I [shall] live and tell him to his teeth,
        "Thus didst thou."
55   KING   If it be so, Laertes—
        As how should it be so? how otherwise?—
        Will you be rul'd by me?
        LAER.   Ay, my lord,
        So you will not o'errule me to a peace.
        KING To thine own peace. If he be now returned
60   As [checking] at his voyage, and that he means
        No more to undertake it, I will work him
        To an exploit, now ripe in my device,
        Under the which he shall not choose but fall;
        And for his death no wind of blame shall breathe,
65   But even his mother shall uncharge the practice,
        And call it accident.
        LAER.   My lord, I will be rul'd,
        The rather if you could devise it so
        That I might be the organ.
        KING   It falls right.
        You have been talk'd of since your travel much,
70   And that in Hamlet's hearing, for a quality
        Wherein they say you shine. Your sum of parts
        Did not together pluck such envy from him
        As did that one, and that, in my regard,
        Of the unworthiest siege.
        LAER.   What part is that, my lord?
75   KING A very riband in the cap of youth,
        Yet needful too, for youth no less becomes
        The light and careless livery that it wears
        Than settled age his sables and his weeds,
        Importing health and graveness. Two months since
80   Here was a gentleman of Normandy:

---

49 **character:** handwriting.
51 **devise me:** explain it to me.
56 **As . . . otherwise:** How can he have come back? Yet he obviously has.
58 **So:** provided that.
60 **checking at:** turning from (like a falcon diverted from its quarry by other prey).
65 **uncharge the practice:** adjudge the plot no plot, i.e. fail to see the plot.
68 **organ:** instrument, agent.
70 **quality:** skill.
71 **Your . . . parts:** all your (other) accomplishments put together.
74 **unworthiest:** i.e. least important (with no implication of unsuitableness).   **siege:** status, position.
78 **weeds:** (characteristic) garb.
79 **Importing . . . graveness:** signifying prosperity and dignity.

I have seen myself, and serv'd against, the French,
And they can well on horseback, but this gallant
Had witchcraft in't, he grew unto his seat,
And to such wondrous doing brought his horse,
85 As had he been incorps'd and demi-natur'd
With the brave beast. So far he topp'd [my] thought,
That I in forgery of shapes and tricks
Come short of what he did.
LAER.   A Norman was't?
KING A Norman.
LAER. Upon my life, Lamord.
90 KING   The very same.
LAER. I know him well. He is the brooch indeed
And gem of all the nation.
KING He made confession of you,
And gave you such a masterly report
95 For art and exercise in your defense,
And for your rapier most especial,
That he cried out 'twould be a sight indeed
If one could match you. The scrimers of their nation
He swore had neither motion, guard, nor eye,
100 If you oppos'd them. Sir, this report of his
Did Hamlet so envenom with his envy
That he could nothing do but wish and beg
Your sudden coming o'er to play with you.
Now, out of this—
LAER.   What out of this, my lord?
105 KING Laertes, was your father dear to you?
Or are you like the painting of a sorrow,
A face without a heart?
LAER.   Why ask you this?
KING Not that I think you did not love your father,
But that I know love is begun by time,
110 And that I see, in passages of proof,
Time qualifies the spark and fire of it.
There lives within the very flame of love
A kind of week or snuff that will abate it,
And nothing is at a like goodness still,

---

82 **can . . . horseback:** are excellent riders.
85 **incorps'd:** made one body. **demi-natur'd:** i.e. become half of a composite animal.
87 **forgery:** mere imagining.
91 **brooch:** ornament (worn in the hat).
93 **made . . . you:** acknowledged your excellence.
98 **scrimers:** fencers.
103 **sudden:** speedy.
109 **time:** i.e. a particular set of circumstances.
110 **in . . . proof:** i.e. by the test of experience, by actual examples.
111 **qualifies:** moderates.
113 **week:** wick.
114 **nothing . . . still:** nothing remains forever at the same pitch of perfection.

115 For goodness, growing to a plurisy,
Dies in his own too much. That we would do,
We should do when we would; for this "would" changes,
And hath abatements and delays as many
As there are tongues, are hands, are accidents,
120 And then this "should" is like a spendthrift's sigh,
That hurts by easing. But to the quick of th' ulcer:
Hamlet comes back. What would you undertake
To show yourself indeed your father's son
More than in words?
LAER.   To cut his throat i' th' church.
125 KING No place indeed should murther sanctuarize,
Revenge should have no bounds. But, good Laertes,
Will you do this, keep close within your chamber.
Hamlet return'd shall know you are come home.
We'll put on those shall praise your excellence,
130 And set a double varnish on the fame
The Frenchman gave you, bring you in fine together,
And wager o'er your heads. He, being remiss,
Most generous, and free from all contriving,
Will not peruse the foils, so that with ease,
135 Or with a little shuffling, you may choose
A sword unbated, and in a [pass] of practice
Requite him for your father.
LAER.   I will do't,
And for [that] purpose I'll anoint my sword.
I bought an unction of a mountebank,
140 So mortal that, but dip a knife in it,
Where it draws blood, no cataplasm so rare,
Collected from all simples that have virtue
Under the moon, can save the thing from death

---

115 **plurisy:** plethora (a variant spelling of *pleurisy*, which was erroneously related to *plus*, stem *plur-*, "more, overmuch."
116 **too much:** excess.
120 **spendthrift's sigh.** A sigh was supposed to draw blood from the heart.
121 **hurts by easing:** injures us at the same time that it gives us relief.
125 **sanctuarize:** offer asylum to.
127 **Will . . . this:** if you want to undertake this.
129 **put on those:** incite those who.
130 **double varnish:** second coat of varnish.
131 **in fine:** finally.
132 **remiss:** careless, overtrustful.
133 **generous:** noble-minded.   **free . . . contriving:** innocent of sharp practices.
134 **peruse:** examine.
135 **shuffling:** cunning exchange.
136 **unbated:** not blunted.   **pass of practice:** tricky thrust.
139 **unction:** ointment.   **mountebank:** traveling quack-doctor.
140 **mortal:** deadly.
141 **cataplasm:** poultice.
142 **simples:** medicinal herbs.   **virtue:** curative power.

That is but scratch'd withal. I'll touch my point
145 With this contagion, that if I gall him slightly,
It may be death.
KING   Let's further think of this,
Weigh what convenience both of time and means
May fit us to our shape. If this should fail,
And that our drift look through our bad performance,
150 'Twere better not assay'd; therefore this project
Should have a back or second, that might hold
If this did blast in proof. Soft, let me see.
We'll make a solemn wager on your cunnings—
I ha't!
155 When in your motion you are hot and dry—
As make your bouts more violent to that end—
And that he calls for drink, I'll have preferr'd him
A chalice for the nonce, whereon but sipping,
If he by chance escape your venom'd stuck,
160 Our purpose may hold there. But stay, what noise?

Enter QUEEN.

QUEEN One woe doth tread upon another's heel,
So fast they follow. Your sister's drown'd, Laertes.
LAER. Drown'd! O, where?
QUEEN There is a willow grows askaunt the brook,
165 That shows his hoary leaves in the glassy stream,
Therewith fantastic garlands did she make
Of crow-flowers, nettles, daisies, and long purples
That liberal shepherds give a grosser name,
But our cull-cold maids do dead men's fingers call them.
170 There on the pendant boughs her crownet weeds
Clamb'ring to hang, an envious sliver broke,
When down her weedy trophies and herself
Fell in the weeping brook. Her clothes spread wide,

---

¹⁴⁵ **gall:** graze.
¹⁴⁸ **fit . . . shape:** i.e. suit our purposes best.
¹⁴⁹ **drift:** purpose. **look through:** become visible, be detected.
¹⁵¹ **back or second:** i.e. a second plot in reserve for emergency.
¹⁵² **blast in proof:** blow up while being tried (an image from gunnery).
¹⁵⁶ **As:** i.e. and you should.
¹⁵⁷ **preferr'd:** offered to. Most editors adopt the F1 reading *prepar'd*.
¹⁵⁸ **nonce:** occasion.
¹⁵⁹ **stuck:** thrust (from *stoccado*, a fencing term).
¹⁶⁴ **askaunt:** sideways over.
¹⁶⁵ **hoary:** grey-white.
¹⁶⁶ **Therewith:** i.e. with willow branches.
¹⁶⁷ **long purples:** wild orchids.
¹⁶⁸ **liberal:** free-spoken.
¹⁶⁹ **cull-cold:** chaste.
¹⁷⁰ **crownet:** made into coronets.
¹⁷¹ **envious sliver:** malicious branch.

And mermaid-like awhile they bore her up,
175 Which time she chaunted snatches of old lauds,
As one incapable of her own distress,
Or like a creature native and indued
Unto that element. But long it could not be
Till that her garments, heavy with their drink,
180 Pull'd the poor wretch from her melodious lay
To muddy death.
LAER.   Alas, then she is drown'd?
QUEEN Drown'd, drown'd.
LAER. Too much of water hast thou, poor Ophelia,
And therefore I forbid my tears; but yet
185 It is our trick, Nature her custom holds,
Let shame say what it will; when these are gone,
The woman will be out. Adieu, my lord,
I have a speech a' fire that fain would blaze,
But that this folly drowns it.

Exit.

KING   Let's follow, Gertrude.
190 How much I had to do to calm his rage!
Now fear I this will give it start again,
Therefore let's follow.

Exeunt.

ACT V

SCENE I.

Enter two CLOWNS *[with spades and mattocks].*

1 CLO. Is she to be buried in Christian burial when she willfully seeks her own salvation?
2 CLO. I tell thee she is, therefore make her grave straight. The crowner hath sate on her, and finds it Christian burial.
1 CLO. How can that be, unless she drown'd herself in her own defense?
5 2 CLO. Why, 'tis found so.
1 CLO. It must be *[se offendendo]*, it cannot be else. For here lies the point: if I drown myself wittingly, it argues an act, and an act hath three branches—it is to act, to do, to perform; [argal], she drown'd herself wittingly.

---

175 **lauds:** hymns.
176 **incapable:** insensible.
177 **indued:** habituated.
185 **It:** i.e. weeping.   **trick:** natural way.
186 **these:** these tears.
187 **The woman . . . out:** my womanish traits will be gone for good.

V.i. Location: A churchyard.
o.s.d. **Clowns:** rustics.
2 **straight:** immediately.   **crowner:** coroner.
6 **se offendendo:** blunder for *se defendendo,* "in self-defense."
8 **argal:** blunder for *ergo,* "therefore."

2 CLO. Nay, but hear you, goodman delver—

10   1 CLO. Give me leave. Here lies the water; good. Here stands the man; good. If the man
go to this water and drown himself, it is, will he, nill he, he goes, mark you that. But
if the water come to him and drown him, he drowns not himself; argal, he that is not
guilty of his own death shortens not his own life.

2 CLO. But is this law?

15   1 CLO. Ay, marry, is't—crowner's quest law.

2 CLO. Will you ha' the truth an't? If this had not been a gentlewoman, she should have
been buried out a' Christian burial.

1 CLO. Why, there thou say'st, and the more pity that great folk should have count'nance
in this world to drown or hang themselves, more than their even-Christen. Come, my

20   spade. There is no ancient gentlemen but gard'ners, ditchers, and grave-makers; they
hold up Adam's profession.

2 CLO. Was he a gentleman?

1 CLO. 'A was the first that ever bore arms.

[2 CLO. Why, he had none.

25   1 CLO. What, art a heathen? How dost thou understand the Scripture? The Scripture
says Adam digg'd; could he dig without arms?] I'll put another question to thee. If
thou answerest me not to the purpose, confess thyself—

2 CLO. Go to.

1 CLO. What is he that builds stronger than either the mason, the shipwright, or the

30   carpenter?

2 CLO. The gallows-maker, for that outlives a thousand tenants.

1 CLO. I like thy wit well, in good faith. The gallows does well; but how does it well? It
does well to those that do ill. Now thou dost ill to say the gallows is built stronger
than the church; argal, the gallows may do well to thee. To't again, come.

35   2 CLO. Who builds stronger than a mason, a shipwright, or a carpenter?

1 CLO. Ay, tell me that, and unyoke.

2 CLO. Marry, now I can tell.

1 CLO. To't.

2 CLO. Mass, I cannot tell.

Enter HAMLET *and* HORATIO *[afar off]*.

40   1 CLO. Cudgel thy brains no more about it, for your dull ass will not mend his pace
with beating, and when you are ask'd this question next, say "a grave-maker": the houses
he makes lasts till doomsday. Go get thee in, and fetch me a sup of liquor.

[Exit SECOND CLOWN. FIRST CLOWN *digs.]*

10-13 **Here . . . life.** Alluding to a very famous suicide case, that of Sir James Hales, a judge who
drowned himself in 1554; it was long cited in the courts. The clown gives a garbled account
of the defense summing-up and the verdict.
11 **nill he:** he will not.
15 **quest:** inquest.
19 **even-Christen:** fellow Christians.
24 **none:** i.e. no coat of arms.
36 **unyoke:** i.e. cease to labor, call it a day.
39 **Mass:** by the mass.

Song.

>   "In youth when I did love, did love,
>   Methought it was very sweet,
> 45   To contract—O—the time for—a—my behove,
>   O, methought there—a—was nothing—a—meet."

HAM. Has this fellow no feeling of his business? 'a sings in grave-making.
HOR. Custom hath made it in him a property of easiness.
HAM. 'Tis e'en so, the hand of little employment hath the daintier sense.
1 CLO.

Song.

> 50   "But age with his stealing steps
>   Hath clawed me in his clutch,
>   And hath shipped me into the land,
>   As if I had never been such."

[Throws up a shovelful of earth with a skull in it.]

HAM. That skull had a tongue in it, and could sing once. How the knave jowls it to the
55   ground, as if 'twere Cain's jaw-bone, that did the first murder! This might be the pate
of a politician, which this ass now o'erreaches, one that would circumvent God, might
it not?
HOR. It might, my lord.
HAM. Or of a courtier, which could say, "Good morrow, sweet lord! How dost thou,
60   sweet lord?" This might be my Lord Such-a-one, that prais'd my Lord Such-a-one's
horse when 'a [meant] to beg it, might it not?
HOR. Ay, my lord.
HAM. Why, e'en so, and now my Lady Worm's, chopless, and knock'd about the [mazzard]
with a sexton's spade. Here's fine revolution, and we had the trick to see't. Did these
65   bones cost no more the breeding, but to play at loggats with them? Mine ache to
think on't.
1 CLO.

Song.

>   "A pickaxe and a spade, a spade,
>   For and a shrouding sheet:

---

⁴⁵ **contract . . . behove:** shorten, i.e. spend agreeably . . . advantage. The song, punctuated by the grunts of the clown as he digs, is a garbled version of a poem by Thomas Lord Vaux, entitled "The Aged Lover Renounceth Love."
⁴⁸ **Custom:** habit.   **a property of easiness:** i.e. a thing he can do with complete ease of mind.
⁴⁹ **daintier sense:** more delicate sensitivity.
⁵⁴ **jowls:** dashes.
⁵⁶ **politician:** schemer, intriguer.   **o'erreaches:** gets the better of (with play on the literal sense). **circumvent God:** bypass God's law.
⁶³ **chopless:** lacking the lower jaw.   **mazzard:** head.
⁶⁴ **revolution:** change.   **and:** if.   **trick:** knack, ability.
⁶⁴⁻⁶⁵ **Did . . . cost:** were . . . worth.
⁶⁵ **loggats:** a game in which blocks of wood were thrown at a stake.

O, a pit of clay for to be made

For such a guest is meet."

70

[Throws up another skull.]

HAM. There's another. Why may not that be the skull of a lawyer? Where be his quiddities now, his quillities, his cases, his tenures, and his tricks? Why does he suffer this mad knave now to knock him about the sconce with a dirty shovel, and will not tell him of his action of battery? Hum! This fellow might be in 's time a great buyer of land,
75   with his statutes, his recognizances, his fines, his double vouchers, his recoveries. [Is this the fine of his fines, and the recovery of his recoveries,] to have his fine pate full of fine dirt? Will [his] vouchers vouch him no more of his purchases, and [double ones too], than the length and breadth of a pair of indentures? The very conveyances of his lands will scarcely lie in this box, and must th' inheritor himself have no
80   more, ha?

HOR. Not a jot more, my lord.

HAM. Is not parchment made of sheep-skins?

HOR. Ay, my lord, and of calves'-skins too.

HAM. They are sheep and calves which seek out assurance in that. I will speak to this
85   fellow. Whose grave's this, sirrah?

1 CLO. Mine, sir.

[Sings.]

"[O], a pit of clay for to be made

[For such a guest is meet]."

HAM. I think it be thine indeed, for thou liest in't.
90   1 CLO. You lie out on't, sir, and therefore 'tis not yours; for my part, I do not lie in't, yet it is mine.

HAM. Thou dost lie in't, to be in't and say it is thine. 'Tis for the dead, not for the quick; therefore thou liest.

1 CLO. 'Tis a quick lie, sir, 'twill away again from me to you.
95   HAM. What man dost thou dig it for?

1 CLO. For no man, sir.

HAM. What woman then?

1 CLO. For none neither.

HAM. Who is to be buried in't?
100   1 CLO. One that was a woman, sir, but, rest her soul, she's dead.

---

71 **quiddities:** subtleties, quibbles.
72 **quillities:** fine distinctions.   **tenures:** titles to real estate.
73 **sconce:** head.
75 **statutes, recognizances:** bonds securing debts by attaching land and property.   **fines, recoveries:** procedures for converting an entailed estate to freehold.   **double vouchers:** documents guaranteeing title to real estate, signed by two persons.
76 **fine:** end.
78 **pair of indentures:** legal document cut into two parts that fit together on a serrated edge. Perhaps Hamlet thus refers to the two rows of teeth in the skull, or to the bone sutures.   **conveyances:** documents relating to transfer of property.
79 **this box:** i.e. the skull itself.   **inheritor:** owner.
85 **sirrah:** term of address to inferiors.

HAM. How absolute the knave is! we must speak by the card, or equivocation will undo us. By the Lord, Horatio, this three years I have took note of it: the age is grown so pick'd that the toe of the peasant comes so near the heel of the courtier, he galls his kibe. How long hast thou been grave-maker?

105 1 CLO. Of [all] the days i' th' year, I came to't that day that our last king Hamlet overcame Fortinbras.

HAM. How long is that since?

1 CLO. Cannot you tell that? Every fool can tell that. It was that very day that young Hamlet was born—he that is mad, and sent into England.

110 HAM. Ay, marry, why was he sent into England?

1 CLO. Why, because 'a was mad. 'A shall recover his wits there, or if 'a do not, 'tis no great matter there.

HAM. Why?

1 CLO. 'Twill not be seen in him there, there the men are as mad as he.

115 HAM. How came he mad?

1 CLO. Very strangely, they say.

HAM. How strangely?

1 CLO. Faith, e'en with losing his wits.

HAM. Upon what ground?

120 1 CLO. Why, here in Denmark. I have been sexton here, man and boy, thirty years.

HAM. How long will a man lie i' th' earth ere he rot?

1 CLO. Faith, if 'a be not rotten before 'a die—as we have many pocky corses, that will scarce hold the laying in—'a will last you some eight year or nine year. A tanner will last you nine year.

125 HAM. Why he more than another?

1 CLO. Why, sir, his hide is so tann'd with his trade that 'a will keep out water a great while, and your water is a sore decayer of your whoreson dead body. Here's a skull now hath lien you i' th' earth three and twenty years.

HAM. Whose was it?

130 1 CLO. A whoreson mad fellow's it was. Whose do you think it was?

HAM. Nay, I know not.

1 CLO. A pestilence on him for a mad rogue! 'a pour'd a flagon of Rhenish on my head once. This same skull, sir, was, sir, Yorick's skull, the King's jester.

HAM. This?

[Takes the skull.]

135 1 CLO. E'en that.

HAM. Alas, poor Yorick! I knew him, Horatio, a fellow of infinite jest, of most excellent fancy. He hath bore me on his back a thousand times, and now how abhorr'd in my imagination it is! my gorge rises at it. Here hung those lips that I have kiss'd I know not how oft. Where be your gibes now, your gambols, your songs, your flashes of

140 merriment, that were wont to set the table on a roar? Not one now to mock your own

---

101 **absolute:** positive. **by the card:** by the compass, i.e. punctiliously. **equivocation:** ambiguity.
103 **pick'd:** refined.
103–04 **galls his kibe:** rubs the courtier's chilblain.
122 **pocky:** rotten with venereal disease.
123 **hold . . . in:** last out the burial.

grinning—quite chop-fall'n. Now get you to my lady's [chamber], and tell her, let her paint an inch thick, to this favor she must come; make her laugh at that. Prithee, Horatio, tell me one thing.

HOR. What's that, my lord?

145   HAM. Dost thou think Alexander look'd a' this fashion i' th' earth?

HOR. E'en so.

HAM. And smelt so? pah!

[Puts down the skull.]

HOR. E'en so, my lord.

HAM. To what base uses we may return, Horatio! Why may not imagination trace the
150   noble dust of Alexander, till 'a find it stopping a bunghole?

HOR. 'Twere to consider too curiously, to consider so.

HAM. No, faith, not a jot, but to follow him thither with modesty enough and likelihood to lead it: Alexander died, Alexander was buried, Alexander returneth to dust, the dust is earth, of earth we make loam, and why of that loam whereto he was converted
155   might they not stop a beer-barrel?

Imperious Caesar, dead and turn'd to clay,
Might stop a hole to keep the wind away.
O that that earth which kept the world in awe
Should patch a wall t' expel the [winter's] flaw!
160   But soft, but soft awhile, here comes the King,

Enter KING, QUEEN, LAERTES, *and [a* DOCTOR OF DIVINITY, *following] the corse, [with* LORDS *attendant].*

The Queen, the courtiers. Who is this they follow?
And with such maimed rites? This doth betoken
The corse they follow did with desp'rate hand
Foredo it own life. 'Twas of some estate.
165   Couch we a while and mark.

[Retiring with HORATIO.]

LAER. What ceremony else?

HAM. That is Laertes, a very noble youth. Mark.

LAER. What ceremony else?

DOCTOR Her obsequies have been as far enlarg'd
170   As we have warranty. Her death was doubtful,
And but that great command o'ersways the order,

---

141 **chop-fall'n:** (1) lacking the lower jaw; (2) downcast.
142 **favor:** appearance.
151 **curiously:** closely, minutely.
152 **modesty:** moderation.
154 **loam:** a mixture of moistened clay with sand, straw, etc.
156 **Imperious:** imperial.
159 **flaw:** gust.
162 **maimed rites:** lack of customary ceremony.
164 **Foredo:** fordo, destroy.   **it:** its.   **estate:** rank.
165 **Couch we:** let us conceal ourselves.
170 **doubtful:** i.e. the subject of an "open verdict."
171 **order:** customary procedure.

She should in ground unsanctified been lodg'd
Till the last trumpet; for charitable prayers,
[Shards,] flints, and pebbles should be thrown on her.
175 Yet here she is allow'd her virgin crants,
Her maiden strewments, and the bringing home
Of bell and burial.
LAER. Must there no more be done?
DOCTOR   No more be done:
We should profane the service of the dead
180 To sing a requiem and such rest to her
As to peace-parted souls.
LAER.   Lay her i' th' earth,
And from her fair and unpolluted flesh
May violets spring! I tell thee, churlish priest,
A minist'ring angel shall my sister be
When thou liest howling.
185 HAM.   What, the fair Ophelia!
QUEEN [Scattering flowers.] Sweets to the sweet, farewell!
I hop'd thou shouldst have been my Hamlet's wife.
I thought thy bride-bed to have deck'd, sweet maid,
And not have strew'd thy grave.
LAER.   O, treble woe
190 Fall ten times [treble] on that cursed head
Whose wicked deed thy most ingenious sense
Depriv'd thee of! Hold off the earth a while,
Till I have caught her once more in mine arms.

[Leaps in the grave.]

Now pile your dust upon the quick and dead,
195 Till of this flat a mountain you have made
T' o'ertop old Pelion, or the skyish head
Of blue Olympus.
HAM. *[Coming forward.]* What is he whose grief
Bears such an emphasis, whose phrase of sorrow
200 Conjures the wand'ring stars and makes them stand
Like wonder-wounded hearers? This is I,
Hamlet the Dane!

---

172 **should:** would certainly.
173 **for:** instead of.
175 **crants:** garland.
176 **maiden strewments:** flowers scattered on the grave of an unmarried girl.
176–77 **bringing . . . burial:** i.e. burial in consecrated ground, with the bell tolling.
180 **requiem:** dirge.
186 **Sweets:** flowers.
191 **ingenious:** intelligent.
196, 197 **Pelion, Olympus:** mountains in northeastern Greece.
199 **emphasis, phrase.** Rhetorical terms, here used in disparaging reference to Laertes' inflated language.
200 **Conjures:** puts a spell upon. **wand'ring stars:** planets.
202 **the Dane.** This title normally signifies the King.

[HAMLET *leaps in after* LAERTES.]

LAER. The devil take thy soul!

[*Grappling with him.*]

HAM.   Thou pray'st not well.
I prithee take thy fingers from my throat.
205   For though I am not splenitive [and] rash,
Yet have I in me something dangerous,
Which let thy wisdom fear. Hold off thy hand!
KING Pluck them asunder.
QUEEN   Hamlet, Hamlet!
ALL   Gentlemen!
HOR. Good my lord, be quiet.

[*The* ATTENDANTS *part them, and they come out of the grave.*]

210   HAM. Why, I will fight with him upon this theme
Until my eyelids will no longer wag.
QUEEN O my son, what theme?
HAM. I lov'd Ophelia. Forty thousand brothers
Could not with all their quantity of love
215   Make up my sum. What wilt thou do for her?
KING O, he is mad, Laertes.
QUEEN For love of God, forbear him.
HAM. 'Swounds, show me what thou't do.
Woo't weep, woo't fight, woo't fast, woo't tear thyself?
220   Woo't drink up eisel, eat a crocadile?
I'll do't. Dost [thou] come here to whine?
To outface me with leaping in her grave?
Be buried quick with her, and so will I.
And if thou prate of mountains, let them throw
225   Millions of acres on us, till our ground,
Singeing his pate against the burning zone,
Make Ossa like a wart! Nay, and thou'lt mouth,
I'll rant as well as thou.
QUEEN   This is mere madness,
And [thus] a while the fit will work on him;
230   Anon, as patient as the female dove,

---

²⁰⁵ **splenitive:** impetuous.
²¹⁸ **thou't:** thou wilt.
²¹⁹ **Woo't:** wilt thou.
²²⁰ **eisel:** vinegar. **crocadile:** crocodile.
²²⁴ **if . . . mountains.** Referring to lines 194–97.
²²⁶ **burning zone:** sphere of the sun.
²²⁷ **Ossa:** another mountain in Greece, near Pelion and Olympus. **mouth:** talk bombast (synonymous with *rant* in the next line).
²²⁸ **mere:** utter.
²³⁰ **patient:** calm.

When that her golden couplets are disclosed,
His silence will sit drooping.

HAM.   Hear you, sir,
What is the reason that you use me thus?
I lov'd you ever. But it is no matter.
235   Let Hercules himself do what he may,
The cat will mew, and dog will have his day.

Exit HAMLET.

KING I pray thee, good Horatio, wait upon him.

[Exit] HORATIO.

[To LAERTES.*]*   Strengthen your patience in our last night's speech,
We'll put the matter to the present push.—
240   Good Gertrude, set some watch over your son.
This grave shall have a living monument.
An hour of quiet [shortly] shall we see,
Till then in patience our proceeding be.

Exeunt.

SCENE II.

Enter HAMLET *and* HORATIO.

HAM. So much for this, sir, now shall you see the other—
You do remember all the circumstance?
HOR. Remember it, my lord!
5 HAM. Sir, in my heart there was a kind of fighting
That would not let me sleep. [Methought] I lay
Worse than the mutines in the [bilboes]. Rashly—
And prais'd be rashness for it—let us know
Our indiscretion sometime serves us well
10 When our deep plots do pall, and that should learn us
There's a divinity that shapes our ends,
Rough-hew them how we will—

---

²³¹ **golden couplets:** pair of baby birds, covered with yellow down. **disclosed:** hatched.
^{235–36} **Let . . . day:** i.e. nobody can prevent another from making the scenes he feels he has
    a right to.
²³⁸ **in:** i.e. by recalling.
²³⁹ **present push:** immediate test.
²⁴¹ **living:** enduring (?) or in the form of a lifelike effigy (?).

V.ii. Location: The castle.
¹ **see the other:** i.e. hear the other news I have to tell you (hinted at in the letter to Horatio,
   IV.vi.18).
⁶ **mutines:** mutineers (but the term *mutiny* was in Shakespeare's day used of almost any act of
   rebellion against authority). **bilboes:** fetters attached to a heavy iron bar. **Rashly:** on impulse.
⁷ **know:** recognize, acknowledge.
⁹ **pall:** lose force, come to nothing. **learn:** teach.
¹⁰ **shapes our ends:** gives final shape to our designs.
¹¹ **Rough-hew them:** block them out in initial form.

HOR.   That is most certain.

HAM. Up from my cabin,
     My sea-gown scarf'd about me, in the dark
     Grop'd I to find out them, had my desire,
15   Finger'd their packet, and in fine withdrew
     To mine own room again, making so bold,
     My fears forgetting manners, to [unseal]
     Their grand commission; where I found, Horatio—
     Ah, royal knavery!—an exact command,
20   Larded with many several sorts of reasons,
     Importing Denmark's health and England's too,
     With, ho, such bugs and goblins in my life,
     That, on the supervise, no leisure bated,
     No, not to stay the grinding of the axe,
     My head should be strook off.
25 HOR.   Is't possible?

HAM. Here's the commission, read it at more leisure.
     But wilt thou hear now how I did proceed?

HOR. I beseech you.

HAM. Being thus benetted round with [villainies],
30   Or I could make a prologue to my brains,
     They had begun the play. I sat me down,
     Devis'd a new commission, wrote it fair.
     I once did hold it, as our statists do,
     A baseness to write fair, and labor'd much
35   How to forget that learning, but, sir, now
     It did me yeman's service. Wilt thou know
     Th' effect of what I wrote?

HOR.   Ay, good my lord.

HAM. An earnest conjuration from the King,
     As England was his faithful tributary,
40   As love between them like the palm might flourish,
     As peace should still her wheaten garland wear
     And stand a comma 'tween their amities,
     And many such-like [as's] of great charge,

---

15 **Finger'd**: filched, "pinched."
20 **Larded**: garnished.
21 **Importing**: relating to.
22 **bugs . . . life**: terrifying things in prospect if I were permitted to remain alive. *Bugs* = bugaboos.
23 **supervise**: perusal.   **bated**: deducted (from the stipulated speediness).
24 **stay**: wait for.
30 **Or**: before.
32 **fair**: i.e. in a beautiful hand (such as a professional scribe would use).
33 **statists**: statesmen, public officials.
34 **A baseness**: i.e. a skill befitting men of low rank.
36 **yeman's**: yeoman's, i.e. solid, substantial.
37 **effect**: purport, gist.
42 **comma**: connective, link.
43 **as's . . . charge**: (1) weighty clauses beginning with *as*; (2) asses with heavy loads.

That on the view and knowing of these contents,
45 Without debatement further, more or less,
He should those bearers put to sudden death,
Not shriving time allow'd.

HOR.   How was this seal'd?

HAM. Why, even in that was heaven ordinant.
I had my father's signet in my purse,
50 Which was the model of that Danish seal;
Folded the writ up in the form of th' other,
[Subscrib'd] it, gave't th' impression, plac'd it safely,
The changeling never known. Now the next day
Was our sea-fight, and what to this was sequent
55 Thou knowest already.

HOR. So Guildenstern and Rosencrantz go to't.

HAM. [Why, man, they did make love to this employment,]
They are not near my conscience. Their defeat
Does by their own insinuation grow.
60 'Tis dangerous when the baser nature comes
Between the pass and fell incensed points
Of mighty opposites.

HOR.   Why, what a king is this!

HAM. Does it not, think thee, stand me now upon—
He that hath kill'd my king and whor'd my mother,
65 Popp'd in between th' election and my hopes,
Thrown out his angle for my proper life,
And with such coz'nage—is't not perfect conscience
[To quit him with this arm? And is't not to be damn'd,
To let this canker of our nature come
70 In further evil?

HOR. It must be shortly known to him from England
What is the issue of the business there.

---

47 **shriving time:** time for confession and absolution.
48 **ordinant:** in charge, guiding.
50 **model:** small copy.
52 **Subscrib'd:** signed.
53 **changeling:** i.e. Hamlet's letter, substituted secretly for the genuine letter, as fairies substituted
their children for human children.   **never known:** never recognized as a substitution (unlike the
fairies' changelings).
56 **go to't:** i.e. are going to their death.
58 **defeat:** ruin, overthrow.
59 **insinuation:** winding their way into the affair.
60 **baser:** inferior.
61 **pass:** thrust.   **fell:** fierce.
63 **stand . . . upon:** i.e. rest upon me as a duty.
65 **election:** i.e. as King of Denmark.
66 **angle:** hook and line.   **proper:** very.
67 **coz'nage:** trickery.
68 **quit him:** pay him back.
69 **canker:** cancerous sore.
69–70 **come In:** grow into.

HAM. It will be short; the interim's mine,
And a man's life's no more than to say "one."
75   But I am very sorry, good Horatio,
That to Laertes I forgot myself,
For by the image of my cause I see
The portraiture of his. I'll [court] his favors.
But sure the bravery of his grief did put me
Into a tow'ring passion.
80   HOR.   Peace, who comes here?]

Enter [young OSRIC,] a courtier.

OSR. Your lordship is right welcome back to Denmark.
HAM. I humbly thank you, sir.—Dost know this water-fly?
HOR. No, my good lord.
HAM. Thy state is the more gracious, for 'tis a vice to know him. He hath much land,
85   and fertile; let a beast be lord of beasts, and his crib shall stand at the King's mess.
'Tis a chough, but, as I say, spacious in the possession of dirt.
OSR. Sweet lord, if your lordship were at leisure, I should impart a thing to you from
his Majesty.
HAM. I will receive it, sir, with all diligence of spirit. [Put] your bonnet to his right use,
90   'tis for the head.
OSR. I thank your lordship, it is very hot.
HAM. No, believe me, 'tis very cold, the wind is northerly.
OSR. It is indifferent cold, my lord, indeed.
HAM. But yet methinks it is very [sultry] and hot [for] my complexion.
95   OSR. Exceedingly, my lord, it is very sultry—as 'twere—I cannot tell how. My lord, his
Majesty bade me signify to you that 'a has laid a great wager on your head. Sir, this
is the matter—
HAM. I beseech you remember.

[HAMLET moves him to put on his hat.]

OSR. Nay, good my lord, for my ease, in good faith. Sir, here is newly come to court
100   Laertes, believe me, an absolute [gentleman], full of most excellent differences, of very

---

74 **a man's . . . more:** i.e. to kill a man takes no more time.   **say "one."** Perhaps this is equivalent
to "deliver one sword thrust"; see line 237 below, where Hamlet says "One" as he makes the first
hit.
77 **image:** likeness.
79 **bravery:** ostentatious expression.
82 **water-fly:** i.e. tiny, vainly agitated creature.
84 **gracious:** virtuous.
85 **let . . . mess:** i.e. if a beast owned as many cattle as Osric, he could feast with the King.
86 **chough:** jackdaw, a bird that could be taught to speak.
89 **bonnet:** hat.
93 **indifferent:** somewhat.
94 **complexion:** temperament.
99 **for my ease:** i.e. I am really more comfortable with my hat off (a polite insistence on maintaining
ceremony).
100 **absolute:** complete, possessing every quality a gentleman should have.   **differences:** distinguishing characteristics, personal qualities.

soft society, and great showing; indeed, to speak sellingly of him, he is the card or calendar of gentry; for you shall find in him the continent of what part a gentleman would see.

HAM. Sir, his definement suffers no perdition in you, though I know to divide him
105 inventorially would dozy th' arithmetic of memory, and yet but yaw neither in respect of his quick sail; but in the verity of extolment, I take him to be a soul of great article, and his infusion of such dearth and rareness as, to make true diction of him, his semblable is his mirror, and who else would trace him, his umbrage, nothing more.

OSR. Your lordship speaks most infallibly of him.

110 HAM. The concernancy, sir? Why do we wrap the gentleman in our more rawer breath?

OSR. Sir?

HOR. Is't not possible to understand in another tongue? You will to't, sir, really.

HAM. What imports the nomination of this gentleman?

OSR. Of Laertes?

115 HOR. His purse is empty already: all 's golden words are spent.

HAM. Of him, sir.

OSR. I know you are not ignorant—

HAM. I would you did, sir, yet, in faith, if you did, it would not much approve me. Well, sir?

120 OSR. You are not ignorant of what excellence Laertes is—

HAM. I dare not confess that, lest I should compare with him in excellence, but to know a man well were to know himself.

OSR. I mean, sir, for [his] weapon, but in the imputation laid on him by them, in his meed he's unfellow'd.

125 HAM. What's his weapon?

OSR. Rapier and dagger.

HAM. That's two of his weapons—but well.

---

101 **soft:** agreeable.   **great showing:** splendid appearance.   **sellingly:** i.e. like a seller to a prospective buyer; in a fashion to do full justice. Most editors follow Q3 in reading *feelingly* = with exactitude, as he deserves.

101–02 **card or calendar:** chart or register, i.e. compendious guide.

102 **gentry:** gentlemanly behavior.   **the continent . . . part:** one who contains every quality.

104 **perdition:** loss.

105 **dozy:** make dizzy.   **yaw:** keep deviating erratically from its course (said of a ship).   **neither:** for all that.

105–06 **in respect of:** compared with.

106 **in . . . extolment:** to praise him truly.   **article:** scope (?) or importance (?).

107 **infusion:** essence, quality.   **dearth:** scarceness.   **make true diction:** speak truly.

107–08 **his semblable:** his only likeness or equal.

108 **who . . . him:** anyone else who tries to follow him.   **umbrage:** shadow.

110 **concernancy:** relevance.   **more rawer breath:** i.e. words too crude to describe him properly.

112 **in another tongue:** i.e. when someone else is the speaker.   **You . . . really:** i.e. you can do it if you try.

113 **nomination:** naming, mention.

118 **approve:** commend.

121 **compare . . . excellence:** i.e. seem to claim the same degree of excellence for myself.   **but.** The sense seems to require *for*.

122 **himself:** i.e. oneself.

123 **in . . . them:** i.e. in popular estimation.

124 **meed:** merit.

OSR. The King, sir, hath wager'd with him six Barbary horses, against the which he has
impawn'd, as I take it, six French rapiers and poniards, with their assigns, as girdle,
130 [hangers], and so. Three of the carriages, in faith, are very dear to fancy, very responsive
to the hilts, most delicate carriages, and of very liberal conceit.
HAM. What call you the carriages?
HOR. I knew you must be edified by the margent ere you had done.
OSR. The [carriages], sir, are the hangers.
135 HAM. The phrase would be more germane to the matter if we could carry a cannon by
our sides; I would it [might be] hangers till then. But on: six Barb'ry horses against six
French swords, their assigns, and three liberal-conceited carriages; that's the French
bet against the Danish. Why is this all [impawn'd, as] you call it?
OSR. The King, sir, hath laid, sir, that in a dozen passes between yourself and him, he
140 shall not exceed you three hits; he hath laid on twelve for nine; and it would come to
immediate trial, if your lordship would vouchsafe the answer.
HAM. How if I answer no?
OSR. I mean, my lord, the opposition of your person in trial.
HAM. Sir, I will walk here in the hall. If it please his Majesty, it is the breathing time
145 of day with me. Let the foils be brought, the gentleman willing, and the King hold his
purpose, I will win for him and I can; if not, I will gain nothing but my shame and
the odd hits.
OSR. Shall I deliver you so?
HAM. To this effect, sir—after what flourish your nature will.
150 OSR. I commend my duty to your lordship.
HAM. Yours. [Exit OSRIC.] ['A] does well to commend it himself, there are no tongues
else for 's turn.
HOR. This lapwing runs away with the shell on his head.
HAM. 'A did [comply], sir, with his dug before 'a suck'd it. Thus has he, and many more
155 of the same breed that I know the drossy age dotes on, only got the tune of the time,
and out of an habit of encounter, a kind of [yesty] collection, which carries them

---

129 **impawn'd**: staked. **assigns**: appurtenances.
130 **hangers**: straps on which the swords hang from the girdle. **carriages**: properly, gun carriages;
here used affectedly in place of *hangers*. **fancy**: taste.
130–31 **very responsive to**: matching well.
131 **liberal conceit**: elegant design.
133 **must . . . margent**: would require enlightenment from a marginal note.
139 **laid**: wagered.
139–40 **he . . . hits**. Laertes must win by at least eight to four (if none of the "passes" or bouts are
draws), since at seven to five he would be only two up.
140 **he . . . nine**. Not satisfactorily explained despite much discussion. One suggestion is that Laertes
has raised the odds against himself by wagering that out of twelve bouts he will win nine.
141 **answer**: encounter (as Hamlet's following quibble forces Osric to explain in his next speech).
144–45 **breathing . . . me**: my usual hour for exercise.
149 **after what flourish**: with whatever embellishment of language.
150 **commend my duty**: offer my dutiful respects (but Hamlet picks up the phrase in the sense "praise
my manner of bowing").
153 **lapwing**: a foolish bird that upon hatching was supposed to run with part of the eggshell still
over its head. (Osric has put his hat on at last.)
154 **comply . . . dug**: bow politely to his mother's nipple.
155 **drossy**: i.e. worthless. **tune . . . time**: i.e. fashionable ways of talk.
156 **habit of encounter**: mode of social intercourse. **yesty**: yeasty, frothy. **collection**: i.e. anthology
of fine phrases.

through and through the most [profound] and [winnow'd] opinions, and do but blow them to their trial, the bubbles are out.

Enter a LORD.

LORD My lord, his Majesty commended him to you by young Osric, who brings back
160 to him that you attend him in the hall. He sends to know if your pleasure hold to play with Laertes, or that you will take longer time.
HAM. I am constant to my purposes, they follow the King's pleasure. If his fitness speaks, mine is ready; now or whensoever, provided I be so able as now.
LORD The King and Queen and all are coming down.
165 HAM. In happy time.
LORD The Queen desires you to use some gentle entertainment to Laertes before you fall to play.
HAM. She well instructs me.

[Exit LORD.]

HOR. You will lose, my lord.
170 HAM. I do not think so; since he went into France I have been in continual practice. I shall win at the odds. Thou wouldst not think how ill all's here about my heart—but it is no matter.
HOR. Nay, good my lord—
HAM. It is but foolery, but it is such a kind of [gain-]giving, as would perhaps trouble a
175 woman.
HOR. If your mind dislike any thing, obey it. I will forestall their repair hither, and say you are not fit.
HAM. Not a whit, we defy augury. There is special providence in the fall of a sparrow. If it be [now], 'tis not to come; if it be not to come, it will be now; if it be not now,
180 yet it [will] come—the readiness is all. Since no man, of aught he leaves, knows what is't to leave betimes, let be.

A table prepar'd, [and flagons of wine on it. Enter] Trumpets, Drums, and OFFICERS
with cushions, foils, daggers; KING, QUEEN, LAERTES, [OSRIC,] *and all the State.*

KING Come, Hamlet, come, and take this hand from me.

[The KING *puts* LAERTES' *hand into* HAMLET's.]

HAM. Give me your pardon, sir. I have done you wrong,
But pardon't as you are a gentleman.

---

157 **winnow'd:** sifted, choice.   **opinions:** judgments.
157–58 **blow . . . trial:** test them by blowing on them, i.e. make even the least demanding trial of them.
158 **out:** blown away (?) or at an end, done for (?).
162–63 **If . . . ready:** i.e. if this is a good moment for him, it is for me also.
166 **gentle entertainment:** courteous greeting.
174 **gain-giving:** misgiving.
178 **special . . . sparrow.** See Matthew 10:29.
180 **of aught:** i.e. whatever.
180–81 **knows . . . betimes:** knows what is the best time to leave it.
181 s.d. **State:** nobles.

185   This presence knows,
      And you must needs have heard, how I am punish'd
      With a sore distraction. What I have done
      That might your nature, honor, and exception
      Roughly awake, I here proclaim was madness.
190   Was't Hamlet wrong'd Laertes? Never Hamlet!
      If Hamlet from himself be ta'en away,
      And when he's not himself does wrong Laertes,
      Then Hamlet does it not, Hamlet denies it.
      Who does it then? His madness. If 't be so,
195   Hamlet is of the faction that is wronged,
      His madness is poor Hamlet's enemy.
      [Sir, in this audience,]
      Let my disclaiming from a purpos'd evil
      Free me so far in your most generous thoughts,
200   That I have shot my arrow o'er the house
      And hurt my brother.
      LAER.   I am satisfied in nature,
      Whose motive in this case should stir me most
      To my revenge, but in my terms of honor
      I stand aloof, and will no reconcilement
205   Till by some elder masters of known honor
      I have a voice and president of peace
      To [keep] my name ungor'd. But [till] that time
      I do receive your offer'd love like love,
      And will not wrong it.
      HAM.   I embrace it freely,
210   And will this brothers' wager frankly play.
      Give us the foils. [Come on.]
      LAER.   Come, one for me.
      HAM. I'll be your foil, Laertes; in mine ignorance
      Your skill shall like a star i' th' darkest night
      Stick fiery off indeed.
      LAER.   You mock me, sir.
215   HAM. No, by this hand.
      KING Give them the foils, young Osric. Cousin Hamlet,
      You know the wager?

---

185 **presence:** assembled court.
186 **punish'd:** afflicted.
188 **exception:** objection.
198 **my . . . evil:** my declaration that I intended no harm.
199 **Free:** absolve.
201 **in nature:** so far as my personal feelings are concerned.
203 **in . . . honor:** i.e. as a man governed by an established code of honor.
206–07 **have . . . ungor'd:** can secure an opinion backed by precedent that I can make peace with
      you without injury to my reputation.
210 **brothers':** i.e. amicable, as if between brothers.   **frankly:** freely, without constraint.
212 **foil:** thin sheet of metal placed behind a jewel to set it off.
214 **Stick . , . off:** blaze out in contrast.

HAM.   Very well, my lord.
    Your Grace has laid the odds a' th' weaker side.
    KING I do not fear it, I have seen you both;
220   But since he is [better'd], we have therefore odds.
    LAER. This is too heavy; let me see another.
    HAM. This likes me well. These foils have all a length?

[Prepare to play.]

    OSR. Ay, my good lord.
    KING Set me the stoups of wine upon that table.
225   If Hamlet give the first or second hit,
    Or quit in answer of the third exchange,
    Let all the battlements their ord'nance fire.
    The King shall drink to Hamlet's better breath,
    And in the cup an [union] shall he throw,
230   Richer than that which four successive kings
    In Denmark's crown have worn. Give me the cups,
    And let the kettle to the trumpet speak,
    The trumpet to the cannoneer without,
    The cannons to the heavens, the heaven to earth,
235   "Now the King drinks to Hamlet." Come begin;

Trumpets the while.

    And you, the judges, bear a wary eye.
    HAM. Come on, sir.
    LAER.   Come, my lord.

[They play and HAMLET *scores a hit.]*

    HAM.   One.
    LAER.   No.
    HAM.   Judgment.

    OSR. A hit, a very palpable hit.
    LAER.   Well, again.
240   KING Stay, give me drink. Hamlet, this pearl is thine,
    Here's to thy health! Give him the cup.

Drum, trumpets [sound] flourish. A piece goes off [within].

    HAM. I'll play this bout first, set it by a while.
    Come. *[They play again.]* Another hit; what say you?
    LAER. [A touch, a touch,] I do confess't.

    _____

    218 **laid the odds:** i.e. wagered a higher stake (horses to rapiers).
    220 **is better'd:** has perfected his skill.   **odds:** i.e. the arrangement that Laertes must take more bouts
    than Hamlet to win.
    222 **likes:** pleases.   **a length:** the same length.
    224 **stoups:** tankards.
    226 **quit . . . exchange:** pays back wins by Laertes in the first and second bouts by taking the third.
    229 **union:** an especially fine pearl.
    232 **kettle:** kettledrum.

KING Our son shall win.

QUEEN He's fat, and scant of breath.
245 Here, Hamlet, take my napkin, rub thy brows.
The Queen carouses to thy fortune, Hamlet.

HAM. Good madam!

KING Gertrude, do not drink.

QUEEN I will, my lord, I pray you pardon me.

KING [Aside.] It is the pois'ned cup, it is too late.

250 HAM. I dare not drink yet, madam; by and by.

QUEEN Come, let me wipe thy face.

LAER. My lord, I'll hit him now.

KING I do not think't.

LAER. [Aside.] And yet it is almost against my conscience.

HAM. Come, for the third, Laertes, you do but dally.
255 I pray you pass with your best violence;
I am sure you make a wanton of me.

LAER. Say you so? Come on.

[They play.]

OSR. Nothing, neither way.

LAER. Have at you now!

[LAERTES wounds HAMLET; then, in scuffling, they change rapiers.]

KING Part them, they are incens'd.

HAM. Nay, come again.

[HAMLET wounds LAERTES. The QUEEN falls.]

260 OSR. Look to the Queen there ho!

HOR. They bleed on both sides. How is it, my lord?

OSR. How is't, Laertes?

LAER. Why, as a woodcock to mine own springe, Osric:
I am justly kill'd with mine own treachery.

HAM. How does the Queen?

265 KING She sounds to see them bleed.

QUEEN No, no, the drink, the drink—O my dear Hamlet—
The drink, the drink! I am pois'ned.

[Dies.]

HAM. O villainy! Ho, let the door be lock'd!
Treachery! Seek it out.

---

244 **fat:** sweaty.
246 **carouses:** drinks a toast.
256 **make . . . me:** i.e. are holding back in order to let me win, as one does with a spoiled child (*wanton*).
263 **springe:** snare.
265 **sounds:** swoons.

270 LAER. It is here, Hamlet. [Hamlet,] thou art slain.
No med'cine in the world can do thee good;
In thee there is not half an hour's life.
The treacherous instrument is in [thy] hand,
Unbated and envenom'd. The foul practice
275 Hath turn'd itself on me. Lo here I lie,
Never to rise again. Thy mother's pois'ned.
I can no more—the King, the King's to blame.
HAM. The point envenom'd too!
Then, venom, to thy work.

[Hurts the KING.]

280 ALL Treason! treason!
KING O, yet defend me, friends, I am but hurt.
HAM. Here, thou incestious, [murd'rous], damned Dane,
Drink [off] this potion! Is [thy union] here?
Follow my mother!

[KING *dies.*]

LAER.   He is justly served,
285 It is a poison temper'd by himself.
Exchange forgiveness with me, noble Hamlet.
Mine and my father's death come not upon thee,
Nor thine on me!

[Dies.]

HAM. Heaven make thee free of it! I follow thee.
290 I am dead, Horatio. Wretched queen, adieu!
You that look pale, and tremble at this chance,
That are but mutes or audience to this act,
Had I but time—as this fell sergeant, Death,
Is strict in his arrest—O, I could tell you—
295 But let it be. Horatio, I am dead,
Thou livest. Report me and my cause aright
To the unsatisfied.
HOR.   Never believe it;
I am more an antique Roman than a Dane.
Here's yet some liquor left.
HAM.   As th' art a man,
300 Give me the cup. Let go! By heaven, I'll ha't!
O God, Horatio, what a wounded name,
Things standing thus unknown, shall I leave behind me!

---

274 **Unbated:** not blunted.   **foul practice:** vile plot.
279 s.d. **Hurts:** wounds.
285 **temper'd:** mixed.
289 **make thee free:** absolve you.
292 **mutes or audience:** silent spectators.
293 **fell:** cruel.   **sergeant:** sheriff 's officer.
298 **antique Roman:** i.e. one who will commit suicide on such an occasion.

If thou didst ever hold me in thy heart,
Absent thee from felicity a while,
305 And in this harsh world draw thy breath in pain
To tell my story.

A march afar off [and a shot within].

What warlike noise is this?

[OSRIC goes to the door and returns.]

OSR. Young Fortinbras, with conquest come from Poland,
To th' embassadors of England gives
This warlike volley.
HAM.   O, I die, Horatio,
310 The potent poison quite o'er-crows my spirit.
I cannot live to hear the news from England,
But I do prophesy th' election lights
On Fortinbras, he has my dying voice.
So tell him, with th' occurrents more and less
315 Which have solicited—the rest is silence.

[Dies.]

HOR. Now cracks a noble heart. Good night, sweet prince,
And flights of angels sing thee to thy rest!

[March within.]

Why does the drum come hither?

Enter FORTINBRAS *with the* [ENGLISH] EMBASSADORS, *[with* Drum, Colors, *and*
ATTENDANTS].

FORT. Where is this sight?
HOR.   What is it you would see?
320 If aught of woe or wonder, cease your search.
FORT. This quarry cries on havoc. O proud death,
What feast is toward in thine eternal cell,
That thou so many princes at a shot
So bloodily hast strook?
[1] EMB.   The sight is dismal,
325 And our affairs from England come too late.
The ears are senseless that should give us hearing,
To tell him his commandement is fulfill'd,
That Rosencrantz and Guildenstern are dead.
Where should we have our thanks?

---

310 **o'er-crows:** triumphs over (a term derived from cockfighting). **spirit:** vital energy.
313 **voice:** vote.
314 **occurrents:** occurrences.
315 **solicited:** instigated.
321 **This . . . havoc:** this heap of corpses proclaims a massacre.
322 **toward:** in preparation.

HOR.   Not from his mouth,
330   Had it th' ability of life to thank you.
        He never gave commandement for their death.
        But since so jump upon this bloody question,
        You from the Polack wars, and you from England,
        Are here arrived, give order that these bodies
335   High on a stage be placed to the view,
        And let me speak to [th'] yet unknowing world
        How these things came about. So shall you hear
        Of carnal, bloody, and unnatural acts,
        Of accidental judgments, casual slaughters,
340   Of deaths put on by cunning and [forc'd] cause,
        And in this upshot, purposes mistook
        Fall'n on th' inventors' heads: all this can I
        Truly deliver.
FORT.   Let us haste to hear it,
        And call the noblest to the audience.
345   For me, with sorrow I embrace my fortune.
        I have some rights, of memory in this kingdom,
        Which now to claim my vantage doth invite me.
HOR. Of that I shall have also cause to speak,
        And from his mouth whose voice will draw [on] more.
350   But let this same be presently perform'd
        Even while men's minds are wild, lest more mischance
        On plots and errors happen.
FORT.   Let four captains
        Bear Hamlet like a soldier to the stage,
        For he was likely, had he been put on,
355   To have prov'd most royal; and for his passage,
        The soldiers' music and the rite of war
        Speak loudly for him.
        Take up the bodies. Such a sight as this
        Becomes the field, but here shows much amiss.
360   Go bid the soldiers shoot.

        Exeunt [marching; after the which a peal of ordinance are shot off].

---

329 **his:** i.e. the King's.
332 **jump:** precisely, pat.   **question:** matter.
335 **stage:** platform.
339 **judgments:** retributions.   **casual:** happening by chance.
340 **put on:** instigated.
346 **of memory:** unforgotten.
347 **my vantage:** i.e. my opportune presence at a moment when the throne is empty.
349 **his . . . more:** the mouth of one (Hamlet) whose vote will induce others to support your claim.
350 **presently:** at once.
351 **wild:** distraught.
354 **put on:** put to the test (by becoming king).
355 **passage:** death.
359 **Becomes . . . amiss:** befits the battlefield, but appears very much out of place here.

Questions

1. The ghost seems quite real when he appears to everyone in Act I, Scene 4, and when he speaks in Scene 5. Does he seem less real when he is alone with Hamlet? Why?
2. By the end of Act I, the dramatic situation is clear. What is Hamlet's objective? What is his obstacle? Does Hamlet's dramatic situation in any way resemble that of Oedipus?
3. If Hamlet is not crazy, why does he pretend to be? How does his "antic disposition" contribute to the rising action?
4. What are Hamlet's feelings for Gertrude? Are they extreme? To what extent do you sympathize with him? Is she a villain?
5. What are Hamlet's virtues? Virtues aside, what qualities of character make him attractive to you?
6. Hamlet's soliloquy at the end of Act II, Scene 2, shows he is acutely self-conscious, and aware of his major flaw. What is it?
7. Who is the villain of the play? Do you understand his motives in opposing the hero?
8. What recognition results from the "play within the play"? How does it bring Hamlet closer to his objective?
9. Having proved the guilt of Claudius, why doesn't Hamlet kill his uncle at the first opportunity in Act III, Scene 3? Explain how this might be the climax or turning point of the action.
10. Do you fear for Hamlet when he kills Polonius? Why?
11. The scene with the gravedigger (Act V, Scene 1) provides comic relief between the sad events of the falling action and the violence of the catastrophe. In what way does the dialogue here relate to the rest of the play?
12. By the time Hamlet is challenged by Laertes to a duel, he has caused the death of Polonius, as well as the madness and suicide of Ophelia. Yet we still fear for Hamlet, and pity him when he is wounded. Why?
13. The relationship between Hamlet and Laertes undergoes a striking peripeteia in their final scene. Describe it. What is Hamlet's recognition in this scene? How is it a peripeteia for Laertes?

Death of a Salesman—The Tragedy of the Common Man

Oedipus and Hamlet are members of the aristocracy. They have the dignity that ancient Greeks and Tudor Englishmen associated with high social position. Their fates concern not only themselves and their loved ones, but entire nations. Watching aristocrats fall from power is especially moving, because aristocrats have farther to fall and because they will take more people down with them than, say, the corner grocer, should he suffer a similar fate. Some critics, Aristotle among them, have suggested that the tragic hero or heroine must be of noble stature. It is a difficult question. Obviously, if a character is already in a state of ruin or squalor it is not tragic to see him ruined further. On the other hand, if the hero is to be considered noble, the audience must agree on what is noble. This was easier two hundred years ago when class structure was clearly defined and everyone knew a member of the nobility by his or her title.

Willy Loman, the protagonist of *Death of a Salesman*, is not a king or a prince. Yet his son Biff, in a speech that seems like a comment on the above controversy, calls Willy "A fine troubled prince. A hard-working, unappreciated prince. . . . A good companion. Always for his boys." Willy owns property. He is lord and master of his house. He owns his car, his refrigerator, and other household items he has bought on time. He is not a nobleman, but then there are no titled noblemen here; and while Willy is not the richest or most highly bred American, he has enough to lose so that we know it will hurt him to lose it. If he had more money and power, American audiences might be glad to see him destroyed, and then there would be no tragedy either. In short, he is a shrewdly selected figure for our tragic sympathies.

Oedipus Rex and *Hamlet*, whose noble protagonists inspire not only compassion but religious or philosophical awe, are often called "high tragedies." Society having changed so drastically since Shakespeare's time, some critics believe that high tragedy is no longer possible. Northrop Frye, whose comments on the loftiness of tragic heroes were quoted earlier, has this to say about tragedy's place in the history of civilization: "Tragedy belongs chiefly to the two indigenous developments of tragic drama in fifth century Athens and seventeenth century Europe from Shakespeare to Racine. Both belong to a period of social history in which an aristocracy is fast losing its effective power but still retains a good deal of ideological prestige."

The protagonist of *Death of a Salesman* has never stood at the top of the wheel of fortune, at least not in the glorious manner that those aristocrats, Oedipus and Hamlet, have stood "halfway between human society and something greater in the sky." Willy Loman remains a common man; therefore, his struggle and his suffering hold greater human than religious significance. Because he resembles us more closely than do Oedipus and Hamlet, he inspires more pathos, more immediate compassion. We might refer to his story as a domestic tragedy rather than a high tragedy. To create "high tragedy" in the tradition of Sophocles or Shakespeare, a playwright would have to portray a hero more exalted than Willy Loman, a character standing somewhere between heaven and earth. Whether or not this remains possible in a civilization wherein aristocracy has lost both prestige and power, is still a subject for debate.

Reading *Death of a Salesman*

Death of a Salesman has a different structure than the other plays we have read. It maintains the five-part movement of action, but the play covers a much longer time period, more than fifteen years. Most of the action takes place in the present, a two-day period at the end of Willy's life. But the play shifts from the present to the past with little transition. Willy is losing his mind. He is haunted by his past, and sometimes his memories are so vivid they shut out the present. When this happens, the figures from Willy's past appear on the stage and act out entire scenes, until his revery is over or someone interrupts him.

Mielziner's opening set for *Death of a Salesman* (© *Eileen Darby*)

In the theater, these shifts between present and past are sometimes signalled by music or lighting changes, and sometimes by the movement of the actors to the forward area of the stage. The reader must recognize the time shifts by paying special attention to stage directions and Willy's state of mind. The first time shift or flashback occurs on page 1046, when Willy's sons, whom we have just seen as grown men, enter as adolescent boys. The following several pages depict a scene from twenty years earlier, when the boys were promising high school students and Willy was a prosperous salesman. Willy's wife joins the scene as a young woman. Suddenly, on another part of the stage, a mysterious woman appears, with whom Willy plays a love-scene, also from his past. When she disappears, Willy plays another scene with his wife, also in the past. On page 1051, Willy's wife, the mysterious woman, and Willy's neighbor, Bernard, are all talking to Willy at once, having separate conversations with him. The reader must remember that this is all going on in Willy's mind. When his son Happy comes down the stairs, Willy returns to the real present. If, as you are reading, the dialogue becomes confusing, go back to the most recent stage direction to determine whether the action is in the real present or in Willy's memories.

Arthur Miller, along with Tennessee Williams, is considered one of the greatest American playwrights of the post–World War II era. Like Williams, Miller was influenced by the realistic techniques of the Moscow Art Theater. His first Broadway success came with *All My Sons* in 1947, but it was *Death of a Salesman* that made him famous. The play won the Pulitzer Prize in 1949, has been performed all over the world, and is frequently revived on the American stage.

ARTHUR MILLER (1915–)

Death of a Salesman

Certain Private Conversations in Two Acts and a Requiem

CHARACTERS

WILLY LOMAN	UNCLE BEN
LINDA	HOWARD WAGNER
BIFF	JENNY
HAPPY	STANLEY
BERNARD	MISS FORSYTHE
THE WOMAN	LETTA
CHARLEY	

The action takes place in WILLY LOMAN's *house and yard and in various places he visits in the New York and Boston of today.*

Throughout the play, in the stage directions, left and right mean stage left and stage right.

ACT I

AN OVERTURE. *A melody is heard, played upon a flute. It is small and fine, telling of grass and trees and the horizon. The curtain rises.*

Before us is the Salesman's house. We are aware of towering, angular shapes behind it, surrounding it on all sides. Only the blue light of the sky falls upon the house and forestage; the surrounding area shows an angry glow of orange. As more light appears, we see a solid vault of apartment houses around the small, fragile-seeming home. An air of the dream clings to the place, a dream rising out of reality. The kitchen at center seems actual enough, for there is a kitchen table with three chairs, and a refrigerator. But no other fixtures are seen. At the back of the kitchen there is a draped entrance, which leads to the living-room. To the right of the kitchen, on a level raised two feet, is a bedroom furnished only with a brass bedstead and a straight chair. On a shelf over the bed a silver athletic trophy stands. A window opens onto the apartment house at the side.

Behind the kitchen, on a level raised six and a half feet, is the boys' bedroom, at present barely visible. Two beds are dimly seen, and at the back of the room a dormer window. (This bedroom is above the unseen living-room.) At the left a stairway curves up to it from the kitchen.

The entire setting is wholly or, in some places, partially transparent. The roof-line of the house is one-dimensional; under and over it we see the apartment buildings. Before the house lies an apron, curving beyond the forestage into the orchestra. This forward area serves as the back yard as well as the locale of all WILLY'S *imaginings and of his city scenes. Whenever the action is in the present the actors observe the imaginary wall-lines, entering the house only through its door at the left. But in the scenes of the past these boundaries are broken, and characters enter or leave a room by stepping "through" a wall onto the forestage.*

From the right, WILLY LOMAN, *the Salesman, enters, carrying two large sample cases. The flute plays on. He hears but is not aware of it. He is past sixty years of age, dressed quietly. Even as he crosses the stage to the doorway of the house, his exhaustion is apparent. He unlocks the door, comes into the kitchen, and thankfully lets his burden down, feeling the soreness of his palms. A word-sigh escapes his lips—it might be "Oh, boy, oh, boy." He closes the door, then carries his cases out into the living room, through the draped kitchen doorway.*

LINDA, *his wife, has stirred in her bed at the right. She gets out and puts on a robe, listening. Most often jovial, she has developed an iron repression of her exceptions to* WILLY'S *behavior—she more than loves him, she admires him, as though his mercurial nature, his temper, his massive dreams and little cruelties, served her only as sharp reminders of the turbulent longings within him, longings which she shares but lacks the temperament to utter and follow to their end.*

LINDA (*hearing* WILLY *outside the bedroom, calls with some trepidation*) Willy!

WILLY It's all right. I came back.

LINDA Why? What happened? (*Slight pause*) Did something happen, Willy?

WILLY No, nothing happened.

LINDA You didn't smash the car, did you?

WILLY (*with casual irritation*) I said nothing happened. Didn't you hear me?

LINDA Don't you feel well?

WILLY I'm tired to the death. (*The flute has faded away. He sits on the bed beside her, a little numb*) I couldn't make it. I just couldn't make it, Linda.

LINDA (*very carefully, delicately*) Where were you all day? You look terrible.

WILLY I got as far as a little above Yonkers. I stopped for a cup of coffee. Maybe it was the coffee.

LINDA What?

WILLY (*after a pause*) I suddenly couldn't drive any more. The car kept going off onto the shoulder, y'know?

LINDA (*helpfully*) Oh. Maybe it was the steering again. I don't think Angelo knows the Studebaker.

WILLY No, it's me, it's me. Suddenly I realize I'm goin' sixty miles an hour and I don't remember the last five minutes. I'm—I can't seem to—keep my mind to it.

LINDA Maybe it's your glasses. You never went for your new glasses.

WILLY No, I see everything. I came back ten miles an hour. It took me nearly four hours from Yonkers.

LINDA (*resigned*) Well, you'll just have to take a rest, Willy, you can't continue this way.

WILLY I just got back from Florida.

LINDA But you didn't rest your mind. Your mind is overactive, and the mind is what counts, dear.

WILLY I'll start out in the morning. Maybe I'll feel better in the morning. (*She is taking off his shoes*) These goddam arch supports are killing me.

LINDA Take an aspirin. Should I get you an aspirin? It'll soothe you.

WILLY (*with wonder*) I was driving along, you understand? And I was fine. I was even observing the scenery. You can imagine, me looking at scenery, on the road every week of my life. But it's so beautiful up there, Linda, the trees are so thick, and the sun is warm. I opened the windshield and just let the warm air bathe over me. And then all of a sudden I'm goin' off the road! I'm tellin' ya, I absolutely forgot I was driving. If I'd've gone the other way over the white line I might've killed somebody. So I went on again—and five minutes later I'm dreamin' again, and I nearly— (*He presses two fingers against his eyes*) I have such thoughts, I have such strange thoughts.

LINDA Willy, dear. Talk to them again. There's no reason why you can't work in New York.

WILLY They don't need me in New York. I'm the New England man. I'm vital in New England.

LINDA But you're sixty years old. They can't expect you to keep traveling every week.

WILLY I'll have to send a wire to Portland. I'm supposed to see Brown and Morrison tomorrow morning at ten o'clock to show the line. Goddammit, I could sell them! (*He starts putting on his jacket*)

LINDA (*taking the jacket from him*) Why don't you go down to the place tomorrow and tell Howard you've simply got to work in New York? You're too accommodating, dear.

WILLY If old man Wagner was alive I'd a been in charge of New York now! That man was a prince, he was a masterful man. But that boy of his, that Howard, he don't appreciate. When I went north the first time, the Wagner Company didn't know where New England was!

LINDA Why don't you tell those things to Howard, dear?

WILLY (*encouraged*) I will, I definitely will. Is there any cheese?

LINDA I'll make you a sandwich.

WILLY No, go to sleep. I'll take some milk. I'll be up right away. The boys in?

LINDA They're sleeping. Happy took Biff on a date tonight.

WILLY (*interested*) That so?

LINDA It was so nice to see them shaving together, one behind the other, in the bathroom. And going out together. You notice? The whole house smells of shaving lotion.

WILLY Figure it out. Work a lifetime to pay off a house. You finally own it, and there's nobody to live in it.

LINDA Well, dear, life is a casting off. It's always that way.

WILLY No, no, some people—some people accomplish something. Did Biff say anything after I went this morning?

LINDA You shouldn't have criticized him, Willy, especially after he just got off the train. You mustn't lose your temper with him.

WILLY When the hell did I lose my temper? I simply asked him if he was making any money. Is that a criticism?

LINDA But, dear, how could he make any money?

WILLY (*worried and angered*) There's such an undercurrent in him. He became a moody man. Did he apologize when I left this morning.

LINDA He was crestfallen, Willy. You know how he admires you. I think if he finds himself, then you'll both be happier and not fight any more.

WILLY How can he find himself on a farm? Is that a life? A farmhand? In the beginning, when he was young, I thought, well, a young man, it's good for him to tramp around, take a lot of different jobs. But it's more than ten years now and he has yet to make thirty-five dollars a week!

LINDA He's finding himself, Willy.

WILLY Not finding yourself at the age of thirty-four is a disgrace!

LINDA Shh!

WILLY The trouble is he's lazy, goddammit!

LINDA Willy, please!

WILLY Biff is a lazy bum!

LINDA They're sleeping. Get something to eat. Go on down.

WILLY Why did he come home? I would like to know what brought him home.

LINDA I don't know. I think he's still lost, Willy. I think he's very lost.

WILLY Biff Loman is lost. In the greatest country in the world a young man with such—personal attractiveness, gets lost. And such a hard worker. There's one thing about Biff—he's not lazy.

LINDA Never.

WILLY (*with pity and resolve*) I'll see him in the morning; I'll have a nice talk with him. I'll get him a job selling. He could be big in no time. My God! Remember how they used to follow him around in high school? When he smiled at one of them their faces lit up. When he walked down the street . . . (*He loses himself in reminiscences*)

LINDA (*trying to bring him out of it*) Willy, dear, I got a new kind of American-type cheese today. It's whipped.

WILLY Why do you get American when I like Swiss?

LINDA I just thought you'd like a change—

WILLY I don't want a change! I want Swiss cheese. Why am I always being contradicted?

LINDA (*with a covering laugh*) I thought it would be a surprise.

WILLY Why don't you open a window in here, for God's sake?

LINDA (*with infinite patience*) They're all open, dear.

WILLY The way they boxed us in here. Bricks and windows, windows and bricks.

LINDA We should've bought the land next door.

WILLY The street is lined with cars. There's not a breath of fresh air in the neighborhood. The grass don't grow any more, you can't raise a carrot in the back yard. They should've had a law against apartment houses. Remember those two beautiful elm trees out there? When I and Biff hung the swing between them?

LINDA Yeah, like being a million miles from the city.

WILLY They should've arrested the builder for cutting those down. They massacred the neighborhood. (*Lost*) More and more I think of those days, Linda. This time of year it was lilac and wisteria. And then the peonies would come out, and the daffodils. What fragrance in this room!

LINDA Well, after all, people had to move somewhere.

WILLY No, there's more people now.

LINDA I don't think there's more people. I think—

WILLY There's more people! That's what's ruining this country! Population is getting out of control. The competition is maddening! Smell the stink from that apartment house! And another one on the other side . . . How can they whip cheese?

On WILLY's *last line,* BIFF *and* HAPPY *raise themselves up in their beds, listening.*

LINDA Go down, try it. And be quiet.

WILLY (*turning to* LINDA, *guiltily*) You're not worried about me, are you, sweetheart?

BIFF What's the matter?

HAPPY Listen!

LINDA You've got too much on the ball to worry about.

WILLY You're my foundation and my support, Linda.

LINDA Just try to relax, dear. You make mountains out of molehills.

WILLY I won't fight with him any more. If he wants to go back to Texas, let him go.

LINDA He'll find his way.

WILLY Sure. Certain men just don't get started till later in life. Like Thomas Edison, I think. Or B. F. Goodrich. One of them was deaf. (*He starts for the bedroom doorway*) I'll put my money on Biff.

LINDA And Willy—if it's warm Sunday we'll drive in the country. And we'll open the windshield, and take lunch.

WILLY No, the windshields don't open on the new cars.

LINDA But you opened it today.

WILLY Me? I didn't. (*He stops*) Now isn't that peculiar! Isn't that a remarkable— (*He breaks off in amazement and fright as the flute is heard distantly*)

LINDA What, darling?

WILLY That is the most remarkable thing.

LINDA What, dear?

WILLY I was thinking of the Chevvy. (*Slight pause*) Nineteen twenty-eight . . . when I had that red Chevvy— (*Breaks off*) That funny? I coulda sworn I was driving that Chevvy today.

LINDA Well, that's nothing. Something must've reminded you.

WILLY Remarkable. Ts. Remember those days? The way Biff used to simonize that car? The dealer refused to believe there was eighty thousand miles on it. (*He shakes his head*) Heh! (*To* LINDA) Close your eyes, I'll be right up. (*He walks out of the bedroom*)

HAPPY (*to* BIFF) Jesus, maybe he smashed up the car again!

LINDA (*calling after* WILLY) Be careful on the stairs, dear! The cheese is on the middle shelf! (*She turns, goes over to the bed, takes his jacket, and goes out of the bedroom*)

Light has risen on the boys' room. Unseen, WILLY *is heard talking to himself, "Eighty thousand miles," and a little laugh.* BIFF *gets out of bed, comes downstage a bit, and stands attentively.* BIFF *is two years older than his brother* HAPPY, *well built, but in these days bears a worn air and seems less self-assured. He has succeeded less, and his dreams are stronger and less acceptable than* HAPPY's. HAPPY *is tall, powerfully made. Sexuality is like a visible color on him, or a scent that many women have discovered. He, like his brother, is lost, but in a different way, for he has never allowed himself to turn his face toward defeat and is thus more confused and hard-skinned, although seemingly more content.*

HAPPY (*getting out of bed*) He's going to get his license taken away if he keeps that up. I'm getting nervous about him, y'know, Biff?

BIFF His eyes are going.

HAPPY No, I've driven with him. He sees all right. He just doesn't keep his mind on it. I drove into the city with him last week. He stops at a green light and then it turns red and he goes. (*He laughs*)

BIFF Maybe he's color-blind.

HAPPY Pop? Why he's got the finest eye for color in the business. You know that.

BIFF (*sitting down on his bed*) I'm going to sleep.

HAPPY You're not still sour on Dad, are you, Biff?

BIFF He's all right, I guess.

WILLY (*underneath them, in the living-room*) Yes, sir, eighty thousand miles— eighty-two thousand!

BIFF You smoking?

HAPPY (*holding out a pack of cigarettes*) Want one?

BIFF (*taking a cigarette*) I can never sleep when I smell it.

WILLY What a simonizing job, heh!

HAPPY (*with deep sentiment*) Funny, Biff, y'now? Us sleeping in here again? The old beds. (*He pats his bed affectionately*) All the talk that went across those two beds, huh? Our whole lives.

BIFF Yeah. Lotta dreams and plans.

HAPPY (*with a deep and masculine laugh*) About five hundred women would like to know what was said in this room.

They share a soft laugh.

BIFF Remember that big Betsy something—what the hell was her name—over on Bush-wick Avenue?

HAPPY (*combing his hair*) With the collie dog!

BIFF That's the one. I got you in there, remember?

HAPPY Yeah, that was my first time—I think. Boy, there was a pig! (*They laugh, almost crudely*) You taught me everything I know about women. Don't forget that.

BIFF I bet you forgot how bashful you used to be. Especially with girls.

HAPPY Oh, I still am, Biff.

BIFF Oh, go on.

HAPPY I just control it, that's all. I think I got less bashful and you got more so. What happened, Biff? Where's the old humor, the old confidence? (*He shakes* BIFF's *knee.* BIFF *gets up and moves restlessly about the room*) What's the matter?

BIFF Why does Dad mock me all the time?

HAPPY He's not mocking you, he—

BIFF Everything I say there's a twist of mockery on his face. I can't get near him.

HAPPY He just wants you to make good, that's all. I wanted to talk to you about Dad for a long time, Biff. Something's—happening to him. He—talks to himself.

BIFF I noticed that this morning. But he always mumbled.

HAPPY But not so noticeable. It got so embarrassing I sent him to Florida. And you know something? Most of the time he's talking to you.

BIFF What's he say about me?

HAPPY I can't make it out.

BIFF What's he say about me?

HAPPY I think the fact that you're not settled, that you're still kind of up in the air . . .

BIFF There's one or two other things depressing him, Happy.

HAPPY What do you mean?

BIFF Never mind. Just don't lay it all to me.

HAPPY But I think if you just got started—I mean—is there any future for you out there?

BIFF I tell ya, Hap, I don't know what the future is. I don't know—what I'm supposed to want.

HAPPY What do you mean?

BIFF Well, I spent six or seven years after high school trying to work myself up. Shipping clerk, salesman, business of one kind or another. And it's a measly manner of existence. To get on that subway on the hot mornings in summer. To devote your whole life to keeping stock, or making phone calls, or selling or buying. To suffer fifty weeks of the year for the sake of a two-week vacation, when all you really desire is to be outdoors, with your shirt off. And always to have to get ahead of the next fella. And still—that's how you build a future.

HAPPY Well, you really enjoy it on a farm? Are you content out there?

BIFF (*with rising agitation*) Hap, I've had twenty or thirty different kinds of jobs since I left home before the war, and it always turns out the same. I just realized it lately. In Nebraska when I herded cattle, and the Dakotas, and Arizona, and now in Texas. It's why I came home now, I guess, because I realized it. This farm I work on, it's spring there now, see? And they've got about fifteen new colts. There's nothing more inspiring or—beautiful than the sight of a mare and a new colt. And it's cool there now, see? Texas is cool now, and it's spring. And whenever spring comes to where I am, I suddenly get the feeling, my God, I'm not gettin' anywhere! What the hell am I doing, playing around with horses, twenty-eight dollars a week! I'm thirty-four years old, I oughta be makin' my future. That's when I come running home. And now, I get here, and I don't know what to do with myself. (*After a pause*) I've always made a point of not wasting my life, and everytime I come back here I know that all I've done is to waste my life.

HAPPY You're a poet, you know that, Biff? You're a—you're an idealist!

BIFF No, I'm mixed up very bad. Maybe I oughta get married. Maybe I oughta get stuck into something. Maybe that's my trouble. I'm like a boy. I'm not married, I'm not in business, I just—I'm like a boy. Are you content, Hap? You're a success, aren't you? Are you content?

HAPPY Hell, no!

BIFF Why? You're making money, aren't you?

HAPPY (*moving about with energy, expressiveness*) All I can do now is wait for the merchandise manager to die. And suppose I get to be merchandise manager? He's a good friend of mine, and he just built a terrific estate on Long Island. And he lived there about two months and sold it, and now he's building another one. He can't enjoy it once it's finished. And I know that's just what I would do. I don't know what the hell I'm workin' for. Sometimes I sit in my apartment—all alone. And I think of the rent I'm paying. And it's crazy. But then, it's what I always wanted. My own apartment, a car, and plenty of women. And still, goddammit. I'm lonely.

BIFF (*with enthusiasm*) Listen, why don't you come out West with me?

HAPPY You and I, heh?

BIFF Sure, maybe we could buy a ranch. Raise cattle, use our muscles. Men built like we are should be working out in the open.

HAPPY (*avidly*) The Loman Brothers, heh?

BIFF (*with vast affection*) Sure, we'd be known all over the counties!

HAPPY (*enthralled*) That's what I dream about, Biff. Sometimes I want to just rip my clothes off in the middle of the store and outbox that goddam merchandise manager. I mean I can outbox, outrun, and outlift anybody in that store, and I have to take orders from those common, petty sons-of-bitches till I can't stand it any more.

BIFF I'm tellin' you, kid, if you were with me I'd be happy out there.

HAPPY (*enthused*) See, Biff, everybody around me is so false that I'm constantly lowering my ideals . . .

BIFF Baby, together we'd stand up for one another, we'd have someone to trust.

HAPPY If I were around you—

BIFF Hap, the trouble is we weren't brought up to grub for money. I don't know how to do it.

HAPPY Neither can I!

BIFF Then let's go!

HAPPY The only thing is—what can you make out there?

BIFF But look at your friend. Builds an estate and then hasn't the peace of mind to live in it.

HAPPY Yeah, but when he walks into the store the waves part in front of him. That's fifty-two thousand dollars a year coming through the revolving door, and I got more in my pinky finger than he's got in his head.

BIFF Yeah, but you just said—

HAPPY I gotta show some of those pompous, self-important executives over there that Hap Loman can make the grade. I want to walk into the store the way he walks in. Then I'll go with you, Biff. We'll be together yet, I swear. But take those two we had tonight. Now weren't they gorgeous creatures?

BIFF Yeah, yeah, most gorgeous I've had in years.

HAPPY I get that any time I want, Biff. Whenever I feel disgusted. The only trouble is, it gets like bowling or something. I just keep knockin' them over and it doesn't mean anything. You still run around a lot?

BIFF Naa. I'd like to find a girl—steady, somebody with substance.

HAPPY That's what I long for.

BIFF Go on! You'd never come home.

HAPPY I would! Somebody with character, with resistance! Like Mom, y'know? You're gonna call me a bastard when I tell you this. That girl Charlotte I was with tonight is engaged to be married in five weeks. (*He tries on his new hat*)

BIFF No kiddin'!

HAPPY Sure, the guy's in line for the vice-presidency of the store. I don't know what gets into me, maybe I just have an overdeveloped sense of competition or something, but I went and ruined her, and furthermore I can't get rid of her. And he's the third executive I've done that to. Isn't that a crummy characteristic? And to top it all, I go to their weddings! (*Indignantly, but laughing*) Like I'm not supposed to take bribes. Manufacturers offer me a hundred-dollar bill now and then to throw an order their way. You know how honest I am, but it's like this girl, see. I hate myself for it. Because I don't want the girl, and, still, I take it and—I love it!

BIFF Let's go to sleep.

HAPPY I guess we didn't settle anything, heh?

BIFF I just got one idea that I think I'm going to try.

HAPPY What's that?

BIFF Remember Bill Oliver?

HAPPY Sure, Oliver is very big now. You want to work for him again?

BIFF No, but when I quit he said something to me. He put his arm on my shoulder, and he said, "Biff, if you ever need anything, come to me."

HAPPY I remember that. That sounds good.

BIFF I think I'll go to see him. If I could get ten thousand or even seven or eight thousand dollars I could buy a beautiful ranch.

HAPPY I bet he'd back you. 'Cause he thought highly of you, Biff. I mean, they all do. You're well liked, Biff. That's why I say to come back here, and we both have the apartment. And I'm tellin' you, Biff, any babe you want . . .

BIFF No, with a ranch I could do the work I like and still be something. I just wonder though. I wonder if Oliver still thinks I stole that carton of basketballs.

HAPPY Oh, he probably forgot that long ago. It's almost ten years. You're too sensitive. Anyway, he didn't really fire you.

BIFF Well, I think he was going to. I think that's why I quit. I was never sure whether he knew or not. I know he thought the world of me, though. I was the only one he'd let lock up the place.

WILLY (*below*) You gonna wash the engine, Biff?

HAPPY Shh!

BIFF *looks at* HAPPY, *who is gazing down, listening.* WILLY *is mumbling in the parlor.*

HAPPY You hear that?

They listen. WILLY *laughs warmly.*

BIFF (*growing angry*) Doesn't he know Mom can hear that?

WILLY Don't get your sweater dirty, Biff!

A look of pain crosses BIFF's *face.*

HAPPY Isn't that terrible? Don't leave again, will you? You'll find a job here. You gotta stick around. I don't know what to do about him, it's getting embarrassing.

WILLY What a simonizing job!

BIFF Mom's hearing that!

WILLY No kiddin', Biff, you got a date? Wonderful!

HAPPY Go on to sleep. But talk to him in the morning, will you?

BIFF (*reluctantly getting into bed*) With her in the house. Brother!

HAPPY (*getting into bed*) I wish you'd have a good talk with him.

The light on their room begins to fade.

BIFF (*to himself in bed*) That selfish, stupid . . .

HAPPY Sh . . . Sleep, Biff.

Their light is out. Well before they have finished speaking, WILLY's *form is dimly seen below in the darkened kitchen. He opens the refrigerator, searches in there, and takes out a bottle of milk. The apartment houses are fading out, and the entire house and surroundings become covered with leaves. Music insinuates itself as the leaves appear.*

WILLY Just wanna be careful with those girls, Biff, that's all. Don't make any promises. No promises of any kind. Because a girl, y'know, they always believe what you tell 'em, and you're very young, Biff, you're too young to be talking seriously to girls.

Light rises on the kitchen. WILLY, *talking, shuts the refrigerator door and comes downstage to the kitchen table. He pours milk into a glass. He is totally immersed in himself, smiling faintly.*

WILLY Too young entirely, Biff. You want to watch your schooling first. Then when you're all set, there'll be plenty of girls for a boy like you. (*He smiles broadly at a kitchen chair*) That so? The girls pay for you? (*He laughs*) Boy, you must really be makin' a hit.

WILLY *is gradually addressing—physically—a point offstage, speaking through the wall of the kitchen, and his voice has been rising in volume to that of a normal conversation.*

WILLY I been wondering why you polish the car so careful. Ha! Don't leave the hubcaps, boys. Get the chamois to the hubcaps. Happy, use newspaper on the windows, it's the easiest thing. Show him how to do it, Biff! You see, Happy? Pad it up, use it like a pad. That's it, that's it, good work. You're doin' all right, Hap. (*He pauses, then nods in approbation for a few seconds, then looks upward*) Biff, first thing we gotta do when we get time is clip that big branch over the house. Afraid it's gonna fall in a storm and hit the roof. Tell you what. We get a rope and sling her around, and then we climb up there with a couple of saws and take her down. Soon as you finish the car, boys, I wanna see ya. I got a surprise for you, boys.

BIFF (*offstage*) Whatta ya got, Dad?

WILLY No, you finish first. Never leave a job till you're finished—remember that. (*Looking toward the "big trees"*) Biff, up in Albany I saw a beautiful hammock. I think I'll buy it next trip, and we'll hang it right between those two elms. Wouldn't that be something? Just swingin' there under those branches. Boy, that would be . . .

YOUNG BIFF *and* YOUNG HAPPY *appear from the direction* WILLY *was addressing.* HAPPY *carries rags and a pail of water.* BIFF, *wearing a sweater with a block "S," carries a football.*

BIFF (*pointing in direction of the car offstage*) How's that, Pop, professional?

WILLY Terrific. Terrific job, boys. Good work, Biff.

HAPPY Where's the surprise, Pop?

WILLY In the back seat of the car.

HAPPY Boy! (*He runs off*)

BIFF What is it, Dad? Tell me, what'd you buy?

WILLY (*laughing, cuffs him*) Never mind, something I want you to have.

BIFF (*turns and starts off*) What is it, Hap?

HAPPY (*offstage*) It's a punching bag!

BIFF Oh, Pop!

WILLY It's got Gene Tunney's signature on it!

HAPPY *runs onstage with a punching bag.*

BIFF Gee, how'd you know we wanted a punching bag?

WILLY Well, it's the finest thing for the timing.

HAPPY (*lies down on his back and pedals with his feet*) I'm losing weight, you notice, Pop?

WILLY (*to* HAPPY) Jumping rope is good too.

BIFF Did you see the new football I got?

WILLY (*examining the ball*) Where'd you get a new ball?

BIFF The coach told me to practice my passing.

WILLY That so? And he gave you the ball, heh?

BIFF Well, I borrowed it from the locker room. (*He laughs confidentially*)

WILLY (*laughing with him at the theft*) I want you to return that.

HAPPY I told you he wouldn't like it!

BIFF (*angrily*) Well, I'm bringing it back!

WILLY (*stopping the incipient argument, to* HAPPY) Sure, he's gotta practice with a regulation ball, doesn't he? (*To* BIFF) Coach'll probably congratulate you on your initiative!

BIFF Oh, he keeps congratulating my initiative all the time, Pop.

WILLY That's because he likes you. If somebody else took that ball there'd be an uproar. So what's the report, boys, what's the report?

BIFF Where'd you go this time, Dad? Gee we were lonesome for you.

WILLY (*pleased, puts an arm around each boy and they come down to the apron*) Lonesome, heh?

BIFF Missed you every minute.

WILLY Don't say? Tell you a secret, boys. Don't breathe it to a soul. Someday I'll have my own business, and I'll never have to leave home any more.

HAPPY Like Uncle Charley, heh?

WILLY Bigger than Uncle Charley! Because Charley is not—liked. He's liked, but he's not—well liked.

BIFF Where'd you go this time, Dad?

WILLY Well, I got on the road, and I went north to Providence. Met the Mayor.

BIFF The Mayor of Providence!

WILLY He was sitting in the hotel lobby.

BIFF What'd he say?

WILLY He said, "Morning!" And I said, "You got a fine city here, Mayor." And then he had coffee with me. And then I went to Waterbury. Waterbury is a fine city. Big clock city, the famous Waterbury clock. Sold a nice bill there. And then Boston— Boston is the cradle of the Revolution. A fine city. And a couple of other towns in Mass., and on to Portland and Bangor and straight home!

BIFF Gee, I'd love to go with you sometime, Dad.

WILLY Soon as summer comes.

HAPPY Promise?

WILLY You and Hap and I, and I'll show you all the towns. America is full of beautiful towns and fine, upstanding people. And they know me, boys, they know me up and down New England. The finest people. And when I bring you fellas up, there'll be open sesame for all of us, 'cause one thing, boys: I have friends. I can park my car in any street in New England, and the cops protect it like their own. This summer, heh?

BIFF AND HAPPY (together) Yeah! You bet!

WILLY We'll take our bathing suits.

HAPPY We'll carry your bags, Pop!

WILLY Oh, won't that be something! Me comin' into the Boston stores with you boys carryin' my bags. What a sensation!

BIFF *is prancing around, practicing passing the ball.*

WILLY You nervous, Biff, about the game?

BIFF Not if you're gonna be there.

WILLY What do they say about you in school, now that they made you captain?

HAPPY There's a crowd of girls behind him everytime the classes change.

BIFF (*taking* WILLY's *hand*) This Saturday, Pop, this Saturday—just for you, I'm going to break through for a touchdown.

HAPPY You're supposed to pass.

BIFF I'm takin' one play for Pop. You watch me, Pop, and when I take off my helmet, that means I'm breakin' out. Then you watch me crash through that line!

WILLY (*kisses* BIFF) Oh, wait'll I tell this in Boston!

BERNARD *enters in knickers. He is younger than* BIFF, *earnest and loyal, a worried boy.*

BERNARD Biff, where are you? You're supposed to study with me today.

WILLY Hey, looka Bernard. What're you lookin' so anemic about, Bernard?

BERNARD He's gotta study, Uncle Willy. He's got Regents next week.

HAPPY (*tauntingly, spinning* BERNARD *around*) Let's box, Bernard!

BERNARD Biff! (*He gets away from* HAPPY) Listen, Biff, I heard Mr. Birnbaum say that if you don't start studyin' math he's gonna flunk you, and you won't graduate. I heard him!

WILLY You better study with him, Biff. Go ahead now.

BERNARD I heard him!

BIFF Oh, Pop, you didn't see my sneakers! (*He holds up a foot for* WILLY *to look at*)

WILLY Hey, that's a beautiful job of printing!

BERNARD (*wiping his glasses*) Just because he printed University of Virginia on his sneakers doesn't mean they've got to graduate him, Uncle Willy!

WILLY (*angrily*) What're you talking about? With scholarships to three universities they're gonna flunk him?

BERNARD But I heard Mr. Birnbaum say—

WILLY Don't be a pest, Bernard! (*To his boys*) What an anemic!

BERNARD Okay, I'm waiting for you in my house, Biff.

BERNARD *goes off. The* LOMANS *laugh.*

WILLY Bernard is not well liked, is he?

BIFF He's liked, but he's not well liked.

HAPPY That's right, Pop.

WILLY That's just what I mean. Bernard can get the best marks in school, y'understand, but when he gets out in the business world, y'understand, you are going to be five times ahead of him. That's why I thank Almighty God you're both built like Adonises. Because the man who makes an appearance in the business world, the man who creates personal interest, is the man who gets ahead. Be liked and you will never want. You take me, for instance. I never have to wait in line to see a buyer. "Willy Loman is here!" That's all they have to know, and I go right through.

BIFF Did you knock them dead, Pop?

WILLY Knocked 'em cold in Providence, slaughtered 'em in Boston.

HAPPY (*on his back, pedaling again*) I'm losing weight, you notice, Pop?

LINDA *enters, as of old, a ribbon in her hair, carrying a basket of washing.*

LINDA (*with youthful energy*) Hello, dear!

WILLY Sweetheart!

LINDA How'd the Chevvy run?

WILLY Chevrolet, Linda, is the greatest car ever built. (*To the boys*) Since when do you let your mother carry wash up the stairs?

BIFF Grab hold there, boy!

HAPPY Where to, Mom?

LINDA Hang them up on the line. And you better go down to your friends, Biff. The cellar is full of boys. They don't know what to do with themselves.

BIFF Ah, when Pop comes home they can wait!

WILLY (*laughs appreciatively*) You better go down and tell them what to do, Biff.

BIFF I think I'll have them sweep out the furnace room.

WILLY Good work, Biff.

BIFF (*goes through wall-line of kitchen to doorway at back and calls down*) Fellas! Everybody sweep out the furnace room! I'll be right down!

VOICES All right! Okay, Biff.

BIFF George and Sam and Frank, come out back! We're hangin' up the wash! Come on, Hap, on the double! (*He and* HAPPY *carry out the basket*)

LINDA The way they obey him!

WILLY Well, that's training, the training. I'm tellin' you, I was sellin' thousands and thousands, but I had to come home.

LINDA Oh, the whole block'll be at that game. Did you sell anything?

WILLY I did five hundred gross in Providence and seven hundred gross in Boston.

LINDA No! Wait a minute, I've got a pencil. (*She pulls pencil and paper out of her apron pocket*) That makes your commission . . . Two hundred—my God! Two hundred and twelve dollars!

WILLY Well, I didn't figure it yet, but . . .

LINDA How much did you do?

WILLY Well, I—I did—about a hundred and eighty gross in Providence. Well, no—it came to—roughly two hundred gross on the whole trip.

LINDA (*without hesitation*) Two hundred gross. That's . . . (*She figures*)

WILLY The trouble was that three of the stores were half closed for inventory in Boston. Otherwise I woulda broke records.

LINDA Well, it makes seventy dollars and some pennies. That's very good.

WILLY What do we owe?

LINDA Well, on the first there's sixteen dollars on the refrigerator—

WILLY Why sixteen?

LINDA Well, the fan belt broke, so it was a dollar eighty.

WILLY But it's brand new.

LINDA Well, the man said that's the way it is. Till they work themselves in, y'know.

They move through the wall-line into the kitchen.

WILLY I hope we didn't get stuck on that machine.

LINDA They got the biggest ads of any of them!

WILLY I know, it's a fine machine. What else?

LINDA Well, there's nine-sixty for the washing machine. And for the vacuum cleaner there's three and a half due on the fifteenth. Then the roof, you got twenty-one dollars remaining.

WILLY It don't leak, does it?

LINDA No, they did a wonderful job. Then you owe Frank for the carburetor.

WILLY I'm not going to pay that man! That goddam Chevrolet, they ought to prohibit the manufacture of that car!

LINDA Well, you owe him three and a half. And odds and ends, comes to around a hundred and twenty dollars by the fifteenth.

WILLY A hundred and twenty dollars! My God, if business don't pick up I don't know what I'm gonna do!

LINDA Well, next week you'll do better.

WILLY Oh, I'll knock 'em dead next week. I'll go to Hartford. I'm very well liked in Hartford. You know, the trouble is, Linda, people don't seem to take to me.

They move onto the forestage.

LINDA Oh, don't be foolish.

WILLY I know it when I walk in. They seem to laugh at me.

LINDA Why? Why would they laugh at you? Don't talk that way, Willy.

WILLY *moves to the edge of the stage.* LINDA *goes into the kitchen and starts to darn stockings.*

WILLY I don't know the reason for it, but they just pass me by. I'm not noticed.

LINDA But you're doing wonderful, dear. You're making seventy to a hundred dollars a week.

WILLY But I gotta be at it ten, twelve hours a day. Other men—I don't know—they do it easier. I don't know why—I can't stop myself—I talk too much. A man oughta come in with a few words. One thing about Charley. He's a man of few words, and they respect him.

LINDA You don't talk too much, you're just lively.

WILLY (*smiling*) Well, I figure, what the hell, life is short, a couple of jokes. (*To himself*) I joke too much! (*The smile goes*)

LINDA Why? You're—

WILLY I'm fat. I'm very—foolish to look at, Linda. I didn't tell you, but Christmas time I happened to be calling on F. H. Stewarts, and a salesman I know, as I was going in to see the buyer I heard him say something about—walrus. And I—I cracked him right across the face. I won't take that. I simply will not take that. But they do laugh at me. I know that.

LINDA Darling . . .

WILLY I gotta overcome it. I know I gotta overcome it. I'm not dressing to advantage, maybe.

LINDA Willy, darling, you're the handsomest man in the world—

WILLY Oh, no, Linda.

LINDA To me you are. (*Slight pause*) The handsomest.

From the darkness is heard the laughter of a woman. WILLY doesn't turn to it, but it continues through LINDA's lines.

LINDA And the boys, Willy. Few men are idolized by their children the way you are.

Music is heard as behind a scrim, to the left of the house. THE WOMAN, dimly seen, is dressing.

WILLY (*with great feeling*) You're the best there is, Linda, you're a pal, you know that? On the road—on the road I want to grab you sometimes and just kiss the life outa you.

The laughter is loud now, and he moves into a brightening area at the left, where THE WOMAN has come from behind the scrim and is standing, putting on her hat, looking into a "mirror" and laughing.

WILLY 'Cause I get so lonely—especially when business is bad and there's nobody to talk to. I get the feeling that I'll never sell anything again, that I won't make a living for you, or a business, a business for the boys. (*He talks through THE WOMAN's subsiding laughter; THE WOMAN primps at the "mirror"*) There's so much I want to make for—

THE WOMAN Me? You didn't make me, Willy. I picked you.

WILLY (*pleased*) You picked me?

THE WOMAN (*who is quite proper-looking, WILLY's age*) I did. I've been sitting at that desk watching all the salesmen go by, day in, day out. But you've got such a sense of humor, and we do have such a good time together, don't we?

WILLY Sure, sure. (*He takes her in his arms*) Why do you have to go now?

THE WOMAN It's two o'clock . . .

WILLY No, come on in! (*He pulls her*)

THE WOMAN . . . my sisters'll be scandalized. When'll you be back?

WILLY Oh, two weeks about. Will you come up again?

THE WOMAN Sure thing. You do make me laugh. It's good for me. (*She squeezes his arm, kisses him*) And I think you're a wonderful man.

WILLY You picked me, heh?

THE WOMAN Sure. Because you're so sweet. And such a kidder.

WILLY Well, I'll see you next time I'm in Boston.

THE WOMAN I'll put you right through to the buyers.

WILLY (*slapping her bottom*) Right. Well, bottoms up!

THE WOMAN (*slaps him gently and laughs*) You just kill me, Willy. (*He suddenly grabs her and kisses her roughly*) You kill me. And thanks for the stockings. I love a lot of stockings. Well, good night.

WILLY Good night. And keep your pores open!

THE WOMAN Oh, Willy!

THE WOMAN *bursts out laughing, and* LINDA's *laughter blends in.* THE WOMAN *disappears into the dark. Now the area at the kitchen table brightens.* LINDA *is sitting where she was at the kitchen table, but now is mending a pair of her silk stockings.*

LINDA You are, Willy. The handsomest man. You've got no reason to feel that—

WILLY (*coming out of* THE WOMAN's *dimming area and going over to* LINDA) I'll make it all up to you, Linda, I'll—

LINDA There's nothing to make up, dear. You're doing fine, better than—

WILLY (*noticing her mending*) What's that?

LINDA Just mending my stockings. They're so expensive—

WILLY (*angrily, taking them from her*) I won't have you mending stockings in this house! Now throw them out!

LINDA *puts the stockings in her pocket.*

BERNARD (*entering on the run*) Where is he? If he doesn't study!

WILLY (*moving to the forestage, with great agitation*) You'll give him the answers!

BERNARD I do, but I can't on a Regents! That's a state exam! They're liable to arrest me!

WILLY Where is he? I'll whip him, I'll whip him!

LINDA And he'd better give back that football, Willy, it's not nice.

WILLY Biff! Where is he? Why is he taking everything?

LINDA He's too rough with the girls, Willy. All the mothers are afraid of him!

WILLY I'll whip him!

BERNARD He's driving the car without a license!

THE WOMAN's *laugh is heard.*

WILLY Shut up!

LINDA All the mothers—

WILLY Shut up!

BERNARD (*backing quietly away and out*) Mr. Birnbaum says he's stuck up.

WILLY Get outa here!

BERNARD If he doesn't buckle down he'll flunk math! (*He goes off*)

LINDA He's right, Willy, you've gotta—

WILLY (*exploding at her*) There's nothing the matter with him! You want him to be a worm like Bernard? He's got spirit, personality . . .

As he speaks, LINDA, *almost in tears, exits into the living-room.* WILLY *is alone in the kitchen, wilting and staring. The leaves are gone. It is night again, and the apartment houses look down from behind.*

WILLY Loaded with it. Loaded! What is he stealing? He's giving it back, isn't he? Why is he stealing? What did I tell him? I never in my life told him anything but decent things.

HAPPY *in pajamas has come down the stairs;* WILLY *suddenly becomes aware of* HAPPY's *presence.*

HAPPY Let's go now, come on.
WILLY (*sitting down at the kitchen table*) Huh! Why did she have to wax the floors herself? Everytime she waxes the floors she keels over. She knows that!
HAPPY Shh! Take it easy. What brought you back tonight?
WILLY I got an awful scare. Nearly hit a kid in Yonkers. God! Why didn't I go to Alaska with my brother Ben that time! Ben! That man was a genius, that man was success incarnate! What a mistake! He begged me to go.
HAPPY Well, there's no use in—
WILLY You guys! There was a man started with the clothes on his back and ended up with diamond mines!
HAPPY Boy, someday I'd like to know how he did it.
WILLY What's the mystery? The man knew what he wanted and went out and got it! Walked into a jungle, and comes out, the age of twenty-one, and he's rich! The world is an oyster, but you don't crack it open on a mattress!
HAPPY Pop, I told you I'm gonna retire you for life.
WILLY You'll retire me for life on seventy goddam dollars a week? And your women and your car and your apartment, and you'll retire me for life! Christ's sake, I couldn't get past Yonkers today! Where are you guys, where are you? The woods are burning! I can't drive a car!

CHARLEY *has appeared in the doorway. He is a large man, slow of speech, laconic, immovable. In all he says, despite what he says, there is pity, and, now, trepidation. He has a robe over pajamas, slippers on his feet. He enters the kitchen.*

CHARLEY Everything all right?
HAPPY Yeah, Charley, everything's . . .
WILLY What's the matter?
CHARLEY I heard some noise. I thought something happened. Can't we do something about the walls? You sneeze in here, and in my house hats blow off.
HAPPY Let's go to bed, Dad. Come on.

CHARLEY *signals to* HAPPY *to go.*

WILLY You go ahead, I'm not tired at the moment.
HAPPY (*to* WILLY) Take it easy, huh? (*He exits*)
WILLY What're you doin' up?
CHARLEY (*sitting down at the kitchen table opposite* WILLY) Couldn't sleep good. I had a heartburn.
WILLY Well, you don't know how to eat.
CHARLEY I eat with my mouth.
WILLY No, you're ignorant. You gotta know about vitamins and things like that.

CHARLEY Come on, let's shoot. Tire you out a little.

WILLY (*hesitantly*) All right. You got cards?

CHARLEY (*taking a deck from his pocket*) Yeah, I got them. Someplace. What is it with those vitamins?

WILLY (*dealing*) They build up your bones. Chemistry.

CHARLEY Yeah, but there's no bones in a heartburn.

WILLY What are you talkin' about? Do you know the first thing about it?

CHARLEY Don't get insulted.

WILLY Don't talk about something you don't know anything about.

They are playing. Pause.

CHARLEY What're you doin' home?

WILLY A little trouble with the car.

CHARLEY Oh. (*Pause*) I'd like to take a trip to California.

WILLY Don't say.

CHARLEY You want a job?

WILLY I got a job, I told you that. (*After a slight pause*) What the hell are you offering me a job for?

CHARLEY Don't get insulted.

WILLY Don't insult me.

CHARLEY I don't see no sense in it. You don't have to go on this way.

WILLY I got a good job. (*Slight pause*) What do you keep comin' in here for?

CHARLEY You want me to go?

WILLY (*after a pause, withering*) I can't understand it. He's going back to Texas again. What the hell is that?

CHARLEY Let him go.

WILLY I got nothin' to give him, Charley. I'm clean, I'm clean.

CHARLEY He won't starve. None a them starve. Forget about him.

WILLY Then what have I got to remember?

CHARLEY You take it too hard. To hell with it. When a deposit bottle is broken you don't get your nickel back.

WILLY That's easy enough for you to say.

CHARLEY That ain't easy for me to say.

WILLY Did you see the ceiling I put up in the living-room?

CHARLEY Yeah, that's a piece of work. To put up a ceiling is a mystery to me. How do you do it?

WILLY What's the difference?

CHARLEY Well, talk about it.

WILLY You gonna put up a ceiling?

CHARLEY How could I put up a ceiling?

WILLY Then what the hell are you bothering me for?

CHARLEY You're insulted again.

WILLY A man who can't handle tools is not a man. You're disgusting.

CHARLEY Don't call me disgusting, Willy.

UNCLE BEN, *carrying a valise and an umbrella, enters the forestage from around the right corner of the house. He is a stolid man, in his sixties, with a mustache and an authoritative air. He is utterly certain of his destiny, and there is an aura of far places about him. He enters exactly as* WILLY *speaks.*

WILLY I'm getting awfully tired, Ben.

BEN's *music is heard.* BEN *looks around at everything.*

CHARLEY Good, keep playing; you'll sleep better. Did you call me Ben?

BEN *looks at his watch.*

WILLY That's funny. For a second there you reminded me of my brother Ben.

BEN I only have a few minutes. (*He strolls, inspecting the place.* WILLY *and* CHARLEY *continue playing*)

CHARLEY You never heard from him again, heh? Since that time?

WILLY Didn't Linda tell you? Couple of weeks ago we got a letter from his wife in Africa. He died.

CHARLEY That so.

BEN (*chuckling*) So this is Brooklyn, eh?

CHARLEY Maybe you're in for some of his money.

WILLY Naa, he had seven sons. There's just one opportunity I had with that man . . .

BEN I must make a train, William. There are several properties I'm looking at in Alaska.

WILLY Sure, sure! If I'd gone with him to Alaska that time, everything would've been totally different.

CHARLEY Go on, you'd froze to death up there.

WILLY What're you talking about?

BEN Opportunity is tremendous in Alaska, William. Surprised you're not up there.

WILLY Sure, tremendous.

CHARLEY Heh?

WILLY There was the only man I ever met who knew the answers.

CHARLEY Who?

BEN How are you all?

WILLY (*taking a pot, smiling*) Fine, fine.

CHARLEY Pretty sharp tonight.

BEN Is Mother living with you?

WILLY No, she died a long time ago.

CHARLEY Who?

BEN That's too bad. Fine specimen of a lady, Mother.

WILLY (*to* CHARLEY) Heh?

BEN I'd hoped to see the old girl.

CHARLEY Who died?

BEN Heard anything from Father, have you?

WILLY (*unnerved*) What do you mean, who died?

CHARLEY (*taking a pot*) What're you talkin' about?

BEN (*looking at his watch*) William, it's half-past eight!

WILLY (*as though to dispel his confusion he angrily stops* CHARLEY's *hand*) That's my build!

CHARLEY I put the ace—

WILLY If you don't know how to play the game I'm not gonna throw my money away on you!

CHARLEY (*rising*) It was my ace, for God's sake!

WILLY I'm through, I'm through!

BEN When did Mother die?

WILLY Long ago. Since the beginning you never knew how to play cards.

CHARLEY (*picks up the cards and goes to the door*) All right! Next time I'll bring a deck with five aces.

WILLY I don't play that kind of game!

CHARLEY (*turning to him*) You ought to be ashamed of yourself!

WILLY Yeah?

CHARLEY Yeah! (*He goes out*)

WILLY (*slamming the door after him*) Ignoramus!

BEN (*as* WILLY *comes toward him through the wall-line of the kitchen*) So you're William.

WILLY (*shaking* BEN's *hand*) Ben! I've been waiting for you so long! What's the answer? How did you do it?

BEN Oh, there's a story in that.

LINDA *enters the forestage, as of old, carrying the wash basket.*

LINDA Is this Ben?

BEN (*gallantly*) How do you do, my dear.

LINDA Where've you been all these years? Willy's always wondered why you—

WILLY (*pulling* BEN *away from her impatiently*) Where is Dad? Didn't you follow him? How did you get started?

BEN Well, I don't know how much you remember.

WILLY Well, I was just a baby, of course, only three or four years old—

BEN Three years and eleven months.

WILLY What a memory, Ben!

BEN I have many enterprises, William, and I have never kept books.

WILLY I remember I was sitting under the wagon in—was it Nebraska?

BEN It was South Dakota, and I gave you a bunch of wild flowers.

WILLY I remember you walking away down some open road.

BEN (*laughing*) I was going to find Father in Alaska.

WILLY Where is he?

BEN At that age I had a very faulty view of geography, William. I discovered after a few days that I was heading due south, so instead of Alaska, I ended up in Africa.

LINDA Africa!

WILLY The Gold Coast!

BEN Principally diamond mines.

LINDA Diamond mines!

BEN Yes, my dear. But I've only a few minutes—

WILLY No! Boys! Boys! (YOUNG BIFF *and* HAPPY *appear*) Listen to this. This is your Uncle Ben, a great man! Tell my boys, Ben!

BEN Why, boys, when I was seventeen I walked into the jungle, and when I was twenty-one I walked out. (*He laughs*) And by God I was rich.

WILLY (*to the boys*) You see what I been talking about? The greatest things can happen!

BEN (*glancing at his watch*) I have an appointment in Ketchikan Tuesday week.

WILLY No, Ben! Please tell about Dad. I want my boys to hear. I want them to know the kind of stock they spring from. All I remember is a man with a big beard, and I was in Mamma's lap, sitting around a fire, and some kind of high music.

BEN His flute. He played the flute.

WILLY Sure, the flute, that's right!

New music is heard, a high, rollicking tune.

BEN Father was a very great and a very wild-hearted man. We would start in Boston, and he'd toss the whole family into the wagon, and then he'd drive the team right across the country; through Ohio, and Indiana, Michigan, Illinois, and all the Western states. And we'd stop in the towns and sell the flutes that he'd made on the way. Great inventor, Father. With one gadget he made more in a week than a man like you could make in a lifetime.

WILLY That's just the way I'm bringing them up, Ben—rugged, well liked, all-around.

BEN Yeah? (*To* BIFF) Hit that, boy—hard as you can. (*He pounds his stomach*)

BIFF Oh, no, sir!

BEN (*taking boxing stance*) Come on, get to me! (*He laughs*)

WILLY Go to it, Biff! Go ahead, show him!

BIFF Okay! (*He cocks his fists and starts in*)

LINDA (*to* WILLY) Why must he fight, dear?

BEN (*sparring with* BIFF) Good boy! Good boy!

WILLY How's that, Ben, heh?

HAPPY Give him the left, Biff!

LINDA Why are you fighting?

BEN Good boy! (*Suddenly comes in, trips* BIFF, *and stands over him, the point of his umbrella poised over* BIFF's *eye*)

LINDA Look out, Biff!

BIFF Gee!

BEN (*patting* BIFF's *knee*) Never fight fair with a stranger, boy. You'll never get out of the jungle that way. (*Taking* LINDA's *hand and bowing*) It was an honor and a pleasure to meet you, Linda.

LINDA (*withdrawing her hand coldly, frightened*) Have a nice—trip.

BEN (*to* WILLY) And good luck with your—what do you do?

WILLY Selling.

BEN Yes. Well . . . (*He raises his hand in farewell to all*)

WILLY No, Ben, I don't want you to think . . . (*He takes* BEN's *arm to show him*) It's Brooklyn, I know, but we hunt too.

BEN Really, now.

WILLY Oh, sure, there's snakes and rabbits and—that's why I moved out here. Why, Biff can fell any one of these trees in no time! Boys! Go right over to where they're building the apartment house and get some sand. We're gonna rebuild the entire front stoop right now! Watch this, Ben!

BIFF Yes, sir! On the double, Hap!

HAPPY (*as he and* BIFF *run off*) I lost weight, Pop, you notice?

CHARLEY *enters in knickers, even before the boys are gone.*

CHARLEY Listen, if they steal any more from that building the watchman'll put the cops on them!

LINDA (*to* WILLY) Don't let Biff . . .

BEN *laughs lustily.*

WILLY You shoulda seen the lumber they brought home last week. At least a dozen six-by-tens worth all kinds a money.

CHARLEY Listen, if that watchman—

WILLY I gave them hell, understand. But I got a couple of fearless characters there.

CHARLEY Willy, the jails are full of fearless characters.

BEN (*clapping* WILLY *on the back, with a laugh at* CHARLEY) And the stock exchange, friend!

WILLY (*joining in* BEN's *laughter*) Where are the rest of your pants?

CHARLEY My wife bought them.

WILLY Now all you need is a golf club and you can go upstairs and go to sleep. (*To* BEN) Great athlete! Between him and his son Bernard they can't hammer a nail!

BERNARD (*rushing in*) The watchman's chasing Biff!

WILLY (*angrily*) Shut up! He's not stealing anything!

LINDA (*alarmed, hurrying off left*) Where is he? Biff, dear! (*She exits*)

WILLY (*moving toward the left, away from* BEN) There's nothing wrong. What's the matter with you?

BEN Nervy boy. Good!

WILLY (*laughing*) Oh, nerves of iron, that Biff!

CHARLEY Don't know what it is. My New England man comes back and he's bleedin', they murdered him up there.

WILLY It's contacts, Charley, I got important contacts!

CHARLEY (*sarcastically*) Glad to hear it, Willy. Come in later, we'll shoot a little casino. I'll take some of your Portland money. (*He laughs at* WILLY *and exits*)

WILLY (*turning to* BEN) Business is bad, it's murderous. But not for me, of course.

BEN I'll stop by on my way back to Africa.

WILLY (*longingly*) Can't you stay a few days? You're just what I need, Ben, because I— I have a fine position here, but I—well, Dad left when I was such a baby and I never had a chance to talk to him and I still feel—kind of temporary about myself.

BEN I'll be late for my train.

They are at opposite ends of the stage.

WILLY Ben, my boys—can't we talk? They'd go into the jaws of hell for me, see, but I—

BEN William, you're being first-rate with your boys. Outstanding, manly chaps!

WILLY (*hanging on to his words*) Oh, Ben, that's good to hear! Because sometimes I'm afraid that I'm not teaching them the right kind of—Ben, how should I teach them?

BEN (*giving great weight to each word, and with a certain vicious audacity*) William, when I walked into the jungle, I was seventeen. When I walked out I was twenty-one. And, by God, I was rich! (*He goes off into darkness around the right corner of the house*)

WILLY . . . was rich! That's just the spirit I want to imbue them with! To walk into a jungle! I was right! I was right! I was right!

BEN *is gone, but* WILLY *is still speaking to him as* LINDA, *in nightgown and robe, enters the kitchen, glances around for* WILLY, *then goes to the door of the house, looks out and sees him. Comes down to his left. He looks at her.*

LINDA Willy, dear? Willy?

WILLY I was right!

LINDA Did you have some cheese? (*He can't answer*) It's very late, darling. Come to bed, heh?

WILLY (*looking straight up*) Gotta break your neck to see a star in this yard.

LINDA You coming in?

WILLY Whatever happened to that diamond watch fob? Remember? When Ben came from Africa that time? Didn't he give me a watch fob with a diamond in it?

LINDA You pawned it, dear. Twelve, thirteen years ago. For Biff's radio correspondence course.

WILLY Gee, that was a beautiful thing. I'll take a walk.

LINDA But you're in your slippers.

WILLY (*starting to go around the house at the left*) I was right! I was! (*Half to* LINDA, *as he goes, shaking his head*) What a man! There was a man worth talking to. I was right!

LINDA (*calling after* WILLY) But in your slippers, Willy!

WILLY *is almost gone when* BIFF, *in his pajamas, comes down the stairs and enters the kitchen.*

BIFF What is he doing out there?

LINDA Sh!

BIFF God Almighty, Mom, how long has he been doing this?

LINDA Don't, he'll hear you.

BIFF What the hell is the matter with him?

LINDA It'll pass by morning.

BIFF Shouldn't we do anything?

LINDA Oh, my dear, you should do a lot of things, but there's nothing to do, so go to sleep.

HAPPY *comes down the stairs and sits on the steps.*

HAPPY I never heard him so loud, Mom.

LINDA Well, come around more often; you'll hear him. (*She sits down at the table and mends the lining of* WILLY's *jacket*)

BIFF Why didn't you ever write me about this, Mom?

LINDA How would I write to you? For over three months you had no address.

BIFF I was on the move. But you know I thought of you all the time. You know that, don't you, pal?

LINDA I know, dear, I know. But he likes to have a letter. Just to know that there's still a possibility for better things.

BIFF He's not like this all the time, is he?

LINDA It's when you come home he's always the worst.

BIFF When I come home?

LINDA When you write you're coming, he's all smiles, and talks about the future, and— he's just wonderful. And then the closer you seem to come, the more shaky he gets, and then, by the time you get here, he's arguing, and he seems angry at you. I think it's just that maybe he can't bring himself to—to open up to you. Why are you so hateful to each other? Why is that?

BIFF (*evasively*) I'm not hateful, Mom.

LINDA But you no sooner come in the door than you're fighting!

BIFF I don't know why. I mean to change. I'm tryin', Mom, you understand?

LINDA Are you home to stay now?

BIFF I don't know. I want to look around, see what's doin'.

LINDA Biff, you can't look around all your life, can you?

BIFF I just can't take hold, Mom. I can't take hold of some kind of a life.

LINDA Biff, a man is not a bird, to come and go with the springtime.

BIFF Your hair . . . (*He touches her hair*) Your hair got so gray.

LINDA Oh, it's been gray since you were in high school. I just stopped dyeing it, that's all.

BIFF Dye it again, will ya? I don't want my pal looking old. (*He smiles*)

LINDA You're such a boy! You think you can go away for a year and . . . You've got to get it into your head now that one day you'll knock on this door and there'll be strange people here—

BIFF What are you talking about? You're not even sixty, Mom.

LINDA But what about your father?

BIFF (*lamely*) Well, I meant him too.

HAPPY He admires Pop.

LINDA Biff, dear, if you don't have any feeling for him, then you can't have any feeling for me.

BIFF Sure I can, Mom.

LINDA No. You can't just come to see me, because I love him. (*With a threat, but only a threat, of tears*) He's the dearest man in the world to me, and I won't have anyone making him feel unwanted and low and blue. You've got to make up your mind now, darling, there's no leeway any more. Either he's your father and you pay him that respect, or else you're not to come here. I know he's not easy to get along with—nobody knows that better than me—but . . .

WILLY (*from the left, with a laugh*) Hey, hey, Biffo!

BIFF (*starting to go out after* WILLY) What the hell is the matter with him? (HAPPY *stops him*)

LINDA Don't—don't go near him!

BIFF Stop making excuses for him! He always, always wiped the floor with you. Never had an ounce of respect for you.

HAPPY He's always had respect for—

BIFF What the hell do you know about it?

HAPPY (*surlily*) Just don't call him crazy!

BIFF He's got no character—Charley wouldn't do this. Not in his own house—spewing out that vomit from his mind.

HAPPY Charley never had to cope with what he's got to.

BIFF People are worse off than Willy Loman. Believe me, I've seen them!

LINDA Then make Charley your father, Biff. You can't do that, can you? I don't say he's a great man. Willy Loman never made a lot of money. His name was never in the paper. He's not the finest character that ever lived. But he's a human being, and a terrible thing is happening to him. So attention must be paid. He's not to be allowed to fall into his grave like an old dog. Attention, attention must be finally paid to such a person. You called him crazy—

BIFF I didn't mean—

LINDA No, a lot of people think he's lost his—balance. But you don't have to be very smart to know what his trouble is. The man is exhausted.

HAPPY Sure!

LINDA A small man can be just as exhausted as a great man. He works for a company thirty-six years this March, opens up unheard-of territories to their trademark, and now in his old age they take his salary away.

HAPPY (*indignantly*) I didn't know that, Mom.

LINDA You never asked, my dear! Now that you get your spending money someplace else you don't trouble your mind with him.

HAPPY But I gave you money last—

LINDA Christmas time, fifty dollars! To fix the hot water it cost ninety-seven fifty! For five weeks he's been on straight commission, like a beginner, an unknown!

BIFF Those ungrateful bastards!

LINDA Are they any worse than his sons? When he brought them business, when he was young, they were glad to see him. But now his old friends, the old buyers that loved him so and always found some order to hand him in a pinch—they're all dead, retired. He used to be able to make six, seven calls a day in Boston. Now he takes his valises out of the car and puts them back and takes them out again and he's exhausted. Instead of walking he talks now. He drives seven hundred miles, and when he gets there no one knows him any more, no one welcomes him. And what goes through a man's mind, driving seven hundred miles home without having earned a cent? Why shouldn't he talk to himself? Why? When he has to go to Charley and borrow fifty dollars a week and pretend to me that it's his pay? How long can that go on? How long? You see what I'm sitting here and waiting for? And you tell me he has no character? The man who never worked a day but for your benefit? When does he get the medal for that? Is this his reward—to turn around at the age of sixty-three and find his sons, who he loved better than his life, one a philandering bum—

HAPPY Mom!

LINDA That's all you are, my baby! (*To* BIFF) And you! What happened to the love you had for him? You were such pals! How you used to talk to him on the phone every night! How lonely he was till he could come home to you!

BIFF All right, Mom. I'll live here in my room, and I'll get a job. I'll keep away from him, that's all.

LINDA No, Biff. You can't stay here and fight all the time.

BIFF He threw me out of this house, remember that.

LINDA Why did he do that? I never knew why.

BIFF Because I know he's a fake and he doesn't like anybody around who knows!

LINDA Why a fake? In what way? What do you mean?

BIFF Just don't lay it all at my feet. It's between me and him—that's all I have to say. I'll chip in from now on. He'll settle for half my pay check. He'll be all right. I'm going to bed. (*He starts for the stairs*)

LINDA He won't be all right.

BIFF (*turning on the stairs, furiously*) I hate this city and I'll stay here. Now what do you want?

LINDA He's dying, Biff.

HAPPY *turns quickly to her, shocked.*

BIFF (*after a pause*) Why is he dying?

LINDA He's been trying to kill himself.

BIFF (*with great horror*) How?

LINDA I live from day to day.

BIFF What're you talking about?

LINDA Remember I wrote you that he smashed up the car again? In February?

BIFF Well?

LINDA The insurance inspector came. He said that they have evidence. That all these accidents in the last year—weren't—weren't—accidents.

HAPPY How can they tell that? That's a lie.

LINDA It seems there's a woman . . . (*She takes a breath as . . .*)

BIFF (*sharply but contained*) What woman?

LINDA (*simultaneously*) . . . and this woman . . .

LINDA What?

BIFF Nothing. Go ahead.

LINDA What did you say?

BIFF Nothing. I just said what woman?

HAPPY What about her?

LINDA Well, it seems she was walking down the road and saw his car. She says that he wasn't driving fast at all, and that he didn't skid. She says he came to that little bridge, and then deliberately smashed into the railing, and it was only the shallowness of the water that saved him.

BIFF Oh, no, he probably just fell asleep again.

LINDA I don't think he fell asleep.

BIFF Why not?

LINDA Last month . . . (*With great difficulty*) Oh, boys, it's so hard to say a thing like this! He's just a big stupid man to you, but I tell you there's more good in him than in many other people. (*She chokes, wipes her eyes*) I wasa looking for a fuse. The lights blew out, and I went down the cellar. And behind the fuse box—it happened to fall out—was a length of rubber pipe—just short.

HAPPY No kidding?

LINDA There's a little attachment on the end of it. I knew right away. And sure enough, on the bottom of the water heater there's a new little nipple on the gas pipe.

HAPPY (*angrily*) That—jerk.

BIFF Did you have it taken off?

LINDA I'm—I'm ashamed to. How can I mention it to him? Every day I go down and take away that little rubber pipe. But, when he comes home, I put it back where it was. How can I insult him that way? I don't know what to do. I live from day to day, boys. I tell you, I know every thought in his mind. It sounds so old-fashioned and silly, but I tell you he put his whole life into you and you've turned your backs on him. (*She is bent over in the chair, weeping, her face in her hands*) Biff, I swear to God! Biff, his life is in your hands!

HAPPY (*to* BIFF) How do you like that damned fool!

BIFF (*kissing her*) All right, pal, all right. It's all settled now. I've been remiss. I know that, Mom. But now I'll stay, and I swear to you, I'll apply myself. (*Kneeling in front of her, in a fever of self-reproach*) It's just—you see, Mom, I don't fit in business. Not that I won't try. I'll try, and I'll make good.

HAPPY Sure you will. The trouble with you in business was you never tried to please people.

BIFF I know, I—

HAPPY Like when you worked for Harrison's. Bob Harrison said you were tops, and then you go and do some damn fool thing like whistling whole songs in the elevator like a comedian.

BIFF (*against* HAPPY) So what? I like to whistle sometimes.

HAPPY You don't raise a guy to a responsible job who whistles in the elevator!

LINDA Well, don't argue about it now.

HAPPY Like when you'd go off and swim in the middle of the day instead of taking the line around.

BIFF (*his resentment rising*) Well, don't you run off? You take off sometimes, don't you? On a nice summer day?

HAPPY Yeah, but I cover myself!

LINDA Boys!

HAPPY If I'm going to take a fade the boss can call any number where I'm supposed to be and they'll swear to him that I just left. I'll tell you something that I hate to say, Biff, but in the business world some of them think you're crazy.

BIFF (*angered*) Screw the business world!

HAPPY All right, screw it! Great, but cover yourself!

LINDA Hap, Hap!

BIFF I don't care what they think! They've laughed at Dad for years, and you know why? Because we don't belong in this nuthouse of a city! We should be mixing cement on some open plain, or—or carpenters. A carpenter is allowed to whistle!

WILLY *walks in from the entrance of the house, at left.*

WILLY Even your grandfather was better than a carpenter. (*Pause. They watch him*) You never grew up. Bernard does not whistle in the elevator, I assure you.

BIFF (*as though to laugh* WILLY *out of it*) Yeah, but you do, Pop.

WILLY I never in my life whistled in an elevator! And who in the business world thinks I'm crazy?

BIFF I didn't mean it like that, Pop. Now don't make a whole thing out of it, will ya?

WILLY Go back to the West! Be a carpenter, a cowboy, enjoy yourself!

LINDA Willy, he was just saying—

WILLY I heard what he said!

HAPPY (*trying to quiet* WILLY) Hey, Pop, come on now . . .

WILLY (*continuing over* HAPPY's *line*) They laugh at me, heh? Go to Filene's, go to the Hub, go to Slattery's, Boston. Call out the name Willy Loman and see what happens! Big shot!

BIFF All right, Pop.

WILLY Big!

BIFF All right!

WILLY Why do you always insult me?

BIFF I didn't say a word. (*To* LINDA) Did I say a word?

LINDA He didn't say anything, Willy.

WILLY (*going to the doorway of the living-room*) All right, good night, good night.

LINDA Willy, dear, he just decided . . .

WILLY (*to* BIFF) If you get tired hanging around tomorrow, paint the ceiling I put up in the living-room.

BIFF I'm leaving early tomorrow.

HAPPY He's going to see Bill Oliver, Pop.

WILLY (*interestedly*) Oliver? For what?

BIFF (*with reserve, but trying, trying*) He always said he'd stake me. I'd like to go into business, so maybe I can take him up on it.

LINDA Isn't that wonderful?

WILLY Don't interrupt. What's wonderful about it? There's fifty men in the City of New York who'd stake him. (*To* BIFF) Sporting goods?

BIFF I guess so. I know something about it and—

WILLY He knows something about it! You know sporting goods better than Spalding, for God's sake! How much is he giving you?

BIFF I don't know, I didn't even see him yet, but—

WILLY Then what're you talkin' about?

BIFF (*getting angry*) Well, all I said was I'm gonna see him, that's all!

WILLY (*turning away*) Ah, you're counting your chickens again.

BIFF (*starting left for the stairs*) Oh, Jesus, I'm going to sleep!

WILLY (*calling after him*) Don't curse in this house!

BIFF (*turning*) Since when did you get so clean?

HAPPY (*trying to stop them*) Wait a . . .

WILLY Don't use that language to me! I won't have it!

HAPPY (*grabbing* BIFF, *shouts*) Wait a minute! I got an idea. I got a feasible idea. Come here, Biff, let's talk this over now, let's talk some sense here. When I was down in Florida last time, I thought of a great idea to sell sporting goods. It just came back to me. You and I, Biff—we have a line, the Loman Line. We train a couple of weeks, and put on a couple of exhibitions, see?

WILLY That's an idea!

HAPPY Wait! We form two basketball teams, see? Two waterpolo teams. We play each other. It's a million dollars' worth of publicity. Two brothers, see? The Loman Brothers. Displays in the Royal Palms—all the hotels. And banners over the ring and the basketball court: "Loman Brothers." Baby, we could sell sporting goods!

WILLY That is a one-million-dollar idea!

LINDA Marvelous!

BIFF I'm in great shape as far as that's concerned.

HAPPY And the beauty of it is, Biff, it wouldn't be like a business. We'd be out playin' ball again . . .

BIFF (*enthused*) Yeah, that's . . .

WILLY Million-dollar . . .

HAPPY And you wouldn't get fed up with it, Biff. It'd be the family again. There'd be the old honor, and comradeship, and if you wanted to go off for a swim or somethin'—well, you'd do it! Without some smart cooky gettin' up ahead of you!

WILLY Lick the world! You guys together could absolutely lick the civilized world.

BIFF I'll see Oliver tomorrow. Hap, if we could work that out . . .

LINDA Maybe things are beginning to—

WILLY (*wildly enthused, to* LINDA) Stop interrupting! (*To* BIFF) But don't wear sport jacket and slacks when you see Oliver.

BIFF No, I'll—

WILLY A business suit, and talk as little as possible, and don't crack any jokes.

BIFF He did like me. Always liked me.

LINDA He loved you!

WILLY (*to* LINDA) Will you stop! (*To* BIFF) Walk in very serious. You are not applying for a boy's job. Money is to pass. Be quiet, fine, and serious. Everybody likes a kidder, but nobody lends him money.

HAPPY I'll try to get some myself, Biff. I'm sure I can.

WILLY I see great things for you kids, I think your troubles are over. But remember, start big and you'll end big. Ask for fifteen. How much you gonna ask for?

BIFF Gee, I don't know—

WILLY And don't say "Gee." "Gee" is a boy's word. A man walking in for fifteen thousand dollars does not say "Gee!"

BIFF Ten, I think, would be top though.

WILLY Don't be so modest. You always started too low. Walk in with a big laugh. Don't look worried. Start off with a couple of your good stories to lighten things up. It's not what you say, it's how you say it—because personality always wins the day.

LINDA Oliver always thought the highest of him—

WILLY Will you let me talk?

BIFF Don't yell at her, Pop, will ya?

WILLY (*angrily*) I was talking, wasn't I?

BIFF I don't like you yelling at her all the time, and I'm tellin' you, that's all.

WILLY What're you, takin' over this house?

LINDA Willy—

WILLY (*turning on her*) Don't take his side all the time, goddammit!

BIFF (*furiously*) Stop yelling at her!

WILLY (*suddenly pulling on his cheek, beaten down, guilt ridden*) Give my best to Bill Oliver—he may remember me. (*He exits through the living-room doorway*)

LINDA (*her voice subdued*) What'd you have to start that for? (BIFF *turns away*) You see how sweet he was as soon as you talked hopefully? (*She goes over to* BIFF) Come up and say good night to him. Don't let him go to bed that way.

HAPPY Come on, Biff, let's buck him up.

LINDA Please, dear. Just say good night. It takes so little to make him happy. Come. (*She goes through the living-room doorway, calling upstairs from within the living-room*) Your pajamas are hanging in the bathroom, Willy!

HAPPY (*looking toward where* LINDA *went out*) What a woman! They broke the mold when they made her. You know that, Biff?

BIFF He's off salary. My God, working on commission!

HAPPY Well, let's face it: he's no hot-shot selling man. Except that sometimes, you have to admit, he's a sweet personality.

BIFF (*deciding*) Lend me ten bucks, will ya? I want to buy some new ties.

HAPPY I'll take you to a place I know. Beautiful stuff. Wear one of my striped shirts tomorrow.

BIFF She got gray. Mom got awful old. Gee, I'm gonna go in to Oliver tomorrow and knock him for a—

HAPPY Come on up. Tell that to Dad. Let's give him a whirl. Come on.

BIFF (*steamed up*) You know, with ten thousand bucks, boy!

HAPPY (*as they go into the living-room*) That's the talk, Biff, that's the first time I've heard the old confidence out of you! (*From within the living-room, fading off*) You're gonna live with me, kid, and any babe you want just say the word . . .

The last lines are hardly heard. They are mounting the stairs to their parents' bedroom.

LINDA (*entering her bedroom and addressing* WILLY, *who is in the bathroom. She is straightening the bed for him*) Can you do anything about the shower? It drips.

WILLY (*from the bathroom*) All of a sudden everything falls to pieces! Goddam plumbing, oughta be sued, those people. I hardly finished putting it in and the thing . . . (*His words rumble off*)

LINDA I'm just wondering if Oliver will remember him. You think he might?

WILLY (*coming out of the bathroom in his pajamas*) Remember him? What's the matter with you, you crazy? If he'd've stayed with Oliver he'd be on top by now! Wait'll Oliver gets a look at him. You don't know the average caliber any more. The average young man today—(*he is getting into bed*)—is got a caliber of zero. Greatest thing in the world for him was to bum around.

BIFF *and* HAPPY *enter the bedroom. Slight pause.*

WILLY (*stops short, looking at* BIFF) Glad to hear it, boy.

HAPPY He wanted to say good night to you, sport.

WILLY (*to* BIFF) Yeah. Knock him dead, boy. What'd you want to tell me?

BIFF Just take it easy, Pop. Good night. (*He turns to go*)

WILLY (*unable to resist*) And if anything falls off the desk while you're talking to him—like a package or something—don't you pick it up. They have office boys for that.

LINDA I'll make a big breakfast—

WILLY Will you let me finish? (*To* BIFF) Tell him you were in the business in the West. Not farm work.

BIFF All right, Dad.

LINDA I think everything—

WILLY (*going right through her speech*) And don't undersell yourself. No less than fifteen thousand dollars.

BIFF (*unable to bear him*) Okay. Good night, Mom. (*He starts moving*)

WILLY Because you got a greatness in you, Biff, remember that. You got all kinds a greatness . . . (*He lies back, exhausted.* BIFF *walks out*)

LINDA (*calling after* BIFF) Sleep well, darling!

HAPPY I'm gonna get married, Mom. I wanted to tell you.

LINDA Go to sleep, dear.

HAPPY (*going*) I just wanted to tell you.

WILLY Keep up the good work. (HAPPY *exits*) God . . . remember that Ebbets Field game? The championship of the city?

LINDA Just rest. Should I sing to you?

WILLY Yeah. Sing to me. (LINDA *hums a soft lullaby*) When that team came out—he was the tallest, remember?

LINDA Oh, yes. And in gold.

BIFF *enters the darkened kitchen, takes a cigarette, and leaves the house. He comes downstage into a golden pool of light. He smokes, staring at the night.*

WILLY Like a young god. Hercules—something like that. And the sun, the sun all around him. Remember how he waved to me? Right up from the field, with the representatives of three colleges standing by? And the buyers I brought, and the cheers when he came out—Loman, Loman, Loman! God almighty, he'll be great yet. A star like that, magnificent, can never really fade away!

The light on WILLY *is fading. The gas heater begins to glow through the kitchen wall, near the stairs, a blue flame beneath red coils.*

LINDA (*timidly*) Willy dear, what has he got against you?

WILLY I'm so tired. Don't talk any more.

BIFF *slowly returns to the kitchen. He stops, stares toward the heater.*

LINDA Will you ask Howard to let you work in New York?

WILLY First thing in the morning. Everything'll be all right.

BIFF *reaches behind the heater and draws out a length of rubber tubing. He is horrified and turns his head toward* WILLY's *room, still dimly lit, from which the strains of* LINDA's *desperate but monotonous humming rise.*

WILLY (*staring through the window into the moonlight*) Gee, look at the moon moving between the buildings!

BIFF *wraps the tubing around his hand and quickly goes up the stairs.*

Curtain

ACT II

Music is heard, gay and bright. The curtain rises as the music fades away. WILLY, *in shirt sleeves, is sitting at the kitchen table, sipping coffee, his hat in his lap.* LINDA *is filling his cup when she can.*

WILLY Wonderful coffee. Meal in itself.

LINDA Can I make you some eggs?

WILLY No. Take a breath.

LINDA You look so rested, dear.

WILLY I slept like a dead one. First time in months. Imagine, sleeping till ten on a Tuesday morning. Boys left nice and early, heh?

LINDA They were out of here by eight o'clock.

WILLY Good work!

LINDA It was so thrilling to see them leaving together. I can't get over the shaving lotion in this house!

WILLY (*smiling*) Mmm—

LINDA Biff was very changed this morning. His whole attitude seemed to be hopeful. He couldn't wait to get downtown to see Oliver.

WILLY He's heading for a change. There's no question, there simply are certain men that take longer to get—solidified. How did he dress?

LINDA His blue suit. He's so handsome in that suit. He could be a—anything in that suit!

WILLY *gets up from the table.* LINDA *holds his jacket for him.*

WILLY There's no question, no question at all. Gee, on the way home tonight I'd like to buy some seeds.

LINDA (*laughing*) That'd be wonderful. But not enough sun gets back there. Nothing'll grow any more.

WILLY You wait, kid, before it's all over we're gonna get a little place out in the country, and I'll raise some vegetables, a couple of chickens . . .

LINDA You'll do it yet, dear.

WILLY *walks out of his jacket.* LINDA *follows him.*

WILLY And they'll get married, and come for a weekend. I'd build a little guest house. 'Cause I got so many fine tools, all I'd need would be a little lumber and some peace of mind.

LINDA (*joyfully*) I sewed the lining . . .

WILLY I could build two guest houses, so they'd both come. Did he decide how much he's going to ask Oliver for?

LINDA (*getting him into the jacket*) He didn't mention it, but I imagine ten or fifteen thousand. You going to talk to Howard today?

WILLY Yeah. I'll put it to him straight and simple. He'll just have to take me off the road.

LINDA And Willy, don't forget to ask for a little advance, because we've got the insurance premium. It's the grace period now.

WILLY That's a hundred . . . ?

LINDA A hundred and eight, sixty-eight. Because we're a little short again.

WILLY Why are we short?

LINDA Well, you had the motor job on the car . . .

WILLY That goddam Studebaker!

LINDA And you got one more payment on the refrigerator . . .

WILLY But it just broke again!

LINDA Well, it's old, dear.

WILLY I told you we should've bought a well-advertised machine. Charley bought a General Electric and it's twenty years old and it's still good, that son-of-a-bitch.

LINDA But, Willy—

WILLY Whoever heard of a Hastings refrigerator? Once in my life I would like to own something outright before it's broken! I'm always in a race with the junkyard! I just finished paying for the car and it's on its last legs. The refrigerator consumes belts like a goddam maniac. They time those things. They time them so when you finally paid for them, they're used up.

LINDA (*buttoning up his jacket as he unbuttons it*) All told, about two hundred dollars would carry us, dear. But that includes the last payment on the mortgage. After this payment, Willy, the house belongs to us.

WILLY It's twenty-five years!

LINDA Biff was nine years old when we bought it.

WILLY Well, that's a great thing. To weather a twenty-five year mortgage is—

LINDA It's an accomplishment.

WILLY All the cement, the lumber, the reconstruction I put in this house! There ain't a crack to be found in it any more.

LINDA Well, it served its purpose.

WILLY What purpose? Some stranger'll come along, move in, and that's that. If only Biff would take this house, and raise a family . . . (*He starts to go*) Good-by, I'm late.

LINDA (*suddenly remembering*) Oh, I forgot! You're supposed to meet them for dinner.

WILLY Me?

LINDA At Frank's Chop House on Forty-eighth near Sixth Avenue.

WILLY Is that so! How about you?

LINDA No, just the three of you. They're gonna blow you to a big meal!

WILLY Don't say! Who thought of that?

LINDA Biff came to me this morning, Willy, and he said, "Tell Dad, we want to blow him to a big meal." Be there six o'clock. You and your two boys are going to have dinner.

WILLY Gee whiz! That's really somethin'. I'm gonna knock Howard for a loop, kid. I'll get an advance, and I'll come home with a New York job. Goddammit, now I'm gonna do it!

LINDA Oh, that's the spirit, Willy!

WILLY I will never get behind a wheel the rest of my life!

LINDA It's changing, Willy, I can feel it changing!

WILLY Beyond a question. G'by, I'm late. (*He starts to go again*)

LINDA (*calling after him as she runs to the kitchen table for a handkerchief*) You got your glasses?

WILLY (*feels for them, then comes back in*) Yeah, yeah, got my glasses.

LINDA (*giving him the handkerchief*) And a handkerchief.

WILLY Yeah, handkerchief.

LINDA And your saccharine?

WILLY Yeah, my saccharine.

LINDA Be careful on the subway stairs.

She kisses him, and a silk stocking is seen hanging from her hand. WILLY *notices it.*

WILLY Will you stop mending stockings? At least while I'm in the house. It gets me nervous. I can't tell you. Please.

LINDA *hides the stocking in her hand as she follows* WILLY *across the forestage in front of the house.*

LINDA Remember, Frank's Chop House.
WILLY (*passing the apron*) Maybe beets would grow out there.
LINDA (*laughing*) But you tried so many times.
WILLY Yeah. Well, don't work hard today. (*He disappears around the right corner of the house*)
LINDA Be careful!

As WILLY *vanishes,* LINDA *waves to him. Suddenly the phone rings. She runs across the stage and into the kitchen and lifts it.*

LINDA Hello? Oh, Biff! I'm so glad you called, I just . . . Yes, sure, I told him. Yes, he'll be there for dinner at six o'clock, I didn't forget. Listen, I was just dying to tell you. You know that little rubber pipe I told you about? That he connected to the gas heater? I finally decided to go down the cellar this morning and take it away and destroy it. But it's gone! Imagine? He took it away himself, it isn't there! (*She listens*) When? Oh, then you took it. Oh—nothing, it's just that I'd hoped he'd taken it away himself. Oh, I'm not worried, darling, because this morning he left in such high spirits, it was like the old days! I'm not afraid any more. Did Mr. Oliver see you? . . . Well, you wait there then. And make a nice impression on him, darling. Just don't perspire too much before you see him. And have a nice time with Dad. He may have big news too! . . . That's right, a New York job. And be sweet to him tonight, dear. Be loving to him. Because he's only a little boat looking for a harbor. (*She is trembling with sorrow and joy*) Oh, that's wonderful, Biff, you'll save his life. Thanks, darling. Just put your arm around him when he comes into the restaurant. Give him a smile. That's the boy . . . Good-by, dear. . . . You got your comb? . . . That's fine. Good-by, Biff dear.

In the middle of her speech, HOWARD WAGNER, *thirty-six, wheels on a small typewriter table on which is a wire-recording machine and proceeds to plug it in. This is on the left forestage. Light slowly fades on* LINDA *as it rises on* HOWARD. HOWARD *is intent on threading the machine and only glances over his shoulder as* WILLY *appears.*

WILLY Pst! Pst!
HOWARD Hello, Willy, come in.
WILLY Like to have a little talk with you, Howard.
HOWARD Sorry to keep you waiting. I'll be with you in a minute.
WILLY What's that, Howard?
HOWARD Didn't you ever see one of these? Wire recorder.
WILLY Oh. Can we talk a minute?
HOWARD Records things. Just got delivery yesterday. Been driving me crazy, the most terrific machine I ever saw in my life. I was up all night with it.
WILLY What do you do with it?
HOWARD I bought it for dictation, but you can do anything with it. Listen to this. I had it home last night. Listen to what I picked up. The first one is my daughter. Get this.

(*He flicks the switch and "Roll out the Barrel" is heard being whistled*) Listen to that kid whistle.

WILLY That is lifelike, isn't it?

HOWARD Seven years old. Get that tone.

WILLY Ts, ts. Like to ask a little favor of you . . .

The whistling breaks off, and the voice of HOWARD's *daughter is heard.*

HIS DAUGHTER "Now you, Daddy."

HOWARD She's crazy for me! (*Again the same song is whistled*) That's me! Ha! (*He winks*)

WILLY You're very good!

The whistling breaks off again. The machine runs silent for a moment.

HOWARD Sh! Get this now, this is my son.

HIS SON "The capital of Alabama is Montgomery; the capital of Arizona is Phoenix; the capital of Arkansas is Little Rock; the capital of California is Sacramento . . ." (*and on, and on*)

HOWARD (*holding up five fingers*) Five years old, Willy!

WILLY He'll make an announcer some day!

HIS SON (*continuing*) "The capital . . ."

HOWARD Get that—alphabetical order! (*The machine breaks off suddenly*) Wait a minute. The maid kicked the plug out.

WILLY It certainly is a—

HOWARD Sh, for God's sake!

HIS SON "It's nine o'clock, Bulova watch time. So I have to go to sleep."

WILLY That really is—

HOWARD Wait a minute! The next is my wife.

They wait.

HOWARD'S VOICE "Go on, say something." (*Pause*) "Well, you gonna talk?"

HIS WIFE "I can't think of anything."

HOWARD'S VOICE "Well, talk—it's turning."

HIS WIFE (*shyly, beaten*) "Hello." (*Silence*) "Oh, Howard, I can't talk into this . . ."

HOWARD (*snapping the machine off*) That was my wife.

WILLY That is a wonderful machine. Can we—

HOWARD I tell you, Willy, I'm gonna take my camera, and my bandsaw, and all my hobbies, and out they go. This is the most fascinating relaxation I ever found.

WILLY I think I'll get one myself.

HOWARD Sure, they're only a hundred and a half. You can't do without it. Supposing you wanna hear Jack Benny, see? But you can't be at home at that hour. So you tell the maid to turn the radio on when Jack Benny comes on, and this automatically goes on with the radio . . .

WILLY And when you come home you . . .

HOWARD You can come home twelve o'clock, one o'clock, any time you like, and you get yourself a Coke and sit yourself down, throw the switch, and there's Jack Benny's program in the middle of the night!

WILLY I'm definitely going to get one. Because lots of time I'm on the road, and I think to myself, what I must be missing on the radio!

HOWARD Don't you have a radio in the car?

WILLY Well, yeah, but who ever thinks of turning it on?

HOWARD Say, aren't you supposed to be in Boston?

WILLY That's what I want to talk to you about, Howard. You got a minute? (*He draws a chair in from the wing*)

HOWARD What happened? What're you doing here?

WILLY Well . . .

HOWARD You didn't crack up again, did you?

WILLY Oh, no. No . . .

HOWARD Geez, you had me worried there for a minute. What's the trouble?

WILLY Well, tell you the truth, Howard. I've come to the decision that I'd rather not travel any more.

HOWARD Not travel! Well, what'll you do?

WILLY Remember, Christmas time, when you had the party here? You said you'd try to think of some spot for me here in town.

HOWARD With us?

WILLY Well, sure.

HOWARD Oh, yeah, yeah. I remember. Well, I couldn't think of anything for you, Willy.

WILLY I tell ya, Howard. The kids are all grown up, y'know. I don't need much any more. If I could take home—well, sixty-five dollars a week, I could swing it.

HOWARD Yeah, but Willy, see I—

WILLY I tell ya why, Howard. Speaking frankly and between the two of us, y'know—I'm just a little tired.

HOWARD Oh, I could understand that, Willy. But you're a road man, Willy, and we do a road business. We've only got a half-dozen salesmen on the floor here.

WILLY God knows, Howard, I never asked a favor of any man. But I was with the firm when your father used to carry you in here in his arms.

HOWARD I know that, Willy, but—

WILLY Your father came to me the day you were born and asked me what I thought of the name of Howard, may he rest in peace.

HOWARD I appreciate that, Willy, but there just is no spot here for you. If I had a spot I'd slam you right in, but I just don't have a single solitary spot.

He looks for his lighter. WILLY *has picked it up and gives it to him. Pause.*

WILLY (*with increasing anger*) Howard, all I need to set my table is fifty dollars a week.

HOWARD But where am I going to put you, kid?

WILLY Look, it isn't a question of whether I can sell merchandise, is it?

HOWARD No, but it's a business, kid, and everybody's gotta pull his own weight.

WILLY (*desperately*) Just let me tell you a story, Howard—

HOWARD 'Cause you gotta admit, business is business.

WILLY (*angrily*) Business is definitely business, but just listen for a minute. You don't understand this. When I was a boy—eighteen, nineteen—I was already on the road. And there was a question in my mind as to whether selling had a future for me. Because in those days I had a yearning to go to Alaska. See, there were three gold strikes in one month in Alaska, and I felt like going out. Just for the ride, you might say.

HOWARD (*barely interested*) Don't say.

WILLY Oh, yeah, my father lived many years in Alaska. He was an adventurous man. We've got quite a little streak of self-reliance in our family. I thought I'd go out with my older brother and try to locate him, and maybe settle in the North with the old man. And I was almost decided to go, when I met a salesman in the Parker House. His name was Dave Singleman. And he was eighty-four years old, and he'd drummed merchandise in thirty-one states. And old Dave, he'd go up to his room, y'understand, put on his green velvet slippers—I'll never forget—and pick up his phone and call the buyers, and without ever leaving his room, at the age of eighty-four, he made his living. And when I saw that, I realized that selling was the greatest career a man could want. 'Cause what could be more satisfying than to be able to go, at the age of eighty-four, into twenty or thirty different cities, and pick up a phone, and be remembered and loved and helped by so many different people? Do you know? when he died— and by the way he died the death of a salesman, in his green velvet slippers in the smoker of the New York, New Haven and Hartford, going into Boston—when he died, hundreds of salesmen and buyers were at his funeral. Things were sad on a lotta trains for months after that. (*He stands up.* HOWARD *has not looked at him*) In those days there was personality in it, Howard. There was respect, and comradeship, and gratitude in it. Today, it's all cut and dried, and there's no chance for bringing friendship to bear—or personality. You see what I mean? They don't know me any more.

HOWARD (*moving away, to the right*) That's just the thing, Willy.

WILLY If I had forty dollars a week—that's all I'd need. Forty dollars, Howard.

HOWARD Kid, I can't take blood from a stone, I—

WILLY (*desperation is on him now*) Howard, the year Al Smith was nominated, your father came to me and—

HOWARD (*starting to go off*) I've got to see some people, kid.

WILLY (*stopping him*) I'm talking about your father! There were promises made across this desk! You mustn't tell me you've got people to see—I put thirty-four years into this firm, Howard, and now I can't pay my insurance! You can't eat the orange and throw the peel away—a man is not a piece of fruit! (*After a pause*) Now pay attention. Your father—in 1928 I had a big year. I averaged a hundred and seventy dollars a week in commissions.

HOWARD (*impatiently*) Now, Willy, you never averaged—

WILLY (*banging his hand on the desk*) I averaged a hundred and seventy dollars a week in the year of 1928! And your father came to me—or rather, I was in the office here— it was right over this desk—and he put his hand on my shoulder—

HOWARD (*getting up*) You'll have to excuse me, Willy, I gotta see some people. Pull yourself together. (*Going out*) I'll be back in a little while.

On HOWARD's *exit, the light on his chair grows very bright and strange.*

WILLY Pull myself together! What the hell did I say to him? My God, I was yelling at him! How could I! (WILLY *breaks off, staring at the light, which occupies the chair, animating it. He approaches this chair, standing across the desk from it*) Frank, Frank, don't you remember what you told me that time? How you put your hand on my shoulder, and Frank . . . (*He leans on the desk and as he speaks the dead man's name he accidentally switches on the recorder, and instantly*)

HOWARD's SON " . . . of New York is Albany. The capital of Ohio is Cincinnati, the capital of Rhode Island is . . ." (*The recitation continues*)

WILLY (*leaping away with fright, shouting*) Ha! Howard! Howard! Howard!

HOWARD (*rushing in*) What happened?

WILLY (*pointing at the machine, which continues nasally, childishly, with the capital cities*) Shut it off! Shut it off!

HOWARD (*pulling the plug out*) Look, Willy . . .

WILLY (*pressing his hands to his eyes*) I gotta get myself some coffee. I'll get some coffee . . .

WILLY *starts to walk out.* HOWARD *stops him.*

HOWARD (*rolling up the cord*) Willy, look . . .

WILLY I'll go to Boston.

HOWARD Willy, you can't go to Boston for us.

WILLY Why can't I go?

HOWARD I don't want you to represent us. I've been meaning to tell you for a long time now.

WILLY Howard, are you firing me?

HOWARD I think you need a good long rest, Willy.

WILLY Howard—

HOWARD And when you feel better, come back, and we'll see if we can work something out.

WILLY But I gotta earn money, Howard. I'm in no position to—

HOWARD Where are your sons? Why don't your sons give you a hand?

WILLY They're working on a very big deal.

HOWARD This is no time for false pride, Willy. You go to your sons and you tell them that you're tired. You've got two great boys, haven't you?

WILLY Oh, no question, no question, but in the meantime . . .

HOWARD Then that's that, heh?

WILLY All right, I'll go to Boston tomorrow.

HOWARD No, no.

WILLY I can't throw myself on my sons. I'm not a cripple!

HOWARD Look, kid, I'm busy this morning.

WILLY (*grasping* HOWARD's *arm*) Howard, you've got to let me go to Boston!

HOWARD (*hard, keeping himself under control*) I've got a line of people to see this morning. Sit down, take five minutes, and pull yourself together, and then go home, will ya? I need the office, Willy. (*He starts to go, turns, remembering the recorder, starts to push off the table holding the recorder*) Oh, yeah. Whenever you can this week, stop by and drop off the samples. You'll feel better, Willy, and then come back and we'll talk. Pull yourself together, kid, there's people outside.

HOWARD *exits, pushing the table off left.* WILLY *stares into space, exhausted. Now the music is heard—*BEN's *music—first distantly, then closer, closer. As* WILLY *speaks,* BEN *enters from the right. He carries valise and umbrella.*

WILLY Oh, Ben, how did you do it? What is the answer? Did you wind up the Alaska deal already?

BEN Doesn't take much time if you know what you're doing. Just a short business trip. Boarding ship in an hour. Wanted to say good-by.

WILLY Ben, I've got to talk to you.

BEN (*glancing at his watch*) Haven't the time, William.

WILLY (*crossing the apron to* BEN) Ben, nothing's working out. I don't know what to do.

BEN Now, look here, William. I've bought timberland in Alaska and I need a man to look after things for me.

WILLY God, timberland! Me and my boys in those grand outdoors!

BEN You've a new continent at your doorstep, William. Get out of these cities, they're full of talk and time payments and courts of law. Screw on your fists and you can fight for a fortune up there.

WILLY Yes, yes! Linda, Linda!

LINDA *enters as of old, with the wash.*

LINDA Oh, you're back?

BEN I haven't much time.

WILLY No, wait! Linda, he's got a proposition for me in Alaska.

LINDA But you've got— (*To* BEN) He's got a beautiful job here.

WILLY But in Alaska, kid, I could—

LINDA You're doing well enough, Willy!

BEN (*to* LINDA) Enough for what, my dear?

LINDA (*frightened of* BEN *and angry at him*) Don't say those things to him! Enough to be happy right here, right now. (*To* WILLY, *while* BEN *laughs*) Why must everybody conquer the world? You're well liked, and the boys love you, and someday—(*to* BEN)—why, old man Wagner told him just the other day that if he keeps it up he'll be a member of the firm, didn't he, Willy?

WILLY Sure, sure. I am building something with this firm, Ben, and if a man is building something he must be on the right track, mustn't he?

BEN What are you building? Lay your hand on it. Where is it?

WILLY (*hesitantly*) That's true, Linda, there's nothing.

LINDA Why? (*To* BEN) There's a man eighty-four years old—

WILLY That's right, Ben, that's right. When I look at that man I say, what is there to worry about?

BEN Bah!

WILLY It's true, Ben. All he has to do is go into any city, pick up the phone, and he's making his living and you know why?

BEN (*picking up his valise*) I've got to go.

WILLY (*holding* BEN *back*) Look at this boy!

BIFF, *in his high school sweater, enters carrying suitcase.* HAPPY *carries* BIFF's *shoulder guards, gold helmet, and football pants.*

WILLY Without a penny to his name, three great universities are begging for him, and from there the sky's the limit, because it's not what you do, Ben. It's who you know and the smile on your face! It's contacts, Ben, contacts! The whole wealth of Alaska passes over the lunch table at the Commodore Hotel, and that's the wonder, the wonder of this country, that a man can end with diamonds here on the basis of being liked! (*He turns to* BIFF) And that's why when you get out on that field today it's important. Because thousands of people will be rooting for you and loving you. (*To* BEN, *who has again begun to leave*) And Ben! when he walks into a business office his name will sound out like a bell and all the doors will open to him! I've seen it, Ben, I've seen it a thousand times! You can't feel it with your hand like timber, but it's there!

BEN Good-by, William.

WILLY Ben, am I right? Don't you think I'm right? I value your advice.

BEN There's a new continent at your doorstep, William. You could walk out rich. Rich! (*He is gone*)

WILLY We'll do it here, Ben! You hear me? We're gonna do it here!

YOUNG BERNARD *rushes in. The gay music of the boys is heard.*

BERNARD Oh, gee, I was afraid you left already!

WILLY Why? What time is it?

BIFF It's half-past one!

WILLY Well, come on, everybody! Ebbets Field next stop! Where's the pennants? (*He rushes through the wall-line of the kitchen and out into the living-room*)

LINDA (*to* BIFF) Did you pack fresh underwear?

BIFF (*who has been limbering up*) I want to go!

BERNARD Biff, I'm carrying your helmet, ain't I?

HAPPY No, I'm carrying the helmet.

BERNARD Oh, Biff, you promised me.

HAPPY I'm carrying the helmet.

BERNARD How am I going to get in the locker room?

LINDA Let him carry the shoulder guards. (*She puts her coat and hat on in the kitchen*)

BERNARD Can I, Biff? 'Cause I told everybody I'm going to be in the locker room.

HAPPY In Ebbets Field it's the clubhouse.

BERNARD I meant the clubhouse. Biff!

HAPPY Biff!

BIFF (*grandly, after a slight pause*) Let him carry the shoulder guards.

HAPPY (*as he gives* BERNARD *the shoulder guards*) Stay close to us now.

WILLY *rushes in with the pennants.*

WILLY (*handing them out*) Everybody wave when Biff comes out on the field. (HAPPY *and* BERNARD *run off*) You set now, boy?

The music has died away.

BIFF Ready to go, Pop. Every muscle is ready.

WILLY (*at the edge of the apron*) You realize what this means?

BIFF That's right, Pop.

WILLY (*feeling* BIFF'S *muscles*) You're comin' home this afternoon captain of the All-Scholastic Championship Team of the City of New York.

BIFF I got it, Pop. And remember, pal, when I take off my helmet, that touchdown is for you.

WILLY Let's go! (*He is starting out, with his arm around* BIFF, *when* CHARLEY *enters, as of old, in knickers*) I got no room for you, Charley.

CHARLEY Room? For what?

WILLY In the car.

CHARLEY You goin' for a ride? I wanted to shoot some casino.

WILLY (*furiously*) Casino! (*Incredulously*) Don't you realize what today is?

LINDA Oh, he knows, Willy. He's just kidding you.

WILLY That's nothing to kid about!

CHARLEY No, Linda, what's goin' on?

LINDA He's playing in Ebbets Field.

CHARLEY Baseball in this weather?

WILLY Don't talk to him. Come on, come on! (*He is pushing them out*)

CHARLEY Wait a minute, didn't you hear the news?

WILLY What?

CHARLEY Don't you listen to the radio? Ebbets Field just blew up.

WILLY You go to hell! (CHARLEY *laughs*) (*Pushing them out*) Come on, come on! We're late.

CHARLEY (*as they go*) Knock a homer, Biff, knock a homer!

WILLY (*the last to leave, turning to* CHARLEY) I don't think that was funny, Charley. This is the greatest day of his life.

CHARLEY Willy, when are you going to grow up?

WILLY Yeah, heh? When this game is over, Charley, you'll be laughing out of the other side of your face. They'll be calling him another Red Grange. Twenty-five thousand a year.

CHARLEY (*kidding*) Is that so?

WILLY Yeah, that's so.

CHARLEY Well, then, I'm sorry, Willy. But tell me something.

WILLY What?

CHARLEY Who is Red Grange?

WILLY Put up your hands. Goddam you, put up your hands!

CHARLEY, *chuckling, shakes his head and walks away, around the left corner of the stage.* WILLY *follows him. The music rises to a mocking frenzy.*

WILLY Who the hell do you think you are, better than everybody else? You don't know everything, you big, ignorant, stupid . . . Put up your hands!

Light rises, on the right side of the forestage, on a small table in the reception room of CHARLEY'S *office. Traffic sounds are heard.* BERNARD, *now mature, sits whistling to himself. A pair of tennis rackets and an overnight bag are on the floor beside him.*

WILLY (*offstage*) What are you walking away for? Don't walk away! If you're going to say something say it to my face! I know you laugh at me behind my back. You'll laugh out of the other side of your goddam face after this game. Touchdown! Touchdown! Eighty thousand people! Touchdown! Right between the goal posts.

BERNARD *is a quiet, earnest, but self-assured young man.* WILLY'S *voice is coming from right upstage now.* BERNARD *lowers his feet off the table and listens.* JENNY, *his father's secretary, enters.*

JENNY (*distressed*) Say, Bernard, will you go out in the hall?

BERNARD What is that noise? Who is it?

JENNY Mr. Loman. He just got off the elevator.

BERNARD (*getting up*) Who's he arguing with?

JENNY Nobody. There's nobody with him. I can't deal with him any more, and your father gets all upset everytime he comes. I've got a lot of typing to do, and your father's waiting to sign it. Will you see him?

WILLY (*entering*) Touchdown! Touch— (*He sees* JENNY) Jenny, Jenny, good to see you. How're ya? Workin'? Or still honest?

JENNY Fine. How've you been feeling?

WILLY Not much any more, Jenny. Ha, ha! (*He is surprised to see the rackets*)

BERNARD Hello, Uncle Willy.

WILLY (*almost shocked*) Bernard! Well, look who's here! (*He comes quickly, guiltily, to* BERNARD *and warmly shakes his hand*)

BERNARD How are you? Good to see you.

WILLY What are you doing here?

BERNARD Oh, just stopped by to see Pop. Get off my feet till my train leaves. I'm going to Washington in a few minutes.

WILLY Is he in?

BERNARD Yes, he's in his office with the accountant. Sit down.

WILLY (sitting down) What're you going to do in Washington?

BERNARD Oh, just a case I've got there, Willy.

WILLY That so? (Indicating the rackets) You going to play tennis there?

BERNARD I'm staying with a friend who's got a court.

WILLY Don't say. His own tennis court. Must be fine people, I bet.

BERNARD They are, very nice. Dad tells me Biff's in town.

WILLY (with a big smile) Yeah, Biff's in. Working on a very big deal, Bernard.

BERNARD What's Biff doing?

WILLY Well, he's been doing very big things in the West. But he decided to establish himself here. Very big. We're having dinner. Did I hear your wife had a boy?

BERNARD That's right. Our second.

WILLY Two boys! What do you know!

BERNARD What kind of a deal has Biff got?

WILLY Well, Bill Oliver—very big sporting-goods man—he wants Biff very badly. Called him in from the West. Long distance, carte blanche, special deliveries. Your friends have their own private tennis court?

BERNARD You still with the old firm, Willy?

WILLY (after a pause) I'm—I'm overjoyed to see how you made the grade, Bernard, overjoyed. It's an encouraging thing to see a young man really—really—Looks very good for Biff—very—(He breaks off, then) Bernard—(He is so full of emotion, he breaks off again)

BERNARD What is it, Willy?

WILLY (small and alone) What—what's the secret?

BERNARD What secret?

WILLY How—how did you? Why didn't he ever catch on?

BERNARD I wouldn't know that, Willy.

WILLY (confidentially, desperately) You were his friend, his boyhood friend. There's something I don't understand about it. His life ended after that Ebbets Field game. From the age of seventeen nothing good ever happened to him.

BERNARD He never trained himself for anything.

WILLY But he did, he did. After high school he took so many correspondence courses. Radio mechanics; television; God knows what, and never made the slightest mark.

BERNARD (taking off his glasses) Willy, do you want to talk candidly?

WILLY (rising, faces BERNARD) I regard you as a very brilliant man, Bernard. I value your advice.

BERNARD Oh, the hell with the advice, Willy. I couldn't advise you. There's just one thing I've always wanted to ask you. When he was supposed to graduate, and the math teacher flunked him—

WILLY Oh, that son-of-a-bitch ruined his life.

BERNARD Yeah, but, Willy, all he had to do was go to summer school and make up that subject.

WILLY That's right, that's right.

BERNARD Did you tell him not to go to summer school?

WILLY Me? I begged him to go. I ordered him to go!

BERNARD Then why wouldn't he go?

WILLY Why? Why! Bernard, that question has been trailing me like a ghost for the last fifteen years. He flunked the subject, and laid down and died like a hammer hit him!

BERNARD Take it easy, kid.

WILLY Let me talk to you—I got nobody to talk to. Bernard, Bernard, was it my fault? Y'see? It keeps going around in my mind, maybe I did something to him. I got nothing to give him.

BERNARD Don't take it so hard.

WILLY Why did he lay down? What is the story there? You were his friend!

BERNARD Willy, I remember, it was June, and our grades came out. And he'd flunked math.

WILLY That son-of-a-bitch!

BERNARD No, it wasn't right then. Biff just got very angry, I remember, and he was ready to enroll in summer school.

WILLY (surprised) He was?

BERNARD He wasn't beaten by it at all. But then, Willy, he disappeared from the block for almost a month. And I got the idea that he'd gone up to New England to see you. Did he have a talk with you then?

WILLY *stares in silence.*

BERNARD Willy?

WILLY (with a strong edge of resentment in his voice) Yeah, he came to Boston. What about it?

BERNARD Well, just that when he came back—I'll never forget this, it always mystifies me. Because I'd thought so well of Biff, even though he'd always taken advantage of me. I loved him, Willy, y'know? And he came back after that month and took his sneakers—remember those sneakers with "University of Virginia" printed on them? He was so proud of those, wore them every day. And he took them down in the cellar, and burned them up in the furnace. We had a fist fight. It lasted at least half an hour. Just the two of us, punching each other down the cellar, and crying right through it. I've often thought of how strange it was that I knew he'd given up his life. What happened in Boston, Willy?

WILLY *looks at him as at an intruder.*

BERNARD I just bring it up because you asked me.

WILLY (angrily) Nothing. What do you mean, "What happened?" What's that got to do with anything?

BERNARD Well, don't get sore.

WILLY What are you trying to do, blame it on me? If a boy lays down is that my fault?

BERNARD Now, Willy, don't get—

WILLY Well, don't—don't talk to me that way! What does that mean, "What happened?"

CHARLEY *enters. He is in his vest, and he carries a bottle of bourbon.*

CHARLEY Hey, you're going to miss that train. (He waves the bottle)

BERNARD Yeah, I'm going. (He takes the bottle) Thanks, Pop. (He picks up his rackets and bag) Good-by, Willy, and don't worry about it. You know, "If at first you don't succeed . . . ."

WILLY Yes, I believe in that.

BERNARD But sometimes, Willy, it's better for a man just to walk away.

WILLY Walk away?

BERNARD That's right.

WILLY But if you can't walk away?

BERNARD (*after a slight pause*) I guess that's when it's tough. (*Extending his hand*) Good-by, Willy.

WILLY (*shaking* BERNARD's *hand*) Good-by, boy.

CHARLEY (*an arm on* BERNARD's *shoulder*) How do you like this kid? Gonna argue a case in front of the Supreme Court.

BERNARD (*protesting*) Pop!

WILLY (*genuinely shocked, pained, and happy*) No! The Supreme Court!

BERNARD I gotta run. 'By, Dad!

CHARLEY Knock 'em dead, Bernard!

BERNARD *goes off.*

WILLY (*as* CHARLEY *takes out his wallet*) The Supreme Court! And he didn't even mention it!

CHARLEY (*counting out money on the desk*) He don't have to—he's gonna do it.

WILLY And you never told him what to do, did you? You never took any interest in him.

CHARLEY My salvation is that I never took any interest in anything. There's some money—fifty dollars. I got an accountant inside.

WILLY Charley, look . . . (*With difficulty*) I got my insurance to pay. If you can manage it—I need a hundred and ten dollars.

CHARLEY *doesn't reply for a moment; merely stops moving.*

WILLY I'd draw it from my bank but Linda would know, and I . . .

CHARLEY Sit down, Willy.

WILLY (*moving toward the chair*) I'm keeping an account of everything, remember. I'll pay every penny back. (*He sits*)

CHARLEY Now listen to me, Willy.

WILLY I want you to know I appreciate . . .

CHARLEY (*sitting down on the table*) Willy, what're you doin'? What the hell is goin' on in your head?

WILLY Why? I'm simply . . .

CHARLEY I offered you a job. You can make fifty dollars a week. And I won't send you on the road.

WILLY I've got a job.

CHARLEY Without pay? What kind of a job is a job without pay? (*He rises*) Now, look, kid, enough is enough. I'm no genius but I know when I'm being insulted.

WILLY Insulted!

CHARLEY Why don't you want to work for me?

WILLY What's the matter with you? I've got a job.

CHARLEY Then what're you walkin' in here every week for?

WILLY (*getting up*) Well, if you don't want me to walk in here—

CHARLEY I am offering you a job.

WILLY I don't want your goddam job!

CHARLEY When the hell are you going to grow up?

WILLY (*furiously*) You big ignoramus, if you say that to me again I'll rap you one! I don't care how big you are! (*He's ready to fight*)

Pause.

CHARLEY (*kindly, going to him*) How much do you need, Willy?

WILLY Charley, I'm strapped. I'm strapped. I don't know what to do. I was just fired.

CHARLEY Howard fired you?

WILLY That snotnose. Imagine that? I named him. I named him Howard.

CHARLEY Willy, when're you gonna realize that them things don't mean anything? You named him Howard, but you can't sell that. The only thing you got in this world is what you can sell. And the funny thing is that you're a salesman, and you don't know that.

WILLY I've always tried to think otherwise, I guess. I always felt that if a man was impressive, and well liked, that nothing—

CHARLEY Why must everybody like you? Who liked J. P. Morgan? Was he impressive? In a Turkish bath he'd look like a butcher. But with his pockets on he was very well liked. Now listen, Willy, I know you don't like me, and nobody can say I'm in love with you, but I'll give you a job because—just for the hell of it, put it that way. Now what do you say?

WILLY I—I just can't work for you, Charley.

CHARLEY What're you, jealous of me?

WILLY I can't work for you, that's all, don't ask me why.

CHARLEY (*angered, takes out more bills*) You been jealous of me all your life, you damned fool! Here, pay your insurance. (*He puts the money in* WILLY's *hand*)

WILLY I'm keeping strict accounts.

CHARLEY I've got some work to do. Take care of yourself. And pay your insurance.

WILLY (*moving to the right*) Funny, y'know? After all the highways, and the trains, and the appointments, and the years, you end up worth more dead than alive.

CHARLEY Willy, nobody's worth nothin' dead. (*After a slight pause*) Did you hear what I said?

WILLY *stands still, dreaming.*

CHARLEY Willy!

WILLY Apologize to Bernard for me when you see him. I didn't mean to argue with him. He's a fine boy. They're all fine boys, and they'll end up big—all of them. Someday they'll all play tennis together. Wish me luck, Charley. He saw Bill Oliver today.

CHARLEY Good luck.

WILLY (*on the verge of tears*) Charley, you're the only friend I got. Isn't that a remarkable thing? (*He goes out*)

CHARLEY Jesus!

CHARLEY *stares after him a moment and follows. All light blacks out. Suddenly raucous music is heard, and a red glow rises behind the screen at right.* STANLEY, *a young waiter, appears, carrying a table, followed by* HAPPY, *who is carrying two chairs.*

STANLEY (*putting the table down*) That's all right, Mr. Loman, I can handle it myself. (*He turns and takes the chairs from* HAPPY *and places them at the table*)

HAPPY (*glancing around*) Oh, this is better.

STANLEY Sure, in the front there you're in the middle of all kinds a noise. Whenever you got a party, Mr. Loman, you just tell me and I'll put you back here. Y'know, there's a lotta people they don't like it private, because when they go out they like to see a lotta action around them because they're sick and tired to stay in the house by theirself. But I know you, you ain't from Hackensack. You know what I mean?

HAPPY (*sitting down*) So how's it coming, Stanley?

STANLEY Ah, it's a dog's life. I only wish during the war they'd a took me in the Army. I coulda been dead by now.

HAPPY My brother's back, Stanley.

STANLEY Oh, he come back, heh? From the Far West.

HAPPY Yeah, big cattle man, my brother, so treat him right. And my father's coming too.

STANLEY Oh, your father too!

HAPPY You got a couple of nice lobsters?

STANLEY Hundred per cent, big.

HAPPY I want them with the claws.

STANLEY Don't worry, I don't give you no mice. (HAPPY *laughs*) How about some wine? It'll put a head on the meal.

HAPPY No. You remember, Stanley, that recipe I brought you from overseas? With the champagne in it?

STANLEY Oh, yeah, sure. I still got it tacked up yet in the kitchen. But that'll have to cost a buck apiece anyways.

HAPPY That's all right.

STANLEY What'd you, hit a number or somethin'?

HAPPY No, it's a little celebration. My brother is—I think he pulled off a big deal today. I think we're going into business together.

STANLEY Great! That's the best for you. Because a family business, you know what I mean?—that's the best.

HAPPY That's what I think.

STANLEY 'Cause what's the difference? Somebody steals? It's in the family. Know what I mean? (*Sotto voce*) Like this bartender here. The boss is goin' crazy what kinda leak he's got in the cash register. You put it in but it don't come out.

HAPPY (*raising his head*) Sh!

STANLEY What?

HAPPY You notice I wasn't lookin' right or left, was I?

STANLEY No.

HAPPY And my eyes are closed.

STANLEY So what's the—?

HAPPY Strudel's comin'.

STANLEY (*catching on, looks around*) Ah, no, there's no—

He breaks off as a furred, lavishly dressed girl enters and sits at the next table. Both follow her with their eyes.

STANLEY Geez, how'd ya know?

HAPPY I got radar or something. (*Staring directly at her profile*) Oooooooo . . . Stanley.

STANLEY I think that's for you, Mr. Loman.

HAPPY Look at that mouth. Oh, God. And the binoculars.

STANLEY Geez, you got a life, Mr. Loman.

HAPPY Wait on her.

STANLEY (*going to the* GIRL'S *table*) Would you like a menu, ma'am?

GIRL I'm expecting someone, but I'd like a—

HAPPY Why don't you bring her—excuse me, miss, do you mind? I sell champagne, and I'd like you to try my brand. Bring her a champagne, Stanley.

GIRL That's awfully nice of you.

HAPPY Don't mention it. It's all company money. (*He laughs*)

GIRL That's a charming product to be selling, isn't it?

HAPPY Oh, gets to be like everything else. Selling is selling, y'know.

GIRL I suppose.

HAPPY You don't happen to sell, do you?

GIRL No, I don't sell.

HAPPY Would you object to a compliment from a stranger? You ought to be on a magazine cover.

GIRL (*looking at him a little archly*) I have been.

STANLEY *comes in with a glass of champagne.*

HAPPY What'd I say before, Stanley? You see? She's a cover girl.

STANLEY Oh, I could see, I could see.

HAPPY (*to the* GIRL) What magazine?

GIRL Oh, a lot of them. (*She takes the drink*) Thank you.

HAPPY You know what they say in France, don't you? "Champagne is the drink of the complexion"—Hya, Biff!

BIFF *has entered and sits with* HAPPY.

BIFF Hello, kid. Sorry I'm late.

HAPPY I just got here. Uh, Miss—?

GIRL Forsythe.

HAPPY Miss Forsythe, this is my brother.

BIFF Is Dad here?

HAPPY His name is Biff. You might've heard of him. Great football player.

GIRL Really? What team?

HAPPY Are you familiar with football?

GIRL No, I'm afraid I'm not.

HAPPY Biff is quarterback with the New York Giants.

GIRL Well, that is nice, isn't it? (*She drinks*)

HAPPY Good health.

GIRL I'm happy to meet you.

HAPPY That's my name. Hap. It's really Harold, but at West Point they called me Happy.

GIRL (*now really impressed*) Oh, I see. How do you do? (*She turns her profile*)

BIFF Isn't Dad coming?

HAPPY You want her?

BIFF Oh, I could never make that.

HAPPY I remember the time that idea would never come into your head. Where's the old confidence, Biff?

BIFF I just saw Oliver—

HAPPY Wait a minute. I've got to see that old confidence again. Do you want her? She's on call.

BIFF Oh, no. (*He turns to look at the* GIRL)

HAPPY I'm telling you. Watch this. (*Turning to the* GIRL) Honey? (*She turns to him*) Are you busy?

GIRL Well, I am . . . but I could make a phone call.

HAPPY Do that, will you, honey? And see if you can get a friend. We'll be here for a while. Biff is one of the greatest football players in the country.

GIRL (*standing up*) Well, I'm certainly happy to meet you.

HAPPY Come back soon.

GIRL I'll try.

HAPPY Don't try, honey, try hard.

The GIRL *exits.* STANLEY *follows, shaking his head in bewildered admiration.*

HAPPY Isn't that a shame now? A beautiful girl like that? That's why I can't get married. There's not a good woman in a thousand. New York is loaded with them, kid!

BIFF Hap, look—

HAPPY I told you she was on call!

BIFF (*strangely unnerved*) Cut it out, will ya? I want to say something to you.

HAPPY Did you see Oliver?

BIFF I saw him all right. Now look, I want to tell Dad a couple of things and I want you to help me.

HAPPY What? Is he going to back you?

BIFF Are you crazy? You're out of your goddam head, you know that?

HAPPY Why? What happened?

BIFF (*breathlessly*) I did a terrible thing today, Hap. It's been the strangest day I ever went through. I'm all numb, I swear.

HAPPY You mean he wouldn't see you?

BIFF Well, I waited six hours for him, see? All day. Kept sending my name in. Even tried to date his secretary so she'd get me to him, but no soap.

HAPPY Because you're not showin' the old confidence, Biff. He remembered you, didn't he?

BIFF (*stopping* HAPPY *with a gesture*) Finally, about five o'clock, he comes out. Didn't remember who I was or anything. I felt like such an idiot, Hap.

HAPPY Did you tell him my Florida idea?

BIFF He walked away. I saw him for one minute. I got so mad I could've torn the walls down! How the hell did I ever get the idea I was a salesman there? I even believed myself that I'd been a salesman for him! And then he gave me one look and—I realized what a ridiculous lie my whole life has been! We've been talking in a dream for fifteen years. I was a shipping clerk.

HAPPY What'd you do?

BIFF (*with great tension and wonder*) Well, he left, see. And the secretary went out. I was all alone in the waiting-room. I don't know what came over me, Hap. The next thing I know I'm in his office—paneled walls, everything. I can't explain it. I—Hap, I took his fountain pen.

HAPPY Geez, did he catch you?

BIFF I ran out. I ran down all eleven flights. I ran and ran and ran.

HAPPY That was an awful dumb—what'd you do that for?

BIFF (*agonized*) I don't know, I just—wanted to take something, I don't know. You gotta help me, Hap. I'm gonna tell Pop.

HAPPY You crazy? What for?

BIFF Hap, he's got to understand that I'm not the man somebody lends that kind of money to. He thinks I've been spiting him all these years and it's eating him up.

HAPPY That's just it. You tell him something nice.

BIFF I can't.

HAPPY Say you got a lunch date with Oliver tomorrow.

BIFF So what do I do tomorrow?

HAPPY You leave the house tomorrow and come back at night and say Oliver is thinking
it over. And he thinks it over for a couple of weeks, and gradually it fades away and
nobody's the worse.
BIFF But it'll go on forever!
HAPPY Dad is never so happy as when he's looking forward to something!

WILLY *enters.*

HAPPY Hello, scout!
WILLY Gee, I haven't been here in years!

STANLEY *has followed* WILLY *in and sets a chair for him.* STANLEY *starts off but* HAPPY
stops him.

HAPPY Stanley!

STANLEY *stands by, waiting for an order.*

BIFF (*going to* WILLY *with guilt, as to an invalid*) Sit down, Pop. You want a drink?
WILLY Sure, I don't mind.
BIFF Let's get a load on.
WILLY You look worried.
BIFF N-no. (*To* STANLEY) Scotch all around. Make it doubles.
STANLEY Doubles, right. (*He goes*)
WILLY You had a couple already, didn't you?
BIFF Just a couple, yeah.
WILLY Well, what happened, boy? (*Nodding affirmatively, with a smile*) Everything go
all right?
BIFF (*takes a breath, then reaches out and grasps* WILLY's *hand*) Pal . . . (*He is smiling
bravely, and* WILLY *is smiling too*) I had an experience today.
HAPPY Terrific, Pop.
WILLY That so? What happened?
BIFF (*high, slightly alcoholic, above the earth*) I'm going to tell you everything from first
to last. It's been a strange day. (*Silence. He looks around, composes himself as best he
can, but his breath keeps breaking the rhythm of his voice*) I had to wait quite a while
for him, and—
WILLY Oliver?
BIFF Yeah, Oliver. All day, as a matter of cold fact. And a lot of—instances—facts, Pop,
facts about my life came back to me. Who was it, Pop? Who ever said I was a salesman
with Oliver?
WILLY Well, you were.
BIFF No, Dad, I was a shipping clerk.
WILLY But you were practically—
BIFF (*with determination*) Dad, I don't know who said it first, but I was never a salesman
for Bill Oliver.
WILLY What're you talking about?
BIFF Let's hold on to the facts tonight, Pop. We're not going to get anywhere bullin'
around. I was a shipping clerk.
WILLY (*angrily*) All right, now listen to me—
BIFF Why don't you let me finish?

WILLY I'm not interested in stories about the past or any crap of that kind because the woods are burning, boys, you understand? There's a big blaze going on all around. I was fired today.

BIFF (*shocked*) How could you be?

WILLY I was fired, and I'm looking for a little good news to tell your mother, because the woman has waited and the woman has suffered. The gift of it is that I haven't got a story left in my head, Biff. So don't give me a lecture about facts and aspects. I am not interested. Now what've you got to say to me?

STANLEY *enters with three drinks. They wait until he leaves.*

WILLY Did you see Oliver?

BIFF Jesus, Dad!

WILLY You mean you didn't go up there?

HAPPY Sure he went up there.

BIFF I did. I—saw him. How could they fire you?

WILLY (*on the edge of his chair*) What kind of a welcome did he give you?

BIFF He won't even let you work on commission?

WILLY I'm out! (*Driving*) So tell me, he gave you a warm welcome?

HAPPY Sure, Pop, sure!

BIFF (*driven*) Well, it was kind of—

WILLY I was wondering if he'd remember you. (*To* HAPPY) Imagine, man doesn't see him for ten, twelve years and gives him that kind of a welcome!

HAPPY Damn right!

BIFF (*trying to return to the offensive*) Pop, look—

WILLY You know why he remembered you, don't you? Because you impressed him in those days.

BIFF Let's talk quietly and get this down to the facts, huh?

WILLY (*as though* BIFF *had been interrupting*) Well, what happened? It's great news, Biff. Did he take you into his office or'd you talk in the waiting-room?

BIFF Well, he came in, see, and—

WILLY (*with a big smile*) What'd he say? Betcha he threw his arm around you.

BIFF Well, he kinda—

WILLY He's a fine man. (*To* HAPPY) Very hard man to see, y'know.

HAPPY (*agreeing*) Oh, I know.

WILLY (*to* BIFF) Is that where you had the drinks?

BIFF Yeah, he gave me a couple of—no, no!

HAPPY (*cutting in*) He told him my Florida idea.

WILLY Don't interrupt. (*To* BIFF) How'd he react to the Florida idea?

BIFF Dad, will you give me a minute to explain?

WILLY I've been waiting for you to explain since I sat down here! What happened? He took you into his office and what?

BIFF Well—I talked. And—and he listened, see.

WILLY Famous for the way he listens, y'know. What was his answer?

BIFF His answer was— (*He breaks off, suddenly angry*) Dad, you're not letting me tell you what I want to tell you!

WILLY (*accusing, angered*) You didn't see him, did you?

BIFF I did see him!

WILLY What'd you insult him or something? You insulted him, didn't you?

BIFF Listen, will you let me out of it, will you just let me out of it!

HAPPY What the hell!

WILLY Tell me what happened!

BIFF (*to* HAPPY) I can't talk to him!

A single trumpet note jars the ear. The light of green leaves stains the house, which holds the air of night and a dream. YOUNG BERNARD *enters and knocks on the door of the house.*

YOUNG BERNARD (*frantically*) Mrs. Loman, Mrs. Loman!

HAPPY Tell him what happened!

BIFF (*to* HAPPY) Shut up and leave me alone!

WILLY No, no! You had to go and flunk math!

BIFF What math? What're you talking about?

YOUNG BERNARD Mrs. Loman, Mrs. Loman!

LINDA *appears in the house, as of old.*

WILLY (*wildly*) Math, math, math!

BIFF Take it easy, Pop!

YOUNG BERNARD Mrs. Loman!

WILLY (*furiously*) If you hadn't flunked you'd've been set by now!

BIFF Now, look, I'm gonna tell you what happened, and you're going to listen to me.

YOUNG BERNARD Mrs. Loman!

BIFF I waited six hours—

HAPPY What the hell are you saying?

BIFF I kept sending in my name but he wouldn't see me. So finally he . . . (*He continues unheard as light fades low on the restaurant*)

YOUNG BERNARD Biff flunked math!

LINDA No!

YOUNG BERNARD Birnbaum flunked him! They won't graduate him!

LINDA But they have to. He's gotta go to the university. Where is he? Biff! Biff!

YOUNG BERNARD No, he left. He went to Grand Central.

LINDA Grand— You mean he went to Boston!

YOUNG BERNARD Is Uncle Willy in Boston?

LINDA Oh, maybe Willy can talk to the teacher. Oh, the poor, poor boy!

Light on house area snaps out.

BIFF (*at the table, now audible, holding up a gold fountain pen*) . . . so I'm washed up with Oliver, you understand? Are you listening to me?

WILLY (*at a loss*) Yeah, sure. If you hadn't flunked—

BIFF Flunked what? What're you talking about?

WILLY Don't blame everything on me! I didn't flunk math—you did! What pen?

HAPPY That was awful dumb, Biff, a pen like that is worth—

WILLY (*seeing the pen for the first time*) You took Oliver's pen?

BIFF (*weakening*) Dad, I just explained it to you.

WILLY You stole Bill Oliver's fountain pen!

BIFF I didn't exactly steal it! That's just what I've been explaining to you!

HAPPY He had it in his hand and just then Oliver walked in, so he got nervous and stuck it in his pocket.

WILLY My God, Biff!

BIFF I never intended to do it, Dad!

OPERATOR'S VOICE Standish Arms, good evening!

WILLY (*shouting*) I'm not in my room!

BIFF (*frightened*) Dad, what's the matter? (*He and* HAPPY *stand up*)

OPERATOR Ringing Mr. Loman for you!

WILLY I'm not there, stop it!

BIFF (*horrified, gets down on one knee before* WILLY) Dad, I'll make good, I'll make good. (WILLY *tries to get to his feet.* BIFF *holds him down*) Sit down now.

WILLY No, you're no good, you're no good for anything.

BIFF I am, Dad, I'll find something else, you understand? Now don't worry about anything. (*He holds up* WILLY's *face*) Talk to me, Dad.

OPERATOR Mr. Loman does not answer. Shall I page him?

WILLY (*attempting to stand, as though to rush and silence the* OPERATOR) No, no, no!

HAPPY He'll strike something, Pop.

WILLY No, no . . .

BIFF (*desperately, standing over* WILLY) Pop, listen! Listen to me! I'm telling you something good. Oliver talked to his partner about the Florida idea. You listening? He—he talked to his partner, and he came to me . . . I'm going to be all right, you hear? Dad, listen to me, he said it was just a question of the amount!

WILLY Then you . . . got it?

HAPPY He's gonna be terrific, Pop!

WILLY (*trying to stand*) Then you got it, haven't you? You got it! You got it!

BIFF (*agonized, holds* WILLY *down*) No, no. Look, Pop. I'm supposed to have lunch with them tomorrow. I'm just telling you this so you'll know that I can still make an impression, Pop. And I'll make good somewhere, but I can't go tomorrow, see?

WILLY Why not? You simply—

BIFF But the pen, Pop!

WILLY You give it to him and tell him it was an oversight!

HAPPY Sure, have lunch tomorrow!

BIFF I can't say that—

WILLY You were doing a crossword puzzle and accidentally used his pen!

BIFF Listen, kid, I took those balls years ago, now I walk in with his fountain pen? That clinches it, don't you see? I can't face him like that! I'll try elsewhere.

PAGE'S VOICE Paging Mr. Loman!

WILLY Don't you want to be anything?

BIFF Pop, how can I go back?

WILLY You don't want to be anything, is that what's behind it?

BIFF (*now angry at* WILLY *for not crediting his sympathy*) Don't take it that way! You think it was easy walking into that office after what I'd done to him? A team of horses couldn't have dragged me back to Bill Oliver!

WILLY Then why'd you go?

BIFF Why did I go? Why did I go! Look at you! Look at what's become of you!

Off left, THE WOMAN *laughs.*

WILLY Biff, you're going to go to that lunch tomorrow, or—

BIFF I can't go. I've got no appointment!

HAPPY Biff, for . . . !

WILLY Are you spiting me?

BIFF Don't take it that way! Goddammit!

WILLY (*strikes* BIFF *and falters away from the table*) You rotten little louse! Are you spiting me?

THE WOMAN Someone's at the door, Willy!

BIFF I'm no good, can't you see what I am?

HAPPY (*separating them*) Hey, you're in a restaurant! Now cut it out, both of you! (*The girls enter*) Hello, girls, sit down.

THE WOMAN *laughs, off left.*

MISS FORSYTHE I guess we might as well. This is Letta.

THE WOMAN Willy, are you going to wake up?

BIFF (*ignoring* WILLY) How're ya, miss, sit down. What do you drink?

MISS FORSYTHE Letta might not be able to stay long.

LETTA I gotta get up very early tomorrow. I got jury duty. I'm so excited! Were you fellows ever on a jury?

BIFF No, but I been in front of them! (*The girls laugh*) This is my father.

LETTA Isn't he cute? Sit down with us, Pop.

HAPPY Sit him down, Biff!

BIFF (*going to him*) Come on, slugger, drink us under the table. To hell with it! Come on, sit down, pal.

On BIFF's *last insistence,* WILLY *is about to sit.*

THE WOMAN (*now urgently*) Willy, are you going to answer the door!

THE WOMAN's *call pulls* WILLY *back. He starts right, befuddled.*

BIFF Hey, where are you going?

WILLY Open the door.

BIFF The door?

WILLY The washroom . . . the door . . . where's the door?

BIFF (*leading* WILLY *to the left*) Just go straight down.

WILLY *moves left.*

THE WOMAN Willy, Willy, are you going to get up, get up, get up, get up?

WILLY *exits left.*

LETTA I think it's sweet you bring your daddy along.

MISS FORSYTHE Oh, he isn't really your father!

BIFF (*at left, turning to her resentfully*) Miss Forsythe, you've just seen a prince walk by. A fine, troubled prince. A hard-working, unappreciated prince. A pal, you understand? A good companion. Always for his boys.

LETTA That's so sweet.

HAPPY Well, girls, what's the program? We're wasting time. Come on, Biff. Gather round. Where would you like to go?

BIFF Why don't you do something for him?

HAPPY Me!

BIFF Don't you give a damn for him, Hap?

HAPPY What're you talking about? I'm the one who—

BIFF I sense it, you don't give a good goddam about him. (*He takes the rolled-up hose from his pocket and puts it on the table in front of* HAPPY) Look what I found in the cellar, for Christ's sake. How can you bear to let it go on?

HAPPY Me? Who goes away? Who runs off and—

BIFF Yeah, but he doesn't mean anything to you. You could help him—I can't! Don't you understand what I'm talking about? He's going to kill himself, don't you know that?

HAPPY Don't I know it! Me!

BIFF Hap, help him! Jesus . . . help him . . . Help me, help me, I can't bear to look at his face! (*Ready to weep, he hurries out, up right*)

HAPPY (*starting after him*) Where are you going?

MISS FORSYTHE What's he so mad about?

HAPPY Come on, girls, we'll catch up with him.

MISS FORSYTHE (*as* HAPPY *pushes her out*) Say, I don't like that temper of his!

HAPPY He's just a little overstrung, he'll be all right!

WILLY (*off left, as* THE WOMAN *laughs*) Don't answer! Don't answer!

LETTA Don't you want to tell your father—

HAPPY No, that's not my father. He's just a guy. Come on, we'll catch Biff, and, honey, we're going to paint this town! Stanley, where's the check! Hey, Stanley!

They exit. STANLEY *looks toward left.*

STANLEY (*calling to* HAPPY *indignantly*) Mr. Loman! Mr. Loman!

STANLEY *picks up a chair and follows them off. Knocking is heard off left.* THE WOMAN *enters, laughing.* WILLY *follows her. She is in a black slip; he is buttoning his shirt. Raw, sensuous music accompanies their speech.*

WILLY Will you stop laughing? Will you stop?

THE WOMAN Aren't you going to answer the door? He'll wake the whole hotel.

WILLY I'm not expecting anybody.

THE WOMAN Whyn't you have another drink, honey, and stop being so damn self-centered?

WILLY I'm so lonely.

THE WOMAN You know you ruined me, Willy? From now on, whenever you come to the office, I'll see that you go right through to the buyers. No waiting at my desk any more, Willy. You ruined me.

WILLY That's nice of you to say that.

THE WOMAN Gee, you are self-centered! Why so sad? You are the saddest, self-centeredest soul I ever did see-saw. (*She laughs. He kisses her*) Come on inside, drummer boy. It's silly to be dressing in the middle of the night. (*As knocking is heard*) Aren't you going to answer the door?

WILLY They're knocking on the wrong door.

THE WOMAN But I felt the knocking. And he heard us talking in here. Maybe the hotel's on fire!

WILLY (*his terror rising*) It's a mistake.

THE WOMAN Then tell him to go away!

WILLY There's nobody there.

THE WOMAN It's getting on my nerves, Willy. There's somebody standing out there and it's getting on my nerves!

WILLY (*pushing her away from him*) All right, stay in the bathroom here, and don't come out. I think there's a law in Massachusetts about it, so don't come out. It may be that new room clerk. He looked very mean. So don't come out. It's a mistake, there's no fire.

The knocking is heard again. He takes a few steps away from her, and she vanishes into the wing. The light follows him, and now he is facing YOUNG BIFF, *who carries a suitcase.* BIFF *steps toward him. The music is gone.*

BIFF Why didn't you answer?

WILLY Biff! What are you doing in Boston?

BIFF Why didn't you answer? I've been knocking for five minutes, I called you on the phone—

WILLY I just heard you. I was in the bathroom and had the door shut. Did anything happen home?

BIFF Dad—I let you down.

WILLY What do you mean?

BIFF Dad . . .

WILLY Biffo, what's this about? (*Putting his arm around* BIFF) Come on, let's go downstairs and get you a malted.

BIFF Dad, I flunked math.

WILLY Not for the term?

BIFF The term. I haven't got enough credits to graduate.

WILLY You mean to say Bernard wouldn't give you the answers?

BIFF He did, he tried, but I only got a sixty-one.

WILLY And they wouldn't give you four points?

BIFF Birnbaum refused absolutely. I begged him, Pop, but he won't give me those points. You gotta talk to him before they close the school. Because if he saw the kind of man you are, and you just talked to him in your way, I'm sure he'd come through for me. The class came right before practice, see, and I didn't go enough. Would you talk to him? He'd like you, Pop. You know the way you could talk.

WILLY You're on. We'll drive right back.

BIFF Oh, Dad, good work! I'm sure he'll change it for you!

WILLY Go downstairs and tell the clerk I'm checkin' out. Go right down.

BIFF Yes, sir! See, the reason he hates me, Pop—one day he was late for class so I got up at the blackboard and imitated him. I crossed my eyes and talked with a lithp.

WILLY (*laughing*) You did? The kids like it?

BIFF They nearly died laughing!

WILLY Yeah? What'd you do?

BIFF The thquare root of thixthy twee is . . . (WILLY *bursts out laughing*; BIFF *joins him*) And in the middle of it he walked in!

WILLY *laughs and* THE WOMAN *joins in offstage.*

WILLY (*without hesitation*) Hurry downstairs and—

BIFF Somebody in there?

WILLY No, that was next door.

THE WOMAN *laughs offstage.*

BIFF Somebody got in your bathroom!

WILLY No, it's the next room, there's a party—

THE WOMAN (*enters, laughing. She lisps this*) Can I come in? There's something in the bathtub, Willy, and it's moving!

WILLY *looks at* BIFF, *who is staring open-mouthed and horrified at* THE WOMAN.

WILLY Ah—you better go back to your room. They must be finished painting by now. They're painting her room so I let her take a shower here. Go back, go back . . . (*He pushes her*)
THE WOMAN (*resisting*) But I've got to get dressed, Willy, I can't—
WILLY Get out of here! Go back, go back . . . (*Suddenly striving for the ordinary*) This is Miss Francis, Biff, she's a buyer. They're painting her room. Go back, Miss Francis, go back . . .
THE WOMAN But my clothes, I can't go out naked in the hall!
WILLY (*pushing her offstage*) Get outa here! Go back, go back!

BIFF *slowly sits down on his suitcase as the argument continues offstage.*

THE WOMAN Where's my stockings? You promised me stockings, Willy!
WILLY I have no stockings here!
THE WOMAN You had two boxes of size nine sheers for me, and I want them!
WILLY Here, for God's sake, will you get outa here!
THE WOMAN (*enters holding a box of stockings*) I just hope there's nobody in the hall. That's all I hope. (*To* BIFF) Are you football or baseball?
BIFF Football.
THE WOMAN (*angry, humiliated*) That's me too. G'night. (*She snatches her clothes from* WILLY, *and walks out*)
WILLY (*after a pause*) Well, better get going. I want to get to the school first thing in the morning. Get my suits out of the closet. I'll get my valise. (BIFF *doesn't move*) What's the matter? (BIFF *remains motionless, tears falling*) She's a buyer. Buys for J. H. Simmons. She lives down the hall—they're painting. You don't imagine— (*He breaks off. After a pause*) Now listen, pal, she's just a buyer. She sees merchandise in her room and they have to keep it looking just so . . . (*Pause. Assuming command*) All right, get my suits. (BIFF *doesn't move*) Now stop crying and do as I say. I gave you an order. Biff, I gave you an order! Is that what you do when I give you an order? How dare you cry! (*Putting his arm around* BIFF) Now look, Biff, when you grow up you'll understand about these things. You mustn't—you mustn't overemphasize a thing like this. I'll see Birnbaum first thing in the morning.
BIFF Never mind.
WILLY (*getting down beside* BIFF) Never mind! He's going to give you those points. I'll see to it.
BIFF He wouldn't listen to you.
WILLY He certainly will listen to me. You need those points for the U. of Virginia.
BIFF I'm not going there.
WILLY Yeh? If I can't get him to change that mark you'll make it up in summer school. You've got all summer to—
BIFF (*his weeping breaking from him*) Dad . . .
WILLY (*infected by it*) Oh, my boy . . .
BIFF Dad . . .
WILLY She's nothing to me, Biff. I was lonely, I was terribly lonely.
BIFF You—you gave her Mama's stockings! (*His tears break through and he rises to go*)

WILLY (*grabbing for* BIFF) I gave you an order!

BIFF Don't touch me, you—liar!

WILLY Apologize for that!

BIFF You fake! You phony little fake! You fake! (*Overcome, he turns quickly and weeping fully goes out with his suitcase.* WILLY *is left on the floor on his knees*)

WILLY I gave you an order! Biff, come back here or I'll beat you! Come back here! I'll whip you!

STANLEY *comes quickly in from the right and stands in front of* WILLY.

WILLY (*shouts at* STANLEY) I gave you an order . . .

STANLEY Hey, let's pick it up, pick it up, Mr. Loman. (*He helps* WILLY *to his feet*) Your boys left with the chippies. They said they'll see you home.

A *second waiter watches some distance away.*

WILLY But we were supposed to have dinner together.

Music is heard, WILLY's *theme.*

STANLEY Can you make it?

WILLY I'll—sure, I can make it. (*Suddenly concerned about his clothes*) Do I—I look all right?

STANLEY Sure, you look all right. (*He flicks a speck off* WILLY's *lapel*)

WILLY Here—here's a dollar.

STANLEY Oh, your son paid me. It's all right.

WILLY (*putting it in* STANLEY's *hand*) No, take it. You're a good boy.

STANLEY Oh, no, you don't have to . . .

WILLY Here—here's some more, I don't need it any more. (*After a slight pause*) Tell me—is there a seed store in the neighborhood?

STANLEY Seeds? You mean like to plant?

As WILLY *turns,* STANLEY *slips the money back into his jacket pocket.*

WILLY Yes. Carrots, peas . . .

STANLEY Well, there's hardware stores on Sixth Avenue, but it may be too late now.

WILLY (*anxiously*) Oh, I'd better hurry. I've got to get some seeds. (*He starts off to the right*) I've got to get some seeds, right away. Nothing's planted. I don't have a thing in the ground.

WILLY *hurries out as the light goes down.* STANLEY *moves over to the right after him, watches him off. The other waiter has been staring at* WILLY.

STANLEY (*to the waiter*) Well, whatta you looking at?

The waiter picks up the chairs and moves off right. STANLEY *takes the table and follows him. The light fades on this area. There is a long pause, the sound of the flute coming over. The light gradually rises on the kitchen, which is empty.* HAPPY *appears at the door of the house, followed by* BIFF. HAPPY *is carrying a large bunch of long-stemmed roses. He enters the kitchen, looks around for* LINDA. *Not seeing her, he turns to* BIFF, *who is just outside the house door, and makes a gesture with his hands, indicating "Not here, I guess." He looks into the living-room and freezes. Inside,* LINDA, *unseen, is seated,* WILLY's *coat on her lap. She rises ominously and quietly and moves toward* HAPPY, *who backs up into the kitchen, afraid.*

HAPPY Hey, what're you doing up? (LINDA *says nothing but moves toward him implacably*) Where's Pop? (*He keeps backing to the right, and now* LINDA *is in full view in the doorway to the living-room*) Is he sleeping?

LINDA Where were you?

HAPPY (*trying to laugh it off*) We met two girls, Mom, very fine types. Here, we brought you some flowers. (*Offering them to her*) Put them in your room, Ma.

She knocks them to the floor at BIFF's *feet. He has now come inside and closed the door behind him. She stares at* BIFF, *silent.*

HAPPY Now what'd you do that for? Mom, I want you to have some flowers—

LINDA (*cutting* HAPPY *off, violently to* BIFF) Don't you care whether he lives or dies?

HAPPY (*going to the stairs*) Come upstairs, Biff.

BIFF (*with a flare of disgust, to* HAPPY) Go away from me! (*To* LINDA) What do you mean, lives or dies? Nobody's dying around here, pal.

LINDA Get out of my sight! Get out of here!

BIFF I wanna see the boss.

LINDA You're not going near him!

BIFF Where is he? (*He moves into the living-room and* LINDA *follows*)

LINDA (*shouting after* BIFF) You intvie him for dinner. He looks forward to it all day— (BIFF *appears in his parents' bedroom, looks around, and exits*)—and then you desert him there. There's no stranger you'd do that to!

HAPPY Why? He had a swell time with us. Listen, when I— (LINDA *comes back into the kitchen*)—desert him I hope I don't outlive the day!

LINDA Get out of here!

HAPPY Now look, Mom . . .

LINDA Did you have to go to women tonight? You and your lousy rotten whores!

BIFF *re-enters the kitchen.*

HAPPY Mom, all we did was follow Biff around trying to cheer him up! (*To* BIFF) Boy, what a night you gave me!

LINDA Get out of here, both of you, and don't come back! I don't want you tormenting him any more. Go on now, get your things together! (*To* BIFF) You can sleep in his apartment. (*She starts to pick up the flowers and stops herself*) Pick up this stuff, I'm not your maid any more. Pick it up, you bum, you!

HAPPY *turns his back to her in refusal.* BIFF *slowly moves over and gets down on his knees, picking up the flowers.*

LINDA You're a pair of animals! Not one, not another living soul would have had the cruelty to walk out on that man in a restaurant!

BIFF (*not looking at her*) Is that what he said?

LINDA He didn't have to say anything. He was so humiliated he nearly limped when he came in.

HAPPY But, Mom, he had a great time with us—

BIFF (*cutting him off violently*) Shut up!

Without another word, HAPPY *goes upstairs.*

LINDA You! You didn't even go in to see if he was all right!

BIFF (*still on the floor in front of* LINDA, *the flowers in his hand; with self-loathing*) No. Didn't. Didn't do a damned thing. How do you like that, heh? Left him babbling in a toilet.

LINDA You louse. You . . .

BIFF Now you hit it on the nose! (*He gets up, throws the flowers in the wastebasket*) The scum of the earth, and you're looking at him!

LINDA Get out of here!

BIFF I gotta talk to the boss, Mom. Where is he?

LINDA You're not going near him. Get out of this house!

BIFF (*with absolute assurance, determination*) No. We're gonna have an abrupt conversation, him and me.

LINDA You're not talking to him!

Hammering is heard from outside the house, off right. BIFF *turns toward the noise.*

LINDA (*suddenly pleading*) Will you please leave him alone?

BIFF What's he doing out there?

LINDA He's planting the garden!

BIFF (*quietly*) Now? Oh, my God!

BIFF *moves outside,* LINDA *following. The light dies down on them and comes up on the center of the apron as* WILLY *walks into it. He is carrying a flashlight, a hoe, and a handful of seed packets. He raps the top of the hoe sharply to fix it firmly, and then moves to the left, measuring off the distance with his foot. He holds the flashlight to look at the seed packets, reading off the instructions. He is in the blue of night.*

WILLY Carrots . . . quarter-inch apart. Rows . . . one-foot rows. (*He measures it off*) One foot. (*He puts down a package and measures off*) Beets. (*He puts down another package and measures again*) Lettuce. (*He reads the package, puts it down*) One foot— (*He breaks off as* BEN *appears at the right and moves slowly down to him*) What a proposition, ts, ts. Terrific, terrific. 'Cause she's suffered, Ben, the woman has suffered. You understand me? A man can't go out the way he came in, Ben, a man has got to add up to something. You can't, you can't— (BEN *moves toward him as though to interrupt*) You gotta consider, now. Don't answer so quick. Remember, it's a guaranteed twenty-thousand-dollar proposition. Now look, Ben, I want you to go through the ins and outs of this thing with me. I've got nobody to talk to, Ben, and the woman has suffered, you hear me?

BEN (*standing still, considering*) What's the proposition?

WILLY It's twenty thousand dollars on the barrelhead. Guaranteed, gilt-edged, you understand?

BEN You don't want to make a fool of yourself. They might not honor the policy.

WILLY How can they dare refuse? Didn't I work like a coolie to meet every premium on the nose? And now they don't pay off? Impossible!

BEN It's called a cowardly thing, William.

WILLY Why? Does it take more guts to stand here the rest of my life ringing up a zero?

BEN (*yielding*) That's a point, William. (*He moves, thinking, turns*) And twenty thousand—that *is* something one can feel with the hand, it is there.

WILLY (*now assured, with rising power*) Oh, Ben, that's the whole beauty of it! I see it like a diamond, shining in the dark, hard and rough, that I can pick up and touch in my hand. Not like—like an appointment! This would not be another damned-fool appointment, Ben, and it changes all the aspects. Because he thinks I'm nothing, see, and so he spites me. But the funeral— (*Straightening up*) Ben, that funeral will be massive! They'll come from Maine, Massachusetts, Vermont, New Hampshire! All the old-timers with the strange license plates—that boy will be thunderstruck, Ben, because he never realized—I am known! Rhode Island, New York, New Jersey—I am known, Ben, and he'll see it with his eyes once and for all. He'll see what I am, Ben! He's in for a shock, that boy!

BEN (*coming down to the edge of the garden*) He'll call you a coward.

WILLY (*suddenly fearful*) No, that would be terrible.

BEN Yes. And a damned fool.

WILLY No, no, he mustn't, I won't have that! (*He is broken and desperate*)

BEN He'll hate you, William.

The gay music of the boys is heard.

WILLY Oh, Ben, how do we get back to all the great times? Used to be so full of light, and comradeship, the sleigh-riding in winter, and the ruddiness on his cheeks. And always some kind of good news coming up, always something nice coming up ahead. And never even let me carry the valises in the house, and simonizing, simonizing that little red car! Why, why can't I give him something and not have him hate me?

BEN Let me think about it. (*He glances at his watch*) I still have a little time. Remarkable proposition, but you've got to be sure you're not making a fool of yourself.

BEN *drifts off upstage and goes out of sight.* BIFF *comes down from the left.*

WILLY (*suddenly conscious of* BIFF, *turns and looks up at him, then begins picking up the packages of seeds in confusion*) Where the hell is that seed? (*Indignantly*) You can't see nothing out here! They boxed in the whole goddam neighborhood!

BIFF There are people all around here. Don't you realize that?

WILLY I'm busy. Don't bother me.

BIFF (*taking the hoe from* WILLY) I'm saying good-by to you, Pop. (WILLY *looks at him, silent, unable to move*) I'm not coming back any more.

WILLY You're not going to see Oliver tomorrow?

BIFF I've got no appointment, Dad.

WILLY He put his arm around you, and you've got no appointment?

BIFF Pop, get this now, will you? Everytime I've left it's been a fight that sent me out of here. Today I realized something about myself and I tried to explain it to you and I—I think I'm just not smart enough to make any sense out of it for you. To hell with whose fault it is or anything like that. (*He takes* WILLY's *arm*) Let's just wrap it up, heh? Come on in, we'll tell Mom. (*He gently tries to pull* WILLY *to left*)

WILLY (*frozen, immobile, with guilt in his voice*) No, I don't want to see her.

BIFF Come on! (*He pulls again, and* WILLY *tries to pull away*)

WILLY (*highly nervous*) No, no, I don't want to see her.

BIFF (*tries to look into* WILLY's *face, as if to find the answer there*) Why don't you want to see her?

WILLY (*more harshly now*) Don't bother me, will you?

BIFF What do you mean, you don't want to see her? You don't want them calling you yellow, do you? This isn't your fault; it's me, I'm a bum. Now come inside! (WILLY *strains to get away*) Did you hear what I said to you?

WILLY *pulls away and quickly goes by himself into the house.* BIFF *follows.*

LINDA (*to* WILLY) Did you plant, dear?

BIFF (*at the door, to* LINDA) All right, we had it out. I'm going and I'm not writing any more.

LINDA (*going to* WILLY *in the kitchen*) I think that's the best way, dear. 'Cause there's no use drawing it out, you'll just never get along.

WILLY *doesn't respond.*

BIFF People ask where I am and what I'm doing, you don't know, and you don't care. That way it'll be off your mind and you can start brightening up again. All right? That clears it, doesn't it? (WILLY *is silent, and* BIFF *goes to him*) You gonna wish me luck, scout? (*He extends his hand*) What do you say?

LINDA Shake his hand, Willy.

WILLY (*turning to her, seething with hurt*) There's no necessity to mention the pen at all, y'know.

BIFF (*gently*) I've got no appointment, Dad.

WILLY (*erupting fiercely*) He put his arm around . . . ?

BIFF Dad, you're never going to see what I am, so what's the use of arguing? If I strike oil I'll send you a check. Meantime forget I'm alive.

WILLY (*to* LINDA) Spite, see?

BIFF Shake hands, Dad.

WILLY Not my hand.

BIFF I was hoping not to go this way.

WILLY Well, this is the way you're going. Good-by.

BIFF *looks at him a moment, then turns sharply and goes to the stairs.*

WILLY (*stops him with*) May you rot in hell if you leave this house!

BIFF (*turning*) Exactly what is it that you want from me?

WILLY I want you to know, on the train, in the mountains, in the valleys, wherever you go, that you cut down your life for spite!

BIFF No, no.

WILLY Spite, spite, is the word of your undoing! And when you're down and out, remember what did it. When you're rotting somewhere beside the railroad tracks, remember, and don't you dare blame it on me!

BIFF I'm not blaming it on you!

WILLY I won't take the rap for this, you hear?

HAPPY *comes down the stairs and stands on the bottom step, watching.*

BIFF That's just what I'm telling you!

WILLY (*sinking into a chair at the table, with full accusation*) You're trying to put a knife in me—don't think I don't know what you're doing!

BIFF All right, phony! Then let's lay it on the line. (*He whips the rubber tube out of his pocket and puts it on the table*)

HAPPY You crazy—

LINDA Biff! (*She moves to grab the hose, but* BIFF *holds it down with his hand*)

BIFF Leave it there! Don't move it!

WILLY (*not looking at it*) What is that?

BIFF You know goddam well what that is.

WILLY (*caged, wanting to escape*) I never saw that.

BIFF You saw it. The mice didn't bring it into the cellar! What is this supposed to do, make a hero out of you? This supposed to make me sorry for you?

WILLY Never heard of it.

BIFF There'll be no pity for you, you hear it? No pity!

WILLY (*to* LINDA) You hear the spite!

BIFF No, you're going to hear the truth—what you are and what I am!

LINDA Stop it!

WILLY Spite!

HAPPY (*coming down toward* BIFF) You cut it now!

BIFF (*to* HAPPY) The man don't know who we are! The man is gonna know! (*To* WILLY) We never told the truth for ten minutes in this house!

HAPPY We always told the truth!

BIFF (*turning on him*) You big blow, are you the assistant buyer? You're one of the two assistants to the assistant, aren't you?

HAPPY Well, I'm practically—

BIFF You're practically full of it! We all are! And I'm through with it. (*To* WILLY) Now hear this, Willy, this is me.

WILLY I know you!

BIFF You know why I had no address for three months? I stole a suit in Kansas City and I was in jail. (*To* LINDA, *who is sobbing*) Stop crying. I'm through with it.

LINDA *turns away from them, her hands covering her face.*

WILLY I suppose that's my fault.

BIFF I stole myself out of every good job since high school!

WILLY And whose fault is that?

BIFF And I never got anywhere because you blew me so full of hot air I could never stand taking orders from anybody! That's whose fault it is!

WILLY I hear that!

LINDA Don't, Biff!

BIFF It's goddam time you heard that! I had to be boss big shot in two weeks, and I'm through with it!

WILLY Then hang yourself! For spite, hang yourself!

BIFF No! Nobody's hanging himself, Willy! I ran down eleven flights with a pen in my hand today. And suddenly I stopped, you hear me? And in the middle of that office building, do you hear this? I stopped in the middle of that building and I saw—the sky. I saw the things that I love in this world. The work and the food and time to sit and smoke. And I looked at the pen and said to myself, what the hell am I grabbing this for? Why am I trying to become what I don't want to be? What am I doing in an office, making a contemptuous, begging fool of myself, when all I want is out there, waiting for me the minute I say I know who I am! Why can't I say that, Willy? (*He tries to make* WILLY *face him, but* WILLY *pulls away and moves to the left*)

WILLY (*with hatred, threateningly*) The door of your life is wide open!

BIFF Pop! I'm a dime a dozen, and so are you!

WILLY (*turning on him now in an uncontrolled outburst*) I am not a dime a dozen! I am Willy Loman, and you are Biff Loman!

BIFF *starts for* WILLY, *but is blocked by* HAPPY. *In his fury,* BIFF *seems on the verge of attacking his father.*

BIFF I am not a leader of men, Willy, and neither are you. You were never anything but a hard-working drummer who landed in the ash can like all the rest of them! I'm one dollar an hour, Willy! I tried seven states and couldn't raise it. A buck an hour! Do you gather my meaning? I'm not bringing home any prizes any more, and you're going to stop waiting for me to bring them home!

WILLY (*directly to* BIFF) You vengeful, spiteful mut!

BIFF *breaks from* HAPPY. WILLY, *in fright, starts up the stairs.* BIFF *grabs him.*

BIFF (*at the peak of his fury*) Pop, I'm nothing! I'm nothing, Pop. Can't you understand that? There's no spite in it any more. I'm just what I am, that's all.

BIFF's *fury has spent itself, and he breaks down, sobbing, holding on to* WILLY, *who dumbly fumbles for* BIFF's *face.*

WILLY (*astonished*) What're you doing? What're you doing? (*To* LINDA) Why is he crying?

BIFF (*crying, broken*) Will you let me go, for Christ's sake? Will you take that phony dream and burn it before something happens? (*Struggling to contain himself, he pulls away and moves to the stairs*) I'll go in the morning. Put him—put him to bed. (*Exhausted,* BIFF *moves up the stairs to his room*)

WILLY (*after a long pause, astonished, elevated*) Isn't that—isn't that remarkable? Biff—he likes me!

LINDA He loves you, Willy!

HAPPY (*deeply moved*) Always did, Pop.

WILLY Oh, Biff! (*Staring wildly*) He cried! Cried to me. (*He is choking with his love, and now cries out his promise*) That boy—that boy is going to be magnificent!

BEN *appears in the light just outside the kitchen.*

BEN Yes, outstanding, with twenty thousand behind him.

LINDA (*sensing the racing of his mind, fearfully, carefully*) Now come to bed, Willy. It's all settled now.

WILLY (*finding it difficult not to rush out of the house*) Yes, we'll sleep. Come on. Go to sleep, Hap.

BEN And it does take a great kind of a man to crack the jungle.

In accents of dread, BEN's *idyllic music starts up.*

HAPPY (*his arm around* LINDA) I'm getting married, Pop, don't forget it. I'm changing everything. I'm gonna run that department before the year is up. You'll see, Mom. (*He kisses her*)

BEN The jungle is dark but full of diamonds, Willy.

WILLY *turns, moves, listening to* BEN.

LINDA Be good. You're both good boys, just act that way, that's all.

HAPPY 'Night, Pop. (*He goes upstairs*)

LINDA (*to* WILLY) Come, dear.

BEN (*with greater force*) One must go in to fetch a diamond out.

WILLY (*to* LINDA, *as he moves slowly along the edge of the kitchen, toward the door*) I just want to get settled down, Linda. Let me sit alone for a little.

LINDA (*almost uttering her fear*) I want you upstairs.

WILLY (*taking her in his arms*) In a few minutes, Linda. I couldn't sleep right now. Go on, you look awful tired. (*He kisses her*)

BEN Not like an appointment at all. A diamond is rough and hard to the touch.

WILLY Go on now. I'll be right up.

LINDA I think this is the only way, Willy.

WILLY Sure, it's the best thing.

BEN Best thing!

WILLY The only way. Everything is gonna be—go on, kid, get to bed. You look so tired.

LINDA Come right up.

WILLY Two minutes.

LINDA *goes into the living-room, then reappears in her bedroom.* WILLY *moves just outside the kitchen door.*

WILLY Loves me. (*Wonderingly*) Always loved me. Isn't that a remarkable thing? Ben, he'll worship me for it!

BEN (*with promise*) It's dark there, but full of diamonds.

WILLY Can you imagine that magnificence with twenty thousand dollars in his pocket?

LINDA (*calling from her room*) Willy! Come up!

WILLY (*calling into the kitchen*) Yes! Yes. Coming! It's very smart, you realize that, don't you, sweetheart? Even Ben sees it. I gotta go, baby. 'By! 'By! (*Going over to* BEN, *almost dancing*) Imagine? When the mail comes he'll be ahead of Bernard again!

BEN A perfect proposition all around.

WILLY Did you see how he cried to me? Oh, if I could kiss him, Ben!

BEN Time, William, time!

WILLY Oh, Ben, I always knew one way or another we were gonna make it, Biff and I!

BEN (*looking at his watch*) The boat. We'll be late. (*He moves slowly off into the darkness*)

WILLY (*elegiacally, turning to the house*) Now when you kick off, boy, I want a seventy-yard boot, and get right down the field under the ball, and when you hit, hit low and hit hard, because it's important, boy. (*He swings around and faces the audience*) There's all kinds of important people in the stands, and the first thing you know . . . (*Suddenly realizing he is alone*) Ben! Ben, where do I . . . ? (*He makes a sudden movement of search*) Ben, how do I . . . ?

LINDA (*calling*) Willy, you coming up?

WILLY (*uttering a gasp of fear, whirling about as if to quiet her*) Sh! (*He turns around as if to find his way; sounds, faces, voices, seem to be swarming in upon him and he flicks at them, crying*) Sh! Sh! (*Suddenly music, faint and high, stops him. It rises in intensity, almost to an unbearable scream. He goes up and down on his toes, and rushes off around the house*) Shhh!

LINDA Willy?

There is no answer. LINDA *waits.* BIFF *gets up off his bed. He is still in his clothes.* HAPPY *sits up.* BIFF *stands listening.*

LINDA (*with real fear*) Willy, answer me! Willy!

There is the sound of a car starting and moving away at full speed.

LINDA No!

BIFF (*rushing down the stairs*) Pop!

As the car speeds off, the music crashes down in a frenzy of sound, which becomes the soft pulsation of a single cello string. BIFF slowly returns to his bedroom. He and HAPPY gravely don their jackets. LINDA slowly walks out of her room. The music has developed into a dead march. The leaves of day are appearing over everything. CHARLEY and BERNARD, somberly dressed, appear and knock on the kitchen door. BIFF and HAPPY slowly descend the stairs to the kitchen as CHARLEY and BERNARD enter. All stop a moment when LINDA, in clothes of mourning, bearing a little bunch of roses, comes through the draped doorway into the kitchen. She goes to CHARLEY and takes his arm. Now all move toward the audience, through the wall-line of the kitchen. At the limit of the apron, LINDA lays down the flowers, kneels, and sits back on her heels. All stare down at the grave.

REQUIEM

CHARLEY It's getting dark, Linda.

LINDA *doesn't react. She stares at the grave.*

BIFF How about it, Mom? Better get some rest, heh? They'll be closing the gate soon.

LINDA *makes no move. Pause.*

HAPPY (*deeply angered*) He had no right to do that. There was no necessity for it. We would've helped him.

CHARLEY (*grunting*) Hmmm.

BIFF Come along, Mom.

LINDA Why didn't anybody come?

CHARLEY It was a very nice funeral.

LINDA But where are all the people he knew? Maybe they blame him.

CHARLEY Naa. It's a rough world, Linda. They wouldn't blame him.

LINDA I can't understand it. At this time especially. First time in thirty-five years we were just about free and clear. He only needed a little salary. He was even finished with the dentist.

CHARLEY No man only needs a little salary.

LINDA I can't understand it.

BIFF There were a lot of nice days. When he'd come home from a trip; or on Sundays, making the stoop; finishing the cellar; putting on the new porch; when he built the extra bathroom; and put up the garage. You know something, Charley, there's more of him in that front stoop than in all the sales he ever made.

CHARLEY Yeah. He was a happy man with a batch of cement.

LINDA He was so wonderful with his hands.

BIFF He had the wrong dreams. All, all, wrong.

HAPPY (*almost ready to fight BIFF*) Don't say that!

BIFF He never knew who he was.

CHARLEY (*stopping HAPPY's movement and reply. To BIFF*) Nobody dast blame this man. You don't understand: Willy was a salesman. And for a salesman, there is no rock bottom to the life. He don't put a bolt to a nut, he don't tell you the law or give you medicine. He's a man way out there in the blue, riding on a smile and a shoeshine. And when they start not smiling back—that's an earthquake. And then you get yourself a couple of spots on your hat, and you're finished. Nobody dast blame this man. A salesman is got to dream, boy. It comes with the territory.

BIFF Charley, the man didn't know who he was.

HAPPY (*infuriated*) Don't say that!

BIFF Why don't you come with me, Happy?

HAPPY I'm not licked that easily. I'm staying right in this city, and I'm gonna beat this racket! (*He looks at* BIFF, *his chin set*) The Loman Brothers!

BIFF I know who I am, kid.

HAPPY All right, boy. I'm gonna show you and everybody else that Willy Loman did not die in vain. He had a good dream. It's the only dream you can have—to come out number-one man. He fought it out here, and this is where I'm gonna win it for him.

BIFF (*with a hopeless glance at* HAPPY, *bends toward his mother*) Let's go, Mom.

LINDA I'll be with you in a minute. Go on, Charley. (*He hesitates*) I want to, just for a minute. I never had a chance to say good-by.

CHARLEY *moves away, followed by* HAPPY. BIFF *remains a slight distance up and left of* LINDA. *She sits there, summoning herself. The flute begins, not far away, playing behind her speech.*

LINDA Forgive me, dear. I can't cry. I don't know what it is, but I can't cry. I don't understand it. Why did you ever do that? Help me, Willy, I can't cry. It seems to me that you're just on another trip. I keep expecting you. Willy, dear, I can't cry. Why did you do it? I search and search and I search, and I can't understand it, Willy. I made the last payment on the house today. Today, dear. And there'll be nobody home. (*A sob rises in her throat*) We're free and clear. (*Sobbing more fully, released*) We're free. (BIFF *comes slowly toward her*) We're free . . . We're free . . .

BIFF *lifts her to her feet and moves out up right with her in his arms.* LINDA *sobs quietly.* BERNARD *and* CHARLEY *come together and follow them, followed by* HAPPY. *Only the music of the flute is left on the darkening stage as over the house the hard towers of the apartment buildings rise into sharp focus, and*

The Curtain Falls

Questions

1. Part of the suspense of *Death of a Salesman* comes from the threat of Willy's suicide. But is this central to the dramatic situation? Is suicide Willy's main objective?
2. Describe Willy's objective with regard to his job. What is standing in his way?
3. Is Howard a villain? Does he seem real to you?
4. What is Willy's objective with regard to his sons?
5. What qualities of character does Willy most value and encourage in Biff and Happy? Are these virtues? To what extent is Willy responsible for Biff's failure?
6. On page 1047, Willy says to his sons, "Someday I'll have my own business and I'll never have to leave home any more." Does he ever do this? Find other examples of Willy's actions contradicting his words.
7. Why does Willy accept loans from Charley, but refuse the job he offers? Do you like Charley? Do you think Willy appreciates him?
8. Biff's confession in the restaurant that he is a thief and a failure brings on Willy's memory of a terrible scene of recognition in the past. Tell how the scene in the

restaurant is the climax of the present action, and how the scene in the hotel is the climax of action in the past. Describe these scenes as reversals for Willy and Biff.

9. Think of Linda Loman as heroine of *Death of a Salesman*. What are her virtues? What is her tragic flaw?

10. Do you fear for Willy when he is in the garden? Why? At what point do you most pity him?

11. Charlie says, on page 1079, "The only thing you got in this world is what you can sell. And the funny thing is that you're a salesman, and you don't know that." Biff says in the Requiem: "the man didn't know who he was." Do you agree with these comments on Willy's character? How do they point to his tragic flaw?

Suggestions for Dramatists

1. Try to think of a figure in American history who has sufficient stature to be considered a tragic hero, as the hero is described on p. 1034.

2. Plot that hero's rise and fall, using Freytag's pyramid of action.

6  Comedy

Veterans of the stage often remark that audiences come to the theater to laugh, cry, or be frightened out of their wits. Notice that they mention laughter first. For every successful tragedy, there are ten comedies that usually have longer commercial runs and play to larger audiences. Tragedy produces *catharsis*, the relief of tension that comes when we have witnessed what we most dreaded. Comedy provides a purer delight—laughter in the face of danger, and serenity as we find that everything we hoped for comes true. The villain gets trapped and punished. The boy gets the girl, gold is found in a flowerpot, and everyone lives happily ever after.

But comedy is much more than an entertainment that makes us laugh, much more than an exciting story with a happy ending. Comedy originates from a source as deep and complex as the origin of tragedy. The novelist Thackeray said that "humor is the mistress of tears," and indeed great comedies often make us laugh at human situations that, if they happened to us, we would consider very serious. The subjects of comedy are frequently tragic, as you will soon discover in reading *The Misanthrope*, which relates the misadventures of an honest man in a corrupt society. The genius of the comic dramatist encourages us to view difficulties of life with a sense of humor.

Let us consider the difference between the tragic vision and the comic. Tragedy, with its noble heroes, concerns us with the moral government of the universe, and all that is godlike in our efforts to live in it. Comedy, with its clowns and lovesick youths, has always mocked at any attempt of humans to behave like gods. You may have seen Charlie Chaplin aping the imperious scowls of Hitler, or Groucho Marx in a professor's robes and mortarboard doing a jig at a mock commencement. Comedy looks at the individual from the outside, viewing the folly, injustice, and misery of humans with critical detachment. From a distance the worst troubles and heartaches seem smaller, lighter. We are relieved that they are not ours. As the American cowboy humorist Will Rogers once said: "Everything is funny as long as it is happening to someone else."

The historical origins of comedy are dim. The word *comedy* comes from the Greek *Komos*, meaning "revel," and we believe that comic drama began with the festivities to celebrate spring and Dionysus, the god of fertility and wine. Mating rituals and drunkenness have always been rich sources of humor. In the ancient satyr plays of Euripides and others, the chorus consists of goatlike, horsetailed satyrs who leap and cavort drunkenly on the stage. Such plays provided comic relief after a series of tragedies at the festival of Dionysus. Later the satyr plays developed into the sophisticated Old Comedy, as practiced by Aristophanes.

High and Low Comedy

When the cook puts a foot in the soap-bucket and then slides into the ashbin, that is low comedy. It appeals to our lowest sense of humor, the impulse to laugh when someone else suffers a temporary physical discomfort or indignity.

High comedy appeals to the intellect. When Algernon in *The Importance of Being Earnest* gains entrance to his friend Jack's house under the guise of being Jack's imaginary brother, Ernest, that is high comedy. When Alceste, the hero of *The Misanthrope*, is summoned to court for having criticized the sonnet of a rival suitor, that is high comedy. There is high comedy in mistaken identity, in excessive or mechanical behavior, and in frustrated expectations. High comedy onstage often relies heavily on displays of verbal wit. Molière's verbal humor shines throughout *The Misanthrope*. Alceste's attack on Oronte's sonnet provokes the following dialogue:

Oronte. And I maintain my sonnet's very good.
Alceste. It's not at all surprising that you should.
   You have your reasons; permit me to have mine
   For thinking that you cannot write a line.
Oronte. Others have praised my sonnet to the skies.
Alceste. I lack their art of telling pleasant lies.
Oronte. You seem to think you've got no end of wit.
Alceste. To praise your verse, I'd need still more of it.

High and *low* comedy, as the words suggest, are relative terms; most comic plays are a blend of both. Although *The Importance of Being Earnest* turns upon the high comic predicament of mistaken identity, there are elements of low humor in the circumstances: the central character John Worthing was orphaned at birth, having been mistaken for a three-volume novel and left in a hand-bag in Victoria Station.

Farce is the genre of dramatic comedy that relies most heavily upon clowning, slapstick, and low humor. Originating in medieval France, the farce reached its full expressions in the romantic plays of Georges Feydeau (1862–1921). The characters of farce are less realistic and complex than those of high comedy, and the situations are less probable. In these particulars the farce resembles Italian commedia dell'arte, with its stock characters Lucinda (the beautiful young lady), Scaramuccia (the braggart captain), and Pantalone (the rich, foolish father), and its fantastic turns of plot.

High comedy reaches its zenith in the English *comedy of manners*, a form developed during the Restoration, after 1660, when Charles II opened the theaters that the Puritan Cromwell had closed. The subtle wit and ingenious dramatic situations of these comedies deflate the pretensions of the most civilized behavior. Many critics consider the comic playwright William Congreve (1670–1729) to be the greatest dramatist of the Restoration period. He wrote *The Way of the World, Love for Love* and other great comedies of manners. Richard Brinsley Sheridan (1751–1816), who wrote *The School for Scandal,* and Oscar Wilde (1854–1900), who wrote *The Importance of Being Earnest,* have made enduring contributions to the form.

Satire

One of the most important social functions of comedy is *satire*. Satire is the ridiculing of any human vice or folly. But it is particularly useful in ridiculing people and institutions whose esteem exceeds their true value. Satire deflates the overblown and pompous, cuts them down to size. The oldest comedies extant, called the Greek Old Comedy, attacked the political and cultural institutions of Athens with a savage wit. These comedies of Aristophanes (477–380 B.C.) were performed in the same Theater of Dionysus as the tragedies of Sophocles. In his hilarious *Lysistrata* (411 B.C.) Aristophanes portrays a group of Greek wives who sexually blackmail their warrior husbands into declaring peace. The play is a relentless satire of the Peloponnesian War, the Athenian magistrate, and the whole masculine political establishment. In one of the scenes Lysistrata and her disciples transform the obnoxious magistrate into a woman. Comedy can be subtle or gentle when it deals with humble or romantic subjects. But satire, when it chooses vicious and powerful subjects, can be brutally cruel.

Most comedies depend upon a certain element of satire. Satire requires an object of attack, and we can always depend upon the villain to display some mean quality worthy of ridicule, even in romantic comedies, where the heroes are admirable. In some comedies such as Molière's *the Misanthrope, The Miser,* and *Tartuffe,* the protagonist becomes the main object of ridicule. Many critics prefer to call these dramas satires or tragicomedies, reserving the term comedy for romantic plays with virtuous heroes.

Romantic Comedy

The fantastical satires of the Greek Old Comedy gave way to the New Comedy in the third century B.C. The New Comedy, as practiced by Menander (342–292 B.C.), portrays ordinary domestic situations and contemporary manners and usually involves a love affair which begins in trouble and ends in happiness. Menander's romantic plays served as models for the Roman playwrights Plautus (254–184 B.C.) and Terence (185–159 B.C.), who wrote romantic comedies that were both amusing and moral. In a typical plot the young gentleman falls in love with the servant girl. He schemes to buy her, but in the course of the play discovers she is the lost child of noble parents. Through all her trials she has preserved her chastity, in keeping with traditional morals, so they can be married. Many of the stock characters of Roman comedy entered into the Renaissance Italian commedia dell'arte and into Elizabethan and classical French comedy. The plots from Shakespeare's *Comedy of Errors* as well as Molière's *The Miser* come from Plautus, who probably got them from Menander.

Romantic comedies culminate in marriage as surely as tragedies end in isolation and death for their protagonists. Since Menander, the lovers in classical comedy have struggled to be together in the face of societies that frown upon their love. Again and again the lovers overcome the objections of society, either by altering it or by changing themselves, and achieve an integration—of themselves into society, and of the conflicting social forces that kept the lovers apart. The success of the lovers in romantic comedy is an affirmation of life. Comedy, which had its origins in a fertility ritual, celebrates humanity and the future through love and marriage.

The Importance of Being Earnest

Oscar Wilde's *The Importance of Being Earnest* is a delightful blend of romantic comedy and social satire. In the ancient tradition of romantic comedy, two pairs of lovers struggle to overcome conventions that threaten their happiness. But, in the zany society of Wilde's theater, those conventions—parental consent and legitimate courtship—are rendered utterly ridiculous. Lady Bracknell, who alone can give consent to the marriage between her daughter Gwendolen and Jack Worthy, interviews the prospective bridegroom as follows:

> LADY BRACKNELL I have always been of the opinion that a man who desires to get married should know either everything or nothing. Which do you know?
> JACK (*after some hesitation*) I know nothing, Lady Bracknell.
> LADY BRACKNELL I am pleased to hear it. I do not approve of anything that tampers with natural ignorance. Ignorance is like a delicate exotic fruit; touch it and the bloom is gone.

With such epigrammatic humor Wilde reduces the conventions of courtship to absurdity. And the lovers themselves are in a predicament worthy of a farce. Each heroine has fallen in love with a man she believes to be named Ernest, and both profess as much love for the name as for the man. The discovery that neither man is named Ernest presents a major obstacle to the two marriages.

Oscar Wilde was the most extravagantly gifted all-around man of letters of the late nineteenth century, one of the few writers ever to have created masterpieces in the novel, drama, and verse. Born in Ireland in 1854, Wilde studied at Oxford, where he came under the influence of the critic Walter Pater. Wilde

led an aesthetic movement that advocated "Art for Art's sake," the doctrine that the aim of art should be the perfection of expression rather than any moral or political effect. *The Importance of Being Earnest* (1895) is his greatest work for the stage. He is also known for his short novel *The Picture of Dorian Gray* (1891) and *The Ballad of Reading Gaol,* a poem.

OSCAR WILDE (1854–1900)

The Importance of Being Earnest

CHARACTERS

JOHN WORTHING, J.P.
ALGERNON MONCRIEFF
REV. CANON CHASUBLE, D.D.
MERRIMAN, *butler*
LANE, *manservant*

LADY BRACKNELL
HON. GWENDOLEN FAIRFAX
CECILY CARDEW
MISS PRISM, *governess*

THE SCENES OF THE PLAY

ACT I. *Algernon Moncrieff's Flat in Half-Moon Street, W.*
ACT II. *The Garden at the Manor House, Woolton.*
ACT III. *Drawing-Room of the Manor House, Woolton.*

TIME—*The Present.*
PLACE—*London.*

SCENE. *Morning-room in* ALGERNON'S *flat in Half-Moon Street. The room is luxuriously and artistically furnished. The sound of a piano is heard in the adjoining room.*

(LANE *is arranging afternoon tea on the table, and after the music has ceased,* ALGERNON *enters.*)

ALGERNON. Did you hear what I was playing, Lane?

LANE. I didn't think it polite to listen, sir.

ALGERNON. I'm sorry for that, for your sake. I don't play accurately—any one can play accurately—but I play with wonderful expression. As far as the piano is concerned, sentiment is my forte. I keep science for Life.

LANE. Yes, sir.

ALGERNON. And, speaking of the science of Life, have you got the cucumber sandwiches cut for Lady Bracknell?

LANE. Yes, sir. (*Hands them on a salver.*)

ALGERNON (*inspects them, takes two, and sits down on the sofa*) Oh! . . . by the way, Lane, I see from your book that on Thursday night, when Lord Shoreman and Mr. Worthing were dining with me, eight bottles of champagne are entered as having been consumed.

LANE Yes, sir; eight bottles and a pint.

ALGERNON Why is it that at a bachelor's establishment the servants invariably drink the champagne? I ask merely for information.

LANE I attribute it to the superior quality of the wine, sir. I have often observed that in married households the champagne is rarely of a first-rate brand.

ALGERNON Good Heavens! Is marriage so demoralizing as that?

LANE I believe it *is* a very pleasant state, sir. I have had very little experience of it myself up to the present. I have only been married once. That was in consequence of a misunderstanding between myself and a young woman.

ALGERNON (*languidly*) I don't know that I am much interested in your family life, Lane.

LANE No, sir; it is not a very interesting subject. I never think of it myself.

ALGERNON Very natural, I am sure. That will do, Lane, thank you.

LANE Thank you, sir.(LANE *goes out.*)

ALGERNON Lane's views on marriage seem somewhat lax. Really, if the lower orders don't set us a good example, what on earth is the use of them? They seem, as a class, to have absolutely no sense of moral responsibility.

Enter LANE.

LANE Mr. Ernest Worthing.

Enter JACK. LANE *goes out.*

ALGERNON How are you, my dear Ernest? What brings you up to town?

JACK Oh, pleasure, pleasure! What else should bring one anywhere? Eating as usual, I see, Algy!

ALGERNON (*stiffly*) I believe it is customary in good society to take some slight refreshment at five o'clock. Where have you been since last Thursday?

JACK (*sitting down on the sofa*) In the country.

ALGERNON What on earth do you do there?

JACK (*pulling off his gloves*) When one is in town one amuses oneself. When one is in the country one amuses other people. It is excessively boring.

ALGERNON And who are the people you amuse?

JACK (*airily*) Oh, neighbors, neighbors.

ALGERNON Got nice neighbors in your part of Shropshire?

JACK Perfectly horrid! Never speak to one of them.

ALGERNON How immensely you must amuse them! (*Goes over and takes sandwich.*) By the way, Shropshire is your county, is it not?

JACK Eh? Shropshire? Yes, of course. Hallo! Why all these cups? Why cucumber sandwiches? Why such reckless extravagance in one so young? Who is coming to tea?

ALGERNON Oh! merely Aunt Augusta and Gwendolen.

JACK How perfectly delightful!

ALGERNON Yes, that is all very well; but I am afraid Aunt Augusta won't quite approve of your being here.

JACK May I ask why?

ALGERNON My dear fellow, the way you flirt with Gwendolen is perfectly disgraceful. It is almost as bad as the way Gwendolen flirts with you.

JACK I am in love with Gwendolen. I have come up to town expressly to propose to her.

ALGERNON I thought you had come up for pleasure? . . . I call that business.

JACK How utterly unromantic you are!

ALGERNON I really don't see anything romantic in proposing. It is very romantic to be in love. But there is nothing romantic about a definite proposal. Why, one may be accepted. One usually is, I believe. Then the excitement is all over. The very essence of romance is uncertainty. If ever I get married, I'll certainly try to forget the fact.

JACK I have no doubt about that, dear Algy. The Divorce Court was specially invented for people whose memories are so curiously constituted.

ALGERNON Oh! there is no use speculating on that subject. Divorces are made in Heaven—(JACK *puts out his hand to take a sandwich.* ALGERNON *at once interferes.*) Please don't touch the cucumber sandwiches. They are ordered specially for Aunt Augusta. (*Takes one and eats it.*)

JACK Well, you have been eating them all the time.

ALGERNON That is quite a different matter. She is my aunt. (*Takes plate from below.*) Have some bread and butter. The bread and butter is for Gwendolen. Gwendolen is devoted to bread and butter.

JACK (*advancing to table and helping himself*) And very good bread and butter it is, too.

ALGERNON Well, my dear fellow, you need not eat as if you were going to eat it all. You behave as if you were married to her already. You are not married to her already, and I don't think you ever will be.

JACK Why on earth do you say that?

ALGERNON Well, in the first place girls never marry the men they flirt with. Girls don't think it right.

JACK Oh, that is nonsense!

ALGERNON It isn't. It is a great truth. It accounts for the extraordinary number of bachelors that one sees all over the place. In the second place, I don't give my consent.

JACK Your consent!

ALGERNON My dear fellow, Gwendolen is my first cousin. And before I allow you to marry her, you will have to clear up the whole question of Cecily. (*Rings bell.*)

JACK Cecily! What on earth do you mean? What do you mean, Algy, by Cecily? I don't know any one of the name of Cecily.

Enter LANE.

ALGERNON Bring me that cigarette case Mr. Worthing left in the smoking-room the last time he dined here.

LANE Yes, sir. (LANE *goes out.*)

JACK Do you mean to say you have had my cigarette case all this time? I wish to goodness you had let me know. I have been writing frantic letters to Scotland Yard about it. I was very nearly offering a large reward.

ALGERNON Well, I wish you would offer one. I happen to be more than usually hard up.

JACK There is no good offering a large reward now that the thing is found.

Enter LANE *with the cigarette case on a salver.* ALGERNON *takes it at once.* LANE *goes out.*

ALGERNON I think that is rather mean of you, Ernest, I must say. (*Opens case and examines it.*) However, it makes no matter, for, now that I look at the inscription, I find that the thing isn't yours after all.

JACK Of course it's mine. (*Moving to him.*) You have seen me with it a hundred times, and you have no right whatsoever to read what is written inside. It is a very ungentlemanly thing to read a private cigarette case.

ALGERNON Oh! it is absurd to have a hard-and-fast rule about what one should read and what one shouldn't. More than half of modern culture depends on what one shouldn't read.

JACK I am quite aware of the fact, and I don't propose to discuss modern culture. It isn't the sort of thing one should talk of in private. I simply want my cigarette case back.

ALGERNON Yes; but this isn't your cigarette case. This cigarette case is a present from some one of the name of Cecily, and you said you didn't know any one of that name.

JACK Well, if you want to know, Cecily happens to be my aunt.

ALGERNON Your aunt!

JACK Yes. Charming old lady she is, too. Lives at Tunbridge Wells. Just give it back to me, Algy.

ALGERNON (*retreating to back of sofa*) But why does she call herself little Cecily if she is your aunt and lives at Tunbridge Wells? (*Reading.*) "From little Cecily with her fondest love."

JACK (*moving to sofa and kneeling upon it*) My dear fellow, what on earth is there in that? Some aunts are tall, some aunts are not tall. That is a matter that surely an aunt may be allowed to decide for herself. You seem to think that every aunt should be exactly like your aunt! That is absurd! For Heaven's sake give me back my cigarette case. (*Follows* ALGERNON *round the room.*)

ALGERNON Yes. But why does your aunt call you her uncle? "From little Cecily, with her fondest love to her dear Uncle Jack." There is no objection, I admit, to an aunt being a small aunt, but why an aunt, no matter what her size may be, should call her own nephew her uncle, I can't quite make out. Besides, your name isn't Jack at all; it is Ernest.

JACK It isn't Ernest; it's Jack.

ALGERNON You have always told me it was Ernest. I have introduced you to every one as Ernest. You answer to the name of Ernest. You look as if your name was Ernest. You are the most earnest looking person I ever saw in my life. It is perfectly absurd your saying that your name isn't Ernest. It's on your cards. Here is one of them. (*Taking it from case.*) "Mr. Ernest Worthing, B 4, The Albany." I'll keep this as a proof your name is Ernest if ever you attempt to deny it to me, or to Gwendolen, or to any one else. (*Puts the card in his pocket.*)

JACK Well, my name is Ernest in town and Jack in the country, and the cigarette case was given to me in the country.

ALGERNON Yes, but that does not account for the fact that your small Aunt Cecily, who lives at Tunbridge Wells, calls you her dear uncle. Come, old boy, you had much better have the thing out at once.

JACK My dear Algy, you talk exactly as if you were a dentist. It is very vulgar to talk like a dentist when one isn't a dentist. It produces a false impression.

ALGERNON Well, that is exactly what dentists always do. Now, go on! Tell me the whole thing. I may mention that I have always suspected you of being a confirmed and secret Bunburyist; and I am quite sure of it now.

JACK Bunburyist? What on earth do you mean by a Bunburyist?

ALGERNON I'll reveal to you the meaning of that incomparable expression as soon as you are kind enough to inform me why you are Ernest in town and Jack in the country.

JACK Well, produce my cigarette case first.

ALGERNON Here it is. (*Hands cigarette case.*) Now produce your explanation, and pray make it improbable. (*Sits on sofa.*)

JACK My dear fellow, there is nothing improbable about my explanation at all. In fact it's perfectly ordinary. Old Mr. Thomas Cardew, who adopted me when I was a little boy, made me in his will guardian to his grand-daughter, Miss Cecily Cardew. Cecily, who addresses me as her uncle from motives of respect that you could not possibly appreciate, lives at my place in the country under the charge of her admirable governess, Miss Prism.

ALGERNON Where is that place in the country, by the way?

JACK That is nothing to you, dear boy. You are not going to be invited. . . . I may tell you candidly that the place is not in Shropshire.

ALGERNON I suspected that, my dear fellow! I have Bunburyed all over Shropshire on two separate occasions. Now, go on. Why are you Ernest in town and Jack in the country?

JACK My dear Algy, I don't know whether you will be able to understand my real motives. You are hardly serious enough. When one is placed in the position of guardian, one has to adopt a very high moral tone on all subjects. It's one's duty to do so. And as a high moral tone can hardly be said to conduce very much to either one's health or one's happiness, in order to get up to town I have always pretended to have a younger brother of the name of Ernest, who lives in the Albany, and gets into the most dreadful scrapes. That, my dear Algy, is the whole truth pure and simple.

ALGERNON The truth is rarely pure and never simple. Modern life would be very tedious if it were either, and modern literature a complete impossibility!

JACK That wouldn't be at all a bad thing.

ALGERNON Literary criticism is not your forte, my dear fellow. Don't try it. You should leave that to people who haven't been at a University. They do it so well in the daily papers. What you really are is a Bunburyist. I was quite right in saying you were a Bunburyist. You are one of the most advanced Bunburyists I know.

JACK What on earth do you mean?

ALGERNON You have invented a very useful younger brother called Ernest, in order that you may be able to come up to town as often as you like. I have invented an invaluable permanent invalid called Bunbury, in order that I may be able to go down into the country whenever I choose. Bunbury is perfectly invaluable. If it wasn't for Bunbury's extraordinary bad health, for instance, I wouldn't be able to dine with you at Willis's to-night, for I have been really engaged to Aunt Augusta for more than a week.

JACK I haven't asked you to dine with me anywhere tonight.

ALGERNON I know. You are absolutely careless about sending out invitations. It is very foolish of you. Nothing annoys people so much as not receiving invitations.

JACK You had much better dine with your Aunt Augusta.

ALGERNON I haven't the smallest intention of doing anything of the kind. To begin with, I dined there on Monday, and once a week is quite enough to dine with one's own relatives. In the second place, whenever I do dine there I am always treated as a member of the family, and sent down with either no woman at all, or two. In the third place, I know perfectly well whom she will place me next to, tonight. She will place me next Mary Farquhar, who always flirts with her own husband across the dinner-table. That is not very pleasant. Indeed, it is not even decent . . . and that sort of thing is enormously on the increase. The amount of women in London who flirt with their own husbands is perfectly scandalous. It looks so bad. It is simply washing one's clean linen in public. Besides, now that I know you to be a confirmed Bunburyist I naturally want to talk to you about Bunburying. I want to tell you the rules.

JACK I'm not a Bunburyist at all. If Gwendolen accepts me, I am going to kill my brother, indeed I think I'll kill him in any case. Cecily is a little too much interested in him. It is rather a bore. So I am going to get rid of Ernest. And I strongly advise you to do the same with Mr. ——— with your invalid friend who has the absurd name.

ALGERNON Nothing will induce me to part with Bunbury, and if you ever get married, which seems to me extremely problematic, you will be very glad to know Bunbury. A man who marries without knowing Bunbury has a very tedious time of it.

JACK That is nonsense. If I marry a charming girl like Gwendolen, and she is the only girl I ever saw in my life that I would marry, I certainly won't want to know Bunbury.

ALGERNON Then your wife will. You don't seem to realize, that in married life three is company and two is none.

JACK (*sententiously*) That, my dear young friend, is the theory that the corrupt French Drama has been propounding for the last fifty years.

ALGERNON Yes; and that the happy English home has proved in half the time.

JACK For heaven's sake, don't try to be cynical. It's perfectly easy to be cynical.

ALGERNON My dear fellow, it isn't easy to be anything now-a-days. There's such a lot of beastly competition about. (*The sound of an electric bell is heard.*) Ah! that must be Aunt Augusta. Only relatives, or creditors, ever ring in that Wagnerian manner. Now, if I get her out of the way for ten minutes, so that you can have an opportunity for proposing to Gwendolen, may I dine with you to-night at Willis's?

JACK I suppose so, if you want to.

ALGERNON Yes, but you must be serious about it. I have people who are not serious about meals. It is so shallow of them.

Enter LANE.

LANE Lady Bracknell and Miss Fairfax. (ALGERNON *goes forward to meet them. Enter* LADY BRACKNELL *and* GWENDOLEN.)

LADY BRACKNELL Good afternoon, dear Algernon, I hope you are behaving very well.

ALGERNON I'm feeling very well, Aunt Augusta.

LADY BRACKNELL That's not quite the same thing. In fact the two things rarely go together. (*Sees* JACK *and bows to him with icy coldness.*)

ALGERNON (*to* GWENDOLEN) Dear me, you are smart!

GWENDOLEN I am always smart! Aren't I, Mr. Worthing?

JACK You're quite perfect, Miss Fairfax.

GWENDOLEN Oh! I hope I am not that. It would leave no room for developments, and I intend to develop in *many directions*. (GWENDOLEN *and* JACK *sit down together in the corner.*)

LADY BRACKNELL I'm sorry if we are a little late, Algernon, but I was obliged to call on dear Lady Harbury. Hadn't been there since her poor husband's death. I never saw a woman so altered; she looks quite twenty years younger. And now I'll have a cup of tea, and one of those nice cucumber sandwiches you promised me.

ALGERNON Certainly, Aunt Augusta. (*Goes over to tea-table.*)

LADY BRACKNELL Won't you come and sit here, Gwendolen?

GWENDOLEN Thanks, mamma, I'm quite comfortable where I am.

ALGERNON (*picking up empty plate in horror*) Good heavens! Lane! Why are there no cucumber sandwiches? I ordered them specially.

LANE (*gravely*) There were no cucumbers in the market this morning, sir. I went down twice.

ALGERNON No cucumbers!

LANE No, sir. Not even for ready money.

ALGERNON That will do, Lane, thank you.

LANE Thank you, sir. (*Goes out.*)

ALGERNON I am greatly distressed, Aunt Augusta, about there being no cucumbers, not even for ready money.

LADY BRACKNELL It really makes no matter, Algernon. I had some crumpets with Lady Harbury, who seems to me to be living entirely for pleasure now.

ALGERNON I hear her hair has turned quite gold from grief.

LADY BRACKNELL It certainly has changed its color. From what cause I, of course, cannot say. (ALGERNON *crosses and hands tea.*) Thank you. I've quite a treat for you to-night, Algernon. I am going to send you down with Mary Farquhar. She is such a nice woman, and so attentive to her husband. It's delightful to watch them.

ALGERNON I am afraid, Aunt Augusta, I shall have to give up the pleasure of dining with you to-night after all.

LADY BRACKNELL (*frowning*) I hope not, Algernon. It would put my table completely out. Your uncle would have to dine upstairs. Fortunately he is accustomed to that.

ALGERNON It is a great bore, and, I need hardly say, a terrible disappointment to me, but the fact is I have just had a telegram to say that my poor friend Bunbury is very ill again. (*Exchanges glances with* JACK.) They seem to think I should be with him.

LADY BRACKNELL It is very strange. This Mr. Bunbury seems to suffer from curiously bad health.

ALGERNON Yes; poor Bunbury is a dreadful invalid.

LADY BRACKNELL Well, I must say, Algernon, that I think it is high time that Mr. Bunbury made up his mind whether he was going to live or to die. This shilly-shallying with the question is absurd. Nor do I in any way approve of the modern sympathy with invalids. I consider it morbid. Illness of any kind is hardly a thing to be encouraged in others. Health is the primary duty of life. I am always telling that to your poor uncle, but he never seems to take much notice . . . as far as any improvement in his ailments goes. I should be much obliged if you would ask Mr. Bunbury, from me, to be kind enough not to have a relapse on Saturday, for I rely on you to arrange my music for me. It is my last reception and one wants something that will encourage conversation, particularly at the end of the season when every one has practically said whatever they had to say, which, in most cases, was probably not much.

ALGERNON I'll speak to Bunbury, Aunt Augusta, if he is still conscious, and I think I can promise you he'll be all right by Saturday. You see, if one plays good music, people don't listen, and if one plays bad music people don't talk. But I'll run over the program I've drawn out, if you will kindly come into the next room for a moment.

LADY BRACKNELL Thank you, Algernon. It is very thoughtful of you. (*Rising, and following* ALGERNON.) I'm sure the program will be delightful, after a few expurgations. French songs I cannot possibly allow. People always seem to think that they are improper, and either look shocked, which is vulgar, or laugh, which is worse. But German sounds a thoroughly respectable language, and indeed, I believe is so. Gwendolen, you will accompany me.

GWENDOLEN Certainly, mamma. (LADY BRACKNELL AND ALGERNON *go into the music-room,* GWENDOLEN *remains behind.*)

JACK Charming day it has been, Miss Fairfax.

GWENDOLEN Pray don't talk to me about the weather, Mr. Worthing. Whenever people talk to me about the weather, I always feel quite certain that they mean something else. And that makes me so nervous.

JACK I do mean something else.

GWENDOLEN I thought so. In fact, I am never wrong.

JACK And I would like to be allowed to take advantage of Lady Bracknell's temporary absence . . .

GWENDOLEN I would certainly advise you to do so. Mamma has a way of coming back suddenly into a room that I have often had to speak to her about.

JACK (*nervously*) Miss Fairfax, ever since I met you I have admired you more than any girl . . . I have ever met since . . . I met you.

GWENDOLEN Yes, I am quite aware of the fact. And I often wish that in public, at any rate, you had been more demonstrative. For me you have always had an irresistible fascination. Even before I met you I was far from indifferent to you. (JACK *looks at her in amazement.*) We live, as I hope you know, Mr. Worthing, in an age of ideals. The fact is constantly mentioned in the more expensive monthly magazines, and has reached the provincial pulpits I am told: and my ideal has always been to love some one of the name of Ernest. There is something in that name that inspires absolute confidence. The moment Algernon first mentioned to me that he had a friend called Ernest, I knew I was destined to love you.

JACK You really love me, Gwendolen?

GWENDOLEN Passionately!

JACK Darling! You don't know how happy you've made me.

GWENDOLEN My own Ernest!

JACK But you don't really mean to say that you couldn't love me if my name wasn't Ernest?

GWENDOLEN But your name is Ernest.

JACK Yes, I know it is. But supposing it was something else? Do you mean to say you couldn't love me then?

GWENDOLEN (*glibly*) Ah! that is clearly a metaphysical speculation, and like most metaphysical speculations has very little reference at all to the actual facts of real life, as we know them.

JACK Personally, darling, to speak quite candidly, I don't much care about the name of Ernest . . . I don't think that name suits me at all.

GWENDOLEN It suits you perfectly. It is a divine name. It has a music of its own. It produces vibrations.

JACK Well, really, Gwendolen, I must say that I think there are lots of other much nicer names. I think, Jack, for instance, a charming name.

GWENDOLEN Jack? . . . No, there is very little music in the name Jack, if any at all, indeed. It does not thrill. It produces absolutely no vibrations. . . . I have known several Jacks, and they all, without exception, were more than usually plain. Besides, Jack is a notorious domesticity for John! And I pity any woman who is married to a man called John. She would probably never be allowed to know the entrancing pleasure of a single moment's solitude. The only really safe name is Ernest.

JACK Gwendolen, I must get christened at once—I mean we must get married at once. There is no time to be lost.

GWENDOLEN Married, Mr. Worthing?

JACK (astounded) Well . . . surely. You know that I love you, and you led me to believe, Miss Fairfax, that you were not absolutely indifferent to me.

GWENDOLEN I adore you. But you haven't proposed to me yet. Nothing has been said at all about marriage. The subject has not even been touched on.

JACK Well . . . may I propose to you now?

GWENDOLEN I think it would be an admirable opportunity. And to spare you any possible disappointment, Mr. Worthing, I think it only fair to tell you quite frankly beforehand that I am fully determined to accept you.

JACK Gwendolen!

GWENDOLEN Yes, Mr. Worthing, what have you got to say to me?

JACK You know what I have got to say to you.

GWENDOLEN Yes, but you don't say it.

JACK Gwendolen, will you marry me? (Goes on his knees.)

GWENDOLEN Of course I will, darling. How long you have been about it! I am afraid you have had very little experience in how to propose.

JACK My own one, I have never loved any one in the world but you.

GWENDOLEN Yes, but men often propose for practice. I know my brother Gerald does. All my girl-friends tell me so. What wonderfully blue eyes you have, Ernest! They are quite, quite blue. I hope you will always look at me just like that, especially when there are other people present.

Enter LADY BRACKNELL.

LADY BRACKNELL Mr. Worthing! Rise, sir, from this semi-recumbent posture. It is most indecorous.

GWENDOLEN Mamma! (*He tries to rise; she restrains him.*) I must beg you to retire. This is no place for you. Besides, Mr. Worthing has not quite finished yet.

LADY BRACKNELL Finished what, may I ask?

GWENDOLEN I am engaged to Mr. Worthing, mamma. (*They rise together.*)

LADY BRACKNELL Pardon me, you are not engaged to any one. When you do become engaged to some one, I, or your father, should his health permit him, will inform you of the fact. An engagement should come on a young girl as a surprise, pleasant or unpleasant, as the case may be. It is hardly a matter that she could be allowed to arrange for herself. . . . And now I have a few questions to put to you, Mr. Worthing. While I am making these inquiries, you, Gwendolen, will wait for me below in the carriage.

GWENDOLEN (*reproachfully*) Mamma!

LADY BRACKNELL In the carriage, Gwendolen! (GWENDOLEN *goes to the door. She and* JACK *blow kisses to each other behind* LADY BRACKNELL'S *back.* LADY BRACKNELL *looks vaguely about as if she could not understand what the noise was. Finally turns round.*) Gwendolen, the carriage!

GWENDOLEN Yes, mamma. (*Goes out, looking back at* JACK.)

LADY BRACKNELL (*sitting down*) You can take a seat, Mr. Worthing. (*Looks in her pocket for note-book and pencil.*)

JACK Thank you, Lady Bracknell, I prefer standing.

LADY BRACKNELL (*pencil and note-book in hand*) I feel bound to tell you that you are not down on my list of eligible young men, although I have the same list as the dear Duchess of Bolton has. We work together, in fact. However, I am quite ready to enter your name, should your answers be what a really affectionate mother requires. Do you smoke?

JACK Well, yes, I must admit I smoke.

LADY BRACKNELL I am glad to hear it. A man should always have an occupation of some kind. There are far too many idle men in London as it is. How old are you?

JACK Twenty-nine.

LADY BRACKNELL A very good age to be married at. I have always been of opinion that a man who desires to get married should know either everything or nothing. Which do you know?

JACK (*after some hesitation*) I know nothing, Lady Bracknell.

LADY BRACKNELL I am pleased to hear it. I do not approve of anything that tampers with natural ignorance. Ignorance is like a delicate exotic fruit; touch it and the bloom is gone. The whole theory of modern education is radically unsound. Fortunately in England, at any rate, education produces no effect whatsoever. If it did, it would prove a serious danger to the upper classes, and probably lead to acts of violence in Grosvenor Square. What is your income?

JACK Between seven and eight thousand a year.

LADY BRACKNELL (*makes a note in her book*) In land, or in investments?

JACK In investments, chiefly.

LADY BRACKNELL That is satisfactory. What between the duties expected of one during one's life-time, and the duties exacted from one after one's death, land has ceased to be either a profit or a pleasure. It gives one position, and prevents one from keeping it up. That's all that can be said about land.

JACK I have a country house with some land, of course, attached to it, about fifteen hundred acres, I believe; but I don't depend on that for my real income. In fact, as far as I can make out, the poachers are the only people who make anything out of it.

LADY BRACKNELL A country house! How many bedrooms? Well, that point can be cleared up afterwards. You have a town house, I hope? A girl with a simple, unspoiled nature, like Gwendolen, could hardly be expected to reside in the country.

JACK Well, I own a house in Belgrave Square, but it is let by the year to Lady Bloxham. Of course, I can get it back whenever I like, at six months' notice.

LADY BRACKNELL Lady Bloxham? I don't know her.

JACK Oh, she goes about very little. She is a lady considerably advanced in years.

LADY BRACKNELL Ah, now-a-days that is no guarantee of respectability of character. What number in Belgrave Square?

JACK 149.

LADY BRACKNELL (*shaking her head*) The unfashionable side. I thought there was something. However, that could easily be altered.

JACK Do you mean the fashion, or the side?

LADY BRACKNELL (*sternly*) Both, if necessary, I presume. What are your politics?

JACK Well, I am afraid I really have none. I am a Liberal Unionist.

LADY BRACKNELL Oh, they count as Tories. They dine with us. Or come in the evening, at any rate. Now to minor matters. Are your parents living?

JACK I have lost both my parents.

LADY BRACKNELL Both? . . . That seems like carelessness. Who was your father? He was evidently a man of some wealth. Was he born in what the Radical papers call the purple of commerce, or did he rise from the ranks of the aristocracy?

JACK I am afraid I really don't know. The fact is, Lady Bracknell, I said I had lost my parents. It would be nearer the truth to say that my parents seem to have lost me . . . I don't actually know who I am by birth. I was . . . well, I was found.

LADY BRACKNELL Found!

JACK The late Mr. Thomas Cardew, an old gentleman of a very charitable and kindly disposition, found me, and gave me the name of Worthing, because he happened to have a first-class ticket for Worthing in his pocket at the time. Worthing is a place in Sussex. It is a seaside resort.

LADY BRACKNELL Where did the charitable gentleman who had a first-class ticket for this seaside resort find you?

JACK (*gravely*) In a hand-bag.

LADY BRACKNELL A hand-bag?

JACK (*very seriously*) Yes, Lady Bracknell. I was in a hand-bag—a somewhat large, black leather hand-bag, with handles to it—an ordinary hand-bag in fact.

LADY BRACKNELL In what locality did this Mr. James, or Thomas, Cardew come across this ordinary hand-bag?

JACK In the cloak-room at Victoria Station. It was given to him in mistake for his own.

LADY BRACKNELL The cloak-room at Victoria Station?

JACK Yes. The Brighton line.

LADY BRACKNELL The line is immaterial. Mr. Worthing, I confess I feel somewhat bewildered by what you have just told me. To be born, or at any rate bred, in a hand-bag, whether it had handles or not, seems to me to display a contempt for the ordinary decencies of family life that remind one of the worst excesses of the French Revolution. And I presume you know what that unfortunate movement led to? As for the particular locality in which the hand-bag was found, a cloak-room at a railway station might serve to conceal a social indiscretion—has probably, indeed, been used for that purpose before now—but it could hardly be regarded as an assured basis for a recognized position in good society.

JACK May I ask you then what you would advise me to do? I need hardly say I would do anything in the world to ensure Gwendolen's happiness.

LADY BRACKNELL I would strongly advise you, Mr. Worthing, to try and acquire some relations as soon as possible, and to make a definite effort to produce at any rate one parent, of either sex, before the season is quite over.

JACK Well, I don't see how I could possibly manage to do that. I can produce the hand-bag at any moment. It is in my dressing-room at home. I really think that should satisfy you, Lady Bracknell.

LADY BRACKNELL Me, sir! What has it to do with me? You can hardly imagine that I and Lord Bracknell would dream of allowing our only daughter—a girl brought up with the utmost care—to marry into a cloak-room, and form an alliance with a parcel? Good morning, Mr. Worthing! (LADY BRACKNELL *sweeps out in majestic indignation.*)

JACK Good morning! (ALGERNON, *from the other room, strikes up the Wedding March.* JACK *looks perfectly furious, and goes to the door.*) For goodness' sake don't play that ghastly tune, Algy! How idiotic you are! (*The music stops, and* ALGERNON *enters cheerily.*)

ALGERNON Didn't it go off all right, old boy? You don't mean to say Gwendolen refused you? I know it is a way she has. She is always refusing people. I think it is most ill-natured of her.

JACK Oh, Gwendolen is as right as a trivet. As far as she is concerned, we are engaged. Her mother is perfectly unbearable. Never met such a Gorgon . . . I don't really know what a Gorgon is like, but I am quite sure that Lady Bracknell is one. In any case, she is a monster, without being a myth, which is rather unfair. . . . I beg your pardon, Algy, I suppose I shouldn't talk about your own aunt in that way before you.

ALGERNON My dear boy, I love hearing my relations abused. It is the only thing that makes me put up with them at all. Relations are simply a tedious pack of people, who haven't got the remotest knowledge of how to live, nor the smallest instinct about when to die.

JACK Oh, that is nonsense!

ALGERNON It isn't!

JACK Well, I won't argue about the matter. You always want to argue about things.

ALGERNON That is exactly what things were originally made for.

JACK Upon my word, if I thought that, I'd shoot myself . . . (*A pause.*) You don't think there is any chance of Gwendolen becoming like her mother in about a hundred and fifty years, do you, Algy?

ALGERNON All women become like their mothers. That is their tragedy. No man does. That's his.

JACK Is that clever?

ALGERNON It is perfectly phrased! and quite as true as any observation in civilized life should be.

JACK I am sick to death of cleverness. Everybody is clever now-a-days. You can't go anywhere without meeting clever people. The thing has become an absolute public nuisance. I wish to goodness we had a few fools left.

ALGERNON We have.

JACK I should extremely like to meet them. What do they talk about?

ALGERNON The fools? Oh! about the clever people, of course.

JACK What fools!

ALGERNON By the way, did you tell Gwendolen the truth about your being Ernest in town, and Jack in the country?

JACK (*in a very patronizing manner*) My dear fellow, the truth isn't quite the sort of thing one tells to a nice, sweet, refined girl. What extraordinary ideas you have about the way to behave to a woman!

ALGERNON The only way to behave to a woman is to make love to her, if she is pretty, and to some one else if she is plain.

JACK Oh, that is nonsense.

ALGERNON What about your brother? What about the profligate Ernest?

JACK Oh, before the end of the week I shall have got rid of him. I'll say he died in Paris of apoplexy. Lots of people die of apoplexy, quite suddenly, don't they?

ALGERNON Yes, but it's hereditary, my dear fellow. It's a sort of thing that runs in families. You had much better say a severe chill.

JACK You are sure a severe chill isn't hereditary, or anything of that kind?

ALGERNON Of course it isn't!

JACK Very well, then. My poor brother Ernest is carried off suddenly in Paris, by a severe chill. That gets rid of him.

ALGERNON But I thought you said that . . . Miss Cardew was a little too much interested in your poor brother Ernest? Won't she feel his loss a good deal?

JACK Oh, that is all right. Cecily is not a silly, romantic girl, I am glad to say. She has got a capital appetite, goes for long walks, and pays no attention at all to her lessons.

ALGERNON I would rather like to see Cecily.

JACK I will take very good care you never do. She is excessively pretty, and she is only just eighteen.

ALGERNON Have you told Gwendolen yet that you have an excessively pretty ward who is only just eighteen?

JACK Oh, one doesn't blurt these things out to people. Cecily and Gwendolen are perfectly certain to be extremely great friends. I'll bet you anything you like that half an hour after they have met, they will be calling each other sister.

ALGERNON Women only do that when they have called each other a lot of other things first. Now, my dear boy, if we want to get a good table at Willis's, we really must go and dress. Do you know it is nearly seven?

JACK (*irritably*) Oh! it always is nearly seven.

ALGERNON Well, I'm hungry.

JACK I never knew you when you weren't. . . .

ALGERNON What shall we do after dinner? Go to a theater?

JACK Oh, no! I loathe listening.

ALGERNON Well, let us go to the Club?

JACK Oh, no! I hate talking.

ALGERNON Well, we might trot round to the Empire at ten?

JACK Oh, no! I can't bear looking at things. It is so silly.

ALGERNON Well, what shall we do?

JACK Nothing!

ALGERNON It is awfully hard work doing nothing. However, I don't mind hard work where there is no definite object of any kind.

Enter LANE.

LANE Miss Fairfax.

Enter GWENDOLEN. LANE *goes out.*

ALGERNON Gwendolen, upon my word!

GWENDOLEN Algy, kindly turn your back. I have something very particular to say to Mr. Worthing.

ALGERNON Really, Gwendolen, I don't think I can allow this at all.

GWENDOLEN Algy, you always adopt a strictly immoral attitude towards life. You are not quite old enough to do that. (ALGERNON *retires to the fireplace.*)

JACK My own darling!

GWENDOLEN Ernest, we may never be married. From the expression on mamma's face I fear we never shall. Few parents now-a-days pay any regard to what their children say to them. The old-fashioned respect for the young is fast dying out. Whatever influence I ever had over mamma, I lost at the age of three. But although she may prevent us from becoming man and wife, and I may marry some one else, and marry often, nothing that she can possibly do can alter my eternal devotion to you.

JACK Dear Gwendolen.

GWENDOLEN The story of your romantic origin, as related to me by mamma, with unpleasing comments, has naturally stirred the deeper fibers of my nature. Your Christian name has an irresistible fascination. The simplicity on your character makes you exquisitely incomprehensible to me. Your town address at the Albany I have. What is your address in the country?

JACK The Manor House, Woolton, Hertfordshire. (ALGERNON, *who has been carefully listening, smiles to himself, and writes the address on his shirt-cuff. Then picks up the Railway Guide.*)

GWENDOLEN There is a good postal service, I suppose? It may be necessary to do something desperate. That, of course, will require serious consideration. I will communicate with you daily.

JACK My own one!

GWENDOLEN How long do you remain in town?

JACK Till Monday.

GWENDOLEN Good! Algy, you may turn round now.

ALGERNON Thanks, I've turned round already.

GWENDOLEN You may also ring the bell.

JACK You will let me see you to your carriage, my own darling?

GWENDOLEN Certainly.

JACK (*to* LANE, *who now enters*) I will see Miss Fairfax out.

LANE Yes, sir. (JACK *and* GWENDOLEN *go off.* LANE *presents several letters on a salver to* ALGERNON. *It is to be surmised that they are bills, as* ALGERNON, *after looking at the envelopes, tears them up.*)

ALGERNON A glass of sherry, Lane.

LANE Yes, sir.

ALGERNON To-morrow, Lane, I'm going Bunburying.

LANE Yes, sir.

ALGERNON I shall probably not be back till Monday. You can put up my dress clothes, my smoking jacket, and all the Bunbury suits . . .

LANE Yes, sir. (*Handing sherry.*)

ALGERNON I hope to-morrow will be a fine day, Lane.

LANE It never is, sir.

ALGERNON Lane, you're a perfect pessimist.

LANE I do my best to give satisfaction, sir.

Enter JACK. LANE *goes off.*

JACK There's a sensible, intellectual girl! the only girl I ever cared for in my life. (AL- GERNON *is laughing immoderately.*) What on earth are you so amused at?

ALGERNON Oh, I'm a little anxious about poor Bunbury, that's all.

JACK If you don't take care, your friend Bunbury will get you into a serious scrape some day.

ALGERNON I love scrapes. They are the only things that are never serious.

JACK Oh, that's nonsense, Algy. You never talk anything but nonsense.

ALGERNON Nobody ever does. (JACK *looks indignantly at him, and leaves the room.* ALGERNON *lights a cigarette, reads his shirt-cuff and smiles.*)

CURTAIN

SCENE *Garden at the Manor House. A flight of gray stone steps leads up to the house. The garden, an old-fashioned one, full of roses. Time of year, July. Basket chairs, and a table covered with books, are set under a large yew tree.*

(MISS PRISM *discovered seated at the table.* CECILY *is at the back watering flowers.*)

MISS PRISM (*calling*) Cecily, Cecily! Surely such a utilitarian occupation as the watering of flowers is rather Moulton's duty than yours? Especially at a moment when intellectual pleasures await you. Your German grammar is on the table. Pray open it at page fifteen. We will repeat yesterday's lesson.

CECILY (*coming over very slowly*) But I don't like German. It isn't at all a becoming language. I know perfectly well that I look quite plain after my German lesson.

MISS PRISM Child, you know how anxious your guardian is that you should improve yourself in every way. He laid particular stress on your German, as he was leaving for town yesterday. Indeed, he always lays stress on your German when he is leaving for town.

CECILY Dear Uncle Jack is so very serious! Sometimes he is so serious that I think he cannot be quite well.

MISS PRISM (*drawing herself up*) Your guardian enjoys the best of health, and his gravity of demeanor is especially to be commended in one so comparatively young as he is. I know no one who has a higher sense of duty and responsibility.

CECILY I suppose that is why he often looks a little bored when we three are together.

MISS PRISM Cecily! I am surprised at you. Mr. Worthing has many troubles in his life. Idle merriment and triviality would be out of place in his conversation. You must remember his constant anxiety about that unfortunate young man, his brother.

CECILY I wish Uncle Jack would allow that unfortunate young man, his brother, to come down here sometimes. We might have a good influence over him, Miss Prism. I am sure you certainly would. You know German, and geology, and things of that kind influence a man very much. (CECILY *begins to write in her diary.*)

MISS PRISM (*shaking her head*) I do not think that even I could produce any effect on a character that, according to his own brother's admission, is irretrievably weak and vacillating. Indeed, I am not sure that I would desire to reclaim him. I am not in favor of this modern mania for turning bad people into good people at a moment's notice. As a man sows so let him reap. You must put away your diary, Cecily. I really don't see why you should keep a diary at all.

CECILY I keep a diary in order to enter the wonderful secrets of my life. If I didn't write them down I should probably forget all about them.

MISS PRISM Memory, my dear Cecily, is the diary that we all carry about with us.

CECILY Yes, but it usually chronicles the things that have never happened, and couldn't possibly have happened. I believe that Memory is responsible for nearly all the three-volume novels that Mudie sends us.

MISS PRISM Do not speak slightingly of the three-volume novel, Cecily. I wrote one myself in earlier days.

CECILY Did you really, Miss Prism? How wonderfully clever you are! I hope it did not end happily? I don't like novels that end happily. They depress me so much.

MISS PRISM The good ended happily, and the bad unhappily. That is what Fiction means.

CECILY I suppose so. But it seems very unfair. And was your novel ever published?

MISS PRISM Alas! no. The manuscript unfortunately was abandoned. I use the word in the sense of lost or mislaid. To your work, child, these speculations are profitless.

CECILY (*smiling*) But I see dear Dr. Chasuble coming up through the garden.

MISS PRISM (*rising and advancing*) Dr. Chasuble! This is indeed a pleasure.

Enter CANON CHASUBLE.

CHASUBLE And how are we this morning? Miss Prism, you are, I trust, well?

CECILY Miss Prism has just been complaining of a slight headache. I think it would do her so much good to have a short stroll with you in the park, Dr. Chasuble.

MISS PRISM Cecily, I have not mentioned anything about a headache.

CECILY No, dear Miss Prism, I know that, but I felt instinctively that you had a headache. Indeed I was thinking about that, and not about my German lesson, when the Rector came in.

CHASUBLE I hope, Cecily, you are not inattentive.

CECILY Oh, I am afraid I am.

CHASUBLE That is strange. Were I fortunate enough to be Miss Prism's pupil, I would hang upon her lips. (Miss Prism *glares.*) I spoke metaphorically.—My metaphor was drawn from bees. Ahem! Mr. Worthing, I suppose, has not returned from town yet?

MISS PRISM We do not expect him till Monday afternoon.

CHASUBLE Ah, yes, he usually likes to spend his Sunday in London. He is not one of those whose sole aim is enjoyment, as, by all accounts, that unfortunate young man, his brother, seems to be. But I must not disturb Egeria and her pupil any longer.

MISS PRISM Egeria? My name is Laetitia, Doctor.

CHASUBLE (*bowing*) A classical allusion merely, drawn from the Pagan authors. I shall see you both no doubt at Evensong.

MISS PRISM I think, dear Doctor, I will have a stroll with you. I find I have a headache after all, and a walk might do it good.

CHASUBLE With pleasure, Miss Prism, with pleasure. We might go as far as the schools and back.

MISS PRISM That would be delightful. Cecily, you will read your Political Economy in my absence. The chapter on the Fall of the Rupee you may omit. It is somewhat too sensational. Even these metallic problems have their melodramatic side. (*Goes down the garden with* DR. CHASUBLE.)

CECILY (*picks up books and throws them back on table*) Horrid Political Economy! Horrid Geography! Horrid, horrid German!

Enter MERRIMAN *with a card on a salver.*

MERRIMAN Mr. Ernest Worthing has just driven over from the station. He has brought his luggage with him.

CECILY (*takes the card and reads it*) "Mr. Ernest Worthing, B 4, The Albany, W." Uncle Jack's brother! Did you tell him Mr. Worthing was in town?

MERRIMAN Yes, Miss. He seemed very much disappointed. I mentioned that you and Miss Prism were in the garden. He said he was anxious to speak to you privately for a moment.

CECILY Ask Mr. Ernest Worthing to come here. I suppose you had better talk to the housekeeper about a room for him.

MERRIMAN Yes, Miss. (MERRIMAN *goes off.*)

CECILY I have never met any really wicked person before. I feel rather frightened. I am so afraid he will look just like every one else.

Enter ALGERNON, *very gay and debonair.*

He does!

ALGERNON (*raising his hat*) You are my little cousin Cecily, I'm sure.

CECILY You are under some strange mistake. I am not little. In fact, I am more than usually tall for my age. (ALGERNON *is rather taken aback.*) But I am your cousin Cecily. You, I see from your card, are Uncle Jack's brother, my cousin Ernest, my wicked cousin Ernest.

ALGERNON Oh! I am not really wicked at all, cousin Cecily. You mustn't think that I am wicked.

CECILY If you are not, then you have certainly been deceiving us all in a very inexcusable manner. I hope you have not been leading a double life, pretending to be wicked and being really good all the time. That would be hypocrisy.

ALGERNON (*looks at her in amazement*) Oh! of course I have been rather reckless.

CECILY I am glad to hear it.

ALGERNON In fact, now you mention the subject, I have been very bad in my own small way.

CECILY I don't think you should be so proud of that, though I am sure it must have been very pleasant.

ALGERNON It is much pleasanter being here with you.

CECILY I can't understand how you are here at all. Uncle Jack won't be back till Monday afternoon.

ALGERNON That is a great disappointment. I am obliged to go up by the first train on Monday morning. I have a business appointment that I am anxious . . . to miss.

CECILY Couldn't you miss it anywhere but in London?

ALGERNON No; the appointment is in London.

CECILY Well, I know, of course, how important it is not to keep a business engagement, if one wants to retain any sense of the beauty of life, but still I think you had better wait till Uncle Jack arrives. I know he wants to speak to you about your emigrating.

ALGERNON About my what?

CECILY Your emigrating. He has gone up to buy your outfit.

ALGERNON I certainly wouldn't let Jack buy my outfit. He has no taste in neckties at all.

CECILY I don't think you will require neckties. Uncle Jack is sending you to Australia.

ALGERNON Australia! I'd sooner die.

CECILY Well, he said at dinner on Wednesday night, that you would have to choose between this world, the next world, and Australia.

ALGERNON Oh, well! The accounts I have received of Australia and the next world, are not particularly encouraging. This world is good enough for me, cousin Cecily.

CECILY Yes, but are you good enough for it?

ALGERNON I'm afraid I'm not that. That is why I want you to reform me. You might make that your mission, if you don't mind, cousin Cecily.

CECILY I'm afraid I've not time, this afternoon.

ALGERNON Well, would you mind my reforming myself this afternoon?

CECILY That is rather Quixotic of you. But I think you should try.

ALGERNON I will. I feel better already.

CECILY You are looking a little worse.

ALGERNON That is because I am hungry.

CECILY How thoughtless of me. I should have remembered that when one is going to lead an entirely new life, one requires regular and wholesome meals. Won't you come in?

ALGERNON Thank you. Might I have a button-hole first? I never have any appetite unless I have a button-hole first.

CECILY A Maréchal Niel? (*Picks up scissors.*)

ALGERNON No, I'd sooner have a pink rose.

CECILY Why? (*Cuts a flower.*)

ALGERNON Because you are like a pink rose, cousin Cecily.

CECILY I don't think it can be right for you to talk to me like that. Miss Prism never says such things to me.

ALGERNON Then Miss Prism is a short-sighted old lady. (CECILY *puts the rose in his button-hole.*) You are the prettiest girl I ever saw.

CECILY Miss Prism says that all good looks are a snare.

ALGERNON They are a snare that every sensible man would like to be caught in.

CECILY Oh! I don't think I would care to catch a sensible man. I shouldn't know what to talk to him about. (*They pass into the house.* MISS PRISM *and* DR. CHASUBLE *return*)

MISS PRISM You are too much alone, dear Dr. Chasuble. You should get married. A misanthrope I can understand—a womanthrope, never!

CHASUBLE (*with a scholar's shudder*) Believe me, I do not deserve so neologistic a phrase. The precept as well as the practice of the Primitive Church was distinctly against matrimony.

MISS PRISM (*sententiously*) That is obviously the reason why the Primitive Church has not lasted up to the present day. And you do not seem to realize, dear Doctor, that by persistently remaining single, a man converts himself into a permanent public temptation. Men should be careful; this very celibacy leads weaker vessels astray.

CHASUBLE But is a man not equally attractive when married?

MISS PRISM No married man is ever attractive except to his wife.

CHASUBLE And often, I've been told, not even to her.

MISS PRISM That depends on the intellectual sympathies of the woman. Maturity can always be depended on. Ripeness can be trusted. Young women are green. (DR. CHASUBLE *starts.*) I spoke horticulturally. My metaphor was drawn from fruits. But where is Cecily?

CHASUBLE Perhaps she followed us to the schools.

Enter JACK *slowly from the back of the garden. He is dressed in the deepest mourning, with crape hatband and black gloves.*

MISS PRISM Mr. Worthing!

CHASUBLE Mr. Worthing?

MISS PRISM This is indeed a surprise. We did not look for you till Monday afternoon.

JACK (*shakes* MISS PRISM'S *hand in a tragic manner*) I have returned sooner than I expected. Dr. Chasuble, I hope you are well?

CHASUBLE Dear Mr. Worthing, I trust this garb of woe does not betoken some terrible calamity?

JACK My brother.

MISS PRISM More shameful debts and extravagance?

CHASUBLE Still leading his life of pleasure?

JACK (*shaking his head*) Dead!

CHASUBLE Your brother Ernest dead?

JACK Quite dead.

MISS PRISM What a lesson for him! I trust he will profit by it.

CHASUBLE Mr. Worthing, I offer you my sincere condolence. You have at least the consolation of knowing that you were always the most generous and forgiving of brothers.

JACK Poor Ernest! He had many faults, but it is a sad, sad blow.

CHASUBLE Very sad indeed. Were you with him at the end?

JACK No. He died abroad; in Paris, in fact. I had a telegram last night from the manager of the Grand Hotel.

CHASUBLE Was the cause of death mentioned?

JACK A severe chill, it seems.

MISS PRISM As a man sows, so shall he reap.

CHASUBLE (*raising his hand*) Charity, dear Miss Prism, charity! None of us are perfect. I myself am peculiarly susceptible to draughts. Will the interment take place here?

JACK No. He seems to have expressed a desire to be buried in Paris.

CHASUBLE In Paris! (*Shakes his head.*) I fear that hardly points to any very serious state of mind at the last. You would no doubt wish me to make some slight allusion to this tragic domestic affliction next Sunday. (JACK *presses his hand convulsively.*) My sermon on the meaning of the manna in the wilderness can be adapted to almost any occasion, joyful, or, as in the present case, distressing. (*All sigh.*) I have preached it at harvest celebrations, christenings, confirmations, on days of humiliation and festal days. The last time I delivered it was in the Cathedral, as a charity sermon on behalf of the Society for the Prevention of Discontentment among the Upper Orders. The Bishop, who was present, was much struck by some of the analogies I drew.

JACK Ah, that reminds me, you mentioned christenings I think, Dr. Chasuble? I suppose you know how to christen all right? (DR. CHASUBLE *looks astounded.*) I mean, of course, you are continually christening, aren't you?

MISS PRISM It is, I regret to say, one of the Rector's most constant duties in this parish. I have often spoken to the poorer classes on the subject. But they don't seem to know what thrift is.

CHASUBLE But is there any particular infant in whom you are interested, Mr. Worthing? Your brother was, I believe, unmarried, was he not?

JACK Oh, yes.

MISS PRISM (*bitterly*) People who live entirely for pleasure usually are.

JACK But it is not for any child, dear Doctor. I am very fond of children. No! the fact is, I would like to be christened myself, this afternoon, if you have nothing better to do.

CHASUBLE But surely, Mr. Worthing, you have been christened already?

JACK I don't remember anything about it.

CHASUBLE But have you any grave doubts on the subject?

JACK I certainly intend to have. Of course, I don't know if the thing would bother you in any way, or if you think I am a little too old now.

CHASUBLE Not at all. The sprinkling, and, indeed, the immersion of adults is a perfectly canonical practice.

JACK Immersion!

CHASUBLE You need have no apprehensions. Sprinkling is all that is necessary, or indeed I think advisable. Our weather is so changeable. At what hour would you wish the ceremony performed?

JACK Oh, I might trot around about five if that would suit you.

CHASUBLE Perfectly, perfectly! In fact I have two similar ceremonies to perform at that time. A case of twins that occurred recently in one of the outlying cottages on your own estate. Poor Jenkins the carter, a most hard-working man.

JACK Oh! I don't see much fun in being christened along with other babies. It would be childish. Would half-past five do?

CHASUBLE Admirably! Admirably! (*Takes out watch.*) And now, dear Mr. Worthing, I will not intrude any longer into a house of sorrow. I would merely beg you not to be too much bowed down by grief. What seem to us bitter trials at the moment are often blessings in disguise.

MISS PRISM This seems to me a blessing of an extremely obvious kind.

Enter CECILY *from the house.*

CECILY Uncle Jack! Oh, I am pleased to see you back. But what horrid clothes you have on! Do go and change them.

MISS PRISM Cecily!

CHASUBLE My child! my child! (CECILY *goes towards* JACK; *he kisses her brow in a melancholy manner.*)

CECILY What is the matter, Uncle Jack? Do look happy! You look as if you had a toothache and I have such a surprise for you. Who do you think is in the dining-room? Your brother!

JACK Who?

CECILY Your brother Ernest. He arrived about half an hour ago.

JACK What nonsense! I haven't got a brother.

CECILY Oh, don't say that. However badly he may have behaved to you in the past he is still your brother. You couldn't be so heartless as to disown him. I'll tell him to come out. And you will shake hands with him, won't you, Uncle Jack? (*Runs back into the house.*)

CHASUBLE These are very joyful tidings.

MISS PRISM After we had all been resigned to his loss, his sudden return seems to me peculiarly distressing.

JACK My brother is in the dining-room? I don't know what it all means. I think it is perfectly absurd.

Enter ALGERNON *and* CECILY *hand in hand. They come slowly up to* JACK.

JACK Good heavens! (*Motions* ALGERNON *away.*)

ALGERNON Brother John, I have come down from town to tell you that I am very sorry for all the trouble I have given you, and that I intend to lead a better life in the future. (JACK *glares at him and does not take his hand.*)

CECILY Uncle Jack, you are not going to refuse your own brother's hand?

JACK Nothing will induce me to take his hand. I think his coming down here disgraceful. He knows perfectly well why.

CECILY Uncle Jack, do be nice. There is some good in every one. Ernest has just been telling me about his poor invalid friend, Mr. Bunbury, whom he goes to visit so often. And surely there must be much good in one who is kind to an invalid, and leaves the pleasures of London to sit by a bed of pain.

JACK Oh, he has been talking about Bunbury, has he?

CECILY Yes, he has told me all about poor Mr. Bunbury, and his terrible state of health.

JACK Bunbury! Well, I won't have him talk to you about Bunbury or about anything else. It is enough to drive one perfectly frantic.

ALGERNON Of course I admit that the faults were all on my side. But I must say that I think that Brother John's coldness to me is peculiarly painful. I expected a more enthusiastic welcome, especially considering it is the first time I have come here.

CECILY Uncle Jack, if you don't shake hands with Ernest I will never forgive you.

JACK Never forgive me?

CECILY Never, never, never!

JACK Well, this is the last time I shall ever do it. (*Shakes hands with* ALGERNON *and glares.*)

CHASUBLE It's pleasant, is it not, to see so perfect a reconciliation? I think we might leave the two brothers together.

MISS PRISM Cecily, you will come with us.

CECILY Certainly, Miss Prism. My little task of reconciliation is over.

CHASUBLE You have done a beautiful action to-day, dear child.

MISS PRISM We must not be premature in our judgments.

CECILY I feel very happy. (*They all go off.*)

JACK You young scoundrel, Algy, you must get out of this place as soon as possible. I don't allow any Bunburying here.

Enter MERRIMAN.

MERRIMAN I have put Mr. Ernest's things in the room next to yours, sir. I suppose that is all right?

JACK What?

MERRIMAN Mr. Ernest's luggage, sir. I have unpacked it and put it in the room next to your own.

JACK His luggage?

MERRIMAN Yes, sir. Three portmanteaus, a dressing-case, two hat-boxes, and a large luncheon-basket.

ALGERNON I am afraid I can't stay more than a week this time.

JACK Merriman, order the dog-cart at once. Mr. Ernest has been suddenly called back to town.

MERRIMAN Yes, sir. (*Goes back into the house.*)

ALGERNON What a fearful liar you are, Jack. I have not been called back to town at all.

JACK Yes, you have.

ALGERNON I haven't heard any one call me.

JACK Your duty as a gentleman calls you back.

ALGERNON My duty as a gentleman has never interfered with my pleasures in the smallest degree.

JACK I can quite understand that.

ALGERNON Well, Cecily is a darling.

JACK You are not to talk of Miss Cardew like that. I don't like it.

ALGERNON Well, I don't like your clothes. You look perfectly ridiculous in them. Why on earth don't you go up and change? It is perfectly childish to be in deep mourning for a man who is actually staying for a whole week with you in your house as a guest. I call it grotesque.

JACK You are certainly not staying with me for a whole week as a guest or anything else. You have got to leave . . . by the four-five train.

ALGERNON I certainly won't leave you so long as you are in mourning. It would be most unfriendly. If I were in mourning you would stay with me, I suppose. I should think it very unkind if you didn't.

JACK Well, will you go if I change my clothes?

ALGERNON Yes, if you are not too long. I never saw anybody take so long to dress, and with such little result.

JACK Well, at any rate, that is better than being always over-dressed as you are.

ALGERNON If I am occasionally a little over-dressed, I make up for it by being always immensely over-educated.

JACK Your vanity is ridiculous, your conduct an outrage, and your presence in my garden utterly absurd. However, you have got to catch the four-five, and I hope you will have a pleasant journey back to town. This Bunburying, as you call it, has not been a great success for you. (*Goes into the house.*)

ALGERNON I think it has been a great success. I'm in love with Cecily, and that is everything. (*Enter* CECILY *at the back of the garden. She picks up the can and begins to water the flowers.*) But I must see her before I go, and make arrangements for another Bunbury. Ah, there she is.

CECILY Oh, I merely came back to water the roses. I thought you were with Uncle Jack.

ALGERNON He's gone to order the dog-cart for me.

CECILY Oh, is he going to take you for a nice drive?

ALGERNON He's going to send me away.

CECILY Then have we got to part?

ALGERNON I am afraid so. It's a very painful parting.

CECILY It is always painful to part from people whom one has known for a very brief space of time. The absence of old friends one can endure with equanimity. But even a momentary separation from any one to whom one has just been introduced is almost unbearable.

ALGERNON Thank you.

Enter MERRIMAN.

MERRIMAN The dog-cart is at the door, sir. (ALGERNON *looks appealingly at* CECILY.)

CECILY It can wait, Merriman . . . for . . . five minutes.

MERRIMAN Yes, miss.

Exit MERRIMAN.

ALGERNON I hope, Cecily, I shall not offend you if I state quite frankly and openly that you seem to me to be in every way the visible personification of absolute perfection.

CECILY I think your frankness does you great credit, Ernest. If you will allow me I will copy your remarks into my diary. (*Goes over to table and begins writing in diary.*)

ALGERNON Do you really keep a diary? I'd give anything to look at it. May I?

CECILY Oh, no. (*Puts her hand over it.*) You see it is simply a very young girl's record of her own thoughts and impressions, and consequently meant for publication. When it appears in volume form I hope you will order a copy. But pray, Ernest, don't stop. I delight in taking down from dictation. I have reached "absolute perfection." You can go on. I am quite ready for more.

ALGERNON (*somewhat taken aback*) Ahem! Ahem!

CECILY Oh, don't cough, Ernest. When one is dictating one should speak fluently and not cough. Besides, I don't know how to spell a cough. (*Writes as* ALGERNON *speaks.*)

ALGERNON (*speaking very rapidly*) Cecily, ever since I first looked upon your wonderful and incomparable beauty, I have dared to love you wildly, passionately, devotedly, hopelessly.

CECILY I don't think that you should tell me that you love me wildly, passionately, devotedly, hopelessly. Hopelessly doesn't seem to make much sense, does it?

ALGERNON Cecily!

Enter MERRIMAN.

MERRIMAN The dog-cart is waiting, sir.
ALGERNON Tell it to come round next week, at the same hour.
MERRIMAN (*looks at* CECILY, *who makes no sign*) Yes, sir.

MERRIMAN *retires.*

CECILY Uncle Jack would be very much annoyed if he knew you were staying on till
   next week, at the same hour.
ALGERNON Oh, I don't care about Jack. I don't care for anybody in the whole world but
   you. I love you, Cecily. You will marry me, won't you?
CECILY You silly you! Of course. Why, we have been engaged for the last three months.
ALGERNON For the last three months?
CECILY Yes, it will be exactly three months on Thursday.
ALGERNON But how did we become engaged?
CECILY Well, ever since dear Uncle Jack first confessed to us that he had a younger
   brother who was very wicked and bad, you of course have formed the chief topic of
   conversation between myself and Miss Prism. And of course a man who is much talked
   about is always very attractive. One feels there must be something in him after all. I
   daresay it was foolish of me, but I fell in love with you, Ernest.
ALGERNON Darling! And when was the engagement actually settled?
CECILY On the 4th of February last. Worn out by your entire ignorance of my existence,
   I determined to end the matter one way or the other, and after a long struggle with
   myself I accepted you under this dear old tree here. The next day I bought this little
   ring in your name, and this is the little bangle with the true lovers' knot I promised
   you always to wear.
ALGERNON Did I give you this? It's very pretty, isn't it?
CECILY Yes, you've wonderfully good taste, Ernest. It's the excuse I've always given for
   your leading such a bad life. And this is the box in which I keep all your dear letters.
   (*Kneels at table, opens box, and produces letters tied up with blue ribbon.*)
ALGERNON My letters! But my own sweet Cecily, I have never written you any letters.
CECILY You need hardly remind me of that, Ernest. I remember only too well that I
   was forced to write your letters for you. I wrote always three times a week, and sometimes
   oftener.
ALGERNON Oh, do let me read them, Cecily?
CECILY Oh, I couldn't possibly. They would make you far too conceited. (*Replaces box.*)
   The three you wrote me after I had broken off the engagement are so beautiful, and
   so badly spelled, that even now I can hardly read them without crying a little.
ALGERNON But was our engagement ever broken off?
CECILY Of course it was. On the 22nd of last March. You can see the entry if you like.
   (*Shows diary.*) "To-day I broke off my engagement with Ernest. I feel it is better to do
   so. The weather still continues charming."
ALGERNON But why on earth did you break it off? What had I done? I had done nothing
   at all. Cecily, I am very much hurt indeed to hear you broke it off. Particularly when
   the weather was so charming.
CECILY It would hardly have been a really serious engagement if it hadn't been broken
   off at least once. But I forgave you before the week was out.
ALGERNON (*crossing to her, and kneeling*). What a perfect angel you are, Cecily.

CECILY You dear romantic boy. (*He kisses her, she puts her fingers through his hair.*) I hope your hair curls naturally, does it?

ALGERNON Yes, darling, with a little help from others.

CECILY I am so glad.

ALGERNON You'll never break off our engagement again, Cecily?

CECILY I don't think I could break it off now that I have actually met you. Besides, of course, there is the question of your name.

ALGERNON Yes, of course. (*Nervously.*)

CECILY You must not laugh at me, darling, but it had always been a girlish dream of mine to love some one whose name was Ernest. (ALGERNON *rises*, CECILY *also.*) There is something in that name that seems to inspire absolute confidence. I pity any poor married woman whose husband is not called Ernest.

ALGERNON But, my dear child, do you mean to say you could not love me if I had some other name?

CECILY But what name?

ALGERNON Oh, any name you like—Algernon, for instance. . . .

CECILY But I don't like the name of Algernon.

ALGERNON Well, my own dear, sweet, loving little darling, I really can't see why you should object to the name of Algernon. It is not at all a bad name. In fact, it is rather an aristocratic name. Half of the chaps who get into the Bankruptcy Court are called Algernon. But seriously, Cecily . . . (*moving to her*) . . . if my name was Algy, couldn't you love me?

CECILY (*rising*) I might respect you, Ernest, I might admire your character, but I fear that I should not be able to give you my undivided attention.

ALGERNON Ahem! Cecily! (*Picking up hat.*) Your Rector here is, I suppose, thoroughly experienced in the practice of all the rites and ceremonials of the church?

CECILY Oh, yes. Dr. Chasuble is a most learned man. He has never written a single book, so you can imagine how much he knows.

ALGERNON I must see him at once on a most important christening—I mean on most important business.

CECILY Oh!

ALGERNON I sha'n't be away more than half an hour.

CECILY Considering that we have been engaged since February the 14th, and that I only met you to-day for the first time, I think it is rather hard that you should leave me for so long a period as half an hour. Couldn't you make it twenty minutes?

ALGERNON I'll be back in no time (*Kisses her and rushes down the garden.*)

CECILY What an impetuous boy he is. I like his hair so much. I must enter his proposal in my diary.

Enter MERRIMAN.

MERRIMAN A Miss Fairfax has just called to see Mr. Worthing. On very important business, Miss Fairfax states.

CECILY Isn't Mr. Worthing in his library?

MERRIMAN Mr. Worthing went over in the direction of the Rectory some time ago.

CECILY Pray ask the lady to come out here; Mr. Worthing is sure to be back soon. And you can bring tea.

MERRIMAN Yes, miss. (*Goes out.*)

CECILY Miss Fairfax! I suppose one of the many good elderly women who are associated with Uncle Jack in some of his philanthropic work in London. I don't quite like women who are interested in philanthropic work. I think it is so forward of them.

Enter MERRIMAN.

MERRIMAN Miss Fairfax.

Enter GWENDOLEN. *Exit* MERRIMAN.

CECILY (*advancing to meet her*) Pray let me introduce myself to you. My name is Cecily Cardew.

GWENDOLEN Cecily Cardew? (*Moving to her and shaking hands.*) What a very sweet name! Something tells me that we are going to be great friends. I like you already more than I can say. My first impressions of people are never wrong.

CECILY How nice of you to like me so much after we have known each other such a comparatively short time. Pray sit down.

GWENDOLEN (*still standing up*) I may call you Cecily, may I not?

CECILY With pleasure!

GWENDOLEN And you will always call me Gwendolen, won't you?

CECILY If you wish.

GWENDOLEN Then that is all quite settled, is it not?

CECILY I hope so. (*A pause. they both sit down together.*)

GWENDOLEN Perhaps this might be a favorable opportunity for my mentioning who I am. My father is Lord Bracknell. You have never heard of papa, I suppose?

CECILY I don't think so.

GWENDOLEN Outside the family circle, papa, I am glad to say, is entirely unknown. I think that is quite as it should be. The home seems to me to be the proper sphere for the man. And certainly once a man begins to neglect his domestic duties he becomes painfully effeminate, does he not? And I don't like that. It makes men so very attractive. Cecily, mamma, whose views on education are remarkably strict, has brought me up to be extremely short-sighted; it is part of her system; so do you mind my looking at you through my glasses?

CECILY Oh, not at all, Gwendolen. I am very fond of being looked at.

GWENDOLEN (*after examining* CECILY *carefully through a lorgnette*) You are here on a short visit, I suppose.

CECILY Oh, no, I live here.

GWENDOLEN (*severely*) Really? Your mother, no doubt, or some female relative of advanced years, resides here also?

CECILY Oh, no. I have no mother, nor, in fact, any relations.

GWENDOLEN Indeed?

CECILY My dear guardian, with the assistance of Miss Prism, has the arduous task of looking after me.

GWENDOLEN Your guardian?

CECILY Yes, I am Mr. Worthing's ward.

GWENDOLEN Oh! It is strange he never mentioned to me that he had a ward. How secretive of him! He grows more interesting hourly. I am not sure, however, that the news inspires me with feelings of unmixed delight (*Rising and going to her.*) I am very fond of you, Cecily; I have liked you ever since I met you. But I am bound to state that now that I know that you are Mr. Worthing's ward, I cannot help expressing a wish you were—well, just a little older than you seem to be—and not quite so very alluring in appearance. In fact, if I may speak candidly—

CECILY Pray do! I think that whenever one has anything unpleasant to say, one should always be quite candid.

GWENDOLEN Well, to speak with perfect candor, Cecily, I wish that you were fully forty-two, and more than usually plain for your age. Ernest has a strong upright nature. He is the very soul of truth and honor. Disloyalty would be as impossible to him as deception. But even men of the noblest possible moral character are extremely susceptible to the influence of the physical charms of others. Modern, no less than Ancient History, supplies us with many most painful examples of what I refer to. If it were not so, indeed, History would be quite unreadable.

CECILY I beg your pardon, Gwendolen, did you say Ernest?

GWENDOLEN Yes.

CECILY Oh, but it is not Mr. Ernest Worthing who is my guardian. It is his brother—his elder brother.

GWENDOLEN (*sitting down again*) Ernest never mentioned to me that he had a brother.

CECILY I am sorry to say they have not been on good terms for a long time.

GWENDOLEN Ah! that accounts for it. And now that I think of it I have never heard any man mention his brother. The subject seems distasteful to most men. Cecily, you have lifted a load from my mind. I was growing almost anxious. It would have been terrible if any cloud had come across a friendship like ours, would it not? Of course you are quite, quite sure that it is not Mr. Ernest Worthing who is your guardian?

CECILY Quite sure (*A pause.*) In fact, I am going to be his.

GWENDOLEN (*enquiringly*) I beg your pardon?

CECILY (*rather shy and confidingly*) Dearest Gwendolen, there is no reason why I should make a secret of it to you. Our little county newspaper is sure to chronicle the fact next week. Mr. Ernest Worthing and I are engaged to be married.

GWENDOLEN (*quite politely, rising*) My darling Cecily, I think there must be some slight error. Mr. Ernest Worthing is engaged to me. The announcement will appear in the *Morning Post* on Saturday at the latest.

CECILY (*very politely, rising*) I am afraid you must be under some misconception. Ernest proposed to me exactly ten minutes ago. (*Shows diary.*)

GWENDOLEN (*examines diary through her lorgnette carefully*) It is certainly very curious, for he asked me to be his wife yesterday afternoon at 5:30. If you would care to verify the incident, pray do so. (*Produces diary of her own.*) I never travel without my diary. One should always have something sensational to read in the train. I am so sorry, dear Cecily, if it is any disappointment to you, but I'm afraid *I* have the prior claim.

CECILY It would distress me more than I can tell you, dear Gwendolen, if it caused you any mental or physical anguish, but I feel bound to point out that since Ernest proposed to you he clearly has changed his mind.

GWENDOLEN (*meditatively*) If the poor fellow has been entrapped into any foolish promise I shall consider it my duty to rescue him at once, and with a firm hand.

CECILY (*thoughtfully and sadly*) Whatever unfortunate entanglement my dear boy may have got into, I will never reproach him with it after we are married.

GWENDOLEN Do you allude to me, Miss Cardew, as an entanglement? You are presumptuous. On an occasion of this kind it becomes more than a moral duty to speak one's mind. It becomes a pleasure.

CECILY Do you suggest, Miss Fairfax, that I entrapped Ernest into an engagement? How dare you? This is no time for wearing the shallow mask of manners. When I see a spade I call it a spade.

GWENDOLEN (*satirically*) I am glad to say that I have never seen a spade. It is obvious that our social spheres have been widely different.

Enter MERRIMAN, *followed by the footman. He carries a salver, tablecloth, and plate-stand.* CECILY *is about to retort. The presence of the servants exercises a restraining influence, under which both girls chafe.*

MERRIMAN Shall I lay tea here as usual, miss?

CECILY (*sternly, in a calm voice*) Yes, as usual. (MERRIMAN *begins to clear and lay cloth. A long pause.* CECILY *and* GWENDOLEN *glare at each other.*)

GWENDOLEN Are there many interesting walks in the vicinity, Miss Cardew?

CECILY Oh, yes, a great many. From the top of one of the hills quite close one can see five counties.

GWENDOLEN Five counties! I don't think I should like that. I hate crowds.

CECILY (*sweetly*) I suppose that is why you live in town? (GWENDOLEN *bites her lip, and beats her foot nervously with her parasol.*)

GWENDOLEN (*looking round*) Quite a well-kept garden this is, Miss Cardew.

CECILY So glad you like it, Miss Fairfax.

GWENDOLEN I had no idea there were any flowers in the country.

CECILY Oh, flowers are as common here, Miss Fairfax, as people are in London.

GWENDOLEN Personally I cannot understand how anybody manages to exist in the country, if anybody who is anybody does. The country always bores me to death.

CECILY Ah! This is what the newspapers call agricultural depression, is it not? I believe the aristocracy are suffering very much from it just at present. It is almost an epidemic amongst them, I have been told. May I offer you some tea, Miss Fairfax?

GWENDOLEN (*with elaborate politeness*) Thank you. (*Aside.*) Detestable girl! But I require tea!

CECILY (*sweetly*) Sugar?

GWENDOLEN (*superciliously*) No, thank you. Sugar is not fashionable any more. (CECILY *looks angrily at her, takes up the tongs and puts four lumps of sugar into the cup.*)

CECILY (*severely*) Cake or bread and butter?

GWENDOLEN (*in a bored manner*) Bread and butter, please. Cake is rarely seen at the best houses now-a-days.

CECILY (*cuts a very large slice of cake, and puts it on the tray*). Hand that to Miss Fairfax. (MERRIMAN *does so, and goes out with footman.* GWENDOLEN *drinks the tea and makes a grimace. Puts down cup at once, reaches out her hand to the bread and butter, looks at it, and finds it is cake. Rises in indignation.*)

GWENDOLEN You have filled my tea with lumps of sugar, and though I asked most distinctly for bread and butter, you have given me cake. I am known for the gentleness of my disposition, and the extraordinary sweetness of my nature, but I warn you, Miss Cardew, you may go too far.

CECILY (*rising*) To save my poor, innocent, trusting boy from the machinations of any other girl there are no lengths to which I would not go.

GWENDOLEN From the moment I saw you I distrusted you. I felt that you were false and deceitful. I am never deceived in such matters. My first impressions of people are invariably right.

CECILY It seems to me, Miss Fairfax, that I am trespassing on your valuable time. No doubt you have many other calls of a similar character to make in the neighborhood.

Enter JACK.

GWENDOLEN (*catching sight of him*) Ernest! My own Ernest!

JACK Gwendolen! Darling! (*Offers to kiss her.*)

GWENDOLEN (*drawing back*) A moment! May I ask if you are engaged to be married to this young lady? (*Points to* CECILY.)

JACK (*laughing*) To dear little Cecily! Of course not! What could have put such an idea into your pretty little head?

GWENDOLEN Thank you. You may. (*Offers her cheek.*)

CECILY (*very sweetly*) I knew there must be some misunderstanding, Miss Fairfax. The gentleman whose arm is at present around your waist is my dear guardian, Mr. John Worthing.

GWENDOLEN I beg your pardon?

CECILY This is Uncle Jack.

GWENDOLEN (*receding*) Jack! Oh!

Enter ALGERNON.

CECILY Here is Ernest.

ALGERNON (*goes straight over to* CECILY *without noticing any one else*). My own love! (*Offers to kiss her.*)

CECILY (*drawing back*) A moment, Ernest! May I ask you—are you engaged to be married to this young lady?

ALGERNON (*looking round*) To what young lady? Good heavens! Gwendolen!

CECILY Yes, to good heavens, Gwendolen, I mean to Gwendolen.

ALGERNON (*laughing*) Of course not! What could have put such an idea into your pretty little head?

CECILY Thank you. (*Presenting her cheek to be kissed.*) You may. (ALGERNON *kisses her.*)

GWENDOLEN I felt there was some slight error, Miss Cardew. The gentleman who is now embracing you is my cousin, Mr. Algernon Moncrieff.

CECILY (*breaking away from* ALGERNON) Algernon Moncrieff! Oh! (*The two girls move towards each other and put their arms round each other's waists as if for protection.*)

CECILY Are you called Algernon?

ALGERNON I cannot deny it.

CECILY Oh!

GWENDOLEN Is your name really John?

JACK (*standing rather proudly*) I could deny it if I liked. I could deny anything if I liked. But my name certainly is John. It has been John for years.

CECILY (*to* GWENDOLEN) A gross deception has been practiced on both of us.

GWENDOLEN My poor wounded Cecily!

CECILY My sweet, wronged Gwendolen!

GWENDOLEN (*slowly and seriously*) You will call me sister, will you not? (*They embrace.* JACK *and* ALGERNON *groan and walk up and down.*)

CECILY (*rather brightly*) There is just one question I would like to be allowed to ask my guardian.

GWENDOLEN An admirable idea! Mr. Worthing, there is just one question I would like to be permitted to put to you. Where is your brother Ernest? We are both engaged to be married to your brother Ernest, so it is a matter of some importance to us to know where your brother Ernest is at present.

JACK (*slowly and hesitatingly*) Gwendolen—Cecily—it is very painful for me to be forced to speak the truth. It is the first time in my life that I have ever been reduced to such a painful position, and I am really quite inexperienced in doing anything of the kind. However I will tell you quite frankly that I have no brother Ernest. I have no brother at all. I never had a brother in my life, and I certainly have not the smallest intention of ever having one in the future.

CECILY (*surprised*) No brother at all?

JACK (*cheerily*) None!

GWENDOLEN (*severely*) Had you never a brother of any kind?

JACK (*pleasantly*) Never. Not even of any kind.

GWENDOLEN I am afraid it is quite clear, Cecily, that neither of us is engaged to be married to any one.

CECILY It is not a very pleasant position for a young girl suddenly to find herself in. Is it?

GWENDOLEN Let us go into the house. They will hardly venture to come after us there.

CECILY No, men are so cowardly, aren't they? (*They retire into the house with scornful looks.*)

JACK This ghastly state of things is what you call Bunburying, I suppose?

ALGERNON Yes, and a perfectly wonderful Bunbury it is. The most wonderful Bunbury I have ever had in my life.

JACK Well, you've no right whatsoever to Bunbury here.

ALGERNON That is absurd. One has a right to Bunbury anywhere one chooses. Every serious Bunburyist knows that.

JACK Serious Bunburyist! Good heavens!

ALGERNON Well, one must be serious about something, if one wants to have any amusement in life. I happen to be serious about Bunburying. What on earth you are serious about I haven't got the remotest idea. About everything, I should fancy. You have such an absolutely trivial nature.

JACK Well, the only small satisfaction I have in the whole of this wretched business is that your friend Bunbury is quite exploded. You won't be able to run down to the country quite so often as you used to do, dear Algy. And a very good thing, too.

ALGERNON Your brother is a little off color, isn't he, dear Jack? You won't be able to disappear to London quite so frequently as your wicked custom was. And not a bad thing, either.

JACK As for your conduct towards Miss Cardew, I must say that your taking in a sweet, simple, innocent girl like that is quite inexcusable. To say nothing of the fact that she is my ward.

ALGERNON I can see no possible defense at all for your deceiving a brillant, clever, thoroughly experienced young lady like Miss Fairfax. To say nothing of the fact that she is my cousin.

JACK I wanted to be engaged to Gwendolen, that is all. I love her.

ALGERNON Well, I simply wanted to be engaged to Cecily. I adore her.

JACK There is certainly no chance of your marrying Miss Cardew.

ALGERNON I don't think there is much likelihood, Jack, of you and Miss Fairfax being united.

JACK Well, that is no business of yours.

ALGERNON If it was my business, I wouldn't talk about it. (*Begins to eat muffins.*) It is very vulgar to talk about one's business. Only people like stock-brokers do that, and then merely at dinner parties.

JACK How you can sit there, calmly eating muffins, when we are in this horrible trouble, I can't make out. You seem to me to be perfectly heartless.

ALGERNON Well, I can't eat muffins in an agitated manner. The butter would probably get on my cuffs. One should always eat muffins quite calmly. It is the only way to eat them.

JACK I say it's perfectly heartless your eating muffins at all, under the circumstances.

ALGERNON When I am in trouble, eating is the only thing that consoles me. Indeed, when I am in really great trouble, as any one who knows me intimately will tell you, I refuse everything except food and drink. At the present moment I am eating muffins because I am unhappy. Besides, I am particularly fond of muffins. (*Rising.*)

JACK (*rising*) Well, that is no reason why you should eat them all in that greedy way. (*Takes muffins from* ALGERNON.)

ALGERNON (*offering tea-cake*) I wish you would have tea-cake instead. I don't like tea-cake.

JACK Good heavens! I suppose a man may eat his own muffins in his own garden.

ALGERNON But you have just said it was perfectly heartless to eat muffins.

JACK I said it was perfectly heartless of you, under the circumstances. That is a very different thing.

ALGERNON That may be. But the muffins are the same. (*He seizes the muffin-dish from* JACK.)

JACK Algy, I wish to goodness you would go.

ALGERNON You can't possibly ask me to go without having some dinner. It's absurd. I never go without my dinner. No one ever does, except vegetarians and people like that. Besides I have just made arrangements with Dr. Chasuble to be christened at a quarter to six under the name of Ernest.

JACK My dear fellow, the sooner you give up that nonsense the better. I made arrangements this morning with Dr. Chasuble to be christened myself at 5.30, and I naturally will take the name of Ernest. Gwendolen would wish it. We can't both be christened Ernest. It's absurd. Besides, I have a perfect right to be christened if I like. There is no evidence at all that I ever have been christened by anybody. I should think it extremely probable I never was, and so does Dr. Chasuble. It is entirely different in your case. You have been christened already.

ALGERNON Yes, but I have not been christened for years.

JACK Yes, but you have been christened. That is the important thing.

ALGERNON Quite so. So I know my constitution can stand it. If you are not quite sure about your ever having been christened, I must say I think it rather dangerous your venturing on it now. It might make you very unwell. You can hardly have forgotten that some one very closely connected with you was very nearly carried off this week in Paris by a severe chill.

JACK Yes, but you said yourself that a severe chill was not hereditary.

ALGERNON It usedn't to be, I know—but I daresay it is now. Science is always making wonderful improvements in things.

JACK (*picking up the muffin-dish*) Oh, that is nonsense; you are always talking nonsense.

ALGERNON Jack, you are at the muffins again! I wish you wouldn't. There are only two left. (*Takes them.*) I told you I was particularly fond of muffins.

JACK But I hate tea-cake.

ALGERNON Why on earth then do you allow tea-cake to be served up for your guests? What ideas you have of hospitality!

JACK Algernon! I have already told you to go. I don't want you here. Why don't you go?

ALGERNON I haven't quite finished my tea yet, and there is still one muffin left. (JACK *groans, and sinks into a chair.* ALGERNON *still continues eating.*)

CURTAIN

ACT III

SCENE *Morning-room at the Manor House.* GWENDOLEN *and* CECILY *are at the window, looking out into the garden.*

GWENDOLEN The fact that they did not follow us at once into the house, as any one else would have done, seems to me to show that they have some sense of shame left.

CECILY They have been eating muffins. That looks like repentance.

GWENDOLEN (*after a pause*) They don't seem to notice us at all. Couldn't you cough?

GWENDOLEN They're looking at us. What effrontery!

CECILY They're approaching. That's very forward of them.

GWENDOLEN Let us preserve a dignified silence.

CECILY Certainly. It's the only thing to do now.

Enter JACK, *followed by* ALGERNON. *They whistle some dreadful popular air from a British opera.*

GWENDOLEN This dignified silence seems to produce an unpleasant effect.

CECILY A most distasteful one.

GWENDOLEN But we will not be the first to speak.

CECILY Certainly not.

GWENDOLEN Mr. Worthing, I have something very particular to ask you. Much depends on your reply.

CECILY Gwendolen, your common sense is invaluable. Mr. Moncrieff, kindly answer me the following question. Why did you pretend to be my guardian's brother?

ALGERNON In order that I might have an opportunity of meeting you.

CECILY (*to* GWENDOLEN) That certainly seems a satisfactory explanation, does it not?

GWENDOLEN Yes, dear, if you can believe him.

CECILY I don't. But that does not affect the wonderful beauty of his answer.

GWENDOLEN True. In matters of grave importance, style, not sincerity, is the vital thing. Mr. Worthing, what explanation can you offer to me for pretending to have a brother? Was it in order that you might have an opportunity of coming up to town to see me as often as possible?

JACK Can you doubt it, Miss Fairfax?

GWENDOLEN I have the gravest doubts upon the subject. But I intend to crush them. This is not the moment for German skepticism. (*Moving to* CECILY.) Their explanations appear to be quite satisfactory, especially Mr. Worthing's. That seems to me to have the stamp of truth upon it.

CECILY I am more than content with what Mr. Moncrieff said. His voice alone inspires one with absolute credulity.

GWENDOLEN Then you think we should forgive them?

CECILY Yes. I mean no.

GWENDOLEN True! I had forgotten. There are principles at stake that one cannot surrender. Which of us should tell them? The task is not a pleasant one.

CECILY Could we not both speak at the same time?

GWENDOLEN An excellent idea! I nearly always speak at the same time as other people. Will you take the time from me?

CECILY Certainly. (GWENDOLEN *beats time with uplifted finger.*)

GWENDOLEN and CECILY (*speaking together*) Your Christian names are still an insuperable barrrier. That is all!

JACK and ALGERNON (*speaking together*) Our Christian names! Is that all? But we are going to be christened this afternoon.

GWENDOLEN (*to* JACK) For my sake you are prepared to do this terrible thing?

JACK I am.

CECILY (*to* ALGERNON) To please me you are ready to face this fearful ordeal?

ALGERNON I am!

GWENDOLEN How absurd to talk of the equality of the sexes! Where questions of self-sacrifice are concerned, men are infinitely beyond us.

JACK We are. (*Clasps hands with* ALGERNON.)

CECILY They have moments of physical courage of which we women know absolutely nothing.

GWENDOLEN (*to* JACK) Darling!

ALGERNON (*to* CECILY) Darling! (*They fall into each other's arms.*)

Enter MERRIMAN. *When he enters he coughs loudly, seeing the situation.*

MERRIMAN Ahem! Ahem! Lady Bracknell!

JACK Good heavens!

Enter LADY BRACKNELL. *The couples separate in alarm. Exit* MERRIMAN.

LADY BRACKNELL Gwendolen! What does this mean?

GWENDOLEN Merely that I am engaged to be married to Mr. Worthing, Mamma.

LADY BRACKNELL Come here. Sit down. Sit down immediately. Hesitation of any kind is a sign of mental decay in the young, of physical weakness in the old. (*Turns to* JACK.) Apprised, sir, of my daughter's sudden flight by her trusty maid, whose confidence I purchased by means of a small coin, I followed her at once by a luggage train. Her unhappy father is, I am glad to say, under the impression that she is attending a more than usually lengthy lecture by the University Extension Scheme on the Influence of a Permanent Income on Thought. I do not propose to undeceive him. Indeed I have never undeceived him on any question. I would consider it wrong. But of course you will clearly understand that all communication between yourself and my daughter must cease immediately from this moment. On this point, as indeed on all points, I am firm.

JACK I am engaged to be married to Gwendolen, Lady Bracknell!

LADY BRACKNELL You are nothing of the kind, sir. And now, as regards Algernon! . . . Algernon!

ALGERNON Yes, Aunt Augusta.

LADY BRACKNELL May I ask if it is in this house that your invalid friend Mr. Bunbury resides?

ALGERNON (*stammering*) Oh, no! Bunbury doesn't live here. Bunbury is somewhere else at present. In fact, Bunbury is dead.

LADY BRACKNELL Dead! When did Mr. Bunburry die? His death must have been extremely sudden.

ALGERNON (*airily*) Oh, I killed Bunbury this afternoon. I mean poor Bunbury died this afternoon.

LADY BRACKNELL What did he die of?

ALGERNON Bunbury? Oh, he was quite exploded.

LADY BRACKNELL Exploded! Was he the victim of a revolutionary outrage? I was not aware that Mr. Bunbury was interested in social legislation. If so, he is well punished for his morbidity.

ALGERNON My dear Aunt Augusta, I mean he was found out! The doctors found out that Bunbury could not live, that is what I mean—so Bunbury died.

LADY BRACKNELL He seems to have had great confidence in the opinion of his physicians. I am glad, however, that he made up his mind at the last to some definite course of action, and acted under proper medical advice. And now that we have finally got rid of this Mr. Bunbury, may I ask, Mr. Worthing, who is that young person whose hand my nephew Algernon is now holding in what seems to me a peculiarly unnecessary manner?

JACK That lady is Miss Cecily Cardew, my ward. (LADY BRACKNELL *bows coldy to* CECILY.)

ALGERNON I am engaged to be married to Cecily, Aunt Augusta.

LADY BRACKNELL I beg your pardon?

CECILY Mr. Moncrieff and I are engaged to be married, Lady Bracknell.

LADY BRACKNELL (*with a shiver, crossing to the sofa and sitting down*) I do not know whether there is anything peculiarly exciting in the air of this particular part of Hertfordshire, but the number of engagements that go on seems to me considerably above the proper average that statistics have laid down for our guidance. I think some preliminary enquiry on my part would not be out of place. Mr. Worthing, is Miss Cardew at all connected with any of the larger railway stations in London? I merely desire information. Until yesterday I had no idea that there were any families or persons whose origin was a Terminus. (JACK *looks perfectly furious, but restrains himself.*)

JACK (*in a clear, cold voice*) Miss Cardew is the granddaughter of the late Mr. Thomas Cardew of 149, Belgrave Square, S.W.; Gervase Park, Dorking, Surrey; and the Sporran, Fifeshire, N.B.

LADY BRACKNELL That sounds not unsatisfactory. Three addresses always inspire confidence, even in tradesmen. But what proof have I of their authenticity?

JACK I have carefully preserved the Court Guide of the period. They are open to your inspection, Lady Bracknell.

LADY BRACKNELL (*grimly*) I have known strange errors in that publication.

JACK Miss Cardew's family solicitors are Messrs. Markby, Markby, and Markby.

LADY BRACKNELL Markby, Markby, and Markby? A firm of the very highest position in their profession. Indeed I am told that one of the Mr. Markbys is occasionally to be seen at dinner parties. So far I am satisfied.

JACK (*very irritably*) How extremely kind of you, Lady Bracknell! I have also in my possession, you will be pleased to hear, certificates of Miss Cardew's birth, baptism, whooping cough, registration, vaccination, confirmation, and the measles; both the German and the English variety.

LADY BRACKNELL Ah! A life crowded with incident, I see; though perhaps somewhat too exciting for a young girl. I am not myself in favor of premature experiences. (*Rises, looks at her watch.*) Gwendolen! the time approaches for our departure. We have not a moment to lose. As a matter of form, Mr. Worthing, I had better ask you if Miss Cardew has any little fortune?

JACK Oh, about a hundred and thirty thousand pounds in the Funds. That is all. Goodby, Lady Bracknell. So pleased to have seen you.

LADY BRACKNELL (*sitting down again*) A moment, Mr. Worthing. A hundred and thirty thousand pounds! And in the Funds! Miss Cardew seems to me a most attractive young lady, now that I look at her. Few girls of the present day have any really solid qualities, any of the qualities that last, and improve with time. We live, I regret to say, in an age of surfaces. (*To* CECILY.) Come over here, dear. (CECILY *goes across.*) Pretty child! your dress is sadly simple, and your hair seems almost as Nature might have left it. But we can soon alter all that. A thoroughly experienced French maid produces a really marvelous result in a very brief space of time. I remember recommending one to young Lady Lancing, and after three months her own husband did not know her.

JACK (*aside*) And after six months nobody knew her.

LADY BRACKNELL (*glares at* JACK *for a few moments, then bends, with a practiced smile, to* CECILY) Kindly turn round, sweet child. (CECILY *turns completely round.*) No, the side view is what I want. (CECILY *presents her profile.*) Yes, quite as I expected. There are distinct social possibilities in your profile. The two weak points in our age are its want of principle and its want of profile. The chin a little higher, dear. Style largely depends on the way the chin is worn. They are worn very high, just at present, Algernon!

ALGERNON Yes, Aunt Augusta!

LADY BRACKNELL There are distinct social possibilities in Miss Cardew's profile.

ALGERNON Cecily is the sweetest, dearest, prettiest girl in the whole world. And I don't care twopence about social possibilities.

LADY BRACKNELL Never speak disrespectfully of society, Algernon. Only people who can't get into it do that. (*To* CECILY.) Dear child, of course you know that Algernon has nothing but his debts to depend upon. But I do not approve of mercenary marriages. When I married Lord Bracknell I had no fortune of any kind. But I never dreamed for a moment of allowing that to stand in my way. Well, I suppose I must give my consent.

ALGERNON Thank you, Aunt Augusta.

LADY BRACKNELL Cecily, you may kiss me!

CECILY (*kisses her*) Thank you, Lady Bracknell.

LADY BRACKNELL You may also address me as Aunt Augusta for the future.

CECILY Thank you, Aunt Augusta.

LADY BRACKNELL The marriage, I think, had better take place quite soon.

ALGERNON Thank you, Aunt Augusta.

CECILY Thank you, Aunt Augusta.

LADY BRACKNELL To speak frankly, I am not in favor of long engagements. They give people the opportunity of finding out each other's character before marriage, which I think is never advisable.

JACK I beg your pardon for interrupting you, Lady Bracknell, but this engagement is quite out of the question. I am Miss Cardew's guardian, and she cannot marry without my consent until she comes of age. That consent I absolutely decline to give.

LADY BRACKNELL Upon what grounds, may I ask? Algernon is an extremely, I may almost say an ostentatiously, eligible young man. He has nothing, but he looks everything. What more can one desire?

JACK It pains me very much to have to speak frankly to you, Lady Bracknell, about your nephew, but the fact is that I do not approve at all of his moral character. I suspect him of being untruthful. (ALGERNON *and* CECILY *look at him in indignant amazement.*)

LADY BRACKNELL Untruthful! My nephew Algernon? Impossible! He is an Oxonian.

JACK I fear there can be no possible doubt about the matter. This afternoon, during my temporary absence in London on an important question of romance, he obtained admission to my house by means of the false pretense of being my brother. Under an assumed name he drank, I've just been informed by my butler, an entire pint bottle of my Perrier-Jouet, Brut, '89; a wine I was specially reserving for myself. Continuing his disgraceful deception, he succeeded in the course of the afternoon in alienating the affections of my only ward. He subsequently stayed to tea, and devoured every single muffin. And what makes his conduct all the more heartless is, that he was perfectly well aware from the first that I have no brother, that I never had a brother, and that I don't intend to have a brother, not even of any kind. I distinctly told him so myself yesterday afternoon.

LADY BRACKNELL Ahem! Mr. Worthing, after careful consideration I have decided entirely to overlook my nephew's conduct to you.

JACK That is very generous of you, Lady Bracknell. My own decision, however, is unalterable. I decline to give my consent.

LADY BRACKNELL (*to* CECILY) Come here, sweet child. (CECILY *goes over.*) How old are you, dear?

CECILY Well, I am really only eighteen, but I always admit to twenty when I go to evening parties.

LADY BRACKNELL You are perfectly right in making some slight alteration. Indeed, no woman should ever be quite accurate about her age. It looks so calculating. . . . (*In meditative manner.*) Eighteen, but admitting to twenty at evening parties. Well, it will not be very long before you are of age and free from the restraints of tutelage. So I don't think your guardian's consent is, after all, a matter of any importance.

JACK Pray excuse me, Lady Bracknell, for interrupting you again, but it is only fair to tell you that according to the terms of her grandfather's will Miss Cardew does not come legally of age till she is thirty-five.

LADY BRACKNELL That does not seem to me to be a grave objection. Thirty-five is a very attractive age. London society is full of women of the very highest birth who have, of their own free choice, remained thirty-five for years. Lady Dumbleton is an instance in point. To my own knowledge she has been thirty-five ever since she arrived at the age of forty, which was many years ago now. I see no reason why our dear Cecily should not be even still more attractive at the age you mention than she is at present. There will be a large accumulation of property.

CECILY Algy, could you wait for me till I was thirty-five?

ALGERNON Of course I could, Cecily. You know I could.

CECILY Yes, I felt it instinctively, but I couldn't wait all that time. I hate waiting even five minutes for anybody. It always makes me rather cross. I am not punctual myself, I know, but I do like punctuality in others, and waiting, even to be married, is quite out of the question.

ALGERNON Then what is to be done, Cecily?

CECILY I don't know, Mr. Moncrieff.

LADY BRACKNELL My dear Mr. Worthing, as Miss Cardew states positively that she cannot wait till she is thirty-five—a remark which I am bound to say seems to me to show a somewhat impatient nature—I would beg of you to reconsider your decision.

JACK But, my dear Lady Bracknell, the matter is entirely in your own hands. The moment you consent to my marriage with Gwendolen, I will most gladly allow your nephew to form an alliance with my ward.

LADY BRACKNELL (*rising and drawing herself up*) You must be quite aware that what you propose is out of the question.

JACK Then a passionate celibacy is all that any of us can look forward to.

LADY BRACKNELL That is not the destiny I propose for Gwendolen. Algernon, of course, can choose for himself. (*Pulls out her watch.*) Come, dear (GWENDOLEN *rises*), we have already missed five, if not six, trains. To miss any more might expose us to comment on the platform.

Enter DR. CHASUBLE.

CHASUBLE Everything is quite ready for the christenings.

LADY BRACKNELL The christenings, sir! Is not that somewhat premature?

CHASUBLE (*looking rather puzzled, and pointing to* JACK *and* ALGERNON) Both these gentlemen have expressed a desire for immediate baptism.

LADY BRACKNELL At their age? The idea is grotesque and irreligious! Algernon, I forbid you to be baptized. I will not hear of such excesses. Lord Bracknell would be highly displeased if he learned that that was the way in which you wasted your time and money.

CHASUBLE Am I to understand then that there are to be no christenings at all this afternoon?

JACK I don't think that, as things are now, it would be of much practical value to either of us, Dr. Chasuble.

CHASUBLE I am grieved to hear such sentiments from you, Mr. Worthing. They savor of the heretical views of the Anabaptists, views that I have completely refuted in four of my unpublished sermons. However, as your present mood seems to be one peculiarly secular, I will return to the church at once. Indeed, I have just been informed by the pewopener that for the last hour and a half Miss Prism has been waiting for me in the vestry.

LADY BRACKNELL (*starting*) Miss Prism! Did I hear you mention a Miss Prism?

CHASUBLE Yes, Lady Bracknell. I am on my way to join her.

LADY BRACKNELL Pray allow me to detain you for a moment. This matter may prove to be one of vital importance to Lord Bracknell and myself. Is this Miss Prism a female of repellent aspect, remotely connected with education?

CHASUBLE (*somewhat indignantly*) She is the most cultivated of ladies, and the very picture of respectability.

LADY BRACKNELL It is obviously the same person. May I ask what position she holds in your household?

CHASUBLE (*severely*) I am a celibate, madam.

JACK (*interposing*) Miss Prism, Lady Bracknell, has been for the last three years Miss Cardew's esteemed governess and valued companion.

LADY BRACKNELL In spite of what I hear of her, I must see her at once. Let her be sent for.

CHASUBLE (*looking off*) She approaches; she is nigh.

Enter MISS PRISM *hurriedly.*

MISS PRISM I was told you expected me in the vestry, dear Canon. I have been waiting for you there for an hour and three-quarters. (*Catches sight of* LADY BRACKNELL, *who has fixed her with a stony glare.* MISS PRISM *grows pale and quails. She looks anxiously round as if desirous to escape.*)

LADY BRACKNELL (*in a severe, judicial voice*) Prism! (MISS PRISM *bows her head in shame.*) Come here, Prism! (MISS PRISM *approaches in a humble manner.*) Prism! Where is that baby? (*General consternation. The Canon starts back in horror.* ALGERNON *and* JACK *pretend to be anxious to shield* CECILY *and* GWENDOLEN *from hearing the details of a terrible public scandal.*) Twenty-eight years ago, Prism, you left Lord Bracknell's house, Number 104, Upper Grosvenor Street, in charge of a perambulator that contained a baby, of the male sex. You never returned. A few weeks later, through the elaborate investigations of the Metropolitan police, the perambulator was discovered at midnight, standing by itself in a remote corner of Bayswater. It contained the manuscript of a three-volume novel of more than usually revolting sentimentality. (MISS PRISM *starts in involuntary indignation.*) But the baby was not there! (*Every one looks at* MISS PRISM.) Prism, where is that baby? (*A pause.*)

MISS PRISM Lady Bracknell, I admit with shame that I do not know. I only wish I did. The plain facts of the case are these. On the morning of the day you mention, a day that is forever branded on my memory, I prepared as usual to take the baby out in its perambulator. I had also with me a somewhat old but capacious hand-bag in which I had intended to place the manuscript of a work of fiction that I had written during my few unoccupied hours. In a moment of mental abstraction, for which I never can forgive myself, I deposited the manuscript in the bassinet, and placed the baby in the hand-bag.

JACK (*who has been listening attentively*) But where did you deposit the hand-bag?

MISS PRISM Do not ask me, Mr. Worthing.

JACK Miss Prism, this is a matter of no small importance to me. I insist on knowing where you deposited the hand-bag that contained that infant.

MISS PRISM I left it in the cloak-room of one of the larger railway stations in London.

JACK What railway station?

MISS PRISM (*quite crushed*) Victoria. The Brighton line. (*Sinks into a chair.*)

JACK I must retire to my room for a moment. Gwendolen, wait here for me.

GWENDOLEN If you are not too long, I will wait here for you all my life.

Exit JACK *in great excitement.*

CHASUBLE What do you think this means, Lady Bracknell?

LADY BRACKNELL I dare not even suspect, Dr. Chasuble. I need hardly tell you that in families of high position strange coincidences are not supposed to occur. They are hardly considered the thing. (*Noises heard overhead as if some one was throwing trunks about. Everybody looks up.*)

CECILY Uncle Jack seems strangely agitated.

CHASUBLE Your guardian has a very emotional nature.

LADY BRACKNELL This noise is extremely unpleasant. It sounds as if he was having an argument. I dislike arguments of any kind. They are always vulgar, and often convincing.

CHASUBLE (*looking up*) It has stopped now. (*The noise is redoubled.*)

LADY BRACKNELL I wish he would arrive at some conclusion.

GWENDOLEN This suspense is terrible. I hope it will last.

Enter JACK *with a hand-bag of black leather in his hand.*

JACK (*rushing over to* MISS PRISM) Is this the hand-bag, Miss Prism? Examine it carefully before you speak. The happiness of more than one life depends on your answer.

MISS PRISM (*calmly*) It seems to be mine. Yes, here is the injury it received through the upsetting of a Gower Street omnibus in younger and happier days. Here is the stain on the lining caused by the explosion of a temperance beverage, an incident that occurred at Leamington. And here, on the lock, are my initials. I had forgotten that in an extravagant mood I had had them placed there. The bag is undoubtedly mine. I am delighted to have it so unexpectedly restored to me. It has been a great inconvenience being without it all these years.

JACK (*in a pathetic voice*) Miss Prism, more is restored to you than this hand-bag. I was the baby you placed in it.

MISS PRISM (*amazed*) You?

JACK (*embracing her*) Yes . . . mother!

MISS PRISM (*recoiling in indignant astonishment*) Mr. Worthing! I am unmarried!

JACK Unmarried! I do not deny that is a serious blow. But after all, who has the right to cast a stone against one who has suffered? Cannot repentance wipe out an act of folly? Why should there be one law for men and another for women? Mother, I forgive you. (*Tries to embrace her again.*)

MISS PRISM (*still more indignant*) Mr. Worthing, there is some error. (*Pointing to* LADY BRACKNELL.) There is the lady who can tell you who you really are.

JACK (*after a pause*) Lady Bracknell, I hate to seem inquisitive, but would you kindly inform me who I am?

LADY BRACKNELL I am afraid that the news I have to give you will not altogether please you. You are the son of my poor sister, Mrs. Moncrieff, and consequently Algernon's elder brother.

JACK Algy's elder brother! Then I have a brother after all. I knew I had a brother! I always said I had a brother! Cecily,—how could you have ever doubted that I had a brother? (*Seizes hold of* ALGERNON.) Dr. Chasuble, my unfortunate brother. Miss Prism, my unfortunate brother. Gwendolen, my unfortunate brother. Algy, you young scoundrel, you will have to treat me with more respect in the future. You have never behaved to me like a brother in all your life.

ALGERNON Well, not till to-day, old boy, I admit. I did my best, however, though I was out of practice. (*Shakes hands.*)

GWENDOLEN (*to* JACK) My own! but what own are you? What is your Christian name, now that you have become some one else?

JACK Good heavens! . . . I had quite forgotten that point. Your decision on the subject of my name is irrevocable, I suppose?

GWENDOLEN I never change, except in my affections.

CECILY What a noble nature you have, Gwendolen!

JACK Then the question had better be cleared up at once. Aunt Augusta, a moment. At the time when Miss Prism left me in the hand-bag, had I been christened already?

LADY BRACKNELL Every luxury that money could buy, including christening, had been lavished on you by your fond and doting parents.

JACK Then I was christened! That is settled. Now, what name was I given? Let me know the worst.

LADY BRACKNELL Being the eldest son you were naturally christened after your father.

JACK (*irritably*) Yes, but what was my father's Christian name?

LADY BRACKNELL (*meditatively*) I cannot at the present moment recall what the General's Christian name was. But I have no doubt he had one. He was eccentric, I admit. But only in later years. And that was the result of the Indian climate, and marriage, and indigestion, and other things of that kind.

JACK Algy! Can't you recollect what our father's Christian name was?

ALGERNON My dear boy, we were never even on speaking terms. He died before I was a year old.

JACK His name would appear in the Army Lists of the period, I suppose, Aunt Augusta?

LADY BRACKNELL The General was essentially a man of peace, except in his domestic life. But I have no doubt his name would appear in any military directory.

JACK The Army Lists of the last forty years are here. These delightful records should have been my constant study. (*Rushes to bookcase and tears the books out.*) M. Generals . . . Mallam, Maxbohm, Magley, what ghastly names they have—Markby, Migsby, Mobbs, Moncrieff! Lieutenant 1840, Captain, Lieutenant-Colonel, Colonel, General 1869, Christian names, Ernest John. (*Puts book very quietly down and speaks quite calmly.*) I always told you, Gwendolen, my name was Ernest, didn't I? Well, it is Ernest after all. I mean it naturally is Ernest.

LADY BRACKNELL Yes, I remember that the General was called Ernest. I knew I had some particular reason for disliking the name.

GWENDOLEN Ernest! My own Ernest! I felt from the first that you could have no other name!

JACK Gwendolen, it is a terrible thing for a man to find out suddenly that all his life he has been speaking nothing but the truth. Can you forgive me?

GWENDOLEN I can. For I feel that you are sure to change.

JACK My own one!

CHASUBLE (*to* MISS PRISM) Laetitia! (*Embraces her.*)

MISS PRISM (*enthusiastically*) Frederick! At last!

ALGERNON Cecily! (*Embraces her.*) At last!

JACK Gwendolen! (*Embraces her.*) At last!

LADY BRACKNELL My nephew, you seem to be displaying signs of triviality.

JACK On the contrary, Aunt Augusta, I've now realized for the first time in my life the vital Importance of Being Earnest.

TABLEAU

CURTAIN

Questions

1. The tone of the first conversation between Algernon and Jack (pp. 1107–08) alerts us that this is not a serious drama, but a comedy. Identify specific instances of humorous irony.

2. Oscar Wilde—and his characters—delight in word-play and the invention of neologisms (new words). "Bunburyist" and "Bunburying" are instances of neologisms. Define "Bunburying" in your own words, and explain how "Bunburying" contributes to the dramatic situation of this play.

3. How much of what Lady Bracknell says can be taken seriously? How do her attitudes satirize the English upper class?

4. *The Importance of Being Earnest* burlesques not only the manners of society but also the clichés of nineteenth-century melodrama. Discuss the love-scene between Jack and Gwendolen (pp. 1113–14) and how it burlesques a conventional, sentimental love-scene.

5. Foreshadowing, in the theater, is a clue or suggestion that some important event will transpire or that some secret will be revealed. Is there any foreshadowing early in the play of the fact that Miss Prism left Jack in the hand-bag at Victoria Station?

6. To what extent do the opinions and behavior of Canon Chasuble satirize the Church of England?

7. A common form of comic irony occurs when a character suffers embarrassment because he does not immediately understand his predicament. How is Jack an object of comic irony in Act II (p. 1125)?

8. In ancient Greek drama, threatened characters were sometimes rescued by a *deus ex machina*, or god from the machine, who would swoop down on the stage to carry them out of harm's way. The term has come to refer to any last-minute action or revelation that improves a character's fortune. Explain how Jack benefits from the *deus ex machina* effect in Act III.

Tragicomedy

The dramas of Aeschylus and Sophocles are tragic throughout, and the comedies of Aristophanes maintain their comic tone even in scenes that reveal an underlying seriousness. Such consistency in the playwright's attitude toward his characters and story is called consistency of tone. Most classical drama and some modern plays have such consistency. *The Importance of Being Earnest* is so thoroughly funny that we do not doubt for a moment that the play we are reading is a comedy.

Not all plays maintain such evenness of tone. Starting with Euripides, the classical consistency of tone begins to dissolve, giving rise to tragicomedy. In a tragicomedy serious scenes alternate with comic scenes, providing comic relief and a richly ironic blend of emotions. Euripides' first play, *Alcestis* (434 B.C.), dramatizes the story of a king's wife who voluntarily descends into Hades in place of her doomed husband. Heracles goes to rescue her. His drunken, wise-cracking character lends comic relief to a play that is otherwise quite serious. We find it difficult to call *Alcestis* a tragedy or a comedy, so we call it a tragicomedy. The Elizabethan playwrights were great masters of tragicomedy, particularly Shakespeare in *Measure for Measure, A Winter's Tale,* and *Troilus and Cressida.* Some critics consider *Hamlet,* with its amusing graveyard scene and the protagonist's antics, to be a tragicomedy. *King Lear,* with its hilarious Fool, and *Macbeth,* with its drunken Porter, also mingle serious and comic scenes. Yet these plays remain fundamentally tragic because they compel sympathy for their ill-fated protagonists.

The Misanthrope

It is difficult to sympathize with the protagonist of Molière's *The Misanthrope.* Although his honesty and forthrightness lend him a certain stature, Alceste is so thoroughly egotistical that we are more likely to find him a fit object for satire than a figure to inspire fear and pity. Molière maintains a comic distance from Alceste through alternating scenes of humor and high seriousness. The scenes in which Alceste complains to his friend Philinte of the falsity of humankind, and the scenes in which he scolds his beloved Célimène for her fickleness, are quite bitter. Taken out of context, they look almost like passages from a tragedy. Alceste's insistence on truth in a dishonest world, and his demand that people love him on his own terms, defy the laws of his society, and lead him as fatally toward isolation as any tragic hero. Yet his behavior seems so absurd among his frivolous peers, that we laugh instead of feeling sorry for him. Because of the alternation of serious and comic scenes in *The Misanthrope,* we may rightly call it a tragicomedy. Since the protagonist as well as the society around him becomes an object of ridicule, we may properly consider the play a satire as well.

Molière and the Palais Royal

As a writer of witty epigrams as well as broad jokes, a deviser of hilarious situations, and a critic of human nature and manners, Molière is without rival. He is to French comedy what Shakespeare is to English tragedy. Shakespeare wrote many kinds of plays, but Molière concentrated on comedy, producing a literature of extraordinary range, from buffoonish farces in prose to the most elegant tragicomedies in perfectly balanced verses. Molière had the sublime ability to create comic characters embodying essential flaws or inconsistencies in human nature. These characters—The Miser, The Misanthrope, The Imposter, and others—have become immortal to theatergoers and readers the world over.

From his youth Molière was a man of the theater; he knew all of the madness, deep frustration, and joys of the profession. Born and christened Jean Baptiste Poquelin in Paris in 1622, he was the son of an upholsterer who served Louis XV. He studied with the Jesuits, then in 1643 became an actor, adopting the name by which we know him. With the encouragement of a famous French actress, Molière co-founded the theater company for which he wrote his first plays. The company failed in Paris, then went on the road where it experienced some success and considerable hardship, returning to the capital in 1658 when the King granted Molière a theater near the Louvre.

The King liked Molière, but his patronage of the young playwright has been exaggerated. The pension promised Molière after the success of *The Doctor in Love* was never paid. Even after the company moved to the Palais Royal, where Molière staged such triumphs as *The School for Husbands*, *The Misanthrope*, and *The School for Wives*, he had to fight for survival. The barbs of his satire kept him in trouble with one Parisian faction or other for most of his career. His free-thinking *Don Juan* caused such scandal that after fifteen performances it was banned from the repertory. *Tartuffe*, the satire of a religious hypocrite, was banned after one performance, and the archbishop supported the ban with ecclesiastical censure. Despite these troubles, Molière's personality and genius held his actors together, as well as his audience. In the fourteen years from 1660 to 1673, Molière wrote thirty-one of the ninety-five plays acted by his players, many of them dazzling masterpieces. While acting the lead in the premiere of *The Imaginary Invalid*, Molière was taken ill on stage, and died the same night. Since he had not had time enough to renounce the actor's profession and receive the sacraments, he was buried without ceremony after sunset on February 21, 1673.

Madeline Renaud and Jean-Louis Barrault in *Le Misanthrope* *(Performing Arts Research Center, The New York Public Library)*

The Palais Royal was even more intimate than Shakespeare's Globe, seating about six hundred. An indoor theater, it was lighted by candles. The stage was the proscenium style most familiar to modern theater audiences, with painted, shaped scenery and a curtain between the playing area and the orchestra.

French Scenes

French scripts do not indicate entrances and exits in the same manner as the English. For the French, a scene consists of a conversation among certain characters; as soon as one of the characters exits or a new one enters, the script declares a new scene. Thus Act I, Scene 1 of *The Misanthrope* finds Philinte and Alceste in conversation in a drawing room of Célimène's house. Then Oronte enters. But the script doesn't say "Oronte enters," rather it indicates:

> SCENE II. ORONTE, ALCESTE, PHILINTE

When Oronte exits, the script doesn't say "Oronte exits," but marks a new scene:

> SCENE III. PHILINTE, ALCESTE

The reader must pay careful attention to these scene indications in order to keep track of who is on stage at any given time.

MOLIÈRE (1622–1673)

The Misanthrope

English version by Richard Wilbur

CHARACTERS

ALCESTE, *in love with Célimène*	ACASTE ⎱ *Marquesses*
PHILINTE, *Alceste's friend*	CLITANDRE ⎰
ORONTE, *in love with Célimène*	BASQUE, *Célimène's servant*
CÉLIMÈNE, *Alceste's beloved*	A GUARD *of the Marshalsea*
ÉLIANTE, *Célimène's cousin*	DUBOIS, *Alceste's valet*
ARSINOÉ, *a friend of Célimène's*	

The Scene throughout is in CÉLIMÈNE's *house at Paris*

ACT I

SCENE I. PHILINTE, ALCESTE

PHILINTE Now, what's got into you?
ALCESTE (*seated*)   Kindly leave me alone.
PHILINTE Come, come, what is it? This lugubrious tone . . .
ALCESTE Leave me, I said; you spoil my solitude.
PHILINTE Oh, listen to me, now, and don't be rude.
5 ALCESTE I choose to be rude, Sir, and to be hard of hearing.
PHILINTE These ugly moods of yours are not endearing;

Friends though we are, I really must insist . . .
ALCESTE (*abruptly rising*) Friends? Friends, you say? Well, cross me off your list.
I've been your friend till now, as you well know;
10   But after what I saw a moment ago
I tell you flatly that our ways must part.
I wish no place in a dishonest heart.
PHILINTE Why, what have I done, Alceste? Is this quite just?
ALCESTE My God, you ought to die of self-disgust.
15   I call your conduct inexcusable, Sir,
And every man of honor will concur.
I see you almost hug a man to death,
Exclaim for joy until you're out of breath,
And supplement these loving demonstrations
20   With endless offers, vows, and protestations;
Then when I ask you "Who was that?" I find
That you can barely bring his name to mind!
Once the man's back is turned, you cease to love him,
And speak with absolute indifference of him!
25   By God, I say it's base and scandalous
To falsify the heart's affections thus;
If I caught myself behaving in such a way,
I'd hang myself for shame, without delay.
PHILINTE It hardly seems a hanging matter to me;
30   I hope that you will take it graciously
If I extend myself a slight reprieve,
And live a little longer, by your leave.
ALCESTE How dare you joke about a crime so grave?
PHILINTE What crime? How else are people to behave?
35   ALCESTE I'd have them be sincere, and never part
With any word that isn't from the heart.
PHILINTE When someone greets us with a show of pleasure,
It's but polite to give him equal measure,
Return his love the best that we know how,
40   And trade him offer for offer, vow for vow.
ALCESTE No, no, this formula you'd have me follow,
However fashionable, is false and hollow,
And I despise the frenzied operations
Of all these barterers of protestations,
45   These lavishers of meaningless embraces,
These utterers of obliging commonplaces,
Who court and flatter everyone on earth
And praise the fool no less than the man of worth.
Should you rejoice that someone fondles you,
50   Offers his love and service, swears to be true,
And fills your ears with praises of your name,
When to the first damned fop he'll say the same?
No, no: no self-respecting heart would dream
Of prizing so promiscuous an esteem;
55   However high the praise, there's nothing worse

Than sharing honors with the universe.
Esteem is founded on comparison:
To honor all men is to honor none.
Since you embrace this indiscriminate vice,
60 Your friendship comes at far too cheap a price;
I spurn the easy tribute of a heart
Which will not set the worthy man apart:
I choose, Sir, to be chosen; and in fine,
The friend of mankind is no friend of mine.
65 PHILINTE But in polite society, custom decrees
That we show certain outward courtesies. . . .
ALCESTE Ah, no! we should condemn with all our force
Such false and artificial intercourse.
Let men behave like men; let them display
70 Their inmost hearts in everything they say;
Let the heart speak, and let our sentiments
Not mask themselves in silly compliments.
PHILINTE In certain cases it would be uncouth
And most absurd to speak the naked truth;
75 With all respect for your exalted notions,
It's often best to veil one's true emotions.
Wouldn't the social fabric come undone
If we were wholly frank with everyone?
Suppose you met with someone you couldn't bear;
80 Would you inform him of it then and there?
ALCESTE Yes.
PHILINTE   Then you'd tell old Emilie it's pathetic
The way she daubs her features with cosmetic
And plays the gay coquette at sixty-four?
ALCESTE I would.
PHILINTE   And you'd call Dorilas a bore,
85 And tell him every ear at court is lame
From hearing him brag about his noble name?
ALCESTE Precisely.
PHILINTE   Ah, you're joking.
ALCESTE   Au contraire:
In this regard there's none I'd choose to spare.
All are corrupt; there's nothing to be seen
90 In court or town but aggravates my spleen.
I fall into deep gloom and melancholy
When I survey the scene of human folly,
Finding on every hand base flattery,
Injustice, fraud, self-interest, treachery. . . .
95 Ah, it's too much; mankind has grown so base,
I mean to break with the whole human race.
PHILINTE This philosophic rage is a bit extreme;
You've no idea how comical you seem;
Indeed, we're like those brothers in the play
100 Called *School for Husbands*, one of whom was prey . . .

ALCESTE Enough, now! None of your stupid similes.
PHILINTE Then let's have no more tirades, if you please.
    The world won't change, whatever you say or do;
    And since plain speaking means so much to you,
105   I'll tell you plainly that by being frank
    You've earned the reputation of a crank,
    And that you're thought ridiculous when you rage
    And rant against the manners of the age.
ALCESTE So much the better; just what I wish to hear.
110   No news could be more grateful to my ear.
    All men are so detestable in my eyes,
    I should be sorry if they thought me wise.
PHILINTE Your hatred's very sweeping, is it not?
ALCESTE Quite right: I hate the whole degraded lot.
115 PHILINTE Must all poor human creatures be embraced,
    Without distinction, by your vast distaste?
    Even in these bad times, there are surely a few . . .
ALCESTE No, I include all men in one dim view:
    Some men I hate for being rogues: the others
120   I hate because they treat the rogues like brothers,
    And, lacking a virtuous scorn for what is vile,
    Receive the villain with a complaisant smile.
    Notice how tolerant people choose to be
    Toward that bold rascal who's at law with me.
125   His social polish can't conceal his nature;
    One sees at once that he's a treacherous creature;
    No one could possibly be taken in
    By those soft speeches and that sugary grin.
    The whole world knows the shady means by which
130   The low-brow's grown so powerful and rich,
    And risen to a rank so bright and high
    That virtue can but blush, and merit sigh.
    Whenever his name comes up in conversation,
    None will defend his wretched reputation;
135   Call him knave, liar, scoundrel, and all the rest,
    Each head will nod, and no one will protest.
    And yet his smirk is seen in every house,
    He's greeted everywhere with smiles and bows,
    And when there's any honor that can be got
140   By pulling strings, he'll get it, like as not.
    My God! It chills my heart to see the ways
    Men come to terms with evil nowadays;
    Sometimes, I swear, I'm moved to flee and find
    Some desert land unfouled by humankind.
145 PHILINTE Come let's forget the follies of the times
    And pardon mankind for its petty crimes;
    Let's have an end of rantings and of railings,
    And show some leniency toward human failings.
    This world requires a pliant rectitude;

150   Too stern a virtue makes one stiff and rude;
        Good sense views all extremes with detestation,
        And bids us to be noble in moderation.
        The rigid virtues of the ancient days
        Are not for us; they jar with all our ways
155   And ask of us too lofty a perfection.
        Wise men accept their times without objection,
        And there's no greater folly, if you ask me,
        Than trying to reform society.
        Like you, I see each day a hundred and one
160   Unhandsome deeds that might be better done,
        But still, for all the faults that meet my view,
        I'm never known to storm and rave like you.
        I take men as they are, or let them be,
        And teach my soul to bear their frailty;
165   And whether in court or town, whatever the scene,
        My phlegm's as philosophic as your spleen.
   ALCESTE This phlegm which you so eloquently commend,
        Does nothing ever rile it up, my friend?
        Suppose some man you trust should treacherously
170   Conspire to rob you of your property,
        And do his best to wreck your reputation?
        Wouldn't you feel a certain indignation?
   PHILINTE Why, no. These faults of which you so complain
        Are part of human nature, I maintain,
175   And it's no more a matter for disgust
        That men are knavish, selfish and unjust,
        Than that the vulture dines upon the dead,
        And wolves are furious, and apes ill-bred.
   ALCESTE Shall I see myself betrayed, robbed, torn to bits,
180   And not . . . Oh, let's be still and rest our wits.
        Enough of reasoning, now. I've had my fill.
   PHILINTE Indeed, you would do well, Sir, to be still.
        Rage less at your opponent, and give some thought
        To how you'll win this lawsuit that he's brought.
185 ALCESTE I assure you I'll do nothing of the sort.
   PHILINTE Then who will plead your case before the court?
   ALCESTE Reason and right and justice will plead for me.
   PHILINTE Oh, Lord. What judges do you plan to see?
   ALCESTE Why, none. The justice of my cause is clear.
190 PHILINTE Of course, man; but there's politics to fear. . . .
   ALCESTE No, I refuse to lift a hand. That's flat.
        I'm either right, or wrong.
   PHILINTE   Don't count on that.
   ALCESTE No, I'll do nothing.
   PHILINTE   Your enemy's influence
        Is great, you know . . .
   ALCESTE   That makes no difference.
   PHILINTE It will; you'll see.

195 ALCESTE   Must honor bow to guile?
    If so, I shall be proud to lose the trial.
    PHILINTE Oh, really . . .
    ALCESTE   I'll discover by this case
    Whether or not men are sufficiently base
    And impudent and villainous and perverse
200   To do me wrong before the universe.
    PHILINTE What a man!
    ALCESTE   Oh, I could wish, whatever the cost,
    Just for the beauty of it, that my trial were lost.
    PHILINTE If people heard you talking so, Alceste,
    They'd split their sides. Your name would be a jest.
    ALCESTE So much the worse for jesters.
205 PHILINTE   May I enquire
    Whether this rectitude you so admire,
    And these hard virtues you're enamored of
    Are qualities of the lady whom you love?
    It much surprises me that you, who seem
210   To view mankind with furious disesteem,
    Have yet found something to enchant your eyes
    Amidst a species which you so despise.
    And what is more amazing, I'm afraid,
    Is the most curious choice your heart has made.
215   The honest Éliante is fond of you,
    Arsinoé, the prude, admires you too;
    And yet your spirit's been perversely led
    To choose the flighty Célimène instead,
    Whose brittle malice and coquettish ways
220   So typify the manners of our days.
    How is it that the traits you most abhor
    Are bearable in this lady you adore?
    Are you so blind with love that you can't find them?
    Or do you contrive, in her case, not to mind them?
225 ALCESTE My love for that young widow's not the kind
    That can't perceive defects; no, I'm not blind.
    I see her faults, despite my ardent love,
    And all I see I fervently reprove.
    And yet I'm weak; for all her falsity,
230   That woman knows the art of pleasing me,
    And though I never cease complaining of her,
    I swear I cannot manage not to love her.
    Her charm outweighs her faults; I can but aim
    To cleanse her spirit in my love's pure flame.
235 PHILINTE That's no small task; I wish you all success.
    You think then that she loves you?
    ALCESTE   Heavens, yes!
    I wouldn't love her did she not love me.
    PHILINTE Well, if her taste for you is plain to see,
    Why do these rivals cause you such despair?

240 ALCESTE True love, Sir, is possessive, and cannot bear
       To share with all the world. I'm here today
       To tell her she must send that mob away.
     PHILINTE If I were you, and had your choice to make,
       Éliante, her cousin, would be the one I'd take;
245   That honest heart, which cares for you alone,
       Would harmonize far better with your own.
     ALCESTE True, true: each day my reason tells me so;
       But reason doesn't rule in love, you know.
     PHILINTE I fear some bitter sorrow is in store;
       This love . . .

     SCENE II. ORONTE, ALCESTE, PHILINTE

250 ORONTE (to ALCESTE) The servants told me at the door
       That Éliante and Célimène were out,
       But when I heard, dear Sir, that you were about,
       I came to say, without exaggeration,
       That I hold you in the vastest admiration,
255   And that it's always been my dearest desire
       To be the friend of one I so admire.
       I hope to see my love of merit requited,
       And you and I in friendship's bond united.
       I'm sure you won't refuse—if I may be frank—
260   A friend of my devotedness—and rank.

     During this speech of ORONTE's, ALCESTE *is abstracted, and seems unaware that he is
     being spoken to. He only breaks off his reverie when* ORONTE *says:*

       It was for you, if you please, that my words were intended.
     ALCESTE For me, Sir?
     ORONTE   Yes, for you. You're not offended?
     ALCESTE By no means. But this much surprises me. . . .
       The honor comes most unexpectedly. . . .
265 ORONTE My high regard should not astonish you;
       The whole world feels the same. It is your due.
     ALCESTE Sir . . .
     ORONTE   Why, in all the State there isn't one
       Can match your merits; they shine, Sir, like the sun.
     ALCESTE Sir . . .
     ORONTE   You are higher in my estimation
270   Than all that's most illustrious in the nation.
     ALCESTE Sir . . .
     ORONTE   If I lie, may heaven strike me dead!
       To show you that I mean what I have said,
       Permit me, Sir, to embrace you most sincerely,
       And swear that I will prize our friendship dearly.
275   Give me your hand. And now, Sir, if you choose,
       We'll make our vows.
     ALCESTE   Sir . . .

ORONTE   What! You refuse?

ALCESTE Sir, it's a very great honor you extend:
          But friendship is a sacred thing, my friend;
          It would be profanation to bestow
280   The name of friend on one you hardly know.
          All parts are better played when well-rehearsed;
          Let's put off friendship, and get acquainted first.
          We may discover it would be unwise
          To try to make our natures harmonize.
285 ORONTE By heaven! You're sagacious to the core;
          This speech has made me admire you even more.
          Let time, then, bring us closer day by day;
          Meanwhile, I shall be yours in every way.
          If, for example, there should be anything
290   You wish at court, I'll mention it to the King.
          I have his ear, of course; it's quite well known
          That I am much in favor with the throne.
          In short, I am your servant. And now, dear friend,
          Since you have such fine judgment, I intend
295   To please you, if I can, with a small sonnet
          I wrote not long ago. Please comment on it,
          And tell me whether I ought to publish it.
     ALCESTE You must excuse me, Sir; I'm hardly fit
          To judge such matters.
     ORONTE   Why not?
     ALCESTE   I am, I fear,
300   Inclined to be unfashionably sincere.
     ORONTE Just what I ask; I'd take no satisfaction
          In anything but your sincere reaction.
          I beg you not to dream of being kind.
     ALCESTE Since you desire it, Sir, I'll speak my mind.
305 ORONTE *Sonnet.* It's a sonnet . . . *Hope* . . . The poem's addressed
          To a lady who wakened hopes within my breast.
          Hope . . . this is not the pompous sort of thing,
          Just modest little verses, with a tender ring.
     ALCESTE Well, we shall see.
     ORONTE   *Hope* . . . I'm anxious to hear
310   Whether the style seems properly smooth and clear,
          And whether the choice of words is good or bad.
     ALCESTE We'll see, we'll see.
     ORONTE   Perhaps I ought to add
          That it took me only a quarter-hour to write it.
     ALCESTE The time's irrelevant, Sir: kindly recite it.
     ORONTE (*reading*)

315   *Hope comforts us awhile, 'tis true,*
                 Lulling our cares with careless laughter,
                 And yet such joy is full of rue,
                 My Phyllis, if nothing follows after.

PHILINTE I'm charmed by this already; the style's delightful.
320 ALCESTE (*sotto voice, to* PHILINTE) How can you say that? Why, the thing is frightful.
ORONTE

> Your fair face smiled on me awhile,
> But was it kindness so to enchant me?
> 'Twould have been fairer not to smile,
> If hope was all you meant to grant me.

325 PHILINTE What a clever thought! How handsomely you phrase it!
ALCESTE (*sotto voce, to* PHILINTE) You know the thing is trash. How dare you praise it?
ORONTE

> If it's to be my passion's fate
> Thus everlastingly to wait,
> Then death will come to set me free:
330 > For death is fairer than the fair;
> Phyllis, to hope is to despair
> When one must hope eternally.

PHILINTE The close is exquisite—full of feeling and grace.
ALCESTE (*sotto voce, aside*) Oh, blast the close; you'd better close your face
335 Before you send your lying soul to hell.
PHILINTE I can't remember a poem I've liked so well.
ALCESTE (*sotto voce, aside*) Good Lord!
ORONTE (*to* PHILINTE)   I fear you're flattering me a bit.
PHILINTE Oh, no!
ALCESTE (*sotto voce, aside*) What else d'you call it, you hypocrite?
ORONTE (*to* ALCESTE) But you, Sir, keep your promise now: don't shrink
340 From telling me sincerely what you think.
ALCESTE Sir, these are delicate matters; we all desire
To be told that we've the true poetic fire.
But once, to one whose name I shall not mention,
I said, regarding some verse of his invention,
345 That gentlemen should rigorously control
That itch to write which often afflicts the soul;
That one should curb the heady inclination
To publicize one's little avocation;
And that in showing off one's works of art
350 One often plays a very clownish part.
ORONTE Are you suggesting in a devious way
That I ought not . . .
ALCESTE   Oh, that I do not say.
Further, I told him that no fault is worse
Than that of writing frigid, lifeless verse,
355 And that the merest whisper of such a shame
Suffices to destroy a man's good name.
ORONTE D'you mean to say my sonnet's dull and trite?
ALCESTE I don't say that. But I went on to cite
Numerous cases of once-respected men
360 Who came to grief by taking up the pen.

ORONTE And am I like them? Do I write so poorly?
ALCESTE I don't say that. But I told this person, "Surely
       You're under no necessity to compose;
       Why you should wish to publish, heaven knows.
365   There's no excuse for printing tedious rot
       Unless one writes for bread, as you do not.
       Resist temptation, then, I beg of you;
       Conceal your pastimes from the public view;
       And don't give up, on any provocation,
370   Your present high and courtly reputation,
       To purchase at a greedy printer's shop
       The name of silly author and scribbling fop."
       These were the points I tried to make him see.
ORONTE I sense that they are also aimed at me;
375   But now—about my sonnet—I'd like to be told . . .
ALCESTE Frankly, that sonnet should be pigeonholed.
       You've chosen the worst models to imitate.
       The style's unnatural. Let me illustrate:
       For example, *Your fair face smiled on me awhile,*
380   Followed by, *'Twould have been fairer not to smile!*
       Or this: *such joy is full of rue;*
       Or this: *For death is fairer than the fair;*
       Or, *Phyllis, to hope is to despair*
       When one must hope eternally!
385   This artificial style, that's all the fashion,
       Has neither taste, nor honesty, nor passion;
       It's nothing but a sort of wordy play,
       And nature never spoke in such a way.
       What, in this shallow age, is not debased?
390   Our fathers, though less refined, had better taste;
       I'd barter all that men admire today
       For one old love song I shall try to say:

            If the King had given me for my own
            Paris, his citadel,
395   *And I for that must leave alone*
            Her whom I love so well,
            I'd say then to the Crown,
            Take back your glittering town;
            My darling is more fair, I swear,
400   *My darling is more fair.*

       The rhyme's not rich, the style is rough and old,
       But don't you see that it's the purest gold
       Beside the tinsel nonsense now preferred,
       And that there's passion in its every word?

405   *If the King had given me for my own*
            Paris, his citadel,
            And I for that must leave alone

> Her whom I love so well,
> I'd say then to the Crown,
> Take back your glittering town;
> My darling is more fair, I swear,
> My darling is more fair.

There speaks a loving heart. (*To* PHILINTE.) You're laughing, eh?
Laugh on, my precious wit. Whatever you say,
I hold that song's worth all the bibelots
That people hail today with ah's and oh's.

ORONTE And I maintain my sonnet's very good.

ALCESTE It's not at all surprising that you should.
You have your reasons; permit me to have mine
For thinking that you cannot write a line.

ORONTE Others have praised my sonnet to the skies.

ALCESTE I lack their art of telling pleasant lies.

ORONTE You seem to think you've got no end of wit.

ALCESTE To praise your verse, I'd need still more of it.

ORONTE I'm not in need of your approval, Sir.

ALCESTE That's good; you couldn't have it if you were.

ORONTE Come now, I'll lend you the subject of my sonnet;
I'd like to see you try to improve upon it.

ALCESTE I might, by chance, write something just as shoddy;
But then I wouldn't show it to everybody.

ORONTE You're most opinionated and conceited.

ALCESTE Go find your flatterers, and be better treated.

ORONTE Look here, my little fellow, pray watch your tone.

ALCESTE My great big fellow, you'd better watch your own.

PHILINTE (*stepping between them*) Oh, please, please, gentlemen! This will never do.

ORONTE The fault is mine, and I leave the field to you.
I am your servant, Sir, in every way.

ALCESTE And I, Sir, am your most abject valet.

SCENE III. PHILINTE, ALCESTE

PHILINTE Well, as you see, sincerity in excess
Can get you into a very pretty mess;
Oronte was hungry for appreciation. . . .

ALCESTE Don't speak to me.

PHILINTE   What?

ALCESTE   No more conversation.

PHILINTE Really, now . . .

ALCESTE   Leave me alone.

PHILINTE   If I . . .

ALCESTE   Out of my sight!

PHILINTE But what . . .

ALCESTE   I won't listen.

PHILINTE   But . . .

ALCESTE   Silence!

PHILINTE   Now, is it polite . . .

445   ALCESTE By heaven, I've had enough. Don't follow me.

PHILINTE Ah, you're just joking. I'll keep you company.

ACT II

SCENE I. ALCESTE, CÉLIMÈNE

ALCESTE Shall I speak plainly, Madam? I confess
    Your conduct gives me infinite distress,
    And my resentment's grown too hot to smother.
    Soon, I foresee, we'll break with one another.
5   If I said otherwise, I should deceive you;
    Sooner or later, I shall be forced to leave you,
    And if I swore that we shall never part,
    I should misread the omens of my heart.
CÉLIMÈNE You kindly saw me home, it would appear,
10   So as to pour invectives in my ear.
ALCESTE I've no desire to quarrel. But I deplore
    Your inability to shut the door
    On all these suitors who beset you so.
    There's what annoys me, if you care to know.
15   CÉLIMÈNE Is it my fault that all these men pursue me?
    Am I to blame if they're attracted to me?
    And when they gently beg an audience,
    Ought I to take a stick and drive them hence?
ALCESTE Madam, there's no necessity for a stick;
20   A less responsive heart would do the trick.
    Of your attractiveness I don't complain;
    But those your charms attract, you then detain
    By a most melting and receptive manner,
    And so enlist their hearts beneath your banner.
25   It's the agreeable hopes which you excite
    That keep these lovers round you day and night;
    Were they less liberally smiled upon,
    That sighing troop would very soon be gone.
    But tell me, Madam, why it is that lately
30   This man Clitandre interests you so greatly?
    Because of what high merits do you deem
    Him worthy of the honor of your esteem?
    Is it that your admiring glances linger
    On the splendidly long nail of his little finger?
35   Or do you share the general deep respect
    For the blond wig he chooses to affect?
    Are you in love with his embroidered hose?
    Do you adore his ribbons and his bows?
    Or is it that this paragon bewitches
40   Your tasteful eye with his vast German breeches?
    Perhaps his giggle, or his falsetto voice,
    Makes him the latest gallant of your choice?

CÉLIMÈNE You're much mistaken to resent him so.
Why I put up with him you surely know:
45   My lawsuit's very shortly to be tried,
And I must have his influence on my side.
ALCESTE Then lose your lawsuit, Madam, or let it drop;
Don't torture me by humoring such a fop.
CÉLIMÈNE You're jealous of the whole world, Sir.
ALCESTE   That's true,
50   Since the whole world is well-received by you.
CÉLIMÈNE That my good nature is so unconfined
Should serve to pacify your jealous mind;
Were I to smile on one, and scorn the rest,
Then you might have some cause to be distressed.
55   ALCESTE Well, if I mustn't be jealous, tell me, then,
Just how I'm better treated than other men.
CÉLIMÈNE You know you have my love. Will that not do?
ALCESTE What proof have I that what you say is true?
CÉLIMÈNE I would expect, Sir, that my having said it
60   Might give the statement a sufficient credit.
ALCESTE But how can I be sure that you don't tell
The selfsame thing to other men as well?
CÉLIMÈNE What a gallant speech! How flattering to me!
What a sweet creature you make me out to be!
65   Well then, to save you from the pangs of doubt,
All that I've said I hereby cancel out;
Now, none but yourself shall make a monkey of you:
Are you content?
ALCESTE   Why, why am I doomed to love you?
I swear that I shall bless the blissful hour
70   When this poor heart's no longer in your power!
I make no secret of it: I've done my best
To exorcise this passion from my breast;
But thus far all in vain; it will not go;
It's for my sins that I must love you so.
75   CÉLIMÈNE Your love for me is matchless, Sir; that's clear.
ALCESTE Indeed, in all the world it has no peer;
Words can't describe the nature of my passion,
And no man ever loved in such a fashion.
CÉLIMÈNE Yes, it's a brand-new fashion, I agree:
80   You show your love by castigating me,
And all your speeches are enraged and rude.
I've never been so furiously wooed.
ALCESTE Yet you could calm that fury, if you chose.
Come, shall we bring our quarrels to a close?
85   Let's speak with open hearts, then, and begin . . .

SCENE II. CÉLIMÈNE, ALCESTE, BASQUE

CÉLIMÈNE What is it?
BASQUE   Acaste is here.
CÉLIMÈNE   Well, send him in.

SCENE III. CÉLIMÈNE, ALCESTE

ALCESTE What! Shall we never be alone at all?
    You're always ready to receive a call,
    And you can't bear, for ten ticks of the clock,
90   Not to keep open house for all who knock.
CÉLIMÈNE I couldn't refuse him: he'd be most put out.
ALCESTE Surely that's not worth worrying about.
CÉLIMÈNE Acaste would never forgive me if he guessed
    That I consider him a dreadful pest.
95 ALCESTE If he's a pest, why bother with him then?
CÉLIMÈNE Heavens! One can't antagonize such men;
    Why, they're the chartered gossips of the court,
    And have a say in things of every sort.
    One must receive them, and be full of charm;
100   They're no great help, but they can do you harm,
    And though your influence be ever so great,
    They're hardly the best people to alienate.
ALCESTE I see, dear lady, that you could make a case
    For putting up with the whole human race;
105   These friendships that you calculate so nicely . . .

SCENE IV. ALCESTE, CÉLIMÈNE, BASQUE

BASQUE Madam, Clitandre is here as well.
ALCESTE   Precisely.
CÉLIMÈNE Where are you going?
ALCESTE   Elsewhere.
CÉLIMÈNE   Stay.
ALCESTE   No, no.
CÉLIMÈNE Stay, Sir.
ALCESTE   I can't.
CÉLIMÈNE   I wish it.
ALCESTE   No, I must go.
    I beg you, Madam, not to press the matter;
110   You know I have no taste for idle chatter.
CÉLIMÈNE Stay. I command you.
ALCESTE   No, I cannot stay.
CÉLIMÈNE Very well; you have my leave to go away.

SCENE V. ÉLIANTE, PHILINTE, ACASTE, CLITANDRE, ALCESTE, CÉLIMÈNE, BASQUE

ÉLIANTE (to CÉLIMÈNE) The Marquesses have kindly come to call.
    Were they announced?
CÉLIMÈNE   Yes. Basque, bring chairs for all.

BASQUE *provides the chairs, and exits.*

    (To ALCESTE.) You haven't gone?
115 ALCESTE   No; and I shan't depart
    Till you decide who's foremost in your heart.
CÉLIMÈNE Oh, hush.
ALCESTE   It's time to choose; take them, or me.

CÉLIMÈNE You're mad.

ALCESTE   I'm not, as you shall shortly see.

CÉLIMÈNE Oh?

ALCESTE   You'll decide.

CÉLIMÈNE   You're joking now, dear friend.

120 ALCESTE No, no; you'll choose; my patience is at an end.

CLITANDRE Madam, I come from court, where poor Cléonte
    Behaved like a perfect fool, as is his wont.
    Has he no friend to counsel him, I wonder,
    And teach him less unerringly to blunder?

125 CÉLIMÈNE It's true, the man's a most accomplished dunce;
    His gauche behavior charms the eye at once;
    And every time one sees him, on my word,
    His manner's grown a trifle more asburd.

ACASTE Speaking of dunces, I've just now conversed
130   With old Damon, who's one of the very worst;
    I stood a lifetime in the broiling sun.
    Before his dreary monologue was done.

CÉLIMÈNE Oh, he's a wondrous talker, and has the power
    To tell you nothing hour after hour:
135   If, by mistake, he ever came to the point,
    The shock would put his jawbone out of joint.

ÉLIANTE (to PHILINTE) The conversation takes its usual turn,
    And all our dear friends' ears will shortly burn.

CLITANDRE Timante's a character, Madam.

CÉLIMÈNE   Isn't he, though?
140   A man of mystery from top to toe,
    Who moves about in a romantic mist
    On secret missions which do not exist.
    His talk is full of eyebrows and grimaces;
    How tired one gets of his momentous faces;
145   He's always whispering something confidential
    Which turns out to be quite inconsequential;
    Nothing's too slight for him to mystify;
    He even whispers when he says "good-by."

ACASTE Tell us about Géralde.

CÉLIMÈNE   That tiresome ass.
150   He mixes only with the titled class,
    And fawns on dukes and princes, and is bored
    With anyone who's not at least a lord.
    The man's obsessed with rank, and his discourses
    Are all of hounds and carriages and horses;
155   He uses Christian names with all the great,
    And the word Milord, with him, is out of date.

CLITANDRE He's very taken with Bélise, I hear.

CÉLIMÈNE She is the dreariest company, poor dear.
    Whenever she comes to call, I grope about
160   To find some topic which will draw her out,
    But, owing to her dry and faint replies,

The conversation wilts, and droops, and dies.
In vain one hopes to animate her face
By mentioning the ultimate commonplace;
165   But sun or shower, even hail or frost
Are matters she can instantly exhaust.
Meanwhile her visit, painful though it is,
Drags on and on through mute eternities,
And though you ask the time, and yawn, and yawn,
170   She sits there like a stone and won't be gone.

ACASTE Now for Adraste.

CÉLIMÈNE   Oh, that conceited elf
Has a gigantic passion for himself;
He rails against the court, and cannot bear it
That none will recognize his hidden merit;
175   All honors given to others give offense
To his imaginary excellence.

CLITANDRE What about young Cléon? His house, they say,
Is full of the best society, night and day.

CÉLIMÈNE His cook has made him popular, not he:
180   It's Cléon's table that people come to see.

ÉLIANTE He gives a splendid dinner, you must admit.

CÉLIMÈNE But must he serve himself along with it?
For my taste, he's a most insipid dish
Whose presence sours the wine and spoils the fish.

185 PHILINTE Damis, his uncle, is admired no end.
What's your opinion, Madam?

CÉLIMÈNE   Why, he's my friend.

PHILINTE He seems a decent fellow, and rather clever.

CÉLIMÈNE He works too hard at cleverness, however.
I hate to see him sweat and struggle so
190   To fill his conversation with bons mots.
Since he's decided to become a wit
His taste's so pure that nothing pleases it;
He scolds at all the latest books and plays,
Thinking that wit must never stoop to praise,
195   That finding fault's a sign of intellect,
That all appreciation is abject,
And that by damning everything in sight
One shows oneself in a distinguished light.
He's scornful even of our conversations:
200   Their trivial nature sorely tries his patience;
He folds his arms, and stands above the battle,
And listens sadly to our childish prattle.

ACASTE Wonderful, Madam! You've hit him off precisely.

CLITANDRE No one can sketch a character so nicely.

205 ALCESTE How bravely, Sirs, you cut and thrust at all
These absent fools, till one by one they fall:
But let one come in sight, and you'll at once
Embrace the man you lately called a dunce,

Telling him in a tone sincere and fervent
210 How proud you are to be his humble servant.
CLITANDRE Why pick on us? *Madame's* been speaking, Sir.
And you should quarrel, if you must, with her.
ALCESTE No, no, by God, the fault is yours, because
You lead her on with laughter and applause,
215 And make her think that she's the more delightful
The more her talk is scandalous and spiteful.
Oh, she would stoop to malice far, far less
If no such claque approved her cleverness.
It's flatterers like you whose foolish praise
220 Nourishes all the vices of these days.
PHILINTE But why protest when someone ridicules
Those you'd condemn, yourself, as knaves or fools?
CÉLIMÈNE Why, Sir? Because he loves to make a fuss.
You don't expect him to agree with us,
225 When there's an opportunity to express
His heaven-sent spirit of contrariness?
What other people think, he can't abide;
Whatever they say, he's on the other side;
He lives in deadly terror of agreeing;
230 'Twould make him seem an ordinary being.
Indeed, he's so in love with contradiction,
He'll turn against his most profound conviction
And with a furious eloquence deplore it,
If only someone else is speaking for it.
235 ALCESTE Go on, dear lady, mock me as you please;
You have your audience in ecstasies.
PHILINTE But what she says is true: you have a way
Of bridling at whatever people say;
Whether they praise or blame, your angry spirit
240 Is equally unsatisfied to hear it.
ALCESTE Men, Sir, are always wrong, and that's the reason
That righteous anger's never out of season;
All that I hear in all their conversation
Is flattering praise or reckless condemnation.
CÉLIMÈNE But . . .
245 ALCESTE   No, no, Madam, I am forced to state
That you have pleasures which I deprecate,
And that these others, here, are much to blame
For nourishing the faults which are your shame.
CLITANDRE I shan't defend myself, Sir; but I vow
250 I'd thought this lady faultless until now.
ACASTE I see her charms and graces, which are many;
But as for faults, I've never noticed any.
ALCESTE I see them, Sir; and rather than ignore them,
I strenuously criticize her for them.
255 The more one loves, the more one should object
To every blemish, every least defect.

Were I this lady, I would soon get rid
Of lovers who approved of all I did,
And by their slack indulgence and applause
260   Endorsed my follies and excused my flaws.
    CÉLIMÈNE If all hearts beat according to your measure,
    The dawn of love would be the end of pleasure;
    And love would find its perfect consummation
    In ecstasies of rage and reprobation.
265   ÉLIANTE Love, as a rule, affects men otherwise,
    And lovers rarely love to criticize.
    They see their lady as a charming blur,
    And find all things commendable in her.
    If she has any blemish, fault, or shame,
270   They will redeem it by a pleasing name.
    The pale-faced lady's lily-white, perforce;
    The swarthy one's a sweet brunette, of course;
    The spindly lady has a slender grace;
    The fat one has a most majestic pace;
275   The plain one, with her dress in disarray,
    They classify as *beauté négligée*;
    The hulking one's a goddess in their eyes,
    The dwarf, a concentrate of Paradise;
    The haughty lady has a noble mind;
280   The mean one's witty, and the dull one's kind;
    The chatterbox has liveliness and verve,
    The mute one has a virtuous reserve.
    So lovers manage, in their passion's cause,
    To love their ladies even for their flaws.
    ALCESTE But I still say . . .
285   CÉLIMÈNE   I think it would be nice
    To stroll around the gallery once or twice.
    What! You're not going, Sirs?
    CLITANDRE AND ACASTE   No, Madam, no.
    ALCESTE You seem to be in terror lest they go.
    Do what you will, Sirs; leave, or linger on,
290   But I shan't go till after you are gone.
    ACASTE I'm free to linger, unless I should perceive
    Madame is tired, and wishes me to leave.
    CLITANDRE And as for me, I needn't go today
    Until the hour of the King's *coucher.*
    CÉLIMÈNE (*to* ALCESTE) You're joking, surely?
295   ALCESTE   Not in the least; we'll see
    Whether you'd rather part with them, or me.

SCENE VI. ALCESTE, CÉLIMÈNE, ÉLIANTE, ACASTE, PHILINTE, CLITANDRE, BASQUE

    BASQUE (*to* ALCESTE) Sir, there's a fellow here who bids me state
    That he must see you, and that it can't wait.
    ALCESTE Tell him that I have no such pressing affairs.

300 BASQUE It's a long tailcoat that this fellow wears,
    With gold all over.
CÉLIMÈNE (*to* ALCESTE) You'd best go down and see.
    Or—have him enter.

SCENE VII. ALCESTE, CÉLIMÈNE, ÉLIANTE, ACASTE, PHILINTE, CLITANDRE, GUARD

ALCESTE (*confronting the* GUARD) Well, what do you want with me?
    Come in, Sir.
GUARD   I've a word, Sir, for your ear.
ALCESTE Speak it aloud, Sir; I shall strive to hear.
305 GUARD The Marshals have instructed me to say
    You must report to them without delay.
ALCESTE Who? Me, Sir?
GUARD   Yes, Sir; you.
ALCESTE   But what do they want?
PHILINTE (*to* ALCESTE) To scotch your silly quarrel with Oronte.
CÉLIMÈNE (*to* PHILINTE) What quarrel?
PHILINTE   Oronte and he have fallen out
310 Over some verse he spoke his mind about;
    The Marshals wish to arbitrate the matter.
ALCESTE Never shall I equivocate or flatter!
PHILINTE You'd best obey their summons; come, let's go.
ALCESTE How can they mend our quarrel, I'd like to know?
315 Am I to make a cowardly retraction,
    And praise those jingles to his satisfaction?
    I'll not recant; I've judged that sonnet rightly.
    It's bad.
PHILINTE But you might say so more politely. . . .
ALCESTE I'll not back down; his verses make me sick.
320 PHILINTE If only you could be more politic!
    But come, let's go.
ALCESTE   I'll go, but I won't unsay
    A single word.
PHILINTE   Well, let's be on our way.
ALCESTE Till I am ordered by my lord the King
    To praise that poem, I shall say the thing
325 Is scandalous, by God, and that the poet
    Ought to be hanged for having the nerve to show it.
    (*To* CLITANDRE *and* ACASTE, *who are laughing.*) By heaven, Sirs, I really didn't know
    That I was being humorous.
CÉLIMÈNE   Go, Sir, go;
    Settle your business.
ALCESTE   I shall, and when I'm through,
330 I shall return to settle things with you.

ACT III

SCENE I. CLITANDRE, ACASTE

CLITANDRE Dear Marquess, how contented you appear;
    All things delight you, nothing mars your cheer.

Can you, in perfect honesty, declare
That you've a right to be so debonair?

5 ACASTE By Jove, when I survey myself, I find
No cause whatever for distress of mind.
I'm young and rich; I can in modesty
Lay claim to an exalted pedigree;
And owing to my name and my condition
10 I shall not want for honors and position.
Then as to courage, that most precious trait,
I seem to have it, as was proved of late
Upon the field of honor, where my bearing,
They say, was very cool and rather daring.
15 I've wit, of course; and taste in such perfection
That I can judge without the least reflection,
And at the theater, which is my delight,
Can make or break a play on opening night,
And lead the crowd in hisses or bravos,
20 And generally be known as one who knows.
I'm clever, handsome, gracefully polite;
My waist is small, my teeth are strong and white;
As for my dress, the world's astonished eyes
Assure me that I bear away the prize.
25 I find myself in favor everywhere,
Honored by men, and worshiped by the fair;
And since these things are so, it seems to me
I'm justified in my complacency.
CLITANDRE Well, if so many ladies hold you dear,
30 Why do you press a hopeless courtship here?
ACASTE Hopeless, you say? I'm not the sort of fool
That likes his ladies difficult and cool.
Men who are awkward, shy, and peasantish
May pine for heartless beauties, if they wish,
35 Grovel before them, bear their cruelties,
Woo them with tears and sighs and bended knees,
And hope by dogged faithfulness to gain
What their poor merits never could obtain.
For men like me, however, it makes no sense
40 To love on trust, and foot the whole expense.
Whatever any lady's merits be,
I think, thank God, that I'm as choice as she;
That if my heart is kind enough to burn
For her, she owes me something in return;
45 And that in any proper love affair
The partners must invest an equal share.
CLITANDRE You think, then, that our hostess favors you?
ACASTE I've reason to believe that that is true.
CLITANDRE How did you come to such a mad conclusion?
50 You're blind, dear fellow. This is sheer delusion.
ACASTE All right, then: I'm deluded and I'm blind.

CLITANDRE Whatever put the notion in your mind?
ACASTE Delusion.
CLITANDRE   What persuades you that you're right?
ACASTE I'm blind.
CLITANDRE   But have you any proofs to cite?
ACASTE I tell you I'm deluded.
55 CLITANDRE   Have you, then,
   Received some secret pledge from Célimène?
ACASTE On, no: she scorns me.
CLITANDRE   Tell me the truth, I beg.
ACASTE She just can't bear me.
CLITANDRE   Ah, don't pull my leg.
   Tell me what hope she's given you, I pray.
60 ACASTE I'm hopeless, and it's you who win the day.
   She hates me thoroughly, and I'm so vexed
   I mean to hang myself on Tuesday next.
CLITANDRE Dear Marquess, let us have an armistice
   And make a treaty. What do you say to this?
65   If ever one of us can plainly prove
   That Célimène encourages his love,
   The other must abandon hope, and yield,
   And leave him in possession of the field.
ACASTE Now, there's a bargain that appeals to me;
70   With all my heart, dear Marquess, I agree.
   But hush.

SCENE II. CÉLIMÈNE, ACASTE, CLITANDRE

CÉLIMÈNE Still here?
CLITANDRE   'Twas love that stayed our feet.
CÉLIMÈNE I think I heard a carriage in the street.
   Whose is it? D'you know?

SCENE III. CÉLIMÈNE, ACASTE, CLITANDRE, BASQUE

BASQUE   Arsinoé is here,
   Madame.
CÉLIMÈNE Arsinoé, you say? Oh, dear.
75 BASQUE Éliante is entertaining her below.
CÉLIMÈNE What brings the creature here, I'd like to know?
ACASTE They say she's dreadfully prudish, but in fact
   I think her piety . . .
CÉLIMÈNE   It's all an act.
   At heart she's worldly, and her poor success
80   In snaring men explains her prudishness.
   It breaks her heart to see the beaux and gallants
   Engrossed by other women's charms and talents,
   And so she's always in a jealous rage
   Against the faulty standards of the age.
85   She lets the world believe that she's a prude
   To justify her loveless solitude,

And strives to put a brand of moral shame
On all the graces that she cannot claim.
But still she'd love a lover; and Alceste
90   Appears to be the one she'd love the best.
His visits here are poison to her pride;
She seems to think I've lured him from her side;
And everywhere, at court or in the town,
The spiteful, envious woman runs me down.
95   In short, she's just as stupid as can be,
Vicious and arrogant in the last degree,
And . . .

SCENE IV. ARSINOÉ, CÉLIMÈNE, CLITANDRE, ACASTE

CÉLIMÈNE Ah! What happy chance has brought you here?
I've thought about you ever so much, my dear.
ARSINOÉ I've come to tell you something you should know.
100 CÉLIMÈNE How good of you to think of doing so!

CLITANDRE *and* ACASTE *go out, laughing.*

SCENE V. ARSINOÉ, CÉLIMÈNE

ARSINOÉ It's just as well those gentlemen didn't tarry.
CÉLIMÈNE Shall we sit down?
ARSINOÉ   That won't be necessary.
Madam, the flame of friendship ought to burn
Brightest in matters of the most concern,
105 And as there's nothing which concerns us more
Than honor, I have hastened to your door
To bring you, as your friend, some information
About the status of your reputation.
I visited, last night, some virtuous folk,
110 And, quite by chance, it was of you they spoke;
There was, I fear, no tendency to praise
Your light behavior and your dashing ways.
The quantity of gentlemen you see
And your by now notorious coquetry
115 Were both so vehemently criticized
By everyone, that I was much surprised.
Of course, I needn't tell you where I stood;
I came to your defense as best I could,
Assured them you were harmless, and declared
120 Your soul was absolutely unimpaired.
But there are some things, you must realize,
One can't excuse, however hard one tries,
And I was forced at last into conceding
That your behavior, Madam, is misleading,
125 That it makes a bad impression, giving rise
To ugly gossip and obscene surmise,
And that if you were more *overtly* good,

You wouldn't be so much misunderstood.
Not that I think you've been unchaste—no! no!
130 The saints preserve me from a thought so low!
But mere good conscience never did suffice:
One must avoid the outward show of vice.
Madam, you're too intelligent, I'm sure,
To think my motives anything but pure
135 In offering you this counsel—which I do
Out of a zealous interest in you.
CÉLIMÈNE Madam, I haven't taken you amiss;
I'm very much obliged to you for this;
And I'll at once discharge the obligation
140 By telling you about *your* reputation.
You've been so friendly as to let me know
What certain people say of me, and so
I mean to follow your benign example
By offering you a somewhat similar sample.
145 The other day, I went to an affair
And found some most distinguished people there
Discussing piety, both false and true.
The conversation soon came round to you.
Alas! Your prudery and bustling zeal
150 Appeared to have a very slight appeal.
Your affectation of a grave demeanor,
Your endless talk of virtue and of honor,
The aptitude of your suspicious mind
For finding sin where there is none to find,
155 Your towering self-esteem, that pitying face
With which you contemplate the human race,
Your sermonizings and your sharp aspersions
On people's pure and innocent diversions—
All these were mentioned, Madam, and, in fact,
160 Were roundly and concertedly attacked.
"What good," they said, "are all these outward shows,
When everything belies her pious pose?
She prays incessantly; but then, they say,
She beats her maids and cheats them of their pay;
165 She shows her zeal in every holy place,
But still she's vain enough to paint her face;
She holds that naked statues are immoral,
But with a naked *man* she'd have no quarrel."
Of course, I said to everybody there
170 That they were being viciously unfair;
But still they were disposed to criticize you,
And all agreed that someone should advise you
To leave the morals of the world alone,
And worry rather more about your own.
175 They felt that one's self-knowledge should be great
Before one thinks of setting others straight;
That one should learn the art of living well

Before one threatens other men with hell,
And that the Church is best equipped, no doubt,
180   To guide our souls and root our vices out.
Madam, you're too intelligent, I'm sure,
To think my motives anything but pure
In offering you this counsel—which I do
Out of a zealous interest in you.
185 ARSINOÉ I dared not hope for gratitude, but I
Did not expect so acid a reply;
I judge, since you've been so extremely tart,
That my good counsel pierced you to the heart.
CÉLIMÈNE Far from it, Madam. Indeed, it seems to me
190   We ought to trade advice more frequently.
One's vision of oneself is so defective
That it would be an excellent corrective.
If you are willing, Madam, let's arrange
Shortly to have another frank exchange
195   In which we'll tell each other, *entre nous*,
What you've heard tell of me, and I of you.
ARSINOÉ Oh, people never censure you, my dear;
It's me they criticize. Or so I hear.
CÉLIMÈNE Madam, I think we either blame or praise
200   According to our taste and length of days.
There is a time of life for coquetry,
And there's a season, too, for prudery.
When all one's charms are gone, it is, I'm sure,
Good strategy to be devout and pure:
205   It makes one seem a little less forsaken.
Some day, perhaps, I'll take the road you've taken:
Time brings all things. But I have time aplenty,
And see no cause to be a prude at twenty.
ARSINOÉ You give your age in such a gloating tone
210   That one would think I was an ancient crone;
We're not so far apart, in sober truth,
That you can mock me with a boast of youth!
Madam, you baffle me. I wish I knew
What moves you to provoke me as you do.
215 CÉLIMÈNE For my part, Madam, I should like to know
Why you abuse me everywhere you go.
Is it my fault, dear lady, that your hand
Is not, alas, in very great demand?
If men admire me, if they pay me court
220   And daily make me offers of the sort
You'd dearly love to have them make to you,
How can I help it? What would you have me do?
If what you want is lovers, please feel free
To take as many as you can from me.
225 ARSINOÉ Oh, come. D'you think the world is losing sleep
Over the flock of lovers which you keep,
Or that we find it difficult to guess

What price you pay for their devotedness?
Surely you don't expect us to suppose
230 Mere merit could attract so many beaux?
It's not your virtue that they're dazzled by;
Nor is it virtuous love for which they sigh.
You're fooling no one, Madam; the world's not blind;
There's many a lady heaven has designed
235 To call men's noblest, tenderest feelings out,
Who has no lovers dogging her about;
From which it's plain that lovers nowadays
Must be acquired in bold and shameless ways,
And only pay one court for such reward
240 As modesty and virtue can't afford.
Then don't be quite so puffed up, if you please,
About your tawdry little victories;
Try, if you can, to be a shade less vain,
And treat the world with somewhat less disdain.
245 If one were envious of your amours,
One soon could have a following like yours;
Lovers are no great trouble to collect
If one prefers them to one's self-respect.
CÉLIMÈNE Collect them then, my dear; I'd love to see
250 You demonstrate that charming theory;
Who knows, you might . . .
ARSINOÉ   Now, Madam, that will do;
It's time to end this trying interview.
My coach is late in coming to your door.
Or I'd have taken leave of you before.
255 CÉLIMÈNE Oh, please don't feel that you must rush away;
I'd be delighted, Madam, if you'd stay.
However, lest my conversation bore you,
Let me provide some better company for you;
This gentleman, who comes most apropos,
260 Will please you more than I could do, I know.

SCENE VI. ALCESTE, CÉLIMÈNE, ARSINOÉ

CÉLIMÈNE Alceste, I have a little note to write
Which simply must go out before tonight;
Please entertain *Madame*; I'm sure that she
Will overlook my incivility.

SCENE VII. ALCESTE, ARSINOÉ

265 ARSINOÉ Well, Sir, our hostess graciously contrives
For us to chat until my coach arrives;
And I shall be forever in her debt
For granting me this little tête-à-tête.
We women very rightly give our hearts
270 To men of noble character and parts,
And your especial merits, dear Alceste,

Have roused the deepest sympathy in my breast.
Oh, how I wish they had sufficient sense
At court, to recognize your excellence!
275 They wrong you greatly, Sir. How it must hurt you
Never to be rewarded for your virtue!
ALCESTE Why, Madam, what cause have I to feel aggrieved?
What great and brilliant thing have I achieved?
What service have I rendered to the King
280 That I should look to him for anything?
ARSINOÉ Not everyone who's honored by the State
Has done great services. A man must wait
Till time and fortune offer him the chance.
Your merit, Sir, is obvious at a glance,
And . . .
285 ALCESTE Ah, forget my merit; I am not neglected.
The court, I think, can hardly be expected
To mine men's souls for merit, and unearth
Our hidden virtues and our secret worth.
ARSINOÉ *Some* virtues, though, are far too bright to hide;
290 Yours are acknowledged, Sir, on every side.
Indeed, I've heard you warmly praised of late
By persons of considerable weight.
ALCESTE This fawning age has praise for everyone,
And all distinctions, Madam, are undone.
295 All things have equal honor nowadays,
And no one should be gratified by praise.
To be admired, one only need exist,
And every lackey's on the honors list.
ARSINOÉ I only wish, Sir, that you had your eye
300 On some position at court, however high;
You'd only have to hint at such a notion
For me to set the proper wheels in motion;
I've certain friendships I'd be glad to use
To get you any office you might choose.
305 ALCESTE Madam, I fear that any such ambition
Is wholly foreign to my disposition.
The soul God gave me isn't of the sort
That prospers in the weather of a court.
It's all too obvious that I don't possess
310 The virtues necessary for success.
My only great talent is for speaking plain;
I've never learned to flatter or to feign;
And anyone so stupidly sincere
Had best not seek a courtier's career.
315 Outside the court, I know, one must dispense
With honors, privilege, and influence;
But still one gains the right, foregoing these,
Not to be tortured by the wish to please.
One needn't live in dread of snubs and slights,

320   Nor praise the verse that every idiot writes,
         Nor humor silly Marquesses, nor bestow
         Politic sighs on Madam So-and-So.
     ARSINOÉ Forget the court, then; let the matter rest.
         But I've another cause to be distressed
325   About your present situation, Sir.
         It's to your love affair that I refer.
         She whom you love, and who pretends to love you,
         Is, I regret to say, unworthy of you.
     ALCESTE Why, Madam? Can you seriously intend
330   To make so grave a charge against your friend?
     ARSINOÉ Alas, I must. I've stood aside too long
         And let that lady do you grievous wrong;
         But now my debt to conscience shall be paid:
         I tell you that your love has been betrayed.
335 ALCESTE I thank you, Madam; you're extremely kind.
         Such words are soothing to a lover's mind.
     ARSINOÉ Yes, though she *is* my friend, I say again
         You're very much too good for Célimène.
         She's wantonly misled you from the start.
340 ALCESTE You may be right; who knows another's heart?
         But ask yourself if it's the part of charity
         To shake my soul with doubts of her sincerity.
     ARSINOÉ Well, if you'd rather be a dupe than doubt her,
         That's your affair. I'll say no more about her.
345 ALCESTE Madam, you know that doubt and vague suspicion
         Are painful to a man in my position;
         It's most unkind to worry me this way
         Unless you've some real proof of what you say.
     ARSINOÉ Sir, say no more: all doubts shall be removed,
350   And all that I've been saying shall be proved.
         You've only to escort me home, and there
         We'll look into the heart of this affair.
         I've ocular evidence which will persuade you
         Beyond a doubt, that Célimène's betrayed you.
355   Then, if you're saddened by that revelation,
         Perhaps I can provide some consolation.

ACT IV

SCENE I. ÉLIANTE, PHILINTE

PHILINTE Madam, he acted like a stubborn child;
         I thought they never would be reconciled;
         In vain we reasoned, threatened, and appealed;
         He stood his ground and simply would not yield.
5   The Marshals, I feel sure, have never heard
         An argument so splendidly absurd.
         "No, gentlemen," said he, "I'll not retract.
         His verse is bad: extremely bad, in fact.
         Surely it does the man no harm to know it.

10   Does it disgrace him, not to be a poet?
      A gentleman may be respected still,
      Whether he writes a sonnet well or ill.
      That I dislike his verse should not offend him;
      In all that touches honor, I commend him;
15   He's noble, brave, and virtuous—but I fear
      He can't in truth be called a sonneteer.
      I'll gladly praise his wardrobe; I'll endorse
      His dancing, or the way he sits a horse;
      But, gentlemen, I cannot praise his rhyme.
20   In fact, it ought to be a capital crime
      For anyone so sadly unendowed
      To write a sonnet and read the thing aloud."
      At length he fell into a gentler mood
      And, striking a concessive attitude,
25   He paid Oronte the following courtesies:
      "Sir, I regret that I'm so hard to please,
      And I'm profoundly sorry that your lyric
      Failed to provoke me to a panegyric."
      After these curious words, the two embraced,
30   And then the hearing was adjourned—in haste.
      ÉLIANTE His conduct has been very singular lately;
      Still, I confess that I respect him greatly.
      The honesty in which he takes such pride
      Has—to my mind—its noble, heroic side.
35   In this false age, such candor seems outrageous;
      But I could wish that it were more contagious.
      PHILINTE What most intrigues me in our friend Alceste
      Is the grand passion that rages in his breast.
      The sullen humors he's compounded of
40   Should not, I think, dispose his heart to love;
      But since they do, it puzzles me still more
      That he should choose your cousin to adore.
      ÉLIANTE It does, indeed, belie the theory
      That love is born of gentle sympathy,
45   And that the tender passion must be based
      On sweet accords of temper and of taste.
      PHILINTE Does she return his love, do you suppose?
      ÉLIANTE Ah, that's a difficult question, Sir. Who knows?
      How can we judge the truth of her devotion?
50   Her heart's a stranger to its own emotion.
      Sometimes it thinks it loves, when no love's there;
      At other times it loves quite unaware.
      PHILINTE I rather think Alceste is in for more
      Distress and sorrow than he's bargained for;
55   Were he of my mind, Madam, his affection
      Would turn in quite a different direction,
      And we would see him more responsive to
      The kind regard which he receives from you.

ÉLIANTE Sir, I believe in frankness, and I'm inclined,
60   In matters of the heart, to speak my mind.
     I don't oppose his love for her; indeed,
     I hope with all my heart that he'll succeed,
     And were it in my power, I'd rejoice
     In giving him the lady of his choice.
65   But if, as happens frequently enough
     In love affairs, he meets with a rebuff—
     If Célimène should grant some rival's suit—
     I'd gladly play the role of substitute;
     Nor would his tender speeches please me less
70   Because they'd once been made without success.
PHILINTE Well, Madam, as for me, I don't oppose
     Your hopes in this affair; and heaven knows
     That in my conversations with the man
     I plead your cause as often as I can.
75   But if those two should marry, and so remove
     All chance that he will offer you his love,
     Then I'll declare my own, and hope to see
     Your gracious favor pass from him to me.
     In short, should you be cheated of Alceste,
80   I'd be most happy to be second best.
ÉLIANTE Philinte, you're teasing.
PHILINTE   Ah, Madam, never fear;
     No words of mine were ever so sincere,
     And I shall live in fretful expectation
     Till I can make a fuller declaration.

SCENE II. ALCESTE, ÉLIANTE, PHILINTE

85 ALCESTE Avenge me, Madam! I must have satisfaction,
     Or this great wrong will drive me to distraction!
ÉLIANTE Why, what's the matter? What's upset you so?
ALCESTE Madam, I've had a mortal, mortal blow.
     If Chaos repossessed the universe,
90   I swear I'd not be shaken any worse.
     I'm ruined. . . . I can say no more. . . . My soul . . .
ÉLIANTE Do try, Sir, to regain your self-control.
ALCESTE Just heaven! Why were so much beauty and grace
     Bestowed on one so vicious and so base?
ÉLIANTE Once more, Sir, tell us. . . .
95 ALCESTE   My world has gone to wrack;
     I'm—I'm betrayed; she's stabbed me in the back:
     Yes, Célimène (who would have thought it of her?)
     Is false to me, and has another lover.
ÉLIANTE Are you quite certain? Can you prove these things?
100 PHILINTE Lovers are prey to wild imaginings
     And jealous fancies. No doubt there's some mistake. . . .
ALCESTE Mind your own business, Sir, for heaven's sake.
     (To ÉLIANTE.) Madam, I have the proof that you demand

Here in my pocket, penned by her own hand.
105 Yes, all the shameful evidence one could want
Lies in this letter written to Oronte—
Oronte! whom I felt sure she couldn't love,
And hardly bothered to be jealous of.
PHILINTE Still, in a letter, appearances may deceive;
110 This may not be so bad as you believe.
ALCESTE Once more I beg you, Sir, to let me be;
Tend to your own affairs; leave mine to me.
ÉLIANTE Compose yourself; this anguish that you feel . . .
ALCESTE Is something, Madam, you alone can heal.
115 My outraged heart, beside itself with grief,
Appeals to you for comfort and relief.
Avenge me on your cousin, whose unjust
And faithless nature has deceived my trust;
Avenge a crime your pure soul must detest.
ÉLIANTE But how, Sir?
120 ALCESTE   Madam, this heart within my breast
Is yours; pray take it; redeem my heart from her,
And so avenge me on my torturer.
Let her be punished by the fond emotion,
The ardent love, the bottomless devotion,
125 The faithful worship which this heart of mine
Will offer up to yours as to a shrine.
ÉLIANTE You have my sympathy, Sir, in all you suffer;
Nor do I scorn the noble heart you offer;
But I suspect you'll soon be mollified,
130 And this desire for vengeance will subside.
When some belovèd hand has done us wrong
We thirst for retribution—but not for long;
However dark the deed that she's committed,
A lovely culprit's very soon acquitted.
135 Nothing's so stormy as an injured lover,
And yet no storm so quickly passes over.
ALCESTE No, Madam, no—this is no lovers' spat;
I'll not forgive her; its gone too far for that;
My mind's made up; I'll kill myself before
140 I waste my hopes upon her any more.
Ah, here she is. My wrath intensifies.
I shall confront her with her tricks and lies,
And crush her utterly, and bring you then
A heart no longer slave to Célimène.

SCENE III. CÉLIMÈNE, ALCESTE

145 ALCESTE (aside) Sweet heaven, help me to control my passion.
CÉLIMÈNE (aside) Oh, Lord.
(To ALCESTE.)   Why stand there staring in that fashion?
And what d'you mean by those dramatic sighs,
And that malignant glitter in your eyes?

ALCESTE I mean that sins which cause the blood to freeze
150   Look innocent beside your treacheries;
       That nothing Hell's or Heaven's wrath could do
       Ever produced so bad a thing as you.
       CÉLIMÈNE Your compliments were always sweet and pretty.
       ALCESTE Madam, it's not the moment to be witty.
155   No, blush and hang your head; you've ample reason,
       Since I've the fullest evidence of your treason.
       Ah, this is what my sad heart prophesied;
       Now all my anxious fears are verified;
       My dark suspicion and my gloomy doubt
160   Divined the truth, and now the truth is out.
       For all your trickery, I was not deceived;
       It was my bitter stars that I believed.
       But don't imagine that you'll go scot-free;
       You shan't misuse me with impunity.
165   I know that love's irrational and blind;
       I know the heart's not subject to the mind,
       And can't be reasoned into beating faster;
       I know each soul is free to choose its master;
       Therefore had you but spoken from the heart,
170   Rejecting my attentions from the start,
       I'd have no grievance, or at any rate
       I could complain of nothing but my fate.
       Ah, but so falsely to encourage me—
       That was a treason and a treachery
175   For which you cannot suffer too severely,
       And you shall pay for that behavior dearly.
       Yes, now I have no pity, not a shred;
       My temper's out of hand; I've lost my head;
       Shocked by the knowledge of your double-dealings,
180   My reason can't restrain my savage feelings;
       A righteous wrath deprives me of my senses,
       And I won't answer for the consequences.
       CÉLIMÈNE What does this outburst mean? Will you please explain?
       Have you, by any chance, gone quite insane?
185   ALCESTE Yes, yes, I went insane the day I fell
       A victim to your black and fatal spell,
       Thinking to meet with some sincerity
       Among the treacherous charms that beckoned me.
       CÉLIMÈNE Pooh. Of what treachery can you complain?
190   ALCESTE How sly you are, how cleverly you feign!
       But you'll not victimize me any more.
       Look: here's a document you've seen before.
       This evidence, which I acquired today,
       Leaves you, I think, without a thing to say.
195   CÉLIMÈNE Is this what sent you into such a fit?
       ALCESTE You should be blushing at the sight of it.
       CÉLIMÈNE Ought I to blush? I truly don't see why.

ALCESTE Ah, now you're being bold as well as sly;
    Since there's no signature, perhaps you'll claim . . .
200 CÉLIMÈNE I wrote it, whether or not it bears my name.
ALCESTE And you can view with equanimity
    This proof of your disloyalty to me!
CÉLIMÈNE Oh, don't be so outrageous and extreme.
ALCESTE You take this matter lightly, it would seem.
205   Was it no wrong to me, no shame to you,
    That you should send Oronte this billet-doux?
CÉLIMÈNE Oronte! Who said it was for him?
ALCESTE   Why, those
    Who brought me this example of your prose.
    But what's the difference? If you wrote the letter
210   To someone else, it pleases me no better.
    My grievance and your guilt remain the same.
CÉLIMÈNE But need you rage, and need I blush for shame,
    If this was written to a *woman* friend?
ALCESTE Ah! Most ingenious. I'm impressed no end;
215   And after that incredible evasion
    Your guilt is clear. I need no more persuasion.
    How dare you try so clumsy a deception?
    D'you think I'm wholly wanting in perception?
    Come, come, let's see how brazenly you'll try
220   To bolster up so palpable a lie:
    Kindly construe this ardent closing section
    As nothing more than sisterly affection!
    Here, let me read it. Tell me, if you dare to,
    That this is for a woman . . .
CÉLIMÈNE   I don't care to.
225   What right have you to badger and berate me,
    And so highhandedly interrogate me?
ALCESTE Now, don't be angry; all I ask of you
    Is that you justify a phrase or two . . .
CÉLIMÈNE No, I shall not. I utterly refuse,
230   And you may take those phrases as you choose.
ALCESTE Just show me how this letter could be meant
    For a woman's eyes, and I shall be content.
CÉLIMÈNE No, no, it's for Oronte; you're perfectly right.
    I welcome his attentions with delight,
235   I prize his character and his intellect,
    And everything is just as you suspect.
    Come, do your worst now; give your rage free rein;
    But kindly cease to bicker and complain.
ALCESTE (*aside*) Good God! Could anything be more inhuman?
240   Was ever a heart so mangled by a woman?
    When I complain of how she has betrayed me,
    She bridles, and commences to upbraid me!
    She tries my tortured patience to the limit;
    She won't deny her guilt; she glories in it!

245   And yet my heart's too faint and cowardly
      To break these chains of passion, and be free,
      To scorn her as it should, and rise above
      This unrewarded, mad, and bitter love.
      (*To* CÉLIMÈNE.) Ah, traitress, in how confident a fashion
250   You take advantage of my helpless passion,
      And use my weakness for your faithless charms
      To make me once again throw down my arms!
      But do at least deny this black transgression;
      Take back that mocking and perverse confession;
255   Defend this letter and your innocence,
      And I, poor fool, will aid in your defense.
      Pretend, pretend, that you are just and true,
      And I shall make myself believe in you.
      CÉLIMÈNE Oh, stop it. Don't be such a jealous dunce,
260   Or I shall leave off loving you at once.
      Just why should I *pretend?* What could impel me
      To stoop so low as that? And kindly tell me
      Why, if I loved another, I shouldn't merely
      Inform you of it, simply and sincerely!
265   I've told you where you stand, and that admission
      Should altogether clear me of suspicion;
      After so generous a guarantee,
      What right have you to harbor doubts of me?
      Since women are (from natural reticence)
270   Reluctant to declare their sentiments,
      And since the honor of our sex requires
      That we conceal our amorous desires,
      Ought any man for whom such laws are broken
      To question what the oracle has spoken?
275   Should he not rather feel an obligation
      To trust that most obliging declaration?
      Enough, now. Your suspicions quite disgust me;
      Why should I love a man who doesn't trust me?
      I cannot understand why I continue,
280   Fool that I am, to take an interest in you.
      I ought to choose a man less prone to doubt,
      And give you something to be vexed about.
      ALCESTE Ah, what a poor enchanted fool I am;
      These gentle words, no doubt, were all a sham,
285   But destiny requires me to entrust
      My happiness to you, and so I must.
      I'll love you to the bitter end, and see
      How false and treacherous you dare to be.
      CÉLIMÈNE No, you don't really love me as you ought.
290   ALCESTE I love you more than can be said or thought;
      Indeed, I wish you were in such distress
      That I might show my deep devotedness.
      Yes, I could wish that you were wretchedly poor,

Unloved, uncherished, utterly obscure;
295 That fate had set you down upon the earth
Without possessions, rank, or gentle birth;
Then, by the offer of my heart, I might
Repair the great injustice of your plight;
I'd raise you from the dust, and proudly prove
300 The purity and vastness of my love.
CÉLIMÈNE This is a strange benevolence indeed!
God grant that I may never be in need. . . .
Ah, here's Monsieur Dubois, in quaint disguise.

SCENE IV. CÉLIMÈNE, ALCESTE, DUBOIS

ALCESTE Well, why this costume? Why those frightened eyes?
What ails you?
305 DUBOIS   Well, Sir, things are most mysterious.
ALCESTE What do you mean?
DUBOIS   I fear they're very serious.
ALCESTE What?
DUBOIS   Shall I speak more loudly?
ALCESTE   Yes; speak out.
DUBOIS Isn't there someone here, Sir?
ALCESTE   Speak, you lout!
Stop wasting time.
DUBOIS   Sir, we must slip away.
ALCESTE How's that?
310 DUBOIS   We must decamp without delay.
ALCESTE Explain yourself.
DUBOIS   I tell you we must fly.
ALCESTE What for?
DUBOIS   We mustn't pause to say good-by.
ALCESTE Now what d'you mean by all of this, you clown?
DUBOIS I mean, Sir, that we've got to leave this town.
315 ALCESTE I'll tear you limb from limb and joint from joint
If you don't come more quickly to the point.
DUBOIS Well, Sir, today a man in a black suit,
Who wore a black and ugly scowl to boot,
Left us a document scrawled in such a hand
320 As even Satan couldn't understand.
It bears upon your lawsuit, I don't doubt;
But all hell's devils couldn't make it out.
ALCESTE Well, well, go on. What then? I fail to see
How this event obliges us to flee.
325 DUBOIS Well, Sir, an hour later, hardly more,
A gentleman who's often called before
Came looking for you in an anxious way.
Not finding you, he asked me to convey
(Knowing I could be trusted with the same)
330 The following message. . . . Now, what *was* his name?
ALCESTE Forget his name, you idiot. What did he say?

DUBOIS Well, it was one of your friends, Sir, anyway.
    He warned you to begone, and he suggested
    That if you stay, you may well be arrested.
335 ALCESTE What? Nothing more specific? Think, man, think!
DUBOIS No, Sir. He had me bring him pen and ink,
    And dashed you off a letter which, I'm sure,
    Will render things distinctly less obscure.
ALCESTE Well—let me have it!
CÉLIMÈNE   What *is* this all about?
340 ALCESTE God knows; but I have hopes of finding out.
    How long am I to wait, you blitherer?
DUBOIS (*after a protracted search for the letter*) I must have left it on your table, Sir.
ALCESTE I ought to . . .
CÉLIMÈNE   No, no, keep your self-control;
    Go find out what's behind his rigmarole.
345 ALCESTE It seems that fate, no matter what I do,
    Has sworn that I may not converse with you;
    But, Madam, pray permit your faithful lover
    To try once more before the day is over.

ACT V

SCENE I. ALCESTE, PHILINTE

ALCESTE No, it's too much. My mind's made up, I tell you.
PHILINTE Why should this blow, however hard, compel you . . .
ALCESTE No, no, don't waste your breath in argument;
    Nothing you say will alter my intent;
5   This age is vile, and I've made up my mind
    To have no further commerce with mankind.
    Did not truth, honor, decency, and the laws
    Oppose my enemy and approve my cause?
    My claims were justified in all men's sight;
10   I put my trust in equity and right;
    Yet, to my horror and the world's disgrace,
    Justice is mocked, and I have lost my case!
    A scoundrel whose dishonesty is notorious
    Emerges from another lie victorious!
15   Honor and right condone his brazen fraud,
    While rectitude and decency applaud!
    Before his smirking face, the truth stands charmed,
    And virtue conquered, and the law disarmed!
    His crime is sanctioned by a court decree!
20   And not content with what he's done to me,
    The dog now seeks to ruin me by stating
    That I composed a book now circulating,
    A book so wholly criminal and vicious
    That even to speak its title is seditious!
25   Meanwhile Oronte, my rival, lends his credit
    To the same libelous tale, and helps to spread it!
    Oronte! a man of honor and of rank,

With whom I've been entirely fair and frank;
Who sought me out and forced me, willy nilly,
30 To judge some verse I found extremely silly;
And who, because I properly refused
To flatter him, or see the truth abused,
Abets my enemy in a rotten slander!
There's the reward of honesty and candor!
35 The man will hate me to the end of time
For failing to commend his wretched rhyme!
And not this man alone, but all humanity
Do what they do from interest and vanity;
They prate of honor, truth, and righteousness,
40 But lie, betray, and swindle nonetheless.
Come then: man's villainy is too much to bear;
Let's leave this jungle and this jackal's lair.
Yes! treacherous and savage race of men,
You shall not look upon my face again.
45 PHILINTE Oh, don't rush into exile prematurely;
Things aren't as dreadful as you make them, surely.
It's rather obvious, since you're still at large,
That people don't believe your enemy's charge.
Indeed, his tale's so patently untrue
50 That it may do more harm to him than you.
ALCESTE Nothing could do that scoundrel any harm:
His frank corruption is his greatest charm,
And, far from hurting him, a further shame
Would only serve to magnify his name.
55 PHILINTE In any case, his bald prevarication
Has done no injury to your reputation,
And you may feel secure in that regard.
As for your lawsuit, it should not be hard
To have the case reopened, and contest
This judgment . . .
60 ALCESTE   No, no, let the verdict rest.
Whatever cruel penalty it may bring,
I wouldn't have it changed for anything.
It shows the times' injustice with such clarity
That I shall pass it down to our posterity
65 As a great proof and signal demonstration
Of the black wickedness of this generation.
It may cost twenty thousand francs; but I
Shall pay their twenty thousand, and gain thereby
The right to storm and rage at human evil,
70 And send the race of mankind to the devil.
PHILINTE Listen to me . . .
ALCESTE   Why? What can you possibly say?
Don't argue, Sir; your labor's thrown away.
Do you propose to offer lame excuses
For men's behavior and the times' abuses?

75 PHILINTE No, all you say I'll readily concede:
　　　This is a low, conniving age indeed;
　　　Nothing but trickery prospers nowadays,
　　　And people ought to mend their shabby ways.
　　　Yes, man's a beastly creature; but must we then
80　　Abandon the society of men?
　　　Here in the world, each human frailty
　　　Provides occasion for philosophy,
　　　And that is virtue's noblest exercise;
　　　If honesty shone forth from all men's eyes,
85　　If every heart were frank and kind and just.
　　　What could our virtues do but gather dust
　　　(Since their employment is to help us bear
　　　The villainies of men without despair)?
　　　A heart well-armed with virtue can endure . . .
90 ALCESTE Sir, you're a matchless reasoner, to be sure;
　　　Your words are fine and full of cogency;
　　　But don't waste time and eloquence on me.
　　　My reason bids me go, for my own good.
　　　My tongue won't lie and flatter as it should;
95　　God knows what frankness it might next commit,
　　　And what I'd suffer on account of it.
　　　Pray let me wait for Célimène's return
　　　In peace and quiet. I shall shortly learn,
　　　By her response to what I have in view,
100　　Whether her love for me is feigned or true.
　　PHILINTE Till then, let's visit Éliante upstairs.
　　ALCESTE No, I am too weighed down with somber cares.
　　　Go to her, do; and leave me with my gloom
　　　Here in the darkened corner of this room.
105 PHILINTE Why, that's no sort of company, my friend;
　　　I'll see if Éliante will not descend.

SCENE II. CÉLIMÈNE, ORONTE, ALCESTE

　　ORONTE Yes, Madam, if you wish me to remain
　　　Your true and ardent lover, you must deign
　　　To give me some more positive assurance.
110　　All this suspense is quite beyond endurance.
　　　If your heart shares the sweet desires of mine,
　　　Show me as much by some convincing sign;
　　　And here's the sign I urgently suggest:
　　　That you no longer tolerate Alceste,
115　　But sacrifice him to my love, and sever
　　　All your relations with the man forever.
　　CÉLIMÈNE Why do you suddenly dislike him so?
　　　You praised him to the skies not long ago.
　　ORONTE Madam, that's not the point. I'm here to find
120　　Which way your tender feelings are inclined.

Choose, if you please, between Alceste and me,
And I shall stay or go accordingly.
ALCESTE (*emerging from the corner*) Yes, Madam, choose; this gentleman's demand
Is wholly just, and I support his stand.
125 I too am true and ardent; I too am here
To ask you that you make your feelings clear.
No more delays, now; no equivocation;
The time has come to make your declaration.
ORONTE Sir, I've no wish in any way to be
130 An obstacle to your felicity.
ALCESTE Sir, I've no wish to share her heart with you;
That may sound jealous, but at least it's true.
ORONTE If, weighing us, she leans in your direction . . .
ALCESTE If she regards you with the least affection . . .
135 ORONTE I swear I'll yield her to you there and then.
ALCESTE I swear I'll never see her face again.
ORONTE Now, Madam, tell us what we've come to hear.
ALCESTE Madam, speak openly and have no fear.
ORONTE Just say which one is to remain your lover.
140 ALCESTE Just name one name, and it will all be over.
ORONTE What! Is it possible that you're undecided?
ALCESTE What! Can your feelings possibly be divided?
CÉLIMÈNE Enough: this inquisition's gone too far:
How utterly unreasonable you are!
145 Not that I couldn't make the choice with ease;
My heart has no conflicting sympathies;
I know full well which one of you I favor,
And you'd not see me hesitate or waver.
But how can you expect me to reveal
150 So cruelly and bluntly what I feel?
I think it altogether too unpleasant
To choose between two men when both are present;
One's heart has means more subtle and more kind
Of letting its affections be divined,
155 Nor need one be uncharitably plain
To let a lover know he loves in vain.
ORONTE No, no, speak plainly; I for one can stand it.
I beg you to be frank.
ALCESTE   And I demand it.
The simple truth is what I wish to know,
160 And there's no need for softening the blow.
You've made an art of pleasing everyone,
But now your days of coquetry are done:
You have no choice now, Madam, but to choose,
For I'll know what to think if you refuse;
165 I'll take your silence for a clear admission
That I'm entitled to my worst suspicion.
ORONTE I thank you for this ultimatum, Sir,
And I may say I heartily concur.

CÉLIMÈNE Really, this foolishness is very wearing:
170   Must you be so unjust and overbearing?
      Haven't I told you why I must demur?
      Ah, here's Éliante; I'll put the case to her.

SCENE III.   ÉLIANTE, PHILINTE, CÉLIMÈNE, ORONTE, ALCESTE

CÉLIMÈNE Cousin, I'm being persecuted here
      By these two persons, who, it would appear,
175   Will not be satisfied till I confess
      Which one I love the more, and which the less,
      And tell the latter to his face that he
      Is henceforth banished from my company.
      Tell me, has ever such a thing been done?
180 ÉLIANTE You'd best not turn to me; I'm not the one
      To back you in a matter of this kind:
      I'm all for those who frankly speak their mind.
      ORONTE Madam, you'll search in vain for a defender.
      ALCESTE You're beaten, Madam, and may as well surrender.
185 ORONTE Speak, speak, you must; and end this awful strain.
      ALCESTE Or don't, and your position will be plain.
      ORONTE A single word will close this painful scene.
      ALCESTE But if you're silent, I'll know what you mean.

SCENE IV.   ARSINOÉ, CÉLIMÈNE, ÉLIANTE, ALCESTE, PHILINTE, ACASTE, CLITANDRE,
            ORONTE

ACASTE (to CÉLIMÈNE) Madam, with all due deference, we two
190   Have come to pick a little bone with you.
      CLITANDRE (to ORONTE and ALCESTE) I'm glad you're present,
          Sirs, as you'll soon learn,
      Our business here is also your concern.
      ARSINOÉ (to CÉLIMÈNE) Madam, I visit you so soon again
      Only because of these two gentlemen,
195   Who came to me indignant and aggrieved
      About a crime too base to be believed.
      Knowing your virtue, having such confidence in it,
      I couldn't think you guilty for a minute,
      In spite of all their telling evidence;
200   And, rising above our little difference,
      I've hastened here in friendship's name to see
      You clear yourself of this great calumny.
      ACASTE Yes, Madam, let us see with what composure
      You'll manage to respond to this disclosure.
205   You lately sent Clitandre this tender note.
      CLITANDRE And this one, for Acaste, you also wrote.
      ACASTE (to ORONTE and ALCESTE) You'll recognize this writing, Sirs, I think;
      The lady is so free with pen and ink
      That you must know it all too well, I fear.
210   But listen: this is something you should hear.

1186   Comedy

"How absurd you are to condemn my lightheartedness in society, and to accuse me of being happiest in the company of others. Nothing could be more unjust; and if you do not come to me instantly and beg pardon for saying such a thing, I shall never forgive you as long as I live. Our big bumbling friend the Viscount . . . "

215   What a shame that he's not here.

"Our big bumbling friend the Viscount, whose name stands first in your complaint, is hardly a man to my taste; and ever since the day I watched him spend three-quarters of an hour spitting into a well, so as to make circles in the water, I have been unable to think highly of him. As for the little Marquess . . . "

220   In all modesty, gentlemen, that is I.

"As for the little Marquess, who sat squeezing my hand for such a long while yesterday, I find him in all respects the most trifling creature alive; and the only things of value about him are his cape and his sword. As for the man with the green ribbons . . . "

225   (*To* ALCESTE.) It's your turn now, Sir.

"As for the man with the green ribbons, he amuses me now and then with his bluntness and his bearish ill-humor; but there are many times indeed when I think him the greatest bore in the world. And as for the sonneteer . . . "

(*To* ORONTE.) Here's your helping.

230   "And as for the sonneteer, who has taken it into his head to be witty, and insists on being an author in the teeth of opinion, I simply cannot be bothered to listen to him, and his prose wearies me quite as much as his poetry. Be assured that I am not always so well-entertained as you suppose; that I long for your company, more than I dare to say, at all these entertainments to which people drag me; and
235   that the presence of those one loves is the true and perfect seasoning to all one's pleasures."

CLITANDRE   And now for me.

"Clitandre, whom you mention, and who so pesters me with his saccharine speeches, is the last man on earth for whom I could feel any affection. He is quite mad to
240   suppose that I love him, and so are you, to doubt that you are loved. Do come to your senses; exchange your suppositions for his; and visit me as often as possible, to help me bear the annoyance of his unwelcome attentions."

It's sweet character that these letters show,
And what to call it, Madam, you well know.
245   Enough. We're off to make the world acquainted
With this sublime self-portrait that you've painted.
ACASTE   Madam, I'll make you no farewell oration;
No, you're not worthy of my indignation.
Far choicer hearts than yours, as you'll discover,
250   Would like this little Marquess for a lover.

SCENE V.   CÉLIMÈNE, ÉLIANTE, ARSINOÉ, ALCESTE, ORONTE, PHILINTE

ORONTE   So! After all those loving letters you wrote,
You turn on me like this, and cut my throat!

And your dissembling, faithless heart, I find,
Has pledged itself by turns to all mankind!
255 How blind I've been! But now I clearly see;
I thank you, Madam, for enlightening me.
My heart is mine once more, and I'm content;
The loss of it shall be your punishment.
(*To* ALCESTE.) Sir, she is yours; I'll seek no more to stand
260 Between your wishes and this lady's hand.

SCENE VI. CÉLIMÈNE, ÉLIANTE, ARSINOÉ, ALCESTE, PHILINTE

ARSINOÉ (*to* CÉLIMÈNE) Madam, I'm forced to speak. I'm far too stirred
To keep my counsel, after what I've heard.
I'm shocked and staggered by your want of morals.
It's not my way to mix in others' quarrels;
265 But really, when this fine and noble spirit,
This man of honor and surpassing merit,
Laid down the offering of his heart before you,
How *could* you . . .
ALCESTE   Madam, permit me, I implore you,
To represent myself in this debate.
270 Don't bother, please, to be my advocate.
My heart, in any case, could not afford
To give your services their due reward;
And if I chose, for consolation's sake,
Some other lady, 'twould not be you I'd take.
275 ARSINOÉ What makes you think you could, Sir? And how dare you
Imply that I've been trying to ensnare you?
If you can for a moment entertain
Such flattering fancies, you're extremely vain.
I'm not so interested as you suppose
280 In Célimène's discarded gigolos.
Get rid of that absurd illusion, do.
Women like me are not for such as you.
Stay with this creature, to whom you're so attached;
I've never seen two people better matched.

SCENE VII. CÉLIMÈNE, ÉLIANTE, ALCESTE, PHILINTE

285 ALCESTE (*to* CÉLIMÈNE) Well, I've been still throughout this exposé,
Till everyone but me has said his say.
Come, have I shown sufficient self-restraint?
And may I now . . .
CÉLIMÈNE   Yes, make your just complaint.
Reproach me freely, call me what you will;
290 You've every right to say I've used you ill.
I've wronged you, I confess it; and in my shame
I'll make no effort to escape the blame.
The anger of those others I could despise;
My guilt toward you I sadly recognize.

295 Your wrath is wholly justified, I fear;
I know how culpable I must appear,
I know all things bespeak my treachery,
And that, in short, you've grounds for hating me.
Do so; I give you leave.
ALCESTE   Ah, traitress—how,
300 How should I cease to love you, even now?
Though mind and will were passionately bent
On hating you, my heart would not consent.
(To ÉLIANTE *and* PHILINTE.) Be witness to my madness, both of you;
See what infatuation drives one to;
305 But wait; my folly's only just begun,
And I shall prove to you before I'm done
How strange the human heart is, and how far
From rational we sorry creatures are.
(To CÉLIMÈNE.) Woman, I'm willing to forget your shame,
310 And clothe your treacheries in a sweeter name;
I'll call them youthful errors, instead of crimes,
And lay the blame on these corrupting times.
My one condition is that you agree
To share my chosen fate, and fly with me
315 To that wild, trackless, solitary place
In which I shall forget the human race.
Only by such a course can you atone
For those atrocious letters; by that alone
Can you remove my present horror of you,
320 And make it possible for me to love you.
CÉLIMÈNE What! I renounce the world at my young age,
And die of boredom in some hermitage?
ALCESTE Ah, if you really loved me as you ought,
You wouldn't give the world a moment's thought;
325 Must you have me, and all the world beside?
CÉLIMÈNE Alas, at twenty one is terrified
Of solitude. I fear I lack the force
And depth of soul to take so stern a course.
But if my hand in marriage will content you,
330 Why, there's a plan which I might well consent to,
And . . .
ALCESTE   No, I detest you now. I could excuse
Everything else, but since you thus refuse
To love me wholly, as a wife should do,
And see the world in me, as I in you,
335 Go! I reject your hand, and disenthrall
My heart from your enchantments, once for all.

SCENE VIII. ÉLIANTE, ALCESTE, PHILINTE

ALCESTE (*to* ÉLIANTE) Madam, your virtuous beauty has no peer;
Of all this world you only are sincere;
I've long esteemed you highly, as you know;

340   Permit me ever to esteem you so,
      And if I do not now request your hand,
      Forgive me, Madam, and try to understand.
      I feel unworthy of it; I sense that fate
      Does not intend me for the married state,
345   That I should do you wrong by offering you
      My shattered heart's unhappy residue,
      And that in short . . .
      ÉLIANTE   Your argument's well taken:
      Nor need you fear that I shall feel forsaken.
      Were I to offer him this hand of mine,
350   Your friend Philinte, I think, would not decline.
      PHILINTE Ah, Madam, that's my heart's most cherished goal,
      For which I'd gladly give my life and soul.
      ALCESTE (to ÉLIANTE and PHILINTE) May you be true to all you now profess,
      And so deserve unending happiness.
355   Meanwhile, betrayed and wronged in everything,
      I'll flee this bitter world where vice is king,
      And seek some spot unpeopled and apart
      Where I'll be free to have an honest heart.
      PHILINTE Come, Madam, let's do everything we can
360   To change the mind of this unhappy man.

Questions

1. What qualities of character do you admire in Alceste in the first scene? What qualities are not admirable?
2. In this scene Philinte advises Alceste, "Come, let's forget the follies of the times/And pardon mankind for its petty crimes." How much of the ensuing speech do you agree with?
3. Of the seven scenes in Act III, which are clearly comic? Which ones are serious? Of the eight scenes in Act V, which are comic and which are not?
4. Are there any characters in the play that you would want to have as friends? Which ones? Why?
5. Why do you suppose Alceste has such a great affection for Célimène? Does she care about him? Whom does she really love?
6. Are there any instances of low comedy in *The Misanthrope*? Are there any elements of farce?
7. Compare this play with *She Stoops to Conquer* as a romantic comedy.
8. Are there any characters in *The Misanthrope* who escape satire?
9. The play is written in rhymed couplets. How is that form of versification particularly suitable for the play's subject and characters?

Suggestions for Dramatists

1. A frequent technique of comic irony is called "talk at cross-purposes." This occurs when two characters think they are talking about the same thing, but actually are talking about totally different matters.

Create a situation likely to breed misunderstanding between two people. For instance, the two may attempt to discuss an object that they both think they have seen when actually they have seen two different things, or one character may have stumbled into a scene thinking it is familiar and the other character is forced to correct him. Write a dialogue between two characters who talk at cross-purposes.

2. Think of someone you would like to satirize. Imagine a scene in which he or she might be made to look ridiculous. Write a short skit based upon that scene, using as few characters as possible.

7 ❧ The Rise of Realism

In art and literature, realism is the accurate representation of the real world and human nature. In drama, realism avoids all that is improbable in events and characters, and all that is visionary in theatrical presentation. We have grown so accustomed to realism in modern theater and film, we may forget that most drama before the twentieth century, and a good deal of drama since, is not at all realistic. Consider the plays we have read. The plot of *Oedipus Rex*, as well as the character of Teiresias, is highly improbable. So is the acting and chanting of the chorus. The events of *Hamlet* are quite probable, but the appearance of the ghost in Act I is not. Nor is the manner of speech probable. No one ever spoke as beautifully as the characters in *Hamlet*. Then there are Hamlet's asides, his stage whispers only the audience can hear, and soliloquies where he speaks at length to himself and the audience. Have you ever heard of anybody speaking so long and eloquently to himself? Of course not. You accept these things because the theater is a world of illusion, and these are accepted conventions within that world of illusion.

Realism is just such a convention. It has roots in the Greek New Comedy that portrayed ordinary people and domestic situations, instead of demigods struggling against fate. These comedies and their European successors, with their stock characters and happy endings, may be more probable than the tragedies of Sophocles and Marlowe. Yet they are not truly realistic. Realism as we know it is largely the invention of a nineteenth-century Norwegian, Henrik Ibsen.

In the early nineteenth century the spirit of Romanticism swept through the arts in Europe and England. Romanticism emphasizes the emotions and imagination above reason and intellect. The plays of Lord Byron, Victor Hugo, and Heinrich von Kleist dramatized historical and sentimental subjects in a grand style that often verged on melodrama. Ibsen's realism was partly a reaction to romantic excess. In his most influential plays, both the characters and the situations seem highly probable, and the language is natural prose. There are no choruses, soliloquies, ghosts, nor other "stagey" trappings—just real people with serious personal and social problems. This approach was totally shocking to the audiences of the time. They went to the theater expecting a show, and what they found was embarrassingly lifelike.

Ibsen's achievement is all the more stunning when you recall that before the nineteenth century only comic playwrights dared to be realistic, and in that case only to make people laugh at human folly. Ibsen's plays are not funny. They show the frailties of real people and society in a tragic light.

Social Realism

We have mentioned the effectiveness of theater as an incubator of manners and morals during revolutionary times. Ibsen's plays of the late nineteenth century correspond with a cultural revolution. Society had changed enormously since the Renaissance, but theater had not kept pace with the change. The Napoleonic Wars, the Industrial Revolution, and the rise of the middle class had bred a new audience that longed for serious criticism of outmoded social institutions. They wanted exploration of their psychology. Henrik Ibsen, contemporary of Marx and Freud, was able to provide both. He created a new kind of hero. The tragic heroes of Sophocles and Shakespeare struggle with their fates and against the gods. They are exalted, universal figures. Ibsen's characters are middle-class, flesh-and-blood, struggling against social and economic systems, and with psychological problems clearly provoked by those systems. Drama that portrays such characters and situations has been called *social realism.*

A Doll's House

A Doll's House (1879) was one of the first and most controversial plays of social realism. In Norway, as in much of Europe at the time, women's rights was a hot topic. The heroine of Ibsen's play, Nora, has been petted, spoiled, and humiliated by her father and her husband. Millions of middle-class women saw themselves in Nora Helmer. Nora's slamming of the door on her husband and their outmoded ideal of marriage echoed around the world. The play was damned and praised in journals, in pamphlets and books, and at public meetings. Preachers denounced it from the pulpit. *A Doll's House* was a scandalous success; by the end of the eighties, it had been staged in nearly every civilized country. In England the play was first performed privately in a Bloomsbury lodging house, with Karl Marx's daughter as Nora, and Krogstad played by Bernard Shaw. The latter was a great fan and advocate of Ibsen, and obviously learned a good deal from him.

Henrik Ibsen was born in Skien, Norway, in 1828, the son of a businessman whose reversals of fortune kept the family in financial straits. Ibsen worked as a pharmacist's assistant and later studied medicine in Oslo. He was not a good student. Though he managed to write his first play, *Catilina*, during those years

(1848–1850) he failed to matriculate at the University. In 1851 Ibsen accepted a position as producer of the National theater in Bergen. Later he was invited to write a play yearly for the theater's anniversary. In 1857 he became the manager of the Norwegian Theater at Christiania. In 1858 the playwright married Suzannah Thoresen.

Ibsen's early works are not realistic. *The Vikings of Helgoland* (1858) and *The Pretenders* (1864) are romantic histories characteristic of the period. *Brand* (1865) and *Peer Gynt* (1867) are symbolic and mock-heroic. Although *The League of Youth* has elements of the prose drama, his first decisive play of social realism is *Pillars of Society*, about the double-dealings of a successful, hypocritical businessman. It established his fame in Europe and was followed by *A Doll's House* in 1879.

Shortly after the failure of the Norwegian theater in 1862, Ibsen left Norway for Rome. He lived abroad for the next twenty-seven years—mostly in Rome, Dresden, and Munich—and like the novelists James Joyce and Henry James, did his greatest work in exile, including *Ghosts*, *Hedda Gabler*, *The Master Builder*, and *The Wild Duck*.

In 1891 Ibsen returned to Norway and took up residence in Christiania. By then he was world famous. In 1901 he suffered a stroke that left him helpless. He wrote no more, and died in Christiania in 1906.

The Drama of Catastrophe

Ibsen's mastery of psychological portraiture resulted partly from the innovative plotting of his plays. During his years at Bergen, Ibsen became quite familiar with classic plot structure through the works of Eugène Scribe (1791–1861). More than half of the hundred and forty-five plays Ibsen produced were French, and were influenced by Scribe's *well-made-play*, a kind of comedy full of suspense and reversals, based on the classic five-part plot. Restless action, constant play and counterplay, expressed the changing attitudes of Scribe's shallow characters. Ibsen adopted the dynamic movement of Scribe's drama, but internalized the changes in his characters, making them mental rather than physical. To achieve this end, he had to re-order the narrative and create what is called the *catastrophic* plot.

Classic drama shows us the protagonist moving toward the central action of his story. We see Hamlet working to prove his uncle's guilt. We watch Oedipus search for the murderer of Laios. Then we see the central action, which makes the play's turning point: Hamlet fails to murder Claudius at his prayers; Oedipus begins to suspect he, himself, is the murderer. After the climax we get the catastrophe, or dénouement.

Ibsen's plot is quite different. The central event of *A Doll's House*, Nora's forging of a contract, occurs eight years before the curtain goes up. In the classical sense the whole play is catastrophe, or dénouement. There is little action, but a great deal of reflection, a marvelous opportunity to see how the characters

Liv Ullman with Sam Waterston in A Doll's House (Photograph by Friedman-Abeles from Performing Arts Research Center, The New York Public Library)

have been spiritually affected by the past action. The emotional climax of A Doll's House comes, at last, with the *discovery* of the central action rather than the dramatization of it.

A Doll's House is considered the first great drama of catastrophe. You have already seen its mark on Arthur Miller's *Death of a Salesman*. Eugene O'Neill's *Long Day's Journey into Night* is another highly regarded drama of catastrophe.

HENRIK IBSEN (1828–1906)

A Doll's House

Newly translated from the Norwegian by Michael Meyer

CHARACTERS

TORVALD HELMER, *a lawyer*	THE HELMERS' THREE SMALL CHILDREN
NORA, *his wife*	ANNE-MARIE, *their nurse*
DR. RANK	HELEN, *the maid*
MRS. LINDE	A PORTER
NILS KROGSTAD, *also a lawyer*	

The action takes place in the Helmers' apartment.

This translation of A DOLL'S HOUSE *was first performed on 16 October 1964 at the Oxford Playhouse with the following cast:*

TORVALD HELMER	Richard Gale
NORA	Barbara Young
DR. RANK	James Cairncross
MRS. LINDE	Pamela Lane
KROGSTAD	John Warner
ANNE-MARIE	Gabrielle Hamilton
HELEN	Yvette Byrne

Directed by Robert Chetwyn

ACT I

A comfortably and tastefully, but not expensively furnished room. Backstage right a door leads out to the hall; backstage left, another door to HELMER's *study. Between these two doors stands a piano. In the middle of the left-hand wall is a door, with a window downstage of it. Near the window, a round table with armchairs and a small sofa. In the right-hand wall, slightly upstage, is a door; downstage of this, against the same wall, a stove lined with porcelain tiles, with a couple of armchairs and a rocking-chair in front of it. Between the stove and the side door is a small table. Engravings on the wall. A what-not with china and other bric-a-brac; a small bookcase with leather-bound books. A carpet on the floor; a fire in the stove. A winter day.*

A bell rings in the hall outside. After a moment, we hear the front door being opened. NORA *enters the room, humming contentedly to herself. She is wearing outdoor clothes and carrying a lot of parcels, which she puts down on the table right. She leaves the door to the hall open; through it, we can see a* PORTER *carrying a Christmas tree and a basket. He gives these to the* MAID, *who has opened the door for them.*

NORA Hide that Christmas tree away, Helen. The children mustn't see it before I've decorated it this evening. (*To the* PORTER, *taking out her purse.*) How much—?
PORTER A shilling.
NORA Here's half a crown. No, keep it.

The PORTER *touches his cap and goes.* NORA *closes the door. She continues to laugh happily to herself as she removes her coat, etc. She takes from her pocket a bag containing macaroons and eats a couple. Then she tiptoes across and listens at her husband's door.*

NORA Yes, he's here. (*Starts humming again as she goes over to the table, right.*)
HELMER (*from his room*) Is that my skylark twittering out there?
NORA (*opening some of the parcels*) It is!
HELMER Is that my squirrel rustling?
NORA Yes!
HELMER When did my squirrel come home?
NORA Just now. (*Pops the bag of macaroons in her pocket and wipes her mouth.*) Come out here, Torvald, and see what I've bought.
HELMER You mustn't disturb me! (*Short pause; then he opens the door and looks in, his pen in his hand.*) Bought, did you say? All that? Has my little squanderbird been overspending again?
NORA Oh, Torvald, surely we can let ourselves go a little this year! It's the first Christmas we don't have to scrape.
HELMER Well, you know, we can't afford to be extravagant.
NORA Oh yes, Torvald, we can be a little extravagant now. Can't we? Just a tiny bit? You've got a big salary now, and you're going to make lots and lots of money.
HELMER Next year, yes. But my new salary doesn't start till April.

NORA Pooh; we can borrow till then.

HELMER Nora! (*Goes over to her and takes her playfully by the ear.*) What a little spend-thrift you are! Suppose I were to borrow fifty pounds today, and you spent it all over Christmas, and then on New Year's Eve a tile fell off a roof on to my head—

NORA (*puts her hand over his mouth*) Oh, Torvald! Don't say such dreadful things!

HELMER Yes, but suppose something like that did happen? What then?

NORA If anything as frightful as that happened, it wouldn't make much difference whether I was in debt or not.

HELMER But what about the people I'd borrowed from?

NORA Them? Who cares about them? They're strangers.

HELMER Oh, Nora, Nora, how like a woman! No, but seriously, Nora, you know how I feel about this. No debts! Never borrow! A home that is founded on debts can never be a place of freedom and beauty. We two have stuck it out bravely up to now; and we shall continue to do so for the short time we still have to.

NORA (*goes over towards the stove*) Very well, Torvald. As you say.

HELMER (*follows her*) Now, now! My little songbird mustn't droop her wings. What's this? Is little squirrel sulking? (*Takes out his purse.*) Nora; guess what I've got here!

NORA (*turns quickly*) Money!

HELMER Look. (*Hands her some banknotes.*) I know how these small expenses crop up at Christmas.

NORA (*counts them*) One—two—three—four. Oh, thank you, Torvald, thank you! I should be able to manage with this.

HELMER You'll have to.

NORA Yes, yes, of course I will. But come over here, I want to show you everything I've bought. And so cheaply! Look, here are new clothes for Ivar—and a sword. And a horse and a trumpet for Bob. And a doll and a cradle for Emmy—they're nothing much, but she'll pull them apart in a few days. And some bits of material and hand-kerchiefs for the maids. Old Anne-Marie ought to have had something better, really.

HELMER And what's in that parcel?

NORA (*cries*) No, Torvald, you mustn't see that before this evening!

HELMER Very well. But now, tell me, you little spendthrift, what do you want for Christmas?

NORA Me? Oh, pooh, I don't want anything.

HELMER Oh, yes, you do. Now tell me, what, within reason, would you most like?

NORA No, I really don't know. Oh, yes—Torvald—!

HELMER Well?

NORA (*plays with his coat-buttons; not looking at him*) If you really want to give me something, you could—you could—

HELMER Come on, out with it.

NORA (*quickly*) You could give me money, Torvald. Only as much as you feel you can afford; then later I'll buy something with it.

HELMER But, Nora—

NORA Oh yes, Torvald dear, please! Please! Then I'll wrap up the notes in pretty gold paper and hang them on the Christmas tree. Wouldn't that be fun?

HELMER What's the name of that little bird that can never keep any money?

NORA Yes, yes, squanderbird; I know. But let's do as I say, Torvald; then I'll have time to think about what I need most. Isn't that the best way? Mm?

HELMER (*smiles*) To be sure it would be, if you could keep what I give you and really buy yourself something with it. But you'll spend it on all sorts of useless things for the house, and then I'll have to put my hand in my pocket again.

NORA Oh, but Torvald—

HELMER You can't deny it, Nora dear. (*Puts his arm round her waist.*) The squanderbird's a pretty little creature, but she gets through an awful lot of money. It's incredible what an expensive pet she is for a man to keep.

NORA For shame! How can you say such a thing? I save every penny I can.

HELMER (*laughs*) That's quite true. Every penny you can. But you can't.

NORA (*hums and smiles, quietly gleeful*) Hm. If you only knew how many expenses we larks and squirrels have, Torvald.

HELMER You're a funny little creature. Just like your father used to be. Always on the look-out for some way to get money, but as soon as you have any it just runs through your fingers, and you never know where it's gone. Well, I suppose I must take you as you are. It's in your blood. Yes, yes, yes, these things are hereditary, Nora.

NORA Oh, I wish I'd inherited more of Papa's qualities.

HELMER And I wouldn't wish my darling little songbird to be any different from what she is. By the way, that reminds me. You look awfully—how shall I put it?—awfully guilty today.

NORA Do I?

HELMER Yes, you do. Look me in the eyes.

NORA (*looks at him*) Well?

HELMER (*wags his finger*) Has my little sweet-tooth been indulging herself in town today, by any chance?

NORA No, how can you think such a thing?

HELMER Not a tiny little digression into a pastry shop?

NORA No, Torvald, I promise—

HELMER Not just a wee jam tart?

NORA Certainly not.

HELMER Not a little nibble at a macaroon?

NORA No, Torvald—I promise you, honestly—

HELMER There, there. I was only joking.

NORA (*goes over to the table, right*) You know I could never act against your wishes.

HELMER Of course not. And you've given me your word— (*Goes over to her.*) Well, my beloved Nora, you keep your little Christmas secrets to yourself. They'll be revealed this evening, I've no doubt, once the Christmas tree has been lit.

NORA Have you remembered to invite Dr. Rank?

HELMER No. But there's no need; he knows he'll be dining with us. Anyway, I'll ask him when he comes this morning. I've ordered some good wine. Oh, Nora, you can't imagine how I'm looking forward to this evening.

NORA So am I. And, Torvald, how the children will love it!

HELMER Yes, it's a wonderful thing to know that one's position is assured and that one has an ample income. Don't you agree? It's good to know that, isn't it?

NORA Yes, it's almost like a miracle.

HELMER Do you remember last Christmas? For three whole weeks you shut yourself away every evening to make flowers for the Christmas tree, and all those other things you were going to surprise us with. Ugh, it was the most boring time I've ever had in my life.

NORA I didn't find it boring.

HELMER (*smiles*) But it all came to nothing in the end, didn't it?

NORA Oh, are you going to bring that up again? How could I help the cat getting in and tearing everything to bits?

HELMER No, my poor little Nora, of course you couldn't. You simply wanted to make us happy, and that's all that matters. But it's good that those hard times are past.

NORA Yes, it's wonderful.

HELMER I don't have to sit by myself and be bored. And you don't have to tire your pretty eyes and your delicate little hands—

NORA (*claps her hands*) No, Torvald, that's true, isn't it—I don't have to any longer? Oh, it's really all just like a miracle. (*Takes his arm.*) Now, I'm going to tell you what I thought we might do, Torvald. As soon as Christmas is over— (*A bell rings in the hall.*) Oh, there's the doorbell. (*Tidies up one or two things in the room.*) Someone's coming. What a bore.

HELMER I'm not at home to any visitors. Remember!

MAID (*in the doorway*) A lady's called, madam. A stranger.

NORA Well, ask her to come in.

MAID And the doctor's here too, sir.

HELMER Has he gone to my room?

MAID Yes, sir.

HELMER *goes into his room. The* MAID *shows in* MRS. LINDE, *who is dressed in travelling clothes, and closes the door.*

MRS. LINDE (*shyly and a little hesitantly*) Good evening, Nora.

NORA (*uncertainly*) Good evening—

MRS. LINDE I don't suppose you recognize me.

NORA No, I'm afraid I— Yes, wait a minute—surely— (*Exclaims.*) Why, Christine! Is it really you?

MRS. LINDE Yes, it's me.

NORA Christine! And I didn't recognize you! But how could I—? (*More quietly.*) How you've changed, Christine!

MRS. LINDE Yes, I know. It's been nine years—nearly ten—

NORA Is it so long? Yes, it must be. Oh, these last eight years have been such a happy time for me! So you've come to town? All that way in winter! How brave of you!

MRS. LINDE I arrived by the steamer this morning.

NORA Yes, of course—to enjoy yourself over Christmas. Oh, how splendid! We'll have to celebrate! But take off your coat. You're not cold, are you? (*Helps her off with it.*) There! Now let's sit down here by the stove and be comfortable. No, you take the armchair. I'll sit here in the rocking-chair. (*Clasps* MRS. LINDE's *hands.*) Yes, now you look like your old self. It was just at first that—you've got a little paler, though, Christine. And perhaps a bit thinner.

MRS. LINDE And older, Nora. Much, much older.

NORA Yes, perhaps a little older. Just a tiny bit. Not much. (*Checks herself suddenly and says earnestly.*) Oh, but how thoughtless of me to sit here and chatter away like this! Dear, sweet Christine, can you forgive me?

MRS. LINDE What do you mean, Nora?

NORA (*quietly*) Poor Christine, you've become a widow.

MRS. LINDE Yes. Three years ago.

NORA I know, I know—I read it in the papers. Oh, Christine, I meant to write to you so often, honestly. But I always put it off, and something else always cropped up.

MRS. LINDE I understand, Nora dear.

NORA No, Christine, it was beastly of me. Oh, my poor darling, what you've gone through! And he didn't leave you anything?

MRS. LINDE No.

NORA No children, either?

MRS. LINDE No.

NORA Nothing at all, then?

MRS. LINDE Not even a feeling of loss or sorrow.

NORA (looks incredulously at her) But, Christine, how is that possible?

MRS. LINDE (smiles sadly and strokes NORA's hair) Oh, these things happen, Nora.

NORA All alone. How dreadful that must be for you. I've three lovely children. I'm afraid you can't see them now, because they're out with nanny. But you must tell me everything—

MRS. LINDE No, no, no. I want to hear about you.

NORA No, you start. I'm not going to be selfish today, I'm just going to think about you. Oh, but there's one thing I *must* tell you. Have you heard of the wonderful luck we've just had?

MRS. LINDE No. What?

NORA Would you believe it—my husband's just been made manager of the bank!

MRS. LINDE Your husband? Oh, how lucky—!

NORA Yes, isn't it? Being a lawyer is so uncertain, you know, especially if one isn't prepared to touch any case that isn't—well—quite nice. And of course Torvald's been very firm about that—and I'm absolutely with him. Oh, you can imagine how happy we are! He's joining the bank in the New Year, and he'll be getting a big salary, and lots of percentages too. From now on we'll be able to live quite differently—we'll be able to do whatever we want. Oh, Christine, it's such a relief! I feel so happy! Well, I mean, it's lovely to have heaps of money and not to have to worry about anything. Don't you think?

MRS. LINDE It must be lovely to have enough to cover one's needs, anyway.

NORA Not just our needs! We're going to have heaps and heaps of money!

MRS. LINDE (smiles) Nora, Nora, haven't you grown up yet? When we were at school you were a terrible little spendthrift.

NORA (laughs quietly) Yes, Torvald still says that. (Wags her finger.) But "Nora, Nora" isn't as silly as you think. Oh, we've been in no position for me to waste money. We've both had to work.

MRS. LINDE You too?

NORA Yes, little things—fancy work, crocheting, embroidery and so forth. (Casually.) And other things too. I suppose you know Torvald left the Ministry when we got married? There were no prospects of promotion in his department, and of course he needed more money. But the first year he overworked himself quite dreadfully. He had to take on all sorts of extra jobs, and worked day and night. But it was too much for him, and he became frightfully ill. The doctors said he'd have to go to a warmer climate.

MRS. LINDE Yes, you spent a whole year in Italy, didn't you?

NORA Yes. It wasn't easy for me to get away, you know. I'd just had Ivar. But of course we had to do it. Oh, it was a marvellous trip! And it saved Torvald's life. But it cost an awful lot of money, Christine.

MRS. LINDE I can imagine.

NORA Two hundred and fifty pounds. That's a lot of money, you know.

MRS. LINDE How lucky you had it.

NORA Well, actually, we got it from my father.

MRS. LINDE Oh, I see. Didn't he die just about that time?

NORA Yes, Christine, just about then. Wasn't it dreadful, I couldn't go and look after him. I was expecting little Ivar any day. And then I had my poor Torvald to care for— we really didn't think he'd live. Dear, kind Papa! I never saw him again, Christine. Oh, it's the saddest thing that's happened to me since I got married.

MRS. LINDE I know you were very fond of him. But you went to Italy—?

NORA Yes. Well, we had the money, you see, and the doctors said we mustn't delay. So we went the month after Papa died.

MRS. LINDE And your husband came back completely cured?

NORA Fit as a fiddle!

MRS. LINDE But—the doctor?

NORA How do you mean?

MRS. LINDE I thought the maid said that the gentleman who arrived with me was the doctor.

NORA Oh yes, that's Doctor Rank, but he doesn't come because anyone's ill. He's our best friend, and he looks us up at least once every day. No, Torvald hasn't had a moment's illness since we went away. And the children are fit and healthy and so am I. (*Jumps up and claps her hands.*) Oh God, oh God, Christine, isn't it a wonderful thing to be alive and happy! Oh, but how beastly of me! I'm only talking about myself. (*Sits on a footstool and rests her arms on* MRS. LINDE*'s knee.*) Oh, please don't be angry with me! Tell me, is it really true you didn't love your husband? Why did you marry him, then?

MRS. LINDE Well, my mother was still alive; and she was helpless and bedridden. And I had my two little brothers to take care of. I didn't feel I could say no.

NORA Yes, well, perhaps you're right. He was rich then, was he?

MRS. LINDE Quite comfortably off, I believe. But his business was unsound, you see, Nora. When he died it went bankrupt, and there was nothing left.

NORA What did you do?

MRS. LINDE Well, I had to try to make ends meet somehow, so I started a little shop, and a little school, and anything else I could turn my hand to. These last three years have been just one endless slog for me, without a moment's rest. But now it's over, Nora. My poor dear mother doesn't need me any more; she's passed away. And the boys don't need me either; they've got jobs now and can look after themselves.

NORA How relieved you must feel—

MRS. LINDE No, Nora. Just unspeakably empty. No one to live for any more. (*Gets up restlessly.*) That's why I couldn't bear to stay out there any longer, cut off from the world. I thought it'd be easier to find some work here that will exercise and occupy my mind. If only I could get a regular job—office work of some kind—

NORA Oh but, Christine, that's dreadfully exhausting; and you look practically finished already. It'd be much better for you if you could go away somewhere.

MRS. LINDE (*goes over to the window*) I have no Papa to pay for my holidays, Nora.

NORA (*gets up*) Oh, please don't be angry with me.

MRS. LINDE My dear Nora, it's I who should ask you not to be angry. That's the worst thing about this kind of situation—it makes one so bitter. One has no one to work for; and yet one has to be continually sponging for jobs. One has to live; and so one becomes completely egocentric. When you told me about this luck you've just had with Torvald's new job—can you imagine?—I was happy not so much on your account, as on my own.

NORA How do you mean? Oh, I understand. You mean Torvald might be able to do something for you?

MRS. LINDE Yes, I was thinking that.

NORA He will too, Christine. Just you leave it to me. I'll lead up to it so delicately, so delicately; I'll get him in the right mood. Oh, Christine, I do so want to help you.

MRS. LINDE It's sweet of you to bother so much about me, Nora. Especially since you know so little of the worries and hardships of life.

NORA I? You say I know little of—?

MRS. LINDE (smiles) Well, good heavens—those bits of fancy work of yours—well, really—! You're a child, Nora.

NORA (tosses her head and walks across the room) You shouldn't say that so patronisingly.

MRS. LINDE Oh?

NORA You're like the rest. You all think I'm incapable of getting down to anything serious—

MRS. LINDE My dear—

NORA You think I've never had any worries like the rest of you.

MRS. LINDE Nora dear, you've just told me about all your difficulties—

NORA Pooh—that! (Quietly.) I haven't told you about the big thing.

MRS. LINDE What big thing? What do you mean?

NORA You patronise me, Christine; but you shouldn't. You're proud that you've worked so long and so hard for your mother.

MRS. LINDE I don't patronise anyone, Nora. But you're right—I am both proud and happy that I was able to make my mother's last months on earth comparatively easy.

NORA And you're also proud of what you've done for your brothers.

MRS. LINDE I think I have a right to be.

NORA I think so too. But let me tell you something, Christine. I too have done something to be proud and happy about.

MRS. LINDE I don't doubt it. But—how do you mean?

NORA Speak quietly! Suppose Torvald should hear! He mustn't, at any price—no one must know, Christine—no one but you.

MRS. LINDE But what is this?

NORA Come over here. (Pulls her down on to the sofa beside her.) Yes, Christine—I too have done something to be happy and proud about. It was I who saved Torvald's life.

MRS. LINDE Saved his—? How did you save it?

NORA I told you about our trip to Italy. Torvald couldn't have lived if he hadn't managed to get down there—

MRS. LINDE Yes, well—your father provided the money—

NORA (smiles) So Torvald and everyone else thinks. But—

MRS. LINDE Yes?

NORA Papa didn't give us a penny. It was I who found the money.

MRS. LINDE You? All of it?

NORA Two hundred and fifty pounds. What do you say to that?

MRS. LINDE But Nora, how could you? Did you win a lottery or something?

NORA (scornfully) Lottery? (Sniffs.) What would there be to be proud of in that?

MRS. LINDE But where did you get it from, then?

NORA (hums and smiles secretively) Hm; tra-la-la-la!

MRS. LINDE You couldn't have borrowed it.

NORA Oh? Why not?

MRS. LINDE Well, a wife can't borrow money without her husband's consent.

NORA (tosses her head) Ah, but when a wife has a little business sense, and knows how to be clever—

MRS. LINDE But Nora, I simply don't understand—

NORA You don't have to. No one has said I borrowed the money. I could have got it in some other way. (*Throws herself back on the sofa.*) I could have got it from an admirer. When a girl's as pretty as I am—

MRS. LINDE Nora, you're crazy!

NORA You're dying of curiosity now, aren't you, Christine?

MRS. LINDE Nora dear, you haven't done anything foolish?

NORA (*sits up again*) Is it foolish to save one's husband's life?

MRS. LINDE I think it's foolish if without his knowledge you—

NORA But the whole point was that he mustn't know! Great heavens, don't you see? He hadn't to know how dangerously ill he was. I was the one they told that his life was in danger and that only going to a warm climate could save him. Do you suppose I didn't try to think of other ways of getting him down there? I told him how wonderful it would be for me to go abroad like other young wives; I cried and prayed; I asked him to remember my condition, and said he ought to be nice and tender to me; and then I suggested he might quite easily borrow the money. But then he got almost angry with me, Christine. He said I was frivolous, and that it was his duty as a husband not to pander to my moods and caprices—I think that's what he called them. Well, well, I thought, you've got to be saved somehow. And then I thought of a way—

MRS. LINDE But didn't your husband find out from your father that the money hadn't come from him?

NORA No, never. Papa died just then. I'd thought of letting him into the plot and asking him not to tell. But since he was so ill—! And as things turned out, it didn't become necessary.

MRS. LINDE And you've never told your husband about this?

NORA For heaven's sake, no! What an idea! He's frightfully strict about such matters. And besides—he's so proud of being a *man*—it'd be so painful and humiliating for him to know that he owed anything to me. It'd completely wreck our relationship. This life we have built together would no longer exist.

MRS. LINDE Will you never tell him?

NORA (*thoughtfully, half-smiling*) Yes—some time, perhaps. Years from now, when I'm no longer pretty. You mustn't laugh! I mean of course, when Torvald no longer loves me as he does now; when it no longer amuses him to see me dance and dress up and play the fool for him. Then it might be useful to have something up my sleeve. (*Breaks off.*) Stupid, stupid, stupid! That time will never come. Well, what do you think of my big secret, Christine? I'm not completely useless, am I? Mind you, all this has caused me a frightful lot of worry. It hasn't been easy for me to meet my obligations punctually. In case you don't know, in the world of business there are things called quarterly instalments and interest, and they're a terrible problem to cope with. So I've had to scrape a little here and save a little there as best I can. I haven't been able to save much on the housekeeping money, because Torvald likes to live well; and I couldn't let the children go short of clothes—I couldn't take anything out of what he gives me for them. The poor little angels!

MRS. LINDE So you've had to stint yourself, my poor Nora?

NORA Of course. Well, after all, it was my problem. Whenever Torvald gave me money to buy myself new clothes, I never used more than half of it; and I always bought what was cheapest and plainest. Thank heaven anything suits me, so that Torvald's never noticed. But it made me a bit sad sometimes, because it's lovely to wear pretty clothes. Don't you think?

MRS. LINDE Indeed it is.

NORA And then I've found one or two other sources of income. Last winter I managed to get a lot of copying to do. So I shut myself away and wrote every evening, late into the night. Oh, I often got so tired, so tired. But it was great fun, though, sitting there working and earning money. It was almost like being a man.

MRS. LINDE But how much have you managed to pay off like this?

NORA Well, I can't say exactly. It's awfully difficult to keep an exact check on these kind of transactions. I only know I've paid everything I've managed to scrape together. Sometimes I really didn't know where to turn. (*Smiles.*) Then I'd sit here and imagine some rich old gentleman had fallen in love with me—

MRS. LINDE What! What gentleman?

NORA Silly! And that now he'd died and when they opened his will it said in big letters: "Everything I possess is to be paid forthwith to my beloved Mrs. Nora Helmer in cash."

MRS. LINDE But, Nora dear, who was this gentleman?

NORA Great heavens, don't you understand? There wasn't any old gentleman; he was just something I used to dream up as I sat here evening after evening wondering how on earth I could raise some money. But what does it matter? The old bore can stay imaginary as far as I'm concerned, because now I don't have to worry any longer! (*Jumps up.*) Oh, Christine, isn't it wonderful? I don't have to worry any more! No more troubles! I can play all day with the children, I can fill the house with pretty things, just the way Torvald likes. And, Christine, it'll soon be spring, and the air'll be fresh and the skies blue,—and then perhaps we'll be able to take a little trip somewhere. I shall be able to see the sea again. Oh, yes, yes, it's a wonderful thing to be alive and happy!

The bell rings in the hall.

MRS. LINDE (*gets up*) You've a visitor. Perhaps I'd better go.

NORA No, stay. It won't be for me. It's someone for Torvald—

MAID (*in the doorway*) Excuse me, madam, a gentleman's called who says he wants to speak to the master. But I didn't know—seeing as the doctor's with him—

NORA Who is this gentleman?

KROGSTAD (*in the doorway*) It's me, Mrs. Helmer.

MRS. LINDE *starts, composes herself and turns away to the window.*

NORA (*takes a step towards him and whispers tensely*) You? What is it? What do you want to talk to my husband about?

KROGSTAD Business—you might call it. I hold a minor post in the bank, and I hear your husband is to become our new chief—

NORA Oh—then it isn't—?

KROGSTAD Pure business, Mrs. Helmer. Nothing more.

NORA Well, you'll find him in his study.

Nods indifferently as she closes the hall door behind him. Then she walks across the room and sees to the stove.

MRS. LINDE Nora, who was that man?

NORA A lawyer called Krogstad.

MRS. LINDE It was him, then.

NORA Do you know that man?

MRS. LINDE I used to know him—some years ago. He was a solicitor's clerk in our town, for a while.

NORA Yes, of course, so he was.

MRS. LINDE How he's changed!

NORA He was very unhappily married, I believe.

MRS. LINDE Is he a widower now?

NORA Yes, with a lot of children. Ah, now it's alight.

She closes the door of the stove and moves the rocking-chair a little to one side.

MRS. LINDE He does—various things now, I hear?

NORA Does he? It's quite possible—I really don't know. But don't let's talk about business. It's so boring.

DR. RANK *enters from* HELMER'*s study.*

RANK (*still in the doorway*) No, no, my dear chap, don't see me out. I'll go and have a word with your wife. (*Closes the door and notices* MRS. LINDE.) Oh, I beg your pardon. I seem to be *de trop* here too.

NORA Not in the least. (*Introduces them.*) Dr. Rank. Mrs. Linde.

RANK Ah! A name I have often heard in this house. I believe I passed you on the stairs as I came up.

MRS. LINDE Yes. Stairs tire me; I have to take them slowly.

RANK Oh, have you hurt yourself?

MRS. LINDE No, I'm just a little run down.

RANK Ah, is that all? Then I take it you've come to town to cure yourself by a round of parties?

MRS. LINDE I have come here to find work.

RANK Is that an approved remedy for being run down?

MRS. LINDE One has to live, Doctor.

RANK Yes, people do seem to regard it as a necessity.

NORA Oh, really, Dr. Rank. I bet you want to stay alive.

RANK You bet I do. However miserable I sometimes feel, I still want to go on being tortured for as long as possible. It's the same with all my patients; and with people who are morally sick, too. There's a moral cripple in with Helmer at this very moment—

MRS. LINDE (*softly*) Oh!

NORA Whom do you mean?

RANK Oh, a lawyer fellow called Krogstad—you wouldn't know him. He's crippled all right; morally twisted. But even he started off by announcing, as though it were a matter of enormous importance, that he had to live.

NORA Oh? What did he want to talk to Torvald about?

RANK I haven't the faintest idea. All I heard was something about the bank.

NORA I didn't know that Krog—that this man Krogstad had any connection with the bank.

RANK Yes, he's got some kind of job down there. (*To* MRS. LINDE.) I wonder if in your part of the world you too have a species of human being that spends its time fussing around trying to smell out moral corruption? And when they find a case they give him some nice, comfortable position so that they can keep a good watch on him. The healthy ones just have to lump it.

MRS. LINDE But surely it's the sick who need care most?

RANK (*shrugs his shoulders*) Well, there we have it. It's that attitude that's turning human society into a hospital.

NORA, *lost in her own thoughts, laughs half to herself and claps her hands.*

RANK Why are you laughing? Do you really know what society is?

NORA What do I care about society? I think it's a bore. I was laughing at something else—something frightfully funny. Tell me, Dr. Rank—will everyone who works at the bank come under Torvald now?

RANK Do you find that particularly funny?

NORA (*smiles and hums*) Never you mind! Never you mind! (*Walks around the room.*) Yes, I find it very amusing to think that we—I mean, Torvald—has obtained so much influence over so many people. (*Takes the paper bag from her pocket.*) Dr. Rank, would you like a small macaroon?

RANK Macaroons! I say! I thought they were forbidden here.

NORA Yes, well, these are some Christine gave me.

MRS. LINDE What? I—?

NORA All right, all right, don't get frightened. You weren't to know Torvald had forbidden them. He's afraid they'll ruin my teeth. But, dash it—for once—! Don't you agree, Dr. Rank? Here! (*Pops a macaroon into his mouth.*) You too, Christine. And I'll have one too. Just a little one. Two at the most. (*Begins to walk round again.*) Yes, now I feel really, really happy. Now there's just one thing in the world I'd really love to do.

RANK Oh? And what is that?

NORA Just something I'd love to say to Torvald.

RANK Well, why don't you say it?

NORA No, I daren't. It's too dreadful.

MRS. LINDE Dreadful?

RANK Well, then, you'd better not. But you can say it to us. What is it you'd so love to say to Torvald?

NORA I've the most extraordinary longing to say: "Bloody hell!"

RANK Are you mad?

MRS. LINDE My dear Nora—!

RANK Say it. Here he is

NORA (*hiding the bag of macaroons*). Ssh! Ssh!

HELMER, *with his overcoat on his arm and his hat in his hand, enters from his study.*

NORA (*goes to meet him*) Well, Torvald dear, did you get rid of him?

HELMER Yes, he's just gone.

NORA May I introduce you—? This is Christine. She's just arrived in town.

HELMER Christine—? Forgive me, but I don't think—

NORA Mrs. Linde, Torvald dear. Christine Linde.

HELMER Ah. A childhood friend of my wife's, I presume?

MRS. LINDE Yes, we knew each other in earlier days.

NORA And imagine, now she's travelled all this way to talk to you.

HELMER Oh?

MRS. LINDE Well, I didn't really—

NORA You see, Christine's frightfully good at office work, and she's mad to come under some really clever man who can teach her even more than she knows already—

HELMER Very sensible, madam.

NORA So when she heard you'd become head of the bank—it was in her local paper—she came here as quickly as she could and—Torvald, you will, won't you? Do a little something to help Christine? For my sake?

HELMER Well, that shouldn't be impossible. You are a widow, I take it, Mrs. Linde?

MRS. LINDE Yes.

HELMER And you have experience of office work?

MRS. LINDE Yes, quite a bit.

HELMER Well then, it's quite likely I may be able to find some job for you—

NORA (*claps her hands*) You see, you see!

HELMER You've come at a lucky moment, Mrs. Linde.

MRS. LINDE Oh, how can I ever thank you—?

HELMER There's absolutely no need. (*Puts on his overcoat.*) But now I'm afraid I must ask you to excuse me—

RANK Wait. I'll come with you.

He gets his fur coat from the hall and warms it at the stove.

NORA Don't be long, Torvald dear.

HELMER I'll only be an hour.

NORA Are you going too, Christine?

MRS. LINDE (*puts on her outdoor clothes*) Yes, I must start to look round for a room.

HELMER Then perhaps we can walk part of the way together.

NORA (*helps her*) It's such a nuisance we're so cramped here—I'm afraid we can't offer to—

MRS. LINDE Oh, I wouldn't dream of it. Goodbye, Nora dear, and thanks for everything.

NORA *Au revoir.* You'll be coming back this evening, of course. And you too, Dr. Rank. What? If you're well enough? Of course you'll be well enough. Wrap up warmly, though.

They go out, talking, into the hall. CHILDREN's *voices are heard from the stairs.*

NORA Here they are! Here they are!

She runs out and opens the door. ANNE-MARIE, *the* NURSE, *enters with the* CHILDREN.

NORA Come in, come in! (*Stoops down and kisses them.*) Oh, my sweet darlings—! Look at them, Christine! Aren't they beautiful?

RANK Don't stand here chattering in this draught!

HELMER Come, Mrs. Linde. This is for mothers only.

DR. RANK, HELMER *and* MRS. LINDE *go down the stairs. The* NURSE *brings the* CHILDREN *into the room.* NORA *follows, and closes the door to the hall.*

NORA Now well you look! What red cheeks you've got! Like apples and roses! (*The* CHILDREN *answer her inaudibly as she talks to them.*) Have you had fun? That's splendid. You gave Emmy and Bob a ride on the sledge? What, both together? I say! What a clever boy you are, Ivar! Oh, let me hold her for a moment, Anne-Marie! My sweet little baby doll! (*Takes the smallest child from the* NURSE *and dances with her.*) Yes, yes, Mummy will dance with Bob too. What? Have you been throwing snowballs? Oh, I wish I'd been there! No, don't—I'll undress them myself, Anne-Marie. No, please let me; it's such fun. Go inside and warm yourself; you look frozen.

There's some hot coffee on the stove. (*The* NURSE *goes into the room on the left.* NORA *takes off the* CHILDREN's *outdoor clothes and throws them anywhere while they all chatter simultaneously.*) What? A big dog ran after you? But he didn't bite you? No, dogs don't bite lovely little baby dolls. Leave those parcels alone, Ivar. What's in them? Ah, wouldn't you like to know! No, no; it's nothing nice. Come on, let's play a game. What shall we play? Hide and seek. Yes, let's play hide and seek. Bob shall hide first. You want me to? All right, let me hide first.

NORA *and the* CHILDREN *play around the room, and in the adjacent room to the left, laughing and shouting. At length* NORA *hides under the table. The* CHILDREN *rush in, look, but cannot find her. Then they hear her half-stifled laughter, run to the table, lift up the cloth and see her. Great excitement. She crawls out as though to frighten them. Further excitement. Meanwhile, there has been a knock on the door leading from the hall, but no one has noticed it. Now the door is half-opened and* KROGSTAD *enters. He waits for a moment; the game continues.*

KROGSTAD Excuse me, Mrs. Helmer—
NORA (*turns with a stifled cry and half jumps up*) Oh! What do you want?
KROGSTAD I beg your pardon; the front door was ajar. Someone must have forgotten to close it.
NORA (*gets up*) My husband is not at home, Mr. Krogstad.
KROGSTAD I know.
NORA Well, what do want here, then?
KROGSTAD A word with you.
NORA With—? (*To the* CHILDREN, *quietly.*) Go inside to Anne-Marie. What? No, the strange gentleman won't do anything to hurt Mummy. When he's gone we'll start playing again.

She takes the CHILDREN *into the room on the left and closes the door behind them.*

NORA (*uneasy, tense*) You want to speak to me?
KROGSTAD Yes.
NORA Today? But it's not the first of the month yet.
KROGSTAD No, it is Christmas Eve. Whether or not you have a merry Christmas depends on you.
NORA What do you want? I can't give you anything today—
KROGSTAD We won't talk about that for the present. There's something else. You have a moment to spare?
NORA Oh, yes. Yes, I suppose so; though—
KROGSTAD Good. I was sitting in the café down below and I saw your husband cross the street—
NORA Yes.
KROGSTAD With a lady.
NORA Well?
KROGSTAD Might I be so bold as to ask: was not that lady a Mrs. Linde?
NORA Yes.
KROGSTAD Recently arrived in town?
NORA Yes, today.
KROGSTAD She is a good friend of yours, is she not?
NORA Yes, she is. But I don't see—
KROGSTAD I used to know her too once.

NORA I know.

KROGSTAD Oh? You've discovered that. Yes, I thought you would. Well then, may I ask you a straight question: is Mrs. Linde to be employed at the bank?

NORA How dare you presume to cross-examine me, Mr. Krogstad? You, one of my husband's employees? But since you ask, you shall have an answer. Yes, Mrs. Linde is to be employed by the bank. And I arranged it, Mr. Krogstad. Now you know.

KROGSTAD I guessed right, then.

NORA (*walks up and down the room*) Oh, one has a little influence, you know. Just because one's a woman it doesn't necessarily mean that— When one is in a humble position, Mr. Krogstad, one should think twice before offending someone who—hm—

KROGSTAD —who has influence?

NORA Precisely.

KROGSTAD (*changes his tone*) Mrs. Helmer, will you have the kindness to use your influence on my behalf?

NORA What? What do you mean?

KROGSTAD Will you be so good as to see that I keep my humble position at the bank?

NORA What do you mean? Who is thinking of removing you from your position?

KROGSTAD Oh, you don't need to play innocent with me. I realize it can't be very pleasant for your friend to risk bumping into me; and now I also realize whom I have to thank for being hounded out like this.

NORA But I assure you—

KROGSTAD Look, let's not beat about the bush. There's still time, and I'd advise you to use your influence to stop it.

NORA But, Mr. Krogstad, I have no influence!

KROGSTAD Oh? I thought you just said—

NORA But I didn't mean it like that! I? How on earth could you imagine that I would have any influence over my husband?

KROGSTAD Oh, I've known your husband since we were students together. I imagine he has his weaknesses like other married men.

NORA If you speak impertinently of my husband, I shall show you the door.

KROGSTAD You're a bold woman, Mrs. Helmer.

NORA I'm not afraid of you any longer. Once the New Year is in, I'll soon be rid of you.

KROGSTAD (*more controlled*) Now listen to me, Mrs. Helmer. If I'm forced to, I shall fight for my little job at the bank as I would fight for my life.

NORA So it sounds.

KROGSTAD It isn't just the money; that's the last thing I care about. There's something else—well, you might as well know. It's like this, you see. You know of course, as everyone else does, that some years ago I committed an indiscretion.

NORA I think I did hear something—

KROGSTAD It never came into court; but from that day, every opening was barred to me. So I turned my hand to the kind of business you know about. I had to do something; and I don't think I was one of the worst. But now I want to give up all that. My sons are growing up; for their sake, I must try to regain what respectability I can. This job in the bank was the first step on the ladder. And now your husband wants to kick me off that ladder back into the dirt.

NORA But my dear Mr. Krogstad, it simply isn't in my power to help you.

KROGSTAD You say that because you don't want to help me. But I have the means to make you.

NORA You don't mean you'd tell my husband that I owe you money?

KROGSTAD And if I did?

NORA That'd be a filthy trick! (*Almost in tears.*) This secret that is my pride and my joy—that he should hear about it in such a filthy, beastly way—hear about it from you! It'd involve me in the most dreadful unpleasantness—

KROGSTAD Only—unpleasantness?

NORA (*vehemently*) All right, do it! You'll be the one who'll suffer. It'll show my husband the kind of man you are, and then you'll never keep your job.

KROGSTAD I asked you whether it was merely domestic unpleasantness you were afraid of.

NORA If my husband hears about it, he will of course immediately pay you whatever is owing. And then we shall have nothing more to do with you.

KROGSTAD (*takes a step closer*) Listen, Mrs. Helmer. Either you've a bad memory or else you know very little about financial transactions. I had better enlighten you.

NORA What do you mean?

KROGSTAD When your husband was ill, you came to me to borrow two hundred and fifty pounds.

NORA I didn't know anyone else.

KROGSTAD I promised to find that sum for you—

NORA And you did find it.

KROGSTAD I promised to find that sum for you on certain conditions. You were so worried about your husband's illness and so keen to get the money to take him abroad that I don't think you bothered much about the details. So it won't be out of place if I refresh your memory. Well—I promised to get you the money in exchange for an I.O.U., which I drew up.

NORA Yes, and which I signed.

KROGSTAD Exactly. But then I added a few lines naming your father as security for the debt. This paragraph was to be signed by your father.

NORA Was to be? He did sign it.

KROGSTAD I left the date blank for your father to fill in when he signed this paper. You remember, Mrs. Helmer?

NORA Yes, I think so—

KROGSTAD Then I gave you back this I.O.U. for you to post to your father. Is that not correct?

NORA Yes.

KROGSTAD And of course you posted it at once; for within five or six days you brought it along to me with your father's signature on it. Whereupon I handed you the money.

NORA Yes, well. Haven't I repaid the instalments as agreed?

KROGSTAD Mm—yes, more or less. But to return to what we were speaking about—that was a difficult time for you just then, wasn't it, Mrs. Helmer?

NORA Yes, it was.

KROGSTAD And your father was very ill, if I am not mistaken.

NORA He was dying.

KROGSTAD He did in fact die shortly afterwards?

NORA Yes.

KROGSTAD Tell me, Mrs. Helmer, do you by any chance remember the date of your father's death? The day of the month, I mean.

NORA Papa died on the twenty-ninth of September.

KROGSTAD Quite correct; I took the trouble to confirm it. And that leaves me with a curious little problem— (*Takes out a paper.*) —which I simply cannot solve.

NORA Problem? I don't see—

KROGSTAD The problem, Mrs. Helmer, is that your father signed this paper three days after his death.

NORA What? I don't understand—

KROGSTAD Your father died on the twenty-ninth of September. But look at this. Here your father has dated his signature the second of October. Isn't that a curious little problem, Mrs. Helmer? (NORA *is silent.*) Can you suggest any explanation? (*She remains silent.*) And there's another curious thing. The words "second of October" and the year are written in a hand which is not your father's, but which I seem to know. Well, there's a simple explanation to that. Your father could have forgotten to write in the date when he signed, and someone else could have added it before the news came of his death. There's nothing criminal about that. It's the signature itself I'm wondering about. It *is* genuine, I suppose, Mrs. Helmer? It was your father who wrote his name here?

NORA (*after a short silence, throws back her head and looks defiantly at him*) No, it was not. It was I who wrote Papa's name there.

KROGSTAD Look, Mrs. Helmer, do you realize this is a dangerous admission?

NORA Why? You'll get your money.

KROGSTAD May I ask you a question? Why didn't you send this paper to your father?

NORA I couldn't. Papa was very ill. If I'd asked him to sign this, I'd have had to tell him what the money was for. But I couldn't have told him in his condition that my husband's life was in danger. I couldn't have done that!

KROGSTAD Then you would have been wiser to have given up your idea of a holiday.

NORA But I couldn't! It was to save my husband's life. I couldn't put it off.

KROGSTAD But didn't it occur to you that you were being dishonest towards me?

NORA I couldn't bother about that. I didn't care about you. I hated you because of all the beastly difficulties you'd put in my way when you knew how dangerously ill my husband was.

KROGSTAD Mrs. Helmer, you evidently don't appreciate exactly what you have done. But I can assure you that it is no bigger nor worse a crime than the one I once committed, and thereby ruined my whole social position.

NORA You? Do you expect me to believe that you would have taken a risk like that to save your wife's life?

KROGSTAD The law does not concern itself with motives.

NORA Then the law must be very stupid.

KROGSTAD Stupid or not, if I show this paper to the police, you will be judged according to it.

NORA I don't believe that. Hasn't a daughter the right to shield her father from worry and anxiety when he's old and dying? Hasn't a wife the right to save her husband's life? I don't know much about the law, but there must be something somewhere that says that such things are allowed. You ought to know about that, you're meant to be a lawyer, aren't you? You can't be a very good lawyer, Mr. Krogstad.

KROGSTAD Possibly not. But business, the kind of business we two have been transacting—I think you'll admit I understand something about that? Good. Do as you please. But I tell you this. If I get thrown into the gutter for a second time, I shall take you with me.

He bows and goes out through the hall.

NORA (*stands for a moment in thought, then tosses her head*) What nonsense! He's trying to frighten me! I'm not that stupid. (*Busies herself gathering together the* CHILDREN's *clothes; then she suddenly stops.*) But—? No, it's impossible. I did it for love, didn't I?

CHILDREN (*in the doorway, left*) Mummy, the strange gentleman's gone out into the street.

NORA Yes, yes, I know. But don't talk to anyone about the strange gentleman. You hear? Not even to Daddy.

CHILDREN No, Mummy. Will you play with us again now?

NORA No, no. Not now.

CHILDREN Oh but, Mummy, you promised!

NORA I know, but I can't just now. Go back to the nursery. I've a lot to do. Go away, my darlings, go away. (*She pushes them gently into the other room, and closes the door behind them. She sits on the sofa, takes up her embroidery, stitches for a few moments, but soon stops.*) No! (*Throws the embroidery aside, gets up, goes to the door leading to the hall and calls.*) Helen! Bring in the Christmas tree! (*She goes to the table on the left and opens the drawer in it; then pauses again.*) No, but it's utterly impossible!

MAID (*enters with the tree*) Where shall I put it, madam?

NORA There, in the middle of the room.

MAID Will you be wanting anything else?

NORA No, thank you. I have everything I need.

The MAID *puts down the tree and goes out.*

NORA (*busy decorating the tree*) Now—candles here—and flowers here. That loathsome man! Nonsense, nonsense, there's nothing to be frightened about. The Christmas tree must be beautiful. I'll do everything that you like, Torvald. I'll sing for you, dance for you—

HELMER, *with a bundle of papers under his arm, enters.*

NORA Oh—are you back already?

HELMER Yes. Has anyone been here?

NORA Here? No.

HELMER That's strange. I saw Krogstad come out of the front door.

NORA Did you? Oh yes, that's quite right—Krogstad was here for a few minutes.

HELMER Nora, I can tell from your face, he's been here and asked you to put in a good word for him.

NORA Yes.

HELMER And you were to pretend you were doing it of your own accord? You weren't going to tell me he'd been here? He asked you to do that too, didn't he?

NORA Yes, Torvald. But—

HELMER Nora, Nora! And you were ready to enter into such a conspiracy? Talking to a man like that, and making him promises—and then, on top of it all, to tell me an untruth!

NORA An untruth?

HELMER Didn't you say no one had been here? (*Wags his finger.*) My little songbird must never do that again. A songbird must have a clean beak to sing with; otherwise she'll start twittering out of tune. (*Puts his arm round her waist*). Isn't that the way we want things? Yes, of course it is. (*Lets go of her.*) So let's hear no more about that. (*Sits down in front of the stove.*) Ah, how cosy and peaceful it is here. (*Glances for a few moments at his papers.*)

NORA (*busy with the tree; after a short silence*) Torvald.

HELMER Yes.

NORA I'm terribly looking forward to that fancy dress ball at the Stenborgs on Boxing Day.

HELMER And I'm terribly curious to see what you're going to surprise me with.

NORA Oh, it's so maddening.

HELMER What is?

NORA I can't think of anything to wear. It all seems so stupid and meaningless.

HELMER So my little Nora's come to that conclusion, has she?

NORA (*behind his chair, resting her arms on its back*) Are you very busy, Torvald?

HELMER Oh—

NORA What are those papers?

HELMER Just something to do with the bank.

NORA Already?

HELMER I persuaded the trustees to give me authority to make certain immediate changes in the staff and organization. I want to have everything straight by the New Year.

NORA Then that's why this poor man Krogstad—

HELMER Hm.

NORA (*still leaning over his chair, slowly strokes the back of his head*) If you hadn't been so busy, I was going to ask you an enormous favour, Torvald.

HELMER Well, tell me. What was it to be?

NORA You know I trust your taste more than anyone's. I'm so anxious to look really beautiful at the fancy dress ball. Torvald, couldn't you help me to decide what I shall go as, and what kind of costume I ought to wear?

HELMER Aha! So little Miss Independent's in trouble and needs a man to rescue her, does she?

NORA Yes, Torvald. I can't get anywhere without your help.

HELMER Well, well, I'll give the matter thought. We'll find something.

NORA Oh, how kind of you! (*Goes back to the tree. Pause.*) How pretty these red flowers look! But, tell me, is it so dreadful, this thing that Krogstad's done?

HELMER He forged someone else's name. Have you any idea what that means?

NORA Mightn't he have been forced to do it by some emergency?

HELMER He probably just didn't think—that's what usually happens. I'm not so heartless as to condemn a man for an isolated action.

NORA No, Torvald, of course not!

HELMER Men often succeed in re-establishing themselves if they admit their crime and take their punishment.

NORA Punishment?

HELMER But Krogstad didn't do that. He chose to try and trick his way out of it; and that's what has morally destroyed him.

NORA You think that would—?

HELMER Just think how a man with that load on his conscience must always be lying and cheating and dissembling; how he must wear a mask even in the presence of those who are dearest to him, even his own wife and children! Yes, the children. That's the worst danger, Nora.

NORA Why?

HELMER Because an atmosphere of lies contaminates and poisons every corner of the home. Every breath that the children draw in such a house contains the germs of evil.

NORA (*comes closer behind him*) Do you really believe that?

HELMER Oh, my dear, I've come across it so often in my work at the bar. Nearly all young criminals are the children of mothers who are constitutional liars.

NORA Why do you say mothers?

HELMER It's usually the mother; though of course the father can have the same influence. Every lawyer knows that only too well. And yet this fellow Krogstad has been sitting at home all these years poisoning his children with his lies and pretences. That's why I say that, morally speaking, he is dead. (*Stretches out his hands towards her.*) So my pretty little Nora must promise me not to plead his case. Your hand on it. Come, come, what's this? Give me your hand. There. That's settled, now. I assure you it'd be quite impossible for me to work in the same building as him. I literally feel physically ill in the presence of a man like that.

NORA (*draws her hand from his and goes over to the other side of the Christmas tree*) How hot it is in here! And I've so much to do.

HELMER (*gets up and gathers his papers*) Yes, and I must try to get some of this read before dinner. I'll think about your costume too. And I may even have something up my sleeve to hang in gold paper on the Christmas tree. (*Lays his hand on her head.*) My precious little songbird!

He goes into his study and closes the door.

NORA (*softly, after a pause*) It's nonsense. It must be. It's impossible. It *must* be impossible!

NURSE (*in the doorway, left*) The children are asking if they can come in to Mummy.

NORA No, no, no; don't let them in! You stay with them, Anne-Marie.

NURSE Very good, madam. (*Closes the door.*)

NORA (*pale with fear*) Corrupt my little children—! Poison my home! (*Short pause. She throws back her head.*) It isn't true! It *couldn't* be true!

ACT II

The same room. In the corner by the piano the Christmas tree stands, stripped and dishevelled, its candles burned to their sockets. NORA'S *outdoor clothes lie on the sofa. She is alone in the room, walking restlessly to and fro. At length she stops by the sofa and picks up her coat.*

NORA (*drops the coat again*) There's someone coming! (*Goes to the door and listens.*) No, it's no one. Of course—no one'll come today, it's Christmas Day. Nor tomorrow. But perhaps—! (*Opens the door and looks out.*) No. Nothing in the letter-box. Quite empty. (*Walks across the room.*) Silly, silly. Of course he won't do anything. It couldn't happen. It isn't possible. Why, I've three small children.

The NURSE, *carrying a large cardboard box, enters from the room on the left.*

NURSE I found those fancy dress clothes at last, madam.

NORA Thank you. Put them on the table.

NURSE (*does so*) They're all rumpled up.

NORA Oh, I wish I could tear them into a million pieces!

NURSE Why, madam! They'll be all right. Just a little patience.

NORA Yes, of course. I'll go and get Mrs. Linde to help me.

NURSE What, out again? In this dreadful weather? You'll catch a chill, madam.

NORA Well, that wouldn't be the worst. How are the children?

NURSE Playing with their Christmas presents, poor little dears. But—

NORA Are they still asking to see me?

NURSE They're so used to having their Mummy with them.

NORA Yes, but, Anne-Marie, from now on I shan't be able to spend so much time with them.

NURSE Well, children get used to anything in time.

NORA Do you think so? Do you think they'd forget their mother if she went away from them—for ever?

NURSE Mercy's sake, madam! For ever!

NORA Tell me, Anne-Marie—I've so often wondered. How could you bear to give your child away—to strangers?

NURSE But I had to when I came to nurse my little Miss Nora.

NORA Do you mean you wanted to?

NURSE When I had the chance of such a good job? A poor girl what's got into trouble can't afford to pick and choose. That good-for-nothing didn't lift a finger.

NORA But your daughter must have completely forgotten you.

NURSE Oh no, indeed she hasn't. She's written to me twice, once when she got confirmed and then again when she got married.

NORA (hugs her) Dear old Anne-Marie, you were a good mother to me.

NURSE Poor little Miss Nora, you never had any mother but me.

NORA And if my little ones had no one else, I know you would—no, silly, silly, silly! (Opens the cardboard box.) Go back to them, Anne-Marie. Now I must— Tomorrow you'll see how pretty I shall look.

NURSE Why, there'll be no one at the ball as beautiful as my Miss Nora.

She goes into the room, left.

NORA (begins to unpack the clothes from the box, but soon throws them down again) Oh, if only I dared to go out! If I could be sure no one would come, and nothing would happen while I was away! Stupid, stupid! No one will come. I just mustn't think about it. Brush this muff. Pretty gloves, pretty gloves! Don't think about it, don't think about it! One, two, three, four, five, six— (Cries.) Ah—they're coming—!

She begins to run towards the door, but stops uncertainly. MRS. LINDE enters from the hall, where she has been taking off her outdoor clothes.

NORA Oh, it's you, Christine. There's no one else out there, is there? Oh, I'm so glad you've come.

MRS. LINDE I hear you were at my room asking for me.

NORA Yes, I just happened to be passing. I want to ask you to help me with something. Let's sit down here on the sofa. Look at this. There's going to be a fancy dress ball tomorrow night upstairs at Consul Stenborg's, and Torvald wants me to go as a Neapolitan fisher-girl and dance the tarantella. I learned it on Capri.

MRS. LINDE I say, are you going to give a performance?

NORA Yes, Torvald says I should. Look, here's the dress. Torvald had it made for me in Italy; but now it's all so torn, I don't know—

MRS. LINDE Oh, we'll soon put that right; the stitching's just come away. Needle and thread? Ah, here we are.

NORA You're being awfully sweet.

MRS. LINDE (*sews*) So you're going to dress up tomorrow, Nora? I must pop over for a moment to see how you look. Oh, but I've completely forgotten to thank you for that nice evening yesterday.

NORA (*gets up and walks across the room*) Oh, I didn't think it was as nice as usual. You ought to have come to town a little earlier, Christine. . . . Yes, Torvald understands how to make a home look attractive.

MRS. LINDE I'm sure you do, too. You're not your father's daughter for nothing. But, tell me. Is Dr. Rank always in such low spirits as he was yesterday?

NORA No, last night it was very noticeable. But he's got a terrible disease; he's got spinal tuberculosis, poor man. His father was a frightful creature who kept mistresses and so on. As a result Dr. Rank has been sickly ever since he was a child—you understand—

MRS. LINDE (*puts down her sewing*) But, my dear Nora, how on earth did you get to know about such things?

NORA (*walks about the room*) Oh, don't be silly, Christine—when one has three children, one comes into contact with women who—well, who know about medical matters, and they tell one a thing or two.

MRS. LINDE (*sews again; a short silence*) Does Dr. Rank visit you every day?

NORA Yes, every day. He's Torvald's oldest friend, and a good friend to me too. Dr. Rank's almost one of the family.

MRS. LINDE But, tell me—is he quite sincere? I mean, doesn't he rather say the sort of thing he thinks people want to hear?

NORA No, quite the contrary. What gave you that idea?

MRS. LINDE When you introduced me to him yesterday, he said he'd often heard my name mentioned here. But later I noticed your husband had no idea who I was. So how could Dr. Rank—?

NORA Yes, that's quite right, Christine. You see, Torvald's so hopelessly in love with me that he wants to have me all to himself—those were his very words. When we were first married, he got quite jealous if I as much as mentioned any of my old friends back home. So naturally, I stopped talking about them. But I often chat with Dr. Rank about that kind of thing. He enjoys it, you see.

MRS. LINDE Now listen, Nora. In many ways you're still a child; I'm a bit older than you and have a little more experience of the world. There's something I want to say to you. You ought to give up this business with Dr. Rank.

NORA What business?

MRS. LINDE Well, everything. Last night you were speaking about this rich admirer of yours who was going to give you money—

NORA Yes, and who doesn't exist—unfortunately. But what's that got to do with—?

MRS. LINDE Is Dr. Rank rich?

NORA Yes.

MRS. LINDE And he has no dependants?

NORA No, no one. But—

MRS. LINDE And he comes here to see you every day?

NORA Yes, I've told you.

MRS. LINDE But how dare a man of his education be so forward?

NORA What on earth are you talking about?

MRS. LINDE Oh, stop pretending, Nora. Do you think I haven't guessed who it was who lent you that two hundred pounds?

NORA Are you out of your mind? How could you imagine such a thing? A friend, someone who comes here every day! Why, that'd be an impossible situation!

MRS. LINDE Then it really wasn't him?

NORA No, of course not. I've never for a moment dreamed of—anyway, he hadn't any money to lend then. He didn't come into that till later.

MRS. LINDE Well, I think that was a lucky thing for you, Nora dear.

NORA No, I could never have dreamed of asking Dr. Rank—Though I'm sure that if I ever did ask him—

MRS. LINDE But of course you won't.

NORA Of course not. I can't imagine that it should ever become necessary. But I'm perfectly sure that if I did speak to Dr. Rank—

MRS. LINDE Behind your husband's back?

NORA I've got to get out of this other business; and *that's* been going on behind his back. I've *got* to get out of it.

MRS. LINDE Yes, well, that's what I told you yesterday. But—

NORA (*walking up and down*) It's much easier for a man to arrange these things than a woman—

MRS. LINDE One's own husband, yes.

NORA Oh, bosh. (*Stops walking.*) When you've completely repaid a debt, you get your I.O.U. back, don't you?

MRS. LINDE Yes, of course.

NORA And you can tear it into a thousand pieces and burn the filthy, beastly thing!

MRS. LINDE (*looks hard at her, puts down her sewing and gets up slowly*) Nora, you're hiding something from me.

NORA Can you see that?

MRS. LINDE Something has happened since yesterday morning. Nora, what is it?

NORA (*goes towards her*) Christine! (*Listens.*) Ssh! There's Torvald. Would you mind going into the nursery for a few minutes? Torvald can't bear to see sewing around. Anne-Marie'll help you.

MRS. LINDE (*gathers some of her things together*) Very well. But I shan't leave this house until we've talked this matter out.

She goes into the nursery, left. As she does so, HELMER *enters from the hall.*

NORA (*runs to meet him*) Oh, Torvald dear, I've been so longing for you to come back!

HELMER Was that the dressmaker?

NORA No, it was Christine. She's helping me mend my costume. I'm going to look rather splendid in that.

HELMER Yes, that was quite a bright idea of mine, wasn't it?

NORA Wonderful! But wasn't it nice of me to give in to you?

HELMER (*takes her chin in his hand*) Nice—to give in to your husband? All right, little silly, I know you didn't mean it like that. But I won't disturb you. I expect you'll be wanting to try it on.

NORA Are you going to work now?

HELMER Yes. (*Shows her a bundle of papers.*) Look at these. I've been down to the bank— (*Turns to go into his study.*)

NORA Torvald.

HELMER (*stops*) Yes.

NORA If little squirrel asked you really prettily to grant her a wish—

HELMER Well?

NORA Would you grant it to her?

HELMER First I should naturally have to know what it was.

NORA Squirrel would do lots of pretty tricks for you if you granted her wish.

HELMER Out with it, then.

NORA Your little skylark would sing in every room—

HELMER My little skylark does that already.

NORA I'd turn myself into a little fairy and dance for you in the moonlight, Torvald.

HELMER Nora, it isn't that business you were talking about this morning?

NORA (comes closer) Yes, Torvald—oh, please! I beg of you!

HELMER Have you really the nerve to bring that up again?

NORA Yes, Torvald, yes, you must do as I ask! You must let Krogstad keep his place at the bank!

HELMER My dear Nora, his is the job I'm giving to Mrs. Linde.

NORA Yes, that's terribly sweet of you. But you can get rid of one of the other clerks instead of Krogstad.

HELMER Really, you're being incredibly obstinate. Just because you thoughtlessly promised to put in a word for him, you expect me to—

NORA No, it isn't that, Helmer. It's for your own sake. That man writes for the most beastly newspapers—you said so yourself. He could do you tremendous harm. I'm so dreadfully frightened of him—

HELMER Oh, I understand. Memories of the past. That's what's frightening you.

NORA What do you mean?

HELMER You're thinking of your father, aren't you?

NORA Yes, yes. Of course. Just think what those dreadful men wrote in the papers about Papa! The most frightful slanders. I really believe it would have lost him his job if the Ministry hadn't sent you down to investigate, and you hadn't been so kind and helpful to him.

HELMER But my dear little Nora, there's a considerable difference between your father and me. Your father was not a man of unassailable reputation. But I am; and I hope to remain so all my life.

NORA But no one knows what spiteful people may not dig up. We could be so peaceful and happy now, Torvald—we could be free from every worry—you and I and the children. Oh, please, Torvald, please—!

HELMER The very fact of your pleading his cause makes it impossible for me to keep him. Everyone at the bank already knows that I intend to dismiss Krogstad. If the rumour got about that the new manager had allowed his wife to persuade him to change his mind—

NORA Well, what then?

HELMER Oh, nothing, nothing. As long as my little Miss Obstinate gets her way—! Do you expect me to make a laughing-stock of myself before my entire staff—give people the idea that I am open to outside influence? Believe me, I'd soon feel the consequences! Besides—there's something else that makes it impossible for Krogstad to remain in the bank while I am its manager.

NORA What is that?

HELMER I might conceivably have allowed myself to ignore his moral obloquies—

NORA Yes, Torvald, surely?

HELMER And I hear he's quite efficient at his job. But we—well, we were schoolfriends. It was one of those friendships that one enters into over-hastily and so often comes to regret later in life. I might as well confess the truth. We—well, we're on Christian name terms. And the tactless idiot makes no attempt to conceal it when other people are present. On the contrary, he thinks it gives him the right to be familiar with me. He shows off the whole time, with "Torvald this," and "Torvald that." I can tell you, I find it damned annoying. If he stayed, he'd make my position intolerable.

NORA Torvald, you can't mean this seriously.

HELMER Oh? And why not?

NORA But it's so petty.

HELMER What did you say? Petty? You think *I* am petty?

NORA No, Torvald dear, of course you're not. That's just why—

HELMER Don't quibble! You call my motives petty. Then I must be petty too. Petty! I see. Well, I've had enough of this. (*Goes to the door and calls into the hall.*) Helen!

NORA What are you going to do?

HELMER (*searching among his papers*) I'm going to settle this matter once and for all. (*The* MAID *enters.*) Take this letter downstairs at once. Find a messenger and see that he delivers it. Immediately! The address is on the envelope. Here's the money.

MAID Very good, sir. (*Goes out with the letter.*)

HELMER (*putting his papers in order*) There now, little Miss Obstinate.

NORA (*tensely*) Torvald—what was in that letter?

HELMER Krogstad's dismissal.

NORA Call her back, Torvald! There's still time. Oh, Torvald, call her back! Do it for my sake—for your own sake—for the children! Do you hear me, Torvald? Please do it! You don't realize what this may do to us all!

HELMER Too late.

NORA Yes. Too late.

HELMER My dear Nora, I forgive you this anxiety. Though it is a bit of an insult to me. Oh, but it is! Isn't it an insult to imply that I should be frightened by the vindictiveness of a depraved hack journalist? But I forgive you, because it so charmingly testifies to the love you bear me. (*Takes her in his arms.*) Which is as it should be, my own dearest Nora. Let what will happen, happen. When the real crisis comes, you will not find me lacking in strength or courage. I am man enough to bear the burden for us both.

NORA (*fearfully*) What do you mean?

HELMER The whole burden, I say—

NORA (*calmly*) I shall never let you do that.

HELMER Very well. We shall share it, Nora—as man and wife. And that is as it should be. (*Caresses her.*) Are you happy now? There, there, there; don't look at me with those frightened little eyes. You're simply imagining things. You go ahead now and do your tarantella, and get some practice on that tambourine. I'll sit in my study and close the door. Then I won't hear anything, and you can make all the noise you want. (*Turns in the doorway.*) When Dr. Rank comes, tell him where to find me. (*He nods to her, goes into his room with his papers and closes the door.*)

NORA (*desperate with anxiety, stands as though transfixed, and whispers*) He said he'd do it. He will do it. He will do it, and nothing'll stop him. No, never that. I'd rather anything. There must be some escape—! Some way out—! (*The bell rings in the hall.*) Dr. Rank—! Anything but that! Anything, I don't care—!

She passes her hand across her face, composes herself, walks across and opens the door to the hall. DR. RANK *is standing there, hanging up his fur coat. During the following scene it begins to grow dark.*

NORA Good evening, Dr. Rank. I recognized your ring. But you mustn't go in to Torvald yet. I think he's busy.

RANK And—you?

NORA (*as he enters the room and she closes the door behind him*) Oh, you know very well I've always time to talk to you.

RANK Thank you. I shall avail myself of that privilege as long as I can.

NORA What do you mean by that? As long as you *can?*

RANK Yes. Does that frighten you?

NORA Well, it's rather a curious expression. Is something going to happen?

RANK Something I've been expecting to happen for a long time. But I didn't think it would happen quite so soon.

NORA (*seizes his arm*) What is it? Dr. Rank, you must tell me!

RANK (*sits down by the stove*) I'm on the way out. And there's nothing to be done about it.

NORA (*sighs with relief*) Oh, it's you—?

RANK Who else? No, it's no good lying to oneself. I am the most wretched of all my patients, Mrs. Helmer. These last few days I've been going through the books of this poor body of mine, and I find I am bankrupt. Within a month I may be rotting up there in the churchyard.

NORA Ugh, what a nasty way to talk!

RANK The facts aren't exactly nice. But the worst is that there's so much else that's nasty to come first. I've only one more test to make. When that's done I'll have a pretty accurate idea of when the final disintegration is likely to begin. I want to ask you a favour. Helmer's a sensitive chap, and I know how he hates anything ugly. I don't want him to visit me when I'm in hospital—

NORA Oh but, Dr. Rank—

RANK I don't want him there. On any pretext. I shan't have him allowed in. As soon as I know the worst, I'll send you my visiting card with a black cross on it, and then you'll know that the final filthy process has begun.

NORA Really, you're being quite impossible this evening. And I did hope you'd be in a good mood.

RANK With death on my hands? And all this to atone for someone else's sin? Is there justice in that? And in every single family, in one way or another, the same merciless law of retribution is at work—

NORA (*holds her hands to her ears*) Nonsense! Cheer up! Laugh!

RANK Yes, you're right. Laughter's all the damned thing's fit for. My poor innocent spine must pay for the fun my father had as a gay young lieutenant.

NORA (*at the table, left*) You mean he was too fond of asparagus and *foie gras?*

RANK Yes; and truffles too.

NORA Yes, of course, truffles, yes. And oysters too, I suppose?

RANK Yes, oysters, oysters. Of course.

NORA And all that port and champagne to wash them down. It's too sad that all those lovely things should affect one's spine.

RANK Especially a poor spine that never got any pleasure out of them.

NORA Oh yes, that's the saddest thing of all.

RANK (*looks searchingly at her*) Hm—

NORA (*after a moment*) Why did you smile?

RANK No, it was you who laughed.

NORA No, it was you who smiled, Dr. Rank!

RANK (*gets up*) You're a worse little rogue than I thought.

NORA Oh, I'm full of stupid tricks today.

RANK So it seems.

NORA (*puts both her hands on his shoulders*) Dear, dear Dr. Rank, you mustn't die and leave Torvald and me.

RANK Oh, you'll soon get over it. Once one is gone, one is soon forgotten.

NORA (*looks at him anxiously*) Do you believe that?

RANK One finds replacements, and then—

NORA Who will find a replacement?

RANK You and Helmer both will, when I am gone. You seem to have made a start already, haven't you? What was this Mrs. Linde doing here yesterday evening?

NORA Aha! But surely you can't be jealous of poor Christine?

RANK Indeed I am. She will be my successor in this house. When I have moved on, this lady will—

NORA Ssh—don't speak so loud! She's in there!

RANK Today again? You see!

NORA She's only come to mend my dress. Good heavens, how unreasonable you are! (*Sits on the sofa.*) Be nice now, Dr. Rank. Tomorrow you'll see how beautifully I shall dance; and you must imagine that I'm doing it just for you. And for Torvald, of course; obviously. (*Takes some things out of the box.*) Dr. Rank, sit down here and I'll show you something.

RANK (*sits*) What's this?

NORA Look here! Look!

RANK Silk stockings!

NORA Flesh-coloured. Aren't they beautiful? It's very dark in here now, of course, but tomorrow—! No, no, no; only the soles. Oh well, I suppose you can look a bit higher if you want to.

RANK Hm—

NORA Why are you looking so critical? Don't you think they'll fit me?

RANK I can't really give you a qualified opinion on that.

NORA (*looks at him for a moment*) Shame on you! (*Flicks him on the ear with the stockings.*) Take that. (*Puts them back in the box.*)

RANK What other wonders are to be revealed to me?

NORA I shan't show you anything else. You're being naughty.

She hums a little and looks among the things in the box.

RANK (*after a short silence*) When I sit here like this being so intimate with you, I can't think—I cannot imagine what would have become of me if I had never entered this house.

NORA (*smiles*) Yes, I think you enjoy being with us, don't you?

RANK (*more quietly, looking into the middle distance*) And now to have to leave it all—

NORA Nonsense. You're not leaving us.

RANK (*as before*) And not to be able to leave even the most wretched token of gratitude behind; hardly even a passing sense of loss; only an empty place, to be filled by the next comer.

NORA Suppose I were to ask you to—? No—

RANK To do what?

NORA To give me proof of your friendship—

RANK Yes, yes?

NORA No, I mean—to do me a very great service—

RANK Would you really for once grant me that happiness?

NORA But you've no idea what it is.

RANK Very well, tell me, then.

NORA No, but, Dr. Rank, I can't. It's far too much—I want your help and advice, and I want you to do something for me.

RANK The more the better. I've no idea what it can be. But tell me. You do trust me, don't you?

NORA Oh, yes, more than anyone. You're my best and truest friend. Otherwise I couldn't tell you. Well then, Dr. Rank—there's something you must help me to prevent. You know how much Torvald loves me—he'd never hesitate for an instant to lay down his life for me—

RANK (*leans over towards her*) Nora—do you think he is the only one—?

NORA (*with a slight start*) What do you mean?

RANK Who would gladly lay down his life for you?

NORA (*sadly*) Oh, I see.

RANK I swore to myself I would let you know that before I go. I shall never have a better opportunity. . . . Well, Nora, now you know that. And now you also know that you can trust me as you can trust nobody else.

NORA (*rises; calmly and quietly*) Let me pass, please.

RANK (*makes room for her but remains seated*) Nora—

NORA (*in the doorway to the hall*) Helen, bring the lamp. (*Goes over to the stove.*) Oh, dear Dr. Rank, this was really horrid of you.

RANK (*gets up*) That I have loved you as deeply as anyone else has? Was that horrid of me?

NORA No—but that you should go and tell me. That was quite unnecessary—

RANK What do you mean? Did you know, then—?

The MAID *enters with the lamp, puts it on the table and goes out.*

RANK Nora—Mrs. Helmer—I am asking you, did you know this?

NORA Oh, what do I know, what did I know, what didn't I know—I really can't say. How could you be so stupid, Dr. Rank? Everything was so nice.

RANK Well, at any rate now you know that I am ready to serve you, body and soul. So—please continue.

NORA (*looks at him*) After this?

RANK Please tell me what it is.

NORA I can't possibly tell you now.

RANK Yes, yes! You mustn't punish me like this. Let me be allowed to do what I can for you.

NORA You can't do anything for me now. Anyway, I don't need any help. It was only my imagination—you'll see. Yes, really. Honestly. (*Sits in the rocking-chair, looks at him and smiles.*) Well, upon my word you *are* a fine gentleman, Dr. Rank. Aren't you ashamed of yourself, now that the lamp's been lit?

RANK Frankly, no. But perhaps I ought to say—*adieu*?

NORA Of course not. You will naturally continue to visit us as before. You know quite well how Torvald depends on your company.

RANK Yes, but you?

NORA Oh, I always think it's enormous fun having you here.

RANK That was what misled me. You're a riddle to me, you know. I'd often felt you'd just as soon be with me as with Helmer.

NORA Well, you see, there are some people whom one loves, and others whom it's almost more fun to be with.

RANK Oh yes, there's some truth in that.

NORA When I was at home, of course I loved Papa best. But I always used to think it was terribly amusing to go down and talk to the servants; because they never told me what I ought to do; and they were such fun to listen to.

RANK I see. So I've taken their place?

NORA *(jumps up and runs over to him)* Oh, dear, sweet Dr. Rank, I didn't mean that at all. But I'm sure you understand—I feel the same about Torvald as I did about Papa.

MAID *(enters from the hall)* Excuse me, madam. *(Whispers to her and hands her a visiting card.)*

NORA *(glances at the card)* Oh! *(Puts it quickly in her pocket.)*

RANK Anything wrong?

NORA No, no, nothing at all. It's just something that—it's my new dress.

RANK What? But your costume is lying over there.

NORA Oh—that, yes—but there's another—I ordered it specially—Torvald mustn't know—

RANK Ah, so that's your big secret?

NORA Yes, yes. Go in and talk to him—he's in his study—keep him talking for a bit—

RANK Don't worry. He won't get away from me. *(Goes into* HELMER's *study.)*

NORA *(to the* MAID) Is he waiting in the kitchen?

MAID Yes, madam, he came up the back way—

NORA But didn't you tell him I had a visitor?

MAID Yes, but he wouldn't go.

NORA Wouldn't go?

MAID No, madam, not until he'd spoken with you.

NORA Very well, show him in; but quietly. Helen, you mustn't tell anyone about this. It's a surprise for my husband.

MAID Very good, madam. I understand. *(Goes.)*

NORA It's happening. It's happening after all. No, no, no, it can't happen, it mustn't happen.

She walks across and bolts the door of HELMER's *study. The* MAID *opens the door from the hall to admit* KROGSTAD, *and closes it behind him. He is wearing an overcoat, heavy boots and a fur cap.*

NORA *(goes towards him)* Speak quietly. My husband's at home.

KROGSTAD Let him hear.

NORA What do you want from me?

KROGSTAD Information.

NORA Hurry up, then. What is it?

KROGSTAD I suppose you know I've been given the sack.

NORA I couldn't stop it, Mr. Krogstad. I did my best for you, but it didn't help.

KROGSTAD Does your husband love you so little? He knows what I can do to you, and yet he dares to—

NORA Surely you don't imagine I told him?

KROGSTAD No, I didn't really think you had. It wouldn't have been like my old friend Torvald Helmer to show that much courage—

NORA Mr. Krogstad, I'll trouble you to speak respectfully of my husband.

KROGSTAD Don't worry, I'll show him all the respect he deserves. But since you're so anxious to keep this matter hushed up, I presume you're better informed than you were yesterday of the gravity of what you've done?

NORA I've learned more than you could ever teach me.

KROGSTAD Yes, a bad lawyer like me—

NORA What do you want from me?

KROGSTAD I just wanted to see how things were with you, Mrs. Helmer. I've been thinking about you all day. Even duns and hack journalists have hearts, you know.

NORA Show some heart, then. Think of my little children.

KROGSTAD Have you and your husband thought of mine? Well, let's forget that. I just wanted to tell you, you don't need to take this business too seriously. I'm not going to take any action, for the present.

NORA Oh, no—you won't, will you? I knew it.

KROGSTAD It can all be settled quite amicably. There's no need for it to become public. We'll keep it among the three of us.

NORA My husband must never know about this.

KROGSTAD How can you stop him? Can you pay the balance of what you owe me?

NORA Not immediately.

KROGSTAD Have you any means of raising the money during the next few days?

NORA None that I would care to use.

KROGSTAD Well, it wouldn't have helped anyway. However much money you offered me now I wouldn't give you back that paper.

NORA What are you going to do with it?

KROGSTAD Just keep it. No one else need ever hear about it. So in case you were thinking of doing anything desperate—

NORA I am.

KROGSTAD Such as running away—

NORA I am.

KROGSTAD Or anything more desperate—

NORA How did you know?

KROGSTAD —just give up the idea.

NORA How did you know?

KROGSTAD Most of us think of that at first. I did. But I hadn't the courage—

NORA (dully) Neither have I.

KROGSTAD (relieved) It's true, isn't it? You haven't the courage either?

NORA No. I haven't. I haven't.

KROGSTAD It'd be a stupid thing to do anyway. Once the first little domestic explosion is over. . . . I've got a letter in my pocket here addressed to your husband—

NORA Telling him everything?

KROGSTAD As delicately as possible.

NORA (quickly) He must never see that letter. Tear it up. I'll find the money somehow—

KROGSTAD I'm sorry, Mrs. Helmer, I thought I'd explained—

NORA Oh, I don't mean the money I owe you. Let me know how much you want from my husband, and I'll find it for you.

KROGSTAD I'm not asking your husband for money.

NORA What do you want, then?

KROGSTAD I'll tell you. I want to get on my feet again, Mrs. Helmer. I want to get to the top. And your husband's going to help me. For eighteen months now my record's been clean. I've been in hard straits all that time; I was content to fight my way back inch by inch. Now I've been chucked back into the mud, and I'm not going to be satisfied with just getting back my job. I'm going to get to the top, I tell you. I'm going to get back into the bank, and it's going to be higher up. Your husband's going to create a new job for me—

NORA He'll never do that!

KROGSTAD Oh, yes he will. I know him. He won't dare to risk a scandal. And once I'm in there with him, you'll see! Within a year I'll be his right-hand man. It'll be Nils Krogstad who'll be running that bank, not Torvald Helmer!

NORA That will never happen.

KROGSTAD Are you thinking of—?

NORA Now I *have* the courage.

KROGSTAD Oh, you can't frighten me. A pampered little pretty like you—

NORA You'll see! You'll see!

KROGSTAD Under the ice? Down in the cold, black water? And then, in the spring, to float up again, ugly, unrecognizable, hairless—?

NORA You can't frighten me.

KROGSTAD And you can't frighten me. People don't do such things, Mrs. Helmer. And anyway, what'd be the use? I've got him in my pocket.

NORA But afterwards? When I'm no longer—?

KROGSTAD Have you forgotten that then your reputation will be in my hands? (*She looks at him speechlessly.*) Well, I've warned you. Don't do anything silly. When Helmer's read my letter, he'll get in touch with me. And remember, it's your husband who's forced me to act like this. And for that I'll never forgive him. Goodbye, Mrs. Helmer. (*He goes out through the hall*).

NORA (*runs to the hall door, opens it a few inches and listens*) He's going. He's not going to give him the letter. Oh, no, no, it couldn't possibly happen. (*Opens the door a little wider.*) What's he doing? Standing outside the front door. He's not going downstairs. Is he changing his mind? Yes, he—!

A *letter falls into the letter-box.* KROGSTAD's *footsteps die away down the stairs.*

NORA (*with a stifled cry, runs across the room towards the table by the sofa. A pause*) In the letter-box. (*Steals timidly over towards the hall door.*) There it is! Oh, Torvald, Torvald! Now we're lost!

MRS. LINDE (*enters from the nursery with* NORA's *costume*) Well, I've done the best I can. Shall we see how it looks—?

NORA (*whispers hoarsely*) Christine, come here.

MRS. LINDE (*throws the dress on the sofa*) What's wrong with you? You look as though you'd seen a ghost!

NORA Come here. Do you see that letter? There—look—through the glass of the letter-box.

MRS. LINDE Yes, yes, I see it.

NORA That letter's from Krogstad—

MRS. LINDE Nora! It was Krogstad who lent you the money!

NORA Yes. And now Torvald's going to discover everything.

MRS. LINDE Oh, believe me, Nora, it'll be best for you both.

NORA You don't know what's happened. I've committed a forgery—

MRS. LINDE But, for heaven's sake—!

NORA Christine, all I want is for you to be my witness.

MRS. LINDE What do you mean? Witness what?

NORA If I should go out of my mind—and it might easily happen—

MRS. LINDE Nora!

NORA Or if anything else should happen to me—so that I wasn't here any longer—

MRS. LINDE Nora, Nora, you don't know what you're saying!

NORA If anyone should try to take the blame, and say it was all his fault—you understand—?

MRS. LINDE Yes, yes—but how can you think—?

NORA Then you must testify that it isn't true, Christine. I'm not mad—I know exactly what I'm saying—and I'm telling you, no one else knows anything about this. I did it entirely on my own. Remember that.

MRS. LINDE All right. But I simply don't understand—

NORA Oh, how could you understand? A—miracle—is about to happen.

MRS. LINDE Miracle?

NORA Yes. A miracle. But it's so frightening, Christine. It *mustn't* happen, not for anything in the world.

MRS. LINDE I'll go over and talk to Krogstad.

NORA Don't go near him. He'll only do something to hurt you.

MRS. LINDE Once upon a time he'd have done anything for my sake.

NORA He?

MRS. LINDE Where does he live?

NORA Oh, how should I know—? Oh, yes, wait a moment—! (*Feels in her pocket.*) Here's his card. But the letter, the letter—!

HELMER (*from his study, knocks on the door*) Nora!

NORA (*cries in alarm*) What is it?

HELMER Now, now, don't get alarmed. We're not coming in; you've closed the door. Are you trying on your costume?

NORA Yes, yes—I'm trying on my costume. I'm going to look so pretty for you, Torvald.

MRS. LINDE (*who has been reading the card*) Why, he lives just around the corner.

NORA Yes; but it's no use. There's nothing to be done now. The letter's lying there in the box.

MRS. LINDE And your husband has the key?

NORA Yes, he always keeps it.

MRS. LINDE Krogstad must ask him to send the letter back unread. He must find some excuse—

NORA But Torvald always opens the box at just about this time—

MRS. LINDE You must stop him. Go in and keep him talking. I'll be back as quickly as I can.

She hurries out through the hall.

NORA (*goes over to* HELMER's *door, opens it and peeps in*) Torvald!

HELMER (*offstage*) Well, may a man enter his own drawing-room again? Come on, Rank, now we'll see what— (*In the doorway.*) But what's this?

NORA What, Torvald dear?

HELMER Rank's been preparing me for some great transformation scene.

RANK (*in the doorway*) So I understood. But I seem to have been mistaken.

NORA Yes, no one's to be allowed to see me before tomorrow night.

HELMER But, my dear Nora, you look quite worn out. Have you been practising too hard?

NORA No, I haven't practised at all yet.

HELMER Well, you must.

NORA Yes, Torvald, I must, I know. But I can't get anywhere without your help. I've completely forgotten everything.

HELMER Oh, we'll soon put that to rights.

NORA Yes, help me, Torvald. Promise me you will? Oh, I'm so nervous. All those people—! You must forget everything except me this evening. You mustn't think of business—I won't even let you touch a pen. Promise me, Torvald?

HELMER I promise. This evening I shall think of nothing but you—my poor, helpless little darling. Oh, there's just one thing I must see to—(*Goes towards the hall door.*)

NORA What do you want out there?

HELMER I'm only going to see if any letters have come.

NORA No, Torvald, no!

HELMER Why, what's the matter?

NORA Torvald, I beg you. There's nothing there.

HELMER Well, I'll just make sure.

He moves towards the door. NORA *runs to the piano and plays the first bars of the tarantella.*

HELMER (*at the door, turns*) Aha!

NORA I can't dance tomorrow if I don't practise with you now.

HELMER (*goes over to her*) Are you really so frightened, Nora dear?

NORA Yes, terribly frightened. Let me start practising now, at once—we've still time before dinner. Oh, do sit down and play for me, Torvald dear. Correct me, lead me, the way you always do.

HELMER Very well, my dear, if you wish it.

He sits down at the piano. NORA *seizes the tambourine and a long multi-coloured shawl from the cardboard box, wraps the latter hastily around her, then takes a quick leap into the centre of the room.*

NORA Play for me! I want to dance!

HELMER *plays and* NORA *dances.* DR. RANK *stands behind* HELMER *at the piano and watches her.*

HELMER (*as he plays*) Slower, slower!

NORA I can't!

HELMER Not so violently, Nora.

NORA I must!

HELMER (*stops playing*) No, no, this won't do at all.

NORA (*laughs and swings her tambourine*) Isn't that what I told you?

RANK Let me play for her.

HELMER (*gets up*) Yes, would you? Then it'll be easier for me to show her.

RANK *sits down at the piano and plays.* NORA *dances more and more wildly.* HELMER *has stationed himself by the stove and tries repeatedly to correct her, but she seems not to hear him. Her hair works loose and falls over her shoulders; she ignores it and continues to dance.* MRS. LINDE *enters.*

MRS. LINDE (*stands in the doorway as though tongue-tied*) Ah—!

NORA (*as she dances*) Oh, Christine, we're having such fun!

HELMER But, Nora darling, you're dancing as if your life depended on it.

NORA It does.

HELMER Rank, stop it! This is sheer lunacy. Stop it, I say!

RANK *ceases playing.* NORA *suddenly stops dancing.*

HELMER (*goes over to her*) I'd never have believed it. You've forgotten everything I taught you.

NORA (*throws away the tambourine*) You see!

HELMER I'll have to show you every step.

NORA You see how much I need you! You must show me every step of the way. Right to the end of the dance. Promise me you will, Torvald?

HELMER Never fear. I will.

NORA You mustn't think about anything but me—today or tomorrow. Don't open any letters—don't even open the letter-box—

HELMER Aha, you're still worried about that fellow—

NORA Oh, yes, yes, him too.

HELMER Nora, I can tell from the way you're behaving, there's a letter from him already lying there.

NORA I don't know. I think so. But you mustn't read it now. I don't want anything ugly to come between us till it's all over.

RANK (*quietly, to* HELMER) Better give her her way.

HELMER (*puts his arm round her*) My child shall have her way. But tomorrow night, when your dance is over—

NORA Then you will be free.

MAID (*appears in the doorway, right*) Dinner is served, madam.

NORA Put out some champagne, Helen.

MAID Very good, madam. (*Goes.*)

HELMER I say! What's this, a banquet?

NORA We'll drink champagne until dawn! (*Calls.*) And, Helen! Put out some macaroons! Lots of macaroons—for once!

HELMER (*takes her hands in his*) Now, now, now. Don't get so excited. Where's my little songbird, the one I know?

NORA All right. Go and sit down—and you too, Dr. Rank. I'll be with you in a minute. Christine, you must help me put my hair up.

RANK (*quietly, as they go*) There's nothing wrong, is there? I mean, she isn't—er—expecting—?

HELMER Good heavens no, my dear chap. She just gets scared like a child sometimes—I told you before—

They go out right.

NORA Well?

MRS. LINDE He's left town.

NORA I saw it from your face.

MRS. LINDE He'll be back tomorrow evening. I left a note for him.

NORA You needn't have bothered. You can't stop anything now. Anyway, it's wonderful really, in a way—sitting here and waiting for the miracle to happen.

MRS. LINDE Waiting for what?

NORA Oh, you wouldn't understand. Go in and join them. I'll be with you in a moment.

MRS. LINDE *goes into the dining-room.*

NORA *(stands for a moment as though collecting herself. Then she looks at her watch)* Five
o'clock. Seven hours till midnight. Then another twenty-four hours till midnight
tomorrow. And then the tarantella will be finished. Twenty-four and seven? Thirty-
one hours to live.

HELMER *(appears in the doorway, right)* What's happened to my little songbird?

NORA *(runs to him with her arms wide)* Your songbird is here!

ACT III

*The same room. The table which was formerly by the sofa has been moved into the centre
of the room; the chairs surround it as before. The door to the hall stands open. Dance
music can be heard from the floor above.* MRS. LINDE *is seated at the table, absent-
mindedly glancing through a book. She is trying to read, but seems unable to keep her
mind on it. More than once she turns and listens anxiously towards the front door.*

MRS. LINDE *(looks at her watch)* Not here yet. There's not much time left. Please God
he hasn't—! *(Listens again.)* Ah, here he is. *(Goes out into the hall and cautiously
opens the front door. Footsteps can be heard softly ascending the stairs. She whispers.)*
Come in. There's no one here.

KROGSTAD *(in the doorway)* I found a note from you at my lodgings. What does this
mean?

MRS. LINDE I must speak with you.

KROGSTAD Oh? And must our conversation take place in this house?

MRS. LINDE We couldn't meet at my place; my room has no separate entrance. Come
in. We're quite alone. The maid's asleep, and the Helmers are at the dance upstairs.

KROGSTAD *(comes into the room)* Well, well! So the Helmers are dancing this evening?
Are they indeed?

MRS. LINDE Yes, why not?

KROGSTAD True enough. Why not?

MRS. LINDE Well, Krogstad. You and I must have a talk together.

KROGSTAD Have we two anything further to discuss?

MRS. LINDE We have a great deal to discuss.

KROGSTAD I wasn't aware of it.

MRS. LINDE That's because you've never really understood me.

KROGSTAD Was there anything to understand? It's the old story, isn't it—a woman chuck-
ing a man because something better turns up?

MRS. LINDE Do you really think I'm so utterly heartless? You think it was easy for me
to give you up?

KROGSTAD Wasn't it?

MRS. LINDE Oh, Nils, did you really believe that?

KROGSTAD Then why did you write to me the way you did?

MRS. LINDE I had to. Since I had to break with you, I thought it my duty to destroy all
the feelings you had for me.

KROGSTAD *(clenches his fists)* So that was it. And you did this for money!

MRS. LINDE You mustn't forget I had a helpless mother to take care of, and two little
brothers. We couldn't wait for you, Nils. It would have been so long before you'd had
enough to support us.

KROGSTAD Maybe. But you had no right to cast me off for someone else.

MRS. LINDE Perhaps not. I've often asked myself that.

KROGSTAD (*more quietly*) When I lost you, it was just as though all solid ground had been swept from under my feet. Look at me. Now I am a shipwrecked man, clinging to a spar.

MRS. LINDE Help may be near at hand.

KROGSTAD It was near. But then you came, and stood between it and me.

MRS. LINDE I didn't know, Nils. No one told me till today that this job I'd found was yours.

KROGSTAD I believe you, since you say so. But now you know, won't you give it up?

MRS. LINDE No—because it wouldn't help you even if I did.

KROGSTAD Wouldn't it? I'd do it all the same.

MRS. LINDE I've learned to look at things practically. Life and poverty have taught me that.

KROGSTAD And life has taught me to distrust fine words.

MRS. LINDE Then it's taught you a useful lesson. But surely you still believe in actions?

KROGSTAD What do you mean?

MRS. LINDE You said you were like a shipwrecked man clinging to a spar.

KROGSTAD I have good reason to say it.

MRS. LINDE I'm in the same position as you. No one to care about, no one to care for.

KROGSTAD You made your own choice.

MRS. LINDE I had no choice—then.

KROGSTAD Well?

MRS. LINDE Nils, suppose we two shipwrecked souls could join hands?

KROGSTAD What are you saying?

MRS. LINDE Castaways have a better chance of survival together than on their own.

KROGSTAD Christine!

MRS. LINDE Why do you suppose I came to this town?

KROGSTAD You mean—you came because of me?

MRS. LINDE I must work if I'm to find life worth living. I've always worked, for as long as I can remember; it's been the greatest joy of my life—my only joy. But now I'm alone in the world, and I feel so dreadfully lost and empty. There's no joy in working just for oneself. Oh, Nils, give me something—someone—to work for.

KROGSTAD I don't believe all that. You're just being hysterical and romantic. You want to find an excuse for self-sacrifice.

MRS. LINDE Have you ever known me to be hysterical?

KROGSTAD You mean you really—? Is it possible? Tell me—you know all about my past?

MRS. LINDE Yes.

KROGSTAD And you know what people think of me here?

MRS. LINDE You said just now that with me you might have become a different person.

KROGSTAD I know I could have.

MRS. LINDE Couldn't it still happen?

KROGSTAD Christine—do you really mean this? Yes—you do—I see it in your face. Have you really the courage—?

MRS. LINDE I need someone to be a mother to; and your children need a mother. And you and I need each other. I believe in you, Nils. I am afraid of nothing—with you.

KROGSTAD (*clasps her hands*) Thank you, Christine—thank you! Now I shall make the world believe in me as you do! Oh—but I'd forgotten—

MRS. LINDE (*listens*) Ssh! The tarantella! Go quickly, go!

KROGSTAD Why? What is it?

MRS. LINDE You hear that dance? As soon as it's finished, they'll be coming down.

KROGSTAD All right, I'll go. It's no good, Christine. I'd forgotten—you don't know what I've just done to the Helmers.

MRS. LINDE Yes, Nils. I know.

KROGSTAD And yet you'd still have the courage to—?

MRS. LINDE I know what despair can drive a man like you to.

KROGSTAD Oh, if only I could undo this!

MRS. LINDE You can. Your letter is still lying in the box.

KROGSTAD Are you sure?

MRS. LINDE Quite sure. But—

KROGSTAD (*looks searchingly at her*) Is that why you're doing this? You want to save your friend at any price? Tell me the truth. Is that the reason?

MRS. LINDE Nils, a woman who has sold herself once for the sake of others doesn't make the same mistake again.

KROGSTAD I shall demand my letter back.

MRS. LINDE No, no.

KROGSTAD Of course I shall. I shall stay here till Helmer comes down. I'll tell him he must give me back my letter—I'll say it was only to do with my dismissal, and that I don't want him to read it—

MRS. LINDE No, Nils, you mustn't ask for that letter back.

KROGSTAD But—tell me—wasn't that the real reason you asked me to come here?

MRS. LINDE Yes—at first, when I was frightened. But a day has passed since then, and in that time I've seen incredible things happen in this house. Helmer must know the truth. This unhappy secret of Nora's must be revealed. They must come to a full understanding; there must be an end of all these shiftings and evasions.

KROGSTAD Very well. If you're prepared to risk it. But one thing I can do—and at once—

MRS. LINDE (*listens*) Hurry! Go, go! The dance is over. We aren't safe here another moment.

KROGSTAD I'll wait for you downstairs.

MRS. LINDE Yes, do. You can see me home.

KROGSTAD I've never been so happy in my life before!

He goes out through the front door. The door leading from the room into the hall remains open.

MRS. LINDE (*tidies the room a little and gets her hat and coat*) What a change! Oh, what a change! Someone to work for—to live for! A home to bring joy into! I won't let this chance of happiness slip through my fingers. Oh, why don't they come? (*Listens.*) Ah, here they are. I must get my coat on.

She takes her hat and coat. HELMER'S *and* NORA'S *voices become audible outside. A key is turned in the lock and* HELMER *leads* NORA *almost forcibly into the hall. She is dressed in an Italian costume with a large black shawl. He is in evening dress, with a black cloak.*

NORA (*still in the doorway, resisting him*) No, no, no—not in here! I want to go back upstairs. I don't want to leave so early.

HELMER But my dearest Nora—

NORA Oh, please, Torvald, please! Just another hour!

HELMER Not another minute, Nora, my sweet. You know what we agreed. Come along, now. Into the drawing-room. You'll catch cold if you stay out here.

He leads her, despite her efforts to resist him, gently into the room.

MRS. LINDE Good evening.

NORA Christine!

HELMER Oh, hullo, Mrs. Linde. You still here?

MRS. LINDE Please forgive me. I did so want to see Nora in her costume.

NORA Have you been sitting here waiting for me?

MRS. LINDE Yes. I got here too late, I'm afraid. You'd already gone up. And I felt I really couldn't go back home without seeing you.

HELMER (*takes off* NORA'*s shawl*) Well, take a good look at her. She's worth looking at, don't you think? Isn't she beautiful, Mrs. Linde?

MRS. LINDE Oh, yes, indeed—

HELMER Isn't she unbelievably beautiful? Everyone at the party said so. But dreadfully stubborn she is, bless her pretty little heart. What's to be done about that? Would you believe it, I practically had to use force to get her away!

NORA Oh, Torvald, you're going to regret not letting me stay—just half an hour longer.

HELMER Hear that, Mrs. Linde? She dances her tarantella—makes a roaring success— and very well deserved—though possibly a trifle too realistic—more so than was aesthetically necessary, strictly speaking. But never mind that. Main thing is—she had a success—roaring success. Was I going to let her stay on after that and spoil the impression? No, thank you. I took my beautiful little Capri signorina—my capricious little Capricienne, what?—under my arm—a swift round of the ballroom, a curtsey to the company, and, as they say in novels, the beautiful apparition disappeared! An exit should always be dramatic, Mrs. Linde. But unfortunately that's just what I can't get Nora to realize. I say, it's hot in here. (*Throws his cloak on a chair and opens the door to his study.*) What's this? It's dark in here. Ah, yes, of course—excuse me. (*Goes in and lights a couple of candles.*)

NORA (*whispers swiftly, breathlessly*) Well?

MRS. LINDE (*quietly*) I've spoken to him.

NORA Yes?

MRS. LINDE Nora—you must tell your husband everything.

NORA (*dully*) I knew it.

MRS. LINDE You've nothing to fear from Krogstad. But you must tell him.

NORA I shan't tell him anything.

MRS. LINDE Then the letter will.

NORA Thank you, Christine. Now I know what I must do. Ssh!

HELMER (*returns*) Well, Mrs. Linde, finished admiring her?

MRS. LINDE Yes. Now I must say good night.

HELMER Oh, already? Does this knitting belong to you?

MRS. LINDE (*takes it*) Thank you, yes. I nearly forgot it.

HELMER You knit, then?

MRS. LINDE Why, yes.

HELMER Know what? You ought to take up embroidery.

MRS. LINDE Oh? Why?

HELMER It's much prettier. Watch me, now. You hold the embroidery in your left hand, like this, and then you take the needle in your right hand and go in and out in a slow, easy movement—like this. I am right, aren't I?

MRS. LINDE Yes, I'm sure—

HELMER But knitting, now—that's an ugly business—can't help it. Look—arms all huddled up—great clumsy needles going up and down—makes you look like a damned
Chinaman. I say, that really was a magnificent champagne they served us.

MRS. LINDE Well, good night, Nora. And stop being stubborn. Remember!

HELMER Quite right, Mrs. Linde!

MRS. LINDE Good night, Mr. Helmer.

HELMER (*accompanies her to the door*) Good night, good night! I hope you'll manage to
get home all right? I'd gladly—but you haven't far to go, have you? Good night, good
night. (*She goes. He closes the door behind her and returns.*) Well, we've got rid of her
at last. Dreadful bore that woman is!

NORA Aren't you very tired, Torvald?

HELMER No, not in the least.

NORA Aren't you sleepy?

HELMER Not a bit. On the contrary, I feel extraordinarily exhilarated. But what about
you? Yes, you look very sleepy and tired.

NORA Yes, I am very tired. Soon I shall sleep.

HELMER You see, you see! How right I was not to let you stay longer!

NORA Oh, you're always right, whatever you do.

HELMER (*kisses her on the forehead*) Now my little songbird's talking just like a real big
human being. I say, did you notice how cheerful Rank was this evening?

NORA Oh? Was he? I didn't have a chance to speak with him.

HELMER I hardly did. But I haven't seen him in such a jolly mood for ages. (*Looks at
her for a moment, then comes closer.*) I say, it's nice to get back to one's home again,
and be all alone with you. Upon my word, you're a distractingly beautiful young
woman.

NORA Don't look at me like that, Torvald!

HELMER What, not look at my most treasured possession? At all this wonderful beauty
that's mine, mine alone, all mine.

NORA (*goes round to the other side of the table*) You mustn't talk to me like that tonight.

HELMER (*follows her*) You've still the tarantella in your blood, I see. And that makes you
even more desirable. Listen! Now the other guests are beginning to go. (*More quietly.*)
Nora—soon the whole house will be absolutely quiet.

NORA Yes, I hope so.

HELMER Yes, my beloved Nora, of course you do! Do you know—when I'm out with
you among other people like we were tonight, do you know why I say so little to you,
why I keep so aloof from you, and just throw you an occasional glance? Do you know
why I do that? It's because I pretend to myself that you're my secret mistress, my
clandestine little sweetheart, and that nobody knows there's anything at all between
us.

NORA Oh, yes, yes, yes—I know you never think of anything but me.

HELMER And then when we're about to go, and I wrap the shawl round your lovely
young shoulders, over this wonderful curve of your neck—then I pretend to myself
that you are my young bride, that we've just come from the wedding, that I'm taking
you to my house for the first time—that, for the first time, I am alone with you—
quite alone with you, as you stand there young and trembling and beautiful. All
evening I've had no eyes for anyone but you. When I saw you dance the tarantella,
like a huntress, a temptress, my blood grew hot, I couldn't stand it any longer! That
was why I seized you and dragged you down here with me—

NORA Leave me, Torvald! Get away from me! I don't want all this.

HELMER What? Now, Nora, you're joking with me. Don't want, don't want—? Aren't I your husband—?

There is a knock on the front door.

NORA (*starts*) What was that?

HELMER (*goes towards the hall*) Who is it?

RANK (*outside*) It's me. May I come in for a moment?

HELMER (*quietly, annoyed*) Oh, what does he want now? (*Calls.*) Wait a moment. (*Walks over and opens the door.*) Well! Nice of you not to go by without looking in.

RANK I thought I heard your voice, so I felt I had to say goodbye. (*His eyes travel swiftly around the room.*) Ah, yes—these dear rooms, how well I know them. What a happy, peaceful home you two have.

HELMER You seemed to be having a pretty happy time yourself upstairs.

RANK Indeed I did. Why not? Why shouldn't one make the most of this world? As much as one can, and for as long as one can. The wine was excellent—

HELMER Especially the champagne.

RANK You noticed that too? It's almost incredible how much I managed to get down.

NORA Torvald drank a lot of champagne too, this evening.

RANK Oh?

NORA Yes. It always makes him merry afterwards.

RANK Well, why shouldn't a man have a merry evening after a well-spent day?

HELMER Well-spent? Oh, I don't know that I can claim that.

RANK (*slaps him across the back*) I can, though, my dear fellow!

NORA Yes, of course, Dr. Rank—you've been carrying out a scientific experiment today, haven't you?

RANK Exactly.

HELMER Scientific experiment! Those are big words for my little Nora to use!

NORA And may I congratulate you on the finding?

RANK You may indeed.

NORA It was good, then?

RANK The best possible finding—both for the doctor and the patient. Certainty.

NORA (*quickly*) Certainty?

RANK Absolute certainty. So aren't I entitled to have a merry evening after that?

NORA Yes, Dr. Rank. You were quite right to.

HELMER I agree. Provided you don't have to regret it tomorrow.

RANK Well, you never get anything in this life without paying for it.

NORA Dr. Rank—you like masquerades, don't you?

RANK Yes, if the disguises are sufficiently amusing.

NORA Tell me. What shall we two wear at the next masquerade?

HELMER You little gadabout! Are you thinking about the next one already?

RANK We two? Yes, I'll tell you. You must go as the Spirit of Happiness—

HELMER You try to think of a costume that'll convey that.

RANK Your wife need only appear as her normal, everyday self—

HELMER Quite right! Well said! But what are you going to be? Have you decided that?

RANK Yes, my dear friend. I have decided that.

HELMER Well?

RANK At the next masquerade, I shall be invisible.

HELMER Well, that's a funny idea.

RANK There's a big, black hat—haven't you heard of the invisible hat? Once it's over your head, no one can see you any more.

HELMER (*represses a smile*) Ah yes, of course.

RANK But I'm forgetting what I came for. Helmer, give me a cigar. One of your black Havanas.

HELMER With the greatest pleasure. (*Offers him the box.*)

RANK (*takes one and cuts off the tip*) Thank you.

NORA (*strikes a match*) Let me give you a light.

RANK Thank you. (*She holds out the match for him. He lights his cigar.*) And now— goodbye.

HELMER Goodbye, my dear chap, goodbye.

NORA Sleep well, Dr. Rank.

RANK Thank you for that kind wish.

NORA Wish me the same.

RANK You? Very well—since you ask. Sleep well. And thank you for the light. (*He nods to them both and goes.*)

HELMER (*quietly*) He's been drinking too much.

NORA (*abstractedly*) Perhaps.

HELMER *takes his bunch of keys from his pocket and goes out into the hall.*

NORA Torvald, what do you want out there?

HELMER I must empty the letter-box. It's absolutely full. There'll be no room for the newspapers in the morning.

NORA Are you going to work tonight?

HELMER You know very well I'm not. Hullo, what's this? Someone's been at the lock.

NORA At the lock—?

HELMER Yes, I'm sure of it. Who on earth—? Surely not one of the maids? Here's a broken hairpin. Nora, it's yours—

NORA (*quickly*) Then it must have been the children.

HELMER Well, you'll have to break them of that habit. Hm, hm. Ah, that's done it. (*Takes out the contents of the box and calls into the kitchen.*) Helen! Put out the light on the staircase. (*Comes back into the drawing-room with the letters in his hand and closes the door to the hall.*) Look at this! You see how they've piled up? (*Glances through them.*) What on earth's this?

NORA (*at the window*) The letter! Oh, no, Torvald, no!

HELMER Two visiting cards—from Rank.

NORA From Dr. Rank?

HELMER (*looks at them*) Peter Rank, M.D. They were on top. He must have dropped them in as he left.

NORA Has he written anything on them?

HELMER There's a black cross above his name. Look. Rather gruesome, isn't it? It looks just as though he was announcing his death.

NORA He is.

HELMER What? Do you know something? Has he told you anything?

NORA Yes. When these cards come, it means he's said goodbye to us. He wants to shut himself up in his house and die.

HELMER Ah, poor fellow. I knew I wouldn't be seeing him for much longer. But so soon—! And now he's going to slink away and hide like a wounded beast.

NORA When the time comes, it's best to go silently. Don't you think so, Torvald?

HELMER (*walks up and down*) He was so much a part of our life. I can't realize that he's gone. His suffering and loneliness seemed to provide a kind of dark background to the happy sunlight of our marriage. Well, perhaps it's best this way. For him, anyway. (*Stops walking.*) And perhaps for us too, Nora. Now we have only each other. (*Embraces her.*) Oh, my beloved wife—I feel as though I could never hold you close enough. Do you know, Nora, often I wish some terrible danger might threaten you, so that I could offer my life and my blood, everything, for your sake.

NORA (*tears herself loose and says in a clear, firm voice*) Read your letters now, Torvald.

HELMER No, no. Not tonight. Tonight I want to be with you, my darling wife—

NORA When your friend is about to die—?

HELMER You're right. This news has upset us both. An ugliness has come between us; thoughts of death and dissolution. We must try to forget them. Until then—you go to your room; I shall go to mine.

NORA (*throws her arms round his neck*) Good night, Torvald! Good night!

HELMER (*kisses her on the forehead*) Good night, my darling little songbird. Sleep well, Nora. I'll go and read my letters.

He goes into the study with the letters in his hand, and closes the door.

NORA (*wild-eyed, fumbles around, seizes* HELMER's *cloak, throws it round herself and whispers quickly, hoarsely*) Never see him again. Never. Never. Never. (*Throws the shawl over her head.*) Never see the children again. Them too. Never. Never. Oh— the icy black water! Oh—that bottomless—that—! Oh, if only it were all over! Now he's got it—he's reading it. Oh, no, no! Not yet! Goodbye, Torvald! Goodbye, my darlings!

She turns to run into the hall. As she does so, HELMER *throws open his door and stands there with an open letter in his hand.*

HELMER Nora!

NORA (*shrieks*) Ah—!

HELMER What is this? Do you know what is in this letter?

NORA Yes, I know. Let me go! Let me go!

HELMER (*holds her back*) Go? Where?

NORA (*tries to tear herself loose*) You mustn't try to save me, Torvald!

HELMER (*staggers back*) Is it true? Is it true, what he writes? Oh, my God! No, no—it's impossible, it can't be true!

NORA It *is* true. I've loved you more than anything else in the world.

HELMER Oh, don't try to make silly excuses.

NORA (*takes a step towards him*) Torvald—

HELMER Wretched woman! What have you done?

NORA Let me go! You're not going to suffer for my sake. I won't let you!

HELMER Stop being theatrical. (*Locks the front door.*) You're going to stay here and explain yourself. Do you understand what you've done? Answer me! Do you understand?

NORA (*looks unflinchingly at him and, her expression growing colder, says*) Yes. Now I am beginning to understand.

HELMER (*walking round the room*) Oh, what a dreadful awakening! For eight whole years—she who was my joy and my pride—a hypocrite, a liar—worse, worse—a criminal! Oh, the hideousness of it! Shame on you, shame!

NORA *is silent and stares unblinkingly at him.*

HELMER (*stops in front of her*) I ought to have guessed that something of this sort would happen. I should have foreseen it. All your father's recklessness and instability—be quiet!—I repeat, all your father's recklessness and instability he has handed on to you. No religion, no morals, no sense of duty! Oh, how I have been punished for closing my eyes to his faults! I did it for your sake. And now you reward me like this.

NORA Yes. Like this.

HELMER Now you have destroyed all my happiness. You have ruined my whole future. Oh, it's too dreadful to contemplate! I am in the power of a man who is completely without scruples. He can do what he likes with me, demand what he pleases, order me to do anything—I dare not disobey him. I am condemned to humiliation and ruin simply for the weakness of a woman.

NORA When I am gone from this world, you will be free.

HELMER Oh, don't be melodramatic. Your father was always ready with that kind of remark. How would it help me if you were "gone from this world," as you put it? It wouldn't assist me in the slightest. He can still make all the facts public; and if he does, I may quite easily be suspected of having been an accomplice in your crime. People may think that I was behind it—that it was I who encouraged you! And for all this I have to thank you, you whom I have carried on my hands through all the years of our marriage! Now do you realize what you've done to me?

NORA (*coldly calm*) Yes.

HELMER It's so unbelievable I can hardly credit it. But we must try to find some way out. Take off that shawl. Take it off, I say! I must try to buy him off somehow. This thing must be hushed up at any price. As regards our relationship—we must appear to be living together just as before. Only *appear*, of course. You will therefore continue to reside here. That is understood. But the children shall be taken out of your hands. I dare no longer entrust them to you. Oh, to have to say this to the woman I once loved so dearly—and whom I still—! Well, all that must be finished. Henceforth there can be no question of happiness; we must merely strive to save what shreds and tatters— (*The front door bell rings.* HELMER *starts.*) What can that be? At this hour? Surely not—? He wouldn't—? Hide yourself, Nora. Say you're ill.

NORA *does not move.* HELMER *goes to the door of the room and opens it. The* MAID *is standing half-dressed in the hall.*

MAID A letter for madam.

HELMER Give it to me. (*Seizes the letter and shuts the door.*) Yes, it's from him. You're not having it. I'll read this myself.

NORA Read it.

HELMER (*by the lamp*) I hardly dare to. This may mean the end for us both. No I must know. (*Tears open the letter hastily; reads a few lines; looks at a piece of paper which is enclosed with it; utters a cry of joy.*) Nora! (*She looks at him questioningly.*) Nora! No—I must read it once more. Yes, yes, it's true! I am saved! Nora, I am saved!

NORA What about me?

HELMER You too, of course. We're both saved, you and I. Look! He's returning your I.O.U. He writes that he is sorry for what has happened—a happy accident has changed his life—oh, what does it matter what he writes? We are saved, Nora! No one can harm you now. Oh, Nora, Nora—no, first let me destroy this filthy thing. Let me see—! (*Glances at the I.O.U.*) No, I don't want to look at it. I shall merely regard the whole business as a dream. (*He tears the I.O.U. and both letters into pieces, throws them into the stove and watches them burn.*) There. Now they're destroyed. He wrote that ever since Christmas Eve you've been—oh, these must have been three dreadful days for you, Nora.

NORA Yes. It's been a hard fight.

HELMER It must have been terrible—seeing no way out except—no, we'll forget the whole sordid business. We'll just be happy and go on telling ourselves over and over again: "It's over! It's over!" Listen to me, Nora. You don't seem to realize. It's over! Why are you looking so pale? Ah, my poor little Nora, I understand. You can't believe that I have forgiven you. But I have, Nora. I swear it to you. I have forgiven you everything. I know that what you did you did for your love of me.

NORA That is true.

HELMER You have loved me as a wife should love her husband. It was simply that in your inexperience you chose the wrong means. But do you think I love you any the less because you don't know how to act on your own initiative? No, no. Just lean on me. I shall counsel you. I shall guide you. I would not be a true man if your feminine helplessness did not make you doubly attractive in my eyes. You mustn't mind the hard words I said to you in those first dreadful moments when my whole world seemed to be tumbling about my ears. I have forgiven you, Nora. I swear it to you; I have forgiven you.

NORA Thank you for your forgiveness.

She goes out through the door, right.

HELMER No, don't go—(*Looks in.*) What are you doing there?

NORA (*offstage*) Taking off my fancy dress.

HELMER (*by the open door*) Yes, do that. Try to calm yourself and get your balance again, my frightened little songbird. Don't be afraid. I have broad wings to shield you. (*Begins to walk around near the door.*) How lovely and peaceful this little home of ours is, Nora. You are safe here; I shall watch over you like a hunted dove which I have snatched unharmed from the claws of the falcon. Your wildly beating little heart shall find peace with me. It will happen, Nora; it will take time, but it will happen, believe me. Tomorrow all this will seem quite different. Soon everything will be as it was before. I shall no longer need to remind you that I have forgiven you; your own heart will tell you that it is true. Do you really think I could ever bring myself to disown you, or even to reproach you? Ah, Nora, you don't understand what goes on in a husband's heart. There is something indescribably wonderful and satisfying for a husband in knowing that he has forgiven his wife—forgiven her unreservedly, from the bottom of his heart. It means that she has become his property in a double sense; he has, as it were, brought her into the world anew; she is now not only his wife but also his child. From now on that is what you shall be to me, my poor, helpless, bewildered little creature. Never be frightened of anything again, Nora. Just open your heart to me. I shall be both your will and your conscience. What's this? Not in bed? Have you changed?

NORA (*in her everyday dress*) Yes, Torvald. I've changed.

HELMER But why now—so late—?

NORA I shall not sleep tonight.

HELMER But, my dear Nora—

NORA (*looks at her watch*) It isn't that late. Sit down here, Torvald. You and I have a lot to talk about.

She sits down on one side of the table.

HELMER Nora, what does this mean? You look quite drawn—

NORA Sit down. It's going to take a long time. I've a lot to say to you.

HELMER (*sits down on the other side of the table*) You alarm me, Nora. I don't understand you.

NORA No, that's just it. You don't understand me. And I've never understood you— until this evening. No, don't interrupt me. Just listen to what I have to say. You and I have got to face facts, Torvald.

HELMER What do you mean by that?

NORA (*after a short silence*) Doesn't anything strike you about the way we're sitting here?

HELMER What?

NORA We've been married for eight years. Does it occur to you that this is the first time that we two, you and I, man and wife, have ever had a serious talk together?

HELMER Serious? What do you mean, serious?

NORA In eight whole years—no, longer—ever since we first met—we have never exchanged a serious word on a serious subject.

HELMER Did you expect me to drag you into all my worries—worries you couldn't possibly have helped me with?

NORA I'm not talking about worries. I'm simply saying that we have never sat down seriously to try to get to the bottom of anything.

HELMER But, my dear Nora, what on earth has that got to do with you?

NORA That's just the point. You have never understood me. A great wrong has been done to me, Torvald. First by Papa, and then by you.

HELMER What? But we two have loved you more than anyone in the world!

NORA (*shakes her head*) You have never loved me. You just thought it was fun to be in love with me.

HELMER Nora, what kind of a way is this to talk?

NORA It's the truth, Torvald. When I lived with Papa, he used to tell me what he thought about everything, so that I never had any opinions but his. And if I did have any of my own, I kept them quiet, because he wouldn't have liked them. He called me his little doll, and he played with me just the way I played with my dolls. Then I came here to live in your house—

HELMER What kind of a way is that to describe our marriage?

NORA (*undisturbed*) I mean, then I passed from Papa's hands into yours. You arranged everything the way you wanted it, so that I simply took over your taste in everything— or pretended I did—I don't really know—I think it was a little of both—first one and then the other. Now I look back on it, it's as if I've been living here like a pauper, from hand to mouth. I performed tricks for you, and you gave me food and drink. But that was how you wanted it. You and Papa have done me a great wrong. It's your fault that I have done nothing with my life.

HELMER Nora, how can you be so unreasonable and ungrateful? Haven't you been happy here?

NORA No; never. I used to think I was; but I haven't ever been happy.

HELMER Not—not happy?

NORA No. I've just had fun. You've always been very kind to me. But our home has never been anything but a playroom. I've been your doll-wife, just as I used to be Papa's doll-child. And the children have been my dolls. I used to think it was fun when you came in and played with me, just as they think it's fun when I go in and play games with them. That's all our marriage has been, Torvald.

HELMER There may be a little truth in what you say, though you exaggerate and romanticize. But from now on it'll be different. Playtime is over. Now the time has come for education.

NORA Whose education? Mine or the children's?

HELMER Both yours and the children's, my dearest Nora.

NORA Oh, Torvald, you're not the man to educate me into being the right wife for you.

HELMER How can you say that?

NORA And what about me? Am I fit to educate the children?

HELMER Nora!

NORA Didn't you say yourself a few minutes ago that you dare not leave them in my charge?

HELMER In a moment of excitement. Surely you don't think I meant it seriously?

NORA Yes. You were perfectly right. I'm not fitted to educate them. There's something else I must do first. I must educate myself. And you can't help me with that. It's something I must do by myself. That's why I'm leaving you.

HELMER (*jumps up*) What did you say?

NORA I must stand on my own feet if I am to find out the truth about myself and about life. So I can't go on living here with you any longer.

HELMER Nora, Nora!

NORA I'm leaving you now, at once. Christine will put me up for tonight—

HELMER You're out of your mind! You can't do this! I forbid you!

NORA It's no use your trying to forbid me any more. I shall take with me nothing but what is mine. I don't want anything from you, now or ever.

HELMER What kind of madness is this?

NORA Tomorrow I shall go home—I mean, to where I was born. It'll be easiest for me to find some kind of a job there.

HELMER But you're blind! You've no experience of the world—

NORA I must try to get some, Torvald.

HELMER But to leave your home, your husband, your children! Have you thought what people will say?

NORA I can't help that. I only know that I must do this.

HELMER But this is monstrous! Can you neglect your most sacred duties?

NORA What do you call my most sacred duties?

HELMER Do I have to tell you? Your duties towards your husband, and your children.

NORA I have another duty which is equally sacred.

HELMER You have not. What on earth could that be?

NORA My duty towards myself.

HELMER First and foremost you are a wife and a mother.

NORA I don't believe that any longer. I believe that I am first and foremost a human being, like you—or anyway, that I must try to become one. I know most people think as you do, Torvald, and I know there's something of the sort to be found in books. But I'm no longer prepared to accept what people say and what's written in books. I must think things out for myself, and try to find my own answer.

HELMER Do you need to ask where your duty lies in your own home? Haven't you an infallible guide in such matters—your religion?

NORA Oh, Torvald, I don't really know what religion means.

HELMER What are you saying?

NORA I only know what Pastor Hansen told me when I went to confirmation. He explained that religion meant this and that. When I get away from all this and can think things out on my own, that's one of the questions I want to look into. I want to find out whether what Pastor Hansen said was right—or anyway, whether it is right for me.

HELMER But it's unheard of for so young a woman to behave like this! If religion cannot guide you, let me at least appeal to your conscience. I presume you have some moral feelings left? Or—perhaps you haven't? Well, answer me.

NORA Oh, Torvald, that isn't an easy question to answer. I simply don't know. I don't know where I am in these matters. I only know that these things mean something quite different to me from what they do to you. I've learned now that certain laws are different from what I'd imagined them to be; but I can't accept that such laws can be right. Has a woman really not the right to spare her dying father pain, or save her husband's life? I can't believe that.

HELMER You're talking like a child. You don't understand how society works.

NORA No, I don't. But now I intend to learn. I must try to satisfy myself which is right, society or I.

HELMER Nora, you're ill; you're feverish. I almost believe you're out of your mind.

NORA I've never felt so sane and sure in my life.

HELMER You feel sure that it is right to leave your husband and your children?

NORA Yes. I do.

HELMER Then there is only one possible explanation.

NORA What?

HELMER That you don't love me any longer.

NORA No, that's exactly it.

HELMER Nora! How can you say this to me?

NORA Oh, Torvald, it hurts me terribly to have to say it, because you've always been so kind to me. But I can't help it. I don't love you any longer.

HELMER (*controlling his emotions with difficulty*) And you feel quite sure about this too?

NORA Yes, absolutely sure. That's why I can't go on living here any longer.

HELMER Can you also explain why I have lost your love?

NORA Yes, I can. It happened this evening, when the miracle failed to happen. It was then that I realized you weren't the man I'd thought you to be.

HELMER Explain more clearly. I don't understand you.

NORA I've waited so patiently, for eight whole years—well, good heavens, I'm not such a fool as to suppose that miracles occur every day. Then this dreadful thing happened to me, and then I *knew*: "Now the miracle will take place!" When Krogstad's letter was lying out there, it never occurred to me for a moment that you would let that man trample over you. I *knew* that you would say to him: "Publish the facts to the world." And when he had done this—

HELMER Yes, what then? When I'd exposed my wife's name to shame and scandal—

NORA Then I was certain that you would step forward and take all the blame on yourself, and say: "I am the one who is guilty!"

HELMER Nora!

NORA You're thinking I wouldn't have accepted such a sacrifice from you? No, of course I wouldn't! But what would my word have counted for against yours? That was the miracle I was hoping for, and dreading. And it was to prevent it happening that I wanted to end my life.

HELMER Nora, I would gladly work for you night and day, and endure sorrow and hardship for your sake. But no man can be expected to sacrifice his honour, even for the person he loves.

NORA Millions of women have done it.

HELMER Oh, you think and talk like a stupid child.

NORA That may be. But you neither think nor talk like the man I could share my life with. Once you'd got over your fright—and you weren't frightened of what might threaten me, but only of what threatened you—once the danger was past, then as far as you were concerned it was exactly as though nothing had happened. I was your little songbird just as before—your doll whom henceforth you would take particular care to protect from the world because she was so weak and fragile. (*Gets up.*) Torvald, in that moment I realized that for eight years I had been living here with a complete stranger, and had borne him three children—! Oh, I can't bear to think of it! I could tear myself to pieces!

HELMER (*sadly*) I see it, I see it. A gulf has indeed opened between us. Oh, but Nora— couldn't it be bridged?

NORA As I am now, I am no wife for you.

HELMER I have the strength to change.

NORA Perhaps—if your doll is taken from you.

HELMER But to be parted—to be parted from you! No, no, Nora, I can't conceive of it happening!

NORA (*goes into the room, right*) All the more necessary that it should happen.

She comes back with her outdoor things and a small travelling-bag, which she puts down on a chair by the table.

HELMER Nora, Nora, not now! Wait till tomorrow!

NORA (*puts on her coat*) I can't spend the night in a strange man's house.

HELMER But can't we live here as brother and sister, then—?

NORA (*fastens her hat*) You know quite well it wouldn't last. (*Puts on her shawl.*) Goodbye, Torvald. I don't want to see the children. I know they're in better hands than mine. As I am now, I can be nothing to them.

HELMER But some time, Nora—some time—?

NORA How can I tell? I've no idea what will happen to me.

HELMER But you are my wife, both as you are and as you will be.

NORA Listen, Torvald. When a wife leaves her husband's house, as I'm doing now, I'm told that according to the law he is freed of any obligations towards her. In any case, I release you from any such obligations. You mustn't feel bound to me in any way, however small, just as I shall not feel bound to you. We must both be quite free. Here is your ring back. Give me mine.

HELMER That too?

NORA That too.

HELMER Here it is.

NORA Good. Well, now it's over. I'll leave the keys here. The servants know about everything to do with the house—much better than I do. Tomorrow, when I have left town, Christine will come to pack the things I brought here from home. I'll have them sent on after me.

HELMER This is the end then! Nora, will you never think of me any more?

NORA Yes, of course. I shall often think of you and the children and this house.

HELMER May I write to you, Nora?

NORA No. Never. You mustn't do that.

HELMER But at least you must let me send you—

NORA Nothing. Nothing.

HELMER But if you should need help?—

NORA I tell you, no. I don't accept things from strangers.

HELMER Nora—can I never be anything but a stranger to you?

NORA (*picks up her bag*) Oh, Torvald! Then the miracle of miracles would have to happen.

HELMER The miracle of miracles?

NORA You and I would both have to change so much that—oh, Torvald, I don't believe in miracles any longer.

HELMER But I want to believe in them. Tell me. We should have to change so much that—?

NORA That life together between us two could become a marriage. Goodbye.

She goes out through the hall.

HELMER (*sinks down on a chair by the door and buries his face in his hands*) Nora! Nora! (*Looks round and gets up.*) Empty! She's gone! (*A hope strikes him.*) The miracle of miracles—?

The street door is slammed shut downstairs.

Questions

1. What do you think of the way Helmer addresses Nora? How much are his pet names for her an expression of affection, and how much do they express condescension?
2. What is Nora's attitude toward money? Is it realistic? Does her attitude toward money point to a significant flaw in her character?
3. What is the dramatic situation? Describe it in terms of Nora as protagonist, her objective, and obstacles.
4. Nora wants to help Mrs. Linde, and yet in certain ways she is unable to comprehend Mrs. Linde's plight. Cite instances of Nora's naiveté in her first scene with Mrs. Linde.
5. Describe the differences in character between Dr. Rank and Helmer. Why do you suppose Ibsen included Dr. Rank in the story?
6. With the dialogue between Nora and Krogstad at the end of Act I we become aware of the play's problem. What is it? Why did Nora forget the I.O.U.? Would you have done the same?
7. Is Krogstad a villain? Explain his change of heart in Act III. Does it seem realistic?
8. In Act II (p. 1219) Helmer tells Nora "Let what will happen, happen. When the real crisis comes, you will not find me lacking in strength or courage. I am man enough to bear the burden for us both." How do these words contradict his actions in Act III? What does this contradiction tell you about Helmer's character?
9. Discuss the irony of Helmer's response to Krogstad's first letter. Discuss the irony of his response to the second letter.
10. What is the "miracle" Nora was hoping for?
11. The most famous dialogue in *A Doll's House* comes near the end of Act III:

    NORA What do you call my most sacred duties?
    HELMER Do I have to tell you? Your duties towards your husband, and your children.
    NORA I have another duty which is equally sacred.

HELMER You have not. What on earth could that be?
NORA My duty towards myself.

Do you think Nora is right in leaving her husband and children?
12. Discuss the symbolic significance of the play's title.

Realism in America

Before 1900, drama in this country was the least sophisticated of the arts. Melo-dramas, sentimental comedies, and revivals of Shakespeare were about all the commercial theater had to offer. But then young Americans traveling abroad saw the plays of Ibsen, Shaw, and Chekhov. They returned to establish the Little Theater Movement—small theaters, far from the pressures of the commercial stage, where they could experiment with techniques discovered in Europe. This movement, spawning groups like the Washington Square Players and The Provincetown Players, began to attract talented actors, professional producers, and playwrights such as Eugene O'Neill.

At the same time, the popular critic H. L. Mencken was championing the realistic works of Ibsen and Shaw in America. By the early twenties one could see their influence on Eugene O'Neill in his plays *Anna Christie* (1922) and *Desire under the Elms* (1924). O'Neill's psychological dramas benefited most from Ibsen's sensitive portraiture and the "catastrophic" plot. Other playwrights, such as Clifford Odets, followed in Ibsen's footsteps as social realists, as critics of ideas and morals. Realism became the dominant mode of drama in twentieth-century America. The plays of Tennessee Williams are a kind of poetic realism, their characters and situations generally probable, their language occasionally elevated and figurative. With the exception of Willy Loman's scenes from his past, *Death of a Salesman* is highly realistic, as are most of Arthur Miller's plays.

One of the most successful realistic dramas of our time is Lorraine Hansberry's *A Raisin in the Sun*. The first effort of a twenty-nine-year old black playwright, the play opened on Broadway in 1959 and was a spectacular hit. *Raisin* ran for 530 performances. It made a star of Sidney Poitier in the role of Walter Lee Younger, and thrust Lorraine Hansberry into the national spotlight. Not only was she the youngest American ever to win the Drama Critic's Circle Award, she also was the first black woman to have her work produced on Broadway. Hansberry became an advocate of human rights during a decade of racial strife, a role for which she was well prepared.

Born in Chicago in 1930, she was the daughter of Carl Augustus Hansberry, who sued to break the covenants that barred blacks from living in certain neighborhoods. He argued the case before the Supreme Court in 1940 and won. When Lorraine was a child, she received verbal and physical threats as a result of her father's courage. In the early fifties she took a job in New York as a reporter for her friend Paul Robeson's radical magazine *Freedom*. Later, while she was developing her skills as a playwright, she studied history with W. E. B. Du Bois.

Hansberry wrote other plays, including *Les Blancs* and *The Sign in Sidney Brustein's Window,* and continued her political activities into the mid-sixties in spite of fatigue and failing health. Her death from cancer on January 12, 1965, was a tragic loss to the theater in America.

LORRAINE HANSBERRY (1930–1965)

A Raisin in the Sun

To Mama: in gratitude for the dream

CHARACTERS

RUTH YOUNGER	JOSEPH ASAGAI
TRAVIS YOUNGER	GEORGE MURCHISON
WALTER LEE YOUNGER (*Brother*)	KARL LINDNER
BENEATHA YOUNGER	BOBO
LENA YOUNGER (*Mama*)	MOVING MEN

Sidney Poitier and Claudia McNeil in A *Raisin in the Sun (Photograph by Friedman-Abeles from Performing Arts Research Center, The New York Public Library)*

The action of the play is set in Chicago's Southside, sometime between World War II and the present.

ACT I
SCENE I. *Friday morning*
SCENE II. *The following morning*

ACT II
SCENE I. *Later, the same day*
SCENE II. *Friday night, a few weeks later*
SCENE III. *Saturday, moving day, one week later*

ACT III
An hour later

> What happens to a dream deferred?
> Does it dry up
> Like a raisin in the sun?
> Or fester like a sore—
>
> And then run?
> Does it stink like rotten meat?
> Or crust and sugar over—
> Like a syrupy sweet?
>
> Maybe it just sags
> Like a heavy load.
>
> *Or does it explode?*
>
> Langston Hughes[1]

ACT I

SCENE I.

The Younger living room would be a comfortable and well-ordered room if it were not for a number of indestructible contradictions to this state of being. Its furnishings are typical and undistinguished and their primary feature now is that they have clearly had to accommodate the living of too many people for too many years—and they are tired. Still, we can see that at some time, a time probably no longer remembered by the family (except perhaps for MAMA*), the furnishings of this room were actually selected with care and love and even hope—and brought to this apartment and arranged with taste and pride.*

That was a long time ago. Now the once loved pattern of the couch upholstery has to fight to show itself from under acres of crocheted doilies and couch covers which have themselves finally come to be more important than the upholstery. And here a table or a chair has been moved to disguise the worn places in the carpet; but the carpet has fought back by showing its weariness, with depressing uniformity, elsewhere on its surface.

Weariness has, in fact, won in this room. Everything has been polished, washed, sat on, used, scrubbed too often. All pretenses but living itself have long since vanished from the very atmosphere of this room.

---

[1] From "Dream Deferred." Copyright 1951 by Langston Hughes. Reprinted from *The Panther and the Lash* by Langston Hughes, by permission of Alfred A. Knopf, Inc.

Moreover, a section of this room, for it is not really a room unto itself, though the landlord's lease would make it seem so, slopes backward to provide a small kitchen area, where the family prepares the meals that are eaten in the living room proper, which must also serve as dining room. The single window that has been provided for these "two" rooms is located in this kitchen area. The sole natural light the family may enjoy in the course of a day is only that which fights its way through this little window.

At left, a door leads to a bedroom which is shared by MAMA *and her daughter,* BENEATHA. *At right, opposite, is a second room (which in the beginning of the life of this apartment was probably a breakfast room), which serves as a bedroom for* WALTER *and his wife,* RUTH.

Time: Sometime between World War II and the present.

Place: Chicago's Southside.

At rise: It is morning dark in the living room. TRAVIS *is asleep on the make-down bed at center. An alarm clock sounds from within the bedroom at right, and presently* RUTH *enters from that room and closes the door behind her. She crosses sleepily toward the window. As she passes her sleeping son she reaches down and shakes him a little. At the window she raises the shade and a dusky Southside morning light comes in feebly. She fills a pot with water and puts it on to boil. She calls to the boy, between yawns, in a slightly muffled voice.*

RUTH *is about thirty. We can see that she was a pretty girl, even exceptionally so, but now it is apparent that life has been little that she expected, and disappointment has already begun to hang in her face. In a few years, before thirty-five even, she will be known among her people as a "settled woman."*

She crosses to her son and gives him a good, final, rousing shake.

RUTH Come on now, boy, it's seven thirty! (*Her son sits up at last, in a stupor of sleepiness.*) I say hurry up, Travis! You ain't the only person in the world got to use a bathroom! (*The child, a sturdy, handsome little boy of ten or eleven, drags himself out of the bed and almost blindly takes his towels and "today's clothes" from drawers and a closet and goes out to the bathroom, which is in an outside hall and which is shared by another family or families on the same floor.* RUTH *crosses to the bedroom door at right and opens it and calls in to her husband.*) Walter Lee! . . . It's after seven thirty! Lemme see you do some waking up in there now! (*She waits.*) You better get up from there, man! It's after seven thirty I tell you. (*She waits again.*) All right, you just go ahead and lay there and next thing you know Travis be finished and Mr. Johnson'll be in there and you'll be fussing and cussing round here like a mad man! And be late too! (*She waits, at the end of patience.*) Walter Lee—it's time for you to get up!

She waits another second and then starts to go into the bedroom, but is apparently satisfied that her husband has begun to get up. She stops, pulls the door to, and returns to the kitchen area. She wipes her face with a moist cloth and runs her fingers through her sleep-disheveled hair in a vain effort and ties an apron around her housecoat. The bedroom door at right opens and her husband stands in the doorway in his pajamas, which are rumpled and mismated. He is a lean, intense young man in his middle thirties, inclined to quick nervous movements and erratic speech habits—and always in his voice there is a quality of indictment.

WALTER Is he out yet?

RUTH What you mean *out?* He ain't hardly got in there good yet.

WALTER (*wandering in, still more oriented to sleep than to a new day*) Well, what was you doing all that yelling for if I can't even get in there yet? (*Stopping and thinking*) Check coming today?

RUTH They *said* Saturday and this is just Friday and I hopes to God you ain't going to get up here first thing this morning and start talking to me 'bout no money—'cause I 'bout don't want to hear it.

WALTER Something the matter with you this morning?

RUTH No—I'm just sleepy as the devil. What kind of eggs you want?

WALTER Not scrambled. (RUTH *starts to scramble eggs.*) Paper come? (RUTH *points impatiently to the rolled up* Tribune *on the table, and he gets it and spreads it out and vaguely reads the front page.*) Set off another bomb yesterday.

RUTH (*maximum indifference*) Did they?

WALTER (*looking up*) What's the matter with you?

RUTH Ain't nothing the matter with me. And don't keep asking me that this morning.

WALTER Ain't nobody bothering you. (*Reading the news of the day absently again*) Say Colonel McCormick is sick.

RUTH (*affecting tea-party interest*) Is he now? Poor thing.

WALTER (*sighing and looking at his watch*) Oh, me. (*He waits.*) Now what is that boy doing in that bathroom all this time? He just going to have to start getting up earlier. I can't be being late to work on account of him fooling around in there.

RUTH (*turning on him*) Oh, no he ain't going to be getting up no earlier no such thing! It ain't his fault that he can't get to bed no earlier nights 'cause he got a bunch of crazy good-for-nothing clowns sitting up running their mouths in what is supposed to be his bedroom after ten o'clock at night. . . .

WALTER That's what you mad about, ain't it? The things I want to talk about with my friends just couldn't be important in your mind, could they?

He rises and finds a cigarette in her handbag on the table and crosses to the little window and looks out, smoking and deeply enjoying this first one.

RUTH (*almost matter of factly, a complaint too automatic to deserve emphasis*) Why you always got to smoke before you eat in the morning?

WALTER (*at the window*) Just look at 'em down there. . . . Running and racing to work . . . (*He turns and faces his wife and watches her a moment at the stove, and then, suddenly*) You look young this morning, baby.

RUTH (*indifferently*) Yeah?

WALTER Just for a second—stirring them eggs. It's gone now—just for a second it was— you looked real young again. (*Then, drily*) It's gone now—you look like yourself again.

RUTH Man, if you don't shut up and leave me alone.

WALTER (*looking out to the street again*) First thing a man ought to learn in life is not to make love to no colored woman first thing in the morning. You all some evil people at eight o'clock in the morning.

TRAVIS *appears in the hall doorway, almost fully dressed and quite wide awake now, his towels and pajamas across his shoulders. He opens the door and signals for his father to make the bathroom in a hurry.*

TRAVIS (*watching the bathroom*) Daddy, come on!

WALTER *gets his bathroom utensils and flies out to the bathroom.*

RUTH Sit down and have your breakfast, Travis.

TRAVIS Mama, this is Friday. (*Gleefully*) Check coming tomorrow, huh?

RUTH You get your mind off money and eat your breakfast.

TRAVIS (*eating*) This is the morning we supposed to bring the fifty cents to school.

RUTH Well, I ain't got no fifty cents this morning.

TRAVIS Teacher say we have to.

RUTH I don't care what teacher say. I ain't got it. Eat your breakfast, Travis.

TRAVIS I *am* eating.

RUTH Hush up now and just eat!

The boy gives her an exasperated look for her lack of understanding, and eats grudgingly.

TRAVIS You think Grandmama would have it?

RUTH No! And I want you to stop asking your grandmother for money, you hear me?

TRAVIS (*outraged*) Gaaaleee! I don't ask her, she just gimme it sometimes!

RUTH Travis Willard Younger—I got too much on me this morning to be—

TRAVIS Maybe Daddy—

RUTH *Travis!*

The boy hushes abruptly. They are both quiet and tense for several seconds.

TRAVIS (*presently*) Could I maybe go carry some groceries in front of the supermarket for a little while after school then?

RUTH Just hush, I said. (TRAVIS *jabs his spoon into his cereal bowl viciously, and rests his head in anger upon his fists.*) If you through eating, you can get over there and make up your bed.

The boy obeys stiffly and crosses the room, almost mechanically, to the bed and more or less carefully folds the covering. He carries the bedding into his mother's room and returns with his books and cap.

TRAVIS (*sulking and standing apart from her unnaturally*) I'm gone.

RUTH (*looking up from the stove to inspect him automatically*) Come here. (*He crosses to her and she studies his head.*) If you don't take this comb and fix this here head, you better! (TRAVIS *puts down his books with a great sigh of oppression, and crosses to the mirror. His mother mutters under her breath about his "slubbornness."*) 'Bout to march out of here with that head looking just like chickens slept in it! I just don't know where you get your slubborn ways. . . . And get your jacket, too. Looks chilly out this morning.

TRAVIS (*with conspicuously brushed hair and jacket*) I'm gone.

RUTH Get carfare and milk money—(*waving one finger*)—and not a single penny for no caps, you hear me?

TRAVIS (*with sullen politeness*) Yes'm.

He turns in outrage to leave. His mother watches after him as in his frustration he approaches the door almost comically. When she speaks to him, her voice has become a very gentle tease.

RUTH (*mocking; as she thinks he would say it*) Oh, Mama makes me so mad sometimes, I don't know what to do! (*She waits and continues to his back as he stands stock-still in front of the door.*) I wouldn't kiss that woman good-bye for nothing in this world this morning! (*The boy finally turns around and rolls his eyes at her, knowing the mood has changed and he is vindicated; he does not, however, move toward her yet.*) Not for nothing in this world! (*She finally laughs aloud at him and holds out her arms to him and we see that it is a way between them, very old and practiced. He crosses to her and allows her to embrace him warmly but keeps his face fixed with masculine rigidity. She holds him back from her presently and looks at him and runs her fingers over the features of his face. With utter gentleness—*) Now—whose little old angry man are you?

TRAVIS (*the masculinity and gruffness start to fade at last*) Aw gaalee—Mama . . .

RUTH (*mimicking*) Aw—gaaaaalleeeee, Mama! (*She pushes him, with rough playfulness and finality, toward the door.*) Get on out of here or you going to be late.

TRAVIS (*in the face of love, new aggressiveness*) Mama, could I *please* go carry groceries?

RUTH Honey, it's starting to get so cold evenings.

WALTER (*coming in from the bathroom and drawing a make-believe gun from a make-believe holster and shooting at his son*) What is it he wants to do?

RUTH Go carry groceries after school at the supermarket.

WALTER Well, let him go . . .

TRAVIS (*quickly, to the ally*) I *have* to—she won't gimme the fifty cents. . . .

WALTER (*to his wife only*) Why not?

RUTH (*simply, and with flavor*) 'Cause we don't have it.

WALTER (*to RUTH only*) What you tell the boy things like that for? (*Reaching down into his pants with a rather important gesture*) Here, son—

He hands the boy the coin, but his eyes are directed to his wife's. TRAVIS *takes the money happily.*

TRAVIS Thanks, Daddy.

He starts out. RUTH *watches both of them with murder in her eyes.* WALTER *stands and stares back at her with defiance, and suddenly reaches into his pocket again on an afterthought.*

WALTER (*without even looking at his son, still staring hard at his wife*) In fact, here's another fifty cents. . . . Buy yourself some fruit today—or take a taxicab to school or something!

TRAVIS Whoopee—

He leaps up and clasps his father around the middle with his legs, and they face each other in mutual appreciation; slowly WALTER LEE *peeks around the boy to catch the violent rays from his wife's eyes and draws his head back as if shot.*

WALTER You better get down now—and get to school, man.

TRAVIS (*at the door*) O.K. Good-bye. (*He exits.*)

WALTER (*after him, pointing with pride*) That's my boy. (*She looks at him in disgust and turns back to her work.*) You know what I was thinking 'bout in the bathroom this morning?

RUTH No.

WALTER How come you always try to be so pleasant!

RUTH What is there to be pleasant 'bout!

WALTER You want to know what I was thinking 'bout in the bathroom or not!

RUTH I know what you thinking 'bout.

WALTER (*ignoring her*) 'Bout what me and Willy Harris was talking about last night.

RUTH (*immediately—a refrain*) Willy Harris is a good-for-nothing loud mouth.

WALTER Anybody who talks to me has got to be a good-for-nothing loud mouth, ain't he? And what you know about who is just a good-for-nothing loud mouth? Charlie Atkins was just a "good-for-nothing loud mouth" too, wasn't he! When he wanted me to go in the dry-cleaning business with him. And now—he's grossing a hundred thousand a year. A hundred thousand dollars a year! You still call *him* a loud mouth!

RUTH (*bitterly*) Oh, Walter Lee. . . . (*She folds her head on her arms over the table.*)

WALTER (*rising and coming to her and standing over her*) You tired, ain't you? Tired of everything. Me, the boy, the way we live—this beat-up hole—everything. Ain't you? (*She doesn't look up, doesn't answer.*) So tired—moaning and groaning all the time, but you wouldn't do nothing to help, would you? You couldn't be on my side that long for nothing, could you?

RUTH Walter, please leave me alone.

WALTER A man needs for a woman to back him up. . . .

RUTH Walter—

WALTER Mama would listen to you. You know she listen to you more than she do me and Bennie. She think more of you. All you have to do is just sit down with her when you drinking your coffee one morning and talking 'bout things like you do and—(*he sits down beside her and demonstrates graphically what he thinks her methods and tone should be*)—you just sip your coffee, see, and say easy like that you been thinking 'bout that deal Walter Lee is so interested in, 'bout the store and all, and sip some more coffee, like what you saying ain't really that important to you—And the next thing you know, she be listening good and asking you questions and when I come home—I can tell her the details. This ain't no fly-by-night proposition, baby. I mean we figured it out, me and Willy and Bobo.

RUTH (*with a frown*) Bobo?

WALTER Yeah. You see, this little liquor store we got in mind cost seventy-five thousand and we figured the initial investment on the place be 'bout thirty thousand, see. That be ten thousand each. Course, there's a couple of hundred you got to pay so's you don't spend your life just waiting for them clowns to let your license get approved—

RUTH You mean graft?

WALTER (*frowning impatiently*) Don't call it that. See there, that just goes to show you what women understand about the world. Baby, don't *nothing* happen for you in this world 'less you pay *somebody* off!

RUTH Walter, leave me alone! (*She raises her head and stares at him vigorously—then says, more quietly*) Eat your eggs, they gonna be cold.

WALTER (*straightening up from her and looking off*) That's it. There you are. Man say to his woman: I got me a dream. His woman say: Eat your eggs. (*Sadly, but gaining in power*) Man say: I got to take hold of this here world, baby! And a woman will say: Eat your eggs and go to work. (*Passionately now*) Man say: I got to change my life, I'm choking to death, baby! And his woman say—(*in utter anguish as he brings his fists down on his thighs*)—Your eggs is getting cold!

RUTH (*softly*) Walter, that ain't none of our money.

WALTER (*not listening at all or even looking at her*) This morning, I was lookin' in the mirror and thinking about it. . . . I'm thirty-five years old; I been married eleven years and I got a boy who sleeps in the living room—(*very, very quietly*)—and all I got to give him is stories about how rich white people live. . . .

RUTH Eat your eggs, Walter.

WALTER Damn my eggs . . . damn all the eggs that ever was!

RUTH Then go to work.

WALTER (*looking up at her*) See— I'm trying to talk to you 'bout myself—(*shaking his head with the repetition*)—and all you can say is eat them eggs and go to work.

RUTH (*wearily*) Honey, you never say nothing new. I listen to you every day, every night and every morning, and you never say nothing new. (*Shrugging*) So you would rather be Mr. Arnold than be his chauffeur. So—I would *rather* be living in Buckingham Palace.

WALTER That is just what is wrong with the colored woman in this world. . . . Don't understand about building their men up and making 'em feel like they somebody. Like they can do something.

RUTH (*drily, but to hurt*) There *are* colored men who do things.

WALTER No thanks to the colored woman.

RUTH Well, being a colored woman, I guess I can't help myself none.

She rises and gets the ironing board and sets it up and attacks a huge pile of rough-dried clothes, sprinkling them in preparation for the ironing and then rolling them into tight fat balls.

WALTER (*mumbling*) We one group of men tied to a race of women with small minds.

His sister BENEATHA *enters. She is about twenty, as slim and intense as her brother. She is not as pretty as her sister-in-law, but her lean, almost intellectual face has a handsomeness of its own. She wears a bright-red flannel nightie, and her thick hair stands wildly about her head. Her speech is a mixture of many things; it is different from the rest of the family's insofar as education has permeated her sense of English—and perhaps the Midwest rather than the South has finally—at last—won out in her inflection; but not altogether, because over all of it is a soft slurring and transformed use of vowels which is the decided influence of the Southside. She passes through the room without looking at either* RUTH *or* WALTER *and goes to the outside door and looks, a little blindly, out to the bathroom. She sees that it has been lost to the Johnsons. She closes the door with a sleepy vengeance and crosses to the table and sits down a little defeated.*

BENEATHA I am going to start timing those people.

WALTER You should get up earlier.

BENEATHA (*her face in her hands. She is still fighting the urge to go back to bed*) Really— would you suggest dawn? Where's the paper?

WALTER (*pushing the paper across the table to her as he studies her almost clinically, as though he has never seen her before*) You a horrible-looking chick at this hour.

BENEATHA (*drily*) Good morning, everybody.

WALTER (*senselessly*) How is school coming?

BENEATHA (*in the same spirit*) Lovely. Lovely. And you know, biology is the greatest. (*Looking up at him*) I dissected something that looked just like you yesterday.

WALTER I just wondered if you've made up your mind and everything.

BENEATHA (*gaining in sharpness and impatience*) And what did I answer yesterday morning—and the day before that?

RUTH (*from the ironing board, like someone disinterested and old*) Don't be so nasty, Bennie.

BENEATHA (*still to her brother*) And the day before that and the day before that!

WALTER (*defensively*) I'm interested in you. Something wrong with that? Ain't many girls who decide—

WALTER AND BENEATHA (*in unison*) —"to be a doctor."

Silence.

WALTER Have we figured out yet just exactly how much medical school is going to cost?

RUTH Walter Lee, why don't you leave that girl alone and get out of here to work?

BENEATHA (*exits to the bathroom and bangs on the door*) Come on out of there, please! (*She comes back into the room.*)

WALTER (*looking at his sister intently*) You know the check is coming tomorrow.

BENEATHA (*turning on him with a sharpness all her own*) That money belongs to Mama, Walter, and it's for her to decide how she wants to use it. I don't care if she wants to buy a house or a rocket ship or just nail it up somewhere and look at it. It's hers. Not ours—*hers.*

WALTER (*bitterly*) Now ain't that fine! You just got your mother's interest at heart, ain't you, girl? You such a nice girl—but if Mama got that money she can always take a few thousand and help you through school too—can't she?

BENEATHA I have never asked anyone around here to do anything for me!

WALTER No! And the line between asking and just accepting when the time comes is big and wide—ain't it!

BENEATHA (*with fury*) What do you want from me, Brother—that I quit school or just drop dead, which!

WALTER I don't want nothing but for you to stop acting holy 'round here. Me and Ruth done made some sacrifices for you—why can't you do something for the family?

RUTH Walter, don't be dragging me in it.

WALTER You are in it—Don't you get up and go work in somebody's kitchen for the last three years to help put clothes on her back?

RUTH Oh, Walter—that's not fair. . . .

WALTER It ain't that nobody expects you to get on your knees and say thank you, Brother; thank you, Ruth; thank you, Mama—and thank you, Travis, for wearing the same pair of shoes for two semesters—

BENEATHA (*dropping to her knees*) Well—I *do*—all right?—thank everybody . . . and forgive me for ever wanting to be anything at all . . . forgive me, forgive me!

RUTH Please stop it! Your mama'll hear you.

WALTER Who the hell told you you had to be a doctor? If you so crazy 'bout messing 'round with sick people—then go be a nurse like other women—or just get married and be quiet. . . .

BENEATHA Well—you finally got it said. . . . It took you three years but you finally got it said. Walter, give up; leave me alone—it's Mama's money.

WALTER *He was my father, too!*

BENEATHA So what? He was mine, too—and Travis' grandfather—but the insurance money belongs to Mama. Picking on me is not going to make her give it to you to invest in any liquor stores—(*underbreath, dropping into a chair*)—and I for one say, God bless Mama for that!

WALTER (*to* RUTH) See—did you hear? Did you hear!

RUTH Honey, please go to work.

WALTER Nobody in this house is ever going to understand me.

BENEATHA Because you're a nut.

WALTER Who's a nut?

BENEATHA You—you are a nut. Thee is mad, boy.

WALTER (*looking at his wife and his sister from the door, very sadly*) The world's most backward race of people, and that's a fact.

BENEATHA (*turning slowly in her chair*) And then there are all those prophets who would lead us out of the wilderness—(WALTER *slams out of the house.*)—into the swamps!

RUTH Bennie, why you always gotta be pickin' on your brother? Can't you be a little sweeter sometimes? (*Door opens. WALTER walks in.*)

WALTER (*to* RUTH) I need some money for carfare.

RUTH (*looks at him, then warms; teasing, but tenderly*) Fifty cents? (*She goes to her bag and gets money.*) Here, take a taxi.

WALTER *exits.* MAMA *enters. She is a woman in her early sixties, full-bodied and strong. She is one of those women of a certain grace and beauty who wears it so unobtrusively that it takes a while to notice. Her dark-brown face is surrounded by the total whiteness of her hair, and, being a woman who has adjusted to many things in life and overcome many more, her face is full of strength. She has, we can see, wit and faith of a kind that keep her eyes lit and full of interest and expectancy. She is, in a word, a beautiful woman. Her bearing is perhaps most like the noble bearing of the women of the Hereros of Southwest Africa—rather as if she imagines that as she walks she still bears a basket or a vessel upon her head. Her speech, on the other hand, is as careless as her carriage is precise—she is inclined to slur everything—but her voice is perhaps not so much quiet as simply soft.*

MAMA Who that 'round here slamming doors at this hour?

She crosses through the room, goes to the window, opens it, and brings in a feeble little plant growing doggedly in a small pot on the window sill. She feels the dirt and puts it back out.

RUTH That was Walter Lee. He and Bennie was at it again.

MAMA My children and they tempers. Lord, if this little old plant don't get more sun than it's been getting it ain't never going to see spring again. (*She turns from the window.*) What's the matter with you this morning, Ruth? You looks right peaked. You aiming to iron all them things? Leave some for me. I'll get to 'em this afternoon. Bennie honey, it's too drafty for you to be sitting 'round half dressed. Where's your robe?

BENEATHA In the cleaners.

MAMA Well, go get mine and put it on.

BENEATHA I'm not cold, Mama, honest.

MAMA I know—but you so thin. . . .

BENEATHA (*irritably*) Mama, I'm not cold.

MAMA (*seeing the make-down bed as* TRAVIS *has left it*) Lord have mercy, look at that poor bed. Bless his heart—he tries, don't he? (*She moves to the bed* TRAVIS *has sloppily made up.*)

RUTH No—he don't half try at all 'cause he knows you going to come along behind him and fix everything. That's just how come he don't know how to do nothing right now— you done spoiled that boy so.

MAMA Well—he's a little boy. Ain't supposed to know 'bout housekeeping. My baby, that's what he is. What you fix for his breakfast this morning?

RUTH (*angrily*) I feed my son, Lena!

MAMA I ain't meddling—(*underbreath; busy-bodyish*) *I just noticed all last week he had cold cereal, and when it starts getting this chilly in the fall a child ought to have some hot grits or something when he goes out in the cold—*

RUTH (*furious*) I gave him hot oats—is that all right!

MAMA I ain't meddling. (*Pause*) Put a lot of nice butter on it? (RUTH *shoots her an angry look and does not reply.*) He likes lots of butter.

RUTH (*exasperated*) Lena—

MAMA (*to* BENEATHA. MAMA *is inclined to wander conversationally sometimes*) What was you and your brother fussing 'bout this morning?

BENEATHA It's not important, Mama.

She gets up and goes to look out at the bathroom, which is apparently free, and she picks up her towels and rushes out.

MAMA What was they fighting about?

RUTH Now you know as well as I do.

MAMA (*shaking her head*) Brother still worrying his self sick about that money?

RUTH You know he is.

MAMA You had breakfast?

RUTH Some coffee.

MAMA Girl, you better start eating and looking after yourself better. You almost thin as Travis.

RUTH Lena—

MAMA Un-hunh?

RUTH What are you going to do with it?

MAMA Now don't you start, child. It's too early in the morning to be talking about money. It ain't Christian.

RUTH It's just that he got his heart set on that store—

MAMA You mean that liquor store that Willy Harris want him to invest in?

RUTH Yes—

MAMA We ain't no business people, Ruth. We just plain working folks.

RUTH Ain't nobody business people till they go into business. Walter Lee say colored people ain't never going to start getting ahead till they start gambling on some different kinds of things in the world—investments and things.

MAMA What done got into you, girl? Walter Lee done finally sold you on investing.

RUTH No. Mama, something is happening between Walter and me. I don't know what it is—but he needs something—something I can't give him any more. He needs this chance, Lena.

MAMA (*frowning deeply*) But liquor, honey—

RUTH Well—like Walter say—I spec people going to always be drinking themselves some liquor.

MAMA Well—whether they drinks it or not ain't none of my business. But whether I go into business selling it to 'em *is*, and I don't want that on my ledger this late in life. (*Stopping suddenly and studying her daughter-in-law*) Ruth Younger, what's the matter with you today? You look like you could fall over right there.

RUTH I'm tired.

MAMA Then you better stay home from work today.

RUTH I can't stay home. She'd be calling up the agency and screaming at them, "My girl didn't come in today—send me somebody! My girl didn't come in!" Oh, she just have a fit. . . .

MAMA Well, let her have it. I'll just call her up and say you got the flu—

RUTH (*laughing*) Why the flu?

MAMA 'Cause it sounds respectable to 'em. Something white people get, too. They know 'bout the flu. Otherwise they think you been cut up or something when you tell 'em you sick.

RUTH I got to go in. We need the money.

MAMA Somebody would of thought my children done all but starved to death the way they talk about money here late. Child, we got a great big old check coming tomorrow.

RUTH (*sincerely, but also self-righteously*) Now that's your money. It ain't got nothing to do with me. We all feel like that—Walter and Bennie and me—even Travis.

MAMA (*thoughtfully, and suddenly very far away*) Ten thousand dollars—

RUTH Sure is wonderful.

MAMA Ten thousand dollars.

RUTH You know what you should do, Miss Lena? You should take yourself a trip somewhere. To Europe or South America or someplace—

MAMA (*throwing up her hands at the thought*) Oh, child!

RUTH I'm serious. Just pack up and leave! Go on away and enjoy yourself some. Forget about the family and have yourself a ball for once in your life—

MAMA (*drily*) You sound like I'm just about ready to die. Who'd go with me? What I look like wandering 'round Europe by myself?

RUTH Shoot—these here rich white women do it all the time. They don't think nothing of packing up they suitcases and piling on one of them big steamships and—swoosh!— they gone, child.

MAMA Something always told me I wasn't no rich white woman.

RUTH Well—what are you going to do with it then?

MAMA I ain't rightly decided. (*Thinking. She speaks now with emphasis.*) Some of it got to be put away for Beneatha and her schoolin'—and ain't nothing going to touch that part of it. Nothing. (*She waits several seconds, trying to make up her mind about something, and looks at* RUTH *a little tentatively before going on.*) Been thinking that we maybe could meet the notes on a little old two-story somewhere, with a yard where Travis could play in the summertime, if we use part of the insurance for a down payment and everybody kind of pitch in. I could maybe take on a little day work again, few days a week—

RUTH (*studying her mother-in-law furtively and concentrating on her ironing, anxious to encourage without seeming to*) Well, Lord knows, we've put enough rent into this here rat trap to pay for four houses by now. . . .

MAMA (*looking up at the words "rat trap" and then looking around and leaning back and sighing—in a suddenly reflective mood—*) "Rat trap"—yes, that's all it is. (*Smiling*) I remember just as well the day me and Big Walter moved in here. Hadn't been married but two weeks and wasn't planning on living here no more than a year. (*She shakes her head at the dissolved dream.*) We was going to set away, little by little, don't you know, and buy a little place out in Morgan Park. We had even picked out the house. (*Chuckling a little*) Looks right dumpy today. But Lord, child, you should know all the dreams I had 'bout buying that house and fixing it up and making me a little garden in the back— (*She waits and stops smiling.*) And didn't none of it happen. (*Dropping her hands in a futile gesture*)

RUTH (*keeps her head down, ironing*) Yes, life can be a barrel of disappointments, sometimes.

MAMA Honey, Big Walter would come in here some nights back then and slump down on that couch there and just look at the rug, and look at me and look at the rug and then back at me—and I'd know he was down then . . . really down. (*After a second very long and thoughtful pause; she is seeing back to times that only she can see.*) And then, Lord, when I lost that baby—little Claude—I almost thought I was going to lose Big Walter too. Oh, that man grieved hisself! He was one man to love his children.

RUTH Ain't nothin' can tear at you like losin' your baby.

MAMA I guess that's how come that man finally worked hisself to death like he done. Like he was fighting his own war with this here world that took his baby from him.

RUTH He sure was a fine man, all right. I always liked Mr. Younger.

MAMA Crazy 'bout his children! God knows there was plenty wrong with Walter Younger— hard-headed, mean, kind of wild with women—plenty wrong with him. But he sure loved his children. Always wanted them to have something—be something. That's where Brother gets all these notions, I reckon. Big Walter used to say, he'd get right wet in the eyes sometimes, lean his head back with the water standing in his eyes and say, "Seem like God didn't see fit to give the black man nothing but dreams—but He did give us children to make them dreams seem worth while." (*She smiles.*) He could talk like that, don't you know.

RUTH Yes, he sure could. He was a good man, Mr. Younger.

MAMA Yes, a fine man—just couldn't never catch up with his dreams, that's all.

BENEATHA *comes in, brushing her hair and looking up to the ceiling, where the sound of a vacuum cleaner has started up.*

BENEATHA What could be so dirty on that woman's rugs that she has to vacuum them every single day?

RUTH I wish certain young women 'round here who I could name would take inspiration about certain rugs in a certain apartment I could also mention.

BENEATHA (*shrugging*) How much cleaning can a house need, for Christ's sakes.

MAMA (*not liking the Lord's name used thus*) Bennie!

RUTH Just listen to her—just listen!

BENEATHA Oh, God!

MAMA If you use the Lord's name just one more time—

BENEATHA (*a bit of a whine*) Oh, Mama—

RUTH Fresh—just fresh as salt, this girl!

BENEATHA (*drily*) Well—if the salt loses its savor—

MAMA Now that will do. I just ain't going to have you 'round here reciting the scriptures in vain—you hear me?

BENEATHA How did I manage to get on everybody's wrong side by just walking into a room?

RUTH If you weren't so fresh—

BENEATHA Ruth, I'm twenty years old.

MAMA What time you be home from school today?

BENEATHA Kind of late. (*With enthusiasm*) Madeline is going to start my guitar lessons today.

MAMA *and* RUTH *look up with the same expression.*

MAMA Your *what* kind of lessons?

BENEATHA Guitar.

RUTH Oh, Father!

MAMA How come you done taken it in your mind to learn to play the guitar?

BENEATHA I just want to, that's all.

MAMA (*smiling*) Lord, child, don't you know what to do with yourself? How long it going to be before you get tired of this now—like you got tired of that little play-acting group you joined last year? (*Looking at* RUTH) And what was it the year before that?

RUTH The horseback-riding club for which she bought that fifty-five-dollar riding habit that's been hanging in the closet ever since!

MAMA (*to* BENEATHA) Why you got to flit so from one thing to another, baby?

BENEATHA (*sharply*) I just want to learn to play the guitar. Is there anything wrong with that?

MAMA Ain't nobody trying to stop you. I just wonders sometimes why you has to flit so from one thing to another all the time. You ain't never done nothing with all that camera equipment you brought home—

BENEATHA I don't flit! I—I experiment with different forms of expression—

RUTH Like riding a horse?

BENEATHA —People have to express themselves one way or another.

MAMA What is it you want to express?

BENEATHA (*angrily*) Me! (MAMA *and* RUTH *look at each other and burst into raucous laughter*.) Don't worry—I don't expect you to understand.

MAMA (*to change the subject*) Who you going out with tomorrow night?

BENEATHA (*with displeasure*) George Murchison again.

MAMA (*pleased*) Oh—you getting a little sweet on him?

RUTH You ask me, this child ain't sweet on nobody but herself— (*Underbreath*) Express herself!

They laugh.

BENEATHA Oh—I like George all right, Mama. I mean I like him enough to go out with him and stuff, but—

RUTH (*for devilment*) What does *and stuff* mean?

BENEATHA Mind your own business.

MAMA Stop picking at her now, Ruth. (A *thoughtful pause, and then a suspicious sudden look at her daughter as she turns in her chair for emphasis*) What *does* it mean?

BENEATHA (*wearily*) Oh, I just mean I couldn't ever really be serious about George. He's—he's so shallow.

RUTH Shallow—what do you mean he's shallow? He's *rich!*

MAMA Hush, Ruth.

BENEATHA I know he's rich. He knows he's rich, too.

RUTH Well—what other qualities a man got to have to satisfy you, little girl?

BENEATHA You wouldn't even begin to understand. Anybody who married Walter could not possibly understand.

MAMA (*outraged*) What kind of way is that to talk about your brother?

BENEATHA Brother is a flip—let's face it.

MAMA (*to* RUTH, *helplessly*) What's a flip?

RUTH (*glad to add kindling*) She's saying he's crazy.

BENEATHA Not crazy. Brother isn't really crazy yet—he—he's an elaborate neurotic.

MAMA Hush your mouth!

BENEATHA As for George. Well. George looks good—he's got a beautiful car and he takes me to nice places and, as my sister-in-law says, he is probably the richest boy I will ever get to know and I even like him sometimes—but if the Youngers are sitting around waiting to see if their little Bennie is going to tie up the family with the Murchisons, they are wasting their time.

RUTH You mean you wouldn't marry George Murchison if he asked you someday? That pretty, rich thing? Honey, I knew you was odd—

BENEATHA No I would not marry him if all I felt for him was what I feel now. Besides, George's family wouldn't really like it.

MAMA Why not?

BENEATHA Oh, Mama—The Murchisons are honest-to-God-real-*live*-rich colored people, and the only people in the world who are more snobbish than rich white people are rich colored people. I thought everybody knew that. I've met Mrs. Murchison. She's a scene!

MAMA You must not dislike people 'cause they well off, honey.

BENEATHA Why not? It makes just as much sense as disliking people 'cause they are poor, and lots of people do that.

RUTH (*a wisdom-of-the-ages manner. To* MAMA) Well, she'll get over some of this—

BENEATHA Get over it? What are you talking about, Ruth? Listen, I'm going to be a doctor. I'm not worried about who I'm going to marry yet—if I ever get married.

MAMA AND RUTH *If!*

MAMA Now, Bennie—

BENEATHA Oh, I probably will . . . but first I'm going to be a doctor, and George, for one, still thinks that's pretty funny. I couldn't be bothered with that, I am going to be a doctor and everybody around here better understand that!

MAMA (*kindly*) 'Course you going to be a doctor, honey, God willing.

BENEATHA (*drily*) God hasn't got a thing to do with it.

MAMA Beneatha—that just wasn't necessary.

BENEATHA Well—neither is God. I get sick of hearing about God.

MAMA Beneatha!

BENEATHA I mean it! I'm just tired of hearing about God all the time. What has He got to do with anything? Does He pay tuition?

MAMA You 'bout to get your fresh little jaw slapped!

RUTH That's just what she needs, all right!

BENEATHA Why? Why can't I say what I want to around here, like everybody else?

MAMA It don't sound nice for a young girl to say things like that—you wasn't brought up that way. Me and your father went to trouble to get you and Brother to church every Sunday.

BENEATHA Mama, you don't understand. It's all a matter of ideas, and God is just one idea I don't accept. It's not important, I am not going out and be immoral or commit crimes because I don't believe in God. I don't even think about it. It's just that I get tired of Him getting credit for all the things the human race achieves through its own stubborn effort. There simply is no blasted God—there is only man and it is he who makes miracles!

MAMA *absorbs this speech, studies her daughter and rises slowly and crosses to* BENEATHA *and slaps her powerfully across the face. After, there is only silence and the daughter drops her eyes from her mother's face, and* MAMA *is very tall before her.*

MAMA Now—you say after me, in my mother's house there is still God. (*There is a long pause and* BENEATHA *stares at the floor wordlessly.* MAMA *repeats the phrase with precision and cool emotion.*) In my mother's house there is still God.

BENEATHA In my mother's house there is still God.

A long pause.

MAMA (*walking away from* BENEATHA, *too disturbed for triumphant posture. Stopping and turning back to her daughter*) There are some ideas we ain't going to have in this house. Not long as I am at the head of this family.

BENEATHA Yes, ma'am.

MAMA *walks out of the room.*

RUTH (*almost gently, with profound understanding*) You think you a woman, Bennie—but you still a little girl. What you did was childish—so you got treated like a child.

BENEATHA I see. (*Quietly*) I also see that everybody thinks it's all right for Mama to be a tyrant. But all the tyranny in the world will never put a God in the heavens! (*She picks up her books and goes out.*)

RUTH (*goes to* MAMA's *door*) She said she was sorry.

MAMA (*coming out, going to her plant*) They frightens me, Ruth. My children.

RUTH You got good children, Lena. They just a little off sometimes—but they're good.

MAMA No—there's something come down between me and them that don't let us understand each other and I don't know what it is. One done almost lost his mind thinking 'bout money all the time and the other done commence to talk about things I can't seem to understand in no form or fashion. What is it that's changing, Ruth?

RUTH (*soothingly, older than her years*) Now . . . you taking it all too seriously. You just got strong-willed children and it takes a strong woman like you to keep 'em in hand.

MAMA (*looking at her plant and sprinkling a little water on it*) They spirited all right, my children. Got to admit they got spirit—Bennie and Walter. Like this little old plant that ain't never had enough sunshine or nothing—and look at it. . . .

She has her back to RUTH, *who has had to stop ironing and lean against something and put the back of her hand to her forehead.*

RUTH (*trying to keep* MAMA *from noticing*) You . . . sure . . . loves that little old thing, don't you? . . .

MAMA Well, I always wanted me a garden like I used to see sometimes at the back of the houses down home. This plant is close as I ever got to having one. (*She looks out of the window as she replaces the plant.*) Lord, ain't nothing as dreary as the view from this window on a dreary day, is there? Why ain't you singing this morning, Ruth? Sing that "No Ways Tired." That song always lifts me up so—(*She turns at last to see that* RUTH *has slipped quietly into a chair, in a state of semiconsciousness.*) Ruth! Ruth honey—what's the matter with you . . . Ruth!

Curtain

SCENE II.

It is the following morning; a Saturday morning, and house cleaning is in progress at the Youngers. Furniture has been shoved hither and yon and MAMA *is giving the kitchen-area walls a washing down.* BENEATHA, *in dungarees, with a handkerchief tied around her face, is spraying insecticide into the cracks in the walls. As they work, the radio is on and a Southside disc-jockey program is inappropriately filling the house with a rather exotic saxophone blues.* TRAVIS, *the sole idle one, is leaning on his arms, looking out of the window.*

TRAVIS Grandmama, that stuff Bennie is using smells awful. Can I go downstairs, please?

MAMA Did you get all them chores done already? I ain't see you doing much.

TRAVIS Yes'm—finished early. Where did mama go this morning?

MAMA (*looking at* BENEATHA) She had to go on a little errand.

TRAVIS Where?

MAMA To tend to her business.

TRAVIS Can I go outside then?

MAMA Oh, I guess so. You better stay right in front of the house, though . . . and keep a good lookout for the postman.

TRAVIS Yes'm. (*He starts out and decides to give his* AUNT BENEATHA *a good swat on the legs as he passes her.*) Leave them poor little old cockroaches alone, they ain't bothering you none.

He runs as she swings the spray gun at him both viciously and playfully. WALTER *enters from the bedroom and goes to the phone.*

MAMA Look out there, girl, before you be spilling some of that stuff on that child!

TRAVIS (*teasing*) That's right—look out now! (*He exits.*)

BENEATHA (*drily*) I can't imagine that it would hurt him—it has never hurt the roaches.

MAMA Well, little boys' hides ain't as tough as Southside roaches.

WALTER (*into phone*) Hello—Let me talk to Willy Harris.

MAMA You better get over there behind the bureau. I seen one marching out of there like Napoleon yesterday.

WALTER Hello. Willy? It ain't come yet. It'll be here in a few minutes. Did the lawyer give you the papers?

BENEATHA There's really only one way to get rid of them, Mama—

MAMA How?

BENEATHA Set fire to this building.

WALTER Good. Good. I'll be right over.

BENEATHA Where did Ruth go, Walter?

WALTER I don't know. (*He exits abruptly.*)

BENEATHA Mama, where did Ruth go?

MAMA (*looking at her with meaning*) To the doctor, I think.

BENEATHA The doctor? What's the matter? (*They exchange glances.*) You don't think—

MAMA (*with her sense of drama*) Now I ain't saying what I think. But I ain't never been wrong 'bout a woman neither.

The phone rings.

BENEATHA (*at the phone*) Hay-lo . . . (*Pause, and a moment of recognition*) Well—when did you get back! . . . And how was it? . . . Of course I've missed you—in my way. . . . This morning? No . . . house cleaning and all that and Mama hates it if I let people come over when the house is like this. . . . You *have?* Well, that's different. . . . What is it—Oh, what the hell, come on over. . . . Right, see you then. (*She hangs up.*)

MAMA (*who has listened vigorously, as is her habit*) Who is that you inviting over here with this house looking like this? You ain't got the pride you was born with!

BENEATHA Asagai doesn't care how houses look, Mama—he's an intellectual.

MAMA *Who?*

BENEATHA Asagai—Joseph Asagai. He's an African boy I met on campus. He's been studying in Canada all summer.

MAMA What's his name?

BENEATHA Asagai, Joseph. Ah-sah-guy . . . He's from Nigeria.

MAMA Oh, that's the little country that was founded by slaves way back. . . .

BENEATHA No, Mama—that's Liberia.

MAMA I don't think I never met no African before.

BENEATHA Well, do me a favor and don't ask him a whole lot of ignorant questions about Africans. I mean, do they wear clothes and all that—

MAMA Well, now, I guess if you think we so ignorant 'round here maybe you shouldn't bring your friends here—

BENEATHA It's just that people ask such crazy things. All anyone seems to know about when it comes to Africa is Tarzan—

MAMA (*indignantly*) Why should I know anything about Africa?

BENEATHA Why do you give money at church for the missionary work?

MAMA Well, that's to help save people.

BENEATHA You mean to save them from *heathenism*—

MAMA (*innocently*) Yes.

BENEATHA I'm afraid they need more salvation from the British and the French.

RUTH *comes in forlornly and pulls off her coat with dejection. They both turn to look at her.*

RUTH (*dispiritedly*) Well, I guess from all the happy faces—everybody knows.

BENEATHA You pregnant?

MAMA Lord have mercy, I sure hope it's a little old girl. Travis ought to have a sister.

BENEATHA *and* RUTH *give her a hopeless look for this grandmotherly enthusiasm.*

BENEATHA How far along are you?

RUTH Two months.

BENEATHA Did you mean to? I mean did you plan it or was it an accident?

MAMA What do you know about planning or not planning?

BENEATHA Oh, Mama.

RUTH (*wearily*) She's twenty years old, Lena.

BENEATHA Did you plan it, Ruth?

RUTH Mind your own business.

BENEATHA It is my business—where is he going to live, on the *roof*? (*There is silence following the remark as the three women react to the sense of it.*) Gee—I didn't mean that, Ruth, honest. Gee, I don't feel like that at all. I—I think it is wonderful.

RUTH (*dully*) Wonderful.

BENEATHA Yes—really.

MAMA (*looking at* RUTH, *worried*) Doctor say everything going to be all right?

RUTH (*far away*) Yes—she says everything is going to be fine. . . .

MAMA (*immediately suspicious*) "She"—What doctor you went to?

RUTH *folds over, near hysteria.*

MAMA (*worriedly hovering over* RUTH) Ruth honey—what's the matter with you—you sick?

RUTH *has her fists clenched on her thighs and is fighting hard to suppress a scream that seems to be rising in her.*

BENEATHA What's the matter with her, Mama?

MAMA (*working her fingers in* RUTH's *shoulder to relax her*) She be all right. Women gets right depressed sometimes when they get her way. (*Speaking softly, expertly, rapidly*) Now you just relax. That's right . . . just lean back, don't think 'bout nothing at all . . . nothing at all—

RUTH I'm all right. . . .

The glassy-eyed look melts and then she collapses into a fit of heavy sobbing. The bell rings.

BENEATHA Oh, my God—that must be Asagai.

MAMA (to RUTH) Come on now, honey. You need to lie down and rest awhile . . . then have some nice hot food.

They exit, RUTH's weight on her mother-in-law. BENEATHA, herself profoundly disturbed, opens the door to admit a rather dramatic-looking young man with a large package.

ASAGAI *Hello, Alaiyo*—

BENEATHA (*holding the door open and regarding him with pleasure*) Hello . . . (*Long pause*) Well—come in. And please excuse everything. My mother was very upset about my letting anyone come here with the place like this.

ASAGAI (*coming into the room*) You look disturbed too. . . . Is something wrong?

BENEATHA (*still at the door, absently*) Yes . . . we've all got acute ghetto-itus. (*She smiles and comes toward him, finding a cigarette and sitting.*) So—sit down! How was Canada?

ASAGAI (*a sophisticate*) Canadian.

BENEATHA (*looking at him*) I'm very glad you are back.

ASAGAI (*looking back at her in turn*) Are you really?

BENEATHA Yes—very.

ASAGAI Why—you were quite glad when I went away. What happened?

BENEATHA You went away.

ASAGAI Ahhhhhhhhh.

BENEATHA Before—you wanted to be so serious before there was time.

ASAGAI How much time must there be before one knows what one feels?

BENEATHA (*stalling this particular conversation. Her hands pressed together, in a deliberately childish gesture*) What did you bring me?

ASAGAI (*handing her the package*) Open it and see.

BENEATHA (*eagerly opening the package and drawing out some records and the colorful robes of a Nigerian woman*) Oh, Asagai! . . . You got them for me! . . . How beautiful . . . and the records too! (*She lifts out the robes and runs to the mirror with them and holds the drapery up in front of herself.*)

ASAGAI (*coming to her at the mirror*) I shall have to teach you how to drape it properly. (*He flings the material about her for the moment and stands back to look at her.*) Ah— Oh-pay-gay-day, oh-gbah-mu-shay. (*A Yoruba exclamation for admiration*) You wear it well . . . very well . . . mutilated hair and all.

BENEATHA (*turning suddenly*) My hair—what's wrong with my hair?

ASAGAI (*shrugging*) Were you born with it like that?

BENEATHA (*reaching up to touch it*) No . . . of course not. (*She looks back to the mirror, disturbed.*)

ASAGAI (*smiling*) How then?

BENEATHA You know perfectly well how . . . as crinkly as yours . . . that's how.

ASAGAI And it is ugly to you that way?

BENEATHA (*quickly*) Oh, no—not ugly . . . (*More slowly, apologetically*) But it's so hard to manage when it's, well—raw.

ASAGAI And so to accommodate that—you mutilate it every week?

BENEATHA It's not mutilation!

ASAGAI (*laughing aloud at her seriousness*) Oh . . . please! I am only teasing you because you are so very serious about these things. (*He stands back from her and folds his arms across his chest as he watches her pulling at her hair and frowning in the mirror.*) Do you remember the first time you met me at school? . . . (*He laughs.*) You came up to me and you said—and I thought you were the most serious little thing I had ever seen—you said: (*He imitates her.*) "Mr. Asagai—I want very much to talk with you. About Africa. You see, Mr. Asagai, I am looking for my *identity!*" (*He laughs.*)

BENEATHA (*turning to him, not laughing*) Yes—(*Her face is quizzical, profoundly disturbed.*)

ASAGAI (*still teasing and reaching out and taking her face in his hands and turning her profile to him*) Well . . . it is true that this is not so much a profile of a Hollywood queen as perhaps a queen of the Nile—(*A mock dismissal of the importance of the question*) But what does it matter? Assimilationism is so popular in your country.

BENEATHA (*wheeling, passionately, sharply*) I am not an assimilationist!

ASAGAI (*the protest hangs in the room for a moment and* ASAGAI *studies her, his laughter fading*) Such a serious one. (*There is a pause.*) So—you like the robes? You must take excellent care of them—they are from my sister's personal wardrobe.

BENEATHA (*with incredulity*) You—you sent all the way home—for me?

ASAGAI (*with charm*) For you—I would do much more. . . . Well, that is what I came for. I must go.

BENEATHA Will you call me Monday?

ASAGAI Yes . . . We have a great deal to talk about. I mean about identity and time and all that.

BENEATHA Time?

ASAGAI Yes. About how much time one needs to know what one feels.

BENEATHA You never understood that there is more than one kind of feeling which can exist between a man and a woman—or, at least, there should be.

ASAGAI (*shaking his head negatively but gently*) No. Between a man and a woman there need be only one kind of feeling. I have that for you. . . . Now even . . . right this moment. . . .

BENEATHA I know—and by itself—it won't do. I can find that anywhere.

ASAGAI For a woman it should be enough.

BENEATHA I know—because that's what it says in all the novels that men write. But it isn't. Go ahead and laugh—but I'm not interested in being someone's little episode in America or—(*with feminine vengeance*)—one of them! (ASAGAI *has burst into laughter again.*) That's funny as hell, huh!

ASAGAI It's just that every American girl I have known has said that to me. White— black—in this you are all the same. And the same speech, too!

BENEATHA (*angrily*) Yuk, yuk, yuk!

ASAGAI It's how you can be sure that the world's most liberated women are not liberated at all. You all talk about it too much!

MAMA *enters and is immediately all social charm because of the presence of a guest.*

BENEATHA Oh—Mama—this is Mr. Asagai.

MAMA How do you do?

ASAGAI (*total politeness to an elder*) How do you do, Mrs. Younger. Please forgive me for coming at such an outrageous hour on a Saturday.

MAMA Well, you are quite welcome. I just hope you understand that our house don't always look like this. (*Chatterish*) You must come again. I would love to hear all about—(*not sure of the name*)—your country. I think it's so sad the way our American Negroes don't know nothing about Africa 'cept Tarzan and all that. And all that money they pour into these churches when they ought to be helping you people over there drive out them French and Englishmen done taken away your land.

The mother flashes a slightly superior look at her daughter upon completion of the recitation.

ASAGAI (*taken aback by this sudden and acutely unrelated expression of sympathy*) Yes
. . . yes. . . .

MAMA (*smiling at him suddenly and relaxing and looking him over*) How many miles is
it from here to where you come from?

ASAGAI Many thousands.

MAMA (*looking at him as she would* WALTER) I bet you don't half look after yourself,
being away from your mama either. I spec you better come 'round here from time to
time and get yourself some decent home-cooked meals. . . .

ASAGAI (*moved*) Thank you. Thank you very much. (*They are all quiet, then—*) Well
. . . I must go. I will call you Monday, Alaiyo.

MAMA What's that he call you?

ASAGAI Oh—"Alaiyo." I hope you don't mind. Is it what you would call a nickname,
I think. It is a Yoruba word. I am a Yoruba.

MAMA (*looking at* BENEATHA) I—I thought he was from—

ASAGAI (*understanding*) Nigeria is my country. Yoruba is my tribal origin—

BENEATHA You didn't tell us what Alaiyo means . . . for all I know, you might be calling
me Little Idiot or something. . . .

ASAGAI Well . . . let me see . . . I do not know how just to explain it. . . . The sense
of a thing can be so different when it changes languages.

BENEATHA You're evading.

ASAGAI No—really it is difficult. . . . (*Thinking*) It means . . . it means One for Whom
Bread—Food—Is Not Enough. (*He looks at her.*) Is that all right?

BENEATHA (*understanding, softly*) Thank you.

MAMA (*looking from one to the other and not understanding any of it*) Well . . . that's
nice. . . . You must come see us again—Mr.—

ASAGAI Ah-sah-guy . . .

MAMA Yes . . . Do come again.

ASAGAI Good-bye. (*He exits.*)

MAMA (*after him*) Lord, that's a pretty thing just went out here! (*Insinuatingly, to her
daughter*) Yes, I guess I see why we done commence to get so interested in Africa
'round here. Missionaries my aunt Jenny! (*She exits.*)

BENEATHA Oh, Mama! . . .

*She picks up the Nigerian dress and holds it up to her in front of the mirror again. She
sets the headdress on haphazardly and then notices her hair again and clutches at it and
then replaces the headdress and frowns at herself. Then she starts to wriggle in front of
the mirror as she thinks a Nigerian woman might.* TRAVIS *enters and regards her.*

TRAVIS You cracking up?

BENEATHA Shut up.

*She pulls the headdress off and looks at herself in the mirror and clutches at her hair
again and squinches her eyes as if trying to imagine something. Then, suddenly, she gets
her raincoat and kerchief and hurriedly prepares for going out.*

MAMA (*coming back into the room*) She's resting now. Travis, baby, run next door and
ask Miss Johnson to please let me have a little kitchen cleanser. This here can is empty
as Jacob's kettle.

TRAVIS I just come in.

MAMA Do as you told. (*He exits and she looks at her daughter.*) Where you going?

BENEATHA (*halting at the door*) To become a queen of the Nile!

She exits in a breathless blaze of glory. RUTH *appears in the bedroom doorway.*

MAMA Who told you to get up?

RUTH Ain't nothing wrong with me to be lying in no bed for. Where did Bennie go?

MAMA (*drumming her fingers*) Far as I could make out—to Egypt. (RUTH *just looks at her.*) What time is it getting to?

RUTH Ten twenty. And the mailman going to ring that bell this morning just like he done every morning for the last umpteen years.

TRAVIS *comes in with the cleanser can.*

TRAVIS She say to tell you that she don't have much.

MAMA (*angrily*) Lord, some people I could name sure is tight-fisted! (*Directing her grandson*) Mark two cans of cleanser down on the list there. If she that hard up for kitchen cleanser, I sure don't want to forget to get her none!

RUTH Lena—maybe the woman is just short on cleanser—

MAMA (*not listening*) —Much baking powder as she done borrowed from me all these years, she could of done gone into the baking business!

The bell sounds suddenly and sharply and all three are stunned—serious and silent— mid-speech. In spite of all the other conversations and distractions of the morning, this is what they have been waiting for, even TRAVIS, *who looks helplessly from his mother to his grandmother.* RUTH *is the first to come to life again.*

RUTH (*to* TRAVIS) *Get down them steps, boy!*

TRAVIS *snaps to life and flies out to get the mail.*

MAMA (*her eyes wide, her hand to her breast*) You mean it done really come?

RUTH (*excitedly*) Oh, Miss Lena!

MAMA (*collecting herself*) Well . . . I don't know what we all so excited about 'round here for. We known it was coming for months.

RUTH That's a whole lot different from having it come and being able to hold it in your hands . . . a piece of paper worth ten thousand dollars. . . . (TRAVIS *bursts back into the room. He holds the envelope high above his head, like a little dancer, his face is radiant and he is breathless. He moves to his grandmother with sudden slow ceremony and puts the envelope into her hands. She accepts it, and then merely holds it and looks at it.*) Come on! Open it . . . Lord have mercy, I wish Walter Lee was here!

TRAVIS Open it, Grandmama!

MAMA (*staring at it*) Now you all be quiet. It's just a check.

RUTH *Open it.* . . .

MAMA (*still staring at it*) Now don't act silly. . . . We ain't never been no people to act silly 'bout no money—

RUTH (*swiftly*) We ain't never had none before—*open it!*

MAMA *finally makes a good strong tear and pulls out the thin blue slice of paper and inspects it closely. The boy and his mother study it raptly over* MAMA's *shoulders.*

MAMA *Travis!* (*She is counting off with doubt.*) Is that the right number of zeros.

TRAVIS Yes'm . . . ten thousand dollars. Gaalee, Grandmama, you rich.

MAMA (*she holds the check away from her, still looking at it. Slowly her face sobers into a mask of unhappiness*) Ten thousand dollars. (*She hands it to* RUTH.) Put it away somewhere, Ruth. (*She does not look at* RUTH; *her eyes seem to be seeing something somewhere very far off.*) Ten thousand dollars they give you. Ten thousand dollars.

TRAVIS (*to his mother, sincerely*) What's the matter with Grandmama—don't she want to be rich?

RUTH (*distractedly*) You go on out and play now, baby. (TRAVIS *exits.* MAMA *starts wiping dishes absently, humming intently to herself.* RUTH *turns to her, with kind exasperation.*) You're gone and got yourself upset.

MAMA (*not looking at her*) I spec if it wasn't for you all . . . I would just put that money away or give it to the church or something.

RUTH Now what kind of talk is that. Mr. Younger would just be plain mad if he could hear you talking foolish like that.

MAMA (*stopping and staring off*) Yes . . . he sure would. (*Sighing*) We got enough to do with that money, all right. (*She halts then, and turns and looks at her daughter-in-law hard;* RUTH *avoids her eyes and* MAMA *wipes her hands with finality and starts to speak firmly to* RUTH.) Where did you go today, girl?

RUTH To the doctor.

MAMA (*impatiently*) Now, Ruth . . . you know better than that. Old Doctor Jones is strange enough in his way but there ain't nothing 'bout him make somebody slip and call him "she"—like you done this morning.

RUTH Well, that's what happened—my tongue slipped.

MAMA You went to see that woman, didn't you?

RUTH (*defensively, giving herself away*) What woman you talking about?

MAMA (*angrily*) That woman who—

WALTER *enters in great excitement.*

WALTER Did it come?

MAMA (*quietly*) Can't you give people a Christian greeting before you start asking about money?

WALTER (*to* RUTH) Did it come? (RUTH *unfolds the check and lays it quietly before him, watching him intently with thoughts of her own.* WALTER *sits down and grasps it close and counts off the zeros.*) Ten thousand dollars—(*He turns suddenly, frantically to his mother and draws some papers out of his breast pocket.*) Mama—look. Old Willy Harris put everything on paper—

MAMA Son—I think you ought to talk to your wife. . . . I'll go on out and leave you alone if you want—

WALTER I can talk to her later—Mama, look—

MAMA Son—

WALTER WILL SOMEBODY PLEASE LISTEN TO ME TODAY!

MAMA (*quietly*) I don't 'low no yellin' in this house, Walter Lee, and you know it—(WALTER *stares at them in frustration and starts to speak several times.*) And there ain't going to be no investing in no liquor stores. I don't aim to have to speak on that again.

A *long pause.*

WALTER Oh—so you don't aim to have to speak on that again? So *you* have decided. . . . (*Crumpling his papers*) Well, *you* tell that to my boy tonight when you put him to sleep on the living-room couch. . . . (*Turning to* MAMA *and speaking directly to her*) Yeah—and tell it to my wife, Mama, tomorrow when she has to go out of here to look after somebody else's kids. And tell it to *me*, Mama, every time we need a new pair of curtains and I have to watch *you* go out and work in somebody's kitchen. Yeah, you tell me then!

WALTER *starts out.*

RUTH Where you going?
WALTER I'm going out!
RUTH Where?
WALTER Just out of this house somewhere—
RUTH (*getting her coat*) I'll come too.
WALTER I don't want you to come!
RUTH I got something to talk to you about, Walter.
WALTER That's too bad.
MAMA (*still quietly*) Walter Lee— (*She waits and he finally turns and looks at her.*) Sit down.
WALTER I'm a grown man, Mama.
MAMA Ain't nobody said you wasn't grown. But you still in my house and my presence. And as long as you are—you'll talk to your wife civil. Now sit down.
RUTH (*suddenly*) Oh, let him go on out and drink himself to death! He makes me sick to my stomach! (*She flings her coat against him.*)
WALTER (*violently*) And you turn mine too, baby! (RUTH *goes into their bedroom and slams the door behind her.*) That was my greatest mistake—
MAMA (*still quietly*) Walter, what is the matter with you?
WALTER Matter with me? Ain't nothing the matter with *me*!
MAMA Yes there is. Something eating you up like a crazy man. Something more than me not giving you this money. The past few years I been watching it happen to you. You get all nervous acting and kind of wild in the eyes— (WALTER *jumps up impatiently at her words.*) I said sit there now, I'm talking to you!
WALTER Mama—I don't need no nagging at me today.
MAMA Seem like you getting to a place where you always tied up in some kind of knot about something. But if anybody ask you 'bout it you just yell at 'em and bust out the house and go out and drink somewheres. Walter Lee, people can't live with that. Ruth's a good, patient girl in her way—but you getting to be too much. Boy, don't make the mistake of driving that girl away from you.
WALTER Why—what she do for me?
MAMA She loves you.
WALTER Mama—I'm going out. I want to go off somewhere and be by myself for a while.
MAMA I'm sorry 'bout your liquor store, son. It just wasn't the thing for us to do. That's what I want to tell you about—
WALTER I got to go out, Mama— (*He rises.*)
MAMA It's dangerous, son.
WALTER What's dangerous?
MAMA When a man goes outside his home to look for peace.
WALTER (*beseechingly*) Then why can't there never be no peace in this house then?
MAMA You done found it in some other house?

WALTER No—there ain't no woman! Why do women always think there's a woman somewhere when a man gets restless. (*Coming to her*) Mama—Mama—I want so many things. . . .

MAMA Yes, son—

WALTER I want so many things that they are driving me kind of crazy. . . . Mama—look at me.

MAMA I'm looking at you. You a good-looking boy. You got a job, a nice wife, a fine boy and—

WALTER A job. (*Looks at her*) Mama, a job? I open and close car doors all day long. I drive a man around in his limousine and I say, "Yes, sir; no, sir; very good, sir; shall I take the Drive, sir?" Mama, that ain't no kind of job . . . that ain't nothing at all. (*Very quietly*) Mama, I don't know if I can make you understand.

MAMA Understand what, baby?

WALTER (*quietly*) Sometimes it's like I can see the future stretched out in front of me—just plain as day. The future, Mama. Hanging over there at the edge of my days. Just waiting for me—a big, looming blank space—full of *nothing*. Just waiting for *me*. (*Pause*) Mama—sometimes when I'm downtown and I pass them cool, quiet-looking restaurants where them white boys are sitting back and talking 'bout things . . . sitting there turning deals worth millions of dollars . . . sometimes I see guys don't look much older than me—

MAMA Son—how come you talk so much 'bout money?

WALTER (*with immense passion*) Because it is life, Mama!

MAMA (*quietly*) Oh— (*Very quietly*) So now it's life. Money is life. Once upon a time freedom used to be life—now it's money. I guess the world really do change. . . .

WALTER No—it was always money, Mama. We just didn't know about it.

MAMA No . . . something has changed. (*She looks at him.*) You something new, boy. In my time we was worried about not being lynched and getting to the North if we could and how to stay alive and still have a pinch of dignity too. . . . Now here come you and Beneatha—talking 'bout things we ain't never even thought about hardly, me and your daddy. You ain't satisfied or proud of nothing we done. I mean that you had a home; that we kept you out of trouble till you was grown; that you don't have to ride to work on the back of nobody's streetcar—You my children—but how different we done become.

WALTER You just don't understand, Mama, you just don't understand.

MAMA Son—do you know your wife is expecting another baby? (WALTER *stands, stunned, and absorbs what his mother has said.*) That's what she wanted to talk to you about. (WALTER *sinks down into a chair.*) This ain't for me to be telling—but you ought to know. (*She waits.*) I think Ruth is thinking 'bout getting rid of that child.

WALTER (*slowly understanding*) No—no—Ruth wouldn't do that.

MAMA When the world gets ugly enough—a woman will do anything for her family. *The part that's already living.*

WALTER You don't know Ruth, Mama, if you think she would do that.

RUTH *opens the bedroom door and stands there a little limp.*

RUTH (*beaten*) Yes I would too, Walter. (*Pause*) I gave her a five-dollar down payment.

There is total silence as the man stares at his wife and the mother stares at her son.

MAMA (*presently*) Well— (*Tightly*) Well—son, I'm waiting to hear you say something.

. . . I'm waiting to hear how you be your father's son. Be the man he was. . . . (*Pause*)
Your wife say she going to destroy your child. And I'm waiting to hear you talk like
him and say we a people who give children life, not who destroys them— (*She rises.*)
I'm waiting to see you stand up and look like your daddy and say we done give up one
baby to poverty and that we ain't going to give up nary another one. . . . I'm waiting.

WALTER Ruth—

MAMA If you a son of mine, tell her! (WALTER *turns, looks at her and can say nothing.
She continues, bitterly.*) You . . . you are a disgrace to your father's memory. Somebody
get me my hat.

Curtain

ACT II

SCENE I.

Time: Later the same day.

At rise: RUTH *is ironing again. She has the radio going. Presently* BENEATHA's *bedroom
door opens and* RUTH's *mouth falls and she puts down the iron in fascination.*

RUTH What have we got on tonight!

BENEATHA (*emerging grandly from the doorway so that we can see her thoroughly robed
in the costume* ASAGAI *brought*) You are looking at what a well-dressed Nigerian woman
wears— (*She parades for* RUTH, *her hair completely hidden by the headdress; she is
coquettishly fanning herself with an ornate oriental fan, mistakenly more like Butterfly
than any Nigerian that ever was.*) Isn't it beautiful? (*She promenades to the radio and,
with an arrogant flourish, turns off the good loud blues that is playing.*) Enough of
this assimilationist junk! (RUTH *follows her with her eyes as she goes to the phonograph
and puts on a record and turns and waits ceremoniously for the music to come up.
Then, with a shout—*) OCOMOGOSIAY!

RUTH *jumps. The music comes up, a lovely Nigerian melody.* BENEATHA *listens, enrap-
tured, her eyes far away—"back to the past." She begins to dance.* RUTH *is dumbfounded.*

RUTH What kind of dance is that?

BENEATHA A folk dance.

RUTH (*Pearl Bailey*) What kind of folks do that, honey?

BENEATHA It's from Nigeria. It's a dance of welcome.

RUTH Who you welcoming?

BENEATHA The men back to the village.

RUTH Where they been?

BENEATHA How should I know—out hunting or something. Anyway, they are coming
back now. . . .

RUTH Well, that's good.

BENEATHA (*with the record*)

*Alundi, alundi
Alundi alunya
Jop pu a jeepua
Ang gu sooooooooooo*

*Ai yai yae . . .
Ayehaye—alundi . . .*

WALTER *comes in during this performance; he has obviously been drinking. He leans against the door heavily and watches his sister, at first with distaste. Then his eyes look off—"back to the past"—as he lifts both his fists to the roof, screaming.*

WALTER YEAH . . . AND ETHIOPIA STRETCH FORTH HER HANDS AGAIN!. . .

RUTH (*drily, looking at him*) Yes—and Africa sure is claiming her own tonight. (*She gives them both up and starts ironing again.*)

WALTER (*all in a drunken, dramatic shout*) Shut up! . . . . I'm digging them drums . . . them drums move me! . . . (*He makes his weaving way to his wife's face and leans in close to her.*) In my *heart of hearts*—(*he thumps his chest*)—I am much warrior!

RUTH (*without even looking up*) In your heart of hearts you are much drunkard.

WALTER (*coming away from her and starting to wander around the room, shouting*) Me and Jomo . . . (*Intently, in his sister's face. She has stopped dancing to watch him in this unknown mood.*) That's my man, Kenyatta. (*Shouting and thumping his chest*) FLAMING SPEAR! HOT DAMN! (*He is suddenly in possession of an imaginary spear and actively spearing enemies all over the room.*) OCOMOGOSIAY . . . THE LION IS WAKING . . . OWIMOWEH! (*He pulls his shirt open and leaps up on a table and gestures with his spear. The bell rings.* RUTH *goes to answer.*)

BENEATHA (*to encourage* WALTER, *thoroughly caught up with this side of him*) OCOMOGOSIAY, FLAMING SPEAR!

WALTER (*on the table, very far gone, his eyes pure glass sheets. He sees what we cannot, that he is a leader of his people, a great chief, a descendant of Chaka, and that the hour to march has come*) Listen, my black broth—ers—

BENEATHA OCOMOGOSIAY!

WALTER —Do you hear the waters rushing against the shores of the coastlands—

BENEATHA OCOMOGOSIAY!

WALTER —Do you hear the screeching of the cocks in yonder hills beyond where the chiefs meet in council for the coming of the mighty war—

BENEATHA OCOMOGOSIAY!

WALTER —Do you hear the beating of the wings of the birds flying low over the mountains and the low places of our land—

RUTH *opens the door.* GEORGE MURCHISON *enters.*

BENEATHA OCOMOGOSIAY!

WALTER —Do you hear the singing of the women, singing the war songs of our fathers to the babies in the great houses . . . singing the sweet war songs? OH, DO YOU HEAR, MY BLACK BROTHERS!

BENEATHA (*completely gone*) We hear you, Flaming Spear—

WALTER Telling us to prepare for the greatness of the time— (*To* GEORGE) Black Brother! (*He extends his hand for the fraternal clasp.*)

GEORGE Black Brother, hell!

RUTH (*having had enough, and embarrassed for the family*) Beneatha, you got company— what's the matter with you? Walter Lee Younger, get down off that table and stop acting like a fool. . . .

WALTER *comes down off the table suddenly and makes a quick exit to the bathroom.*

RUTH He's had a little to drink. . . . I don't know what her excuse is.

GEORGE (*to* BENEATHA) Look honey, we're going *to* the theater—we're not going to be *in* it . . . so go change, huh?

RUTH You expect this boy to go out with you looking like that?

BENEATHA (*looking at* GEORGE) That's up to George. If he's ashamed of his heritage—

GEORGE Oh, don't be so proud of yourself, Bennie—just because you look eccentric.

BENEATHA How can something that's natural be eccentric?

GEORGE That's what being eccentric means—being natural. Get dressed.

BENEATHA I don't like that, George.

RUTH Why must you and your brother make an argument out of everything people say?

BENEATHA Because I hate assimilationist Negroes!

RUTH Will somebody please tell me what assimila-whoever means!

GEORGE Oh, it's just a college girl's way of calling people Uncle Toms—but that isn't what it means at all.

RUTH Well, what does it mean?

BENEATHA (*cutting* GEORGE *off and staring at him as she replies to* RUTH) It means someone who is willing to give up his own culture and submerge himself completely in the dominant, and in this case, *oppressive* culture!

GEORGE Oh, dear, dear, dear! Here we go! A lecture on the African past! On our Great West African Heritage! In one second we will hear all about the great Ashanti empires; the great Songhay civilizations; and the great sculpture of Bénin—and then some poetry in the Bantu—and the whole monologue will end with the word *heritage!* (*Nastily*) Let's face it, baby, your heritage is nothing but a bunch of raggedy-assed spirituals and some grass huts!

BENEATHA *Grass huts!* (RUTH *crosses to her and forcibly pushes her toward the bedroom.*) See there . . . you are standing there in your splendid ignorance talking about people who were the first to smelt iron on the face of the earth! (RUTH *is pushing her through the door.*) The Ashanti were performing surgical operations when the English—(RUTH *pulls the door to, with* BENEATHA *on the other side, and smiles graciously at* GEORGE. BENEATHA *opens the door and shouts the end of the sentence defiantly at* GEORGE)— were still tattooing themselves with blue dragons. . . . (*She goes back inside.*)

RUTH Have a seat, George. (*They both sit.* RUTH *folds her hands rather primly on her lap, determined to demonstrate the civilization of the family.*) Warm, ain't it? I mean for September. (*Pause*) Just like they always say about Chicago weather: If it's too hot or cold for you, just wait a minute and it'll change. (*She smiles happily at this cliché of clichés.*) Everybody say it's got to do with them bombs and things they keep setting off. (*Pause*) Would you like a nice cold beer?

GEORGE No, thank you. I don't care for beer. (*He looks at his watch*). I hope she hurries up.

RUTH What time is the show?

GEORGE It's an eight-thirty curtain. That's just Chicago, though. In New York standard curtain time is eight forty. (*He is rather proud of this knowledge.*)

RUTH (*properly appreciating it*) You get to New York a lot?

GEORGE (*offhand*) Few times a year.

RUTH Oh—that's nice. I've never been to New York.

WALTER *enters. We feel he has relieved himself, but the edge of unreality is still with him.*

WALTER New York ain't got nothing Chicago ain't. Just a bunch of hustling people all squeezed up together—being "Eastern." (*He turns his face into a screw of displeasure.*)

GEORGE Oh—you've been?

WALTER *Plenty* of times.

RUTH (*shocked at the lie*) Walter Lee Younger!

WALTER (*staring her down*) Plenty! (*Pause*) What we got to drink in this house? Why don't you offer this man some refreshment? (*To* GEORGE) They don't know how to entertain people in this house, man.

GEORGE Thank you—I don't really care for anything.

WALTER (*feeling his head; sobriety coming*) Where's Mama?

RUTH She ain't come back yet.

WALTER (*looking* MURCHISON *over from head to toe, scrutinizing his carefully casual tweed sports jacket over cashmere V-neck sweater over soft eyelet shirt and tie, and soft slacks, finished off with white buckskin shoes*) Why all you college boys wear them fairyish-looking white shoes?

RUTH Walter Lee!

GEORGE MURCHISON *ignores the remark.*

WALTER (*to* RUTH) Well, they look crazy as hell—white shoes, cold as it is.

RUTH (*crushed*) You have to excuse him—

WALTER No he don't! Excuse me for what? What you always excusing me for! I'll excuse myself when I needs to be excused! (*A pause*) They look as funny as them black knee socks Beneatha wears out of here all the time.

RUTH It's the college *style*, Walter.

WALTER Style, hell. She looks like she got burnt legs or something!

RUTH Oh, Walter—

WALTER (*an irritable mimic*) Oh, Walter! Oh, Walter! (*To* MURCHISON) How's your old man making out? I understand you all going to buy that big hotel on the Drive? (*He finds a beer in the refrigerator, wanders over to* MURCHISON, *sipping and wiping his lips with the back of his hand, and straddling a chair backwards to talk to the other man.*) Shrewd move. Your old man is all right, man. (*Tapping his head and half winking for emphasis*) I mean he knows how to operate. I mean he thinks *big*, you know what I mean, I mean for a *home*, you know? But I think he's kind of running out of ideas now. I'd like to talk to him. Listen, man, I got some plans that could turn this city upside down. I mean I think like he does. *Big*. Invest big, gamble big, hell, lose *big* if you have to, you know what I mean. It's hard to find a man on this whole Southside who understands my kind of thinking—you dig? (*He scrutinizes* MURCHISON *again, drinks his beer, squints his eyes and leans in close, confidential, man to man.*) Me and you ought to sit down and talk sometimes, man. Man, I got me some ideas. . . .

GEORGE (*with boredom*) Yeah—sometimes we'll have to do that, Walter.

WALTER (*understanding the indifference, and offended*) Yeah—well, when you get the time, man. I know you a busy little boy.

RUTH Walter, please—

WALTER (*bitterly, hurt*) I know ain't nothing in this world as busy as you colored college boys with your fraternity pins and white shoes. . . .

RUTH (*covering her face with humiliation*) Oh, Walter Lee—

WALTER I see you all all the time—with the books tucked under your arms—going to your (*British A—a mimic*) "clahsses." And for what! What the hell you learning over there? Filling up your heads—(*counting off on his fingers*)—with the sociology and the psychology—but they teaching you how to be a man? How to take over and run the world? They teaching you how to run a rubber plantation or a steel mill? Naw—just to talk proper and read books and wear white shoes. . . .

GEORGE (*looking at him with distaste, a little above it all*) You're all wacked up with bitterness, man.

WALTER (*intently, almost quietly, between the teeth, glaring at the boy*) And you—ain't you bitter, man? Ain't you just about had it yet? Don't you see no stars gleaming that you can't reach out and grab? You happy?—You contented son-of-a-bitch—you happy? You got it made? Bitter? Man, I'm a volcano. Bitter? Here I am a giant—surrounded by ants! Ants who can't even understand what it is the giant is talking about.

RUTH (*passionately and suddenly*) Oh, Walter—ain't you with nobody!

WALTER (*violently*) No! 'Cause ain't nobody with me! Not even my own mother!

RUTH Walter, that's a terrible thing to say!

BENEATHA *enters, dressed for the evening in a cocktail dress and earrings.*

GEORGE Well—hey, you look great.

BENEATHA Let's go, George. See you all later.

RUTH Have a nice time.

GEORGE Thanks. Good night. (*To* WALTER, *sarcastically*) Good night, *Prometheus.* (BENEATHA *and* GEORGE *exit.*)

WALTER (*to* RUTH) Who is Prometheus?

RUTH I don't know. Don't worry about it.

WALTER (*in fury, pointing after* GEORGE) See there—they get to a point where they can't insult you man to man—they got to go talk about something ain't nobody never heard of!

RUTH How do you know it was an insult? (*To humor him*) Maybe Prometheus is a nice fellow.

WALTER Prometheus! I bet there ain't even no such thing! I bet that simple-minded clown—

RUTH Walter— (*She stops what she is doing and looks at him.*)

WALTER (*yelling*) Don't start!

RUTH Start what?

WALTER Your nagging! Where was I? Who was I with? How much money did I spend?

RUTH (*plaintively*) Walter Lee—why don't we just try to talk about it. . . .

WALTER (*not listening*) I been out talking with people who understand me. People who care about the things I got on my mind.

RUTH (*wearily*) I guess that means people like Willy Harris.

WALTER Yes, people like Willy Harris.

RUTH (*with a sudden flash of impatience*) Why don't you all just hurry up and go into the banking business and stop talking about it!

WALTER Why? You want to know why? 'Cause we all tied up in a race of people that don't know how to do nothing but moan, pray and have babies!

The line is too bitter even for him and he looks at her and sits down.

RUTH Oh, Walter . . . (*Softly*) Honey, why can't you stop fighting me?

WALTER (*without thinking*) Who's fighting you? Who even cares about you?

This line begins the retardation of his mood.

RUTH Well— (*She waits a long time, and then with resignation starts to put away her things.*) I guess I might as well go on to bed. . . . (*More or less to herself*) I don't know where we lost it . . . but we have. . . . (*Then, to him*) I—I'm sorry about this new baby, Walter. I guess maybe I better go on and do what I started . . . I guess I just didn't realize how bad things was with us . . . I guess I just didn't really realize— (*She starts out to the bedroom and stops.*) You want some hot milk?

WALTER Hot milk?

RUTH Yes—hot milk.

WALTER Why hot milk?

RUTH 'Cause after all that liquor you come home with you ought to have something hot in your stomach.

WALTER I don't want no milk.

RUTH You want some coffee then?

WALTER No, I don't want no coffee. I don't want nothing hot to drink. (*Almost plaintively*) Why you always trying to give me something to eat?

RUTH (*standing and looking at him helplessly*) What else can I give you, Walter Lee Younger?

She stands and looks at him and presently turns to go out again. He lifts his head and watches her going away from him in a new mood which began to emerge when he asked her "Who cares about you?"

WALTER It's been rough, ain't it, baby? (*She hears and stops but does not turn around and he continues to her back.*) I guess between two people there ain't never as much understood as folks generally thinks there is. I mean like between me and you— (*She turns to face him.*) How we gets to the place where we scared to talk softness to each other. (*He waits, thinking hard himself.*) Why you think it got to be like that? (*He is thoughtful, almost as a child would be.*) Ruth, what is it gets into people ought to be close?

RUTH I don't know, honey. I think about it a lot.

WALTER On account of you and me, you mean? The way things are with us. The way something done come down between us.

RUTH There ain't so much between us, Walter. . . . Not when you come to me and try to talk to me. Try to be with me . . . a little even.

WALTER (*total honesty*) Sometimes . . . sometimes . . . I don't even know how to try.

RUTH Walter—

WALTER Yes?

RUTH (*coming to him, gently and with misgiving, but coming to him*) Honey . . . life don't have to be like this. I mean sometimes people can do things so that things are better. . . . You remember how we used to talk when Travis was born . . . about the way we were going to live . . . the kind of house . . . (*She is stroking his head.*) Well, it's all starting to slip away from us. . . .

MAMA *enters, and* WALTER *jumps up and shouts at her.*

WALTER Mama, where have you been?

MAMA My—them steps is longer than they used to be. Whew! (*She sits down and ignores him.*) How you feeling this evening, Ruth?

RUTH *shrugs, disturbed some at having been prematurely interrupted and watching her husband knowingly.*

WALTER Mama, where have you been all day?

MAMA (*still ignoring him and leaning on the table and changing to more comfortable shoes*) Where's Travis?

RUTH I let him go out earlier and he ain't come back yet. Boy, is he going to get it!

WALTER Mama!

MAMA (*as if she has heard him for the first time*) Yes, son?

WALTER Where did you go this afternoon?

MAMA I went downtown to tend to some business that I had to tend to.

WALTER What kind of business?

MAMA You know better than to question me like a child, Brother.

WALTER (*rising and bending over the table*) Where were you, Mama? (*Bringing his fists down and shouting*) Mama, you didn't go do something with that insurance money, something crazy?

The front door opens slowly, interrupting him, and TRAVIS *peeks his head in, less than hopefully.*

TRAVIS (*to his mother*) Mama, I—

RUTH "Mama I" nothing! You're going to get, it boy! Get on in that bedroom and get yourself ready!

TRAVIS But I—

MAMA Why don't you all never let the child explain hisself.

RUTH Keep out of it now, Lena.

MAMA *clamps her lips together, and* RUTH *advances toward her son menacingly.*

RUTH A thousand times I have told you not to go off like that—

MAMA (*holding out her arms to her grandson*) Well—at least let me tell him something. I want him to be the first one to hear. . . . Come here, Travis. (*The boy obeys, gladly.*) Travis—(*she takes him by the shoulder and looks into his face*)—you know that money we got in the mail this morning?

TRAVIS Yes'm—

MAMA Well—what you think your grandmama gone and done with that money?

TRAVIS I don't know, Grandmama.

MAMA (*putting her finger on his nose for emphasis*) She went out and she bought you a house! (*The explosion comes from* WALTER *at the end of the revelation and he jumps up and turns away from all of them in a fury.* MAMA *continues, to* TRAVIS) You glad about the house? It's going to be yours when you get to be a man.

TRAVIS Yeah—I always wanted to live in a house.

MAMA All right, gimme some sugar then— (TRAVIS *puts his arms around her neck as she watches her son over the boy's shoulder. Then to* TRAVIS, *after the embrace*) Now when you say your prayers tonight, you thank God and your grandfather—'cause it was him who give you the house—in his way.

RUTH (*taking the boy from* MAMA *and pushing him toward the bedroom*) Now you get out of here and get ready for your beating.

TRAVIS Aw, Mama—

RUTH Get on in there— (*Closing the door behind him and turning radiantly to her mother-in-law*) So you went and did it!

MAMA (*quietly, looking at her son with pain*) Yes, I did.

RUTH (*raising both arms classically*) Praise God! (*Looks at* WALTER *a moment, who says nothing. She crosses rapidly to her husband.*) Please honey—let me be glad . . . you be glad too. (*She has laid her hands on his shoulders, but he shakes himself free of her roughly, without turning to face her.*) Oh, Walter . . . a home . . . a home. (*She comes back to* MAMA.) Well—where is it? How big is it? How much it going to cost?

MAMA Well—

RUTH When we moving?

MAMA (*smiling at her*) First of the month.

RUTH (*throwing back her head with jubilance*) Praise God!

MAMA (*tentatively, still looking at her son's back turned against her and* RUTH) It's—it's a nice house too. . . . (*She cannot help speaking directly to him. An imploring quality in her voice, her manner, makes her almost like a girl now.*) Three bedrooms—nice big one for you Ruth. . . . Me and Beneatha still have to share our room, but Travis have one of his own—and (*with difficulty*) I figure if the—new baby—is a boy, we could get one of them double-decker outfits. . . . And there's a yard with a little patch of dirt where I could maybe get to grow me a few flowers. . . . And a nice big basement. . . .

RUTH Walter honey, be glad—

MAMA (*still to his back, fingering things on the table*) 'Course I don't want to make it sound fancier than it is. . . . It's just a plain little old house—but it's made good and solid—and it will be *ours*. Walter Lee—it makes a difference in a man when he can walk on the floors that belong to *him*. . . .

RUTH Where is it?

MAMA (*frightened at this telling*) Well—well—it's out there in Clybourne Park—

RUTH'S *radiance fades abruptly, and* WALTER *finally turns slowly to face his mother with incredulity and hostility.*

RUTH Where?

MAMA (*matter-of-factly*) Four o six Clybourne Street, Clybourne Park.

RUTH Clybourne Park? Mama, there ain't no colored people living in Clybourne Park.

MAMA (*almost idiotically*) Well, I guess there's going to be some now.

WALTER (*bitterly*) So that's the peace and comfort you went out and bought for us today!

MAMA (*raising her eyes to meet his finally*) Son—I just tried to find the nicest place for the least amount of money for my family.

RUTH (*trying to recover from the shock*) Well—well—'course I ain't one never been 'fraid of no crackers, mind you—but—well, wasn't there no other houses nowhere?

MAMA Them houses they put up for colored in them areas way out all seem to cost twice as much as other houses. I did the best I could.

RUTH (*struck senseless with the news, in its various degrees of goodness and trouble, she sits a moment, her fists propping her chin in thought, and then she starts to rise, bringing her fists down with vigor, the radiance spreading from cheek to cheek again*) Well—well!—All I can say is—if this is my time in life—*my time*—to say good-bye—(*and she builds with momentum as she starts to circle the room with an exuberant, almost tearfully happy release*)—to these Goddamned cracking walls!—(*she pounds the walls*)—and these marching *roaches!*—(*she wipes at an imaginary army of marching roaches*)—and this cramped little closet which ain't now or never was no kitchen! . . . then I say it loud and good, *Hallelujah! and good-bye misery. . . . I don't never want to see your ugly face again!* (*She laughs joyously, having practically destroyed the apartment, and flings her arms up and lets them come down happily, slowly, reflectively, over her abdomen, aware for the first time perhaps that the life therein pulses with happiness and not despair.*) Lena?

MAMA moved, watching her happiness) Yes, honey?

RUTH (*looking off*) Is there—is there a whole lot of sunlight?

MAMA (*understanding*) Yes, child, there's a whole lot of sunlight.

Long pause.

RUTH (*collecting herself and going to the door of the room* TRAVIS *is in*) Well—I guess I better see 'bout Travis. (*To* MAMA) Lord, I sure don't feel like whipping nobody today! (*She exits.*)

MAMA (*the mother and son are left alone now and the mother waits a long time, considering deeply, before she speaks*) Son—you—you understand what I done, don't you? (WAL-TER *is silent and sullen.*) I—I just seen my family falling apart today . . . just falling to pieces in front of my eyes. . . . We couldn't of gone on like we was today. We was going backwards 'stead of forwards—talking 'bout killing babies and wishing each other was dead. . . . When it gets like that in life—you just got to do something different, push on out and do something bigger. . . . (*She waits.*) I wish you say something, son . . . I wish you'd say how deep inside you you think I done the right thing—

WALTER (*crossing slowly to his bedroom door and finally turning there and speaking measuredly*) What you need me to say you done right for? You the head of this family. You run our lives like you want to. It was your money and you did what you wanted with it. So what you need for me to say it was all right for? (*Bitterly, to hurt her as deeply as he knows is possible*) So you butchered up a dream of mine—you—who always talking 'bout your children's dreams. . . .

MAMA Walter Lee—

He just closes the door behind him. MAMA *sits alone, thinking heavily.*

Curtain

SCENE II.

Time: Friday night, a few weeks later.
    At rise: Packing crates mark the intention of the family to move. BENEATHA *and* GEORGE *come in, presumably from an evening out again.*

GEORGE O.K. . . . O.K., whatever you say. . . . (*They both sit on the couch. He tries to kiss her. She moves away.*) Look, we've had a nice evening; let's not spoil it, huh? . . .

He again turns her head and tries to nuzzle in and she turns away from him, not with distaste but with momentary lack of interest; in a mood to pursue what they were talking about.

BENEATHA I'm *trying* to talk to you.

GEORGE We always talk.

BENEATHA Yes—and I love to talk.

GEORGE (*exasperated; rising*) I know it and I don't mind it sometimes . . . I want you to cut it out, see—The moody stuff, I mean. I don't like it. You're a nice-looking girl . . . all over. That's all you need, honey, forget the atmosphere. Guys aren't going to go for the atmosphere—they're going to go for what they see. Be glad for that. Drop the Garbo routine. It doesn't go with you. As for myself, I want a nice—(*groping*)—simple (*thoughtfully*)—sophisticated girl . . . not a poet—O.K.?

She rebuffs him again and he starts to leave.

BENEATHA Why are you angry?

GEORGE Because this is stupid! I don't go out with you to discuss the nature of "quiet desperation" or to hear all about your thoughts—because the world will go on thinking what it thinks regardless—

BENEATHA Then why read books? Why go to school?

GEORGE (*with artificial patience, counting on his fingers*) It's simple. You read books— to learn facts—to get grades—to pass the course—to get a degree. That's all—it has nothing to do with thoughts.

A long pause.

BENEATHA I see. (*A longer pause as she looks at him*) Good night, George.

GEORGE *looks at her a little oddly, and starts to exit. He meets* MAMA *coming in.*

GEORGE Oh—hello, Mrs. Younger.

MAMA Hello, George, how you feeling?

GEORGE Fine—fine, how are you?

MAMA Oh, a little tired. You know them steps can get you after a day's work. You all have a nice time tonight?

GEORGE Yes—a fine time. Well, good night.

MAMA Good night. (*He exits.* MAMA *closes the door behind her.*) Hello, honey. What you sitting like that for?

BENEATHA I'm just sitting.

MAMA Didn't you have a nice time?

BENEATHA No.

MAMA No? What's the matter?

BENEATHA Mama, George is a fool—honest. (*She rises.*)

MAMA (*hustling around unloading the packages she has entered with. She stops*) Is he, baby?

BENEATHA Yes.

BENEATHA *makes up* TRAVIS' *bed as she talks.*

MAMA You sure?

BENEATHA Yes.

MAMA Well—I guess you better not waste your time with no fools.

BENEATHA *looks up at her mother, watching her put groceries in the refrigerator. Finally she gathers up her things and starts into the bedroom. At the door she stops and looks back at her mother.*

BENEATHA Mama—

MAMA Yes, baby—

BENEATHA Thank you.

MAMA For what?

BENEATHA For understanding me this time.

She exits quickly and the mother stands, smiling a little, looking at the place where BENEATHA *just stood.* RUTH *enters.*

RUTH Now don't you fool with any of this stuff, Lena—

MAMA Oh, I just thought I'd sort a few things out.

The phone rings. RUTH *answers.*

RUTH (*at the phone*) Hello—Just a minute. (*Goes to the door*) Walter, it's Mrs. Arnold. (*Waits. Goes back to the phone. Tense*) Hello. Yes, this is his wife speaking . . . He's lying down now. Yes . . . well, he'll be in tomorrow. He's been very sick. Yes—I know we should have called, but we were so sure he'd be able to come in today. Yes— yes, I'm very sorry. Yes . . . Thank you very much. (*She hangs up.* WALTER *is standing in the doorway of the bedroom behind her.*) That was Mrs. Arnold.

WALTER (*indifferently*) Was it?

RUTH She said if you don't come in tomorrow that they are getting a new man. . . .

WALTER Ain't that sad—ain't that crying sad.

RUTH She said Mr. Arnold has had to take a cab for three days. . . . Walter, you ain't been to work for three days! (*This is a revelation to her.*) Where you been, Walter Lee Younger? (WALTER *looks at her and starts to laugh.*) You're going to lose your job.

WALTER That's right . . .

RUTH Oh, Walter, and with your mother working like a dog every day—

WALTER That's sad too—Everything is sad.

MAMA What you been doing for these three days, son?

WALTER Mama—you don't know all the things a man what got leisure can find to do in this city. . . . What's this—Friday night? Well—Wednesday I borrowed Willy Harris' car and I went for a drive . . . just me and myself and I drove and drove . . . Way out . . . way past South Chicago, and I parked the car and I sat and looked at the steel mills all day long. I just sat in the car and looked at them big black chimneys for hours. Then I drove back and I went to the Green Hat. (*Pause*) And Thursday— Thursday I borrowed the car again and I got in it and I pointed it the other way and I drove the other way—for hours—way, way up to Wisconsin, and I looked at the farms. I just drove and looked at the farms. Then I drove back and I went to the Green Hat. (*Pause*) And today—today I didn't get the car. Today I just walked. All over the South side. And I looked at the Negroes and they looked at me and finally I just sat down on the curb at Thirty-ninth and South Parkway and I just sat there and watched the Negroes go by. And then I went to the Green Hat. You all sad? You all depressed? And you know where I am going right now—

RUTH *goes out quietly.*

MAMA Oh, Big Walter, is this the harvest of our days?

WALTER You know what I like about the Green Hat? (*He turns the radio on and a steamy, deep blues pours into the room.*) I like this little cat they got there who blows a sax. . . . He blows. He talks to me. He ain't but 'bout five feet tall and he's got a conked head and his eyes is always closed and he's all music—

MAMA (*rising and getting some papers out of her handbag*) Walter—

WALTER And there's this other guy who plays the piano . . . and they got a sound. I mean they can work on some music. . . . They got the best little combo in the world in the Green Hat. . . . You can just sit there and drink and listen to them three men play and you realize that don't nothing matter worth a damn, but just being there—

MAMA I've helped do it to you, haven't I, son? Walter, I been wrong.

WALTER Naw—you ain't never been wrong about nothing, Mama.

MAMA Listen to me, now. I say I been wrong, son. That I been doing to you what the rest of the world been doing to you. (*She stops and he looks up slowly at her and she meets his eyes pleadingly.*) Walter—what you ain't never understood is that I ain't got nothing, don't own nothing, ain't never really wanted nothing that wasn't for you. There ain't nothing as precious to me. . . . There ain't nothing worth holding on to, money, dreams, nothing else—if it means—if it means it's going to destroy my boy. (*She puts her papers in front of him and he watches her without speaking or moving.*) I paid the man thirty-five hundred dollars down on the house. That leaves sixty-five hundred dollars. Monday morning I want you to take this money and take three thousand dollars and put it in a savings account for Beneatha's medical schooling. The rest you put in a checking account—with your name on it. And from now on any penny that come out of it or that go in it is for you to look after. For you to decide. (*She drops her hands a little helplessly.*) It ain't much, but it's all I got in the world and I'm putting it in your hands. I'm telling you to be the head of this family from now on like you supposed to be.

WALTER (*stares at the money*) You trust me like that, Mama?

MAMA I ain't never stop trusting you. Like I ain't never stop loving you.

She goes out, and WALTER *sits looking at the money on the table as the music continues in its idiom, pulsing in the room. Finally, in a decisive gesture, he gets up, and, in mingled joy and desperation, picks up the money. At the same moment,* TRAVIS *enters for bed.*

TRAVIS What's the matter, Daddy? You drunk?

WALTER (*sweetly, more sweetly than we have ever known him*) No, Daddy ain't drunk. Daddy ain't going to never be drunk again. . . .

TRAVIS Well, good night, Daddy.

The father has come from behind the couch and leans over, embracing his son.

WALTER Son, I feel like talking to you tonight.

TRAVIS About what?

WALTER Oh, about a lot of things. About you and what kind of man you going to be when you grow up. . . . Son—son, what do you want to be when you grow up?

TRAVIS A bus driver.

WALTER (*laughing a little*) A what? Man, that ain't nothing to want to be!

TRAVIS Why not?

WALTER 'Cause, man—it ain't big enough—you know what I mean.

TRAVIS I don't know then. I can't make up my mind. Sometimes Mama asks me that too. And sometimes when I tell her I just want to be like you—she says she don't want me to be like that and sometimes she says she does. . . .

WALTER (*gathering him up in his arms*) You know what, Travis? In seven years you going to be seventeen years old. And things is going to be very different with us in seven years, Travis. . . . One day when you are seventeen I'll come home—home from my office downtown somewhere—

TRAVIS You don't work in no office, Daddy.

WALTER No—but after tonight. After what your daddy gonna do tonight, there's going to be offices—a whole lot of offices. . . .

TRAVIS What you gonna do tonight, Daddy?

WALTER You wouldn't understand yet, son, but your daddy's gonna make a transaction . . . a business transaction that's going to change our lives. . . . That's how come one day when you 'bout seventeen years old I'll come home and I'll be pretty tired, you know what I mean, after a day of conferences and secretaries getting things wrong the way they do . . . 'cause an executive's life is hell, man— (*The more he talks, the farther away he gets.*) And I'll pull the car up on the driveway . . . just a plain black Chrysler, I think, with white walls—no—black tires. More elegant. Rich people don't have to be flashy . . . though I'll have to get something a little sportier for Ruth—maybe a Cadillac convertible to do her shopping in. . . . And I'll come up the steps to the house and the gardener will be clipping away at the hedges and he'll say, "Good evening, Mr. Younger." And I'll say, "Hello, Jefferson, how are you this evening?" And I'll go inside and Ruth will come downstairs and meet me at the door and we'll kiss each other and she'll take my arm and we'll go up to your room to see you sitting on the floor with the catalogues of all the great schools in America around you. . . . All the great schools in the world! And—and I'll say, all right son—it's your seventeenth birthday, what is it you've decided? . . . Just tell me where you want to go to school and you'll *go.* Just tell me, what it is you want to be—and you'll *be* it. . . . Whatever you want to be—Yessir! (*He holds his arms open for* TRAVIS.) You just name it, son . . . (TRAVIS *leaps into them.*) and I hand you the world!

WALTER's *voice has risen in pitch and hysterical promise and on the last line he lifts* TRAVIS *high.*

Blackout

SCENE III.

Time: Saturday, moving day, one week later.

Before the curtain rises, RUTH's *voice, a strident, dramatic church alto cuts through the silence.*

It is, in the darkness a triumphant surge, a penetrating statement of expectation: "Oh, Lord, I don't feel no ways tired! Children, oh, glory hallelujah!"

As the curtain rises we see that RUTH *is alone in the living room, finishing up the family's packing. It is moving day. She is nailing crates and tying cartons.* BENEATHA *enters, carrying a guitar case, and watches her exuberant sister-in-law.*

RUTH Hey!

BENEATHA (*putting away the case*) Hi.

RUTH (*pointing at a package*) Honey—look in that package there and see what I found on sale this morning at the South Center. (RUTH *gets up and moves to the package and draws out some curtains.*) Lookahere—hand-turned hems!

BENEATHA How do you know the window size out there?

RUTH (*who hadn't thought of that*) Oh—Well, they bound to fit something in the whole house. Anyhow, they was too good a bargain to pass up. (RUTH *slaps her head, suddenly remembering something.*) Oh, Bennie—I meant to put a special note on that carton over there. That's your mamma's good china and she wants 'em to be very careful with it.

BENEATHA I'll do it.

BENEATHA *finds a piece of paper and starts to draw large letters on it.*

RUTH You know what I'm going to do soon as I get in that new house?

BENEATHA What?

RUTH Honey—I'm going to run me a tub of water up to here. . . . (*With her fingers practically up to her nostrils*) And I am going to get in it—and I am going to sit . . . and sit in that hot water and the first person who knocks to tell *me* to hurry up and come out—

BENEATHA Gets shot at sunrise.

RUTH (*laughing happily*) You said it, sister! (*Noticing how large* BENEATHA *is absent-mindedly making the note*) Honey, they ain't going to read that from no airplane.

BENEATHA (*laughing herself*) I guess I always think things have more emphasis if they are big, somehow.

RUTH (*looking up at her and smiling*) You and your brother seem to have that as a philosophy of life. Lord, that man—done changed so 'round here. You know—you know what we did last night? Me and Walter Lee?

BENEATHA What?

RUTH (*smiling to herself*) We went to the movies. (*Looking at* BENEATHA *to see if she understands*) We went to the movies. You know the last time me and Walter went to the movies together?

BENEATHA No.

RUTH Me neither. That's how long it been. (*Smiling again*) But we went last night. The picture wasn't much good, but that didn't seem to matter. We went—and we held hands.

BENEATHA Oh, Lord!

RUTH We held hands—and you know what?

BENEATHA What?

RUTH When we come out of the show it was late and dark and all the stores and things was closed up . . . and it was kind of chilly and there wasn't many people on the streets . . . and we was still holding hands, me and Walter.

BENEATHA You're killing me.

WALTER *enters with a large package. His happiness is deep in him; he cannot keep still with his new-found exuberance. He is singing and wiggling and snapping his fingers. He puts his package in a corner and puts a phonograph record, which he has brought in with him, on the record player. As the music comes up he dances over to* RUTH *and tries to get her to dance with him. She gives in at last to his raunchiness and in a fit of giggling allows herself to be drawn into his mood and together they deliberately burlesque an old social dance of their youth.*

BENEATHA (*regarding them a long time as they dance, then drawing in her breath for a deeply exaggerated comment which she does not particularly mean*) Talk about—oldddddddddd-fashionedddddddd—Negroes!

WALTER (*stopping momentarily*) What kind of Negroes?

He says this in fun. He is not angry with her today, nor with anyone. He starts to dance with his wife again.

BENEATHA Old-fashioned.

WALTER (*as he dances with* RUTH) You know, when these *New Negroes* have their convention—(*pointing at his sister*)—that is going to be the chairman of the Committee on Unending Agitation. (*He goes on dancing, then stops.*) Race, race, race! . . . Girl, I do believe you are the first person in the history of the entire human race to successfully brainwash yourself. (BENEATHA *breaks up and he goes on dancing. He stops again, enjoying his tease.*) Damn, even the N double A C P takes a holiday sometimes! (BENEATHA *and* RUTH *laugh. He dances with* RUTH *some more and starts to laugh and stops and pantomimes someone over an operating table.*) I can just see that chick someday looking down at some poor cat on an operating table before she starts to slice him, saying . . . (*pulling his sleeves back maliciously*) "By the way, what are your views on civil rights down there? . . ."

He laughs at her again and starts to dance happily. The bell sounds.

BENEATHA Sticks and stones may break my bones but . . . words will never hurt me!

BENEATHA *goes to the door and opens it as* WALTER *and* RUTH *go on with the clowning.* BENEATHA *is somewhat surprised to see a quiet-looking middle-aged white man in a business suit holding his hat and a briefcase in his hand and consulting a small piece of paper.*

MAN Uh—how do you do, miss. I am looking for a Mrs.— *(he looks at the slip of paper)* Mrs. Lena Younger?

BENEATHA *(smoothing her hair with slight embarrassment)* Oh—yes, that's my mother. Excuse me. *(She closes the door and turns to quiet the other two.)* Ruth! Brother! Somebody's here. *(Then she opens the door. The man casts a curious quick glance at all of them.)* Uh—come in please.

MAN *(coming in)* Thank you.

BENEATHA My mother isn't here just now. Is it business?

MAN Yes . . . well, of a sort.

WALTER *(freely, the Man of the House)* Have a seat. I'm Mrs. Younger's son. I look after most of her business matters.

RUTH *and* BENEATHA *exchange amused glances.*

MAN *(regarding* WALTER, *and sitting)* Well—My name is Karl Lindner . . .

WALTER *(stretching out his hand)* Walter Younger. This is my wife—*(*RUTH *nods politely)*—and my sister.

LINDNER How do you do.

WALTER *(amiably, as he sits himself easily on a chair, leaning with interest forward on his knees and looking expectantly into the newcomer's face)* What can we do for you, Mr. Lindner!

LINDNER *(some minor shuffling of the hat and briefcase on his knees)* Well—I am a representative of the Clybourne Park Improvement Association—

WALTER *(pointing)* Why don't you sit your things on the floor?

LINDNER Oh—yes. Thank you. *(He slides the briefcase and hat under the chair.)* And as I was saying—I am from the Clybourne Park Improvement Association and we have had it brought to our attention at the last meeting that you people—or at least your mother—has bought a piece of residential property at—*(he digs for the slip of paper again)*—four o six Clybourne Street. . . .

WALTER That's right. Care for something to drink? Ruth, get Mr. Lindner a beer.

LINDNER *(upset for some reason)* Oh—no, really. I mean thank you very much, but no thank you.

RUTH *(innocently)* Some coffee?

LINDNER Thank you, nothing at all.

BENEATHA *is watching the man carefully.*

LINDNER Well, I don't know how much you folks know about our organization. *(He is a gentle man; thoughtful and somewhat labored in his manner.)* It is one of those community organizations set up to look after—oh, you know, things like block upkeep and special projects and we also have what we call our New Neighbors Orientation Committee. . . .

BENEATHA (*drily*) Yes—and what do they do?

LINDNER (*turning a little to her and then returning the main force to* WALTER) Well—it's what you might call a sort of welcoming committee, I guess. I mean they, we, I'm the chairman of the committee—go around and see the new people who move into the neighborhood and sort of give them the lowdown on the way we do things out in Clybourne Park.

BENEATHA (*with appreciation of the two meanings, which escape* RUTH *and* WALTER) Un-huh.

LINDNER And we also have the category of what the association calls—(*he looks elsewhere*)—uh—special community problems. . . .

BENEATHA Yes—and what are some of those?

WALTER Girl, let the man talk.

LINDNER (*with understated relief*) Thank you. I would like to explain this thing in my own way. I mean I want to explain to you in a certain way.

WALTER Go ahead.

LINDNER Yes. Well. I'm going to try to get right to the point. I'm sure we'll all appreciate that in the long run.

BENEATHA Yes.

LINDNER Well—

WALTER Be still now!

LINDNER Well—

RUTH (*still innocently*) Would you like another chair—you don't look comfortable.

LINDNER (*more frustrated than annoyed*) No, thank you very much. Please. Well—to get right to the point I—(*a great breath, and he is off at last*) I am sure you people must be aware of some of the incidents which have happened in various parts of the city when colored people have moved into certain areas— (BENEATHA *exhales heavily and starts tossing a piece of fruit up and down in the air.*) Well—because we have what I think is going to be a unique type of organization in American community life—not only do we deplore that kind of thing—but we are trying to do something about it. (BENEATHA *stops tossing and turns with a new and quizzical interest to the man.*) We feel—(*gaining confidence in his mission because of the interest in the faces of the people he is talking to*)—we feel that most of the trouble in this world, when you come right down to it—(*he hits his knee for emphasis*)—most of the trouble exists because people just don't sit down and talk to each other.

RUTH (*nodding as she might in church, pleased with the remark*) You can say that again, mister.

LINDNER (*more encouraged by such affirmation*) That we don't try hard enough in this world to understand the other fellow's problem. The other guy's point of view.

RUTH Now that's right.

BENEATHA *and* WALTER *merely watch and listen with genuine interest.*

LINDNER Yes—that's the way we feel out in Clybourne Park. And that's why I was elected to come here this afternoon and talk to you people. Friendly like, you know, the way people should talk to each other and see if we couldn't find some way to work this thing out. As I say, the whole business is a matter of *caring* about the other fellow. Anybody can see that you are a nice family of folks, hard-working and honest I'm sure. (BENEATHA *frowns slightly, quizzically, her head tilted regarding him.*) Today everybody knows what it means to be on the outside of *something*. And of course, there is always somebody who is out to take the advantage of people who don't always understand.

WALTER What do you mean?

LINDNER Well—you see our community is made up of people who've worked hard as the dickens for years to build up that little community. They're not rich and fancy people; just hard-working, honest people who don't really have much but those little homes and a dream of the kind of community they want to raise their children in. Now, I don't say we are perfect and there is a lot wrong in some of the things they want. But you've got to admit that a man, right or wrong, has the right to want to have the neighborhood he lives in a certain kind of way. And at the moment the overwhelming majority of our people out there feel that people get along better, take more of a common interest in the life of the community, when they share a common background. I want you to believe me when I tell you that race prejudice simply doesn't enter into it. It is a matter of the people of Clybourne Park believing, rightly or wrongly, as I say, that for the happiness of all concerned that our Negro families are happier when they live in their *own* communities.

BENEATHA (*with a grand and bitter gesture*) This, friends, is the Welcoming Committee!

WALTER (*dumbfounded, looking at* LINDER) Is this what you came marching all the way over here to tell us?

LINDNER Well, now we've been having a fine conversation. I hope you'll hear me all the way through.

WALTER (*tightly*) Go ahead, man.

LINDNER You see—in the face of all the things I have said, we are prepared to make your family a very generous offer. . . .

BENEATHA Thirty pieces and not a coin less!

WALTER Yeah?

LINDNER (*putting on his glasses and drawing a form out of the briefcase*) Our association is prepared, through the collective effort of our people, to buy the house from you at a financial gain to your family.

RUTH Lord have mercy, ain't this the living gall!

WALTER All right, you through?

LINDNER Well, I want to give you the exact terms of the financial arrangement—

WALTER We don't want to hear no exact terms of no arrangements. I want to know if you got any more to tell us 'bout getting together?

LINDNER (*taking off his glasses*) Well—I don't suppose that you feel. . . .

WALTER Never mind how I feel—you got any more to say 'bout how people ought to sit down and talk to each other? . . . Get out of my house, man. (*He turns his back and walks to the door.*)

LINDNER (*looking around at the hostile faces and reaching and assembling his hat and briefcase*) Well—I don't understand why you people are reacting this way. What do you think you are going to gain by moving into a neighborhood where you just aren't wanted and where some elements—well—people can get awful worked up when they feel that their whole way of life and everything they've ever worked for is threatened.

WALTER Get out.

LINDNER (*at the door, holding a small card*) Well—I'm sorry it went like this.

WALTER Get out.

LINDNER (*almost sadly, regarding* WALTER) You just can't force people to change their hearts, son.

He turns and puts his card on the table and exits. WALTER *pushes the door to with stinging hatred, and stands looking at it.* RUTH *just sits and* BENEATHA *just stands. They say nothing.* MAMA *and* TRAVIS *enter.*

MAMA Well—this all the packing got done since I left out of here this morning. I testify before God that my children got all the energy of the dead. What time the moving men due?

BENEATHA Four o'clock. You had a caller, Mama. (*She is smiling, teasingly.*)

MAMA Sure enough—who?

BENEATHA (*her arms folded saucily*) The Welcoming Committee.

WALTER *and* RUTH *giggle.*

MAMA (*innocently*) Who?

BENEATHA The Welcoming Committee. They said they're sure going to be glad to see you when you get there.

WALTER (*devilishly*) Yeah, they said they can't hardly wait to see your face.

Laughter.

MAMA (*sensing their facetiousness*) What's the matter with you all?

WALTER Ain't nothing the matter with us. We just telling you 'bout the gentleman who came to see you this afternoon. From the Clybourne Park Improvement Association.

MAMA What he want?

RUTH (*in the same mood as* BENEATHA *and* WALTER) To welcome you, honey.

WALTER He said they can't hardly wait. He said the one thing they don't have, that they just *dying* to have out there is a fine family of colored people! (*To* RUTH *and* BENEATHA) Ain't that right!

RUTH AND BENEATHA (*mockingly*) Yeah! He left his card in case—

They indicate the card, and MAMA *picks it up and throws it on the floor—understanding and looking off as she draws her chair up to the table on which she has put her plant and some sticks and some cord.*

MAMA Father, give us strength. (*Knowingly—and without fun*) Did he threaten us?

BENEATHA Oh—Mama—they don't do it like that any more. He talked Brotherhood. He said everybody ought to learn how to sit down and hate each other with good Christian fellowship.

She and WALTER *shake hands to ridicule the remark.*

MAMA (*sadly*) Lord, protect us. . . .

RUTH You should hear the money those folks raised to buy the house from us. All we paid and then some.

BENEATHA What they think we going to do—eat 'em?

RUTH No, honey, marry 'em.

MAMA (*shaking her head*) Lord, Lord, Lord. . . .

RUTH Well—that's the way the crackers crumble. Joke.

BENEATHA (*laughingly noticing what her mother is doing*) Mama, what are you doing?

MAMA Fixing my plant so it won't get hurt none on the way. . . .

BENEATHA Mama, you going to take *that* to the new house?

MAMA Un-huh—

BENEATHA That raggedy-looking old thing?

MAMA (*stopping and looking at her*) It expresses *me*.

RUTH (*with delight, to* BENEATHA) So there, Miss Thing!

WALTER *comes to* MAMA *suddenly and bends down behind her and squeezes her in his arms with all his strength. She is overwhelmed by the suddenness of it and, though delighted, her manner is like that of* RUTH *with* TRAVIS.

MAMA Look out now, boy! You make me mess up my thing here!

WALTER (*his face lit, he slips down on his knees beside her, his arms still about her*) Mama . . . you know what it means to climb up in the chariot?

MAMA (*gruffly, very happy*) Get on away from me now. . . .

RUTH (*near the gift-wrapped package, trying to catch* WALTER's *eye*) Psst—

WALTER What the old song say, Mama. . . .

RUTH Walter—Now? (*She is pointing at the package.*)

WALTER (*speaking the lines, sweetly, playfully, in his mother's face*)

> I got wings . . . you got wings . . .
> All God's children got wings . . .

MAMA Boy—get out of my face and do some work. . . .

WALTER

> When I get to heaven gonna put on my wings.
> Gonna fly all over God's heaven . . .

BENEATHA (*teasingly, from across the room*) Everybody talking 'bout heaven ain't going there!

WALTER (*to* RUTH, *who is carrying the box across to them*) I don't know, you think we ought to give her that. . . . Seems to me she ain't been very appreciative around here.

MAMA (*eyeing the box, which is obviously a gift*) What is that?

WALTER (*taking it from* RUTH *and putting it on the table in front of* MAMA) Well— what you all think? Should we give it to her?

RUTH Oh—she was pretty good today.

MAMA I'll good you— (*She turns her eyes to the box again.*)

BENEATHA Open it, Mama.

She stands up, looks at it, turns and looks at all of them, and then presses her hands together and does not open the package.

WALTER (*sweetly*) Open it, Mama. It's for you. (MAMA *looks in his eyes. It is the first present in her life without its being Christmas. Slowly she opens her package and lifts out, one by one, a brand-new sparkling set of gardening tools.* WALTER *continues, prodding*) Ruth made up the note—read it . . .

MAMA (*picking up the card and adjusting her glasses*) "To our own Mrs. Miniver—Love from Brother, Ruth and Beneatha." Ain't that lovely. . . .

TRAVIS (*tugging at his father's sleeve*) Daddy, can I give her mine now?

WALTER All right, son. (TRAVIS *flies to get his gift.*) Travis didn't want to go in with the rest of us, Mama. He got his own. (*Somewhat amused*) We don't know what it is. . . .

TRAVIS (*racing back in the room with a large hatbox and putting it in front of his grandmother*) Here!

MAMA Lord have mercy, baby. You done gone and bought your grandmother a hat?

TRAVIS (*very proud*) Open it!

She does and lifts out an elaborate, but very elaborate, wide gardening hat, and all the adults break up at the sight of it.

RUTH Travis, honey, what is that?

TRAVIS (*who thinks it is beautiful and appropriate*) It's a gardening hat! Like the ladies always have on in the magazines when they work in their gardens.

BENEATHA (*giggling fiercely*) Travis—we were trying to make Mama Mrs. Miniver—not Scarlett O'Hara!

MAMA (*indignantly*) What's the matter with you all! This here is a beautiful hat! (*Absurdly*) I always wanted me one just like it!

She pops it on her head to prove it to her grandson, and the hat is ludicrous and considerably oversized.

RUTH Hot dog! Go, Mama!

WALTER (*doubled over with laughter*) I'm sorry, Mama—but you look like you ready to go out and chop you some cotton sure enough!

They all laugh except MAMA, *out of deference to* TRAVIS' *feelings.*

MAMA (*gathering the boy up to her*) Bless your heart—this is the prettiest hat I ever owned— (WALTER, RUTH, *and* BENEATHA *chime in noisily, festively and insincerely congratulating* TRAVIS *on his gift.*) What are we all standing around here for? We ain't finished packin' yet. Bennie, you ain't packed one book.

The bell rings.

BENEATHA That couldn't be the movers . . . it's not hardly two good yet—

BENEATHA *goes into her room.* MAMA *starts for door.*

WALTER (*turning, stiffening*) Wait—wait—I'll get it. (*He stands and looks at the door.*)

MAMA You expecting company, son?

WALTER (*just looking at the door*) Yeah—yeah. . . .

MAMA *looks at* RUTH, *and they exchange innocent and unfrightened glances.*

MAMA (*not understanding*) Well, let them in, son.

BENEATHA (*from her room*) We need some more string.

MAMA Travis—you run to the hardware and get me some string cord.

MAMA *goes out and* WALTER *turns and looks at* RUTH. TRAVIS *goes to a dish for money.*

RUTH Why don't you answer the door, man?

WALTER (*suddenly bounding across the floor to her*) 'Cause sometimes it hard to let the future begin! (*Stooping down in her face*)

I got wings! You got wings!
All God's children got wings!

(*He crosses to the door and throws it open. Standing there is a very slight little man in a not too prosperous business suit and with haunted frightened eyes and a hat pulled*

down tightly, brim up, around his forehead. TRAVIS passes between the men and exits.
WALTER *leans deep in the man's face, still in his jubilance.*)

When I get to heaven gonna put on my wings.
Gonna fly all over God's heaven . . .

(*The little man just stares at him.*)

Heaven—

(*Suddenly he stops and looks past the little man into the empty hallway.*) Where's
Willy, man?

BOBO He ain't with me.

WALTER (*not disturbed*) Oh—come on in. You know my wife.

BOBO (*dumbly, taking off his hat*) Yes—h'you, Miss Ruth.

RUTH (*quietly, a mood apart from her husband already, seeing* BOBO) Hello, Bobo.

WALTER You right on time today. . . . Right on time. That's the way! (*He slaps* BOBO
on his back.) Sit down . . . lemme hear.

RUTH *stands stiffly and quietly in back of them, as though somehow she senses death, her
eyes fixed on her husband.*

BOBO (*his frightened eyes on the floor, his hat in his hands*) Could I please get a drink of
water, before I tell you about it, Walter Lee?

WALTER *does not take his eyes off the man.* RUTH *goes blindly to the tap and gets a glass
of water and brings it to* BOBO.

WALTER There ain't nothing wrong, is there?

BOBO Lemme tell you—

WALTER Man—didn't nothing go wrong?

BOBO Lemme tell you—Walter Lee. (*Looking at* RUTH *and talking to her more than to*
WALTER) You know how it was. I got to tell you how it was. I mean first I got to tell
you how it was all the way . . . I mean about the money I put in, Walter Lee. . . .

WALTER (*with taut agitation now*) What about the money you put in?

BOBO Well—it wasn't much as we told you—me and Willy— (*He stops.*) I'm sorry,
Walter. I got a bad feeling about it. I got a real bad feeling about it. . . .

WALTER Man, what you telling me about all this for? . . . Tell me what happened in
Springfield. . . .

BOBO Springfield.

RUTH (*like a dead woman*) What was supposed to happen in Springfield?

BOBO (*to her*) This deal that me and Walter went into with Willy—Me and Willy was
going to go down to Springfield and spread some money 'round so's we wouldn't have
to wait so long for the liquor license. . . . That's what we were going to do. Everybody
said that was the way you had to do, you understand, Miss Ruth?

WALTER Man—what happened down there?

BOBO (*a pitiful man, near tears*) I'm trying to tell you, Walter.

WALTER (*screaming at him suddenly*) THEN TELL ME, GODDAMMIT . . . WHAT'S
THE MATTER WITH YOU?

BOBO Man . . . I didn't go to no Springfield, yesterday.

WALTER (*halted, life hanging in the moment*) Why not?

BOBO (*the long way, the hard way to tell*) 'Cause I didn't have no reasons to. . . .

WALTER Man, what are you talking about!

BOBO I'm talking about the fact that when I got to the train station yesterday morning—eight o'clock like we planned . . . Man—*Willy didn't never show up.*

WALTER Why . . . where was he . . . where is he?

BOBO That's what I'm trying to tell you . . . I don't know . . . I waited six hours . . . I called his house . . . and I waited . . . six hours . . . I waited in that train station six hours . . . (*Breaking into tears*) That was all the extra money I had in the world. . . . (*Looking up at* WALTER *with the tears running down his face*) Man, *Willy is gone.*

WALTER Gone, what you mean Willy is gone? Gone where? You mean he went by himself. You mean he went off to Springfield by himself—to take care of getting the license— (*Turns and looks anxiously at* RUTH) You mean maybe he didn't want too many people in on the business down there? (*Looks to* RUTH *again, as before*) You know Willy got his own ways. (*Looks back to* BOBO) Maybe you was late yesterday and he just went on down there without you. Maybe—maybe—he's been callin' you at home tryin' to tell you what happened or something. Maybe—maybe—he just got sick. He's somewhere—he's got to be somewhere. We just got to find him—me and you got to find him. (*Grabs* BOBO *senselessly by the collar and starts to shake him*) We got to!

BOBO (*in sudden angry, frightened agony*) What's the matter with you, Walter! *When a cat take off with your money he don't leave you no maps!*

WALTER (*turning madly, as though he is looking for* WILLY *in the very room*) Willy! . . . Willy . . . don't do it. . . . Please don't do it. . . . Man, not with that money . . . Man, please, not with that money . . . Oh, God . . . Don't let it be true. . . . (*He is wandering around, crying out for* WILLY *and looking for him or perhaps for help from God.*) Man . . . I trusted you . . . Man, I put my life in your hands. . . . (*He starts to crumple down on the floor as* RUTH *just covers her face in horror.* MAMA *opens the door and comes into the room, with* BENEATHA *behind her.*) Man . . . (*He starts to pound the floor with his fists, sobbing wildly.*) That money is made out of my father's flesh. . . .

BOBO (*standing over him helplessly*) I'm sorry, Walter. . . . (*Only* WALTER's *sobs reply.* BOBO *puts on his hat.*) I had my life staked on this deal, too. . . . (*He exits.*)

MAMA (*to* WALTER) Son— (*She goes to him, bends down to him, talks to his bent head.*) Son . . . Is it gone? Son, I gave you sixty-five hundred dollars. Is it gone? All of it? Beneatha's money too?

WALTER (*lifting his head slowly*) Mama . . . I never . . . went to the bank at all. . . .

MAMA (*not wanting to believe him*) You mean . . . your sister's school money . . . you used that too . . . Walter? . . .

WALTER Yessss! . . . All of it. . . . It's all gone. . . .

There is total silence. RUTH *stands with her face covered with her hands;* BENEATHA *leans forlornly against a wall, fingering a piece of red ribbon from the mother's gift.* MAMA *stops and looks at her son without recognition and then, quite without thinking about it, starts to beat him senselessly in the face.* BENEATHA *goes to them and stops it.*

BENEATHA Mama!

MAMA *stops and looks at both of her children and rises slowly and wanders vaguely, aimlessly away from them.*

MAMA I seen . . . him . . . night after night . . . come in . . . and look at that rug . . . and then look at me . . . the red showing in his eyes . . . the veins moving in his head. . . . I seen him grow thin and old before he was forty . . . working and working and working like somebody's old horse . . . killing himself . . . and you—you give it all away in a day. . . .

BENEATHA Mama—

MAMA Oh, God . . . (*She looks up to Him.*) Look down here—and show me the strength.

BENEATHA Mama—

MAMA (*folding over*) Strength . . .

BENEATHA (*plaintively*) Mama . . .

MAMA Strength!

Curtain

ACT III

An hour later.

At curtain, there is a sullen light of gloom in the living room, gray light not unlike that which began the first scene of Act I. At left we can see WALTER within his room, alone with himself. He is stretched out on the bed, his shirt out and open, his arms under his head. He does not smoke, he does not cry out, he merely lies there, looking up at the ceiling, much as if he were alone in the world.

In the living room BENEATHA sits at the table, still surrounded by the now almost ominous packing crates. She sits looking off. We feel that this is a mood struck perhaps an hour before, and it lingers now, full of the empty sound of profound disappointment. We see on a line from her brother's bedroom the sameness of their attitudes. Presently the bell rings and BENEATHA rises without ambition or interest in answering. It is ASAGAI, smiling broadly, striding into the room with energy and happy expectation and conversation.

ASAGAI I came over . . . I had some free time. I thought I might help with the packing. Ah, I like the look of packing crates! A household in preparation for a journey! It depresses some people . . . but for me . . . it is another feeling. Something full of the flow of life, do you understand? Movement, progress . . . It makes me think of Africa.

BENEATHA Africa!

ASAGAI What kind of a mood is this? Have I told you how deeply you move me?

BENEATHA He gave away the money, Asagai. . . .

ASAGAI Who gave away what money?

BENEATHA The insurance money. My brother gave it away.

ASAGAI Gave it away?

BENEATHA He made an investment! With a man even Travis wouldn't have trusted.

ASAGAI And it's gone?

BENEATHA Gone!

ASAGAI I'm very sorry. . . . And you, now?

BENEATHA Me? . . . Me? . . . Me I'm nothing. . . . Me. When I was very small . . . we used to take our sleds out in the wintertime and the only hills we had were the ice-covered stone steps of some houses down the street. And we used to fill them in with snow and make them smooth and slide down them all day . . . and it was very dangerous you know . . . far too steep . . . and sure enough one day a kid named Rufus came down too fast and hit the sidewalk . . . and we saw his face just split open right there in front of us. . . . And I remember standing there looking at his bloody open face thinking that was the end of Rufus. But the ambulance came and they took him to the hospital and they fixed the broken bones and they sewed it all up . . . and the next time I saw Rufus he just had a little line down the middle of his face. . . . I never got over that. . . .

WALTER *sits up, listening on the bed. Throughout this scene it is important that we feel his reaction at all times, that he visibly respond to the words of his sister and* ASAGAI.

ASAGAI What?

BENEATHA That was what one person could do for another, fix him up—sew up the problem, make him all right again. That was the most marvelous thing in the world. . . . I wanted to do that. I always thought it was the one concrete thing in the world that a human being could do. Fix up the sick, you know—and make them whole again. This was truly being God. . . .

ASAGAI You wanted to be God?

BENEATHA No—I wanted to cure. It used to be so important to me. I wanted to cure. It used to matter. I used to care. I mean about people and how their bodies hurt. . . .

ASAGAI And you've stopped caring?

BENEATHA Yes—I think so.

ASAGAI Why?

WALTER *rises, goes to the door of his room and is about to open it, then stops and stands listening, leaning on the door jamb.*

BENEATHA Because it doesn't seem deep enough, close enough to what ails mankind— I mean this thing of sewing up bodies or administering drugs. Don't you understand? It was a child's reaction to the world. I thought that doctors had the secret to all the hurts. . . . That's the way a child sees things—or an idealist.

ASAGAI Children see things very well sometimes—and idealists even better.

BENEATHA I know that's what you think. Because you are still where I left off—you still care. This is what you see for the world, for Africa. You with the dreams of the future will patch up all Africa—you are going to cure the Great Sore of colonialism with Independence—

ASAGAI Yes!

BENEATHA Yes—and you think that one word is the penicillin of the human spirit: "Independence!" But then what?

ASAGAI That will be the problem for another time. First we must get there.

BENEATHA And where does it end?

ASAGAI End? Who even spoke of an end? To life? To living?

BENEATHA An end to misery!

ASAGAI (*smiling*) You sound like a French intellectual.

BENEATHA No! I sound like a human being who just had her future taken right out of her hands! While I was sleeping in my bed in there, things were happening in this world that directly concerned me—and nobody asked me, consulted me—they just went out and did things—and changed my life. Don't you see there isn't any real progress, Asagai, there is only one large circle that we march in, around and around, each of us with our own little picture—in front of us—our own little mirage that we think is the future.

ASAGAI That is the mistake.

BENEATHA What?

ASAGAI What you just said—about the circle. It isn't a circle—it is simply a long line— as in geometry, you know, one that reaches into infinity. And because we cannot see the end—we also cannot see how it changes. And it is very odd but those who see the changes are called "idealists"—and those who cannot, or refuse to think, they are the "realists." It is very strange, and amusing too, I think.

BENEATHA You—you are almost religious.

ASAGAI Yes . . . I think I have the religion of doing what is necessary in the world—and of worshipping man—because he is so marvelous, you see.

BENEATHA Man is foul! And the human race deserves its misery!

ASAGAI You see: *you* have become the religious one in the old sense. Already, and after such a small defeat, you are worshipping despair.

BENEATHA From now on, I worship the truth—and the truth is that people are puny, small and selfish. . . .

ASAGAI Truth? Why is it that you despairing ones always think that only you have the truth? I never thought to see *you* like that. You! Your brother made a stupid, childish mistake—and you are grateful to him. So that now you can give up the ailing human race on account of it. You talk about what good is struggle; what good is anything? Where are we all going? And why are we bothering?

BENEATHA *And you cannot answer it!* All your talk and dreams about Africa and Independence. Independence and then what? What about all the crooks and petty thieves and just plain idiots who will come into power to steal and plunder the same as before—only now they will be black and do it in the name of the new Independence— You cannot answer that.

ASAGAI (*shouting over her*) I *live the answer!* (*Pause*) In my village at home it is the exceptional man who can even read a newspaper . . . or who ever *sees* a book at all. I will go home and much of what I will have to say will seem strange to the people of my village. . . . But I will teach and work and things will happen, slowly and swiftly. At times it will seem that nothing changes at all . . . and then again . . . the sudden dramatic events which make history leap into the future. And then quiet again. Retrogression even. Guns, murder, revolution. And I even will have moments when I wonder if the quiet was not better than all that death and hatred. But I will look about my village at the illiteracy and disease and ignorance and I will not wonder long. And perhaps . . . perhaps I will be a great man. . . . I mean perhaps I will hold on to the substance of truth and find my way always with the right course . . . and perhaps for it I will be butchered in my bed some night by the servants of the empire. . . .

BENEATHA *The martyr!*

ASAGAI . . . or perhaps I shall live to be a very old man, respected and esteemed in my new nation. . . . And perhaps I shall hold office and this is what I'm trying to tell you, Alaiyo; perhaps the things I believe now for my country will be wrong and outmoded, and I will not understand and do terrible things to have things my way or merely to keep my power. Don't you see that there will be young men and women, not British soldiers then, but my own black countrymen . . . to step out of the shadows some evening and slit my then useless throat? Don't you see they have always been there . . . that they always will be. And that such a thing as my own death will be an advance? They who might kill me even . . . actually replenish me!

BENEATHA Oh, Asagai, I know all that.

ASAGAI Good! Then stop moaning and groaning and tell me what you plan to do.

BENEATHA Do?

ASAGAI I have a bit of a suggestion.

BENEATHA What?

ASAGAI (*rather quietly for him*) That when it is all over—that you come home with me—

BENEATHA (*slapping herself on the forehead with exasperation born of misunderstanding*) Oh—Asagai—at this moment you decide to be romantic!

ASAGAI (*quickly understanding the misunderstanding*) My dear, young creature of the New World—I do not mean across the city—I mean across the ocean; home—to Africa.

BENEATHA (*slowly understanding and turning to him with murmured amazement*) To—to Nigeria?

ASAGAI Yes! . . . (*Smiling and lifting his arms playfully*) Three hundred years later the African Prince rose up out of the seas and swept the maiden back across the middle passage over which her ancestors had come—

BENEATHA (*unable to play*) Nigeria?

ASAGAI Nigeria. Home. (*Coming to her with genuine romantic flippancy*) I will show you our mountains and our stars; and give you cool drinks from gourds and teach you the old songs and the ways of our people—and, in time, we will pretend that—(*very softly*)—you have only been away for a day—

She turns her back to him, thinking. He swings her around and takes her full in his arms in a long embrace which proceeds to passion.

BENEATHA (*pulling away*) You're getting me all mixed up—

ASAGAI Why?

BENEATHA Too many things—too many things have happened today. I must sit down and think. I don't know what I feel about anything right this minute. (*She promptly sits down and props her chin on her fist.*)

ASAGAI (*charmed*) All right, I shall leave you. No—don't get up. (*Touching her, gently, sweetly*) Just sit awhile and think. . . . Never be afraid to sit awhile and think. (*He goes to door and looks at her.*) How often I have looked at you and said, "Ah—so this is what the New World hath finally wrought. . . ."

He exits. BENEATHA *sits on alone. Presently* WALTER *enters from his room and starts to rummage through things, feverishly looking for something. She looks up and turns in her seat.*

BENEATHA (*hissingly*) Yes—just look at what the New World hath wrought! . . . Just look! (*She gestures with bitter disgust.*) There he is! *Monsieur le petit bourgeois noir*—himself! There he is—Symbol of a Rising Class! Entrepreneur! Titan of the system! (WALTER *ignores her completely and continues frantically and destructively looking for something and hurling things to floor and tearing things out of their place in his search.* BENEATHA *ignores the eccentricity of his actions and goes on with the monologue of insult.*) Did you dream of yachts on Lake Michigan, Brother? Did you see yourself on that Great Day sitting down at the Conference Table, surrounded by all the mighty bald-headed men in America? All halted, waiting, breathless, waiting for your pronouncements on industry? Waiting for you—Chairman of the Board? (WALTER *finds what he is looking for—a small piece of white paper—and pushes it in his pocket and puts on his coat and rushes out without ever having looked at her. She shouts after him.*) I look at you and I see the final triumph of stupidity in the world!

The door slams and she returns to just sitting again. RUTH *comes quickly out of* MAMA's *room.*

RUTH Who was that?

BENEATHA Your husband.

RUTH Where did he go?

BENEATHA Who knows—maybe he has an appointment at U.S. Steel.

RUTH (*anxiously, with frightened eyes*) You didn't say nothing bad to him, did you?

BENEATHA Bad? Say anything bad to him? No—I told him he was a sweet boy and full of dreams and everything is strictly peachy keen, as the ofay kids say!

MAMA *enters from her bedroom. She is lost, vague, trying to catch hold, to make some sense of her former command of the world, but it still eludes her. A sense of waste overwhelms her gait; a measure of apology rides on her shoulders. She goes to her plant, which has remained on the table, looks at it, picks it up and takes it to the window sill and sits it outside, and she stands and looks at it a long moment. Then she closes the window, straightens her body with effort and turns around to her children.*

MAMA Well—ain't it a mess in here, though? (*A false cheerfulness, a beginning of something*) I guess we all better stop moping around and get some work done. All this unpacking and everything we got to do. (RUTH *raises her head slowly in response to the sense of the line; and* BENEATHA *in similar manner turns very slowly to look at her mother.*) One of you all better call the moving people and tell 'em not to come.

RUTH Tell 'em not to come?

MAMA Of course, baby. Ain't no need in 'em coming all the way here and having to go back. They charges for that too. (*She sits down, fingers to her brow, thinking.*) Lord, ever since I was a little girl, I always remembers people saying, "Lena—Lena Eggleston, you aims too high all the time. You needs to slow down and see life a little more like it is. Just slow down some." That's what they always used to say down home—"Lord, that Lena Eggleston is a high-minded thing. She'll get her due one day!"

RUTH No, Lena. . . .

MAMA Me and Big Walter just didn't never learn right.

RUTH Lena, no! We gotta go. Bennie—tell her. . . . (*She rises and crosses to* BENEATHA *with her arms outstretched.* BENEATHA *doesn't respond.*) Tell her we can still move . . . the notes ain't but a hundred and twenty-five a month. We got four grown people in this house—we can work. . . .

MAMA (*to herself*) Just aimed too high all the time—

RUTH (*turning and going to* MAMA *fast—the words pouring out with urgency and desperation*) Lena—I'll work. . . . I'll work twenty hours a day in all the kitchens in Chicago. . . . I'll strap my baby on my back if I have to and scrub all the floors in America and wash all the sheets in America if I have to—but we got to move. . . . We got to get out of here. . . .

MAMA *reaches out absently and pats* RUTH's *hand.*

MAMA No—I see things differently now. Been thinking 'bout some of the things we could do to fix this place up some. I seen a second-hand bureau over on Maxwell Street just the other day that could fit right there. (*She points to where the new furniture might go.* RUTH *wanders away from her.*) Would need some new handles on it and then a little varnish and then it look like something brand-new. And—we can put up them new curtains in the kitchen. . . . Why this place be looking fine. Cheer us all up so that we forget trouble ever came. . . . (*To* RUTH) And you could get some nice screens to put up in your room round the baby's bassinet. . . . (*She looks at both of them, pleadingly.*) Sometimes you just got to know when to give up some things . . . and hold on to what you got.

WALTER *enters from the outside, looking spent and leaning against the door, his coat hanging from him.*

MAMA Where you been, son?

WALTER (*breathing hard*) Made a call.

MAMA To who, son?

WALTER To The Man.

MAMA What man, baby?

WALTER The Man, Mama. Don't you know who The Man is?

RUTH Walter Lee?

WALTER *The Man.* Like the guys in the streets say—The Man. Captain Boss—Mistuh Charley . . . Old Captain Please Mr. Bossman . . .

BENEATHA (*suddenly*) Lindner!

WALTER That's right! That's good. I told him to come right over.

BENEATHA (*fiercely, understanding*) For what? What do you want to see him for!

WALTER (*looking at his sister*) We going to do business with him.

MAMA What you talking 'bout, son?

WALTER Talking 'bout life, Mama. You all always telling me to see life like it is. Well— I laid in there on my back today . . . and I figured it out. Life just like it is. Who gets and who don't get. (*He sits down with his coat on and laughs.*) Mama, you know it's all divided up. Life is. Sure enough. Between the takers and the "tooken." (*He laughs.*) I've figured it out finally. (*He looks around at them.*) Yeah. Some of us always getting "tooken." (*He laughs.*) People like Willy Harris, they don't never get "tooken." And you know why the rest of us do? 'Cause we all mixed up. Mixed up bad. We get to looking 'round for the right and the wrong; and we worry about it and cry about it and stay up nights trying to figure out 'bout the wrong and the right of things all the time. . . . And all the time, man, them takers is out there operating, just taking and taking. Willy Harris? Shoot—Willy Harris don't even count. He don't even count in the big scheme of things. But I'll say one thing for old Willy Harris . . . he's taught me something. He's taught me to keep my eye on what counts in this world. Yeah— (*shouting out a little*) Thanks, Willy!

RUTH What did you call that man for, Walter Lee?

WALTER Called him to tell him to come on over to the show. Gonna put on a show for the man. Just what he wants to see. You see, Mama, the man came here today and he told us that them people out there where you want us to move—well they so upset they willing to pay us not to move out there. (*He laughs again.*) And—and oh, Mama— you would of been proud of the way me and Ruth and Bennie acted. We told him to get out . . . Lord have mercy! We told the man to get out. Oh, we was some proud folks this afternoon, yeah. (*He lights a cigarette.*) We were still full of that old-time stuff. . . .

RUTH (*coming toward him slowly*) You talking 'bout taking them people's money to keep us from moving in that house?

WALTER I ain't just talking 'bout it, baby—I'm telling you that's what's going to happen.

BENEATHA Oh, God! Where is the bottom! Where is the real honest-to-God bottom so he can't go any farther!

WALTER See—that's old stuff. You and that boy that was here today. You all want everybody to carry a flag and a spear and sing some marching songs, huh? You wanna spend your life looking into things and trying to find the right and the wrong part, huh? Yeah. You know what's going to happen to that boy someday—he'll find himself sitting in a dungeon, locked in forever—and the takers will have the key! Forget it, baby! There ain't no causes—there ain't nothing but taking in this world, and he who takes most is smartest—and it don't make a damn bit of difference *how.*

MAMA You making something inside me cry, son. Some awful pain inside me.

WALTER Don't cry, Mama. Understand. That white man is going to walk in that door able to write checks for more money than we ever had. It's important to him and I'm going to help him . . . I'm going to put on the show, Mama.

MAMA Son—I come from five generations of people who was slaves and sharecroppers—but ain't nobody in my family never let nobody pay 'em no money that was a way of telling us we wasn't fit to walk the earth. We ain't never been that poor. (*Raising her eyes and looking at him*) We ain't never been that dead inside.

BENEATHA Well—we are dead now. All the talk about dreams and sunlight that goes on in this house. All dead.

WALTER What's the matter with you all! I didn't make this world! It was give to me this way! Hell, yes, I want me some yachts someday! Yes, I want to hang some real pearls 'round my wife's neck. Ain't she supposed to wear no pearls? Somebody tell me—tell me, who decides which women is suppose to wear pearls in this world. I tell you I am a *man*—and I think my wife should wear some pearls in this world!

This last line hangs a good while and WALTER *begins to move about the room. The word "man" has penetrated his consciousness; he mumbles it to himself repeatedly between strange agitated pauses as he moves about.*

MAMA Baby, how you going to feel on the inside?

WALTER Fine! . . . Going to feel fine . . . a man. . . .

MAMA You won't have nothing left then, Walter Lee.

WALTER (*coming to her*) I'm going to feel fine, Mama. I'm going to look that son-of-a-bitch in the eyes and say—(*he falters*)—and say, "All right, Mr. Lindner—(*he falters even more*)—that's your neighborhood out there. You got the right to keep it like you want. You got the right to have it like you want. Just write the check and—the house is yours." And, and I am going to say— (*His voice almost breaks.*) And you—you people just put the money in my hand and you won't have to live next to this bunch of stinking niggers! . . . (*He straightens up and moves away from his mother, walking around the room.*) Maybe—maybe I'll just get down on my black knees. . . . (*He does so;* RUTH *and* BENNIE *and* MAMA *watch him in frozen horror.*) Captain, Mistuh, Bossman. (*He starts crying.*) A-hee-hee-hee! (*Wringing his hands in profoundly anguished imitation*) Yassssssuh! Great White Father, just gi' ussen de money, fo' God's sake, and we's ain't gwine come out deh and dirty up yo' white folks neighborhood. . . .

He breaks down completely, then gets up and goes into the bedroom.

BENEATHA That is not a man. That is nothing but a toothless rat.

MAMA Yes—death done come in this here house. (*She is nodding, slowly, reflectively.*) Done come walking in my house. On the lips of my children. You what supposed to be my beginning again. You—what supposed to be my harvest. (*To* BENEATHA) You—you mourning your brother?

BENEATHA He's no brother of mine.

MAMA What you say?

BENEATHA I said that that individual in that room is no brother of mine.

MAMA That's what I thought you said. You feeling like you better than he is today? (BENEATHA *does not answer.*) Yes? What you tell him a minute ago? That he wasn't a man? Yes? You give him up for me? You done wrote his epitaph too—like the rest of the world? Well, who give you the privilege?

BENEATHA Be on my side for once! You saw what he just did, Mama! You saw him—down on his knees. Wasn't it you who taught me—to despise any man who would do that. Do what he's going to do.

MAMA Yes—I taught you that. Me and your daddy. But I thought I taught you something else too . . . I thought I taught you to love him.

BENEATHA Love him? There is nothing left to love.

MAMA There is always something left to love. And if you ain't learned that, you ain't learned nothing. (*Looking at her*) Have you cried for that boy today? I don't mean for yourself and for the family 'cause we lost the money. I mean for him; what he been through and what it done to him. Child, when do you think is the time to love somebody the most; when they done good and made things easy for everybody? Well then, you ain't through learning—because that ain't the time at all. It's when he's at his lowest and can't believe in hisself 'cause the world done whipped him so. When you starts measuring somebody, measure him right, child, measure him right. Make sure you done taken into account what hills and valleys he come through before he got to wherever he is.

TRAVIS *bursts into the room at the end of the speech, leaving the door open.*

TRAVIS Grandmama—the moving men are downstairs! The truck just pulled up.

MAMA (*turning and looking at him*) Are they, baby? They downstairs?

She sighs and sits. LINDNER *appears in the doorway. He peers in and knocks lightly, to gain attention, and comes in. All turn to look at him.*

LINDNER (*hat and briefcase in hand*) Uh—hello . . .

RUTH *crosses mechanically to the bedroom door and opens it and lets it swing open freely and slowly as the lights come up on* WALTER *within, still in his coat, sitting at the far corner of the room. He looks up and out through the room to* LINDNER.

RUTH He's here.

A long minute passes and WALTER *slowly gets up.*

LINDNER (*coming to the table with efficiency, putting his briefcase on the table and starting to unfold papers and unscrew fountain pens*) Well, I certainly was glad to hear from you people. (WALTER *has begun the trek out of the room, slowly and awkwardly, rather like a small boy, passing the back of his sleeve across his mouth from time to time.*) Life can really be so much simpler than people let it be most of the time. Well—with whom do I negotiate? You, Mrs. Younger, or your son here? (MAMA *sits with her hands folded on her lap and her eyes closed as* WALTER *advances.* TRAVIS *goes close to* LINDNER *and looks at the papers curiously.*) Just some official papers, sonny.

RUTH Travis, you go downstairs.

MAMA (*opening her eyes and looking into* WALTER's) No. Travis, you stay right here. And you make him understand what you doing, Walter Lee. You teach him good. Like Willy Harris taught you. You show where our five generations done come to. Go ahead, son—

WALTER (*looks down into his boy's eyes.* TRAVIS *grins at him merrily and* WALTER *draws him beside him with his arm lightly around his shoulders*) Well, Mr. Lindner. (BENEATHA *turns away.*) We called you—(*there is a profound, simple groping quality in his speech*)—because, well, me and my family— (*He looks around and shifts from one foot to the other.*) Well—we are very plain people. . . .

LINDNER Yes—

WALTER I mean—I have worked as a chauffeur most of my life—and my wife here, she does domestic work in people's kitchens. So does my mother. I mean—we are plain people. . . .

LINDNER Yes, Mr. Younger—

WALTER (*really like a small boy, looking down at his shoes and then up at the man*) And— uh—well, my father, well, he was a laborer most of his life.

LINDNER (*absolutely confused*) Uh, yes—

WALTER (*looking down at his toes once again*) My father almost beat a man to death once because this man called him a bad name or something, you know what I mean?

LINDNER No, I'm afraid I don't.

WALTER (*finally straightening up*) Well, what I mean is that we come from people who had a lot of pride. I mean—we are very proud people. And that's my sister over there and she's going to be a doctor—and we are very proud—

LINDNER Well—I am sure that is very nice, but—

WALTER (*starting to cry and facing the man eye to eye*) What I am telling you is that we called you over here to tell you that we are very proud and that this is—this is my son, who makes the sixth generation of our family in this country, and that we have all thought about your offer and we have decided to move into our house because my father—my father—he earned it. (MAMA *has her eyes closed and is rocking back and forth as though she were in church, with her head nodding the amen yes.*) We don't want to make no trouble for nobody or fight no causes—but we will try to be good neighbors. That's all we got to say. (*He looks the man absolutely in the eyes.*) We don't want your money. (*He turns and walks away from the man.*)

LINDNER (*looking around at all of them*) I take it then that you have decided to occupy.

BENEATHA That's what the man said.

LINDNER (*to* MAMA *in her reverie*) Then I would like to appeal to you, Mrs. Younger. You are older and wiser and understand things better I am sure. . . .

MAMA (*rising*) I am afraid you don't understand. My son said we was going to move and there ain't nothing left for me to say. (*Shaking her head with double meaning*) You know how these young folks is nowadays, mister. Can't do a thing with 'em. Goodbye.

LINDNER (*folding up his materials*) Well—if you are that final about it. . . . There is nothing left for me to say. (*He finishes. He is almost ignored by the family, who are concentrating on* WALTER LEE. *At the door* LINDNER *halts and looks around.*) I sure hope you people know what you're doing. (*He shakes his head and exits.*)

RUTH (*looking around and coming to life*) Well, for God's sake—if the moving men are here—LET'S GET THE HELL OUT OF HERE!

MAMA (*into action*) Ain't it the truth! Look at all this here mess. Ruth, put Travis' good jacket on him. . . . Walter Lee, fix your tie and tuck your shirt in, you look just like somebody's hoodlum. Lord have mercy, where is my plant? (*She flies to get it amid the general bustling of the family, who are deliberately trying to ignore the nobility of the past moment.*) You all start on down. . . . Travis child, don't go empty-handed. . . . Ruth, where did I put that box with my skillets in it? I want to be in charge of it myself. . . . I'm going to make us the biggest dinner we ever ate tonight. . . . Beneatha, what's the matter with them stockings? Pull them things up, girl. . . .

The family starts to file out as two moving men appear and begin to carry out the heavier pieces of furniture, bumping into the family as they move about.

BENEATHA Mama, Asagai—asked me to marry him today and go to Africa—

MAMA (*in the middle of her getting-ready activity*) He did? You ain't old enough to marry nobody— (*Seeing the moving men lifting one of her chairs precariously*) Darling, that ain't no bale of cotton, please handle it so we can sit in it again. I had that chair twenty-five years. . . .

The movers sigh with exasperation and go on with their work.

BENEATHA (*girlishly and unreasonably trying to pursue the conversation*) To go to Africa, Mama—be a doctor in Africa. . . .

MAMA (*distracted*) Yes, baby—

WALTER Africa! What he want you to go to Africa for?

BENEATHA To practice there. . . .

WALTER Girl, if you don't get all them silly ideas out your head! You better marry yourself a man with some loot. . . .

BENEATHA (*angrily, precisely as in the first scene of the play*) What have you got to do with who I marry!

WALTER Plenty. Now I think George Murchison—

He and BENEATHA *go out yelling at each other vigorously;* BENEATHA *is heard saying that she would not marry* GEORGE MURCHISON *if he were Adam and she were Eve, etc. The anger is loud and real till their voices diminish.* RUTH *stands at the door and turns to* MAMA *and smiles knowingly.*

MAMA (*fixing her hat at last*) Yeah—they something all right, my children. . . .

RUTH Yeah—they're something. Let's go, Lena.

MAMA (*stalling, starting to look around at the house*) Yes—I'm coming. Ruth—

RUTH Yes?

MAMA (*quietly, woman to woman*) He finally come into his manhood today, didn't he? Kind of like a rainbow after the rain. . . .

RUTH (*biting her lip lest her own pride explode in front of* MAMA) Yes, Lena.

WALTER's *voice calls for them raucously.*

MAMA (*waving* RUTH *out vaguely*) All right, honey—go on down. I be down directly.

RUTH *hesitates, then exits.* MAMA *stands, at last alone in the living room, her plant on the table before her as the lights start to come down. She looks around at all the walls and ceilings and suddenly, despite herself, while the children call below, a great heaving thing rises in her and she puts her fist to her mouth, takes a final desperate look, pulls her coat about her, pats her hat and goes out. The lights dim down. The door opens and she comes back in, grabs her plant, and goes out for the last time.*

Curtain

Questions

1. Who is the protagonist of the play? Does it have a single protagonist or is it a play of "atmosphere"?

2. Which character do you most admire? Why?
3. Consider the dramatic situation with Mama as protagonist, stating her objective and the obstacles that stand in her way. Then consider the dramatic situation with Walter Lee as protagonist. What does he want? What is standing in his way?
4. What is Mama's major flaw? What is Walter's?
5. Compare Beneatha's sense of values with Walter Lee's. What does each value most in the world? Whose sense of values is most like your own?
6. One of the most powerful scenes in the play comes when Mama slaps Beneatha in Act I. Do you think Beneatha deserves it? Why is Mama so furious?
7. Do you think it was wrong for Walter Lee to invest Beneatha's school money in the liquor store? How does this action show the weaknesses and/or strengths of his character?
8. What is the play's climax?
9. Mama's triumph in A Raisin in the Sun is that she has managed to instill in her children certain virtues that enable them to survive as a family. What lessons has she strived to teach them?
10. Is the play a comedy, a tragedy, or a tragicomedy?

8 🌿 New Directions

In adopting the conventions of realism, twentieth-century theater was giving up certain traditional sources of dramatic power. For instance poetry, which had been the most effective medium of communication on the stage for centuries, lost favor because "people don't talk like that." Popular theater audiences grew accustomed to lifelike behavior and probable events in new plays. Bizarre happenings like the ghost's appearance in *Hamlet* were discouraged because they destroyed the illusion of realism. It was as if playwrights and audiences had forgotten that what matters most in the theater is the illusion itself, not the fashionable convention of realism. What happens on the stage need not be probable in order to move us to tears or laughter.

Several modern dramatists were well aware of this. Their plays reflect a reaction to realism, as well as a development of ancient techniques of communication and illusion in the theater.

Symbolist Drama

We are familiar with symbolism as a technique of poetry and fiction. A symbol is an object or word that stands for something else, as the rose stands for the eternal beauty of womanhood, and the cross represents suffering and deliverance. In a symbolist drama the actions as well as the characters, props, and setting, refer to eternal ideas and states of being in a "higher" world. Thus, a person walking down a road in a symbolist play might represent Humankind's progress through Time. If that character should trip over a corpse, the corpse might symbolize the obstacles that Ancestors leave in Humankind's way.

If we work at it, we can interpret almost any dramatic action in symbolic terms. But we should not. Most plays are not so intended, preferring to focus our attention on the immediate event. There are symbols in *Oedipus Rex* and

Death of a Salesman, but the world to which they refer is not nearly as important to us as the play's setting. A thoroughgoing Symbolist Drama shows a dreamlike indifference to the particulars of the present scene. Characters often have figurative names—Mr. Cactus or Mrs. Ablebody—and there is a liberal use of traditional poetic symbols.

Geography of a Horse Dreamer

The play you are about to read, Sam Shepard's *Geography of a Horse Dreamer,* declares its nonrealistic intentions in its title, in the description of the scene, and, as the play develops, in the symbolic meaning of the principal characters. Shepard subtitles the play "A Mystery in Two Acts," and yet it is not a mystery in the modern sense of a detective novel or play. Shepard's title alludes to a medieval form of drama based on Christ's life and resurrection and intended to explore the religious "mysteries," those questions that defy human understanding.

Though the characters in Shepard's play speak a highly idiomatic lingo, the dramatic situation is wholly unrealistic, which invites us to interpret it symbolically. The principal character, Cody, is supposed to be able to name the winners of horse races in his dreams. The bookmaking gangsters and their henchmen are holding Cody captive in a manner utterly inhuman, in a tormented slavery that would be counterproductive even if a man possessed the kind of gift the play ascribes to him. Cody has many of the traditional characteristics of the artist, and continual references to him as "Beethoven" insist that we see the play as allegorical, a symbolic picture of the artist in an unsympathetic society. But you will find the play rich in other interpretive possibilities.

Few playwrights in the history of American theater have shown the prolific energy and versatility of Sam Shepard. Born Samuel Shepard Rogers in 1943, Shepard grew up on a ranch and enjoyed working with horses, an enthusiasm reflected in *Geography of a Horse Dreamer.* He left college after one year to join a touring repertory group, the Bishop's Company, which played primarily in churches. In 1963 he arrived in New York, where he quickly established himself as a vibrant force in the Off-Off Broadway theater movement with two one-act plays, *Cowboy* and *The Rock Garden.* Between 1964 and 1970 he received six Obie Awards for playwriting. Shepard reached full maturity with *Curse of the Starving Class,* a superrealistic play depicting the collapse of a Western family. In 1979 he received the Pulitzer Prize for another play about a dissolving family, *Buried Child,* which is in a more conventionally realistic stage manner. His more recent works, *True West* and *A Lie of the Mind,* have established him as the most influential playwright working in America today, with works running on Broadway, on Off-Broadway, and around the world. Also an accomplished actor, Sam Shepard is the only American ever to enjoy the distinction of winning the Pulitzer Prize and a nomination for an Academy Award, for his role as Chuck Yeager in *The Right Stuff.* He is married to the actress Jessica Lange.

Sam Shepard (*Sygma*)

SAM SHEPARD (1943–)

Geography of a Horse Dreamer
A *Mystery in Two Acts*

GEOGRAPHY OF A HORSE DREAMER *was first performed at the Theatre Upstairs in London on February 21, 1974, directed by the author with the following cast:*

CODY: *Steven Rea*
BEAUJO: *Bob Hoskins*
SANTEE: *Kenneth Cranham*
FINGERS: *Neil Johnston*

THE DOCTOR: *George Silver*
THE WAITER: *Alfred Hoffman*
JASPER: *Bill Bailey*
JASON: *Raymond Skipp*

ACT 1: THE SLUMP

SCENE   *An old sleazy hotel room. Semirealistic with a beat-up brass bed, cracked mirror, broken-down chairs, small desk, etc. It's the dead of winter. A small paraffin heater provides the only heat.* CODY *lies spreadeagled on his back on the bed with his arms and legs handcuffed to each bedpost. He's asleep with dark glasses on. He wears jeans and a cowboy shirt.* SANTEE *sits in a chair stage right of the bed reading the* Racing Form. *He wears a long dark overcoat, shiny black shoes and a gangster-type hat. In his lap is a Colt .45.* BEAUJO *is practicing his pool shots with a cue and three balls on the floor. He wears a forties-type pinstriped suit with white shoes. His clothes are very wrinkled like he's been sleeping in them for a month. The stage should be dark or hidden before the opening. In the darkness the sound of horses galloping at a distance is heard. A slow-motion color film clip of a horse race is projected just above* CODY'S *head on the rear wall. No screen. The film begins out of focus and slowly is pulled into a sharp picture as the sound of galloping horses grows louder. The film clip lasts for a short while with the sound then* CODY *wakes up with a yell. The film goes off and the lights onstage bang up.* SANTEE *and* BEAUJO *continue their routines.*

CODY Silky Sullivan in the seventh! By a neck. By a short head. Silky Sullivan in the seventh!

BEAUJO He's got one, Santee.

SANTEE (*without moving from behind his paper*) He's lost it. I told ya' he's lost it.

SANTEE Sounds very certain to me.

SANTEE Silky Sullivan was a fly-by-night C.V. Whitney nag outa' Santa Anita. Won a couple a' stakes back in sixty-two. Retired to stud shortly thereafter. Known chiefly for his dramatic closing rushes.

BEAUJO I'll be darned. He's sure slippin' bad ain't he.

SANTEE Slippin' ain't the word for it. He's almost disappeared.

CODY (*waking up*) I need a better situation. It's too jagged in here. This wallpaper, the smell. You gotta take these things into consideration.

BEAUJO Maybe he's right, Santee.

SANTEE Sure he's right. I'd be the first to agree that he's right. But it's his own damn fault. We was set up pretty in California weren't we. The Beverly Wilshire. Room service. The whole fandango.

BEAUJO Yeah. Couldn't even hear yerself walk down the halls.

SANTEE So what're we doin' here then?

BEAUJO Fingers.

SANTEE Naw, you numbskull. It ain't Fingers. That's a byproduct of the situation. The reason we is here is on account of Mr. Artistic Cowboy here. Backslidin' on his system. That's the reason. If he was still dreamin' the winners we'd still be in California. In the money. Now ain't that right.

BEAUJO I suppose so.

SANTEE No supposin' about it. It's him that put us on the skids.

CODY Could I have a cigarette?

SANTEE We're runnin' low, pal.

CODY Just a puff then.

SANTEE All right, give him a smoke.

BEAUJO Could I have the keys.

SANTEE *reaches in his pocket and pulls out a ring of keys. He tosses them to* BEAUJO.

SANTEE Just the right arm.

BEAUJO *unlocks the handcuffs on* CODY'S *right arm and gives him a cigarette then lights it.* CODY *smokes.*

SANTEE You gotta remember that I ain't the source a' this caper, Beaujo. I been askin' Fingers for a new dreamer for months now. It ain't my idea of a good time beatin' a dead horse ya' know.

BEAUJO What's Fingers' angle keepin' Cody on then?

CODY 'Cause I'm the best. He knows that. I'm the best.

SANTEE (to CODY) Aw shaddup! (to BEAUJO) You know a big time gamblin' man can't forget his early wins. All those memories when it was pourin' in like a flood. A quarter of a million bucks in a day. That ain't shootin' chicken ya' know.

BEAUJO Yeah, but he must have other dreamers workin' for him. He's gotta pay the rent.

SANTEE Sure he does but they're all mediocre. No class. I'll have to hand it to Mr. Artistic here, once upon a time he had some class.

CODY I could regain my form if I got some decent treatment.

SANTEE You had your shot at the red carpet routine and you blew it.

CODY Nothin' fancy. Just some free movement during the day. A chance to get my blood moving again.

SANTEE A chance to escape you mean.

CODY I been with it too long, Santee. I couldn't run out on ya' now. I'd be lost. It's been years. I been blindfolded and shuffled from one hotel to another for as long as I can remember. I ain't seen Great Nature for years now. The sun would probably blind me. Where would I go if I did escape?

SANTEE Wherever you was headed last time you cut loose.

CODY I don't remember that. I musta' been off my cake. I'd never try it again. I promise.

SANTEE No dice, Beethoven.

BEAUJO Wouldn't hurt to just let him walk around the room here, Santee. Just to get his circulation going.

SANTEE Well if it ain't the soft-hearted gangster type. Go ahead then! Turn him loose. I'm gettin' sick of his corny mug and his crucified position. Go ahead! Just remember if he gets loose it's your ass, not mine.

BEAUJO (as he unlocks CODY) Sure, sure. The last time Fingers bothered with us was last Christmas when he gave us each an Indian-head nickel. We could be mistaken about this whole deal ya' know, Santee. I mean what if Fingers has just cut out on us. Left us here like a bunch a' saps.

SANTEE He wouldn't do that.

BEAUJO What's to stop him. He ain't exactly a man of high morals or nothin'.

SANTEE Don't start bad-mouthin' Fingers now. Just 'cause things get tough is no reason to commit mutiny. Fingers's been good to us right along.

BEAUJO Yeah, well I wouldn't exactly describe our present situation as the berries.

SANTEE You got no faith. No gamblin' heart.

BEAUJO I figure it's more like a game a' pool. You know, the way sometimes you got the feel. You got the touch. All the practice and technique in the world can't beat ya' 'cause you got magic. There's no trace a' tension. Then it goes. Just like that. No way to pin it down. It just slides away from ya'. I figure that's how it is with Cody here.

SANTEE Maybe.

CODY Yeah. That's how it is all right. The dreams are jagged. I get a fuzzy picture. Sometimes the numbers blur.

SANTEE (to CODY) You'd agree with anything to get yerself off the hook. Come on, take a walk, Mr. Artist. It may be yer last for a while.

CODY *begins to get up from the bed. He struggles to gain muscular control, moving his limbs very slowly and trying to figure out how they work.* BEAUJO *backs away and lights a cigarette.* SANTEE *waves the pistol at* CODY.

SANTEE Just remember the old iron here. She gets very ticklish in a nervous situation.

BEAUJO What if we was to make a real effort to treat him decent for a change. You know, steak and eggs in the morning, maybe a walk down the hallway, maybe even bring in a little chippie to warm his heart.

SANTEE None a' that stuff. First thing you know he'll be crying about his record again. That's what got him started in his present slump if you'll recall.

CODY My record? You still got my record don't ya', Santee?

SANTEE What'd I tell ya'? Yeah, yeah. I still got yer record.

CODY Just don't bust it or nothin'. You wouldn't bust it wouldya'?

SANTEE I'll bust yer damn neck if ya' don't start walking around this room pretty soon. Come on, start hoofin'.

CODY I gotta take it slow. Everything's like mush. It feels like Jell-O in my veins.

SANTEE Yeah, yeah. The Champeen Complainer.

CODY *finally gets to his feet and moves very slowly around the room trying to adjust to walking. Every once in a while he loses his balance and* BEAUJO *helps him stay upright.*

BEAUJO I know you got somethin' against art, Santee, but maybe he's right ya' know. I mean maybe his dreamin' does take on a kind of an art form, the way he does it. It might need some special stuff to get him back in top form.

SANTEE Like what special stuff?

CODY Like a decent bed for one thing.

BEAUJO Yeah. I mean that's important. A thing like that. After all, the bed is where he does his work. This thing's like sleepin' on a week-old griddle cake. (*kicking the bed*)

SANTEE We can't afford it. It's not within the budget.

CODY Some fresh air.

BEAUJO Now you can't begrudge a man a little fresh air once in a while.

SANTEE We might arrange some fresh air. Maybe. He's gotta be blindfolded though. He can't know where he is. That's the chief thing that Fingers impressed upon us. He can't for a second know where he is outside the room he's locked up in. Otherwise it spoils the dreaming. He can't know the time either.

CODY We've come a long way from the Beverly Wilshire haven't we?

SANTEE A long way down.

CODY No, I mean we're on a whole different continent here aren't we? I can feel it.

SANTEE How can you feel it, Mr. Sensitive?

CODY We took a ship.

SANTEE Don't start guessing. There's no way you can find out.

CODY You've blocked up all the windows again.

SANTEE That ain't so unusual. That's standard procedure.

CODY They speak English here though. They speak English don't they?

SANTEE No guessing goddammit! Or it's back in the sack and no dinner!

BEAUJO Take it easy, Cody. No need to get Santee worked up.

SANTEE Just keep walkin', meatball.

CODY It's all right. Fingers' theory was good for the beginning but now it sucks dogs.

SANTEE How's that?

CODY He don't understand the area I have to dream in.

BEAUJO There's nothing we can do about that now.

CODY Not this area. The inside one. The space inside where the dream comes. It's gotta be created. That's what Fingers don't understand. He thinks it's just like it was when I started.

SANTEE So what's different now?

CODY He's blocked up my senses. Everything forces itself on the space I need. There's too much chaos now. He'll never get a winner out of me till the space comes back.

SANTEE What a crock a' shit. I never heard so much gobbledygook in my whole life.

CODY What do you dream about, Santee?

SANTEE I don't dream. I'm one a' those rare dreamless sleepers. I got no worries, no troubles to work out. Everything's hunky-dory.

CODY I dream about the Great Plains.

SANTEE Well that's yer whole damn trouble! That ain't what yer gettin' paid for. Yer paid to dream about racehorses. That's all.

BEAUJO Yeah, Cody. Shit man, you gotta get down to business. We're going' down the tubes in this dump while you dream about the Great Plains.

CODY It'll get worse.

SANTEE What! It can't get worse! Put him back in the cuffs! Go on! Back in the sack! I ain't gonna tolerate that kinda' stuff!

BEAUJO Now take it easy, Santee.

SANTEE Back in the sack! I ain't takin' no more crap from this hick! I can't stand the sight of him. Back in the sack!

BEAUJO *leads* CODY *back to the bed and helps him back into the position he was in before. Then he puts the handcuffs back on him and locks them all.* CODY *doesn't resist.*

SANTEE (*pacing around the room with his gun*) I'm goin' straight to the top. No more fartin' around. Tomorrow morning I'm gonna' call Fingers and get the lowdown. This whole situation stinks. It's driving me crazy. It's useless keepin' this creep here. He ain't gonna' come up with a horse. He ain't come up with a horse for over six months. One bum dream after another. He's lucky if he even dreams a horse in this century let alone a winner tomorrow. I can't stand it. I'm goin' down there now and call him. Right now. You got some change Beaujo? Gimme some change.

BEAUJO All right, all right. Take it easy though, Santee. You don't want him comin' down on us too hard. You might catch him in a bad mood.

BEAUJO *hands* SANTEE *some change for the phone.*

SANTEE I don't care how I catch him. We just gotta get outa' this slump somehow. I'm just goin' down the block to a phone booth. Don't let this jerk loose for a second.

BEAUJO You got the keys.

SANTEE (*remembering he's in a position of power*) Yeah. Right, I got the keys and don't you forget it. I got the keys.

SANTEE *exits.* BEAUJO *speaks to* CODY.

BEAUJO What the hell are you tryin' to pull? You know better than to get Santee pissed off like that. We're all in this together ya' know.

CODY Yeah. Sorry.

BEAUJO I mean it's mostly up to you ya' know. I mean the dreaming end of it. You're actually the big shot in the situation. You can call all the shots. All you gotta do is dream right.

CODY It ain't so easy, Beaujo. I'm dried up. I need a break.

BEAUJO Yeah, I can see that and I'm doin' everything I can to make that happen. But in the meantime you gotta play it cool. When Santee's nerves are on edge you gotta go slow.

CODY If I could just talk to Fingers myself maybe I could convince him. I can't talk to Santee. He hates my guts. He don't understand my position. It's very delicate work, dreaming a winner. You can't just close your eyes and bingo! it's there in front of you. It takes certain special conditions. A certain internal environment.

BEAUJO Well how did it happen before? It used to be a snap for you.

CODY I don't know. It was accidental. It just sort of came to me outa' the blue. You know how that is. At first it's all instinct. Now it's work.

BEAUJO Yeah, but you can't explain that kinda' stuff to mugs like Santee and Fingers. They don't buy it. All they understand is results. The process don't interest them.

BEAUJO *lights a cigarette and walks around.*

CODY If I could just listen to my record again. That's all. Just a couple of tracks off my record.

BEAUJO No show. It drives Santee crazy. Besides, like he says, that's part of what got you goin' downhill.

CODY He's nuts. In the beginning I came up with six fifteen-to-one shots in a row. Six of 'em. And all of 'em came from the music. It's a source of inspiration, Beaujo.

BEAUJO It's just impossible right now. We gotta go slow. Maybe later we can sneak the music back into it.

CODY Then tell me where we are at least. What country is this?

BEAUJO Can't do it, Cody. It's strictly against the rules.

CODY It's stupid! It's really stupid! I'm dreaming American horses and we're probably in Morocco somewhere. It don't make sense. I gotta know where we are so's I can adjust. I've lost track of everything. I need some landmarks.

BEAUJO Fingers says the dreams are a gift from God. It don't matter what country you dream in.

CODY Fuck Fingers! I'm the dreamer. I oughta' know.

BEAUJO I could describe the general area to you maybe. The neighborhood around the hotel.

CODY That'd help. Anything would help.

BEAUJO It's a city. We're in a certain area of a city. The workers wear handkerchiefs around their heads. Their main concern is getting laid. They use rough language and swagger their manhood around.

CODY That could be anywhere.

BEAUJO It's a gambling town. Racing all year round. It's the poor people who lose. Dozens of big bookmakers for every block. A few shysters work a system. All of 'em work with high stakes. The government has hooks directly into the bookmakers. There's protection on every level except for the bums. The police are paid of by high syndicates. For the rich it's a sport. For the poor it's a disease.

CODY That doesn't help. It don't put me in touch with anything. I need firm ground to stand on.

BEAUJO That's all I can give you.

CODY What kind of cars do they drive?

BEAUJO No more. I overstepped my bounds already.

CODY What do the cops look like?

BEAUJO That's it, Cody. No more.

CODY If I could just take a walk. You think you can talk Santee into letting me have a short walk?

BEAUJO We'll see.

CODY Oh man, I wish I was dead.

BEAUJO It'll pass.

CODY I got a feeling I'll never see daylight again.

BEAUJO Now come on. Don't go gettin' morbid about it. This is just a slump we're in. Fingers'll pull us out of it.

CODY Fingers is in the same boat as us. We're like his mirror. We never see him but we're always in touch. When he's winning we're in the Beverly Wilshire. When he's losing we're in a dump like this.

BEAUJO He's got other dreamers. As soon as things pick up he'll move us.

CODY Why is he keepin' me on! I wanna go back to Wyoming and raise sheep. That's all I wanna do. I got no more tips. I'm from the Great Plains not the city. He's poisoned my dreams with these cities.

BEAUJO You want a sleeper?

CODY Yeah. Gimme four of 'em. The blue ones.

BEAUJO Oh no. Last time you had four you didn't come around for three days. We thought we lost ya'.

CODY Gimme three then.

BEAUJO Two's enough. Put you in a nice light sleep. Who knows, you might even dream a winner.

CODY Just gimme the pills!

BEAUJO *hands* CODY *two sleeping pills and a glass of water.* CODY *gobbles them down.*

BEAUJO You know your problem Cody? You don't accept the situation. There's no way out. Even if your could escape you're too weak to get very far. Even if you got very far we'd know where to find you. You gotta give in to it, boy.

CODY Yeah. Maybe you're right.

BEAUJO You gotta use some smarts. If you just relaxed into it and accepted it then everything would come to you. We might even let you have a little more freedom. No blindfolds. Walks in the park. All that stuff would come to you.

CODY Yeah. I keep thinking this is temporary. How long's it been going on anyway?

BEAUJO No time hints. Just forget about the other possibilities. This is all you got.

CODY I can't remember how it started.

BEAUJO You had a dream.

CODY Yeah. I had that big dream.

BEAUJO Then you got publicized.

CODY Yeah. *Life* magazine. Then my folks started cashin' in. My brothers.

BEAUJO Then half the state of Wyoming. You were the hottest thing in the West. Then we nabbed you.

CODY I was kidnapped.

BEAUJO Well, not exactly.

CODY I was wined and dined. Where was that?

Through this CODY *is getting drowsy until he finally falls asleep.*

BEAUJO Hollywood Park. Aqueduct. Yonkers.

CODY What happened?

BEAUJO We had to keep you secret. Too many scabbies cashin' in.

CODY I used to wake up and not know where I was. As long as I can remember.

BEAUJO It'll be all right now. It'll all come back to you. (*melodramatically*) You'll find that special area. A huge blue space. In the distance you'll see 'em approaching the quarter-mile pole. The thunder of hooves. Whips flying. The clubhouse turn. You'll get a sense of it again. It'll all come back just like it used to. You'll see. You got magic Cody. You'll see.

CODY *falls into a deep sleep.* BEAUJO *gets up and walks around. He comes to a stop and looks around the room.*

BEAUJO (*to himself*) Huh, for a second there I thought I was lost.

SANTEE *enters and shuts the door behind him. He goes to the heater shivering from the cold and rubbing his arms.*

BEAUJO Did ya' talk to Fingers?
SANTEE More or less.
BEAUJO What do ya' mean? What'd he say?
SANTEE He wasn't there. I had to talk to Zonka.
BEAUJO Zonka? What's he know?
SANTEE He gave me a message direct from Fingers.
BEAUJO What's the scoop?
SANTEE Dogs.
BEAUJO Dogs?
SANTEE Dogs. Greyhounds.
BEAUJO Greyhounds?!
SANTEE We been relegated to the dog tracks. It's the most humiliatin' experience of my whole career. All on account a' that meathead!
BEAUJO There must be some mistake.
SANTEE Ain't no mistake. It come from the top. He's gotta start dreamin' dogs. That's all there is to it.
BEAUJO But he don't know a greyhound from a crocodile. This kid's strictly a horse man.
SANTEE I know, I know. It ain't my idea.
BEAUJO He can't suddenly change his whole style a' dreaming like that. It might kill him.
SANTEE Well he's gonna' have to or our ass is grass! Wake him up.
BEAUJO I just gave him two sleepers.
SANTEE Wake him up! Here, take the keys and unlock him.

BEAUJO *takes the keys and unlocks* CODY. CODY *stays asleep.*

BEAUJO Jesus Christ, Santee, we're gonna kill him with this kind of treatment. I'm tellin' ya'.
SANTEE I could care less. As far as I can tell it's him that got us into this mess and it's him that'll get us out. All my life I been proud a' my position. I've carried a certain sense of honor with me but I'll be damned if I'm gonna carry it to the goddamn dog track.
BEAUJO He's out cold Santee.
SANTEE Wake him up! I don't care how ya' do it. I want him on his feet. I'm gonna' drill him with dogs till he hears 'em barkin' in his ears.

BEAUJO *slaps* CODY'S *face and tries to bring him around.*

BEAUJO It's no good, Santee. He's out like a light.
SANTEE Great! That's just great. Now we're sunk. We're really sunk.

BEAUJO *leaves* CODY *sleeping on the bed. His arms and legs are free.*

BEAUJO It might mean we're being let off the hook, Santee. Eased-in grade.

SANTEE Can't you understand that this is serious business. What's a' matter with you. Zonka told me if there's no results within the week that Fingers is sendin' the Doctor over here.

BEAUJO The Doctor?

SANTEE Yeah. You know what that means.

BEAUJO He can't do that.

SANTEE Yeah, well that's what's gonna' happen if Cowboy don't pop up with some winners and fast.

BEAUJO The Doctor? Fingers must be crazy. He was goin' to the pay the window every day for a month and now he can turn on us like this?

SANTEE That's the way it falls, Beaujo.

CODY *lets out a loud voice then goes right back into sleep.*

CODY Native Dancer in the eighth!

SANTEE He's gettin' more and more pathetic. Native Dancer musta' died in the fifties.

BEAUJO I got faith in him, Santee.

SANTEE Faith! What good is that gonna' do us? We need results! Right now. There's only one thing we can do.

SANTEE *goes to the* Racing Form *and leafs through it.*

SANTEE We gotta take the gamble. We gotta try to pick some dogs ourselves and pass 'em off as his dreams. That's the only thing.

BEAUJO But we don't even know how to read the form for greyhounds. You don't know the first thing about it.

SANTEE We can learn. Look, it says here: "Black Banjo, the young Walthamstow hopeful, has been unlucky in his last six outings. With the advantage of trap one and a slow starter to his right, Black Banjo could get to the first bend and go clear."

CODY Man o' War by a neck!

SANTEE Can you do something about him?

BEAUJO He'll come around in a while.

SANTEE Look, write these down. Get a piece a' paper and write.

BEAUJO I don't know Santee. We're takin' quite a risk.

BEAUJO *goes to a small desk and gets a pad and pencil. He writes down what* SANTEE *says.*

SANTEE It's worth a try. We might even pick us some winners. Put down: "Harringay. 7.45, Sgt. Mick. 8.00, Go Astray, 8.15, Zeitung. 8.30, Lemon Castle. 8.45, Come Dark Night. 9.00—"

CODY (*speaking in an even, cool voice*) Black Banjo will win the seventh race at Wimbledon by two and a half lengths on the trot.

SANTEE Can you shut him up. I can't concentrate.

BEAUJO Wait a minute! Did you hear what he said. Black Banjo! That's a dog. A greyhound!

SANTEE I know. I just read it in the paper.

BEAUJO He just picked him to win at Wimbledon.

SANTEE So what. The power of suggestion. He musta' heard me read it.

CODY Black Banjo, a young son of the great Irish stud dog Monalee Champion, has all the looks and speed of a top-class dog. His early speed and clever tracking has told the tale on more than one occasion. Although unlucky in most of his recent deciders he will definitely win by two and a half lengths tonight at Wimbledon.

BEAUJO Listen to that! Where'd he get information like that? Look it up. See if that's his breeding.

SANTEE What'd he say?

BEAUJO Monalee Champion. Look it up.

SANTEE (*looking in the paper*) Monalee Champion. Let's see. Yeah. What do ya' know. Monalee Champion. How'd he know that?

BEAUJO He's back on, Santee! He's back on the winners! We're gonna' be in the money again!

SANTEE You think so? I'd hate to risk it.

BEAUJO I know it. I can feel it. He's havin' a breakthrough.

CODY Black Banjo will break in front with Shara Dee close up at the first bend. There'll be some bad crowding going around and Stow Welcome will be thrown to the outside. From there to the wire Black Banjo will have it all his own way. Shara Dee will be closing in the final stages but will not come to terms with the winner. She will be second with another length back to Seaman's Pride.

SANTEE Go call Fingers. If Zonka answers pass on the message. Black Banjo to win, Shara Dee to place. Forecast, one and three. Tell him it's a certainty.

BEAUJO Right.

SANTEE And grab me a fifth of Scotch on the way back. I'm gonna' need it if we lose.

BEAUJO This is it, Santee. I feel in it my bones. The slump is over. Tomorrow we'll be sittin' pretty!

SANTEE It ain't happened yet.

BEAUJO *exits.* SANTEE *talks quietly to* CODY, *who remains asleep.*

SANTEE Okay Mr. Artistic. Maybe I was wrong. Maybe I was pushin' it too hard. This better be it boy or we're all gonna be cut up in little pieces and mailed to our mommas. I know you ain't used to workin' under pressure but that's how it is. It's like a snake bitin' its own tail. We keep infecting each other. The Doctor's on our back. The pressure's there. It comes from the outside. Somewhere out there. We wind up with the effects. I don't understand how you work, Beethoven, that's how come I got no patience. To me it's a lot a' mumbo jumbo. Like I said, I don't even have no dreams. All I know is that you was right once. For a solid month you was right. You was so right that you had somebody out there eatin' turtle soup and filet mignon three times a day. Being chauffeur-driven to the grocery store. That's how it is. You got the genius, somebody else got the power. That's how it always is, Beethoven. The most we can hope for is a little room service and a color T.V.

CODY *sits up. He talks with another voice; slightly Irish, as though he's been inhabited by a spirit.*

CODY The main mistake is watching the race in an emotional way. As though the dog you've gambled on is a piece of yourself. That way you only see one-sixth of the race and miss the other five dogs. You might go a dozen races gambling on dogs you've seen before but never watched.

SANTEE Say, what is this? Are you awake now or what?

CODY *gets up off the bed and moves easily around the room.*

CODY You gotta take mental photographs of each dog. You gotta draw back from the race, take an indifferent attitude. Memorize forty-eight dogs a night. Don't gamble for a week of racing. Just take photographs.

SANTEE Don't try nothin' funny! I still got the rod.

CODY Once you've built up an interior form you attack in a calculated way. Never let the odds influence you. Go about it cold-blooded. Make definite decisions and stick to them. Forget the Quinellas and Duellas. They're for suckers. Stick with £5 reverse forecasts, tenners each way on the selection.

SANTEE What's got into you. Get back over there on the bed!

CODY Keep a record of the seasonal dates of bitches. One week before they're due in season back 'em to the hilt. Don't be fooled by fast-improving pups but don't be afraid to have a gamble in the middle of their form. Forget Yellow Printer sons in the Derby. They're jinxed. Too difficult to tune them up. Look at Super Rory. Donemark Printer. Tremendous class but see how fast they blew up.

SANTEE Shaddup!

CODY *snaps out of it back into his old self. He's barely able to stand up. A short silence then* BEAUJO *bursts in the door.*

BEAUJO Fingers is comin'!

SANTEE What! Now?

CODY Lemme talk to him.

BEAUJO After the race. He's comin' right after the race.

SANTEE (*threatening* CODY) You better be right, Schmoe.

CODY I gotta talk to him.

BEAUJO He's bringin' the Doctor if he loses.

SANTEE Where's my Scotch?

CODY *collapses on the floor.* BEAUJO *hands* SANTEE *a fifth of Scotch.* SANTEE *breaks it open and takes a long swig. They both stare at* CODY *on the floor as the lights dim and the sound of an* ANNOUNCER'S VOICE *is heard over the speakers.*

ANNOUNCER'S VOICE The hare is running at Wimbledon. Black Banjo breaks clear of Shara Dee in trap three followed closely by Stow Welcome and Seaman's Pride. As they go into the first turn it's Black Banjo by a length and a half. There's some bad crowding. Stow Welcome is knocked out of it. Down the back straight it's Black Banjo going four lengths clear from Shara Dee, followed by Seaman's Pride. It's Black Banjo into the third bend still well clear of Shara Dee who is making up ground on the outside. Coming for home it's Black Banjo with Shara Dee closing very fast. It's Shara Dee and Black Banjo!

The swelling sound of a huge crowd drowns out the ANNOUNCER'S VOICE *as the lights go to black.*

ACT II: THE HUMP

SCENE *A fancy hotel room with the furniture in the same position as in Act One. A color T.V. with a flickering image, the sound off. A record player on top of a chest of drawers. The characters all have new clothes but all in the same styles as Act One.* CODY *still wears his shades and speaks with a slight Irish accent. He stands center stage holding a fishing pole at arm's length with a white rabbit skin tied to the end of the line so it just touches the floor. He turns slowly in a tight circle so that the rabbit skin drags across the floor around him. He watches a litter of imaginary greyhound pups chasing the skin. This is the method for schooling puppies to chase the mechanical hare in a circle. SANTEE sits on a chair in the same position as Act One, reading the* Racing Form. BEAUJO *sits at a table down-left dealing a hand of five-card stud to himself and an imaginary partner across from him. In the darkness, before the action begins, the sound of dogs yapping is heard faintly and grows louder as a color film clip of greyhounds racing in slow motion is projected on the rear wall. It's done in the same way as the film of the horses at the beginning of Act One. CODY yells at his imaginary puppies, the film goes off and the lights onstage bang up. CODY turns in a circle and talks. SANTEE and BEAUJO ignore him.*

CODY You gotta watch that brindle. He's a devil. The biggest in the litter. Thinks he can get away with murder. It's very crucial to catch them at an early age. Once they get the taste for fightin' there's the seed of a bad habit. It's usually the big ones that get pushy. You don't want to take the fire out of 'em. Just let 'em know that you'll have none of it.

He strikes out at one of the puppies then goes on in a circle.

SANTEE I notice he missed the fifth at Catford yesterday.
BEAUJO Seven out of eight ain't so bad.
SANTEE Just hope it's not a bad omen.
BEAUJO We're in the pink, Santee. He's locked into it this time.
SANTEE Yeah. It gives me the creeps. Like being a nurse at a flip house.

CODY *reverses direction with the pole and keeps moving in a tight circle.*

CODY It's important to reverse your direction once in a while. To balance out the muscles. Too much counterclockwise action makes 'em soft on the right side. You watch the Irish dogs. You'll never see near as many dogs breaking down in Ireland as you do in England. The schooling's different. We take more time in Ireland. More patience.
SANTEE He still don't know where he is.
BEAUJO He's gettin' closer though.
SANTEE If ya' ask me he's further away than ever. He's off his cake, Beaujo.
BEAUJO Lucky for us.
SANTEE What do ya' supposed happened to him?
BEAUJO You got me. Some kinda' weird mental disorder. I told ya' he was a genius. There's a very fine line between madness and genius ya' know.
SANTEE Yeah, yeah. Cut the baloney. He's gone bananas and that's all there is to it. It just happens to coincide with our needs.
BEAUJO Well, leastwise Fingers is happy. That's all that counts right now.

A loud knock at the door. SANTEE and BEAUJO leap to their feet. CODY keeps turning in a circle and mumbling to the puppies. SANTEE has his gun out.

SANTEE You expectin' company?
BEAUJO Not me. Must be room service.
SANTEE I didn't order nothin'.
BEAUJO Me neither.

More loud knocking.

SANTEE Well answer it! Go on!

BEAUJO *goes to the door.*

BEAUJO Who is it?
DOCTOR'S VOICE Fingers! Open up!
BEAUJO (*to* SANTEE) Oh shit, it's Fingers!
SANTEE Well let him in.
BEAUJO (*to the door*) Hold on a second!

BEAUJO *unlocks three or four locks on the door as* SANTEE *grabs the fishing pole out of* CODY'S *hand and hides it under the bed. He grabs* CODY *by the back of the neck and throws him onto the bed.* BEAUJO *swings the door open and* FINGERS *sweeps into the room with the* DOCTOR *behind him.* FINGERS *is tall, thin and rather effete wearing a bowler hat, tweed cape with matching trousers, black vest with a white carnation, thin pencil-line mustache, spats, black cane and gaudy rings on every finger including the thumbs. The* DOCTOR *is very fat and looks like Sydney Greenstreet. He wears all black in the style of the thirties and carries a doctor's ominous-looking black bag.*

FINGERS Good God man, you'd think it was Fort Knox in here the way you carry on with the bloody locks. Where's my boy?
BEAUJO Sorry, Fingers. We was takin' precautionary measures.

FINGERS *spots* CODY *on the bed and moves toward him.* CODY *runs frantically to the other side of the room. He seems terrified of* FINGERS' *every move.*

FINGERS Ah yes! Yes, yes, yes! I should have known he'd have the look of eagles. Absolutely. Look at him, Doctor. Just look. Splendid.
DOCTOR Hmm. So that's him.
SANTEE We been keepin' him good, Fingers. Three squares a day. Free movement through the room. Just like you said.
FINGERS Those eyes. It almost hurts to look in his face.
SANTEE You ain't kiddin'. I was just tellin' Beaujo how sick I was gettin' a' his mug.

The DOCTOR *takes his coat off and throws it on the bed, then he helps* FINGERS *off with his cape.*

FINGERS (*to* CODY) At last we meet. Like the tail and the head of a great dragon. This calls for a celebration. Order some sherry and cognac. The finest in the house. (*to* CODY). You do drink I trust?
SANTEE He ain't being too communicative lately, Fingers. He's slipped into some kinda' depression or something.

BEAUJO *rings for the* WAITER. *The* DOCTOR *sinks into a chair and watches T.V. He turns the sound up very loud.* FINGERS *glares at him.*

FINGERS Doctor! I say, Doctor!

FINGERS *crosses briskly to the T.V. and turns the sound off. The* DOCTOR *just stares into the screen.*

FINGERS Do you mind? We're trying to conduct a conversation.

FINGERS *crosses back to* SANTEE.

FINGERS Now then. Where are we? Oh yes. Depression. Depression? Good Lord, we can't have that. Let me feel his temperature.

FINGERS *moves toward* CODY. CODY *leaps over the bed and crashes into a wall trying to get away from him. The* DOCTOR *is unmoved.*

FINGERS Is he always this hypertensive?
BEAUJO Only around strangers. He's only seen me and Santee for the past year and a half now. He don't know what to make of you.
SANTEE Yeah, he should settle down in a little while. Then you can pet him.
FINGERS I see. Poor chap. I dare say he does look a bit at odds with himself doesn't he. Has he been sleeping well?
SANTEE In spurts. He'll fall dead asleep for fifteen minutes in the middle of the floor and then wham, he'll be up and prowling the room again.
FINGERS I don't like the sound of that at all. Doctor, did you hear that?
DOCTOR I wasn't listening.
FINGERS Santee says the poor fellow only sleeps for fifteen minutes at a stretch and then he's up and about.
DOCTOR So what? It's not unusual in cases like this. People in his state can go a week without sleeping a wink.
FINGERS I see. I rather thought it was more serious than that.
DOCTOR 'Course they don't live long.
FINGERS Then it is serious.
DOCTOR Maybe, maybe not. Depends on the particular case.
FINGERS Well I do wish you'd examine the poor chap and make some sort of diagnosis. After all our livelihood hinges upon his well-being.
DOCTOR Later. Right now I'm gonna' take in a little viewing.
FINGERS Well I suppose it can wait. Now then, where's the champagne?

SANTEE *and* BEAUJO *seem surprised by* FINGERS' *lack of authority over the* DOCTOR.

BEAUJO I thought you said sherry.
FINGERS Did I? Ah yes, sherry. So I did.
CODY Just two tablespoonsful. That's all. Otherwise you blow 'em out.
FINGERS Is he speaking to me?
SANTEE We're never certain Fingers. It could be any of us.
FINGERS I see. How long has this been going on?
BEAUJO Ever since the switchover.
FINGERS Switchover?
SANTEE To greyhounds.
BEAUJO You upset something very fragile, Fingers. He may never come back from it.
FINGERS I'm afraid I don't understand.
BEAUJO He's a horse dreamer, Mr. Fingers. A horse dreamer. When you had us switch over to dogs something snapped in him. The mind is a very mysterious thing ya' know.
FINGERS Yes, I see. I had no idea. Poor devil.
SANTEE He's doin' all right though. He's still on the winners and everything.
BEAUJO But it won't last for long.
SANTEE Will you shut up!

BEAUJO I'm only trying to give ya' fair warning so it don't come as too much of a shock.

SANTEE Beaujo's talkin' through his hat, Fingers. He don't know nothin' for certain.

FINGERS It's all my fault. I should have brought a stop to this insanity long ago. I should have known something like this would happen.

SANTEE Nothing's happened. We've been in the money for three weeks straight now. Everything's hunky-dory, Fingers. All we gotta do is ride him out. When he hits another slump we just give him a breather. Simple as that.

A knock at the door.

SANTEE That must be the waiter. You just set yourself down on the bed there and I'll order us some drinks. You just relax, Fingers. Everything's gonna' be okay, Beaujo, help him onto the bed. Take his shoes off, loosen his tie.

BEAUJO *helps* FINGERS *to the bed.* FINGERS *has gone all weak and sickly now. Every time* FINGERS *moves,* CODY *moves frantically to get away from him, crashing over furniture and smashing into the walls. The* DOCTOR *remains indifferent, staring into the T.V. with the sound off.* SANTEE *opens the door and lets the* WAITER *in. The* WAITER *wears white gloves and tails. He looks a big apprehensive about the situation.*

WAITER Uh, you rang, sir?

SANTEE Yeah, get us a coupla' bottles of yer best cognac and some sherry. Nothin' but the best. Oh yeah, and some glasses. Here's a tenner. Keep the change.

WAITER Very good sir. Thank you very much sir.

SANTEE Don't mention it. Now scram.

He shoves the WAITER *out the door and bolts it.* FINGERS *is lying on the bed as* BEAUJO *takes* FINGERS' *shoes off and massages his feet.*

FINGERS I had a feeling it would end like this. I've committed a terrible sin.

SANTEE Nothing's ended. It's all going on right now. We're on top. Nothing's ended, Fingers.

CODY The sickness is sweeping through the kennel! There's no escape! Intestinal Catarrh is on the march! Sprinters and stayers! Everyone's equal in this.

FINGERS What in God's name is he on about?

SANTEE It's nothin' Fingers. He's practicin' up for White City tonight.

FINGERS Oh my God!

SANTEE I'll have him under control in just a minute. Come here you!

SANTEE *moves toward* CODY. CODY *leaps away again crashing into things like a frightened animal.*

FINGERS Don't you touch him! Don't you lay a hand on him! Enough damage has been done already.

CODY (*panting like a dog*) Didn't you give me enough stick already! At Dundalk! Shelbourne Park! Trucked around half of Ireland like so much hamburger.

FINGERS (*to* SANTEE) Now you've done it! You've pushed him too far. He's over the edge.

CODY (*to* SANTEE) I kept crying for trap one. Over and over again I asked for trap one. I could've won from the inside! But no, I was forced to go wide. You couldn't understand why I'd check at the third bend. Time and again I'd check at the third bend. How stupid can you get. I was schooled on the inside hare and you put me in trap six. Trap six! Trap six! Trap six! I'm bloody tired of trap six!

SANTEE Aw fuck off, ya' nut-case! (*to* FINGERS) I wash my hands a' this whole deal. I warned ya' right from the start about this country bumpkin. He's a weirdo. Unreliable. I coulda' found ya' plenty a' good dreamers from the city but no, we had to go to the middle of the goddamn Great Plains and bring back a dodo. A fruitcake. Well I've had it. From here on it's your ballgame. I'm watchin' T.V. with the Doc.

SANTEE *goes and stands behind the* DOCTOR *and watches T.V.*

BEAUJO (*to* FINGERS) Maybe after White City tonight we should give him a rest, Fingers. Let him get his strength back.

FINGERS (*sitting up on the edge of the bed*) There'll be no White City tonight or any other night. I'm setting him free.

SANTEE You're what! You can't do that! He's still worth millions even though he is crazy.

FINGERS (*getting up and moving toward the* DOCTOR) I don't care what he's worth. He's going back tonight. Doctor, would you be so kind as to arrange air passage for two to Wyoming. I'm taking him back personally.

The DOCTOR *stays staring at the T.V.* FINGERS *moves back to* BEAUJO. SANTEE *follows him.*

SANTEE Fingers, wait a minute. I take back what I said before.

FINGERS We must gather his personal effects together.

BEAUJO All he's got is what he's wearing and an old beat-up record.

FINGERS Very well. Get it.

BEAUJO *goes to a drawer and pulls out an old album with no cover.*

SANTEE This is a real mistake, Fingers. Why don't we just keep him on until he starts slippin' again. No harm in that. He's a gold mine right now.

FINGERS Gold mine. Yes. By the way, what was the name of that town we took him from. Do you remember?

BEAUJO Somewhere in the High Mountain country. Above the Big Horns.

FINGERS That's quite a large piece of real estate as I recall. Can't you be more specific.

BEAUJO Something like Pawnee or Cheyenne. Something like that.

SANTEE Cheyenne's in the southeast. It was north of there.

BEAUJO Something like Arapahoe or Mitchell. Was it Mitchell?

FINGERS Does anyone have a map?

SANTEE Look, Fingers, just leave him to us for a while. Give him another chance. We'll bring him around.

BEAUJO Well look, we can figure it out easy enough. We left Salt Lake City on a Friday night and drove all night. We crossed the Utah state line about two in the morning.

FINGERS Yes, I remember that. I remember thinking, now we're in Wyoming, it can't be far now. On the map it looked to be no further than Brighton is from London. Then all the next day we drove and drove. I'd never seen such country. Nothing as far as the eye could see. Nothing.

BEAUJO We hit the Wind River Reservation about noon. We had lunch in the Silver Star. Fingers bought a cowboy hat and a pair of spurs.

FINGERS Yes! I remember that! I remember thinking this is the West! This is really The West! Then we got to that town where Buffalo Bill lived. I forgot the name of it. Oh what a town! Saloons with Winchester rifles tacked up on the walls. Real cowboys in leather chaps. Indians shuffling through the dusty streets. Buffalo Bill's name plastered on everything. And at night. At night it was magical. Like praying. I'd never heard such a silence as that. Nowhere on the earth. So vast and lonely. Just the brisk cold night blowing in through the hotel window. And outside, the blue peaks of the Big Horn mountains. The moon shining on their snowy caps. The prairie stretching out and out like a great ocean. I felt that God was with me then. The earth held me in its arms.

A short pause as FINGERS *reflects.*

BEAUJO That was the town.
FINGERS What was.
BEAUJO The town we nabbed him in. That was it.
FINGERS Yes! That's right! What was it called? Doctor, do you remember the name of that charming town. The one where Buffalo Bill lived. Doctor?

FINGERS *turns to the* DOCTOR *who is sitting very still in a kind of trance.*

FINGERS For heaven's sake, man, snap out of it.
SANTEE What's eatin' him now.

FINGERS *goes to the* DOCTOR *and shakes his shoulder.*

FINGERS I say. Doctor! I asked you to go and arrange our passage to Wyoming. Doctor!

FINGERS *shakes him again. The* DOCTOR *lets out a bloodcurdling yell and throws* FINGERS *across the room.* CODY *screams like a dog who's being whipped. He whimpers in a corner.* BEAUJO *and* SANTEE *stand facing the* DOCTOR, *who stands center stage.* FINGERS *moans on the floor holding his leg in pain. The* DOCTOR *quickly gains control of himself.*

SANTEE Say, look, Doc. I'm with you in this. I never wanted to let Cody off the hook. I'm with you.
DOCTOR Yes, I can see that. Fetch my bag.
SANTEE What?
DOCTOR My bag!
SANTEE Yessir. You bet. I'm with you in this.

SANTEE *gets the* DOCTOR'S *bag and gives it to him.*

DOCTOR And stop repeating foolish platitudes. I've grown quite tired of all this trivia. Something drastic must take place.
BEAUJO Drastic?
DOCTOR Yes, that's right. Something rather more adventurous. You're a man of adventure aren't you, Beaujo?
BEAUJO Well, not exactly. I mean I been around but—
DOCTOR You've been around?
BEAUJO Yessir. I mean, the States, you know. I've seen the States.
DOCTOR I see. Did you discover anything of particular interest in your travels?
BEAUJO Well, you know, the usual stuff. Card games, pool halls, that kinda' stuff.

DOCTOR Then you're a man who can recognize gifts.

BEAUJO Gifts? Well, I don't—I don't exactly get what you mean.

DOCTOR What I mean very simply is that perhaps in a card game you noticed a particular player who seemed to have more luck than the others. Perhaps even yourself. Something more than luck. A gift we might say.

BEAUJO Yeah. You might say that.

SANTEE Say, what's goin' on here anyway?

DOCTOR Please be silent until you're spoken to!

SANTEE Yessir.

During all this the DOCTOR *has placed his black bag on the bed and opened it. As he talks he handles various unseen objects in the bag.*

DOCTOR I'm not speaking superstitiously you understand. Luck is no accident. It's a phenomenon. Luck is a living thing. The problem of course is tracking it down.

BEAUJO Yeah, I see what you mean.

DOCTOR Do you? You see, in Cody here we had actually tracked it down. We had placed it on the map. We combed the planet for someone like him and we finally found him. In Wyoming of all places.

FINGERS That's enough Doctor! Enough!

DOCTOR These dreams, these visions that he has, do you suppose they are purely accident? Mere coincidence?

BEAUJO Well, I don't know. I couldn't say for sure. Look, I'm just a sidekick here. I don't know anything important.

DOCTOR Fair enough, but there's no harm in investigating a few details.

BEAUJO I'd rather you talked to Santee about it. I'm liable to get a headache and go right out on ya'!

DOCTOR Santee has no space between his ears for anything new. I was hoping perhaps you would.

FINGERS (*still on the floor*) You can't do this! No one's prepared.

DOCTOR I recognized you immediately, Beaujo, as a man of adventure.

BEAUJO You did?

DOCTOR Yes. A man who's been around as you say. A man who's looked life in the face. You have dreams, don't you, Beaujo?

BEAUJO Sure. Santee's the only one that don't have dreams.

DOCTOR What do you dream about?

BEAUJO Pool mostly. Fast cars. Money.

DOCTOR Yes. Pool, fast cars and money. Probably women too?

BEAUJO Sure.

DOCTOR You can see the difference between your dreams and someone like Cody's. You can recognize that you're worlds apart.

BEAUJO I guess so. I never thought about it too much.

DOCTOR Of course not. No reason to think about it. That's my job. I'm the doctor. You're simply the bodyguard.

SANTEE Could I say somethin' here?

DOCTOR No! Be quiet! Come here and look in this bag, Beaujo. I want you to see something.

FINGERS NO! Don't look! Don't look, Beaujo!

DOCTOR You are a man of adventure aren't you, Beaujo? I wasn't wrong in that was I?

BEAUJO I'm feelin' a little paralyzed, Doc. I don't know what it is. I'm afraid.

DOCTOR There's nowhere to run. Besides, it could turn out to be something quite extraordinary. Come have a look.

SANTEE I'll look.

DOCTOR Stay where you are! Beaujo?

BEAUJO What's in it?

DOCTOR Come and look.

BEAUJO What if I can't take it. I'm not a very strong person.

DOCTOR It doesn't matter. Nothing will hurt you. Just come and look in the bag.

A *moment of silence while* BEAUJO *decides.* BEAUJO *slowly crosses to the bag where the* DOCTOR *is and looks into it.*

FINGERS Oh God. Oh my God.

BEAUJO What are they?

DOCTOR Take one in your hand. Go ahead. Nothing will happen, I promise.

BEAUJO *reaches into the bag and pulls out a small white bone the size of a large marble. He holds it in the palm of his hand.*

BEAUJO What is it?

DOCTOR A bone from the back of the neck. A dreamer's bone.

BEAUJO Human?

DOCTOR Yes.

BEAUJO You mean you cut it out of somebody?

DOCTOR In a dreamer's prime he collects certain valuable substances from his dreams in the back of his neck. Even when he loses his touch these substances remain imbedded in these magical bones. A man in possession of enough of these bones becomes eternally linked to the dreamer's magic. His gift lives on.

BEAUJO You mean these are from dead dreamers?

DOCTOR I wouldn't say dead exactly. Out of their bodies perhaps but not dead.

BEAUJO And they help you pick the winners?

DOCTOR Infallibly.

BEAUJO Then what's the point in having live dreamers all the time.

DOCTOR Unfortunately the bones tend to fade in strength. Their power has to continually be replenished. This is where the adventure comes in. It's a very delicate process finding the correct dreamer to restore the power. It has to be one who has experienced a certain stretch of genius. One who is beginning to fade but not to such an extent as to have lost all his magic. Like Cody here for instance. He appears to be the perfect choice.

CODY Oh no ya' don't. Not me, boy. Not this kid. I ain't gettin' cut up and put in no bag. This has gone far enough. I've played ball with you right down the line but this is the limit. No more.

DOCTOR Santee, strap him to the bed!

SANTEE With pleasure.

SANTEE *goes after* CODY. *There's a mad chase around the room.* FINGERS *weeps and moans on the floor. The* DOCTOR *pulls a huge syringe out of his bag.* BEAUJO *is frozen.*

DOCTOR You see the territory he travels in. He's perfectly capable of living in several worlds at the same time. This is his genius.

CODY I was just bluffin'! Honest! I made it all up! I got no magic! I was just pretending!

DOCTOR Right now he'll do anything to deny his gifts. His gifts are poison to him now. If he knew his power he could even make us disappear. Fortunately he's just a slave for us.

SANTEE Come here you greaseball! (CODY *keeps getting away from* SANTEE)

FINGERS Stop it! You've got to stop it! Beaujo, do something!

DOCTOR You see how we're each on our own territory right now. Each of us paralyzed within certain boundaries. We'd do anything to cross the border but we're stuck. Quite stuck.

BEAUJO You're gonna' operate on him?

DOCTOR I'm simply going to alter the balance of things. Like a great chef. A pinch of this with a pinch of that. You'd be amazed at how little it takes to create an explosion. Santee, put him on the bed.

SANTEE *has* CODY *in a firm grip.* CODY *squeals and squirms but* SANTEE *is too strong. He hauls* CODY *over to the bed and throws him down on his back then straddles his stomach and holds his arms down.*

BEAUJO Maybe there's some other way. I mean maybe we could hypnotize him or something. I keep putting myself in his place.

DOCTOR That's quite impossible, Beaujo. You see there's no way for you to be in his place. There's no way for any of us to be in any place but the one we're in right now. Each of us. Quite separate from each other and yet connected. It's quite extraordinary isn't it? Now hold him down Santee. It's important to get a direct hit.

SANTEE *holds* CODY'S *arm and slowly injects the serum.* CODY *becomes calm and speaks very evenly.* BEAUJO *looks on.*

CODY The white buffalo. Approach him in a sacred manner. He is Wakan. The ground he walks is Wakan. This day has sent a spirit gift. You must take it. Clean your heart of evil thoughts. Take him in a sacred way. If one bad thought is creeping in you it will mean your death. You will crumble to the earth. You will vanish from this time.

DOCTOR Santee, hand me my scalpel please. It's in my bag.

SANTEE Sure thing, Doc.

SANTEE *hands the* DOCTOR *a scalpel from out of the bag. A series of knocks at the door. The* DOCTOR *remains cool.*

DOCTOR Beaujo, would you mind answering that. It's probably our waiter.

BEAUJO *crosses to the door as the* DOCTOR *cuts into the back of* CODY'S *neck with the scalpel.* CODY *makes no sound.* BEAUJO *swings the door open. A shotgun blast throws him clear across the room. He lies in a heap.* CODY'S *two brothers,* JASPER *and* JASON, *enter. They're both about six foot five and weigh 250 lbs. each. They wear Wyoming cowboy gear with dust covering them from head to foot. Their costumes should be well used and authentic without looking like dime-store cowboys. They both carry double-barreled twelve-gauge shotguns and wear side guns on their waists. The* DOCTOR *turns suddenly toward them. Another shotgun blast from* JASPER. *The* DOCTOR *sinks to the floor.* SANTEE *reaches for his pistol and is cut down by both shotguns at once.* FINGERS *whimpers on the floor.* JASPER *and* JASON *look at him stony-faced.* CODY *sits on the bed with the back of his neck bleeding. He doesn't know where he is.* JASPER *crosses slowly over to* FINGERS *with his spurs jangling. He peers down at him.*

JASPER We come fer our brother, mister. You so much as make a twitch and you can kiss tomorrow goodbye.

JASON (*crossing to* CODY) Come on, boy. We're goin' home now.

CODY One bad thought. A clean heart.

JASON (*helping* CODY *to his feet*) Come on now. You gather yerself together. A little beef stew in yer gullet, you'll be good as new.

CODY (*standing*) In a sacred way. This day. Sacred. I was walking in my dream. A great circle. I was walking and I stopped. Even after the smoke cleared I couldn't see my home. Not even a familiar rock. You could tell me it was anywhere and I'd believe ya'. You could tell me it was any old where.

JASON *leads* CODY *slowly out the door as* JASPER *backs out keeping his eye on* FINGERS. *They disappear out the door. A short pause. The* WAITER *enters briskly into the room carrying a silver serving tray with three bottles of booze and sparkling glasses. He stops short center stage and looks around the room at all the corpses. His eyes finally fall on* FINGERS *who moans softly.*

WAITER Is there something I could get you, sir?

FINGERS The record. (*gesturing to the album*) Put the record on.

WAITER Very good sir.

The WAITER *puts down his tray and picks up the record. He puts it on the record player. The song plays. It is "Zydeco et pas sale" on Side 2 of Clifton Chenier's Very Best, on EMI, Harvest Recordings. The* WAITER *stands and listens to the tune as the lights fade. The music continues as the audience leaves.*

Questions

1. The conversation between Santee, Beaujo, and Cody makes constant comparisons between the horse dreamer's selection of horses and the act of artistic creation. How are they shown to be similar?
2. Why is Santee so reluctant to allow Cody any comfort or movement?
3. Santee says (p. 1308): "He can't know where he is. . . . He can't for a second know where he is outside the room he's locked up in. Otherwise it spoils the dreaming. He can't know the time either." Why do you suppose Santee believes this?
4. What is Cody's theory of how to make his accurate dreams return?
5. When Cody first started dreaming winners, he became famous. How did that affect his life? How did it affect his work?
6. Word comes from Fingers that Cody must shift his range of operations from the horse track to the dog track. How does this affect Cody's performance? Why?
7. Cody's sudden mastery of dog racing in Act II is clearly not realistic, yet it has symbolic significance. What do you suppose Shepard intends to convey by this symbolic transformation?
8. What is the relationship between Fingers and the Doctor? Who is in authority?
9. Why does the Doctor want to remove Cody's dreaming bone?

American Gothic—*Crimes of the Heart*

We have remarked that realism avoids all that is improbable in events and characters and all that is visionary in theatrical presentation. The symbolic play you have just read, *Geography of a Horse Dreamer*, is clearly unrealistic, for its main character has miraculous powers of prophecy. A more common and subtle reaction to the realism in modern drama may be seen in Beth Henley's *Crimes of the Heart*. The central character, Babe Botrelle, has shot her husband because she "didn't like his looks." Her sister Lenny's pet horse has just been struck dead by lightning. A young lawyer, Barnette Lloyd, has taken on Babe's defense, despite its hopelessness, because he fell in love with her years ago when she sold him pound cake at a bazaar. These situations are more and less probable when we consider each one singly; considered together they make an altogether bizarre and improbable picture. In the manner of Eudora Welty, Beth Henley is working in a great tradition of Gothic American storytelling, in which characters and situations are exaggerated up to the point of incredibility. She also shares with many contemporary playwrights a penchant for black humor, the comic treatment of subjects that are not in themselves very funny. In fact, Babe's shooting of her husband, which sets the play in motion, is never taken at all seriously. The more the characters refer to the assault in their flippant manner, the more humorous it seems. What rescues the play from silliness, or plain bad taste, is the characters' innocence—the sisters seem utterly unaware of their own shortcomings and have a true affection for one another that we, as readers, are invited to share.

Beth Henley, born in Mississippi in 1952, studied at Southern Methodist University and the University of Illinois. In 1979 her *Crimes of the Heart* was the co-winner of the great American Play Contest, Actors Theatre of Louisville; a year later it opened Off-Broadway at the Manhattan Theatre Club. It won the Pulitzer Prize and New York Drama Critics Circle Award before its successful run on Broadway.

BETH HENLEY (1952–)

Crimes of the Heart

"For Len, C.C., and Kayo."

THE CAST

LENNY MAGRATH, 30, *the oldest sister*
CHICK BOYLE, 29, *the sisters' first cousin*
DOC PORTER, 30, *Meg's old boyfriend*

MEG MAGRATH, 27, *the middle sister*
BABE BOTRELLE, 24, *the youngest sister*
BARNETTE LLOYD, 26, *Babe's lawyer*

THE SETTING

The setting of the entire play is the kitchen in the Magrath sisters' house in Hazlehurst, Mississippi, a small southern town. The oldfashioned kitchen is unusually spacious, but there is a lived-in, cluttered look about it. There are four different entrances and exits to the kitchen: the back door; the door leading to the dining room and the front of the house; a door leading to the downstairs bedroom; and a staircase leading to the upstairs room. There is a table near the center of the room, and a cot has been set up in one of the corners.

THE TIME

In the fall; five years after Hurricane Camille

ACT I

The lights go up on the empty kitchen. It is late afternoon. LENNY MAGRATH, *a thirty-year-old woman with a round figure and face, enters from the back door carrying a white suitcase, a saxophone case, and a brown paper sack. She sets the suitcase and the sax case down and takes the brown sack to the kitchen table. After glancing quickly at the door, she gets the cookie jar from the kitchen counter, a box of matches from the stove and then brings both objects back down to the kitchen table. Excitedly, she reaches into the brown sack and pulls out a package of birthday candles. She quickly opens the package and removes a candle. She tries to stick the candle into a cookie—it falls off. She sticks the candle in again but the cookie is too hard and it crumbles. Frantically, she gets a second cookie from the jar. She strikes a match, lights the candle and begins dripping wax onto the cookie. Just as she is beginning to smile we hear* CHICK'S *voice from Offstage.*

CHICK'S VOICE Lenny! Oh, Lenny! (LENNY *quickly blows out the candle and stuffs the cookie and candle into her dress pocket.* CHICK, 29, *enters from the back door. She is a brightly dressed matron with yellow hair and shiny, red lips.*)

CHICK Hi! I saw your car pull up.

LENNY Hi.

CHICK Well, did you see today's paper? (LENNY *nods.*) It's just too awful! It's just way too awful! How I'm gonna continue holding my head up high in this community, I do not know. Did you remember to pick up those pantyhose for me?

LENNY They're in the sack.

CHICK Well, thank goodness, at least I'm not gonna have to go into town wearing holes in my stockings. (CHICK *gets the package, tears it open and proceeds to take off one pair of stockings and put on another, throughout the following scene. There should be something slightly grotesque about this woman changing her stockings in the kitchen.*)

LENNY Did Uncle Watson call?

CHICK Yes, Daddy has called me twice already. He said Babe's ready to come home. We've got to get right over and pick her up before they change their simple minds.

LENNY (*hesitantly*) Oh, I know, of course, it's just—

CHICK What?

LENNY Well, I was hoping Meg would call.

CHICK Meg?

LENNY Yes, I sent her a telegram: about Babe, and—

CHICK A telegram?! Couldn't you just phone her up?

LENNY Well, no, 'cause her phone's . . . out of order.

CHICK Out of order?

LENNY Disconnected. I don't know what.

CHICK Well, that sounds like Meg. My, these are snug. Are your sure you bought my right size?

LENNY (*looking at the box*) Size extra petite.

CHICK Well, they're skimping on the nylon material. (*Struggling to pull up the stockings.*) That's all there is to it. Skimping on the nylon. (*She finishes on one leg and starts on the other.*) Now, just what all did you say in this "telegram" to Meg?

LENNY I don't recall exactly. I, well, I just told her to come on home.

CHICK To come on home! Why, Lenora Josephine, have you lost your only brain, or what?

LENNY (*nervously, as she begins to pick up the mess of dirty stockings and plastic wrappings*) But Babe wants Meg home. She asked me to call her.

CHICK I'm not talking about what Babe wants.

LENNY Well, what then?

CHICK Listen, Lenora, I think it's pretty accurate to assume that after this morning's paper, Babe's gonna be incurring some mighty negative publicity around this town. And Meg's appearance isn't gonna help out a bit.

LENNY What's wrong with Meg?

CHICK She had a loose reputation in high school.

LENNY (*weakly*) She was popular.

CHICK She was known all over Copiah County as cheap Christmas trash, and that was the least of it. There was that whole sordid affair with Doc Porter, leaving him a cripple.

LENNY A cripple—he's got a limp. Just, kind of, barely a limp.

CHICK Well, his mother was going to keep *me* out of the Ladies' Social League because of it.

LENNY What?

CHICK That's right. I never told you, but I had to go plead with that mean, old woman and convince her that I was just as appalled and upset with what Meg had done as she was, and that I was only a first cousin anyway and I could hardly be blamed for all the skeletons in the Magraths' closet. It was humiliating. I tell you, she even brought up your mother's death. And that poor cat.

LENNY Oh! Oh! Oh, please, Chick! I'm sorry. But you're in the Ladies' League now.

CHICK Yes. That's true, I am. But frankly, if Mrs. Porter hadn't developed that tumor in her bladder, I wouldn't be in the club today, much less a committee head. (*As she brushes her hair.*) Anyway, you be a sweet potato and wait right here for Meg to call, so's you can convince her not to come back home. It would make things a whole lot easier on everybody. Don't you think it really would?

LENNY Probably.

CHICK Good, then suit yourself. How's my hair?

LENNY Fine.

CHICK Not pooching out in the back, is it?

LENNY No.

CHICK (*cleaning the hair from her brush*) All right then, I'm on my way. I've got Annie May over there keeping an eye on Peekay and Buck Jr., but I don't trust her with them for long periods of time. (*Dropping the ball of hair onto the floor.*) Her mind is like a loose sieve. Honestly it is. (*She puts the brush back into her purse.*) Oh! Oh! Oh! I almost forgot. Here's a present for you. Happy Birthday to Lenny, from the Buck Boyles! (CHICK *takes a wrapped package from her bag and hands it to* LENNY.)

LENNY Why, thank you, Chick. It's so nice to have you remember my birthday every year like you do.

CHICK (*modestly*) Oh well, now, that's just the way I am, I suppose. That's just the way I was brought up to be. Well, why don't you go on and open up the present?

LENNY All right. (*She starts to unwrap the gift.*)

CHICK It's a box of candy—assorted cremes.

LENNY Candy—that's always a nice gift.

CHICK And you have a sweet tooth, don't you?

LENNY I guess.

CHICK Well, I'm glad you like it.

LENNY I do.

CHICK Oh, speaking of which, remember that little polka dot dress you got Peekay for her fifth birthday last month?

LENNY The red and white one?

CHICK Yes; well, the first time I put it in the washing machine, I mean the very first time, it fell all to pieces. Those little polka dots just dropped right off in the water.

LENNY (*crushed*) Oh, no. Well, I'll get something else for her then—a little toy.

CHICK Oh, no, no, no, no, no! We wouldn't hear of it! I just wanted to let you know so you wouldn't go and waste any more of your hard-earned money on that make of dress. Those inexpensive brands just don't hold up. I'm sorry but not in these modern washing machines.

DOC PORTER'S VOICE Hello! Hello, Lenny!

CHICK (*taking over*) Oh, look, it's Doc Porter! Come on in, Doc! Please come right on in! (DOC PORTER *enters through the back door. He is carrying a large sack of pecans. DOC is an attractively worn man with a slight limp that adds rather than detracts from his quiet seductive quality. He is 30 years old, but appears slightly older.*) Well, how are you doing? How in the world are you doing?

DOC Just fine, Chick.

CHICK And how are you liking it now that you're back in Hazlehurst?

DOC Oh, I'm finding it somewhat enjoyable.

CHICK Somewhat! Only somewhat! Will you listen to him! What a silly, silly, silly man! Well, I'm on my way. I've got some people waiting on me. (*Whispering to* DOC.) It's Babe. I'm on my way to pick her up.

DOC Oh.

CHICK Well, goodbye! Farewell and goodbye!

LENNY Bye. (CHICK *exits.*)

DOC Hello.

LENNY Hi. I guess you heard about the thing with Babe.

DOC Yeah.

LENNY It was in the newspaper.

DOC Uh huh.

LENNY What a mess.

DOC Yeah.

LENNY Well, come on and sit down. I'll heat us up some coffee.

DOC That's okay. I can only stay a minute. I have to pick up Scott; he's at the dentist's.

LENNY Oh; well, I'll heat some up for myself. I'm kinda thirsty for a cup of hot coffee.

(LENNY *puts the coffeepot on the burner.*)

DOC Lenny—

LENNY What?

DOC (*not able to go on*) Ah . . .

LENNY Yes?

DOC Here, some pecans for you (*He hands her the sack.*)

LENNY Why, thank you, Doc. I love pecans.

DOC My wife and Scott picked them up around the yard.

LENNY Well, I can use them to make a pie. A pecan pie.

DOC Yeah. Look, Lenny, I've got some bad news for you.

LENNY What?

DOC Well, you know, you've been keeping Billy Boy out on our farm; he's been grazing out there.

LENNY Yes—

DOC Well, last night, Billy Boy died.

LENNY He died?

DOC Yeah. I'm sorry to tell you when you've got all this on you; but I thought you'd want to know.

LENNY Well, yeah. I do. He died?

DOC Uh huh. He was struck by lightning.

LENNY Struck by lightning? In that storm yesterday?

DOC That's what we think.

LENNY Gosh, struck by lightning. I've had Billy Boy so long. You know. Ever since I was ten years old.

DOC Yeah. He was a mighty old horse.

LENNY (stung) Mighty old.

DOC Almost twenty years old.

LENNY That's right, twenty years. 'Cause; ah; I'm thirty years old today. Did you know that?

DOC No, Lenny, I didn't know. Happy Birthday.

LENNY Thanks. (She begins to cry.)

DOC Oh, come on now, Lenny. Come on. Hey, hey, now. You know I can't stand it when you Magrath women start to cry. You know it just gets me.

LENNY Oh-ho! Sure! You mean when Meg cries! Meg's the one you could never stand to watch cry! Not me! I could fill up a pig's trough!

DOC Now, Lenny . . . stop it. Come on. Jesus!

LENNY Okay! Okay! I don't know what's wrong with me. I don't mean to make a scene. I've been on this crying jag. (She blows her nose.) All this stuff with Babe and old Granddaddy's gotten worse in the hospital and I can't get in touch with Meg.

DOC You tried calling Meggy?

LENNY Yes.

DOC Is she coming home?

LENNY Who knows. She hasn't called me. That's what I'm waiting here for—hoping she'll call.

DOC She still living in California?

LENNY Yes; in Hollwood.

DOC Well, give me a call if she gets in. I'd like to see her.

LENNY Oh, you would, huh?

DOC Yeah, Lenny, sad to say, but I would.

LENNY It is sad. It's very sad indeed. (They stare at each other, then look away. There is a moment of tense silence.)

DOC Hey, Jello Face, your coffee's boiling.

LENNY (going to check) Oh, it is? Thanks. (After she checks the pot.) Look, you'd better go on and pick Scott up. You don't want him to have to wait for you.

DOC Yeah, you're right. Poor kid. It's his first time at the dentist.

LENNY Poor thing.

DOC Well, 'bye. I'm sorry to have to tell you about your horse.

LENNY Oh, I know. Tell Joan thanks for picking up the pecans.

DOC I will. (He starts to leave.)

LENNY Oh, how's the baby?

DOC She's fine. Real pretty. She, ah, holds your finger in her hand; like this.

LENNY Oh, that's cute.

DOC Yeah. 'Bye, Lenny.

LENNY 'Bye. (DOC *exits.* LENNY *stares after him for a moment, then goes and sits back down at the kitchen table. She reaches into her pocket and pulls out a somewhat crumbled cookie and a wax candle. She lights the candle again, lets the wax drip onto the cookie, then sticks the candle on top of the cookie. She begins to sing the "Happy Birthday Song" to herself. At the end of the song she pauses, silently makes a wish, and blows out the candle. She waits a moment, then re-lights the candle, and repeats her actions, only this time making a different wish at the end of the song. She starts to repeat the procedure for the third time, as the phone begins to ring. She goes to answer it.*) Hello . . . oh, hello, Lucille, how's Zackery? . . . Oh, no! . . . Oh, I'm so sorry. Of course, it must be grueling for you . . . Yes, I understand. Your only brother . . . no, she's not here yet. Chick just went to pick her up . . . oh, now, Lucille, she's still his wife, I'm sure she'll be interested . . . Well, you can just tell me the information and I'll relate it all to her . . . Uh-hum, his liver's saved. Oh, that's good news! . . . Well, of course, when you look at it like that . . . Breathing stabilized . . . Damage to the spinal column, not yet determined . . . Okay . . . Yes, Lucille, I've got it all down . . . Uh-huh, I'll give her that message. 'Bye, 'bye. (LENNY *drops the pencil and paper down. She sighs deeply, wipes her cheeks with the back of her hand, and goes to the stove to pour herself a cup of coffee. After a few moments, the front door is heard slamming.* LENNY *starts. A whistle is heard, then* MEG'S *voice.*)

MEG'S VOICE I'm home! (*She whistles the family whistle.*) Anybody home?!!

LENNY Meg? Meg! (MEG, 27, *enters from the dining room. She has sad, magic eyes and wears a hat. She carries a worn-out suitcase.*)

MEG (*dropping her suitcase, running to hug* LENNY) Lenny—

LENNY Well, Meg! Why, Meg! Oh, Meggy! Why didn't you call? Did you fly in? You didn't take a cab, did you? Why didn't you give us a call?

MEG (*overlapping*) Oh, Lenny! Why, Lenny! Dear, Lenny! (*Then she looks at* LENNY'S *face.*) My God, we're getting so old! Oh, I called for heaven's sake. Of course, I called!

LENNY Well, I never talked to you—

MEG Well, I know! I let the phone ring right off the hook!

LENNY Well, as a matter of fact, I was out most of the morning seeing to Babe—!

MEG Now just what's all this business about Babe? How could you send me such a telegram about Babe? And Zackery! You say somebody's shot Zackery?!

LENNY Yes; they have.

MEG Well, good Lord! Is he dead?

LENNY No. But he's in the hospital. He was shot in his stomach.

MEG In his stomach! How awful! Do they know who shot him? (LENNY *nods.*) Well, who? Who was it? Who? Who?

LENNY Babe! They're all saying Babe shot him! They took her to jail! And they're saying she shot him! They're all saying it! It's horrible! It's awful!

MEG (*overlapping*) Jail! Good Lord, jail! Well, who? Who's saying it? Who?!!

LENNY Everyone!! The policemen, the sheriff, Zackery, even Babe's saying it! Even Babe herself!!

MEG Well, for God's sake. For God's sake.

LENNY (*overlapping as she falls apart*) It's horrible! It's horrible! It's just horrible!!!

MEG Now calm down, Lenny. Just calm down. Would you like a Coke? Here, I'll get you some Coke. (MEG *gets a Coke from the refrigerator. She opens it and downs a large swig.*) Why? Why would she shoot him? Why? (MEG *hands the Coke bottle to* LENNY.)

LENNY I talked to her this morning and I asked her that very question. I said, "Babe, why would you shoot Zackery? He was your own husband. Why would you shoot him?" And do you know what she said? (MEG *shakes her head.*) She said, " 'Cause I didn't like his looks. I just didn't like his looks."

MEG (*after a pause*) Well, I don't like his looks.

LENNY But you didn't shoot him! You wouldn't shoot a person 'cause you didn't like their looks! You wouldn't do that! Oh, I hate to say this—I do hate to say this—but I believe Babe is ill. I mean in-her-head-ill.

MEG Oh, now, Lenny, don't you say that! There're plenty of good sane reasons to shoot another person and I'm sure that Babe had one. Now what we've got to do is get her the best lawyer in town. Do you have any ideas on who's the best lawyer in town?

LENNY Well, Zackery is, of course; but he's been shot!

MEG Well, count him out! Just count him and his whole firm out!

LENNY Anyway, you don't have to worry, she's already got her lawyer.

MEG She does? Who?

LENNY Barnette Lloyd. Annie Lloyd's boy. He just opened his office here in town. And Uncle Watson said we'd be doing Annie a favor by hiring him up.

MEG Doing Annie a favor? Doing Annie a favor?! Well, what about Babe? Have you thought about Babe? Do we want to do her a favor of thirty or forty years in jail?! Have you thought about that?

LENNY Now, don't snap at me! Just don't snap at me! I try to do what's right! All this responsibility keeps falling on my shoulders, and I try to do what's right!

MEG Well, boo hoo, hoo, hoo! And how in the hell could you send me such a telegram about Babe!

LENNY Well, if you had a phone, or if you didn't live way out there in Hollywood and not even come home for Christmas maybe I wouldn't have to pay all that money to send you a telegram!!!

MEG (*overlapping*) 'Babe's in terrible trouble—Stop! Zackery's been shot—Stop! Come home immediately—Stop! Stop! Stop!'

LENNY And what was that you said about how old we're getting? When you looked at my face, you said, "My God, we're getting so old!" But you didn't mean we—you meant me! Didn't you? I'm thirty years old today and my face is getting all pinched up and my hair is falling out in the comb.

MEG Why, Lenny! It's your birthday, October 23rd. How could I forget. Happy Birthday!

LENNY Well, it's not. I'm thirty years old and Billy Boy died last night. He was struck by lightning. He was struck dead.

MEG (*reaching for a cigarette*) Struck dead. Oh, what a mess. What a mess. Are you really thirty? Then I must be twenty-seven and Babe is twenty-four. My God, we're getting so old. (*They are silent for several moments as* MEG *drags off her cigarette and* LENNY *drinks her Coke.*) What's the cot doing in the kitchen?

LENNY Well, I rolled it out when Old Granddaddy got sick. So I could be close and hear him at night if he needed something.

MEG (*glancing toward the door leading to the downstairs bedroom*) Is Old Granddaddy here?

LENNY Why, no. Old Granddaddy's at the hospital.

MEG Again?

LENNY Meg!

MEG What?

LENNY I wrote you all about it. He's been in the hospital over three months straight.

MEG He has?

LENNY Don't you remember? I wrote you about all those blood vessels popping in his brain?

MEG Popping—

LENNY And how he was so anxious to hear from you and to find out about your singing career. I wrote it all to you. How they have to feed him through those tubes now. Didn't you get my letters?

MEG Oh, I don't know, Lenny. I guess I did. To tell you the truth, sometimes I kinda don't read your letters.

LENNY What?

MEG I'm sorry. I used to read them. It's just since Christmas reading them gives me these slicing pains right here in my chest.

LENNY I see. I see. Is that why you didn't use that money Old Granddaddy sent you to come home Christmas; because you hate us so much? We never did all that much to make you hate us. We didn't!

MEG Oh, Lenny! Do you think I'd be getting slicing pains in my chest, if I didn't care about you? If I hated you? Honestly, now, do you think I would?

LENNY No.

MEG Okay, then. Let's drop it. I'm sorry I didn't read your letters. Okay?

LENNY Okay.

MEG Anyway, we've got this whole thing with Babe to deal with. The first thing is to get her a good lawyer and get her out of jail.

LENNY Well, she's out of jail.

MEG She is?

LENNY That young lawyer, he's gotten her out.

MEG Oh, he has?

LENNY Yes, on bail. Uncle Watson's put it up. Chick's bringing her back right now— she's driving her home.

MEG Oh; well, that's a relief.

LENNY Yes, and they're due home any minute now; so we can just wait right here for 'em.

MEG Well, good. That's good. (*As she leans against the counter.*) So, Babe shot Zackery Botrelle, the richest and most powerful man in all of Hazlehurst, slap in the gut. It's hard to believe.

LENNY It certainly is. Little Babe—shooting off a gun.

MEG Little Babe.

LENNY She was always the prettiest and most perfect of the three of us. Old Granddaddy used to call her his Dancing Sugar Plum. Why, remember how proud and happy he was the day she married Zackery.

MEG Yes, I remember. It was his finest hour.

LENNY He remarked how Babe was gonna skyrocket right to the heights of Hazlehurst society. And how Zackery was just the right man for her whether she knew it now or not.

MEG Oh, Lordy, Lordy. And what does Old Granddaddy say now?

LENNY Well, I haven't had the courage to tell him all about this as yet. I thought maybe tonight we could go to visit him at the hospital and you could talk to him and . . .

MEG Yeah, well, we'll see. We'll see. Do we have anything to drink around here—to the tune of straight bourbon?

LENNY No. There's no liquor.

MEG Hell. (MEG *gets a Coke from the refrigerator and opens it.*)

LENNY Then you will go with me to see Old Granddaddy at the hospital tonight?

MEG Of course. (MEG *goes to her purse and gets out a bottle of Empirin Compound. She takes out a tablet and puts it on her tongue.*) Brother, I know he's gonna go on about my singing career. Just like he always does.

LENNY Well, how is your career going?

MEG It's not.

LENNY Why, aren't you still singing at the club down on Malibu beach?

MEG No. Not since Christmas.

LENNY Well, then, are you singing some place new?

MEG No, I'm not singing. I'm not singing at all.

LENNY Oh. Well, what do you do then?

MEG What I do is I pay cold storage bills for a dog food company. That's what I do.

LENNY (*trying to be helpful*) Gosh, don't you think it'd be a good idea to stay in the show business field?

MEG Oh, maybe.

LENNY Like Old Granddaddy says, "With your talent all you need is exposure. Then you can make your own breaks!" Did you hear his suggestion about getting your foot put in one of those blocks of cement they've got out here? He thinks that's real important.

MEG Yeh. I think I've heard that. And I'll probably hear it again when I go to visit him at the hospital tonight; so let's just drop it. Okay? (*She noticed the sack of pecans.*) What's this? Pecans? Great, I love pecans! (MEG *takes out two pecans and tries to open them by cracking them together.*) Come on . . . Crack, you demons! Crack!

LENNY We have a nutcracker!

MEG (*trying with her teeth*) Ah, where's the sport in a nutcracker? Where's the challenge?

LENNY (*getting up to get the nutcracker*) It's over here in the utensil drawer. (As LENNY *gets the nutcracker*, MEG *opens the pecan by stepping on it with her shoe.*)

MEG There! Open! (MEG *picks up the crumbled pecan and eats it.*) Mmmm, delicious. Delicious. Where'd you get the fresh pecans?

LENNY Oh . . . I don't know.

MEG They sure are tasty.

LENNY Doc Porter brought them over.

MEG Doc. What's Doc doing here in town?

LENNY Well, his father died a couple of months ago. Now he's back home seeing to his property.

MEG Gosh, the last I heard of Doc, he was up in the East painting the walls of houses to earn a living. (*Amused.*) Heard he was living with some Yankee woman who made clay pots.

LENNY Joan.

MEG What?

LENNY Her name's Joan. She came down here with him. That's one of her pots. Doc's married to her.

MEG Married—

LENNY Uh huh.

MEG Doc married a Yankee?

LENNY That's right; and they've got two kids.

MEG Kids—

LENNY A boy and a girl.

MEG God. Then his kids must be half-Yankee.

LENNY I suppose.

MEG God. That really gets me. I don't know why, but somehow that really gets me.

LENNY I don't know why it should.

MEG And what a stupid-looking pot! Who'd buy it anyway?

LENNY Wait—I think that's them. Yeah, that's Chick's car! Oh, there's Babe! Hello, Babe! They're home, Meg! They're home. (MEG *hides.*)

BABES VOICE Lenny! I'm home! I'm free! (BABE, *24, enters exuberantly. She has an angelic face and fierce, volatile eyes. She carries a pink pocketbook.*) I'm home! (MEG *jumps out of hiding.*) Oh, Meg—Look it's Meg! (*Running to hug her.*) Meg! When did you get home?

MEG Just now!

BABE Well, it's so good to see you! I'm so glad you're home! I'm so relieved. (CHICK *enters.*)

MEG Why, Chick; hello.

CHICK Hello, Cousin Margaret. What brings you back to Hazlehurst?

MEG Oh, I came on home . . . (*turning to* BABE) I came on home to see about Babe.

BABE (*running to hug* MEG) Oh, Meg—

MEG How are things with you, Babe?

CHICK Well, they are dismal, if you want my opinion. She is refusing to cooperate with her lawyer, that nice-looking young Lloyd boy. She won't tell any of us why she committed this heinous crime, except to say that she didn't like Zackery's looks—

BABE Oh, look, Lenny brought my suitcase from home! And my saxophone! Thank you! (BABE *runs over to the cot and gets out her saxophone.*)

CHICK Now that young lawyer is coming over here this afternoon, and when he gets here he expects to get some concrete answers! That's what he expects! No more of this nonsense and stubborness from you, Rebecca Magrath, or they'll put you in jail and throw away the key!

BABE Meg, come look at my new saxophone. I went to Jackson and bought it used. Feel it. I'ts so heavy.

MEG It's beautiful. (*The room goes silent.*)

CHICK Isn't that right, won't they throw away the key?

LENNY Well, honestly, I don't know about that—

CHICK They will! And leave you there to rot. So, Rebecca, what are you going to tell Mr. Lloyd about shooting Zackery when he gets here? What are your reasons going to be?

BABE (*glaring*) That I didn't like his looks! I just didn't like his stinking looks! And I don't like yours much either, Chick-the-Stick! So, just leave me alone! I mean it! Leave me alone! Oooh! (BABE *exits up the stairs. There is a long moment of silence.*)

CHICK Well, I was only trying to warn her that she's going to have to help herself. It's just that she doesn't understand how serious the situation is. Does she? She doesn't have the vaguest idea. Does she now?

LENNY Well, it's true, she does seem a little confused.

CHICK And that's putting it mildly, Lenny honey. That's putting it mighty mild. So, Margaret, how's your singing career going? We keep looking for your picture in the movie magazines. (MEG *moves to light a cigarette.*) You know, you shouldn't smoke. It causes cancer. Cancer of the lungs. They say each cigarette is just a little stick of cancer. A little death stick.

MEG That's what I like about it, Chick—taking a drag off of death. (MEG *takes a long, deep drag.*) Mmm! Gives me a sense of controlling my own destiny. What power! What exhilaration! Want a drag?

LENNY (*trying to break the tension*) Ah, Zackery's liver's been saved! His sister called up and said his liver was saved. Isn't that good news?

MEG Well, yes, that's fine news. Mighty fine news. Why I've been told that the liver's a powerful important bodily organ. I believe it's used to absorb all our excess bile.

LENNY Yes—well—it's been saved. (*The phone rings.* LENNY *gets it.*)

MEG So! Did you hear all that good news about the liver, Litttle Chicken?

CHICK I heard it. And don't you call me Chicken! (MEG *clucks like a chicken.*) I've told you a hundred times if I've told you once not to call me Chicken. You cannot call me Chicken.

LENNY . . . Oh, no! . . . Of course, we'll be right over! Bye! (*She hangs up the phone.*) That was Annie May—Peekay and Buck Jr. have eaten paints!

CHICK Oh, no! Are they all right? They're not sick? They're not sick, are they?

LENNY I don't know. I don't know. Come on. We've got to run on next door.

CHICK (*overlapping.*) Oh, God! Oh, please! Please let them be all right! Don't let them die!! Please, don't let them die!!

CHICK *runs Off howling with* LENNY *following after.* MEG *sits alone, finishing her cigarette. After a moment,* BABE'S *voice is heard.*

BABE'S VOICE Pst—Psst!

MEG *looks around. Babe comes tiptoeing down the stairs.*

BABE Has she gone?

MEG She's gone. Peekay and Buck Jr. just ate their paints.

BABE What idiots.

MEG Yeah.

BABE You know, Chick's hated us ever since we had to move here from Vicksburg to live with Old Grandmama and Old Granddaddy.

MEG She's an idiot.

BABE Yeah. Do you know what she told me this morning while I was still behind bars and couldn't get away?

MEG What?

BABE She told me how embarrassing it was for her all those years ago, you know, when mama—

MEG Yeah, down in the cellar.

BABE She said our mama had shamed the entire family, and we were known notoriously all through Hazelhurst. (*About to cry.*) Then she went on to say how I would now be getting just as much bad publicity and humiliating her and the family all over again.

MEG Ah, forget it, Babe. Just forget it.

BABE I told her, "Mama got national coverage! National!" And if Zackery wasn't a senator from Copiah County, I probably wouldn't even be getting state-wide.

MEG Of course you wouldn't.

BABE (*after a pause.*) Gosh, sometimes I wonder . . .

MEG What?

BABE Why she did it. Why mama hung herself.

MEG I don't know. She had a bad day. A real bad day. You know how it feels on a real bad day.

BABE And that old yellow cat. It was sad about that old cat.

MEG Yeah.

BABE I bet if Daddy hadn't of left us, they'd still be alive.

MEG Oh, I don't know.

BABE 'Cause it was after he left that she started spending whole days just sitting there and smoking on the back porch steps. She'd sling her ashes down onto the different bugs and ants that'd be passing by.

MEG Yeah. Well, I'm glad he left.

BABE That old yellow cat'd stay back there with her.

MEG God, he was a bastard.

BABE I thought if she felt something for anyone it would a been that old cat. Guess I musta been mistaken.

MEG Really, with his white teeth, Daddy was such a bastard.

BABE Was he? I don't remember. (MEG *blows out a mouthful of smoke. After a moment, uneasily.*) I think I'm gonna make some lemonade. You want some?

MEG Sure. (BABE *cuts lemons, dumps sugar, stirs ice cubes, etc. throughout the following exchange.*) Babe. Why won't you talk? Why won't you tell anyone about shooting Zackery?

BABE Oooh—

MEG Why not? You must have had a good reason. Didn't you?

BABE I guess I did.

MEG Well, what was it?

BABE I . . . I can't say.

MEG Why not? (*Pause.*) Babe, why not? You can tell me.

BABE 'Cause . . . I'm sort of . . . protecting someone.

MEG Protecting someone? Oh, Babe, then you really didn't shoot him?! I knew you couldn't have done it!! I knew it!!!

BABE No, I shot him. I shot him all right. I meant to kill him. I was aiming for his heart, but I guess my hands were shaking and I—just got him in the stomach.

MEG (*collapsing*) I see.

BABE (*stirring the lemonade*) So I'm guilty. And I'm just gonna have to take my punishment and go on to jail.

MEG Oh, Babe—

BABE Don't worry, Meg, jail's gonna be a relief to me. I can learn to play my new saxophone. I won't have to live with Zackery anymore. And I won't have his snoopy old sister, Lucille, coming over and pushing me around. Jail will be a relief. Here's your lemonade.

MEG Thanks.

BABE It taste okay?

MEG Perfect.

BABE I like a lot of sugar in mine. I'm gonna add some more sugar. (BABE *goes to add more sugar to her lemonade, as* LENNY *bursts through the back door in a state of excitement and confusion.*)

LENNY Well, it looks like the paint is primarily on their arms and faces; but Chick wants me to drive them all over to Doctor Winn's just to make sure. (LENNY *grabs her car keys off of the counter and as she does so, she notices the mess of lemons and sugar.*) Oh, now, Babe, try not to make a mess here; and be careful with this sharp knife. Honestly, all that sugar's gonna get you sick. Well, 'bye, 'bye. I'll be back as soon as I can.

MEG Bye, Lenny.

BABE 'Bye. (LENNY *exits.*) Boy, I don't know what's happening to Lenny.

MEG What do you mean?

BABE "Don't make a mess; don't make yourself sick; don't cut yourself with that sharp knife." She's turning into Old Grandmama.

MEG You think so?

BABE More and more. Do you know she's taken to wearing Old Grandmama's torn sunhat and her green garden gloves?

MEG Those old lime green ones?

BABE Yeah; she works out in the garden wearing the lime green gloves of a dead woman. Imagine wearing those gloves on your hands.

MEG Poor Lenny. She needs some love in her life. All she does is work out at that brick yard and take care of Old Granddaddy.

BABE Yeah. But she's so shy with men.

MEG (*biting into an apple*) Probably because of that *shrunken* ovary she has.

BABE (*slinging ice cubes*) Yeah, that *deformed* ovary.

MEG Old Granddaddy's the one who's made her feel self-conconscious about it. It's his fault. The old fool.

BABE It's so sad.

MEG God—you know what?

BABE What?

MEG I bet Lenny's never even slept with a man. Just think, thirty years old and never even had it once.

BABE (*slyly*) Oh; I don't know. Maybe she's . . . had it once?

MEG She has?

BABE Maybe. I think so.

MEG When? When?

BABE Well . . . maybe I shouldn't say—

MEG Babe!

BABE (*rapidly telling the story*) All right then; it was after Old Granddaddy went back to the hospital this second time. Lenny was really in a state of deep depression. I could tell that she was. Then one day she calls me up and asks me to come over and to bring along my polaroid camera. Well, when I arrive she's waiting for me out there in the sun parlour wearing her powder blue Sunday dress and this old curled up wig. She confided that she was gonna try sending in her picture to one of those lonely hearts clubs.

MEG Oh, my God.

BABE Lonely Hearts of the South. She'd seen their ad in a magazine.

MEG Jesus.

BABE Anyway, I take some snapshots and she sends them on in to the club, and about two weeks later she receives in the mail this whole load of pictures of available men, most of 'em fairly odd looking. But of course she doesn't call any of 'em up 'cause she's real shy. But one of 'em, this Charlie Hill from Memphis, Tennessee, he calls her.

MEG He does?

BABE Yeah. And time goes on and she says he's real funny on the phone; so they decide to get together to meet.

MEG Yeah?!

BABE Well, he drives down here to Hazlehurst 'bout three or four different times and has supper with her, then one weekend she goes up to Memphis to visit him; and I think that is where it happened.

MEG What makes you think so?

BABE Well, when I went to pick her up from the bus depot, she ran off the bus and threw her arms around me and started crying and sobbing as though she'd like to never stop. I asked her, I said, "Lenny, what's the matter?" And she said, "I've done it, Babe! Honey, I've done it!"

MEG (*whispering*) And you think she meant that she'd done *it?*

BABE (*whispering back, slyly*) I think so.

MEG Well, goddamn! (*They laugh with glee.*)

BABE But she didn't say anything else about it. She just went on to tell me about the boot factory where Charlie worked and what a nice city Memphis was.

MEG So, what happened to this Charlie?

BABE Well, he came to Hazlehurst just one more time. Lenny took him over to meet Old Granddaddy at the hospital and after that they broke it off.

MEG 'Cause of Old Granddaddy?

BABE Well, she said it was on account of her missing ovary. That Charlie didn't want to marry her on account of it.

MEG Ah, how mean. How hateful.

BABE Oh, it was. He seemed like such a nice man, too—kinda chubby with red hair and freckles, always telling these funny jokes.

MEG Hmmm, that just doesn't seem right. Something about that doesn't seem exactly right. (MEG *paces about the kitchen and comes across the box of candy* LENNY *got for her birthday.*) Oh, God. "Happy Birthday to Lenny from the Buck Boyles."

BABE Oh, no! Today's Lenny's birthday!

MEG That's right.

BABE I forgot all about it!

MEG I know. I did too.

BABE Gosh, we'll have to order up a big cake for her. She always loves to make those wishes on her birthday cake.

MEG Yeah, let's get her a big cake! A huge one! (*Suddenly noticing the plastic wrapper on the candy box.*) Oh, God, that Chick's so cheap!

BABE What do you mean?

MEG This plastic has poinsettias on it!

BABE (*running to see*) Oh, let me see—(*She looks at the package with disgust.*) Boy, oh, boy! I'm calling that bakery and ordering the very largest size cake they have! That Jumbo Deluxe!

MEG Good!

BABE Why, I imagine they can make one up to be about—*this* big. (*She demonstrates.*)

MEG Oh, at least; at least that big. Why, maybe, it'll even be *this* big. (*She makes a very, very, very, large size cake.*)

BABE You think it could be *that* big?

MEG Sure!

BABE (*after a moment, getting the idea*) Or, or what if it were *this* big? (*She maps out a cake that covers the room.*) What if we get the cake and it's *this* big?!! (*She gulps down a fistful of cake.*) Gulp! Gulp! Gulp! Tasty treat!

MEG Hmmm—I'll have me some more! Give me some more of that birthday cake!

Suddenly there is a loud knock at the door.

BARNETTE'S VOICE Hello . . . hello! May I come in?

BABE (*to Meg, in a whisper, as she takes cover*) Who's that?

MEG I don't know.

BARNETTE'S VOICE (*still knocking*) Hello! Hello, Mrs. Botrelle!

BABE Oh, shoot! It's that lawyer. I don't want to see him.

MEG Oh, Babe, come on. You've got to see him sometime.

BABE No, I don't! (*She starts up the stairs.*) Just tell him I died—I'm going upstairs.

MEG Oh, Babe! Will you come back here!

BABE (*as she exits*) You talk to him, please, Meg. Please! I just don't want to see him—

MEG Babe—Babe! Oh, shit . . . ah, come on in! Door's open!

BARNETTE LLOYD, 26, *enters carrying a briefcase. He is a slender, intelligent young man with an almost fanatical intensity that he subdues by sheer will.*

BARNETTE How do you do? I'm Barnette Lloyd.

MEG Pleased to meet you. I'm Meg Magrath, Babe's older sister.

BARNETTE Yes, I know. You're the singer.

MEG Well, yes . . .

BARNETTE I came to hear you five different times when you were singing at the club in Biloxi. Greeny's I believe was the name of it.

MEG Yes, Greeny's.

BARNETTE You were very good. There was something sad and moving about how you sang those songs. It was like you had some sort of vision. Some special sort of vision.

MEG Well, thank you. You're very kind. Now . . . about Babe's case—

BARNETTE Yes?

MEG We've just got to win it.

BARNETTE I intend to.

MEG Of course. But, ah . . . (*She looks at him.*) Ah, you know, you're very young.

BARNETTE Yes. I am. I'm young.

MEG It's just, I'm concerned, Mr. Lloyd—

BARNETTE Barnette. Please.

MEG Barnette; that, ah, just maybe we need someone with, well, with more experience. Someone totally familiar with all the ins and outs and the this and thats of the legal dealings and such. As that.

BARNETTE Ah, you have reservations.

MEG (*relieved*) Reservations. Yes, I have . . . reservations.

BARNETTE Well, possibly it would help you to know that I graduated first in my class from Ole Miss Law School. I also spent three different summers taking advanced courses in criminal law at Harvard Law School. I made A's in all the given courses. I was fascinated!

MEG I'm sure.

BARNETTE And even now, I've just completed one year working with Jackson's top criminal law firm, Manchester and Wayne. I was invaluable to them. Indispensable. They offered to double my percentage, if I'd stay on; but I refused. I wanted to return to Hazlehurst and open my own office. The reason being, and this is a key point, that I have a personal vendetta to settle with one Zackery F. Botrelle.

MEG A personal vendetta?

BARNETTE Yes, ma'am. You are correct. Indeed, I do.

MEG Hmmm. A personal vendetta . . . I think I like that. So you have some sort of a personal vendetta to settle with Zackery?

BARNETTE Precisely. Just between the two of us, I not only intend to keep that sorry S.O.B. from ever being re-elected to the state senate by exposing his shady, criminal dealings; but I also intend to decimate his personal credibility by exposing him as a bully, a brute, and a red-neck thug!

MEG Well; I can see that you're—fanatical about this.

BARNETTE Yes; I am. I'm sorry, if I seem outspoken. But, for some reason, I feel I can talk to you . . . those songs you sang. Excuse me; I feel like a jackass.

MEG It's all right. Relax. Relax, Barnette. Let me think this out a minute. (*She takes out a cigarette. He lights it for her.*) Now just exactly how do you intend to get Babe off? You know, keep her out of jail.

BARNETTE It seems to me that we can get her off with a plea of self-defense, or possibly we could go with innocent by reason of temporary insanity. But basically, I intend to prove that Zackery Botrelle brutalized and tormented this poor woman to such an extent that she had no recourse but to defend herself in the only way she knew how!

MEG I like that!

BARNETTE Then, of course, I'm hoping this will break the ice and we'll be able to go on to prove that the man's a total criminal, as well as an abusive bully and contemptible slob!

MEG That sounds good! To me that sounds very good!

BARNETTE It's just our basic game plan.

MEG But, now, how are you going to prove all this about Babe being brutalized? We don't want anyone perjured. I mean to commit perjury.

BARNETTE Perjury? According to my sources, the'll be no need for perjury.

MEG You mean it's the truth?

BARNETTE This is a small town, Miss Magrath. The word gets out.

MEG It's really the truth?

BARNETTE (*opening his briefcase*) Just look at this. It's a photostatic copy of Mrs. Botrelle's medical chart over the past four years. Take a good look at it, if you want your blood to boil!

MEG (*looking over the chart*) What! What! This is maddening. This is madness! Did he do this to her? I'll kill him; I will—I'll fry his blood!! Did he do this?

BARNETTE (*alarmed*) To tell you the truth, I can't say for certain what was accidental and what was not. That's why I need to talk with Mrs. Botrelle. That's why it's very important that I see her!

MEG (*her eyes are wild, as she shoves him toward the door*) Well, look, I've got to see her first. I've got to talk to her first. What I'll do is I'll give you a call. Maybe you can come back over later on—

BARNETTE Well, then, here's my card—

MEG Okay. Goodbye.

BARNETTE 'Bye!

MEG Oh, wait! Wait! There's one problem with you.

BARNETTE What?

MEG What if you get so fanatically obsessed with this vendetta thing that you forget about Babe? You forget about her and sell her down the river just to get at Zackery. What about that?

BARNETTE I—wouldn't do that.

MEG You wouldn't?

BARNETTE No.

MEG Why not?

BARNETTE Because, I'm—I'm fond of her.

MEG What do you mean you're fond of her?

BARNETTE Well, she . . . she sold me a pound cake at a bazaar once. And I'm fond of her.

MEG All right; I believe you. Goodbye.

BARNETTE Goodbye. (BARNETTE *exits.*)

MEG Babe! Babe, come down here! Babe!

BABE *comes hurrying down the stairs.*

BABE What? What is it? I called about the cake—

MEG What did Zackery do to you?

BABE They can't have it for today.

MEG Did he hurt you? Did he? Did he do that?

BABE Oh, Meg, please—

MEG Did he? Goddamnit, Babe—

BABE Yes, he did.

MEG Why? Why?

BABE I don't know! He started hating me, 'cause I couldn't laugh at his jokes. I just started finding it impossible to laugh at his jokes the way I used to. And then the sound of his voice got to where it tired me out awful bad to hear it. I'd fall asleep just listening to him at the dinner table. He'd say, "Hand me some of that gravy!" Or, "This roast beef is too damn bloody." And suddenly I'd be out cold like a light.

MEG Oh, Babe. BABE, this is very important. I want you to sit down here and tell me what all happened right before you shot Zackery. That's right, just sit down and tell me.

BABE (*after a pause*) I told you I can't tell you on account of I'm protecting someone.

MEG But Babe, you've just got to talk to someone about all this. You just do.

BABE Why?

MEG Because it's a human need. To talk about our lives. It's an important human need.

BABE Oh. Well, I do feel like I want to talk to someone. I do.

MEG Then talk to me; please.

BABE (*a decision*) All right. (*After thinking a minute.*) I don't know where to start.

MEG Just start at the beginning. Just there at the beginning.

BABE (*after a moment*) Well, do you remember Willie Jay? (MEG *shakes her head.*) Cora's youngest boy?

MEG Oh, yeah, that little kid we used to pay a nickel to, to run down to the drugstore and bring us back a cherry Coke.

BABE Right. Well, Cora irons at my place on Wednesdays now, and she just happened to mention that Willie Jay'd picked up this old stray dog and that he'd gotten real fond of him. But now they couldn't afford to feed him anymore, so she was gonna have to tell Willie Jay to set him loose in the woods.

MEG (*trying to be patient*) Uh huh.

BABE Well, I said I liked dogs and if he wanted to bring the dog over here, I'd take care of him. You see, I was alone by myself most of the time 'cause the senate was in session, and Zackery was up in Jackson.

MEG Uh huh. (MEG *reaches for* LENNY'S *box of birthday candy. She takes little nibbles out of each piece, throughout the rest of the scene.*)

BABE So the next day, Willie Jay brings over this skinny, old dog with these little crossed-eyes. Well, I asked Willie Jay what his name was, and he said they called him Dog. Well, I liked the name; so I thought I'd keep it.

MEG (*getting up*) Uh huh. I'm listening. I'm just gonna get me a glass of cold water; do you want one?

BABE Okay.

MEG So you kept the name—Dog.

BABE Yeah. Anyway, when Willie Jay was leaving he gave Dog a hug and said, "Goodbye, Dog. You're a fine ole dog." Well, I felt something for him, so I told Willie Jay he could come back and visit with Dog any time he wanted, and his face just kinda lit right up.

MEG (*offering the candy*) Candy—

BABE No thanks. Anyhow, time goes on and Willie Jay keeps coming over and over. And we talk about Dog and how fat he's getting and then, well, you know, things start up.

MEG No, I don't know. What things start up?

BABE Well, things start up. Like sex. Like that.

MEG Babe, wait a minute—Willie Jay's a boy. A small boy, about this tall. He's about this tall!

BABE No! Oh, no! He's taller now! He's fifteen now. When you knew him he was only about seven or eight.

MEG But, even so—fifteen. And he's a black boy; a colored boy; a Negro.

BABE (*flustered*) Well, I realize that, Meg. Why do you think I'm so worried about his getting public exposure? I don't want to ruin his reputation!

MEG I'm amazed, Babe. I'm really, completely amazed. I didn't even know you were a liberal.

BABE Well, I'm not! I'm not a liberal! I'm a democratic! I was just lonely! I was so lonely. And he was good. Oh, he was so, so good. I'd never had it that good. We'd always go out into the garage and—

MEG It's okay. I've got the picture; I've got the picture! Now, let's just get back to the story. To yesterday, when you shot Zackery.

BABE All right, then. Let's see . . . Willie Jay was over. And it was after we'd—

MEG Yeah! Yeah.

BABE And we were just standing around on the back porch playing with Dog. Well, suddenly, Zackery comes from around the side of the house. And he startled me 'cause he's supposed to be away at the office, and there he is coming from 'round the side of the house. Anyway, he says to Willie Jay, "Hey, boy, what are you doing back here?" And I said, "He's not doing anything. You just go on home, Willie Jay! You just run right on home." Well, before he can move, Zackery comes up and knocks him once right across the face and then shoves him down the porch steps, causing him to skin up his elbow real bad on that hard concrete. Then he says, "Don't you ever come around here again, or I'll have them cut out your gizzard!" Well, Willie Jay starts crying, these tears come streaming down his face, then he gets up real quick and runs away with Dog following off after him. After that, I don't remember much too clearly; let's see . . . I went into the living room, and I went right up to the davenport and opened the drawer where we keep the burglar gun . . . I took it out. Then I—I brought it up to my ear. That's right. I put it right inside my ear. Why, I was gonna shoot off my own head! That's what I was gonna do. Then I heard the back door slamming and suddenly, for some reason, I thought about mama . . . how she'd hung herself. And here I was about ready to shoot myself. Then I realized—that's right I realized how I didn't want to kill myself! And she—she probably didn't want to kill herself. She wanted to kill him, and I wanted to kill him, too. I wanted to kill

Zackery, not myself 'Cause I—I wanted to live! So I waited for him to come on into the living room. Then I held out the gun, and I pulled the trigger. aiming for his heart, but getting him in the stomach. (*After a pause.*) It's funny that I really did that.

MEG It's a good thing that you did. It's a damn good thing that you did.

BABE It was.

MEG Please, Babe, talk to Barnette Lloyd. Just talk to him and see if he can help.

BABE But how about Willie Jay?

MEG (*starting towards the phone*) Oh, he'll be all right. You just talk to that lawyer like you did to me. (*Looking at the number on the card, she begins dialing.*) See, 'cause he's gonna be on your side.

BABE No! Stop, Meg, stop! Don't call him up! Please don't call him up! You can't! It's too awful. (*She runs over and jerks the bottom half of the phone away from* MEG. MEG *stands, holding the receiver.*)

MEG Babe! (BABE *slams her half of the phone into the refrigerator.*)

BABE I just can't tell some stranger all about my personal life. I just can't.

MEG Well, hell, Babe; you're the one who said you wanted to live.

BABE That's right. I did. (*She takes the phone out of the refrigerator and hands it to* MEG.) Here's the other part of the phone. (BABE *moves to sit at the kitchen table.* MEG *takes the phone back to the counter. Babe, as she fishes a lemon out of her glass and begins sucking on it.*) Meg.

MEG What?

BABE I called the bakery. They're gonna have Lenny's cake ready first thing tomorrow morning. That's the earliest they can get it.

MEG All right.

BABE I told them to write on it, "Happy Birthday Lenny—A Day Late." That sound okay?

MEG (*at the phone*) It sounds nice.

BABE I ordered up the very largest size cake they have. I told them chocolate cake with white icing and red trim. Think she'll like that?

MEG (*dialing on the phone*) Yeah, I'm sure she will. She'll like it.

BABE I'm hoping.

BLACKOUT

END OF ACT I

ACT II

The lights go up on the kitchen. It is later that evening on the same day. MEG's *suitcase has been moved upstairs.* BABE's *saxophone has been taken out of the case and put together.* BABE *and* BARNETTE *are sitting at the kitchen table.* BARNETTE *is writing and re-checking notes with explosive intensity.* BABE, *who has changed into a casual shift, sits eating a bowl of oatmeal, slowly.*

BARNETTE (*to himself*) Mmm-huh! Yes! I see, I see! Well, we can work on that! And of course, this is mere conjecture! Difficult, if not impossible, to prove. Ha! Yes. Yes, indeed. Indeed—

BABE Sure you don't want any oatmeal?

BARNETTE What? Oh, no. No, thank you. Let's see, ah, where were we?

BABE I just shot Zackery.

BARNETTE (*looking at his notes*) Right. Correct. You've just pulled the trigger.

BABE Tell me, do you think Willie Jay can stay out of all this?

BARNETTE Believe me, it is in our interest to keep him as far out of this as possible.

BABE Good.

BARNETTE (*throughout the following,* BARNETTE *stays glued to* BABE'S *every word*) All right, you've just shot one Zackery Botrelle, as a result of his continual physical and mental abuse—what happens now?

BABE Well, after I shot him, I put the gun down on the piano bench and then I went out into the kitchen and made up a pitcher of lemonade.

BARNETTE Lemonade?

BABE Yes, I was dying of thirst. My mouth was just as dry as a bone.

BARNETTE So in order to quench this raging thirst that was choking you dry and preventing any possibility of you uttering intelligible sounds or phrases, you went out to the kitchen and made up a pitcher of lemonade?

BABE Right. I made it just the way I like it with lots of sugar and lots of lemon—about ten lemons in all. Then I added two trays of ice and stirred it up with my wooden stirring spoon.

BARNETTE Then what?

BABE Then I drank three glasses, one right after the other. They were large glasses, about this tall. Then suddenly, my stomach kind of swoll all up. I guess what caused it was all that sour lemon.

BARNETTE Could be.

BABE Then what I did was . . . I wiped my mouth off with the back of my hand, like this . . . (*She demonstrates.*)

BARNETTE Hmmm.

BABE I did it to clear off all those little beads of water that had settled there.

BARNETTE I see.

BABE Then I called out to Zackery. I said, "Zackery, I've made some lemonade. Can you use a glass?"

BARNETTE Did he answer? Did you hear an answer?

BABE No. He didn't answer.

BARNETTE So, what'd you do?

BABE I poured him a glass anyway and took it out to him.

BARNETTE You took it out to the living room?

BABE I did. And there he was; lying on the rug. He was looking up at me trying to speak words. I said, "What? . . . Lemonade? . . . You don't want it? Would you like a Coke instead?" Then I got the idea, he was telling me to call on the phone for medical help. So I got on the phone and called up the hospital. I gave my name and address and I told them my husband was shot and he was lying on the rug and there was plenty of blood. (BABE *pauses a minute, as* BARNETTE *works frantically on his notes.*) I guess that's gonna look kinda bad.

BARNETTE What?

BABE Me fixing that lemonade, before I called the hospital.

BARNETTE Well, not . . . necessarily.

BABE I tell you, I think the reason I made up the lemonade, I mean besides the fact that my mouth was bone dry, was that I was afraid to call the authorities. I was afraid. I— I really think I was afraid they would see that I had tried to shoot Zackery, in fact, that I had shot him, and they would accuse me of possible murder and send me away to jail.

BARNETTE Well, that's understandable.

BABE I think so. I mean, in fact, that's what did happen. That's what is happening—'cause here I am just about ready to go right off to the Parchment Prison Farm. Yes, here I am just practically on the brink of utter doom. Why, I feel so all alone.

BARNETTE Now, now, look—Why, there's no reason for you to get yourself so all upset and worried. Please, don't. Please. (*They look at each other for a moment.*) You just keep filling in as much detailed information as you can about those incidents on the medical reports. That's all you need to think about. Don't you worry, Mrs. Botrelle, we're going to have a solid defense.

BABE Please, don't call me Mrs. Botrelle.

BARNETTE All right.

BABE My name's Becky. People in the family call me Babe; but my real name's Becky.

BARNETTE All right, Becky. (BARNETTE *and* BABE *stare at each other for a long moment.*)

BABE Are you sure you didn't go to Hazlehurst High?

BARNETTE No, I went away to a boarding school.

BABE Gosh, you sure do look familiar. You sure do.

BARNETTE Well, I—I doubt you'll remember, but I did meet you once.

BABE You did? When?

BARNETTE At the Christmas bazaar, year before last. You were selling cakes and cookies and . . . candy.

BABE Oh, yes! You bought the orange pound cake!

BARNETTE Right.

BABE Of course, and then we talked for a while. We talked about the Christmas angel.

BARNETTE You do remember.

BABE I remember it very well. You were even thinner then than you are now.

BARNETTE Well, I'm surprised. I'm certainly . . . surprised. (*The phone begins to ring.*)

BABE (*as she goes to answer the phone*) This is quite a coincidence! Don't you think it is? Why, it's almost a fluke. (*She answers the phone.*) Hello . . . Oh, hello, Lucille . . . Oh, he is? . . . Oh, he does? . . . Okay. Oh, Lucille, wait! Has Dog come back to the house? . . . Oh, I see . . . Okay. Okay. (*After a brief pause.*) Hello, Zackery? How are you doing? . . . Uh huh . . . uh huh . . . oh, I'm sorry . . . Please, don't scream . . . uh huh . . . uh huh . . . You want what? . . . No, I can't come up there now . . . Well, for one thing, I don't even have the car. Lenny and Meg are up at the hospital right now, visiting with Old Granddaddy . . . What? . . . Oh, really? . . . Oh, really? . . . Well, I've got me a lawyer that's over here right now, and he's building me up a solid defense! . . . Wait just a minute, I'll see. (*To* BARNETTE.) He wants to talk to you. He says he's got some blackening evidence that's gonna convict me of attempting to murder him on the first degree!

BARNETTE (*disgustedly*) Oh, bluff! He's bluffing! Here, hand me the phone. (*He takes the phone and becomes suddenly cool and suave.*) Hello, this is Mr. Barnette Lloyd speaking. I'm Mrs. . . . ah, Becky's attorney . . . Why, certainly, Mr. Botrelle, I'd be more than glad to check out any pertinent information that you may have . . . Fine, then I'll be right over. Goodbye. (*He hangs up the phone.*)

BABE What did he say?

BARNETTE He wants me to come to see him at the hospital this evening. Says he's got some sort of evidence. Sounds highly suspect to me.

BABE Oooh! Didn't you just hate his voice? Doesn't he have the most awful voice! I just hate it! I can't bear to hear it!

BARNETTE Well, now—now, wait. Wait just a minute.

BABE What?

BARNETTE I have a solution. From now on I'll handle all communications between you two. You can simply refuse to speak with him.

BABE All right—I will. I'll do that.

BARNETTE (*starting to pack his briefcase*) Well, I'd better get over there and see just what he's got up his sleeve.

BABE (*after a pause*) Barnette.

BARNETTE Yes?

BABE What's the personal vendetta about? You know, the one you have to settle with Zackery.

BARNETTE Oh, it's—it's complicated. It's a very complicated matter.

BABE I see.

BARNETTE The major thing he did was to ruin my father's life. He took away his job, his home, his health, his respectability. I don't like to talk about it.

BABE I'm sorry. I just wanted to say—I hope you win it. I hope you win your vendetta.

BARNETTE Thank you.

BABE I think it's an important thing that a person could win a life long vendetta.

BARNETTE Yes. Well, I'd better be going.

BABE All right. Let me know what happens.

BARNETTE I will. I'll get back to you right away.

BABE Thanks.

BARNETTE Goodbye, Becky.

BABE Goodbye, Barnette. (BARNETTE *exits*. BABE *looks around the room for a moment, then goes over to her white suitcase and opens it up. She takes out her pink hair curlers and a brush. She begins brushing her hair.*) Goodbye, Becky. Goodbye, Barnette. Goodbye Becky. Oooh. (LENNY *enters. She is fuming.* BABE *is rolling her hair throughout most of the following scene.*) Lenny, hi!

LENNY Hi.

BABE Where's Meg?

LENNY Oh, she had to go by the store and pick some things up. I don't know what.

BABE Well, how's Old Granddaddy?

LENNY (*as she picks up Babe's bowl of oatmeal*) He's fine. Wonderful! Never been better!

BABE Lenny, what's wrong? What's the matter?

LENNY It's Meg! I could just wring her neck! I could just wring it!

BABE Why? Wha'd she do?

LENNY She lied! She sat in that hospital room and shamelessly lied to Old Granddaddy. She went on and on telling such untrue stories and lies.

BABE Well, what? What did she say?

LENNY Well, for one thing she said she was gonna have a RCA record coming out with her picture on the cover, eating pineapples under a palm tree.

BABE Well, gosh, Lenny, maybe she is! Don't you think she really is?

LENNY Babe, she sat here this very afternoon and told me how all that she's done this whole year is work as a clerk for a dog food company.

BABE Oh, shoot. I'm disappointed.

LENNY And then she goes on to say that she'll be appearing on the "Johnny Carson Show" in two weeks' time. Two weeks' time! Why, Old Granddaddy's got a TV set right in his room. Imagine what a letdown it's gonna be.

BABE Why, mercy me.

LENNY (*slamming the coffeepot on*) Oh, and she told him the reason she didn't use the money he sent her to come home Christmas was that she was right in the middle of making a huge multi-million-dollar motion picture and was just under too much pressure.

BABE My word!

LENNY The movie's coming out this spring. It's called, "Singing in a Shoe Factory." But she only has a small leading role—not a large leading role.

BABE (*laughing*) For heaven's sake—

LENNY I'm sizzling. Oh, I just can't help it! I'm sizzling!

BABE Sometimes Meg does such strange things.

LENNY (*slowly, as she picks up the opened box of birthday candy*) Who ate this candy?

BABE (*hesitantly*) Meg.

LENNY My one birthday present, and look what she does! Why, she's taken one little bite out of each piece and then just put it back in! Ooh! That's just like her! That is just like her!

BABE Lenny, please—

LENNY I can't help it! It gets me mad! It gets me upset! Why, Meg's always run wild— she started smoking and drinking when she was fourteen years old, she never made good grades—never made her own bed! But somehow she always seemed to get what she wanted. She's the one who got singing and dancing lessons; and a store-bought dress to wear to her senior prom. Why do you remember how Meg always got to wear twelve jingle bells on her petticoats, while we were only allowed to wear three apiece? Why?! Why should Old Grandmama let her sew twelve golden jingle bells on her petticoats and us only three!!!

BABE (*who has heard all this before*) I don't know!! Maybe she didn't jingle them as much!

LENNY I can't help it! It gets me mad! I resent it. I do.

BABE Oh, don't resent Meg. Things have been hard for Meg. After all, she was the one who found Mama.

LENNY Oh, I know; she's the one who found Mama. But that's always been the excuse.

BABE But, I tell you, Lenny, after it happened, Meg started doing all sorts of these strange things.

LENNY She did? Like what?

BABE Like things I never wanted to tell you about.

LENNY What sort of things?

BABE Well, for instance, back when we used to go over to the library, Meg would spend all her time reading and looking through this old, black book called *Diseases of the Skin*. It was full of the most sickening pictures you'd ever seen. Things like rotting-away noses and eyeballs drooping off down the sides of people's faces and scabs and sores and eaten-away places all over *all* parts of people's bodies.

LENNY (*trying to pour her coffee*) Babe, please! That's enough.

BABE Anyway, she'd spend hours and hours just forcing herself to look through this book. Why, it was the same way she'd force herself to look at the poster of crippled children stuck up in the window at Dixieland Drugs. You know, that one where they want you to give a dime. Meg would stand there and stare at their eyes and look at the braces on their little crippled-up legs—then she'd purposely go and spend her dime on a double scoop ice cream cone and eat it all down. She'd say to me, "See, I can stand it. I can stand it. Just look how I'm gonna be able to stand it."

LENNY That's awful.

BABE She said she was afraid of being a weak person. I guess 'cause she cried in bed every night for such a long time.

LENNY Goodness mercy. (*After a pause.*) Well, I suppose you'd have to be a pretty hard person to be able to do what she did to Doc Porter.

BABE (*exasperated*) Oh, shoot! It wasn't Meg's fault that hurricane wiped Biloxi away. I never understood why people were blaming all that on Meg—just because that roof fell in and crunched Doc's leg. It wasn't her fault.

LENNY Well, it was Meg who refused to evacuate. Jim Craig and some of Doc's other friends were all down there and they kept trying to get everyone to evacuate. But Meg refused. She wanted to stay on because she thought a hurricane would be—oh, I don't know—a lot of fun. Then everyone says she baited Doc into staying with her. She said she'd marry him if he'd stay.

BABE (*taken aback by this new information*) Well, he has a mind of his own. He could have gone.

LENNY But he didn't. 'Cause . . . 'cause he loved her. And then after the roof caved, and they got Doc to the high school gym, Meg just left. She just left him there to leave for California—'cause of her career, she says. I think it was a shameful thing to do. It took almost a year for his leg to heal and after that he gave up his medical career altogether. He said he was tired of hospitals. It's such a sad thing. Everyone always knew he was gonna be a doctor. We've called him Doc for years.

BABE I don't know. I guess, I don't have any room to talk; 'cause I just don't know. (*Pause.*) Gosh, you look so tired.

LENNY I feel tired.

BABE They say women need a lot of iron . . . so they won't feel tired.

LENNY What's got iron in it? Liver?

BABE Yeah, liver's got it. And vitamin pills.

After a moment, MEG *enters. She carries a bottle of bourbon that is already minus a few slugs and a newspaper. She is wearing black boots, a dark dress, and a hat. The room goes silent.*

MEG Hello.

BABE (*fooling with her hair*) Hi, Meg. (LENNY *quietly sips her coffee.*)

MEG (*handing the newspaper to* BABE) Here's your paper.

BABE Thanks. (*She opens it.*) Oh, here it is, right on the front page. (MEG *lights a cigarette.*) Where's the scissors, Lenny?

LENNY Look in there in the ribbon drawer.

BABE Okay. (BABE *gets the scissors and glue out of the drawer and slowly begins cutting out the newspaper article.*)

MEG (*after a few moments, filled only with the snipping of scissors*) All right—I lied! I lied! I couldn't help it . . . these stories just came pouring out of my mouth! When I saw how tired and sick Old Granddaddy'd gotten—they just flew out! All I wanted was to see him smiling and happy. I just wasn't going to sit there and look at him all miserable and sick and sad! I just wasn't!

BABE Oh, Meg, he is sick, isn't he—

MEG Why, he's gotten all white and milky—he's almost evaporated!

LENNY (*gasping and turning to* MEG) But still you shouldn't have lied! It just was wrong for you to tell such lies—

MEG Well, I know that! Don't you think I know that? I hate myself when I lie for that old man. I do. I feel so weak. And then I have to go and do at least three or four things that I know he'd despise just to get even with that miserable, old, bossy man!

LENNY Oh, Meg, please, don't talk so about Old Granddaddy! It sounds so ungrateful. Why, he went out of his way to make a home for us; to treat us like we were his very own children. All he ever wanted was the best for us. That's all he ever wanted.

MEG Well, I guess it was; but sometimes I wonder what we wanted.

BABE (*taking the newspaper article and glue over to her suitcase*) Well, one thing I wanted was a team of white horses to ride Mama's coffin to her grave. That's one thing I wanted. (LENNY *and* MEG *exchange looks.*) Lenny, did you remember to pack my photo album?

LENNY It's down there at the bottom, under all that night stuff.

BABE Oh, I found it.

LENNY Really, Babe, I don't understand why you have to put in the articles that are about the unhappy things in your life. Why would you want to remember them?

BABE (*pasting the article in*) I don't know. I just like to keep an accurate record, I suppose. There. (*She begins flipping through the book.*) Look, here's a picture of me when I got married.

MEG Let's see.

BABE *brings the photo album over to the table. They all look at it.*

LENNY My word, you look about twelve years old.

BABE I was just eighteen.

MEG You're smiling, Babe. Were you happy then?

BABE (*laughing*) Well, I was drunk on champagne punch. I remember that! (*They turn the page.*)

LENNY Oh, there's Meg singing at Greeny's!

BABE Oooh, I wish you were still singing at Greeny's! I wish you were!

LENNY You're so beautiful!

BABE Yes, you are. You're beautiful.

MEG Oh, stop! I'm not—

LENNY Look, Meg's starting to cry.

BABE Oh, Meg—

MEG I'm not—

BABE Quick, better turn the page; we don't want Meg crying—(*She flips the pages.*)

LENNY Why, it's Daddy.

MEG Where'd you get that picture, Babe? I thought she burned them all.

BABE Ah, I just found it around.

LENNY What does it say here? What's that inscription?

BABE It says "Jimmy—clowning at the beach—1952."

LENNY Well, will you look at that smile.

MEG Jesus, those white teeth—turn the page, will you; we can't do any worse than this! (*They turn the page. The room goes silent.*)

BABE It's Mama and the cat.

LENNY Oh, turn the page—

BABE That old yellow cat. You know, I bet if she hadn't of hung that old cat along with her, she wouldn't have gotten all that national coverage.

MEG (*after a moment, hopelessly*) Why are we talking about this?

LENNY Meg's right. It was so sad. It was awfully sad. I remember how we all three just sat up on that bed the day of the service all dressed up in our black velveteen suits crying the whole morning long.

BABE We used up one whole big box of Kleenexes.

MEG And then Old Granddaddy came in and said he was gonna take us out to breakfast. Remember, he told us not to cry anymore 'cause he was gonna take us out to get banana splits for breakfast.

BABE That's right—banana splits for breakfast!

MEG Why, Lenny was fourteen years old and he thought that would make it all better—

BABE Oh, I remember he said for us to eat all we wanted. I think I ate about five! He kept shoving them down us!

MEG God, we were so sick!

LENNY Oh, we were!

MEG (laughing) Lenny's face turned green—

LENNY I was just as sick as a dog!

BABE Old Grandmama was furious!

LENNY Oh, she was!

MEG The thing about Old Granddaddy is he keeps trying to make us happy and we end up getting stomach aches and turning green and throwing up in the flower arrangements.

BABE Oh, that was me! I threw up in the flowers! Oh, no! How embarrassing!

LENNY (laughing) Oh, Babe—

BABE (hugging her sisters) Oh, Lenny! Oh, Meg!

MEG Oh, Babe! Oh, Lenny! It's so good to be home!

LENNY Hey, I have an idea—

BABE What?

LENNY Let's play cards!!

BABE Oh, let's do!

MEG All right!

LENNY Oh, good! It'll be just like when we used to sit around the table playing hearts all night long.

BABE I know! (getting up) I'll fix us up some popcorn and hot chocolate—

MEG (getting up) Here, let me get out that old black popcorn pot.

LENNY (getting up) Oh, yes! Now, let's see, I think I have a deck of cards around here somewhere.

BABE Gosh, I hope I remember all the rules—Are hearts good or bad?

MEG Bad, I think. Aren't they, Lenny?

LENNY That's right. Hearts are bad, but the Black Sister is the worst of all—

MEG Oh, that's right! And the Black Sister is the Queen of Spades.

BABE (figuring it out) And spades are the black cards that aren't the puppy dog feet?

MEG (thinking a moment) Right. And she counts a lot of points.

BABE And points are bad?

MEG Right. Here, I'll get some paper so we can keep score.

The phone begins to ring.

LENNY Oh, here they are!

MEG I'll get it—

LENNY Why, look at these cards! They're years old!

BABE Oh, let me see!

MEG Hello . . . No, this is Meg Magrath . . . Doc. How are you? . . . Well, good . . . You're where? . . . Well, sure. Come on over . . . Sure, I'm sure. Yeah, come right on over . . . All right. Bye. (*She hangs up.*) That was Doc Porter. He's down the street at Al's Grill. He's gonna come on over.

LENNY He is?

MEG He said he wanted to come see me.

LENNY Oh. (*after a pause*) Well, do you still want to play?

MEG No, I don't think so.

LENNY All right. (LENNY *starts to shuffle the cards, as* MEG *brushes her hair.*) You know, it's really not much fun playing Hearts with only two people.

MEG I'm sorry; maybe after Doc leaves, I'll join you.

LENNY I know; maybe Doc'll want to play, then we can have a game of bridge.

MEG I don't think so. Doc never liked cards. Maybe we'll just go out somewhere.

LENNY (*putting down the cards;* BABE *picks them up*) Meg—

MEG What?

LENNY Well, Doc's married now.

MEG I know. You told me.

LENNY Oh. Well, as long as you know that. (*Pause*) As long as you know that.

MEG (*still primping*) Yes, I know. She made the pot.

BABE How many cards do I deal out?

LENNY (*leaving the table*) Excuse me.

BABE All of 'em, or what?

LENNY Ah, Meg? Could I—could I ask you something? (BABE *proceeds to deal out all the cards.*)

MEG What?

LENNY I just wanted to ask you—

MEG What?

Unable to go on with what she really wants to say, LENNY *runs up and picks up the box of candy.*

LENNY Well, just why did you take one little bite out of each piece of candy in this box and then just put it back in?

MEG Oh. Well, I was looking for the ones with nuts.

LENNY The ones with nuts.

MEG Yeah.

LENNY But there are none with nuts. It's a box of assorted cremes—all it has in it are cremes!

MEG Oh.

LENNY Why couldn't you just read the box? It says right here, "Assorted Cremes," not nuts! Besides this was a birthday present to me! My one and only birthday present; my only one!

MEG I'm sorry. I'll get you another box.

LENNY I don't want another box. That's not the point!

MEG What is the point?

LENNY I don't know; it's—it's—You have no respect for other people's property! You just take whatever you want. You just take it! Why, remember how you had layers and layers of jingle bells sewed onto your petticoats while Babe and I only had three apiece?!

MEG Oh, God! She's starting up about those stupid jingle bells!

LENNY Well, it's an example! A specific example of how you always got what you wanted!

MEG Oh, come on, Lenny, you're just upset because Doc called.

LENNY Who said anything about Doc? Do you think I'm upset about Doc? Why, I've long since given up worrying about you and all your men.

MEG (turning in anger) Look, I know I've had too many men. Believe me, I've had way too many men. But it's not my fault you haven't had any—or maybe just that one from Memphis.

LENNY (stopping) What one from Memphis?

MEG (slowly) The one Babe told me about. From the—club.

LENNY Babe!!!

BABE Meg!!!

LENNY How could you?!! I asked you not to tell anyone! I'm so ashamed! How could you?! Who else have you told? Did you tell anyone else?

BABE (overlapping, to MEG) Why'd you have to open your big mouth?!

MEG (overlapping) How am I supposed to know? You never said not to tell!

BABE Can't you use your head just for once?!! (Then to LENNY.) No, I never told anyone else. Somehow it just slipped out to Meg. Really, it just flew out of my mouth—

LENNY What do you two have—wings on your tongues?

BABE I'm sorry, Lenny. Really sorry.

LENNY I'll just never, never, never be able to trust you again—

MEG (furiously, coming to BABE's defense) Oh, for heaven's sake, Lenny, we were just worried about you! We wanted to find a way to make you happy!

LENNY Happy! Happy! I'll never be happy!

MEG Well, not if you keep living your life as Old Granddaddy's nursemaid—

BABE Meg, shut up!

MEG I can't help it! I just know that the reason you stopped seeing this man from Memphis was because of Old Granddaddy.

LENNY What—Babe didn't tell you the rest of the story—

MEG Oh, she said it was something about your shrunken ovary.

BABE Meg!!

LENNY Babe!!

BABE I just mentioned it!

MEG But I don't believe a word of that story!

LENNY Oh, I don't care what you believe! It's so easy for you—you always have men falling in love with you! But I have this underdeveloped ovary and I can't have children and my hair is falling out in the comb—so what man can love me?! What man's gonna love me?

MEG A lot of men!

BABE Yeah, a lot! A whole lot!

MEG Old Granddaddy's the only one who seems to think otherwise.

LENNY 'Cause he doesn't want to see me hurt! He doesn't want to see me rejected and humiliated.

MEG Oh, come on now, Lenny, don't be so pathetic! God, you make me angry when you just stand there looking so pathetic! Just tell me, did you really ask the man from Memphis? Did you actually ask that man from Memphis all about it?

LENNY (breaking apart) No; I didn't. I didn't. Because I just didn't want him not to want me—

MEG Lenny—

LENNY (*furious*) Don't talk to me anymore! Don't talk to me! I think I'm gonna vomit—
I just hope all this doesn't cause me to vomit! (LENNY *exits up the stairs sobbing.*)

MEG See! See! She didn't even ask him about her stupid ovary! She just broke it all off
'cause of Old Granddaddy! What a jackass fool!

BABE Oh, Meg, shut up! Why do you have to make Lenny cry? I just hate it when you
make Lenny cry! (BABE *runs up the stairs.*) Lenny! Oh, Lenny—(MEG *takes a long
sigh and goes to get a cigarette and a drink.*)

MEG I feel like hell. (MEG *sits in despair—smoking and drinking bourbon. There is a
knock at the back door. MEG starts. She brushes her hair out of her face and goes to
answer the door. It is* DOC.)

DOC Hello, Meggy.

MEG Well, Doc. Well, it's Doc.

DOC (*after a pause*) You're home, Meggy.

MEG Yeah; I've come home. I've come on home to see about Babe.

DOC And how's Babe?

MEG Oh, fine. Well, fair. She's fair. (DOC *nods.*) Hey, do you want a drink?

DOC Whatcha got?

MEG Bourbon.

DOC Oh, don't tell me Lenny's stocking bourbon.

MEG Well, no. I've been to the store. (MEG *gets him a glass and pours them each a
drink. They click glasses.*) So, how's your wife?

DOC She's fine.

MEG I hear ya got two kids.

DOC Yeah. Yeah, I got two kids.

MEG A boy and a girl.

DOC That's right, Meggy, a boy and a girl.

MEG That's what you always said you wanted, wasn't it? A boy and a girl.

DOC Is that what I said?

MEG I don't know. I thought it's what you said. (*They finish their drinks in silence.*)

DOC Whose cot?

MEG Lenny's. She's taken to sleeping in the kitchen.

DOC Ah. Where is Lenny?

MEG She's in the upstairs room. I made her cry. Babe's up there seeing to her.

DOC How'd you make her cry?

MEG I don't know. Eating her birthday candy; talking on about her boyfriend from
Memphis. I don't know. I'm upset about it. She's got a lot on her. Why can't I keep
my mouth shut?

DOC I don't know, Meggy. Maybe it's because you don't want to.

MEG Maybe. (*They smile at each other.* MEG *pours each of them another drink.*)

DOC Well, it's been a long time.

MEG It has been a long time.

DOC Let's see—when was the last time we saw each other?

MEG I can't quite recall.

DOC Wasn't it in Biloxi?

MEG Ah, Biloxi. I believe so.

DOC And wasn't there a—a hurricane going on at the time?

MEG Was there?

DOC Yes, there was, one hell of a hurricane. Camille, I believe they called it. Hurricane
Camille.

MEG Yes, now I remember. It was a beautiful hurricane.

DOC We had a time down there. We had quite a time. Drinking vodka, eating oysters on the half shell, dancing all night long. And the wind was blowing.

MEG Oh, God, was it blowing.

DOC Goddamn, was it blowing.

MEG There never has been such a wind blowing.

DOC Oh, God, Meggy. Oh, God.

MEG I know, Doc. It was my fault to leave you. I was crazy. I thought I was choking. I felt choked!

DOC I felt like a fool.

MEG No.

DOC I just kept on wondering why.

MEG I don't know why . . . 'Cause I didn't want to care. I don't know. I did care though. I did.

DOC (after a pause) Ah, hell—(He pours them both another drink.) Are you still singing those sad songs?

MEG No.

DOC Why not?

MEG I don't know, Doc. Things got worse for me. After a while, I just couldn't sing anymore. I tell you, I had one hell of a time over Christmas.

DOC What do you mean?

MEG I went nuts. I went insane. Ended up in L.A. County Hospital. Psychiatric ward.

DOC Hell. Ah, hell, Meggy. What happened?

MEG I don't really know. I couldn't sing anymore; so I lost my job. And I had a bad toothache. I had this incredibly painful toothache. For days I had it, but I wouldn't do anything about it. I just stayed inside my apartment. All I could do was sit around in chairs, chewing on my fingers. Then one afternoon I ran screaming out of the apartment with all my money and jewelry and valuables and tried to stuff it all into one of those March of Dimes collection boxes. That was when they nabbed me. Sad story. Meg goes mad. (DOC stares at her for a long moment. He pours them both another drink.)

DOC (after quite a pause) There's a moon out.

MEG Is there?

DOC Wanna go take a ride in my truck and look out at the moon?

MEG I don't know, Doc. I don't wanna start up. It'll be too hard, if we start up.

DOC Who says we're gonna start up? We're just gonna look at the moon. For one night just you and me are gonna go for a ride in the country and look out at the moon.

MEG One night?

DOC Right.

MEG Look out at the moon?

DOC You got it.

MEG Well . . . all right. (She gets up.)

DOC Better take your coat. (He helps her into her coat.) And the bottle—(He takes the bottle. Meg picks up the glasses.) Forget the glasses—

MEG (laughing) Yeah—forget the glasses. Forget the goddamn glasses.

MEG shuts off the kitchen lights, leaving the kitchen lit by only a dim light over the kitchen sink. MEG and DOC leave. After a moment, BABE comes down the stairs in her slip.

BABE Meg—Meg?

She stands for a moment in the moonlight wearing only a slip. She sees her saxophone then moves to pick it up. She plays a few shrieking notes. There is a loud knock on the back door.

BARNETTE'S VOICE Becky! Becky, is that you? (*BABE puts down the saxophone.*)

BABE Just a minute. I'm coming. (*She puts a raincoat on over her slip and goes to answer the door. It is* BARNETTE.) Hello, Barnette. Come on in. (BARNETTE *comes in. He is troubled but is making a great effort to hide the fact.*)

BARNETTE Thank you.

BABE What is it?

BARNETTE I've, ah, I've just come from seeing Zackery at the hospital.

BABE Oh?

BARNETTE It seems . . . Well, it seems his sister, Lucille, was somewhat suspicious.

BABE Suspicious?

BARNETTE About you?

BABE Me?

BARNETTE She hired a private detective, he took these pictures. (*He hands* BABE *a small envelope containing several photographs.* BABE *opens the envelope and begins looking at the pictures in stunned silence.*) They were taken about two weeks ago. It seems, she wasn't going to show them to Botrelle straight away. She, ah, wanted to wait till the time was right. (*The phone rings one and a half times.* BARNETTE *glances uneasily towards the phone.*) Becky? (*The phone stops ringing.*)

BABE (*looking up at* BARNETTE, *slowly*) These are pictures of Willie Jay and me . . . out in the garage.

BARNETTE (*looking away*) I know.

BABE You looked at these pictures?

BARNETTE Yes—I—well . . . professionally, I looked at them.

BABE Oh, mercy. Oh, mercy! We can burn them, can't we? Quick, we can burn them—

BARNETTE It won't do any good. They have the negatives.

BABE (*holding the pictures, as she bangs herself hopelessly into the stove, table, cabinets, etc.*) Oh, no; oh, no; oh, no! Oh, no—

BARNETTE There—there, now—there—

LENNY'S VOICE Babe? Are you all right? Babe—

BABE (*hiding the pictures*) What? I'm all right. Go on back to bed. (LENNY *comes down the stairs. She is wearing a coat and wiping white night cream off of her face with a wash rag.*)

LENNY What's the matter? What's going on down here?

BABE Nothin! (*Then as she begins dancing ballet style around the room.*) We're—we're just dancing. We were just dancing around down here. (*Signaling to* BARNETTE *to dance.*)

LENNY Well, you'd better get your shoes on, 'cause we've got—

BABE All right, I will! That's a good idea! (*As she goes to get her shoes, she hides the pictures.*) Now, you go on back to bed. It's pretty late and—

LENNY Babe, will you listen a minute—

BABE (*holding up her shoes*) I'm putting 'em on—

LENNY That was the hospital that just called. We've got to get over there. Old Grand-daddy's had himself another stroke.

BABE Oh. All right. My shoes are on. (*She stands. They all look at each other as the lights blackout.*)

END OF ACT II

ACT III

The lights go up on the empty kitchen. It is the following morning. After a few moments, BABE *enters from the back door. She is carrying her hair curlers in her hands. She goes and lies down on the cot. A few moments later,* LENNY *enters. She is tired and weary.* CHICK'S *voice is heard.*

CHICK'S VOICE Lenny! Oh, Lenny! (LENNY *turns to the door.* CHICK *enters energetically.*) Well . . . how is he?

LENNY He's stabilized; they say for now his functions are all stabilized.

CHICK Well, is he still in the coma?

LENNY Uh huh.

CHICK Hmmm. So do they think he's gonna be . . . passing on?

LENNY He may be. He doesn't look so good. They said they'd phone us if there were any sudden changes.

CHICK Well, it seems to me we'd better get busy phoning on the phone ourselves. (*Removing a list from her pocket.*) Now I've made out this list of all the people we need to notify about Old Granddaddy's predicament. I'll phone half if you'll phone half.

LENNY But—what would we say?

CHICK Just tell them the facts; that Old Granddaddy's got himself in a coma, and it could be, he doesn't have long for this world.

LENNY I—I don't know. I don't feel like phoning.

CHICK Why, Lenora, I'm surprised, how can you be this way? I went to all the trouble of making up the list. And I offered to phone half of the people on it, even though I'm only one-fourth of the granddaughters. I mean, I just get tired of doing more than my fair share, when people like Meg can suddenly just disappear to where they can't even be reached in case of emergency!

LENNY All right; give me the list. I'll phone half.

CHICK Well, don't do it just to suit me.

LENNY (*she wearily tears the list into two halves*) I'll phone these here.

CHICK (*taking her half of the list*) Fine then. Suit yourself. Oh, wait—let me call Sally Bell. I need to talk to her anyway.

LENNY All right.

CHICK So you add Great Uncle Spark Dude to your list.

LENNY Okay.

CHICK Fine. Well, I've got to get on back home and see to the kids. It is gonna be an uphill struggle till I can find someone to replace that good-for-nothing Annie May Jenkins. Well, you let me know if you hear anymore.

LENNY All right.

CHICK Goodbye, Rebecca. I said goodbye. (BABE *blows her sax.* CHICK *starts to exit in a flurry then pauses to add:*) And you really ought to try to get that phoning done before twelve noon. (CHICK *exits.*)

LENNY (*after a long pause*) Babe; I feel bad. I feel real bad.

BABE Why, Lenny?

LENNY Because yesterday I—I wished it.

BABE You wished what?

LENNY I wished that Old Granddaddy would be put out of his pain. I wished on one of my birthday candles. I did. And now he's in this coma, and they say he's feeling no pain.

BABE Well, when did you have a cake yesterday? I don't remember you having any cake.

LENNY Well, I didn't . . . have a cake. But I just blew out the candles anyway.

BABE Oh. Well, those birthday wishes don't count unless you have a cake.

LENNY They don't?

BABE No. A lot of times they don't even count when you do have a cake. It just depends.

LENNY Depends on what?

BABE On how deep your wish is, I suppose.

LENNY Still, I just wish I hadn't of wished it. Gosh, I wonder when Meg's coming home.

BABE Should be soon.

LENNY I just wish we wouldn't fight all the time. I don't like it when we do.

BABE Me, neither.

LENNY I guess it hurts my feelings, a little, the way Old Granddaddy's always put so much stock in Meg and all her singing talent. I think I've been, well, envious of her 'cause I can't seem to do too much.

BABE Why, sure you can.

LENNY I can?

BABE Sure. You just have to put your mind to it; that's all. It's like how I went out and bought that saxophone, just hoping I'd be able to attend music school and start up my own career. I just went out and did it. Just on hope. Of course, now it looks like . . . Well, it just doesn't look like things are gonna work out for me. But I know they would for you.

LENNY Well, they'll work out for you, too.

BABE I doubt it.

LENNY Listen, I heard up at the hospital that Zackery's already in fair condition. They say soon he'll probably be able to walk and everything.

BABE Yeah. And life sure can be miserable.

LENNY Well, I know, 'cause—day before yesterday, Billy Boy was struck down by lightning.

BABE He was?

LENNY (nearing sobs) Yeah. He was struck dead.

BABE (crushed) Life sure can be miserable.

(They sit together for several moments in morbid silence. MEG is heard singing a loud happy song. She suddenly enters through the dining room door. She is exuberant! Her hair is a mess and the heel of one shoe has broken off. She is laughing radiantly and limping as she sings into the broken heel.)

MEG (spotting her sisters) Good morning! Good morning! Oh, it's a wonderful morning! I tell you, I am surprised I feel this good. I should feel like hell. By all accounts, I should feel like utter hell! (She is looking for the glue.) Where's that glue? This damn heel has broken off my shoe. La, la, la, la, la! Ah, here it is! Now let me just get these shoes off. Zip, zip, zip, zip, zip! Well, what's wrong with you two? My God, you look like doom! (BABE and LENNY stare helplessly at MEG.) Oh, I know, you're mad at me 'cause I stayed out all night long. Well, I did.

LENNY No, we're—we're not mad at you. We're just . . . depressed. (She starts to sob.)

MEG Oh, Lenny, listen to me, now, everything's all right with Doc. I mean nothing happened. Well, actually a lot did happen, but it didn't come to anything. Not because of me, I'm afraid. (Smearing glue on her heel.) I mean, I was out there thinking, "What will I say when he begs me to run away with him? Will I have pity on his wife and those two half-Yankee children? I mean, can I sacrifice their happiness for mine? Yes!

Oh, yes! Yes, I can!" But . . . he didn't ask me. He didn't even want to ask me. I could tell by this certain look in his eyes that he didn't even want to ask me. Why aren't I miserable! Why aren't I morbid! I should be humiliated! Devastated! Maybe these feelings are coming—I don't know. But for now it was . . . just such fun. I'm happy. I realized I could care about someone. I could want someone. And I sang! I sang all night long! I sang right up into the trees! But not for Old Granddaddy. None of it was to please Old Granddaddy! (LENNY and BABE look at each other.)

BABE Ah, Meg—

MEG What—

BABE Well, it's just—It's . . .

LENNY It's about Old Granddaddy—

MEG Oh, I know; I know. I told him all those stupid lies. Well, I'm gonna go right over there this morning and tell him the truth. I mean every horrible thing. I don't care if he wants to hear it or not. He's just gonna have to take me like I am. And if he can't take it, if it sends him into a coma, that's just too damn bad!

BABE and LENNY look at each other; BABE cracks a smile. LENNY cracks a smile.

BABE You're too late—Ha, ha, ha! (They both break up laughing.)

LENNY Oh, stop! Please! Ha, ha, ha!

MEG What is it? What' so funny?

BABE (still laughing) It's not—It's not funny!

LENNY (still laughing) No, it's not! It's not a bit funny!

MEG Well, what is it then? What?

BABE (trying to calm down) Well, it's just—it's just—

MEG What?

BABE Well, Old Granddaddy—he—he's in a coma! (BABE and LENNY break up laughing.)

MEG He's what?

BABE (shrieking) In a coma!

MEG My God! That's not funny!

BABE (calming down) I know. I know. For some reason it just struck us as funny.

LENNY I'm sorry. It's—it's not funny. It's sad. It's very sad. We've been up all night long.

BABE We're really tired.

MEG Well, my God. How is he? Is he gonna live?

(BABE and LENNY look at each other.)

BABE They don't think so! (They both break up again)

LENNY Oh, I don't know why we're laughing like this. We're just sick! We're just awful!

BABE We are—we're awful!

LENNY (as she collects herself) Oh, good; now I feel bad. Now, I feel like crying. I do; I feel like crying.

BABE Me, too. Me, too.

MEG Well, you've gotten me depressed!

LENNY I'm sorry. I'm sorry. It, ah happened last night. He had another stroke. (They laugh again.)

MEG I see.

LENNY But he's stabilized now. (She chokes up once more.)

MEG That's good. You two okay? (BABE *and* LENNY *nod.*) You look like you need some rest. (BABE *and* LENNY *nod again.* MEG *goes on, about her heel.*) I hope that'll stay. (MEG *puts the top on the glue. A realization*—) Oh, of course, now I won't be able to tell him the truth about all those lies I told. I mean, finally, I get my wits about me, and he conks out. It's just like him. Babe, can I wear your slippers till this glue dries?

BABE Sure.

LENNY (*after a pause*) Things sure are gonna be different around here . . . when Old Granddaddy dies. Well, not for you two really, but for me.

BABE (*depressed*) Yeah. It'll work out.

LENNY I hope so. I'm afraid of being here all by myself. All alone.

MEG Well, you don't have to be alone. Maybe Babe'll move back in here.

(LENNY *looks at* BABE *hopefully.*)

BABE No; I don't think I'll be living here.

MEG (*realizing her mistake*) Well, anyway, you're your own woman. Invite some people over. Have some parties. Go out with strange men.

LENNY I don't know any strange men.

MEG Well you know that Charlie.

LENNY (*shaking her head*) Not anymore.

MEG Why not?

LENNY (*breaking down*) I told him we should never see each other again.

MEG Well; if you told him, you can just untell him.

LENNY Oh, no I couldn't. I'd feel like a fool.

MEG Oh, that's not a good enough reason! All people in love feel like fools. Don't they, Babe?

BABE Sure.

MEG Look, why don't you give him a call right now? See how things stand?

LENNY Oh, no! I'd be too scared—

MEG But what harm could it possibly do? I mean, it's not gonna make things any worse than this never seeing him again, at all, forever.

LENNY I suppose that's true.

MEG Of course it is; so call him up! Take a chance, will you? Just take some sort of chance!

LENNY You think I should?

MEG Of course! You've got to try—You do! (LENNY *looks over at* BABE.)

BABE You do, Lenny—I think you do.

LENNY Really? Really, really?

MEG Yes! Yes!

BABE You should!

LENNY All right. I will! I will!

MEG Oh, good!

BABE Good!

LENNY I'll call him right now, while I've got my confidence up!

MEG Have you got the number?

LENNY Uh huh. But, ah, I think I wanna call him upstairs. It'll be more private.

MEG Ah, good idea.

LENNY I'm just gonna go on; and call him up; and see what happens—(*She has started up the stairs.*) Wish me good luck!

MEG Good luck!

BABE Good luck, Lenny!

LENNY Thanks.

(LENNY *gets almost out of sight, when the phone begins to ring. She stops,* MEG *picks up the phone.*)

MEG Hello? (*Then in a whisper.*) Oh, thank you very much . . . Yes, I will. 'Bye, 'bye.

LENNY Who was it?

MEG Wrong number. They wanted Weed's Body Shop.

LENNY Oh. Well, I'll be right back down in a minute. (LENNY *exits.*)

MEG (*after a moment, whispering to* BABE) That was the bakery; Lenny's cake is ready!

BABE (*who has become increasingly depressed*) Oh.

MEG I think I'll sneak on down to the corner and pick it up. (*She starts to leave.*)

BABE Meg—

MEG What?

BABE Nothing.

MEG You okay? (BABE *shakes her head.*) What is it?

BABE It's just—

MEG What?

(BABE *gets up and goes to her suitcase. She opens it and removes the envelope containing the photographs.*)

BABE Here. Take a look.

MEG (*taking the envelope*) What is it?

BABE It's some evidence Zackery's collected against me. Looks like my goose is cooked. (MEG *opens the envelope and looks at the photographs.*)

MEG My God, it's—it's you and . . . is *that* Willie Jay?

BABE Yeh.

MEG Well, he certainly *has* grown. You were right about that. My, oh, my.

BABE Please don't tell Lenny. She'd hate me.

MEG I won't. I won't tell Lenny. (*Putting the pictures back into the envelope.*) What are you gonna do?

BABE What can I do? (*There is a knock on the door.* BABE *grabs the envelope and hides it.*)

MEG Who is it?

BARNETTE'S VOICE It's Barnette Lloyd.

MEG Oh. Come on in, Barnette.

(BARNETTE *enters. His eyes are ablaze with excitement.*)

BARNETTE (*as he paces around the room*) Well; good morning! (*Shaking* MEG'S *hand.*) Good morning, Miss Magrath. (*Touching* BABE *on the shoulder.*) Becky. (*Moving away.*) What I meant to say is . . . how are you doing this morning?

MEG Ah—fine. Fine.

BARNETTE Good. Good. I—I just had time to drop by for a minute.

MEG Oh.

BARNETTE So, ah, how's your Granddad doing?

MEG Well, not very, ah—ah, he's in this coma. (*She breaks up laughing.*)

BARNETTE I see . . . I see. (*To* BABE.) Actually, the primary reason I came by was to pick up that—envelope. I left it here last night in all the confusion. (*Pause.*) You, ah, still do have it? (BABE *hands him the envelope.*) Yes. (*Taking the envelope.*) That's the one. I'm sure it'll be much better off in my office safe. (*He puts the envelope into his coat pocket.*)

MEG I'm sure it will.

BARNETTE Beg your pardon?

BABE It's all right. I showed her the pictures.

BARNETTE Ah; I see.

MEG So what's going to happen now, Barnette? What are those pictures gonna mean?

BARNETTE (*after pacing a moment*) Hmmm. May I speak frankly and openly?

BABE Uh huh.

MEG Please do—

BARNETTE Well, I tell you now, at first glance, I admit those pictures had me considerably perturbed and upset. Perturbed to the point that I spent most of last night going over certain suspect papers and reports that had fallen into my hands—rather recklessly.

BABE What papers do you mean?

BARNETTE Papers that pending word from three varied and unbiased experts, could prove graft, fraud, forgery, as well as a history of unethical behavior.

MEG You mean about Zackery?

BARNETTE Exactly. You see, I now intend to make this matter just as sticky and gritty for one Z. Botrelle as it is for us. Why, with the amount of scandal I'll dig up, Botrelle will be forced to settle this affair on our own terms!

MEG Oh, Babe! Did you hear that?!

BABE Yes! Oh, yes! So you've won it! You've won your lifelong vendetta!

BARNETTE Well . . . well, now of course it's problematic in that, well, in that we won't be able to expose him openly in the courts. That was the original game plan.

BABE But why not? Why?

BARNETTE Well, it's only that if, well, if a jury were to—to get, say, a glance at these, ah, photographs, well . . . well possibly . . .

BABE We could be sunk.

BARNETTE In a sense. But! On the other hand, if a newspaper were to get a hold of our little item, Mr. Zackery Botrelle could find himself boiling in some awfully hot water. So what I'm looking for very simply, is—a deal.

BABE A deal?

MEG Thank you, Barnette. It's a sunny day, Babe. (*Realizing she is in the way.*) Ooh, where's that broken shoe? (*She grabs her boots and runs upstairs.*)

BABE So, you're having to give up your vendetta?

BARNETTE Well, in a way. For the time. It, ah, seems to me you shouldn't always let your life be ruled by such things as, ah, personal vendettas. (*Looking at BABE with meaning.*) Other things can be important.

BABE I don't know, I don't exactly know. How 'bout Willie Jay? Will he be all right?

BARNETTE Yes, it's all been taken care of. He'll be leaving incognito on the midnight bus—heading north.

BABE North.

BARNETTE I'm sorry, it seemed the only . . . way. (BARNETTE *moves to her—She moves away.*)

BABE Look, you'd better be getting on back to your work.

BARNETTE (*awkwardly*) Right—'cause I—I've got those important calls out. (*Full of hope for her.*) They'll be pouring in directly. (*He starts to leave, then says to her with love.*) We'll talk.

MEG (*reappearing in her boots*) Oh, Barnette—

BARNETTE Yes?

MEG Could you give me a ride just down to the corner? I need to stop at Helen's Bakery.

BARNETTE Be glad to.

MEG Thanks. Listen, Babe, I'll be right back with the cake. We're gonna have the best celebration! Now, ah, if Lenny asks where I've gone, just say I'm . . . just say, I've gone out back to, ah, pick up some paw paws! Okay?

BABE Okay.

MEG Fine; I'll be back in a bit. Goodbye.

BABE 'Bye.

BARNETTE Goodbye, Becky.

BABE Goodbye, Barnette. Take care. (MEG *and* BARNETTE *exit.* BABE *sits staring ahead, in a state of deep despair.*) Goodbye, Becky. Goodbye, Barnette. Goodbye, Becky. (*She stops when* LENNY *comes down the stairs in a fluster.*)

LENNY Oh! Oh! Oh! I'm so ashamed! I'm such a coward! I'm such a yellow-bellied chicken! I'm so ashamed! Where's Meg?

BABE (*suddenly bright*) She's, ah—gone out back—to pick up some paw paws.

LENNY Oh. Well, at least I don't have to face her! I just couldn't do it! I couldn't make the call!! My heart was pounding like a hammer. Pound! Pound! Pound! Why, I looked down and I could actually see my blouse moving back and forth! Oh, Babe, you look so disappointed. Are you?

BABE (*despondently*) Uh huh.

LENNY Oh, no! I've disappointed Babe! I can't stand it! I've gone and disappointed my little sister, Babe! Oh, no! I feel like howling like a dog!

CHICK'S VOICE Oooh, Lenny! (CHICK *enters dramatically; dripping with sympathy.*) Well, I just don't know what to say! I'm so sorry! I am so sorry for you! And for Little Babe, here, too. I mean to have such a sister as that!

LENNY What do you mean?

CHICK Oh, you don't need to pretend with me. I saw it all from over there in my own backyard; I saw Meg stumbling out of Doc Porter's pickup truck, not 15 minutes ago. And her looking such a disgusting mess. You must be so ashamed! You must just want to die! Why, I always said that girl was nothing but cheap Christmas trash!

LENNY Don't talk that way about Meg.

CHICK Oh, come on now. Lenny, honey, I know exacly how you feel about Meg. Why, Meg's a low-class tramp and you need not have one more blessed thing to do with her and her disgusting behavior.

LENNY I said don't you ever talk that way about my sister Meg again.

CHICK Well, my goodness gracious, Lenora, don't be such a noodle—it's the truth!

LENNY I don't care if it's the Ten Commandments. I don't want to hear it in my home. Not ever again.

CHICK In your home?! Why, I never in all my life—This is my Grandfather's home! And you're just living here on his charity; so don't you get high-falutin' with me, Miss Lenora Josephine Magrath!

LENNY Get out of here—

CHICK Don't you tell me to get out! What makes you think you can order me around? Why, I've had just about my fill of you trashy Magraths and your trashy ways; hanging your selves in cellars; carrying on with married men; shooting your own husbands!

LENNY Get out!

CHICK (*to* BABE) And don't think she's not gonna end up at the state prison farm or in some—mental institution. Why it's a clear-cut case of manslaughter with intent to kill!

LENNY Out! Get out!

CHICK (*running on*) That's what everyone's saying, deliberate intent to kill! And you'll pay for that! Do you hear me? You'll pay!

LENNY (*she picks up a broom and threatens* CHICK *with it*) And I'm telling you to get out!

CHICK You—you put that down this minute—are you a raving lunatic?

LENNY (*beating* CHICK *with the broom*) I said for you to get out! That means out! And never, never, never come back!

CHICK (*overlapping, as she runs around the room*) Oh! Oh! Oh! You're crazy! You're crazy!

LENNY (*chasing* CHICK *out the door*) Do you hear me, Chick the Stick! This is my home! This is my house! Get out! Out!

CHICK (*overlapping*) Oh! Oh! Police! Police! You're crazy! Help! Help! (LENNY *chases* CHICK *out of the house. They are both screaming. The phone rings.* BABE *goes and picks it up.*)

BABE Hello? . . . Oh, hello, Zackery! . . . Yes, he showed them to me! . . . You're what! . . . What do you mean? . . . What! . . . You can't put me out to Whitfield . . . 'Cause I'm not crazy . . . I'm not! I'm not! . . . She wasn't crazy either . . . Don't you call my mother crazy! . . . No, you're not! You're not gonna. You're not! (*She slams the phone down and stares wildly ahead.*) He's not. He's not. (*As she walks over to the ribbon drawer.*) I'll do it. I will. And he won't . . . (*She opens the drawer; pulls out the rope; becomes terrified; throws the rope back in the drawer and slams it shut.* LENNY *enters from the back door swinging the broom and laughing.*)

LENNY Oh, my! Oh, my! You should have seen us! Why, I chased Chick the Stick right up the mimosa tree. I did! I left her right up there screaming in the tree!

BABE (*laughing; she is insanely delighted*) Oh, you did!

LENNY Yes, I did! And I feel so good! I do! I feel good! I feel good!

BABE (*overlapping*) Good! Good, Lenny! Good for you! (*They dance around the kitchen.*)

LENNY (*stopping*) You know what—

BABE What?

LENNY I'm gonna call Charlie!!! I'm gonna call him right now!

BABE You are?

LENNY Yeah, I feel like I can really do it!

BABE You do?

LENNY My courage is up; my heart's in it; the time is right! No more beating around the bush! Let's strike while the iron is hot!

BABE Right! Right! No more beating around the bush! Strike while the iron is hot! (LENNY *goes to the phone.* BABE *rushes over to the ribbon drawer. She begins tearing through it.*)

LENNY (*with the receiver in her hand*) I'm calling him up, BABE—I'm really gonna do it!

BABE (*still tearing through the drawer*) Good! Do it! Good!

LENNY (*as she dials*) Look. My hands aren't even shaking.

BABE (*pulling out a red cord of rope*) Don't we have any stronger rope than this?

LENNY I guess not. All the rope we've got's in that drawer. (*About her hands.*) Now they're shaking a little. (BABE *takes the rope and goes up the stairs.* LENNY *finishes dialing the number. She waits for an answer.*) Hello? . . . Hello, Charlie. This is Lenny Magrath . . . Well, I'm fine. I'm just fine. (*An awkward pause.*) I was, ah, just calling to see—how you're getting on . . . Well, good. Good . . . Yes, I know I said that. Now I wish I didn't say it . . . Well, the reason I said that before, about not seeing each other again, was 'cause of me, not you . . . Well, it's just I—can't have any children. I—have this ovary problem . . . Why, Charlie, what a thing to say! . . . Well, they're not all little snot-nosed pigs! . . . You think they are! . . . Oh, Charlie, stop, stop! You're making me laugh . . . Yes, I guess I was. I can see now that I was . . . You are? . . . Well, I'm dying to see you, too . . . Well, I don't know when, Charlie . . . soon. How about, well, how about tonight? . . . You will? . . . Oh, you will! . . . All right, I'll be here. I'll be right here . . . Goodbye, then, Charlie. Goodbye for now. (*She hangs up the phone in a daze.*) Babe. Oh, Babe! He's coming. He's coming! Babe! Oh, Babe, where are you? Meg! Oh . . . out back—picking up paw paws. (*As she exits through the back door.*) And those paw paws are just ripe for picking up!

(*There is a moment of silence, then a loud, horrible thud is heard coming from upstairs. The telephone begins ringing immediately. It rings five times before* BABE *comes hurrying down the stairs with a broken piece of rope hanging around her neck. The phone continues to ring.*)

BABE (*to the phone*) Will you shut up! (*She is jerking the rope from around her neck. She grabs a knife to cut it off.*) Cheap! Miserable! I hate you! I hate you! (*She throws the rope violently around the room. The phone stops ringing.*) Thank God. (*She looks at the stove, goes over to it, and turns the gas on. The sound of gas escaping is heard.* BABE *sniffs at it.*) Come on. Come on . . . Hurry up . . . I beg of you—hurry up! (*Finally,* BABE *feels the oven is ready; she takes a deep breath and opens the oven door to stick her head into it. She spots the rack and furiously jerks it out. Taking another breath, she sticks her head into the oven. She stands for several moments tapping her fingers furiously on top of the stove. She speaks from inside the oven . . .*) Oh, please. Please. (*After a few moments, she reaches for the box of matches with her head still in the oven. She tries to strike a match. It doesn't catch.*) Oh, Mama, please! (*She throws the match away and is getting a second one.*) Mama . . . Mama . . . So that's why you done it!

(*In her excitement she starts to get up, bangs her head and falls back in the stove.* MEG *enters from the back door, carrying a birthday cake in a pink box.*)

MEG Babe! (MEG *throws the box down and runs to pull* BABE'S *head out of the oven.*) Oh, my God! What are you doing? What the hell are you doing?
BABE (*dizzily*) Nothing. I don't know. Nothing. (MEG *turns off the gas and moves* BABE *to a chair near the open door.*)
MEG Sit down. Sit down! Will you sit down!
BABE I'm okay. I'm okay.
MEG Put your head between your knees and breathe deep!
BABE Meg—
MEG Just do it! I'll get you some water. (MEG *gets some water for* BABE.) Here.
BABE Thanks.
MEG Are you okay?
BABE Uh-huh.
MEG Are you sure?
BABE Yeah, I'm sure. I'm okay.
MEG (*getting a damp rag and putting it over her own face*) Well good. That's good.

BABE Meg—

MEG Yes?

BABE I know why she did it.

MEG What? Why who did what?

BABE (*with joy*) Mama. I know why she hung that cat along with her.

MEG You do?

BABE (*with enlightenment*) It's 'cause she was afraid of dying all alone.

MEG Was she?

BABE She felt so unsure, you know, as to what was coming. It seems the best thing coming up would be a lot of angels and all of them singing. But I imagine they have high, scary voices and little gold pointed fingers that are as sharp as blades and you don't want to meet 'em all alone. You'd be afraid to meet 'em all alone. So it wasn't like what people were saying about her hating that cat. Fact is, she loved that cat. She needed him with her 'cause she felt so all alone.

MEG Oh, Babe . . . Babe. Why, Babe? Why?

BABE Why what?

MEG Why did you stick your head into the oven?!

BABE I don't know, Meg. I'm having a bad day. It's been a real bad day; those pictures; and Barnette giving up his vendetta; then Willie Jay, heading north; and—Zackery called me up. (*Trembling with terror.*) He says he's gonna have me classified insane and send me on out to the Whitfield asylum.

MEG What! Why, he could never do that!

BABE Why not?

MEG 'Cause you're not insane.

BABE I'm not?

MEG No! He's trying to bluff you. Don't you see it? Barnette's got him running scared.

BABE Really?

MEG Sure. He's scared to death—calling you insane. Ha! Why, you're just as perfectly sane as anyone walking the streets of Hazlehurst, Mississippi.

BABE I am?

MEG More so! A lot more so!

BABE Good!

MEG But, Babe, we've just got to learn how to get through these real bad days here. I mean, it's getting to be a thing in our family. (*Slight pause as she looks at* BABE.) Come on now. Look, we've got Lenny's cake right here. I mean don't you wanna be around to give her her cake; watch her blow out the candles?

BABE (*realizing how much she wants to be here*) Yeah, I do, I do. Cause she always loves to make her birthday wishes on those candles.

MEG Well, then we'll give her her cake and maybe you won't be so miserable.

BABE Okay.

MEG Good. Go on and take it out of the box.

BABE Okay. (*She takes the cake out of the box. It is a magical moment.*) Gosh, it's a pretty cake.

MEG (*handing her some matches*) Here now. You can go on and light up the candles.

BABE All right. (*She starts to light the candles.*) I love to light up candles. And there are so many here. Thirty pink ones in all plus one green one to grow on.

MEG (*watching her light the candles*) They're pretty.

BABE They are. (*She stops lighting the candles.*) And I'm not like Mama. I'm not so all alone.

MEG You're not.

BABE (*as she goes back to lighting candles*) Well, you'd better keep an eye out for Lenny. She's supposed to be surprised.

MEG All right. Do you know where she's gone?

BABE Well, she's not here inside—so she must have gone on outside.

MEG Oh, well, then I'd better run and find her.

BABE Okay 'cause these candles are gonna melt down. (MEG *starts out the door.*)

MEG Wait—there she is coming. Lenny! Oh, Lenny! Come on! Hurry up!

BABE (*overlapping and improvising as she finishes lighting candles*) Oh, no! No! Well, yes—yes! No, wait! Wait! Okay! (LENNY *enters.* MEG *covers* LENNY's *eyes with her hands.*)

LENNY (*terrified*) What?! What is it?!! What?!!

MEG & BABE Surprise! Happy Birthday! Happy Birthday to Lenny!!

LENNY Oh, no! Oh me!!! What a surprise! I could just cry! Oh, look, "Happy Birthday to Lenny—A Day Late!" How cute! My! Will you look at all those candles—it's absolutely frightening.

BABE (*spontaneous thought*) Oh, no, Lenny, it's good! 'Cause—'cause the more candles you have on your cake, the stronger your wish is.

LENNY Really?

BABE Sure!

LENNY Mercy. (*They start the song.* LENNY, *interrupting the song.*) Oh, but wait! I—I can't think of my wish! My body's gone all nervous inside.

MEG For God's sake, Lenny—come on!

BABE The wax is all melting!

LENNY My mind is just a blank, a total blank!

MEG Will you please just—

BABE (*overlapping*) Lenny, hurry! Come on!

LENNY Okay! Okay! Just go!! (MEG *and* BABE *burst into the "Happy Birthday Song."* As it ends LENNY *blows out all of the candles on the cake.* MEG *and* BABE *applaud loudly.*)

MEG Oh, you made it!

BABE Hurray!

LENNY Oh, me! Oh, me! I hope that wish comes true! I hope it does!

BABE Why? What did you wish for?

LENNY (*as she removes the candles from the cake*) Why. I can't tell you that.

BABE Oh, sure you can—

LENNY Oh, no! Then it won't come true.

BABE Why, that's just superstition! Of course it will, if you made it deep enough.

MEG Really? I didn't know that.

LENNY Well, Babe's the regular expert on birthday wishes.

BABE It's just I get these feelings. Now come on and tell us. What was it you wished for?

MEG Yes, tell us. What was it?

LENNY Well, I guess, it wasn't really a specific wish. This—this vision just sort of came into my mind.

BABE A vision? What was it of?

LENNY I don't know exactly. It was something about the three of us smiling and laughing together.

BABE Well, when was it? Was it far away or near?

LENNY I'm not sure, but it wasn't forever; it wasn't for every minute. Just this one moment and we were all laughing.

BABE What were we laughing about?

LENNY I don't know. Just nothing I guess.

MEG Well, that's a nice wish to make. (LENNY *and* MEG *look at each other a moment.*) Here, now, I'll get a knife so we can go ahead and cut the cake in celebration of Lenny being born!

BABE Oh, yes! And give each one of us a rose. A whole rose apiece!

LENNY (*cutting the cake nervously*) Well, I'll try—I'll try!

MEG (*licking the icing off a candle*) Mmmm—this icing is delicious! Here, try some!

BABE Mmmm! It's wonderful! Here, Lenny!

LENNY (*laughing joyously as she licks icing from her fingers and cuts huge pieces of cake that her sisters bite into ravenously*) Oh, how I do love having birthday cake for breakfast! How I do! (*The sisters freeze for a moment laughing and eating cake; the lights change and frame them in a magical, golden, sparkling glimmer; saxophone music is heard. The lights dim to blackout, and the saxophone continues to play.*)

END OF PLAY

Questions

1. What is the relationship between Chick and Lenny? Why does Chick look down on the Magraths?
2. Why do you suppose Babe shot Zackery?
3. What is particularly comic about Babe's entrance on p. 1335 and the several lines of dialogue following?
4. What is Meg's chief character flaw? Do you like her in spite of it?
5. Explain the relationship between Meg and Doc.
6. The Magraths have inherited a capacity for suffering. How does their family history relate to their present misfortunes?
7. How does Lenny change over the course of the drama?
8. *The New York Times* drama critic wrote that "*Crimes of the Heart* is finally the story of how its young characters escape the past to seize the future." Do you agree or not? Explain.

Appendix

Writing about Literature

From time to time most of us will have occasion to write about something we have read. Such an exercise will not be confined to literature courses for which we will compose essays and exams. Business employees often have to write reports based on other documents. Lawyers must write briefs based on their interpretations of laws and depositions. Although these other sorts of writing may not require precisely the skills required of a literary text, the practice of writing about literature is exceptionally helpful. Indeed, law schools consider the study of literature one of the most valuable preparations for legal training. The care, concentration, and judgment needed to evaluate and write about a literary work is a discipline useful in any number of demanding professions and fields.

Nevertheless, some students balk at writing essays about literature. They feel that literature should be enjoyed and that writing about it dampens their enjoyment. Although it is true that people take a certain degree of pleasure in what comes easily, many readers find that they do not fully appreciate what they read until they force themselves to formulate their responses in writing. Writing about literature, therefore, can aid in a more profound and lasting enjoyment of literature.

Writing about literature is not significantly different from writing on any other subject. A critical essay demands the same clarity and coherence of expression as any other type of writing. For your convenience, however, we have broken down the process into five stages: (1) understanding the work, (2) choosing a thesis, (3) choosing supporting material, (4) organizing the essay, and (5) writing the essay.

Understanding the Work

Before writing anything, you must be certain that you understand the work. You must understand not only each word, but also the relationship of various parts to each other. You must understand not only what is present, but also why certain things are excluded from the text. This book has given you many skills needed to analyze literature, and it would be redundant to attempt to summarize these skills here.

When assigned to write a paper on a literary subject, you should start by reading the works carefully on your own rather than by reading criticism, biographies, or reader's guides. Your essays should reflect your own emotional and intellectual comprehension of the work. Outside sources are useful *only* insofar as they enhance your understanding. To repeat critical positions we neither understand nor agree with leads to a muddle of half-formed thoughts and comments.

Moreover, criticism is usually more difficult to understand than the work it discusses. By reading criticism first, you may succeed only in confusing yourself and in making your task harder. Most works are written for the average literate reader, but most scholarship is written by scholars for scholars. Thus critics tend to assume that their readers have a wide familiarity with history, literary methodology, and other works of literature.

The Qualities of a Good Thesis

Before you can write an outline for your essay, you must formulate a *thesis* or central idea. Every essay has a thesis, and typically it is stated in the first paragraph of a short theme. This *thesis statement* is the single most important sentence in your essay and will determine its entire composition. A thesis gives an essay unity and coherence. All other sentences either support it, restrict it, or place it in context. Any sentence that does not help prove the thesis is irrelevant and ought to be rewritten or removed.

What sort of statement is a thesis? A *thesis is a statement that needs to be proved.* Thus it is something controversial, questionable, or in need of substantiation. Facts rarely make good theses. For example, one hardly needs to prove this statement: "Lorraine Hansberry wrote *A Raisin in the Sun.*" No one has questioned her authorship. A better thesis would read: "*A Raisin in the Sun* is based upon events in which Hansberry's family was personally involved." If you used this thesis, you would need to describe those family events—which are not common knowledge—and then indicate how those events were used in the play. An essayist using such a thesis has a clear point that needs substantiation.

Good theses also need to be *restrictive* and *precise.* An essay will be much more convincing if it has a clear, limited point it wishes to prove.

Here are three theses written for the same essay. Let us evaluate them to see which one would make the best paper.

1. "Young Goodman Brown" is a good story.
2. "Young Goodman Brown" clearly and powerfully shows the mind at work.
3. "Young Goodman Brown" vividly depicts the anxiety and suspicion of the Puritan mind.

The first thesis is very broad. By what standard is "Young Goodman Brown" a good story? Is it a good adventure story, psychological portrait, or social commentary? The second thesis is clearer. The story is praised for its psychological clarity and power. But the second thesis does not tell us what psychological conditions the story so "clearly and powerfully shows." Does the story show us a variety of different psychological types? The third thesis is far more precise and restrictive. The story is now praised for its depiction of the anxiety and suspicion of the Puritan mind. This last is a far easier point to prove than the vague statement that "Young Goodman Brown" is merely good.

Two other factors go into making a good thesis. A writer must choose a thesis that he or she can prove in the allotted space and time. Some theses demand so much research that they require years of study to accumulate the necessary proof. Some theses need pages of development before they can be convincingly demonstrated. A writer facing a specific deadline with specific page requirements must consider whether he or she can successfully and convincingly substantiate and defend the thesis. If not, it is better to choose a less difficult notion to write about. In *Hamlet* Shakespeare investigates the manipulation of royal succession that fascinated the Elizabethan Court. While this thesis may be true, it demands a detailed knowledge of British history. Most writers would choose a less specialized topic.

Exercise

Of the ten statements that follow, some are good thesis statements, some are poor, and some are not thesis statements at all. Indicate the thesis statements and improve those that seem weak.

1. Ray Bradbury wrote "There Will Come Soft Rains."
2. Bradbury's "There Will Come Soft Rains" reflects his anxiety of nuclear holocaust.
3. There are some striking similarities between Hawthorne's "The Haunted Mind" and "Young Goodman Brown."
4. Dylan Thomas's "Do Not Go Gentle into That Good Night" is a villanelle.
5. "Do Not Go Gentle into That Good Night" is a very moving poem.
6. *Oedipus Rex* ends tragically for the hero.
7. Although the couple in George Meredith's *Modern Love* is married, the sequence is typical of Elizabethan sonnet sequences because it traces the dissolution of their love.
8. The comparison between the beloved and nature in Shakespeare's sonnets underscores the supernatural quality of human beauty.
9. *The Importance of Being Earnest* made me laugh again and again.
10. Ibsen's *A Doll's House* depicts the suffocating conditions in which middle-class Victorian women lived.

Formulating a Thesis

Writers often have difficulty formulating thesis statements. Where do you find a thesis? How do you come up with a good thesis? These are questions writers frequently ask. Here are some questions whose answers will help you formulate thesis statements.

1. Since the thesis is the most important statement in your essay, it should contain the most important idea you wish to share with your reader. Ask yourself, "If I had only one notion I wanted my reader to understand, what would it be?"
2. The endings of literary works frequently contain crucial actions or statements. Ask yourself, "Why does the literary work end in the way it does?"
3. Often a story, play, or poem contains a section we find particularly puzzling. Instead of ignoring the section, ask yourself, "Why is this section here?" or "What does this section mean?"
4. Stories and plays usually contain at least one important action before the work concludes. Ask yourself, "What is the significance of this action?" For example, critics have long debated why Hamlet refrains from killing Claudius when they are alone in the chapel. Answering such a problem will generate an interesting paper.

In general, the most interesting essays are those that try to solve some literary problem. A good way to proceed is by exploring what you find problematic, and trying to solve that problem yourself.

In addition, there are specific types of papers that one could write. For example, one could write a character analysis, a comparison between two works, or an essay which relates historical information to a literary work. Each of these specific essay types is developed in a particular way.

Developing the Comparison Thesis

Many students like to compare two literary works. But it is never enough to say that two works are alike or different. A central idea that is so vague and general is sure to lead to a vague and general essay. The more specific your central idea, the more specific your essay will be.

Let us say you are intrigued by two of Shakespeare's sonnets, the ones beginning "Shall I compare thee to a summer's day," and "My mistress' eyes are nothing like the sun." You have read them carefully and have consulted the critics. You are now ready to formulate a thesis. To aid in the process, you may compare them point by point by dividing a piece of paper into two columns, one for each poem. At the end of the process, your paper looks like this:

Summer's day	*Nothing like the sun*
1. sonnet	1. sonnet
2. compares beloved to nature	2. compares beloved to nature

3. beloved is "fair" (l. 7) golden complexion (l. 6)	3. beloved is dark black hair (l. 4) skin "dun" (l. 3)
4. the beloved's eye is better than the sun (l. 5)	4. beloved's eye inferior to sun (l. 1)
5. the beloved will become the poem in the future (l. 12)	5. the beloved stands beyond the poem (l. 14)
6. beloved's beauty made eternal in poetry (l. 14)	6. beloved's beauty greater than poem can represent (l. 14)
7. beloved possesses more typical beauty	7. beloved has atypical beauty
8. tone: serious throughout, laudatory	8. tone: sometimes comic, insulting; laudatory at end
9. poem emphasizes the lasting condition of poetry and the mutable condition of nature	9. poem emphasizes the false condition of poetry and the indefinable beauty of human beings

This list does not exhaust the points of comparison, but it does give you enough material with which to begin formulating your thesis.

You notice that some of your points are facts about the poems. For example, Shakespeare is writing about two different people, one light, the other dark. Both poems speak of the sun as an eye. Could these facts be the basis of an essay? No. A thesis *must be a statement that needs proof, something controversial or uncertain.* Facts, unless they are revolutionary discoveries, are not sufficiently in need of support to be adequate statements for a thesis.

However, some of the statements are interpretive, and these might be useful in formulating a thesis. For example, the entry under "tone" indicates that both poems end by praising the beloved but that the second poem arrives at its praise in a more complicated manner. One might argue as follows: "Though both poems conclude by praising their subjects, 'My mistress' eyes are nothing like the sun,' approaches the subject in a richer, more complicated way." Because this thesis is both interpretive and evaluative, it needs to be supported. It would make a good thesis.

There are other statements one could use as the basis for a thesis. Entry 9 is interesting. One might argue: "In 'My mistress' eyes,' Shakespeare acknowledges a beauty so peculiarly human that it eludes the criteria of nature and poetry." Or, perhaps, one might wish to argue: "In these two poems Shakespeare suggests that nature is not an adequate measure by which to judge human beauty." Your list of comparisons could lead to a number of interesting theses. Critics and scholars have been studying Shakespeare's sonnets for centuries without exhausting their richness and variety. Clearly, you might formulate many different theses comparing these sonnets. You must decide which thesis most interests you and is within your capacity to support.

A good thesis, then, should incorporate a number of characteristics:

1. It should grow out of your understanding of the poem and should not be imposed on a work it may not fit.

2. It should be evaluative or interpretive. It cannot be a statement of fact, unless the fact is not yet accepted.
3. It should be precise. The reader must know what you are trying to prove. Imprecise or vague terms obscure your point and make it difficult to defend your position adequately.
4. It should be restrictive. Think of your thesis as a sort of fort under attack by the skeptical mind of your reader. If you try to protect too wide an area, your supporting forces will be too widely dispersed. A tight defense of a small territory is more likely to succeed. Never argue any point *you* do not thoroughly believe.
5. Finally, your thesis should contain one central idea. One good idea is hard enough to support and defend. More than one compels you to scatter your forces.

Developing the Character Analysis

As we have stated in our chapters on characterization, there are two sorts of characters: round and flat. Flat characters are poor choices for literary analysis because their behavior can be summarized in a sentence or two. Flat characters do not leave one much to say or explore. Successful essays are usually written about rounded characters.

In developing a thesis about a character, you must decide whether the character changes over the course of the work or remains the same. If the character changes, one can compare the character's earlier personality to his or her later personality. As you did with the comparison essay, you can develop a worksheet. Here is one for Dimitry Dmitrich Gurov in Chekhov's "Lady with Lapdog."

Early Gurov

1. contempt for women
2. thinks himself above life
3. careless of affection
4. lots of superficial friends
5. alone in a resort
6. confident
7. brags of sexual conquests
8. works in bank
9. dresses well
10. concerned for social acceptance

Later Gurov

1. love for a woman
2. sees difficulties ahead
3. careful of affection
4. one love
5. mostly alone in Moscow
6. less confident
7. silent about love
8. works in bank
9. dresses well
10. still concerned about acceptance

We notice that Gurov has not changed in every respect. Both at the beginning and at the end of the story he works for a bank, dresses well, and wants social acceptance. Love does not entirely change him. But we note some clear differences. We notice at the beginning that he is contemptuous, careless, and self-important, while at the close of the story he is respectful, careful, and sympathetic. How can we word a thesis that might indicate this change? Let's look at three attempts:

1. Gurov changes during the course of the story.
2. The love of Anna has made Gurov a better person.
3. Through his love of Anna, Gurov has lost his unfeeling confidence and gained a richer appreciation of the difficulties of life.

Clearly the last of these is more precise and restrictive. Can you focus the thesis even more sharply?

Yet another strategy in developing a character analysis is to review the conflicts within a character's personality. Here, for example, is a work sheet on the conflicts in Hamlet's character:

1. avoids involvement in court
2. wants to revenge father
3. wants to be close to mother
4. wants to be close to Ophelia
5. believes ghost

1. drawn into intrigue
2. afraid to kill uncle
3. wants to hurt mother
4. drives Ophelia away
5. doubts ghost

Again from the work sheet, we can begin to formulate a thesis. At first we are general:

"Hamlet is in conflict with himself."

We try to make it more precise:

"Hamlet tries to be close to people but cannot be."

Last we try to be as precise as possible:

"Because of the 'rotten . . . state of Denmark,' Hamlet forces himself to keep at a distance the very people he would like to show affection to."

This thesis develops only one important conflict in Hamlet's personality. For example, one might argue that Hamlet is in conflict between the desire to revenge his father and his own tendency to do nothing. Or one might argue that Hamlet is in conflict between hating his uncle and being just to him. In restricting your thesis, you have moved from general conflicts to one specific conflict.

Developing a Historical Thesis

Among the more difficult theses to write is one that relates historical conditions to works of literature. No doubt writers, like other people, are affected by historical events. But since these effects are so subtle, various, and personal, their relation to a literary text is difficult to pin down unless the literary work specifically refers to some event. For example, Frances Harper's "The Slave Auction" refers to American slavery practices and was written at a time of Abolitionist agitation. But other works are more allusive. W.H. Auden's "Musée des Beaux Arts" never refers to the political events of 1939 or the beginnings of World War II, but the topic of suffering is made more urgent by those events. A student of the period might know that an important issue of the late thirties was how writers should respond to the approaching war. Should they become soldiers, propagandists, or stop writing completely? One might have as a thesis: "In 'Musée des Beaux Arts' Auden indicates that the artist's role is to put suffering in its proper perspective, an act necessary in the face of the rise of fascism."

Choosing Supporting Material

Although you have now formulated your thesis, you are not yet ready to start writing. First you must consider the best way to defend and support your thesis.

The best evidence for supporting your thesis is the text of the work itself. This may seem obvious, but it is surprising how easily writers overlook the source while writing about it. *Never make a statement about a work that cannot be corroborated by a passage in it.* You should quote frequently and extensively. Before stating any opinion, you should be aware of the word, line, or passage that led you to that opinion.

One of the chief complaints teachers make about student literary essays is that they are *impressionistic*; that is, they make general comments about a story, play, or poem without indicating what in the work gave rise to those ideas, feelings, or evaluations. No matter how true, well worded, or insightful such impressions are, they are nearly worthless if the writer does not connect them to the text. Students concerned about improving their writing should guard against impressionistic writing.

Your second source of support material comes from what other critics and scholars have said about the work. As we cautioned earlier, your essay should not be a collage of other people's thoughts. A critic's work should be used only when it furthers your own understanding. You should quote or paraphrase a critic or scholar only in three situations:

1. When the critic makes a point so well that it is worthy of repetition. Some critics are especially articulate and polished writers. Make use of their beautifully turned observations.
2. When the critic supplies you with an idea, a fact (not of common knowledge), a method of presentation, or an opinion that is not your own but whose truth you both recognize and need for your own essay. It is any scholar's duty to acknowledge the intellectual debt by quoting the critic and/or noting the source of the observation.
3. When you believe your own evaluation needs support. By quoting a critic, you are saying indirectly, "See, I'm not alone in this belief. X believes it, too!" Such support is especially needed when you are evaluating a piece's literary merit. It is good to have someone on your side when either praising or disparaging someone's work.

In the following paragraphs we can observe all three uses of quotation and paraphrase. The passage is part of an essay on John Milton's use of the sonnet.

(You will find one of his sonnets on page 468.) The author, James G. Mengert, wishes to show that Milton effectively used traditional aspects of the sonnet in his own special way. Mengert's aim is threefold: it is factual, interpretive, and evaluative. First, Mengert must establish the facts of the sonnet tradition. Second, he must interpret Milton's use of the tradition. Third, he must evaluate Milton's use of the tradition. Mengert cannot do all this work in one paragraph, but this excerpt shows how he goes about supporting his thesis.

> It was not until J. S. Smart's edition of the sonnets in 1921 that Milton was fully allowed to have a conception of the sonnet that was in any sense traditional rather than merely or substantially idiosyncratic.[1] The roots of Milton's sonnet form in traditional, especially Italian, practice were further explored by F. T. Prince.[2] Although there have since been refinements or qualifications of the work of these men, their basic contentions still stand; and studies of individual sonnets can now take for granted Milton's firm grasp of the tradition and resources of the sonnet and go on to examine the interaction of his own powerful, reshaping genius with that tradition. Indeed, it is possible to see this very reshaping as itself a participation in a flexible sonnet tradition. Thus Taylor Stroehr introduces his own analysis of the sonnets with this comment: "He chose the form, one supposes, exactly because it was demanding, suited by its brevity to the expression of occasional thoughts and feelings, by its complexity and sinewy movement to the development of powerful emotion and tough logic." And he concludes his essay with the observation that "Milton plays the conventional elements of linguistic structure off against the less flexible conventions of the sonnet form itself, to produce a compelling expression of poetic feeling, beyond the reach of less self-conscious art."[3]

Mengert refers to the historical work of J. S. Smart and F. T. Prince and summarizes their findings. He then quotes Taylor Stoehr twice, first because Stroehr so beautifully articulates Mengert's position and later to support Mengert's evaluation that Milton's sonnets are great works of art. This passage is more scholarly than the writing you may be called on to produce, but it clearly indicates how the skillful use of quotation, reference, and paraphrase can support and advance an argument.

Biographical information is perhaps the most difficult information to use in an essay. Some professors absolutely forbid it and may go so far as to remove the author's name from the literary work. They argue that the reader should be concerned only with the text and that biographical information is merely sophisticated gossip that has no place in serious literary discussion. Other teachers do recognize a place for biographical information. The rule of thumb to use is that *no biographical information should be included unless it illuminates the literature.* For example, it does help the reader to know that Sylvia Plath's father

---

[1] John S. Smart, ed., *The Sonnets of Milton* (Glasgow: Maclehose, Jackson, 1921).
[2] F. T. Prince, *The Italian Element in Milton's Verse* (Oxford: Clarendon Press, 1954), esp. pp. 89–107.
[3] Taylor Stroehr, "Syntax and Poetic Form in Milton's Sonnets," *English Studies* 45 (1964), pp. 289, 301.

was a German professor in order to understand why there are German words in her poem "Daddy" and why he is associated with fascism. But the poem is not illuminated by the fact that Plath went to Smith College on a scholarship. Thus one biographical fact may be relevant, another irrelevant. Considerate and interesting writers typically do not set aside a paragraph to give a biographical summary of the author. They do not wish to waste precious space or their reader's time with irrelevant information.

Organizing the Essay

The literary essay, like most essays, is generally divided into three basic parts: an introduction, a body, and a conclusion. Each part has its own structure and purpose.

The chief feature of the introduction is the thesis, which typically appears as the last sentence of the introductory paragraph. The rest of the paragraph sets the stage for the thesis by raising the issue the thesis attempts to answer. Indeed, one could say that the opening or introductory paragraph tries to answer the following questions: Why should a reader be interested in the thesis? Does it answer some unsolved problem? Does the thesis assert something unusual?

Like the introduction, the conclusion is usually a single paragraph in smaller essays. Conclusions generally contain no new material. They summarize what has been said in the essay. They can also project from the material discussed to the further issues it raises. But writers should be careful not to let the conclusion be too provocative. Too many threads left hanging leave the reader dissatisfied.

Most of the essay, then, is made up of body paragraphs. A body paragraph contains three parts. It begins with a topic sentence. The topic sentence is followed by supporting material. An optional concluding sentence either summarizes the paragraph or serves as a transition to the next paragraph.

Before writing an essay, you should first prepare an outline. Even a brief outline can be helpful. For example, let us outline a possible essay based on Tennyson's "Ulysses." The thesis we developed earlier was: "In 'Ulysses,' Tennyson explores the hero's obsessive search for knowledge." We might break this down in three ways:

1. Ulysses' earlier wanderings were a quest for new experiences.
2. Ulysses sees life as a constant quest for knowledge.
3. Ulysses' dissatisfaction with his Ithaca is derived from intellectual boredom.

If we go back through the poem, we can find textual evidence to support our contentions.

1. Ulysses' earlier wanderings were a quest for new experiences:
   a. ll. 11–12 speak of "roaming with a hungry heart."
   b. ll. 13–17 speak of the various experiences he has had on his travels.
   c. l. 64 speaks of Achilles, the hero whom he knew.

2. Ulysses sees life as a constant quest for knowledge:
   a. ll. 19–21 speak of "experience as an archway."
   b. ll. 30–33 speak of the desire "to follow knowledge like a sinking star."
   c. ll. 56–57 speak of the wish to "seek a newer world."
   d. l. 70 speaks of wanting "to strive, to seek, to find."
3. Ulysses is dissatisfied with Ithaca because it is intellectually boring:
   a. ll. 35–43 speak of the slow labor of civilizing people.
   b. ll. 4–5 speak of people as crude and uninteresting.
   c. ll. 22–24 speak of the boredom of a life that is not challenging.
   d. l. 3 suggests that his wife does not interest him.

To this basic outline you could add references to critics and scholars who support your interpretation of "Ulysses."

Several things about this outline are noteworthy. Every point you make about the work is directly supported by several key phrases in the text. One could diagram the relationship between the thesis and the text as a pyramid whose footing is the poem.

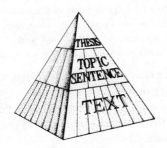

If the text were not there at every point, the entire structure would come crashing to the ground.

Another point you should notice about the outline is that we have chosen quotes from all over the text, but we have not necessarily followed the order of the poem. Under heading 3, we first begin with a quotation from the end of the poem; we then go to a quotation from the beginning, then to one from the middle, and finally to another reference to the opening lines. As a writer, you are busy proving your point. Your essay follows *your* organization, not Tennyson's.

Writing the Essay

Before discussing specific problems of composition, we would like to discuss a general problem with writing literary essays.

An annoying habit in critical writing is speaking of the story, play, or poem as if the reader has not read the work. In book reviews that appear in newspapers, the writer is obliged to narrate the plot of the story because the reader presumably has *not* read the book. In literary essays, however, *the author should assume that the reader is familiar with the work.* Thus there is no reason to summarize the contents. Yet time and again, student essays contain such paragraphs as the following:

> Tennyson's "Ulysses" is a dramatic monologue. The poem begins with Ulysses home in Ithaca after traveling ten years. However, Ulysses is not content to remain home. He turns his kingdom over to his son Telemachus, and summons his men back to his ship. Though he admits to being old, Ulysses still believes he can perform "some work of noble note" (l. 52).

Such a summary paragraph is useless and time-consuming. It reveals only the most superficial understanding of the poem. Authors concerned about improving their writing avoid such unnecessary passages.

Introductions

Even professional writers have difficulty deciding where to begin their discussions. Most often, students start the discussion far from their thesis statements and therefore never lead up to them clearly or adequately. Here, for example, is a typical opening of a student paper on "Ulysses."

> Alfred, Lord Tennyson was one of the greatest English poets of the nineteenth century. He was fascinated by Greek epics and mythology. He wrote about the Greeks in such poems as "The Lotus-Eaters," "Tithonus," and "Ulysses." In "Ulysses," Tennyson explores the hero's obsessive search for knowledge.

Notice the jump between the thesis statement and the rest of the paragraph. The opening sentences are very general. They do not discuss Ulysses as either a man or a poem, nor do they mention his quest for knowledge. The key ideas of the thesis are not developed in this poor introductory paragraph. Let us rewrite the opening so that it more suitably prepares for the thesis.

> The Ulysses of Tennyson's poem has a problem understanding his own motives, for after struggling ten years to return to Ithaca, he is seized by the desire to go traveling again. He attempts to explain this desire in many ways. He feels useless in Ithaca; he is not a patient administrator; he is misunderstood by his people, who "hoard, and sleep, and feed, and know not me" (l. 5). But the heart of his dissatisfaction is a desire for knowledge. In "Ulysses," Tennyson explores the hero's obsessive desire for knowledge.

Notice how in this second version, the author has gotten straight down to business by eliminating any superfluous discussion of Tennyson in general and focusing immediately on the issue of Ulysses' motives for leaving Ithaca. The thesis, then, is a summary of the discussion in the introduction. Clear and to the point, this new introduction well prepares the reader for the discussion that follows.

Conclusions

Sophisticated writers will attempt to conclude an essay by suggesting the significance of the observations for a wider understanding of life or of the author's work. First, let us look at an adequate conclusion to our paper on "Ulysses."

Ulysses is not a king satisfied with being an executive, a manager, a bureaucrat. In his past wanderings, Ulysses has accustomed himself to constantly-changing experience and ever-increasing knowledge. Ithaca has given him all of the experiences it contains, and now he feels compelled to "seek a newer world." (1. 57). With his band of aging mariners, he determinedly sets out, "to strive, to seek, to find, and not to yield." (1. 70)

Here is another conclusion, one that extends the meaning of the poem while summarizing the argument.

Through the poem, we come to understand Ulysses' needs better. For Ulysses, power is not enough, comfort is not enough; food, drink, shelter are insufficient for life. Ulysses has become aware of a great human emotion—curiosity, a desire for new knowledge and experience. Once that appetite is developed, it is not forgotten or easily sated. Ulysses' curiosity elevates him above the swashbuckling heroism of his fellow warriors like Achilles, and makes him a new hero for an age yet to come.

Body Paragraphs

Body paragraphs are used to support the thesis. Topic sentences break down the thesis into smaller, defendable units. For example, in the following paragraph Michael Ferber discusses William Blake's poem "London" (the text of which is on page 510). Ferber's thesis is that "London" is basically a political poem, despite the claims of some critics. He hopes to show in part how political the poem is by explaining some of the political implications of the words used in the poem. Here is the paragraph that explains the phrase "charter'd street."

We meet *charter'd street* right away. I have little to add to the discussions by David Erdman and E. P. Thompson of the connotations of *charter'd* which emerge when we set the poem in its historical context. London had a charter, granting it certain privileges or liberties, and so did many commercial associations in the City such as the East India Company, prominent along the banks of the Thames. Yet one man's charter is another's manacle; charters are exclusive. It was over just this two-sidedness of "charter" and its synonyms that Burke, Paine, and many others fought their pamphlet wars. In Part II of *Rights of Man*, published the year Blake probably wrote his poem (1792), Paine wrote, "It is a perversion of terms to say, that a charter gives rights. It operates by a contrary effect, that of taking rights away." The adjective "chartered" had as it still does the sense of "hired" or "leased," which combines with Paine's pejorative political nuance to suggest the monopolistic and exploitative practices of England's commercial empire. Under the regime of Pitt, as under every regime at least since the Conqueror, all Englishmen are "chartered," and the second half of the poem is a litany of typical cases: they are sold into slavery as chimney sweepers by their fathers, impressed into the army or navy for a few shillings, hired for a few hours as harlots, or bought and sold on the London marriage market.

Notice how full and yet economical the paragraph is. Ferber does not quote David Erdman and E. P. Thompson directly. He is content merely to refer to their work. His longest quotation is an elegant sentence from Thomas Paine, who perfectly exemplifies both Ferber's and Blake's position.

Quotations

One difficulty in writing a body paragraph lies in intergrating quotations into the flow of your own words. There are two general types of quotations: direct and indirect. An indirect quotation is a paraphrase of the author's words. For example, you might write:

> Ulysses says *that* his wife is old.

The word *that* indicates you are not quoting Ulysses' precise words. However, you might have written:

> Ulysses complains of being "matched with an aged wife."

This second version is a direct quotation; consequently, the quoted phrase is enclosed by quotation marks. Indirect quotations save both space and explanation. Often one can more easily paraphrase an author than integrate direct quotations. However, indirect quotations are of limited use. Because the words are yours, they are less convincing than the poet's own words. You open yourself to the charge of altering the poet's meaning to suit your own purposes.

Direct quotations may be either short or extensive. Short quotations can be as brief as one word or as long as two lines, and they are placed within the text of the essay. For example, the sentence "Ulysses complains of being 'matched with an aged wife,' " represents a short quotation. Extensive quotations are any that are longer than two lines of poetry or two sentences in length. They are generally isolated from the main text and distinguished from it in some way, as in this example of an essay that discusses Robert Frost's "Out, Out—." (The text of "Out, Out—" can be found on pages 440–41.)

> The most painful of these encounters [with the physical world], of course, takes place in "Out, Out—," where a boy helping some adults work with a power saw loses his right hand to the saw and then, as a result, life itself. The implicit epigraph to this poem is contained in the passage in *Macbeth* that follows the words of the title:
>
> > Out, out, brief candle!
> > Life's . . . a tale
> > Told by an idiot, full of sound and fury,
> > Signifying nothing.
>
> These lines, as I have pointed out in another connection, express not Frost's cynical view of life, but his tacit condemnation of a world in which people make things go wrong, starting with the refusal of the unnamed "they" to allow the boy an extra half-hour at the end of the day to watch the sunset.

Notice that since the quotation begins in the middle of the poetic line, the quotation is placed in a way that indicates its position. Indeed, a writer is always expected to indicate where each line ends. In short quotations the slash is used to indicate line breaks, as in this discussion of Wordsworth's "The Solitary Reaper."

> The aloneness of the singer is intensified in the second stanza when she is compared to the lone nightingale singing in far-off Arabia and to the solitary cuckoo "Breaking the silence of the seas/Among the farthest Hebrides." The melancholy tone and rhythm established in the first stanza are developed in the third stanza.

The foregoing passage indicates several aspects of quoting. When you quote, you *must* quote the passage exactly as it is written, without making any alterations. In the foregoing passage, the line break is indicated and Wordsworth's punctuation is preserved precisely as it was published.

Occasionally you will want to delete or add words to a quotation. Deletions must be indicated by an *ellipsis*, or three dots. Notice that in the quotation from Shakespeare, the author has deleted several words. The omission is indicated by an ellipsis. One should delete only unimportant words or phrases. You do not want to alter the meaning of the text by eliminating essential words. Additions are indicated by placing the inserted words in brackets. For example, note the addition in this sentence about "Out, Out—":

> The boy in Frost's poem has his life snuffed "out [like a] brief candle."

In quotations one may also replace pronouns with their antecedent nouns. One must be careful to preserve the original meaning, however. For example, in Tennyson's poem, Ulysses always speaks of himself in the first person. Such references may not be clear when quoted. In the following passage, note how a proper name has been substituted for the pronoun *me*.

> The people of Ithaca are lazy, stupid and barely civilized. They "hoard, and sleep, and feed, and know not [Ulysses]."

Deletions and additions are often necessary to integrate quotations into the text. Many writers prefer numerous short quotations over long ones. By quoting frequently, an essayist can constantly refer to the text and keep the poet's words in the reader's mind.

Not all quotations need to be preceded by a comma. A comma is not necessary if the quotation is part of the sentence's flow. Study the punctuation of the following two sentences.

1. Ulysses says, "I cannot rest from travel."
2. Ulysses is a man who "cannot rest from travel."

In the first sentence there is a grammatical break between the sentence and the quotation. In the second the quotation is part of the sentence's flow; thus no commas are needed in sentence 2. Examine how quotations are used in the passages we have studied. You will notice that careful writers try to integrate their quotations into the flow of their sentences.

Documentation

Writers should acknowledge the source of any ideas or quotations they have used by parenthetical notations in text and by a list of works cited at the end of the essay.

Why do authors document their sources? The practice may seem tedious, troublesome, and unnecessary, but it does serve important functions.

The first reason for documentation is to help the reader. Because most quotations are relatively short, the reader may wish to understand the context of the quotation or more of what the original author has to say. Without a citation, the reader would have no way to find the source of the quotation.

Second, documentation is a means of maintaining intellectual honesty. We are all indebted to others for ideas, skills, and knowledge, and it is only proper to acknowledge that debt. Without such acknowledgment we would be claiming other people's thoughts and language as our own. To the educated person, stealing people's ideas is as heinous as stealing their property. Indeed, copyright and patent laws make it a punishable offense to steal someone's words and ideas without compensation and permission.

Documentation must contain the author's name, the title of the work, and the page number citing where the quotation appears. In the case of an article, you must note the name of the journal in which it appeared and the volume and date of its appearance. For books, you must note the place of publication, the publisher, and the date of publication.

We cannot give a complete list of all the items you may need to document. For a complete list, consult the latest edition of the *MLA Handbook for Writers of Research Papers*.

PREPARING A LIST OF WORKS

On a separate page at the end of your essay or report, you must prepare a list of works cited. The page should be headed "Works Cited," and the list arranged in alphabetical order. Here are several of the commonest kinds of entries:

A book by a single author

> Huberman, Elizabeth. *The Poetry of Edwin Muir: The Field of Good and Ill.* New York: Oxford UP, 1971.

An article

> Mengert, James G. "The Resistance of Milton's Sonnets," *English Literary Renaissance* 11 (1981): 81–95.

A work in an anthology

> García Márquez, Gabriel. "A Very Old Man with Enormous Wings." *The Heath Guide to Literature.* Ed. David Bergman and Daniel Mark Epstein. 2nd ed. Lexington: Heath, 1987. 000–000.

PREPARING PARENTHETICAL REFERENCES

When a list of works are cited at the end of the essay or report, you need only refer in parentheses to the name of the author followed by a page number to let the reader know where you obtained a specific idea or found a particular quotation. Sometimes if the author's name is not mentioned in the text, you will have to indicate both the author's name and the page number to identify the work. The following examples illustrate the most common types of citation:

Parenthetical note when author is not mentioned in the text

> Latin American authors have developed out of folk traditions and popular culture a style called "magical realism." One story includes a molting angel and a woman transformed into a spider as punishment for disobeying her parents (García Márquez 186).

Parenthetical note when author is mentioned

> Latin American authors have developed out of folk traditions and popular culture a style called "magical realism." In one story of Gabriel García Márquez, a molting angel falls to earth and a woman who appears in a carnival is transformed into a spider for disobeying her parents (186).

Parenthetical note of direct quotation

> Latin American authors have developed out of folk traditions and popular culture a style called "magical realism." In Gabriel García Márquez's a "A Very Old Man with Enormous Wings," a traveling carnival contains a "woman who had been changed into a spider for having disobeyed her parents" (186).

Parenthetical note of direct quotation without author's name

> Latin American authors have developed out of folk traditions and popular culture a style called "magical realism." In one instance, for example, a fallen angel competes for popularity with a "woman who had been changed into a spider for having disobeyed her parents" (García Márquez 186).

Bibliographies

Short essays do not need bibliographies. However, teachers may require bibliographies in order to give students practice in writing them. A bibliography lists alphabetically by the author's last name all the works consulted. Thus our list of books and articles would look like this.

> Huberman, Elizabeth. *The Poetry of Edwin Muir: The Field of Good and Evil.* New York: Oxford UP, 1971.
> Mengert, James G. "The Resistance of Milton's Sonnets," *English Literary Renaissance* 11 (1981). 81–95.
> Tennyson, Alfred Lord. "Ulysses," in *The Poems of Tennyson.* Ed. Christopher Ricks, London: Longman's, 1969. 560–566.

Five Complete Essays

Here are five different essays for you to read and study. Two are by scholars and are written for scholars. However, they can show you valuable techniques for writing about literature. The essay on Robert Lowell's "Skunk Hour" was written by an advanced student of literature. The last two essays were written by beginning students of literature. All in all, the essays should provide you with a spectrum of techniques and sophistication. All the stories, plays, and poems mentioned in the essays may be found in this book.

ERNEST W. SULLIVAN, II

The Cur in "The Chrysanthemums"

Anyone reading John Steinbeck's "The Chrysanthemums" cannot help being struck by the repeated association of unpleasant canine characteristics with the otherwise attractive Elisa Allen. These associations identify her with the visiting tinker's mongrel dog, further suggesting a parallel between the Allens' two ranch shepherds and the tinker and Elisa's husband, Henry. The correspondences between people and dogs elucidate the social and sexual relationships of the three humans, as well as foreshadow and explain Elisa's failure at the end of the story to escape from her unproductive and sterile lifestyle.

The dog imagery related to Elisa is uncomplimentary. In her garden, she destroys unpleasant creatures such as "aphids," "bugs," "snails," "cutworms," and similar "pests" with her "terrier fingers."[1] When aroused by the tinker, she "crouched low like a fawning dog" (p. 18). Finally, in response to the tinker's assertion that his life of freedom "ain't the right kind of life for a woman," she bares her teeth in hostile fashion: "Her upper lip raised a little, showing her teeth" (p. 19). Burrowing in flower gardens, fawning, snarling—not a very pleasant picture of man's best friend.

The last two images directly link Elisa to the tinker's mongrel, and their physical descriptions clearly parallel these two unfortunates. She kneels before the tinker like a dog would to shake hands: "Kneeling there, her hand went out toward his legs in the greasy black trousers. Her hesitant fingers almost touched the cloth. Then her hand dropped to the ground. She crouched low like a fawning dog" (p. 18). As Elisa bared her teeth in resistance to the tinker, so his mongrel resisted the two Allen ranch shepherds "with raised hackles and bared teeth" (p. 13). Additionally, the cur is "lean and rangy" (p. 13); Elisa is "lean and strong" (p. 10). Finally, of course, the tinker's mongrel, unlike the ranch shepherds, contains a mixture of dog breeds, and Elisa's personality mixes masculine and feminine elements.[2]

Whereas Elisa shares several characteristics with the cur, the tinker and Henry resemble the two ranch shepherds. The two shepherds were born to their jobs, which they perform instinctively. Confident that "Pots, pans, knives, sisors, lawn mores" can all be "Fixed" (p. 13), the tinker feels at home in his occupation and world: " 'I ain't in any hurry, ma'am. I go from Seattle to San Diego and back every year. Takes all my time. About six months each way. I aim to follow nice weather' " (p. 14). Henry Allen is also successful at his job and derives satisfaction from it: "I sold those thirty head of three-year-old steers. Got nearly my own price, too" (p. 11). On the other hand, Elisa, like the mongrel, does not participate in the main work on which her livelihood depends,

---

[1] John Steinbeck, the *The Long Valley* (New York: Viking Press, 1956), pp. 10–11. All quotations are from this text.

[2] The mixed elements of Elisa's personality are also suggested in the " 'good bitter smell' " (p. 16) of the chrysanthemums with which she is usually identified.

even though her husband suggests that she should become useful: "I wish you'd work out in the orchard and raise some apples that big" (p. 11). Both Elisa and the cur are merely companions for their respective breadwinners, their subservient position suggested by Elisa's kneeling before the tinker: "She was kneeling on the ground looking up at him" (p. 18).

The interaction of the three dogs closely parallels that of the three people and foreshadows Elisa's eventual failure to escape her confined lifestyle. When the mongrel darts from its accustomed position beneath the tinker's wagon, the two ranch dogs shepherd it back. The mongrel considers fighting, but, aware that it could not overcome the two dogs secure on their home ground, retreats angrily back under the wagon and protection of its owner: "The rangy dog darted from between the wheels and ran ahead. Instantly the two ranch shepherds flew out at him. Then all three stopped, and with stiff and quivering tails, with taut straight legs, with ambassadorial dignity, they slowly circled, sniffing daintily. . . . The newcomer dog, feeling out-numbered, lowered his tail and retired under the wagon with raised hackles and bared teeth" (p. 13).

Elisa, in the course of the story, moves out of her accustomed role to challenge Henry and the tinker on their home ground, their occupations and sexuality. In response to Henry's comment that she could put her skills to productive use in the orchards, "Elisa's eyes sharpened. 'Maybe I could do it, too' " (p. 11). But she never does. Her challenge to his sexuality is equally unfulfilled; in response to her appearance in "the dress which was the symbol of her prettiness" (p. 21), Henry observes that "You look strong enough to break a calf over your knee, happy enough to eat it like a watermelon" (pp. 21–22) and goes to turn on the car. Elisa directly expresses an urge to compete in the tinker's occupation: " 'You might be surprised to have a rival some time. I can sharpen scissors, too. And I can beat the dents out of little pots. I could show you what a woman might do' " (p. 19). The tinker rebuts her challenge: " 'It ain't the right kind of a life for a woman' " (p. 19), and her career as a tinker never gets started. The tinker's feigned interest in the chrysanthemums clearly arouses Elisa's sexual instincts: "Her breast swelled passionately" (p. 18), and she does her unconscious best to arouse his: "Elisa's voice grew husky. . . . 'When the night is dark—why, the stars are sharp-pointed, and there's quiet. Why, you rise up and up! Every pointed star gets driven into your body. It's like that. Hot and sharp and—lovely' " (p. 18). And, as had her husband, the tinker deflects the conversation to one involving a less carnal appetite: " 'It's nice, just like you say. Only when you don't have no dinner, it ain't' " (p. 18).

In each case, when Elisa threatened to encroach upon male territory, she was rebuffed and shepherded back to the refuge of her submissive and unproductive place. Elisa, like the cur, might be " 'a bad dog in a fight when he gets started' " (p. 13), but, like the cur, she rarely, if ever, gets started: " 'sometimes [he does] not [get started] for weeks and weeks' " (p. 13). The positions of the dogs after the meeting between Elisa and the tinker foreshadow her final defeat. The cur "took his place between the back wheels" (p. 20), and, with Elisa's occupational and sexual challenge to the tinker rebuffed, the ranch shepherds could cease their watchfulness: "Only the dogs had heard. They lifted their heads toward her from their sleeping in the dust, and then stretched out their chins and settled asleep again" (p. 20).

Interestingly, neither the mongrel nor Elisa gives up until "out-numbered." Any previous challenges to her husband's role as breadwinner and sexual aggressor have apparently been frustrated; the story offers no evidence of her doing farm work; they have no children; and Henry responds unromantically to Elisa's effort to make herself sexually attractive. Yet her occupational and sexual challenges to the tinker show that she has not given up. After the tinker also rejects her by discarding the chrysanthemums that she had given him, Elisa, like the out-numbered cur baring his teeth at the two shepherds, vents her anger and frustration over her defeat through her description of the pain inflicted upon men in fights: " 'I've read how they break noses, and blood runs down their chests. I've read how the fighting gloves get heavy and soggy with blood' " (p. 23). Overcome by the two men, Elisa never gets started in the fight to escape her role; she even decides against vicarious participation in the fight: " 'I don't want to go [to the fights]. I'm sure I don't' " (p. 23). She retreats to the safety of her accustomed unproductive and sexless role, "crying weakly—like an old woman" (p. 23).

DAVID MATTHEW ROSEN

Time, Identity, and Context in Wyatt's Verse

In reading Thomas Wyatt's poem "They Flee from Me," one is struck by the power of the human voice speaking in its lines. Though a lithe and simple lyric, "They Flee from Me" resonates with nuances of emotion that encompass not only the speaker's distress at the loss of love, but also his distress at the irrevocable passage of time.[1] How does Wyatt create this remarkable voice full of the evanescence of beautiful moments? It is through the layering of time, the juxtaposition of incident in a way that suggests the dissolution of one moment into the next, and so conveys impermanence, frustration, despair.

In "They Flee from Me" each stanza creates a context for the next. In the opening stanza, the poet relates his experience with some ambiguous creatures in an unclear past by juxtaposing their former tameness with their present return to a wilder state. The fragility of their momentary tameness is heightened by its distance in time and by our awareness of its extraordinary character. The preciousness of this experience and the poignancy of its loss serve as the context for our understanding of what follows.

The second stanza recreates a more particular time when unexpectedly the beloved kissed her lover. When the woman embraces the poet, the moment is sweet for being both unexpected and desired. Yet we are aware that, although longed for, the moment is disconnected from what appears to be the natural flow of things—the woman's usual behaviour, her distance. Like the creatures', it is the possibility of the woman's reversion to a wilder state, the sense of her underlying wildness that is brought to the moment, that, in fact, makes the moment precious. The woman and the creatures are so desirable because they can never be fully possessed.[2] They are, like creatures in much of Wyatt's verse, too complex to be contained by any person or any arbitrary set of rules.

The moment of the kiss, nonetheless, remains for the poet a sacred moment, fixed and transcendent, as he exclaims at the beginning of the second stanza. But this transcendent past, this luminous moment—that in religion would begin a new era and order different from the temporal one—remains unfulfilled expectation. In a world pressed forward by time, the kiss is inevitably juxtaposed with events as they actually turn out. Like the past changing to a present with which it is both connected and disconnected, the woman changes. Like time itself, she recognizes her relationship with her lover, but like time, she invites "newfangledness." Although to the poet's idealistic mind the woman's actions seem cruel and unexpected, they are no more cruel and unexpected than the creatures' actions with which they are linked. Only the poet's static position

---

[1] For an amusingly jaundiced review of critical background, see Richard L. Greene, "Wyatt's 'They Flee from Me' and the Busily Seeking Critics," *Bucknell Review* 12, no. 3 (Fall 1964), pp. 17–30. Some have not been intimidated: Leonard E. Nathan, "Tradition and Newfangledness in Wyatt's 'They Flee from Me,'" *ELH* 32, no. 1 (1965), pp. 1–16; Leigh Winser, "The Question of Love Tradition in Wyatt's 'They Flee from Me,'" *Essays in Literature (Western Illinois University)* 2, no. 1 (Spring 1975), pp. 3–9; Carolyn Chiapelli, "A Late Gothic Vein in Wyatt's 'They Flee from Me,'" *Renaissance and Reformation* 1 (New Series), no. 2 (1977), pp. 95–102.

[2] Michael McCanles, "Love and Power in the Poetry of Sir Thomas Wyatt," *Modern Language Quarterly* 29, no. 2 (June 1968), pp. 145–160.

makes them seem unexpected. In terms of the general lesson of the creatures and the poem's special logic, the poet should have anticipated what would happen.

This conflict of expectation and event is the crux of the poem, then. The poet, unlike the changing and complex world about him, remains rigid in his view of things. As a result things out of his control seem to happen to him. His sense of his own helplessness and our sense of it as well is heightened by the awareness that we develop and share as the poem develops, the awareness that time moves, that past and present do not form a pattern, that the world is complex and therefore its moments of simplicity are precious.

This sense of the distance of moments in a continuous time is intensified by the lover's static position, layering the final question of the poem with real emotion: "I would fain know what she has deserved." It is useless to answer, useless to ask. One might as properly inquire what "they" which flee deserve. There is no way for the speaker to ask for judgment, to assume control. By recourse to what system of rules? The question is heavy with emotion, vibrating sadness, cynicism, argumentativeness and more.

Thus when we examine the events of the poem, we find that they lead to complications that result in the poet's despair. And if we look again we will find that even the poet, though he won't admit it, has the same complexities and changeableness; he too is human and affected by time. We see this when he is taken in the woman's arms, for then it is he who is like the creatures who fed at his hand. However, when the woman gives him leave to fly, unlike the creatures and unlike her, he cannot. In spite of, or because of these various poses, the lover exposes his own complexity, a complexity he shares with all creatures. Although the speaker tries to maintain a steadfast position, we can see that his view continuously evolves as it copes with the contexts of past actions. This forced complexity of the lover's view grinds against his static faith and only serves to isolate him further in a world he cannot account for, control, or accept. In this way time past becomes more precious and more hopelessly lost. In the end, his final words are rather unconvincing as a call for justice, unconvincing to himself as well, it seems. Yet they are convincing as an expression of his mixed and authentic emotions. Our appreciation of the emotions that shape these simple words attests to the thickening of experience that the progress of the poem and Wyatt's handling of time have achieved.

From this poem we learn that the past acts like an after-image of a continuous action. The after-image continues to affect our view of the present moment from which it is now disjoined and which it can only partly explain. The progress of the poem is a process of accumulating detail, of accumulating these images that create a context for a present in which it becomes clear how time works and how complex things are. Reading becomes a process of changing or modifying our own viewpoints so that reading resembles the time which it often contemplates and in which it takes place. In other words, our sense of loss develops as the poem develops; as the reader must give up one beautiful word or image to go on to the next, so the poet has given up each moment of his life, savoring it and unwillingly losing it. Our sense of loss when the poem stops is like the poet's own sense of loss. Although the poet can never recover the beautiful moments that he has lost, luckily we may reread the poem and through it reexperience the beauty of Wyatt's own evanescent human voice expressing his poignant sense of loss, beauty and isolation.

ELEANOR LESTER

Skunk Hour: An Explication

Robert Lowell's poem ''Skunk Hour'' is dedicated to
Elizabeth Bishop, whose poem ''The Armadillo'' Lowell
used as a model (On ''Skunk Hour'' 109).[1] The poems do
indeed contain many similarities. But whereas Bishop
concludes her poem with the armadillo clenching ''a weak
mailed fist/ . . . ignorant against the sky,'' (123) a
sign of impotent resistance against man's invasion,
Lowell's skunk ''jabs her wedge—head in a cup/of sour
cream'' (46—47) and will not be frightened away. The
skunk triumphs over both man and time not by resisting
them, but by adapting herself to them. For Richard Wilbur, ''they stand for stubborn, unabashed livingness,
and for [Lowell's] own refusal . . . to cease desiring a
world of vitality, freedom, and love,'' (87). The skunk
may not be the sweetest creature, but she survives.

The skunk's acceptance is in marked contrast to the
people who inhabit Nautilus Island. The ''heiress'' who
is '' in her dotage'' (6) fights the encroachment of civilization, and thus

> she buys up all
> the eyesores facing her shore
> and lets them fall. [10—12]

The result does not improve nature but increases the
number of ruins. Like the heiress, the decorator fights a
futile battle to improve the drab world by decorating
his shop. Nevertheless, ''there's no money in the
work,'' and ''he'd rather marry'' (23—24). The decorator's resistance achieves nothing.

The people of Nautilus Island are not regenerative.
The decorator is homosexual. The heiress has produced
one child, but he is a bishop with vows of celibacy.
''The summer millionaire/who seemed to leap from an
L. L. Bean/catalogue'' (14—16) is lost, either bankrupt
or dead. In either case, his holdings are not passed
down to his offspring, but sold off to the highest bid-
der. Lowell himself commented that in ''Skunk Hour,''
''Sterility howls through the scenery'' (On ''Skunk
Hour'' 107).

However, the most desperate character of all is the
speaker of the poem, Lowell himself. He admits that his

''mind's not right'' (30) and believes that like Milton's Satan, he himself is hell. A Puritan and a peeping
Tom, he prowls the local lovers' lane hoping to catch
some couple making love. Yet the locale of the lovers'
lane is not particularly auspicious; it tops the
''hill's skull'' (26) at the place ''where the graveyard
shelves in the town'' (29). In short it is a place not of
regeneration but of death, a location which Lowell
ghoulishly haunts.

Only the skunks thrive; in fact, they have taken over
the town:

> They march on their soles up Main Street,
> white stripes, moonstruck eyes' red fire
> under the chalk-dry and spar spire
> of the Trinitarian Church [39–42]

There may be something sinister in the ''red fire'' of
their eyes, but at least they show more life than the
''chalk-dry'' Trinitarian Church. Indeed, the skunk
does not march alone; she leads ''her column of kittens'' (45).

The skunks' triumph is not wholly laudable. They are
smelly. They are scavengers; they swill ''the garbage
pail'' (45). Their eyes are sinister. But they are not
merely bad. They have beautiful ostrich plume tails and
''moonstruck'' eyes. Yet, their survival rests not on
their beauty but on their adaptability to the world
around them. Unlike the humans, they are not caught up
in any of the outdated beliefs, fashions, or
hierarchies.

The choice Lowell seems to be giving us is not very attractive. We can either hold on to our cherished beliefs
and kill ourselves off, or we can become that somewhat
stinky and homely scavenger and flourish. Lowell is
trying to frighten us with this choice, but I for one
''will not scare'' (48) and hold out for a better
bargain.

Works Cited

Bishop, Elizabeth. *The Complete Poems.* New York: Farrar, 1969.

Lowell, Robert. ''On 'Skunk Hour.' '' *The Contemporary Poet as Artist and Critic.* Ed. Anthony Ostroff. Boston: Little, 1964.

———. *Life Studies.* New York: Noonday, 1964.

Wilbur, Richard. ''On Robert Lowell's 'Skunk Hour.' '' *The Contemporary Poet as Artist and Critic.* Ed. Anthony Ostroff. Boston: Little, 1964.

JOHN LESSNER

Hamlet and the Gravedigger

Hamlet reveals his thoughts on death in Act V when he
speaks to the gravedigger. This discussion is not the
first time the Dane shows his fascination with death and
decay. For example in the ''To be or not to be'' soliloquy, he speaks of his own death, and in the scene in
which Claudius prays (III, iii), he contemplates killing his uncle. But in his conversation with the gravedigger, he most clearly shows the tension in his ideas.
On the one hand, he wants to grow easy with death. On the
other, he is afraid and repulsed by it.

Hamlet is unusually concerned about the decaying process. He asks the gravedigger, ''How long will a man lie
i' the earth ere he rot?'' (157). He also inquires why a
tanner's body lasts longer than most people's. In fact
Hamlet becomes so interested in the scientific questions
of decay that he forgets his original question to the
sexton—for whom is he digging the grave? This morbid
curiosity is also revealed in Hamlet's question over the
identity of Yorick's skull.

Hamlet's discussion leads him to the recognition that
death is an equalizing force, affecting everyone and
reducing all to the same level. Alexander the Great
surely rotted as quickly as Yorick and smelled just as
bad. A tanner's body would last longer than Alexander's,
even though Alexander was a great conqueror. Death knows
no social or political class. After his death, Hamlet
will no longer be the Prince of Denmark. Like Caesar, he
is likely to end up as a stopper in a beer barrel.

In strong contrast to Hamlet's obsession with death is
the gravedigger's nonchalance. This country fellow has
been sexton and gravedigger for thirty years. He is not
at all intrigued or awed by, or afraid of death and decay. It is part of his job and everyday life. He takes
his task so lightly that he sings and jokes while digging. When he comes across a skull, he throws it aside
and goes on digging.

The gravedigger is so comfortable with death that he
can look beyond the foulness of decay and see in the
corpses the lives they once contained. When Hamlet handles the skull, he says his ''gorge rises'' (181).

Hamlet is repulsed by and afraid of this all-too-real reminder of death. Hamlet tells the skull, ''get you to my lady's chamber, and tell her, let her paint an inch thick to this favour she must come.'' But death cannot be disguised or avoided. Death dressed up is still death.

We can also see Hamlet's uneasiness when he discusses the uses of the dead. Three times he alludes to the uses. He imagines them as stoppers or plugs: a bunghole for a cask, a stopper for a beer barrel, and a patch in the wall to keep the wind out. But it is important to note that the dead are merely parts of a larger whole and not Hamlet's primary object. The dead do not make up the cask, barrel, or wall; they are merely placed in them. The dead have no true value in themselves, but only as patches or plugs. This observation returns Hamlet to his central recognition that great and obscure alike are reduced to insignificance by death.

Through his encounter with the gravedigger Hamlet comes more to terms with death. His reconciliation with death is one of the major movements of the play. Death is an alien and powerful force for Hamlet, but in his conversation with the gravedigger he comes to grips with his fears.

LESLIE MILLER

O'Hara's Conversation with the Sun

Before his death in 1966, Frank O'Hara was known as a
poet only to a small group of friends and to the few who
occasionally stumbled upon him in periodicals. ''A True
Account of Talking to the Sun at Fire Island'' is an affirmation of his importance as a poet. The Sun is Faith,
the faith that someday the public will notice him and be
convinced of his value.

The Sun is the faith that O'Hara seems to be lacking.
According to the Sun, O'Hara is under attack from both
conservative and avant-garde poets. He tells O'Hara:

> Now, I've heard some
> say you're crazy, they being excessively
> calm themselves to my mind, and other
> crazy poets think that you're a boring
> reactionary. (11.31–35)

But the Sun wishes to awaken O'Hara to his particular
virtues and tells him not to pay attention to critics.
''Just keep right on,'' the Sun encourages him. ''I like
it.'' (44)

The Sun also gives O'Hara faith in his subject matter.
O'Hara wrote about his friends and the events happening
right around him, but he could not believe that outsiders would recognize the value of those experiences. The
Sun, however, urges O'Hara to make his poetry out of his
common experiences. ''Always embrace things, people,
earth / sky stars, as I do, freely and with / the appropriate sense of space,'' (11.65–67) the Sun advises.

Furthermore, The Sun advises O'Hara not to be worried
about his poetic predecessors who wrote to philoso-
phize. O'Hara must keep faith that he does not have to
write like the famous poets of the past. The Sun has democratic taste, and tells O'Hara:

> And don't worry about your lineage
> poetic or natural. The Sun shines on
> the jungle, you know, on the tundra
> the sea, the ghetto. Wherever you were
> I knew it and saw you moving. (46–49)

Inspiration is not limited to only a few poets in a few
places. The Sun's faith and inspiration can smile on
O'Hara anywhere.

At the poem's conclusion, the Sun leaves because ''they're calling / me.'' (ll.77–78) When O'Hara asks, ''Who are they?'' the Sun mysteriously answers, ''They're calling to you / too.'' (ll.81–82) Destiny speaks to both O'Hara and the Sun and through them as well. The ''tiny poem'' (l.74) left in O'Hara's brain is a colossal one that shows his importance not only to himself and his friends, but to all of us who stumble upon him and stay for a while.

Glossary of Literary Terms

Action. In a drama, the behavior of characters and succession of events that tell the story. 797–98, 816–822

Allegory. A literary or dramatic device in which the events of a narrative or an implied narrative obviously and continuously refer to another simultaneous structure of events or ideas, whether historical events, moral or philosophical ideas, or natural phenomena. 540–543

Alliteration. The repetition of an initial consonant sound in two or more words of a line (or line group), to produce a noticeable artistic effect, as in "The sails did sigh like sedge" (Coleridge). 593–97

Allusion. Tacit reference to another literary work, to another art, to history, to contemporary figures, and the like. 567–568

Amphitheater. An outdoor theater with tiers of seats rising gradually outward from the central playing area. 821

Amplificatio. The Latin term in classical rhetoric for amplification of style or the expansion of detail and elaboration of effects. 270

Anagnorisis. See *Recognition.*

Anapest. A metrical unit of three syllables, of which the first two are unstressed and the last is stressed. 579

Anaphora. Repetition of the initial word in several successive lines of poetry. 462

Antagonist. A character who forms an obstacle to the protagonist's completion of his goal. See *Villain.* 119

Antistrophe. See *Pindaric ode.*

Note: Page numbers following definitions refer to discussion in the text.

Anti-utopia. See *Utopia.*

Aside. See *Stage whisper.*

Assonance. As distinguished from rhyme, the repetition of vowel sounds preceded by unlike consonants, as in "Be near me when my light is low." 593–97

Ballad. Usually a narrative poem in quatrains in which the second and fourth lines rhyme. In a ballad, the first and third lines are typically four feet long, and the second and fourth lines three feet long. 434–35, 625–26

Ballade. A form that consists of three eight-line stanzas and an envoi.

Bard. A poet-reciter in a preliterate or semiliterate society; more loosely, a poet or poet-singer. 432, 436

Blank verse. Unrhymed iambic pentameter lines. 578

Brevitas. The Latin term in classical rhetoric for brevity—for concise, to-the-point writing. 270

Caesura. A rhetorical pause within a poetic line, usually in the middle. 586

Carpe diem. A theme in many love poems, in which a lover is implored not to be hesitant in affection (Latin for "seize the day"). 458

Casting. The selection of actors for a drama.

Catastrophe. The outcome of a tragedy; from the Greek, meaning "a downward turn." 819–20

Catastrophic plot. A drama where the action begins *after* the climactic event, and the emotional climax comes in the discovery of that event.

Catharsis. From Greek "cleansing." The relief that comes after witnessing the catastrophe of a tragedy. 914

A character. The performer of a fictional action. 115, 863

The Character. A literary form in which a character type is described. The form was orginated by the Greek writer Theophrastus. 116

Chiasmus. A rhetorical device in which words initially presented are restated in reverse order. An example is the sentence, "For we that live to please, must please to live." 678

Chorus. In ancient Greek drama, a group of actors who sang and danced in unison, predicting and commenting upon the actions of the main characters. 820

Climax. The point in the story at which protagonists have definitely achieved or failed to achieve their central goal. 74

Climax of dramatic action (turning point). The point at which the hero's fortune turns from good to bad in a tragedy, and from bad to good in a comedy. 818–19

Climax of emotion. The point in a drama that moves the audience most deeply.

Comedy. From the Greek *komos*, meaning revel. A drama that shows the change in the protagonist's fortune from bad to good.

Comedy of ideas. Comedies that support philosophical or political dialogue.

Comedy of manners. High comedy developed during the Restoration, characterized by subtle wit and ingenious dramatic situations that satirize prevailing manners and morals. 1104

Comic relief. In a tragedy, a scene of light humor that provides relief for the spectator after a violent or pathetic scene.

Complication. The introduction of an obstacle to the goal of the protagonist of a drama.

Conceit. An intricate, extended, or far-fetched metaphor or simile that arouses a feeling of surprise, shock, or amusement. 527–31

Concrete poem. A poem in which the visual arrangement of the letters and words suggests the meaning. 649–53

Conflict. The obstacles which prevent the protagonist from achieving his or her goal. In drama, the disagreement between characters or within a character that precipitates the play's action. 74

Connotative meaning. See *Denotative meaning.*

Consistency of character. A convention in which a character's actions are consistent with his or her behavioral traits. 119

Corpus. A Latin term used to refer to an author's entire "body" of work. 230

Costume designer. The member of the artistic staff of a dramatic production who creates or appropriates whatever the actors wear in the play. 800

Cothurnus. An elevator shoe used by actors in ancient Greek drama. 822

Couplet. A two-line stanza, usually rhymed. 626–28

Crisis. In drama, the most intense moment of any scene. 818

Cross-purposes. A technique of comic irony, in which two characters think they are discussing the same thing, but are not.

Dactyl. A metrical unit of three syllables, of which the first is stressed and the second two are not. 579

Denotative meaning. Literal meaning; the dictionary meaning as opposed to connotative meaning, which is the associations (historical, evaluative, and economic) the word conveys. For example, *car* and *automobile* refer to the same object, but *automobile* is more formal and old-fashioned than *car.* 507

Denouement. French for "untying." In fiction, the end of the story in which the fate of the characters is clearly set out. In drama, the part of a play that answers our questions. In a comedy, the solving of the problems of the protagonists. 76, 819–20

Deus ex machina. Latin for "the god from the machine." In ancient drama, a god who descended upon the stage to rescue the protagonist from doom. Hence, any unexpected or unlikely event that changes the outcome of a drama.

Developing characters. Characters whose personality traits alter in the course of a story, usually as a result of events narrated in the story. 119

Diction. The writer's choice of words. 618–20

Didactic poetry. Poetry whose purpose is to teach. 611–614

Dimeter. A metrical line with two feet. 578

Director. The head of the artistic staff of a dramatic production. It is the director's responsibility to see that all aspects of production—casting, scenery, lighting, etc.—express the playwright's intention. 800

Doggerel. Rough, poorly constructed verse, characterized by strong and monotonous rhyme and rhythm, cheap sentiment, triviality, and lack of dignity. 589–90, 673

Double dactyl. A complicated comic form of eight lines, the fourth and eighth of which rhyme.

Drama of character. A drama in which the development of character is more important than the plotting or progress of action.

Dramatic irony (also called *irony of situation*). A situation in which the author and the audience share knowledge by which they can recognize the characters' actions as wholly inappropriate, or the characters' words as possessing a significance unknown to the characters themselves. 548, 866

Dramatic monologue. A poem in which the poet adopts a fictive or historical voice, or persona, and from which an entire dramatic scene may be inferred. 478–79

Dramatic situation. The dynamic relation of a character to an objective and its intervening obstacles. 805–06, 816

Dramatis personae. Latin for "the persons in the play." 802–04

Dystopia. See *Utopia.*

Elegy. A lyric, usually formal in tone and diction, suggested either by the death of an actual person or by the poet's contemplation of tragic aspects of life. 462–67

Encomium. A song praising not a god but a hero, sung at the *komos*, the jubilant procession or revels that celebrated the victor in the Olympic games. 459–62

End rhyme. Rhymes at the ends of lines of poetry. 589

End-stopped line. A line that ends where the syntactic unit ends, at a clear pause, or at the end of a sentence. 586

English or Shakespearean sonnet. A fourteen-line poem rhyming *abab cdcd efef gg*. It consists of three quatrains and a closing couplet. 630–31

Enjambment. The employment of run-on lines that carry the sense of statement from one line to another without rhetorical or syntactic pause at the end of the line. 586

Envoi. A short concluding section of a poem that bids the poem farewell or contains concluding remarks.

Epic. A long narrative poem. Primary epics are passed down orally and have a legendary author (for example, the *Iliad* and the *Odyssey*, which are traditionally ascribed to Homer). A secondary epic is one written by a known author. 436

Epigram. A poem with the qualities of an inscription, and thus short, pointed, and often with a witty or surprising turn of thought. 469

Epistolary poem. A letter in verse. 485–87

Epode. See *Pindaric ode.* 640

Exposition. In fiction, those narrative passages that establish the basic details of the story, such as the setting, time, and characters. In drama, the scenes that introduce the characters and the dramatic situation. 74, 817–18, 917–18

Expressionism. In theater, the dramatization of a character's emotion or thought at the expense of realism. Characters of expressionist dramas tend to be types, the scenes roughly or mysteriously defined.

Extras. Minor characters in a drama who have neither specific names nor significant roles in the progress of the action. 803–04

Fable. A story in which animals are given human attributes and represent moral, philosophic, psychological, or political positions. Fables typically have morals as their conclusions. 543–545

Falling action (also called *declining action,* or *the return*). The scenes of a tragedy that show the hero or heroine as they fall from power. In a comedy, those scenes that show the villains or forces of adversity in decline. 819

Farce. Dramatic comedy relying heavily upon clowning, slap-stick, and improbable romantic situations. 1103–04

Feminine ending. An unstressed syllable at the end of a line. 584

Feminine rhyme. A rhyme in which the similarity of sound is in both of the last two syllables—for example, *dreary/weary.* 590

Figurative language. Language that uses figures of speech and that cannot be taken literally. 519

First-person narrative. A story told in the voice of one of the characters who participates in the action. 22–24

Flat character. A character with a single behavioral trait or a stereotyped group of behaviors. 115–16

Foot. A measurable, patterned unit of poetic rhythm usually consisting of one stressed syllable and one or more unstressed syllables. 578

Formulae. Stock phrases used by poets in reciting oral poems. 432–34

Framed story. A story in which another story is told, frequently by one of the characters. In Chaucer's *Canterbury Tales,* a band of pilgrims journeying to Canterbury Cathedral amuse each other on the way with short tales. The framed story is made up of two parts: (1) the frame, and (2) the tale-within-a-tale. 162–63

Free verse. Poetry that is both unrhymed and without a regular meter, although it may be more or less rhythmical. 623–25

French scene. A unit of dramatic action uninterrupted by exits or entrances. 1148

Freytag's pyramid. A diagram of the five-part movement of plot in classic drama. 817

Genre. A term used to describe various types of literature. For example, prose can be divided into fiction, autobiography, biography, history, essays, letters, etc. These genres can be further divided into smaller genres or *sub-genres.* 801–02

Greek Old Comedy. The fantastical satires of Aristophanes (447–380 B.C.). 1103

Groundlings. The spectators who sat or stood on the ground at performances of Elizabethan plays. 918

Haiku. An Oriental lyric form of seventeen syllables in three lines of five, seven, and five syllables, respectively. The haiku must state or imply a season and, except for modern innovations, is almost wholly restricted to natural images. 498–99, 587, 644–48

Heptameter. A metrical line with seven feet. 578

Hero. In Greek literature, a noble warrior. The principal male character in a story, poem, or play. 119, 863, 914–15

Heroic couplet. A rhymed couplet in iambic pentameter whose second line is end-stopped. 626–27

Heroine. The principal female character in a story, poem, or play. 863, 914–15

Hexameter. A metrical line with six feet. 578

High comedy. Comedy appealing to the intellect, depending upon ingenuity of plot and verbal wit. 1103

High diction. Formal literary language. 618–20

High tragedy. Tragedy concerning the fall of noble heroes or heroines. 913, 1035

Horatian ode. An ode that repeats the same irregular stanza pattern throughout. It is personal rather than public, general rather than occasional, tranquil rather than intense, and is intended for the reader in privacy rather than for the spectator in the theater. 639, 641–44

Hyperbole. An exaggeration; a statement that something has either much more or much less of a quality than it truly has. 559–562

Iamb. A metrical unit of two syllables in which the second is stressed. 578

Image. A direct presentation of sensory experience. 497–504

In medias res. Literally, "in the middle of things"—the way in which epics traditionally start. Classical plays, like epics, frequently begin in the middle of a story, *in medias res.* 434

Internal rhyme. Rhyme that occurs in the middle of a line. 591

Invective. See *Satire.*

Irony of situation. See *Dramatic irony.*

Irregular ode. An ode in which each stanza has a different irregular shape. 639

Italian or Petrarchan sonnet. A poem fourteen lines long and divided between an opening octet and a closing sestet. The rhyme scheme is *abba abba//cdc cdc.* 629–32

Lighting. The illumination of the acting area for purposes of clarity and artistic effect. 800

Lighting designer. The member of the artistic staff of a dramatic production who creates illusions of daylight or nightlight, who specifies changes in light color and intensity contributing to the mood of the play. 800

Limerick. A five-line comic form rhyming *aabba,* of which the first, second, and fifth lines are trimeter and the third and fourth dimeter. 649

Limited third-person narrative. A story told by a voice which is outside the action, but which limits itself to the thoughts and perceptions of one of the characters. 26

Literary ballad. A ballad intended to be read rather than sung. 625

Low comedy. Comedy that plays upon the audience's lowest sense of humor, the impulse to laugh when someone else suffers physical discomfort or indignity. 1103

Low diction. Street language; simple or vulgar words. 618–20

Lyric. A highly concentrated poem of direct personal emotion, most often written in the first person. Lyric poetry is generally considered the most intense genre of poetry, the form that most honors its musical origins. The love poem, the elegy, and the meditation are all forms of lyric poetry. 454–59

Main plot. The principal sequence of actions of a narrative or drama. 271

Masculine ending. A stressed syllable at the end of a line. 584

Masculine rhyme. A rhyme in which the similarity of sounds is in the final syllables of the words involved. 590

Melodrama. A sensational form of nineteenth-century drama, in which organ music often accompanied the action. Thus, any sensational and romantic drama, usually with a happy ending. 865

Metaphor. A figure of speech in which a person, an object, or an idea is imaginatively transformed, as in "The grass is itself a child, the produced babe of the vegetation" (Whitman). A metaphor may be suggested by comparison, but it need not be. 519–25, 569

Meter. The measure of stressed and unstressed syllables in lines of poetry. When stresses occur at regular intervals, the poetry is said to have regular meter. 578–83

Metonymy. A figure of speech in which a single name of a person, place, or thing comes to stand for a more complex situation or experience with which the name is associated—for example, *Washington* for the U.S. government, *the press* for the enterprise of journalism. 563–567

Microcosm. Means "a small world." In fiction it refers to a model which, in miniature, depicts events and processes going on in the larger world. For example, a family squabble might be a microcosm of a disagreement between nations. 270

Monometer. A metrical line of one foot. 578

Motivation. The reason a character performs an action. 119

Narrative. The recounting of actions in prose or poetic form. 22–27, 50–52, 74–75

Narrative focus. Occurs when less important narrative events are subordinated to the more important ones. 73

Narrator. The voice that tells the story. See *First-person narrative, Limited third-person narrative,* and *Omniscient third-person narrative.*

Near rhyme. Two words or syllables that have approximate sounds, such as "lids" and "lads." 591

The New Comedy. Ancient Greek comedy as first practiced by Menander (342–292 B.C.), portraying domestic situations and contemporary manners, and usually involving a love affair. 1104–05

Novel. A lengthy work of prose fiction depicting a number of characters in various settings covering a relatively long period of time. 269

Novella. A combination of the short story and novel. It usually develops one aspect as completely as does a novel, but compresses other aspects, as in a short story. 269–72

Objective. In drama, the goal that motivates a character's actions. 863

Obstacle. In a dramatic situation, a person or circumstance that comes between the protagonist and his or her objective. 863

Octave. An eight-line stanza or section; often, the first eight lines of an Italian or Petrarchan sonnet. 629

Octometer. A metrical line with eight feet, rare in English. 578

Ode. The name of the most formal, ceremonious, and complexly organized form of lyric poetry, usually of considerable length. The ode is often used as a poem of praise for a formal occasion such as a marriage, a funeral, or a state ceremonial. 469–71, 639–644

Off rhyme. See *Near rhyme.*

Offstage. The area beyond that which the audience sees on stage—the rest of the imaginary world from which the characters enter and into which they exit. 804

Omniscient third-person narrative. A story told by the voice of a person outside the action who can read the thoughts of the characters and is aware of everything that takes place. 23

One act play. A play performed without intermission, with a few characters, a single setting, and (usually) a single story. 802

Onomatopoeia. A word whose sound imitates the actual sound to which it refers, such as *pop, sizzle,* and *crash.* 594–97

Onstage. The acting or playing area of a theater. 804

Orchestra. In the ancient Greek theater, the playing area, located between the scene proper and the audience, where the chorus performed. 821

Oxymoron. A phrase that combines two seemingly contradictory elements, such as *icy heat, loud silence, painful ease.* 569

Paradox. A seemingly contradictory statement. 568–571

Partial rhyme. See *Near rhyme.*

Pastoral. An artistic work that contains an urbane nostalgia for the simplicity of the shepherd's life and of country conventions, and which thus depicts rural living in a highly idealized and stylized manner; a classical dialogue between shepherds.

Pathos. Feelings of tender sympathy often evoked by the closing scenes of a drama. 820

Pentameter. A metrical line with five feet. 578

Peripeteia. See *Reversal.*

Persona. The speaker of the poem, who may or may not be the same as the poet. 427–31

Personification. The granting of human attributes to things that are not human. 538–39

Petrarchan sonnet. See *Italian sonnet.*

Pindaric ode. An ode of three parts—strophe, antistrophe, and epode. The strophe and antistrophe are the same irregularly shaped form, invented by the poet for each ode. The epode contrasts in shape. 469, 639–40

Play of atmosphere. A drama which has several equally important characters, instead of an obvious protagonist. 865

Playwright. The writer of the play script, the composer of the dialogue and action of a play. 799–800

Plot. The choice and arrangement of events within a story, the order of scenes in a drama. In classical drama, the articulation of a story in scenes of exposition, rising action, climax, falling action, and catastrophe or denouement. 72–75, 817

Popular ballad. A ballad passed on orally, with no known author. 433–34

Posthumous monologue. A poem spoken by the dead. 489

Premiere. The first performance of a drama.

Primary epic. See *Epic.*

Producer. The individual responsible for bringing a play to an audience. The producer selects the script, hires the artistic staff, and provides the performance space for the play. 800

Production. All the elements contributing to the presentation of a drama to an audience.

Proscenium. The part of the stage in front of the curtain. The proscenium arch is the structure separating the playing area from the audience. The "proscenium" stage is the sort in most school auditoriums. 804

Prose poem. A form that uses imagery and figurative language but forfeits the effects of versification, meter, and line endings.

Protagonist. The central character of a drama or other literary work. See *Hero.* 74, 864

Psalm. A sacred song or hymn, such as any of the sacred songs collected in the Old Testament Book of Psalms. Psalms are organized through a complex series of parallel and opposed ideas. 624

Psychomachia. Literally, "conflict of the soul"; a work in which parts of the personality or mind are in conflict with one another, sometimes depicted as an inner debate or quarrel.

Pun. A play on words with similar sounds or on a single word with different meanings. 617–18

Pyrrhic. A metrical unit of two unaccented syllables. 580

Quantitative meter. Meter determined by the duration of syllables rather than by their accents. 598

Quatrain. A stanza of four lines, rhymed or unrhymed. 435, 625

Realism. A quality in fiction and drama in which the events depicted correspond to events that might occur in real life. Realistic art avoids supernatural occurrences or improbable coincidences. In drama, realism is a 19th and 20th century theatrical convention. Dramatic realism avoids all that is improbable in events and characters, and all that is fantastic in presentation. 5, 1192, 1244

Recognition. A scene in which a dramatic character becomes aware of the nature of his predicament, or the weakness of character that has caused it. 913–14

Reversal. A change from bad to good fortune in a comedy, from good to bad in a tragedy. 913–14

Rhyme. The occurrence of the same stressed vowel sounds in two words, such as in *spring–sing, dies–eyes, day–gray.* This is known as perfect rhyme and assumes that the accented vowel sounds involved are preceded by different consonant sounds. For variations, see *Feminine rhyme, Internal rhyme, Near rhyme,* and *Masculine rhyme.* 588–92

Rhyme scheme. A pattern of rhyme throughout a stanza or poem. 589–90

Rising action. The scenes in which the chief characters of a drama begin pursuing their objectives in earnest. 818

Romance. A drama or story of adventure in which characters possess extraordinary powers and attributes. In romances, people are braver, kinder, handsomer, meaner than they are in real life. 190

Romantic comedy. A comic drama in which there is a love interest. 1104–05

Round characters. Characters who have a variety of personality traits and seem to have a life that extends beyond the story. 117–18

Satire. The ridiculing of any human vice or folly, frequently by means of exaggeration. When such attacks lose their humor, they become *invective.* 190–91, 1104

Scansion. The system of describing more or less conventional poetic rhythms by visual symbols for purposes of metrical analysis and study. 577–78

Scene. A unit of dramatic action which tells one part of the play's story. An action that takes place in a specific time and place. See *Set.* 804–05

Science fiction. A story usually set in the future or distant past dealing with issues raised by scientific or technological discoveries or possibilities. 189–92

Script. The dialogue and stage directions of a play. The blueprint and record of a play, the printed text of dialogue and stage directions. 801–06

Secondary epic. See *Epic.*

Sestet. A six-line unit that can stand alone as a stanza or as the concluding six lines of an Italian or Petrarchan sonnet. 629

Sestina. A verse form that consists of six six-line stanzas and a concluding tercet. The end words of each line of the first stanza are repeated in subsequent stanzas.

Set. The acting or playing area of the theater; the props and scenery for a particular scene or act of a drama. 804

Setting. The place, time, or circumstance in which the action of a story takes place. 141–45

Shakespearean sonnet. See *English sonnet.*

Shaped form. A poem whose lines, taken together, form a visual representation of its subject. 649–53

Short story. A work of prose fiction which generally involves a small number of characters in a limited number of settings, and is condensed into a short span of time.

Simile. A comparison of one thing with another, explictly announced by the word *like* or *as.* 525–27

Skit. An informal dramatic exercise that has neither the depth nor completeness of a play.

Social realism. In drama, a play that portrays characters struggling with social and economic problems. 1193

Soliloquy. A speech to oneself. 477–85

Sonnet. A fourteen-line poem in iambic pentameter whose rhyme scheme has, in practice, been widely varied. Sonnets concern themselves with love, death, politics, and other topics that evoke intense personal feelings. 629–34

Spondee. A metrical unit of two accented syllables. 580

Stage designer. The member of the artistic staff of a dramatic production who plans the layout, architecture, and colors of the stage scenery. 800

Stage direction. Any description in a script of an actor's behavior that is not indicated by dialogue. 805

Stage props. Furniture and other movable effects that make up the scene of a play. 805

Stage whisper. Words spoken by an actor which, by dramatic convention, are supposed not to be heard by the other actors onstage.

Stanza. A sequence of lines that form a metrical, tonal, or intellectual unit. 435, 456, 625

Static characters. Characters that do not change during the course of a narrative. 119

Stock characters. Characters, usually found in comedy and melodrama, whose qualities are so exaggerated and common that they represent a type of human nature. 865

Stream-of-consciousness. A narrative technique which gives the reader the impression of listening to a character's innermost thoughts. 118–19

Stress. Emphasis given to a word or syllable. There are two forms of stress: stress of accent and stress of emphasis. Stress of accent occurs in polysyllabic words. Thus we say beaúty rather than beauty. Stress of emphasis is the stress we give to particular words in a sentence. In the sentence, "I have a bad headache," the word *bad* is stressed. 577–78

Strophe. See *Pindaric ode.*

Sub-plot. One or more sequences of action subordinated to the main plot. 271

Supporting character. In drama, a character who helps to forward the action but is neither the cause nor the major victim of it. 865

Surprise. An aspect of plot construction in which events are sprung upon the unsuspecting reader. Surprise is frequently a function of point-of-view. 73

Suspense. The feeling of pleasurable tension experienced by the reader or spectator in anticipation of learning the outcome of a narrative situation. 73–74

Syllabic verse. A poem whose line lengths are calculated by the number of syllables in each line rather than the number of feet per line. 587–88

Symbol. An object, person, action, or situation that signifies more than itself and thus may be read both literally and metaphorically. 173–75, 545–50

Symbolist drama. Plays in which actions as well as characters, props, and setting refer to eternal ideas and states of being in a "higher" world. 1303–04

Synecdoche. A figure of speech wherein part of a thing is employed to suggest the whole, or a larger concept is used to suggest something specific. *Example:* "All hands were on deck." 562–563

Synesthesia. The manner of speaking about one sense in terms of another. "He wore a *screaming* yellow necktie" is an example of synesthesia because *yellow* is described as if it were a sound. 502

Tale-within-a-tale. See *Framed story.*

Talon. The last word of the line of a sestina.

Tanka. A Japanese lyric form of thirty-one syllables, in lines of five, seven, five, seven, seven. Historically, its diction has been traditional and elevated, and its subjects most often include love, lament, felicitations, travel, and nature. 644–48

Tercet. A three-line stanza. 634

Terza rima. A form of interconnected three-line stanzas that rhyme *aba bcb cdc ded efe.* . . . 634–36

Tetrameter. A metrical line with four feet. 578

Theater of the absurd. A twentieth-century school of drama concerned with human alienation, the death of God, and the futility of language.

Third-person narrative. A story told by a voice outside the action. See also *Omniscient third-person narrative* and *Limited third-person narrative.* 23

Tone. The writer's attitude toward a subject as exhibited through rhythms, sounds, and the selection of words. 606–22

Tragedy. A stage play that shows the change in the protagonist's fortune from good to bad, inspiring fear and pity. 912–15

Tragic flaw. In drama, the flaw in the character of the protagonist that leads to his or her downfall. 864

Tragic irony. In drama, a misfortune contrary to the expectations of the protagonist. 914

Tragicomedy. A drama that alternates comic and serious scenes, producing a richly ironic blend of emotions. 1145–46

Trimeter. A metrical line with three feet. 578

Triplet. A verse unit of three lines, usually containing rhyme, employed as a stanzaic form, as a variation on the couplet, or occasionally as a complete poem in itself. 626

Trochee. A metrical unit of two syllables in which the first is stressed. 578

Turning point. See *Climax of action.*

Twist ending. The surprise conclusion of a narrative, often the result of an odd or unexpected turn of events. 164

Unreliable narrator. A narrator whose account of events is recognized by the reader as being faulty, distorted, or untrustworthy. 50–53

Utopia. An imaginary ideal place—a paradise, an Eden. A *dystopia* or *anti-utopia* is its opposite—a place of horror and evil. 191–92

Villain. An antagonist who is deliberately evil. 119, 865

Villanelle. A poem made up of five tercets, all rhyming *aba*, and a concluding quatrain, rhyming *abaa*. Lines 6, 12, and 18 repeat line 1; lines 9, 15, and 19 repeat line 3. 637–39

Acknowledgments *(continued)*

Gabriel García Márquez. "A Very Old Man with Enormous Wings" (pp. 105–112) from *Leaf Storm and Other Stories* by Gabriel García Márquez. English translation © 1972 by Gabriel García Márquez. Reprinted by permission of Harper & Row, Publishers, Inc.

Ernest Hemingway. "The Short Happy Life of Francis Macomber" from *The Short Stories of Ernest Hemingway.* Copyright 1936 Ernest Hemingway; copyright renewed © 1964 Mary Hemingway. Reprinted with the permission of Charles Scribner's Sons.

James Joyce. "Araby" from *Dubliners* by James Joyce. Originally published in 1916 by B. W. Huebsch. Definitive text © 1967 by the Estate of James Joyce. Reprinted by permission of Viking Penguin Inc.

Franz Kafka. "A Hunger Artist." Reprinted by permission of Schocken Books Inc. from *The Penal Colony* by Franz Kafka, trans, Willa & Edwin Muir. Copyright © 1948, 1976 by Schocken Books, Inc.

Maxine Hong Kingston. "On Mortality" from *China Men,* by Maxine Hong Kingston. Copyright © 1980 by Maxine Hong Kingston. Reprinted by permission of Alfred A. Knopf, Inc.

D. H. Lawrence. "The Horse-Dealer's Daughter" from *Complete Short Stories of D. H. Lawrence.* Copyright 1922 by Thomas Seltzer, Inc. Copyright renewed 1950 by Frieda Lawrence. Reprinted by permission of Viking Penguin Inc. Also from *The Collected Short Stories of D. H. Lawrence.* Copyright © 1974 by The Estate of Frieda Lawrence Ravagli. Reprinted by permission of Laurence Pollinger Ltd. and The Estate of Frieda Lawrence Ravagli.

Ursula K. Le Guin. "The New Atlantis." Copyright © 1975 by Ursula K. Le Guin; reprinted by permission of the author and the author's agent, Virginia Kidd.

Doris Lessing. "Homage to Isaac Babel" from *A Man and Two Women* by Doris Lessing. Copyright © 1958, 1962, 1963 by Doris Lessing. Reprinted by permission of Simon & Schuster, Inc. and Jonathan Clowes, Ltd., London, on behalf of Doris Lessing.

Sinclair Lewis. "Virga Vay & Allan Cedar" from *Cass Timberlane,* by Sinclair Lewis. Copyright 1945 by Sinclair Lewis. Reprinted by permission of Random House, Inc.

Bernard Malamud. "The Jewbird" from *Idiots First* by Bernard Malamud. Copyright © 1963 by Bernard Malamud. Reprinted by permission of Farrar, Straus and Giroux, Inc.

Bobbie Ann Mason. "Shiloh" from *Shiloh and Other Stories* by Bobbie Ann Mason. Copyright © 1982 by Bobbie Ann Mason. Reprinted by permission of Harper & Row, Publishers, Inc.

V. S. Naipaul. "The Night Watchman's Occurrence Book" from *A Flag on the Island* by V. S. Naipaul. Reprinted by permission of Gillon Aitken, Ltd.

Flannery O'Connor. "Everything That Rises Must Converge" from *Everything That Rises Must Converge* by Flannery O'Connor. Copyright © 1961, 1965 by the Estate of Mary Flannery O'Connor. Reprinted by permission by Farrar, Straus & Giroux, Inc.

Grace Paley. "A Conversation with My Father" from *Enormous Changes at the Minute* by Grace Paley. Copyright © 1972, 1974 by Grace Paley. Reprinted by permission of Farrar, Straus and Giroux, Inc.

Katherine Anne Porter. "The Jilting of Granny Weatherall." Copyright 1930, 1958 by Katherine Anne Porter. Reprinted from her volume *Flowering Judas and Other Stories* by permission of Harcourt Brace Jovanovich, Inc.

Raymond Queneau. Exercises in Style. Copyright © 1947 Editions Gallimard, © Barbara Wright 1958. Reprinted by permission of New Directions Publishing Corporation.

Jean Rhys. "I Used to Live Here" from *Sleep It Off, Lady* by Jean Rhys. Copyright © by Jean Rhys. Reprinted by permission of Harper & Row, Publishers, Inc.

John Steinbeck. "Chrysanthemums" from *The Long Valley* by John Steinbeck. Copyright 1938 by John Steinbeck. Copyright renewed 1965 by John Steinbeck. Reprinted by permission of Viking Penguin Inc.

Anne Tyler. "The Artificial Heart" by Anne Tyler, published in *The Southern Review,* 1975, Summer Issue. Copyright © 1975 by Anne Tyler. Reprinted by permission of Russell & Volkening, Inc. as agents for the author.

John Updike. "Separating" from *Problems and Other Stories* by John Updike. Copyright © 1975 by John Updike. Reprinted by permission of Alfred A. Knopf, Inc. Originally appeared in *The New Yorker.*

Alice Walker. "How Did I Get Away with Killing One of the Biggest Lawyers in the State? It Was Easy" from *You Can't Keep A Good Woman Down* by Alice Walker. Copyright © by Alice Walker. Reprinted by permission of Harcourt Brace Jovanovich, Inc.

Eudora Welty. "Lily Daw and the Three Ladies" from *A Curtain of Green and Other Stories* by Eudora Welty. Copyright 1937 by University of Nebraska; renewed 1965 by Eudora Welty. Reprinted by permission of Harcourt Brace Jovanovich, Inc.

POETRY AND ESSAYS

A. R. Ammons. "The Visit" is reprinted from *Collected Poems,1951–1971,* by A. R. Ammons, with permission of W. W. Norton & Company, Inc. Copyright © 1972 by A. R. Ammons.

Archilochus. From *Fragments of Archilochus,* translated by Guy Davenport, p. 87, fragment 262. Copyright © 1980 by the Regents of the University of California. Reprinted by permission of University of California Press.

John Ashbery. "Paradoxes and Oxymorons" from *Shadow Train* by John Ashbery. Copyright © 1980, 1981 by John Ashbery. Reprinted by permission of Viking Penguin Inc.

Margaret Atwood. "You Are Happy" from *You Are Happy* by Margaret Atwood. Copyright © 1974 by Margaret Atwood. Reprinted by permission of Harper & Row, Publishers, Inc., and Phoebe Larmore.

W. H. Auden. "Musée des Beaux Arts," "In Memory of W. B. Yeats," "Fleet Visit," "Lay Your Sleeping Head, My Love," "As I Walked Out One Evening" from *W. H. Auden: Collected Poems,* edited by Edward Mendelson. Copyright 1940, 1955, and renewed 1968 by W. H. Auden. Reprinted by permission of Random House, Inc. "Musée des Beaux Arts," "In Memory of W. B. Yeats," "Lay Your Sleeping Head, My Love," "As I Walked Out One Evening" from *Collected Poems* by W. H. Auden. Reprinted by permission of Faber and Faber Ltd.

Imamu Amiri Baraka (LeRoi Jones). "Preface to a Twenty Volume Suicide Note" from *Preface to a Twenty Volume Suicide Note* by LeRoi Jones. Copyright 1961 by LeRoi Jones. Reprinted by permission of The Sterling Lord Agency, Inc.

Matsuo Basho. "Nine Haiku" from *The Penguin Book of Japanese Verse,* translated by Geoffrey Bownas and Anthony Thwaite (The Penguin Poets, 1964), pp. 58–59. Copyright © 1964 by Geoffrey Bownas and Anthony Thwaite. Reprinted by permission of Penguin Books Ltd.

Harry Behn. From *Cricket Songs: Japanese Haiku*, translated by Harry Behn. All rights reserved. Reprinted by permission of Marian Reiner.

Hillaire Belloc. "On His Books." Reprinted by permission of Sheed & Ward Ltd., London.

Wendell Berry. "The Old Elm Tree by the River" from *The Country of Marriage* by Wendell Berry. Copyright © 1971 by Wendell Berry. Reprinted by permission of Harcourt Brace Jovanovich, Inc.

John Berryman. "Young Woman's Song" from *Short Poems* by John Berryman. Copyright 1948 by John Berryman and renewed © 1976 by Kate Berryman. Reprinted by permission of Farrar, Straus and Giroux, Inc.

Louise Bogan. "Night" from *The Blue Estuaries* by Louise Bogan. Copyright © 1923, 1929, 1930, 1931, 1933, 1934, 1935, 1936, 1937, 1938, 1941, 1949, 1951, 1952, 1954, 1957, 1958, 1962, 1963, 1964, 1965, 1966, 1967 by Louise Bogan. Reprinted by permission of Farrar, Straus and Giroux, Inc.

Arna Bontemps. Southern Mansion" from *Personals* by Arna Bontemps, published by Paul Breman. Copyright © 1963 by Arna Bontemps. Reprinted by permission of Harold Ober Associates Incorporated.

Marie Borroff. "Robert Frost: To Earthward" from *Frost: Centennial Essays II* (1976), edited by Jac Tharp, pp. 24–25. Courtesy of the University Press of Mississippi.

Gwendolyn Brooks. "Sadie and Maud" from *The World of Gwendolyn Brooks* by Gwendolyn Brooks. Copyright 1944 by Gwendolyn Brooks Blakely. Reprinted by permission of Harper & Row, Publishers, Inc.

Charles Bukowski. "Yellow," copyright © 1969. From *The Days Run Away like Wild Horses over the Hills* by Charles Bukowski, published by Black Shadow Press. Reprinted by permission.

Catullus. "LXXXV," translated by Daniel Mark Epstein.

Amy Clampitt. "The Sun Underfoot Among the Sundews" from *The Kingfisher* by Amy Clampitt. Copyright © 1983 by Amy Clampitt. Reprinted by permission of Alfred A. Knopf, Inc.

Lucille Clifton. "Good Times" from *Good Times* by Lucille Clifton. Copyright © 1969 by Lucille Clifton. Reprinted by permission of Random House, Inc.

Alfred Corn. "Fifty-Seventh Street and Fifth" from *A Call in the Midst of the Crowd* by Alfred Corn. Copyright © 1977 by Alfred Corn. Reprinted by permission of Viking Penguin Inc.

H. D. (Hilda Doolittle). "Never More Will the Wind," "Oread" from *Selected Poems of H. D.* copyright 1925, 1953, © 1957 by Norman Holmes Pearson. Reprinted by permission of New Directions Publishing Corporation.

Hart Crane. "My Grandmother's Love Letters." Reprinted from *The Complete Poems and Selected Letters and Prose of Hart Crane*, edited by Brom Weber, by permission of Liveright Publishing Corporation. Copyright 1933, 1958, 1966 by Liveright Publishing Corporation.

Robert Creeley. "If You" from *For Love: Poems 1950–1960* by Robert Creeley. Copyright 1962 by Robert Creeley (New York: Charles Scribner's Sons, 1962). Reprinted with the permission of Charles Scribner's Sons.

Countee Cullen. "Incident" from *On These I Stand* by Countee Cullen. Copyright 1925 by Harper & Row, Publishers, Inc., and renewed 1953 by Ida M. Cullen. Reprinted by permission of Harper & Row, Publishers, Inc.

E. E. Cummings. "somewhere i have never travelled, gladly beyond," Reprinted from *ViVa*, poems by E. E. Cummings, by permission of Liveright Publishing Corporation. Copyright © 1979, 1973 by the Trustees for the E. E. Cummings Trust. Copyright © 1979, 1973 by George James Firmage. "next to of course god america i." Reprinted from *IS 5* poems by E. E. Cummings, by permission of Liveright Publishing Corporation. Copyright 1926 by Horace Liveright. Copyright renewed 1953 by E. E. Cummings. "the Cambridge ladies," "in Just-" Reprinted from *Tulips & Chimneys* by E. E. Cummings by permission of Liveright Publishing Corporation. Copyright 1923, 1925, and renewed 1951, 1953 by E. E. Cummings. Copyright © 1973, 1976 by the Trustees for the E. E. Cummings Trust. Copyright © 1973, 1976 by George James Firmage.

James Dickey. "Buckdancer's Choice" from *Buckdancer's Choice* by James Dickey. Copyright © 1965 by James Dickey. "Buckdancer's Choice" first appeared in *The New Yorker*. Reprinted by permission of Wesleyan University Press.

Emily Dickinson. "I Felt a Funeral in My Brain," "Hope Is the Thing with Feathers," "Because I Could Not Stop for Death," "Success Is Counted Sweetest," "Apparently with No Surprise," "I Heard a Fly Buzz—When I Died" from *The Poems of Emily Dickinson*, edited by Thomas H. Johnson (Cambridge, Mass.: The Belknap Press of Harvard University Press). Copyright 1951, © 1955, 1979 by the President and Fellows of Harvard College. Reprinted by permission of the publishers and the Trustees of Amherst College. "My Life Had Stood, a Loaded Gun," "After Great Pain, a Formal Feeling Comes" from *The Complete Poems of Emily Dickinson*, edited by Thomas H. Johnson. Copyright 1929 by Martha Dickinson Bianchi, © renewed 1957 by Mary L. Hampson. Reprinted by permission of Little, Brown and Company.

Alan Dugan. "Morning Song" copyright © 1961 by Alan Dugan. From *New and Collected Poems: 1961–1983* by Alan Dugan, published by The Ecco Press in 1983. Reprinted by permission.

Paul Laurence Dunbar. "In the Morning" from *The Complete Poems of Paul Laurence Dunbar* (1970). Reprinted by permission of Dodd, Mead & Company, Inc.

Robert Duncan. "My Mother Would Be a Falconress" from *Bending the Bow* by Robert Duncan. Copyright © 1966 by Robert Duncan. Reprinted by permission of New Directions Publishing Corporation.

Bob Dylan. "Boots of Spanish Leather" by Bob Dylan. Copyright © 1963 by Warner Brothers, Inc. All rights reserved. Used by permission.

T. S. Eliot. "Preludes," "Aunt Helen," "The Love Song of J. Alfred Prufrock" from *Collected Poems 1909–1962* by T. S. Eliot. Copyright 1936 by Harcourt Brace Jovanovich, Inc., copyright © 1963, 1964 by T. S. Eliot. Reprinted by permission of Harcourt Brace Jovanovich, Inc., and Faber & Faber, Ltd.

William Empson. "Villanelle" from *Collected Poems of William Empson*. Copyright 1949, 1977 by William Empson. Reprinted by permission of Harcourt Brace Jovanovich, Inc., and Chatto & Windus Ltd.

Daniel Mark Epstein. "Madonna (with Child Missing)." Reprinted from *No Vacancies in Hell*, Poems by Daniel Mark Epstein, by permission of Liveright Publishing Corporation. Copyright © 1971, 1972, 1973 by Daniel Mark Epstein.

Louise Erdrich. "Windigo" from *Jacklight* by Louise Erdrich. Copyright © 1984 by Louise Erdrich. Reprinted by permission of Henry Holt and Company.

Michael Ferber. " 'London' and Its Politics" from *English Literary History*, Vol. 48, No. 2 (Summer 1981), pp. 310–338. Reprinted by permission of Johns Hopkins University Press.

Lawrence Ferlinghetti. "In Goya's Greatest Scenes We Seem to See" from *Coney Island of the Mind* by Lawrence Ferlinghetti. Copyright © 1958 by Lawrence Ferlinghetti. Reprinted by permission of New Directions Publishing Corporation.

Edward Field. "My Polish Grandmother." Reprinted by permission of Edward Field.

Charles Henri Ford. "Somebody's Gone" from *The Overturned Lake* by Charles Henri Ford, published by New Directions Publishing Corporation. Reprinted by permission of Charles Henri Ford.

Robert Frost. "Out, Out—," "Fire and Ice," "For Once, Then, Something," "The Road Not Taken," "Provide, Provide," "Mending Wall," "After Apple-Picking," "A Peck of Gold," "The Silken Tent" from *The Poetry of Robert Frost*, edited by Edward Connery Lathem. Copyright 1916, 1923, 1928, 1930, 1939, © 1969 by Holt, Rinehart and Winston. Copyright 1936, 1942, 1944, 1951, © 1956, 1958 by Robert Frost. Copyright © 1964, 1967, 1970 by Lesley Frost Ballantine. Reprinted by permission of Holt, Rinehart and Winston, Publishers.

Federico García Lorca. "Half Moon" from *The Selected Poems of Federico García Lorca.* Copyright © 1955 by New Directions Publishing Corporation. Reprinted by permission of New Directions Publishing Corporation.

Allen Ginsberg. "A Supermarket in California" from *Collected Poems 1947–1980.* Copyright © 1955, 1984 by Allen Ginsberg. Reprinted by permission of Harper & Row, Publishers, Inc.

Nikki Giovanni. "Nikki-Rosa" from *Black Feeling, Black Talk, Black Judgement.* Copyright © 1968, 1970 by Nikki Giovanni. By permission of William Morrow & Company.

Louise Glück. "The Pond" from *The House on Marshland* by Louise Glück. Copyright © 1975 by Louise Glück. Reprinted by permission of The Ecco Press.

Paul Goodman. "To My Only World" from *Collected Poems* edited by Taylor Stoehr. Copyright © 1973 by The Estate of Paul Goodman. Reprinted by permission of Random House, Inc.

Edward Gorey. "There Was A Young Woman Named Plunnery" from *Listing Attic*, 1954, by Duell, Sloane and Pearce. From *Oxford Anthology of Light Verse*, edited by William Harmon. Reprinted by permission of Edward Gorey.

Thom Gunn. "Moly" from *Moly* and *My Sad Captains* by Thom Gunn. Copyright © 1961, 1971, 1973 by Thom Gunn. Reprinted by permission of Farrar, Straus and Giroux, Inc., and Faber and Faber Ltd.

Marilyn Hacker. "Villanelle" from *Presentation Piece* by Marilyn Hacker, published by the Viking Press. Copyright © 1972 by Marilyn Hacker. Reprinted by permission of Marilyn Hacker.

Donald Hall. "Ox Cart Man" from *The Ox Cart Man* by Donald Hall. Copyright © 1977 by Donald Hall.

Thomas Hardy. "The Subalterns" from *The Complete Poems of Thomas Hardy*, edited by James Gibson (1978). Reprinted by permission of Macmillan Company, Inc.

Michael Harper. "A Mother Speaks: The Algiers Motel Incident, Detroit" from *Dear John, Dear Coltrane* by Michael Harper. Copyright 1970 by the University of Pittsburgh Press. Reprinted by permission of the University of Illinois Press.

Jim Harrison. "Sound" from *Outlyers and Ghazals* by Jim Harrison, published by Liveright Publishing Corporation. Copyright © 1969, 1971 by Jim Harrison. Reprinted by permission of Jim Harrison.

Robert Hayden. First 68 lines from "Middle Passage" from *Angle of Ascent, New and Selected Poems* by Robert Hayden, by permission of Liveright Publishing Corporation. Copyright © 1975, 1972, 1970, 1966 by Robert Hayden.

Seamus Heaney. "The Forge" from *Poems 1965–1975* by Seamus Heaney. Copyright © 1969 by Seamus Heaney. Reprinted by permission of Farrar, Straus and Giroux, Inc. Also from *Door into the Dark* by Seamus Heaney. Reprinted by permission of Faber and Faber Ltd.

Anthony Hecht. "The Dover Bitch, A Criticism of Life" in *The Hard Hours.* Copyright © 1967 by Anthony Hecht (New York: Atheneum, 1967) Reprinted with permission of Atheneum Publishers.

Daryl Hine. "The Survivors," in *Minutes.* Copyright © 1968 by Daryl Hine (New York: Atheneum, 1968). Reprinted with the permission of Atheneum Publishers.

Edward Hirsch. "A Letter" from *For The Sleepwalkers* by Edward Hirsch. Copyright © 1981 by Edward Hirsch. Reprinted by permission of Alfred A. Knopf, Inc.

Billie Holiday. "God Bless the Child" by Billie Holiday and Arthur Herzog, Jr. © 1941, Edward B. Marks Music Company, Copyright renewed. All rights reserved. Used by permission.

John Hollander. "Swan and Shadow," from *Forms of Shape.* Copyright © 1969 by John Hollander (New York: Atheneum 1969). Reprinted with permission of Atheneum Publishers.

Homer. From the *Odyssey*, translated by Robert Fitzgerald. Copyright © 1961 by Robert Fitzgerald. Reprinted by permission of Doubleday & Company, Inc.

Garrett Kaoru Hongo. "The Hongo Store" from *Yellow Light.* Copyright © 1977 by Garrett Kaoru Hongo. Reprinted by permission of Wesleyan University Press.

A. E. Houseman. "To an Athlete Dying Young," "With Rue My Heart Is Laden," "Loveliest of Trees, the Cherry Now," "When I Was One-and-Twenty," from "A Shropshire Lad"—authorized edition—from *The Collected Poems of A. E. Houseman.* Copyright 1939, 1940, © 1965 by Holt, Rinehart and Winston. Copyright © 1967, 1968 by Robert E. Symons. Reprinted by permission of Henry Holt and Company; the Society of Authors as the literary representative of the Estate of A. E. Houseman; Jonathan Cape Ltd., publishers of A. E. Houseman's *Collected Poems.*

Richard Howard. "Giovanni da Fiesole on the Sublime, or Fra Angelico's 'Last Judgment'" in *Findings.* Copyright © 1971 by Richard Howard (New York: Atheneum, 1971). Reprinted by permission of Atheneum Publishers.

Langston Hughes. "Sylvester's Dying Bed," "Who but the Lord?" from *Selected Poems of Langston Hughes.* Copyright © 1959 by Langston Hughes. Reprinted by permission of Alfred A. Knopf, Inc.

Ted Hughes. "Hawk Roosting" from *Selected Poems* by Ted Hughes. Copyright © 1959 by Ted Hughes. Reprinted by permission of Harper & Row, Publishers, Inc. Also from *Lupercal* by Ted Hughes. Reprinted by permission of Faber and Faber Ltd.

Richard Hugo. "Driving Montana" is reprinted from *The Lady Kicking Horse Reservoir*, Poems by Richard Hugo, by permission of W. W. Norton & Company, Inc. Copyright © 1973 by Richard Hugo.

T. E. Hulme. "Autumn" from *Personae* by Ezra Pound. Copyright 1926 by Ezra Pound. Reprinted by permission of New Directions Publishing Corporation.

Colette Inez. "Spanish Heaven" from *Alive and Taking Names* by Collette Inez (Athens, Ohio: Ohio University Press, 1977). "Spanish Heaven" was first published by Salt Creek Reader. Reprinted by permission of Windflower Press.

Randall Jarrell. "The Death of the Ball Turret Gunner" from *Randall Jarrell: Complete Poems.* Copyright © 1945, 1969 by Mrs. Randall Jarrell and renewed 1973 by Mrs. Randall Jarrell. Reprinted by permission of Farrar, Straus and Giroux, Inc. "The Mocking Bird" from *The Bat-Poet.* Copyright © 1963, 1964 by Macmillan Publishing

1414   Acknowledgments (continued)

Co., Inc. "The Mocking Bird" first appeared in *The New York*. Reprinted by permission of Macmillan Publishing Co., Inc. "The Woman at the Washington Zoo," from *The Woman at the Washington Zoo: Poems and Translations*. Copyright © 1960 by Randall Jarrell. Reprinted with the permission of Atheneum Publishers.

Robinson Jeffers. "Rock and Hawk" from *Selected Poems* by Robinson Jeffers. Copyright 1934 and renewed 1962 by Donnan Jeffers and Garth Jeffers. Reprinted by permission of Random House, Inc.

Erica Jong. "How You Get Born" from *Half-Lives* by Erica Jong. Copyright © 1971, 1972, 1973 by Erica Mann Jong. Reprinted by permission of Holt, Rinehart and Winston, Publishers.

June Jordan. "My Sadness Sits Around Me" from *Some Changes* by June Jordan, published by E. P. Dutton (1971). Reprinted by permission Richard W. Baron Publishing Co.

James Joyce. "All Day I Hear the Noise of Waters" from *Chamber Music*, Stanza XXXV, by James Joyce. Copyright © 1918 by B. W. Huebsch. Reprinted by permission of Viking Penguin Inc. and the Society of Authors as the literary representative of the Estate of James Joyce.

Lady Kasa. "Six Tanka" from *The Penguin Book of Japanese Verse*, translated by Geoffrey Bownas and Anthony Thwaite (The Penguin Poets, 1964), pp. 112, 113. Copyright © 1964 by Geoffrey Bownas and Anthony Thwaite. Reprinted by permission of Penguin Books Ltd.

Bob Kaufman. "Blues Note" from *Solitudes Filled with Loneliness* by Bob Kaufman. Copyright © 1965 by Bob Kaufman. Reprinted by permission of New Directions Publishing Corporation.

Patrick Kavanagh. "Tinker's Wife." Copyright © 1964 by Patrick Kavanagh. Reprinted by permission of Devin-Adair Co., Old Greenwich, Ct.

Weldon Kees. "Aspects of Robinson" from *The Selected Poems of Weldon Kees*, edited by Donald Justice. Copyright © 1975 by the University of Nebraska Press. Reprinted by permission of the University of Nebraska Press.

Peter Klappert. "Mail at Your New Address" from *Lugging Vegetables to Nantucket* by Peter Klappert, published by Yale University Press. Reprinted by permission of Yale University Press.

Etheridge Knight. "Haiku" from *Poems from Prison* by Etheridge Knight. Reprinted by permission of the author.

Bill Knott. "The Hair Poem," "Death" from *The Naomi Poems* by Bill Knott. Copyright © 1968 by William Knott. Reprinted by permission of Follett Publishing Company.

Kenneth Koch. "Mending Sump" from *The New American Poetry*, edited by Donald M. Allen. Copyright © 1960 by Kenneth Koch. Reprinted by permission of Kenneth Koch.

Maxine Kumin. "For a Shetland Pony Brood Mare Who Died in Her Barren Year" from *Our Ground Time Here Will Be Brief* by Maxine Kumin. Copyright © 1969 by Maxine Kumin. Reprinted by permission of Viking Penguin Inc.

Stanley Kunitz. "The Portrait" from *The Poems of Stanley Kunitz 1928–1978*. Copyright © 1971 by Stanley Kunitz. Reprinted by permission of Little, Brown and Company in association with the Atlantic Monthly Press.

Philip Larkin. "Faith Healing" from *The Witsun Weddings* by Philip Larkin. Reprinted by permission of Faber and Faber Ltd.

D. H. Lawrence. "Sorrow," "Snake," "Gloire de Dijon" from *The Complete Poems* by D. H. Lawrence, edited by Vivan de Sola Pinto and F. Warren Roberts. Copyright © 1964, 1971 by Angelo Ravagli and C. M. Weekley, Executors of the Estate of Frieda Lawrence Ravagli. Reprinted by permission of Viking Pengiun Inc. Also from *The Complete Poems of D. H. Lawrence*, published by William Heinemann Ltd. Reprinted by permission of Laurence Pollinger Ltd. and the Estate of Frieda Lawrence Ravagli.

Irving Layton. "Cain" from *The Selected Poems of Irving Layton*. Reprinted by permission of the Canadian Publishers, McClelland and Stewart Limited, Toronto.

John Lessner. "Hamlet and the Gravedigger." Reprinted by permission of the author.

Denise Levertov. "To the Snake" from *Collected Earlier Poems 1940–1960*. Copyright 1958 by Denise Levertov Goodman. First printed in *Poetry*. "The Ache of Marriage" from *O Taste and See* by Denise Levertov. Copyright © 1964 by Denise Levertov Goodman. Reprinted by permission of New Directions Publishing Corporation.

Philip Levine. "To a Child Trapped in a Barber Shop" from *Not This Pig* by Philip Levine. Copyright © 1966 by Philip Levine. Reprinted by permission of Wesleyan University Press.

Audre Lorde. "Now That I Am Forever with Child" is reprinted from *CFoal*, poems by Audre Lorde, with permission of W. W. Norton & Company, Inc. Copyright © 1968, 1970, 1976 by Audre Lorde.

Amy Lowell. "Chinoiseries" from *The Complete Poetical works of Amy Lowell*. Copyright 1955 by Houghton Mifflin Company. Reprinted by permission of Houghton Mifflin Company.

Robert Lowell. "Skunk Hour" from *Life Studies* by Robert Lowell. Copyright © 1956, 1959 by Robert Lowell. "Robert Frost" from *History* by Robert Lowell. Copyright © 1967, 1968, 1969, 1970, 1973 by Robert Lowell. All reprinted by permission of Farrar, Straus and Giroux, Inc.

Claude McKay. "If We Must Die" from *Selected Poems of Claude McKay*. Copyright 1981 by Twayne Publishers, a Division of G. K. Hall & Co. Reprinted by permission of Twayne Publishers, a Division of G. K. Hall & Co., Boston.

Archibald MacLeish. "Ars Poetica" from *New and Collected Poems 1917–1976* by Archibald MacLeish. Copyright © 1976 by Archibald MacLeish. Reprinted by permission of Houghton Mifflin Company.

Edgar Lee Masters. "Fiddler Jones" from *The Spoon River Anthology* by Edgar Lee Masters, published by Macmillan Publishing Co., Inc. Reprinted by permission of Ellen C. Masters.

James G. Mengert. "The Resistance to Milton's Sonnets" in *English Literary Renaissance* (Winter 1981), pp. 81–82. Reprinted by permission of *English Literary Renaissance*.

James Merrill. "Charles on Fire" from *From The First Nine Poems 1946–1976*. Copyright © 1982 James Merrill. From "McKane's Falls," in *Divine Comedies*, copyright © 1976 by James Merrill (New York: Atheneum, 1976). Reprinted with the permission of Atheneum Publishers.

Thomas Merton. "The Regret," "Elegy of the Monastery Barn" from *Collected Poems of Thomas Merton*. Copyright 1944 by Our Lady of Gethsemani Monastery. Copyright © 1962 by The Abbey of Gethsemani, Inc. Reprinted by permission of New Directions Publishing Corporation.

W. S. Merwin. "For the Anniversary of My Death," in *The Lice*. Copyright © 1967 by W. S. Merwin (New York: Atheneum, 1967). Reprinted with the permission of Atheneum Publishers.

Edna St. Vincent Millay. "Recuerdo," "Pity Me Not Because the Light of Day" from *Collected Poems* by Edna St. Vincent Millay, published by Harper & Row, Publishers, Inc. Copyright 1922, 1923, 1950, 1951 by Edna St. Vincent Millay and Norma Millay Ellis. Reprinted by permission of Norma Millay Ellis.

Leslie Miller. "O'Hara's Conversation with the Sun." Reprinted by permission of the author.

N. Scott Momaday. "The Delight Song of Tsoai-Talee," "Earth and I Gave You Turquoise" from *The Gourd Dancer* by N. Scott Momaday. Copyright © 1975 by N. Scott Momaday. Reprinted by permission of Harper & Row, Publishers, Inc.

Marianne Moore. "The Wood-Weasel" from *Collected Poems* by Marianne Moore. Copyright 1944, renewed 1972 by Marianne Moore. "The Monkey Puzzle" from *Collected Poems* by Marianne Moore. Copyright 1935 by Marianne Moore, renewed 1963 by Marianne Moore and T. S. Eliot. "The Steeple-Jack" from *Collected Poems* by Marianne Moore. Copyright 1951 by Marianne Moore, renewed 1979 by Lawrence E. Brinn and Louise Crane. All reprinted by permission of Macmillan Publishing Co., Inc.

Howard Moss. "Water Island," in *Finding Them Lost*. Copyright © 1965 by Howard Moss (New York: Atheneum, 1965). Reprinted with the permission of Atheneum Publishers.

Michael Mott. "Adam Names the Animals" from *Absence of Unicorns, Presence of Lions* by Michael Mott. Copyright © 1976 by Michael Mott. Reprinted by permission of Little, Brown and Company.

Edwin Muir. "The Horses" from *Collected Poems* by Edwin Muir. Copyright © 1960 by Willa Muir. Reprinted by permission of Oxford University Press, Inc. Also from *The Collected Poems of Edwin Muir*. Reprinted by permission of Faber and Faber Ltd.

Ogden Nash. "Requiem" (formerly titled "Gervaise"), "Edouard" from *Verses from 1929 On* by Ogden Nash. Copyright 1940 by Ogden Nash. Reprinted by permission of Little, Brown and Company.

Russell Noyes. From *William Wordsworth*, p. 140. Reprinted by permission of Twayne Publishers, a Division of G. K. Hall & Co., Boston.

Frank O'Hara. "A True Account of Talking to the Sun at Fire Island" from *The Collected Poems of Frank O'Hara*, edited by Donald Allen. Copyright © 1968 by Maureen Granville Smith, Administratrix of the Estate of Frank O'Hara. Reprinted by permission of Alfred A. Knopf, Inc.

Sharon Olds. "The Race" Copyright © 1985 by Sharon Olds. Reprinted by permission. Originally in *The New Yorker*.

Charles Olson. "Maximus, to Himself" from *The Maximus Poems* by Charles Olson, published by Jargon/Cornith Books. Copyright © 1960 by Charles Olson. Reprinted by permission of Corinth Books, Inc.

Gregory Orr. "All Morning" from *Gathering the Bones Together* by Gregory Orr. Copyright © 1975 by Gregory Orr. Reprinted by permission of Harper & Row, Publishers, Inc.

Wilfred Owen. "Anthem for Doomed Youth" from *The Collected Poems of Wilfred Owen*, edited by C. Day Lewis. Copyright © 1963 by Chatto & Windus. Reprinted by permission of New Directions Publishing Corporation, the Owen Estate, and Chatto & Windus Ltd.

Linda Pastan. "25th High School Reunion" from *The Five Stages of Grief*, Poems of Linda Pastan, by permission of W. W. Norton & Company, Inc. Copyright © 1978 by Linda Pastan.

Cesare Pavese. "Encounter" from *Hard Labor* by Cesare Pavese. Copyright 1943 by Einaudi editore, Torino. English translation copyright © 1976 by William Arrowsmith. Reprinted by permission of Viking Penguin Inc.

Molly Peacock. "Petting and Being a Pet" from *Raw Heaven* by Molly Peacock. Copyright © 1984 by Molly Peacock. Reprinted by permission of Random House, Inc.

Pindar. "Olympian 11," translated by Frank J. Nisetich from *Pindar's Victory Songs* by Frank J. Nisetich. Reprinted by permission of The Johns Hopkins University Press.

Sylvia Plath. "Daddy," "Lady Lazarus" from *Ariel* by Sylvia Plath. Copyright © 1963 by Ted Hughes. Reprinted by permission of Harper & Row Publishers, Inc. Also from *Ariel*, published by Faber & Faber, London. Copyright 1965 by Ted Hughes. Reprinted by permission of Faber & Faber Ltd.

Cole Porter. "My Heart Belongs to Daddy." Copyright © 1938 by Chappell and Co., Inc. Copyright Renewed, assigned to Robert H. Montgomery, Trustee of the Cole Porter Musical and Literary Property Trust. Chapell and Co., Inc., publisher. International copyright secured. All rights reserved. Reprinted by permission.

Ezra Pound. "In a Station of the Metro," and "The Bath Tub," from *Personae* by Ezra Pound. Reprinted by permission of New Directions Publishing Corporation.

Dudley Randall. "Ballad of Birmingham" from *Poems, Counterpoems* by Dudley Randall, published by Broadside Press. Reprinted by permission of Dudley Randall.

John Crowe Ransom. "Here Lies a Lady," "Piazza Piece," "Winter Remembered" from *Selected Poems*, Third Edition, Revised and Enlarged by John Crowe Ransom. Copyright 1924, 1927 by Alfred A. Knopf Inc., and renewed 1952, 1955 by John Crowe Ransom. Reprinted by permission of Alfred A. Knopf, Inc.

Henry Reed. "Naming of Parts" from *A Map of Verona* by Henry Reed, published by Jonathan Cape Ltd. Reprinted by permission of Jonathan Cape Ltd.

Ishmael Reed. "beware: do not read this poem" from *Catechism of a Neo-American* (too-doo Church). Copyright © 1969. Reprinted by permission of International Publishers, Inc., NY.

Pierre Reverdy. "Departure" from *The Poetry of Surrealism*, edited by Michael Benedikt. Copyright © 1974 by Michael Benedikt. Reprinted by permission of Georges Borchardt, Inc.

Adrienne Rich. "A Woman Mourned by Daughters." Reprinted from *Poems*, Selected and New, 1950–1974, by Adrienne Rich, by permission of W. W. Norton & Company, Inc. Copyright © 1975, 1973, 1971, 1969, 1966 by W. W. Norton & Company, Inc. 1967, 1963, 1962, 1961, 1960, 1959, 1958, 1957, 1956, 1955, 1954, 1953, 1952, 1951 by Adrienne Rich.

Rihaku. "The River Merchant's Wife, A Letter" from *Personae* by Ezra Pound. Copyright 1926 by Ezra Pound. Reprinted by permission of New Directions Publishing Corporation.

Edwin Arlington Robinson. "Mr. Flood's Party" from *Collected Poems* by Edwin Arlington Robinson. Copyright 1921 by Edwin Arlington Robinson, renewed 1949 by Ruth Nivison. Reprinted by permission of Macmillan Publishing Co., Inc.

Theodore Roethke. "The Lady and the Bear" from *The Collected Poems of Theodore Roethke*. Copyright 1951 by Theodore Roethke. "Elegy for Jane," "Child on Top of a Greenhouse," "My Papa's Waltz," "I Knew a Woman" from *The Collected Poems of Theodore Roethke*. Copyright 1950, 1954 by Theodore Roethke, Copyright 1946 by Editorial Publications, Inc., Copyright 1942 by Hearst Magazines, Inc. "The Waking" from *The Collected Poems of Theodore Roethke*. Copyright 1953 by Theodore Roethke. All reprinted by permission of Doubleday & Company, Inc.

David Matthew Rosen. "Time, Identity and Context in Wyatt's Verse" from *Studies in English Literature, 1500–1900*, Vol. 21 (Winter 1981), pp. 5, 12–13. Reprinted by permission of *Studies in English Literature* and David Matthew Rosen.

Derek Walcott. "Sea Grapes" from *Sea Grapes* by Derek Walcott. Copyright © 1971, 1973, 1974, 1975, 1976 by Derek Walcott. Reprinted by permission of Farrar, Straus and Giroux, Inc. Also from *Sea Grapes*, published by Jonathan Cape Ltd. Reprinted by permission of Jonathan Cape Ltd.

Margaret Walker. "Lineage" from *For My People* by Margaret Walker, published by Yale Younger Poets, 1942. Copyright 1942 by Margaret Walker. Reprinted by permission of Margaret Walker.

Alice Walker. "My Daughter is Coming" from *Horses Make a Landscape Look More Beautiful* by Alice Walker. Copyright © 1979 by Alice Walker. Reprinted by permission of Harcourt Brace Jovanovich, Inc.

Robert Penn Warren. "Bearded Oaks" from *Selected Poems 1923–1975* by Robert Penn Warren. Copyright 1942 and renewed 1970 by Robert Penn Warren. Reprinted by permission of Random House, Inc.

Tom Wayman. "Unemployment" from *Waiting for Wayman* by Tom Wayman. Reprinted by permission of the Canadian publishers, McClelland and Stewart Limited, Toronto.

Richard Wilbur. "The Death of a Toad" from *Ceremony and Other Poems* by Richard Wilbur. Copyright 1950, 1978 by Richard Wilbur. "The Beautiful Changes" from *The Beautiful Changes and Other Poems* by Richard Wilbur. Copyright 1947, 1975 by Richard Wilbur. "Love Calls Us to the Things of This World" from *Things of the World* by Richard Wilbur. Copyright © 1956 by Richard Wilbur. All reprinted by permission of Harcourt Brace Jovanovich, Inc.

William Carlos Williams. "Danse Russe" from *Collected Later Poems* by William Carlos Williams. Copyright 1938 by New Directions Publishing Corporation. "The Widow's Lament in Springtime," "The Great Figure," "The Red Wheelbarrow," "The Young Housewife" from *Collected Earlier Poems* by William Carlos Williams. Copyright 1938 by New Directions Publishing Corporation. "The Dance" from *Collected Later Poems* by William Carlos Williams. Copyright 1944 by William Carlos Williams. All reprinted by permission of New Directions Publishing Corporation.

James Wright. "A Blessing," "Lying in a Hammock at Williams Duffy's Farm in Pine Island, Minnesota" from *The Branch Will Not Break* by James Wright. "A Blessing" first appeared in *Poetry*. Reprinted by permission of Wesleyan University Press.

Richard Wright. "Four Haiku" © by Richard Wright. Reprinted by permission of John-Hawkins & Associates, Inc., 71 West 23rd Street, NY, NY 10010.

William Butler Yeats. "He Wishes for the Cloths of Heaven," "The Rose of Peace," "The Lake Isle of Innisfree" from *Collected Poems* by William Butler Yeats (New York: Macmillan, 1956). Reprinted by permission of M. B. Yeats, Anne Yeats, and Macmillan London Limited. "The Great Day" from *Collected Poems* by William Butler Yeats. Copyright 1940 by Georgie Yeats, renewed 1968 by Bertha Georgie Yeats, Michael Butler Yeats, and Anne Yeats. "Sailing to Byzantium" from *Collected Poems* by William Butler Yeats. Copyright 1928 by Macmillan Publishing Co., Inc., renewed 1956 by Georgie Yeats. "Crazy Jane Talks with the Bishop" from *Collected Poems* by William Butler Yeats. Copyright 1933 by Macmillan Publishing Co., Inc., renewed 1961 by Bertha Georgie Yeats. All reprinted by permission of Macmillan Publishing Co., Inc., M. B. Yeats, Anne Yeats, and Macmillan London Limited. "An Irish Airman Foresees His Death" from *Collected Poems* by William Butler Yeats. Copyright 1919 by Macmillan Publishing Co., Inc., renewed 1947 by Bertha Georgie Yeats. Reprinted by permission of Macmillan Publishing Co., Inc.

John Yau. "For Alexander Pope's Garden" from *Corpse and Mirror* by John Yau. Copyright © 1983 by John Yau. Reprinted by permission of Henry Holt and Company.

DRAMA

Lorraine Hansberry. *A Raisin in the Sun* by Lorraine Hansberry. Copyright © 1958, 1959 by Robert Nemiroff as Executor of the Estate of Lorraine Hansberry. Reprinted by permission of Random House, Inc.

Beth Henley. CRIMES OF THE HEART by Beth Henley. Copyright © 1981, 1982 by Beth Henley. Reprinted by permission of Viking Penguin, Inc.

Henrik Ibsen. *A Doll's House,* translated by Michael Meyer. Reprinted by permission of Harold Ober Associates Incorporated. Copyright © 1966 by Michael Meyer.

Arthur Miller. *Death of a Salesman* by Arthur Miller. Copyright 1949 by Arthur Miller. Copyright renewed 1977 by Arthur Miller. Reprinted by permission of Viking Penguin Inc.

Molière. THE MISANTHROPE translated by Richard Wilbur, copyright © 1954, 1955 by Richard Wilbur. Reprinted by permission of Harcourt Brace Jovanovich, Inc. CAUTION: Professionals and amateurs are hereby warned that this translation, being fully protected under the copyright laws of the United States of America, the British Commonwealth, including the Dominion of Canada, and all other countries which are signatories to the Universal Copyright Convention and the International Copyright Union, is subject to royalty. All rights, including professional, amateur, motion picture, recitation, lecturing, public reading, radio broadcasting, and television, are strictly reserved. Particular emphasis is laid on the question of readings, permission for which must be secured from the author's agent in writing. Inquiries on professional rights (except for amateur rights) should be addressed to Curtis Brown Ltd., Ten Astor Place, New York, NY 10003; inquiries on translation rights should be addressed to Harcourt Brace Jovanovich, Inc., Orlando, FL 32887. The amateur acting rights of THE MISANTHROPE are controlled exclusively by the Dramatists Play Service, Inc., 440 Park Avenue South, New York 10016. No amateur performance of the play may be given without obtaining in advance the written permission of the Dramatists Play Service, Inc. and paying the requisite fee.

Sam Shepard. GEOGRAPHY OF A HORSE DREAMER from the collection FOOL FOR LOVE AND OTHER PLAYS by Sam Shepard. Copyright © 1984 by Sam Shepard. Reprinted by permission of Bantam Books, Inc. All rights reserved.

Sophocles. THE OEDIPUS REX OF SOPHOCLES: An English Version by Dudley Fitts and Robert Fitzgerald, copyright 1949 by Harcourt Brace Jovanovich, Inc.; renewed 1977 by Cornelia Fitts and Robert Fitzgerald. Reprinted by permission of the publisher. CAUTION: All rights, including professional, amateur, motion picture, recitation, lecturing, performance, public reading, radio broadcasting, and television are strictly reserved. Inquiries on all rights should be addressed to Harcourt Brace Jovanovich, Inc., Orlando, FL 32887.

J. M. Synge. *Riders to the Sea.* From *The Complete Works of John Millington Synge* (New York: Random House, Inc., 1935).

Tennessee Williams. *The Glass Menagerie,* by Tennessee Williams. Copyright 1945 by Tennessee Williams and Edwina D. Williams and renewed 1973 by Tennessee Williams. Reprinted by permission of Random House, Inc.

Index of First Lines

As an ant, of his talents superiorly vain, 556
As I in hoary winter's night stood shivering in the snow, 557
As I walked out one evening, 748
A snake came to my water-trough, 554
As some fond virgin, whom her mother's care, 715
As though an aged person were to wear, 532
As virtuous men pass mildly away, 530
A sweet disorder in the dress, 711
At dawn I squat on the garage, 501
At midnight, 498
A toad the power mower caught, 618
A touch of cold in the Autumn night— 526
At ten A.M. the young housewife, 606
Ay, man is manly. Here you see, 727

Barely a twelvemonth after, 442
Because I could not stop for Death— 540
Because you are old and departing I have wetted my handkerchief, 563
Behold her, single in the field, 459
Blind with love, my daughter, 770

Chieftain Iffucan of Azcan in caftan, 658
Child, the current of your breath is six days long. 481
childhood remembrances are always a drag, 787
Come live with me and be my love, 423

Dark house, by which once more I stand, 463
Dear mother, dear mother, the Church is cold, 480
Death, be not proud, though some have calléd thee, 711
Did your car get you to Florida? 495
Does it mean anything, 782
Dogs, lambs, chickens, women—pets of all nations! 790
Do not go gentle into that good night, 637
Do you have a lion in your house? 668
Dürer would have seen a reason for living, 697
Dusk, 652
Dust always blowing about the town, 740

Earth and I gave you turquoise, 779
Eastern guard tower, 517
emerges daintily, the skunk— 587
Every day brings a ship, 563
Every day our bodies separate, 785
Every year without knowing it I have passed the day, 769

Farewell, thou child of my right hand, and joy; 430